DISCOVERING

Lewis & Clark

FROM THE AIR

DISCOVERING
Lewis & Clark
from the AIR

Photography by JIM WARK

Text by JOSEPH A. MUSSULMAN

Mountain Press Publishing Company
Missoula, Montana
2004

Library of Congress Cataloging-in-Publication Data

Wark, Jim.
    Discovering Lewis and Clark from the air / photography Jim Wark ; text
by Joseph A. Mussulman.
        p. cm.

    Includes bibliographical references and index.
    ISBN 0-87842-489-X (pbk. : alk. paper) — ISBN 0-87842-490-3
(cloth : alk. paper)
    1. Lewis and Clark National Historic Trail—Aerial photographs. 2. West
(U.S.)—History, Local—Aerial photographs. 3. Lewis and Clark Expedition
(1804-1806) 4. West (U.S.)—Description and travel.   I. Mussulman, Joseph.
II. Title.
    F592.7.W365 2004
      917.8′0022′2—dc22

                                        2003027641

PRINTED IN HONG KONG BY MANTEC PRODUCTION COMPANY

MOUNTAIN PRESS PUBLISHING COMPANY
Post Office Box 2399
Missoula, Montana 59801
406-728-1900

With gratitude to my wife Judy, as always, for her patience and encouragement, and to my good friend Debra Lappin for planting the seed.

—J.W.

Contents

Photographer's Preface

ON THE MORNING OF FRIDAY, May 14, 1999, I began my westward retracing of the Lewis and Clark route from St. Louis to the Pacific Ocean in my Christen A-1 Husky, a single-engine, high-wing, bush-type airplane. The day marked the 195th anniversary of the departure of the Corps of Discovery from this point. I had spent five months planning and plotting the route, and I had entered geographic coordinates of known Corps of Discovery campsites and points of interest into the airplane's Global Positioning System (GPS). I also entered many potential camping sites. The nights spent camping with my airplane are treasured times, and I put much thought into selecting locations.

The National Park Service reckons the distance of the Lewis and Clark Trail at 3,700 miles. My GPS flight plan showed 2,473 miles. The point-to-point traverse of the GPS planned route eliminated many miles of river and trail meandering, so the distances are not necessarily at odds. The trip took seven flying days, with eighty hours of flight time. For Lewis and Clark, the time in actual travel was twelve months. In 2001, at the urging of Dr. Joseph Mussulman, I flew the eastern portion of the Lewis and Clark route, as well as all the principal side journeys.

My trips produced a total of 3,182 images, all of which were shot with Leica 35mm cameras and Fuji Velvia film. The heights at which the pictures were shot varied from 500 to 3000 feet, with most taken between 1000 and 1500 feet.

Helping to create this book was a wonderful experience for me. I hope you enjoy the results.

JIM WARK

Introduction

SOMETIME DURING 1804, the year the Lewis and Clark expedition began, an event of similarly far-reaching import occurred in Yorkshire, England. A young inventor named George Cayley, of about the same age as the two American explorers, launched the first successful tests of a small glider, initiating the science of aerodynamics and demonstrating the practicality of fixed-wing flight. Those two synchronous threads of history have come together in this book of aerial photographs of selected places along the route traced by Meriwether Lewis, William Clark, and the Corps of Volunteers for North Western Discovery. It is my privilege to provide some commentary connecting these scenes with incidents from the history of the expedition.

The book also rests on a fabric of less momentous experiences and coincidences. Over the years, having lived and traveled along the Lewis and Clark trail from childhood, I had developed an eye-level familiarity with much of its scenery. But it was not until the spring of 1999 that I saw much of it from the air, except from a commercial airliner. Beginning on 14 May 1999, serving as a personal tour guide for Tom Arthur of Tampa, Florida, I studied the trail from St. Louis to the Rockies through the windows of his Pilatus Porter PC-6, cruising at a leisurely pace of eighty knots, a thousand feet or so above the Missouri, Jefferson, Beaverhead, and Bitterroot Rivers. The experience was exhilarating. In the span of four days I saw more than half of the official Lewis and Clark Trail from an altitude that paralleled the geographical sensibility from which William Clark drew his remarkable maps.

Unbeknown to Tom or me, another aircraft climbed into the airspace above St. Louis at almost the same hour on the same day, the 195th anniversary of the expedition's departure from the mouth of the Wood River, a few miles away. At the controls of the small, sturdy Christen Husky was Jim Wark, a professional aerial photographer from Pueblo, Colorado.

Two years later, in April 2001, I was searching for some oblique aerial views of certain points along the trail for my Web site, Discovering Lewis & Clark®, which had been under development since 1993, when I happened upon Jim's rich catalog of photos on the Web and arranged to use several of them. When we eventually met, I expressed my interest in writing about the expedition from an aerial perspective; he responded by showing me his own concept for such a book. This collaboration was the outcome.

Although Meriwether Lewis declared that the mouth of the Missouri River should be considered the start of the expedition, one might say that its true birthplace was Thomas Jefferson's home, Monticello. In more practical terms, the months of planning and preparation for the journey took place in Washington, D.C.; at Harpers Ferry in West Virginia; and in Philadephia, Lancaster, and Pittsburgh, Pennsylvania. Lewis's journey down the Ohio in the fall of 1803 was the time for recruitment, climaxing with his reunion at Louisville, Kentucky, with his friend and former army commander William Clark. For these reasons, and because the popular perception of the expedition has recently changed from that of a Western adventure to an epic of continental dimensions, this photographic essay extends from coast to coast.

Early photographic records of portions of the expedition's route date from the 1880s, culminating first in 1904 with the more than two dozen scenic views with which Olin Wheeler illustrated his "heritage tourism" guide, *The Trail of Lewis and Clark*. The next benchmark in the idiom was Albert and Jane Salisbury's *Two Captains West*, in 1950, followed by Ingvard Eide's 1969 photo-essay, *American Odyssey*. Since then, numerous photographers have similarly captured intimations of the splendorous wilderness Lewis and Clark saw. More recently, a few aerial views have also emerged.

Out of the library of some 3,200 photos Jim shot during his numerous flights, we chose the ones for this book primarily for their esthetic qualities, some more for their documentary or narrative functions, and most for both reasons. Together, they help us comprehend the Corps' journey by embracing a wider range of vision than ground-based photos. On a hypothetically level plain, the field of view for a six-footer like Lewis is only about three miles. From a thousand feet up, where Jim usually cruised, the horizon is a little over forty-two miles distant—about as far as the Corps of Discovery traveled upriver, on average, in four dawn-to-dusk days. At three thousand feet above the ground, where several of these photos were taken, the horizon is almost seventy-five miles away.

Low-elevation oblique aerial photos show the land from an unusual perspective, minimizing or eliminating many details and introducing different qualities and values than we customarily apply on the ground. For example, I had viewed Beaverhead Rock (cover photo), one of the expedition's most famous landmarks, many times from Montana Highway 41, and I had often stopped to study it from the nearby historic-marker pullout at the crest of a rise in the road. When Jim showed me his shot of it, I was convinced he had missed the mark. There was no sere, juniper-and-sagebrush-mantled mountain behind the Beaverhead Rock I thought I knew. The highway was in the wrong place, and the little hump with the interpretive marker was missing. So Jim made a special trip to try again. He had been right the first time, of course. Information transmitted direct to his plane's GPS receiver from a group of satellites can be relied upon; our eyes cannot. Though I had often looked at the scene, its total setting had never soaked in.

Through these pictures we may also gain a greater appreciation of some of the rigors the explorers endured. We can see, for instance, that their river routes were often many times longer than an overland route might have been. Furthermore, we can appreciate the actual scope of the journey in a daily context. Whereas Clark measured his journey in terms of estimated straight-line distances between successive landmarks, the Corps' daily work led them over a much broader path. To search for fresh meat, hunters went out nearly every day, at times ranging many miles on either side of the rivers' courses. Only from above can we see beyond the thin line of a trail map and appreciate what they really saw.

Many of these pictures challenge us to imagine the realities of northwestern exploration in the early 1800s. They remind us of how many intricate cityscapes and sprawling suburbs, and how many industrial, agricultural and resource-extractive efforts now overlie the path Lewis and Clark took two centuries ago. Jefferson's primary directive, to find a water route to the Pacific Ocean "for purposes of commerce," ensured that their main highways would be rivers. Today, between Pittsburgh and Portland, the ancient riverbeds are filled with the sluggish backwaters of forty-three twentieth-century dams. The Ohio River, for instance, through whose shallow, gravelly bed Lewis sometimes had to drag his keelboat with oxen, is today a nine-hundred-mile chain of artificial lakes. In addition, changing issues, values, and visions have obliterated the few Indian trails the Corps used and have displaced the people who trod them into the land. Modern travelers cannot actually retrace much of Lewis and Clark's line of march, but merely intersect with it at some of the places pictured or briefly parallel it at varying distances.

Yet none of the photos is meant to imply that Lewis and Clark were responsible for the repopulation and development of the Northwest. They did not "open the West." In the

4

journals of the expedition there is ample evidence that Euro-American claims on the West began generations before Congress authorized Thomas Jefferson's enterprise. They prove also that American traders and fur trappers were already heading that direction, and the Corps of Discovery met that vanguard both coming and going. In short, the cities that crowd some of these photos were not built simply because Lewis and Clark passed by. Each of the pictures simply frames the modern setting in which some memorable moments occurred in the lives of the young men of the Corps of Discovery.

Most of the stories are recounted here partly through quotations from the journals of Captain Lewis, Captain Clark, Sergeants Floyd, Ordway, and Gass, and Private Whitehouse.[1] It must be remembered that, as originally written, those documents were not meant for the general reader. For the most part they were notes and reports written in haste under conditions totally inconsistent with serious literary efforts. They were the raw material for a work in progress. When Lewis sent his and Clark's first set of diaries back to Jefferson from Fort Mandan in April of 1805, he assured the president they were "of course incorrect," surely meaning uncorrected. Furthermore, he wrote, "Capt. Clark dose not wish this journal exposed in it's present state, but has no objection that one or more copies of it be made by some confidential person under your direction, correcting it's grammatical errors &c."[2]

Yet those unrefined phrases and plainly phonetic spellings convey a sense of immediacy, like the emotion-soaked spontaneity of street talk or on-the-scene news reports. They lend human weight to the now invisible footsteps of one of the great exploratory expeditions in American history. They are worth reading not for the sake of historical authenticity, nor just because many readers have come to expect them, but because those rough-hewn words convey the spirit of the courageous "band of brothers" that made its way through these scenes toward history, and safely home again.

---

[1] All quotations are from *The Definitive Journals of Lewis & Clark*, the paperback edition of volumes two through eleven of *The Journals of the Lewis and Clark Expedition*, edited by Gary E. Moulton, 13 vols. (Lincoln: University of Nebraska Press, 1983–2001).

[2] Donald Jackson, ed., *Letters of the Lewis and Clark Expedition, with Related Documents, 1783–1854*, 2nd ed., 2 vols. (Champaign: University of Illinois Press, 1978), 1:231.

Part I

Gathering Forces

MONTICELLO to ST. LOUIS

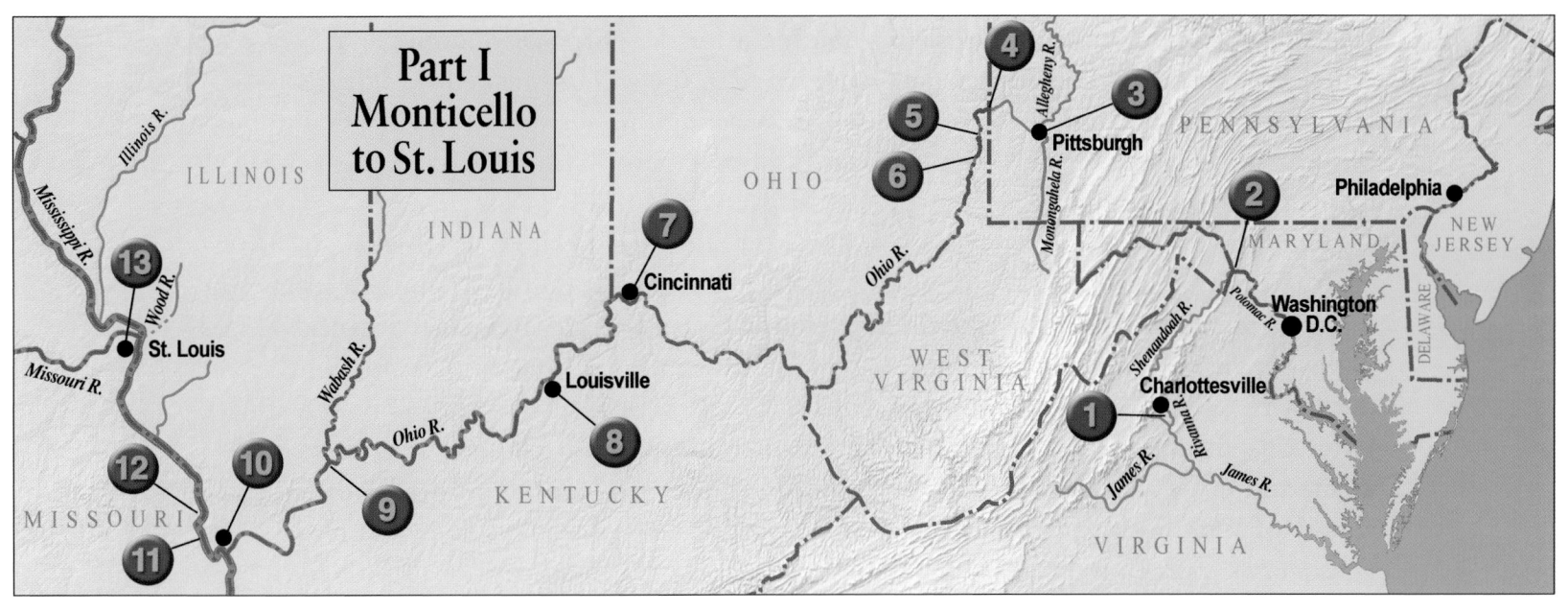

Part I
Monticello
to St. Louis

Source and Paradigm

ON 20 JUNE 1804, President Thomas Jefferson handed his secretary, Captain Meriwether Lewis of the First Infantry Regiment, a letter with instructions for one of the first and most significant exploratory expeditions in American history. "The object of your mission is to explore the Missouri river, & such principal stream of it, as, by it's course and communication with the waters of the Pacific ocean . . . may offer the most direct & practicable water communication across this continent for the purposes of commerce."

The two former Virginia neighbors were living in the still unfinished President's House—not yet named the White House—in Washington, but the president's real home, physical and spiritual, was Monticello, his hilltop plantation on the east slope of the Appalachian Mountains.

Beginning in 1769 at age twenty-six, Jefferson built Monticello over a period of forty years. The house and grounds stand as a physical manifestation of the mind of its creator, the man one French admirer called "Musician, Draftsman, Surveyor, Astronomer, Natural Philosopher, Jurist, and Statesman." Jefferson framed the house with "roundabout" roads lined with "allées" of mulberry and honey locust trees. Inside, Monticello bursts with Jefferson's inventions and experiments in architecture, furniture design, scientific equipment, and more. The crafter of the Declaration of Independence and founder of the University of Virginia was, in other words, a born explorer—of ideas. The Corps of Discovery's journey west was yet another expression of his genius.

In Monticello's entrance hall, Jefferson displayed some of the Indian artifacts and animal specimens the expedition sent and brought back, reflecting his interests in natural history and ethnography. He was a farmer, too, and even planted some of the seeds Lewis brought from the West at Monticello: Indian corn and beans from Fort Mandan, orange honeysuckle from the Bitterroot Mountains.

(1) *Monticello, near Charlottesville, Virginia* (view east) →

Wedge of History

IN 1747 ENTREPRENEUR Robert Harper settled on the point of land where the Shenandoah River (left) meets the Potomac (right) and took over the ferryboat service. Yet the area was still a wilderness in the early 1780s when Thomas Jefferson described it in his *Notes on the State of Virginia* as "perhaps one of the most stupendous scenes in nature."

Wedged between the two rocky rivers and the steep slopes of Schoolhouse Ridge, Harpers Ferry's tiny footprint belies the richness of its history—it would become a center of American industrialization and commerce and would play a pivotal role in the unfolding of the Civil War. George Washington, during his second term as president, first determined Harpers Ferry's place in American history when he established the new federal armory and arsenal here.

In mid-March of 1803, two weeks after Congress authorized the expedition, it was to this place that Meriwether Lewis went first, securing supplies of rifles, pipe-tomahawks, knives, and other goods. He also supervised the construction of the iron framework for a collapsible thirty-six-foot boat that could be carried across the anticipated one-day portage between the Missouri and the Columbia River headwaters, then assembled and covered with a hull of animal hides. Lewis referred to it variously as "the Leather boat," "the iron boat," or in a more scientific tone, "the Experiment."

In the months that followed, Lewis's men hauled nearly two hundred pounds of hardware for the boat down the Ohio, up the Missouri, and around the Great Falls. There they set up the frame, stitched hides together, assembled the craft, and cast off. The hull leaked badly and the boat quickly sank. Lewis's experiment was a washout.

Golden Triangle

THE MONONGAHELA RIVER (right) joins the Allegheny River at the apex of Pittsburgh's "golden triangle" to form the river called the Ohio—an Iroquois word meaning "big and beautiful." When Meriwether Lewis set out from here at 11 A.M. on 31 August 1803, the rivers were lower than anyone could remember. On many gravel bars, the water was a scant six inches deep, while Lewis's new custom-built, fifty-five-foot keelboat needed two and a half feet and would have to be dragged.

Just three miles down the Ohio from Pittsburgh, Lewis went ashore to visit friends, who asked to see the pneumatic gun he had purchased for the expedition. Suddenly he came within a fraction of an inch of a tragedy. When a bystander unintentionally discharged the weapon, the ball struck a woman forty yards away. She fell to the ground, blood gushing from her temple. "We were all in the greatest consternation," Lewis confided in his journal. But in a moment she revived, "to our enespressable satisfaction, and by examination we found the wound by no means mortal or even dangerous."

Considering that each man in the Corps of Discovery carried at least one firearm, many used daily by the hunters, the expedition came out with a remarkably good safety record. They had only one other gun accident that drew blood on the entire trip.

(3) *The Monongahela and Allegheny Rivers meet to form the Ohio, Pittsburgh, Pennsylvania* (view east) →

The Old Frontier

ON 2 SEPTEMBER 1803 the keelboat high-centered on a "riffle," or shallow rapid, which a farmer and his horse and ox helped them through. "Payd the man his charge which was one dollar," Lewis wrote, adding, "The inhabitants who live near these riffles live much by the distressed situation of traveler[s], are generally lazy, charge extravagantly when they are called on for assistance, and have no filantrophy or contience [conscience]."

Two days later Lewis and his skeleton crew of eleven hands crossed the boundary between Pennsylvania and Ohio, officially entering the Old Northwest. The boundary line, wrote Lewis, "is made visible from the timber having been felled about sixty feet in width." At Georgetown, Pennsylvania, Lewis paid eleven dollars for a canoe "compleat with two paddles and two poles." The canoe leaked badly and was eventually abandoned.

Most of Little Blue Lake is in Pennsylvania, except for the arm at far right, which is in West Virginia; below the lake is Lawrenceville, West Virginia, and part of East Liverpool, Ohio, is visible at far left.

(4) *Ohio River and Little Blue Lake, Lawrenceville, West Virginia; Pennsylvania at top, West Virginia at bottom and center right, and Ohio at left* (view east)

Weather Report

THE FIFTH OF SEPTEMBER 1803 was the third day in a row that dawned under a fog, delaying the expedition's departure, as it would for many mornings to come. Thomas Jefferson, who systematically recorded his own daily weather observations for more than fifty years, had directed Lewis to make careful notes on weather conditions throughout the journey. Now Lewis speculated on the cause of the fog. He correctly deduced that it was the result of cool dawn air over warm river water, the condensation rising "like steem from boiling water."

That night, the party camped on Brown's Island, named for a nearby landowner of the time. When darkness fell, the two canoes carrying most of Lewis's most valuable supplies had not appeared. "Ordered the trumpet to be sound[ed]," Lewis wrote, "and . . . they came up in a few minutes." Quite different from the musical instrument of the same name, this trumpet was a small, loud, one-note horn that boatmen used for signaling. The four horns Lewis had purchased in Philadelphia would prove useful for keeping track of the boats and calling in hunters. They also made dandy noisemakers for New Year's celebrations.

On the afternoon of the sixth, after another foggy morning and many more shallow riffles, they passed Steubenville, Ohio (beyond the bend in photo). "Stewbenville," Lewis reported, was a "small well built thriving place" that had "several respectable families residing in it, five years since it was a wildernesss." Weirton, West Virginia, is on the bluffs at upper left.

19

"Point of Embarkation"

Wheeling (left; Martins Ferry, Ohio, right) was in the state of Virginia when Lewis and his crew stepped ashore here on 7 September 1803. "This is a pretty considerable Village [that] contains about fifty houses," Lewis wrote. It was "remarkable for being the point of embarkation for merchants and Emegrants who are about to descend the river, particularly if they are late in getting on and the water gets low as it most commonly is from the beginning of July to the last of September; the water from hence being much deeper and the navigation better than it is from Pittsburgh or any point above it."

Though the keelboat, which was the expedition's flagship, could probably carry up to fifteen tons, Lewis kept it light for this shallow stretch of the river by having part of his freight hauled overland by wagon to Wheeling. In 1803 most travel routes were narrow paths best suited to foot and horse traffic. There were only a few thousand miles of decent, if mostly unpaved, wagon roads in the seventeen states. Wheeling was the western terminus of one of the newest of these.

◄— (6) *Ohio River at Wheeling, West Virginia* (view southeast, downstream)

Letart's Falls

ON 18 SEPTEMBER 1803 Lewis and his little flotilla passed Letart's Falls, then an important milepost on the upper Ohio but which has since been removed. Possibly relying on a recent edition of Zadok Cramer's guidebook *The Ohio and Mississippi Navigator*, Lewis wrote, "The descent at Letart's falls"—actually more of a rapid than a fall—"is a little more than . . . four feet in two hundred fifty yards." Thus concluded Lewis's last journal entry for the next fifty-four days and seven hundred river miles. No one knows why.

We know Lewis arrived in Cincinnati on 28 September from a letter he wrote to Jefferson, in which he remarked with relief that the river was somewhat deeper below the falls. From that point on, he must have covered about twenty-three miles per day, compared to the twelve- to fifteen-mile daily average from Wheeling to the falls. In contrast, on the return trip in September 1806, descending the lower Missouri River, the expedition raced along at an estimated fifty miles or more per day.

On the Kentucky side of the river (left), across from Cincinnati, is the city of Covington. On 3 October 1803, knowing Jefferson's interest in the new science of paleontology, Lewis wrote the president detailing his observations of some fossils recently excavated at Big Bone Lick in Kentucky, twenty-two miles southwest of Covington. Lewis's information so intrigued Jefferson that in 1807 he sent William Clark back to Big Bone Lick to supervise a special excavation in his behalf.

Recruits

WILLIAM CLARK, having retired from the army in 1796, had recently moved across the Ohio River from Louisville, Kentucky, to Clarksville, Indiana (not pictured). There he received a long letter, dated 19 June 1803, from his old army friend, Meriwether Lewis, inviting him to share command of the expedition and outlining his plans. "When descending the Ohio it shall be my duty by enquiry to find out and engage some good hunters, stout, healthy, unmarried men, accustomed to the woods, and capable of bearing bodily fatigue in a pretty considerable degree: should any young men answering this discription be found in your neighborhood I would thank you to give information of them on my arivall at the falls of the Ohio."

Lewis is believed to have recruited John Colter in Maysville, Kentucky, on his way downriver to meet with Clark in Louisville. When Lewis arrived at the rendezvous on 14 October 1803, Clark was waiting with seven young prospects from the area, all of whom became permanent members of the Corps of Discovery: William Bratton, Joseph and Reubin Field, Charles Floyd, George Gibson, Nathaniel Pryor, and John Shields.

In 1778 Clark's older brother, George Rogers Clark, established a fort in Louisville, named in 1780 for Louis XVI of France, a staunch supporter of the American War for Independence. Here lay the Falls of the Ohio, a two-mile-long series of rapids with a total drop of twenty-four feet. Lewis stepped ashore at a landing just behind the bridge in the picture, George Rogers Clark Bridge.

(8) *Ohio River at Louisville, Kentucky; Waterfront Park and Slugger Field in foreground* (view southwest, downstream) →

Familiar Water

INDIANS NAMED THIS RIVER Wah-Bah Shik-Ki, meaning "Pure [or Shining] White" or "Water over White Stones." The French spelled the name Quabache; Anglo-American settlers and mapmakers, Wabash. Swerving through the prairie, this river today scribes a crooked boundary between Indiana and Illinois, from near Terre Haute to the Ohio River.

The meadows along the Wabash were familiar to both expedition captains. As a surveyor, Clark covered much of the lower Ohio, and both he and Lewis had crisscrossed the area in the course of their military duties. In fact, Clark had gained one of his first experiences in river boating here during his military service, as commander of a detail hauling supplies up the Wabash in wintertime.

Lewis, Clark, and their crew left the Falls of the Ohio on 26 October 1803. The next journal entry on record was Lewis's, dated 11 November, the day they arrived at Fort Massac, a frontier outpost about 325 miles down the Ohio from Louisville. At a pace averaging nearly 20 miles per day, they must have passed the mouth of the Wabash about 7 November.

In the photo, the Wabash meanders from beyond the horizon through rich farmland to join the Ohio (at right). Today, the Wabash washes agricultural and industrial pollution into the Ohio along with its mud-tinted spring flow.

Meeting of the Waters

ON THE EVENING OF 14 November 1803, Lewis and Clark camped on the point between the Ohio (right) and Mississippi Rivers near today's Cairo, Illinois—or wherever it actually was two hundred years ago. By now they had rowed, poled, dragged, and occasionally sailed their boats a total of 981 miles in 76 days, including rest stops.

Two days later, an admiring Shawnee Indian offered Lewis three beaver skins for his Newfoundland dog, Seaman, but "of course there was no bargain." The dog, Lewis wrote, "I prised much for his docility and qualifications generally for my journey." These qualifications included a comfort with water: Newfoundlands had long been bred to help trawlers retrieve their nets and to guide shipwrecked sailors through surf. The journals contain no hint that the Corps' mascot was ever called on to help with a water rescue, though there were several occasions when he could have been.

Clark had been to this place at least three times in the 1790s, and in 1795 drew a map of the confluence. In 1780 Clark's brother George had built a fort about four miles down the Mississippi from here. On 18 November 1803, the two captains and eight men paddled a canoe down the Mississippi on a sentimental journey to the abandoned post, Fort Jefferson. To men of Clark's day, American history was largely personal history.

← (10) *Confluence of the Ohio and Mississippi Rivers, near Cairo, Illinois* (view west, upstream)

Tywappity Bottom

"ARRIVED OPOSITE THREE NEW habitation of some Americans who had settled under the spanish government," wrote Lewis on 22 November 1803. "This settlement is on a bottom called, *Tywappety.*"

France had ceded Louisiana to Spain in 1762. Napoleon regained nominal ownership in 1800, but under the secret Treaty of San Ildelfonso, Spain retained legal control of the huge and mostly unmapped territory. In 1790 some Spanish families established a village called Zewapeta—a name of uncertain meaning—on the west bank of the Mississippi above the mouth of the Ohio. Seven years later, enticed by generous Spanish land grants, American farmers from east of the Mississippi moved in, quickly anglicizing the Spanish name to the lilting Tywappity, which has since disappeared.

The social complexion of this eastern fringe of Louisiana Territory was richly varied in 1803. Up the Mississippi at Cape Girardeau, Missouri, the next day, the captains found what they perceived as unsavory characters, a population "almost entirely emegrant from the frontiers of Kentuckey & Tennessee . . . [who] are the most dessolute and abandoned even among these people; they are men of desperate fortunes, [with] but little to lose, either character or property." However, a nearby settlement of German-Swiss immigrants from North Carolina struck Lewis as "temperate, laborious and honest people."

(11) *Mississippi River near Charleston, Missouri* (view west, upstream) →

Demons

ON 25 NOVEMBER 1803 Lewis wrote, "Arrived at the *Grand Tower* a little before sunset, passed above it and came too on the Lard. [left] shore for the night." He was referring to the tree-capped island just below the center of the photo. In 1673 French explorers Père Marquette and Louis Joliet listened to local Indians' warnings about this place and erected a cross atop the ninety-foot-high rock to disempower the demons said to be lurking in the treacherous whirlpool at its base. Lewis explained: "This seems among the watermen of the Mississippi to be what the . . . Equinoxial line is with regard to the Sailors; those who have never passed it before are always compelled to pay or furnish some sperits to drink or be ducked."

In fact, the river around the Grand Tower can be devilishly dangerous, as Lewis was told: "When the river is high the courent setts in with great violence . . . this courent meets the other portion of the river which runs E. of the Tower . . . ; these strong courants thus meeting each other form an immence and dangerous whirlpool which no boat dare approach . . . ; the counter courent driving with grat force against the E. side of the rock would instandly dash them to attoms and the whirlpool would as quickly take them to the bottom."

However, Lewis observed, "In the present state of the water there is no danger in approaching it." Every few years, when the water is low, it is briefly possible to walk to the Grand Tower—or Tower Rock—on dry sand, but when the Mississippi is high, even modern towboat pilots shy away from it.

Western Gate

ON 7 DECEMBER, after stopping at old Cahokia, Illinois (population then about seven hundred), the expedition moved past "the American bottom"—on the U.S. side of the Mississippi—to the vicinity of today's East St. Louis, Illinois. On the eleventh they "proceeded on," as Clark later wrote to his brother—the first use of the phrase that was to become a motif in the journals—across the Mississippi "to a landing opposite the center of the Town." That would have been at the foot of St. Louis's Market Street, which extended to the river's edge, just inside the south (left, in the photo) leg of the famous Gateway Arch. The arch was built in the early 1960s to commemorate significant events in America's westward expansion.

Word of the expedition had spread quickly. "The admiration of the people were So great, that hundreds Came to the bank to view us," Clark later wrote. St. Louis's population was around one thousand at the time.

When the Corps of Discovery returned on 23 September 1806, crammed into five canoes and one of the two original pirogues, they were "met by all the village and received a harty welcom from its inhabitants." In the last of his 863 consecutive daily entries, Sgt. John Ordway wrote that the men "drew out the canoes then the party all considerable much rejoiced that we have the Expedition Completed . . . we entend to return to our native homes to See our parents once more as we have been So long from them."

The next morning Lewis and Clark began writing to their commander-in-chief and to their families, and the story took root in American history. On the same ground where the Corps landed, beneath today's Gateway Arch, the two captains resided the rest of their lives.

Familiar Ground

CAMP DUBOIS to KNIFE RIVER VILLAGES

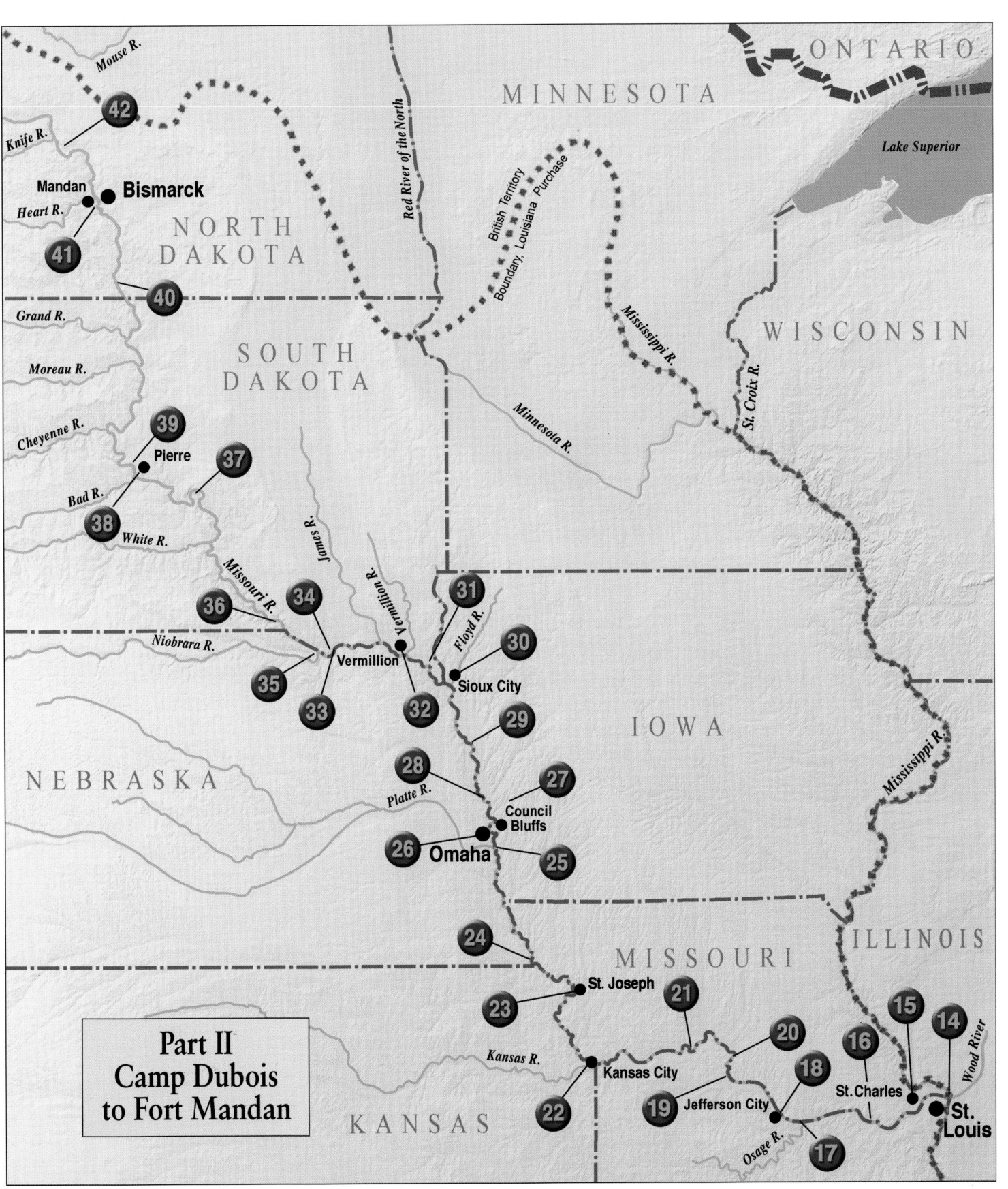

ONTARIO

MINNESOTA

Lake Superior

Mouse R.

Knife R.

42

Mandan **Bismarck**

Heart R.

41

NORTH
DAKOTA

40

Grand R.

Red River of the North

British Territory
Boundary, Louisiana Purchase

WISCONSIN

Mississippi R.

St. Croix R.

SOUTH
DAKOTA

Moreau R.

Cheyenne R.

39

Pierre

37

Minnesota R.

Bad R.

38

White R.

James R.

Vermillion R.

Missouri R.

34

31

Floyd R.

30

36

Niobrara R.

35

Vermillion

32

Sioux City

IOWA

Mississippi R.

33

29

NEBRASKA

28

27

Platte R.

Council
Bluffs

26 **Omaha**

25

24

ILLINOIS

MISSOURI

St. Joseph

21

23

20

15

16

14

Wood River

Kansas R.

18

Pierre

Part II
Camp Dubois
to Fort Mandan

Kansas City

19 Jefferson City

St. Charles

**St.
Louis**

22

KANSAS

Osage R.

17

Starting Point

SOMETIME BEFORE THEY SAILED west on 14 May 1804, Clark recorded: "Capts. Lewis & Clark wintered at the enterance of a Small river opposite the Mouth of Missouri Called wood River, where they formed their party, Composed of robust Young Backwoodsmen of Character." Reconsidering the difficult hours some of those "characters" had caused him with their resistance to the rigorous military disipline imposed upon them, he crossed out the last four words and substituted, "helthy hardy young men."

The expedition began building their winter camp on 13 December 1803. Owing to the shifting of the rivers' confluence, the actual site has never been determined. One study places it near the left side of the bridge at the top center of this photo. In a compromise between history and hydrology, an observation point commemorating their visit (lower center) stands opposite the Missouri's muddy mouth, at a diversion channel that carries two streams—neither of which is Wood River—to the Mississippi.

On their return in 1806, after spending the night of 22 September at the recently built Fort Bellefontaine (in the photo, a few miles around the bend at left), the Corps revisited the Wood River camp. There, according to Sergeant Ordway, they called on a widow who had worked for them on their way west in 1804, and who now had "a plantation under tollarable good way." Her name is unknown.

(14) *Monument to the Lewis and Clark Expedition, on the Mississippi River at its confluence with the Missouri, near Wood River, Illinois* (view northwest) →

Petites Côtes

WITH CAPTAIN CLARK in sole command, the Corps of Volunteers for North Western Discovery, as it was soon to be dubbed, left the mouth of Wood River at 4 P.M. on 14 May 1804. The flotilla comprised the keelboat and two pirogues (large rowboats), one painted red and the other white to distinguish them from afar, of six oars and seven oars, respectively. The expedition also had two horses at the start, to be used for hunting.

Clark and the men "proceeded on under a jentle brease," bound for St. Charles. Arriving there on the sixteenth, they had already learned two things—to load each boat heavy in the bow, and that they needed more manpower.

St. Charles was a single, mile-long main street with 100 dwellings, 450 "pore, polite & harmonious" inhabitants, and a chapel. The settlement occupied a narrow bench between the river and a range of small hills—hence its French name, Petites Côtes, or "Little Hills."

On Sunday, 20 May—anticipating the dangerous mission, and perhaps desirous of all the divine help they could summon—Sergeant Ordway "and a nomber of the party went to the Mass." As Pvt. Joseph Whitehouse wrote, the Roman Catholic service "was a novelty to them."

Captain Lewis arrived from St. Louis that afternoon, and the next morning the Corps set out in earnest, having gained two enlistees who would prove extremely valuable: interpreter François Labiche and boatman Pierre Cruzatte. The expedition now comprised more than forty men—soldiers, civilian employees, and perhaps a dozen French-Canadian hired hands, or engagés.

← (15) *St. Charles, Missouri* (view northeast)

Outpost

ON 25 MAY 1804, seven travel days and about seventy miles above St. Charles, the expedition camped near a small village at the mouth of a creek called Charrette. Its seven French families had arrived only a few years before, drawn by good hunting, opportunities for Indian trade, and the security of the small fort established there around 1796 by the Spanish. Daniel Boone, the famous frontiersman from Kentucky, would move there sometime after 1804.

"The people at this Village is pore, houses Small," Clark observed, but they were hospitable, for "they Sent us milk & eggs to eat." Their little community was the last settlement of whites on the Missouri River.

Passing this way again on 20 September 1806, the Corps knew they were finally back in home territory when they saw some cows on the bank, "which was a joyfull Sight to the party," said Clark. Soon they saw the village, and "the men raised a Shout and Sprung upon their ores." To celebrate, "they discharged 3 rounds with a harty Cheer, which was returned from five tradeing boats" that were moored there. Two young Scotsmen gave the men some beef, pork, and flour, and treated the captains to "a very agreeable supper." The people there "Seem to express great pleasure at our return, and acknowledged them selves much astonished in Seeing us. . . . . they informed us that we were Supposed to have been lost long Since."

The Missouri River washed away all remains of the village many years ago. When Lewis and Clark were there, the mouth of Charrette Creek was perhaps seven miles upriver from where it is now.

(16) *Charrette Creek opposite Washington, Missouri*
(view northwest, upstream) →

"*Delightfull Prospect*"

AT 4 P.M. ON 1 JUNE 1804, the expedition arrived at the mouth of the Osage River (left fork in photo), one of the major Indian trail intersections on the lower Missouri. From a promontory between the rivers, Clark wrote: "I had a delightfull prospect of the Missouries up & down, also the Osage R. up." The point of land on which he stood may have been nearly four miles west and two miles south of where it is in the photo.

That night and the next morning Lewis took astronomical observations to measure the latitude and longitude of the place. The raw numbers for longitude would be passed on to a mathematician after the expedition, since the formula for that was complex. Lewis determined the latitude, which was easier to compute, as 38°31'6.9" north.

Seven days before, thirty-five miles downriver, George Drouillard and Pvt. John Shields had been sent ahead with the expedition's two horses to hunt for two days, but they missed their rendezvous with the boats. On this day they finally caught up with the main party, "much worsted" but giving "a flattering account of the Countrey" they had seen. Their experience reminds us that the Corps of Discovery's trek through the Northwest was anything but an orderly march. Frequently hunters, or even an officer, ranged many miles on either side of a river. Nearly every step each man took was exploratory.

The Corps passed the Osage River again, without comment, on their journey eastward on 20 September 1806—three days from home.

"Nightingale" Song

ON SUNDAY, 3 JUNE 1804, the expedition left its camp at the mouth of the Osage River and proceeded five miles upstream to the mouth of the Moreau River (in the photo, near and parallel to the top, around the curve, going off to the right). There, Clark wrote, he and his men "Saw much sign of war parties of Inds. having Crossed from the mouth of this Creek."

That night was especially memorable, for the next day Clark named a small creek a mile upstream from their camp Nightingale Creek, "from a Bird of that discription which Sang for us all last night, and is the first of the kind I ever heard." But the nightingale is not a North American bird, and it is uncertain what they heard.

That afternoon, several miles upstream, Sergeant Ordway, at the helm of the keelboat, snagged the rigging on an overhanging tree and broke the mast. The big, lumbering craft was fifty-five feet long, with an eight-foot, four-inch beam and a three-foot draft. With most of its weight above the waterline, it must have been difficult to handle in the Missouri's brisk, unpredictable current. Clark commemorated the accident by naming a nearby stream Mast Creek, where they may have cut lumber to mend the break.

On the return trip in 1806, riding a current that tumbled along at nearly seven miles an hour, the Corps raced past Nightingale Creek and the Moreau River. "The men ply their oares," wrote Clark, "& we decended with great velocity."

Jefferson City was not yet established when the expedition passed by. By 1826, however, Missouri Territory had enough citizens to enter the Union as the twenty-first state, and "the City of Jefferson" became the capital.

"Handsome Spot"

IT WAS A HARD AND DANGEROUS day's work getting past the wooded bluff called Arrow Rock (center of photo) on 9 June 1804. The river was about three hundred yards wide and full of treacherous logs driven by a strong current. The keelboat struck one of the logs, then caught on a cluster of them. It was a "disagreeable and Dangerous situation," wrote Clark.

Some of the men leaped into the water, swam ashore with a rope, and pulled the boat out of harm's way. "I can Say with Confidence," declared Clark, "that our party is not inferior to any that was ever on the waters of the Missoppie."

After the expedition, in 1807, Clark would pass through here again, en route to build Fort Osage. He would remark on Arrow Rock as "a handsome Spot for a town." The place was destined to become the first jumping-off point for westering settlers and entre-preneurs—the beginning of the Santa Fe Trail, pioneered by William Becknell in 1821. In 1829 a trader named Marmaduke platted a town here, which with typical frontier hubris he called New Philadelphia, but the name soon reverted to Arrow Rock.

(19) *Arrow Rock, Missouri* (view north, upstream) →

Driftwood

IN LEWIS AND CLARK'S DAY, a lexicon of hazards made up an intimate dialog between the riverman and the river—snag, sweep, sawyer, preacher, rapid, riffle, eddy, and whirlpool; rolling sands, rocky shoals, collapsing banks, and overhanging trees. The photo shows a drift or raft of logs—an *embarras,* or "obstacle," as the French engagés called it. Rising waters in the spring dislodged downed timber, then carried it to places where it caught and collected. Huge drifts could accumulate rapidly. Receding waters left them beached in the mud, to be picked up again the following spring. The Missouri spawned countless hazards such as these throughout its length.

Drifts like the one pictured were even more dangerous on the downstream journey than they were going upstream, with the current in this part of the Missouri running at an estimated six and a half to seven miles per hour. To maintain control and avoid slamming into them, the men of the Corps had to keep the boats moving faster than the current. If a craft caught against the leading edge of a drift, it would be next to impossible for the crew to get away.

"Butifull Prarie"

THE LOWER REACHES OF THE Missouri River already had a long history of European presence when Lewis and Clark came through. One of their most helpful informants in St. Louis had been James Mackay, a veteran in the Missouri River fur trade and, since 1795, a manager for the Spanish-controlled Missouri Fur Company. Mackay also gave Lewis copies of maps for the lower and middle Missouri made by one of his employees, a Welshman named John Evans.

On 16 June 1804 Clark took a long walk through this "butifull extensive Prarie" to look for an old fort on Evans's map, built by the French thereabouts more than eighty years earlier. "I could See no traces of a Settlement of any kind," Clark concluded. Nevertheless, the party spent three days here making new oars, repairing ropes, and hunting.

Two years and three months later, on 16 September 1806, they drifted through this same scene in less than one day—a day "excessively worm and disagreeable, so much So that the men rowed but little," Clark wrote. Still, the navigator, presumably Pvt. Pierre Cruzatte, considered this stretch to be the worst place on the river.

Today the Missouri shows no trace of the treachery its shifting sands and unpredictable currents imposed on the expedition's fleet, and well-groomed farmlands flourish where Clark saw seas of rich tall grass. However, mosquitos and ticks remain relatively "noumerous & bad."

"Great River of the Kansas"

TODAY, THE KANSAS RIVER (at bottom)—also known as the Kaw—is closer to its probable 1804 location than the Missouri River, which at that time may have met it at nearly a right angle somewhere near the petroleum depot at upper center. In the photo, Kansas City, Kansas, is to the left and lower right of the two rivers; Kansas City, Missouri, founded in 1821, is at upper right.

The expedition's campsite from 26 to 28 June 1804 was near the wooded point that protrudes at the confluence. They knew that the Kansas River—named for the resident Indian tribe—was important, but they would not be able to explore it to the extent they would have liked. Its full length and character were still conjectural. "To Describe the most probable of the various accounts of this great river of the Kansas," wrote Clark, "would be too lengthy & uncertain to insert here."

Still, they decided to stay for several days to "recruit"—which to them meant *rest*—and at least get acquainted with this part of it. After building a defensive line of logs and brush against the possibility of an Indian attack during the night—one of the engagés had indicated the area natives could be unfriendly—they proceeded to the business of discovery, determining the latitude of the place, recording the contours of the floodplain and uplands, and measuring the rivers' widths, flows, temperatures, and silt content. Clark found only one fault: "The waters of the Kansas is verry disagreeably tasted to me."

The Corps noticed flocks of the diminutive Carolina parakeet in the neighborhood. Common at that time throughout the southeast, the only North American species of parrot has been extinct since about 1920, when hunting and the cutting down of their forest habitat brought about their demise.

(22) Confluence of the Kansas (bottom) and Missouri Rivers, Kansas City (view northeast, down the Kansas into the Missouri) →

Bad Medicine

WE DON'T KNOW HOW HIGH the temperature rose on 7 July, only that it started out, as Sergeant Floyd remarked, a "Clear morning verry warm." Indeed, before day's end Pvt. Robert Frazer might have become the expedition's first fatality, for he was "verry Sick, struck with the Sun."

We know nothing of Frazer's symptoms, but probably his affliction would be diagnosed today as either heat exhaustion or sunstroke, and the treatment would be to give fluids in the one case, or to cool his body in the other. Lewis did the best he knew, but what he did could have killed his patient.

With full faith in the theory propounded by Dr. Benjamin Rush, the leading physician of the era, that every illness was caused by irritation in the blood vessels, Lewis began by draining some blood from a vein, which only lowered Frazer's blood pressure and reduced his body fluids. Then he administered a dose of niter, which is a diuretic, and thus diminished his body fluids even more. In Clark's opinion, Lewis's treatment had "revived [Frazer] much," when in fact it must have been the man's youth and physical resilience that saved him.

Returning on 12 September 1806, the expedition camped at St. Michael's Prairie, opposite today's St. Joseph, Missouri. That day they met Robert McClellan, an old army acquaintance of Lewis and Clark, who was outbound with a keelboat full of Indian trade goods. He "gave our officers wine and the party as much whiskey as we all could drink," Sergeant Ordway reported.

←— (23) *St. Joseph, Missouri* (view southeast)

High Ground

THE CORPS CAMPED for the night of 11 July 1804 on "Newfound Island," opposite the mouth of the Big Nemaha ("miry water" in Oto) River, about six miles downstream from today's Rulo, Nebraska. The next morning the captains decided to take a day off from traveling, "to tak Some Observations and rest the men who are much fatigued."

After an early breakfast Clark and five of his men explored the Big Nemaha River about three miles up and climbed to the top of "a high artificial Noal"—an Indian burial site—to gain "an emence, extensive & pleasing prospect of the Countrey around." Clark noted, parenthetically, "The Indians of the Missouris Still Keep up the Custom of Burrying their dead on high ground." In the photo, contour plowing accentuates some of this "high ground" on the left side of the Missouri. On his way back to camp, Clark stopped at a rock. "I marked my name & day of the month near an Indian Mark or Image of animals & a boat," he noted. The rock has never been identified.

At one in the afternoon the captains convened a court-martial to try Pvt. Alexander Hamilton Willard, charged by the sergeant of the guard with falling asleep on sentry duty the previous night. They might well have recognized Willard's dereliction as a symptom of the men's general state of fatigue, but it was a crime punishable by death under the Rules and Articles of War and a potential threat to the safety and security of the whole party. They had to make an example of Willard, so they sentenced him to receive one hundred lashes on his bare back, twenty-five at a time, at sunset on four successive evenings.

(24) *Rulo, Nebraska* (view north, upstream) →

High Road Junction

THE CORPS OF DISCOVERY ARRIVED at the mouth of the Platte at ten in the morning on 21 July 1804, noting first of all that "the Current of This river Comes with great Velocity roleing its Sands into the Missouri, filling up its Bend" and "we found great dificuelty in passing around the Sand at the mouth." The problems they encountered have been wiped away by twentieth-century river engineering. It's possible that the Missouri River at this confluence was four to eight times wider and much shallower in 1804 than it is today.

They stopped just long enough for the two captains to take a short side trip a mile or two up the Platte and record some simple hydrological observations—depths, widths, current, the character of its bed—then they pushed on up the Missouri. During the winter at Fort Mandan, Lewis wrote a 250-word summary of what he learned about the Platte River, drawing most of his information from the best secondhand source available, "one of our Party who wintered two winters on this river."

The river named Platte—French for "flat"—drains nearly the entire state of Nebraska, whose name also means "flat," in the Omaha and Oto languages. The comparatively safe and easy terrain is one reason that, beginning in the 1820s, the high road to the Southwest, California, and Oregon was not Lewis and Clark's trail, but overland along the Great Platte River Road, which began in Omaha.

Nobody Home

ON THE EVENING OF 21 JULY 1804, the expedition made camp not far from the Platte River's mouth, then set out early the next day in search of a place "Calculated to make our party Comfortabl in a situation where they Could recive the benifit of a Shade." Ten miles upriver—about eight miles south (right) of this photo—they settled down for five days to rest and take celestial observations. More importantly, they expected to make contact with some Indian tribes at last and try out their diplomatic strategies.

On the twenty-third the captains sent George Drouillard and Pierre Cruzatte eighteen miles west to an Oto Indian village to invite the chiefs to come hear of the change of national allegiance from Spain to the United States and to learn "the wishes of our Government to Cultivate friendship with them." The emissaries returned on the twenty-fifth and reported that the Oto village was empty. It was hunting season, and the residents were following the buffalo herds.

On the twenty-seventh the boatmen worked their way upstream to a campsite in present-day Omaha (in the photo, left of the bridge). Clark and Drouillard walked on shore all day, "with a view of examoning Som mounds on the L. S. of the river," which were the remains of a long-abandoned earth-lodge Oto village.

Eastbound on 8 September 1806, the men "ply'd their orers very well" as they passed here, covering seventy-eight miles that day by Clark's estimate. "The Missouri at this place does not appear to Contain more water than it did 1000 miles above," Clark observed, surmising that "the evaperation must be emence."

64

"Dreadful Haricane"

IT WAS ANOTHER BAD DAY for Pvt. Alexander Willard. About noon on 29 July 1804 he realized he'd left his tomahawk at the previous night's camp. He had to walk more than three miles, alone, over land he had seen only from the river, to retrieve the tomahawk, then walk back to rejoin the company. On his way back, hurrying across the Boyer River on a log, Willard dropped his rifle, which sank deep into the mud. Unable to recover the vital item himself, he had to catch up with the party to get help. The captains sent a few men back with him in a boat, and Reubin Field dived in to get Willard's rifle.

That same day, Clark reported "much fallen timber, apparently the ravages of a dreadful haricane which had passed obliquely across the river from N. W. to S. E. about twelve months since. Many trees were broken off near the ground the trunks of which were sound and four feet in diameter." In today's terms, it was a tornado, not a hurricane, that caused the damage, but in those days the two words were practically synonymous. In a remarkable coincidence, just two days before this photo was taken a tornado crossed the Lewis and Clark route near here, felling trees and killing two women.

(27) *Tornado damage near Logan, Iowa* →

Froth of Feathers

TODAY, SLICING CLEANLY BETWEEN Iowa (left of river) and Nebraska (right), the Missouri River is kept tidily groomed for river commerce. But when the expedition passed this way on 8 August 1804—and again on 6 September 1806—the river was broad and brawny. Sometimes it held driftwood big enough to damage hulls, and sometimes it formed sandbars that impeded forward momentum and put boats and boatmen at the current's mercy.

A highlight of 8 August was a profusion of feathers floating like froth on the water. The feathers went on for three miles "in such quantities as to cover pretty generally sixty or seventy yards of the breadth of the river." Finally, wrote Lewis, they came upon a flock of pelicans on a sandbar, "the number of which would if estimated appear almost in credible; they appeared to cover several acres of ground." As the birds took flight at his approach, Lewis brought one down with his gun. He described the specimen meticulously, adding information from one of the reference books he carried: "They are a bird of clime [They] remain on the coast of Floriday and the borders of the Gulph of mexico & even the lower portion of the Mississippi during the winter and in the Spring . . . [They] visit this country and that farther north for the purpose of raising their young."

Ever alert to the soundscapes around him, Lewis noted in a postscript to his bird tale that "the green insect known in the U' States by the name of the *sawyer* or *chittediddle* [a.k.a. katydid] was first heard to cry on the 27th of July."

69

Meander

THIS OXBOW WAS ONCE PART of the main channel of the Missouri, but by 1804 the river had already cut it off, turning it into a lake "6 leagues [eighteen miles] around." On 9 August 1804 the Corps probably camped on the river, just visible on the far upper right side of the picture. Ordway remarked that the "Grapes are verry pleanty," and Clark observed a "great deel of Beaver Sign." On the downside, the captain recorded, "Musquetors worse this evening than ever I have Seen them."

Today, the former riverbend is known as Blue Lake—named not for the color of the water but for nearby bluffs of blue-gray shale. Blue Lake is the centerpiece of Lewis and Clark State Park, where replicas of the keelboat and pirogues today sail without threat of collapsing banks, rolling sandbars, or treacherous snags.

Homeward bound, the Corps camped near the end of the oxbow's left leg on 5 September 1806. Captain Lewis was "still in a Convelesent State," recovering from the wound Pierre Cruzatte inflicted in a hunting accident on 11 August, when he mistook the buckskin-clad Lewis for an elk and shot him in the buttocks.

(29) *Blue Lake, near Onawa, Iowa* (view south)

"Much Lamented"

ON SATURDAY, 18 AUGUST 1804, Sgt. Charles Floyd wrote his ninety-seventh and last consecutive daily journal entry: "our men Returnd and Brot with them the man and Brot with
them the *Grand Chief* of the *ottoes* and 2 Loer ones and 6 youers [warriors?] of thare
nathion." The man referred to was deserter Pvt. Moses Reed, who had deserted on 4
August and this afternoon was tried and convicted despite the three Oto chiefs' pleas for
leniency. Reed was sentenced to run the gauntlet four times, then dishonorably discharged.

It was Meriwether Lewis's thirtieth birthday, so "the evening was Closed with an extra
Gill of Whiskey & a Dance untill 11 oClock." The next morning, twenty-two-year-old
Charles Floyd "was taken violently bad with the Beliose Cholick and is dangerously ill—
we attempt in Vain to releive him, I am much concerned for his Situation . . . nature
appear exosting fast in him."

On the twentieth the Corps proceeded thirteen miles, while young Floyd quickly grew
worse. A little past noon they landed, and presently Floyd said, "I am going away." He
died, perhaps of perotinitis from a ruptured appendix, "with a great deel of Composure."
His comrades buried him atop a nearby bluff overlooking the Missouri River, "with the
Honors of War, much lamented." Clark continued, "After paying all the honor to our
Decesed brother, we Camped in the mouth of *floyds* river . . . a butifull evening."

The hundred-foot-tall sandstone obelisk in the photo was dedicated to Sergeant Floyd's
memory on Memorial Day 1901.

Names

CAMPED A FEW MILES UPSTREAM from today's Sioux City on 21 August 1804, Clark received a cryptic dream-name in the night—"Roloje." The next day he applied it to a nearby stream, which is now known by its Omaha Indian name, Aowa.

The next day, as the Corps camped somewhere near the center of this photo, the captains allowed the enlisted men to express their preferences about who should replace the late Charles Floyd as sergeant, and on 26 August the commanding officers "thought it proper to appoint Patric Gass a Sergeant in *the corps of volunteers for North Western Discovery.*" This was the earliest written use of that name for the expedition, shortened to Corps of Discovery in Gass's journal, published in 1807.

Here, in the vicinity of Elk Point, South Dakota (upper right), the captains found a variety of unfamiliar minerals, including what Clark believed were arsenic and cobalt. "Capt. Lewis in proveing the quality of those minerals was near poisoning himself by the fumes & taste" of the cobalt, Clark wrote, and took "a dose of salts to carry off the effects." Two days later Lewis was still sick, not from the poison but from the medication.

Lewis had merely been poking around in a cliff of soft white limestone. The "cobalt" was just silky, lustrous selenite gypsum, and the other rocks he found were secondary minerals from interactions between calcareous chalk and iron pyrite—"fool's gold." They may not have pleased Lewis's nose or palate, but they weren't poisonous.

In the photo, the scallops in the riverbank were created by wingdams, built to settle silt and help keep the river from changing course.

(31) *Missouri River near Elk Point, South Dakota* (view northwest, upstream) ➔

"Unusial Spirits"

ON 25 AUGUST 1804, obedient to Jefferson's direction to observe the Indians' traditions and monuments, Lewis and Clark went inland to visit a "conic form" rising from the plain. Local Sioux, Omaha, and Oto Indians related its fascinating legend with enough passion and color to beguile the explorers into going there, despite the oppressive late August heat, and gave them enough detail to lead them precisely nine miles north and twenty degrees west from the mouth of the Vermillion River. The storytellers called it the Mountain of *little people* or Spirits," knee-high, big-headed demons who repelled mortals with "murceyless fury."

Unmolested by the "unusial Spirits," the party climbed to the top of the hill, from which they saw herds of buffalo grazing among distant hills. They made note of the cloud of insects in the mound's lee and the swallows that feasted on them. Clark described the shape and dimensions of the mound, as well as the character of the surrounding landscape, in considerable detail.

Over the past two centuries, the surface of Spirit Mound has changed from shortgrass prairie to farmland and feedlot, then back to expedition-era grassland, thanks to the pride and energy of local residents. Since this photo was taken in 2001, the farmhouse and sheltering trees on the right have been removed and the furrowed ground now blooms each May with prairie grasses and wildflowers.

Peace Parley

THE CORPS MOVED eight and a half miles through this stretch of the Missouri on 27 August 1804. They went ashore on the south side of the river below Calumet Bluff—just above the river's bend, near the left edge of the photo. Here they "formed a camp in a Butifull Plain," erected a flagpole, and settled in to wait for the Sioux, whom they had invited to meet with them. On the thirtieth, seventy-five Sioux men of the Yankton tribe, or *E-hank-ton-wan*, "People of the End Village," ceremoniously entered the expedition's camp, eager to parley. They had managed to get along with the British and the Spanish and were ready to play ball with the Americans.

Lewis delivered a long speech, translated by his recently hired interpreter and peace envoy, Pierre Dorion, Sr., then distributed peace medals and sundry gifts. That night there was a war dance by firelight, with boastful harangues from some of the leading warriors. Early the next morning, the Yankton chiefs promised they'd make peace with the Otos and Missouris. Easily said.

The captains thought it went pretty well. On 1 September they set sail "under a gentle Breeze from the South" toward another band of the Sioux Nation, the Teton. In less than a month, their romance with diplomatic success would turn sour.

There was no settlement here at the time, but by 1860 Yankton would be on the western edge of white settlement on the Great Plains, and would be named capital of the huge Dakota Territory a year later. On this part of the Missouri today, the river is essentially a chain of dam-created reservoirs. The one farthest downstream, visible just below the horizon, is Lewis and Clark Lake, the impoundment of the Gavins Point Dam at Yankton.

Knotty Problem

THIS LABYRINTH IS MADE of sandy silt deposited as the Missouri's current slows upon entering Lewis and Clark Lake near Springfield, South Dakota. Gavins Point Dam created the twenty-five-mile-long, forty-five-foot-deep reservoir in 1957. Such dams have squeezed, shaped, and disciplined the Missouri for so long that it is hard to say how much of it may have been this complex before.

The task of piloting the expedition's boats smoothly through such morasses was the principal responsibility of Pierre Cruzatte, a French Canadian and Omaha Indian mixed-blood who, as a riverman, had the respect and confidence of every member of the party. The many-talented Cruzatte was also admired as an interpreter, a cache digger, and a fiddler.

On 2 September, the men came upon the remains of an "antient fortification" of elaborate form and impressive dimensions, which Clark mapped and described in precise detail. Cruzatte informed him "that a great number of those antint works . . . are in Different parts of this Countrey." But it was all a misconception. The supposed bastions were merely old sandbars left high and dry by the errant river.

The Corps camped that night somewhere near the area shown in the bottom of this picture. Now two days after the captains concluded their council with the Yankton Sioux, the men were still "all in high spirits" despite blustery weather that slowed their progress. But the good mood was tempered by concern about Pvt. George Shannon, who was seven days overdue from a hunting trip. He had hurried ahead, thinking he was behind his comrades. The nineteen-year-old Shannon, the youngest member of the Corps, would rejoin them at last on 11 September, after surviving for twelve days on wild grapes and one rabbit.

(34) *Sandbars near Springfield, South Dakota* (view west, upstream) →

Rushing River

THE EXPEDITION SET OUT from camp on the morning of 4 September 1804 in a "verry Cold" southeast wind, which soon "Shifted to the South," according to Sergeant Ordway, "& blew verry hard we hoisted Sail ran verry fast a Short time. Broke our mast." That was the fourth such mishap since the Corps left Camp Dubois on 14 May. The men later made a new mast of tall, sturdy red cedar, which apparently served them at least until they reached Fort Mandan.

After the mast broke, the Corps "came to"—landed—on the arrow-shaped point (foreground) on the west side of this river, which French travelers had named L'Eau qui Court, or "River that Rushes," but which Indians called Niobrara—"Wide River." Clark described it as "152 yards wide at the mouth & 4 feet Deep Throwing out Sands like the Platt (only Corser) forming bars in its mouth." It was, he later wrote, "not navigable a single mile." He himself explored the river three miles "to a butifull Plain on the upper Side" where the Ponca Indians once had a large village.

The Niobrara apparently hasn't changed its course much here, but the Missouri may have meandered nearly a mile to the south sometime within the past two hundred years, leaving a deposit of rich bottomland in the present state of South Dakota.

The point on which Lewis and Clark camped is now a state park. Near the opposite point, just beyond the photo at lower right, is the village of Niobrara, Nebraska, headquarters of the small Santee Sioux Indian Reservation, shared by the Santee Sioux and the Poncas.

(35) *Niobrara River at its confluence with the Missouri, near Niobrara, Nebraska* (view north, down the Niobrara, up the Missouri) →

Wolf Tricks

THE CORPS' CAMP ON THE NIGHT of 7 September 1804 was perhaps near the river's bend at the horizon in the photograph. On the eighth they sailed before a "gentle Breese" past an abandoned trading post built nine years earlier by Jean Baptiste Truteau, a French Canadian trader. Truteau's house stood on the plain at left, below the Fort Randall Dam (left center). Completed in 1956, the dam transformed the next 108 miles of the river into a reservoir called Lake Francis Case.

Sergeant Gass reported a curious incident from that morning: "At 9 I went out with one of our men, who had killed a buffaloe and left his hat to keep off the vermin and beasts of prey," apparently thinking the scent of humans would keep them away. "But when we came to the place, we found the wolves had devoured the carcase and carried off the hat. Here we found a white wolf, supposed to have been killed in a contest for the buffaloe."

The wind favored the expedition's progress the whole day, and they logged an exceptional seventeen miles before camping.

◄— (36) *Fort Randall Dam on the Missouri, near Pickstown, South Dakota* (view southeast, downstream)

Around the Bend

THE HUGE RIVERINE OXBOW called Big Bend, or Grand Detour, was already a well-known Missouri River landmark when the Corps of Discovery reached it on 20 September 1805. They paced off the distance across "the gouge," wrote Clark, and found it to be about a mile and a quarter; he estimated the distance around the oxbow to be thirty miles. This part of the Missouri is now Lake Sharpe, the reservoir created by Big Bend Dam at Fort Thompson, a few miles below the bend.

The light-colored circles on the peninsula are newly planted fields, plowed in circles around center-pivot irrigation systems. The darker circles are fallow fields. The land is part of the Lower Brule Indian Reservation, home of the 1,095 members of the Sicangu, or Lower Brule Sioux tribe, whose ancestors Lewis and Clark had encountered downriver from here in August 1804. On the left side of the river is the Crow Creek Sioux Reservation, home to about one-third of the 3,521 enrolled Wiciyela (Nakota) Sioux.

The river was shallow here and the sandbars very thick. About 1:30 A.M. on 21 September, awakened by a strange sound, the men of the Corps discovered that the bar they were camped on was washing out from under them. Within minutes, they fled to the boats and moved to safety at the river's edge, watching the bank where their keelboat and pirogues had been moored dissolve into the inky water.

Standoff

AT FORT PIERRE, the main meeting and market center for area tribes, Lewis and Clark first met the Teton Sioux on 25 September 1804. One of Jefferson's primary political objectives for the expedition was to create a peace treaty and trade agreement with the Tetons, the most potent military and economic force on the lower Missouri. Now face-to-face with them, the captains practiced their diplomacy clumsily and at arms' length, exchanging both pleasantries and warnings while shoring up their self-confidence with military posturing. Drawing on a considerable ration of luck, they got through the tense meeting without violence.

Later, while waiting out the winter of 1805-6 at Fort Clatsop, Lewis and Clark conceived a plan to seek the aid of Hugh Heney, a Canadian trader they had met at Fort Mandan, in persuading some Teton Sioux to accompany them back to Washington. But that scheme fell apart too, and on 30 August 1806, a few miles downriver from here, they paddled past the watchdogs of the middle Missouri, exchanging from a safe distance a volley of insults and rude gestures.

As American technology and western commerce accelerated, the city of Pierre (at left) successively became a post on the main route of the Western fur trade, a port of call in the steamboat era, a railroad bridgehead, and the capital of the growing union's fortieth state.

(38) *Missouri River* (Lake Sharpe) *at Pierre, South Dakota* (view east, downstream) →

Change of Heart

ON THE EVENING OF 25 September 1804, after the determination of the Teton Sioux to turn the expedition back had collided with the captains' awkward diplomacy and firm resolve to move on, nearly igniting warfare, the Corps camped on a nearby island Clark called "bad humered Island as we were in a bad humer." The next morning, the Indians had a change of heart, and the captains consented at "the particular request of the Chiefs to let their Womin & Boys See the Boat, and Suffer them to Show us some friendship."

Nicholas Biddle condensed Clark's extensive notes on the evening's festivities: "Captains Lewis and Clark, who went on shore one after the other, were met on landing by ten well dressed young men, who took them up in a robe highly decorated and carried them to a large council house, where they were placed on a dressed buffalo skin by the side of the grand chief. . . . Under this shelter sat about seventy men, forming a circle round the chief, before whom were placed a Spanish flag and the one we had given them yesterday."

The peace pipe was passed, and speeches were "harangued." Then the men gorged themselves on buffalo meat and tasty treats such as "the most delicate parts of the dog, which was cooked for the festival." At dusk, dancing commenced and continued into the night. The Corps stayed at the Tetons' village another day, then continued on their way on the twenty-eighth.

Today, one-third of the Missouri River is confined to reservoirs. Here at the Oahe Dam, six miles north of Pierre, Lake Sharpe ends and Lake Oahe begins. Lake Oahe, 231 miles long, is one of the largest manmade lakes in the United States.

Hunting Party

ON 15 OCTOBER 1804 Lewis and Clark and their party camped somewhere near the island seen at upper right. For the past two weeks they had been in the homeland of the Arikara, or Sahnish, people, who lived in earth lodges and raised corn, beans, pumpkins, watermelons, squashes, and mild Indian tobacco. To these friendly people, Sergeant Ordway reported, "the Greatest Curiosity . . . was York," Clark's black slave. "The children would follow after him, & if he turned towards them they would run from him & hollow as if they were terreyfied, & afraid of him."

Proceeding upriver the following day, the Corps observed an Indian strategy for hunting game. As men on horseback herded pronghorns—"goats or Antelope," Clark called them—into the river, boys swam among them and killed some with sticks, while others on shore shot them with bows and arrows. "I saw 58 Killed in this way," wrote Clark.

By 1845 the ravages of disease and ongoing warfare with the Sioux forced the Arikaras to move up the Missouri and settle among the Mandans and Hidatsas in North Dakota. In 1868 the Great Sioux Nation took over this land under the terms of the Fort Laramie Treaty. However the boundaries of their once vast domain were steadily reduced over the subsequent forty years until only today's isolated and impoverished Standing Rock Reservation was left. Its headquarters are here at Fort Yates, North Dakota, on an island in Lake Oahe. Today, four bands of Sioux subsist marginally on the 562,000-acre reservation: Sihasapa, Hunkpapa, Lower Yanktonai, and Upper Yanktonai.

Main Attraction

THE CORPS OF DISCOVERY arrived in the vicinity of this picture on 20 October 1804, having worked their way some 1,450 miles up the Missouri in 155 days. They camped on the west side of the river, probably several miles downstream, to the right of this view.

That day, wildlife was the main attraction. The men had recently seen signs of the dreaded grizzly, or "White bear," and now Clark saw "Several fresh track of those animals which is 3 times as large as a mans track." He also saw "great numbers of buffalow Swimming the river."

Lewis's short entry for the day recounted two misadventures between Pierre Cruzatte and the local fauna. After he wounded a bear, its "formidable appearance" prompted him to drop his tomahawk and gun and run for it. When he returned to retrieve his weapons, he saw evidence that the bear had run in the opposite direction. Later, Cruzatte took a shot at a buffalo cow, breaking one of her legs. She ran threateningly in his direction, and he ducked for cover in a small ravine.

Returning on 18 August 1806, after bucking headwinds and high waves all day, the Corps camped for the night on the far side of the river, across from today's Bismarck, North Dakota. Now accompanying them was the Mandan chief Sheheke and his family, who had joined the homeward-bound expedition during its stop at their village. The chief had agreed to go with the captains to meet President Jefferson. In Washington, Sheheke indeed met Jefferson and was lavishly feted. He was to return home in 1807, but interference from the Sioux and Arikara delayed him two more years.

(41) *Bismarck and Mandan, North Dakota* (view northeast, flow left to right) →

Marketplace

REACHING THE MOUTH of the Knife River, a little over sixteen hundred miles from the mouth of the Mississippi, the expedition arrived in the midst of a major agricultural center and marketplace for a huge midcontinental region. The five permanent earth-lodge communities there offered a panorama of contemporary Indian life.

Two of the villages were occupied by Mandan families that included about 700 adult males. Two others were Hidatsa, or Minitaree, communities with a total of 650 adult males. The fifth was a small village of Amahamis, refugees from regional war and pestilence. The combined populations totaled about 4,400 persons, according to the American travelers' estimates.

The small bumps in the field on the near-right side of the photograph are the remains of earth lodges in the Hidatsa village the captains knew as Metaharta. The Knife River turns south for about a mile before joining the Missouri a little beyond Stanton, North Dakota (upper left), which grew over the site of the Amahami community.

Today, most of the descendants of the Indians Lewis and Clark met here, plus the few surviving Arikara people, live on the Fort Berthold Reservation; its headquarters are in New Town, North Dakota. Ironically, the Knife River Indian Villages National Historic Site is not on the reservation.

◄— (42) *Knife River Village site, near Stanton, North Dakota* (view southwest)

Part III

Mastering the Unknown Missouri

FORT MANDAN to LOST TRAIL PASS

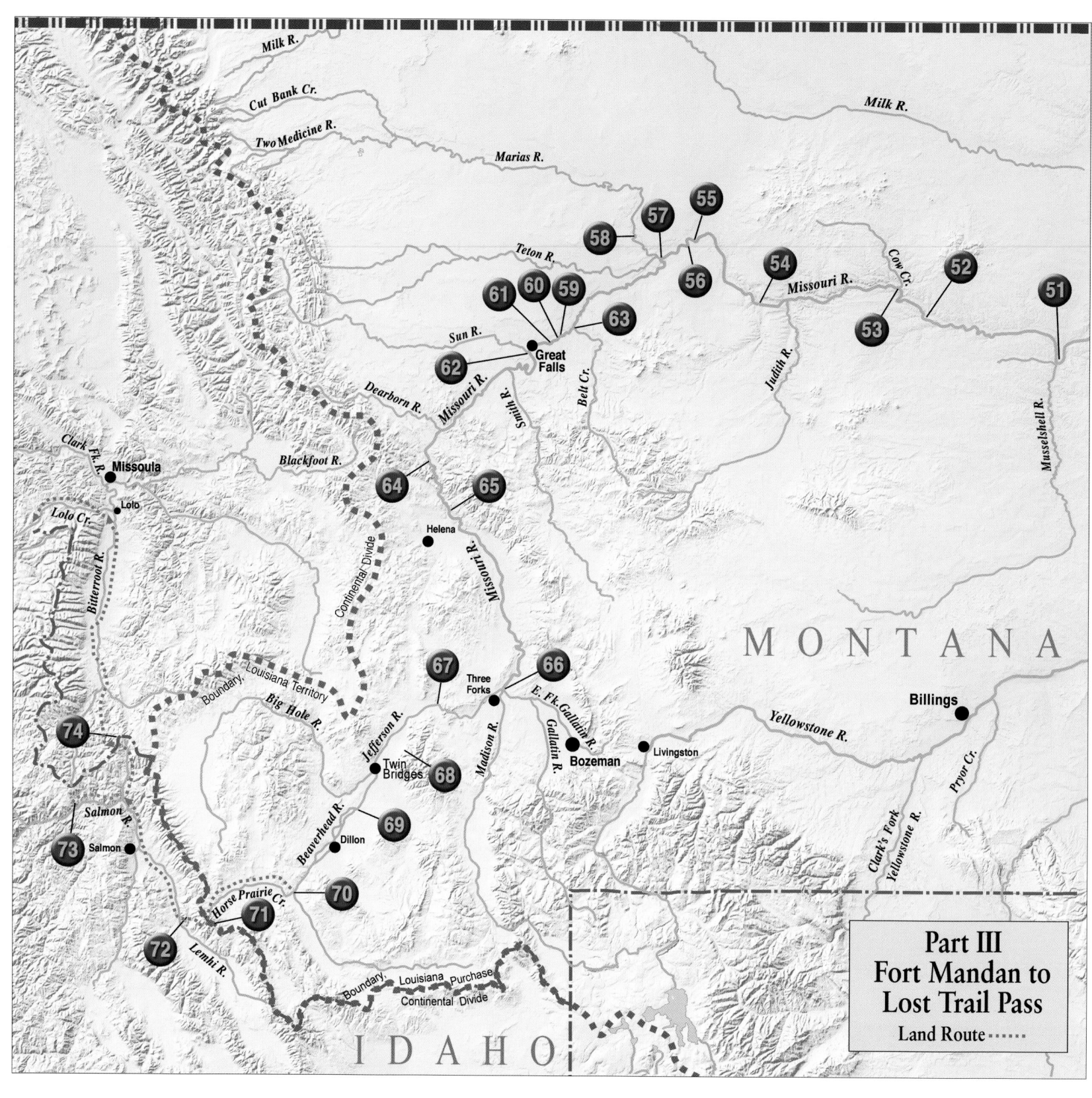

Milk R.

Cut Bank Cr.

Two Medicine R.

Marias R.

Milk R.

Teton R.

Cow Cr.

55

57

58

59

60

61

56

54

52

53

51

Missouri R.

Judith R.

Sun R.

62

63

Great Falls

Belt Cr.

Smith R.

Dearborn R.

Missouri R.

Musselshell R.

Blackfoot R.

Clark Fk. R.

Missoula

Lolo

Lolo Cr.

Bitterroot R.

Continental Divide

64

65

Helena

Missouri R.

M O N T A N A

67

Three Forks

66

Billings

Boundary, Louisiana Territory

Big Hole R.

Jefferson R.

E. Fk. Gallatin R.

Madison R.

Gallatin R.

Yellowstone R.

Livingston

74

Twin Bridges

68

Bozeman

Salmon R.

Beaverhead R.

69

Dillon

73

Salmon

Clark's Fork Yellowstone R.

Pryor Cr.

Horse Prairie Cr.

70

71

72

Lemhi R.

Boundary, Louisiana Purchase
Continental Divide

I D A H O

Part III
Fort Mandan to
Lost Trail Pass

Land Route ······

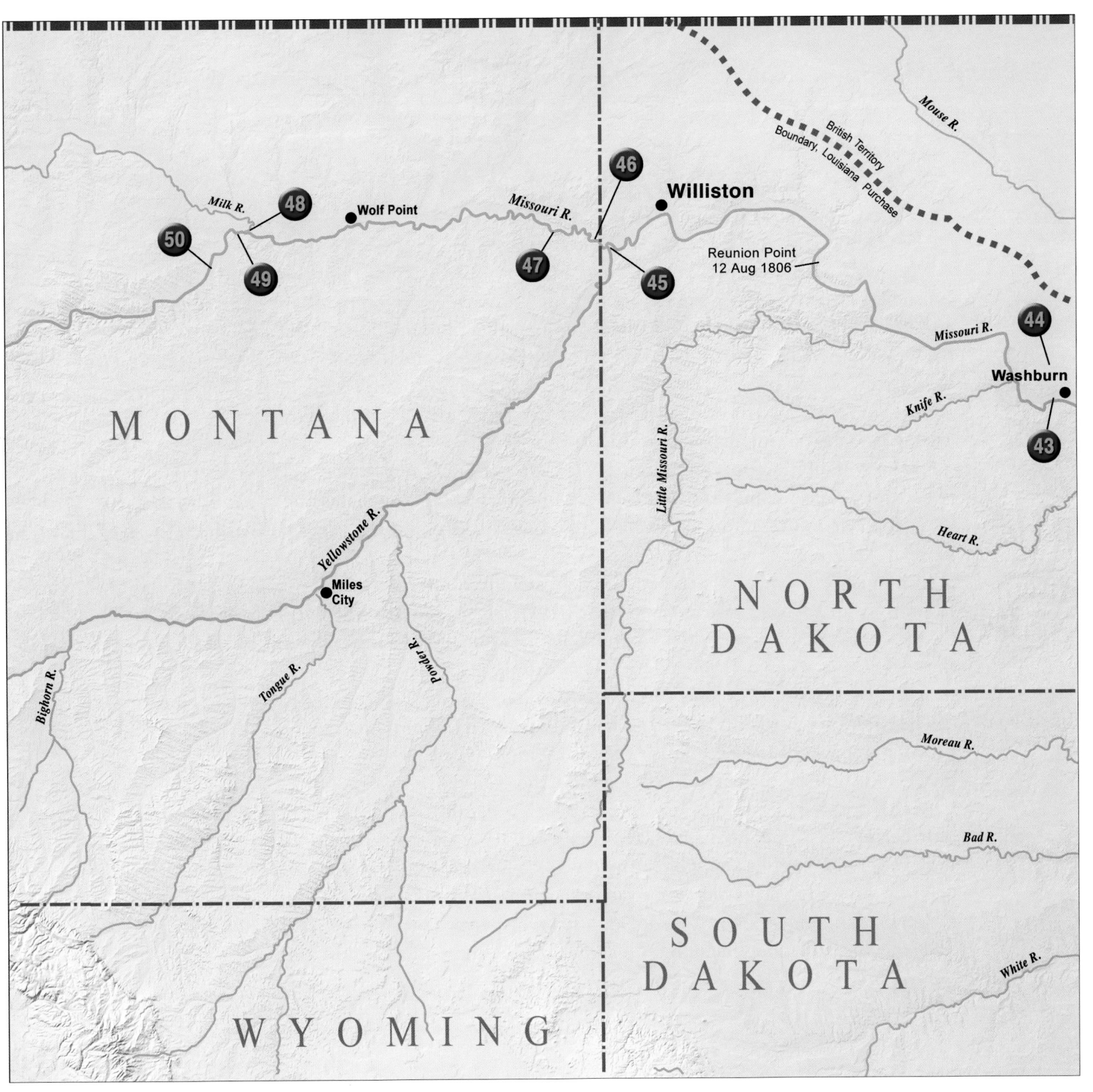

Mouse R.

British Territory
Boundary, Louisiana Purchase

Milk R.

Williston

Missouri R.

Wolf Point

Reunion Point
12 Aug 1806

Missouri R.

Washburn

Knife R.

M O N T A N A

Yellowstone R.

Little Missouri R.

Heart R.

Miles
City

N O R T H
D A K O T A

Tongue R.

Powder R.

Bighorn R.

Moreau R.

Bad R.

S O U T H
D A K O T A

W Y O M I N G

White R.

"Most Perfect Harmony"

AT FORT MANDAN, the most carefully and sturdily constructed of their three winter encampments, the captains prepared reports for President Jefferson on all they had observed and done so far and arranged botanical, biological, and mineralogical specimens for shipment back East. They quizzed their neighbors, the Mandans, about the land that lay westward and visited with traders from Fort Assiniboine, 150 miles north, to ask them as well. They drew the first draft of the new map of the Northwest that ultimately would be one of the most useful outcomes of their expedition.

In short, it all came together at Fort Mandan, even the travel schedule. "You may . . . expect me to meet you at Montachello in September 1806," Lewis wrote to Jefferson in a letter that accompanied the specimens and papers he sent in the spring of 1805. He almost made it.

In January the expedition gained two new members, interpreter and boatman Toussaint Charbonneau and one of his two wives, the teenage Shoshone Sacagawea (also spelled Sakakawea and Sacajawea). On February 11 she added another, her infant boy, Jean Baptiste. Lewis ultimately judged Charbonneau to be "a man of no particular merit," though he had, overall, a long and productive career in the West.

The Mandans were "the most friendly, well disposed Indians inhabiting the Missouri. . . . brave, humane and hospitable," in Clark's opinion. Over the winter, the captains talked peace and commerce, American style, to all who would listen.

Rested and refreshed, the Corps, having been tested by the rigors of a winter on the Northern Plains, embarked again on 7 April 1805, "to penetrate a country at least two thousand miles in width on which the foot of civilized man had never trodden." Lewis proudly attested that his men were "in excellent health and sperits, zealously attached to the enterprise, and anxious to proceed; not a whisper of murmur [grumbling] or discontent to be heard among them, but all act in unison, and with the most perfect harmony."

102

Brilliant Blaze

BY THE END OF the eighteenth century, forests on the Atlantic seaboard, where most Americans lived, were rapidly being used up. However, in places where coal could be picked out of embankments or shallow caves, people came to prefer it for domestic fuel and light, "the blaze being so brilliant" as one traveler remarked, "as to supersede the use of candles, even for sewing."

Obedient to President Jefferson's orders, the captains noted the presence of "pitcoal," or "carbonated wood," whenever they saw it—or fancied they saw it, since neither explorer was well educated in the new science of mineralogy. Just two days after leaving Fort Mandan in April 1805, the explorers began noticing coal in the Missouri's banks, and later Clark found lots of it on his trip down the Yellowstone River, starting a little below Pompeys Pillar. They had no reason to suspect they were looking at cross sections of one of the largest low-sulfur lignite coal beds in the world. Geologists began mapping the bed in the late 1850s, naming it the Fort Union Formation. They found that it covered a massive area in parts of Montana, Wyoming, North Dakota, South Dakota, and Saskatchewan.

Lewis and Clark could never have imagined a coal pit like the one in this photograph. Opened in 1997, the pit is about twelve miles east of the Missouri River and sixty miles north of Bismarck, North Dakota. In the background is a postglacial tarn called Coal Lake.

←— (44) *Strip mine near Falkirk, North Dakota* (view northeast)

"Long Wished for Spot"

STRONG NORTHWEST WINDS had slowed the expedition's progress for several days. Late in the morning of 25 April 1805, Lewis decided to proceed overland to the mouth of the Yellowstone River, which he had learned from the Indians was "at no very great distance." Within a few hours, with time out for a lunch of buffalo calf, the Missouri's greatest tributary came in sight. "I ascended the hills," Lewis wrote, "from whence I had a most pleasing view of the country, particularly of the wide and fertile vallies formed by the Missouri and the Yellowstone rivers."

That night Lewis's party camped a short distance up the Yellowstone. We could guess from Lewis's description that the site was near the third island from the bottom in this photo, but the meeting place of the two rivers has changed so much over the past two centuries that it is impossible to pinpoint the location. The orderly rows of trees on the near shore and on the point between the rivers record the successive high-water marks of recent decades.

The Crow people still call the river *Meé,-ah'-zah*, Elk River, but sometime late in the eighteenth century it acquired the French name, Roche Jaune, or Yellowstone. Here, flowing northward, it runs almost parallel with the North Dakota–Montana border, completing its unimpeded six-hundred-mile flow from the mountains south of Yellowstone National Park.

The next day, 26 August 1805, the Corps reunited on the point of land between the two rivers, "all in good health, and much pleased at having arrived at this long wished for spot." The captains issued "a dram"—four ounces of whiskey—to each person, which generated song, dance, and general hilarity, and the men "seemed as perfectly to forget their past toils, as they appeared regardless of those to come."

Upper Missouri Developers

ON 26 APRIL 1805 strong winds and blowing sand again impeded the main party, but they still managed to cover eight miles before dark. Meanwhile, Lewis and a small party, traveling half a day ahead of the others, explored the Missouri River on foot, looking for a suitable trading-post site. The north side opposite the mouth of the Yellowstone was, Lewis observed, twelve to eighteen feet above water level, less likely to be flooded by these "capricious and versatile" rivers, "except in extreme high water, which dose not appear to be very frequent." And that is where, in 1828, John Jacob Astor's American Fur Company—one of the first corporate monopolies in American business history—built Fort Union, which remained the axis of Indian-American commerce on the Upper Missouri until the late 1860s.

Manpowered boats somewhat like the ones the Corps of Discovery used continued to inch up the Missouri for decades, until the first steamboat, the *Yellow Stone*, reached Fort Union in 1832. By the 1840s, travel time from St. Louis to Fort Union had shrunk to a breathtaking forty-eight days, seven hours. The keelboat era became but a memory—no doubt a painful one for all the men who had waded up the mighty, muddy river, dragging tons of dead weight against the current.

This photograph shows the National Park Service's reconstruction of Fort Union. The parking lot would scarcely have been adequate for the crowds of Mandans, Hidatsas, Assiniboines, Blackfeet, Crows, and others who camped near its riverfront gate or grazed their ponies on the vast prairie to the north.

(46) *Fort Union reconstruction, near Buford, North Dakota* (view north) →

Abundance

AT THE CENTER OF THIS PICTURE, a gravel road circles a well, whose pump-jack bobs for petroleum as far as seven thousand feet down. The green fields surrounding the well are of safflower, a European import whose seeds are processed at a mill in nearby Culbertson, Montana.

Somewhere in this vicinity, on 5 May 1805, Lewis shot his first grizzly bear and promptly began his detailed study of the fascinating species. Confident of the skill and firepower of his hunters, he declared that the bears "are by no means as formidable or dangerous as they have been represented." On 6 May he reported, "I find that the curiossity of our party is pretty well satisfied with rispect to this anamal," but within a few days, his tone had changed towards *Ursus horribilis*. On the eleventh he wrote: "I must confess that I do not like the gentlemen and had reather fight two Indians than one bear."

Other game was astonishingly abundant, too. The expedition had entered a game sink, a huge zone where Indians hunted but did not stay. As Lewis recorded, "We can scarcely cast our eyes in any direction without perceiving deer Elk Buffaloe or Antelopes," as well as beaver and bighorn sheep. Wolves, in packs of six to ten, intrigued Lewis with their collective strategy for killing antelope. "They appear to decoy a single one from a flock," he observed, "and then pursue it, alternately relieving each other until they take it." His Newfoundland dog used a different tactic, catching an antelope calf in the river, drowning it, and dragging it ashore.

Milky Blend

"WE NOONED IT," wrote Lewis on 8 May 1805, "just above the entrance of a large river which disembogues on the Lard. Side"—he meant the starboard side. He "took the advantage of this leasure moment and examined the river about 3 miles." The water of this river, he observed, "possesses a peculiar whiteness, being about the colour of a cup of tea with the admixture of a tablespoonful of milk." Thus, he concluded, "from the colour of it's water we called it Milk river." He wondered whether this might be the river the Hidatsas had called "the river which scoalds at all others." The meaning of the Hidatsas' name for it was less obvious than the one Lewis gave it.

They couldn't be certain, but Clark thought he saw smoke and Indian tepees in the distance, up the Milk. "We do not wish to see those gentlemen just now," said Lewis, "as we presume they would most probably be the Assinniboins and might be troublesome to us." The trouble never materialized.

The captains speculated that, judging from its size at the mouth, the Milk might begin far enough to the north to parallel the Saskatchewan River. If so, it might intersect with the line that had been agreed upon in the treaty following the American Revolutionary War, at 49°37' north latitude, which would add a considerable amount of land to the Louisiana Purchase of 1803. He never had the time to find out.

← (48) *Confluence of the Milk and Missouri Rivers, near Fort Peck, Montana* (view northeast, downstream)

Varied Landscape

AT THE UPPER RIGHT of this photograph, the Milk River snakes through the floodplain to join the Missouri, perhaps two miles upstream from the 1805 confluence. "The countrey on the North Side of the Missouri is one of the handsomest plains we have yet Seen on the river," Clark declared. Lewis described the ragged badlands on the south side as "high broken hills, with much broken, grey black and brown granite scattered on the surface of the earth in a confused manner."

The spillway was built in 1940 to accommodate surplus water from Fort Peck Dam, three miles west on the Missouri. Up to 250,000 cubic feet of water per second can be eased down its tapered, mile-long concrete chute. Fort Peck Lake, the reservoir behind the dam and spillway, stretches 134 miles upstream. The Corps of Discovery spent fourteen days battling the river's swift current to cover that distance. The typically strong, gusty winds that scour the High Plains often slowed their progress, too. On the evening of 21 May, for instance, Lewis wrote, "we found ourselves so invelloped with clouds of dust and sand that we could neither cook, eat, nor sleep." They abandoned their camp on the sandbar they called "windy Island" and dashed for shelter in the lee of a nearby coulee.

Every delay, every frustration elevated the party's stress level. "I begin to feel extreemly anxious to get in view of the rocky mountains," Lewis confessed.

Close Calls

THE FOURTEENTH OF MAY, 1805, was a day of close calls. That evening, six men—"all good hunters"—took on a large grizzly. Employing a tested battle strategy, four concealed gunners hit it almost simultaneously from forty paces. As "this monster ran at them with open mouth, the two who had reserved their fires discharged their pieces at him," one shot breaking the bear's shoulder. This, however, "retarded his motion for a moment only." With no time to reload their weapons, the hunters flung them aside and leaped over a twenty-foot bank into the river. "So enraged was this anamal that he plunged into the river only a few feet behind the second man . . . when one of those who still remained on shore shot him through the head and finally killed him."

When the chastened hunters caught up with the rest of the party after sunset, they found their comrades shaken from their own hairbreadth escape. For the second time in a month, a combination of violent wind, vulnerable sail, and helmsman Toussaint Charbonneau—perhaps trying this time not to be "the most timid waterman in the world"—had nearly sunk the white pirogue and "almost every article indispensibly necessary to . . . insure the success of the enterprize," while the captains, three hundred yards away on the far shore, looked on helplessly. Fortunately, as Lewis reported, "the articles which floated out was nearly all caught" by Sacagawea.

The Missouri River the Corps saw that May averaged perhaps a quarter of a mile in width, and its banks were more or less parallel. But the fractal geometry of today's Fort Peck Lake shoreline, officially 1,520 miles in extent, defies meaningful measurement. The river was dangerous enough in 1805; this lake can be much rougher sailing.

(50) *Fort Peck Lake, Fort Peck, Montana* (view northwest) →

Sharp Curve

On 19 May 1805 the expedition camped on the east side of the neck, or "gouge," at the confluence of the Missouri and Musselshell Rivers, left of the lake in the photo. It had been an exhausting day. "The river," Lewis complained, "was croked, rappid and containing more sawyers than we have seen in the same space" since they passed the Platte River.

To top it off, earlier in the day, when Lewis's dog had swum "as usual" into the river to retrieve a beaver one of the men had shot, the big, wounded rodent bit the dog's hind leg, severing an artery. "It was with great difficulty that I could stop the blood," Lewis wrote. "I fear it will yet prove fatal to him." Fortunately it did not.

During the next two fair, balmy days, the Corps explored a few miles of the Musselshell. Lewis named one of its lower tributaries "Sâh-câ-gar me-âh or bird womans River, after our interpreter the Snake [Shoshone] woman."

Lewis remarked that the water of the Missouri had become semitransparent, "but still retains it's whitish hue." The photograph captures it at a moment when a buttermilk sky dapples both lake and land with shadows, and at an angle that tints the water with a rich green. All the journalists crooned about the beauty and fertility of the land they entered in May 1805, but returning here in the pouring rain on 1 and 2 August 1806, Lewis took no pains to remark on what must have been a muddy brown landscape.

Today, the expedition's campsite lies beneath some fifty feet of water at Fort Peck Lake.

119

Missouri Breaks

THE WIND AGAINST THEM again on 25 May 1805, the Corps had to tow their boats with ropes among islands such as those in the photograph. Early that morning they "passed a Creek 20 yard wide affording no running water," now called Two Calf Creek, seen at left. Springtime rivulets had washed rocks into the Missouri at the mouths of streams and gullies, creating obstacles for the men as they waded through the shallows close to shore. Around these submerged hazards, Lewis observed, "the water run with great violence, and compelled us in some instances to double our force in order to get a perorogue or canoe by them."

Separately, the captains explored the "high broken and rockey" terrain that hemmed in the river on both sides. This rugged area, known as the Missouri Breaks, was created when glaciers forced the Missouri River southward from its original course down today's Milk River basin. "In my walk of this day, " wrote Clark, "I saw mountts. on either side of the river at no great distance . . . I also think I saw a range of high mounts. at a great distance to the S S W. but am not certain as the horozon was not clear enough to view it with Certainty."

That evening Clark shot the expedition's first specimen of bighorn sheep, a new species they had spotted a month earlier. They called it an ibex, from its resemblance to a Eurasian animal. Remembering Jefferson's instruction to watch for fauna that might have been thought extinct, Lewis remarked that he had obtained some bones from the head of a similar animal at Big Bone Lick in Kentucky, on his trip down the Ohio in 1803.

"Deserts of America"

THE EXPLORERS' GRASP of the geography of the interior of the Northwest continued to evolve. At water level they estimated the distances between riverside landmarks and recorded their compass bearings, which were logged in daily lists of "courses and distances." On 26 May 1805, they traveled twenty-two and three-quarter miles in twenty-one courses, pausing at the end of the eleventh course, "Windsor's Creek" (far lower right), now called Cow Creek.

Looking around, the Corps absorbed the shapes and colors of the river's borderlands. Here they noticed that the black rock in yesterday's bluffs had given way to soft, light sandstone overlaid by "a hard freestone of a brownish yellow colour." They were passing through a flicker of geological time, the ancestry of the mighty river, the ebbs and flows of glaciers. In practical terms, Clark judged that "this Countrey may with propriety . . . be termed the Deserts of America, as I do not Conceive any part can ever be Settled, as it is deficent in water, Timber & too Steep to be tilled."

From the summits of riverside hills such as these, they studied the horizons. On this day, from one of the hills near the center of this photo, Lewis thought he glimpsed the sun-glinted Rocky Mountains for the first time. His first thought was of "the difficulties which this snowey barrier would most probably throw in my way to the Pacific," though he was willing to expect "a good comfortable road untill I am compelled to beleive differently." His sentiments were premature. What he saw (seen here in the distance) was an outlying range known today as the Highwoods, nearly a hundred miles east of the Rocky Mountain front.

(53) *Upper Missouri National Wild and Scenic River, twenty-eight miles northeast of Winifred, Montana* (view west, upstream)

White Cliffs

ON THE CLOUDY MORNING OF 31 May 1805, the expedition "proceeded at an early hour," entering into one of the most famous riverscapes on the Missouri, the White Cliffs. It took them by surprise, and Lewis was enchanted by its "most romantic appearance." He reasoned, correctly, that water had "woarn it into a thousand groteasque figures, which with the help of a little imagination and an oblique view at a distance, are made to represent elegant ranges of lofty freestone buildings, having their parapets well stocked with statuary. As we passed on it seemed as if those seens of visionary enchantment would never have an end."

Viewed from a quarter of a mile up in the sky, the architecture and statuary blur into a chalky white line through a green and tan landscape, and much of the romance dissolves.

Amid the fanciful stone shapes, Lewis admired cliff swallows, bighorn sheep, and "the most beautifull fox that I ever beheld." Both he and Clark expressed their sympathy for the crewmen who waded barefoot all day in the cold water through heavy, sucking sand and mud and over sharp rocks.

(54) *White Cliffs of the Upper Missouri National Wild and Scenic River, twenty-five miles south of Big Sandy, Montana* (view west, upstream)

Citadel Rock

CLARK REMARKED ON THIS "high Steep black rock riseing from the waters edge" as they passed it on 31 May 1805, but he did not give it a name. Citadel Rock, so named during the steamboat era for its fortresslike presence, was an igneous intrusion into a layer of sandstone that had washed away, leaving the harder basalt pillar standing.

The ill-fated white pirogue logged another narrow escape that day when the tow rope broke and the boat struck a rock, nearly turning over. "I fear," Lewis lamented, "her evil gennii will play so many pranks with her that she will go to the bottomm some of those days." Against expectations, it would survive to haul the explorers all the way back to St. Louis from the Falls of the Missouri, where it would spend the winter hidden in the willows.

On the return trip the following summer, Lewis and his party raced through "that very interesting part of the Missouri where the natural walls appear" on 30 July 1806. They were to have met Clark and his contingent at the mouth of the Yellowstone on 1 August, but at the end of this day they still had four hundred miles to go. Averaging sixty miles per day, they made it to the meeting point by 7 August and caught up with Clark on the twelfth.

Great Wall

ON THE EVENING OF 31 MAY 1805, Lewis took a walk to examine the array of thin, high rock walls along the White Cliffs close up. Anchored as he was in the mind-set of the Enlightenment, he rhapsodized: "So perfect indeed are those walls that I should have thought that nature had attempted here to rival the human art of masonry had I not recollected that she had first began her work."

He estimated the formations were from ten to a hundred feet high and one to twelve feet thick, their sides perfectly parallel. "The stone of which these walls are formed," he noted, "is black, dence and dureable, and appears to be composed of a large portion of earth intermixed or cemented with a small quantity of sand and a considerable portion of talk or quarts."

Actually, he was looking at igneous dikes, or fins, originating as pasty magma from the earth's fiery core and extruded through cracks in the crust, cooling into layers of dark granular rock geologists call shonkinite. There is no talc or quartz in them.

Some of the walls seemed to bisect the river, "rising from the water's edge much above the sandstone bluffs, which they seem to penetrate." Sometimes two or more walls ran parallel; at other times they intersected one another at right angles, "having the appearance of the walls of ancient houses or gardens."

Decision Point

ON THE EVENING OF SUNDAY, 2 June 1805, the Corps of Discovery "came too on the Lard. [larboard; their left] side in a handsome bottom of small cottonwood timber opposite to the entrance of a very considerable river." Early the next morning they "passed over and formed a camp on the point formed by the junction of the two large rivers." They now faced a crucial question: Which river was the Missouri?

Lewis admitted that the deeper waters of the north fork (entering from left in this photo) "run in the same boiling and roling manner which has uniformly characterized the Missouri throughout it's whole course so far; its waters are of a whitish brown colour very thick and terbid, also characteristic of the Missouri." Nevertheless, he was unconvinced that it was the true Missouri. The rest of the party, however, "with very few exceptions," agreed with their chief waterman, Pierre Cruzatte: the north fork was the one to follow.

The captains noted that the south fork was clearer, smoother, and more rapid, and its bottom was "composed of round and flat smooth stones like most rivers issueing from a mountainous country." They needed to reach the Rocky Mountains, where they hoped to find Sacagawea's tribe and get horses from them, and the south fork seemed more likely to lead there. Nevertheless, just to be sure, they decided to spend a few days reconnoitering both forks. Meanwhile, Lewis named the north fork for his cousin, Maria Wood.

Today, the situation that vexed the Corps of Discovery is hard to appreciate, for a dam built eighty miles upstream in 1970 has restrained, calmed, and cleared "Maria's River," leaving part of its history etched in the broad floodplain at its mouth. Nevertheless, the true course of the Missouri can be confounding even from the air. The photographer flew up the north fork twenty miles before realizing it was the Marias.

Narrow Escape

ON THE MORNING OF 4 JUNE 1805, while Clark and a detail of five men set out on foot to reconnoiter the south "fork" (the Missouri River), Lewis and six men marched up the north one (the Marias). On their way back two days later, Lewis and his detail camped somewhere in this vicinity. The next morning, headed downriver along the brink of the bluffs on the right, they had another of the numerous hairsbreadth escapes from disaster that were almost routine throughout the journey.

"In passing along the face of one of these bluffs today," Lewis wrote, "I sliped at a narrow pass of about 30 yards in length and but for a quick and fortunate recovery by means of my espontoon [six-foot-long lance] I should have been precipitated into the river down a craggy pricipice of about ninety feet." He had just reached a safe place when the man behind him cried out in anguish. He turned to find that Pvt. Richard Windsor had fallen in the slippery gumbo about halfway across the narrow ridge and was hanging by his left hand, arm, and leg.

Stifling his own alarm, Lewis coached Windsor in rescuing himself from the "dreadful situation" by carving a niche for his right foot with his knife to raise himself to comparative safety, then crawling on his hands and knees to a more secure spot. Lewis continued, "those who were some little distance behind returned by my orders and waded the river at the foot of the bluff where the water was breast deep."

On the eighth, after a round trip of 120 miles, Lewis and his men rejoined the main party at the mouth of the Marias. After further deliberations, the Corps struck camp on the eleventh and moved up the clearer of the two rivers toward the Rocky Mountains.

← (58) *Marias River, northern Montana* (view northwest, upstream)

"Sublimely Grand"

THE FRUITS OF THE CAPTAINS' inquiries in and around St. Louis during the winter of 1804 included copies of maps and journals made by one John Evans while on a Spanish-sponsored expedition to find a Northwest Passage in 1795–97. Evans got no farther than the Knife River villages, but there he queried his Indian hosts about Western geography and learned of a waterfall "of an astonishing height" about six hundred miles west of the Mandans.

Lewis and Clark similarly mined the knowledge of the Mandans and Hidatsas while at Fort Mandan. They left with the information that confirmed an earlier report of "a most tremendious Cataract" many miles farther up the Missouri, and that "the nois it makes can be heard at a great distance."

On 10 June 1805, Lewis proceeded ahead of Clark and the canoes, accompanied by Drouillard and Pvts. Joseph Field, George Gibson, and Silas Goodrich. Shortly before noon on the thirteenth, Lewis's ears "were saluted with the agreeable sound of a fall of water," which "soon began to make a roaring too tremendious to be mistaken for any cause short of the great falls of the Missouri." Probably somewhere to the right of the powerhouse in the photo, he then "hurryed down the hill which was about 200 feet high and difficult of access, to gaze on this sublimely grand specticle."

Lewis wrote a detailed description of "this majestically grand scenery," and even sketched "some of the stronger features of this seen" (the sketch has never been found), in hope that he could "give to the world some faint idea of an object which at this moment fills me with such pleasure and astonishment."

The dam in the photo, Ryan Dam, was completed in 1915. The penstock and power-house at right displaced about one-third of the original cataract. In early spring, the orderly overflow at the spillway dwarfs all that remains of the sight that thrilled Meriwether Lewis.

(59) *Great Falls of the Missouri, Great Falls, Montana* →
(view northwest, upstream)

"A Thousand Conjectures"

FRIDAY, 14 JUNE 1805, began placidly beneath a clear sky, the temperature a balmy sixty degrees. At about 10 A.M. Lewis began a solitary walk to check out the rapids above the falls, which he had noticed the day before. After five miles, passing "one continued rappid and three small cascades of abut for or five feet each," he "arrived at a fall of about 19 feet," which he suitably named "the crooked falls" and proceeded to describe its geometry.

Upon reaching the Great Falls, Lewis had still been reasonably confident that the expedition was facing a one-day portage, but during the course of this day he discovered with growing astonishment four more waterfalls and a succession of rapids. It was well after dark before he rejoined his companions at camp. "They had," he wrote, "formed a thousand conjectures, all of which equally forboding my death, which they had so far settled among them, that they had already agreed on the rout which each should take in the morning to surch for me."

The following week, Clark spent three days surveying the river from the mouth of Portage Creek to White Bear Islands. He measured five falls and seventeen separate rapids, cataracts, and pitches, calculating that the river dropped a total of about 360 feet in fifteen miles.

"Pleasingly Beautifull"

AFTER BRIEFLY CONTEMPLATING the Crooked Falls on 14 June, Lewis followed the sound of "a tremendious roaring" to "one of the most beautifull objects in nature," a fifty-foot-high cascade "with an edge as regular and as straight as if formed by art."

Its stunning beauty made him wonder to himself which was the more awesome, the huge waterfall he had seen the day before (the Great Falls), or this. "I now thought," Lewis wrote rapturously in his journal, "that if a skillfull painter had been asked to make a beautifull cascade that he would most probably have presented the precise image of this one; nor could I for some time determine on which of those two great cataracts to bestoe the palm, on this or that which I had discovered yesterday; at length I determined between these two great rivals for glory that this was *pleasingly beautifull*, while the other was *sublimely grand*."

Today, Lewis's "pleasingly beautifull" cascade goes by the name Rainbow Falls. The falls were shortened on the north end when Rainbow Dam was built in 1910. Half a mile farther upstream, Lewis discovered a "cascade of about 14 feet possessing a perpendicular pitch of about 6 feet." Later named Colter Falls, it was submerged beneath the reservoir behind Rainbow Dam.

← (61) *Rainbow Falls, one-third mile above Crooked Falls* (view northwest, upstream)

"Curious Adventures"

AFTER PASSING THE SERIES of waterfalls during his walk of 14 June, Lewis spied a river he surmised to be the one the Hidatsas called Mah-pah-pah,-ah-zhah, "Medicine River" (today called the Sun River). He strode down from the low hills on the north (left in photo) side of the Missouri and headed toward the bend, "near which there was a herd of at least a thousand buffaloe." Just after he shot one, he was startled by a grizzly bear only twenty steps away. The bear charged him, and Lewis, having carelessly neglected to reload his rifle, resorted to a defensive strategy he had been contemplating for some time. He hurried to the river, wading in "to such debth that I could stand and he would be obliged to swim," and turned to defend himself with his espontoon.

The bear followed him to the bank and then, for reasons "misterious and unaccountable," suddenly spun around and ran away. "So it was," Lewis concluded wryly, "and I felt myself not a little gratified that he had declined the combat."

En route back to camp, Lewis was threatened by an animal he could not identify (possibly a wolverine) and a short time later was rushed by three bull bison. The day's "succession of curious adventures wore the impression on my mind of inchantment," he wrote. "It now seemed to me that all the beasts of the neighbourhood had made a league to distroy me." After a hearty supper and a good night's rest, Lewis awoke to find a large rattlesnake sunning itself on a tree just ten feet away.

In this photo, the Missouri flows from right to left, and the Sun River joins it from the northwest. The mountains at the center of the hazy horizon are the Highwoods, flanked by the overlapping Big Belt Mountains at right.

Good News, Bad News

BY THE EVENING OF 15 June, Clark had gotten the boats as close to the Great Falls as possible, and the next afternoon Lewis joined him at the "lower portage camp," a mile below the mouth of Portage Creek (now Belt Creek), at bottom center of the photograph. Just above the creek is Morony Dam, completed in 1930; there is no natural waterfall there. Next upstream is Ryan Dam, completed in 1915, at the "Grand Cataract."

The good news was that the captains had chosen the correct fork back at the Missouri's confusing confluence with the Marias. The bad news was that the shortest way around the falls, on the south side, would be at least fifteen miles long, Lewis thought. Worse yet was the fact that Sacagawea was gravely ill. Lewis sent a detail to the sulfur spring opposite the mouth of Portage Creek for some of the supposedly medicinal water. She recovered quickly, nonetheless.

On 21 June the men wrestled their six dugout canoes up Portage Creek as far as the pictured road crossing, placed them on improvised wooden trucks, and dragged them up onto the prairie. Their eighteen-mile route crossed the deep coulees at left, cut westward through today's Malmstrom Air Force Base, and turned southwest to the upper portage camp, on the riverbank opposite White Bear Islands (no longer in existence), beyond the view in the photo. The portage began on 16 June and was completed on 2 July.

On the voyage home in July 1806, Sergeants Ordway and Gass and fourteen enlisted men, enjoying the benefit of four horses to pull their two crude wagons, completed the downstream portage in just five days.

142

Land and Water

ONCE PAST THE FALLS, on 18 July, the captains agreed that Lewis would take the flotilla on upstream while Clark, with York and Pvts. Joseph Field and John Potts, walked parallel to the river on the right side in the hope of meeting some Shoshones. Continuing along a wide and sometimes very crooked road that in some places appeared to have been dug out of the steep mountainsides, Clark's party saw plenty of evidence that Indians had passed through recently, but they saw not a soul.

Lewis and the rest of the party "proceeded on tolerably well." As the current became stronger, they rowed, towed, and pushed with setting poles. Though there was snow on some of the surrounding peaks, they "were almost suffocated in this confined vally with heat."

The landmark now called Oxbow Bend, which Lewis rounded on the nineteenth, is now nearly submerged under the 26.5-mile-long Holter Lake, the impoundment of the Holter Dam, built in 1916. The river as he saw it was about thirty feet lower, and maybe one-fourth as wide.

If anyone noticed the landmark now known officially as Beartooth Mountain and unofficially as the Sleeping Giant (the "face" is upper left along the ridge, with the "torso" at center), none of the journalists mentioned it. It is conspicuous from certain angles at a considerable distance, but not from the river.

"Gloomy Aspect"

LATE IN THE DAY ON 19 July 1805, Lewis and his party entered a canyon with "the most remarkable clifts that we have yet seen." They seemed to rise "from the waters edge on either side perpendicularly to the hight of 1200 feet," and the entire scene wore "a dark and gloomy aspect." "From the singular appearance of this place," Lewis called it "the gates of the rocky mountains"—one of only 17 place names that have survived from the 128 new names they inscribed on their maps of what is now Montana.

Having approached the cliffs in the evening, Lewis can be forgiven for inaccuracy in his observations. The "clifts" were only half as high as he thought, they were not black granite but pale gray limestone, and the mountaintops out of sight behind him rose two thousand feet above his head.

"The river appears to have forced it's way through this immence body of solid rock for the distance of 5-3/4 miles," Lewis observed. Journal editor Nicholas Biddle paraphrased him, with almost mythic overtones: "The convulsion of the passage must have been terrible, since at its outlet are vast columns of rock, torn from the mountain, which are strewn on both sides of the river—the trophies, as it were, of a victory."

Clark, on foot, missed the whole experience. Beyond the cliffs to the right, he and his detail were suffering from blistered feet, worsened by prickly pear cactus spines and sharp "flint" rocks. Their discomfort was overshadowed, however, by ample evidence of Indians nearby.

◄— (65) *Gates of the Mountains, north of Helena, Montana* (view north, downstream)

"Essential Point"

FOR THOUSANDS OF YEARS, Indian travelers had mapped the geography of North America in their minds. Appreciating this resource, Lewis and Clark had been the Mandans' avid students throughout the winter at Fort Mandan. One feature the Indians described was the coming together of "three noble rivers." Upon the Corps's arrival at this confluence on 27 July 1805, Lewis quickly recognized it as "an essential point in the geography of this western part of the Continent."

The Madison and Jefferson Rivers, which the captains named for the Secretary of State and "the author of our enterprise," respectively, converge at the sandbars just to the right of center in the picture. The Gallatin River, named for Secretary of the Treasury Albert Gallatin, meets them at bottom left. At the center of the horizon are the Tobacco Root Mountains. To their left are the more distant Madison and Gravelly Ranges. Interstate 90 etches its way across the center of the photo, and an abandoned railroad bends toward the town of Three Forks, Montana, established in 1881. Near the center of the picture's right edge is the place where, only four years before, Hidatsa warriors took Sacagawea captive, effecting her destiny as an immortal American icon.

Eastbound on 13 July 1806, Clark and his twenty-two-man contingent, along with Sacagawea and seventeen-month-old Pomp, wended their way through here again. At the confluence Sergeant Ordway led ten men in five canoes down the Missouri to the Upper Portage Camp above the Great Falls, while Clark and the remaining party of thirteen, including the Charbonneaus and their son, headed overland to explore the Yellowstone River.

(66) *Headwaters of the Missouri River, near Three Forks, Montana* (view southwest, upstream)

Third Gap

ON 1 AUGUST 1805, Clark and the expedition's flotilla of eight dugout canoes pushed up the Jefferson River through "a verrey high mountain which jutted its tremedious Clifts on either Side for 9 Miles, the rocks ragide." They emerged into this "wide extesive vallie," and camped that night on the south (right) side of the river, opposite the mouth of "R Fields Valley Creek"—today's Boulder River (left).

The maps of John Evans, which Lewis and Clark had gotten in St. Louis, depicted the Rocky Mountains as four or five separate ridges, among which the headwaters of the Missouri River flowed. From their water-level perspective, the captains had already identified two portals, one being the place Lewis named "the gates of the rocky mountains." This canyon merely bisected a relatively isolated group of low, rugged mountains now known as the London Hills, but Clark regarded it as the "3rd mountain gap," and so labeled it on his sketch map of the area.

Meanwhile Lewis, Drouillard, Charbonneau, and Gass, traveling overland in search of Shoshones, were struggling across the "rough high range of mountains" at left. "Our rout lay through the steep valleys exposed to the head of the sun without shade and scarcely a breath of air," Lewis complained. Without noticing it, he and his men passed the great limestone cave that in 1908 came to be called Lewis and Clark Caverns.

The tiny settlement at the lower center of the photograph is Cardwell, Montana. On the horizon are the Gallatin (left) and Madison (right) Mountains.

150

Beautiful Prairies

"WE PROCEEDED ON and passed a large beautiful bottom," wrote Pvt. Joseph Whitehouse on 2 August 1805, "and Priaries lying on both sides of the River." On each side of the valley, Sergeant Gass observed, "there is a high range of mountains . . . with some spots of snow on their tops."

The Jefferson River was still "crouded with Islands Sholey [shallow] rapid & clear," according to Clark. Coming ashore on 3 August to look for Indians, he found a barefoot track and followed it, discovering "that the person had ascended a point of a hill from which his camp of the last evening was visible." Unidentified Indians had been shadowing them off and on for more than two weeks, but there were as yet no clues as to whether the sign was ominous or hopeful.

Meanwhile, Lewis and his small detail continued southward overland on the opposite side of the river, in advance of Clark and the canoes. They were still anxiously hoping to find Sacagawea's people and buy horses from them so they could renew their westward trek, but the furtive Indians continued to elude them.

When Clark and his detachment passed through here again eleven months later, northwest winds chilled by the snowcapped mountains "rendered it very difficuelt to keep the canoes from running against the Shore."

In the background are the Tobacco Root Mountains. Twenty of this range's jagged glacial summits are above ten thousand feet. The upland slopes of thin, rocky soil are green only for a few weeks in early spring. The dark green areas on the slope at the right of the photo are hayfields irrigated from the little creek at center. The lines across the plain are farm lanes.

152

Home Ground

WITH WHAT SATISFACTION and relief Lewis must have written, on 8 August 1805: "The Indian woman recognized the point of a high plain to our right which she informed us was not very distant from the summer retreat of her nation on a river beyond the mountains which runs to the west." The Corps, reunited again, were traveling up today's Beaverhead River, and the landmark Sacagawea recognized was Beaverhead Rock (near center of photo, about one-third from top). From the right perspective, in good light, and with a willing imagination, this prominent tilt of limestone is said to look like the head of a swimming beaver.

As welcome as Sacagawea's announcement was, it couldn't relieve all the men's frustrations. The going here was slow and tedious. As Clark noted, "[The river] forms itself into smaller circular bends, which are so numerous that within the last fourteen miles we passed thirty-five of them." Worse yet, with the river at its late-summer lowest, the men had to drag the canoes over one gravelly riffle after another. Several days later Clark acknowledged, "[They] complain verry much of the emence labour they are obliged to undergo & wish much to leave the river. I passify them," he ended cryptically.

Upon hearing Sacagawea's confirmation that her people were likely nearby, the expedition split up once more. Lewis took a small party overland to search out the Shoshones while Clark continued up the river.

The following July, the Beaverhead was somewhat deeper, and the return trip was much easier. The Corps averaged forty-seven miles a day for three and a half days.

(69) *Beaverhead Rock, on the Beaverhead River, north of Dillon, Montana* (view northeast, downstream)

Western Road

On 10 August 1805 Captain Lewis, George Drouillard, Hugh McNeal, and John Shields were more than fifty river miles ahead of Clark and the canoes. Following a well-traveled Indian road in search of the Shoshones, Lewis and his men arrived at this "hadsome open and leavel vally where the river divided itself nearly into two equal branches." Today the confluence of the Beaverhead River and Horse Prairie Creek is submerged at left of the large island (photo center) in Clark Canyon Reservoir, beneath eighty feet of water when the reservoir is full.

The Indian road that turned up Horse Prairie Creek (toward right in photo) was more heavily traveled, which confirmed Sacagawea's assertion that it would lead them to her people. "I therefore did not hesitate about changing my rout," said Lewis, "but determined to take the western road." Three days later he would make the long-hoped-for contact with the Shoshones.

The main party arrived at the confluence at noon on the seventeenth. "We had the satisfaction once more to find ourselves all together," Lewis wrote, "with a flattering prospect of being able to obtain as many horses shortly as would enable us to prosicute our voyage by land." Everyone was "transported with joy," and in that spirit they set up here the bivouac they named "Camp Fortunate."

(70) *Clark Canyon Dam and Reservoir, south of Dillon, Montana* (view southeast, upstream) ➤

Division Point

THE GRAVEL ROAD WINDING through the center of the picture parallels Trail Creek, which is lined by low willows. It corresponds roughly to the Indian road that Lewis, Drouillard, Shields, and McNeal followed westward from the forks of the Beaverhead River.

On 12 August 1805, somewhere near the uppermost grove of trees on the right, Private McNeal "exultingly stood with a foot on each side of this little rivulet and thanked his god that he had lived to bestride the mighty & heretofore deemed endless Missouri," wrote Lewis. Two miles farther, the four men found the spring that was the creek's source, hidden in the large grove of trees at far right center of the photo, "the most distant fountain of the waters of the mighty Missouri in surch of which we have spent so many toilsome days and wristless nights."

The four men "proceeded on to the top of the dividing ridge" where the several gravel roads converge today (lower center)—Lemhi Pass. They then descended the steep west side of the pass about three-quarters of a mile "to a handsome bold running creek of cold Clear water" among the trees at lower right, where they "first tasted the water of the great Columbia river."

Hospitable People

WITH THE PEAKS AND RIDGES of the partially snow-clad Beaverhead Range on the eastern horizon, Lewis and his four companions crossed over the divide between the two river drainages and descended a dusty and well-traveled Indian road for some miles down into a deep, "handsome little valley." Lewis recorded that the soil was very poor and "produces little else but prickly pears, and bearded grass about 3 inches high."

In his journal entry for 13 August 1805, Lewis wrote a detailed record of the discoveries he made that pivotal Tuesday. In addition to notations on the area's geography and flora, he wrote accounts of his first three encounters with the Shoshones. The day climaxed with an elaborate pipe-smoking ceremony and led to long diplomatic exchanges via sign language.

Chief Cameahwait (who would prove to be Sacagawea's brother) disclosed that there was no viable riverine route out of the valley. He also reported on a recent raid by some Blackfeet, in which twenty Shoshones were killed or captured, all but one of their leather tepees were destroyed, and many horses were stolen. Nevertheless, it appeared to Lewis that they might still have enough horses to share with the Corps should a long overland portage be necessary.

Finally, a bit of roasted fresh salmon Lewis was served "perfectly convinced me that we were on the waters of the Pacific Ocean."

"Gloomey Picture"

THE EXPEDITION HOPED that the Salmon River was the link in the water route to the Pacific Ocean they had been sent to find. But Chief Cameahwait of the Shoshones painted a "gloomey picture" of it, the details of which, as Clark said, "fell far short of my expectation or wishes." Nonetheless, on the chance the starving Shoshones were merely scheming to keep them and their guns around for a while, the captains persuaded their new Shoshone guide, Old Toby, to conduct Clark on an exploratory trek westward down what would later be called the River of No Return, to see for himself.

In the four days between 21 and 24 August, Clark explored fifty-two miles down the Salmon River (he named it Lewis's River) from today's North Fork, Idaho. All he saw was a continuous series of rapids. Moreover, Old Toby told him that the impediments he had seen were "Small & trifleing in comparison to the rocks & rapids below," and that around the next bend "the Hills or mountains were . . . like the Side of a tree Streight up."

There weren't any trees nearby large enough to make dugout canoes, and portages would have been impossible in many places anyway. Nor was there any food to be had for man or horse.

He and Lewis may have been disappointed, but they couldn't have been surprised. They knew that the Rockies were closer to the ocean than to the Mississippi, so the waters of the Columbia would have to be steeper and faster than those of the Missouri. What they couldn't have guessed is that the river route would have been only fifty miles shorter than the land route Toby recommended.

On 24 August the captains began trading seriously for more horses. On the thirtieth, they turned northward, overland.

← (73) *Salmon River near Shoup, Idaho* (view southwest, downstream)

Uncertainty

"ENCAMPMENT ON A BRAN[C]H of the Creek we assended after crossing several steep points and one mountain," Clark's journal of 3 September 1805 tells us. We can't say for sure that they were lost, and they didn't admit to it in so many words, but Sergeant Gass's laconic summary gives us a hint: "This was not the creek our guide wished to have come upon."

Clark continued, "but little to eat I killed 5 Pheasents [grouse] & The huntes 4 with a little Corn afforded us a kind of Supper." They struggled over "emence hils and Some of the worst roade that ever horses passed." Frequently the horses fell, and in one such instance, lamented Clark, "we met with a great misfortune, in having our last Thmometer broken by accident." At dusk that day it began to snow, and misery piled upon misery— "Snow about 2 inches deep when it began to rain which termonated in a Sleet."

The Corps of Discovery was fortunate to have made it over this ridge before winter set in. The snow depth at today's Lost Trail Powder Mountain Ski Resort, shown on the left in the photo, can exceed fifteen feet.

Lost Trail Pass got its name when U.S. Highway 93, shown at bottom center of the photo, was completed in the 1930s, at the urging of a local rancher who was acquainted with the journals. The pass is not on the Continental Divide, but it separates two major drainages of the Columbia River basin—the Salmon to the south, and the Clark Fork to the north.

(74) *Lost Trail Pass, Montana-Idaho border* (view northwest) →

Part IV

Over the Mountains and Down to the Sea

TRAVELERS' REST to FORT CLATSOP

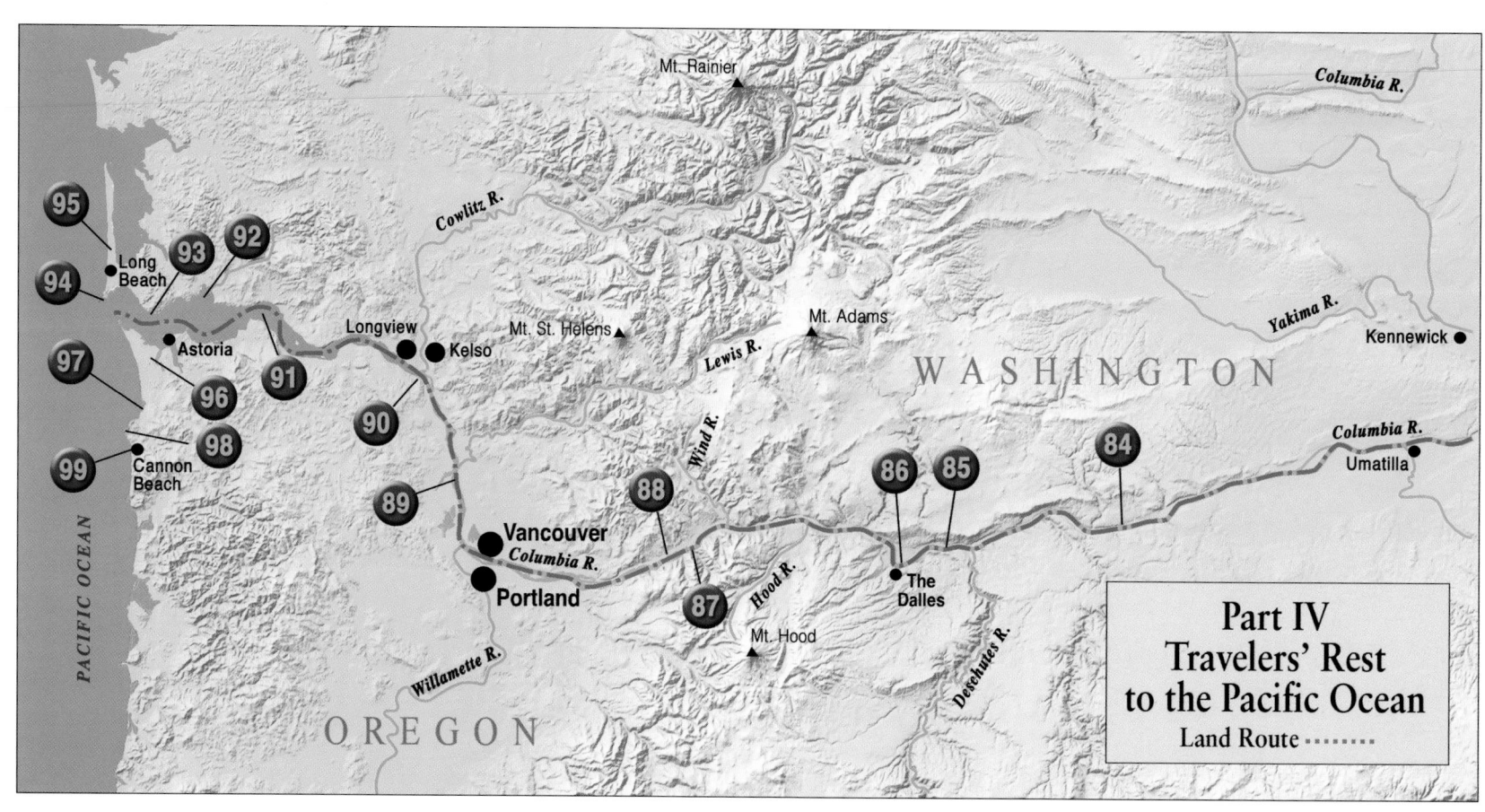

Mt. Rainier

Columbia R.

Cowlitz R.

95

93   92

Long
Beach

94

Astoria

Longview

Mt. St. Helens

Mt. Adams

Yakima R.

WASHINGTON

Kennewick

97

91

Kelso

96

Lewis R.

98

90

99   Cannon
Beach

Wind R.

Columbia R.

Umatilla

84

89

86   85

88

Vancouver
Columbia R.

PACIFIC OCEAN

Portland

87

Hood R.

The
Dalles

Mt. Hood

Deschutes R.

Willamette R.

OREGON

Part IV
Travelers' Rest
to the Pacific Ocean
Land Route ········

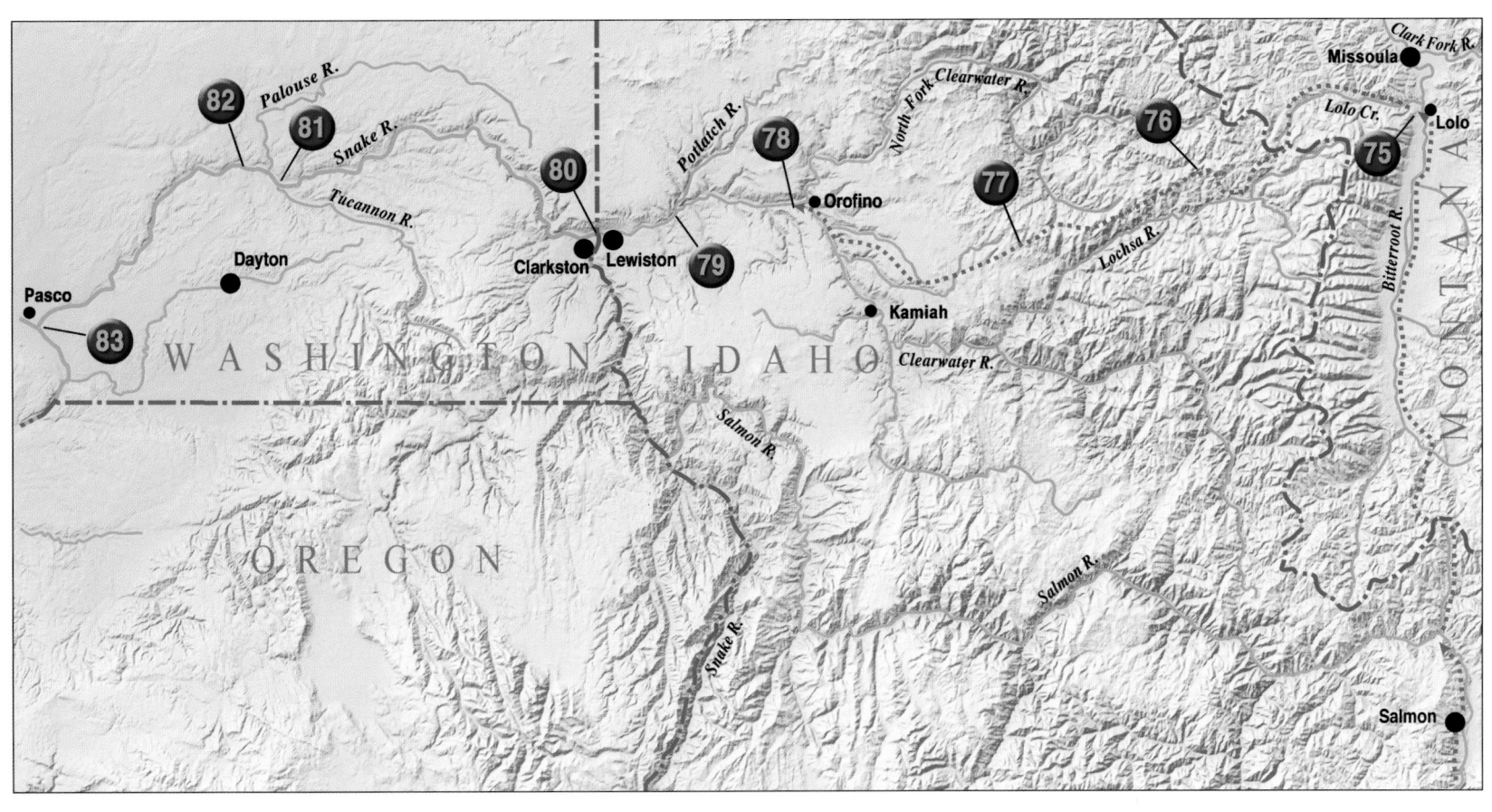

Turning Point

LED BY THEIR SHOSHONE GUIDE Old Toby, the Corps of Discovery walked along the Bitterroot River—they called it "Clark's River"—between snow-covered mountains. In the afternoon of 9 September 1805, they turned westward at a creek they dubbed Travelers' Rest, today known as Lolo Creek. They stopped at a gathering place that Indians had been using for thousands of years, on the creek about two miles above the Bitterroot River. The captains soon recognized it as a focal point in Western geography and inter-tribal politics.

For three days the Corps rested here, gathering strength for the arduous 150-mile trek across the Bitterroot Mountains. The campsite was about two-thirds down in the photo, among the cottonwoods that shelter Lolo Creek, which snakes up from the bottom center toward the right. Archaeological evidence uncovered at Travelers' Rest in summer 2002 has established the precise location of the Corps's camps of 9 through 11 September 1805 and 30 June through 3 July 1806.

Traveling eastward in spring 1806 over "those tremendious mountanes," the Corps arrived back at Travelers' Rest on 30 June. There they prepared their equipment and supplies for the next leg of the trip. They also rested and gathered courage for what would be the most perilous phase of the entire journey.

Ready to depart on the morning of 3 July 1806, the expedition—thirty-three souls and a dog, with sixty-seven horses—split into two detachments. The captains' intricate and risky plan would at times divide the Corps into five units, making them potentially vulnerable to Indian attacks. Independently, the various detachments would retrace the Beaverhead, Jefferson, and Missouri Rivers and explore the Marias and Yellowstone.

(75) *Lolo Creek* (beneath the trees), *Travelers' Rest State Park, Lolo, Montana* (view west, upstream) →

"Tremendious Mountanes"

IN THE CORPS' WESTWARD CROSSING of the Bitterroots, 16 September 1805 was one of the worst days of the expedition. "I have been wet and as cold in every part as I ever was in my life," Clark complained. "Indeed I was at one time fearfull my feet would freeze in the thin mockersons which I wore."

Recrossing these mountains on the way back was no less tough. With home on their minds, the Corps left Weippe Prairie, 140 miles west of Travelers' Rest, on 15 June 1806 only to find snow "in every derection from 6 to 8 feet deep," obscuring the path and covering the forage for their sixty horses. Prudence required them to send two men back to hire Indian guides. On 24 June they set out again, led by three Nez Perce whom Clark called "most admirable pilots." On the thirtieth Clark triumphantly reported: "Descended the mountain to Travellers rest leaveing those tremendious mountanes behind us—in passing of which we have experienced Cold and hunger of which I shall ever remember."

Among these nameless peaks, where the Corps measured progress one crisis at a time, Lewis, Clark, and their crew reached the highest point on their entire journey—7,036 feet above sea level. They could not have known this, however. Since the barometer was still too delicate an instrument for such a journey, they had no way to measure altitude.

The Bitterroot Mountains are not high compared to the Colorado or Canadian Rockies. Their highest peak, in northern Idaho, tops out at only 8,817 feet. Yet the range was twice as high as Easterners had supposed the Rocky Mountains to be, and they were also wider. As Lewis ultimately summarized, their portage across the Bitterroots consisted of "140 miles of high Steep ruged Mountain, 60 miles of which is Covered from 2 to 8 feet deep with Snow in the last of June."

"Tryumph"

FOR COUNTLESS GENERATIONS, Weippe Prairie (pronounced WEE-ipe), like Travelers' Rest, was a major node in the transportation, trade, and social networks of the Rocky Mountain West. Indians routinely covered the 140 miles between these two terminuses in "five sleeps," or six days, but it took the Corps of Discovery eleven cold, wet, painfully hungry days on their late-season westbound journey. On 18 September, two-thirds of the way through the mountains, Clark and six hunters pushed ahead of the main party in search of fresh meat. Two days later they left the mountains and "proceeded on through a beautifull Countrey . . . to a Small Plain" in which there were many Indian lodges. On the twenty-second, Lewis and the rest of the Corps arrived here, elated at having "tryumphed over the rocky Mountains."

At Weippe Prairie, the explorers also experienced the hospitality—albeit tentative—of the people called, in a misinterpretation of a sign-language gesture, the Pierced Noses. Subsequently French traders translated this to *Nez Perce,* pronounced in current English "nez-PURSE." The Nez Perce call themselves Tsoop-nit-peloo, the Walking-Out People, or Nee-me-poo, which means "The People."

On their homeward journey, the Corps returned to Weippe Prairie on 11 June 1806. At the time, the prairie was awash in camas flowers; the blue blossoms rippling in the breeze reminded Lewis of "lakes of fine, clear water." Indeed, this was a major source of the delicious, nutritious bulb of the camas—a wild vegetable equal in status to the potato for many Americans today. Ordway noticed that the soil was "very rich and lays delightful for cultivation," and agriculture has since altered the prairie's ecology.

Canoe Camp

STILL SICK AND EXHAUSTED from their recent crossing of the Bitterroot Mountains, Lewis, Clark, and their crew arrived on 26 September 1805, at what they called Canoe Camp, on the Clearwater River. In the photo, the camp was near the point of the triangle at lower right, between the highway and the south (right) bank of the river. The stream entering from the left is the North Fork of the Clearwater. For the next twelve days, in oppressive heat, the Corps burned and hacked, with axes "Small & badly Calculated" for the task, six dugout canoes from large ponderosa pine logs.

They also established firm friendships with several generous and helpful Nez Perce Indian leaders who lived nearby: We-ark-koomt, or Apash Wyakaikt (Flint Necklace); Tun-nach'-e-moo-toolt (Broken Arm); Walamottinin (Twisted Hair); Neesh-ne-park-ke-ook (Cut Nose); and Te-toh ar sky, who, with one of his sons, would guide the expedition as far as the Great Falls of the Columbia, at today's The Dalles, Oregon. Both captains, always listening closely to unfamiliar tongues, labored to write, phonetically, the approximations of Indian names and words.

On their return trip, the Corps camped about twenty miles upstream from here from 13 May to 10 June 1806. Lewis's 17 May diary entry reflects the homesickness and frustration all the men endured. "I am pleased at finding the river rise so rapidly," for it signified the steady progress of the spring thaw in the mountains, "that icy barrier which separates me from my friends and Country, from all which makes life esteemable." He chided himself: "Patience, patience."

(78) *Clearwater River, five miles west of Orofino, Idaho* (view east, upstream) →

"Doleful Situation"

At 3 p.m. on 7 October 1805, the Corps loaded their five new dugout canoes—four large ones, plus a small one "to look ahead"—and set out down the Clearwater River. After just one mile they passed through the first of ten rapids they would encounter before they pitched camp that day.

On the eighth they repaired the canoes that had been damaged the day before, then proceeded on, racing through fifteen more rapids within twenty miles. The last one was just below the mouth of a stream the captains named for John Colter—now the Potlatch River—the drainage on the right of the photo, near the bridge. It was the site of what Joseph Whitehouse recorded as a "Sad axident." One of the canoes "Struck a rock in the middle of the rapid," Sergeant Ordway explained, "and Swang round and Struck another rock and cracked hir So that it filled with water." Several nonswimmers clung to the damaged canoe, and "their they Stayed in this doleful Situation" until other men, including two Indians, could get them and the baggage safely to shore. Everything was wet, "perticularly the greater part of our Small Stock of merchindize" for trading, according to Clark.

The officers took the precaution of posting sentries to guard the drying items—the Indians, Clark observed, were "enclined to thiave," but he admitted that they "appeared disposed to give us every assistance in their power dureing our distress."

They passed this way again on horseback on 5 May 1806, virtually destitute of trade goods. Reluctantly, they became traveling health-care providers for the Indians. "My friend Capt. C. is their favorite phisician," wrote Lewis, explaining, "in our present situation I think it pardonable to continue this deseption for they will not give us any provision without compensation."

(79) *Clearwater River near Spalding, Idaho* (view west, downstream) →

178

Water Color

"THE SOUTH FORK [the Snake] is a greenish blue, the north as clear as cristial" Clark wrote when the Corps of Discovery arrived at the mouth of the Clearwater on 10 October 1805. Sergeant Gass described the color of the Snake as "goslin-green."

The Corps' four-day trip to this point from Canoe Camp on the Clearwater in their five crowded dugouts was a taste of things to come. As the steep, seasonably shallow river bore the crew down nearly three hundred feet in forty-five miles, it exposed thirty-nine rapids, the last of which was approximately where the bridge is in the photo. Earlier, some Nez Perces had assured them this would be "the last of the bad water" for quite a distance, but the Corps still had 465 miles to float and 738 feet to descend before reaching tidewater.

Proving his ability to put information together to imagine the larger geography around him, Clark realized that the Snake, or Kimooenem, as the Nez Perces called it, was part of the river he had named for Lewis three months and 250 miles earlier, when they were among the Shoshones.

Clark described the land here as a treeless, "high level plain," where Nez Perces were harvesting camas and cous (pronounced "cows") roots, both of which were staple foods and valuable trade goods. Lewiston, Idaho (center and left), named for Meriwether Lewis, was founded in 1860 as a supply center for the nearby goldfields. In the lower right corner of the picture is a fragment of Clarkston, Washington.

← (80) *Clearwater River at its confluence with the Snake* (right), *Lewiston, Idaho* (view east, upstream)

(81) Snake River at the mouth of the Tucannon, downstream of the mouth of the Palouse, north of Waitsburg, Washington (view northwest, downstream)

"Rugid Rocks"

LATE IN THE "windey dark raney morning" of 13 October 1805, traveling down the Snake (Lewis's) River (flowing from bottom to top in the center of the picture), the Corps passed the mouth of the Tucannon River, which they called "Ki-moo-ee-nimm Creek," shown at left center in this view. The river entering from the right, near the top of the photo, is the Palouse River (which Lewis and Clark named "Drewyer's [Drouillard's] River"). The Snake River today is a chain of five lakes beginning near Lewiston, Idaho. Pictured is Lake Herbert G. West, impounded by the Lower Monumental Dam, twenty miles downstream. Its upper end is at Little Goose Dam, eight miles upstream of the Tucannon.

In autumn 1805, however, the Snake was an almost continuous series of rapids. By the time they reached the Tucannon, the explorers had already made it through two bad ones, with "rocks in every derection." Now they entered a four-mile-long torrent, its climax a "narrows or narrow rapid" through which a twenty-five-yard-wide channel was confined between "rugid rocks" for a solid mile and a half. The water "ran as swift as a mill tale [millrace]," said Joseph Whitehouse. "We Should make more portages," Clark confessed, "if the Season was not So far advanced and time precious with us."

The expedition had interacted with Indian people daily since setting out from Canoe Camp on the seventh, and some of them were especially friendly and helpful. This day, two Indian men on horseback caught up with the Americans and indicated they wished to accompany them. The Corps had become steadily more aware of the value of Sacagawea's presence. "The wife of Shabono our interpetr we find reconciles all the Indians, as to our friendly intentions," Clark testified. "A woman with a party of men is a token of peace."

183

"Stuk Fast"

THE BOATING WASN'T ANY better the next day. At the head of a particularly bad three-mile-long rapid, three canoes "Stuk fast for Some time . . . and one Struk a rock in the worst part." At the end of the rapid they went ashore, dined on duck, and proceeded on. At about one o'clock, while passing through a short rapid, one canoe swamped and sank. "A number of articles floated out, Such as the mens bedding clothes & Skins, the Lodge &c. &c." The occupants of two other canoes retrieved some of the flotsam, and one of the Indian volunteers dove in and saved some other items. Fortunately, the waterproof powder canisters in the canoe were tied down, but the company's entire store of roots "prepared in the Indian way"—possibly baked camas bulbs—was ruined.

From the day they arrived at the confluence of the Clearwater and Snake Rivers, firewood had been scarce. This day, however, they found a stash some Indians had secured with rocks, and although they had "made it a point at all times not to take any thing belonging to the Indians even their wood," the temptation was too great to resist, so they took a little of it, as Private Whitehouse put it, "to dress our victuals with."

Today, once-scanty wisps of willow, never very desirable as firewood, thrive in dense patches along the riverbanks, and diesel-powered cruise ships can come and go on the Snake in no danger of getting "Stuk fast."

184

Welcoming Fanfare

IN THE AFTERNOON of 16 October 1805, the expedition portaged around "the last bad rapid as the Indians Sign to us"—the last on the Snake River, that is—and soon arrived at the "Great River of the West," the Columbia.

They camped on the point between the Columbia (left) and Snake Rivers, about where the grove shading Sacajawea State Park in Pasco, Washington (upper right), now stands. Kennewick is on the left in the picture. On the bottom right is McNary National Wildlife Refuge and the town of Burbank.

"The Country around these forks is level Smooth plain," wrote Ordway, "not a tree to be Seen as far as our Eyes could extend." Clark measured the width of the Snake at 575 yards, the Columbia at 960 and three-quarters. Since 1953 McNary Dam, thirty-two miles down the Columbia, has broadened the confluence into Lake Walula.

The Indians—Yakamas and Wanapams—considerately kept their distance until the Corps had finished setting up camp. Then "a Chief came from their Camp . . . at the head of about 200 men Singing and beeting on their drums . . . and keeping time to the musik, they formed a half circle around us and Sung for Some time," Clark reported. Afterward, he added, "the 2 old Chiefs who accompanied us from the head of the river procured us Some fuil such as the Stalks of weed or plant and willow bushes," and one man "made me a present of . . . about 20 lb. of verry fat Dried horse meat," exceptionally magnanimous gifts.

187

Greatest Chief

ROADS AND RIVERINE ENGINEERING have obliterated most of the details Lewis and Clark saw as they passed by on the Columbia. Yet this scene's most arresting feature is still the "high mountain of emence hight covered with Snow" on the photo's horizon. Clark mistook it for Mount St. Helens. The Indians called the mountain Pahtoe. Since 1838 it has been known as Mount Adams.

In this vicinity on 19 October 1805, the Corps met Yelleppit, chief of the Walulas, whom Clark described as "a bold handsom Indian, with a dignified countenance about 35 years of age, about 5 feet 8 inches high and well perpotioned." He was, Clark later said, "the greatest we met with."

From the mouth of the Snake River to the Lewis River, 240 miles away, the banks were crowded with people. On the return trip, the congestion even caused traffic jams. The Corps's stress was sometimes made worse by the shortage of food and knowing that the salmon were not yet running.

In addition to the crowds, rough terrain made the expedition's trip up the Columbia the following year at least as arduous as the downstream run had been. By the time they camped for the night on 24 April 1806, perhaps near the bend on the north (right) side of the river, the Corps had exchanged their dugout canoes for horses to carry their supplies. The men's feet and legs grew sore from trudging over rough stones and through deep sand, after being "for some months past accustomed to a soft soil."

◄— (84) *Columbia River near Blalock, Oregon* (view northwest, downstream)

River of the Falls

ON THE NORTH (right) side of Miller Island, which Private Whitehouse described as "an Island of Rocks, which had towers of solid Rock on it," the Columbia's main channel was obstructed by "a very rough roaring rapid." Thus on that day—22 October 1805—the Corps took the narrower south channel. The once rough, steep channels of the Columbia River now lie beneath the wind-ruffled waters of Lake Celilo, which begins at The Dalles Dam, ten miles downstream.

Near the west end of the island, they passed a sizeable tributary local Indians called To war ne hi ooks. The explorers renamed it Clark's River, but fur traders in the 1820s came to know it as the "River of the Falls." Today, it's the Deschutes. The falls the river's name probably refers to, three miles down the Columbia, were later called Celilo Falls.

Headed upstream on 21 April 1806, most of the Corps camped on the north side of the river opposite the island's west end. The men were somewhat scattered, most of the company leading the ten pack horses they had so far, the rest manning the two remaining canoes. While here, Lewis purchased one more horse "for a trifle"—the equivalent, he said, of ten shillings, Virginia currency.

Food was still scarce for native and traveler alike. So was firewood. Lewis characterized the local natives as "poor, dirty, proud, haughty, inhospitable, parsimonious and faithless in every rispect," and he felt it necessary to treat them menacingly. Out of spite he ordered the spare paddles and poles to be burned in an evening bonfire—a vindictive gesture in this treeless desert.

(85) *Miller Island on the Columbia River, near The Dalles, Oregon* (view southwest, downstream)

Through the Narrows

FROM THE LOCAL INDIANS' point of view, these thirty-three strangers and their dog put on quite a spectacle for four days in late October 1805, easing their clumsy dugouts down by ropes through the Great Falls (Celilo Falls) and the Short and Long Narrows—later called "The Dalles"—a French Canadian term denoting rapids confined by rock walls.

On the twenty-fifth, the Corps coasted by the last few rocky spots into "a butifull jentle Stream of about half a mile wide," and beached their battered canoes at "a high point of rocks" below today's Mill Creek (just around the bend, top center in the picture). It provided, Clark observed with satisfaction, a secure redoubt against any "designs of the natives, Should They be enclined to attack us." Better yet, the hunting thereabouts was promising, for a change.

There really was no need for him to have been on the defensive. On the twenty-sixth, two chiefs and fifteen Indian men in a single canoe crossed the river for a visit. That evening, Pierre Cruzatte and his fiddle cast a spell, more unifying than any diplomatic talk, over the assembly. "At night a fire was made in the middle of our camp, and as the Indians sat round it our men danced to the music of the violin, which so delighted them that several resolved to remain with us all night."

Beyond the farthest bend, the Columbia Gorge rifts the Cascade Range, which separates the desert of the Columbia Plateau from the continent's moist coastal margin. On the way home in April 1806, Lewis noticed the climatic change when he emerged from the gorge. "Even at this place which is merely on the border of the plains of Columbia," he wrote, "the climate seems to have changed; the air feels dryer and more pure."

"Great Shute"

ON A "CLOUDY DARK and disagreeable" 30 October 1805, the Corps "passed Several places where the rocks . . . have the appearance of haveing Separated from the mountains and fallen promiscuisly into the river." Dead tree stumps stood in the water, giving it, Clark said, "every appearance of the rivers being damed up below from Some cause which I am not at this time acquainted with." In fact, about A.D. 1250 a mountainside slid into the Columbia from the north; eventually, the river broke through and spilled over a forty-five-foot-high staircase of rubble some four miles long, creating the Cascades of the Columbia at the west end of the Columbia Gorge.

That evening the Corps camped in the vicinity of today's Stevenson, Washington, around the big bend in the distance. They spent the next day scouting the river and found the obstacle Clark had anticipated—a half-mile-long chute 150 paces wide, "water passing with great velocity forming [foaming] & boiling in a most horriable manner."

On 1 November, the expedition hauled their baggage in the rain for 940 yards around the chute, struggling along slippery riverbanks and through swarms of fleas and lice. The next day they left their last natural impediment behind them. With 146 miles of "Smoth gentle Stream" ahead, the worst that was left to endure was the weather.

The Bonneville Dam, completed in 1938, raised the level of this part of the Columbia seventy-two feet and permanently obliterated the place Lewis and Clark called the "Great Shute."

(87) *Bonneville Dam, Bonneville, Oregon; Mount Adams on the horizon* (view northeast, upstream)

Tidewater Mark

ON 31 OCTOBER 1805 Clark first saw this "remarkable high detached rock," the eroded core of an ancient volcano, which he estimated stood eight hundred feet above the riverbank and was four hundred yards in circumference. Here the river widened "and had everry appearance of being effected by the tide."

Camped on 2 November about five miles downstream from the Beacon Rock, Clark thought he noticed a tidal change, although today it is scarcely measurable. Lewis had a copy of a map that showed the part of the Columbia River that had been explored by George Vancouver and his lieutenant, William Broughton, in 1792. It was perhaps that resource, as sketchy as it was, plus the knowledge they had just gone through the last rapid, that enabled the captains to conclude that they had reached tidewater.

When the explorers passed this landmark again on 6 April 1806, Lewis suggested that "it is only in the fall of the year when the river is low that the tides are persceptable as high as the beacon rock." From evidence near their campsite of the previous November, he figured, "the flood of this spring has been about 12 feet higher than it was at that time."

In 1915 river developments threatened to destroy the rock. Henry J. Biddle, a prominent Washingtonian and descendant of the original editor of Lewis and Clark's journals, bought it and eventually gave it to the state for a park. It was known as Castle Rock from 1811 until Biddle restored Clark's label in 1916.

196

Horrid Noise

ON THE NIGHT OF 4 November 1805, Clark "could not Sleep for the noise kept by the Swans, Geese, white & black brant, Ducks . . . & Sand hill Crane. They were emensely numerous and their noise horrid." The Corps' campsite was a few miles north of Vancouver, Washington.

The party set out again at sunrise. Nine miles downriver, near today's Ridgefield, they passed "an Isld. Covered with tall trees & green briers Seperated from the Stard. Shore by a narrow Chanel." The captains understood from the Indians that the channel (at right, beneath the low cloud bank) was a river called Cah-wâh-nah-hi-ooks, a Chinookan word for "enemies." It received its modern name, Lewis River, not in honor of Meriwether Lewis, but rather for a surveyor and settler named Adolphus Lee Lewes—pronounced as Lewis.

Ridgefield, hidden by the thin cloud at upper right, is headquarters for the 4,600-acre Ridgefield National Wildlife Refuge, which harbors more than 180 species of birds. "This is certainly a fertill and a handsom valley," Clark observed as he passed through the scene in this picture, "at this time Crouded with Indians." However, the camp that night, twenty-three miles farther on, was "the first night which we have been entirely clear of Indians Since our arrival on the waters of the Columbia River."

On the upstream trek, breasting the rising spring freshet, they camped near here again on 29 March 1806. This time, the explorers remarked not on the birds, but on the reptiles. "The garter snakes are innumerable, & are seen entwined arround each other in large bundles of forty or fifty lying about in different directions through the praries."

North Cascades at Dawn

THREE PEAKS RISE ABOVE low cloud banks in this early morning view across the Columbia River near Kelso, Washington. The Corps of Discovery recognized them from several different points on the Columbia.

At center is Mount St. Helens. In 1792, on his expedition in the area, British explorer George Vancouver named the volcano for Baron St. Helens, a prominent British diplomat. There is evidence that it may have erupted just a few years before Lewis and Clark got there. At the time, Mount St. Helens's summit was 9,677 feet above sea level. Nearly two centuries later, on 18 May 1980, an eruption (perhaps the volcano's seventh in forty thousand years) blew away the top 1,300 feet.

Vancouver also named 14,410-foot Mount Rainier (at left edge of photo), after his friend Rear Adml. Peter Rainier. Scientists consider this majestic peak the most dangerous volcano in the Cascade Range because of its proximity to the populous Seattle-Tacoma area.

Partially shown at far right, Mount Adams last erupted about 3,500 years ago. In 1838, a patriotic citizen started a campaign to make the Cascade Mountains a "presidential range." This was to include renaming Mount Hood after John Adams. In a series of mix-ups, however, Adams's name was affixed instead to this 12,276-foot mountain fifty miles north of Mount Hood.

(90) *Columbia River near Kelso, Washington* (view northeast) →

"Great Joy"

WHEN THE SKY CLEARED briefly at about noon on 7 November 1805, a rising cheer may have startled the myriad waterfowl in the area, for Clark wrote, "we are in view of the opening of the Ocian, which Creates great joy." For the first time, their horizon was not totally ringed by land; beyond that opening had to be the Pacific. As expressed later in the published journals, this was "the object of all our labors, the reward of all our anxieties."

The explorers were probably more than twenty miles from the ocean, perhaps somewhere to the right of the bottom of the photo, on the Washington side of the Columbia. To a viewer standing at sea level, the horizon is only about three miles ahead, so they could not possibly have been looking at the opening to the Pacific, but rather at the mountains on either side of the estuary. Most of the islands and wetlands in this photo are now part of the Lewis and Clark National Wildlife Refuge.

Local gossip must have torqued up their hopes even higher that day when, according to Private Whitehouse, residents at two different villages "made signs to us that there were vessells lying at the Mouth of this River." Similar rumors of seagoing ships, along with the Euro-American trade goods they saw among the populace that hovered around them, energized the men for several more days.

The Corps returned to the same vicinity on the twenty-fifth, then threaded their way among the islands in the photo to a small wooded peninsula Clark dubbed Point William, today called Tongue Point. In the photo, Tongue Point is the little knob at the right end of Clatsop Spit, which is on left side near the horizon. There, on this narrow neck, foul weather kept Clark and the Corps pinned down for ten days while Lewis and a small party were out searching for a winter campsite.

(91) *Lower estuary of the Columbia River, Astoria, Oregon* →
(view west, downstream)

Shallow Bay

LATE ON THE MORNING OF 8 November, the Corps' flotilla entered a "nitch" they called Shallow Bay (now called Grays Bay) and paused for their midday meal near the mouth of Deep River (at far right in photo). There they found the remains of an Indian village with "great numbers of flees which [we] treated with the greatest caution and distance."

After lunch, rather than paddle straight across the broad bay, the company took advantage of the ebb tide and proceeded downriver "close under the Stard. Side." It had been routine practice to avoid the swift current in a river's main channel as much as possible, keeping to the slower water close to shore. This made navigation easier and gave ready access to shore. Here in the Columbia's estuary, it was similarly prudent to stay close to shore, except that the driftwood there was bigger than any they had ever seen—some logs were two hundred feet long and seven feet in diameter. Moreover, the waves were too much for their dugouts, as the gunwales reached only a few inches above the water's surface.

That evening, when high waves and swells forced them out of the water several miles downriver, the men confronted the problem of finding a campsite. "We have not leavel land sufficient for an encampment and for our baggage to lie Cleare of the tide," complained Clark, "the High hills jutting in So Close and Steep that we cannot retreat back, and the water of the river too Salt to be used."

In fact, one of the canoes was swamped in the waves before it could be unloaded. In Clark's journal entry of 9 November he noted, "Notwithstanding the disagreeable time of the party for Several days past they are all Chearfull and full of anxiety to See further into the ocian."

204

"Blustering Point"

IT WAS "THE MOST disagreeable time I have experienced," Clark grumbled on 15 November 1805. "Confined on a tempiest [tempestuous?] Coast wet, where I can neither get out to hunt, return to a better Situation, or proceed on." For six days, gigantic swells had held the Corps down near Point Ellice, the clearing at the far left end of the landform in the picture; Clark had yet to see the ocean as pacific as it appears in the photo. The day before, Lewis had set out down the shore with four men "to examine if any white men were below."

In the meantime, when the eleven-day rain spell abated about three P.M. on the fifteenth, the company hastily loaded the canoes and rounded the promontory to which Clark had given three names, all reflecting its treacherousness—"blustering point," "Stormey point," and "Point Distress." On a sandy beach beyond the bridge in the picture, near an abandoned Chinook Indian village at the east end of Haleys Bay—today's Baker Bay—the ocean's swells drove them back to the marshy bottom, where they stayed for ten more days.

"We are now at the end of our voyage," wrote Sergeant Gass, "which has been completely accomplished according to the intention of the expedition, the object of which was to discover a passage by the way of the Missouri and Columbia rivers to the Pacific ocean; notwithstanding the difficulties, privations and dangers, which we had to encounter, endure and surmount."

On 24 November the sky cleared, and that evening the captains deliberated on what to do next. They polled the party, including York and Sacagawea. The decision was "to Cross the river and examine the opposite side," where they could hunt elk, refine sea salt, and watch for ships from which they might refresh their depleted supply of Indian trade goods.

◄— (93) *Point Ellice, near Megler, Washington* (view northwest)

"This Emence Ocian"

ON 18 NOVEMBER, Clark and his party proceeded southwest along the shore of Baker Bay, at upper right in the photo, passing a popular trading-ship anchorage, where they carved their names on trees. They then clambered up onto the narrow peninsula at far right, the tip of Cape Disappointment. Turning north, they climbed McKenzie Head, the tree-covered knob left of the inlet, below the larger wooded hill at upper center, called North Head. McKenzie Head was then "a high open hill projecting into the ocian" but is now surrounded by land that built up during the twentieth century behind the North Jetty, the long line of rocks extending up from the bottom of the picture.

Clark was pleased that his men appeared "much Satisfied with their trip beholding with estonishment the high waves dashing against the rocks & this emence ocian." This view of the sea represented their ultimate triumph.

Private Whitehouse thought his officers had named Cape Disappointment "on account of not finding Vessells there," but in truth it had received the name years earlier. For generations, sailors had sought the entrance to the "Great River of the West." In 1788 the British trader John Meares thought he had found it, but, unable to cross the sandy bar, he concluded that it was not the estuary of a river but just a bay. He named it Deception, and the cape on its north side, Disappointment. Four years later Robert Gray, a trader from Boston, found the river's narrow channel and sailed his ship *Columbia Rediviva* across the bar, discovering that this body of water was indeed a river, which he named after his ship.

Mementos

CLARK AWAKENED EARLY on 19 November "from under a wet blanket caused by a Shower of rain which fell in the latter part of the last night." He and his party "proceeded on thro emencely bad thickets & hills." From the top of the hill today called North Head, he noticed a "Point of high land" twenty miles distant, north of the photograph. "This point," he journaled, "I have taken the Liberty of Calling after my particular friend Lewis." Lewis's Point may have been today's Leadbetter Point, at the northern end of Long Beach Peninsula. On his 1793 map, George Vancouver had drawn a point in this vicinity that may have represented this tip of land, but his rendering was more conspicuous than any landmark in the area today.

Clark's party continued north along the beach for four miles, to the vicinity of today's Long Beach, Washington. Here Clark memorialized their first visit to the Pacific Ocean by marking his name and the date on a small pine tree. Once again proving his keen geographical intuition, he led his contingent back to the hill, overland a few miles through dense forest to Baker Bay, and back to camp.

The following day Sacagawea relinquished her belt of blue beads—"Chief beads," the prime legal tender on the Northwest Coast—so the captains could buy a robe made of two sea otter skins as absolute proof they had reached the Pacific Ocean. Clark wrote, "The fur of them [was] more butifull than any fur I had ever Seen."

Coast Range Winter

ON 29 NOVEMBER, Clark and the main party abided impatiently at Point William, today's Tongue Point, in the rain and wind while Lewis and five men set out to explore the south bank of the Columbia. On 5 December Clark fretted, "Capt. Lewis's long delay below, has been the Sorce of no little uneasness on my part of his probable Situation and Safty," but later that same day Lewis relieved his friend's fears, appearing with the news he had found a suitable place to spend the winter.

Two days later, a slight improvement in the weather permitted the company to paddle past present-day Astoria, Oregon, and onto a river the Clatsop Indians called Netul—now known as Lewis and Clark River. Among the trees opposite the river's sharp bend at left center, they began building their log huts on 10 December and moved in—fleas and all— on Christmas Eve. Today a reconstruction of the fort stands at the site.

During their time at the coast, the Corps saw only six sunny days; the rest brought clouds, fog, rain, and a little snow. Fifty-three were partly clear. That's a normal winter on the west slopes of the Coast Range.

When the expedition left Fort Clatsop on 23 March 1806, the captains gave their fort and furniture to Clatsop Indian chief Coboway. "He has been much more kind an hospitable to us," Lewis wrote gratefully, "than any other Indian in this neighbourhood."

(96) *Lewis and Clark River at Fort Clatsop site, near Warrenton, Oregon* (view north, downstream) →

Salt Works

BY THE TIME THEY REACHED the coast in November 1805, the Corps had already been on short salt rations for some time. Back in October, Sergeant Gass had complained that fish was "poor and insipid" provender without salt. When the captains had asked the company their suggestions in choosing a winter campsite, Private Whitehouse summarized the consensus in his journal: "It would be of an advantage to us, for to stay near the Sea shore, on account of making Salt, which we are nearly out of at this time & the want of it in preserving our Provisions for the Winter, would be an object well worth our attention." Salt was also essential in processing hides for clothing and moccasins.

The tidewater river at their campsite was not salty enough for their purposes, so on 28 December the captains sent five men to the ocean to set up a salt works. To get past the dilution of the freshwater outflow, the salt makers had to go more than fifteen miles south of the Columbia's mouth to find a suitable spot, on the beach near Tillamook Head (the peninsula at upper right in the picture). Here they built an oven of stones and, day and night for a month and a half, scooped perhaps 1,400 gallons of water from the surf, boiling it down to about twenty-eight gallons of salt. The product, Clark confirmed, was "excellent white & fine" and "not So Strong as the rock Salt . . . made in Kentucky."

Today's Seaside, Oregon, is a world-famous summer resort. The area had been Indian wintering grounds for a thousand years or more before the Corps of Discovery came here.

◄— (97) *Seaside, Oregon* (view south)

Delightful View

ON 6 JANUARY 1806, Clark and about half the Corps, with Sacagawea and her little boy, set out from Fort Clatsop to the ocean south of Tillamook Head to see a beached whale. Clark hoped to purchase some blubber and whale oil from the Clatsop and Tillamook Indians who were butchering the carcass.

The next day, after passing the salt works and continuing along the "round Slippery Stones under a high hill," Clark related, "my guide made a Sudin halt, pointed to the top of the mountain and uttered the word *Pe Shack* which means bad, and made Signs that we . . . must pass over that mountain. I hesitated a moment & view this emence mountain the top of which was obscured in the clouds and the assent appeard. to be almost perpindecular."

After two hours of "labour and fatigue," at one point drawing themselves up by bushes and roots, they reached the summit of Bald Mountain. Nicholas Biddle, editor of the first published account of the expedition in 1814, paraphrased Clark's description: "Here one of the most delightful views in nature presents itself. Immediately in front is the ocean, which breaks with fury on the coast, from the rocks of cape Disappointment as far as the eye can discern to the northwest, and against the highlands and irregular piles of rock which diversify the shore to the southeast."

Clark "looked down with estonishment" from Bald Mountain, the high point just left of center in the photo. To the right of it, jutting farther out into the ocean, is Tillamook Head. The mountains in the background at left are part of the Coast Range.

216

Whale Tale

BY THE TIME CLARK and his party got to present-day Cannon Beach, Oregon, on 8 January, Indians had picked the dead whale's 105-foot-long carcass clean. Clark succeeded in bargaining for about three hundred pounds of whale blubber and a few gallons of oil. "Small as this Stock is I prise it highly," he wrote, "and thank providence for directing the whale to us; and think him much more kind to us than he was to jonah, having Sent this monster to be *Swallowed by us* in Sted of *Swallowing of us* as jonah's did."

Late that night, as Clark sat smoking with some Tillamook Indians, he was alarmed by a woman's scream from one of the cabins across the creek. His guide "made Signs that Some one's throat was Cut." Noticing that Hugh McNeal was not around, he dispatched several soldiers to look into the situation.

It turned out that an Indian man had lured McNeal into a cabin with the intent of murdering him for his blanket and other possessions. A Chinook woman who was "an old friend of McNeals" shouted a warning and the Indian man ran off. The detail met the intended victim "comeing across the Creak in great hast." Evidently embarassed, McNeal claimed that "the people were alarmed on the opposite side at Something but what he could not tell."

According to Sergeant Ordway, Clark spoke of naming the creek, shown in the photo at left, "McNeals Folly." In the end, he decided on Ecola, the Chinookan word for "whale."

◄— (99) *Cannon Beach, Oregon* (view southwest)

Part V

Reaching Out

THE JOURNEY HOME

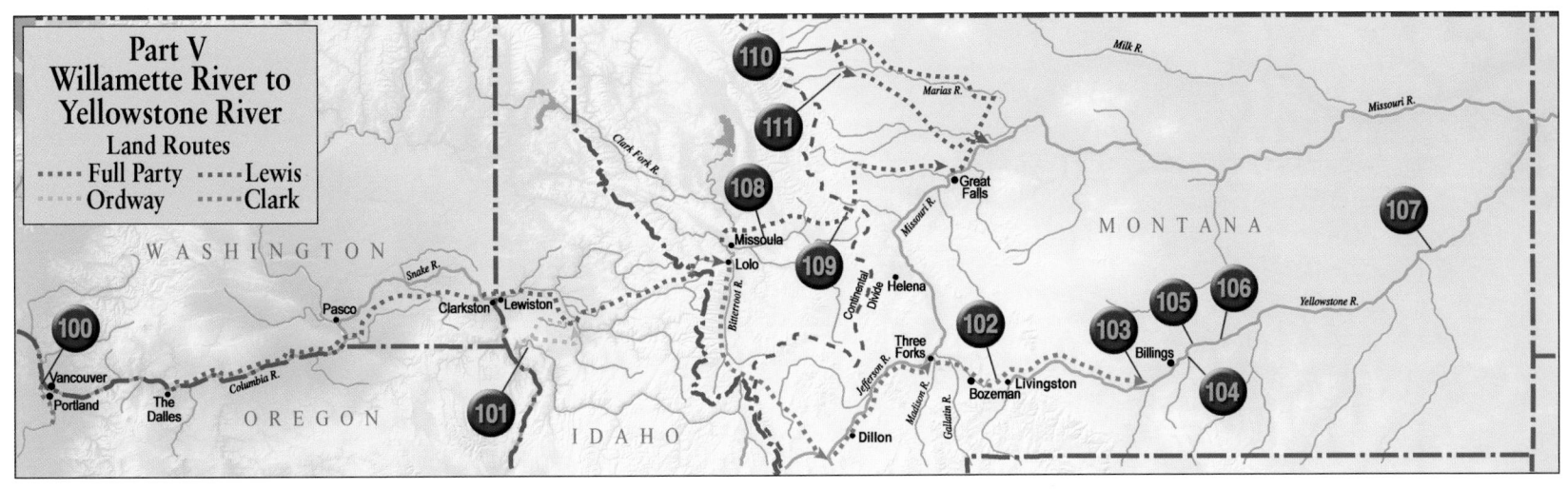

WASHINGTON

OREGON

IDAHO

MONTANA

Clark Fork R.

Snake R.

Columbia R.

Milk R.

Marias R.

Missouri R.

Missouri R.

Yellowstone R.

Bitterroot R.

Continental Divide

Jefferson R.

Madison R.

Gallatin R.

Vancouver
Portland
The Dalles
Pasco
Clarkston
Lewiston
Missoula
Lolo
Helena
Great Falls
Three Forks
Dillon
Bozeman
Livingston
Billings

100
101
102
103
104
105
106
107
108
109
110
111

Filling in the Blank

IN DRAWING HIS FIRST MAP of the continent between the mouth of the Missouri River and that of the Columbia, completed at Fort Clatsop, Clark knew by hearsay that there was "a large river which falls into the Columbia on its south side," but islands had hidden it from view on the westbound trip. Heading home that spring the Corps missed it again for the same reason, but early on 2 April some Indians visiting their camp, which was upstream of the tributary in question, happened to mention it. Later that morning Clark picked six of his soldiers, hired an Indian guide, and went back to explore the lowest ten miles of the river that local residents called the Multnomah.

Clark assumed, mainly on the basis of what he had heard, that the source of the Multnomah was "at no great distance from the Spanish Settlements," around 37° north latitude—almost as far south as Reno, Nevada. He drew it that way on the map he prepared for Nicholas Biddle's 1814 edition of the journals. Actually, the Willamette, as it came to be called after 1841, begins in southern Oregon and is only 189 miles long.

Apart from this miscalculation, Clark's map of the Columbia River basin was remarkably accurate, and it served travelers well for several decades. He had the gift of a great explorer—the ability to sense the land beneath his feet, embrace the moving horizon with his eyes, and extrapolate the rest in his imagination.

225

Side Trip

ON 27 MAY 1806 Lewis remarked, "the dove is cooing which is the signal as the Indians inform us of the approach of the salmon." None of these fish had yet migrated up the Clearwater River to where the explorers were camped, at today's Kamiah, Idaho, but they saw Nez Perces with several fresh salmon, "fat and fine," which the Indians said came from "Lewis's River," known today as the Salmon River. The captains dispatched Sgt. John Ordway, with Pvts. Robert Frazer and Peter Weiser, on horseback to buy some. Indian information put the river only half a day's ride away, but there was a slight miscommunication on that point.

Ordway's journal contains few details of the trip, so the actual route their Nez Perce guides led them on is a matter for conjecture. Ordway told the captains it was "not a direct one." Certainly it led out of Clearwater Canyon, across the high Nez Perce Prairie, and down to the Salmon River, which they reached at the mouth of Deer Creek (just beyond the photo at far upper right) late on the twenty-eighth. While there, Frazer traded his worn-out razor for two Spanish coins that Nez Perce warriors had taken from a Shoshone battle casualty, giving the captains evidence that European goods were reaching Indians who had never seen a white person before.

Unfortunately, the fish had not started up the Salmon River yet, so the party rode down the north bank (left in the photo), climbed back up to the prairie, and descended "the worst hills we ever saw a road made down" to the Snake River. After buying seventeen salmon there, the men headed back to camp. By the time they got there, at noon on 2 June, however, most of the fish had spoiled.

(101) *Salmon River at fifty miles southwest of Kamiah, Idaho* (view northeast, upstream) →

226

"Of Great Service"

ON 3 JULY 1806, at Travelers' Rest, the captains divided the corps into two units. Clark would lead his men on an exploration of the Yellowstone River. Lewis was to take the others to the Great Falls via the Blackfoot River, then, with a detail of three men, explore more of the Marias River. They expected to reunite at the confluence of the Missouri and Yellowstone Rivers about 1 August.

Leaving the Three Forks of the Missouri at 5 P.M. on 13 July 1806, Clark and his contingent followed the east fork of the Gallatin River. The captain observed several Indian and buffalo roads heading northeast across the mountains at the head of the river. However, he noted, "the indian woman who has been of great Service to me as a pilot through this Country recommends a gap in the mountain more South which I shall cross." This was one of the few times Sacagawea acted as the guide that legend has made of her, and it was crucial to Clark's progress down the Yellowstone.

On the fifteenth the party descended a slope (at right in photo) on "a well beaten buffalow road" toward the Yellowstone River. The Yellowstone flows north out of a mountain-bounded valley between low spurs of the Gallatin and Absaroka Ranges (background left), which Clark described as "rugged and covered with Snows."

The party struck the river, "wide bold, rapid and deep," at the bend at about the center of this picture, in present-day Livingston, Montana. From where Clark stood, the fertile river basin now called Paradise Valley was hidden from view, and the party pressed on downstream.

← (102) *Livingston, Montana* (view south, up the Yellowstone)

Horse Thieves

ONE WEEK AND a hundred miles after starting down the Yellowstone River, Clark finally found cottonwood trees large enough for building canoes, though they would not quite meet previous standards. "Those trees," he noted on 20 July 1806, "appeared tolerably Sound and will make Canoes of 28 feet in length and about 16 or 18 inches deep and from 16 to 24 inches wide." The men would have to lash them together, catamaran-style, for stability.

Clark's party made camp at today's Park City, Montana, and settled in to build the new canoes and attend to other business. While a few of the men took turns with the three axes they had along, some of the rest, being nearly naked, made elk- and deer-skin clothing. Clark himself tended Private Gibson, who had punctured a thigh on a fallen tree when bucked off his horse. Some hunted, some dried meat, and others tended the horses. Between chores they rested up.

That night, some Indians, presumably Crows, stole half the company's remaining horses and headed downriver with them. Clark composed a scathing lecture, alternating diplomacy with diatribe, to deliver if and when he caught up with the culprits' chief. On 24 July 1806 Clark and company packed up and took to the river, reaching the Missouri early on 3 August. Clark never came face-to-face with a single Crow Indian.

Ill-Fated Mission

ON 23 JULY 1806, Captain Clark handed written orders to Sgt. Nathaniel Pryor for a mission that, had it succeeded, might have altered both the immediate and the long-term significance of the Lewis and Clark expedition. First, Pryor, with three enlisted men, was to ride ahead and take the expedition's remaining twenty-nine horses to the Mandan villages, where he would leave some for the main party to trade for food. He was then to drive the rest of the horses 150 miles north to the North West Company trading post, on the Assiniboine River. There he was to deliver a letter from the captains to trader Hugh Heney, a good friend they had met at Fort Mandan. The letter asked Heney, who had influence with the refractory Teton Sioux, to induce some of the chiefs to accompany Lewis and Clark east to meet Jefferson. The horses would be partial payment on the contract.

The second night after Pryor and his party set out, Indians, probably Crows again, stole all the horses, and the mission was ruined. Building boats of buffalo hides stretched over bowl-shaped willow-wand frames, the four men drifted down the Yellowstone and caught up with the rest of the party early on 8 August.

In this photograph, a dozen miles northeast of Billings, Montana, the stream Clark named for Nathaniel Pryor (left) descends from its montane sources nearly a hundred miles away. Billings is visible at upper right.

(104) *Pryor Creek near Billings, Montana* (view southwest, upstream) →

Crow Country

IN THE LIST OF NAMES and descriptions of Indian tribes that Lewis and Clark assembled between St. Louis and Fort Mandan, they called the tribe living along the Yellowstone River, "as usially Spelt and pronounc'd by the English," "Ravin nation," later known as the Crows. He wrote down the "primitive" name phonetically as "Arp-Sar-co-gah," and gave the "nick name" that "generally obtained among the Canadian Traders" as "Cor beaus" (i.e., *corbeaux*, French for "crows" or "ravens"). But the people called themselves Absalookas, sometimes heard as Absarokas, or "Children of the Large-beaked Bird." Various early white travelers transcribed the name differently, but the Absalookas maintain it refers to the raven.

The Absalookas called the river that flowed past their doors Iichiilika azah, or Elk River. Indians around Fort Mandan called it Meé,ah'-zah, or Stone River. But French-Canadian fur traders who had been on the lower reaches of it in the 1790s had somehow learned to call it the Roche Jaune, or Yellowstone River.

Barely discernable in the photo at the edge of the woods on the just beyond the bridge is one of the most famous landmarks on Lewis and Clark's route, Pompeys Pillar.

235

Remarkable Rock

FOR COUNTLESS GENERATIONS before William Clark arrived on 25 July 1806, the rock formation on the Yellowstone River now called Pompeys Pillar had been a distinctive feature in the homeland of the Crow Indians. It marked a major trade point, an easy river crossing, a favorite gathering place, and a communications center.

"At 4 P M arrived at a remarkable rock," wrote Clark, "situated in an extensive bottom. . . . This rock I ascended and from it's top had a most extensive view in every direction. This rock which I shall Call Pompy's Tower is 200 feet high and 400 paces in secumphrance and only axcessible on one Side."

The Crows called the rock Iish-biia ah-naac'-he', meaning "Where the Mountain Lion Sits." Unaware of that, Clark memorialized it with his nickname for the Charbonneaus' "butifull promising Child," Jean Baptiste, calling it Pompys Tower. Clark left no clues as to the source or meaning of his pet name for the boy, but Nicolas Biddle incongruously assumed that the landmark's name alluded to Pompey's Pillar, a ninety-nine-foot red granite Corinthian monument in Alexandria, Egypt.

"The natives have ingraved on the face of this rock the figures of animals &c. near which I marked my name and the day of the month & year," Clark noted. His inscription is the only remaining physical evidence anywhere of the passing of the Lewis and Clark expedition, thanks mostly to the Crows, who could have considered it a desecration of one of their sacred places and obliterated it long ago. Meanwhile, the Indian pictographs have weathered away. Today the rock bears about 2,500 marks from more recent passers-by.

Badlands

ON 30 JULY 1806 Clark and his party camped near the mouth of the War har sah, or Powder River, just to the right of the view in this photograph. The next day, eager to reunite with Lewis and his men, Clark and his party covered, by his estimate, sixty-six miles. He remarked on the colors and shapes of the land—"various Coloured earth," some of it red, much of it coal black, all of it "washed into Curious formed mounds & hills and . . . cut much with reveens." In too much of a hurry to climb up and look around, he saw only the ragged river edge of the dramatic Terry Badlands.

Around midday he passed the mouth of a tributary "40 yards wid Shallow and muddy," the banks of which can be faintly discerned near the horizon in the picture, and identified it as the stream the Mandan chief Sheheke had called Oak-tar-pon-er. Years later it came to be called O'Fallon Creek, reportedly after Clark's nephew, Benjamin O'Fallon, who served as a federal Indian agent until the 1820s.

(107) *Yellowstone River near Terry, Montana, in Terry Badlands Special Recreation Management Area* (view east, downstream) →

Prairie of the Knobs

On 6 July 1806, Clark and his contingent were, with Sacagawea's help, threading their way through a maze of Indian roads in the Big Hole Valley, en route back to Camp Fortunate. Meanwhile, 120 miles to the north, Lewis's eleven-man party had broken camp. That day, Lewis's detachment started from the mouth of a Blackfoot River tributary they named Seamans Creek, after Lewis's dog.

That morning the latter party continued through an "extensive high prarie rendered very uneven by a vast number of little hillucks and sinkholes." Lewis wrote, "These plains I called the prarie of the knobs from a number of knobs being irregularly scattered through it." Those "knobs" are mounds of debris deposited by piedmont glaciers during the last ice age, which ended about ten thousand years ago.

Now about halfway through their nine-day journey from Travelers' Rest back to the Great Falls, they seemed to be gaining on a large war party, possibly of Atsinas, compelling them to be "much on our guard both day and night," as Lewis recorded. On 7 July Seaman was "much worried"—either by the proximity of Indians or by the moose Reubin Field wounded near camp earlier that day.

"Dividing Ridge"

LATE IN THE DAY on 7 July 1806, Lewis and his party crossed "the dividing ridge between the waters of the Columbia and Missouri rivers" at today's Lewis and Clark Pass to the headwaters of the Dearborn River. Lewis said little about the area other than that he could see the landmark now called Square Butte—faintly discernable in the photo, just right of center on the horizon—which the Corps had dubbed Fort Mountain the previous July. In the small clearing right of center in the photo, traces of travois poles dragged across the divide by generations of Indians remain to this day faintly etched in the shallow, stony mountain soil.

Lewis and Clark Pass is six miles north of Rogers Pass, where Montana Highway 200 crosses the Continental Divide. The concept of the continental divide, and the term itself, would emerge only after about fifty more years of western exploration. However, the map Clark prepared for the first edition of the expedition's journals would be the first to show, with reasonable accuracy, the mountains separating the two drainages of the Northern Rockies.

Camp Disappointment

LEAVING THE "GRAND FALLS" of the Missouri on 17 July 1806, Lewis and three companions—George Drouillard and Joseph and Reubin Field—headed toward the Marias River. Lewis's sole purpose was to "ascertain whether any branch of that river lies as far north as Latd. 50." If so, it could be used to extend the United States' northern boundary, which had been established by the Paris Peace Treaty of 1783 at 49° 37', enlarging the territory gained through the Louisiana Purchase to include land north of the headwaters of the Mississippi River, as well as most of the Red River of the North drainage.

On 19 July Lewis intersected the Marias River six miles above the point where he had stopped the previous spring. The party continued northwest along the Marias until, on the evening of the twenty-second, the tributary now called Cut Bank Creek appeared to reach its northernmost point. There at "a clump of large cottonwood trees in a beautifull and extensive bottom" (below the bluff at the center of the photo), they made camp, "resolving to rest ourselves and horses a couple of days," Lewis wrote. Inclement weather prevented him from completing the necessary celestial observations, but he had already "lost all hope of the waters of this river ever extending to N. Latitude 50°."

With no game to be found in the vicinity, the four men survived on the remains of some roots and tainted meat they had brought, plus a few passenger pigeons and one small trout. On the twenty-sixth, Lewis and his detail "set out biding a lasting adieu to this place which I now call camp disappointment."

"Accedental Interview"

ON 26 JULY 1806, Lewis and his men left Camp Disappointment and headed for the mouth of the Marias River, where they planned to rendezvous with the rest of their contingent. After about seventeen miles, riding on the south (right) side of the Two Medicine River, Lewis spied eight young Indians "on the top of an eminence"—Flag Butte, the highest point on the ridge above the river in the photograph. The encounter was unwelcome, though not unexpected. Soon, however, Lewis concluded that they "were more allarmed at this accedental interview" than he and his own men were. Lewis assumed the Indians were the dreaded Atsinas, "Minnetarees of Fort de Prarie," but they were Piegan Blackfeet.

The Indians invited the Americans to partake of their shelter. The camp may have been in the vicinity of the wooded area on the far side of the river, just left of center in the picture. Settling in for the night, the two parties smoked and talked, with Drouillard as interpreter. Lewis told the Piegans of his expedition and its purposes, adding that an American post would soon be established in Blackfeet territory. To the youths, this meant that the Salish and other tribes unwelcome to the Blackfeet would come to trade on their turf.

At daybreak, despite the explorers' watchfulness, the Indians tried to steal their guns and horses, inciting a skirmish. Lewis and his men recovered the guns but killed at least one of the Piegans in the process. The rest fled. Quickly, the four Corps members packed their gear, mounted up, and raced toward the Missouri River, covering more than a hundred miles in a little over twenty-four hours. The next morning, as they neared Missouri, they heard rifle fire in the distance, and "on arriving at the bank of the [Missouri] river [we] had the unspeakable satisfaction to see our canoes coming down."

The Corps reunited on 12 August 1806 near today's New Town, North Dakota, and hurried down the Missouri, arriving in St. Louis on 23 September.

(111) *On the Two Medicine River near Cut Bank, Montana* (view east, downstream) →

Acknowledgments

George Berndt
David Borlaug
Butch Bouvier
Bob Doerk
Larry Epstein
Kim Ericsson
Barbara Fifer
Sally Freeman
Kira Gale
James Holmberg
Mimi and Darrold Jackson
Beth Judy
Ken Karsmizki

Jack Lepley
Steve Matz
Gwen McKenna
Robert Moore
Frank Muhly
Charles Parrish
Don Peterson
Eric Plunkett
Charles Raddon
Steve Russell
Roger Wendlick
Harry Windland
Rex Ziak

Recommended Reading

Allen, John Logan. *Lewis and Clark and the Image of the American Northwest*. New York: Dover, 1975.

Ambrose, Stephen. *Undaunted Courage: Meriwether Lewis, Thomas Jefferson, and the Opening of the American West*. New York: Simon & Schuster, 1996.

—————. *Lewis and Clark: Voyage of Discovery*. Photographs by Sam Abell. Washington, D.C.: National Geographic Society, 2002.

Appleman, Roy E. *Lewis and Clark: Historic Places Associated with Their Transcontinental Exploration (1804–06)*. Washington, D.C.: United States Department of the Interior, National Park Service, 1975.

Bergon, Frank. *The Journals of Lewis and Clark*. New York: Viking Penguin, 1989.

Beckham, Stephen Dow. *Lewis and Clark: From the Rockies to the Pacific*. With photographs by Robert M. Reynolds. Portland, Oregon: Graphic Arts Center Publishing Co., 2002.

Burroughs, Raymond Darwin. *The Natural History of the Lewis and Clark Expedition*. Second ed. East Lansing: Michigan State University Press, 1995.

Champagne, Duane, ed. *Native America: Portrait of the Peoples*. Detroit: Visible Ink Press, 1994.

Coues, Elliott, ed. *History of the Expedition Under the Command of Lewis and Clark*. 1893. Reprint. 3 vols. New York: Dover, 1965.

Cutright, Paul Russell. *Lewis and Clark: Pioneering Naturalists*. Urbana: University of Illinois Press, 1969.

Eagle Walking Turtle. *Indian America: A Traveler's Companion*. Fourth ed. Santa Fe: John Muir Publications, 1995.

Fifer, Barbara, and Vicky Soderberg. Maps by Joseph Mussulman. *Along the Trail with Lewis and Clark*. Second ed. Helena, Mont.: Farcountry Press, 2001.

Furtwangler, Albert. *Acts of Discovery: Visions of America in the Lewis and Clark Journals*. Urbana: University of Illinois Press, 1993.

Gilman, Carolyn. *Lewis and Clark Across the Divide*. Washington, D.C.: Smithsonian Books, 2003.

Graetz, Rick, and Suzie Graetz. *Lewis and Clark's Montana Trail*. Helena, Montana: Northern Rockies Publishing, 2001.

Lavender, David. *The Way to the Western Sea*. New York: Anchor-Doubleday, 1988.

Moeller, Bill, and Jan Moeller. *Lewis and Clark: A Photographic Journey*. Missoula, Mont.: Mountain Press, 2003.

Moulton, Gary E., ed. *The Definitive Journals of Lewis and Clark*. 10 vols. Lincoln: University of Nebraska Press, 1986–1997.

_____. *The Lewis and Clark Journals: An American Epic of Discovery*. Lincoln: University of Nebraska Press, 2003.

Peck, David. *Or Perish in the Attempt: Wilderness Medicine in the Lewis and Clark Expedition*. Helena, Mont.: Farcountry Press, 2002.

Plamondon, Martin, II. *Lewis and Clark Trail Maps: A Cartographic Reconstruction*. 3 vols. Pullman: Washington State University Press, 2000–2003.

Ronda, James P. *Lewis and Clark Among the Indians*. Bicentennial ed. Lincoln: University of Nebraska Press, 2002.

Schmidt, Thomas, and Jeremy Schmidt. *Into the Uncharted West: The Saga of Lewis and Clark*. Photographs by Wayne Mumford. New York: Dorling Kindersley Publishing, 2003.

Tubbs, Stephenie Ambrose, and Clay Jenkinson. *The Lewis and Clark Companion: An Encyclopedic Guide to the Voyage of Discovery*. New York: Henry Holt & Company, 2003.

In addition to these books, there are many important texts devoted to Lewis and Clark in specific regions or states, such as *Seeking Western Waters: The Lewis and Clark Trail from the Rockies to the Pacific*, Emory and Ruth Strong (Portland: Oregon Historical Society, 1995); *Lewis and Clark in Missouri*, Ann Rogers (3rd ed. Columbia: University of Missouri Press, 2002); and *Across the Snowy Ranges: The Lewis and Clark Expedition in Idaho and Western Montana*, James R. Fazio, with photography by Mike Venso and cartography by Steve F. Russell (Moscow, Idaho: Woodland Press, 2001). Readers interested in flora may be interested in *Lewis and Clark's Green World: The Expedition and Its Plants*, A. Scott Earle and James L. Reveal (Helena, Mont.: Farcountry Press, 2003), and *Plants of the Lewis & Clark Expedition*, H. Wayne Phillips (Missoula, Mont.: Mountain Press, 2003). There is a steadily growing list of biographical studies, including a reprint of the classic *Men of the Lewis and Clark Expedition*, Charles G. Clark, with an introduction by Dayton Duncan (1970; reprint, Lincoln: Bison Books, 2002); and James Holmberg's, *Dear Brother: Letters of William Clark to Jonathan Clark* (New Haven: Yale University Press, 2002).

Index

Page numbers in **boldface** indicate photographs

257

JIM WARK, a Michigan native, came to Colorado in 1958. He enjoyed careers as a naval aviator, a mining engineer, and a real estate executive before becoming an aerial photographer. Working alone from his small airplane, he has photographed all the states and provinces of North America, along with much of Central America and the Caribbean. He has authored numerous magazine articles and contributed to many books. *Discovering Lewis & Clark from the Air* is the third full volume of his photography.

Wark summarizes his feelings about his photography in this way: "In doing this work, airplane, camera, and photographer are a unit. I love the freedom, mobility, and adventure of aerial photography; to work with the seasons, the weather, and the light; and the ability to seek out hidden places and serendipitous views. It is a constant and compelling challenge to create this work, and it is exciting to share it."

Jim lives in Pueblo, Colorado, with his wife, Judy. Interested readers are invited to visit his Web site at *www.airphotoNA.com.*

JOSEPH A. MUSSULMAN is a teacher, author, cartographer, and lecturer. He is also the producer of the popular Web site *Discovering Lewis & Clark®* *(www.lewis-clark.org)*, an extensive hyperhistory that has been online since 1998 and is expanded regularly. He lives in Missoula, Montana.

We encourage you to patronize your local bookstore. Most stores will order any title that they do not stock. You may also order directly from Mountain Press using the order form provided below or by calling our toll-free number and using your credit card. We will gladly send you a catalog upon request.

Some history titles of interest:

_____ _Discovering Lewis & Clark from the Air_ $24.00/paper $40.00/cloth

_____ _The Journals of Patrick Gass:_
Member of the Lewis and Clark Expedition $20.00/paper

_____ _Geology of the Lewis & Clark Trail in North Dakota_ $18.00/paper

_____ _Lewis & Clark: A Photographic Journey_ $18.00/paper

_____ _Plants of the Lewis & Clark Expedition_ $20.00/paper

_____ _Sacagawea's Son: The Life of Jean Baptiste Charbonneau_ $10.00/paper _(for readers 10 and up)_

Please include $3.00 for 1-4 books or $5.00 for 5 or more books for shipping and handling.

Send the books marked above. I enclose $ _____

Name _____

Address _____

City/State/Zip _____

☐ Payment enclosed (check or money order in U.S. funds)

Bill my: ☐ VISA ☐ MasterCard ☐ American Express ☐ Discover   Exp. Date:_____

Card No. _____

Signature _____

MOUNTAIN PRESS PUBLISHING COMPANY
P.O. Box 2399 • Missoula, MT 59806 • fax: 406-728-1635
Order Toll Free 1-800-234-5308 • Have your credit card ready
e-mail: info@mtnpress.com • website: www.mountain-press.com

Nursing Care Plans

Nursing Diagnosis and Intervention

Meg Gulanick, PhD, APRN, FAAN
Professor
Niehoff School of Nursing
Loyola University Chicago
Chicago, Illinois

Judith L. Myers, MSN, RN
Assistant Professor of Nursing
Grandview College
Des Moines, Iowa

Susan Galanes, MS, RN, CCRN
Clinical Nurse Specialist
Suburban Lung Associates
Winfield, Illinois

Audrey Klopp, PhD, RN, CS, ET, NHA
Administrator
Plymouth Place, Inc.
La Grange Park, Illinois

Deidra Gradishar, RNC, BS
Chicago, Illinois

Michele Knoll Puzas, RNC, MHPE
*Workman's Compensation Coordinator/
Professional Recruiter*
Michael Reese Hospital and Medical Center
Chicago, Illinois

MOSBY

ELSEVIER

MOSBY
ELSEVIER

11830 Westline Industrial Drive
St. Louis, Missouri 63146

NURSING CARE PLANS: NURSING DIAGNOSIS AND
INTERVENTION

ISBN-13: 978-0-323-03954-3
ISBN-10: 0-323-03954-5

Notice

Knowledge and best practice in this field are constantly changing. As new research and experience
broaden our knowledge, changes in practice, treatment and drug therapy may become necessary or
appropriate. Readers are advised to check the most current information provided (i) on procedures
featured or (ii) by the manufacturer of each product to be administered, to verify the recommended
dose or formula, the method and duration of administration, and contraindications. It is the
responsibility of the practitioner, relying on their own experience and knowledge of the patient,
to make diagnoses, to determine dosages and the best treatment for each individual patient, and to
take all appropriate safety precautions. To the fullest extent of the law, neither the Publisher nor
the [Editors/Authors] [delete as appropriate] assumes any liability for any injury and/or damage
to persons or property arising out or related to any use of the material contained in this book.

The Publisher

ISBN-13: 978-0-323-03954-3
ISBN-10: 0-323-03954-5

Acquisitions Editor: Lee Henderson
Senior Developmental Editor: Rae L. Robertson
Publishing Services Manager: Deborah L. Vogel
Senior Project Manager: Jodi M. Willard
Design Direction: Amy Buxton
Cover Designer: Amy Buxton

Printed in the United States of America

Last digit is the print number: 9 8 7 6 5 4 3 2

Contributors

Judy Lau Carino, MSN, CNP
Clinical Instructor
Niehoff School of Nursing
Loyola University Chicago
Chicago, Illinois

Pamela Cianci, MSN, APRN, BC
Clinical Nurse Specialist—Heart Failure
Advocate Christ Medical Center
Oaklawn, Illinois

Marianne T. Cosentino, MSN, CCNS
Clinical Nurse Specialist
Division of Cardiology/Electrophysiology
Loyola University Health System
Maywood, Illinois

Gail DeLuca, MSN, APRN-BC, FNP
Instructor
Niehoff School of Nursing
Loyola University Chicago
Chicago, Illinois;
Family Nurse Practitioner
Poronsky Family Practice
Palos Heights, Illinois

Linda Flemm, RN, MSN, OCN
Clinical Nurse Specialist
Cancer Service Line
Loyola University Medical Center
Maywood, Illinois

Patricia J. Friend, RN, PhD, AOCN
Assistant Professor
Niehoff School of Nursing
Loyola University Chicago
Chicago, Illinois

Katrina Gallagher, MSN, NP-C
Nurse Practitioner, Emergency Room
Greater Elgin Emergency Specialists
Elgin, Illinois

Mary Ellen Hand, RN, BSN
Nurse Coordinator
Pigmented Lesion Center
Division of Hematology/Oncology
Rush University Hospital
Chicago, Illinois

Connie Huberty, MS, APRN-BC
Cardiovascular Clinical Nurse Specialist
Edward Heart Hospital
Naperville, Illinois

Judi Jennrich, RN, PhD, ACNP, CCRN
Associate Professor
Niehoff School of Nursing
Loyola University Chicago
Chicago, Illinois

Linda Kamenjarin, MS, RN
Clinical Nurse Specialist
Cardiovascular Surgery
Advocate Christ Medical Center
Oaklawn, Illinois

Tamara M. Kear, RN, MSN, CNN
Nursing Instructor
Gwynedd-Mercy College
Gwynedd Valley, Pennsylvania

Catherine A. Kefer, RN, MSN
Research Assistant
Niehoff School of Nursing
Loyola University Chicago
Chicago, Illinois

Vicki A. Keough, PhD, ACNP, CCRN
Associate Dean, Master's Program
Associate Professor
Niehoff School of Nursing
Loyola University Chicago
Chicago, Illinois

Marijo Letizia, RN, PhD, APRN-BC
Associate Professor
Niehoff School of Nursing
Loyola University Chicago
Chicago, Illinois

Shelby J. Neel, RN, MSN
Clinical Teaching Associate
Grand View College;
Clinical Nurse
Iowa Methodist Medical Center
Des Moines, Iowa

Linda Denise Oakley, RN, PhD, NP
Professor
School of Nursing
University of Wisconsin—Madison
Madison, Wisconsin

Kelly Oney, MS, APRN, BC-FNP
Board Certified Family Nurse Practitioner
Winfield Family Medicine
Crown Point, Indiana

Judy K. Orth, RN, CHPN, BSN, MA
Adjunct Professor
Grand View College
Des Moines, Iowa

Sue Penckofer, RN, PhD
Professor
Niehoff School of Nursing
Loyola University Chicago
Chicago, Illinois

Lucina M. Sheehy, RN, MSN
Assistant Professor of Nursing
Grand View College
Des Moines, Iowa

Kathy G. Supple, RN, MSN, ACNP, CCRN
Certified Nurse Practitioner
Burn Center
Loyola University Medical Center
Maywood, Illinois

Terry D. Takemoto, RN, MSN, BC
Director of Education
Kindred Chicago Lakeshore
Chicago, Illinois

Geri Tansey, MSN, RN
Clinical Nurse Specialist
Cardiovascular Surgery
Advocate Christ Medical Center
Oak Lawn, Illinois

Carol White, RN, MSN, APN/CNS, AOCN
Advanced Practice Nurse, Hematology-Oncology
Loyola University Medical Center
Maywood, Illinois

Jeffrey Zurlinden, MS
Clinical Coordinator
Northwestern Memorial Hospital
Chicago, Illinois

FIFTH EDITION
Cathy Concert
Peggy Donovan
Marcia J. Hill
Dotti C. James
Lori Klingman
Elaine McLeod
Regina Nicholson
Linda Oakley
Debbie Sanazaro
Melinda Weber
Lynn Wimett
Karen Wiseman

FOURTH EDITION
Sherry Adams
Cynthia Antonio
Linda Arsenault
Lou Ann Ary
Marina Bautista
Kathryn S. Bronstein
Ursula Brozek
Marian D. Cachero-Salavrakos
Mary Leslie Caldwell
Carol Clark
Jan Colip
Eileen Collins
Sue A. Connaughton
Adrian Cooney
Nancy J. Cooney
Margaret A. Cunningham
Maria Dacanay
Catherine Dunning
Linda Ehrlich
Sandra Eungard
Ann Filipski
Sharon Flucus
Robin R. Fortman
Victoria Frazier-Jones
Susan Galanes
Barbara Gallagher
Susan Geoghegan
Margaret Gleason
Cynthia Gordon
Deidra Gradishar
Kathleen L. Grady

Meg Gulanick
Frankie Harper
Lorraine M. Heaney
Jean M. Hughes
Florencia Isidro-Sanchez
Kathleen Jaffry
Vivian Jones
Linda Kamenjarin
Maureen Kangleon
Carol Keeler
Audrey Klopp
Mary Larson
Susan R. Laub
Debbie Lazzara
Cheryl Lefaiver
Evelyn Lyons
Donna MacDonald
Marilyn Magafas
Beth Manglal-Lan
Sheri Martucci
Mary T. McCarthy
Doris M. McNear
Encaracion Mendoza
Anita Morris
Linda Muzio
Carol Nawrocki
Charlotte Niznik
Margaret Norton
Mary O'Leary
Rachel Ongsansoy
Anne Paglinawan

Lumie Perez
Kathleen M. Perry
Gina Marie Petruzzelli
Susan Pische
Judith Popovich
Michele Knoll Puzas
Eileen Raebig
Charlotte Razvi
Dorothy Rhodes
Linda Rosen-Walsh
Rosaline L. Roxas
Carol Ruback
Nancy Ruppman
Marilyn Samson-Hinton
Caroline Sarmiento
Christa M. Schroeder
Nedra Skale
Gail Smith-Jaros
Linda Marie St. Julien
Nancy Staples
Lela Starnes
Christina Stewart-Amidei
Virginia M. Storey
Denise Talley-Lacey
Hope Tolitano
Maureen Weber
Sherry Weber
Lynn Wentz
Gloria Young
Jeff Zurlinden

Reviewers

Sandra K. Brannan, MSN, RN
Assistant Professor, Department of Nursing
Lamar University
Beaumont, Texas

Wendy Brzezny, student reviewer
Big Bend Community College
Ephrata, Washington

Michelle Butler, student reviewer
Bellevue, Nebraska

Olivia Catolico, PhD, MS
Assistant Professor, Department of Nursing
California State University, San Bernardino
San Bernardino, California

Barbara Chamberlain, MSN, APRN, BC,
CCRN, WCC
Critical Care Advanced Practice Nurse
Kennedy Health System
Turnersville, New Jersey

Susan Mott Coles, RN, MSN, AOCN(R),
APRN-BC
Research Nurse
Sarah Cannon Research Institute
Nashville, Tennessee

Nancy W. Darland, RNC, MSN, CNS
Professor, School of Nursing
Louisiana Tech University
Ruston, Louisiana

Leslee D. Edwards, student reviewer
Dillard University
New Orleans, Louisiana

Marianne Fasano, RN, MSN, MEd, CRNI, PCCN,
COCN, CWCN
Assistant Director of Nursing
Pasco-Hernando Community College
New Port Richey, Florida

Margaret Madonna Harkins, RN, MSN, CRNP
Assistant Professor, School of Nursing
LaSalle University;
Adjunct Faculty, School of Nursing
Drexel University
Philadelphia, Pennsylvania

Connie Heflin, MSN, RN
Professor, Nursing Program
West Kentucky Community and Technical College
Paducah, Kentucky

Marilyn Herbert-Ashton, RN, MS, BC
Professor, Department of Nursing
Virginia Western Community College
Roanoke, Virginia

Sarah Morgan Howell, RN, MSN
Assistant Professor of Nursing
Mississippi University for Women
Columbus, Mississippi

Helen Jackson-Ruiz, RN, MSN
Assistant Professor, School of Nursing
Nebraska Methodist College
Omaha, Nebraska

Andrea Knesek, MSN, RN
Professor, Department of Nursing
Macomb Community College
Clinton Township, Michigan

Pamela D. Korte, RN, MS
Associate Professor, Department of Nursing
Monroe Community College
Rochester, New York

Rosemary Macy, PhDc, RN
Assistant Professor, Department of Nursing
Boise State University
Boise, Idaho

Tom Mallon, student reviewer
Wallace Community College
Enterprise, Alabama

Vanessa Mattson, student reviewer
University of North Carolina—Wilmington
Wilmington, North Carolina

Jonathan E. McDonald, student reviewer
UPMC Shadyside School of Nursing
Pittsburgh, Pennsylvania

Amber D. McKenzie, RN, BSN
Memorial Hermann Children's Hospital
Houston, Texas

Heather M. McKnight, student reviewer
Southern Arkansas University
Magnolia, Arkansas

Laurie J. Parks, RN
Greensboro, North Carolina

Michael Perlow, DNS, RN
Professor of Nursing
Murray State University
Murray, Kentucky

Nicole Marie Rall, BSN, RN
Staff Nurse
Banner Good Samaritan Medical Center
Phoenix, Arizona

Sharleen Sawicki, student reviewer
McMaster University
Hamilton, Ontario

Theresa Anne Schmidt, student reviewer
St. Louis Community College
Jewish School of Nursing
St. Louis, Missouri

Deborah Shows-Rushing, RN, MSN
Instructor of Nursing
Troy University
Troy, Alabama

Darrell Spurlock, Jr., MSN, RN, CCRN, CEN
Professor
Mount Carmel College of Nursing
Columbus, Ohio

Wendy Bodendoerfer Stewart, MSN, RN, BA
Professor of Nursing
San Jacinto College—Central
Pasadena, Texas

Lori Theodore, student reviewer
Valencia Community College
Winter Garden, Florida

Melissa Tinnesand, student reviewer
Arizona State University
Goodyear, Arizona

Delrose Tobie, student reviewer
Lake-Sumter Community College
Leesburg, Florida

Sharon Henry Walicek, RN, MEd, MSN, CCNS,
CCRN, ANP-BC
Professor, Department of Nursing
Elgin Community College
Elgin, Illinois

Robert Ware, student reviewer
Clayton College and State University
Atlanta, Georgia

Melissa Yiengst, student reviewer
Alvernia College
Reading, Pennsylvania

Sara Young, RN
Emergency Trauma Staff Nurse
Barnes-Jewish Hospital
St. Louis, Missouri

Preface

Our primary goal for this edition of *Nursing Care Plans: Nursing Diagnosis and Intervention* has been to build on the quality of the previous editions. We want this edition to continue as a state-of-the-art resource used by nurses to plan care for an increasingly diverse population of patients with medical-surgical health problems. The essential format for the book and for the individual care plans has not changed from the 5th edition. Most of the care plans focus on the patient in the acute care setting of the hospital. These care plans include assessments and therapeutic interventions for discharge planning and transition to the community. In addition, some of the care plans have a specific focus on the nursing care of patients in the community.

With this edition, we have included the latest research and nursing science that guides evidence-based nursing practice. Up-to-date information continues to be added to the introductions to the nursing diagnosis care plans in Chapter 2 and to the medical disorder care plans in the remaining chapters. This information provides a foundation for understanding the nursing care for a specific nursing diagnosis or medical disorder. The Ongoing Assessments contain the latest information on methods of assessment and for laboratory and diagnostic tests. The Therapeutic Interventions include up-to-date information on independent and collaborative clinical management and on drug therapy related to nursing diagnoses and medical disorders. The rationales for the Ongoing Assessments and Therapeutic Interventions have been updated and expanded to include current standards and clinical practice guidelines in nursing and other health care disciplines.

Chapter 1 has been revised to provide an expanded discussion of the components of the care plan. Illustrations have been added to this chapter to further clarify the content.

In Chapter 2, four new care plans have been added for the North American Nursing Diagnosis Association (NANDA) International diagnoses of Latex Allergy Response, Risk for Falls, Nausea, and Impaired Memory. The nursing diagnoses used throughout the book have been updated to reflect the NANDA International *Nursing Diagnoses: Definitions and Classification 2005-2006*.

New medical disorder care plans added to this edition include West Nile virus and Lyme disease in the Neurological Care Plans chapter, and SARS and obstructive sleep apnea in the Pulmonary Care Plans chapter.

We give strong support to the development of standardized language to communicate the outcomes and interventions of nursing practice that are represented by the Nursing Intervention Classifications (NIC) and Nursing Outcomes Classifications (NOC). We continue to include the latest editions of NIC and NOC labels at the beginning of each care plan.

The index continues to include entries for all nursing diagnoses, all medical diagnoses, and all synonyms for the medical diagnoses, providing an easy-to-use, practical tool for accessing the book's content.

We continue to use the Evolve website as an adjunct to the printed book. The expanded website now includes 18 additional care plans: amyotrophic lateral sclerosis, myasthenia gravis, near-drowning, adrenal insufficiency, diabetes insipidus, hemophilia, hemorrhoids/hemorrhoidectomy, hematopoietic stem cell collection, vascular access for hemodialysis, blood component therapy, central venous access devices, erectile dysfunction, premenstrual syndrome, dermatitis, anorexia nervosa, bulimia, rape trauma syndrome, and suicide.

The revised Online Care Plan Constructor on the Evolve website contains all nursing diagnosis care plans from Chapter 2. It enables the user to customize the care plan for an individual patient, select from diagnoses, and list specific risk factors, NOC outcomes, NIC interventions and rationales, home care interventions, and specific client/family teaching. This tool has been updated to reflect the additional nursing diagnosis care plans added to the text and is enhanced to allow the user to save customized data. An additional enhancement is the ability to export saved care plans to a word-processing program.

We are grateful to the many contributors to previous editions of this book. Their work continues to be the foundation for the nurses who have contributed to the revisions for this edition.

MEG GULANICK, PHD, APRN, FAAN
JUDITH L. MYERS, MSN, RN

Contents*

*Some care plans are provided on the Evolve website.

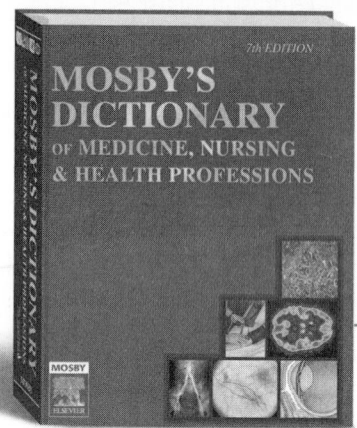

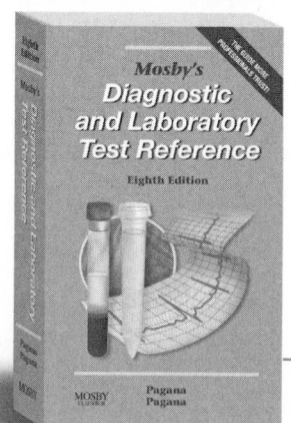

Using Nursing Care Plans to Individualize and Improve Care

Introduction

The diagnosis and treatment of human responses to actual or potential health problems transcend settings, cross the age continuum, and support a wellness philosophy with a focus on self-care. In many ways, they are enhanced by opportunities to provide nursing care in the more natural, less institutional paradigms that are demanded by restructured health care financing.

According to the American Nurses Association (ANA), nursing is the diagnosis and treatment of human responses to actual and potential problems. A broad scope of scientific knowledge, including the biological and behavioral realms, combined with the ability to assist patients, families, and other caregivers in managing their own health needs, has always provided an enormous role for nurses. The current challenges in seizing these opportunities include the following: (1) the ability of the nursing educational system to increasingly prepare future nurses for settings outside the hospital environment, (2) the ability of nurses themselves to be comfortable with the responsibility of their roles, (3) the ability of sufficient numbers of advanced practice nurses to be adequately prepared as primary health care providers, (4) the need to increase the recruitment and retention of nurses from diverse backgrounds to meet the needs of an increasingly diverse population, and (5) the availability of tools to assist nurses in assessing, planning, and providing care. *Nursing Care Plans: Nursing Diagnosis and Intervention* is such a tool.

Components of These Nursing Care Plans

Each care plan in this book begins with an expanded definition of the title problem or diagnosis (Figure 1-1). These definitions include enough information to guide the user in understanding what the problem or diagnosis is, information regarding the incidence or prevalence of the problem or diagnosis, a brief overview of the typical management and/or the focus of nursing care, and a description of the setting in which care for the particular problem or diagnosis can be expected to occur.

Each problem or diagnosis is accompanied by one or several cross-references, some of which may be synonyms (see Figure 1-1). These cross-references assist the user in locating other information that may be helpful and in deciding whether this particular care plan is indeed the one the user needs.

For each care plan, appropriate nursing diagnoses are developed, each with the following components:

- Common related factors (those etiologies associated with a diagnosis for an actual problem) (Figure 1-2)
- Defining characteristics (assessment data that support the nursing diagnosis) (see Figure 1-2)
- Common risk factors (those situations or conditions that contribute to the person's potential to develop a problem or diagnosis) (Figure 1-3)

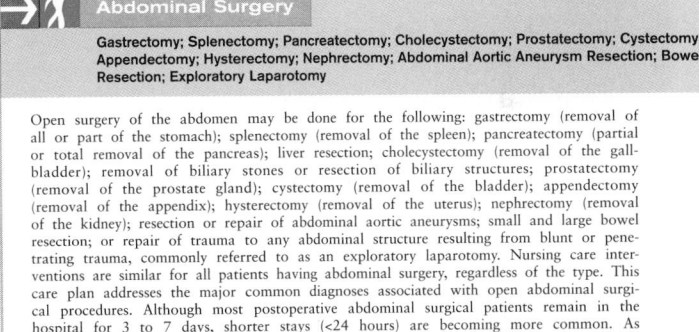

Abdominal Surgery

Gastrectomy; Splenectomy; Pancreatectomy; Cholecystectomy; Prostatectomy; Cystectomy; Appendectomy; Hysterectomy; Nephrectomy; Abdominal Aortic Aneurysm Resection; Bowel Resection; Exploratory Laparotomy

Open surgery of the abdomen may be done for the following: gastrectomy (removal of all or part of the stomach); splenectomy (removal of the spleen); pancreatectomy (partial or total removal of the pancreas); liver resection; cholecystectomy (removal of the gallbladder); removal of biliary stones or resection of biliary structures; prostatectomy (removal of the prostate gland); cystectomy (removal of the bladder); appendectomy (removal of the appendix); hysterectomy (removal of the uterus); nephrectomy (removal of the kidney); resection or repair of abdominal aortic aneurysms; small and large bowel resection; or repair of trauma to any abdominal structure resulting from blunt or penetrating trauma, commonly referred to as an exploratory laparotomy. Nursing care interventions are similar for all patients having abdominal surgery, regardless of the type. This care plan addresses the major common diagnoses associated with open abdominal surgical procedures. Although most postoperative abdominal surgical patients remain in the hospital for 3 to 7 days, shorter stays (<24 hours) are becoming more common. As laparoscopic techniques and instrumentation continue to develop, less open abdominal surgery is being performed.

Figure 1-1 Expanded definition and cross-references of a care plan.

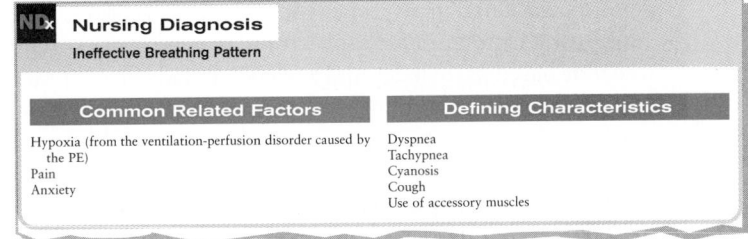

NDx Nursing Diagnosis

Ineffective Breathing Pattern

Common Related Factors	Defining Characteristics
Hypoxia (from the ventilation-perfusion disorder caused by the PE) Pain Anxiety	Dyspnea Tachypnea Cyanosis Cough Use of accessory muscles

Figure 1-2 Common related factors and defining characteristics of the nursing diagnosis.

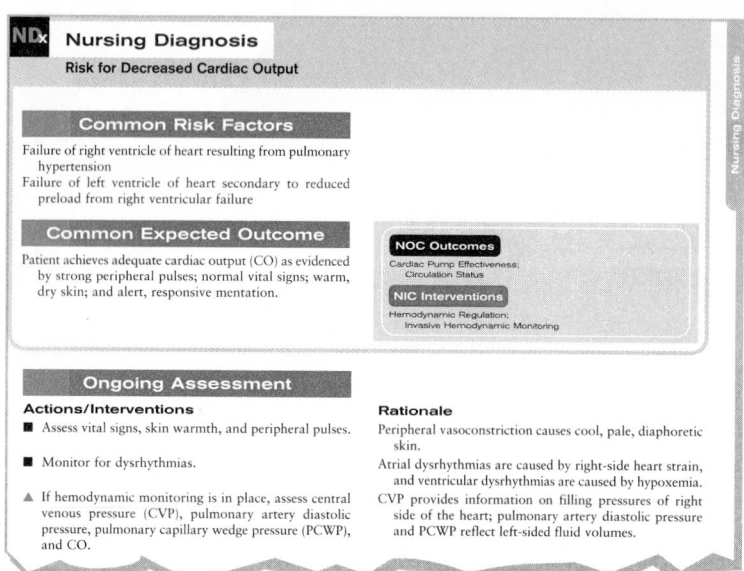

NDx Nursing Diagnosis
Risk for Decreased Cardiac Output

Common Risk Factors

Failure of right ventricle of heart resulting from pulmonary hypertension
Failure of left ventricle of heart secondary to reduced preload from right ventricular failure

Common Expected Outcome

Patient achieves adequate cardiac output (CO) as evidenced by strong peripheral pulses; normal vital signs; warm, dry skin; and alert, responsive mentation.

NOC Outcomes
Cardiac Pump Effectiveness; Circulation Status

NIC Interventions
Hemodynamic Regulation; Invasive Hemodynamic Monitoring

Ongoing Assessment

Actions/Interventions	Rationale
■ Assess vital signs, skin warmth, and peripheral pulses.	Peripheral vasoconstriction causes cool, pale, diaphoretic skin.
■ Monitor for dysrhythmias.	Atrial dysrhythmias are caused by right-side heart strain, and ventricular dysrhythmias are caused by hypoxemia.
▲ If hemodynamic monitoring is in place, assess central venous pressure (CVP), pulmonary artery diastolic pressure, pulmonary capillary wedge pressure (PCWP), and CO.	CVP provides information on filling pressures of right side of the heart; pulmonary artery diastolic pressure and PCWP reflect left-sided fluid volumes.

Figure 1-3 Common risk factors, common expected outcomes, and ongoing assessment of the nursing diagnosis.

Therapeutic Interventions

Actions/Interventions	Rationale
■ Reduce the patient's or significant others' anxiety by explaining all procedures or treatment. Keep explanations basic.	Information helps allay anxiety. Patients who are anxious may not be able to comprehend anything more than simple, clear, brief instruction.
■ Maintain a confident, assured manner.	The staff's anxiety may be easily perceived by patient. The patient's feeling of stability increases in a calm, nonthreatening atmosphere.
■ Encourage the patient to ventilate feelings of anxiety.	Understanding the patient's feelings of anxiety will guide the staff in planning and implementing a care plan to allay individualized anxiety.
■ Provide adequate rest as follows:	
• Organize activities (e.g., morning care, meals, hospital staff rounds, treatments).	Rest improves ability to cope. Organization of tasks can reduce demands on patient's energy level.
• Decrease sensory stimulation as follows:	
• Dim lights when appropriate.	A darkened room can facilitate rest.
• Remove unnecessary equipment from room.	This helps maintain a more relaxed environment.
• Limit visitors and phone calls (to prevent tiring).	Patients feel obligated to entertain, which may be physically and emotionally taxing.
▲ Administer pain medicines or sedatives as indicated.	This assists in allaying anxiety. Anxiety may increase oxygen consumption.
▲ Refer to other support systems (e.g., clergy, social workers, other family or friends) as appropriate.	Specialty exercise may be required.

Figure 1-4 Therapeutic interventions of the nursing diagnosis.

- Common expected outcomes (see Figure 1-3)
- Ongoing assessment (see Figure 1-3)
- Therapeutic interventions (both independent and collaborative) (Figure 1-4)

Wherever possible, expanded rationales assist the user in understanding the information presented; this allows for use of *Nursing Care Plans: Nursing Diagnosis and Intervention* as a singular reference tool. The interventions and supporting rationales for each care plan represent current research-based knowledge and evidence-based clinical practice guidelines for nursing and other health care professionals. Many care plans also refer the user to additional diagnoses that may be pertinent and would assist the user in further developing a care plan. Each diagnosis developed in these care plans also identifies the Iowa Nursing Interventions Classification (NIC) interventions and the Iowa Nursing Outcomes Classifications (NOC) outcomes.

Nursing Diagnosis and Nursing Interventions and Outcomes Classification

As *Nursing Care Plans: Nursing Diagnosis and Intervention* continues to mature and reflect the changing times and needs of its readers, as well as the needs of those for whom care is provided, nursing diagnoses continue to evolve. The body of research to support diagnoses, their definitions, related and risk factors, and defining characteristics is ever increasing and gaining momentum. Nurses continue to study both independent and collaborative interventions for effectiveness and desirable outcomes.

The taxonomy as a whole continues to be refined; its use as an international tool for practice, education, and research is testament to its importance as an organizing framework for the body of knowledge that is uniquely nursing. As a taxonomy, nursing diagnosis and all its components are standardized. Nurses must remember that care plans developed for each diagnosis or cluster of diagnoses for particular patients must be individualized. The tailoring of the care plan is the hallmark of nursing practice.

Nursing Interventions Classification (NIC) presents an additional opportunity for clarifying and organizing what nurses do. With NIC, nursing interventions have been systematically organized to help nurses identify and select interventions. In this sixth edition, NIC information continues to be presented along with each nursing diagnosis within each care plan, giving the user added ability to use NIC taxonomy in planning for individualized patient care. According to the developers of NIC, nursing interventions are "any treatment, based upon clinical judgment and knowledge, that a nurse performs to enhance patient/client outcomes" (Dochterman, Bulechek, 2004, p. 3). These interventions may include direct or indirect care and may be initiated by a nurse, a physician, or another care provider. Student nurses, practicing nurses, advanced practice nurses, and nurse executives can use nursing diagnoses and NIC as tools for learning, organizing, and delivering care; managing care within the framework of redesigned health care and within financial constraints through the development of critical paths; identifying research questions; and monitoring the outcomes of nursing care both at an individual level and at the level of service provision to large populations of patients.

Nurse investigators at the University of Iowa have developed Nursing Outcomes Classification (NOC), a taxonomy of patient outcomes that are sensitive to nursing interventions. The authors of this outcomes taxonomy state, "For nurses to work effectively with managed care organizations to improve quality and reduce costs, nurses must be able to measure and document patient outcomes influenced by nursing care" (Moorhead, Johnson & Maas, 2004, p. 8). In this context, an outcome is defined as the status of the patient or family that follows and is directly influenced by nursing interventions.

The following portion of this chapter guides the user of this text through the steps of individualized care plan development. It also contains recommendations about how this book can be used as the basis of critical path development, for the development of patient education materials, and as a tool for quality improvement work and creating seamless nursing care delivery, regardless of where in the continuum of health care the patient happens to be.

Using *Nursing Care Plans: Nursing Diagnosis and Intervention*

Developing an Individualized Care Plan

The nursing care plan is best thought of as a written reflection of the nursing process: What does the assessment reveal? What should be done? How, when, and where should these planned interventions be carried out? What is the desired outcome? That is, will the delivery of planned interventions result in the desired goal? The nurse's ability to carry out this process in a systematic fashion, using all available information and resources, is the fundamental basis for nursing practice. This process includes correctly identifying existing needs, as well as recognizing potential needs and/or risks. Planning and delivering care in an individualized fashion to address these actual or potential needs, as well as evaluating the effectiveness of that care, is the basis for excellence in nursing practice. Forming a partnership with the patient and/or caregiver in this process and humanizing the experience of being a care recipient is the essence of nursing.

The Assessment

All the information that the nurse collects regarding a particular patient makes up the assessment. This assessment allows a nursing diagnosis, or clinical judgment, to be made. This, in turn, drives the identification of expected outcomes (i.e., what is desired by and for this particular patient in relation to this identified need) and the care plan. Without a comprehensive assessment, all else is a "shot in the dark."

Nurses have always carried out the task of assessment. As science and technology progress, information is more abundant than at any other time in history; however, length of contact with each patient becomes shorter, so astute assessment skills are essential in a nurse's ability to plan and deliver effective nursing care.

Assessment data are abundant in any clinical setting. What the nurse observes, what a history (written or verbal) reveals, what the patient and/or caregiver reports (or fails to report) about a situation, problem, or concern, and what laboratory and other diagnostic information is available are all valid and important data.

Methods useful in gathering these diverse data include interview, direct and indirect observation, physical assessment, medical records review, and analysis and synthesis of available laboratory and other diagnostic studies. The sum of all information obtained through any or all of these means allows the nurse to make a nursing diagnosis.

Gordon's (1976) definition of a nursing diagnosis includes only those problems that nurses are capable of treating, whereas others have expanded the definition to include any health-related issue with which a nurse may interface. In *Nursing Care Plans: Nursing Diagnosis and Intervention*, a sincere attempt is made to use approved North American Nursing Diagnosis Association (NANDA) terminology, although the user will occasionally find problems or health-related issues that do not reflect NANDA terminology. All of the nursing diagnosis terminology in this edition has been revised to conform to the NANDA *Nursing Diagnoses: Definitions & Classification*, 2005-2006. For many of the nursing diagnoses, the modifiers have changed to provide a clearer indication of the type of alteration that has occurred in the diagnostic phenomenon. The reader is reminded that the care plans in this book are written by practicing nurses who form the "front line" in the recognition, identification, and labeling of problems or health-related concerns of their patients.

Performing the Assessment

A nurse has knowledge in the physical and behavioral sciences, is a trusted member of the health care team, and is the interdisciplinary team member who has the most contact with a patient. Because of these qualities, a nurse is in a key position to collect data from the patient and/or caregiver at any point at which the patient enters the health care continuum, whether in the home, in a hospital, in an outpatient clinic, or in a long-term care facility.

Interviewing is an important method of gathering information about a patient. The interview has the added dimensions of providing the nurse with the patient's subjective input on not only the problem but also what the patient may feel about the causes of the problem, how the problem has affected the patient as an individual, what outcomes the patient wants in relation to the particular problem, as well as insight into how the patient and/or caregiver may or may not be capable of participating in management of the problem.

Good interviewing skills are founded on rapport with the patient, the skill of active listening, and preparation in a systematic, thorough format with comprehensive attention given to specific health-related problems. The nurse as the interviewer must be knowledgeable of the patient's overall condition and the environment in which the interview will take place. A comprehensive interview that includes exploration of all the functional health patterns is ideal and will provide the best overall picture of the patient. When time is a limiting factor, the nurse may review existing medical records or other documents before the interview so that the interview can be focused. Care must be taken, however, to not "miss the forest for the trees" by conducting an interview in a fashion that precludes the discovery of important information the patient may have to share.

During an interview the patient may report the following types of information:

- Bothersome or unusual signs and symptoms (e.g., "I have been having cramps and bloody diarrhea for the past month.")
- Changes noticed (e.g., "It's a lot worse when I drink milk.")
- The impact of these problems on his or her ability to carry out desired or necessary activities (e.g., "I know every washroom at the mall. It's tough having lunch with friends.")
- Issues associated with the primary problem (e.g., "It's so embarrassing when my stomach starts to rumble loudly.")
- The impact of these problems on significant others (e.g., "My daughter cannot understand why a trip to the zoo feels like a challenge.")
- What specifically caused the patient to seek attention (e.g., "The amount of blood in the past couple of days really has me worried, and the pain is getting worse.")

In addition, the patient may share the following:

- Previous experiences or history (e.g., "My brother has had Crohn's disease for several years; this is how he started out.")
- Health beliefs and feelings about the problem (e.g., "I have always figured it would catch up with me sooner or later, with all the problems like this in our family.")
- Thoughts on what would help solve the problem (e.g., "Maybe I should watch my diet better.")
- What has been successful in the past in solving similar problems (e.g., "They kept my brother out of surgery for years with just a diet and medicine.")

From this scenario, it is clear that the interviewing nurse would want to explore issues of elimination, pain, nutrition, knowledge, and coping.

Information necessary to begin forming diagnoses has been provided, along with enough additional information to guide further exploration. In this example, the nurse may choose *diarrhea* as the diagnosis. Using NANDA-approved related factors for diarrhea, the nurse will want to explore stress and anxiety, dietary specifics, medications the patient is taking, and the patient's personal and family history of bowel disease.

The defining characteristics for diarrhea (typical signs and symptoms) have been provided by the patient to be cramping; abdominal pain; increased frequency of bowel

movements and sounds; loose, liquid stools; urgency; and changes in the appearance of the stool. These defining characteristics support the nursing diagnosis *diarrhea*.

To explore related concerns such as pain, nutrition, knowledge, and coping, the nurse should refer to defining characteristics for *imbalanced nutrition, less than body requirements; deficient knowledge; acute pain*; and *ineffective coping*. The nurse should then interview the patient further to determine the presence or absence of defining characteristics for these additional diagnoses.

To continue this example, the nurse might ask the patient the following questions: Have you lost weight? Of what does your typical breakfast/lunch/dinner consist? How is your appetite? Describe your abdominal cramping. How frequent is the discomfort? Does it awaken you at night? Does it interfere with your daily routine? On a scale of 1 to 10, with 10 being the worst pain you have ever had, how bad is the cramping? Can you tell me about your brother's Crohn's disease? Have you ever been told by a doctor that you have Crohn's or a similar disease? How are you handling these problems? Have you been able to carry out your usual activities? What do you do to feel better? In asking these questions, the nurse can decide whether the four additional diagnoses (*imbalanced nutrition: less than body requirements; deficient knowledge; acute pain*; and *ineffective coping*) are supported as actual problems or are problems for which the patient may be at risk.

Family, caregivers, and significant others can also be interviewed. When the patient's condition makes him or her incapable of being interviewed, these may be the nurse's only sources of interview information.

Physical assessment provides the nurse with objective data regarding the patient and includes a general survey followed by a systematic assessment of the physical and mental conditions of the patient. Findings of the physical examination may support subjective data already given by the patient or may provide new information that requires additional interviewing. In reality, the interview continues as the physical assessment proceeds and as the patient focuses on particulars. The patient is then able to enhance earlier information, remember new information, become more comfortable with the nurse, and share additional information.

Patient comfort and cooperation are important considerations in performing the physical examination, as is privacy and an undisturbed environment. Explaining the need for assessment and what steps are involved is helpful in putting the patient at ease and gaining cooperation.

Methods used in physical assessment include inspection (performing systematic visual examination), auscultation (using a stethoscope to listen to the heart, lungs, major vessels, and abdomen), percussion (tapping body areas to elicit information about underlying tissues), and palpation (using light or heavy touch to feel for temperature, normal and abnormal structures, and any elicited subjective responses). The usual order of these assessment techniques is inspection, palpation, percussion, and auscultation, except during the abdominal portion of the physical examination. Percussion and palpation may alter a finding by moving gas and bowel fluid and changing bowel sounds. Therefore percussion and palpation should follow inspection and auscultation when the abdomen is being examined.

To continue the example, the nurse may note, through inspection, that the patient is a thin, pale, well-groomed young woman who is shifting her weight often and has a strained facial expression. When asked how she feels at the present, the patient gives additional support to diagnoses *ineffective coping* and *deficient knowledge* ("I don't understand what is wrong with me; I feel tired and stressed out all the time lately"). Physical examination reveals a 10-pound weight loss, hyperactive bowel sounds, and abdominal pain, which is expressed when the nurse palpates the right and left lower quadrants of the patient's abdomen. These findings further support the nursing diagnoses *diarrhea; imbalanced nutrition: less than body requirements;* and *acute pain.*

Using General Versus Specific Care Plan Guides

General

At this point, the nurse has identified five nursing diagnoses: *diarrhea; imbalanced nutrition, less than body requirements; acute pain; deficient knowledge;* and *ineffective coping. Nursing Care Plans: Nursing Diagnosis and Intervention* is organized to allow the nurse to build a care plan by using the primary nursing diagnoses care plans in Chapter 2. A nurse can also select, by medical diagnosis, a set of nursing diagnoses that have been clustered to address a specific medical diagnosis and further individualize it for a particular patient.

Using the first method from Chapter 2, the nurse had every possible related factor and defining characteristic from which to choose to tailor the care plan to the individual patient. It is important to individualize these comprehensive care plans by highlighting those related factors, defining characteristics, assessment suggestions, and interventions that actually pertain to specific patients. Nurses should add any that may not be listed, customize frequencies for assessments and interventions, and specify realistic time frames for outcome achievement. (The blanket application of these standard care plans negates the basic premise of tailoring care to meet individual needs.) To complete the example used to demonstrate individualizing a care plan using this text, the nurse should select the nursing interventions based on the assessment findings and proceed with care delivery.

Specific

Using the clustered diagnoses usually labeled by a medical diagnosis (e.g., *inflammatory bowel disease*), the nurse has the added benefit of a brief definition of the medical diagnosis; an overview of typical management, including the setting (home, hospital, outpatient); synonyms that are useful in locating additional information through cross-referencing; and associated nursing diagnoses with related factors and defining characteristics. Again, it is important that aspects of these care plans be selected and applied (i.e., individualized) based on specific assessment data for a particular patient.

As a tool that guides nursing care delivery, the care plan must be updated and revised periodically to remain useful in care provision. Revisions are based on goal attainment, changes in the patient's condition, and response to interventions. In today's fast-paced, outpatient-oriented health care system, revision will be required often.

As the patient moves through the continuum of care, a well-developed care plan can enhance the continuity of care and contribute to seamless delivery of nursing care, regardless of the setting in which the care is provided. This will serve to replace replication with continuity and ultimately increase the patient's satisfaction with care delivery.

Tools for Performance Improvement

Quality and the notion of constantly improving services have taken a strong hold on health care. As customers have become better informed, more often being responsible for all or part of the financial obligation of their health care, and as managed care providers continuously look for ways of enhancing the bottom line, quality and performance improvement have become essential in managing health care, regardless of the setting.

As consumers demand increasing quality, methods for monitoring and measuring quality have become more complex. The identification of benchmarks has replaced thresholds, regardless of the fact that 90% of the time a particular goal is met. The question now is: How much better, more effective, more satisfying to the customer, or more economical can the service and its outcomes become? The notion of continuously improving outcomes and value has become a standard.

Finding those standards against which comparison and judgment about quality and value can be made has spawned countless outcome measure systems. These systems, to which facilities and practice groups can subscribe and consumers may pay attention, act as sources for identifying the best outcomes and values in health care. This book can be used to identify outcome criteria in quality control studies and in the development of monitoring tools. For example, a nursing department, home health agency, or interdisciplinary pain management team may be interested in monitoring and improving its pain management outcomes. Using the Chapter 2 care plan for Acute Pain, the process of pain management can be monitored simply by using each assessment and intervention as a measurable indicator. The outcome of pain management assessment and intervention can also be studied through direct observation, records review, and/or patient satisfaction measures. There has been increasing focus on the interrelatedness of services and systems (as opposed to the outdated departmental approach). The care plans in this text include independent and collaborative assessment suggestions and interventions, which facilitate use of the care plans as tools for quality improvement activities. Nurses, other health care professionals, clinical managers, and risk management and quality improvement staff will find that the care plans in this text provide specific, measurable detail and language. This aids in the development of monitoring tools for a broad scope of clinical issues.

Finally, when benchmarks are surpassed and there is desire to improve an aspect of care, the plans of care in *Nursing Care Plans: Nursing Diagnosis and Intervention* contain state-of-the-art information that will be helpful in planning corrections or improvements. These outcomes can be measured after implementation. The similarities between the nursing process (assess, plan, intervene, and evaluate) and accepted methods for quality improvement (measure, plan improvements, implement, and remeasure) make these care plan guides natural tools for use in quality and performance improvement activities.

A Basis for Critical Paths

Critical paths (also called *clinical paths* or *pathways, care maps,* or *care passes*) are interdisciplinary care plans to which time frames have been added. The critical path is designed to track the care of a patient based on average and expected lengths of stay in an acute care setting. Critical paths can be developed for the home care and long-term care settings too. The path provides guidelines about the sequence of care provided by the various members of the health care team responsible for the care of the patient. Interventions in a specific critical path may include patient education, diet therapy progression, medications, consultations and referrals to other members of the health care team, activity progression, and discharge planning. The nurse is usually respon-

sible for implementing and monitoring the patient's progress and noting deviations from the suggested time frame.

Critical paths are useful in organizing care delivered to a specific population of patients for whom a measurable sequence of outcomes is readily identifiable. For example, most patients having total hip replacement sit on the edge of their beds by the end of the operative day and are up in a chair by noon on the first postoperative day. They also resume a regular diet intake and stand by the end of the first postoperative day. They progress to oral analgesics by the third postoperative day and are ready for discharge on the fifth postoperative day. Every patient with total hip replacement may not progress according to this path because of individual factors such as other medical diagnoses, development of complications, or simple individual variation. However, most will, and as such, a critical path can be a powerful tool not only in guiding care but also in monitoring use of precious resources and making comparative judgments about outcomes of one physician group, hospital unit, or facility against external benchmarks. This may facilitate consumer decision making and enable those who finance health care to base judgments about referrals on outcome measures of specific physicians, hospitals, surgical centers, and other places. For example, Hospital A can perform a total hip replacement according to the critical path 90% of the time with acceptable outcomes, whereas Hospital B is successful only 80% of the time. A managed care provider can then make informed decisions about "preferred providers," keep costs in line, and provide consumers with confidence based on measurable outcomes.

The clinical care plan forms the basis of a critical path. *Nursing Care Plans: Nursing Diagnosis and Intervention* can be used as the clinical basis from which to begin the development of the critical path. Because nursing care plans in this text are organized by nursing diagnoses, adaptation of these care plans into critical paths may require organizing the information differently.

REFERENCES

Dochterman J, Bulechek G, editors: *Nursing interventions classification (NIC)*, ed 4, St Louis, 2004, Mosby.

Gordon M: Nursing diagnosis and the diagnostic process, *Am J Nurs* 76: 1298, 1976.

Moorhead S, Johnson M, Maas M, editors: *Nursing outcomes classification (NOC)*, ed 2, St Louis, 2004, Mosby.

2

Nursing Diagnosis Care Plans

 **NDx** **Activity Intolerance**

Weakness; Deconditioned; Sedentary

NANDA: Insufficient physiological or psychological energy to endure or complete required or desired daily activities

Most activity intolerance is related to generalized weakness and debilitation secondary to acute or chronic illness and disease. This is especially apparent in older patients with a history of orthopedic, cardiopulmonary, diabetic, or pulmonary-related problems. The aging process itself causes reduction in muscle strength and function, which can impair the ability to maintain activity. Activity intolerance may also be related to factors such as obesity, malnourishment, anemia, side effects of medications (e.g., β-blockers), or emotional states such as depression or lack of confidence to exert oneself. Nursing goals are to reduce the effects of inactivity, promote optimal physical activity, and assist the patient to maintain a satisfactory quality of life.

Common Related Factors

Generalized weakness
Deconditioned state
Sedentary lifestyle
Insufficient sleep or rest periods
Depression or lack of motivation
Prolonged bed rest
Imposed activity restriction
Imbalance between oxygen supply and demand
Pain
Side effects of medications

Defining Characteristics

Verbal report of fatigue or weakness
Inability to begin or perform activity
Abnormal heart rate or blood pressure (BP) response to activity
Exertional discomfort or dyspnea

Common Expected Outcomes

Patient maintains activity level within capabilities, as evidenced by normal heart rate and blood pressure during activity, as well as absence of shortness of breath, weakness, and fatigue.
Patient verbalizes and uses energy-conservation techniques.

NOC Outcomes
Activity Tolerance; Energy Conservation; Knowledge: Treatment Regimen

NIC Interventions
Energy Management; Teaching: Prescribed Activity/Exercise

Activity Intolerance–cont'd

Ongoing Assessment

Actions/Interventions	Rationale
■ Determine the patient's perception of causes of fatigue or activity intolerance.	These may be temporary or permanent, physical or psychological. Assessment guides treatment.
■ Assess the patient's level of mobility.	This aids in defining what the patient is capable of, which is necessary before setting realistic goals.
■ Assess nutritional status.	Adequate energy reserves are required for activity.
■ Assess potential for physical injury with activity, including safety of the immediate environment.	Injury may be related to falls or overexertion. Obstacles such as throw rugs, children's toys, and pets can (further) impede one's ability to ambulate safely.
■ Assess the need for ambulation aids: bracing, cane, walker, equipment modification for activities of daily living (ADLs).	Some aids may require more energy expenditure for patients who have reduced upper arm strength (e.g., walking with crutches). Adequate assessment of energy requirements is indicated.
■ Assess the patient's cardiopulmonary status and stability for exercise before activity using the following measures: • Heart rate	Heart rate should not increase more than 20 to 30 beats/min above resting with routine activities. This number will change depending on the intensity of exercise the patient is attempting (e.g., climbing one flight of stairs versus walking on a flat surface).
• Orthostatic BP changes	Older patients are more susceptible to drops in blood pressure with position changes.
• Need for oxygen with increased activity.	Portable pulse oximetry can be used to assess for oxygen desaturation. Supplemental oxygen may help compensate for the increased oxygen demands.
• How the Valsalva maneuver affects heart rate	The Valsalva maneuver, which requires breath holding and bearing down, can cause bradycardia and related reduced cardiac output.
■ Monitor the patient's sleep pattern and amount of sleep achieved over the past few days.	Difficulties sleeping need to be addressed before activity progression can be achieved.
■ Observe and document response to activity. Report any of the following: • Rapid pulse (20 to 30 beats/min over resting rate or 120 beats/min) • Palpitations/noticeable change in heart rhythm • Significant increase in systolic BP (greater than 20 mm Hg) • Significant decrease in systolic BP (greater than 10 mm Hg) • Dyspnea, labored breathing, wheezing • Weakness, fatigue • Light-headedness, dizziness, pallor, diaphoresis • Chest discomfort	Close monitoring serves as a guide for optimal progression of activity.
■ Assess emotional response to change in physical status.	Depression resulting from the inability to perform required activities can further aggravate activity intolerance.

■ = Independent; ▲ = Collaborative

Activity Intolerance

Therapeutic Interventions

Actions/Interventions

■ Establish guidelines and goals of activity with the patient and caregiver.

■ Encourage adequate rest periods, especially before meals, other ADLs, exercise sessions, and ambulation.

■ Refrain from performing nonessential procedures.

■ Anticipate the patient's needs (e.g., keep telephone and tissues within reach).

■ Assist with ADLs as indicated; however, avoid doing for patients what they can do for themselves.

■ Provide bedside commode as indicated.

■ Encourage physical activity consistent with the patient's energy resources.

■ Assist patients to plan activities for times when they have the most energy.

■ Encourage verbalization of feelings regarding limitations.

■ Progress activity gradually, as with the following:
  • Active range-of-motion (ROM) exercises in bed, progressing to sitting and standing
  • Dangling the legs 10 to 15 minutes three times daily
  • Deep-breathing exercises three or more times daily
  • Sitting up in chair 30 minutes three times daily
  • Walking in room 1 to 2 minutes three times daily
  • Walking in the hall 25 feet or walking through the house, then slowly progressing to walking outside the house, saving energy for return trip

■ Encourage active ROM exercises. If further reconditioning is needed, confer with rehabilitation personnel.

■ Provide emotional support while increasing activity. Promote a positive attitude regarding abilities.

■ Encourage patient to choose activities that gradually build endurance.

■ Provide the patient with the adaptive equipment needed for completing ADL activities.

Rationale

Motivation is enhanced if the patient participates in goal setting. Depending on the etiological factors of the activity intolerance, some patients may be able to live independently and work outside the home. Other patients with chronic debilitating disease may remain homebound.

Rest between activities provides time for energy conservation and recovery. Heart rate recovery following activity is greatest at the beginning of a rest period.

Patients with limited activity tolerance need to prioritize tasks.

This reduces risk for falling while reaching.

Assisting the patient with ADLs allows for conservation of energy. Caregivers need to balance providing assistance with facilitating progressive endurance that will ultimately enhance the patient's activity tolerance and self-esteem.

This reduces energy expenditure. NOTE: Using a bedpan requires more energy than using a commode.

This promotes a sense of autonomy while being realistic about capabilities.

Not all self-care and hygiene activities need to be completed in the morning. Likewise, not all housecleaning needs to be completed in one day.

Acknowledgment that living with activity intolerance is both physically and emotionally difficult aids coping.

This prevents overexerting the heart and promotes attainment of short-range goals.

Exercise maintains muscle strength and joint ROM.

Patients may be fearful of overexertion and potential damage to the heart. Appropriate supervision during early efforts can enhance confidence.

Physically inactive patients need to improve functional capacity through repetitive exercises over a longer period of time. Strength training is valuable in enhancing endurance for many ADLs.

Appropriate aids will enable the patient to achieve optimal independence for self-care.

■ = Independent; ▲ = Collaborative

Activity Intolerance–cont'd

Education/Continuity of Care

Actions/Interventions	Rationale
■ Teach the patient and caregivers to recognize signs of physical overactivity.	This promotes awareness of when to reduce activity.
■ Involve the patient and caregivers in goal setting and care planning.	Setting small, attainable goals can increase self-confidence and self-esteem.
▲ When the patient is hospitalized, arrange for a physical therapist to assess the need for family or significant others to bring in an ambulation aid (e.g., walker, cane) from home.	The patient can begin to make connection/transition to home, and the staff can assess proper functioning and use of assistive devices.
■ Teach the importance of continued activity at home.	This maintains strength, ROM, and endurance gain.
■ Assist in assigning priority to activities to accommodate energy levels.	With a reduced functional capacity, pacing of priority tasks first may better meet the patient's needs.
■ Teach energy conservation techniques, such as the following:	These reduce oxygen consumption, allowing more prolonged activity.
• Sitting to do tasks	Standing requires more work.
• Changing positions often	This distributes work to different muscles to avoid fatigue.
• Pushing rather than pulling	This reduces metabolic work.
• Sliding rather than lifting	This reduces upper body work.
• Working at an even pace	This allows enough time so not all work is completed in a short period.
• Placing frequently used items within easy reach	This avoids bending and reaching.
• Resting for at least 1 hour after meals before starting a new activity	Energy is needed to digest food.
• Using wheeled carts for laundry, shopping, and cleaning needs	These provide a support during walking.
• Organizing a work-rest-work schedule	This reduces strain on energy resources.
■ Teach appropriate use of environmental aids (e.g., bed rails, elevating head of bed while patient gets out of bed, chair in bathroom, hall rails).	These conserve energy and prevent injury from fall.
■ Teach ROM and strengthening exercises.	Exercise promotes increased venous return, prevents contractures, and maintains/increases muscle strength and endurance.
■ Encourage patient to verbalize concerns about discharge and home environment.	This can reduce feelings of anxiety and fear and open doors for ongoing communication.
■ Refer to community resources as indicated.	Continuity of care is facilitated through the use of community resources.

■ = Independent; ▲ = Collaborative

 **NDx Ineffective Airway Clearance**

NANDA: Inability to clear secretions or obstructions from the respiratory tract to maintain airway patency

Maintaining a patent airway is vital to life. Coughing is the main mechanism for clearing the airway. However, the cough may be ineffective in both normal and disease states secondary to factors such as pain from surgical incisions or trauma, respiratory muscle fatigue, or neuromuscular weakness. Other mechanisms that exist in the lower bronchioles and alveoli to maintain the airway include the mucociliary system, macrophages, and the lymphatics. Factors such as anesthesia and dehydration can affect function of the mucociliary system. Likewise, conditions that cause increased production of secretions (e.g., pneumonia, bronchitis, and chemical irritants) can overtax these mechanisms. Ineffective airway clearance can be an acute (e.g., postoperative recovery) or chronic (e.g., from cerebrovascular accident [CVA] or spinal cord injury) problem. Older patients, who have an increased incidence of emphysema and a higher prevalence of chronic cough or sputum production, are at high risk.

Common Related Factors

Decreased energy and fatigue
Ineffective cough
Tracheobronchial infection
Tracheobronchial obstruction (including foreign body aspiration)
Copious and tenacious tracheobronchial secretions
Perceptual/cognitive impairment
Impaired respiratory muscle function
Trauma

Defining Characteristics

Abnormal breath sounds (crackles, rhonchi, wheezes)
Changes in respiratory rate or depth
Ineffective or absent cough
Hypoxemia/cyanosis
Dyspnea
Chest congestion
Fever
Tachycardia
Orthopnea

Common Expected Outcome

Patient's secretions are mobilized and airway is free of excessive secretions, as evidenced by clear lung sounds, eupnea, and ability to effectively cough up secretions after treatments and deep breaths.

NOC Outcome
Respiratory Status: Airway Patency

NIC Interventions
Cough Enhancement; Airway Management; Airway Suctioning

Ongoing Assessment

Actions/Interventions	Rationale
■ Assess airway for patency.	Maintaining the airway is always the first priority, especially in cases of trauma, acute neurological decompensation, or cardiac arrest.
■ Auscultate lungs for presence of normal or adventitious breath sounds, as in the following:	
• Decreased or absent breath sounds	These may indicate presence of a mucous plug or other major airway obstruction.
• Wheezing	This may indicate partial airway obstruction or narrowing.
• Coarse crackles	These may indicate presence of secretions along larger airways.

■ = Independent; ▲ = Collaborative

Ineffective Airway Clearance–cont'd

Actions/Interventions

- Assess respirations; note quality, rate, rhythm, depth, flaring of nostrils, dyspnea on exertion, evidence of splinting, use of accessory muscles, and position for breathing.
- Assess changes in mental status.

- Assess changes in vital signs and temperature.

- Assess cough for effectiveness and productivity.

- Note presence of sputum; assess quality, color, amount, odor, and consistency.

▲ Send a sputum specimen for culture and sensitivity testing, as appropriate.
▲ Monitor arterial blood gases and/or pulse oximetry.

- Assess for abdominal or thoracic pain.

▲ If the patient is on mechanical ventilation, monitor for peak airway pressures and airway resistance.
- Assess use of herbal remedies (e.g., echinacea for upper respiratory infections, goldenseal for pneumonia, ma huang for bronchospasm).

- Assess the patient's knowledge of disease process.

Rationale

Abnormality indicates respiratory compromise.

Increasing confusion, restlessness, and/or irritability can be early signs of cerebral hypoxia. Lethargy and somnolence are late signs.

Tachycardia and hypertension may be related to increased work of breathing or hypoxia. Fever may develop in response to retained secretions or atelectasis or may be a manifestation of an infectious or inflammatory process.

Consider possible causes for ineffective cough (e.g., respiratory muscle fatigue; severe bronchospasm; or thick, tenacious secretions).

Abnormalities may be a result of infection, bronchitis, chronic smoking, or other condition. A sign of infection is discolored sputum (no longer clear or white); an odor may be present.

Respiratory infections increase the work of breathing; antibiotic treatment is indicated.

Increasing $PaCO_2$ and decreasing PaO_2 and pulse oximetry readings are signs of respiratory failure.

Pain can result in shallow breathing and an ineffective cough.

Increases in these parameters signal accumulation of secretions or fluid and potential for ineffective ventilation.

Drug interactions with prescribed medications and contraindications need to be evaluated (e.g., ma huang contains ephedrine, which should not be used by patients with hypertension, heart disease, prostatic hyperplasia, or diabetes).

Patient education will vary depending on the acute or chronic disease state as well as the patient's cognitive level.

Therapeutic Interventions

Actions/Interventions

- Assist the patient in performing coughing and breathing maneuvers.
- Instruct the patient in the following:
  - Optimal positioning (sitting position)
  - Use of pillow or hand splints when coughing
  - Use of abdominal muscles for more forceful cough
  - Use of quad and huff techniques
  - Use of incentive spirometry
  - Importance of ambulation and frequent position changes

Rationale

These improve productivity of the cough.

Controlled coughing techniques help mobilize secretions from smaller airways to larger airways because the coughing is done at varying times. The sitting position and splinting the abdomen promote more effective coughing by increasing abdominal pressure and upward diaphragmatic movement. Ambulation mobilizes secretions and reduces atelectasis.

■ = Independent; ▲ = Collaborative

Nursing Diagnosis Care Plans

Actions/Interventions

- Use upright position (if tolerated, head of bed at 45 degrees; sitting in chair).

- If patient is bedridden, routinely check the patient's position so he or she does not slide down in bed.

▲ If cough is ineffective, use nasotracheal suctioning as needed:
  - Explain procedure to patient.

  - Use soft catheters.
  - Use curved-tip catheters and head positioning (if not contraindicated).

  - Instruct the patient to take several deep breaths before and after each nasotracheal suctioning procedure and use supplemental oxygen, as appropriate.

  - Stop suctioning and provide supplemental oxygen (assisted breaths by resuscitation bag as needed) if the patient experiences bradycardia, an increase in ventricular ectopy, and/or significant desaturation.

  - Use universal precautions: gloves, goggles, and mask, as appropriate.

▲ Institute appropriate isolation precautions for positive cultures (e.g., methicillin-resistant *Staphylococcus aureus* [MRSA] or tuberculosis).

- Use humidity (humidified oxygen or humidifier at bedside).

- Encourage oral intake of up to 3 liters of fluid per day within the limits of cardiac reserve and renal function.

▲ Administer medications (e.g., antibiotics, inhaled steroids, mucolytic agents, bronchodilators, expectorants) as ordered, noting effectiveness and side effects.

▲ Consult a respiratory therapist for chest physiotherapy and nebulizer treatments as indicated (hospital and home care or rehabilitation environments).

▲ Coordinate optimal time for postural drainage and percussion (i.e., at least 1 hour after eating).

- For patients with reduced energy, pace activities. Maintain planned rest periods. Promote energy-conservation techniques.

▲ For acute problems, anticipate bronchoscopy.

▲ If secretions cannot be cleared, anticipate the need for an artificial airway (intubation). After intubation, do the following:

Rationale

This promotes better lung expansion and improved air exchange.

This prevents abdominal contents from pushing upward and inhibiting lung expansion.

Suctioning is indicated when patients are unable to remove secretions from the airways by coughing because of weakness, thick mucous plugs, or excessive or tenacious mucus production.

This prevents trauma to mucous membranes.

These facilitate secretion removal from a specific side (right versus left lung).

This prevents suction-related hypoxia.

Oxygen therapy is indicated to increase oxygen saturation and reduce potential complications.

These prevent transmission of pathogenic micro-organisms.

These prevent transmission of pathogenic microorganisms.

This loosens secretions and facilitates their removal.

Increased fluid intake reduces the viscosity of mucus produced by the goblet cells in the airways. It is easier for the patient to mobilize thinner secretions with coughing.

These promote clearance of airway secretions, and bronchodilation decreases airway resistance.

Chest physiotherapy includes the techniques of postural drainage and chest percussion to loosen and mobilize secretions in smaller airways that cannot be removed by coughing or suctioning. A nebulizer may be used to humidify the airway to thin secretions to facilitate their removal; it may also be used to deliver broncho-dilators and mucolytic agents.

This prevents aspiration.

Fatigue is a contributing factor to ineffective coughing.

Bronchoscopy obtains lavage samples for culture and sensitivity testing, and removes mucous plugs.

This helps facilitate removal of tenacious or copious amounts of secretions.

■ = Independent; ▲ = Collaborative

Ineffective Airway Clearance–cont'd

Actions/Interventions

- Institute suctioning of the airway as determined by the presence of adventitious sounds, increased peak airway pressures, and visible secretions in the tubing.
- Avoid routine sterile saline instillations during suctioning.

▲ For patients with complete airway obstruction, institute appropriate basic life support measures.

Rationale

Saline instillation has an adverse effect on oxygen saturation.

These are used to relieve airway obstructions and to sustain life until definitive treatment can be provided.

Education/Continuity of Care

Actions/Interventions

■ Teach coughing, breathing, and splinting techniques.

■ Instruct the patient on indications for frequency, side effects, and administration requirements of medications.

■ Instruct the patient how to use prescribed inhalers, as appropriate.

■ In the home setting, instruct caregivers regarding the need for humidification and adequate hydration.

■ Instruct caregivers in suctioning techniques. Provide opportunity for return demonstration. Adapt techniques for the home setting.

■ For patients with debilitating disease (e.g., CVA, neuromuscular impairment) being cared for at home, instruct caregivers in chest physiotherapy, as appropriate.

■ Teach the patient about environmental factors that can precipitate respiratory problems.

■ Explain effects of smoking, including secondhand smoke.

■ Refer the patient and/or significant others to smoking-cessation group, as appropriate, and discuss potential use of smoking-cessation aids (e.g., Nicorette Gum, Nicoderm, or Habitrol) to wean off the effects of nicotine.

■ Instruct the patient on the warning signs of impending or recurring pulmonary problems and their appropriate management strategies.

▲ Refer to the pulmonary clinical nurse specialist, home health nurse, or respiratory therapist as indicated.

■ Refer to the American Lung Association Call Center and support groups (e.g., Better Breathers Club).

Rationale

These facilitate clearance of secretions and prevent atelectasis. Dyspnea may be reduced by techniques such as pursed-lip or diaphragmatic breathing.

This promotes safe and effective medication administration.

This promotes safe and effective medication administration.

Thin secretions are easier to clear from the airway.

This promotes safe and effective removal of secretions from the airway.

This loosens and mobilizes secretions.

Chemical irritants and allergens can increase mucus production and bronchospasm.

Chemical irritants and allergens can increase mucus production and bronchospasm.

Supportive groups provide emotional support and information, and smoking cessation aids reduce the unpleasant effects of smoking cessation. These measures may help the patient to stop smoking.

This may reduce emergency department visits, hospitalizations, and mortality.

Use of consultants may be required to ensure that patient needs are met and outcomes achieved.

Support groups provide emotional support and information that may assist patients in coping with chronic illness.

• RELATED CARE PLANS

Pneumonia, p. 477
Tracheostomy, p. 529
Tuberculosis, p. 537

■ = Independent; ▲ = Collaborative

NANDA: Vague uneasy feeling of discomfort or dread accompanied by an autonomic response (the source often nonspecific or unknown to the individual); a feeling of apprehension caused by anticipation of danger. It is an alerting signal that warns of impending danger and enables the individual to take measures to deal with the threat.

Anxiety is probably present at some level in every individual's life, but the degree and the frequency with which it manifests differ broadly. Each individual's response to anxiety is different. Some people are able to use the emotional edge that anxiety provokes to stimulate creativity or problem-solving abilities; others can become immobilized to a pathological degree. The feeling is generally categorized into four levels for treatment purposes: mild, moderate, severe, and panic. Mild anxiety can enhance a person's perception of the environment and his or her readiness to respond. Moderate anxiety is associated with a narrowing of the person's perception of the situation. The person's focus is limited to specific details of the situation. Severe anxiety is associated with increasing emotional and physical feelings of discomfort. Perceptions are further narrowed. The person in a panic stage of anxiety has distorted perceptions of the situation. Their thinking skills become limited and irrational. They may be unable to make decisions. In the severe and panic stages of anxiety, the nurse needs to intervene to promote patient safety. The nurse can encounter the anxious patient anywhere in the hospital or community. The presence of the nurse may lend support to the anxious patient and provide some strategies for traversing anxious moments or panic attacks.

Common Related Factors

Threat or perceived threat to physical and emotional integrity
Changes in role function
Intrusive diagnostic and surgical tests and procedures
Changes in environment and routines
Threat or perceived threat to self-concept
Threat to (or change in) socioeconomic status
Situational and maturational crises
Interpersonal conflicts

Defining Characteristics

Physiological:
- Increase in blood pressure, pulse, and respirations
- Dizziness, light-headedness
- Perspiration
- Frequent urination
- Flushing
- Dyspnea
- Palpitations
- Dry mouth
- Headaches
- Nausea and/or diarrhea
- Restlessness
- Pacing
- Pupil dilation
- Insomnia, nightmares
- Trembling
- Feelings of helplessness and discomfort

Behavioral:
- Expressions of helplessness
- Feelings of inadequacy
- Crying
- Difficulty concentrating
- Rumination
- Inability to problem-solve
- Preoccupation

■ = Independent; ▲ = Collaborative

Anxiety–cont'd

Common Expected Outcomes

Patient is able to recognize signs of anxiety.
Patient demonstrates positive coping mechanisms.
Patient may describe a reduction in the level of anxiety experienced.

NOC Outcomes
Anxiety Self-Control; Coping

NIC Interventions
Anxiety Reduction; Presence; Calming Technique; Emotional Support

Ongoing Assessment

Actions/Interventions

■ Assess patient's level of anxiety.

Rationale

Mild anxiety enhances the patient's awareness and ability to identify and solve problems. Moderate anxiety limits awareness of environmental stimuli. Problem solving can occur but may be more difficult, and the patient may need help. Severe anxiety decreases the patient's ability to integrate information and solve problems. With panic, the patient is unable to follow directions. Hyperactivity, agitation, and immobilization may be observed.

■ Determine how the patient copes with anxiety.

This can be done by interviewing the patient. This assessment helps determine the effectiveness of coping strategies currently used by the patient.

■ Suggest that the patient keep a log of episodes of anxiety. Instruct the patient to describe what is experienced and the events leading up to and surrounding the event. The patient should note how the anxiety dissipates.

The patient may use these notes to begin to identify trends that manifest anxiety. If the patient is comfortable with the idea, the log may be shared with the care provider who may be helpful in problem solving. Symptoms often provide the care provider with information regardng the degree of anxiety being experienced. Physiological symptoms and/or complaints intensify as the level of anxiety increases.

Therapeutic Interventions

Actions/Interventions

■ Acknowledge awareness of the patient's anxiety.

Rationale

Because a cause for anxiety cannot always be identified, the patient may feel as though the feelings being experienced are counterfeit. Acknowledgment of the patient's feelings validates the feelings and communicates acceptance of those feelings.

■ Reassure the patient that he or she is safe. Stay with the patient if this appears necessary.

The presence of a trusted person may be helpful during an anxiety attack.

■ Maintain a calm manner while interacting with the patient.

The health care provider can transmit his or her own anxiety to the hypersensitive patient. The patient's feeling of stability increases in a calm and nonthreatening atmosphere.

■ Establish a working relationship with the patient through continuity of care.

An ongoing relationship establishes a basis for comfort in communicating anxious feelings.

■ = Independent; ▲ = Collaborative

Actions/Interventions

- Orient the patient to the environment and new experiences or people as needed.
- Use simple language and brief statements when instructing the patient about self-care measures or about diagnostic and surgical procedures.
- Reduce sensory stimuli by maintaining a quiet environment; keep "threatening" equipment out of sight.

- Encourage the patient to seek assistance from an understanding significant other or from the health care provider when anxious feelings become difficult.
- Encourage the patient to talk about anxious feelings and examine anxiety-provoking situations if they are identifiable. Assist patient in assessing the situation realistically and recognizing factors leading to the anxious feelings. Avoid false reassurances.
- As the patient's anxiety subsides, encourage exploration of specific events preceding both the onset and reduction of the anxious feelings.

- Assist the patient in developing anxiety-reducing skills (e.g., relaxation, deep breathing, positive visualization, and reassuring self-statements).
- Assist the patient in developing problem-solving abilities.
  - Emphasize the logical strategies that the patient can use when experiencing anxious feelings.
- Instruct the patient in the appropriate use of antianxiety medications.

Rationale

Orientation and awareness of the surroundings promote comfort and may decrease anxiety.

When experiencing moderate to severe anxiety, patients may be unable to comprehend anything more than simple, clear, and brief instructions.

Anxiety may escalate with excessive conversation, noise, and equipment around the patient. This may be evident in both hospital and home environments.

The presence of significant others reinforces feelings of security for the patient.

Talking about anxiety-producing situations and anxious feelings can help the person perceive the situation in a less threatening manner. Expressing emotions can enhance the patient's coping strategies.

Recognition and exploration of factors leading to or reducing anxious feelings are important steps in developing alternative responses. The patient may be unaware of the relationship between emotional concerns and anxiety.

Using anxiety-reduction strategies enhances the patient's sense of personal mastery and confidence.

Learning to identify a problem and to evaluate the alternatives to resolve that problem helps the patient cope.

Short-term use of antianxiety medications can enhance patient coping and reduce physiological manifestations of anxiety.

Education/Continuity of Care

Actions/Interventions

- Assist the patient in recognizing symptoms of increasing anxiety; explore alternatives to use to prevent the anxiety from immobilizing him or her.

- Remind the patient that anxiety at a mild level can encourage growth and development and is important in mobilizing changes.
- Instruct the patient in the proper use of medications and educate him or her to recognize adverse reactions.
- Refer the patient for psychiatric management of anxiety that becomes disabling for an extended period.

Rationale

The ability to recognize anxiety symptoms at lower intensity levels enables the patient to intervene more quickly to manage his or her anxiety. The patient will be able to use problem-solving abilities more effectively when the level of anxiety is low.

Cognitive appraisal of mild anxiety can help the patient perceive the anxiety as an opportunity to develop new strengths that enhance coping.

Medication may be used if the patient's anxiety continues to escalate and the anxiety becomes disabling.

Additional, long-term professional care may be needed when anxiety becomes severe and interferes with daily functioning.

■ = Independent; ▲ = Collaborative

 **Risk for Aspiration**

NANDA: At risk for entry of gastrointestinal secretions, oropharyngeal secretions, solids, or fluids into tracheobronchial passages

Both acute and chronic conditions can place patients at risk for aspiration. Acute conditions, such as postanesthesia effects from surgery or diagnostic tests, occur predominantly in the acute care setting. Chronic conditions, including altered consciousness from head injury, spinal cord injury, neuromuscular weakness, hemiplegia and dysphagia from stroke, use of tube feedings for nutrition, and artificial airway devices such as tracheostomies, may be encountered in the home, rehabilitative, or hospital setting. Older and cognitively impaired patients are at high risk. Aspiration is a common cause of death in comatose patients.

Common Risk Factors

Reduced level of consciousness
Depressed cough and gag reflexes
Presence of tracheostomy or endotracheal tube
Presence of gastrointestinal tubes
Tube feedings
Anesthesia or medication administration
Decreased gastrointestinal motility
Impaired swallowing
Facial, oral, or neck surgery or trauma
Situations hindering elevation of upper body

Common Expected Outcomes

Patient maintains a patent airway.
Patient's risk of aspiration is decreased as a result of ongoing assessment and early intervention.

NOC Outcomes
Aspiration Control; Respiratory Status: Ventilation

NIC Intervention
Aspiration Precautions

Ongoing Assessment

Actions/Interventions

■ Monitor level of consciousness.

■ Assess cough and gag reflexes.

■ Evaluate swallowing ability by assessing for the following:
  • Coughing, choking, throat clearing, gurgling or "wet" voice during or after swallowing
  • Residual food in mouth after eating
  • Regurgitation of food or fluid through the nares
■ In patients with tracheostomies, observe for food particles in tracheal secretions.

Rationale

A decreased level of consciousness is a prime risk factor for aspiration.

A depressed cough or gag reflex increases the risk of aspiration.

Impaired swallowing increases the risk of aspiration.

Coughing and choking are indicative of aspiration.

Pocketed food may be easily aspirated at a later time.

This is a sign of aspiration.

■ = Independent; ▲ = Collaborative

Actions/Interventions

- Auscultate bowel sounds to evaluate bowel motility and assess for abdominal distention and firmness.

- Assess for presence of nausea or vomiting.

- Assess pulmonary status for clinical evidence of aspiration. Auscultate breath sounds for development of crackles and/or wheezes.

▲ In patients with endotracheal or tracheostomy tubes, monitor the effectiveness of the cuff. Collaborate with the respiratory therapist, as needed, to determine cuff pressure.

Rationale

Decreased gastrointestinal motility increases the risk of aspiration because food or fluids accumulate in the stomach. Older patients have a decrease in esophageal motility, which delays esophageal emptying. When combined with the weaker gag reflex of older patients, aspiration is a higher risk.

Antiemetics may be required to prevent aspiration of regurgitated gastric contents.

Aspiration of small amounts can occur without coughing or sudden onset of respiratory distress, especially in patients with a decreased level of consciousness.

An ineffective or overinflated cuff can increase the risk of aspiration.

Therapeutic Interventions

Actions/Interventions

- Keep suction setup available (in both hospital and home settings) and use as needed.
- Notify the physician or other health care provider immediately of noted decrease in cough and/or gag reflexes or difficulty in swallowing.
- Position patients with a decreased level of consciousness on their side.
- Supervise or assist the patient with oral intake. Never give oral fluids to a comatose patient.
- Offer foods with consistency that the patient can swallow. Use thickening agents if recommended by a speech pathologist.
- Encourage the patient to chew thoroughly and eat slowly during meals.
- For patients with reduced cognitive abilities, remove distracting stimuli during mealtimes. Instruct the patient not to talk while eating.
- Place whole or crushed pills in soft foods (e.g., custard). Verify with a pharmacist which pills should not be crushed. Substitute medication in elixir form as indicated.
- Place medication and food on the strong side of the mouth when unilateral weakness or paresis is present.
- Offer liquids after food is eaten.

- Position the patient at a 90-degree angle, whether in bed or in a chair or wheelchair. Use cushions or pillows to maintain position. Maintain the patient in an upright position for 30 to 45 minutes after feeding.

- Provide oral care after meals.

Rationale

This is necessary to maintain a patent airway.

Early intervention protects the patient's airway and prevents aspiration.

This decreases the risk of aspiration by promoting the drainage of secretions away from the airway.

Supervision helps detect abnormalities early and enables implementation of strategies for safe swallowing.

Semisolid foods like pudding and hot cereal are most easily swallowed. Liquids and thin foods like creamed soups are most difficult for patients with dysphagia.

Well-masticated food is easier to swallow; food cut into small pieces may also be easier to swallow.

This facilitates concentration on chewing and swallowing.

Mixing pills with food helps reduce risk of aspiration.

This facilitates chewing and swallowing.

Ingesting food and fluids together increases swallowing difficulties.

The upright position facilitates the gravitational flow of food or fluid through the alimentary tract. If the head of the bed cannot be elevated because of the patient's condition, use a right side-lying position after feedings to facilitate passage of stomach contents into the duodenum.

This removes residual food that can be aspirated at a later time.

■ = Independent; ▲ = Collaborative

Risk for Aspiration–cont'd

Actions/Interventions

■ In patients with artificial airways:
  • Perform oral suctioning as needed.

  • Brush teeth twice a day and swab mouth with sponge applicators every 2 to 4 hours between brushing.

■ In patients with nasogastric (NG) or gastrostomy tubes:
  • Check placement before feeding, using tube markings, x-ray study (most accurate), pH of gastric fluid, and color of aspirate as guides.

  • Check residuals before feeding or every 4 hours if feeding is continuous. Hold feedings if amount of residuals is large, and notify the physician.

  • Test sputum with glucose oxidase reagent strips.

  • Place dye (e.g., methylene blue) in NG feedings only with physician's order.

  • Elevate the head of the bed to 30 to 45 degrees while feeding the patient and for 30 to 45 minutes afterward if feeding is intermittent. Turn off the feeding before lowering the head of the bed.

▲ Consult a speech pathologist, as appropriate.

Rationale

This reduces the volume of oropharyngeal secretions and reduces aspiration risk.

This reduces the risk of ventilator-associated pneumonia by decreasing the number of microorganisms in aspirated oropharyngeal secretions.

A displaced tube may erroneously deliver tube feeding into the airway.

Large amounts of residuals indicate delayed gastric emptying and can cause distention of the stomach, leading to reflux emesis. The amount of residuals may vary depending on the volume and rate of infusion.

Significant amounts of glucose in sputum may be indicative of aspiration.

Detection of the color in pulmonary secretions would indicate aspiration. However, regular amounts of some dyes may discolor skin, body fluids, and tissues, and increase morbidity and mortality, especially in patients with increased intestinal permeability or metabolic disorders such as sepsis. Thus routine use is discouraged without physician's order.

This reduces aspiration by decreasing reflux of gastric contents.

A speech pathologist can be consulted to perform a dysphagia assessment that helps determine the need for videofluoroscopy or modified barium swallow, and to establish specific techniques to prevent aspiration in patients with impaired swallowing.

Education/Continuity of Care

Actions/Interventions

■ Explain to the patient and caregiver the need for proper positioning.

■ Instruct on proper feeding techniques.

■ Instruct on upper airway suctioning techniques to prevent accumulation of secretions in the oral cavity.

■ Instruct on signs and symptoms of aspiration.

■ Instruct the caregiver on what to do in case of emergency.

■ Refer the patient to a home health nurse, rehabilitation specialist, or occupational therapist as indicated.

Rationale

This decreases the risk of aspiration.

An educated patient helps reduce the risk of aspiration.

Patient safety is a priority.

This aids in appropriate assessment of high-risk situations and determination of when to call for further evaluation.

This facilitates appropriate management of potentially life-threatening situations.

Use of consultants may be required to ensure that outcomes are achieved.

■ = Independent; ▲ = Collaborative

 **Disturbed Body Image**

NANDA: Confusion in mental picture of one's physical self

Body image is the attitude a person has about the actual or perceived structure or function of all or parts of his or her body. This attitude is dynamic and is altered through interaction with other persons and situations, and is influenced by age and developmental level. As an important part of one's self-concept, body image disturbance can have a profound impact on how individuals view their overall selves.

Throughout the life span, body image changes as a matter of development, growth, maturation, changes related to childbearing and pregnancy, changes that occur as a result of aging, and changes that occur or are imposed as a result of injury or illness.

In cultures where one's appearance is important, variations from the norm can result in body image disturbance. The importance that an individual places on a body part or function may be more important in determining the degree of disturbance than the actual alteration in the structure or function. Therefore the loss of a limb may result in a greater body image disturbance for an athlete than for a computer programmer. The loss of a breast to a fashion model or a hysterectomy in a nulliparous woman may cause serious body image disturbances even though the overall health of the individual has been improved. Removal of skin lesions, altered elimination resulting from bowel or bladder surgery, and head and neck resections are other examples that can lead to body image disturbance.

The nurse's assessment of the perceived alteration and importance placed by the patient on the altered structure or function will be very important in planning care to address body image disturbance.

Common Related Factors

Situational changes (e.g., pregnancy; temporary presence of a visible drain or tube, dressing, attached equipment)
Permanent alterations in structure and/or function (e.g., mutilating surgery, removal of body part [internal or external])
Malodorous lesions
Change in voice quality

Defining Characteristics

Verbalization about altered structure or function of a body part
Verbal preoccupation with changed body part or function
Naming changed body part or function
Refusal to discuss or acknowledge change
Focusing behavior on changed body part and/or function
Actual change in structure or function
Refusal to look at, touch, or care for altered body part
Change in social behavior (e.g., withdrawal, isolation, flamboyance)
Compensatory use of concealing clothing or other devices

Common Expected Outcome

Patient demonstrates enhanced body image and self-esteem as evidenced by ability to look at, touch, talk about, and care for actual or perceived altered body part or function.

NOC Outcomes
Body Image; Self-Esteem

NIC Interventions
Body Image Enhancement; Grief Work Facilitation; Coping Enhancement

■ = Independent; ▲ = Collaborative

Nursing Diagnosis Care Plans

→ **Disturbed Body Image**–cont'd

Ongoing Assessment

Actions/Interventions

- Assess perception of change in structure or function of body part (also proposed change).

- Assess perceived impact of change on activities of daily living (ADLs), social behavior, personal relationships, and occupational activities.
- Assess impact of body image disturbance in relation to the patient's developmental stage.

- Note the patient's behavior regarding the actual or perceived changed body part or function.

- Note the frequency of the patient's self-critical remarks.

Rationale

The extent of the response is more related to the value or importance the patient places on the part or function than the actual value or importance. Even when an alteration improves the overall health of the individual (e.g., an ileostomy for an individual with precancerous colon polyps), the alteration may result in a body image disturbance.

Changes in body image can have an impact on the person's ability to carry out daily roles and responsibilities.

Adolescents and young adults may be particularly affected by changes in the structure or function of their bodies at a time when developmental changes are normally rapid and at a time when developing social and intimate relationships is particularly important.

There is a broad range of behaviors associated with body image disturbance, ranging from totally ignoring the altered structure or function to preoccupation with it.

Negative statements about the affected body part indicate limited ability to integrate the change into the patient's self-concept.

Therapeutic Interventions

Actions/Interventions

- Acknowledge normalcy of emotional response to actual or perceived change in body structure or function.

- Help the patient identify actual changes.

- Encourage verbalization of positive or negative feelings about the actual or perceived change.

- Assist the patient in incorporating actual changes into ADLs, social life, interpersonal relationships, and occupational activities.
- Demonstrate positive caring in routine activities.

Rationale

Stages of grief over loss of a body part or function is normal and typically involves a period of denial, the length of which varies between individuals.

Patients may perceive changes that are not present or real, or they place an unrealistic value on a body structure or function.

It is worthwhile to encourage the patient to separate feelings about changes in body structure and/or function from feelings about self-worth. Expression of feelings can enhance the person's coping strategies.

Opportunities for positive feedback and success in social situations may hasten adaptation.

Professional caregivers represent a microcosm of society, and their actions and behaviors are scrutinized as the patient plans to return to home, work, and other activities.

Education/Continuity of Care

Actions/Interventions

- Teach the patient about the normalcy of body image disturbance and the grief process.

Rationale

The person experiencing a body image change needs new information to support cognitive appraisal of the change.

■ = Independent; ▲ = Collaborative

Actions/Interventions	Rationale
■ Teach the patient adaptive behavior (e.g., use of adaptive equipment, wigs, cosmetics, clothing that conceals the altered body part or enhances remaining part or function, use of deodorants).	This compensates for the actual changed body structure and function.
■ Help the patient identify ways of coping that have been useful in the past.	Asking patients to remember other body image issues (e.g., getting glasses, wearing orthodontics, being pregnant, having a leg cast) and how they were managed may help the patient adjust to the current issue.
■ Refer the patient and caregivers to support groups composed of individuals with similar alterations.	Lay persons in similar situations offer a different type of support, which is perceived as helpful (e.g., United Ostomy Association, Y Me?, I Can Cope, Mended Hearts).

NDx Risk for Imbalanced Body Temperature

NANDA: At risk for failure to maintain body temperature within a normal range

Risks for altered body temperature exist for all persons, but some situations and individual physical capacities place greater risk on certain individuals. Neonates and older patients are physically incapable of compensating for environmental exposures and are at greater risk in life-threatening events. Infants have trouble conserving body heat because they have a greater ratio of body surface area to body weight. The older adult has difficulty responding to changes in environmental temperature because of slowed circulation, decreased heat-generating activities, changes in skin function, diminished sweating, and impaired perception of temperature changes. People with brain injury that alters the temperature-regulating function of the hypothalamus may have unstable temperature regulation. Healthy persons, such as the athlete who is performing under extremely hot conditions, are also at risk. Prevention is accomplished by providing education specific to individual needs. For the hospitalized patient, the nurse must recognize potential risks related to the diagnosis and the treatment a patient is receiving.

Common Risk Factors

Extremes of weight or age
Dehydration
Illness and/or trauma, especially affecting temperature regulation center
Drugs
Environment: exposure to hot or cold temperatures
Inappropriate clothing
Inactivity or vigorous activity

Common Expected Outcome

Patient maintains body temperature within a normal range.

NOC Outcomes
Risk Control; Risk Detection; Immune Status

NIC Intervention
Temperature Regulation

■ = Independent; ▲ = Collaborative

Nursing Diagnosis Care Plans

> ## Risk for Imbalanced Body Temperature–cont'd

Ongoing Assessment

Actions/Interventions

■ Assess for presence of risk factors such as infection.

■ Assess for precipitating events such as head trauma or surgery near the hypothalamus.

■ Monitor the following other physical indicators:
  • Heart and respiratory rates
  • Fluid balance
  • Blood pressure
  • Skin condition
  • Mental status

▲ Assist with diagnostic examination if needed.

■ For the hospitalized or critically affected patient:
  • Determine the need for continuous temperature monitoring.

  • Measure temperature at frequent intervals. Use the same instrument and method at each interval. If method is changed (e.g., axillary versus rectal), document route.

Rationale

The immune response is fever. The hypothalamus "set point" is higher during fever. The heat-regulating mechanism controls heat production and conservation to maintain body core temperature at a higher level.

The hypothalamus serves as the body's temperature regulatory mechanism.

These may be increased or decreased.

Dehydration may precipitate decrease in temperature.

This may be increased or decreased.

Skin may change in color and temperature.

Changes occur with increase or decrease in core temperature.

Specific diagnosis is necessary for illness and trauma risks to be treated.

Continuous monitoring is indicated when interventions are implemented to adjust core temperature. These measures include cooling blankets and rewarming blankets.

A change of this type usually causes a variance in the temperature obtained.

Therapeutic Interventions

Actions/Interventions

▲ Provide or instruct the patient or caregiver in the following preventive measures as necessary:
  • Control environment.

  • Provide appropriate clothing or covering.

  • Provide adequate fluid and dietary intake.

  • Administer medications as ordered.

■ Notify physician of changes in physical status, especially temperature.

■ Explain prevention of risk factors and consequences of development of temperature alterations.

■ Ensure the patient can read the thermometer being used.

Rationale

Older patients or persons with circulatory disorders may require a warmer environment.

For example, the diabetic must be extremely careful to avoid exposure of hands and feet to extreme cold.

Dehydration can contribute to development of hyperthermia.

Antibiotics and antipyretics may be necessary to prevent febrile response to illness.

Temperature change can be indicative of other serious problems such as hypothermia in the septic patient.

Patients can implement appropriate environmental temperature controls when they understand the risks associated with changes in body temperature.

Older persons may have difficulty visualizing a mercury thermometer.

> • **RELATED CARE PLANS**
>
> Hyperthermia, p. 104
> Hypothermia, p. 106

■ = Independent; ▲ = Collaborative

NDx Bowel Incontinence

Fecal Incontinence

NANDA: Change in normal bowel habits characterized by involuntary passage of stool

Bowel incontinence, also called fecal incontinence, may occur as a result of injury to nerves and other structures involved in normal defecation or as the result of diseases that alter the normal function of defecation. Treatment of bowel incontinence depends on the cause. Injury to rectal, anal, or nervous tissue, such as from trauma, childbirth, radiation, or surgery, can result in bowel incontinence. Infection with resultant diarrhea, or neurological disease such as stroke, multiple sclerosis, and diabetes mellitus can also result in bowel incontinence. In older patients, dementia can contribute to bowel incontinence when the individual cannot respond to normal physiological cues. Normal aging causes changes in the intestinal musculature that may contribute to bowel incontinence. Fecal impaction, as a result of chronic constipation and/or denial of the defecation urge, can result in involuntary leakage of stool past the impaction. Loss of mobility can result in functional bowel incontinence when the person is unable to reach the toilet in a timely manner. Loss of bowel continence is an embarrassing problem that leads to social isolation, and it is one of the most common reasons that older patients are admitted to long-term care facilities. Goals of management include reestablishing a continent bowel elimination pattern, preventing loss of skin integrity, and/or planning management of fecal incontinence in a manner that preserves the individual's self-esteem.

Common Related Factors

Neuromuscular problems:
- Stroke
- Multiple sclerosis
- Diabetes
- Dementia
- Nerve trauma
- Spinal cord injury

Musculoskeletal problems:
- Pelvic floor relaxation
- Nerve trauma
- Damage to sphincters
- Radiation
- Infection
- Postoperative injuries
- Fecal impaction
- Medications
- Hyperosmolar food or fluid intake
- Immobility
- Lack of accessible toileting facilities

Defining Characteristic

Involuntary passage of stool

Common Expected Outcome

Patient is continent of stool or reports decreased episodes of bowel incontinence.

NOC Outcomes
Bowel Continence; Self Care: Toileting

NIC Interventions
Bowel Incontinence Care;
    Bowel Management; Bowel Training;
    Self-Care Assistance: Toileting

■ = Independent; ▲ = Collaborative

Bowel Incontinence

Bowel Incontinence–cont'd

Ongoing Assessment

Actions/Interventions	Rationale
■ Assess the patient's normal bowel elimination pattern.	There is a wide range of "normal" for bowel elimination; some patients have two bowel movements per day, whereas others may have a bowel movement as infrequently as every third or fourth day.
■ If there is current pathology that may affect bowel elimination, determine the premorbid bowel elimination pattern.	Most people feel the urge to defecate shortly after the first oral intake (e.g., coffee or breakfast) of the day; this is a result of the gastrocolic reflex.
■ Determine the cause of incontinence (i.e., review related factors).	Knowledge of causative factors provides direction for subsequent interventions.
■ Perform manual check for fecal impaction.	When the patient has a fecal impaction (hard, dry stool that cannot be expelled normally), liquid stool may leak past the impaction.
■ Assess whether current medications or treatments may be contributing to bowel incontinence.	Hyperosmolar tube feedings, bowel preparation agents, pelvic and/or abdominal irradiation, some chemotherapeutic agents, and certain antibiotic agents may cause explosive diarrhea that the patient cannot control.
■ Assist in preparing the patient for diagnostic measures.	These determine the causes of bowel incontinence. Tests include flexible sigmoidoscopy, barium enema, colonoscopy, and anal manometry (study to determine function of rectal sphincters).
■ Assess the degree to which the patient's daily activities are altered by bowel incontinence.	Patients may restrict their own activity or become isolated from work, family, and friends because they fear odor and embarrassment.
■ Assess the use of diapers, sanitary napkins, incontinence briefs, fecal collection devices, and underpads.	Patients or caregivers may substitute familiar products (e.g., sanitary napkins) for more appropriate incontinence products out of ignorance or embarrassment.
■ Assess perineal skin integrity.	Stool can cause chemical irritation to the skin, which may be exacerbated by the use of diapers, incontinence briefs, and underpads.
■ Assess the patient's ability to go to the bathroom independently.	Soiling accidents that occur as a result of the patient's inability to get to the bathroom may be solved by rearranging the environment, planning for trips to the bathroom, or by providing a bedside commode.
■ Assess the patient's environment for availability of an accessible toilet facility.	Inadequate access to toileting facilities in the home (e.g., bathroom on upper level), in the work environment, at the shopping mall, and the like can aggravate the incontinence experience.
■ Assess fluid and fiber intake.	Both are related to normal bowel evacuation.

Therapeutic Interventions

Actions/Interventions	Rationale
■ Ensure fluid intake of at least 3000 mL/day, unless contraindicated.	Moist stool moves through the bowel more easily than hard, dry stool and prevents impaction. If the patient has a significant amount of diarrhea, fluids provide important volume replacement.

■ = Independent; ▲ = Collaborative

Actions/Interventions	**Rationale**
▲ Provide high-fiber diet under the direction of a dietitian, unless contraindicated.	Fiber aids in bowel elimination because it is insoluble and absorbs fluid as the stool passes through the bowel; this creates bulk. Bulky stool stimulates peristalsis and expulsion of stool from the bowel.
■ Encourage intake of natural bulking agents to thicken stools, for example, foods such as banana, rice, and yogurt.	If bowel incontinence is related to diarrhea, these foods help provide bulk to the stool by absorbing fluids from the stool.
■ Manually remove the fecal impaction, if present	Presence of fecal impaction can interfere with establishment of a regular bowel routine.
■ Encourage mobility or exercise if tolerated.	This enhances gravity, stimulates peristalsis, and aids in bowel evacuation.
■ Provide a bedside commode and assistive devices (e.g., cane, walker) or assistance in reaching the commode or toilet.	Immediate access reduces unnecessary "accidents."
▲ Institute a bowel program.	Facilitating regular time for bowel evacuation prevents the bowel from emptying sporadically (i.e., decreases incontinence).
• Encourage bowel elimination at the same time every day.	Shortly after breakfast is a good time because the gastrocolic reflex is stimulated by food or fluid intake.
• After breakfast (or a warm drink), administer a suppository and perform digital stimulation every 10 to 15 minutes until evacuation occurs.	For some etiologies, direct stimulation of the renal sphincter and lower colon may be required to initiate peristalsis.
• Place patient in an upright position for defecation.	Flexion of the thighs (e.g., sitting upright with feet flat on floor) facilitates muscular movement that aids in defecation.
■ Wash the perineal area after each evacuation with soap and water. Dry thoroughly.	Any fecal material left on the skin can cause skin excoriation and pain.
■ Treat any perianal irritation with a moisture barrier ointment.	Perineal or perianal pain may result in fear of defecating and cause the patient to deny the urge to defecate. Repeated denial of the urge to defecate results in impaction, and eventually in bowel incontinence.
■ Discourage the use of pads, diapers, or collection devices as soon as possible.	Fecal containment devices can be useful in the short term to prevent soiling.
■ Use a fecal incontinence device selectively over pads, diapers, and rectal tubes.	These devices (pouches that adhere to the skin around the rectum) allow for collection and disposal of stool without exposing the perianal skin to stool; odor and embarrassment are controlled because the stool is contained. These devices work best for individuals who are in bed the majority of time.

Education/Continuity of Care

Actions/Interventions	**Rationale**
■ Teach the patient or caregiver the causes of bowel incontinence.	Knowledge of causative factors can clarify appropriate treatment approach.
■ Teach the patient or caregiver the importance of fluid and fiber in maintaining soft, bulky stool.	Teaching the patient or caregiver methods to manage bowel incontinence improves personal efficacy and can enhance compliance with the therapeutic regimen.

■ = Independent; ▲ = Collaborative

Bowel Incontinence–cont'd

Actions/Interventions

- Teach the patient the importance of establishing a regular time for bowel evacuation.
- Teach the caregiver the use of a fecal incontinence device, if appropriate.
- Teach the patient to manage perianal irritation prophylactically by washing with soap and water, drying thoroughly after each bowel movement, and applying a moisture barrier ointment.

Rationale

Information provides rationale for therapy and aids the patient in assuming responsibility for self-care later.

Supportive caregiving may be required. Use of specific devices may be challenging.

Patients and caregivers need to prevent skin irritation and pain that can result from fecal incontinence.

NDx Ineffective Breathing Pattern

NANDA: Inspiration and/or expiration that does not provide adequate ventilation

Ineffective breathing patterns are considered a state in which the rate, depth, timing, rhythm or chest/abdominal wall excursion during inspiration, expiration or both do not maintain optimum ventilation for the individual. Most acute pulmonary deterioration is preceded by a change in breathing pattern. Respiratory failure may be associated with changes in respiratory rate, normal abdominal and thoracic patterns for inspiration and expiration, and in depth of ventilation. Breathing pattern changes may occur in a multitude of conditions: heart failure, diaphragmatic paralysis, airway obstruction, respiratory infection, neuromuscular impairment, trauma or surgery resulting in musculoskeletal impairment and/or pain, cognitive impairment and anxiety, metabolic abnormalities (e.g., diabetic ketoacidosis, uremia, or thyroid dysfunction), peritonitis, drug overdose, pleural inflammation, and chronic respiratory disorders such as asthma or chronic obstructive pulmonary disease (COPD).

Common Related Factors

Inflammatory process: viral or bacterial
Hypoxia
Neuromuscular impairment
Pain
Musculoskeletal impairment
Anxiety
Decreased energy and fatigue
Tracheobronchial obstruction
Perception or cognitive impairment

Defining Characteristics

Dyspnea
Tachypnea/bradypnea
Fremitus
Cyanosis
Cough
Nasal flaring
Respiratory depth changes
Altered chest excursion
Use of accessory muscles
Pursed-lip breathing or prolonged expiratory phase
Increased anteroposterior chest diameter
Irregular or paradoxical breathing
Abnormal arterial blood gas (ABG)
Grunting

■ = Independent; ▲ = Collaborative

Common Expected Outcome

Patient's breathing pattern is effectively maintained as evidenced by eupnea, normal skin color, and minimal or no complaints of dyspnea.

NOC Outcomes
Respiratory Status: Ventilation;
  Vital Sign Status

NIC Interventions
Airway Management;
  Respiratory Monitoring

Ongoing Assessment

Actions/Interventions	Rationale
■ Assess respiratory rate, rhythm, and depth.	Respiratory rate and rhythm changes are early warning signs of impending respiratory difficulties.
■ Assess for the quality, duration, intensity, and distress associated with dyspnea.	This facilitates the evaluation of the patient's response to therapy and activity.
■ Inquire about precipitating and alleviating factors.	Knowledge of these factors is useful in planning interventions to prevent or manage future episodes of dyspnea.
▲ Assess nutritional status (e.g., weight and albumin and electrolyte levels).	Malnutrition may result in premature development of respiratory failure because it reduces respiratory mass and strength. It blunts ventilatory responses to hypoxia and impairs pulmonary and systemic immunity. Overfeeding increases production of CO_2, which increases respiratory drive and respiratory muscle fatigue.
■ Monitor breathing patterns: • Bradypnea (slow respirations) • Tachypnea (increase in respiratory rate) • Hyperventilation (increase in respiratory rate or tidal volume, or both) • Kussmaul's respirations (deep respirations with fast, normal, or slow rate) • Cheyne-Stokes respiration (waxing and waning with periods of apnea between a repetitive pattern) • Apneusis (sustained maximal inhalation with pause) • Biot's respirations (irregular periods of apnea alternating with periods in which four or five breaths of identical depth are taken) • Ataxic patterns (irregular and unpredictable pattern with periods of apnea)	Specific breathing patterns may indicate an underlying disease process or dysfunction. Cheyne-Stokes respiration usually represents bilateral dysfunction in the deep cerebral hemispheres associated with brain injury or metabolic abnormalities. Apneusis and ataxic breathing and Biot's respirations are associated with failure of the respiratory centers in the pons or medulla.
■ Observe for excessive use of accessory muscles (scalene and sternocleidomastoid).	This is indicative of increased respiratory effort.
■ Monitor for diaphragmatic muscle fatigue or weakness (paradoxical motion).	Paradoxical movement of the abdomen (an inward versus outward movement during inspiration) is indicative of respiratory muscle fatigue and weakness.
■ Note retractions or flaring of nostrils.	These signify an increase in respiratory effort.
■ Assess the position that the patient assumes for breathing.	A three-point position or orthopnea is associated with breathing difficulty.
■ Use pulse oximetry to monitor oxygen saturation and heart rate.	Pulse oximetry is a useful tool to detect early changes in oxygenation; however, for CO_2 levels, capnography or ABGs would need to be obtained.

■ = Independent; ▲ = Collaborative

Ineffective Breathing Pattern—cont'd

Actions/Interventions	Rationale
▲ Monitor ABGs as appropriate; note changes.	Increasing $PaCO_2$ and decreasing PaO_2 are signs of respiratory failure. As the patient's condition begins to fail, the respiratory rate decreases and $PaCO_2$ begins to increase.
■ Monitor for changes in orientation, increased restlessness, anxiety, lethargy and somnolence.	Restlessness is an early sign of hypoxia. Lethargy and somnolence are late signs of hypoxia.
▲ Avoid high concentration of oxygen in patients with COPD unless ordered.	Hypoxia stimulates the drive to breathe in the chronic CO_2 retainer patient. When applying oxygen, close monitoring is imperative to prevent unsafe increases in the patient's PaO_2, which could result in apnea.
■ Assess skin color and temperature.	Cyanosis occurs when at least 5 g of hemoglobin is desaturated. Cool pale skin may be secondary to a compensatory/vasoconstrictive response to hypoxemia.
■ Monitor vital capacity in patients with neuromuscular weakness and observe trends.	Monitoring detects changes early so ventilatory support may be initiated before full decompensation occurs.
■ Assess sputum for quantity, color, consistency, and odor.	These may be indicative of an etiology for the alteration in breathing pattern.
▲ If the sputum is discolored (no longer clear or white), send the specimen for culture and sensitivity testing, as appropriate.	An infection may be present. Respiratory infections increase the work of breathing, resulting in fatigue and changes in breathing pattern. Antibiotic treatment may be indicated.
■ Assess ability to clear secretions.	An obstructed airway may cause a change in breathing pattern.
■ Assess for thoracic or upper abdominal pain.	These can result in shallow breathing.
■ Assess use of herbal remedies (e.g., ma huang for bronchospasm, or licorice and hyssop for reducing cough and promoting expectoration).	Drug interactions with prescribed medications and contraindications need to be evaluated (e.g., ma huang contains ephedrine, which should not be used by patients with hypertension, heart disease, prostatic hyperplasia, or diabetes).

Therapeutic Interventions

Actions/Interventions	Rationale
■ Position the patient with proper body alignment for optimal breathing pattern.	If not contraindicated, a sitting position allows for good lung excursion and chest expansion.
▲ Ensure that the oxygen delivery system is applied to the patient.	The appropriate amount of oxygen is continuously delivered so that the patient does not desaturate. An oxygen saturation of 90% provides for adequate oxygenation.
■ Encourage sustained deep breaths by: • Using demonstration (emphasizing slow inhalation, holding end inspiration for a few seconds, and passive exhalation) • Using incentive spirometer (place close for convenient patient use) • Asking the patient to yawn	These techniques promote deep inspiration that increases oxygenation and prevents atelectasis. Controlled breathing techniques may also help slow respirations in patients who are tachypneic.

■ = Independent; ▲ = Collaborative

Actions/Interventions

- Evaluate appropriateness of inspiratory muscle training.

- Encourage the patient to clear his or her own secretions with effective coughing. If secretions cannot be cleared, suction as needed to clear secretions.

- Use universal precautions (e.g., gloves, goggles, and mask) as appropriate. If secretions are purulent, precautions should be instituted before receiving the culture and sensitivity final report. Institute appropriate isolation procedures for positive cultures (e.g., methicillin-resistant *Staphylococcus aureus* or tuberculosis).

- Pace and schedule activities, providing adequate rest periods. Assist with ADLs.

- Provide reassurance and allay anxiety by staying with the patient during acute episodes of respiratory distress.

- Provide relaxation training as appropriate (e.g., biofeedback, imagery, progressive muscle relaxation).

- Encourage diaphragmatic breathing for the patient with chronic disease.

- ▲ Use pain management as appropriate.

- Anticipate the need for intubation and mechanical ventilation if the patient is unable to maintain adequate gas exchange with the present breathing pattern.

Rationale

This improves conscious control of respiratory muscles and inspiratory muscle strength.

This promotes airway patency.

These measures prevent transmission of pathogenic microorganisms.

This prevents dyspnea resulting from fatigue and excessive oxygen demand.

Anxiety can increase dyspnea and respiratory rate.

This reduces pain and anxiety through distraction.

This relaxes muscles and increases the patient's oxygen level.

This allows for pain relief and the ability to deep breathe and cough.

Early intubation and mechanical ventilation are recommended to prevent full decompensation of the patient and a potentially life-threatening situation. Mechanical ventilation may be needed to maintain adequate oxygenation and ventilation.

Education/Continuity of Care

Actions/Interventions

- Explain all procedures before performing.

- Explain effects of wearing restrictive clothing.

- Explain use of oxygen therapy, including the type and use of equipment and why its maintenance is important.

- Instruct about medications: indications, dosage, frequency, and potential side effects. Include review of metered-dose inhaler and nebulizer treatments, as appropriate.

- Review the use of at-home monitoring capabilities and refer to home health nursing, oxygen vendors, and other resources for rental equipment as appropriate.

- Explain environmental factors that may worsen the patient's pulmonary condition (e.g., pollen, secondhand smoke) and discuss possible precipitating factors (e.g., allergens and emotional stress).

- Teach the patient or caregivers appropriate breathing, coughing, and splinting techniques.

Rationale

This decreases patient's anxiety.

Free movement of the chest wall and abdomen is necessary for optimal breathing.

Issues related to home oxygen use, storage, and precautions need to be addressed for safe and effective treatment.

These promote safe and effective medication administration.

Continuity of care is facilitated through the use of community resources.

This prevents recurrence or exacerbation of the patient's condition.

These facilitate adequate clearance of secretions and prevent atelectasis. Dyspnea also may be reduced by techniques such as pursed-lip or diaphragmatic breathing.

■ = Independent; ▲ = Collaborative

Ineffective Breathing Pattern—cont'd

Actions/Interventions

■ Teach patients to pace activities and to avoid unnecessary tasks when dyspneic.

■ Teach the patient when to inhale and exhale while doing strenuous activities.

■ Assist the patient or caregiver in learning signs of respiratory compromise. Refer significant others or caregivers to participate in basic life support class for cardiopulmonary resuscitation, as appropriate.

▲ Refer to social services for further counseling related to the patient's condition and give a list of support groups or a contact person from the support group for the patient to talk with. Suggest use of American Lung Association call center.

Rationale

Energy-conserving methods reduce fatigue, dyspnea, and oxygen consumption.

This reduces fatigue and dyspnea.

This prevents delays in seeking help and facilitate appropriate management in life-threatening situations.

This helps the patient deal with the psychosocial effects of having a chronic respiratory disease and provide a means for the patient to receive additional disease-specific information.

• RELATED CARE PLANS

Ineffective airway clearance, p. 11
Pneumonia, p. 477
Tuberculosis, p. 537

NDx Decreased Cardiac Output

NANDA: Inadequate blood pumped by the heart to meet the metabolic demands of the body

Common causes of reduced cardiac output include myocardial infarction, hypertension, valvular heart disease, congenital heart disease, cardiomyopathy, pulmonary disease, arrhythmias, drug effects, fluid overload, decreased fluid volume, and electrolyte imbalance. Older patients are especially at risk because the aging process causes reduced compliance of the ventricles, which further reduces contractility and cardiac output. Patients may have acute, temporary problems or experience chronic, debilitating effects of decreased cardiac output. Patients may be managed in an acute, ambulatory care, or home care setting. This care plan focuses on the acute management.

Common Related Factors

Increased or decreased ventricular filling (preload)
Alteration in afterload
Impaired contractility
Alteration in heart rate, rhythm, and conduction
Decreased oxygenation
Cardiac muscle disease

Defining Characteristics

Variations in hemodynamic parameters (blood pressure [BP], heart rate, central venous pressure [CVP], pulmonary artery pressures, venous oxygen saturation [SvO$_2$], cardiac output)
Arrhythmias, electrocardiogram (ECG) changes
Rales, tachypnea, dyspnea, orthopnea, cough, abnormal arterial blood gases (ABGs), frothy sputum
Weight gain, edema, decreased urine output
Anxiety, restlessness

■ = Independent; ▲ = Collaborative

Syncope, dizziness
Weakness, fatigue
Abnormal heart sounds
Decreased peripheral pulses, cold clammy skin
Confusion, change in mental status
Angina
Ejection fraction less than 40%
Pulsus alternans

Common Expected Outcome

Patient maintains BP within normal limits; warm, dry skin; regular cardiac rhythm; clear lung sounds; and strong bilateral, equal peripheral pulses.

NOC Outcomes

Cardiac Pump Effectiveness;
   Circulation Status;
      Knowledge: Disease Process;
      Knowledge: Treatment Program

NIC Interventions

Cardiac Care; Hemodynamic Regulation;
   Teaching: Disease Process

Ongoing Assessment

Actions/Interventions

- Assess mentation.

- Assess heart rate and blood pressure.

- Assess skin color and temperature.

- Assess peripheral pulses.
- Assess fluid balance and weight gain.

- Assess heart sounds, noting gallops, S_3, S_4.

- Assess lung sounds. Determine any occurrence of paroxysmal nocturnal dyspnea (PND) or orthopnea.

Rationale

Restlessness is noted in the early stages; severe anxiety and confusion are seen in later stages.

Sinus tachycardia and increased arterial BP are seen in the early stages; BP drops as the condition deteriorates. Older patients have reduced response to catecholamines, thus their response to reduced cardiac output may be blunted, with less increase in heart rate. Pulsus alternans (alternating strong-then-weak pulse) is often seen in heart failure patients.

Cold, clammy skin is secondary to compensatory increase in sympathetic nervous system stimulation and low cardiac output and desaturation.

Pulses are weak with reduced cardiac output.

Compromised regulatory mechanisms may result in fluid and sodium retention. Body weight is a more sensitive indicator of fluid or sodium retention than intake and output.

S_3 denotes reduced left ventricular ejection and is a classic sign of left ventricular failure. S_4 occurs with reduced compliance of the left ventricle, which impairs diastolic filling.

Crackles reflect accumulation of fluid secondary to impaired left ventricular emptying. They are more evident in the dependent areas of the lung. Orthopnea is difficulty breathing when supine; PND is difficulty breathing at night.

■ = Independent; ▲ = Collaborative

Decreased Cardiac Output–cont'd

Actions/Interventions

▲ If hemodynamic monitoring is in place:
  • Monitor CVP, right arterial pressure (RAP), pulmonary artery pressure (PAP) (systolic, diastolic, and mean), and pulmonary capillary wedge pressure (PCWP).
  • Monitor SvO₂ continuously.

  • Perform cardiac output determination.

■ Monitor ECG for rate; rhythm; ectopy; and change in PR, QRS, and QT intervals.

■ Assess response to increased activity.

■ Assess urine output. Determine how often the patient urinates.

■ Assess for chest pain.

■ Assess contributing factors so appropriate care plan can be initiated.

Rationale

Hemodynamic parameters provide information aiding in differentiation of decreased cardiac output secondary to fluid overload versus fluid deficit.

Change in oxygen saturation of mixed venous blood is one of the earliest indicators of reduced cardiac output.

This provides objective numbers to guide therapy.

Tachycardia, bradycardia, and ectopic beats can compromise cardiac output. Older patients are especially sensitive to the loss of atrial kick in atrial fibrillation.

Physical activity increases the demands placed on the heart; fatigue and exertional dyspnea are common problems with low cardiac output states. Close monitoring of the patient's response serves as a guide for optimal progression of activity.

Oliguria can reflect decreased renal perfusion. Diuresis is expected with diuretic therapy.

This indicates an imbalance between oxygen supply and demand.

Specific etiologies guide treatment.

Therapeutic Interventions

Actions/Interventions

▲ Maintain optimal fluid balance. For patients with decreased preload, administer fluid challenge as prescribed, closely monitoring effects.

▲ For patients with increased preload, restrict fluids and sodium as ordered.

▲ Administer medication as prescribed, noting response and watching for side effects and toxicity. Clarify with physician parameters for withholding medications.

▲ Maintain hemodynamic parameters at prescribed levels.

▲ Maintain adequate ventilation and perfusion, as in the following:
  • Place patient in semi- to high-Fowler's position.
  • Place patient in supine position.
  • Administer humidified oxygen as ordered.

▲ Maintain physical and emotional rest, as in the following:
  • Restrict activity.
  • Provide quiet, relaxed environment.
  • Organize nursing and medical care.

Rationale

Administration of fluid increases extracellular fluid volume to raise cardiac output.

This decreases extracellular fluid volume.

Depending on etiological factors, common medications include digitalis therapy, diuretics, vasodilator therapy, antidysrhythmics, angiotensin-converting enzyme inhibitors, and inotropic agents.

For patients in the acute setting, close monitoring of these parameters guides titration of fluids and medications.

This reduces preload and ventricular filling.

This increases venous return and promotes diuresis.

The failing heart may not be able to respond to increased oxygen demands.

This reduces oxygen demands.

Emotional stress increases cardiac demands.

This allows rest periods and optimizes use of the patient's limited energy resources.

■ = Independent; ▲ = Collaborative

Actions/Interventions

- Monitor progressive activity within limits of cardiac function.
- ▲ Administer stool softeners as needed.

- ▲ Monitor sleep patterns; administer sedative.
- ▲ If arrhythmia occurs, determine patient response, document, and report if significant or symptomatic.
  - Have antiarrhythmic drugs readily available.
  - Treat arrhythmias according to medical orders or protocol and evaluate response.
- ▲ If invasive adjunct therapies are indicated (e.g., intra-aortic balloon pump, pacemaker), maintain within prescribed protocol.

Rationale

This prevents overexertion and stress on the cardio-pulmonary system.

Straining for a bowel movement further impairs cardiac output.

Rest is important for conserving energy.

Both tachyarrhythmias and bradyarrhythmias can reduce cardiac output and myocardial tissue perfusion.

Electrical/mechanical assist devices may be indicated when more basic therapies fail. Nurse needs to follow protocols for managing each device.

Education/Continuity of Care

Actions/Interventions

- Explain symptoms and interventions for decreased cardiac output related to etiological factors.

- Explain drug regimen, purpose, dose, and side effects.

- Explain progressive activity schedule and signs of over-exertion.

- Explain diet restrictions (fluid, sodium).

Rationale

Thorough understanding of specific causes for each patient's disease is necessary for appropriate follow-through of treatment plan.

Information provides rationale for therapy and aids the patient in assuming responsibility for self-care later.

Close monitoring of one's response to progressive activity reduces the risk for overexertion.

Diet changes and restrictions can be especially challenging to patients and may require ongoing monitoring.

• RELATED CARE PLANS

Cardiac dysrhythmias, p. 288
Cardiogenic shock, p. 377
Chest trauma, p. 430
Deficient fluid volume, p. 71
Myocardial infarction, p. 310

NDx Caregiver Role Strain

NANDA: Difficulty in performing the caregiver role

The focus of this care plan is on the supportive care rendered by family, significant others, or caregivers responsible for meeting the physical and/or emotional needs of the patient. With limited access to health care for many people, most diseases are diagnosed and managed in the outpatient setting. Rapid hospital discharges for even the most complex health problems result in the care of acute and chronic illnesses being essentially managed in the home environment. Today's health care environment places high expectations on the designated caregiver, whether a family member or someone for hire. For many older patients, the only caregiver is a fragile spouse overwhelmed by his or her own health problems. Even in cultures where care of the ill is the anticipated responsibility of family members, the complexities of today's medical regimens, the chronicity of some

■ = Independent; ▲ = Collaborative

Caregiver Role Strain–cont'd

disease processes, and the burdens of the caregiver's own family or environmental milieu provide an overwhelming challenge. Caregivers have special needs for knowledge and skills in managing the required activities, access to affordable community resources, and recognition that the care they are providing is important and appreciated. Nurses can assist caregivers by providing the requisite education and skill training and offering support through home visits; special clinic sessions; telephone access for questions and comfort; innovative strategies such as telephone or computer support, or "chat groups"; and opportunities for respite care.

Common Related Factors

Illness severity of care receiver
Unpredictable or unstable illness course
Discharge of family member with significant home care needs
Caregiver has health problems
Caregiver has knowledge deficit regarding management of care
Caregiver's personal and social life is disrupted by demands of caregiving
Caregiver has multiple competing roles
Caregiver's time and freedom is restricted because of caregiving.
Past history of poor relationship between caregiver and care recipient
Caregiver feels care is not appreciated
Social isolation of family/caregiver
Caregiver has no respite from caregiving demands
Caregiver is unaware or reluctant to use available community resources
Community resources are not available or not affordable
Economic hardship

Defining Characteristics

Caregiver expresses difficulty in performing patient care
Caregiver verbalizes anger with responsibility of patient care
Caregiver worries that own health will suffer because of caregiving
Caregiver states that formal and informal support systems are inadequate
Caregiver regrets that caregiving responsibility does not allow time for other activities
Caregiver expresses problems in coping with patient's behavior
Caregiver expresses negative feeling about patient or relationship
Caregiver neglects patient care
Caregiver abuses patient

Common Expected Outcomes

Caregiver demonstrates competence and confidence in performing the caregiver role by meeting care recipient's physical and psychosocial needs.
Caregiver expresses satisfaction with caregiver role.
Caregiver verbalizes positive feelings about care recipient and their relationship.
Caregiver reports that formal and informal support systems are adequate and helpful.
Caregiver uses strengths and resources to withstand stress of caregiving.
Caregiver demonstrates flexibility in dealing with problem behavior of care recipient.

NOC Outcomes
Caregiver Well-Being;
    Caregiver–Patient Relationship

NIC Intervention
Caregiver Support

■ = Independent; ▲ = Collaborative

Ongoing Assessment

Actions/Interventions

- Establish relationship with the caregiver and care recipient.
- Assess caregiver–care recipient relationship.

- Assess family communication pattern.

- Assess family resources and support systems.

- Assess the caregiver's appraisal of the caregiving situation, level of understanding, and willingness to assume caregiver role.

- Assess for neglect and abuse of the care recipient and take necessary steps to prevent injury to the care recipient and strain on the caregiver.
- Assess the caregiver's health.

Rationale

This facilitates assessment and intervention.

Dysfunctional relationships can result in ineffective, fragmented care or even lead to neglect or abuse.

Open communication in the family creates a positive environment, whereas concealing feelings creates problems for caregiver and care recipient.

Family and social support is related positively to coping effectiveness. Some cultures are more accepting of this responsibility. However, factors such as blended family units, aging parents, geographical distances between family members, and limited financial resources may hamper coping effectiveness.

Individual responses to potentially stressful situations are mediated by an appraisal of the personal meaning of the situation. For some, caregiving is viewed as "a duty"; for others it may be an act of love.

Safe and appropriate care are priority nursing concerns. The nurse must remain a patient advocate.

Even though strongly motivated to perform the role of caregiver, the person may have physical impairments (e.g., vision problems, musculoskeletal weakness, limited upper body strength) or cognitive impairments that affect the quality of the caregiving activities.

Therapeutic Interventions

Actions/Interventions

- Encourage the caregiver to identify available family and friends who can assist with caregiving.

- Encourage involvement of other family members to relieve pressure on the primary caregiver.
- Suggest that the caregiver use available community resources such as respite, home health care, adult day care, geriatric care, housekeeping services, Home Health Aides, Meals On Wheels, Companion Services, and others, as appropriate.
- Encourage the caregiver to set aside time for self. This could be as simple as a relaxing bath, time to read a book, or going out with friends.
- Teach the caregiver stress-reducing techniques.

- Encourage the caregiver in support group participation.

Rationale

Successful caregiving should not be the sole responsibility of one person. In some situations there may be no readily available resources; however, often family members hesitate to notify other family members or significant others because of unresolved conflicts in the past.

Caring for a family member can be a mutually rewarding and satisfying family experience.

This provides opportunity for multiple competent providers and services on a temporary or more extended period.

Having own "respite" time helps conserve physical and emotional energy.

It is important that the caregiver has the opportunity to relax and reenergize emotionally throughout the day.

Groups that come together for mutual support can be quite beneficial in providing education and anticipatory guidance. Groups can meet in the home, social setting, by telephone, or even through the Internet.

■ = Independent; ▲ = Collaborative

Caregiver Role Strain–cont'd

Actions/Interventions	Rationale
■ Acknowledge the caregiver's role and its value.	Caregivers have identified how important it is to feel appreciated for their efforts.
	Feeling appreciated decreases feelings of strain.
■ Encourage the care recipient to thank the caregiver for care given.	
■ Provide time for the caregiver to discuss problems, concerns, and feelings. Ask the caregiver how he or she is managing.	As a caregiver, the nurse is in an excellent position to provide emotional support and provide guidance throughout this challenging period.
■ Inquire about the caregiver's health. Provide suggestions for ways to adjust the daily routines to meet the physical limitations of the caregiver.	The caregiver may have his or her own health challenges that can become aggravated during the caregiving process.

Education/Continuity of Care

Actions/Interventions	Rationale
■ Provide information on disease process and management strategies.	Accurate information increases understanding of the care recipient's condition and behavior. Caregivers may have an unrealistic picture of the extent of care required at the present time. Home care therapies are becoming increasingly complex (e.g., home dialysis, ventilator care, terminal care, and Alzheimer's care) and require careful attention to the educational process.
■ Instruct the caregiver in management of the care recipient's nursing diagnoses. Demonstrate necessary caregiving skills and allow sufficient time for learning before return demonstration.	Increased knowledge and skills increase the caregiver's confidence and decrease strain.
■ Refer the caregiver to family counseling if the family agrees.	Specialized expertise may be required.
■ Refer the caregiver to a social worker for referral for community resources and/or financial aid, if needed.	Grants or special funds can sometimes be used to assist with physical needs.

 ## Impaired Verbal Communication

NANDA: Decreased, delayed, or absent ability to receive, process, transmit, and use a system of symbols

Human communication takes many forms. Persons communicate verbally through the vocalization of a system of sounds that has been formalized into a language. They communicate using body movements to supplement, emphasize, or even alter what is being verbally communicated. In some cases, such as American Sign Language (the formal language of the deaf community) or Signed English, communication is conducted entirely through hand gestures that may or may not be accompanied by body movements and pantomime. Language can be read by watching an individual's lips to observe words as they are shaped. Humans communicate through touch, intuition, written means, art, and sometimes a combination of all of the mechanisms. Communication implies the sending of information as well as the receiving of information. When communication is received it ceases to be the sole product of the sender as the entire experiential history of the receiver takes over and interprets the information sent. At its best, effective communication is a

■ = Independent; ▲ = Collaborative

dialogue that not only involves the transmission of information but also clarification of points made, expansion of ideas and concepts, and exploration of factors that fall out of the original thoughts transmitted. Communication is a multifaceted, kinetic, reciprocal process. Communication may be impaired for any number of reasons, but rarely are all avenues for communication compromised at one time. The task for the nurse, whether encountering the patient in the hospital or in the community, becomes recognizing when communication has become ineffective and then using strategies to improve transmission of information.

Common Related Factors

Brain injury that adversely affects the transmission, reception, or interpretation of language or other forms of communication
Structural problem (e.g., cleft palate, laryngectomy, tracheostomy, intubation, or wired jaws)
Cultural difference (e.g., speaks different language)
Dyspnea
Fatigue
Sensory challenge involving hearing or vision

Defining Characteristics

Inability to find, recognize, or understand words
Difficulty vocalizing words
Inability to recall familiar words, phrases, or names of known persons, objects, and places
Unable to speak dominant language
Problems in receiving the type of sensory input being sent or sending the type of input necessary for understanding

Common Expected Outcome

Patient is able to use a form of communication to get needs met and to relate effectively with persons and his or her environment.

NOC Outcomes
Communication: Expressive Ability;
Communication: Receptive Ability;
Information Processing

NIC Interventions
Active Listening; Communication Enhancement: Hearing Deficit; Communication Enhancement: Speech Deficit

Ongoing Assessment

Actions/Interventions

■ Assess the following:
  • The patient's primary and preferred means of communication (e.g., verbal, written, gestures)

  • Ability to understand spoken word

Rationale

Patients may have skill with many forms of communication, yet they will prefer one method for important communication.

It is important for health care workers to understand that the construct of gestured language has an entirely different structure from verbal and written English. Signed English is not the true language of the deaf community but an instructional mechanism developed to teach the structure of English so that individuals with hearing impairments may read and write it. Some members of the deaf community learn to do so effectively. American Sign Language is the true language of the deaf community. U.S. federal law requires the use of an official interpreter to communicate with persons who choose to receive informed consent and other important medical information in their own language.

■ = Independent; ▲ = Collaborative

Impaired Verbal Communication—cont'd

Actions/Interventions	**Rationale**
• The patient's preferred language for verbal and written communication	Patients may speak a language quite well without being able to read it effectively. Discharge self-care and follow-up information must be communicated and reinforced with written information that the patient can use. The nurse can no longer assume that it is the patient's responsibility to grasp the information that is being provided. In recognition of the vast array of cultures and physical challenges that patients face, it is the nurse's responsibility to communicate effectively.
• Ability to understand written words, pictures, gestures	In some cases, the only way to be certain that communication has been effective is to arrange for a certified interpreter to validate information from both sides of the dialogue.
■ Assess conditions or situations that may hinder the patient's ability to use or understand language, such as the following:	
• Alternate airway (e.g., tracheostomy, oral or nasal intubation)	When air does not pass over vocal cords, sounds are not produced.
• Orofacial/maxillary problems (e.g., wired jaws)	Words are articulated by coordinated movement of mouth and tongue; when movement is impinged, communication may be ineffective.
■ Assess for presence of expressive dysphasia (inability to convey information verbally) and receptive dysphasia (word meaning may be scrambled during the processing of information by the patient's brain).	The person with expressive dysphagia has nonfluent speech; however, his or her verbal comprehension is often intact. The ability to read and write may be impaired with this type of dysphagia. The person with receptive dysphagia has fluent speech but the content of his or her communication is often meaningless. The primary disturbance is an inability to understand all forms of language.
■ Assess for presence and history of dyspnea.	Patients who are experiencing breathing problems may reduce or cease verbal communication that may complicate their respiratory efforts.
■ Assess energy level.	Fatigue and/or shortness of breath can make communication difficult or impossible.
■ Assess knowledge of patient's, family's, or caregiver's understanding of sign language, as appropriate.	Individuals who have no formal training in sign language usually develop mechanisms for communication, but because communication is such a critical aspect of everyone's life, consider formal training for patients and caregivers to enhance communication.

Therapeutic Interventions

Actions/Interventions	**Rationale**
■ Assist the patient in seeking an evaluation of his or her home and work settings.	This will evaluate the need for assistive devices such as talking computers, telephone typing device, and interpreters.

■ = Independent; ▲ = Collaborative

Actions/Interventions	**Rationale**
■ Anticipate patient needs and pay attention to nonverbal cues.	The nurse should set aside enough time to attend to all of the details of patient care. Care measures may take longer to complete when there is a communication deficit.
■ Place important objects within reach.	This maximizes patient's sense of independence.
■ Provide alternate means of communication for times when interpreters are not available (e.g., a phone contact who can interpret the patient's needs).	Alternate means of communication (e.g., flash cards, symbol boards) can help the person express ideas and communicate needs.
■ Encourage the patient's attempts to communicate; praise attempts and achievements.	Positive feedback enhances the patient's efforts to overcome communication barriers.
■ Listen attentively when the patient attempts to communicate. Clarify your understanding of the patient's communication with the patient or an interpreter.	Patients need feedback about the success of their communication attempts. Feedback promotes effective communication by allowing the sender of the message to verify that the message sent was the message received.
■ Never talk in front of the patient as though he or she comprehends nothing.	This prevents increasing the patient's sense of frustration and feelings of helplessness.
■ Keep distractions such as television and radio at a minimum when talking to the patient.	This keeps the patient focused, decreases stimuli going to the brain for interpretation, and enhances the nurse's ability to listen.
■ Do not speak loudly unless the patient is hearing impaired.	Loud talking does not improve the patient's ability to understand if the barriers are primarily language, dysphasia, or a sensory deficit.
■ Avoid use of medical jargon.	Technical terminology used by health care providers can sound like a foreign language to patients and family.
■ Maintain eye contact with the patient when speaking. Stand close, within the patient's line of vision (generally midline).	Patients may have a defect in their field of vision or may need to see the nurse's face or lips to enhance understanding of what is being communicated.
■ Give the patient ample time to respond.	It may be difficult for patients to respond under pressure; they may need extra time to organize responses, find the correct word, or make necessary language translations.
■ Praise the patient's accomplishments. Acknowledge his or her frustrations.	The inability to communicate enhances a patient's sense of isolation and may promote a sense of helplessness.
■ If the patient's ability to speak is limited to "yes" and "no" answers, try to phrase questions so that the patient can use these responses.	Patients can become easily frustrated when they cannot communicate in a simple manner.
■ Use short sentences and ask only one question at a time.	This allows the patient to stay focused on one thought. Sudden shifts from one subject to another does not allow time for the brain to keep pace with the messages.
■ Speak slowly and distinctly, repeating key words to prevent confusion. Supplement verbal communication with meaningful gestures.	This provides the patient with more channels through which information can be communicated.
■ Give concrete directions that the patient is physically capable of doing (e.g., "point to the pain," "open your mouth," and "turn your head").	Simple, one-action directions enhance comprehension for the patient with language impairment.
■ Avoid finishing sentences for the patient. Allow the patient to complete his or her sentence and thought, but if the patient appears to be having difficulty, ask the patient for permission to help. Say the word or phrase slowly and distinctly if help is requested. Be calm and accepting during attempts; do not say you understand if you do not.	This may reduce frustration and enhance trust.

Impaired Verbal Communication

(■ = Independent; ▲ = Collaborative)

Impaired Verbal Communication—cont'd

Actions/Interventions

- When the patient has difficulty with verbal expressions, support the work the patient is doing in speech therapy by providing practice sessions often throughout the day. Begin with simple words (e.g., "yes," "no," "this is a cup"), then progress.

- When the patient cannot identify objects by name, give practice in receiving word images (e.g., point to an object and clearly enunciate its name: "cup" or "pen").

- Correct errors.

- Provide a list of words that the patient can say; add new words to it. Share this list with family, significant others, and other care providers.

- Provide the patient with word-and-phrase cards, writing pad and pencil, or picture board. Use eye blinks or finger movements for "yes" or "no" responses.

- Carry on a one-way conversation with a totally dysphasic patient.

- ▲ Consult a speech therapist for additional help. See that the patient is well rested before each session with the speech therapist.

- ▲ Consider use of an electronic speech generator in postlaryngectomy patients.

Rationale

Practice with language skills in a supportive environment will increase the patient's communication. Reinforcement by repetition and practice enhances learning.

Visual cueing reinforces language comprehension.

Not correcting errors reinforces undesirable performance and makes correction more difficult later.

This broadens the group of people with whom the patient can communicate.

This is especially helpful for intubated and tracheal patients or those whose jaws are wired.

It may not be possible to determine what information is understood by the patient, but it should not be assumed that the patient understands nothing about his or her environment.

Fatigue may have an adverse effect on learning ability.

Adaptive devices can facilitate communication with patients who cannot produce vocal speech.

Education/Continuity of Care

Actions/Interventions

- Inform the patient, significant others, or caregiver of the type of dysphasia the patient has and how it affects speech, language skills, and understanding.

- Offer significant others the opportunity to ask questions about the patient's communication problem.

- Encourage family members and caregivers to talk to the patient even though the patient may not respond. Suggest that the family engage the patient often throughout the day for short periods. Encourage the family to look for cues that the patient is overstimulated or fatigued.

- Encourage the patient to socialize with family and friends.

Rationale

Many family members assume that a patient's mentation has been affected by a brain injury; this may or may not be true, and if true, some of the effects may be amenable to remediation.

It is important for the family to know that there are many ways to send information to someone and that time may be needed to understand the special needs of the patient.

This decreases the patient's sense of isolation and may assist in recovery from dysphasia. Overstimulation and fatigue hinder effective communication.

Communication should be encouraged despite impairment.

■ = Independent; ▲ = Collaborative

Nursing Diagnosis Care Plans

Actions/Interventions	Rationale
■ Explain that brain injury decreases attention span.	Changes in cognitive function often accompany language dysfunction in the patient with a brain injury. A decreased attention span limits the patient's ability to concentrate during a long conversation.
▲ Provide the patient with an appointment with a speech therapist, if not already done.	Outpatient speech therapy can support the patient's efforts to recover language skills.
■ Inform the patient and significant others to seek information about dysphasia from the American Speech-Language-Hearing Association, 10810 Rockwell Pike, Rockville, MD 20852.	Community resources can offer additional information and support to patients and families coping with impaired language and communication skills.
■ Refer deaf patients and their families to their local hearing society for community support, education, and sign language training.	Specialized services may be required to meet needs.

Chronic Confusion

NANDA: An irreversible, longstanding, and/or progressive deterioration of intellect and personality characterized by decreased ability to interpret environmental stimuli, decreased capacity for intellectual thought process, and manifested by disturbances of memory, orientation, and behavior

Chronic confusion is not limited to any one age group, gender, or clinical problem. Chronic confusion can occur in a variety of settings including the home, hospital, and long-term care facilities. While often associated with older adults with dementia, younger adults with chronic illnesses may also be affected. Depression, multiple sclerosis, brain infections and tumors, repeated head trauma (as seen in athletes), abnormalities resulting from hypertension, diabetes, anemia, endocrine disorders, malnutrition, and vascular disorders are examples of illnesses that may be associated with chronic confusion. Chronic confusion can have a profound impact on family members and family processes as the patient requires more direct supervision and care. This care plan discusses the management of chronic confusion in any setting. It also identifies the importance of addressing the needs of the caregivers.

Common Related Factors

Alzheimer's disease (dementia of the Alzheimer's type)
Multiinfarct dementia
Cerebrovascular accident (CVA)
Acquired immunodeficiency disease
Chronic hepatic encephalopathy
Chronic drug intoxication
Chronic subdural hematoma
Parkinson's disease
Huntington's chorea
Creutzfeldt-Jakob disease

Defining Characteristics

Clinical evidence of organic impairment
Altered interpretation/response to stimuli
Progressive/longstanding cognitive impairment
No change in level of consciousness
Impaired memory (short-term, long-term)
Altered personality

■ = Independent; ▲ = Collaborative

Chronic Confusion–cont'd

Common Expected Outcomes

Patient will remain safe and free from harm.

Family or significant others will verbalize understanding of disease process/prognosis and the patient's needs, identify and participate in interventions to deal effectively with the situation, and provide for maximal independence while meeting safety needs of the patient.

NOC Outcomes

Cognitive Orientation; Decision Making; Distorted Thought Control; Safety Behavior: Home Physical Environment

NIC Interventions

Dementia Management; Environmental Management: Safety; Family Involvement Promotion

Ongoing Assessment

Actions/Interventions

■ Assess degree of impairment:

• Evaluate responses on diagnostic examinations (e.g., memory impairments, reality orientation, attention span, calculations).

• Test ability to receive and send effective communications.

• Note deterioration and changes in personal hygiene or behavior.

• Talk with significant others regarding baseline behaviors, length of time since onset or progression of the problem, their perception of the prognosis, and other pertinent information and concerns for the patient.

■ Evaluate response to care providers and receptiveness to interventions.

■ Determine anxiety level in relation to the situation. Note behavior that may be indicative of potential for violence.

Rationale

This will determine the amount of reorientation and intervention the patient will need to evaluate reality accurately.

Decreased attention span and memory loss can contribute to the person's inability to accurately respond to environmental stimuli. A common screening tool is the Mini-Mental State Examination.

Ability and/or willingness to respond to verbal direction and/or limits may vary with degree of reality orientation.

This information assists in developing a specific plan for grooming and hygiene activities.

Assessment can identify areas of physical care in which the patient needs assistance. These areas include nutrition, elimination, sleep, rest, exercise, bathing, grooming, and dressing. It is important to distinguish ability and motivation in the initiation, performance, and maintenance of self-care activities. Patients may either have the ability and minimal motivation, or motivation and minimal ability.

A patient who has developed trust in a care provider, as well as a relationship with him or her, may be able to accept direction.

Confusion, disorientation, impaired judgment, suspiciousness, and loss of social inhibitions may result in socially inappropriate and/or harmful behaviors to self or others.

Therapeutic Interventions

Actions/Interventions

■ Prevent further deterioration and maximize level of function:
• Provide calm environment; eliminate extraneous noise and stimuli.

Rationale

Increased levels of visual and auditory stimulation can be misinterpreted by the confused patient. Pictures

■ = Independent; ▲ = Collaborative

Actions/Interventions

- Maintain consistency in the person's environment and daily schedule.

- Avoid challenging illogical thinking because defensive reactions may result.

- Encourage the family and significant others to provide ongoing orientation and input about current news and family happenings.

- Maintain reality-oriented relationships and environment (e.g., display clocks, calendars, personal items, seasonal decorations).

- Encourage participation in resocialization groups.

- Allow the patient to reminisce, existing in his or her own reality if not detrimental to the patient's well-being.

- Provide safety measures (e.g., close supervision, identification bracelet, medication lockup, lower temperature on hot water tank).

Rationale

on walls or even shadows can be perceived by the confused patient as threatening. High noise levels can disrupt sleep and add to levels of anxiety and stress.

Consistency in placement of furnishings promotes orientation and memory. Following the same schedule each day reduces stress and anxiety caused by change.

Challenges to the patient's thinking can be perceived as threatening. The confused patient will become more anxious and even combative.

Increased orientation ensures a greater degree of safety for the patient.

Orientation to one's environment increases one's ability to trust others. Encourage the patient to check the calendar and clock often to orient himself or herself. To decrease the sense of alienation that the patient may feel in an environment that is strange, familiar personal possessions increase the patient's comfort level.

Encouraging the patient to assume responsibility for his or her own behavior will increase his or her sense of independence. It is important for the patient to learn socially appropriate behavior through group interactions. This provides an opportunity for the patient to observe the impact his or her behavior has on those around him or her. It also facilitates the development of acceptable social skills.

Depending on etiology, long-term memory is usually retained longer than short-term; reminiscing can be enjoyable to the patient.

These measures promote patient safety.

Education/Continuity of Care

Actions/Interventions

- ■ Assist family and significant others to develop coping strategies.
  - Determine family resources and their availability and willingness to participate in meeting the patient's needs.
  - Identify appropriate community resources (e.g., Alzheimer's or brain injury support groups, respite care).
  - Evaluate attention to own needs, including the grieving process.

  - Provide written information for significant others on living with chronic confusion.

Rationale

Referral of the family for often-needed legal and financial guidance may be necessary.

This provides support, assists with problem solving, and helps the family cope with the long-term stress in caring for the patient.

Caregiver strain can lead to increasing frustration with the confused person. The frustration can precipitate anger and abuse.

This assists significant others with understanding the disorder and its impact on their lives.

■ = Independent; ▲ = Collaborative

Chronic Confusion

Chronic Confusion–cont'd

Actions/Interventions	**Rationale**
■ Promote wellness (teaching and discharge considerations).	
• Determine ongoing treatment needs and appropriate resources.	All these interventions should maximize the patient's level of functioning and quality of life for both the family and the caregivers.
• Develop a care plan with the family to meet the patient's and the family's individual needs.	Instruct the family to let the patient do all that he or she is able to do and encourage the family to increase the patient's activities.
• Provide appropriate referral (e.g., Meals On Wheels, adult home care, home care agency, respite care).	Community resources can support the family and reduce the demands associated with caregiving.

> • RELATED CARE PLAN
>
> Alzheimer's disease/dementia, p. 544

 **Constipation**

Impaction; Obstipation

NANDA: Decrease in normal frequency of defecation accompanied by difficult or incomplete passage of stool and/or passage of excessively hard, dry stool

Constipation is a common, yet complex problem; it is especially prevalent among older patients. Constipation often accompanies pregnancy. Diet, exercise, and daily routine are important factors in maintaining normal bowel patterns. Too little fluid, too little fiber, inactivity or immobility, and disruption in daily routines can result in constipation. Use of medications, particularly narcotic analgesics or overuse of laxatives, can cause constipation. Overuse of enemas can cause constipation, as can ignoring the need to defecate. Psychological disorders such as stress and depression can cause constipation. Because privacy is an issue for most, being away from home, hospitalized, or otherwise being deprived of adequate privacy can result in constipation. Because "normal" patterns of bowel elimination vary so widely from individual to individual, some people believe they are constipated if a day passes without a bowel movement; for others, every third or fourth day is normal. Chronic constipation can result in the development of hemorrhoids; diverticulosis (particularly in older patients who have a high incidence of diverticulitis); straining at stool, which can cause sudden death; and although rare, perforation of the colon. Constipation is usually episodic, although it can become a lifelong, chronic problem. Because tumors of the colon and rectum can result in obstipation (complete lack of passage of stool), it is important to rule out these possibilities. Dietary management (increasing fluid and fiber) remains the most effective treatment for constipation.

Common Related Factors	**Defining Characteristics**
Inadequate fluid intake	Infrequent passage of stool
Low-fiber diet	Passage of hard, dry stool

■ = Independent; ▲ = Collaborative

Inactivity, immobility
Medication use
Lack of privacy
Pain
Fear of pain
Laxative abuse
Pregnancy
Tumor or other obstructing mass
Neurogenic disorders

Straining at stools
Passage of liquid fecal seepage
Frequent but nonproductive desire to defecate
Anorexia
Abdominal distention
Nausea and vomiting
Dull headache, restlessness, and depression
Verbalized pain or fear of pain

Common Expected Outcomes

Patient passes soft, formed stool at a frequency perceived as "normal" by the patient.
Patient or caregiver verbalizes measures that will prevent recurrence of constipation.

NOC Outcomes
Bowel Elimination; Medication Response; Self-Care Toileting

NIC Interventions
Constipation/Impaction Management; Bowel Training; Teaching: Prescribed Medication

Ongoing Assessment

Actions/Interventions

■ Assess usual pattern of elimination; compare with present pattern. Include size, frequency, color, and quality.

■ Evaluate laxative use, type, and frequency.

■ Evaluate reliance on enemas for elimination.

■ Evaluate usual dietary habits, eating habits, eating schedule, and liquid intake.

■ Assess activity level.

■ Evaluate current medication usage that may contribute to constipation.

■ Assess the need for privacy for elimination (e.g., use of bedpan, access to bathroom facilities with privacy during work hours).

■ Evaluate fear of pain.

Rationale

"Normal" frequency of passing stool varies from twice daily to once every third or fourth day. It is important to ascertain what is "normal" for each individual.

Chronic use of laxatives causes the muscles and nerves of the colon to function inadequately in producing an urge to defecate. Over time, the colon becomes atonic and distended.

Abuse or overuse of cathartics and enemas can result in dependence on them for evacuation, because the colon becomes distended and does not respond normally to the presence of stool.

Change in mealtime, type of food, disruption of usual schedule, and anxiety can lead to constipation.

Prolonged bed rest, lack of exercise, and inactivity contribute to constipation.

Drugs that can cause constipation include the following: narcotics, antacids with calcium or aluminum base, antidepressants, anticholinergics, antihypertensives, general anesthetics, hypnotics, and iron and calcium supplements.

Many individuals report that being away from home limits their ability to have a bowel movement. Those who travel or require hospitalization may have difficulty having a bowel movement away from home.

Hemorrhoids, anal fissures, or other anorectal disorders that are painful can cause the patient to ignore the urge to defecate, which over time results in a dilated rectum that no longer responds to the presence of stool.

■ = Independent; ▲ = Collaborative

Constipation—cont'd

Actions/Interventions

- Assess degree to which the patient's procrastination contributes to constipation.

- Assess for history of neurogenic diseases, such as multiple sclerosis or Parkinson's disease.

Rationale

Ignoring the defecation urge eventually leads to chronic constipation, because the rectum no longer senses, or responds to, the presence of stool. The longer the stool remains in the rectum, the drier and harder (and more difficult to pass) it becomes.

Neurogenic disorders may alter the colon's ability to perform peristalsis.

Therapeutic Interventions

Actions/Interventions

- Encourage daily fluid intake of 2000 to 3000 mL/day, if not contraindicated medically.
- Encourage increased fiber in diet (e.g., raw fruits, fresh vegetables, whole grains); a minimum of 20 g of dietary fiber per day is recommended.

- Encourage the patient to consume prunes, prune juice, cold cereal, and bean products.
- Encourage physical activity and regular exercise.

- Encourage a regular time for elimination.

- Encourage isometric abdominal and gluteal exercises.

- Digitally remove fecal impaction.

- Suggest the following measures to minimize rectal discomfort:
  - Warm sitz bath

  - Hemorrhoidal preparations
- For hospitalized patients, the following should be employed:
  - Orient patient to location of bathroom and encourage use, unless contraindicated.

  - Offer a warmed bedpan to bedridden patients; assist patient to assume a high-Fowler's position with knees flexed.
  - Curtain off the area.
  - Allow patient time to relax.

Rationale

Patients, especially older patients, may have cardiovascular limitations that require that less fluid be taken.

Fiber passes through the intestine essentially unchanged. When it reaches the colon, it absorbs water and forms a gel, which adds bulk to the stool and makes defecation easier.

These are "natural" cathartics because of their high-fiber content.

Ambulation and/or abdominal exercises strengthen abdominal muscles that facilitate defecation.

Many persons defecate following the first daily meal or coffee, as a result of the gastrocolic reflex; depending on the person's usual schedule, any time, as long as it is regular, is fine.

Exercises, unless contraindicated, strengthen muscles needed for evacuation.

Stool that remains in the rectum for long periods becomes dry and hard; debilitated patients, especially older patients, may not be able to pass these stools without manual assistance.

The warmth of the water relaxes muscles before defecation attempts.

These shrink swollen hemorrhoidal tissue.

A sitting position with knees flexed straightens the rectum, enhances use of abdominal muscles, and facilitates defecation.

This position best uses gravity and allows for effective Valsalva maneuver.

This provides privacy.

■ = Independent; ▲ = Collaborative

Compromised Family Coping *(vertical, right margin)*

Education/Continuity of Care

Actions/Interventions

▲ Consult dietitian if appropriate.

■ Explain or reinforce to the patient and caregiver the importance of the following:
- A balanced diet that contains adequate fiber, fresh fruits, vegetables, and grains
- Adequate fluid intake (8 glasses per day or 2000 to 3000 mL/day).
- Regular meals
- Regular time for evacuation and adequate time for defecation
- Regular exercise and activity

- Privacy for defecation

■ Teach patients and caregivers to read product labels

▲ Teach use of pharmacological agents as ordered, as in the following:
- Bulk fiber (Metamucil and similar fiber products)

- Stool softeners (e.g., Colace)
- Chemical irritants (e.g., castor oil, cascara, Milk of Magnesia)

- Suppositories

- Oil retention enema

Rationale

A person unaccustomed to a high-fiber diet may experience abdominal discomfort and flatulence; a gradual increase in fiber intake is recommended.

These steps lead to reestablishing regular bowel habits.

Twenty grams of fiber per day is recommended.

Increased hydration promotes a softer fecal mass.

Successful bowel training relies on routine.

Facilitating regular time prevents the bowel from emptying sporadically.

Exercises strengthen abdominal muscles and stimulate peristalsis.

This allows the patient to relax, which can help promote defecation.

It is important for patients and caregivers to determine the fiber content per serving.

These increase fluid, gaseous, and solid bulk of intestinal contents.

These soften stool and lubricate intestinal mucosa.

These irritate the bowel mucosa and cause rapid propulsion of contents of small intestine.

These aid in softening stools and stimulate rectal mucosa; best results occur when given 30 minutes before usual defecation time or after breakfast.

This softens stool.

 **Compromised Family Coping**

Caregiver Role Strain

NANDA: Usually supportive primary person (family member or close friend) provides insufficient, ineffective, or compromised support, comfort, assistance, or encouragement that may be needed by the patient to manage or master adaptive tasks related to his/her health challenge

The changing health care environment places high expectations on family members to assist patients throughout their illness and recovery process. Today's home setting can be challenging because of the expansion of "high-tech" equipment into the home: intravenous therapy, chemotherapy, dialysis, even ventilator care. The expansion of hospice and palliative care programs likewise moves the focus of end-of-life care into the home and the family unit. The "baby boomer" generation is finding itself sandwiched between the demands of their children, many of whom may also have chronic medical problems, and their older parents, many of whom cannot afford care in a nursing home. Older couples

■ = Independent; ▲ = Collaborative

Compromised Family Coping–cont'd

living alone are also finding that the demand for supportive physical and emotional care to one partner are taxing the personal resources and fragile health of the other. Other factors that influence the ability of the family to cope with the demands being placed on the family unit include the following: limited financial and community resources; geographical distance between family members; long, protracted recovery or terminal illness state; and multiple stressors.

Common Related Factors

Knowledge deficit regarding illness prognosis
Inaccurate, incomplete, or conflicting information
Overwhelming situation
Inadequate coping method
Prolonged disease that exhausts supportive capacity of caregiver
Separation of family members
Loss of dominant figure in family structure

Defining Characteristics

Expressed concern inappropriate to need
Verbalization of problem
Disregard for patient's needs
Inappropriate behavior
Limited interaction with patient
Intolerance
Agitation or depression
Abandonment

Common Expected Outcomes

Family members identify the effect the patient's illness has on the family unit.
Family members identify resources available for help with coping.
Family members participate actively in caring for the ill family member.
Family members use supportive services and effective coping strategies.

NOC Outcomes
Family Coping; Family Normalization

NIC Interventions
Family Involvement; Family Process Maintenance; Coping Enhancement

Ongoing Assessment

Actions/Interventions

■ Identify each family member's understanding and beliefs about the patient's health situation.

■ Assess normal coping patterns in the family, including strengths, limitations, and resources.

■ Identify and respect family's coping mechanisms, as appropriate.

■ Identify family members' symptoms related to stress (e.g., fatigue, tearfulness, inability to sleep, irritability).

■ Determine ability of family members to provide necessary care.

Rationale

Misconceptions about the prognosis, expectations for daily care, and the role of family versus patient in managing health problems need to be clarified.

Successful adjustment is influenced by previous coping success. Families with a history of unsuccessful coping may need additional resources.

Not all cultures may display the same response to stress. For example, in some cultures it may be common to yell and slam doors. Although this may be uncomfortable for the nurse, it may not be bothersome for the patient who understands the behavior as normal.

Behavioral and psychological responses to stress can be varied and provide clues to the level of coping difficulty.

Safe and appropriate care are priority nursing concerns. The nurse may have to intervene with suggestions for additional resources, as appropriate.

■ = Independent; ▲ = Collaborative

Nursing Diagnosis Care Plans

Ineffective Coping

Actions/Interventions

- Evaluate resources or support systems available to the family.

- Recognize the primary caregiver's need for relief from continuing care responsibility. Assess the role of the patient in the family structure.

Rationale

In some situations there may be no readily available resources; however, often family members hesitate to notify other family members or significant others because of unresolved conflicts in the past.

The role of family members varies among cultures.

Therapeutic Interventions

Actions/Interventions

- Encourage questions or expressions of concern.

- Provide honest, appropriate answers to family members' questions.

- Discuss ways families can realistically continue to be involved in daily care. Address questions or concerns they have about their involvement in the patient's care.

  • Schedule a multidisciplinary care conference.

  • Help the family develop a realistic action plan.

Rationale

Coping difficulties vary depending on developmental level, extent of social contacts outside the family, and former experience with illness.

Appropriate information and reassurance can relieve stress.

Caregivers may have an unrealistic picture of the extent of care required at the present time, or perhaps the daily routine can be adjusted to facilitate attention to competing demands on the family member.

This may be an important first step to address the impact of family coping

Such a plan may include use of home health nurses, neighbors, Meals On Wheels, or respite care.

Education/Continuity of Care

Actions/Interventions

- Discuss the patient's condition and needed care with the patient and family.
- Provide information on the normal response to stress.
- Provide information about the resources available to assist families under stress (e.g., social services, hot lines, self-help groups, and educational opportunities).
- Offer assistance in notifying clergy, family members, and others of the patient's status.
- Refer the family to social services, pastoral care, and others. Request social work or psychological consults, as indicated.

Rationale

Distorted ideas, if not clarified, may be more frightening than realistic preparation.

This helps families understand what they are experiencing.

Patients may be unaware of services available for questions or problem resolution.

This promotes a sense of connectedness with significant others.

Specialized services may be required to meet specific needs.

NDx Ineffective Coping

NANDA: Inability to form a valid appraisal of the stressors, inadequate choices of practiced responses, and/or inability to use available resources

For most persons, everyday life includes its share of stressors and demands, ranging from family, work, and professional role responsibilities to major life events such as divorce, illness, and the death of loved ones. How one responds to such stressors depends in part

■ = Independent; ▲ = Collaborative

Nursing Diagnosis Care Plans

 Ineffective Coping–cont'd

on the person's coping resources. Such resources can include optimistic beliefs, social support networks, personal health and energy, problem-solving skills, and material resources. Sociocultural and religious factors may influence how people view and handle their problems. Some cultures may prefer privacy and avoid sharing their fears in public, even to health care providers. As resources become limited and problems become more acute, this strategy may prove ineffective. Vulnerable populations such as older patients, those in adverse socioeconomic situations, those with complex medical problems such as substance abuse, or those who find themselves suddenly physically challenged may not have the resources or skills to cope with their acute or chronic stressors. Such problems can occur in any setting (e.g., during hospitalization for an acute event, in the home or rehabilitation environment as a result of chronic illness, or in response to another threat or loss).

Common Related Factors

High degree of threat
Change in or loss of body part
Diagnosis of serious illness
Recent change in health status
Inadequate support system
Inadequate available resources
Personal vulnerability
Inadequate coping method
Situational crises
Maturational crises

Defining Characteristics

Verbalization of inability to cope
Inability to make decisions
Inability to ask for help
Lack of goal-directed behavior
Inadequate problem solving
Inability to meet role expectations
Abuse of chemical agents
Poor concentration
Fatigue
Sleep disturbance
Destructive behavior toward self or others
Inappropriate use of defense mechanisms
Headaches
Irritable bowel
Chronic depression
Emotional tension
High illness rate
Insomnia
General irritability

Common Expected Outcomes

Patient identifies own maladaptive coping behaviors.
Patient identifies available resources and support systems.
Patient describes and initiates alternative coping strategies.
Patient describes positive results from new behaviors.

NOC Outcomes
Coping; Decision Making;
Information Processing

NIC Intervention
Coping Enhancement

Ongoing Assessment

Actions/Interventions

■ Assess for presence of defining characteristics.

■ Assess specific stressors.

Rationale

Behavioral and physiological responses to stress can be varied and provide clues to the level of coping difficulty.

Accurate appraisal can facilitate development of appropriate coping strategies. Because a patient has an altered health status does not mean the coping difficulties he or she exhibits are only (if at all) related to that.

■ = Independent; ▲ = Collaborative

Ineffective Coping

Actions/Interventions

- Assess available or useful past and present coping mechanisms.

- Evaluate resources and support systems available to patient.

- Assess level of understanding and readiness to learn needed lifestyle changes.

- Assess decision-making and problem-solving abilities.

Rationale

Successful adjustment is influenced by previous coping success. Patients with a history of maladaptive coping may need additional resources. Likewise, previously successful coping skills may be inadequate in the present situation.

Patients may have support in one setting, such as during hospitalization, yet be discharged home without sufficient support for effective coping. Resources may include significant others, health care providers such as home health nurses, community resources, and spiritual counseling.

Appropriate problem solving requires accurate information and understanding of options. Often patients who are ineffectively coping are unable to hear or assimilate needed information.

Patients may feel that the threat is greater than their resources to handle it and feel a loss of control over solving the threat or problem.

Therapeutic Interventions

Actions/Interventions

- Establish a working relationship with the patient through continuity of care.
- Provide opportunities to express concerns, fears, feelings, and expectations.
- Convey feelings of acceptance and understanding. Avoid false reassurances.

- Encourage the patient to identify his or her own strengths and abilities.

- Assist patients to accurately evaluate the situation and their own accomplishments.

- Explore attitudes and feelings about required lifestyle changes.
- Encourage the patient to seek information that increases coping skills.
- Provide information the patient wants and needs. Do not provide more than the patient can handle.
- Encourage the patient to set realistic goals.

- Assist the patient to problem solve in a constructive manner.
- Reduce stimuli in an environment that could be misinterpreted as threatening.

Rationale

An ongoing relationship establishes trust, reduces the feeling of isolation, and may facilitate coping.

Verbalization of actual or perceived threats can help reduce anxiety and open doors for ongoing communication.

An honest relationship facilitates problem solving and successful coping. False reassurances are never helpful and only serve to relieve the discomfort of the care provider.

During crises, patients may not be able to recognize their strengths. Fostering awareness can expedite use of these strengths.

It can be helpful to recognize that the patient has the skills and reserves of strength to do the emotional work required.

Each patient is unique. Cultural, religious, ethnic, and individual differences affect attitudes.

Patients who are not coping well may need more guidance initially.

Patients who are coping ineffectively have reduced ability to assimilate information.

Setting realistic goals helps the patient gain control over the situation. Guiding the patient to view the situation in smaller parts may make the problem more manageable.

This can promote independence and a sense of autonomy.

In the acute hospital setting, patients are often exposed to new equipment and environments. This can increase anxiety and make coping more challenging.

■ = Independent; ▲ = Collaborative

Nursing Diagnosis Care Plans

→ Ineffective Coping–cont'd

Actions/Interventions

■ Provide outlets that foster feelings of personal achievement and self-esteem.

■ Point out signs of positive progress or change.

■ Encourage the patient to communicate feelings with significant others.

■ Point out maladaptive behaviors.

■ Assist the patient to grieve and work through the losses of chronic illness and change in body function, if appropriate.

Rationale

Opportunities to role-play or rehearse appropriate actions can increase confidence for behavior in actual situations.

Patients who are coping ineffectively may not be able to assess progress.

Unexpressed feelings can increase stress.

Pointing out observed behaviors helps the patient focus on more appropriate strategies.

The nurse is in an ideal position to guide the patient through this experience.

Education/Continuity of Care

Actions/Interventions

■ Instruct in need for adequate rest and balanced diet.

■ Teach use of relaxation, exercise, and diversional activities as methods to cope with stress.

▲ Involve social services, psychiatric liaison, and pastoral care for additional and ongoing support resources.

■ Assist in development of an alternative support system. Encourage participation in self-help groups, if available.

Rationale

Inadequate diet and fatigue can themselves be stressors.

A variety of brief interventions can be used toward assisting patients to reduce their level of stress.

Specialized services may be required to meet specific needs.

Relationships with persons with common interests and goals can be beneficial.

→ NDx Diarrhea

Loose Stools, *Clostridium difficile (C. difficile)*

NANDA: Passage of loose, unformed stools

Diarrhea may result from a variety of factors, including intestinal absorption disorders, increased secretion of fluid by the intestinal mucosa, and hypermotility of the intestine. Problems associated with diarrhea, which may be acute or chronic, include fluid and electrolyte imbalance and altered skin integrity. In older patients, or those with chronic disease (e.g., acquired immunodeficiency syndrome), diarrhea can be life threatening. Diarrhea may result from infectious (i.e., viral, bacterial, or parasitic) processes; inflammatory bowel diseases (e.g., Crohn's disease); drug therapies (e.g., antibiotics); increased osmotic loads (e.g., tube feedings); radiation; or increased intestinal motility such as with irritable bowel disease. Treatment is based on addressing the cause of the diarrhea, replacing fluids and electrolytes, providing nutrition (if diarrhea is prolonged and/or severe), and maintaining skin integrity. Health care workers and other caregivers must take precautions (e.g., diligent hand washing between patients) to avoid spreading diarrhea from person to person, including self.

■ = Independent; ▲ = Collaborative

Common Related Factors

Stress
Anxiety
Medication use
Bowel disorders: inflammation
Malabsorption
Increased secretion
Enteric infections
Disagreeable dietary intake
Tube feedings
Radiation
Chemotherapy
Bowel resection
Short bowel syndrome
Lactose intolerance

Defining Characteristics

Abdominal pain
Cramping
Frequency of stools
Loose or liquid stools
Urgency
Hyperactive bowel sounds or sensations

Common Expected Outcomes

Patient passes soft, formed stool no more than three
  times per day.
Patient has negative stool cultures.

NOC Outcomes
Bowel Elimination; Fluid Balance;
  Medication Response

NIC Interventions
Diarrhea Management; Enteral Tube Feeding;
  Teaching: Prescribed Medications

Ongoing Assessment

Actions/Interventions	Rationale
■ Assess for abdominal pain, cramping, frequency, urgency, loose or liquid stools, and hyperactive bowel sensations.	These are signs and symptoms associated with diarrhea.
▲ Culture stool.	Testing will identify causative organisms.
■ Inquire about the following:	
• Tolerance to milk and other dairy products	Patients with lactose intolerance have insufficient lactase, the enzyme that digests lactose. The presence of lactose in the intestines increases osmotic pressure and draws water into the intestinal lumen.
• Medications the patient is or has been taking	Laxatives and antibiotics may cause diarrhea. *C. difficile* can colonize the intestine following antibiotic use and lead to pseudomembranous enterocolitis: *C. difficile* is a common cause of nosocomial diarrhea in health care facilities.
• Food intolerances	Spicy, fatty, or high-carbohydrate foods; caffeine; or alcohol may cause diarrhea.
• Method of food preparation	Fried food or food contaminated with bacteria during preparation may cause diarrhea.
• Osmolality of tube feedings	Hyperosmolar food or fluid draws excess fluid into the gut, stimulates peristalsis, and causes diarrhea.
• Change in eating schedule	Changes in eating pattern can result in gastrointestinal manifestations.

■ = Independent; ▲ = Collaborative

Nursing Diagnosis Care Plans *(vertical text, left margin)*

 Diarrhea–cont'd

Actions/Interventions

- Level of activity

- Current stressors

■ Check for history of the following:
- Previous gastrointestinal surgery

- Gastrointestinal diseases

- Abdominal radiation

■ Assess the impact of therapeutic or diagnostic regimens on diarrhea.

■ Assess hydration status, as in the following:
- Input and output

- Skin turgor

- Moisture of mucous membranes
■ Assess condition of perianal skin.

■ Explore emotional impact of illness, hospitalization, and/or soiling accidents by providing privacy and opportunity for verbalization.

Rationale

A sedentary lifestyle can affect irritable bowel syndrome (IBS).

Some individuals respond to stress with hyperactivity of the gastrointestinal tract.

Following bowel resection, a period (1 to 3 weeks) of diarrhea is normal.

Diseases such as IBS and gastroenteritis can result in malabsorption and lead to chronic diarrhea.

Radiation causes sloughing of the intestinal mucosa, decreases usual absorption capacity, and may result in diarrhea.

Preparation for radiography or surgery, and radiation or chemotherapy predispose to diarrhea by altering the mucosal surface and transit time through the bowel.

Diarrhea can lead to profound dehydration and electrolyte imbalance.

Decreased skin turgor and tenting of the skin occur in dehydration.

Dehydration causes dry mucous membranes.

Diarrheal stools may be highly corrosive as a result of increased enzyme content.

Loss of control of bowel elimination that occurs with diarrhea can lead to feelings of embarrassment.

Therapeutic Interventions

Actions/Interventions

■ Give antidiarrheal drugs as ordered.

■ Provide the following dietary alterations as allowed:
- Bulk fiber (e.g., cereal, grains, Metamucil)
- "Natural" bulking agents (e.g., rice, apples, matzos, cheese)
- Avoidance of stimulants (e.g., caffeine, carbonated beverages)
■ Check for fecal impaction by digital examination.

■ Encourage fluids; consider nutritional support.

■ Evaluate appropriateness of physician's radiograph protocols for bowel preparation on basis of age, weight, condition, disease, and other therapies.

■ Assist with or administer perianal care after each bowel movement.

Rationale

Most antidiarrheal drugs suppress gastrointestinal motility, thus allowing for more fluid absorption.

Bulking agents and dietary fibers absorb fluid from the stool and help thicken the stool

Stimulants may increase gastrointestinal motility and worsen diarrhea.

Liquid stool (apparent diarrhea) may seep past a fecal impaction.

Fluids compensate for malabsorption and loss of nutrients.

Older, frail patients or those patients already depleted may require less bowel preparation or additional intravenous fluid therapy during preparation.

This prevents perianal skin excoriation.

■ = Independent; ▲ = Collaborative

Actions/Interventions

■ For patients with enteral tube feeding, employ the following:
  • Change feeding tube equipment according to institutional policy, but no less than every 24 hours.
  • Administer tube feeding at room temperature.
  • Initiate tube feeding slowly.

  • Decrease rate or dilute feeding if diarrhea persists or worsens.

Rationale

Contaminated equipment can cause diarrhea.

Extremes of temperature can stimulate peristalsis.
This allows the gastrointestinal system to accommodate intake.
This prevents hyperosmolar diarrhea.

Education/Continuity of Care

Actions/Interventions

■ Teach the patient or caregiver the following dietary changes that can be controlled:
  • Avoid spicy, fatty foods, alcohol, and caffeine.
  • Broil, bake, or boil foods; avoid frying.
  • Avoid foods that are disagreeable.
■ Encourage reporting of diarrhea that occurs with prescription drugs.

■ Teach the patient or caregiver to use antidiarrheal medications as ordered.
■ Teach the patient or caregiver the importance of fluid replacement during diarrheal episodes.
■ Teach the patient or caregiver the importance of good perianal hygiene after each bowel movement.

Rationale

These dietary changes can slow the passage of stool through the colon and reduce or eliminate diarrhea.

There are usually several antibiotics with which the patient can be treated; if the one prescribed causes diarrhea, this should be reported promptly.

Appropriate use of antidiarrheal medications can promote effective bowel elimination.

Fluids prevent dehydration.

Hygiene controls perianal skin excoriation and minimizes

Deficient Diversional Activity

NANDA: Decreased stimulation from or interest or engagement in recreational or leisure activities

Diversional activity deficit occurs as a result of illness or disability: for example, the pregnant patient who is confined to bed rest, the orthopedic patient who is physically limited, or the geriatric patient who is unable to perform desired activities. It is important for mental and developmental health that individuals in these or similar situations (whether temporary or permanent) maintain some level of productivity and social engagement.

Common Related Factors

Prolonged hospitalization, debilitation, or illness
Environmental lack of diversional activity
Usual hobbies cannot be undertaken
Lack of usual level of socialization
Physical inability to perform tasks
Physical confinement

Defining Characteristics

Verbal expression of boredom
Preoccupation with illness
Desire for activity
Excessive complaints
Withdrawal
Depression

■ = Independent; ▲ = Collaborative

Nursing Diagnosis Care Plans

→ Deficient Diversional Activity—cont'd

Common Expected Outcome

Patient's attention is diverted to interests other than illness and confinement.

> **NOC Outcomes**
> Leisure Participation; Social Involvement
>
> **NIC Intervention**
> Activity Therapy

Ongoing Assessment

Actions/Interventions

For the home care or hospitalized patient, conduct the following:

■ Explore the importance of past or desired activity.

■ Inquire about interest and hobbies before illness or disability (e.g., art, reading, writing, sports).

■ Assess attention span.

■ Assess for physical limitations

■ Observe and document response to activities.

Rationale

Theories of human occupation indicate that the benefits of activities are related to the importance assigned.

Another type of activity, involving a familiar or desired topic, may be acceptable.

Activities requiring extended attention span should not be selected to prevent frustration and feelings of failure.

The patient's physical abilities should be taken into consideration when activities are chosen. Fine needlepoint may not be a good selection for a patient with visual disabilities.

Variety in activities may be desirable to prevent boredom.

Therapeutic Interventions

Actions/Interventions

For the home care or hospitalized patient, instruct the caregiver to:

■ Provide frequent contact. Be certain that patient is aware of your presence.

■ Set up a schedule so that the patient will know when to expect contact or activities.

■ Provide and assist with specific physical, cognitive, social, and/or spiritual activities that can be accomplished in the current situation.

▲ Collaborate with physical, occupational, and/or recreational therapy to plan and implement an acceptable, achievable activity program.

■ Suggest new interests (e.g., crafts, puzzles, Internet).

Rationale

A prolonged confinement resulting from illness or disability may cause the patient to become depressed or to disengage from life by increasing the amount of time spent sleeping or refusing visitors.

Anticipation of a positive activity can provide a hopeful outlook for the patient.

The patient may need assistance to engage in desired activities.

Institutional and community resources can provide a diversity of activities and support for the patient.

Renting or borrowing a computer that can be connected to the World Wide Web may provide both intellectual stimulation and education, as well as access to chat groups.

■ = Independent; ▲ = Collaborative

Actions/Interventions

■ Encourage family and friends to visit and bring diversional materials.

■ Provide dietary changes if possible.

■ Spend time with the patient without providing physical care.

Rationale

Care should be taken to not overload the patient with books, projects, and other items for which the patient has no interest and will not use, providing additional sense of frustration.

Mealtime, especially with family, and menu selection become very important to the confined patient.

Engaging the patient in conversation without focusing on illness will divert the patient's attention and help pass the time.

Education/Continuity of Care

Actions/Interventions

■ Obtain instructional materials for new hobbies and interests.

■ Encourage continuation of education.

■ Explain the benefits of diversional activity (e.g., relaxation, distraction).

■ Suggest contacting church or other social groups for assistance.

Rationale

Providing resources can be a motivation for the patient to engage in activities.

For some patients, this period of time could provide opportunity for self-growth through formal or informal approaches.

Patients are more likely to engage in activities that require expenditure of energy if they see a positive benefit.

Groups such as Libraries on Wheels, companion services, and community support services for older patients often make home visits.

 ## Risk for Falls

NANDA: Increased susceptibility to falling that may cause physical harm

Falls are a major safety risk for adults, especially older adults. Evidence indicates that about 30% to 40% of older adults experience at least one serious fall per year. The consequences of these falls for the older adult represent a major health concern. Injuries sustained as a result of a fall include soft tissue injury, fractures (hip, spine, and wrist), and traumatic brain injury. Fall-related injuries are associated with prolonged hospitalizations for the older adult. The quality of life for older adults is significantly changed following a fall-related injury. The death rate from fall-related injuries and their complications increases with the age of the patient.

Prevention of falls is an important dimension of the nursing care of patients in hospitals and long-term care settings. Implementation of policies and procedures designed to prevent falls is an essential part of nursing care in any health care setting. Fall prevention strategies need to promote patient dignity and functional independence by significantly limiting the use of physical restraints to maintain safety. Nurses also have a major role in educating patients, families, and caregivers about prevention of falls in the home.

■ = Independent; ▲ = Collaborative

Risk for Falls–cont'd

Common Risk Factors

History of falls
Wheelchair use
65 years of age or older
Female (if older)
Lives alone
Use of assistive devices for mobility
Presence of acute illness
Orthostatic hypotension
Visual and/or hearing difficulties
Urinary or bowel incontinence
Impaired physical mobility
Diminished mental status
Polypharmacy
Cluttered environment
Unfamiliar, dimly lit room
Weather conditions (wet floors, ice)

Common Expected Outcomes

Patient will not sustain a fall.
Patient and caregiver will implement strategies to increase
    safety and prevent falls in the home.

> **NOC Outcomes**
> Fall Prevention Behavior; Knowledge: Fall
>   Prevention; Risk Control; Risk Detection
>
> **NIC Interventions**
> Fall Prevention; Environmental Management
>   Safety; Teaching: Prescribed Activity/
>   Exercise; Medication Management

Ongoing Assessment

Actions/Interventions

- Assess the person for factors known to increase fall
  risk:
    - History of falls

    - Mental status changes

    - Age-related physical changes

    - Sensory deficits

    - Use of mobility assistive devices

Rationale

Evidence indicates that a person who has sustained one
    or more falls in the past year is more likely to fall
    again.
Confusion and impaired judgment increase the person's
    risk for falls.
Normal changes associated with aging increase the person's
    risk for falling. These changes include decreased visual
    capacity, impaired color perception, change in center of
    gravity, decreased muscle strength, decreased endurance,
    altered depth perception, and delayed response and
    reaction times.
Impaired vision and hearing limit the person's ability to
    recognize hazards in the environment.
Improper use and maintenance of mobility aids such as
    canes, walkers, and wheelchairs increases the person's
    risk of falls.

■ = Independent; ▲ = Collaborative

Nursing Diagnosis Care Plans

Actions/Interventions

- Disease-related symptoms

- Medications

- Unsafe clothing

■ Assess the person's environment for factors known to increase fall risk such as unfamiliar setting, inadequate lighting, wet surfaces, waxed floors, clutter, and objects on floor.

▲ Refer the person for diagnostic musculoskeletal evaluation.

Rationale

Increased incidence of falls has been demonstrated in persons with symptoms such as orthostatic hypotension, urinary incontinence, reduced cerebral blood flow, edema, dizziness, weakness, fatigue, and confusion.

Side effects of drugs and the drug interactions that occur with polypharmacy increase the person's risk for falls. Drugs that affect blood pressure and level of consciousness are associated with the highest fall risk. Specific drug groups associated with falls include antihypertensives, sedatives, opioid analgesics, tranquilizers, and diuretics.

Poor-fitting shoes, long robes, or long pants legs can limit a person's ambulation and increase fall risk.

Patients who are not familiar with the placement of furniture and equipment in their room are more likely to experience a fall. Anything that blocks or limits a clear, straight path for ambulation can contribute to a person's fall risk.

Patients with musculoskeletal problems such as osteoporosis are at increased risk for serious injury from falls. Bone mineral density testing will help identify the risk for fractures from falls. Physical therapy evaluation can identify problems with balance and gait that can increase a person's fall risk.

Therapeutic Interventions

Actions/Interventions

■ For the patient in the hospital or long-term care setting:
- Post signs to identify the patients at risk for falls and to remind health care providers to implement fall precaution behaviors.

- Place items used by the patient within easy reach.

- Answer call lights immediately.

- Place mechanical beds in the lowest possible position. If needed, place the patient's sleeping surface as close to the floor as possible.

- Use side rails on beds, as needed. For beds with split side rails, leave at least one of the rails at the foot of the bed down.

- Ensure appropriate room lighting, especially at night.

Rationale

All health care providers need to recognize the patient who is at risk for falls. All care providers are responsible for implementing actions to promote patient safety and prevent falls.

Stretching to get items from bedside tables that are out of reach can disrupt the patient's balance and contribute to falls.

Patients who experience delay in having their call lights answered are more likely to get out of bed without assistance. This behavior, especially if they need to go to the bathroom, will increase their risk for falls.

Keeping beds in the lowest position reduces the risk for falls and serious injury. In some health care settings, placing the mattress on the floor significantly reduces fall risk.

Patients who are disoriented or confused have been known to climb over side rails and fall. Research demonstrates that when one of four rails is left down, the patient is less likely to fall.

Older adults with reduced visual capacity will benefit from adequate lighting, especially in an unfamiliar environment. Using a night light helps increase visibility if the patient must get up at night.

■ = Independent; ▲ = Collaborative

Risk for Falls–cont'd

Nursing Diagnosis Care Plans

Actions/Interventions

- Encourage the patient to wear shoes or slippers with nonskid soles when ambulating.

- Orient the patient to the layout of the room. Limit rearranging the furniture in the room.

- Provide heavy furniture that will not tip over if used for support by the patient when ambulating. Keep primary ambulation path clear and as straight as possible. Avoid clutter on the floor surface.

- Use bed and chair alarms to alert staff when the patient gets up without assistance.

- Provide the patient with a chair that has a firm seat and arms on both sides.

- ▲ Collaborate with other health care team members to evaluate the patient's medications that contribute to falling.

- ■ Encourage the patient to participate in a program of regular exercise.

- ■ Encourage the patient to wear eyeglasses and hearing aids.

- ▲ Collaborate with physical therapy and occupational therapy to provide the patient with assistive devices for transfer and ambulation.

Rationale

Nonskid footwear provides sure footing for the patient with diminished foot and toe lift when walking.

The more familiar the patient is with the layout of the room, the less likely the patient is to trip over furniture.

Patients with balance and gait problems are not as skilled at ambulating around objects that obstruct a straight path.

Audible alarms can remind the patient not to get up alone. The use of alarms can be a substitute for physical restraints.

This chair style is easier to get out of, especially when the patient experiences weakness and impaired balance when transferring from bed to chair.

A review of the patient's medications by the prescribing health care provider and the pharmacist can identify side effects and drug interactions that increase the patient's fall risk. The more medications a patient takes, the greater the risk for side effects and interactions such as dizziness, orthostatic hypotension, drowsiness, and incontinence. Polypharmacy in the older adult is a significant risk factor for falls.

Evidence suggests that people who engage in regular exercise and activity will strengthen muscles, improve balance, and increase bone density. Increased physical conditioning reduces the risk of falls and limits injury that is sustained when a fall occurs.

Fall risk can be reduced if the patient uses appropriate aids to promote visual and auditory orientation to the environment.

The use of gait belts by all health care providers can promote safety when assisting patients with transfers from bed to chair. Canes, walkers, and wheelchairs can provide the patient with improved stability and balance when ambulating. Raised toilet seats can facilitate safe transfer on and off the toilet.

Education/Continuity of Care

Actions/Interventions

- ■ Educate the patient and family caregivers about risk factors for falls in the home. Suggest home adaptations to increase safety.
  - Place bright, nonskid strips on the edge of stair treads. Install handrails on both sides of the stairs from top to bottom.

  - Ensure that all rugs are securely fastened to the floor or removed.

Rationale

About 40% of older adults living in the community sustain at least one fall per year. Falls are the leading cause of accidental death in the home setting.

Older adults have problems differentiating shades of the same color and have diminished depth perception. These physiologic changes make it difficult to see the edge of a stair tread that is a uniform color.

Loose throw rugs increase the risk of slipping and falling.

■ = Independent; ▲ = Collaborative

Actions/Interventions

- Install nonslip surfaces in tubs and showers. Place grab bars near the tub or shower and toilet. Consider use of a shower chair.

- Rearrange furniture to have a clear pathway between rooms. Keep traffic patterns free of clutter and electrical cords.

- Increase lighting at the top and bottom of stairs. Use nightlights in bathrooms, bedrooms, and hallways.

▲ Refer the family to community resources for assistance in making home safety modifications.

■ Educate the patient and family caregivers about the correct use and maintenance of mobility assistive devices.

Rationale

Wet surfaces in bathrooms increase the risk of falls.

People with diminished strength or who use mobility devices are less able to negotiate around obstacles in their path.

Older adults have poor vision at night and in dimly lit areas.

Many community service organizations provide financial assistance to help older adults make safety improvements in their homes.

Incorrect use or improper maintenance of canes, walkers, and wheelchairs can increase the risk of falls. The devices need to be properly fitted to the individual. Falls can occur if brakes on wheelchairs are not used correctly.

NDx Interrupted Family Processes

Ineffective Individual Coping

NANDA: Change in family relationships and/or functioning

Altered family processes occur as a result of the inability of one or more members of the family to adjust or perform, resulting in family dysfunction and interruption or prevention of development of the family. Family development is closely related to the developmental changes experienced by adult members. Over time, families must adjust to change within the family structure brought on by both expected and unexpected events, including illness or death of a member, and/or changes in social or economic strengths precipitated by divorce, retirement, and loss of employment. Health care providers must also be aware of the changing constellation of families: gay couples raising children, single parents with children, older grandparents responsible for grandchildren or foster children, and other situations.

Common Related Factors

Illness of family member
Change in socioeconomic status
Births, adoptions, and deaths
Conflict between family members
Situational transition and/or crisis
Developmental transition and/or crisis

Defining Characteristics

Inability to meet needs of family members
Inability to function in larger society (e.g., no job, no community activity)
Inability to meet emotional needs of family members (e.g., feelings of grief, anxiety, or conflict)
Inability to accept or receive needed help
Ineffective family decision-making process
Rigidity in roles, behavior, and beliefs
Inappropriate or poorly communicated family rules, rituals, or symbols
Poor communication
Failure to accomplish current or past developmental task
Social isolation

■ = Independent; ▲ = Collaborative

Interrupted Family Processes—cont'd

Common Expected Outcomes

Family develops improved methods of communication.
Family identifies resources available for problem solving.
Family expresses understanding of mutual problems.

> **NOC Outcomes**
> Family Coping; Family Functioning;
> Family Normalization
>
> **NIC Interventions**
> Family Process Maintenance;
> Normalization Promotion

Ongoing Assessment

Actions/Interventions	Rationale
■ Assess for precipitating events (e.g., divorce, illness, life transition, crisis).	Depending on the stressor, a variety of strategies may be required to facilitate coping.
■ Assess family members' perceptions of the problem.	Resolution is possible only if each person's perceptions are understood. Understanding another's perceptions can lead to clarification and problem solving.
■ Evaluate strengths, coping skills, and current support systems.	This facilitates the use of previously successful techniques.
■ Assess developmental level of family members.	Middle-aged adults may be having difficulty handling the demands of adolescent children and older parents.

Therapeutic Interventions

Actions/Interventions	Rationale
■ Provide opportunities to express concerns, fears, expectations, or questions.	Providing such opportunities promotes communication and support, and may facilitate coping.
■ Explore feelings: identify loneliness, anger, worry, and fear.	The feelings of one family member influence others in the family system.
■ Phrase problems as "family" problems.	This promotes a sense of connectedness and reduces the tendency to blame individual family members.
■ Encourage members to empathize with other family members.	Empathy can increase understanding of others' feelings and fosters mutual respect and support.
■ Assist the family in setting realistic goals.	Setting realistic goals helps the family gain control over the situation.
■ Assist the family in breaking down problems into manageable parts.	Guiding them to view the problems in smaller parts may make the situation more tolerable.
■ Assist with problem-solving process, with delineated responsibilities and follow-through.	This can promote independence and a sense of autonomy.
■ Tailor interventions according to family members' abilities.	This enhances self-efficacy and increases chance for successful resolution.
■ Encourage family members to seek information and resources that increase coping skills.	Practical information and positive role models can be very effective.
■ Investigate cultural norms and factors.	The role of family members varies among cultures.
▲ Refer the family to social services or counseling.	Long-term intervention or assistance may be required.

> ■ = Independent; ▲ = Collaborative

Education/Continuity of Care

Actions/Interventions

■ Provide information regarding stressful situations, as appropriate (e.g., pattern of illness, time frames for recovery, and expectations).

■ Identify community resources that may be helpful in dealing with particular situations (e.g., telephone hotlines, self-help groups, educational opportunities, social services agencies, and counseling centers).

Rationale

Information helps the family understand what they are experiencing and gives them a window to future expectations.

Groups that come together for mutual support or information exchange can be beneficial in helping the family reach goals.

NDx Fatigue

NANDA: An overwhelming sustained sense of exhaustion and decreased capacity for physical and mental work at usual level

Fatigue is a subjective complaint with both acute and chronic illnesses. In an acute illness, fatigue may have a protective function that keeps the person from sustaining injury from overwork in a weakened condition. As a common symptom, fatigue is associated with a variety of physical and psychological conditions. Fatigue is a prominent finding in many viral infections such as hepatitis. Patients with rheumatoid arthritis, fibromyalgia, systemic lupus erythematosus, myasthenia gravis, and depression report fatigue as a profound symptom that reduces their ability to participate in their own care and fulfill role responsibilities. The patient with a chronic illness experiencing fatigue may be unable to work full-time and maintain acceptable performance on the job. The economic impact on the individual and the family can be significant. The social effects of fatigue occur as the person decreases his or her participation in social activities.

Chronic fatigue syndrome is a poorly understood condition that is characterized by prolonged, debilitating fatigue, neurological problems, general pain, gastrointestinal problems, and flulike symptoms. While the exact cause of chronic fatigue syndrome is not known, one theory suggests that the disorder may represent an abnormal response of the immune system to highly stressful physiological or psychological events.

Common Related Factors

Psychological:
  • Boring lifestyle
  • Stress
  • Anxiety
  • Depression
Environmental:
  • Humidity
  • Lights
  • Noise
  • Temperature
Situational:
  • Negative life event
  • Occupation

Defining Characteristics

Inability to restore energy, even after sleep
Lack of energy or inability to maintain usual level of physical activity
Increased rest requirements
Tired
Verbalization of an unremitting and overwhelming lack of energy
Inability to maintain usual routines
Lethargic or listless
Increased physical complaints
Perceived need for additional energy to accomplish routine tasks
Compromised concentration
Feelings of guilt for not keeping up with responsibilities

■ = Independent; ▲ = Collaborative

Fatigue—cont'd

Common Related Factors—cont'd

Physiological:
- Sleep deprivation
- Pregnancy
- Poor physical condition
- Disease states
- Increased physical exertion
- Malnutrition
- Anemia

Common Expected Outcome

Patient verbalizes having sufficient energy to complete desired activities.

NOC Outcomes
Activity Tolerance; Endurance;
   Energy Conservation

NIC Interventions
Energy Management; Exercise Promotion;
   Nutrition Management;
   Sleep Enhancement

Ongoing Assessment

Actions/Interventions

■ Assess the following characteristics of fatigue:
- Severity
- Changes in severity over time
- Aggravating factors
- Alleviating factors

■ Assess for possible causes of fatigue:
- Recent physical illness
- Emotional stress
- Depression
- Medication side effects
- Anemia
- Sleep disorders
- Imbalanced nutritional intake
- Increased responsibilities and demands at home or work

■ Assess the patient's ability to perform activities of daily living (ADLs), instrumental activities of daily living (IADLs), and demands of daily living (DDLs).

■ Assess the patient's emotional response to fatigue.

■ Evaluate the patient's routine prescription and over-the-counter medications.

Rationale

Using a quantitative rating scale (e.g., 0 to 10) can help the patient describe the amount of fatigue experienced. Other rating scales can be developed using pictures or descriptive words. This method allows the nurse to compare changes in the patient's fatigue level over time. It is important to determine if the patient's level of fatigue is constant or if it varies over time.

Identifying the related factors with fatigue can aid in determining possible causes and establishing a collaborative care plan.

Fatigue can limit the person's ability to participate in self-care and perform his or her role responsibilities in the family and society.

Anxiety and depression are the more common emotional responses associated with fatigue. These emotional states can add to the person's fatigue level and create a vicious cycle.

Fatigue may be a medication side effect or an indication of a drug interaction. The nurse should give particular attention to the patient's use of β-blockers, calcium

■ = Independent; ▲ = Collaborative

Actions/Interventions

- Assess the patient's nutritional intake of calories, protein, minerals, and vitamins.

- Evaluate the patient's sleep patterns for quality, quantity, time taken to fall asleep, and feeling upon awakening. Also assess for sleep apnea.

- Assess the patient's usual level of exercise and physical activity.

- Evaluate laboratory/diagnostic test results:
  - Blood glucose
  - Hemoglobin and hematocrit
  - Blood urea nitrogen
  - Oxygen saturation, resting and with activity
  - Thyroid-stimulating hormone

- Assess the patient's expectations for fatigue relief, willingness to participate in strategies to reduce fatigue, and level of family and social support.

Rationale

channel blockers, tranquilizers, alcohol, muscle relaxants, and sedatives.

Fatigue may be a symptom of protein-calorie malnutrition, vitamin deficiencies, or iron deficiencies.

Changes in the person's sleep pattern may be a contributing factor in the development of fatigue.

Both increased physical exertion and limited levels of exercise can contribute to fatigue.

Changes in these physiological measures can be compared with other assessment data to understand possible causes of the patient's fatigue.

The patient will need to be an active participant in planning, implementing, and evaluating therapeutic interventions to relieve fatigue. Social support will be necessary to help the patient implement changes to reduce fatigue.

Therapeutic Interventions

Actions/Interventions

- Encourage the patient to keep a 24-hour fatigue/activity log for at least 1 week.

- Assist the patient to develop a schedule for daily activity and rest.

- ▲ Refer the patient to an occupational therapist.

- Encourage the patient to use assistive devices for ADLs and IADLs:
  - Long-handled sponge for bathing
  - Long shoehorn
  - Sock-puller
  - Long-handled grabber

- Help the patient set priorities for desired activities and role responsibilities.

- Provide recommendations for nutritional intake for adequate energy sources and metabolic requirements.

- Encourage the patient to identify tasks that can be delegated to others.

Rationale

Recognizing relationships between specific activities and levels of fatigue can help the patient identify excessive energy expenditure. The log may indicate times of day when the person feels the least fatigued. This information can help the patient make decisions about arranging his or her activities to take advantage of periods of high energy levels.

A plan that balances periods of activity with periods of rest can help the patient complete desired activities without adding to levels of fatigue.

The occupational therapist can provide the patient with assistive devices and teach the patient energy conservation techniques.

The use of assistive devices can minimize energy expenditure and prevent injury with activities.

Setting priorities is one example of an energy conservation technique that allows the patient to use available energy to accomplish important activities. Achieving desired goals can improve the patient's mood and sense of emotional well-being.

The patient will need adequate, properly balanced intake of carbohydrates, fats, protein, vitamins, and minerals to provide energy resources.

Delegating tasks and responsibilities to others can help the patient conserve energy.

■ = Independent; ▲ = Collaborative

Nursing Diagnosis Care Plans

Fatigue—cont'd

Actions/Interventions

- Minimize environmental stimuli, especially during planned times for rest and sleep.

Rationale

Bright lighting, noise, visitors, frequent distractions, and clutter in the patient's physical environment can inhibit relaxation, interrupt rest/sleep, and contribute to fatigue.

Education/Continuity of Care

Actions/Interventions

- Teach the patient and family task organization techniques and time management strategies.
- Help the patient engage in increasing levels of physical activity and exercise.
- Teach the patient signs and symptoms of overexertion with activity.
- Help the patient develop habits to promote effective rest/sleep patterns.

- Encourage the patient and family to verbalize feelings about the impact of fatigue.

Rationale

Organization and time management can help the patient conserve energy and prevent fatigue.

Exercise can reduce fatigue and help the patient build endurance for physical activity.

Changes in oxygen saturation, respiratory rate, and heart rate will reflect the patient's tolerance for activity.

Promoting relaxation before sleep and providing for several hours of uninterrupted sleep can contribute to energy restoration.

Fatigue can have a profound negative influence on family processes and social interaction.

NDx Fear

NANDA: Response to perceived threat that is consciously recognized as a danger

Fear is a strong and unpleasant emotion caused by the awareness or anticipation of pain or danger. This emotion is primarily externally motivated and source-specific; that is, the individual experiencing the fear can identify the person, place, or thing precipitating this feeling. The factors that precipitate fear are, to some extent, universal; fear of death, pain, and bodily injury are common to most people. Other fears are derived from the life experiences of the individual person. How fear is expressed may be strongly influenced by the culture, age, or gender of the person under consideration. In some cultures it may be unacceptable to express fear regardless of the precipitating factors. Rather than manifesting outward signs of fear as described in the defining characteristics, responses may range from risk-taking behavior to expressions of bravado and defiance of fear as a legitimate feeling. In other cultures fear may be freely expressed and manifestations may be universally accepted. In addition to one's own individual ways of coping with the feeling of fear, there are aspects of coping that are cultural as well. Some cultures control fear through the use of magic, mysticism, or religiosity. Whatever one's mechanism for controlling and coping with fear, it is a normal part of everyone's life. The nurse may encounter the fearful patient in the community, during the performance of diagnostic testing in an outpatient setting, or during hospitalization. The nurse must learn to identify when patients are experiencing fear and must find ways to assist them in a respectful way to negotiate these feelings. The nurse must also learn to identify when fear becomes so persistent and pervasive that it impairs an individual's ability to carry on his or her activities of daily living. Under these circumstances, referral can be made to programs designed to assist the patient in overcoming phobias and other truly debilitating fears.

Common Related Factors

Anticipation of pain
Anticipation or perceived physical threat or danger
Fear of an event
Unfamiliar environment
Environmental stimuli
Separation from support system
Treatments and invasive procedures
Threat of death
Language barrier
Knowledge deficit
Sensory impairment
Specific phobias

Defining Characteristics

Identifies fearful feelings or object of fear
Increased respirations, heart rate, and respiratory rate
Tension
Jitteriness
Apprehension
Impulsivity
Alertness
Avoidance behavior

Common Expected Outcomes

Patient manifests coping behaviors.
Patient verbalizes or manifests a reduction or absence of fear.

NOC Outcomes
Fear Self-Control; Coping

NIC Interventions
Anxiety Reduction; Emotional Support

Ongoing Assessment

Actions/Interventions

- Determine what the patient is fearful of by careful and thoughtful questioning.
- Create an atmosphere that facilitates trust through active listening.

- Assess the degree of fear and the measures the patient uses to cope with that fear. (This can be done by interviewing the patient and significant others.)
- Document behavioral and verbal expression of fear.

- Determine to what degree the patient's fears may be affecting his or her ability to perform activities of daily living (ADLs).

Rationale

The external source of fear can be identified and current responses can be assessed.

Patients who find it unacceptable to express fear may find it helpful to know that someone is willing to listen if they decide to share their feelings at some time in the future.

This helps determine the effectiveness of coping strategies used by the patient.

Physiological symptoms and/or complaints intensify as the level of fear increases. Note that fear differs from anxiety in that it is a response to a recognized and usually external threat. Manifestations of fear are similar to those of anxiety.

Persistent, immobilizing fears may require treatment with antianxiety medications or referral to specially designed treatment programs.

Therapeutic Interventions

Actions/Interventions

- Acknowledge your awareness of the patient's fear

- Stay with the patient to promote safety, especially during frightening procedures or treatments.

Rationale

This validates the feelings the patient is having and communicates an acceptance of those feelings.

The presence of a trusted person increases the patient's sense of security and safety during a period of fear.

■ = Independent; ▲ = Collaborative

Nursing Diagnosis Care Plans

 **Fear**–cont'd

Actions/Interventions

- Maintain a calm and tolerant manner while interacting with the patient.

- Establish a working relationship through continuity of care.

- Orient to the environment as needed.

- Provide safety measures within the home when indicated (e.g., alarm system, safety devices in showers or bathtubs).

- Use simple language and brief statements when instructing the patient regarding diagnostic and surgical procedures. Explain what physical or sensory sensations will be experienced.

- Reduce sensory stimulation by maintaining a quiet environment, whether in the hospital or home situation. Remove unnecessary threatening equipment.

- Assist the patient in identifying strategies used in the past to deal with fearful situations. These measures may be helpful or comforting.

- As the patient's fear subsides, encourage him or her to explore specific events preceding the onset of the fear.

- Encourage rest periods.

- When the patient must be hospitalized or away from home, suggest bringing in comforting objects from home (e.g., music, pillow, blanket, pictures).

- Access appropriate resources to meet the fearful needs of the patient and family (e.g., spiritual counselor or social worker).

Rationale

The patient's feeling of stability increases in a calm and nonthreatening atmosphere.

An ongoing relationship establishes trust and a basis for communicating fearful feelings.

This promotes comfort and a decrease in fear.

If the home environment is unsafe, the patient's fears are not resolved and fear may become disabling.

When experiencing excessive fear or dread, the patient may be unable to comprehend more than simple, clear, and brief instructions. Repetition may be necessary.

Fear may escalate with excessive conversation, noise, and equipment around the patient. Even though the staff or caregiver may be comfortable around "high-tech" or medical equipment, the patient may not be.

This helps the patient focus on fear as a real and natural part of life that has been and can continue to be dealt with successfully.

Recognition and explanation of factors leading to fear are significant in developing alternative responses.

Rest improves ability to cope.

Familiar objects in a new environment can enhance feelings of security.

This provides coordinated patient care that emphasizes supportive health care services.

Education/Continuity of Care

Actions/Interventions

- Reinforce the idea that fear is a normal and appropriate response to situations when pain, danger, or loss of control is anticipated or experienced.

- Instruct the patient in the performance of the following self-calming measures that may reduce fear or make it more manageable:

  • Breathing modifications

  • Exercises in relaxation, meditation, or guided imagery

  • Exercises in the use of affirmations and calming self-talk

Rationale

Knowledge serves to reduce unrealistic expectations.

Educating the patient and significant others to anticipatory coping mechanisms will focus energy on prevention with opportunity for growth rather than reaction to the identified fear.

Controlled, rhythmic breathing can promote relaxation and feelings of being in control.

Exercise reduces the physiological response to fear (i.e., increased BP, pulse, respiration).

These enhance the patient's sense of confidence and reassurance.

■ = Independent; ▲ = Collaborative

Actions/Interventions

▲ Instruct the patient in the use of physician-ordered antianxiety medications.

■ Caution the patient against the use of illicit drugs or the overuse of alcohol to deal with fearful feelings.

Rationale

Short-term use of antianxiety medications can relieve unpleasant feelings.

Abuse of drugs and alcohol limits the effectiveness of the person's coping ability.

> • RELATED CARE PLAN
>
> Anxiety, p. 15

NDx Deficient Fluid Volume

Hypovolemia; Dehydration

NANDA: Decreased intravascular, interstitial, and/or intracellular fluid. This refers to dehydration, water loss alone without change in sodium

Fluid volume deficit, or hypovolemia, occurs from a loss of body fluid or the shift of fluids into the third space, or from a reduced fluid intake. Common sources for fluid loss are the gastrointestinal tract, polyuria, and increased perspiration. Fluid volume deficit may be an acute or chronic condition managed in the hospital, outpatient center, or home setting. The therapeutic goal is to treat the underlying disorder and return the extracellular fluid compartment to normal. Treatment consists of restoring fluid volume and correcting any electrolyte imbalances. Early recognition and treatment are paramount to prevent potentially life-threatening hypovolemic shock. Older patients are more likely to develop fluid imbalances.

Common Related Factors

Inadequate fluid intake
Active fluid loss (diuresis, abnormal drainage or bleeding, diarrhea)
Failure of regulatory mechanisms
Electrolyte and acid-base imbalances
Increased metabolic rate (fever, infection)
Fluid shifts (edema or effusions)

Defining Characteristics

Decreased urine output
Concentrated urine
Output greater than intake
Sudden weight loss
Decreased venous filling
Hemoconcentration
Increased serum sodium
Hypotension
Thirst
Increased pulse rate
Decreased skin turgor
Dry mucous membranes
Weakness
Possible weight gain
Changes in mental status

■ = Independent; ▲ = Collaborative

Deficient Fluid Volume

Nursing Diagnosis Care Plans

 Deficient Fluid Volume–cont'd

Common Expected Outcome

Patient experiences adequate fluid volume and electrolyte balance as evidenced by urine output greater than 30 mL/hr, normotensive blood pressure (BP), heart rate (HR) less than 100 beats/min, consistency of weight, and normal skin turgor.

NOC Outcomes
Fluid Balance; Hydration

NIC Interventions
Fluid Monitoring; Fluid Management; Fluid Resuscitation

Ongoing Assessment

Actions/Interventions

■ Obtain patient history to ascertain the probable cause of the fluid disturbance.

■ Assess or instruct the patient to monitor weight daily and consistently, with the same scale and preferably at the same time of day.

■ Evaluate fluid status in relation to dietary intake. Determine whether the patient has been on fluid restriction.

■ Monitor and document vital signs.

■ Monitor blood pressure for orthostatic changes (from patient lying supine to high-Fowler's).

■ Assess skin turgor and mucous membranes for signs of dehydration.

■ Assess color and amount of urine. Report urine output less than 30 mL/hr for 2 consecutive hours.

■ Monitor temperature.

■ Monitor active fluid loss from wound drainage, tubes, diarrhea, bleeding, and vomiting; maintain accurate input and output record.

▲ Monitor serum electrolytes and urine osmolality, and report abnormal values.

■ Monitor for mental status changes.

Rationale

This can help guide interventions. Causes may include acute trauma and bleeding, reduced fluid intake from changes in cognition, large amount of drainage after surgery, or persistent diarrhea.

This facilitates accurate measurement and follows trends.

Most fluid enters the body through drinking, water in foods, and water formed by oxidation of foods.

Sinus tachycardia may occur with hypovolemia to maintain an effective cardiac output. Usually the pulse is weak and may be irregular if electrolyte imbalance also occurs. Hypotension is evident in hypovolemia.

Postural hypotension is a common manifestation in fluid loss. Note the following orthostatic hypotension significance:
• Greater than 10 mm Hg drop: circulating blood volume is decreased by 20%.
• Greater than 20 to 30 mm Hg drop: circulating blood volume is decreased by 40%.

The skin in older patients loses its elasticity; therefore skin turgor should be assessed over the sternum or on the inner thighs. Longitudinal furrows may be noted along the tongue.

Concentrated urine denotes fluid deficit.

Febrile states decrease body fluids through perspiration and increased respiration.

The most serious problems are related to reduced plasma volume.

Elevated hemoglobin and elevated blood urea nitrogen suggest fluid deficit. Urine specific gravity is likewise increased.

Dehydration may alter mental status, especially among older adults. Manifestations may include restlessness, anxiety, lethargy, and confusion.

■ = Independent; ▲ = Collaborative

Actions/Interventions

■ Evaluate whether the patient has any related heart problem before initiating parenteral therapy.

■ Determine the patient's fluid preferences: type, temperature (hot or cold).

■ During treatment, monitor closely for signs of circulatory overload (headache, flushed skin, tachycardia, venous distention, elevated central venous pressure [CVP], shortness of breath, increased BP, tachypnea, cough).

▲ If hospitalized, monitor hemodynamic status including CVP, pulmonary artery pressure, and pulmonary capillary wedge pressure, if available.

Rationale

Cardiac and older patients often have precarious fluid balances and are susceptible to development of pulmonary edema.

Selecting those fluids that the patient enjoys drinking can facilitate replacement therapy.

Close monitoring for responses during therapy reduces complications associated with fluid replacement.

These direct measurements serve as optimal guides for therapy.

Therapeutic Interventions

Actions/Interventions

▲ Encourage the patient to drink prescribed fluid amounts:
  • Place fluids at bedside within easy reach.
  • Provide fresh water and a straw.
  • Be creative in selecting fluid sources (e.g., flavored gelatin, frozen juice bars, sports drink).

■ Assist the patient if he or she is unable to feed self and encourage the caregiver to assist with feedings, as appropriate.

■ Plan daily activities.

■ Provide oral hygiene.

For more severe hypovolemia:

▲ Obtain and maintain a large-bore intravenous (IV) catheter.

▲ Administer parenteral fluids as ordered. Anticipate the need for an IV fluid challenge with immediate infusion of fluids for patients with abnormal vital signs.

▲ Administer blood products as prescribed.

▲ Assist the physician with insertion of a central venous line and arterial line, as indicated.

▲ Maintain IV flow rate. If signs of fluid overload occur, stop the infusion and have the patient sit up or dangle the legs.

▲ Institute measures to control excessive electrolyte loss (e.g., resting the gastrointestinal tract, administering antipyretics, as ordered). For hypovolemia due to severe diarrhea or vomiting, administer antidiarrheal or antiemetic medications as prescribed, in addition to IV fluids.

▲ Once ongoing fluid losses have stopped, begin to advance the diet in volume and composition.

Rationale

Oral fluid replacement is indicated for mild fluid deficit and is a cost-effective method for replacement treatment. Older patients have a decreased sense of thirst and may need ongoing reminders to drink.

Dehydrated patients may be weak and unable to meet prescribed intake independently.

Planning prevents patient from being too tired at mealtimes.

Attention to mouth care promotes interest in drinking.

Parenteral fluid replacement is indicated to prevent shock.

Determination of the type and amount of fluid to be replaced over a set period of time is based on patient's weight loss and clinical manifestations.

These may be required for active gastrointestinal bleeding.

This allows more effective fluid administration and monitoring.

Older patients are especially susceptible to fluid overload. Upright positioning decreases venous return and optimizes breathing.

Fluid losses from diarrhea should be concomitantly treated with antidiarrheal medications, as indicated. Antipyretics can reduce fever and associated fluid losses from diaphoresis.

Addition of fluid-rich foods can enhance continued interest in eating.

■ = Independent; ▲ = Collaborative

Deficient Fluid Volume–cont'd

Education/Continuity of Care

Actions/Interventions

■ Describe or teach causes of fluid losses or decreased fluid intake.

■ Explain or reinforce rationale and intended effect of treatment program. Inform the patient or caregiver of importance of maintaining prescribed fluid intake and special diet.

■ Teach interventions to prevent future episodes of inadequate intake.

■ If patients are to receive IV fluids at home, instruct the caregiver in managing IV equipment. Allow sufficient time for return demonstration.

▲ Refer to home health agency as appropriate.

Rationale

Information is key to managing the problem.

Follow-up care will be the patient's and/or caregiver's responsibility. Information is needed for making correct choices.

Patients need to understand the importance of drinking extra fluid during bouts of diarrhea, fever, and other conditions causing fluid deficits.

Responsibility for maintaining venous access sites and IV supplies may be overwhelming for the caregiver. In addition, older caregivers may not have the cognitive ability or manual dexterity required for this therapy.

Continuity of care is facilitated through the use of community resources.

> **• RELATED CARE PLAN**
>
> Hypovolemic shock, p. 383

NDx Excess Fluid Volume

Hypervolemia; Fluid Overload

NANDA: Increased isotonic fluid retention

Fluid volume excess, or hypervolemia, occurs from an increase in total body sodium content and an increase in total body water. This fluid excess usually results from compromised regulatory mechanisms for sodium and water as seen in congestive heart failure (CHF), kidney failure, and liver failure. It may also be caused by excessive intake of sodium from foods, intravenous (IV) solutions, medications, or diagnostic contrast dyes. Hypervolemia may be an acute or chronic condition managed in the hospital, outpatient center, or home setting. The therapeutic goal is to treat the underlying disorder and return the extracellular fluid compartment to normal. Treatment consists of fluid and sodium restriction, and the use of diuretics. For acute cases, ultrafiltration or dialysis may be required.

Common Related Factors

Excessive fluid intake
Excessive sodium intake
Renal insufficiency or failure
Steroid therapy
Low protein intake or malnutrition
Decreased cardiac output; chronic or acute heart disease

Defining Characteristics

Weight gain
Edema
Bounding pulse
Shortness of breath; orthopnea
Pulmonary congestion on x-ray
Abnormal breath sounds: crackles (rales)

■ = Independent; ▲ = Collaborative

Head injury
Liver disease
Severe stress
Hormonal disturbances

Change in respiratory pattern
Third heart sound (S_3)
Intake greater than output
Decreased hemoglobin or hematocrit
Increased blood pressure
Increased central venous pressure (CVP)
Increased pulmonary artery pressure (PAP)
Jugular vein distention
Change in mental status (lethargy or confusion)
Oliguria
Specific gravity changes
Azotemia
Change in electrolytes
Restlessness and anxiety

Common Expected Outcome

Patient maintains adequate fluid volume and electrolyte balance as evidenced by vital signs within normal limits, clear lung sounds, pulmonary congestion absent on x-ray study, and resolution of edema.

NOC Outcome
Fluid Balance

NIC Interventions
Fluid Monitoring; Fluid Management

Ongoing Assessment

Actions/Interventions

■ Obtain patient history to ascertain the probable cause of the fluid disturbance.

■ Assess, or instruct the patient to monitor, weight daily and consistently with the same scale, preferably at the same time of day and wearing the same amount of clothing.

■ Monitor for a significant weight change (2 pounds in 1 day).

■ Evaluate weight in relation to nutritional status.

■ If the patient is on fluid restriction, review the daily log or chart for recorded intake.

■ Monitor and document vital signs.

■ Monitor for distended neck veins and ascites. Monitor abdominal girth to follow any ascites accurately.

Rationale

This can help guide interventions. History may include increased fluids or sodium intake, or compromised regulatory mechanisms.

Instruction facilitates accurate measurement and helps follow trends. Sudden weight gain may indicate fluid retention. Different scales or heavier/lighter clothing may slow false weight fluctuations.

Body weight is a more sensitive indicator of fluid or sodium retention than intake and output. A 2- to 3-pound increase in weight normally indicates a need to adjust fluid or diuretic therapy.

In some heart failure patients, weight may be a poor indicator of fluid volume status. Poor nutrition and decreased appetite over time result in a decrease in weight, which may be accompanied by fluid retention even though the net weight remains unchanged.

Patients should be reminded to include items that are liquid at room temperature such as Jell-O, sherbet, and Popsicles.

Sinus tachycardia and increased blood pressure are seen in early stages. Older patients have a reduced response to catecholamines, thus their response to fluid overload may be blunted, with less increase in heart rate.

Patients with hypotonic overhydration exhibit cellular swelling.

■ = Independent; ▲ = Collaborative

Excess Fluid Volume—cont'd

Actions/Interventions	Rationale
■ Auscultate for a third heart sound and assess for bounding peripheral pulses.	These are signs of fluid overload.
■ Assess for crackles in lungs, changes in respiratory pattern, shortness of breath, and orthopnea.	These are early signs of pulmonary congestion from fluid overload.
■ Assess for presence of edema by palpating over the tibia, ankles, feet, and sacrum.	Pitting edema is manifested by a depression that remains after one's finger is pressed over an edematous area and then removed. Grade edema from trace (indicating barely perceptible) to 4 (severe edema). Measurement of an extremity with a measuring tape is another method of following edema.
▲ Monitor chest x-ray reports.	As interstitial edema accumulates, the x-ray studies show cloudy white lung fields.
■ Monitor input and output closely.	Although overall fluid intake may be adequate, shifting of fluid out of the intravascular to the extravascular spaces may result in dehydration. The risk of this occurring increases when diuretics are given. Patients may use diaries for home assessment.
■ Evaluate urine output in response to diuretic therapy.	Focus is on monitoring the response to the diuretics, rather than the actual amount voided. At home, it is unrealistic to expect patients to measure each void. Therefore recording two voids versus six voids after a diuretic medication may provide more useful information. NOTE: Fluid volume excess in the abdomen may interfere with absorption of oral diuretic medications. Medications may need to be given intravenously by a nurse in the home or outpatient setting.
■ Monitor for excessive response to diuretics: 2-pound loss in 1 day, hypotension, weakness, blood urea nitrogen elevated out of proportion to serum creatinine level.	Significantly increased response to diuretic therapy can result in fluid deficit and electrolyte imbalances.
▲ Monitor serum electrolytes, urine osmolality, and urine-specific gravity.	Specific changes will occur depending on whether hypotonic, isotonic, or hypertonic overhydration is present; specific changes guide treatment therapy.
■ Assess the need for an external or indwelling urinary catheter.	Treatment focuses on diuresis of excess fluid. Urinary catheters can make measurement of response to diuretic therapy more accurate.
■ During therapy, monitor for signs of hypovolemia.	Monitoring prevents complications associated with therapy.
▲ If hospitalized, monitor hemodynamic status including CVP, PAP, and PCWP, if available.	These direct measurements serve as optimal guides for therapy.

Therapeutic Interventions

Actions/Interventions	Rationale
▲ Institute and instruct the patient and/or caregiver regarding fluid restrictions, as appropriate.	Fluid restrictions help reduce extracellular volume. For some patients, fluids may need to be restricted to 1000 mL per day. Information is key for patients who will be co-managing fluids.

■ = Independent; ▲ = Collaborative

Excess Fluid Volume

Actions/Interventions

- Provide innovative techniques for monitoring fluid allotment at home. For example, suggest that patients measure out and pour into a large pitcher the prescribed daily fluid allowance (e.g., 1000 mL); then every time the patient drinks some fluid, he or she is to remove that amount from the pitcher.
- ▲ Restrict sodium intake as prescribed.

- ▲ Administer or instruct the patient to take diuretics as prescribed.

- Instruct the patient to avoid medications that may cause fluid retention, such as over-the-counter nonsteroidal antiinflammatory agents, certain vasodilators, and steroids.
- Elevate edematous extremities.
- Reduce constriction of vessels (e.g., use appropriate garments, avoid crossing of legs or ankles).
- ▲ Instruct in need for antiembolic stockings or bandages, as ordered.
- Provide interventions related to specific etiological factors (e.g., inotropic medications for heart failure, paracentesis for liver disease).

For acute cases:
- ▲ Consider admission to an acute care setting for hemofiltration or ultrafiltration.
- ▲ Collaborate with the pharmacist to maximally concentrate IVs and medications.
- Apply saline lock on IV line.

- ▲ Administer IV fluids through infusion pump, if possible.
- Assist with repositioning every 2 hours if the patient is not mobile.

Education/Continuity of Care
Actions/Interventions

- Teach causes of fluid volume excess and/or excess intake to the patient or caregiver.
- Provide information as needed regarding the individual's medical diagnosis (e.g., CHF, renal failure).

- Explain or reinforce rationale and intended effect of the treatment program.
- Identify signs and symptoms of fluid volume excess, and symptoms to report.
- Explain importance of maintaining proper nutrition, hydration, and diet modifications.

Rationale

This provides a visual guide for how much fluid is still allowed throughout the day, enhancing compliance with the regimen.

Restriction decreases extracellular fluid volume. Diets containing 2 to 3 g of sodium are usually prescribed.

Diuretic therapy may include several different types of agents for optimal therapy, depending on the acuteness or chronicity of the patient's problem. For patients with chronic complaints, compliance is often difficult when trying to maintain a normal lifestyle.

Thorough understanding of specific causes, such as medication side effects, is necessary for appropriate follow-up of treatment.

This increases venous return and, in turn, decreases edema.

This prevents venous pooling.

These help promote venous return and minimize fluid accumulation in the extremities.

Knowledge of causative factors provides direction for subsequent interventions.

This is a very effective method to draw off excess fluid.

This decreases use of unnecessary fluids.

This maintains patency but decreases fluid delivered to the patient in a 24-hour period.

This ensures accurate delivery of IV fluids.

This prevents fluid accumulation in dependent areas.

Rationale

Information is key to managing problems.

Patients are better able to ask questions and seek assistance when they know basic information about their condition.

Follow-up care will be the patient's responsibility. Information is needed for making correct choices.

Patients must have information to make correct choices regarding future treatments.

Knowledge enhances compliance with the treatment plan.

■ = Independent; ▲ = Collaborative

Nursing Diagnosis Care Plans

 **NDx** **Impaired Gas Exchange**

Ventilation or Perfusion Imbalance

NANDA: Excess or deficit in oxygenation and/or carbon dioxide elimination at the alveolar-capillary membrane

By the process of diffusion, the exchange of oxygen and carbon dioxide occurs in the alveolar-capillary membrane area. The relationship between ventilation (air flow) and perfusion (blood flow) affects the efficiency of the gas exchange. Normally there is a balance between ventilation and perfusion; however, certain conditions can offset this balance, resulting in impaired gas exchange. Altered blood flow from a pulmonary embolus, or decreased cardiac output or shock can cause ventilation without perfusion. Conditions that cause changes or collapse of the alveoli (e.g., atelectasis, pneumonia, pulmonary edema, and adult respiratory distress syndrome) impair ventilation. Other factors affecting gas exchange include high altitudes, hypoventilation, and altered oxygen-carrying capacity of the blood from reduced hemoglobin. Older patients have a decrease in pulmonary blood flow and diffusion as well as reduced ventilation in the dependent regions of the lung where perfusion is greatest. Chronic conditions such as chronic obstructive pulmonary disease (COPD) put these patients at greater risk for hypoxia. Other patients at risk for impaired gas exchange include those with a history of smoking or pulmonary problems, obesity, prolonged periods of immobility, and chest or upper abdominal incisions.

Common Related Factors

Altered oxygen supply
Alveolar-capillary membrane changes
Altered blood flow
Altered oxygen-carrying capacity of blood

Defining Characteristics

Confusion
Somnolence
Restlessness
Irritability
Inability to move secretions
Hypercapnia
Hypoxia

Common Expected Outcome

Patient maintains optimal gas exchange as evidenced by arterial blood gases (ABGs) within the patient's usual range, alert responsive mentation or no further reduction in mental status, and no signs of respiratory distress.

NOC Outcome
Respiratory Status: Gas Exchange

NIC Interventions
Respiratory Monitoring; Oxygen Therapy;
Airway Management

■ = Independent; ▲ = Collaborative

Ongoing Assessment

Actions/Interventions

- Assess respirations: note quality, rate, rhythm, depth, and breathing effort.

- Assess lung sounds, noting areas of decreased ventilation and the presence of adventitious sounds.

- Assess for tachycardia, restlessness, diaphoresis, headache, visual disturbances, and confusion.

- Assess for signs and symptoms of atelectasis: diminished chest excursion, limited diaphragm excursion, bronchial or tubular breath sounds, crackles, tracheal shift to affected side.

- Assess for signs and symptoms of pulmonary infarction: cough, hemoptysis, pleuritic pain, consolidation, pleural effusion, bronchial breath sounds, pleural friction rub, fever.

- Monitor vital signs.

- Assess for headache, dizziness, lethargy, reduced ability to follow instructions, disorientation, coma.

- ▲ Monitor ABGs and note changes.

- ▲ Use pulse oximetry to monitor oxygen saturation and pulse rate.

- Assess nutritional status.

- ▲ Monitor hemoglobin levels.

- Assess skin color for development of cyanosis.

Rationale

Both rapid, shallow breathing patterns and hypoventilation affect gas exchange. Shallow, "sighless" breathing patterns after surgery (as a result of the effect of anesthesia, pain, and immobility) reduce lung volume and decrease ventilation. Hypoxia is associated with signs of increased breathing effort. (See Defining Characteristics on the previous page.)

Changes in lung sounds may reveal the etiology of impaired gas exchange.

These are early nonpulmonary signs of hypoxia; lethargy and somnolence are late signs. Cognitive changes may occur with chronic hypoxia.

Collapse of alveoli increases shunting (perfusion without ventilation) resulting in hypoxemia.

Hypoxia results from increased dead space ventilation (ventilation without perfusion) and reflex broncho-constriction in areas adjacent to the infarct.

With initial hypoxia and hypercapnia, blood pressure (BP), heart rate, and respiratory rate all increase. As the hypoxia and/or hypercapnia becomes severe, BP and heart rate decrease, and arrhythmias may occur. Respiratory failure may ensue when the patient is unable to maintain the rapid respiratory rate.

These are signs of hypercapnia.

Increasing $PaCO_2$ and decreasing PaO_2 are signs of respiratory failure. As the patient's condition deteriorates, the respiratory rate will decrease and $PaCO_2$ will begin to increase. Some patients, such as those with COPD, have a significant decrease in pulmonary reserves, and additional physiological stress may result in acute respiratory failure.

Pulse oximetry is a useful tool to detect changes in oxygenation. Oxygen saturation should be maintained at 90% or greater.

Malnutrition may reduce respiratory mass and strength, affecting muscle function. Obesity may restrict downward movement of the diaphragm, increasing the risk for atelectasis, hypoventilation, and respiratory infections. Work of breathing is increased in severe obesity due to the excessive weight of the chest wall. Hypercapnia and hypoxia result.

Low levels reduce the uptake of oxygen at the alveolar-capillary membrane and oxygen delivery to the tissues.

For cyanosis to be present, 5 g of hemoglobin must be desaturated. Cool, pale skin may be secondary to a compensatory vasoconstrictive response to hypoxemia.

■ = Independent; ▲ = Collaborative

Impaired Gas Exchange–cont'd

Actions/Interventions	Rationale
■ Monitor chest x-ray reports.	Chest x-ray studies reveal the etiological factors of the impaired gas exchange. Keep in mind that radiographic studies of lung water lag behind clinical presentation by 24 hours.
■ Monitor effects of position changes on oxygenation (ABGs, SvO_2, and pulse oximetry).	Putting the most compromised lung areas in the dependent position (where perfusion is greatest) potentiates ventilation and perfusion imbalances.
■ Assess the patient's ability to cough effectively to clear secretions. Note quantity, color, and consistency of sputum.	Retained secretions impair gas exchange.
■ Evaluate hydration status.	Gas exchange may be impaired by overhydration (in conditions such as heart failure). In conditions associated with increased sputum production (e.g., pneumonia, COPD), insufficient hydration may reduce the ability to clear secretions.
■ Assess use of herbal remedies (e.g., licorice and hyssop to promote expectoration, goldenseal for pneumonia, hawthorn for heart failure).	Drug interactions with prescribed drugs and contraindications need to be evaluated (e.g., licorice should not be used by patients on digitalis preparations and hypertension; sodium loss and retention of water and potassium may occur with long-term use of high doses).

Therapeutic Interventions

Actions/Interventions	Rationale
■ Maintain oxygen administration device as ordered, attempting to maintain oxygen saturation at 90% or greater.	This provides for adequate tissue oxygenation.
• Avoid high concentration of oxygen in patients with COPD unless ordered.	Hypoxia stimulates the drive to breathe in the chronic CO_2 retainer patient. When applying oxygen, close monitoring is imperative to prevent unsafe increases in the patient's PaO_2, which could result in apnea.
• If the patient is allowed to eat, give oxygen to the patient but in a different manner (e.g., changing from mask to a nasal cannula).	Eating is an activity and more oxygen will be consumed than when the patient is at rest. Immediately after the meal, the original oxygen delivery system should be returned.
▲ For patients who should be ambulatory, provide extension tubing or portable oxygen apparatus.	These may improve exercise tolerance by maintaining adequate oxygen levels during activity.
■ Position the patient with proper body alignment for optimal respiratory excursion (if tolerated, head of bed at 45 degrees when supine; for patients with ascites or obesity, try reverse Trendelenburg at 45 degrees if tolerated).	This prevents the abdominal contents from crowding the lungs and preventing their full expansion.
■ Routinely check the patient's position so that he or she does not slide down in bed.	This would cause the abdomen to compress the diaphragm, which would cause respiratory embarrassment.
■ Position the patient to facilitate ventilation-perfusion matching when a side-lying position is used.	When the patient is positioned on the side, the good side should be down (e.g., lung with pulmonary embolus or atelectasis should be up). When lung hemorrhage or abscess is present, the affected lung should be placed downward to avoid drainage to the healthy lung.

■ = Independent; ▲ = Collaborative

Impaired Gas Exchange

Actions/Interventions

■ Pace activities and schedule rest periods to prevent fatigue. Assist with ADLs.

■ Change the patient's position every 2 hours.

■ Suction as needed.

■ Encourage deep breathing, using incentive spirometer as indicated.

■ For postoperative patients, assist with splinting the chest.

■ Encourage or assist with ambulation as indicated.

■ Provide reassurance and allay anxiety:
  • Have an agreed-upon method for the patient to call for assistance (e.g., call light, bell).
  • Stay with the patient during episodes of respiratory distress.
  • Facilitate use of relaxation measures (e.g., meditation, imagery, prayer, music).

■ Anticipate need for intubation and mechanical ventilation if the patient is unable to maintain adequate gas exchange.

▲ Administer medications as prescribed.

Rationale

Even simple activities such as bathing during bed rest can cause fatigue and increase oxygen demand, resulting in dyspnea.

This facilitates secretion movement and drainage and decreases atelectasis.

Suction removes secretions if the patient is unable to effectively clear the airway.

This reduces alveolar collapse.

Splinting optimizes deep breathing and coughing efforts.

This promotes lung expansion, facilitates secretion clearance, and stimulates deep breathing.

Anxiety increases dyspnea and respiratory rate.

Early intubation and mechanical ventilation are recommended to prevent full decompensation of the patient. Mechanical ventilation provides supportive care to maintain adequate oxygenation and ventilation to the patient.

The type depends on the etiological factors of the problem (e.g., antibiotics for pneumonia, bronchodilators for COPD, anticoagulants and thrombolytics for pulmonary embolus, analgesics for thoracic pain).

Education/Continuity of Care

Actions/Interventions

■ Explain the need to restrict and pace activities to decrease oxygen consumption during the acute episode.

■ Explain the type of oxygen therapy being used and why its maintenance is important.

■ Teach the patient appropriate breathing and coughing techniques.

▲ Assist the patient in obtaining a home nebulizer, as appropriate, and instruct in its use in collaboration with the respiratory therapist.

■ Instruct about medications: indications, dosage, frequency, side effects, and administration requirements. Include review of metered-dose inhalers if applicable.

■ Teach the patient or caregivers the signs of early respiratory compromise and their appropriate management.

Rationale

This reduces fatigue and dyspnea.

Issues related to home oxygen use, storage, or precautions need to be addressed for safe and effective treatment.

These facilitate adequate air exchange and secretion clearance.

A nebulizer provides humidification that enhances clearance of secretions and may be used to deliver mucolytics and bronchodilators. Safe and effective use is promoted by patient teaching.

Knowledge promotes safe and effective medication administration.

Early detection and treatment may reduce emergency department visits, hospitalizations, and mortality.

■ = Independent; ▲ = Collaborative

Impaired Gas Exchange–cont'd

Actions/Interventions

■ Discuss the need for lifestyle modifications such as the following:
- Smoking cessation
- Avoidance of persons with respiratory infections
- Need for influenza and pneumococcal vaccines for older adults and patients with lung and other chronic diseases
- Weight loss if applicable
- Avoidance of allergens (respiratory irritants)
- Use of support groups (Better Breather Clubs)

▲ Refer to home health services for nursing care or oxygen management as appropriate.

▲ For chronic respiratory disorders, refer for pulmonary rehabilitation.

Rationale

These strategies prevent recurrence/exacerbation of the condition. Support groups provide emotional support and information that may assist in coping with a chronic condition.

This facilitates continuation of needed services.

Rehabilitation training decreases dyspnea and fatigue, increases exercise capacity and perception of control over condition.

Anticipatory Grieving

NANDA: Intellectual and emotional responses and behaviors by which individuals, families, communities work through the process of modifying self-concept based on the perception of potential loss

Anticipatory grieving is a state in which an individual grieves before an actual loss. It may apply to individuals who have had a perinatal loss or loss of a body part or to patients who have received a terminal diagnosis for themselves or a loved one. Intense mental anguish or a sense of deep sadness may be experienced by patients and their families as they face long-term illness or disability. Grief is an aspect of the human condition that touches every individual, but how an individual or a family system responds to loss and how grief is expressed varies widely. That process is strongly influenced by factors such as age, gender, and culture, as well as personal and intrafamilial reserves and strengths. The nurse must recognize that anticipatory grief is real grief and that, in all likelihood, as the loss actually occurs, it will evolve into grief based on an accomplished event. The nurse will encounter the patient and family experiencing anticipatory grief in the hospital setting, but increasingly, with more hospice services provided in the community, the nurse will find patients struggling with these issues in their own homes where professional help may be limited or fragmented. This care plan discusses measures the nurse can use to help the patient and family members begin the process of grieving.

Common Related Factors

Perceived potential loss of any sort
Perceived potential loss of physiopsychosocial well-being
Perceived potential loss of personal possessions

Defining Characteristics

Patient and family members express feelings reflecting a sense of loss
Patient and family members begin to manifest signs of grief
Denial of potential loss

■ = Independent; ▲ = Collaborative

Sorrow
Crying
Guilt
Anger or hostility
Bargaining
Depression
Acceptance
Changes in eating habits
Alteration in activity level
Altered libido
Altered communication patterns
Fear
Hopelessness
Distortion of reality
Sadness
Loneliness
Social withdrawal

Common Expected Outcome

Patient or family verbalizes feelings, and establishes and maintains functional support systems.

NOC Outcomes
Caregiver Emotional Health;
    Family Coping; Grief Resolution

NIC Interventions
Grief Work Facilitation; Presence;
    Emotional Support

Ongoing Assessment

Actions/Interventions

■ Identify behaviors suggestive of the grieving process. (See Defining Characteristics above and on the previous page.)

■ Assess the phase of grieving being experienced by the patient and significant others. Many theories exist in defining the phases of grief, with the commonalities being the following:
• Notification and shock
• Experience of the loss emotionally and cognitively
• Reintegration

■ Assess the influence of the following factors on coping: past problem-solving abilities, socioeconomic background, educational preparation, cultural beliefs, and spiritual beliefs.

Rationale

Manifestations of grief are strongly influenced by factors such as age, gender, and culture. What the health care provider observes is a product of these feelings after they have been modified through these layers. The health care provider can enter dangerous territory when he or she attempts to categorize grief as appropriate, excessive, or inappropriate. Grief simply is. If its expression is not dangerous to anyone, then it is normal and appropriate.

Although the grief is anticipatory, the patient may move from stage to stage and back again before reintegration occurs.

These factors play a role in how grief will manifest in this particular patient or family. The nurse needs to restrain any notion that individuals of a given culture or age will always manifest predictable grief behaviors. Grief is an individual and exquisitely personal experience.

■ = Independent; ▲ = Collaborative

Anticipatory Grieving–cont'd

Nursing Diagnosis Care Plans

Actions/Interventions

- Assess whether the patient and significant others differ in their stages of grieving.

- Identify available support systems, such as the following: family, peer support, primary physician, consulting physician, nursing staff, clergy, therapist or counselor, and professional or lay support group.
- Identify potential for pathological grieving response.

- Evaluate need for referral to social services, legal consultants, or support groups.

- Observe nonverbal communication.

Rationale

People within the same family system may become impatient when others do not reconcile their feelings as quickly as they do. Older adults may take longer to reconcile their grief.

If the patient's main support is the object of perceived loss, the patient's need for help in identifying support is accentuated.

Anticipatory grief is helpful in preparing an individual to do actual grief work. Those who do not grieve in anticipation may be at higher risk for dysfunctional grief.

It may be helpful to have patients and family members associated with these supports as early as possible so that financial considerations and other special needs are taken care of before the anticipated loss occurs.

Body language may communicate a great deal of information, especially if the patient and his or her family are unable to vocalize their concerns.

Therapeutic Interventions

Actions/Interventions

- Establish rapport with the patient and significant others; try to maintain continuity in care providers. Listen and encourage the patient or significant others to verbalize feelings.

- Recognize stages of grief; apply nursing measures aimed at that specific stage.

- Provide a safe environment for expression of grief. Minimize environmental stresses or stimuli. Provide the mourners with a quiet, private environment with no interruptions.

- Remain with the patient throughout difficult times. This may require the presence of the care provider during procedures, difficult discussions, and conferences with other family members or other members of the health care team.

- Accept the patient's or family's need to deny loss as part of the normal grief process.

Rationale

This may open lines of communication and facilitate eventual resolution of grief. Providing emotional support for a child's grief before death may help validate the child's concerns of anticipatory grief and his or her desire to help at some level.

Shock and disbelief are initial responses to loss. The reality may be overwhelming; denial, panic, and anxiety may be seen.

This assumes a tolerance for the patient's expressions of grief (e.g., the ability to see a man cry, to see mourners make wide gestures with their hands and bodies, to listen to loud vocalizations and crying).

The patient or family may need a trusted person present to represent their interest or feelings if they feel unable to express them. They may require someone to "witness" with them.

The nurse needs to see these events as a time during which the individual or family member consolidates his or her strength to go on to the next plateau of grief. Grief remains a highly dynamic and individualized process. The older adult may take months to years to reach a point of reconciliation and reintegration.

Anticipatory Grieving

Actions/Interventions	Rationale
■ Anticipate increased affective behavior.	All affective behavior may seem increased or exaggerated during this time. Older adults may exhibit a preoccupation with thoughts of the impending death and confusion, especially if multiple losses are anticipated.
■ Recognize the patient's or family's need to maintain hope for the future.	They may continue to deny the inevitability of the loss as a means of maintaining some degree of hope. As the loss begins to manifest, the mourners start accepting aspects of the loss, piece by piece, until the whole is actually grasped.
■ Provide realistic information about health status without false reassurances or taking away hope.	Defensive retreat can occur weeks to months after the loss. The patient attempts to maintain what has been lost; denial, wishful thinking, unwillingness to participate in self-care, and indifference may be seen.
■ Recognize that regression may be an adaptive mechanism.	The sheer volume of emotional reconstituting and reconstruction that must be accomplished after a loss occurs makes it reasonable to assume that time to restore energy will be needed at intervals.
■ Show support and positively reinforce the patient's efforts to go on with his or her life and normal activities of daily living (ADLs), stressing the strength and the reserves that must be present for the patient and family to feel enabled to do this.	This is the same strength and reserve each of them will use to reconstitute their lives after the loss.
• Offer encouragement; point out strengths and progress to date.	Patients often lose sight of their achievements while engaged in the struggle.
■ Discuss the possible need for outside support systems (e.g., peer support, groups, clergy).	Acknowledgment occurs months to years after a loss. The patient slowly realizes the impact of loss; depression, anxiety, and bitterness may be seen. Support groups composed of persons undergoing similar events may be helpful.
■ Help the patient prioritize the importance of rehabilitation needs.	This allows the health care provider and patient to focus rehabilitative energy on those things that are of greatest importance to the patient.
■ Continue to reinforce strengths and progress.	Reintegration occurs during the first year or later, after the loss. The patient continues to reorganize resources, abilities, and self-image. Mourning is a unique and individual process that occurs over time.
■ Recognize the patient's need to review (relive) the illness experience.	This is one way in which the patient or the family integrates the event into their experience. Telling the event allows them an opportunity to hear it described and gain some perspective on the event.
■ Facilitate reorganization by reviewing progress.	When seen as a whole, the process of reorganization after a loss seems enormous, but reviewing the patient's progress toward that end is very helpful and provides perspective on the whole process.
■ Discuss possible involvement with peers or organizations (e.g., stroke support group, arthritis foundation) that work with patient's medical condition.	Support in the grieving process will come in many forms. Patients and family members often find the support of others encountering the same experiences as helpful.
■ Recognize that each patient is unique and will progress at his or her own pace.	Time frames vary widely. Cultural, religious, ethnic, and individual differences affect the manner of grieving.

Carry out the following throughout each stage:

■ Provide as much privacy as possible.	Expression of feelings is more likely to occur in a private setting.

■ = Independent; ▲ = Collaborative

Anticipatory Grieving—cont'd

Actions/Interventions

- Allow use of denial and other defense mechanisms.

- Actively listen and monitor for effective coping mechanisms.
- Avoid judgmental and defensive responses to criticisms of health care providers.
- Do not encourage the use of pharmacological interventions.
- Do not force the patient to make decisions.

- Provide the patient with ongoing information, diagnosis, prognosis, progress, and plan of care. Involve the patient and family in decision making in all issues surrounding care.
- Encourage significant others to assist with the patient's physical care.

- When the patient is hospitalized or housed away from home, facilitate flexible visiting hours and include younger children and extended family.

- Help the patient and significant others share mutual fears, concerns, plans, and hopes for each other, including the patient.

- Encourage significant others to maintain their own self-care needs for rest, sleep, nutrition, leisure activities, and time away from the patient.

If the patient's death is expected:

- Facilitate discussion with the patient and significant others on "final arrangements"; when possible, discuss burial, autopsy, organ donation, funeral, durable power of attorney, and a living will.
- Promote discussion on what to expect when death occurs.
- Encourage significant others and the patient to share their wishes about which family members should be present at the time of death. Help significant others to accept that not being present at the time of death does not indicate a lack of love or caring.

Rationale

Defense mechanisms support coping until the person is ready to acknowledge the pain of the loss.

Early detection of ineffective coping behaviors may offset future dysfunctional grieving.

Displaced anger and hostility may occur when the loss does not occur as anticipated by those grieving.

The use of drugs or alcohol may limit effective coping at this time.

Grief may limit cognitive skills needed for problem solving and decision making.

This acknowledges their right and responsibility for self-direction and autonomy.

The desire to provide care to and for each other does not disappear with illness; involving the family in care is affirming to the relationship the patient has with his or her family.

No individual should be excluded from being with the patient unless that is the wish of the patient. Restricted hospital guidelines for visiting serve staff members who organize care more than they serve patients.

Secrets are rarely helpful during these times of crisis. An open sharing and exchange of information makes it easier to address important issues and facilitates effective family process. These times of stress can be used to facilitate growth and family development. They can be important and sometimes final opportunities for resolving conflict and issues. They can also be used as times for potential personal and intrafamilial growth.

Somatic complaints often accompany mourning; changes in sleep and eating patterns, and interruption of normal routines are a usual occurrence. Care should be taken to treat these symptoms so that emotional reconstitution is not complicated by illness.

The patient and family members can benefit from open communication about these topics. The family may be able to gain confidence about carrying out the patient's wishes.

Knowledge of the dying process can help the family cope with end of life.

These discussions help family members make decisions about being present and fulfilling other responsibilities.

■ = Independent; ▲ = Collaborative

Actions/Interventions

- When the patient is hospitalized, use a visual method to identify the patient's critical status (e.g., color-coded door marker).

- Initiate a process that provides additional support and resources such as clergy.

Rationale

This will inform all personnel of the patient's status in an effort to ensure that staff do not act or respond inappropriately to a crisis situation.

The patient and family may benefit from spiritual support resources.

Education/Continuity of Care

Actions/Interventions

- Involve significant others in discussions.

▲ Refer to other resources (e.g., counseling, pastoral support, or group therapy).

Rationale

This helps reinforce understanding of all individuals involved.

The patient or significant others may need additional help to deal with individual concerns.

> • RELATED CARE PLAN
>
> Death and dying, p. 1131

 **NDx Dysfunctional Grieving**

Failure to Grieve

NANDA: Extended, unsuccessful use of intellectual and emotional responses by which individuals, families, communities attempt to work through the process of modifying self-concept based on the perception of loss

Dysfunctional grieving is a state in which an individual is unable or unwilling to acknowledge or mourn an actual or perceived loss. This may subsequently impair further growth, development, or functioning. Dysfunctional grief may be marked by a broad range of behaviors that may include pervasive denial, or a refusal to partake in self-care measures or the activities of daily living. It may be marked by excessive use of alcohol or drugs, or the inability to maintain one's business or home life. Because all of these behaviors can be seen at one time or another as an emotional response in individuals who are mourning a loss, a distinction must be made between the transient use of these normal adaptive responses and their sustained use, which impedes normal daily functioning and paralyzes one's ability to grow and develop as an individual. Because there is no temporal restriction on the time it takes to mourn a loss, the most reliable indicator may be the mourner himself or herself. When an individual reaches a point when he or she is discomforted by the inability to go on with his or her life, then the issue bears exploration. The nurse may encounter patients experiencing dysfunctional grief in the outpatient setting or in the hospital. They may have physical symptoms reflective of their inability to monitor or care for their own health, or they may have symptoms reflective of chronic emotional or physical illness. Dysfunctional grief may be the outcome of an individual's experience of being at odds with gender, cultural, or their own behavioral norms, which prohibit them from grieving successfully. The nurse may be in a position to help individuals recognize the role that dysfunctional grief has played in their current impasse, and the nurse may be able to help the patient create a framework and environment in which it is safe to begin to mourn. Current literature may categorize dysfunctional grieving as "complicated" or "disenfranchised."

■ = Independent; ▲ = Collaborative

Dysfunctional Grieving

 **Dysfunctional Grieving**–cont'd

Nursing Diagnosis Care Plans

Common Related Factors

Expressed ambivalence toward lost object
Inability to participate in socially sanctioned mourning process and rituals
Concurrent overwhelming stress
Absence of support during the mourning process

Defining Characteristics

Mild to moderate decrease in mood
Constricted affect
Avoidance of affectively charged topics
Somatic complaints
Behavioral regression
Guilt or rumination
Withdrawal from others and/or normal activities
Marked change or deviation from usual behavior pattern
"Acting out" behavior
Patient or significant others report failure to grieve

Common Expected Outcomes

Patient begins to see the role that dysfunctional grief has played in current impasse.
Patient begins process of grieving, as evidenced by ability to discuss loss.
Somatic symptoms may be reduced or become absent.

NOC Outcomes
Coping; Family Coping; Mood Equilibrium; Psychosocial Adjustment: Life Change

NIC Interventions
Grief Work Facilitation; Family Support; Presence

Ongoing Assessment

Actions/Interventions

■ Identify actual or potential losses.

■ Explore the nature of the individual's past attitudes or relationship with lost object or person.

■ Assess the patient's past coping style and mechanisms used in stressful situations.

■ Promote culturally and spiritually competent care while respecting the patient's and family's diversity in the realm of gender, socioeconomic status, and sexual orientation.

■ Assess current affective state:
  • Observe for the presence or absence of emotional distress.

Rationale

A single loss may have resulted in a cascade of events, each of which may be perceived as a loss (e.g., the loss of a limb may have resulted in the loss of a valued job, relationship, or self-concept).

The degree of the patient's avoidance in dealing with his or her grief may be an indicator as to the importance of the lost object in the patient's life. Ambivalence toward the lost object or person may contribute to dysfunctional grief. Do not assume that patients need only to free themselves from their expressive restraints to cure their dysfunctional grief. The factors involved in obstructed grief may be quite complicated.

Avoidance may be the patient's normative style in confronting emotional conflict or pain.

This allows the patient and/or family to accept the grieving process as a life transition, albeit painful.

Factors such as gender or cultural norms may prohibit the free expression of or filter the patient's expressions of grief.

■ = Independent; ▲ = Collaborative

Actions/Interventions

- Observe quality or quantity of communication; observe verbal and nonverbal cues.

- Assess the degree of relatedness to others.

- Assess satisfaction with the ability to cope and implement appropriate safety measures.

- Determine degree of insight in the present situation.

- Identify disturbing topics of conversation or experiences. Consider, however, that individuals may not feel comfortable discussing their issues with you or within the context that you have chosen. Provide patients with options if they seem uninterested in exploring feelings with others.

- Estimate the degree of stress currently experienced.

Rationale

These cues may be an important indicator to the patient's true affective status, especially if the patient's own normative preconceptions about himself or herself, culture, or gender prohibit the free expression of feelings.

A patient with a limited social support network may have difficulty adjusting to a significant loss.

The loss may trigger feelings of powerlessness and hopelessness that are unresolved and may be accompanied by guilt and suicide ideation.

Many patients are able to express sadness but are frozen at this point in their grief. Many patients are able to name or describe what is immobilizing them and inhibiting them from grieving effectively.

Actively listening to the patient and/or family without judgment or interruption is important to the grieving process. Repetition of their stories facilitates healing after the death of a loved one. Team member counseling may prove helpful here.

Patients may feel unable to take on the resolution of complicated emotional issues in times of extreme stress; at the very least, these factors will need to be factored into an understanding of how to progress in the therapeutic approach to be used with the patient.

Therapeutic Interventions

Actions/Interventions

- Communicate comfort in the patient's discussion of loss and grief.

- Offer feedback regarding the patient's expressed feelings.

- Encourage or facilitate expressions of acceptance or offers of emotional support by significant others to the patient.

- Recognize variation and need for individual adjustment to loss and change.

- Provide quiet and privacy when needed or requested.

- Recognize the need for the use of defense mechanisms. Do not personalize negative expression of affect or unduly challenge some use of denial. Patients will have to proceed at their own pace.

Rationale

Patients may be quite sensitive to emotional nuances communicated by the nurse. The nurse should not take on these issues with the patient if he or she is uncomfortable with certain expressions of grief or if grief carries unresolved issues for the nurse. The nurse must assume responsibility for communicating his or her own thoughts and feelings effectively. Dialogue involves mutual honesty, clarification of erroneous messages, and sensitivity to one's self and others.

Dialogue necessitates this kind of reciprocity and promotes understanding of behavior during grief work.

This type of communication is extremely helpful and healing, and it provides the patient with varied sources of support and help.

There is no one norm to conform to; the experience of the patient is perhaps the most important indicator of progress or improvement.

This allows for contemplation and reflection.

The use of defense mechanisms will support coping until the person is ready to integrate the loss.

■ = Independent; ▲ = Collaborative

Dysfunctional Grieving–cont'd

Actions/Interventions

- Reassure the patient and significant others that some negative thoughts and feelings are normal.

- Support the use of adaptive coping mechanisms.

- Discuss the actual loss with patient:
  - Support a realistic assessment of the event or situation.

  - Explore with the patient individual strengths and available resources.

  - Explore reasons for avoidance of feeling or acknowledging loss.

  - Review common changes in behavior associated with normal grieving (e.g., change in appetite and sleep patterns) with the patient and significant others. Explain that although intensity and frequency of behaviors decrease with time, the mourning period may continue for a long time.

  - Discuss normal coping behavior in grief recovery (e.g., the need for contact with others or the need to alternate periods of distraction with quiet time to reflect).

- Encourage sharing of common problems with others.

Rationale

Concern about how others may view one's full range of feelings may lead to further impediments in the grieving process and increase a sense of isolation and loss.

The adaptive coping mechanisms may provide respite for overwhelming pain or grief.

False reassurances are never helpful and only relieve the discomfort of the care provider.

Ultimately, the decision to take on the job of resolving the emotional impasse that the patient has reached is the decision of the patient. This job is certainly difficult and inevitably painful. It may be helpful to recognize that the patient has the skills and reserves of strength necessary to do the emotional work ahead.

These may continue to obstruct progress despite the patient's willingness to proceed. They should be factored into any care plan.

Understanding the range of normal behaviors associated with grieving can enhance family coping with the loss.

This places these needs within the realm of what is needed by all and may sanction the patient's need for the same considerations.

Grief is a universal experience; people who have undergone grief over a loss can be enormously helpful to others undergoing the same feelings.

Education/Continuity of Care

Actions/Interventions

- Explain that emotional response to loss is appropriate and commonly experienced:
  - Describe the "normal" stages of grief and mourning.
  - Offer hope that emotional pain will decrease with time.

- ▲ Initiate referrals to other professional and community resources as appropriate.

Rationale

Many view the overt expression of feelings as a "weakness" or fear that they may lose control if they begin to acknowledge the depth of their emotions.

It is helpful for patients to have more than one resource for helping them in this process.

> • RELATED CARE PLAN
>
> Death and dying, p. 1131

■ = Independent; ▲ = Collaborative

 **Health-Seeking Behaviors**

Health Promotion; Lifestyle Management; Health Education; Patient Education; Smoking Cessation

NANDA: Active seeking (by a person in stable health) of ways to alter personal health habits and/or the environment in order to move toward a higher level of health

Health promotion activities include a wide range of topics, such as smoking cessation; stress management; weight loss; proper diet for prevention of coronary artery disease, cancer, osteoporosis, and others; exercise promotion; prenatal instruction; safe sex practices to prevent sexual transmitted diseases; protective helmets to prevent head trauma; and other practices to reduce risks for diabetes, stroke, and others.

Patients of all ages may be involved in improving health habits. Social cognitive theory identifies factors (e.g., behavior, cognition and other personal factors, and the environment) that influence how and to what extent people are able to change old behaviors and adopt new ones. Psychosocial factors such as stress and anxiety regarding perceived risk for disease, along with social support for engaging in the health-promoting behaviors, must be considered. The action plan must be tailored to fit with the patient's values and belief systems. Opportunities for self-monitoring and receiving feedback enhance the behavior change process.

The setting in which health promotion activities occur may range from the privacy of one's home, group activities such as weight maintenance groups or health clubs, or even the work setting (especially targeted programs for hypertension management and weight reduction). This care plan gives a general overview of health-seeking behaviors and then focuses on one specific type: smoking cessation.

Common Related Factors

New condition, altered health status
Lack of awareness about environmental hazards affecting personal health
Absence of interpersonal support
Limited availability of health care resources
Unfamiliarity with community wellness resources
Lack of knowledge about health promotion behaviors

Defining Characteristics

Perceives optimum health as a primary life purpose
Expresses desire to seek higher level of wellness
Expresses concern about current health status
Demonstrated or observed lack of knowledge of health promotion behaviors
Actively seeks resources to expand wellness knowledge
Expresses sense of self-confidence and personal efficacy toward health promotion
Verbalizes perceived control of health
Anticipates internal and external threats to health status and desires to take preventive action

Common Expected Outcomes

Patient identifies necessary environmental changes to promote a healthier lifestyle.
Patient engages in desired behaviors to promote a healthier lifestyle.

NOC Outcomes
Health-Promoting Behavior;
Health-Seeking Behavior;
Knowledge: Health Resources

NIC Interventions
Self-Modification Assistance;
Health Education; Patient Contracting;
Smoking Cessation

■ = Independent; ▲ = Collaborative

Health-Seeking Behaviors—cont'd

General

Ongoing Assessment

Actions/Interventions	Rationale
■ Assess the patient's individual perceptions of health problems.	According to models such as the Health Belief Model, the patient's perceived susceptibility to and perceived seriousness and threat of disease affect health-seeking behaviors.
■ Question the patient regarding previous experiences and health teaching.	Adults bring many life experiences to learning sessions. Often patients have previously tried unsuccessfully to engage in a specific health practice. Reasons for difficulties need to be explored.
■ Determine at what stage of change the patient is currently.	The Transtheoretical Model emphasizes that interventions for change should be matched with the stage of change at which patients are situated. For example, if the patient is only "contemplating" starting an exercise program, efforts may be directed toward emphasizing the positive aspects of exercise; whereas if the patient is in the "preparation" or "action" stages, more specific directions regarding exercise (e.g., places to exercise, equipment, target heart rate, warm-up activities) can be addressed.
■ Identify priority of learning need within the overall care plan.	Patients learn material most important to them.
■ Identify any misconceptions regarding material to be taught.	Patients must have accurate information to make appropriate behavior changes.
■ Assess the patient's confidence in his or her ability to perform desired behavior.	According to the self-efficacy theory, positive conviction that one can successfully execute a behavior is correlated with performance and successful outcome.
■ Identify the patient's specific strengths and competencies.	Every patient brings unique strengths to the health planning task (e.g., motivation, knowledge, social support).
■ Identify health goals and areas for improvement.	Systematically reviewing areas for potential change can assist patients in making informed choices.
■ Identify possible barriers to change (e.g., lack of motivation, interpersonal support, skills, knowledge, or resources).	If the patient is aware of possible barriers and has formulated plans for dealing with them, then successful behavioral change is more likely to occur. For example, if trying to engage in more exercise, walking in shopping malls can be substituted for outdoor activity during periods of inclement weather.
■ Determine cultural influences on health teaching.	Certain ethnic and religious groups hold unique beliefs and health practices that must be considered when designing educational plans.

Therapeutic Interventions

Actions/Interventions	Rationale
■ Clearly define the specific behavior to be changed.	The more precisely defined the behavior is, the greater the chance of success.

■ = Independent; ▲ = Collaborative

Actions/Interventions	Rationale
■ Guide the patient in setting realistic goals.	Goals that are too global, such as "lose 30 pounds," are difficult to achieve and can foster feelings of failure. Shorter range goals such as "losing 5 pounds in a month" may be more achievable and therefore reinforcing.
■ Promote positive expectations for success.	Patients with stronger self-efficacy to perform a behavior are much more likely to engage in it.
■ Assist the patient in developing a self-contract.	Contracts help clarify the goal and enhance the patient's control over the behavior, creating a sense of independence, competence, and autonomy.
■ Assist in developing a time frame for implementation.	Changes need to be made over a period of time to allow new behaviors to be learned well, integrated into one's lifestyle, and stabilized.
■ Allow periodic evaluation, feedback, and revision of the health plan as necessary.	This provides a systematic approach for movement of the patient toward higher levels of health and promotes adherence to the plan. Appropriately timed feedback is critical to successful behavior change.
■ Reward positive efforts and achievement.	Positive rewards, especially those inherent in the activity, such as the enjoyment of outside walking with a partner, should be encouraged because they continue to reinforce the behavior. Other rewards may consist of verbal praise, monetary rewards, special privileges (e.g., earlier office appointment, free parking), or telephone calls from the health care provider.
■ Inform the patient of appropriate resources in the community; use referrals and agencies that enhance the learning of specific behaviors.	Coordinated use of community resources can enhance effectiveness of efforts.
■ Implement the use of modeling to assist patients.	Observing the behavior of others who have successfully achieved similar goals helps exemplify the exact behaviors that should be developed to reach the goal. The use of videotapes with people performing the desired behavior has been quite effective.
■ Provide a comprehensive approach to health promotion by giving attention to environmental, social, and cultural constraints.	The various health promotion models emphasize that focusing only on behavior change is doomed to failure without simultaneous efforts to alter the environment and collective behavior.
■ Use a variety of teaching methods.	Learning is enhanced when various approaches reinforce the material that is being taught.
■ Prepare for lapses and relapses.	Relapse prevention needs to be addressed early in the treatment plan. The maintenance phase of change is the longest and most challenging to sustain.
■ Encourage participation of family or significant others in proposed changes.	One's significant others can play an important role in providing support over the long term that may enhance overall adaptation to change.

Specific Patient Behaviors for Smoking Cessation

Actions/Interventions	Rationale
■ Determine the patient's history of tobacco use and any prior attempts to quit.	Smoking is considered a chronic disease. Smoking cessation has a high rate of relapse. However, smokers do learn valuable information during each quit attempt.

■ = Independent; ▲ = Collaborative

Health-Seeking Behaviors—cont'd

Actions/Interventions

■ Determine that the patient is interested in quitting smoking.

■ Determine the type of counseling program most appropriate for the patient.

■ Choose an approach to quitting most suitable for the specific patient, as in the following: (1) *cold turkey*—abrupt cessation from one's addictive level of smoking; (2) *tapering*—one smokes fewer cigarettes each day until down to none; (3) *postponing*—one postpones the time to start smoking by a predetermined number of hours each day, eventually leading to no cigarettes; (4) *joining a smoking cessation program*; (5) *pharmacological aids*—nicotine patches, gum; (6) *acupuncture, hypnosis.*

■ Assist the patient to formally set a date to quit smoking, either verbally or by contract.

■ Initiate practical counseling as appropriate.

■ Assist the patient in selecting appropriate support persons.

Rationale

Different approaches are used depending on motivation to quit. The five *R*s (*r*elevance for quitting; *r*isks associated with tobacco use; *r*ewards or benefits of not smoking; *r*oadblocks or barriers to quitting; and *r*epetition of this motivational intervention) will assist in moving patients to begin a cessation program.

Research supports group or individual sessions between 4 and 7 sessions in number. The more intense the treatment, the greater the likelihood of success.

Different approaches appeal to different individuals. Exploration of the most useful treatment options enables the patient to select the approach most acceptable to his or her beliefs, values, and lifestyle. Pharmacological therapies should be encouraged based on their effectiveness (except where contraindicated).

This reinforces the intent and behavior to be changed. A date should be selected within the first 2 weeks to keep the momentum moving forward.

Counseling focused on problem solving, skill training, and use of social support has greatest outcomes.

It is unlikely that one person can meet all types of support that may be required (listening to challenges/frustrations, discussing shared experiences, helping solve problems). The patient needs to appreciate who can serve as the best supporters at various times.

Education/Continuity of Care

Actions/Interventions

■ Provide instruction and counseling on strategies known to be most effective.
  • Avoid temptation or situations associated with the pleasurable aspects of smoking. Suggest the following: (1) instead of smoking after meals, brush teeth or go for walk; (2) instead of smoking while driving, take public transportation; (3) avoid having a cocktail before dinner if it is associated with smoking; (4) limit social activities or situations to those where smoking is prohibited; (5) if in a social situation where others smoke, try to associate with the nonsmokers; (6) develop a clean, fresh, nonsmoking environment at work.

  • Find new activities to make smoking difficult, impossible, or unnecessary (e.g., swimming, jogging, tennis, handball, racquetball, aerobics, biking).

Rationale

Evidence-based guidelines provide rationale for plan.

A change in normal routine is needed to change such a pervasive habit.

These help break the trigger to smoking.

■ = Independent; ▲ = Collaborative

Ineffective Health Maintenance

Actions/Interventions	Rationale
• Maintain a clean taste in the mouth by brushing teeth often and using mouthwash.	This removes nicotine taste and smell and enhances taste buds.
• Do things that require the use of the hands (e.g., crossword puzzles, needlework, gardening, writing letters).	This provides a break in the usual routine.
• Keep oral substitutes handy (e.g., carrots, pickles, sunflower seeds, sugarless gum, celery, apples).	Oral gratification helps reduce the urge to smoke. Low-calorie foods should be chosen because ex-smokers burn fewer calories, and 25% may experience a weight gain when they stop smoking.
• Learn relaxation techniques to reduce the urge to smoke (e.g., make self limp; visualize a soothing, pleasing situation).	Breathing exercises help release tension and overcome the urge to smoke.
• Seek social support.	Commitment to remain a nonsmoker can be made easier by talking with friends and family.
• Mark progress and reward self for not smoking. Each week, month, or more, plan a special celebration. Periodically write down reasons to be glad for quitting and post them.	Positive rewards have been shown to enhance adherence to selected behavior.
■ Instruct the patient that relapses can occur. If they do, recognize the problem, review reasons for quitting, anticipate triggers, and learn how to avoid them.	Identifying high-risk situations likely to cause relapse aids in problem solving.
■ Instruct the patient regarding various coping skills to alleviate further problems; encourage the patient to re-sign a contract to remain an ex-smoker.	It is difficult to remain an ex-smoker. A slip means that a small setback has occurred; it does not mean that the patient will start smoking again. Despite strong resolve to quit, patients often find themselves in situations that may encourage relapse. Being prepared to recognize these and offering other options or sources of assistance enhances the patient's ability to cope and minimizes relapses.
▲ Instruct the patient regarding community resources and self-help groups as appropriate.	Self-help and support groups provide unique perspectives on "being there" and may be effective in providing alternative treatment modalities.

Ineffective Health Maintenance

NANDA: Inability to identify, manage, and/or seek help to maintain health

Altered health maintenance reflects a change in an individual's ability to perform the functions necessary to maintain health or wellness. That individual may already manifest symptoms of existing or impending physical ailment or display behaviors that are strongly or certainly linked to disease. The nurse's role is to identify factors that contribute to an individual's inability to maintain healthy behavior and implement measures that will result in improved health maintenance activities. The nurse may encounter patients who are experiencing an alteration in their ability to maintain health either in the hospital or in the community, and the increased presence of the nurse in the community and home health settings improves the ability to assess patients in their own environment. Patients most likely to experience more than transient alterations in their ability to maintain their health are those whose age or infirmity (either physical or emotional) absorb much of their resources or those for whom the economic challenges of daily life negate an interest in personal health. The task before the nurse is to identify measures that will be successful in empowering patients to maintain their own health within the limits of their ability.

■ = Independent; ▲ = Collaborative

Ineffective Health Maintenance—cont'd

Common Related Factors

Presence of mental retardation, illness, organic brain syndrome

Presence of physical disabilities or challenges

Presence of adverse personal habits:

- Smoking
- Poor diet selection
- Morbid obesity
- Alcohol abuse
- Drug abuse
- Poor hygiene
- Lack of exercise

Evidence of impaired perception

Low income

Lack of access for care

Lack of knowledge

Poor housing conditions

Risk-taking behaviors

Inability to communicate needs adequately (e.g., deafness, speech impediment)

Dramatic change in health status

Lack of support systems

Denial of need to change current habits

Defining Characteristics

Behavioral characteristics:

- Demonstrated lack of knowledge
- Failure to keep appointments
- Expressed interest in improving behaviors
- Failure to recognize or respond to important symptoms reflective of changing health state
- Inability to follow instructions or programs for health maintenance

Physical characteristics:

- Body or mouth odor
- Unusual skin color, pallor
- Poor hygiene
- Soiled clothing
- Frequent infections (e.g., upper respiratory infection, urinary tract infection)
- Frequent toothaches
- Obesity or anorexia
- Anemia
- Chronic fatigue
- Apathetic attitude
- Substance abuse

Common Expected Outcomes

Patient describes positive health maintenance behaviors such as keeping scheduled appointments, participating in smoking and substance abuse programs, making diet and exercise changes, improving home environment, and following treatment regimen.

Patient identifies available resources.

Patient uses available resources.

NOC Outcomes

Health-Promoting Behavior; Self-Direction of Care; Health-Seeking Behavior; Social Support

NIC Interventions

Health System Guidance; Support System Enhancement; Discharge Planning; Health Screening; Risk Identification

Ongoing Assessment

Actions/Interventions

■ Assess for physical defining characteristics.

■ Assess the patient's knowledge of health maintenance behaviors.

■ Assess health history over past 5 years.

Rationale

Changing ability or interest in performing the normal activities of daily living may be an indicator that commitment to health and well-being is waning.

Patients may know that certain unhealthy behaviors can result in poor health outcomes but continue the behavior despite this knowledge. The health care provider needs to ensure that the patient has all of the information needed to make good lifestyle choices.

This may give some perspective on whether poor health habits are recent or chronic in nature.

■ = Independent; ▲ = Collaborative

Nursing Diagnosis Care Plans

Actions/Interventions

- Assess to what degree environmental, social, intrafamilial disruptions, or changes have correlated with poor health behaviors.
- Determine the patient's specific questions related to health maintenance.
- Determine patient's motives for failing to report symptoms reflecting changes in health status.

- Discuss noncompliance with instructions or programs with the patient to determine rationale for failure.
- Assess the patient's educational preparation and ability to integrate and relate to information.

- Assess history of other adverse personal habits, including the following: smoking, obesity, lack of exercise, and alcohol or substance abuse.
- Determine whether the patient's manual dexterity or lack of mobility is a factor in the patient's altered capacity for health maintenance.
- Determine to what degree the patient's cultural beliefs and personality contribute to altered health habits.
- Determine whether the required health maintenance facilities/equipment (e.g., access ramps, motor vehicle modifications, shower bar or chair) are available to the patient.
- Assess whether economic problems present a barrier to maintaining health behaviors.

- Assess hearing, and orientation to time, place, and person to determine the patient's perceptual abilities.
- Make a home visit to determine safety, accessibility, and quality of living conditions.
- Assess the patient's experience of stress and disruptors as they relate to health habits.

Rationale

These changes may be precipitating factors or may be early fallout from a generalized condition reflecting decline.

Patients may have health education needs; meeting these needs may be helpful in mobilizing the patient.

The patient may not want to "bother" the provider, may minimize the importance of the symptoms, or may fear what may be discovered. Language barriers and poor access to care are other common reasons.

The patient may be experiencing obstacles in compliance that can be resolved.

Patients may not have understood information because of a sensory impairment or the inability to read or understand information. Culture, literacy, language barriers, or age may impair a patient's ability to comply with the established treatment plan.

Long-standing habits may be difficult to break; once established, patients may feel that nothing positive can come from a change in behavior.

Patients may need assistive devices for ambulation or to complete tasks of daily living.

Health teaching may need to be modified to be consistent with cultural or religious beliefs.

With adequate assistive devices, the patient may be able to effect enormous changes in maintaining his or her personal health.

Patients may be too proud to ask for assistance or be unaware that Social Security, Medicare, or insurance benefits could be helpful to them. The growing number of uninsured and underinsured Americans is compounding this problem.

Perceptual handicaps may impair an individual's ability to maintain healthy behaviors.

This will help identify and solve problems that complicate health maintenance.

If stressors can be relieved, patients may again be able to resume their self-care activities.

Therapeutic Interventions

Actions/Interventions

- Assist the patient to problem solve specific related factors as able.

- Define your role as patient advocate.

Rationale

Health maintenance is complicated because of the complexities of each individual's circumstance. A "one size fits all" approach will not work.

The nurse is in an ideal position to guide the patient through the health care system.

■ = Independent; ▲ = Collaborative

Ineffective Health Maintenance—cont'd

Actions/Interventions

■ Provide the patient with a means of contacting health care providers.

■ Involve family and friends in health planning conferences.

■ Compliment the patient on positive accomplishments.

Rationale

This will add available resources for questions or problem resolution. An ongoing relationship can establish trust and facilitate change.

Family members need to understand that care is planned to focus on what is most important to the patient. This enables the patient to maintain a sense of autonomy.

Positive reinforcement enhances behavior change.

Education/Continuity of Care

Actions/Interventions

■ Provide the patient with rationale for importance of behaviors such as the following:
- Proper nutrition

- Regular exercise

- Proper hygiene

- Smoking cessation

- Cessation of alcohol and drug abuse

- Stress management

- Regular physical and dental checkups and screenings

- Regular inoculations and immunizations

- Early and regular prenatal care
- Reporting of unusual symptoms to a health professional

▲ Ensure that other agencies (e.g., Department of Children and Family Services, Social Services, Visiting Nurse Association, Meals On Wheels) are following through with plans.

Rationale

The new MyPyramid approved by the Food and Drug Administration provides guidance on recommended food groups across a variety of populations. Cardiovascular disease, cancer, type 2 diabetes, and osteoporosis are but a few of the many medical diseases related to nutrition.

This promotes weight loss and increases agility and stamina. The Surgeon General recommends at least 30 minutes of moderate exercise on most days of the week.

This decreases risk of infection and promotes maintenance and integrity of skin and teeth.

Smoking has been directly linked to cancer and heart disease.

In addition to physical addictions and the social consequences, the physical consequences of substance abuse mitigate against it.

Stress management can be considered a cornerstone to a healthy lifestyle.

Checkups identify and treat problems early. Screening procedures are based on age and prior history (e.g., Papanicolaou, cholesterol, mammogram, blood pressure, prostate, colonoscopy).

These include immunizations for tetanus, diphtheria, hepatitis B as appropriate, pneumonia, and influenza, among others.

This initiates early treatment.

Coordinated efforts are more meaningful and effective.

■ = Independent; ▲ = Collaborative

Impaired Home Maintenance

NANDA: Inability to independently maintain a safe growth-promoting immediate environment

Individuals within a home establish a normative pattern of operation. A vast number of factors can negatively impact on that operational baseline. When this happens, an individual or an entire family may experience a disruption that is significant enough to impair the management of the home environment. Health or safety may be threatened and there may be a threat to relationships or to the physical well-being of the people living in the home. An inability to perform the activities necessary to maintain a home may be the result of the development of chronic mental or physical disabilities, or acute conditions or circumstances that severely affect the vulnerable members of the household. As a result of early hospital discharges, nurses are coordinating complicated recovery regimens in the homes of patients. The patient's home must be safe and suited to the recovery needs of the individual. Patients must have the resources needed to provide for themselves and their families during recovery or following a debilitating illness. Because there is considerable room for cultural and intrafamilial variations in the maintenance of a home, the nurse should be guided by principles of safety when evaluating a home environment.

Common Related Factors

Poor planning and organization
Low income
Inadequate or absent support systems
Lack of knowledge
Illness or injury of the patient or a family member
Death of a significant other
Prolonged recuperation following illness
Substance abuse
Cognitive, perceptual, or emotional disturbance

Defining Characteristics

Patient or family expresses difficulty or lack of knowledge in maintaining home environment
Lack of preventive care such as immunizations
Poor personal habits:
- Soiled clothing
- Frequent illness
- Weight loss
- Body odor
- Substance abuse
- Depressed affect

Poor fiscal management
Risk-taking behaviors
Vulnerable individuals (e.g., infants, children, older adults, infirm) in the home are neglected or often ill
Home visits reveal unsafe home environment or lack of basic hygiene measures (e.g., presence of vermin in the home, accumulation of waste, home in poor repair, improper temperature regulation)

Common Expected Outcomes

Patient maintains a safe home environment.
Patient identifies available resources.
Patient uses available resources.

NOC Outcomes

Family Functioning; Safety Behavior: Home Physical Environment; Social Support

NIC Interventions

Home Maintenance Assistance; Sustenance Support; Discharge Planning

■ = Independent; ▲ = Collaborative

Impaired Home Maintenance–cont'd

Ongoing Assessment

Actions/Interventions

- Assess whether lack of money is a cause for not maintaining the home environment.

- Assess history of substance abuse and determine its impact on the patient's ability to maintain the home.
- Perform a home assessment. Evaluate for accessibility and physical barriers. Assess bathing facilities, temperature regulation, whether windows close and doors lock, presence of screens, trash disposal.
- Evaluate each member of the family to determine whether basic physical and emotional needs are being met.
- Assess the patient's knowledge of the rationale for personal and environmental hygiene and safety.

- Assess the patient's physical ability to perform home maintenance.

- Assess whether the patient has all assistive devices necessary to perform home maintenance.
- Assess the impact of the death of a relative who may have been a significant provider of care.

- Assess the patient's emotional and intellectual preparedness to maintain a home.

- ▲ Enlist assistance from a social worker or community resources that may be helpful to the family or patient.

Rationale

Grants or special funds can sometimes be used to modify the home to suit the need of the physically challenged patient. Other supports and services are available to reduce financial stress.

The financial drain of a substance abuse problem can siphon money from every available resource.

These are basic necessities for a safe environment. Beyond this, evaluate the home to determine if the special needs of the patient can be accommodated.

A distinction must be made between optimal living conditions and a safe home environment.

Although this is an important starting point, knowledge deficit is unlikely to be responsible for poor home maintenance in all cases. The patient's personal priorities, culture, and age may play a role in determining individual preferences.

Accurate assessment guides intervention. For example, patients may not do laundry because they are unable to carry large boxes of detergent from the store, or they may be unable to carry rubbish to the collection site because sidewalks are icy.

If unavailable, other options may need to be explored (e.g., a homemaker, family assistance).

Aspects of home maintenance may have been performed by the deceased, and a new plan to meet these needs may need to be developed.

Some patients who are mentally challenged are capable of living alone if provided with the appropriate supports, whereas the patient with a disease such as Alzheimer's may be unable to care for himself or herself.

Patients may be unaware of the services to which they are entitled.

Therapeutic Interventions

Actions/Interventions

- Begin discharge planning immediately after hospital admission.

- Integrate the family and patient into the discharge planning process.

Rationale

Shortened hospital stays and early discharges require an organized approach to meet individual needs of the family. Patients and their families may be managing more complicated recoveries in the home than were previously encountered.

This ensures patient-centered objectives and promotes compliance.

■ = Independent; ▲ = Collaborative

Actions/Interventions

- Plan a home visit to test the efficacy of discharge plans.

▲ Arrange for ongoing home therapy. Arrange for physical therapy, dietitian, and occupational therapy consultations in the home, as needed.

- Assist the family in arranging for redistribution of the workload. Build in relief for caregivers.

Rationale

The nurse may visit the home to determine its readiness to accommodate the patient, or the patient may go home briefly to help identify potential problems.

Complicated recovery necessitates that services be brought to the patient. Continuity of care is facilitated through the use of community resources.

This prevents fatigue during performance of physically or emotionally exhausting tasks.

Education/Continuity of Care

Actions/Interventions

- Begin care instruction or demonstrations early in the hospital stay.
- Teach care measures to as many family members as possible.
- Ensure that the family, patient, or caregiver has been instructed in the use of all assistive devices.

▲ Arrange for alternate placement when the family is unable to provide care.

- Provide telephone support or support in the form of home visits.

▲ Refer to social services for financial and homemaking concerns. Inform of community resources as appropriate (e.g., drug abuse clinic).

Rationale

Correct techniques need to be reinforced.

This provides multiple competent providers and intrafamilial support.

During the acute period, the family and significant others may require the most teaching in preparation for discharge.

The need for placement may be temporary or extended; the patient's status will determine needs.

This monitors the status of the patient and the well-being of others in the home.

Specialized services may be required to meet specific needs.

NDx Hopelessness

NANDA: Subjective state in which an individual sees limited or no alternatives or personal choices available and is unable to mobilize energy on own behalf

Hopelessness may be expressed anywhere along the illness trajectory. It may occur secondary to an acute event, such as spinal cord injury that leaves the patient permanently paralyzed, or it may be the result of a lifetime of multiple stresses for which the patient is no longer able to mobilize the energy needed to act in his or her own behalf. It is evident in patients living in social isolation, who are lonely and have no social support system or resources. Patients living in poverty, the homeless, and those with limited access to health care all may feel hopeless about changing their health care status and being able to cope with life. Loss of belief in God's care or loss of trust in prior spiritual beliefs may foster a sense of hopelessness.

Common Related Factors

Chronic and/or terminal illness
Prolonged restricted activity
Prolonged isolation
Loss of social support

Defining Characteristics

Passivity
Decreased affect
Decreased verbalization
Lack of initiative

■ = Independent; ▲ = Collaborative

Hopelessness–cont'd

Common Related Factors–cont'd

Lost belief in transcendent values or God
Prolonged discomfort
Impaired functional abilities
Prolonged treatments or diagnostic studies with no positive results
Prolonged dependence on equipment
Long-term stress

Defining Characteristics–cont'd

Decreased response to stimuli
Apathy
Verbalizes that life has no meaning
Feels "empty"
Poor problem solving, decision making
Inability to set goals
Sleep, appetite disturbances
Socially withdrawn
Suicidal thoughts

Common Expected Outcomes

Patient begins to recognize choices and alternatives.
Patient begins to mobilize energy in own behalf (e.g., making decisions).

NOC Outcomes
Hope; Coping; Decision Making

NIC Interventions
Hope Installation; Coping Enhancement

Ongoing Assessment

Actions/Interventions	Rationale
■ Assess the role that illness plays in the patient's hopelessness.	Level of physical functioning, endurance for activities, duration and course of illness, prognosis, and treatments involved can contribute to hopelessness.
■ Assess physical appearance (e.g., grooming, posture, hygiene).	Hopeless patients may not have the energy or interest to engage in self-care activities.
■ Assess appetite, exercise, and sleep patterns.	Deviations from normal patterns are evident during periods of hopelessness.
■ Evaluate the patient's ability to set goals or make decisions and plans.	A patient who feels hopeless will feel that goal-setting is futile and that goals cannot be met.
■ Note whether the patient perceives unachieved outcomes as failures.	Repeated perceptions of failure will reinforce the patient's feelings of hopelessness.
■ Note whether the patient emphasizes failures instead of accomplishments.	This determines the patient's level of control or ability to change the situation.
■ Assess for feelings of hopelessness, lack of self-worth, giving up, suicidal ideas.	Hopelessness is associated with dysfunctional personality characteristics as well as suicidal ideation and behaviors.
■ Assess for potential source of hope (e.g., self, significant others, religion).	Entrusted others (e.g., clergy, family, health team) can support the patient's basic belief system that enhances hope.
■ Assess the person's expectations for the future. Clarify when the situation is only temporary.	Uncertainty about events, duration and course of illness, prognosis, and dependence on others for help and treatments involved can contribute to a feeling of hopelessness.
■ Assess the person's social support network.	Patients in social isolation find it difficult to change their condition. Evaluation of supportive persons from the past may provide the assistance the patient requires at this time. Community groups, church groups, and self-help groups may also be available for assistance.
■ Assess meaning of the illness and treatments to the individual and family.	Certain misconceptions (e.g., patients with cancer always die) may be corrected and hope restored.

■ = Independent; ▲ = Collaborative

Nursing Diagnosis Care Plans

Actions/Interventions

- Assess previous coping strategies used and their effectiveness. Identify patterns of coping related to illness that enhance problem-solving skills and enable the patient to achieve goals.
- Assess patient's belief in self and own abilities. Identify patient's values and satisfaction with his or her role or purpose in life.
- Assess ability for solving problems.

Rationale

Successful coping is influenced by past experiences. Patients with a history of maladaptive coping may require additional resources. Past strategies may not be sufficient in the present situation.

Patients may feel that the threat is greater than their resources to handle it, and feel a loss of control over solving the threat or problem.

Problem solving is a skill that may be taught to decrease hopelessness.

Therapeutic Interventions

Actions/Interventions

- Provide opportunities for the patient to express feelings of pessimism.
- Establish a working relationship with the patient through continuity of care.
- Encourage the patient to identify his or her own strengths and abilities.

- Provide the physical care that the patient is unable to provide for self in a manner that communicates warmth, respect, and acceptance of the patient's abilities.
- Assist the patient in developing a realistic appraisal of the situation.

- Help the patient set realistic goals by identifying short-term goals and revising them as needed.
- Express hope for the patient who feels hopeless.

- Encourage an attitude of realistic hope.

- Support the patient's relationships with significant others; involve them in the patient's care as appropriate.

- Provide opportunities for the patient to control environment.

- Promote ego integrity by the following:
  - Encouraging the patient to reminisce about past life (self-validation).
  - Showing the patient that he or she gives something to you as a clinician.
- Encourage the patient to set realistic goals and acknowledge all accomplishments no matter how small.

Rationale

This creates a supportive environment and sends a message of caring.

An ongoing relationship establishes trust, reduces the feeling of isolation, and may facilitate coping.

During a crisis, patients may not be able to recognize their strengths. Fostering awareness can expedite use of these strengths.

This approach reduces guilt and other negative feelings the person may experience when unable to care for self.

Patients may not be aware of all the support services available to them that can help them move through this stressful situation (e.g., home care aides, financial assistance, free medications, community counseling programs, legal services, companion services).

Guiding the patient to view the situation in smaller parts may make the problem more manageable.

Emphasizing the patient's intrinsic worth and viewing the immediate problem as manageable in time may provide support.

Fostering unrealistic hope is not helpful and may significantly worsen the trust the patient places in the health care provider. Belief in the nurse-patient relationship as a partnership in the journey toward hope is key to fostering hope.

Interest in others may help change the patient's focus from self. Enhancing a sense of connectedness to a caring environment fosters hope.

Hopeless patients may feel they have no control. Yet when given opportunities to make choices, their perception of hopelessness may be reduced.

Older patients especially find value in reviewing life's events and accomplishments.

It is important that the patient set truly realistic goals so as not to be frustrated with the inability to accomplish them.

■ = Independent; ▲ = Collaborative

Nursing Diagnosis Care Plans

Hopelessness—cont'd

Actions/Interventions	Rationale
■ Facilitate problem solving by identifying the problem and appropriate steps.	Small steps that are successful will foster confidence in oneself and may promote a more hopeful outlook. They encourage gradual mastery of the situation.
■ Expand the patient's repertoire of coping skills.	Specialized techniques may be required to help the patient gain control.
■ Encourage the use of spiritual resources as desired.	Religious practices may provide strength and inspiration.

Education/Continuity of Care

Actions/Interventions	Rationale
■ Provide accurate and ongoing information about illness, treatment effects, and care needed.	Misconceptions about diagnosis and prognosis may be contributing to hopelessness.
■ Let the patient or family know when situations are temporary.	The outlook may appear less hopeless when time is limited.
■ Educate the patient or family on using a combination of problem solving and emotive coping.	These skills can enhance the coping ability of the patient and family members.

NDx Hyperthermia

Heat Exhaustion; Heat Stroke; Malignant Hyperthermia

NANDA: Body temperature elevated above normal range

Hyperthermia is a sustained temperature above the normal variance; usually greater than 39° C (core temperature). Many cases of hyperthermia result from activity and from salt and water deprivation in a hot environment, such as when athletes perform in extremely hot weather or when older adults avoid the use of air conditioning because of expense. Hyperthermia may occur more readily in persons who have endocrine disorders; use alcohol; or take diuretics, anticholinergics, or phototoxic agents. Malignant hyperthermia is a life-threatening response to various anesthetic agents. This inherited disorder affects calcium metabolism in muscle cells, causing fever, muscle rigidity, metabolic acidosis, dysrhythmic tachycardia, hypertension, and hypoxia. Careful evaluation of preoperative patients is essential for prevention. Hyperthermia differs from fever in that the hypothalamic set point is not reset at a higher level. Also, hyperthermia is not stimulated by pyrogens, such as occurs with infection.

Common Related Factors
Exposure to hot environment
Vigorous activity
Medications
Anesthesia
Increased metabolic rate
Illness or trauma
Dehydration
Inability to perspire

Defining Characteristics
Body temperature above the normal range
Hot, flushed skin
Diaphoresis
Increased heart rate
Increased respiratory rate
Hypotension with dehydration
Hypertension with malignant hyperthermia
Irritability
Fluid or electrolyte imbalance
Convulsions

■ = Independent; ▲ = Collaborative

Common Expected Outcomes

Patient maintains body temperature below 39° C (102.2° F).

Patient maintains blood pressure, respiratory rate, and heart rate within normal limits.

NOC Outcomes
Thermoregulation; Vital Signs

NIC Interventions
Temperature Regulation; Fever Treatment; Malignant Hyperthermia Precautions

Ongoing Assessment

Actions/Interventions

■ Determine precipitating factors.

■ Assess vital signs, especially tympanic or rectal temperature. Notify physician of significant changes.

■ Obtain age and weight.

■ Measure input and output. If patient is unconscious, central venous pressure or pulmonary artery pressure should be measured to monitor fluid status.

▲ Monitor serum electrolytes, especially serum sodium.

Rationale

Identification and management of underlying cause are essential to recovery.

Vital signs provide more accurate indication of core temperature.

Extremes of age or weight increase the risk for inability to control body temperature.

Fluid resuscitation may be necessary to correct dehydration. The patient who is significantly dehydrated is no longer able to sweat, which allows for evaporative cooling.

Sodium losses occur with profuse sweating and accidental hyperthermia.

Therapeutic Interventions

Actions/Interventions

■ Control environmental temperature. Move heat victim to cooler area, out of direct sunlight. Transport victims with altered consciousness to a health care facility.

■ Remove excess clothing and covers.

▲ Provide antipyretic medications as ordered.

▲ Provide oxygen therapy in extreme cases.

▲ Control excessive shivering with medications such as chlorpromazine (Thorazine) and diazepam (Valium), if necessary.

▲ Provide ample fluids by mouth or intravenously.

▲ Provide additional cooling mechanisms commensurate with significance of fever and related manifestations:
  • Noninvasive: cooling mattress, cold packs applied to major blood vessels

Rationale

Removing sources of heat can begin the cooling process and reduce core temperature. With very high temperature, regulatory centers in the brain begin to fail, leading to cerebral edema and acute tubular necrosis.

This decreases warmth and increases evaporative cooling.

Temperatures above 40° C (104° F) for extended periods can cause cellular damage, delirium, and convulsions.

Hyperthermia increases metabolic demand for oxygen.

Shivering increases metabolic rate and body temperature.

If patient is dehydrated or diaphoretic, fluid loss contributes to fever.

These measures help promote cooling and lower core temperature.

■ = Independent; ▲ = Collaborative

Hyperthermia–cont'd

Actions/Interventions

- Evaporative cooling: cool with tepid bath, do not use alcohol
- Invasive: gastric lavage, peritoneal lavage, cardiopulmonary bypass in an emergency

■ Adjust cooling measures on the basis of physical response.

Rationale

Alcohol cools the skin too rapidly, causing shivering.

These invasive procedures are used to quickly cool core temperature. These patients require cardiopulmonary monitoring.

Cooling too quickly may cause shivering, which burns calories and increases metabolic rate in order to produce heat.

Education/Continuity of Care

Actions/Interventions

■ Explain temperature measurement and all treatments.

■ Provide information regarding normal temperature and control.

■ Discuss precipitating factors and preventive measures, including maintenance of adequate fluid intake, protective skin products, change in environment, taking medications as prescribed (antipyretics, antibiotics).

■ Refer at-risk individuals to the Malignant Hyperthermia Association of the United States.

■ Discuss importance of informing future health care providers of malignant hyperthermia risk; suggest a medical alert bracelet or similar identification.

Rationale

Patients may be initially disoriented, requiring repeated explanations.

This is especially necessary for patients with conditions or in situations putting them at risk for hyperthermia (e.g., those with infection, those subject to extremely hot weather, athletes).

Patients and families need to learn how to prevent future episodes of hyperthermia.

This organization provides information and additional resources.

Alternative anesthetic drugs or methods can be used for these patients. Patient safety is a priority.

NDx Hypothermia

Cold Stress; Cold Injury

NANDA: Body temperature below normal range

Hypothermia is a temperature at a significantly lower level than normal; usually lower than 35° C (95° F) measured by the tympanic/rectal routes. Hypothermia results when the body cannot produce heat at a rate equal to that lost to the environment through conduction, convection, radiation, or evaporation. Core temperature below 32° C (89.6° F) is severe and life threatening. Hypothermia can be classified as inadvertent (seen postoperatively), intentional (for medical purposes), or accidental (exposure related).

■ = Independent; ▲ = Collaborative

Common Related Factors

Exposure to cold environment
Illness or trauma
Inability to shiver
Poor nutrition
Inadequate clothing
Alcohol consumption
Medications: vasodilators
Excessive evaporative heat loss from skin
Decreased metabolic rate

Defining Characteristics

Shivering
Cold appearance
Cool skin
Slow capillary reflexes
Piloerection
Hypertension
Increased heart rate

Common Expected Outcomes

Patient maintains a body temperature above 35° C (95° F) (core).
Patient's vital signs are within normal limits; skin is warm.

NOC Outcomes
Thermoregulation; Vital Sign Status

NIC Interventions
Temperature Regulation;
   Hypothermia Treatment

Ongoing Assessment

Actions/Interventions

- Determine precipitating event and risk factors.

- Assess for extremes in age.

- Monitor temperature.

- Assess vital signs.

- Evaluate for drug use, including psychotherapeutics, narcotics, and alcohol.

- Evaluate peripheral perfusion at frequent intervals.

- Assess nutrition and weight.

- Monitor intake and output (and/or central venous pressure).

- Monitor cardiac rate and rhythm.

▲ Monitor electrolytes, arterial blood gases, and oximetry.

- Evaluate for presence of frostbite, if applicable.

Rationale

Causative factors guide appropriate treatment.

Older patients have a decreased metabolic rate and reduced shivering response; therefore effects of cold may not be immediately apparent.

For alert patients, oral temperature is considered more accurate than tympanic or axillary. For more hypothermic patients, core temperature can be monitored using a temperature-sensitive pulmonary artery catheter or bladder catheter.

Heart and respiratory rates and blood pressure decrease as hypothermia progresses.

These agents cause vasodilation and heat loss.

Hypothermia initially precipitates peripheral vascular constriction as a compensatory mechanism to minimize heat loss from the extremities. As hypothermia progresses, vasodilation occurs, furthering heat loss.

Poor nutrition contributes to decreased energy reserves and limits the body's ability to produce heat by caloric consumption.

Decreased output may indicate dehydration or poor renal perfusion. Avoid fluid overload to prevent pulmonary edema, pneumonia, and taxing an already compromised cardiac and renal status.

Moderate to severe hypothermia increases risk for ventricular fibrillation, along with other arrhythmias.

Acidosis may result from hypoventilation and hypoglycemia.

Severe hypothermia causes ice crystals to form inside cells. The cells then rupture and die.

■ = Independent; ▲ = Collaborative

Nursing Diagnosis Care Plans

 **Hypothermia**–cont'd

Therapeutic Interventions

Actions/Interventions	Rationale
■ Control environmental temperature or move patient to warmer environment.	These techniques provide for a more gradual warming of the body. Rapid warming can induce ventricular fibrillation.
■ Provide the following extra covering: (Passive warming) • Clothing, including head covering.	Heat loss tends to be greatest from the top of the head.
• Blankets; cover postoperative patients with heat-retaining blankets.	Warm blankets provide a passive method for rewarming. A majority of these patients experience mild to moderate hypothermia.
■ Keep patient and linen dry.	Moisture facilitates evaporative heat loss.
■ Provide heated oral fluids for alert patients.	This provides calories as well as a heat source.
▲ Provide extra heat source: • Heat lamp, radiant warmer • Warming mattress, pads, or blankets • Submersion in warm bath • Heated, moisturized oxygen • Warmed intravenous fluids or lavage fluids	These raise core temperature and improve circulation. Because of vasodilation, intravascular volume decreases, dramatically increasing hematocrit.
■ Regulate heat source according to physical response.	Rewarming must be performed carefully to reduce development of life-threatening arrhythmias.
■ Avoid trauma to areas of frostbite.	Rubbing can further damage frozen tissue.

Education/Continuity of Care

Actions/Interventions	Rationale
■ Explain all procedures and treatments.	Keep in mind that the patient is confused from hypothermia and decreased oxygenation; repeated explanations may be necessary.
■ Provide information regarding normal temperature and prevention of hypothermia, once the patient's condition is stable.	Patients and family members need information about how to prevent hypothermia.
■ Enlist support services as appropriate.	Social, mental, or economic problems precipitate many situations where hypothermia occurs, especially when patients are older, poor, or homeless.

NDx Risk for Infection

Universal Precautions; Standard Precautions; CDC Guidelines; OSHA

NANDA: At increased risk for being invaded by pathogenic organisms

Persons at risk for infection are those whose natural defense mechanisms are inadequate to protect them from the inevitable injuries and exposures that occur throughout the course of living. Infections occur when an organism (e.g., bacterium, virus, fungus, or other parasite) invades a susceptible host. Breaks in the integument, the body's first line

 ■ = Independent; ▲ = Collaborative

of defense, and/or the mucous membranes allow invasion by pathogens. If the host's (patient's) immune system cannot combat the invading organism adequately, an infection occurs. Open wounds, traumatic or surgical, can be sites for infection; soft tissues (cells, fat, muscle) and organs (kidneys, lungs) can also be sites for infection either after trauma, invasive procedures, or by invasion of pathogens carried through the bloodstream or lymphatic system. Infections can be transmitted, either by contact or through airborne transmission, sexual contact, or sharing of intravenous (IV) drug paraphernalia. Being malnourished, having inadequate resources for sanitary living conditions, and lacking knowledge about disease transmission place individuals at risk for infection. Health care workers, to protect themselves and others from disease transmission, must understand how to take precautions to prevent transmission. Because identification of infected individuals is not always apparent, standard precautions recommended by the Centers for Disease Control and Prevention are widely practiced. In addition, the Occupational Safety and Health Administration has set forth the Blood Borne Pathogens Standard, developed to protect workers and the public from infection. Ease of and increase in world travel have also increased opportunities for transmission of disease from abroad. Infections prolong healing and can result in death if untreated. Antimicrobials are used to treat infections when susceptibility is present. Organisms may become resistant to antimicrobials, requiring multiple antimicrobial therapy. There are organisms for which no antimicrobial is effective, such as the human immunodeficiency virus.

Common Risk Factors

Inadequate primary defenses: broken skin, injured tissue, body fluid stasis
Inadequate secondary defenses: immunosuppression, leukopenia
Malnutrition
Intubation
Indwelling catheters, drains
IV devices
Invasive procedures
Rupture of amniotic membranes
Chronic disease
Failure to avoid pathogens (exposure)
Inadequate acquired immunity

Common Expected Outcomes

Patient remains free of infection, as evidenced by normal vital signs and absence of purulent drainage from wounds, incisions, and tubes.
Infection is recognized early to allow for prompt treatment.

NOC Outcomes
Immune Status;
Knowledge: Infection Control

NIC Interventions
Infection Control; Infection Protection

■ = Independent; ▲ = Collaborative

Risk for Infection–cont'd

Ongoing Assessment

Actions/Interventions

■ Assess for presence, existence of, and history of risk factors such as open wounds and abrasions; indwelling catheters (Foley, peritoneal); wound drainage tubes (T-tubes, Penrose, Jackson-Pratt); endotracheal or tracheostomy tubes; venous or arterial access devices; and orthopedic fixator pins.

▲ Monitor white blood cell (WBC) count.

■ Monitor the following for signs of infection:
  • Redness, swelling; increased pain; purulent drainage from incisions, injury, and exit sites of tubes, drains, or catheters
  • Elevated temperature

  • Color of respiratory secretions

  • Appearance of urine

■ Assess nutritional status, including weight, history of weight loss, and serum albumin.

■ In pregnant patients, assess intactness of amniotic membranes.

■ Assess for exposure to individuals with active infections.

■ Assess for history of drug use or treatment modalities that may cause immunosuppression.

■ Assess immunization status.

Rationale

Each of these examples represents a break in the body's normal first line of defense.

An increasing WBC count indicates the body's efforts to combat pathogens. Normal values are 4000 to 11,000 mm^3. Very low WBC count (less than 1000 mm^3) indicates severe risk for infection because the patient does not have sufficient WBCs to fight infection. NOTE: In older patients, infection may be present without an increased WBC count.

Any suspicious drainage should be cultured; antibiotic therapy is determined by pathogens identified at culture.

Temperature of up to 38° C (100.4° F) for 48 hours after surgery is related to surgical stress; after 48 hours, temperature greater than 37.7° C (99.8° F) suggests infection; fever spikes that occur and subside are indicative of wound infection; very high temperature accompanied by sweating and chills may indicate septicemia.

Yellow or yellow-green sputum is indicative of respiratory infection.

Cloudy, foul-smelling urine with visible sediment is indicative of urinary tract or bladder infection.

Patients with poor nutritional status may be anergic or unable to muster a cellular immune response to pathogens and are therefore more susceptible to infection.

Prolonged rupture of amniotic membranes before delivery places the mother and infant at increased risk for infection.

This provides warning for potential infection.

Antineoplastic agents and corticosteroids reduce immunocompetence.

Older patients and those not raised in the United States may not have completed immunizations and therefore may not have sufficient acquired immunocompetence.

Therapeutic Interventions

Actions/Interventions

■ Maintain or teach asepsis for dressing changes and wound care, catheter care and handling, and peripheral IV and central venous access management.

Rationale

Use of aseptic technique decreases the chances of transmitting or spreading pathogens to the patient.

■ = Independent; ▲ = Collaborative

Actions/Interventions

- Wash hands and teach other caregivers to wash hands before contact with patients and between procedures with the patient.

- Limit visitors.

- Encourage intake of protein- and calorie-rich foods.
- Encourage fluid intake of 2000 to 3000 mL of water per day (unless contraindicated).

- Encourage coughing and deep breathing; consider use of incentive spirometer.

- ▲ Administer or teach use of antimicrobial (antibiotic) drugs as ordered.

- ▲ Place the patient in protective isolation if he or she is at very high risk.

- Recommend the use of soft-bristled toothbrushes and stool softeners to protect mucous membranes.

Rationale

Friction and running water effectively remove microorganisms from hands. Washing between procedures reduces the risk of transmitting pathogens from one area of the body to another (e.g., perineal care or central line care). Alcohol-based hand sanitizers can be used between hand washing episodes if the hands are not visibly soiled. Use of disposable gloves does not reduce the need for hand washing.

This reduces the number of organisms in the patient's environment and restricts visitation by individuals with any type of infection to reduce the transmission of pathogens to the patient at risk for infection. The most common modes of transmission are by direct contact (touching) and by droplet (airborne).

This maintains optimal nutritional status.

Fluids promote diluted urine and frequent emptying of bladder; reducing stasis of urine, in turn, reduces risk of bladder infection or urinary tract infection.

These measures reduce stasis of secretions in the lungs and bronchial tree. When stasis occurs, pathogens can cause upper respiratory infections, including pneumonia.

Antimicrobial drugs include antibacterial, antifungal, antiparasitic, and antiviral agents. All of these agents are either toxic to the pathogen or retard the pathogen's growth. Ideally, the selection of the drug is based on cultures from the infected area; this is often impossible or impractical, and in these cases, empirical management usually is undertaken with a broad-spectrum drug.

Protective isolation is established when WBC counts indicate neutropenia (less than 500 to 1000 mm^3). Institutional protocols may vary.

Hard-bristled toothbrushes and constipation may compromise the integrity of the mucous membranes and provide a port of entry for pathogens.

Education/Continuity of Care

Actions/Interventions

- Teach the patient or caregiver to wash hands often, especially after toileting, before meals, and before and after administering self-care.

- Teach the patient the importance of avoiding contact with those who have infections or colds. Teach family members and caregivers about protecting susceptible patients from themselves and others with infections or colds.

- Teach the patient, family, and caregivers the purpose and proper technique for maintaining isolation.

Rationale

Patients and caregivers can spread infection from one part of the body to another, as well as pick up surface pathogens; hand washing reduces these risks.

Family members or others can spread infections or colds to a susceptible patient through direct contact, contaminated inanimate objects, or through air currents.

Knowledge about isolation can help patients and family members cooperate with specific precautions.

■ = Independent; ▲ = Collaborative

Risk for Infection–cont'd

Actions/Interventions	Rationale
■ Teach the patient to take antibiotics as prescribed.	Most antibiotics work best when a constant blood level is maintained; a constant blood level is maintained when medications are taken as prescribed. The absorption of some antibiotics is hindered by certain foods; patients should be instructed accordingly.
■ Instruct the patient to take the full course of antibiotics even if symptoms improve or disappear.	Not completing the entire course of the prescribed antibiotic regimen can lead to drug resistance in the pathogens and reactivation of symptoms.
■ Teach the patient and caregiver the signs and symptoms of infection, and when to report these to the physician or nurse.	Patients need to be able to recognize important signs and changes in their condition so early treatment can be initiated.
■ Demonstrate and allow return demonstration of all high-risk procedures that the patient or caregiver will do after discharge, such as dressing changes, peripheral or central IV site care, peritoneal dialysis, and self-catheterization (may use clean technique).	Bladder infection is more related to overdistended bladder resulting from infrequent catheterization than to use of clean versus sterile technique.

ND x Decreased Intracranial Adaptive Capacity

Increased Intracranial Pressure; Altered Level of Consciousness

NANDA: Intracranial fluid dynamic mechanisms that normally compensate for increases in intracranial volumes are compromised, resulting in repeated disproportionate increases in intracranial pressure in response to a variety of noxious and non-noxious stimuli

Intracranial pressure (ICP) reflects the pressure exerted by the intracranial components of blood, brain, and cerebrospinal fluid (CSF), each ordinarily remaining at a constant volume within the rigid skull structure. Any additional fluid or mass (e.g., subdural hematoma, tumor, or abscess) increases the pressure within the cranial vault. Because the total volume cannot change (Monro-Kellie doctrine), blood, CSF, and ultimately brain tissue is forced out of the vault. The normal range of ICP is up to 15 mm Hg; elevations above that level occur normally but readily return to baseline parameters as a result of the adaptive capacity or compensatory mechanisms of the brain and body, such as vasoconstriction and increased venous outflow. In the event of disease, trauma, or a pathological condition, a disturbance in autoregulation occurs, and ICP is increased and sustained. Exceptions include persons with unfused skull fractures (the skull is no longer rigid at the fracture site), infants whose suture lines are not yet fused (this is normal to accommodate growth), and older patients whose brain tissues have shrunk, taking up less volume in the skull (allowing for abnormal tissue growth or intracranial bleeding to occur for a longer period before symptoms appear).

■ = Independent; ▲ = Collaborative

Common Related Factors

Hydrocephalus
Increased cerebral blood flow (CBF), hypercapnia, hyperemia
Injury with cerebral edema
Intracranial mass
Systemic hypotension

Defining Characteristics

Decreased level of consciousness (LOC): confusion, disorientation, somnolence, lethargy, and coma
Headache
Vomiting
Papilledema
Pupil asymmetry
Decreased pupil reactivity
Impaired memory, judgment, thought processes
Glasgow Coma Scale (GCS) score less than 13
Unilateral or bilateral VI nerve palsy
Repeated increases in ICP greater than 10 mm Hg for more than 5 minutes
Elevated ICP waveforms
Baseline ICP greater than 10 mm Hg
Wide amplitude ICP waveform
Volume pressure response test variation
Decreased CBF
Decreased cerebral perfusion pressure (CPP)
Hypertension
Increased or decreased heart rate with arrhythmias
Widening pulse pressure

Common Expected Outcome

Patient maintains optimal cerebral tissue perfusion, as evidenced by ICP less than 10 mm Hg, GCS greater than 13, and CPP from 60 to 90 mm Hg.

NOC Outcomes

Neurological Status: Consciousness; Medication Response; Knowledge: Disease Process; Fluid Balance

NIC Interventions

ICP Monitoring; Neurological Monitoring; Cerebral Edema Management; Teaching: Disease Process; Medication Administration: Parenteral

Ongoing Assessment

Actions/Interventions

■ Assess neurological status as follows: LOC according to GCS—pupil size, symmetry, and reaction to light; extraocular movement; gaze preference; speech and thought processes; memory; motor sensory signs and drift; increased tone; increased reflexes; Babinski reflex.

■ Evaluate presence or absence of protective reflexes (e.g., swallowing, gagging, blinking, and coughing).

■ Monitor vital signs.

▲ Monitor arterial blood gases and/or pulse oximetry (recommended parameters: PaO_2 greater than 80 mm Hg and $PaCO_2$ less than 35 mm Hg with normal ICP). If the patient's lungs are being hyperventilated to decrease ICP, $PaCO_2$ should be between 25 and 30 mm Hg.

Rationale

Deteriorating neurological signs indicate increased cerebral ischemia. A decreased LOC is the first sign of increased ICP.

Loss of protective reflexes increases the person's risk for injuries such as aspiration or corneal abrasions.

Continually increasing ICP results in life-threatening hemodynamic changes; early recognition is essential to survival.

A $PaCO_2$ less than 20 mm Hg may decrease CBF because of profound vasoconstriction that produces hypoxia. $PaCO_2$ greater than 45 mm Hg induces vasodilation with increase in CBF, which may trigger increase in ICP.

■ = Independent; ▲ = Collaborative

Decreased Intracranial Adaptive Capacity–cont'd

Actions/Interventions

■ Monitor input and output with urine-specific gravity. Report urine-specific gravity greater than 1.025 or urine output less than 0.5 mL/kg/hr.

■ Calculate CPP. Calculate CPP by subtracting ICP from the mean arterial pressure (MAP):

$$CPP = MAP - ICP$$

Determine MAP using the following formula:

$$\frac{Systolic\ BP - Diastolic\ BP}{3} + Diastolic\ BP$$

▲ Monitor serum electrolytes, blood urea nitrogen, creatinine, glucose, osmolality, hemoglobin, and hematocrit, as indicated.

▲ Monitor closely when treatment of increased ICP begins to taper.

▲ Monitor ICP if measurement device is in place. Report ICP greater than 15 mm Hg for 5 minutes. Serially monitor ICP pressure and waveforms. Types of ICP waveforms include the following:

• Lundberg A waves (plateau waves) are increased ICP greater than 50 mm Hg sustained for more than 5 minutes.

• B waves are increased ICP, usually 20 to 40 mm Hg, and may precede an A wave.

• C waves are nonpathological and often correlate with heart rate and respiratory rate.

Rationale

Monitoring may indicate decreased renal perfusion and possible associated decrease in CPP.

Pressure should be approximately 90 to 100 mm Hg and not less than 50 mm Hg to ensure blood flow to brain.

These detect treatment complications such as hypovolemia.

ICP may increase as treatment is tapered.

Sustained ICP greater than 15 mm Hg causes transtentorial herniation and brain stem compression/herniation with resultant compression of the respiratory center, apnea, and cardiac arrest. Presence of A and B waves indicates neurological deterioration; the physician should be immediately informed.

These waves indicate a neurological emergency necessitating immediate intervention to avoid brain damage.

These can be seen with changes in respiratory pattern and must be watched as a possible prelude to A waves.

These waves are typically less than 20 mm Hg and occur every 4 to 8 minutes.

Therapeutic Interventions

Actions/Interventions

■ Elevate head of bed 30 degrees and keep head in neutral alignment.

■ Avoid Valsalva maneuver.

■ If ICP is elevated to 12 to 15 mm Hg, reduce nursing and medical procedures to those absolutely necessary.

▲ Maintain normothermia with antipyretics, antibiotics, and cooling blanket.

▲ If ICP increases and fails to respond to repositioning of head in neutral alignment and head elevation, recheck equipment. If ICP is increased, one or more of the following may be prescribed by the physician:

Rationale

Elevation promotes venous outflow. Exceptions include shock and cervical spine injuries. A neutral head position prevents venous obstruction.

Valsalva increases intrathoracic pressure and CBF, thereby increasing ICP.

These procedures can serve as a noxious stimulus that can further increase ICP.

Fever increases cerebral metabolic demand; fever may increase CBF and ICP.

■ = Independent; ▲ = Collaborative

Actions/Interventions

- Hyperventilate the patient.

- Administer mannitol over 30 to 60 minutes.

- Administer barbiturates as needed.

- If the patient is intubated, administer a neuromuscular blocking agent.

- Administer a short-acting pain reliever (e.g., morphine, meperidine [Demerol], or midazolam [Versed]), before painful stimulation or stress-related care such as suctioning or IV line changes.

▲ Drain CSF at ordered rate and amount.

Rationale

This can decrease $Paco_2$ to between 25 and 30 mm Hg and induce vasoconstriction and a decrease in CBF and ICP. Hyperventilation is often reserved for brain-injured patients exhibiting signs of herniation.

This is a hyperosmotic agent that should be used carefully because it can induce cerebral ischemia. It is contraindicated with hypovolemic symptoms. A diuretic response can be anticipated within 30 to 60 minutes. A Foley catheter should be in place. An intravenous (IV) filter should be used when mannitol is infused. Electrolytes, osmolality, and serum glucose must be monitored during mannitol infusion.

Barbiturates reduce cerebral metabolism and reduce cerebral oxygen demand and lower ICP.

This reduces shivering, coughing, bucking, and Valsalva maneuver. However, neuromuscular blocking agents have no effect on cerebration; therefore the patient should receive short-acting sedation before noxious stimulation.

Pain and agitated body movements cause further increases in ICP.

Removal of a small amount of CSF can significantly lower ICP. This can be accomplished intermittently or, as in patients with hydrocephalus, continuously.

Education/Continuity of Care

Actions/Interventions

- Teach patient and family about causes, treatment, and expected outcome.
- Reinforce discussions related to treatment (e.g., head of bed elevated, medication).

- Offer the family frequent feedback regarding the patient's status.
- Encourage family presence and participation in comfort measures.
- Provide social service, community, and/or support group information as appropriate to the primary diagnosis.

Rationale

Knowledge about increased ICP can calm anxieties about this condition.

Patient and family will be able to cooperate with care when they understand the purpose of specific interventions.

This approach will ease anxiety of family members.

This occasionally calms the patient and decreases ICP.

The primary diagnosis (e.g., a resolving head trauma versus repeated stroke) necessitates different levels of postdischarge care needs.

■ = Independent; ▲ = Collaborative

Decreased Intracranial Adaptive Capacity

NDx Deficient Knowledge

Patient Teaching; Health Education

NANDA: Absence or deficiency of cognitive information related to specific topic

Knowledge deficit is a lack of cognitive information or psychomotor skills required for health recovery, maintenance, or health promotion. Teaching may take place in a hospital, ambulatory care, or home setting. The learner may be the patient, a family member, a significant other, or a caregiver unrelated to the patient. Learning may involve any of the three domains: cognitive domain (intellectual activities, problem solving, and others); affective domain (feelings, attitudes, belief); and psychomotor domain (physical skills or procedures). The nurse must decide with the learner what to teach, when to teach, and how to teach the mutually agreed upon content. Adult learning principles guide the teaching-learning process. Information should be made available when the patient wants and needs it, at the pace the patient determines, and using the teaching strategy the patient deems most effective. Many factors influence patient education, including age, cognitive level, developmental stage, physical limitations (e.g., visual, hearing, balance, hand coordination, strength), the primary disease process and comorbidities, and sociocultural factors. Older patients need more time for teaching, and may have sensory-perceptual deficits and/or cognitive changes that may require a modification in teaching techniques. Certain ethnic and religious groups hold unique beliefs and health practices that must be considered when designing a teaching plan. These practices may vary from "home remedies" (e.g., special soups, poultices) and alternative therapies (e.g., massage, biofeedback, energy healing, macrobiotics, or megavitamins in place of prescribed medications) to reliance on an elder in the family to coordinate the care plan. Patients with low literacy skills will require educational programs that include more simplified treatment regimens, simplified teaching tools (e.g., cartoons, lower readability levels), a slower presentation pace, and techniques for cueing patients to initiate certain behaviors (e.g., pill schedule posted on refrigerator, timer for taking medications).

Although the acute hospital setting provides challenges for patient education because of the high acuity and emotional stress inherent in this environment, the home setting can be similarly challenging because of the high expectations for patients or caregivers to self-manage complex procedures such as intravenous therapy, dialysis, or even ventilator care in the home. Caregivers are often overwhelmed by the responsibility delegated to them by the health care professionals. Many have their own health problems and may be unable to perform all the behaviors assigned to them because of visual limitations, generalized weakness, or feelings of inadequacy or exhaustion.

This care plan describes adult learning principles that can be incorporated into a teaching plan for use in any health care setting.

Common Related Factors

New condition, procedure, treatment
Complexity of treatment
Cognitive/physical limitation
Misinterpretation of information
Decreased motivation to learn
Emotional state affecting learning (anxiety, denial, or depression)
Unfamiliarity with information resources

Defining Characteristics

Questioning members of health care team
Verbalizing inaccurate information
Inaccurate follow-through of instruction
Denial of need to learn
Incorrect task performance
Expressing frustration or confusion when performing task
Lack of recall

■ = Independent; ▲ = Collaborative

Deficient Knowledge

Common Expected Outcomes

Patient demonstrates motivation to learn.
Patient identifies perceived learning needs.
Patient verbalizes understanding of desired content and/or performs desired skill.

> ### NOC Outcomes
> Knowledge (Specify Type); Information Processing
>
> ### NIC Interventions
> Learning Facilitation; Teaching: Individual

Ongoing Assessment

Actions/Interventions

- Determine who will be the learner: the patient, family, significant other, or caregiver.

- Assess motivation and willingness of the patient and caregivers to learn.

- Assess ability to learn or perform desired health-related care.

- Identify priority of learning needs within the overall care plan.

- Question the patient regarding previous experience and health teaching.

- Identify any existing misconceptions regarding material to be taught.

- Determine cultural influences on health teaching.

- Determine the patient's learning style, especially if the patient has learned and retained new information in the past.

Rationale

Many older or terminal patients may view themselves as dependent on their caregiver and therefore will not want to be part of the educational process.

Adults must see a need or purpose for learning. Some patients are ready to learn soon after they are diagnosed; others cope better by denying or delaying the need for instruction. Learning also requires energy, which patients may not be ready to use. Patients also have a right to refuse educational services.

Cognitive impairments need to be identified so an appropriate teaching plan can be designed. For example, the Mini-Mental State Examination can be used to identify memory problems that would interfere with learning. Physical limitations such as impaired hearing or vision, or poor hand coordination can likewise compromise learning and must be considered when designing the educational approach. Patients with decreased lens accommodation may require bolder, larger fonts or magnifying lenses for written material.

Adults learn material that is important to them. During the acute stages, the family or significant others may require the most teaching.

Adults bring many life experiences to each learning session. Adults learn best when teaching builds on previous knowledge or experience.

This provides an important starting point in education. Knowledge serves to correct faulty ideas.

Providing a climate of acceptance allows patients to be themselves and to hold their own beliefs as appropriate. Language problems can pose significant barriers to learning.

Some persons may prefer written over visual materials, or they may prefer group versus individual instruction. Matching the learner's preferred style with the educational method will facilitate success in mastery of knowledge.

■ = Independent; ▲ = Collaborative

Deficient Knowledge–cont'd

Actions/Interventions	Rationale
■ Determine the patient's or caregiver's self-efficacy to learn and apply new knowledge.	Self-efficacy refers to one's confidence in his or her ability to perform a behavior. A first step in teaching may be to foster increased self-efficacy in the learner's ability to learn the desired information or skills.

Therapeutic Interventions

Actions/Interventions	Rationale
■ Provide physical comfort for the learner.	This allows the patient to concentrate on what is being discussed or demonstrated. According to Maslow's theory, basic physiological needs must be addressed before patient education.
■ Provide a quiet atmosphere without interruption.	This allows the patient to concentrate more completely.
■ Provide an atmosphere of respect, openness, trust, and collaboration.	This is especially important when providing education to patients with different values and beliefs about health and illness.
■ Establish objectives and goals for learning at the beginning of the session.	This allows the learner to know what will be discussed and expected during the session. Adults tend to focus on here-and-now, problem-centered education.
■ Allow the learner to identify what is most important to him or her.	This clarifies learner expectations and helps the nurse match the information to be presented to the individual's needs. Adult learning is problem oriented. Determine priorities (i.e., what the patient needs to know now versus later). Patients may want to focus only on self-care techniques that facilitate discharge from the hospital or enhance survival at home (e.g., how to take medications, emergency side effects, suctioning a tracheal tube) and are less interested in specifics of the disease process.
■ Explore attitudes and feelings about changes.	This assists the nurse in understanding how the learner may respond to the information and possibly how successful the patient may be with the expected changes.
■ Allow for and support self-directed, self-designed learning.	Adults learn when they feel they are personally involved in the learning process. Patients know what difficulties will be encountered in their own environments, and they must be encouraged to approach learning activities from their priority needs.
■ Assist the learner in integrating information into daily life.	This helps the learner make adjustments in daily life that will result in the desired change in behavior (or learning).
■ Allow adequate time for integration that is in direct conflict with existing values or beliefs.	Information that is in direct conflict with what is already held to be true forces a reevaluation of the old material and is thus integrated more slowly.
■ Give clear, thorough explanations and demonstrations.	Accurate, clear information provides rationale for treatment and aids the patient in assuming responsibility for care at a later time.

■ = Independent; ▲ = Collaborative

Nursing Diagnosis Care Plans

Deficient Knowledge

Actions/Interventions

- Provide information using various media (e.g., explanations, discussions, demonstrations, pictures, written instructions, computer-assisted programs, and videotapes).

- Ensure that required supplies and equipment are available so that the environment is conducive to learning.

- When presenting material, move from familiar, simple, and concrete information to less familiar, complex, or more abstract concepts.

- Focus teaching sessions on a single concept or idea.

- Pace the instruction and keep sessions short.

- Encourage questions.

- Allow learner to practice new skills; provide immediate feedback on performance.

- Encourage repetition of information or new skill.

- Provide positive, constructive reinforcement of learning.

- Document progress of teaching and learning.

Rationale

Different people take in information in different ways. Match the learning style with the educational approach.

This is especially important when teaching in the home setting.

This provides the patient with the opportunity to understand new material in relation to familiar material.

This allows the learner to concentrate more completely on material being discussed. Highly anxious and older patients have reduced short-term memory and benefit from mastery of one concept at a time.

This prevents fatigue. Learning requires energy.

Learners often feel shy or embarrassed about asking questions and often want permission to ask them.

This allows the patient to use new information immediately, thus enhancing retention. Immediate feedback allows the learner to make corrections rather than practicing the skill incorrectly.

This assists in remembering.

A positive approach allows the learner to feel good about learning accomplishments, gain confidence, and maintain self-esteem while correcting mistakes. Incorporate rewards into the learning process.

This allows additional teaching to be based on what the learner has completed, thus enhancing the learner's self-efficacy and encouraging the most cost-effective teaching.

Education/Continuity of Care

Actions/Interventions

- Provide instruction for specific topics.

- ▲ Refer the patient to community resources or support groups, as needed.

- Include significant others whenever possible.

Rationale

Patients must have correct information to make informed choices in their treatment, to identify when therapy adjustments are needed, and to recognize important changes in their condition that could lead to serious outcomes.

These allow the patient to interact with others who have similar problems, learning needs, or specialty resources.

One's partner usually assumes a crucial supportive role when the patient is gathering information and initiating new treatments.

■ = Independent; ▲ = Collaborative

 **Latex Allergy Response**

NANDA: An allergic response to natural latex rubber products

Latex allergy is a hypersensitivity reaction to the proteins in natural rubber latex derived from the sap of the rubber tree, *Hevea brasiliensis*. Products made from synthetic rubber may be called *latex* but do not contain the proteins known to cause an allergic response. The incidence of latex allergy increased after 1985 with the introduction of standard precautions to prevent the spread of bloodborne pathogens such as the human immunodeficiency virus. Soft rubber products such as gloves have the highest content of latex protein and the most potential to cause an allergic response. The people at highest risk for latex allergy include those who wear latex gloves as part of their jobs, such as health care workers, food service workers, housekeepers, and hairdressers. People employed in industries that manufacture latex rubber products are at risk, too. Another group of people at risk are those who undergo repeated surgeries, especially if the surgeries begin in childhood. Evidence indicates a high incidence of latex allergy in people with spina bifida who have had multiple surgeries in childhood. People with a variety of food allergies and sensitivities also have increased risk for latex allergy. Natural latex rubber allergies are IgE-mediated reactions to at least 10 different low–molecular-weight water-soluble proteins contained in the rubber tree sap. The range of hypersensitivity reactions to latex rubber include mild to severe contact dermatitis, respiratory allergic symptoms, and anaphylaxis.

Common Related Factor

No immune response mechanism

Defining Characteristics

Type I hypersensitivity reactions:
Immediate reactions
- Contact urticaria
- Orofacial edema
- Dyspnea
- Wheezing
- Hypotension
- Cardiac arrest
- Abdominal pain
- Flushing and erythema
- Restlessness

Type IV hypersensitivity reactions:
Delayed reactions
- Eczema
- Redness
- Irritation
Irritant reactions
- Erythema
- Chapped, cracked skin
- Blisters

■ = Independent; ▲ = Collaborative

Common Expected Outcomes

Patient verbalizes strategies to avoid exposure to sources of latex rubber.

Patient seeks immediate treatment for symptoms of latex allergy response.

> **NOC Outcomes**
> Allergic Response: Localized; Immune Hypersensitivity Response; Tissue Integrity: Skin and Mucous Membranes
>
> **NIC Interventions**
> Latex Precautions; Allergy Management

Ongoing Assessment

Actions/Interventions

- Assess for history of myelomeningocele or urogenital abnormalities in childhood.

- Assess for history of food allergies to bananas, avocados, tomatoes, kiwi, mangos, and chestnuts.

- Assess for a history of allergic reactions to figs, apples, celery, melon, potatoes, papayas, cherries, and peaches.

- Assess for allergic reactions after contact with products containing latex such as blowing up a balloon, using a condom or diaphragm, undergoing a vaginal or rectal examination, wearing latex gloves, or doing other work-related activities that involved exposure to latex.

▲ Refer the patient for immunological testing for latex sensitivity.

Rationale

Multiple surgeries to correct congenital neural tube defects or urinary tract abnormalities in childhood are associated with increased risk for latex allergy.

These foods have proteins similar to latex rubber. People with these specific food allergies may have a cross sensitivity to latex. These foods are associated with anaphylactic reactions in people with latex sensitivity.

People with sensitivity to these foods have been found to be at higher risk for developing latex allergy.

People may not be aware of latex allergy. Symptoms may have developed after blowing up a balloon, medical or dental procedures where latex products were used, or in the work environment. The person may not have associated the symptoms with exposure to latex. The symptoms may have included skin rash, itching, swelling, hives, shortness of breath, runny nose, or cough.

Diagnostic tests are available to detect IgE immunoglobulins specific to latex and related compounds. Skin prick testing also may be used to identify latex allergy.

Therapeutic Interventions

Actions/Interventions

For the hospitalized patient:

- Place allergy band on the patient.

- Record latex allergy in the patient's medical record and post a sign over the patient's bed about latex allergy.

- Remove latex products from the patient's immediate environment.

- Place latex-free equipment in the patient's room.

Rationale

All health care providers need to be notified of the patient's latex allergy.

Visible signs are used to increase the awareness of all providers and reduce possible exposure to latex.

All latex products need to be removed from the patient's environment to reduce exposure. These products include blood pressure cuffs, gloves, adhesive tape, tourniquets, injection ports, electrode pads, stethoscope tubing, rubber syringe stoppers, and medication vial stoppers.

Most hospitals have latex-free equipment available from the central supply department. It may be necessary to have an emergency crash-cart available with latex-free equipment.

■ = Independent; ▲ = Collaborative

Latex Allergy Response–cont'd

Actions/Interventions

■ Use powder-free, nonlatex gloves for any care activities requiring glove use.

Rationale

Cornstarch powder is added to latex gloves during manufacturing. The powder reduces the stickiness of the latex to increase ease of putting on and removing gloves. Research shows that latex protein adheres to the powder. When the gloves are removed the powder with the attached latex protein is aerosolized. Inhalation of the particles in the air accounts for the respiratory symptoms experienced by the person with a latex allergy.

■ If latex products must be used (tubing, blood pressure cuffs, tourniquets), wrap the patient's extremity with cotton gauze before applying the equipment.

This measure will reduce direct contact between the patient's skin and the latex protein.

▲ Administer medications as prescribed.

Antihistamines, corticosteroids, and H_2-histamine blockers are used as premedications if the patient is undergoing procedures in which latex exposure may occur. Steroids and antihistamines can be used topically or orally to control local allergic reactions such as contact dermatitis.

▲ Initiate appropriate emergency care if the patient shows signs of an acute systemic reaction.

Measures to maintain airway patency, breathing effectiveness, and circulation are priorities. Drug therapy may include epinephrine and steroids to reverse the allergic reaction.

Education/Continuity of Care

Actions/Interventions

■ Educate the patient and family members about signs and symptoms of latex allergy reaction: skin rash; hives; flushing; itching; nasal, eye, or sinus symptoms; asthma; and shock.

Rationale

Recognition of a latex allergy reaction is necessary for prompt treatment, especially to prevent progression of the reaction to anaphylaxis.

■ Educate the patient and family members about emergency treatment, as appropriate.

Patients with a high level of latex sensitivity and their families need to learn to use injectable epinephrine at the onset of respiratory symptoms. This action is necessary to reduce the risk of anaphylaxis.

■ Educate the patient and family about sources of latex in the home and work environment.

Patients and family members need to learn about sources of latex in the home and workplace. Sources of latex include balloons, condoms and diaphragms, rubber bands, adhesive tape, erasers, toys, sports equipment, carpet backing, elastic on clothing, computer mouse pads, buttons on electronic equipment, and shoe soles.

■ Encourage the patient to wear a medical alert tag, carry identification, and notify all health care providers about latex allergy.

Proper identification is necessary to reduce accidental exposure to latex during health care procedures.

■ Encourage the patient to notify his or her employer about latex allergy and ways to reduce workplace exposure.

Modifications in the workplace are necessary to reduce exposure to latex. The National Institute for Occupational Safety and Health has educational material about latex allergy and prevention.

■ = Independent; ▲ = Collaborative

NDx **Impaired Memory**

NANDA: Inability to remember or recall bits of information or behavioral skills

Memory is the result of a complicated cognitive process used by an individual for learning, storing, and retrieving information. Cognitive abilities for reasoning, problem solving, interpreting information, and communication are dependent on the diverse and complex neural network that supports information processing. Structurally, memories are formed by the complex interactions of the hippocampus, thalamus, hypothalamus, and temporal lobes. Any change that disrupts these neural networks may result in problems with transferring information between immediate, short-term, and long-term memory. Amnesia is the complete loss of memory ability. This type of memory impairment represents an inability to recall previously learned information and an inability to learn new information. Memory impairment may be temporary or permanent. Situations that are associated with impaired memory include seizures, head trauma, strokes, cerebral infections, brain tumors, vitamin B_1 deficiency with alcohol abuse, personality disorders, and progressive degenerative dementias. Changes in recent memory often occur with organic disorders such as delirium, dementia, or chronic alcohol abuse. Diminished long-term or remote memory is associated with damage to the area of the cerebral cortex used for storage of that memory. This type of memory loss is seen in Alzheimer's disease. Post-traumatic amnesia is an indicator of the severity of a closed head injury. Slowing of information processing and impaired episodic memory are common problems with head trauma.

Common Related Factors

Fluid and electrolyte imbalance
Neurological disturbances
Excessive environmental disturbances
Anemia
Acute or chronic hypoxia
Decreased cardiac output
Medications

Defining Characteristics

Inability to recall factual information
Inability to recall recent or past events
Inability to learn or retain new skills or information
Inability to determine if a behavior was performed
Observed or reported experience of forgetting
Inability to perform a previously learned skill
Forgets to perform a behavior at a scheduled time

Common Expected Outcomes

Patient is able to recall immediate, recent, and remote information accurately within limits of disease.
Patient is able to maintain attention and respond appropriately to environmental cues within limits of disease.
Patient is oriented to time, person, place, and self within limits of disease.

NOC Outcomes
Memory; Cognitive Orientation; Concentration

NIC Interventions
Memory Training; Reality Orientation

Ongoing Assessment

Actions/Interventions

■ Assess neurological function with special attention to the mental status portion of the examination (e.g., Mini-Mental State Examination)
 • Orientation to time. What is the year, season, month, day, and date?
 • Orientation to place. Where are we now (state, city, and building)?

Rationale

Memory is associated with cognitive information processing. Changes in memory will be most evident during the mental status examination of the patient.
The Mini-Mental State Examination is a simplified scoring tool for assessing changes in cognitive function. The tool will provide information about immediate, recent, and long-term memory function.

■ = Independent; ▲ = Collaborative

Impaired Memory—cont'd

Actions/Interventions	Rationale
• Registration and recall of three words • Serial 7's subtraction • Naming familiar objects • Repetition of a phrase • Following a two-step direction • Reading • Writing a sentence • Copying a figure	
■ Assess for behavioral changes such as anxiety, combativeness, or withdrawal.	The patient with memory loss and diminished orientation may exhibit restlessness, anxiety, agitation, aggressiveness, and combativeness.
■ Include family members and caregivers in the assessment of the patient.	Patients may not be able to provide detailed information about their past history or health status.
■ Assess the impact of memory loss on the patient and family members. Give special attention to assessing safety issues in the patient's living situation.	Memory loss can limit the patient's day-to-day functioning. The patient may be unable to effectively manage family and occupational responsibilities. The patient's safety may be impaired as memory loss interferes with other cognitive abilities to problem solve and make judgments. Patients may forget to turn off stoves or water faucets. Family members may experience increased frustration and stress as they cope with the patient's memory loss and safety concerns.
■ Assess quality of sleep.	Normal sleep plays a role in the consolidation of memories. Inadequate sleep can limit cognitive functions such as formation of memories and new learning.
▲ Refer the patient for diagnostic testing.	Neurological and laboratory testing are indicated to rule out problems that may account for memory loss. Blood tests provide information on electrolyte imbalances or anemia. Hemodynamic assessments provide information on oxygen saturation and cardiac output. Diagnostic testing may include computed tomography scan, magnetic resonance imaging, lumbar puncture, and electroencephalogram. Psychoneurological evaluation by a trained specialist is important to arrive at a diagnosis of conditions such as Alzheimer's disease.

Therapeutic Interventions

Actions/Interventions	Rationale
■ Provide reality orientation for the patient at every contact. For example, address the patient by name, introduce yourself, and review the day, time, location, and activity being completed.	The patient with impaired memory will have difficulty maintaining orientation to the immediate environment. Reality orientation helps the patient remain mentally integrated with the immediate environment. Misinterpretations by the patient can be clarified immediately.
■ Provide a low stimulation environment.	Excessive auditory and visual stimulation can add to disorientation and confusion. The patient needs a setting with limited distractions to enhance accurate information processing.

■ = Independent; ▲ = Collaborative

Nursing Diagnosis Care Plans

Impaired Memory

Actions/Interventions

■ Ask the patient about recent events.

■ Encourage the patient to reminisce about past experiences.

■ Provide opportunities for repeated practice of new information using an errorless learning approach.

■ Encourage use of games and puzzles as appropriate.

▲ Refer the patient to a professional counselor, as needed.

▲ Administer medications as prescribed.

Rationale

Review of events in response to questions assists the patient in encoding information for retrieval at a later time.

The mental stimulation that occurs with recall and review of life events can enhance information retrieval from remote memory.

An errorless learning approach provides the person with the correct information each time it is needed. The person then records the information in a memory aid such as a notebook or computer. When errors occur in learning new information, it impedes memory development of correct information.

Games such as crossword puzzles, jigsaw puzzles, or chess have been shown to aid in stimulating important neural centers that enhance memory function.

The patient with memory loss associated with psychogenic problems may benefit from talk therapy.

Thiamine may be given to patients with memory loss associated with Wernicke encephalopathy from alcohol abuse. Improvement in memory has been seen in patients treated with clonidine and vasopressin. Patients with Alzheimer's disease may receive medications that slow the progression of the disorder and preserve memory function for a short period of time.

Education/Continuity of Care

Actions/Interventions

■ Educate the patient and family about using memory techniques.

• Mnemonic devices

• Imagery

• External memory aids such as calendars, alarms, timers, posted notes, lists, computers, and memory notebooks

▲ Refer the patient and family to community resources to assist in creating safe living environments.

Rationale

Learning to use memory aids is a memory task itself. The patient may need extended time and reinforcement to become successful in using these techniques.

This internal approach to memory rehabilitation uses a variety of verbal and/or visual techniques to facilitate the encoding and retrieval of information.

Visual imagery techniques can be used to assist the patient in organizing and retrieving information.

These external strategies rely on environmental approaches to assist the patient in developing behavioral consistency to compensate for memory loss. Research indicates that external memory aids have more value than internal techniques. Learning to use them can be challenging for the patient.

Patients with impaired memory may no longer be able to live alone or with family members because of safety issues. The family may need help in finding alternative living arrangements for the patient such as supervised group homes or assisted living.

> • RELATED CARE PLANS
>
> Alzheimer's disease/dementia, p. 544
> Chronic confusion, p. 43

■ = Independent; ▲ = Collaborative

Impaired Physical Mobility

Immobility

NANDA: Limitation in independent, purposeful physical movement of the body or of one or more extremities

Alteration in mobility may be a temporary or more permanent problem. Most disease and rehabilitative states involve some degree of immobility (e.g., as seen in strokes, leg fracture, trauma, morbid obesity, and multiple sclerosis). With the longer life expectancy for most Americans, the incidence of disease and disability continues to grow. And with shorter hospital stays, patients are being transferred to rehabilitation facilities or sent home for physical therapy in the home environment.

Mobility is also related to body changes from aging. Loss of muscle mass, reduction in muscle strength and function, stiffer and less mobile joints, and gait changes affecting balance can significantly compromise the mobility of older patients. Mobility is paramount if older patients are to maintain any independent living. Restricted movement affects the performance of most activities of daily living (ADLs). Older patients are also at increased risk for the complications of immobility. Nursing goals are to maintain functional ability, prevent additional impairment of physical activity, and ensure a safe environment.

Common Related Factors

Activity intolerance
Perceptual or cognitive impairment
Musculoskeletal impairment
Neuromuscular impairment
Medical restrictions
Prolonged bed rest
Limited strength
Pain or discomfort
Depression or severe anxiety

Defining Characteristics

Inability to move purposefully within physical environment, including bed mobility, transfers, and ambulation
Reluctance to attempt movement
Limited range of motion (ROM)
Decreased muscle endurance, strength, control, or mass
Imposed restrictions of movement including mechanical, medical protocol, and impaired coordination
Inability to perform action as instructed

Common Expected Outcomes

Patient performs physical activity independently or with assistive devices as needed.
Patient is free of complications of immobility, as evidenced by intact skin, absence of thrombophlebitis, and normal bowel pattern.

NOC Outcomes

Ambulation: Walking;
    Joint Movement: Active; Mobility Level

NIC Interventions

Exercise Therapy: Ambulation;
    Joint Mobility; Fall Precautions;
    Positioning; Bed Rest Care

Ongoing Assessment

Actions/Interventions

■ Assess for impediments to mobility (see Common Related Factors above).

■ Assess the patient's ability to perform ADLs effectively and safely on a daily basis using an appropriate assessment tool, such as the functional independence measures (FIM).

Rationale

Identifying the specific cause (e.g., chronic arthritis versus stroke versus chronic neurological disease) guides design of an optimal treatment plan.

Restricted movement affects the ability to perform most ADLs. A variety of assessment tools are available, depending on the clinical setting. Such tools provide objective data for baselines.

■ = Independent; ▲ = Collaborative

Impaired Physical Mobility

Actions/Interventions

■ Assess ability to perform ROM to all joints.

■ Assess the patient's or caregiver's knowledge of immobility and its implications.

■ Assess for developing thrombophlebitis (e.g., calf pain, Homans' sign, redness, localized swelling, and rise in temperature).

■ Assess skin integrity. Check for signs of redness and tissue ischemia (especially over ears, shoulders, elbows, sacrum, hips, heels, ankles, and toes).

■ Monitor input and output record and nutritional pattern. Assess nutritional needs as they relate to immobility (e.g., possible hypocalcemia, negative nitrogen balance).

■ Assess elimination status (e.g., usual pattern, present patterns, signs of constipation).

■ Assess emotional response to disability or limitation.

■ Evaluate need for home assistance (e.g., physical therapy, visiting nurse).

■ Evaluate the need for assistive devices.

■ Evaluate the safety of the immediate environment.

Rationale

This provides baseline measurement for future evaluation and guides therapy. Testing by a physical therapist may be needed.

Even patients who are temporarily immobile are at risk for effects of immobility such as skin breakdown, muscle weakness, thrombophlebitis, constipation, pneumonia, and depression.

Bed rest or immobility promotes clot formation.

Regular examination of the skin (especially over bony prominences) will allow for prevention or early recognition and treatment of pressure sores.

Pressure sores develop more quickly in patients with a nutritional deficit. Proper nutrition also provides needed energy for participating in an exercise or rehabilitative program.

Immobility promotes constipation.

Acceptance of temporary or more permanent limitations can vary widely among individuals. Each person has his or her own definition of acceptable quality of life.

Obtaining appropriate assistance for the patient can ensure safe and proper progression of activity.

Proper use of wheelchairs, canes, transfer bars, and other assistance can promote activity and reduce danger of falls.

Obstacles such as throw rugs, children's toys, and pets can further impede one's ability to ambulate safely.

Therapeutic Interventions

Actions/Interventions

■ Encourage and facilitate early ambulation and other ADLs when possible. Assist with each initial change: dangling legs, sitting in chair, ambulation.

■ Facilitate transfer training by teaching or using appropriate techniques or devices when transferring patients to bed, chair, or stretcher.

■ Encourage appropriate use of assistive devices in the home setting.

■ Provide positive reinforcement during activity.

■ Allow the patient to perform tasks at his or her own rate. Do not rush the patient. Encourage independent activity as able and safe.

■ Keep side rails up and bed in low position.

Rationale

The sooner the patient becomes mobile, the less chance that debilitation will occur.

This allows the patient to see or use information immediately, thus enhancing retention. The physical or occupational therapist usually provides guidance as to type of transfer required.

Mobility aids can increase level of mobility.

Patients may be reluctant to move or initiate new activity due to a fear of falling. A positive approach allows the learner to feel good about learning accomplishments.

Hospital workers and family caregivers are often in a hurry and do more for patients than needed, thereby slowing the patient's recovery and reducing his or her self-esteem.

This promotes a safe environment.

■ = Independent; ▲ = Collaborative

Impaired Physical Mobility—cont'd

Actions/Interventions

- For inpatients, initiate fall prevention protocol.
- Turn and position the patient every 2 hours or as needed.
- Maintain limbs in functional alignment (e.g., with pillows, sandbags, wedges, or prefabricated splints). Support feet in dorsiflexed position. Use bed cradle.

- Perform passive or active assistive ROM exercises to all extremities.

- Encourage resistance training exercises using light weights when appropriate.

- Turn the patient to prone or semiprone position once daily unless contraindicated.
- Use pressure-relieving devices as indicated (e.g., gel mattresses).
- Use antiembolic stockings and/or sequential compression devices as appropriate.
- Clean, dry, and moisturize skin as needed.

- Encourage coughing and deep-breathing exercises. Use suction as needed. Use incentive spirometer.

- Encourage liquid intake of 2000 to 3000 mL/day unless contraindicated.
- Initiate supplemental high-protein feedings as appropriate. If impairment results from obesity, initiate nutritional counseling as indicated.
- ▲ Set up a bowel program (e.g., adequate fluid, foods high in bulk, physical activity, stool softeners, laxatives) as needed. Record bowel activity level.

- ▲ Administer medications as appropriate.

- Teach energy-saving techniques.
- Assist the patient in accepting limitations. Emphasize abilities.

Rationale

Patient safety is a priority.

Turning patients optimizes circulation to all tissues and relieves pressure.

Maintaining proper alignment of extremities prevents contractures such as footdrop and/or excessive plantar flexion or tightness. Heavy bed linens can cause improper alignment of feet.

Exercise promotes increased venous return, prevents stiffness, and maintains muscle strength and endurance. To be most effective, all joints should be exercised to prevent contractures.

Research supports that strength training and other forms of exercise in older adults can preserve the ability to maintain independent living status and reduce risk of falling.

This positioning drains the bronchial tree.

This prevents tissue breakdown.

These promote increased venous return to prevent thrombophlebitis in the legs.

These measures reduce skin breakdown from prolonged immobility.

These prevent buildup of secretions. Incentive spirometry increases lung expansion. Decreased chest excursions and stasis of secretions are associated with immobility.

Liquids optimize hydration status and prevent hardening of stool.

Proper nutrition is required to maintain adequate energy level.

Prolonged bed rest, lack of exercise, and physical inactivity contribute to constipation. A variety of interventions will promote normal elimination.

Antispasmodic medications may reduce muscle spasms or spasticity that interferes with mobility.

These optimize the patient's limited reserves.

Quality of life is influenced by a variety of factors that can extend beyond only physical function.

Education/Continuity of Care

Actions/Interventions

- Explain progressive activity to the patient. Help the patient or caregivers establish reasonable and obtainable goals.

Rationale

Information promotes awareness of the treatment plan. Setting small, attainable goals helps increase self-confidence and promotes adherence.

■ = Independent; ▲ = Collaborative

Actions/Interventions

- Instruct the patient or caregivers regarding hazards of immobility. Emphasize importance of measures such as position change, ROM, coughing, and exercises.
- Reinforce principles of progressive exercise, emphasizing that joints are to be exercised to the point of pain, not beyond.
- Instruct the patient and family regarding the need to make the home environment safe.
- ▲ Refer the patient to the multidisciplinary health team as appropriate.

Rationale

Information enables the patient to assume some control over the rehabilitative process.

"No pain, no gain" is not always true!

A safe environment will help prevent injury related to falls.

Physical therapists can provide specialized services.

> • **RELATED CARE PLAN**
>
> Risk for falls, p. 59

 **Nausea**

NANDA: An unpleasant, wavelike sensation in the back of the throat, epigastrium, or throughout the abdomen, that may or may not lead to vomiting

Nausea is a common and distressing symptom with a myriad of causes, including intracranial or labyrinthine lesions, chemical stimulation of the vomiting center by most medications, ingestion of toxins (chemotherapy), microorganisms in the gastrointestinal tract, gastrointestinal obstruction, improper gastric emptying, or mucosal diseases. Nausea may have psychogenic origins, which should be considered in cases of chronic nausea or gastroparesis. Nausea can also be associated with severe pain or aberrant motion such as in carsickness or seasickness. During the first trimester of pregnancy, nausea is common and may be related to excessive hormone production. For most women, this subsides by their second trimester; for other women, mild nausea may persist throughout the pregnancy.

Common Related Factors

Treatment related:
- Gastric irritation (drugs, alcohol, iron, blood)
- Gastric distention
- Pharmaceuticals (e.g., analgesics, medications for human immunodeficiency virus, aspirin, opioids, chemotherapy agents)

Biophysical:
- Biochemical disorders (e.g., uremia, pregnancy)
- Cardiac pain
- Cancer of stomach or colon
- Gastrointestinal diseases
- Tumors
- Motion sickness
- Physical factors (e.g., increased intracranial pressure)
- Toxins

Situational:
- Psychological factors (e.g., fear, pain, noxious stimuli)

Defining Characteristics

Reports "nausea" or "sick to stomach." Usually precedes vomiting, but may be experienced after vomiting or when vomiting does occur.

Increased salivation

Increased swallowing movements affected by skeletal muscle

Gagging sensation

Sour taste in mouth

Accompanied by pallor; cold and clammy skin

> ■ = Independent; ▲ = Collaborative

Nursing Diagnosis Care Plans

 **Nausea**–cont'd

Common Expected Outcome

Patient reports diminished severity or elimination of nausea.

> **NOC Outcomes**
> Comfort Level; Symptom Severity; Hydration; Nutritional Status: Food and Fluid Intake
>
> **NIC Interventions**
> Nausea Management; Medication Management; Fluid Monitoring

Ongoing Assessment

Actions/Interventions	Rationale
■ Assess for cause of nausea.	Determining the cause of the nausea will guide the choice of interventions to be used. Surgery may even be required to treat some etiologies.
■ Assess nausea characteristics: • History • Duration • Frequency • Severity • Precipitating factors • Medications • Measures used to alleviate the problem	A comprehensive assessment of the nausea can help determine interventions to minimize or alleviate the problem.
■ Assess hydration status such as measuring daily weights, blood pressure, and intake and output, and assessing skin turgor.	Nausea is often associated with vomiting that can alter a patient's hydration status.

Therapeutic Interventions

Actions/Interventions	Rationale
■ Assist the patient in preparation for diagnostic testing as ordered.	A variety of tests may be used to determine the etiology of the nausea (e.g., upper gastrointestinal study, abdominal computed tomography scan, ultrasound).
■ Keep emesis basin within easy reach of the patient.	Nausea is often associated with vomiting. Keep emesis basin out of sight but in easy reach if nausea has a psychogenic component.
■ Offer and/or assist with oral hygiene every 2 to 4 hours if tolerated.	Nausea is often associated with anorexia and increased salivation. Oral hygiene will help promote comfort.
■ Remove noxious odors from the room (e.g., perfumes, dressings, emesis).	Strong or noxious odors can contribute to nausea.
■ Offer cold water, ice chips, ginger products, room-temperature broth, or bouillon if tolerated and appropriate to diet.	These fluids help with hydration. For some patients, ginger helps relieve nausea whether in ginger ale, ginger tea, or chewed as crystallized ginger. Fluids with extreme temperatures may be difficult to tolerate.
■ Offer frequent, small amounts of foods that appeal to the patient: • Dry foods like toast or crackers	This will help maintain nutritional status; for some patients, an empty stomach exacerbates the nausea. Dry toast or crackers before rising are especially known to be effective for pregnancy-related nausea.

■ = Independent; ▲ = Collaborative

Actions/Interventions

- • Bland, simple foods like broth, rice, bananas, or Jell-O
- • Avoid greasy or fried foods
- ■ Encourage the patient to use nonpharmacological nausea control techniques such as relaxation, guided imagery, music therapy, distraction, or deep breathing.

- ▲ Administer antiemetics as ordered.

- ■ Apply acustimulation bands as ordered or apply acupressure.

Rationale

Patients may tolerate these types of foods. They should try to eat more when nausea is absent.

Fats are difficult to digest and may exacerbate the nausea.

These techniques have helped patients manage their nausea, but they need to be used before nausea occurs or increases, as well as with other nausea control measures.

Most antiemetics act by raising the threshold of the chemoreceptor trigger zone to stimulation. Other drugs that may be used to treat nausea include antihistamines, anticholinergics, dopamine antagonists, and benzodiazepines. A variety of newer antiemetic drugs are available and effective to treat chemotherapy-induced nausea and vomiting.

Stimulation of the Neiguan P6 acupuncture point on the ventral surface of the wrist has been found to control nausea in some patients.

Education/Continuity of Care

Actions/Interventions

- ■ Teach the patient to change positions slowly.
- ■ Teach the patient or caregiver about appropriate fluid and dietary choices for nausea.

- ■ Teach the patient or caregiver nonpharmacological nausea control techniques such as relaxation, guided imagery, music therapy, distraction, or deep breathing.
- ■ Teach the patient to take prescribed medications as ordered.
- ■ Evaluate the patient's response to antiemetics or interventions to alleviate nausea.

- ■ Teach the patient or caregiver how to apply acustimulation bands or acupressure.

- ■ Teach the patient or caregiver to seek medical care if vomiting develops or persists longer than 24 hours.

Rationale

Sudden or gross movement may increase nausea.

Patients and caregivers can promote adequate hydration and nutritional status by knowing dietary considerations to follow when nauseated.

Teaching the patient and caregiver methods to control nausea increases the sense of personal efficacy in managing the nausea.

Appropriate timing for medications can affect outcomes.

It is important to evaluate the interventions used to determine their effectiveness or to find other interventions that may be more effective for the patient.

Patients and caregivers may want to continue with this intervention if it was found effective in controlling nausea.

Persistent vomiting can lead to dehydration, electrolyte imbalance, and nutritional deficiencies.

NDx Noncompliance

Knowledge Deficit; Patient Education

NANDA: Behavior of person and/or caregiver that fails to coincide with a health-promoting or therapeutic plan agreed on by the person (and/or family and/or community) and health care professional. In the presence of an agreed-on health-promoting or therapeutic plan, person's or caregiver's behavior is fully or partially nonadherent and may lead to clinically ineffective or partially ineffective outcomes

■ = Independent; ▲ = Collaborative

Noncompliance–cont'd

The fact that a patient has attained knowledge regarding the treatment plan does not guarantee compliance. Failure to follow the prescribed plan may be related to a number of factors. Much research has been conducted in this area to identify key predictive factors. Several theoretical models, such as the Health Belief Model, Theory of Reasoned Decision Making, and Theory of Planned Behavior, serve to explain those factors that influence patient compliance. Patients are more likely to comply when they believe that they are susceptible to an illness or disease that could seriously affect their health, that certain behaviors will reduce the likelihood of contracting the disease, that the prescribed actions are less threatening than the disease itself, and when normative groups support the change. Factors that may predict noncompliance include past history of non-compliance, stressful lifestyles, contrary cultural or religious beliefs and values, lack of social support, lack of financial resources, and compromised emotional state. People living in adverse social situations (e.g., battered women, homeless individuals, those living amid street violence, the unemployed, or those in poverty) may purposefully defer following medical recommendations until their acute socioeconomic situation is improved. The rising costs of health care, and the growing number of uninsured and underinsured patients often forces patients with limited incomes to choose between food and medications. The problem is especially complex for older patients living on fixed incomes but requiring complex and costly medical therapies.

Common Related Factors

Patient's value system
Health beliefs
Cultural beliefs
Spiritual values
Patient-provider relationships

Defining Characteristics

Behavior indicative of failure to adhere
Objective tests: improper pill counts or missed prescription refills; body fluid analysis inconsistent with compliance
Evidence of development of complications
Evidence of exacerbation of symptoms
"Revolving-door" hospital admissions
Missed appointments
Therapeutic effect not achieved or maintained

Common Expected Outcomes

Patient and/or significant other reports compliance with therapeutic plan.
Patient complies with therapeutic plan, as evidenced by appropriate pill count, appropriate amount of drug in blood or urine, evidence of therapeutic effect, maintained appointments, and/or fewer hospital admissions.

NOC Outcomes

Adherence Behavior; Compliance Behavior; Knowledge: Treatment Regimen; Participation: Health Care Decisions

NIC Interventions

Behavior Modification; Decision-Making Support; Patient Contracting; Health Education

Ongoing Assessment

Actions/Interventions

■ Assess the patient's individual perceptions of health problems.

Rationale

According to the Health Belief Model, a patient's perceived susceptibility to and perceived seriousness and threat of disease affect compliance with the treatment plan.

■ = Independent; ▲ = Collaborative

Actions/Interventions

■ Assess beliefs about current illness.

■ Assess religious beliefs or practices that affect health.

■ Assess beliefs about the treatment plan.

■ Determine reasons for noncompliance in the past.

■ Determine cultural or spiritual influences on importance of health care.

■ Compare actual therapeutic effect with expected effect.

■ Plot pattern of hospitalizations and clinic appointments.

■ Ask the patient to bring prescription drugs to appointments; count remaining pills.

▲ Assess serum or urine drug level.

Rationale

Determining what the patient thinks is causing his or her symptoms or disease, how likely it is that the symptoms may return, and any concerns about the diagnosis or symptoms will provide a basis for planning future care. Persons of other cultures and religious heritages may hold differing views regarding health and illness. For some cultures the causative agent may be a person, not a microbe.

Many people view illness as a punishment from God that must be treated through spiritual healing practices (e.g., prayer, pilgrimage), not medications.

Understanding any worries or misconceptions that the patient may have about the plan or side effects will guide future interventions.

Such reasons may include cognitive impairment, fear of actually experiencing medication side effects, failure to understand instructions regarding the plan (e.g., difficulty understanding a low-sodium diet), impaired manual dexterity (e.g., pill container is too difficult to open), sensory deficit (e.g., unable to read written instructions), and regard for nontraditional treatments (e.g., herbs, liniments, prayer, acupuncture).

Not all persons view maintenance of health the same. For example, some may place trust in God for treatment and refuse pills, blood transfusions, or surgery. Others may only want to follow a "natural" or "health food" regimen.

This provides information on compliance; however, if therapy is ineffective or based on a faulty diagnosis, even perfect compliance will not result in the expected therapeutic effect.

This provides objective information regarding follow-up, but does not necessarily mean the patient is not complying with other prescribed therapies.

This provides some objective evidence of compliance. This technique is commonly used in drug research protocols.

Therapeutic blood levels will not be achieved without consistent ingestion of medication; overdosage or over-treatment can likewise be assessed.

Therapeutic Interventions

Actions/Interventions

■ Develop a therapeutic relationship with the patient and family.

■ Include patient in planning the treatment regimen.

■ Remove disincentives to compliance.

Rationale

Compliance increases when there is a trusting relationship and a consistent caregiver. Use of a skilled interpreter is necessary for patients who do not speak the dominant language.

Patients who become co-managers of their care have a greater stake in achieving a positive outcome.

Actions such as decreasing waiting time in the clinic, recommending lower levels of activity, or suggesting medications that do not cause side effects that are unacceptable to the patient can improve compliance.

■ = Independent; ▲ = Collaborative

Noncompliance–cont'd

Actions/Interventions

▲ Simplify therapy. Suggest long-acting forms of medications and eliminate unnecessary medication. Eliminate unnecessary clinic visits.

■ Tailor the therapy to the patient's lifestyle (e.g., diuretics may be taken with the evening meal for patients who work outside the home) and culture (incorporate herbal medicinal massage or prayer, as appropriate).

■ Increase the amount of supervision provided; as compliance improves, gradually reduce the amount of professional supervision and reinforcement.

■ Develop a behavioral contract.

■ Develop with the patient a system of rewards that follow successful compliance.

Rationale

Compliance increases when therapy is short and includes as few treatments as possible. The physical demands and financial burdens of traveling must be considered.

This will ensure a patient-centered focus and promote compliance. A "one size fits all" approach is usually ineffective.

Home health nurses, telephone monitoring, and frequent return visits or appointments can provide increased supervision as needed that can be tapered as appropriate.

This helps the patient understand and accept his or her role in the care plan and clarifies what the patient can expect from the health care worker or system.

Rewards provide positive reinforcement for compliant behavior.

Education/Continuity of Care

Actions/Interventions

■ Provide specific instruction as indicated.

■ Tailor the information in terms of what the patient feels is the cause of his or her health problem and his or her concerns about therapy.

■ Teach significant others to eliminate disincentives and/or increase rewards to the patient for compliance.

■ Provide social support through the patient's family and self-help groups.

■ Explore community resources.

Rationale

Information enables the patient to better take control in selecting and implementing required changes in behavior.

Adult learning is problem oriented. Focus should be on strategies that reduce barriers to treatment and enhance desired outcome.

Nagging is never effective in promoting change. Incorporating rewards for positive accomplishments is more effective.

Such groups may assist the patient in gaining greater understanding of the benefits of treatment.

Churches, social clubs, and community groups can play a dominant role in some cultures. Outreach workers from a given community may effectively serve as a bridge to the health care provider.

Imbalanced Nutrition: Less Than Body Requirements

Starvation; Weight Loss; Anorexia

NANDA: Intake of nutrients insufficient to meet metabolic needs

Adequate nutrition is necessary to meet the body's demands. Nutritional status can be affected by disease or injury states (e.g., gastrointestinal malabsorption, cancer, burns); physical factors (e.g., muscle weakness, poor dentition, activity intolerance, pain, substance abuse); social factors (e.g., lack of financial resources to obtain nutritious foods); or

■ = Independent; ▲ = Collaborative

psychological factors (e.g., depression, boredom, dementia). During times of illness (e.g., trauma, surgery, sepsis, burns), adequate nutrition plays an important role in healing and recovery. Cultural and religious factors strongly affect the food habits of patients. Women exhibit a higher incidence of voluntary restriction of food intake secondary to anorexia, bulimia, and self-constructed fad dieting. Patients who are older experience problems in nutrition related to lack of financial resources, cognitive impairments causing them to forget to eat, physical limitations that interfere with preparing food, deterioration of their sense of taste and smell, reduction of gastric secretion that accompanies aging and interferes with digestion, and social isolation and boredom that cause a lack of interest in eating. This care plan addresses general concerns related to nutritional deficits for the hospital or home setting.

Common Related Factors

Inability to ingest foods
Inability to digest foods
Inability to absorb or metabolize foods
Inability to procure adequate amounts of food
Knowledge deficit
Unwillingness to eat
Increased metabolic needs caused by disease process or therapy

Defining Characteristics

Loss of weight with or without adequate caloric intake
10% to 20% below ideal body weight
Documented inadequate caloric intake

Common Expected Outcomes

Patient or caregiver verbalizes and demonstrates selection of foods or meals that will achieve a cessation of weight loss.
Patient weighs within 10% of ideal body weight.

NOC Outcomes
Nutritional Status: Food and Fluid Intake;
   Nutritional Status: Nutrient Intake

NIC Interventions
Nutrition Monitoring; Nutrition Therapy;
   Nutrition Management

Ongoing Assessment

Actions/Interventions	Rationale
■ Document actual weight and height; do not estimate.	Patients may be unaware of their actual weight and height or weight loss due to estimating weight.
■ Obtain nutritional history; include family, significant others, or caregiver in assessment.	The patient's perception of actual intake may differ.
■ Determine etiological factors for reduced nutritional intake.	Proper assessment guides intervention. For example, patients with dentition problems require referral to a dentist, whereas patients with memory losses may require services such as Meals On Wheels.
■ Monitor or explore attitudes toward eating and food.	Many psychological, psychosocial, and cultural factors determine the type, amount, and appropriateness of food consumed.
■ Monitor the environment in which eating occurs.	Fewer families today have a general meal together. Many adults find themselves "eating on the run" (e.g., at their desk, in the car) or relying heavily on fast foods with reduced nutritional components.

■ = Independent; ▲ = Collaborative

Imbalanced Nutrition: Less Than Body Requirements

Imbalanced Nutrition: Less Than Body Requirements–cont'd

Actions/Interventions	Rationale
■ Encourage patient participation in recording food intake using a daily log.	Determination of type, amount, and pattern of food or fluid intake is facilitated by accurate documentation by the patient or caregiver as the intake occurs; memory is insufficient.
▲ Monitor laboratory values that indicate nutritional well-being or deterioration:	
• Serum albumin	This indicates degree of protein depletion (2.5 g/dL indicates severe depletion; 3.8 to 4.5 g/dL is normal).
• Transferrin	This is important for iron transfer and typically decreases as serum protein decreases.
• Red blood cell and white blood cell counts	These are usually decreased in malnutrition, indicating anemia and decreased resistance to infection.
• Serum electrolyte values	Potassium is typically increased and sodium is typically decreased in malnutrition.
■ Weigh patient weekly.	During aggressive nutritional support, patient can gain up to 0.5 pound per day.

Therapeutic Interventions

Actions/Interventions	Rationale
▲ Consult dietitian for further assessment and recommendations regarding food preferences and nutritional support.	Dietitians have a greater understanding of the nutritional value of foods and may be helpful in assessing specific ethnic or cultural foods (e.g., "soul foods," Hispanic dishes, kosher foods).
■ Establish appropriate short- and long-range goals.	Depending on the etiological factors of the problem, improvement in nutritional status may take a long time. Without realistic short-term goals to provide tangible rewards, patients may lose interest in addressing this problem.
■ Suggest ways to assist the patient with meals, as needed. Ensure a pleasant environment, facilitate proper position, and provide good oral hygiene and dentition.	Elevating the head of bed 30 degrees aids in swallowing and reduces risk of aspiration.
■ Provide companionship during mealtime.	Attention to the social aspects of eating is important in both the hospital and home settings.
■ For patients with changes in sense of taste, encourage use of seasoning.	Seasoning may enhance the flavor of foods and entice eating.
▲ For patients with physical impairments, refer to occupational therapist for adaptive devices.	The occupational therapist can offer devices such as plate guards and strap-on utensils that can help patients feed themselves.
■ For hospitalized patients, encourage the family to bring food from home as appropriate.	Patients with specific ethnic or religious preferences or restrictions may not be able to eat hospital foods.
■ Suggest liquid drinks for supplemental nutrition.	Such supplements can be used to increase calories and protein without interfering with voluntary food intake.
■ Discourage beverages that are caffeinated or carbonated.	These may decrease appetite and lead to early satiety.

■ = Independent; ▲ = Collaborative

Actions/Interventions

- Discuss possible need for enteral or parenteral nutritional support with patient, family, and caregiver, as appropriate.

- Encourage exercise.

Rationale

Enteral tube feedings are preferred for patients with a functioning gastrointestinal tract. Feedings may be continuous or intermittent (bolus). Parenteral nutrition may be indicated for patients who cannot tolerate enteral feedings. Either solution can be modified to provide required glucose, protein, electrolytes, vitamins, minerals, and trace elements. Fat and fat-soluble vitamins can also be administered two or three times per week. These feedings may be used with in-hospital, long-term care, and subacute care settings, as well as in the home.

Metabolism and utilization of nutrients are enhanced by activity.

Education/Continuity of Care

Actions/Interventions

- Review and reinforce the following to the patient or caregivers:
  - The basic four food groups, as well as the need for specific minerals or vitamins
  - Importance of maintaining adequate caloric intake; an average adult (70 kg) needs 1800 to 2200 kcal/day; patients with burns, severe infections, or draining wounds may require 3000 to 4000 kcal/day
  - Foods high in calories and protein that will promote weight gain and nitrogen balance (e.g., small frequent meals of foods high in calories and protein)
- Provide referral to community nutritional resources such as Meals On Wheels or hot lunch programs for seniors as indicated.

Rationale

Patients may not understand what is involved in a balanced diet. They are better able to ask questions and seek assistance when they know basic information.

Many seniors (especially those living alone) do not take the time or effort to cook for themselves.

NDx Imbalanced Nutrition: More Than Body Requirements

Obesity; Overweight

NANDA: Intake of nutrients that exceeds metabolic needs

Obesity is a growing problem in the United States and is now reaching pandemic proportions, accounting for significant other health problems including cardiovascular disease, insulin-dependent diabetes, sleep disorders, infertility in women, aggravated musculoskeletal problems, and shortened life expectancy. Women are more likely to be overweight than men. African Americans and Hispanic individuals are more likely to be overweight than whites. Factors that affect weight gain include genetics, sedentary lifestyle, emotional factors associated with dysfunctional eating, disease states such as diabetes mellitus and Cushing's syndrome, and cultural or ethnic influences on eating. Overall nutritional requirements of older patients are similar to those of younger individuals, except calories should be reduced because of their leaner body mass.

> ■ = Independent; ▲ = Collaborative

Imbalanced Nutrition: More Than Body Requirements

> ## Imbalanced Nutrition: More Than Body Requirements–cont'd

Common Related Factors

Excessive intake in relation to metabolic need
Lack of knowledge of nutritional needs, food intake, and/or appropriate food preparation
Poor dietary habits
Use of food as coping mechanism
Metabolic disorders
Sedentary activity level

Defining Characteristics

Weight 20% over ideal for height and frame
Triceps skinfold greater than 15 mm in men, 25 mm in women
Reported or observed dysfunctional eating patterns
Eating in response to internal cues other than hunger
Eating in response to external cues such as time of day or social situation

Common Expected Outcomes

Patient verbalizes measures necessary to achieve weight reduction.
Patient demonstrates appropriate selection of meals or menu planning toward the goal of weight reduction.
Patient begins an appropriate program of exercise.

NOC Outcomes
Nutritional Status: Food and Fluid Intake; Weight Control

NIC Interventions
Nutritional Monitoring; Nutrition Counseling; Weight Reduction Assistance

Ongoing Assessment

Actions/Interventions

- Document weight and height; do not estimate.

- Determine body fat composition by skinfold measurements.

- Calculate body mass index (BMI) as a ratio of height and weight.

- Perform a nutritional assessment.

- Explore the importance and meaning of food with the patient.

- Assess knowledge regarding nutritional needs for height and level of activity or other factors (e.g., pregnancy).

- Assess ability to read food labels.

- Assess ability to plan a menu, making appropriate food selections.

Rationale

Patients may be unaware of their actual weight and height.

Skin calipers can be used to estimate amount of fat.

BMI is the person's weight in kilograms divided by the square of his or her height in meters. A BMI between 20 and 24 is associated with healthier outcomes. BMIs greater than 25 are associated with increased morbidity and mortality.

This includes types and amount of food, how food is prepared, intake pattern (e.g., time of day, frequency, other activities patient does while eating).

When food is used as a coping mechanism or as a self-reward, the emotional needs being met by intake of food will need to be addressed as part of the overall plan for weight reduction. In most cultures, eating is a social activity.

A person's height, activity level, or other factors can influence their caloric needs.

Food labels contain information necessary in making appropriate selections, but can be misleading. Patients need to understand that "low-fat" or "fat-free" does not mean that a food item is calorie-free. In addition, attention should be paid to serving size and the number of servings in the food item.

Cultural or ethnic influences need to be identified and addressed.

■ = Independent; ▲ = Collaborative

Imbalanced Nutrition: More Than Body Requirements

Actions/Interventions

- Assess ability to accurately identify appropriate food portions.
- Assess effects or complications of being overweight.

- Assess usual level of activity.

Rationale

Serving sizes must be understood to limit intake according to a planned diet.

Medical complications include cardiovascular and respiratory dysfunction, higher incidence of diabetes mellitus, and aggravation of musculoskeletal disorders. Social complications and poor self-esteem may also result from obesity.

Patients may confuse routine activity with exercise necessary to enhance and maintain weight loss.

Therapeutic Interventions

Actions/Interventions

- ▲ Consult dietitian for further assessment and recommendations regarding a weight loss program.

- Establish appropriate short- and long-range goals.

- Encourage calorie intake appropriate for body type and lifestyle.

- Encourage the patient to keep a daily log of food or liquid ingestion and caloric intake.

- Encourage water intake.

- Encourage the patient to be more aware of nutritional habits that may contribute to or prevent overeating, such as the following:
  - Realize the time needed for eating.

  - Focus on eating and avoid other diversional activities (e.g., reading, television viewing, or telephoning).
  - Observe for cues that lead to eating (e.g., odor, time, depression, or boredom).

  - Eat in a designated place (e.g., at the table rather than in front of the television).
  - Recognize actual hunger versus desire to eat.

- Encourage exercise.

Rationale

Changes in eating patterns are required for weight loss. The type of program may vary (e.g., three balanced meals a day, avoidance of certain high-fat foods). Dietitians have a greater understanding of the nutritional value of foods and may be helpful in assessing or substituting specific high-fat cultural or ethnic foods.

One pound of adipose tissue contains 3500 kcal. Therefore to lose 1 pound per week, the patient must have a calorie deficit of 500 kcal/day.

Diet change is a complicated process that involves changing patterns that have been firmly established by culture, family, and personal factors.

Memory is inadequate for quantification of intake, and a visual record may also help the patient make more appropriate food choices and serving sizes.

Water assists in the excretion of by-products of fat breakdown and helps prevent ketosis.

Hurried eating may result in overeating because satiety is not realized until 15 to 20 minutes after ingestion of food.

Doing several activities at once usually results in less attention being devoted to amount of food eaten.

Identifying triggers or situations that prompt eating behaviors is the first step toward developing alternative coping strategies.

This controls environmental stimuli for eating and other impulse eating.

Eating when not hungry is a commonly recognized symptom among overeaters.

Exercise is an integral part of weight reduction programs. The combination of diet and exercise promotes loss of adipose tissue rather than lean tissue.

■ = Independent; ▲ = Collaborative

Imbalanced Nutrition: More Than Body Requirements–cont'd

Actions/Interventions

- Provide positive reinforcement as indicated. Encourage successes; assist the patient to cope with setbacks.

- Incorporate behavior modification strategies.

Rationale

Positive reinforcement encourages a desired behavior. Patients need to have setbacks reframed as learning opportunities and as a normal step in making lifestyle changes.

Education as the sole intervention is unlikely to achieve and maintain weight loss. Multifactorial programs that include behavioral interventions and counseling are more successful than education alone.

Education/Continuity of Care

Actions/Interventions

- Review and reinforce teaching regarding the following:
  - Four food groups or the food pyramid

  - Proper serving size

  - Caloric content of food

  - Methods of preparation, such as substituting baking and grilling for frying foods
- Include family, caregiver, or food preparer in nutrition counseling.
- ▲ Inform the patient about pharmacological agents such as appetite suppressants that can aid in weight loss.
- Encourage diabetic patients to attend diabetic classes. Review and reinforce principles of dietary management of diabetes.
- Review complications associated with obesity.

- ▲ Refer the patient to commercial weight-loss program as appropriate.

- Remind the patient that significant weight loss requires a long period.

- ▲ Refer to community support groups as indicated.

Rationale

Patients need to learn to eat a variety of foods in appropriate portion sizes when changing their eating pattern to ensure lifelong success at weight maintenance.

Portion distortion is a growing problem in society; consumers often perceive larger portions as more value for their money, further complicating the problem.

Many patients are unaware of the calories present in low-fat foods.

These methods of food preparation decrease the fat content of food.

Success rates are higher when the family incorporates a healthy eating plan.

These drugs act by chemically altering the patient's desire to eat.

Obesity and diabetes are risk factors for coronary artery disease.

Patients need to be aware of long-term health problems as stimulus for change.

Some individuals require the regimented approach or ongoing support during weight loss, whereas others are able (and may prefer) to manage a weight-loss program independently.

Some patients are easily frustrated with the amount of time it takes to lose weight. This frustration can lead to weight loss failure. Remind patients that slow weight loss is associated with permanent weight loss.

Social support is associated with successful weight loss and weight maintenance.

■ = Independent; ▲ = Collaborative

 **ND**x **Impaired Oral Mucous Membrane**

Stomatitis; Mucositis

NANDA: Disruption of the lips and soft tissue of the oral cavity

Minor irritations of the oral mucous membrane occur occasionally in all persons and are usually viral-related, self-limiting, and easily treated. Patients who have severe stomatitis often have an underlying illness. Patients who are immunocompromised, such as the oncology patient receiving chemotherapy, are often affected with severe tissue disruption and pain. Infections such as candidiasis, if left untreated, can spread through the entire gastrointestinal tract, causing further complications and sometimes perineal pain. Oral mucous membrane problems can be encountered in any setting, especially in home care and hospice settings.

Common Related Factors

Pathological conditions—oral cavity (e.g., radiation to head or neck)
Dehydration
Trauma: chemical (e.g., acidic foods, drugs, noxious agents, alcohol); mechanical (e.g., ill-fitting dentures, braces, tubes [endotracheal or nasogastric]); surgery in oral cavity
Nothing by mouth for more than 24 hours
Ineffective oral hygiene
Mouth breathing
Malnutrition
Infection
Lack of or decreased salivation
Medication

Defining Characteristics

Oral pain or discomfort
Coated tongue
Xerostomia (dry mouth)
Stomatitis
Oral lesions or ulcers
Lack of or decreased salivation
Leukoplakia
Edema
Hyperemia
Oral plaque
Desquamation
Vesicles
Hemorrhagic gingivitis
Halitosis
Carious teeth

Common Expected Outcomes

Patient has intact oral mucosa.
Patient demonstrates appropriate oral hygiene.
Patient verbalizes relief from stomatitis.

NOC Outcomes
Oral Health; Tissue Integrity: Skin and Mucous Membranes; Self-Care: Oral Hygiene

NIC Interventions
Oral Health Restoration; Oral Health Maintenance

Ongoing Assessment

Actions/Interventions

■ Assess oral hygiene practices.

■ Assess status of oral mucosa; include tongue, lips, mucous membranes, gums, saliva, and teeth.

Rationale

Information provides direction on possible causative factors and guidance for subsequent education.

These are frequent sites for infection and irritation. Home caregivers also need to be informed of the importance of these assessments.

■ = Independent; ▲ = Collaborative

Nursing Diagnosis Care Plans

> ## Impaired Oral Mucous Membrane–cont'd

Actions/Interventions

- Use adequate source of light.
- Remove dental appliances.

- Use a moist, padded tongue blade to gently pull back the cheeks and tongue.
- Assess for extensiveness of ulcerations involving the intraoral soft tissues, including palate, tongue, gums, and lips.
- Observe for evidence of infection and report to physician or home health nurse. Severe mucositis may manifest as any of the following:
  - Candidiasis: cottage cheese–like white or pale yellowish patches on tongue, buccal mucosa, and palate
  - Herpes simplex: painful itching vesicle (typically on upper lips) that ruptures within 12 hours and becomes encrusted with a dried exudate
  - Gram-positive bacterial infection, specifically staphylococcal and streptococcal infections: dry, raised wart-like yellowish-brown, round plaques on buccal mucosa
  - Gram-negative bacterial infections: creamy to yellow-white, shiny, nonpurulent patches often seated on painful, red, superficial mucosal ulcers and erosions
  - Fevers, chills, rigors
- Assess nutrition status.

- Assess for ability to eat and drink.

Rationale

This facilitates accurate observation.

Lesions may be underlying and further irritated by the appliance.

Tongue blades expose all areas of oral cavity for inspection.

Sloughing of mucosal membrane can progress to ulceration.

Early assessment facilitates prompt treatment. Specific manifestations guide accurate treatment.

Malnutrition can be a contributing cause. Oral fluids are needed for moisture to membranes.

Inability to chew and swallow may occur secondary to pain of inflamed or ulcerated oral and/or oropharyngeal mucous membranes.

> ### Therapeutic Interventions

Actions/Interventions

For hospitalized or home care patients:

- Implement meticulous mouth care regimen after each meal and every 4 hours while awake. Caregivers need to be taught these procedures.
  (See Education/Continuity of Care section for description of oral care.)
- ▲ If signs of mild stomatitis occur (sensation of dryness and burning; mild erythema and edema along the mucocutaneous junction):
  - Increase frequency of oral hygiene by rinsing with one of the suggested solutions between brushings and once during the night.
  - Discontinue flossing if it causes pain.
  - Provide systemic or topical analgesics as ordered.

Rationale

Mouth care prevents buildup of oral plaque and bacteria. Patients with oral catheters and oxygen may require additional care.

These safety measures reduce further damage and may promote comfort.

Optimal oral care reduces buildup of bacteria.

Flossing may further aggravate the problem.

Increased sensitivity to pain is a result of thinning of oral mucosal lining.

■ = Independent; ▲ = Collaborative

Impaired Oral Mucous Membrane

Actions/Interventions	**Rationale**
■ Instruct patient that topical analgesics can be administered as "swish and swallow" or " swish and spit" 15 to 20 minutes before meals, or painted on each lesion immediately before mealtime.	A variety of options are available to patients; each must be performed as prescribed for optimal results.
• Topical analgesics include the following:	These provide a "numbing" feeling.
1. Dyclone 1%	
2. Viscous lidocaine (10 mL per dose up to 120 mL in 24 hours)	
3. Xylocaine (viscous 2%)	
4. Benadryl elixir (12.5 mg/5 mL) and an antacid mixed in equal proportions	
• Instruct the patient to hold solution for several minutes before expectorating, and not to use solution if mucosa is severely ulcerated or if drug sensitivity exists.	This technique enhances full therapeutic effect.
• Caution the patient to chew or swallow after each dose.	Numbness of throat may be experienced.
• Explain use of topical protective agents:	These agents coat the lesions and promote healing as prescribed.
• Zilactin or Zilactin-B	This contains benzocaine for pain and is painted on the lesion and allowed to dry to form a protective seal.
• Substrate of an antacid and kaolin preparation	This substance is prepared by allowing antacid to settle. The pasty residue is swabbed onto the inflamed areas and, after 15 to 20 minutes, rinsed with saline or water. The residue remains as a protectant on the lesion.
• Gelclair	This is a bioadherent oral gel that coats the oral cavity and forms a protective barrier to soothe pain.
• Palifermin	This agent decreases the incidence and duration of severe oral mucositis in patients with hematological cancers undergoing high-dose chemotherapy followed by bone marrow transplantation.
▲ For severe mucositis infection:	
• Administer local antibiotics and/or antifungal agents as ordered.	Mycostatin, nystatin, and Mycelex Troche are commonly prescribed.
• Discontinue use of toothbrush and flossing.	Brushing could increase damage to ulcerated tissues. A disposable foam stick (Toothette) or sterile cotton swab are ways to gently apply cleansing solutions.
• Continue use of lubricating ointment on the lips.	This prevents cracking.
■ For eating problems:	Dietary modifications may be necessary to promote healing and tissue integrity. The patient may need to select food and fluids that are less irritating to oral tissues. Soft, bland foods served at lukewarm or cool temperatures may feel soothing on oral tissues.
• Encourage diet high in protein and vitamins.	
• Serve foods and fluids lukewarm or cold.	
• Serve frequent small meals or snacks spaced throughout the day.	
• Encourage soft foods (e.g., mashed potatoes, puddings, custards, creamy cereals).	
• Encourage use of a straw.	
• Encourage peach, pear, or apricot nectars and fruit drinks instead of citrus juices.	
▲ Refer the patient to the dietitian for instructions on maintenance of a well-balanced diet.	Nutritional expertise may be required to optimize the therapeutic diet needed to promote healing.

■ = Independent; ▲ = Collaborative

Impaired Oral Mucous Membrane—cont'd

Education/Continuity of Care

Actions/Interventions	Rationale
Instruct the patient or caregiver to perform the following:	
■ Gently brush all surfaces of teeth, gums, and tongue with a soft nylon brush.	This loosens debris.
■ Brush with a nonirritating dentifrice such as baking soda.	This promotes further cleaning of teeth.
■ Remove and brush dentures thoroughly during and after meals and as needed.	This reduces risk of infection and improves appetite.
■ Have loose-fitting dentures adjusted.	Rubbing and irritation from ill-fitting dentures promotes disruption of the oral mucous membrane.
■ Rinse the mouth thoroughly during and after brushing.	Removing food particles decreases risk of infection related to trapped decaying food.
■ Avoid alcohol-containing mouthwashes.	Mouthwashes may dry oral mucous membranes, increasing risk for disruption of mucous membrane.
■ Use the following recommended mouth rinses: • Baking soda and water (1 teaspoon in 500 mL) • Salt (½ teaspoon), baking soda (1 teaspoon), and water (100 mL)	Commercial mouthwashes can be irritating; special formulas are better tolerated and may reduce irritation and promote healing.
■ Keep lips moist. Use a lip product or a water-soluble lubricant (e.g., K-Y jelly, Aquaphor Cream).	This prevents drying and cracking. These products minimize risk of aspirating a non–water-soluble agent.
■ Include food items with each meal that require chewing.	This stimulates gingival tissue and promotes circulation.
■ Minimize trauma to mucous membranes. Avoid use of tobacco and alcohol.	These are irritating and drying to the mucosa.
■ Avoid extremely hot or cold foods. Avoid acidic or highly spiced foods.	These are irritating to the mucosa.

NDx Acute Pain

NANDA: Unpleasant sensory and emotional experience arising from actual or potential tissue damage or described in terms of such damage (International Association for the Study of Pain); sudden or slow onset of any intensity from mild to severe with an anticipated or predictable end and a duration of less than 6 months

Pain is a highly subjective state in which a variety of unpleasant sensations and a wide range of distressing factors may be experienced by the sufferer. Pain may be a symptom of injury or illness. Pain may also arise from emotional, psychological, cultural, or spiritual distress. Pain can be very difficult to explain, because it is unique to the individual. Pain should be accepted as described by the sufferer. Pain assessment can be challenging, especially in older patients in whom cognitive impairment and sensory-perceptual deficits are more common.

■ = Independent; ▲ = Collaborative

Common Related Factors

Postoperative pain
Cardiovascular pain
Musculoskeletal pain
Obstetrical pain
Pain resulting from medical problems
Pain resulting from diagnostic procedures or medical treatments
Pain resulting from trauma
Pain resulting from emotional, psychological, spiritual, or cultural distress

Defining Characteristics

Patient reports pain
Guarding behavior, protecting body part
Self-focused
Narrowed focus (e.g., altered time perception, withdrawal from social or physical contact)
Relief or distraction behavior (e.g., moaning, crying, pacing, seeking out other people or activities, restlessness)
Facial mask of pain
Alteration in muscle tone: listlessness or flaccidity; rigidity or tension
Autonomic responses (e.g., diaphoresis; change in blood pressure [BP], pulse rate; pupillary dilation; change in respiratory rate; pallor; nausea)

Common Expected Outcome

Patient verbalizes adequate relief of pain or ability to cope with incompletely relieved pain.

NOC Outcomes
Comfort Level; Medication Response; Pain Control

NIC Interventions
Analgesic Administration; Conscious Sedation; Pain Management; Patient-Controlled Analgesia Assistance

Ongoing Assessment

Actions/Interventions

- Assess pain characteristics.
  - Quality (e.g., sharp, burning, shooting)
  - Severity (scale of 0 [meaning no pain] to 10, with 10 being the most severe)
  - Location (anatomical description)
  - Onset (gradual or sudden)
  - Duration (how long; intermittent or continuous)
  - Precipitating or relieving factors

- Observe or monitor signs and symptoms associated with pain, such as BP, heart rate, temperature, color and moisture of skin, restlessness, and ability to focus.

- Assess for probable cause of pain.

- Assess patient's knowledge of or preference for the array of pain relief strategies available.

- Evaluate the patient's response to pain and medications or therapeutics aimed at abolishing or relieving pain.

Rationale

Assessment of the pain experience is the first step in planning pain management strategies.

Other methods such as a visual analog scale or descriptive scales can be used to identify extent of pain.

Some people deny the experience of pain when it is present. Attention to associated signs may help the nurse in evaluating pain.

Different etiological factors respond better to different therapies.

Some patients may be unaware of the effectiveness of nonpharmacological methods and may be willing to try them, either with or instead of traditional analgesic medications. Often a combination of therapies (e.g., mild analgesics with distraction or heat) may be most effective.

It is important to help patients express as factually as possible (i.e., without the effect of mood, emotion, or anxiety) the effect of pain relief measures. Discrepancies between behavior or appearance and what the

■ = Independent; ▲ = Collaborative

Acute Pain–cont'd

Actions/Interventions

- Assess to what degree cultural, environmental, intrapersonal, and intrapsychic factors may contribute to pain or pain relief.

- Evaluate what the pain means to the individual.

- Assess the patient's expectations for pain relief.

- Assess the patient's willingness or ability to explore a range of techniques aimed at controlling pain.

- Assess appropriateness of the patient as a patient-controlled analgesia (PCA) candidate: no history of substance abuse; no allergy to narcotic analgesics; clear sensorium; cooperative and motivated about use; no history of renal, hepatic, or respiratory disease; manual dexterity; and no history of major psychiatric disorder.

- Monitor the patient for changes in general condition that may herald need for change in pain relief method.

- *If the patient is on PCA, assess the following:*
  - Pain relief

  - Intactness of IV line

  - Amount of pain medication the patient is requesting

  - Possible PCA complications such as excessive sedation, respiratory distress, urinary retention, nausea and vomiting, constipation, and IV site pain, redness, or swelling

- *If the patient is receiving epidural analgesia, assess the following:*
  - Pain relief

Rationale

patient says about pain relief (or lack of it) may be more a reflection of other methods that the patient is using to cope with than pain relief itself.

These variables may modify the patient's expression of his or her experience. For example, some cultures openly express feelings, whereas others restrain such expression. However, health care providers should not stereotype any patient response but rather evaluate the unique response of each patient.

The meaning of the pain will directly influence the patient's response. Some patients, especially the dying, may feel that the "act of suffering" meets a spiritual need.

Some patients may be content to have pain decreased; others will expect complete elimination of pain. This affects their perceptions of the effectiveness of the treatment modality and their willingness to participate in additional treatments.

Some patients will feel uncomfortable exploring alternative methods of pain relief. However, patients need to be informed that there are multiple ways to manage pain.

PCA is the intravenous (IV) infusion of a narcotic (usually morphine or Demerol) through an infusion pump that is controlled by the patient. This allows the patient to manage pain relief within prescribed limits. In the hospice or home setting, a nurse or caregiver may be needed to assist the patient in managing the infusion.

For example, a PCA patient becomes confused and cannot manage PCA, or a successful modality ceases to provide adequate pain relief, as in relaxation breathing.

The basal or lockout dose may need to be increased to cover the patient's pain.

If the IV is not patent, the patient will not receive pain medication.

If demands for medication are quite frequent, the patient's dosage may need to be increased. If demands are very low, the patient may require further instruction to properly use PCA.

Early assessment of complications prompts intervention.

Intermittent epidurals require redosing at intervals. Variations in anatomy may result in a "patch effect."

■ = Independent; ▲ = Collaborative

Actions/Interventions

- Numbness, tingling in extremities, a metallic taste in the mouth

- Possible epidural analgesia complications such as excessive sedation, respiratory distress, urinary retention, or catheter migration

Therapeutic Interventions

Actions/Interventions

■ Anticipate need for pain relief.

■ Respond immediately to complaint of pain.

■ Eliminate additional stressors or sources of discomfort whenever possible.

■ Provide rest periods to facilitate comfort, sleep, and relaxation.

▲ Determine the appropriate pain relief method.

Pharmacological methods include the following:

1. Nonopioids (acetaminophen), a nonselective non-steroidal antiinflammatory drug (NSAID), or a selective NSAID (e.g., COX-2 inhibitor)

2. Opioid analgesics

3. Local anesthetic agents

Nonpharmacological methods include the following:

1. Cognitive-behavioral strategies as follows:
   - Imagery

   - Distraction techniques

Rationale

These symptoms may be indicators of an allergic response to the anesthesia agent or of improper catheter placement.

Respiratory depression and intravascular infusion of anesthesia (resulting from catheter migration) can be potentially life threatening.

Rationale

One can most effectively deal with pain by preventing it. Early intervention may decrease the total amount of analgesic required.

In the midst of painful experiences, a patient's perception of time may become distorted. Prompt responses to complaints may result in decreased anxiety in the patient. Demonstrated concern for the patient's welfare and comfort fosters the development of a trusting relationship.

Patients may experience an exaggeration in pain or a decreased ability to tolerate painful stimuli if environmental, intrapersonal, or intrapsychic factors are further stressing them.

The patient's experiences of pain may become exaggerated as the result of fatigue. In a cyclic fashion, pain may result in fatigue, which may result in exaggerated pain and exhaustion. A quiet environment, a darkened room, and a disconnected phone are all measures geared toward facilitating rest.

Unless contraindicated, all patients with acute pain should receive a nonopioid analgesic around-the-clock.

NSAIDs work in peripheral tissues. Some block synthesis of prostaglandins, which stimulate nociceptors. They are effective in managing mild to moderate pain.

Opioids may be administered orally, intravenously, systemically by PCA systems or epidurally (either by bolus or continuous infusion). Intramuscular injections are not reliably absorbed. Opioids are indicated for severe pain, especially in the hospice or home setting.

Local anesthetics block pain transmission and are used for pain in specific areas of nerve distribution.

The use of a mental picture or an imagined event involves use of the five senses to distract oneself from painful stimuli.

These heighten one's concentration upon nonpainful stimuli to decrease one's awareness and experience of pain. Some methods are breathing modifications and nerve stimulation.

■ = Independent; ▲ = Collaborative

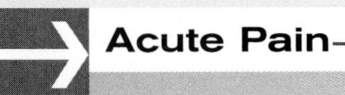

Acute Pain–cont'd

Actions/Interventions

- Relaxation exercises, biofeedback, breathing exercises, music therapy

2. Cutaneous stimulation as follows:
   - Massage of affected area when appropriate

   - Transcutaneous electrical nerve stimulation (TENS) units

   - Hot or cold compress

▲ Give analgesics as ordered, evaluating effectiveness and observing for any signs and symptoms of untoward effects.

■ Notify the physician if interventions are unsuccessful or if the current complaint is a significant change from the patient's past experience of pain.

■ Whenever possible, reassure the patient that pain is time limited and that there is more than one approach to easing pain.

If the patient is on PCA:

▲ Dedicate use of an IV line for PCA only; consult a pharmacist before mixing drug with narcotic being infused.

If the patient is receiving epidural analgesia:

■ Label all tubing (e.g., epidural catheter, IV tubing to epidural catheter) clearly to prevent inadvertent administration of inappropriate fluids or drugs into epidural space.

For the patient with PCA or epidural analgesia:

■ Keep Narcan or other narcotic-reversing agent readily available.

■ Post "No additional analgesia" sign over bed.

Rationale

Techniques are used to bring about a state of physical and mental awareness and tranquility. The goal of these techniques is to reduce tension, subsequently reducing pain.

Massage decreases muscle tension and can promote comfort.

TENS has been shown to reduce pain more commonly for chronic pain. The TENS unit requires patient education to ensure effective use.

Hot, moist compresses have a penetrating effect. The warmth rushes blood to the affected area to promote healing. Cold compresses may reduce total edema and promote some numbing, thereby promoting comfort.

Pain medications are absorbed and metabolized differently by patients, so their effectiveness must be evaluated individually by the patient. Analgesics may cause side effects that range from mild to life threatening.

Patients who request pain medications at more frequent intervals than prescribed may actually require higher doses or more potent analgesics.

When pain is perceived as everlasting and unresolvable, the patient may give up trying to cope with it or experience a sense of hopelessness and loss of control.

IV incompatibilities are possible.

Inappropriate use of an epidural catheter can cause neurological injury or infection.

In case of respiratory depression, these drugs reverse the narcotic effect.

This prevents inadvertent analgesic overdosing.

Education/Continuity of Care

Actions/Interventions

■ Provide anticipatory instruction on pain causes, appropriate prevention, and relief measures.

■ Instruct the patient to report pain.

■ Instruct the patient to evaluate and report effectiveness of measures used.

Rationale

Knowledge about what to expect can help the patient develop effective coping strategies for pain management.

Relief measures may be instituted.

Pain relief strategies can be modified to promote more satisfactory comfort levels.

■ = Independent; ▲ = Collaborative

Actions/Interventions	Rationale
■ Teach the patient effective timing of the medication dose in relation to potentially uncomfortable activities and prevention of peak pain periods.	Patients need to learn to use pain relief strategies to minimize the pain experience.
For patients on PCA or those receiving epidural analgesia:	
■ Teach the patient preoperatively.	Anesthesia effects should not obscure teaching.
■ Teach the patient the purpose, benefits, techniques of use and action, need for IV line (PCA only), other alternatives for pain control, and the need to notify the nurse of machine alarm and occurrence of untoward effects.	Effective pain management with PCA requires patient knowledge of how to use the equipment.

NDx Chronic Pain

NANDA: Unpleasant sensory and emotional experience arising from actual or potential tissue damage or described in terms of such damage (International Association for the Study of Pain); sudden or slow onset of intensity from mild to severe; constant or recurring without an anticipated or predictable end and a duration of greater than 6 months

Chronic pain may be classified as chronic malignant pain or chronic nonmalignant pain. In the former, the pain is associated with a specific cause such as cancer. With chronic nonmalignant pain, the original tissue injury is not progressive or has been healed. Identifying an organic cause for this type of chronic pain is more difficult.

Chronic pain differs from acute pain in that it is harder for the patient to provide specific information about the location and the intensity of the pain. Over time it becomes more difficult for the patient to differentiate the exact location of the pain and clearly identify the intensity of the pain. The patient with chronic pain often does not present with behaviors and physiological changes associated with acute pain. Family members, friends, co-workers, employers, and health care providers question the legitimacy of the patient's pain complaints because the patient may not look like someone in pain. The patient may be accused of using pain to gain attention or to avoid work and family responsibilities. With chronic pain, the patient's level of suffering usually increases over time. Chronic pain can have a profound impact on the patient's activities of daily living, mobility, activity tolerance, ability to work, role performance, financial status, mood, emotional status, spirituality, family interactions, and social interactions.

Common Related Factor

Chronic physical or psychosocial disability

Defining Characteristics

Weight changes
Verbal or coded report or observed evidence of protective behavior, guarding behavior, facial mask, irritability, self-focusing, restlessness, depression
Atrophy of involved muscle group
Changes in sleep pattern
Fatigue
Fear of reinjury
Reduced interaction with people
Altered ability to continue previous activities
Sympathetic mediated responses (e.g., temperature, cold, changes of body position, hypersensitivity)
Anorexia

(■ = Independent; ▲ = Collaborative)

Chronic Pain–cont'd

Common Expected Outcome

Patient verbalizes acceptable level of pain relief and ability to engage in desired activities.

NOC Outcomes

Pain Control; Quality of Life; Family Coping

NIC Interventions

Pain Management; Medication Management; Acupressure; Heat/Cold Application; Progressive Muscle Relaxation; Transcutaneous Electrical Nerve Stimulation (TENS); Simple Massage

Ongoing Assessment

Actions/Interventions

- Assess pain characteristics:
  - Quality (e.g., sharp, burning)
  - Severity (1 to 10 scale)
  - Anatomical location
  - Onset
  - Duration (e.g., continuous, intermittent)
  - Aggravating factors
  - Relieving factors

- Assess for signs and symptoms associated with chronic pain such as fatigue, decreased appetite, weight loss, changes in body posture, sleep pattern disturbance, anxiety, irritability, restlessness, or depression.

- Assess the patient's perception of the effectiveness of methods used for pain relief in the past.

- Evaluate gender, cultural, societal, and religious factors that may influence the patient's pain experience and response to pain relief.

- Assess the patient's expectations about pain relief.

- Assess the patient's attitudes toward pharmacological and nonpharmacological methods of pain management.

- For patients taking opioid analgesics, assess for side effects, dependency, and tolerance.

Rationale

Gathering information about the pain can provide information about the extent of the chronic pain.

Patients with chronic pain may not exhibit the physiological changes and behaviors associated with acute pain. Pulse and blood pressure are usually within normal ranges. The guarding behavior of acute pain may become a persistent change in body posture for the patient with chronic pain. Coping with chronic pain can deplete the patient's energy for other activities. The patient often looks tired with a drawn facial expression that lacks animation.

Patients with chronic pain have a long history of using many pharmacological and nonpharmacological methods to control their pain.

Understanding the variables that affect the patient's pain experience can be useful in developing a care plan that is acceptable to the patient.

The patient with chronic pain may not expect complete absence of pain but may be satisfied with decreasing the severity of the pain and increasing activity level.

Patients may question the effectiveness of nonpharmacological interventions and see medications as the only treatment for pain.

Drug dependence and tolerance to opioid analgesics are concerns in the long-term management of chronic pain.

■ = Independent; ▲ = Collaborative

Actions/Interventions

- Assess the patient's ability to accomplish activities of daily living, instrumental activities of daily living, and demands of daily living.

Rationale

Fatigue, anxiety, and depression associated with chronic pain can limit the person's ability to complete self-care activities and fulfill role responsibilities.

Therapeutic Interventions

Actions/Interventions

- Encourage the patient to keep a pain diary to help in identifying aggravating and relieving factors of chronic pain.

- Acknowledge and convey acceptance of the patient's pain experience.

- Provide the patient and family with information about chronic pain and options available for pain management.

- Assist the patient in making decisions about selecting a particular pain management strategy.

- Refer the patient to a physical therapist for evaluation.

Rationale

Knowledge about factors that influence the pain experience can guide the patient in making decisions about lifestyle modifications that promote more effective pain management.

The patient may have had negative experiences in the past with attitudes of health care providers toward the patient's pain experience. Conveying acceptance of the patient's pain promotes a more cooperative nurse-patient relationship.

Lack of knowledge about the characteristics of chronic pain and pain management strategies can add to the burden of pain in the patient's life.

Guidance and support from the nurse can increase the patient's willingness to choose new interventions to promote pain relief. A combination of nonpharmacological and analgesic medications may be most effective. Nonopioid medications are preferred medications because of their low side-effect profile, especially among the older patient. Medications should be given around-the-clock. The oral route is preferred.

The physical therapist can help the patient with exercises to promote muscle strength and joint mobility, and therapies to promote relaxation of tense muscles. These interventions can contribute to effective pain management.

Education/Continuity of Care

Actions/Interventions

- Teach the patient and family about using nonpharmacological pain management strategies.

  • Cold applications

  • Heat applications

Rationale

Knowledge about how to implement nonpharmacological pain management strategies can help the patient and family gain maximum benefit from these interventions.

Cold reduces pain, inflammation, and muscle spasticity by decreasing the release of pain-inducing chemicals and slowing the conduction of pain impulses. This intervention requires no special equipment and can be cost effective. Cold applications should last about 20 to 30 min/hr.

Heat reduces pain through improved blood flow to the area and through reduction of pain reflexes. This is a cost-effective intervention that requires no special equipment. Heat applications should last no more than 20 min/hr. Special attention needs to be given to preventing burns with this intervention.

■ = Independent; ▲ = Collaborative

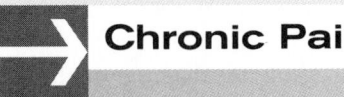

Chronic Pain–cont'd

Actions/Interventions	Rationale
• Massage of the painful area	Massage interrupts pain transmission, increases endorphin levels, and decreases tissue edema. This intervention may require another person to provide the massage. Many health insurance programs will not reimburse for the cost of therapeutic massage.
• Progressive relaxation, imagery, and music	These centrally acting techniques for pain management work through reducing muscle tension and stress. The patient may feel an increased sense of control over his or her pain. Guided imagery can help the patient explore images about pain, pain relief, and healing. These techniques require practice to be effective.
• Distraction	Distraction is a temporary pain management strategy that works by increasing the pain threshold. It should be used for a short duration, usually less than 2 hours at a time. Prolonged use can add to fatigue and increased pain when the distraction is no longer present.
• Acupressure	Acupressure involves finger pressure applied to acupressure points on the body. Using the gate control theory, the technique works to interrupt pain transmission by "closing the gate." This approach requires training and practice.
• Transcutaneous electrical nerve stimulation (TENS)	TENS requires the application of 2 to 4 skin electrodes. Pain reduction occurs through a mild electrical current. The patient is able to regulate the intensity and frequency of the electrical stimulation.
■ Teach the patient and family about the use of pharmacological interventions for pain management:	
• Nonopioids (acetaminophen; nonsteroidal antiinflammatory agents [NSAIDs]; and selective NSAIDs [COX-2 inhibitors])	These drugs are the first step in an analgesic ladder. They work in peripheral tissues by inhibiting the synthesis of prostaglandins that cause pain, inflammation, and edema. The advantages of these drugs are that they can be taken orally and are not associated with dependency and addiction. They should be given around the clock.
• Opioid analgesics (narcotics)	These drugs act on the central nervous system to reduce pain by binding with opiate receptors throughout the body. The side effects associated with this group of drugs tend to be more significant that those with the NSAIDs. Nausea, vomiting, constipation, sedation, respiratory depression, tolerance, and dependency are of concern in patients using these drugs for chronic pain management.
• Antidepressants • Anticonvulsants	These drugs may be useful adjuncts in a total program of pain management, especially for those with chronic neuropathic pain. In addition to their effects on the patient's mood, the antidepressants may have analgesic properties apart from their antidepressant actions.

■ = Independent; ▲ = Collaborative

Actions/Interventions

■ Assist the patient and family in identifying lifestyle modifications that may contribute to effective pain management. Guide the patient to plan activities during periods of greatest relief from pain.

▲ Refer the patient and family to community support groups and self-help groups for people coping with chronic pain.

Rationale

Changes in work routines, household responsibilities, and the home physical environment may be needed to promote more effective pain management. Providing the patient and family with ongoing support and guidance will increase the success of these strategies.

Adding to the patient's network of social support can reduce the burden of suffering associated with chronic pain and provide additional resources.

• RELATED CARE PLANS

Acute pain, p. 144
Fatigue, p. 65

NDx Powerlessness

NANDA: Perception that one's own actions will not significantly affect an outcome; a perceived lack of control over a current situation or immediate happening

Powerlessness may be expressed at any time during a patient's illness. During an acute episode, people used to being in control may temporarily find themselves unable to navigate the health care system and environment. The medical jargon, the swiftness with which decisions are expected to be made, and the vast array of health care providers to which the patient has to relate can all cause a feeling of powerlessness. This response is compounded by patients of cultural, religious, or ethnic backgrounds that differ from those of the dominant health care providers. Patients with chronic, debilitating, or terminal illnesses may have long-term feelings of powerlessness because they are unable to change their inevitable outcomes. Older patients are especially susceptible to the threat of loss of control and independence that comes with aging, as well as the consequences of illness and disease. Patients suffering from feelings of powerlessness may be seen in the hospital, ambulatory care, rehabilitation, or home care environment.

Common Related Factors

Health care environment
Illness-related regimen
Acute or chronic illness
Inability to communicate effectively
Dependence on others for activities of daily living
Inability to perform role responsibilities
Progressive debilitating disease
Terminal prognosis
Loss of control over life decisions
Lack of knowledge

Defining Characteristics

Expression of having no control or influence over situation or outcome
Nonparticipation in care or decision making when opportunities are provided
Reluctance to express true feelings
Diminished patient-initiated interaction
Passivity, submissiveness, apathy
Withdrawal, depression
Aggressive, acting out, and/or violent behavior
Feeling of hopelessness
Decreased participation in activities of daily living

■ = Independent; ▲ = Collaborative

Nursing Diagnosis Care Plans

Powerlessness—cont'd

Common Expected Outcomes

Patient begins to identify ways to achieve control over personal situation.
Patient begins to express sense of personal control.
Patient makes decisions regarding care as appropriate.

> **NOC Outcomes**
> Health Beliefs: Perceived Control;
> Participation: Health Care Decisions
>
> **NIC Interventions**
> Self-Responsibility Facilitation;
> Self-Esteem Enhancement

Ongoing Assessment

Actions/Interventions	**Rationale**
■ Assess the patient's power needs or needs for control.	Patients are usually able to identify those aspects of self-governance that they miss most and that are most important to them.
■ Assess for feelings of hopelessness, depression, and apathy.	These feelings may be a component of powerlessness.
■ Identify the patient's locus of control.	The degree to which people attribute responsibility to themselves (internal control) versus other forces (external control) determines locus of control.
■ Identify situations and/or interactions that may add to the patient's sense of powerlessness.	Many medical routines are superimposed on patients without ever receiving their permission, fostering a sense of powerlessness. It is important for health care providers to recognize the patient's right to refuse procedures such as feeding tubes and intubation.
■ Assess the patient's decision-making ability.	Powerlessness is not the same as the inability to make a decision. It is the feeling that one has lost the implicit power for self-governance.
■ Assess the role the illness plays in the patient's powerlessness.	Uncertainty about events, duration and course of illness, prognosis, and dependence on others for help and treatments involved can contribute to powerlessness.
■ Assess the impact of powerlessness on the patient's physical condition (e.g., appearance, oral intake, hygiene, sleep habits).	Individuals may feel as though they are unable to control very basic aspects of life. Patients most vulnerable to powerlessness are those who are increasingly susceptible to stressful events (e.g., illness with impaired mobility; older age).
■ Note whether the patient demonstrates a need for information about illness, treatment plan, and procedures.	This will differentiate powerlessness from knowledge deficit.
■ Evaluate the effects of the information provided on the patient's behavior and feelings.	A patient experiencing powerlessness may ignore information. A patient simply experiencing a knowledge deficit may be mobilized to act in his or her own best interest after information is given and options are explored. The act of providing information may heighten a patient's sense of autonomy.
■ Assess whether the patient has an advance directive, a durable power of attorney for health care, or a living will.	These legal documents express the patient's desires for health care treatment and designate another person to act on his or her behalf.

> ■ = Independent; ▲ = Collaborative

Actions/Interventions

- Assess the patient's desires or abilities to be an active participant in self-care.

Rationale

Facilitating knowledge needed to improve self-care will make a difference in future health care decision making, especially in older patients. Praise and positive reinforcement for self-care are profound motivators for enhancing self-esteem.

Therapeutic Interventions

Actions/Interventions

- Encourage verbalization of feelings, perceptions, and fears about making decisions.
- Acknowledge the patient's knowledge of self and personal situation.
- Enhance the patient's sense of autonomy. Do this by involving the patient in decision making, by giving information, and by enabling the patient to control the environment as appropriate.

- Encourage the patient to identify strengths.

- Assist the patient to reexamine negative perceptions of the situation.
- Eliminate unpredictability of events by allowing adequate preparation for tests or procedures.
- Encourage increased responsibility for self.

- Implement individualized strategies to provide hygiene, diet, and sleep.

- Give the patient control over his or her environment. Encourage the patient to furnish the environment with those things that he or she finds comforting.

- Assist with creating a timetable to guide increased responsibility in the future.

- Provide positive feedback for making decisions and participating in self-care.
- ▲ Assist the patient to identify the significance of culture, religion, race, gender, and age on his or her sense of powerlessness.

Rationale

This creates a supportive climate and sends a message of caring.

A patient's perception of powerlessness can make a profound alteration in his or her thought processes.

Patients become dependent in the "high-tech" medical environment and may relegate decision making to the health care providers. This may be especially evident in patients of cultures or ethnic heritages different from the dominant health care providers.

Review of past coping experiences and prior decision-making skills may assist the patient to recognize inner strengths. Self-confidence and security come with a sense of control.

The patient may have misconceptions or unrealistic expectations for the situation.

Information can provide a sense of control.

The perception of powerlessness may negate the patient's attention to areas where self-care is attainable; however, the patient may require significant support systems and resources to accomplish goals.

Allowing or helping the patient to decide when and how these things are to be accomplished will increase the patient's sense of autonomy.

This enhances the patient's sense of autonomy and acknowledges his or her right to have dominion over controllable aspects of life. It applies to the hospital as well as the extended care or home care environment.

With short hospital stays, patients may find themselves helpless and dependent on discharge, and they may unrealistically perceive their situation as unchangeable. Use of realistic short-term goals for resuming aspects of self-care may foster confidence in one's abilities.

Success fosters confidence in abilities and a sense of control.

Especially in the hospital environment when the patient does not speak the dominant language, food is different, and customs such as bathing, personal space, and privacy differ, patients may retreat and develop a sense of powerlessness. Use of patient advocates and outreach workers from a given ethnic community may provide a bridge to the health care providers.

■ = Independent; ▲ = Collaborative

Powerlessness

Powerlessness–cont'd

Actions/Interventions

■ Avoid using coercive power when approaching patient.

■ Assist the patient in developing advance directives.

Rationale

This may intensify the patient's feelings of powerlessness and result in decreased self-esteem.

Allowing or helping the patient to decide when and how things are to be accomplished will increase his or her sense of autonomy.

Education/Continuity of Care

Actions/Interventions

■ Assist family members or caregivers to allow independent activities within abilities.

■ Refer to support groups or self-help groups and community resources as appropriate.

Rationale

Caregivers may foster a sense of dependence in their efforts to be helpful and caring.

Persons who have "been there" may be most helpful in providing the supportive empathy necessary to move the patient to the next level of independence and control.

NDx Self-Care Deficit

NANDA: Impaired ability to perform or complete activities of daily living, such as feeding, dressing, bathing, toileting

The nurse may encounter the patient with a self-care deficit in the hospital or in the community. The deficit may be the result of transient limitations, such as those one might experience while recuperating from surgery, or the result of progressive deterioration that erodes the individual's ability or willingness to perform the activities required to care for himself or herself. Careful examination of the patient's deficit is required in order to be certain that the patient is not failing at self-care because of a lack in material resources or a problem with arranging the environment to suit the patient's physical limitations. The nurse coordinates services to maximize the independence of the patient and to ensure that the environment the patient lives in is safe and supportive of his or her special needs. This care plan combines a variety of self-care deficits into one comprehensive plan.

Common Related Factors

Neuromuscular impairment, secondary to cerebrovascular accident (CVA)
Musculoskeletal disorder such as rheumatoid arthritis
Cognitive impairment
Energy deficit
Pain
Severe anxiety
Decreased motivation
Environmental barriers
Impaired mobility or transfer ability

Defining Characteristics

Inability to feed self independently
Inability to dress self independently
Inability to bathe and groom self independently
Inability to perform toileting tasks independently
Inability to transfer from bed to wheelchair
Inability to ambulate independently
Inability to perform miscellaneous common tasks such as telephoning and writing

■ = Independent; ▲ = Collaborative

Common Expected Outcomes

Patient safely performs (to maximum ability) self-care activities.

Resources are identified that are useful in optimizing the autonomy and independence of the patient.

NOC Outcomes

Self-Care: Eating; Self-Care: Bathing; Self-Care: Dressing; Self-Care: Grooming; Self-Care; Hygiene; Self-Care: Toileting

NIC Interventions

Self-Care Assistance: Bathing/Hygiene; Self-Care Assistance: Dressing/Grooming; Self-Care Assistance: Feeding; Self-Care Assistance: Toileting; Environment Management

Ongoing Assessment

Actions/Interventions

- Assess ability to carry out activities of daily living (ADLs), such as feeding, dressing, grooming, bathing, toileting, transferring, and ambulating on a regular basis. Determine the aspects of self-care that are problematic to the patient.

- Assess the specific cause of each deficit (e.g., weakness, visual problems, cognitive impairment).

- Assess the patient's need for assistive devices. Assess the need for home health care after discharge.

- Identify preference for food, personal care items, and other things.

- If indicated, assess for gag reflex or need for swallowing evaluation by speech therapist before initial oral feeding.

Rationale

The patient may only require assistance with some self-care measures.

Different etiological factors may require more specific interventions to enable self-care.

Assistive devices increase independence in performance of ADLs. Shortened hospital stays have resulted in patients being more debilitated on discharge and therefore requiring more assistance at home.

These support the patient's individual and personal preferences.

Absence of gag reflex or inability to chew or swallow properly may lead to choking or aspiration.

Therapeutic Interventions

Actions/Interventions

- Assist the patient in accepting necessary amount of dependence.

- Set short-range goals with the patient.

- Implement measures to facilitate independence, but intervene when the patient cannot perform.

- Use consistent routines and allow adequate time for the patient to complete tasks.

- Provide positive reinforcement for all activities attempted; note partial achievements.

Rationale

If disease, injury, or illness resulting in self-care deficit is recent, the patient may need to grieve before accepting that dependence is necessary.

Assisting the patient to set realistic goals will decrease frustration.

An appropriate level of assistive care can prevent injury from activities without causing frustration.

This helps the patient organize and carry out self-care skills.

This provides the patient with an external source of positive reinforcement and promotes ongoing efforts.

■ = Independent; ▲ = Collaborative

Self-Care Deficit—cont'd

Actions/Interventions	Rationale
Feeding:	
■ Place the patient in optimal position for feeding, preferably sitting up in a chair; support arms, elbows, and wrists, as needed.	Proper positioning can make the task easier while also reducing risk for aspiration.
■ Encourage the patient to feed self as soon as possible (using unaffected hand, if appropriate). Assist with setup as needed.	It is probable that the dominant hand will also be the affected hand if there is upper extremity involvement.
■ Ensure that the patient wears dentures and eyeglasses if needed.	Deficits may be exaggerated if other senses or strengths are not functioning optimally.
▲ Assure that consistency of diet is appropriate for the patient's ability to chew and swallow, as assessed by the speech therapist.	Mechanical problems may prohibit the patient from eating.
■ Provide the patient with appropriate utensils (e.g., drinking straw, food guard, rocking knife, nonskid placemat) to aid in self-feeding.	These items increase opportunities for success.
■ Consider appropriate setting for feeding where the patient has supportive assistance yet is not embarrassed.	Embarrassment or fear of spilling food on self may hinder the patient's attempts to feed self.
■ If the patient has visual problems, advise the patient of the placement of food on the plate.	Following CVA, patients may have unilateral neglect and may ignore half the plate.
Dressing/grooming:	
■ Provide privacy during dressing.	Patients may take longer to dress and may be fearful of breaches in privacy.
■ Provide frequent encouragement and assistance with dressing as needed.	Assistance can reduce energy expenditure and frustration. However, care needs to be taken so the care provider does not rush through tasks, negating the patient's attempts.
■ Plan daily activities so the patient is rested before activity.	A plan that balances periods of activity with periods of rest can help the patient complete the desired activity without undue fatigue and frustration.
▲ Provide appropriate assistive devices for dressing as assessed by the nurse and occupational therapist.	The use of a buttonhook or of loop-and-pile closures on clothes may make it possible for a patient to continue independence in this self-care activity.
■ Place the patient in wheelchair or stationary chair.	This provides more support than sitting on the side of the bed when dressing. Dressing can be fatiguing.
■ Encourage the use of clothing one size larger.	This ensures easier dressing and comfort.
■ Suggest front-opening brassiere and half-slips.	These may be easier to manage.
■ Suggest elastic shoelaces or Velcro closures on shoes.	These eliminate tying, which can add to frustration.
■ Provide makeup and mirror; assist as needed.	Fine motor activities may take more coordinated actions and may be beyond the abilities of the patient.
Bathing/hygiene:	
■ Maintain privacy during bathing as appropriate.	The need for privacy is fundamental for most patients.
■ Ensure that needed utensils are close by.	This conserves energy and optimizes safety.
■ Instruct the patient to select bath time when he or she is rested and unhurried.	Hurrying may result in accidents, and the energy required for these activities may be substantial.

■ = Independent; ▲ = Collaborative

Actions/Interventions	Rationale
■ Provide the patient with appropriate assistive devices (e.g., long-handled bath sponge; shower chair; safety mats for floor; grab bars for bath or shower).	These aid in the ability to bathe self and increase safety.
■ Encourage the patient to bathe self as much as he or she is capable of. Assist with completion of bath, brushing teeth, shaving, and so on, only as needed.	Hospital workers and family caregivers are often in a hurry and do more for patients than needed, thereby slowing the patient's efforts at regaining independence.
■ Encourage the patient to comb own hair (a one-handed task). Suggest hairstyles that are low maintenance.	This enables the patient to maintain autonomy for as long as possible.
■ Assist the patient with care of fingernails and toenails as required.	Patients may require podiatric care to prevent injury to feet during nail trimming or because special implements are required to cut nails.
■ Offer frequent encouragement.	Patients often have difficulty seeing progress.

Toileting:

Actions/Interventions	Rationale
■ Evaluate or document previous and current patterns for toileting; institute a toileting schedule that factors these habits into the program.	The effectiveness of the bowel or bladder program will be enhanced if the natural and personal patterns of the patient are respected.
■ Provide privacy while the patient is toileting.	Lack of privacy may inhibit the patient's ability to evacuate bowel and bladder.
■ Keep the call light within reach and instruct the patient to call as early as possible.	This enables staff members to have time to assist with transfer to commode or toilet.
■ Assist the patient in removing or replacing necessary clothing.	Clothing that is difficult to get into and out of may compromise a patient's ability to be continent.
■ Encourage use of commode or toilet as soon as possible.	Patients are more effective in evacuating bowel and bladder when sitting on a commode. Some patients find it impossible to toilet on a bedpan.
■ Offer bedpan or place patient on toilet every 1 to 1½ hours during the day and three times during the night.	This eliminates incontinence. Time intervals can be lengthened as the patient begins to express the need to toilet on demand.
■ Closely monitor the patient for loss of balance or falls. Keep commode and toilet tissue near the bedside for nighttime use.	Patients may rush readiness to ambulate to the toilet or commode during the night because of fear of soiling themselves and they may fall in the process.

Transferring/ambulation:

Actions/Interventions	Rationale
■ Plan teaching session for transferring/walking when the patient is rested.	Tasks require energy. Fatigued patients may have more difficulty and may become unnecessarily frustrated.
■ Assist with bed mobility by doing the following:	This prevents disabling contractures, pressure sores, and muscle weakness from disuse.
• Encourage the patient to use the stronger side (if appropriate) as best as possible.	If stroke patients experience weakness in their dominant side, it will be necessary for them to develop muscle strength and coordination on the nondominant side.
• Allow the patient to work at own rate of speed.	Many factors may influence a patient's ability to move freely, and each of these factors must be considered when developing or teaching a patient a new system for self-care. It will take time for the patient to learn and then gain confidence in his or her ability to perform these new self-care measures.
• When the patient is sitting up at the side of the bed, instruct him or her not to pull on the caregiver.	This may cause the caregiver to lose balance and fall.
■ When transferring to wheelchair, always place the chair on the patient's stronger side at a slight angle to the bed and lock the brakes.	The patient will weight-bear on the stronger side. Physical or occupational therapists can provide additional guidelines.

■ = Independent; ▲ = Collaborative

Self-Care Deficit—cont'd

Actions/Interventions

Rationale

■ When minimal assistance is needed, stand on the patient's weak side and place a hand under the patient's weak arm. Keep feet well apart; lift with legs, not the back, to prevent back strain.

Proper technique prevents injury to the care provider.

■ For moderate assistance, the caregiver places arms under both the patient's armpits with the caregiver's hands on the patient's back.

This forces the patient to keep his or her weight forward.

■ For patients requiring maximal assistance, use a gait belt.

This technique maximizes patient support while protecting the care provider from injury.

  • Raise the bed to tallest height that still allows patient's feet to be flat on floor.

  • Grasp gait belt with both arms and pull patient forward.

  • Place a knee against the patient's weak knee (if applicable), and encourage the patient to put weight on the strong side during transfer.

  • Encourage the patient to use his or her arms to assist, as able, and to place them on the caregiver's forearms.

■ Assist with ambulation; teach the use of ambulation devices such as canes, walkers, and crutches:

  • Stand on the patient's weak side.

This enhances patient safety.

  • If using a cane, place the cane in the patient's strong hand and ensure proper foot-cane sequence.

This assists with balance and support.

Miscellaneous skills:

■ Telephone: Evaluate need for adaptive equipment through therapy department (e.g., pushbutton phone, larger numbers, increased volume).

Patients will require an effective tool for communicating needs from home.

■ Writing: Supply patient with felt-tip pens. Evaluate need for splint on writing hand.

These pens mark with little pressure and are easier to use. Splints assist in holding the writing device.

■ Provide supervision for each activity until the patient performs the skill competently and is safe in independent care; reevaluate regularly to be certain that the patient is maintaining the skill level and remains safe in environment.

The patient's ability to perform self-care measures may change often over time and will need to be assessed regularly.

■ Encourage maximum independence.

The goal of rehabilitation is one of achieving the highest level of independence as possible.

Education/Continuity of Care

Actions/Interventions

Rationale

■ Plan teaching sessions so the patient has time to practice tasks.

This allows the patient to use new information immediately, thus enhancing retention.

■ Instruct the patient in use of assistive devices as appropriate.

Information enables the patient to take some control.

■ Teach family and caregivers to foster independence and to intervene if the patient becomes fatigued, is unable to perform tasks, or becomes excessively frustrated.

This demonstrates caring and concern but does not interfere with the patient's efforts to achieve independence.

■ = Independent; ▲ = Collaborative

Nursing Diagnosis Care Plans

Situational Low Self-Esteem

NANDA: Development of a negative perception of self-worth in response to current situation (specify)

Mild to marked alteration in an individual's view of himself or herself, including negative self-evaluation or feelings about self or capabilities, is called situational low self-esteem. One's self-esteem is affected by (and may also affect) ability to function in the larger world and relate to others within it. Self-esteem disturbance may be expressed directly or indirectly. Cultural norms, gender, and age are variables that influence how an individual perceives himself or herself. The emotional work that patients do to enhance self-esteem takes weeks, months, or even years, and may require professional help beyond the scope of the bedside or community nurse. A caring individual, who is able to identify the special needs of the patient struggling with self-esteem issues, is in a unique position to provide support and compassion, enhancing the work the patient must do.

Common Related Factors

Alteration in body image
Actual or anticipated loss
Change in relationships with others
Change in social roles (e.g., hospitalization, assumption of the "sick role")
Behavior inconsistent with personal values
Functional impairment

Defining Characteristics

Report by patient of change in self-esteem
Verbally reports current situational challenge to self-worth
Self-negating statements
Indecisive, nonassertive behavior
Verbally reports feeling unable to deal with situation
Expressions of helplessness

Common Expected Outcome

Patient begins to recognize, accept, and verbalize positive aspects of self and self-capabilities.

NOC Outcome
Self-Esteem

NIC Interventions
Self-Esteem Enhancement;
   Body Image Enhancement; Presence

Ongoing Assessment

Actions/Interventions

- Encourage patient to list past and current accomplishments: emotional, social, interpersonal, intellectual, vocational, and physical.

- Listen to or document how the patient describes self and the things he or she says about self.

- Take seriously the patient's reports of changes in self-esteem. Determine if the patient is able to relate these changes to a specific event.

- Determine if these feelings have resulted in a change in patient's behavior.

Rationale

This exercise is sometimes helpful in providing the patient with perspective.

Low self-esteem is often expressed as feeling unloved, unworthy, or incompetent. The person may be self-critical.

The patient may be aware of the events that negatively affect his or her self-concept.

Patients may be able to compensate for low self-esteem through extraordinary performance in work or areas of special interest while still having problems with how he or she envisions self. Fundamentally low self-esteem will not be resolved without factoring these issues into the care plan.

■ = Independent; ▲ = Collaborative

Situational Low Self-Esteem—cont'd

Actions/Interventions

- Assess the degree to which the patient feels "in control" of his or her own behavior.

- Assess the degree to which the patient feels loved and respected by others.

- Assess whether the patient feels satisfied with his or her own behavior.

- Assess how competent patients feel about their ability to perform and/or carry out their own and other's expectations.

- Assess for unresolved grief.

Rationale

Patients may be caught in a vicious cycle of behaviors designed to camouflage the primary self-esteem problem. The acting-out feeds a sense of unworthiness and sabotages attempts at esteem building.

The patient's ability to establish and maintain meaningful relationships is a positive indicator for developing self-esteem. The care and support of others will be helpful in building the patient's self-esteem.

Patients with self-esteem disturbance may feel as though their behaviors are not in keeping with their own personal, moral, or ethical values; they may also deny these behaviors, project blame, and rationalize personal failures.

The patient may have developed the ability to carry out personal responsibilities despite low self-esteem. This may be a positive indicator of the patient's potential for successful enhancement of self-esteem.

Unresolved grief may inhibit patients' ability to move beyond the loss or disability and to accept themselves as they are now.

Therapeutic Interventions

Actions/Interventions

- Provide environment conducive to the expression of feelings:
  - Spend time with the patient; set aside sufficient time so that the encounter is unhurried.

  - Avoid excessive focus on physical tasks.

  - Use active listening and open-ended questions.

  - Provide privacy

- Convey a sense of respect for the patient's abilities and strengths in addition to recognizing problems and concerns.

- Serve as role model for the patient or significant others in healthy expression of feelings or concerns. Assume responsibility for own thoughts and actions by using "I think" language in discussions.

- Discuss "normal" impact of alteration in health status (temporary or permanent) on self-esteem.

Rationale

The patient needs time to express concerns. Spending time with the patient expresses the nurse's interest in and acceptance of the patient's feelings.

Successful resolution of these issues will take considerable time and energy. These issues are deserving of the patient and the nurse's complete attention.

This allows the patient to express concerns, fears, and ideas without interruption.

Sensitive discussions need to take place in a setting where the patient is free to express self without being overheard.

Assistance with problem solving and reality testing is best provided within the context of a trusting relationship.

Patients may need an example of positive ways to express feelings. Self-awareness allows the nurse to demonstrate authentic behavior.

Use of lay support groups or individuals may help the patient with self-esteem disturbance to recognize his or her own self-worth even in the face of injury, disease, or loss.

■ = Independent; ▲ = Collaborative

Actions/Interventions

■ Reassure the patient that such changes often result in a variety of emotional or behavioral responses.

■ Provide anticipatory guidance to minimize anxiety and fear if disturbances in self-esteem are an expected part of the rehabilitation process.
  • Explain routines and procedures in plan of treatment.

  • If hospitalized, orient the patient and significant others to the environment.
  • Use language and terminology that the patient or significant others can understand.
  • Provide opportunities for questions and verbalization of feelings.

  • Include patients and significant others in planning care whenever possible.

  • Observe response to information, caregivers, and environment.

■ Assist the patient in his or her efforts to obtain understanding and mastery of new experiences:
  • Support efforts to maintain independence, reality, positive self-esteem, sense of capability, and problem solving.
  • Provide realistic appraisal of progress.
  • Reinforce efforts at constructive change.
  • Use referral sources such as other professional or lay persons as appropriate.

Rationale

Disturbances in self-esteem are natural responses to significant changes. Reconstitution of the individual's self-esteem occurs after grieving has taken place and acceptance has followed.

This places the shift in self-esteem within the context of the normal recuperative process.

Allowing the patient to maintain a sense of self-determination and autonomy promotes a healthy sense of self-esteem.

Comfort in and mastery of the environment is important to establishing a healthy sense of self-esteem.

Insights gained from self-disclosure of feelings and clarification of information will reduce anxiety and promote coping.

If patients are unable to participate in decisions as they relate to their own care, their self-esteem may be further eroded. Significant others serve as an advocate.

Anxiety (if excessive) may interfere with ability to function.

The patient needs ongoing positive feedback and reinforcement to maintain behaviors to promote self-esteem. Clearly defined goals will help the person see progress.

These support coping efforts.

Education/Continuity of Care

Actions/Interventions

■ Teach the patient to seek and/or plan activities likely to result in a healthy self-esteem.

■ Teach the patient necessary self-care measures related to primary disease.

■ Teach the patient the harmful effects of self-negating talk.

Rationale

The patient needs to explore alternatives to promote self-esteem.

Each success will reinforce positive self-esteem.

Awareness of destructive thoughts can help the patient develop new approaches to coping.

■ = Independent; ▲ = Collaborative

Nursing Diagnosis Care Plans *(side margin)*

 **ND**ₓ **Disturbed Sensory Perception: Auditory**

Hearing Loss; Hearing Impaired; Deafness

NANDA: Change in the amount or patterning of incoming stimuli accompanied by a diminished, exaggerated, distorted, or impaired response to such stimuli

Hearing loss is common among older adults but may also occur as the result of congenital exposure to virus; during childhood after frequent ear infections or trauma; and during adulthood as the result of trauma, infection, or exposure to occupational and/or environmental noise. When hearing loss is profound and precedes language development, the ability to learn speech and interact with hearing peers can be severely impaired. When hearing is impaired or lost later in life, serious emotional and social consequences can occur, including depression and isolation. Some causes of hearing loss are surgically correctable. Many hearing assistive devices and services are available to help hearing-impaired individuals. Nursing interventions with the hearing impaired are aimed at assisting the individual in effective communication despite the loss of normal hearing.

Common Related Factors

Middle ear injuries secondary to penetration of eardrum
History of head trauma, especially direct blow to ear
Prolonged or cumulative exposure to environmental noise greater than 85 dB
Otosclerosis
Ménière's disease
Presbycusis (loss of hearing associated with aging)
Acoustic neuroma
Congenital rubella exposure
Ototoxic drug use
Chronic or recurring otitis media
Inoperative or poorly fitted hearing aids
Accumulated earwax

Defining Characteristics

Asking others to repeat spoken messages
Inappropriate response to questions
Head tilting
Cupping hands around ears
Social avoidance or withdrawal
Irritability
Difficulty learning or following directions
Dizziness
Ear pain

Common Expected Outcome

Patient achieves optimal functioning within limits of hearing impairment as evidenced by ability to communicate effectively and to engage in meaningful activities.

NOC Outcomes
Hearing Compensation Behavior;
Risk Control: Hearing Impairment

NIC Interventions
Communication Enhancement: Hearing
Deficit; Ear Care

Ongoing Assessment

Actions/Interventions

- Assess the patient's ability to hear by performing the following:
  - At screening, note the patient's ability to hear and appropriately respond to normal conversational voice; do this within the patient's sight, then again from out of the patient's sight.

Rationale

Patients may rely on lip-reading to a greater extent than they are aware.

■ = Independent; ▲ = Collaborative

Actions/Interventions	Rationale
• Ask the family or caregivers about their perception of the patient's hearing impairment.	Patients may deny or underestimate the presence of a hearing impairment.
• Review audiogram, if available.	This diagnostic study indicates both type and amount of hearing loss.
■ Assess age.	Neurosensory hearing loss affects many older individuals; inability to hear high-pitched sounds or comprehend some consonants are the earliest effects. Patients may be unaware of progressive hearing loss; family, friends, and caregivers often first notice requests for verbal repetition, lack of response to verbalizations, and mis-answered questions.
■ Assess whether hearing loss is recent, progressive, or present since childhood.	Adults with new or progressive hearing loss require attention to the emotional and social implications of impaired communication, whereas those who have had hearing loss since birth or childhood probably have the skills, tools, and resources available to cope with hearing impairment.
■ Review medical history.	History of head or ear trauma and frequent bouts with ear infections are often associated with hearing loss.
■ Review exposure to environmental noise, either as the result of occupation, recreation, or accident.	The Occupational Safety and Health Act requires hearing protection in workplaces with noise levels exceeding 90 dB. Young persons who frequent rock concerts or listen to very loud music place themselves at risk for hearing loss. Hearing loss that results from noise is not reversible.
■ Review recent use of drugs that are ototoxic.	Aspirin, quinidine, some chemotherapeutic agents, and the aminoglycosides are known ototoxic agents. Withdrawal of these drugs when hearing impairment occurs often allows for full return of hearing.
■ Check ears for earwax.	Wax prevents sound transmission and may clog hearing aids.
■ Investigate and note social and emotional impact of hearing loss.	Loss of hearing may lead to reclusiveness, isolation, depression, and withdrawal from usual activities. The decision to wear a hearing aid is often resisted because of the social stigma perceived in conjunction with aging and loss of abilities.
■ For patients with hearing aids: • Note condition and age of hearing aid. • Note frequency with which patient wears hearing aid. • Check hearing aid for fresh, functional batteries. • Check hearing aid for wax impaction.	A hearing aid that is not functioning correctly may be the cause of decreased hearing acuity. The patient may not wear the hearing aid as needed.
■ Assess for drainage from ear canal.	Purulent, foul-smelling drainage indicates an infection; serous, mucoid, or bloody drainage may indicate effusion of the middle ear after an upper respiratory or sinus infection.
▲ Culture any drainage from the ear canal.	This determines presence of infectious pathogens.
■ Ask the patient whether the ear is painful.	Pain is a symptom of increased pressure behind the eardrum, usually a result of infection.
■ Assess for dizziness, dysequilibrium.	Disorders of the ear (e.g., Ménière's disease) may be accompanied by dizziness because of the inner ear's role in maintenance of equilibrium.

■ = Independent; ▲ = Collaborative

Disturbed Sensory Perception: Auditory—cont'd

Actions/Interventions	Rationale
■ Assess the patient's ability to effectively administer eardrops.	Problems with medication administration may limit effectiveness of the drug.

Therapeutic Interventions

Actions/Interventions	Rationale
■ Use touch and eye contact.	These gain the patient's attention.
■ When speaking, do the following: • Reduce or minimize environmental noise.	The person with a hearing impairment may have difficulty filtering background noises in order to hear the speaker.
• Face the patient in good light and keep hands away from mouth.	This enhances the patient's use of lip-reading, facial expressions, and gesturing.
• Speak close to the patient's "better" ear, as appropriate.	
• Avoid shouting or yelling.	This prevents humiliation.
• Use simple language and short sentences.	
• Speak slowly.	The patient needs additional time to process auditory stimuli.
■ Use grease boards, computers, or other writing tools.	These help communicate with profoundly hearing-impaired individuals.
■ For patients with hearing aids, ensure that hearing aid is in place, clean, and working.	Patients with new hearing aids need time to adjust to the sound produced. Encouragement is often needed, especially among older patients who may decide that the hearing aid is not worth the effort.
■ Provide encouragement to use hearing aid.	Patients may stop using a hearing aid if they think it draws attention to the problem and distorts their body image.
▲ Prepare patient for ear surgery.	Tympanoplasty (removal of dead tissue, restoration of bones with prostheses) and mastoidectomy (removal of all or portions of the middle ear structures) are common surgical treatments for hearing loss.

Education/Continuity of Care

Actions/Interventions	Rationale
■ Teach the patient or caregiver to administer ear medications.	Drops should be administered at room temperature to avoid pain and dizziness; tip of applicator or dropper should not be allowed to come into contact with anything. Head should be positioned to allow medication to flow into ear canal; this position should be maintained for 1 to 2 minutes.
■ Instruct the patient or caregiver in safe techniques for cleaning ears.	Thin washcloths and fingers are best for cleaning ears. Cotton-tipped applicators should be avoided to prevent inadvertent injury to the eardrum.
■ Teach the patient or caregiver use and care of hearing aids and/or other assistive hearing devices.	The patient and caregiver need to be able to care for and maintain the hearing aid in proper working order.

■ = Independent; ▲ = Collaborative

Actions/Interventions

- Explore technology such as amplifiers, modifiers for telephones, and services for the hearing impaired (e.g., closed-caption TV, telephone hearing-impaired assistance).

- Instruct the patient in the importance of routine examination by an audiologist.

Rationale

These may assist the hearing-impaired person function and participate in meaningful activities.

Examinations detect changes in hearing or need for change in hearing aids.

 **Disturbed Sensory Perception: Visual**

Vision Loss; Macular Degeneration; Blindness

NANDA: Change in the amount or patterning of incoming stimuli, accompanied by a diminished, exaggerated, distorted, or impaired response to such stimuli

Visual impairment and/or loss of vision affects more than 100 million Americans. Genetics, aging, and chronic diseases such as diabetes and glaucoma account for the majority of visual impairment. Trauma, usually associated with alcohol use, also accounts for visual impairment or loss to a lesser degree. Some forms of visual impairment can be corrected, either by refraction (glasses, contact lenses), medications (used mainly in the treatment of glaucoma), or surgery (lens implants, keratorefractive procedures). These include myopia (nearsightedness), hyperopia (farsightedness), astigmatism (caused by abnormal corneal curvature), and presbyopia (loss of accommodation as the result of normal, age-related changes in the lens). Other types of visual impairment or loss cannot be corrected. As the American population ages, visual impairment, including noncorrectable loss from progressive macular degeneration, is a growing concern. Nursing interventions in persons with visual impairment are aimed at assisting the individual to cope with the loss and remain functional and safe. An inability to be independent with self-care, especially in the management of medications, may require ongoing supervision and/or institutionalization. This care plan addresses needs of persons who are out of their usual environments (e.g., in outpatient settings, hospitals, or long-term care facilities).

Common Related Factors

Diabetes
Glaucoma
Cataracts
Refractive disorders (myopia, hyperopia, astigmatism, presbyopia)
Macular degeneration
Ocular trauma
Ocular infection
Retinal detachment
Conjunctival Kaposi's sarcoma of acquired immunodeficiency syndrome
Disease or trauma to visual pathways or cranial nerves II, III, IV, and VI, secondary to stroke, intracranial aneurysms, brain tumor, trauma, myasthenia gravis, or multiple sclerosis
Advanced age

Defining Characteristics

Lack of eye-to-eye contact
Abnormal eye movement
Failure to locate distant objects
Squinting, frequent blinking
Bumping into things
Clumsy behavior
Closing of one eye to see
Frequent rubbing of eye
Deviation of eye
Gray opacities in eyes
Head tilting
Disorientation
Reported or measured changes in visual acuity
Anxiety
Change in usual response to visual stimuli
Anger
Visual distortions
Incoordination
History of falls, accidents

■ = Independent; ▲ = Collaborative

Nursing Diagnosis Care Plans

> ## Disturbed Sensory Perception: Visual—cont'd

Common Expected Outcome

Patient achieves optimal functioning within limits of visual impairment as evidenced by ability to care for self, to navigate environment safely, and to engage in meaningful activities.

NOC Outcomes

Visual Compensation Behavior; Risk Control: Visual Impairment

NIC Interventions

Communication Enhancement: Visual Deficit; Environmental Management; Self-Esteem Enhancement

Ongoing Assessment

Actions/Interventions	Rationale
■ Assess age.	The incidence of macular degeneration, cataracts, retinal detachments, diabetic retinopathy, and glaucoma increases with aging.
■ Determine nature of visual symptoms, onset, and degree of visual loss. Inquire about history of visual complaints, eye trauma, or ocular pain.	Recent loss, loss over a long period, or longstanding loss have different implications for nursing intervention and the patient's level of adaptation or resource use. Because visual loss may occur gradually, quantification of loss may be difficult for the patient to articulate.
■ Review medical history. Inquire about patient or family history of systemic or central nervous system disease.	Family or patient history of atherosclerosis, diabetes, thyroid disease, or hypertension should be investigated as possible cause for visual loss.
■ Ask patient about specifics such as ability to read, see television, history of falls, or ability to self-medicate.	Visual impairment can contribute to problems in daily activities. The risk for falls and medication errors increases if the person had diminished visual acuity.
■ Assess central vision with each eye, individually and together.	Vision loss may be unilateral, bilateral, central, and/or peripheral and may not affect both eyes to the same extent.
■ Assess peripheral field of vision and visual acuity.	Glaucoma affects peripheral vision; its onset is insidious and has no associated symptoms. Macular degeneration affects central vision, is more common among cigarette smokers, and is irreversible.
■ Assess eye and lid for inflammation, edema, positional defects, and deviation.	These are correctable problems that can negatively affect vision.
■ Assess factors or aids that improve vision, such as glasses, contact lenses, or bright and/or natural light.	Nursing interventions should include strategies that enhance the patient's adaptive abilities.
■ Evaluate the patient's ability to function within limits of visual impairment.	Personal appearance and condition of clothing and surroundings are good indicators of the patient's adaptation to visual loss.
■ Evaluate psychological response to visual loss.	Anger, depression, and withdrawal are common responses. Self-esteem is often negatively affected.

■ = Independent; ▲ = Collaborative

Therapeutic Interventions

Actions/Interventions

- Introduce self to patient, and acknowledge visual impairment.
- Orient the patient to the environment.
- Do not make unnecessary changes in the environment.
- Provide adequate lighting.
- Place meal tray, tissues, water, and call light within the patient's range of vision or reach.
- Communicate type and degree of impairment to all involved in the patient's care.
- Recommend use of visual aids when appropriate.
- Place food on tray and plate in the same place each meal and explain arrangement of food on tray and plate, using clockwise sequence.
- Encourage use of sense of touch.
- Explain sounds or other unusual stimuli in the environment.
- Encourage use of radios, tapes, and talking books.
- Remove environmental barriers to ensure safety.
- Discourage doors from being left partially open.
- Maintain bed in low position with side rails up, if appropriate. Keep bed in the locked position.
- Guide the patient when ambulating, if appropriate. Describe where you are walking; identify obstacles.
- Instruct the patient to hold both arms of the chair before sitting and to feel for the seat on chairs or sofas without arms.
- ▲ Consult the occupational therapy staff for assistive devices and training in their use.
- Supervise the patient when he or she is smoking.

Rationale

This reduces the patient's anxiety and maintains appropriate orientation.

Orientation reduces fear related to an unfamiliar environment.

This ensures safety and maintains what the patient has arranged.

The use of natural or halogen lighting is preferred to improve vision for patients with diminished vision.

These ensure safety and sense of independence.

This enhances continuity of care.

Visual aids such as a magnifying glass or large-type printed books and magazines encourage reading.

This approach promotes the patient's independence with self-care for feeding.

Touch encourages the patient to become familiar with unfamiliar objects.

Explanations reduce fear.

Diversional activities should be encouraged. Radio and television increase awareness of day and time.

If furniture or wastebaskets are moved, notify patient of changes.

Fully open or closed doors reduce the risk for injury among the vision-impaired.

Side rails help remind the patient not to get up without help when needed.

This approach helps maintain reality orientation to the environment.

These actions reduce the risk of falls.

Adaptive devices such as magnifiers for reading medication vials or syringes used for injections can increase the patient's self-care independence.

Supervision prevents accidental fires.

Education/Continuity of Care

Actions/Interventions

- Involve the caregiver in the patient's care and instructions.
- Reinforce the physician's explanation of medical management and surgical procedures, if any.

Rationale

Help the patient understand the nature and limitations of disease. The patient and family need information to plan strategies for assisting the visually impaired patient to cope.

Patients and their caregivers may need periodic repetition of information to make informed decisions about treatment and procedures.

■ = Independent; ▲ = Collaborative

→ Disturbed Sensory Perception: Visual–cont'd

Actions/Interventions	Rationale
■ Teach general eye care:	
• Maintain sterility of all eyedroppers, tubes of medications, and other items.	These strategies reduce the risk of eye infection or injury.
• Do not share eye makeup.	The patient needs to understand how to prevent contamination of equipment used in or around the eye.
• Care for contact lenses or eyeglasses as recommended by manufacturer.	Care and maintenance of corrective lenses enhances the effectiveness of their use to improve vision.
• Do not rub eyes.	
■ Demonstrate the proper administration of eyedrops or ointments; allow for return demonstration by the patient and/or caregiver.	Repetition of skills after demonstration promotes the patient's level of confidence in administration of eye medications.
■ Help the family or caregiver identify and make arrangements at home.	These provide for the patient's safety and sense of independence, as indicated.
▲ Make appropriate referrals to a home health agency for nursing and social services follow-up.	Evaluation of the home environment can identify the need for additional resources to support the patient's adaptation to visual impairment.
■ Reinforce the need to use community agencies, if indicated (e.g., Lighthouse for the Blind [check local listings] or American Foundation for the Blind, 15 West 16th Street, New York, NY 10011).	These agencies are a source of additional information and resources to support the patient's adaptation to visual impairment.

→ NDx Ineffective Sexuality Patterns

Impotence; Intimacy

NANDA: Expressions of concern regarding own sexuality

A patient or significant other may express concern regarding the means or manner of sexual expression or physical intimacy within their relationship. Alterations in human sexual response may be related to genetic, physiological, emotional, cognitive, religious, and/or sociocultural factors or to a combination of these factors. All of these factors play a role in determining what is normative for each individual within a relationship. The problem of altered patterns of sexuality is not limited to a single gender, age, or cultural group; it is a potential problem for all patients, whether the nurse encounters them in the hospital or in the community. It is probable that most couples encounter some point in their relationship where patterns of sexual expression become altered to the dissatisfaction of one or both members. The ability to communicate effectively, to seek professional help whenever necessary, and to modify existing patterns to the mutual satisfaction of both members are skills that enable the couple to grow and evolve in this aspect of their relationship. The nurse is in a unique position to provide anticipatory guidance relative to altered patterns of sexual function when the problem is an inevitable or probable result of illness or disability. The ability to discuss these issues openly when the patient raises concerns about sexual expression highlights the legitimacy of the couple's feelings and the normalcy of sexual expression as a part of intimacy, as well as emotional and physical well-being.

■ = Independent; ▲ = Collaborative

Ineffective Sexuality Patterns

Common Related Factors

Physical changes or limitations (may be time limited or chronic):
- Acute illness
- Pain or discomfort
- Recent surgery or trauma
- Loss of mobility or normal range of motion
- Decreased activity tolerance
- Hormonal change
- Alcohol or substance abuse
- Medication effects
- Pregnancy
- Infertility

Fear or anxiety:
- Concerns about pregnancy or sexually transmitted infections (STIs)
- Religious or cultural prohibitions
- Lack of privacy
- Social stigma
- Conflicting values

Knowledge deficit:
- Lack of education regarding sexuality
- Means of birth control
- "Safe sex" practices
- Limited social skills

Emotional factors:
- Change in body or self-image
- Recent loss or trauma
- Affective disturbances
- Low self-esteem or poor self-concept
- Dementia
- Discomfort with sexual orientation
- Identity disturbances
- History of traumatic experiences (e.g., rape, sexual abuse)
- Psychosis or other psychiatric disorder

Situational factors:
- Absence of partner
- Social isolation
- Lack of appropriate environment

Defining Characteristics

Verbalized concerns regarding sexual functioning
Questions regarding "normal" sexual functioning
Expressed dissatisfaction with sexuality (e.g., decreased satisfaction, symptoms of sexual dysfunction, concerns about sexual preference or orientation, difficulties in accepting self or others as sexual beings)
Reported changes in relationship with partner
Actual or perceived limitation secondary to diagnosis or therapy
Noncompliance with medications or treatments with associated risk of impaired or altered sexual functioning
Reported changes in previously established sexual patterns
Sexual behavior inappropriate to circumstance or setting
Frequent efforts designed to elicit affirmation of sexual desirability

Common Expected Outcomes

Patient or couple verbalizes satisfaction with the way they express physical intimacy.
Both members of the couple exhibit behavior that is acceptable to his or her partner.

NOC Outcomes
Abuse Recovery: Sexual; Body Image; Sexual Identity: Acceptance

NIC Interventions
Sexual Counseling; Anticipatory Guidance; Teaching: Sexuality

■ = Independent; ▲ = Collaborative

Ineffective Sexuality Patterns–cont'd

Ongoing Assessment

Actions/Interventions

- Assess level of understanding regarding human sexuality and functioning.
- Explore current and past sexual patterns, practices, and degree of satisfaction.
- Identify level of comfort in discussion for patient and/ or significant other.

- Identify potential or actual factors that may contribute to current alteration in sexual functioning (see Common Related Factors on the previous page).
- Solicit information from the patient about the nature, onset, duration, and course of sexual difficulty.

Rationale

Many persons have misconceptions about facts as they relate to sexual intimacy.

This determines a realistic approach to care planning.

It is important for the nurse to create an environment where the couple or patient feels safe and comfortable in discussing feelings.

The care plan will be developed in the context of the patient's overall health status. Different interventions will address specific contributing factors.

Problems with sexuality may be longstanding or of short duration.

Therapeutic Interventions

Actions/Interventions

- Use a relaxed, accepting manner in discussing sexual issues. Convey acceptance and respect for patient concerns.

- Provide privacy and adequate time to discuss sexuality.

- Encourage sharing of concerns, feelings, and information between patient and current or future partner. Whenever possible, involve both in sexual health education and counseling efforts.
- Discuss the multiplicity of influences on sexual functioning (both physiological and emotional). Offer opportunities to ask questions and express feelings.
- Explore awareness of and comfort with a range of sexual expression and activities (not just sexual intercourse).

- Assist the patient and significant other in identifying possible options to overcome situational, temporary, or long-term influences on sexual functioning
- Encourage patient and significant other to locate and read relevant educational materials regarding sexuality.

Rationale

Patients are often hesitant to report such concerns and/ or difficulties because sexuality remains a private matter for many within our culture, and it is uncomfortable to discuss.

Respecting the individual and treating his or her concerns and questions as normal and important may foster greater self-acceptance and decrease anxiety.

For some sexual problems, it is the couple's relationship that provides the focus for intervention.

Patients and couples may have limited knowledge of sexual function and factors that influence sexuality. Open discussion can relieve feelings of guilt or shame.

Patients and couples may have limited knowledge of ways to express their sexuality. They may be uncomfortable with some types of sexual expression based on cultural, social, or religious beliefs.

The nurse can facilitate open discussion by the couple of possible ways to adapt to changes in sexual function. The couple needs to share responsibility for exploring options.

Many excellent books are available that undo myths and errors and promote increased knowledge and communication about sexual concerns.

Education/Continuity of Care

Actions/Interventions

- Provide accurate and timely health teaching regarding the "normal" range of sexual expression and sexual practices throughout the life cycle.

Rationale

Satisfying sexual functioning and practice are not automatic and need to be learned.

■ = Independent; ▲ = Collaborative

Risk for Impaired Skin Integrity

Actions/Interventions	Rationale
■ Discuss range of possibilities and consequences (both positive and negative) associated with sexual expression of all types (e.g., change in relationship, impact on physical and/or emotional health, possibility of pregnancy, STIs).	Information is necessary to support the couple or the individual patient making decisions about sexual activity.
■ Offer information regarding birth control methods and "safe sex" practices.	The patient and significant other need accurate information about preventing unintended pregnancy or transmission of infections through sexual contact.
■ Be specific in providing instruction to the patient and significant other regarding any limitations on sexual activity resulting from illness, surgery, medications, or other events.	The patient needs to understand the relationship between illness, treatment methods, and sexuality.
■ Explain alternative means or forms of expressing intimacy and/or sexual expression (e.g., alternative positions for intercourse) that decrease discomfort or degree of physical exertion for those with impaired mobility or cardiopulmonary disease. Consider concerns imposed by the patient's or significant other's health status, illness, or other situation.	The amount and type of information provided should match the patient or couple's level of interest and comfort. Alternative ways of sexual expression should be mutually pleasing and acceptable to the patient and the significant other.
■ Consider referral for further workup and/or treatment (e.g., primary health care provider, specialized physician or mental health consultant, substance abuse treatment program, or sexual dysfunction clinic).	The counseling needs of the couple or patient may be beyond the skill or training of the nurse.
▲ Consider referral to self-help and/or support groups (e.g., Reach for Recovery, Ostomy Association, Mended Hearts, Huff and Puff, Sexual Impotence Resolved, Us Too, HIV Support Groups, Y Me, Survivors of Abuse, or Resolve).	Self-help support groups are unique sources of empathy, information, and successful role models. These organizations can provide information about sexuality and specific health problems.

Risk for Impaired Skin Integrity

Pressure Ulcers; Decubitus Care

NANDA: At risk for skin being adversely altered

Immobility, which leads to pressure, shear, and friction, is the factor most likely to put an individual at risk for altered skin integrity. Advanced age, the normal loss of elasticity, inadequate nutrition, environmental moisture (especially from incontinence), and vascular insufficiency potentiate the effects of pressure and hasten the development of skin breakdown. Groups of persons with the highest risk for altered skin integrity are those with spinal injuries, those who are confined to bed or wheelchair for prolonged periods of time, those with edema, and those who have altered sensation that triggers the normal protective weight shifting. Pressure relief and pressure reduction devices for the prevention of skin breakdown include a wide range of surfaces, specialty beds and mattresses, and other devices. Preventive measures are usually not reimbursable, even though costs related to treatment once breakdown occurs are greater.

■ = Independent; ▲ = Collaborative

Risk for Impaired Skin Integrity—cont'd

Common Risk Factors

Extremes of age
Immobility
Poor nutrition
Mechanical forces (e.g., pressure, shear, friction)
Pronounced bony prominences
Poor circulation
Altered sensation
Incontinence
Edema
Environmental moisture
History of radiation
Hyperthermia or hypothermia
Acquired immunodeficiency syndrome (AIDS)
NOTE: Risk should be determined by the use of a risk
   assessment tool (e.g., Braden scale).

Common Expected Outcome

Patient's skin remains intact, as evidenced by no redness
   over bony prominences and capillary refill less than 6
   seconds over areas of redness.

NOC Outcomes
Risk Control; Risk Detection; Tissue
   Integrity: Skin And Mucous Membranes

NIC Interventions
Pressure Ulcer Prevention; Skin Surveillance

Ongoing Assessment

Actions/Interventions

■ Determine age.

■ Assess general condition of skin.

■ Specifically assess skin over bony prominences (e.g.,
sacrum, trochanters, scapulae, elbows, heels, inner
and outer malleolus, inner and outer knees, back of
head).
  • Pressure areas initially appear as persistent reddened
areas in light pigmented skin. In darker skin tones,
the area may appear as red, blue, or purple hue spots.

■ Assess the patient's awareness of the sensation of
pressure.

Rationale

Older patients' skin is normally less elastic and has less
moisture, making for higher risk of skin impairment.

Healthy skin varies among individuals but should have
good turgor (an indication of moisture), feel warm
and dry to the touch, be free of impairment (scratches,
bruises, excoriation, rashes), and have quick capillary
refill (less than 6 seconds).

Areas where skin is stretched tautly over bony prominences are at higher risk for breakdown because the
possibility of ischemia to skin is high as a result of
compression of skin capillaries between a hard surface
(e.g., mattress, chair, or table) and the bone.

Normally, individuals shift their weight off pressure areas
every few minutes; this occurs more or less automatically, even during sleep. Patients with decreased
sensation are unaware of unpleasant stimuli (pressure)
and do not shift weight. This results in prolonged
pressure on skin capillaries and ultimately in skin
ischemia.

■ = Independent; ▲ = Collaborative

Actions/Interventions

- Use an objective tool for pressure ulcer risk assessment.
  - Braden scale
  - Gosnell scale
  - Norton scale

- Assess the patient's ability to move (e.g., shift weight while sitting, turn over in bed, move from bed to chair).

- Assess the patient's nutritional status, including weight, weight loss, and serum albumin levels.

- Assess for edema.

- Assess for history of radiation therapy.

- Assess for history or presence of AIDS.

- Assess for fecal and/or urinary incontinence.

- Assess for environmental moisture (e.g., wound drainage, high humidity).

- Assess the surface that the patient spends a majority of time on (e.g., mattress for bedridden patient, cushion for persons in wheelchairs).

- Assess amount of shear (pressure exerted laterally) and friction (rubbing) on the patient's skin.

- Reassess skin often and whenever the patient's condition or treatment plan results in an increased number of risk factors.

Rationale

These are validated tools for risk assessment. Assessment should be carried out on all patients on admission and every 48 hours in acute care settings, or whenever the patient's condition changes.

Immobility is the greatest risk factor in skin breakdown.

An albumin level less than 2.5 g/dL is a grave sign, indicating severe protein depletion. Research has shown that patients whose serum albumin is less than 2.5 g/dL are at high risk for skin breakdown, all other factors being equal.

Skin stretched tautly over edematous tissue is at risk for impairment.

Radiated skin becomes thin and friable, may have less blood supply, and is at higher risk for breakdown.

Early manifestations of diseases related to human immunodeficiency virus may include skin lesions (e.g., Kaposi's sarcoma); additionally, because of their immunocompromised state, patients with AIDS often have skin breakdown.

The urea in urine turns into ammonia within minutes and is caustic to the skin. Stool may contain enzymes that cause skin breakdown. Use of diapers and incontinence pads with plastic liners traps moisture and hastens breakdown.

Moisture may contribute to skin maceration.

Patients who spend the majority of time on one surface need a pressure reduction or pressure relief device to distribute pressure more evenly and lessen the risk for breakdown.

A common cause of shear is elevating the head of the patient's bed: the body's weight is shifted downward onto the patient's sacrum. Common causes of friction include the patient rubbing heels or elbows against bed linen, and moving the patient up in bed without the use of a lift sheet.

The incidence and onset of skin breakdown is directly related to the number of risk factors present.

Therapeutic Interventions

Actions/Interventions

- If patient is restricted to bed:
  - Encourage implementation and posting of a turning schedule, restricting time in one position to 2 hours or less, and customizing the schedule to the patient's routine and caregiver's needs.

Rationale

A schedule that does not interfere with the patient's and caregiver's activities is most likely to be followed.

Risk for Impaired Skin Integrity

■ = Independent; ▲ = Collaborative

 **Risk for Impaired Skin Integrity**—cont'd

Actions/Interventions

- Encourage implementation of pressure-relieving devices commensurate with degree of risk for skin impairment:
  - For low-risk patients: good-quality (dense, at least 5 inches thick) foam mattress overlay

  - For moderate risk patients: water mattress, static or dynamic air mattress

  - For high-risk patients or those with existing stage III or IV pressure ulcers (or with stage II pressure ulcers and multiple risk factors): low–air-loss beds (Mediscus, Flexicare, Kinair) or air-fluidized therapy (Clinitron, Skytron)

- Encourage the patient and/or caregiver to maintain functional body alignment.
- Limit chair sitting to 2 hours at any one time and encourage the patient to shift weight every 15 minutes.

- Encourage ambulation if the patient is able.
- Increase tissue perfusion by massaging **around** affected area.
- Clean, dry, and moisturize skin, especially over bony prominences, twice daily or as indicated by incontinence or sweating. If powder is desirable, use medical grade cornstarch; avoid talc.

- ▲ Encourage adequate nutrition and hydration:
  - 2000 to 3000 kcal/day (more if increased metabolic demands)

  - Fluid intake of 2000 mL/day unless medically restricted

- Encourage use of lift sheets to move patient in bed and discourage patient or caregiver from elevating head of bead repeatedly.
- ▲ Leave blisters intact by wrapping in gauze, or applying a hydrocolloid (DuoDerm, Sween-Appeal) or a vapor-permeable membrane dressing (Op-Site, Tegaderm).

Rationale

Egg crate mattresses less than 4 to 5 inches thick do not relieve pressure. Because they are made of foam, moisture can be trapped. A false sense of security with the use of these mattresses can delay initiation of devices useful in relieving pressure.

Dynamic devices electronically alternate inflation and deflation of the device. Static devices consist of gel, foam, water, or air that remain in a constant state of inflation. In the home, a waterbed is a good alternative.

Low–air-loss beds allow elevated head of bed and patient transfer. These should be used when pulmonary concerns necessitate elevating the head of bed or when getting the patient up is feasible. Air-fluidized therapy supports the patient's weight at well below capillary closing pressure but restricts getting the patient out of bed easily.

Misalignment can lead to discomfort and injury to joints, nerves, or limbs.

Pressure over the sacrum may exceed 100 mm Hg pressure during sitting. The pressure necessary to close skin capillaries is around 32 mm Hg; any pressure greater than 32 mm Hg results in skin ischemia

Ambulation reduces pressure on the skin from immobility.

Massaging the actual reddened area may damage the skin further.

Smooth, supple skin is more resistant to injury. Talc can be inhaled and cause lung injury.

Adequate hydration and nutrition help maintain skin turgor, moisture, and suppleness, which provide resilience to damage caused by pressure.

Hydrated skin is less susceptible to breakdown. Patients with limited cardiovascular reserve may not be able to tolerate this much fluid.

These measures reduce shearing forces on the skin.

Blisters are sterile natural dressings. Leaving them intact maintains the skin's natural function as a barrier to pathogens while the impaired area below the blister heals.

■ = Independent; ▲ = Collaborative

Education/Continuity of Care

Actions/Interventions

▲ Consult dietitian as appropriate.

■ Teach the patient and caregiver the causes of pressure ulcer development:
  • Pressure on skin, especially over bony prominences
  • Incontinence
  • Poor nutrition
  • Shearing or friction against skin

■ Reinforce the importance of mobility, turning, or ambulation in prevention of pressure ulcers.

■ Teach the patient or caregiver the proper use and maintenance of pressure-relieving devices to be used at home.

Rationale

The dietitian can assist the patient and family in food choices to meet adequate nutritional and hydration goals.

This information can assist the patient or caregiver in finding methods to prevent skin breakdown.

Teaching the patient or caregiver methods to prevent pressure ulcers will enhance their sense of self-efficacy and can improve compliance with the prescribed interventions.

Care and maintenance of pressure-relieving devices will promote their ongoing effectiveness.

• RELATED CARE PLAN

Pressure ulcers, p. 1104

NDx Disturbed Sleep Pattern

Insomnia

NANDA: Time-limited disruption of sleep (natural, periodic suspension of consciousness) amount and quality

Sleep is required to provide energy for physical and mental activities. The sleep-wake cycle is complex, consisting of different stages of consciousness: rapid eye movement (REM) sleep, non-REM sleep, and wakefulness. As persons age, the amount of time spent in REM sleep diminishes. The amount of sleep that individuals require varies with age and personal characteristics. In general, the demands for sleep decrease with age. Older patients sleep less during the night, but may take more naps during the day to feel rested. Disruption in the individual's usual diurnal pattern of sleep and wakefulness may be temporary or chronic. Such disruptions may result in both subjective distress and apparent impairment in functional abilities. Sleep patterns can be affected by environment, especially in hospital critical care units. These patients experience sleep disturbance secondary to the noisy, bright environment, and frequent monitoring and treatments. Such sleep disturbance is a significant stressor in the intensive care unit and can affect recovery. Other factors that can affect sleep patterns include temporary changes in routines such as in traveling, jet lag, sharing a room with another, use of medications (especially hypnotic and antianxiety drugs), alcohol ingestion, night-shift rotations that change one's circadian rhythms, acute illness, or emotional problems such as depression or anxiety. This care plan focuses on general disturbances in sleep patterns and does not address organic problems such as narcolepsy or sleep apnea.

■ = Independent; ▲ = Collaborative

Disturbed Sleep Pattern–cont'd

Common Related Factors

Pain/discomfort
Environmental changes
Anxiety/fear
Depression
Medications
Excessive or inadequate stimulation
Abnormal physiological status or symptoms (e.g., dyspnea, hypoxia, or neurological dysfunction)
Normal changes associated with aging

Defining Characteristics

Verbal complaints of difficulty falling asleep
Awakening earlier or later than desired
Interrupted sleep
Verbal complaints of not feeling rested
Restlessness
Irritability
Dozing
Yawning
Altered mental status
Difficulty in arousal
Change in activity level
Altered facial expression (e.g., blank look, fatigued appearance)

Common Expected Outcome

Patient achieves optimal amounts of sleep as evidenced by rested appearance, verbalization of feeling rested, and improvement in sleep pattern.

NOC Outcomes
Anxiety Self-Control; Sleep

NIC Intervention
Sleep Enhancement

Ongoing Assessment

Actions/Interventions

- Assess past patterns of sleep in normal environment: amount, bedtime rituals, depth, length, positions, aids, and interfering agents.
- Assess the patient's perception of cause of sleep difficulty and possible relief measures to facilitate treatment.

- Document nursing or caregiver observations of sleeping and wakeful behaviors. Record number of sleep hours. Note physical (e.g., noise, pain or discomfort, urinary frequency) and/or psychological (e.g., fear, anxiety) circumstances that interrupt sleep.
- Identify factors that may facilitate or interfere with normal patterns.

- Evaluate timing or effects of medications that can disrupt sleep.

Rationale

Sleep patterns are unique to each individual.

For short-term problems, patients may have insight into the etiological factors of the problem (e.g., fear over results of a diagnostic test, concern over a daughter getting divorced, depression over the loss of a loved one). Knowing the specific etiological factor will guide appropriate therapy.

Often the patient's perception of the problem may differ from objective evaluation.

Considerable confusion and myths about sleep exist. Knowledge of its role in health and wellness and the wide variation among individuals may allay anxiety, thereby promoting rest and sleep.

In both the hospital and home care settings, patients may be following medication schedules that require awakening in the early morning hours. Attention to changes in the schedule or changes to once-a-day medication may solve the problem.

■ = Independent; ▲ = Collaborative

Disturbed Sleep Pattern

Therapeutic Interventions

Actions/Interventions

- Instruct the patient to follow as consistent a daily schedule for retiring and arising as possible.

- Instruct the patient to avoid heavy meals, alcohol, caffeine, or smoking before retiring.

- Instruct the patient to avoid large fluid intake before bedtime.

- Increase daytime physical activities as indicated, but instruct the patient to avoid strenuous activity before bedtime.

- Discourage pattern of daytime naps unless deemed necessary to meet sleep requirements or if part of one's usual pattern.

- Suggest use of soporifics such as milk.

- Recommend an environment conducive to sleep or rest (e.g., quiet, comfortable temperature, ventilation, darkness, closed door). Suggest use of earplugs or eye shades as appropriate.

- Suggest engaging in a relaxing activity before retiring (e.g., warm bath, calm music, reading an enjoyable book, relaxation exercises).

- Explain the need to avoid concentrating on the next day's activities or on one's problems at bedtime.

- Encourage patients to journal or write down their problems or activities before going to sleep.

- ▲ Suggest using hypnotics or sedatives as ordered; evaluate effectiveness.

- If unable to fall asleep after about 30 to 45 minutes, suggest getting out of bed and engaging in a relaxing activity.

For patients who are hospitalized:

- Provide nursing aids (e.g., backrub, bedtime care, pain relief, comfortable position, relaxation techniques).

- Organize nursing care:
  - Eliminate nonessential nursing activities.
  - Prepare the patient for necessary anticipated interruptions and disruptions.

- Attempt to allow for sleep cycles of at least 90 minutes.

Rationale

This promotes regulation of the circadian rhythm and reduces the energy required for adaptation to changes.

Although hunger can also keep one awake, gastric digestion and stimulation from caffeine and nicotine can disturb sleep.

This helps patients who otherwise may need to void during the night.

Activity reduces stress and promotes sleep. However, overfatigue may cause insomnia.

Napping can disrupt normal sleep patterns; however, older patients do better with frequent naps during the day to counter their shorter nighttime sleep schedules.

Milk contains L-tryptophan, which facilitates sleep.

Many people sleep better in cool, dark, quiet environments.

These activities provide relaxation and distraction to prepare the body and mind for sleep.

This can interfere with inducing a restful state. Planning a designated time during the next day to address these concerns may provide permission to "let go" of the worries at bedtime.

Journaling allows the patient to "put aside" the mental activities until the morning.

Because of their potential for cumulative effects and generally limited period of benefit, use of hypnotic medications should be thoughtfully considered and avoided if less aggressive means are effective. Different drugs are prescribed depending on whether the patient has trouble falling asleep or staying asleep. Medications that suppress REM sleep should be avoided.

The bed should not be associated with wakefulness, TV watching, or work.

These aids promote rest.

This promotes minimal interruption in sleep or rest.

Experimental studies have indicated that 60 to 90 minutes are needed to complete one sleep cycle and that the completion of an entire cycle is necessary to benefit from sleep.

■ = Independent; ▲ = Collaborative

Disturbed Sleep Pattern—cont'd

Actions/Interventions

- Move the patient to a room farther from the nursing station if noise is a contributing factor.

- Post a "Do not disturb" sign on the door.

Rationale

The nursing station is often the center of noise and activity.

This will alert people to avoid entering the room and interrupting sleep.

Education/Continuity of Care

Actions/Interventions

- Teach about possible causes of sleeping difficulties and optimal ways to treat them.

- Instruct on nonpharmacological sleep enhancement techniques.

Rationale

This allows patients to participate in their care.

Nonpharmacologic sleep enhancement techniques can be used throughout a lifetime. Pharmacological sleep agents should only be used for a limited time.\

NDx Spiritual Distress

NANDA: Disruption in the life principle that pervades a person's entire being and that integrates and transcends one's biological and psychosocial nature

Spiritual distress is an experience of profound disharmony in the person's belief or value system that threatens the meaning of his or her life. During spiritual distress the patient loses hope, questions his or her belief system, or feels separated from his or her personal source of comfort and strength. Pain, chronic or terminal illness, impending surgery, and the death or illness of a loved one are crises that may cause spiritual distress. Being physically separated from family and familiar culture contributes to feeling alone and abandoned. Nurses in the hospital, home care, and ambulatory settings can assist the patient in reestablishing a sense of spiritual well-being.

Common Related Factors

Separation from religious and cultural ties
Challenged belief and value system (e.g., result of moral or ethical implications of therapy or result of intense suffering)

Defining Characteristics

Expresses concern with meaning of life and death and/or belief systems
Expresses anger toward God (as defined by the person)
Questions meaning of suffering
Verbalizes inner conflict about beliefs
Verbalizes concerns about relationship with deity
Questions meaning of own existence
Inability to choose or chooses not to participate in usual religious practices
Seeks spiritual assistance
Questions moral and ethical implications of therapeutic regimen
Displacement of anger toward religious representatives
Description of nightmares or sleep disturbances

■ = Independent; ▲ = Collaborative

Alteration in behavior or mood evidenced by anger, crying, withdrawal, preoccupation, anxiety, hostility, or apathy

Regards illness as punishment

Does not experience that God is forgiving

Inability to accept self

Engages in self-blame

Denies responsibilities for problems

Description of somatic complaints

Common Expected Outcomes

Patient expresses hope in and value of his/her own belief system and inner resources.

Patient expresses a sense of well-being.

NOC Outcomes
Hope; Spiritual Well-Being

NIC Interventions
Spiritual Support; Coping Enhancement; Emotional Support

Ongoing Assessment

Actions/Interventions

■ Assess history of formal religious affiliation and desire for religious contact.

■ Assess cultural beliefs.

■ Assess spiritual meaning of illness or treatment. Questions such as the following provide a basis for future care planning:
- "What is the meaning of your illness?"
- "How does your illness or treatment affect your relationship with God, your beliefs, or other sources of strength?"
- "Does your illness or treatment interfere with expressing your spiritual beliefs?"

■ Assess hope.

■ Assess whether patients have any unfinished business.

Rationale

Information regarding specific religion and importance of rituals or practices may improve understanding of the patient's needs. All people have a spiritual dimension even if they do not express association with a specific religion or faith tradition.

Individuals may have other important beliefs besides religion that provide strength and inspiration. Likewise, physical impairments or suffering may be seen as "punishment from God."

Level of physical functioning, duration and course of illness, prognosis, and treatments involved can contribute to spiritual distress.

Being hopeful provides a link to spiritual well-being.

Patients may not find peace or harmony until business is completed, such as resolving strained family relations.

Therapeutic Interventions

Actions/Interventions

■ Display an understanding and accepting attitude. Encourage verbalization of feelings of anger or loneliness.

■ Structure your interventions in terms of the patient's belief system.

Rationale

When interviewed later, after the crisis is resolved, patients list the nurse's listening to concerns and the nurse's technical competence as two of the most important items that helped create a sense of well-being.

Patients have a right to their beliefs and practices, even if they conflict with the nurse's.

■ = Independent; ▲ = Collaborative

 **Spiritual Distress**–cont'd

Actions/Interventions

- Develop an ongoing relationship with the patient.

- When requested by patient or family, arrange for clergy, religious rituals, or the display of religious objects, especially when the patient is hospitalized.

- If requested, pray with the patient.

- Acknowledge and support the patient's hopes.

- Do not provide logical solutions for spiritual dilemmas.

- Facilitate communication between patient and family, clergy, and other caregivers.

Rationale

An ongoing relationship establishes trust, reduces the feeling of isolation, and may facilitate resolution of spiritual distress.

These help lessen feelings of separation and provide strength and inspiration. If the patient belongs to a highly codified or ritualized religion, such as Orthodox Judaism, clergy is important at times of passage, such as birth or death. In times of crisis the patient may not have the inner strength to call clergy without assistance.

This provides a sense of connectedness to others. Prayer combined with authentic empathy from the nurse can help patients meet their spiritual needs.

Hopes are different from denial or delusions. Supporting a hope for discharge does not mean supporting a denial of the seriousness of the patient's condition. Hope allows the patient to face the seriousness of the situation.

Spiritual beliefs are based on faith and are independent of logic.

The patient may desire privacy or rest, or may not want clergy present, but may find it difficult to express.

Education/Continuity of Care

Actions/Interventions

- Provide information in a way that does not interfere with the patient's beliefs, faith, or hopes.
- Inform the patient and family of how to obtain religious rites or seek spiritual guidance.

Rationale

This demonstrates respect for the patient's individuality.

This may be essential when decisions about prolonging life, organ donation, or some medical therapy (e.g., blood transfusion) is a question in the patient's mind.

 **NDx Impaired Swallowing**

Dysphagia

NANDA: Abnormal functioning of the swallowing mechanism associated with deficits in oral, pharyngeal, or esophageal structure or function

Impaired swallowing can be a temporary or permanent complication from stroke, head trauma, or intracranial infection; or it can be related to facial, neck, or oral trauma or infection. Although older patients are more often affected due to cerebrovascular accident (CVA), this care plan provides information for all patients, as well as specifics for victims of CVA.

■ = Independent; ▲ = Collaborative

Common Related Factors

Neuromuscular:
- Decreased or absent gag reflex
- Decreased strength or excursion of muscles involved in mastication
- Perceptual impairment
- Facial paralysis (cranial nerves VII, IX, X, XII)

Mechanical:
- Edema
- Tracheostomy tube
- Tumor

Fatigue
Limited awareness
Reddened, irritated oropharyngeal cavity (stomatitis)

Defining Characteristics

Observed evidence of difficulty in swallowing:
- Coughing
- Choking
- Pocketing of food along side of mouth

Verbalized difficulty
Evidence of aspiration

Common Expected Outcomes

Patient maintains adequate nutrition, as evidenced by stable weight.
Patient does not experience aspiration.
Patient verbalizes appropriate maneuvers to prevent choking and aspiration: positioning during eating, type of food tolerated, and safe environment.
Patient and caregiver verbalize emergency measures to be enacted should choking occur.

NOC Outcomes
Swallowing Status; Risk Control; Self-Care: Eating

NIC Interventions
Aspiration Precautions; Swallowing Therapy

Ongoing Assessment

Actions/Interventions

- Assess presence or absence of gag and cough reflexes.

- Assess strength of facial muscles.

- Assess coughing or choking during eating and drinking.
- Assess ability to swallow small amount of water.
- Assess for residual food in mouth after eating.
- Assess regurgitation of food or fluid through nares.

- Assess breath sounds and respiratory status.

Rationale

A depressed gag or cough reflex increases the risk of aspiration.
Pathology of cranial nerves, especially VII, IX, X, and XII, affects motor function and control.
These indicate aspiration.
If aspirated, little or no harm to patient occurs.
Pocketed food may be easily aspirated at a later time.
This indicates a decreased ability to swallow food or fluids and an increased risk for aspiration.
These provide clinical evidence of aspiration.

Therapeutic Interventions

Actions/Interventions

For the hospitalized or home care patient:
- Before mealtime, provide adequate rest periods.
- Remove or reduce environmental stimuli (e.g., television, radio).
- Provide oral care before feeding. Clean and insert dentures before each meal.

Rationale

Fatigue can further contribute to swallowing impairment.
The patient can then concentrate on swallowing.

This facilitates appetite.

■ = Independent; ▲ = Collaborative

Nursing Diagnosis Care Plans

Impaired Swallowing—cont'd

Actions/Interventions

- Place suction equipment at bedside, and suction as needed.

- If decreased salivation is a contributing factor:
  - Before feeding, give the patient a lemon wedge, pickle, or tart-flavored hard candy.
  - Use artificial saliva.
- Maintain the patient in high-Fowler's position with head flexed slightly forward during meals.

- Encourage intake of food that the patient can swallow; provide frequent small meals and supplements.

- Instruct the patient to (1) hold food in mouth, (2) close lips, (3) think about swallowing, and then (4) swallow.
- Instruct the patient not to talk while eating.
- Encourage the patient to chew thoroughly, eat slowly, and swallow frequently, especially if extra saliva is produced. Provide patient with direction or reinforcement until he or she has swallowed each mouthful.

- Identify food given to the patient before each spoonful, if the patient is being fed.

- Proceed slowly, giving small amounts; whenever possible, alternate servings of liquids and solids.
- Encourage a high-calorie diet that includes all food groups, as appropriate. Avoid milk and milk products.
- If patients pouch food to one side of their mouth, encourage them to turn their head to the unaffected side and manipulate the tongue to paralyzed side.
- If patient has had a CVA, place food in back of mouth, on unaffected side, and gently massage unaffected side of throat.
- Place whole or crushed pills in custard or gelatin. (First ask a pharmacist which pills should not be crushed.) Substitute medication in elixir form as indicated.
- Encourage the patient to feed self as soon as possible.

- If oral intake is not possible or is inadequate, initiate alternative feedings (e.g., nasogastric feedings, gastrostomy feedings, or hyperalimentation).

Follow-up:
▲ Initiate dietary consultation for calorie count and food preferences.

Rationale

With impaired swallowing reflexes, secretions can rapidly accumulate in the posterior pharynx and upper trachea, increasing risk of aspiration.

Tart flavors stimulate salivation.

Upright position facilitates gravity flow of food or fluid through alimentary tract. Aspiration is less likely to occur with head tilted slightly forward (position narrows airway).

Foods with consistency of pudding, hot cereal, and semisolid food are most easily swallowed because of consistency and weight. Thin foods are most difficult; gravy or sauce added to dry foods facilitates swallowing.

Proper instruction and focused concentration on specific steps reduces risks.

This facilitates concentration on swallowing.

Such directions assist in keeping one's focus on the task.

Knowledge of consistency of food to expect can prepare the patient for appropriate chewing and swallowing technique.

This helps prevent foods from being left in the mouth.

Dairy products can lead to thickened secretions.

This cleans out residual food.

This helps stimulate act of swallowing.

Mixing some pills with foods helps reduce risk of aspiration.

With self-feeding, the patient can control the volume of a food bolus and the timing of each bite to facilitate effective swallowing.

Optimal nutrition is a patient need.

Dietitians have a greater understanding of the nutritional value of foods and may be helpful in guiding treatment.

■ = Independent; ▲ = Collaborative

Ineffective Therapeutic Regimen Management

Actions/Interventions

▲ Initiate speech pathology consultation for swallowing impairment evaluation and patient assistance.

Rationale

A speech pathologist can be consulted to perform a dysphagia assessment that helps determine the need for video fluoroscopy or a modified barium swallow, and specific techniques to prevent aspiration in patients with impaired swallowing.

Education/Continuity of Care

Actions/Interventions

■ Discuss with and demonstrate the following to the patient or caregiver:
  • Avoidance of certain foods or fluids
  • Upright position during eating
  • Allowance of time to eat slowly and chew thoroughly
  • Provision of high-calorie meals
  • Use of fluids to help facilitate passage of solid foods
  • Monitoring of patient for weight loss or dehydration

■ Help the patient or caregiver set realistic goals.

■ Encourage family mealtime to enhance appetite.

■ Facilitate home care aide or meal provision, if needed.

■ Provide name and telephone number of primary nurse and physician and information on when to call.

■ Demonstrate to the patient, caregiver, or family what should be done if the patient aspirates (e.g., chokes, coughs, becomes short of breath). For example, use suction, if available, and the Heimlich maneuver if the patient is unable to speak or breathe. If liquid aspiration, turn the patient three-fourths prone with head slightly lower than chest.
  • If patient has difficulty breathing, call the Emergency Medical System (911).

■ Encourage family members or caregiver to seek out cardiopulmonary resuscitation (CPR) instruction.

Rationale

Both the patient and caregiver may need to be active participants in implementing the treatment plan to optimize safe nutritional intake.

Goals prevent feelings of frustration and disappointment.

Isolation often has a negative effect on appetite and food consumption. For patients living alone, home companions at mealtime could be arranged.

Homebound patients may require additional assistance to maintain adequate nutrition.

This may enhance overall compliance to the therapeutic plan and reduce anxiety.

Being prepared for an emergency helps prevent further complications.

Mastery of emergency measures may provide confidence to both the patient and caregiver.

 **NDx** **Ineffective Therapeutic Regimen Management**

NANDA: Pattern of regulating and integrating into daily living a program for treatment of illness and the sequelae of illness that is unsatisfactory for meeting specific health goals

With the ongoing changes in health care, patients are being expected to be co-managers of their care. They are being discharged from hospitals earlier and are faced with increasingly complex therapeutic regimens to be handled in the home environment. Likewise, patients with chronic illness often have limited access to health care providers and are expected to assume responsibility for managing the nuances of their disease (e.g., heart failure patients taking an extra furosemide [Lasix] tablet for a 2-pound weight gain).

■ = Independent; ▲ = Collaborative

Ineffective Therapeutic Regimen Management–cont'd

Patients with sensory perception deficits, altered cognition, or financial limitations, and those who lack support systems may find themselves overwhelmed and unable to follow the treatment plan. Older patients, who often experience most of the above problems, are especially at high risk for ineffective management of the therapeutic plan. Other vulnerable populations include patients living in adverse social conditions (e.g., poverty, unemployment, little education); patients with emotional problems (e.g., depression over the illness being treated or other life crises or problems); and patients with substance abuse problems. Culture, ethnicity, and religion may influence one's health beliefs, health practices (e.g., folk medicine, alternative therapies), access to health services, and assertiveness in pursuing specific health care services.

Common Related Factors

Complexity of health care
Complexity of therapeutic regimen
Decisional conflicts
Economic difficulties
Excessive demands made on individual or family
Family conflict
Family patterns of health care
Inadequate number and types of cues to action
Knowledge deficit of prescribed regimen
Perceived seriousness
Perceived susceptibility
Perceived barriers
Social support deficits
Perceived powerlessness

Defining Characteristics

Choices of daily living ineffective for meeting the goals of treatment or prescription program
Increased illness
Verbalized desire to manage illness
Verbalized difficulty with prescribed regimen
Verbalization by patient that he or she did not follow prescribed regimen

Common Expected Outcomes

Patient describes intention to follow prescribed regimen.
Patient describes or demonstrates required competencies.
Patient identifies appropriate resources.

NOC Outcomes
Compliance Behavior;
Knowledge: Treatment Regimen

NIC Interventions
Self-Modification Assistance;
Teaching: Individual

Ongoing Assessment

Actions/Interventions

■ Assess prior efforts to follow a regimen.

■ Assess for related factors that may negatively affect success with following the regimen.

Rationale

This knowledge provides an important starting point in understanding any complexities in implementation of the treatment plan.

Knowledge of causative factors provides direction for subsequent intervention. This may range from financial constraints to physical limitations.

■ = Independent; ▲ = Collaborative

Nursing Diagnosis Care Plans

Actions/Interventions

- Assess the patient's individual perceptions of his or her health problems.

- Assess the patient's confidence in his or her ability to perform desired behavior.

- Assess the patient's ability to learn or remember the desired health-related activity.

- Assess the patient's ability to perform the desired activity.

Rationale

According to the Health Belief Model, the patient's perceived susceptibility to and perceived seriousness and threat of disease affect his or her compliance with the program. In addition, factors such as cultural phenomena and heritage can affect how people view their health.

According to the self-efficacy theory, positive conviction that one can successfully execute a behavior is correlated with performance and successful outcome.

Cognitive impairments need to be identified so an appropriate alternative plan can be devised. For example, the Mini-Mental Status Examination can be used to identify memory problems that could interfere with accurate pill taking. Once identified, alternative actions such as using egg cartons to dispense medications, or daily phone reminders, can be instituted.

Patients with limited financial resources may be unable to purchase special diet foods such as those low in fat or low in salt. Patients with arthritis may be unable to open childproof pill containers.

Therapeutic Interventions

Actions/Interventions

- Include the patient in planning the treatment regimen.

- Tailor the therapy to the patient's lifestyle (e.g., taking diuretics at dinner if working during the day).

- Inform the patient of the benefits of adherence to the prescribed regimen.
- Simplify the regimen. Suggest long-acting forms of medications and eliminate unnecessary medication.

- Eliminate unnecessary clinic visits.

- Develop a system for the patient to monitor his or her own progress.

- Develop with the patient a system of rewards that follow successful follow-through.

Rationale

Patients who become co-managers of their care have a greater stake in achieving a positive outcome. They know best their personal and environmental barriers to success.

This will foster a patient-centered focus and promote compliance. A "one size fits all" approach is usually ineffective.

Increased knowledge fosters compliance.

The greater the number of times during the day that patients need to take medications, the greater the risk of not following through. Polypharmacy is a significant problem with older patients. Attempt to reduce non-essential drug usage.

The physical demands of traveling to an appointment, the financial costs incurred (loss of day's work, child care), the negative feelings of being "talked down to" by health care providers not fluent in the patient's language, as well as the commonly long waits can cause patients to avoid follow-ups when they are required. Telephone follow-up may be substituted as appropriate.

Self-monitoring is a key component of a successful change in behavior.

Rewards may consist of verbal praise, monetary rewards, special privileges (e.g., earlier office appointment, free parking), or telephone calls.

Ineffective Therapeutic Regimen Management

■ = Independent; ▲ = Collaborative

Ineffective Therapeutic Regimen Management–cont'd

Actions/Interventions

- Concentrate on the behaviors that will make the greatest contribution to the therapeutic effect.

- If negative side effects of prescribed treatment are a problem, explain that many side effects can be controlled or eliminated.

- If the patient lacks adequate support in following the prescribed treatment plan, initiate referral to a support group (e.g., American Association of Retired Persons [AARP], American Diabetes Association, senior groups, weight loss programs, Y Me, smoking cessation clinics, stress management classes, social services).

Rationale

Behavior change is never easy. Efforts should be directed to activities known to result in specific benefits (e.g., smoking cessation, fluid control in heart failure patients).

Nonadherence because of medication side effects is a commonly reported problem. Health care providers need to determine actual etiological factors for side effects and possible interplay with over-the-counter medications. Similarly, patients may report fatigue or muscle cramps with exercise. If so, the exercise prescription may need to be revised.

Groups that come together for mutual support and information can be beneficial, especially to patients coping with chronic illness.

Education/Continuity of Care

Actions/Interventions

- Use a variety of teaching methods.

- Introduce complicated therapy one step at a time.

- Instruct the patient on the importance of reordering medications 2 to 3 days before running out.

- Include significant others in explanations and teaching. Encourage their support and assistance in following plans.

- Allow the learner to practice new skills; provide immediate feedback on performance.

- Role-play scenarios when nonadherence to the plan may easily occur. Demonstrate appropriate behaviors.

Rationale

Different people learn in different ways. Match the learning style with the educational approach. For some patients this may require grocery shopping for "healthy foods" with a dietitian or a home visit by the nurse to review a psychomotor skill.

This allows the learner to concentrate more completely on one topic at a time.

Although many cultures in the United States are future-oriented and are concerned with measures to prevent illness, other cultures are more oriented to the present. This difference in time orientation may need to be addressed.

This may enhance overall adaptation to the program.

This allows the patient to use new information immediately, thus enhancing retention. Immediate feedback allows the learner to make corrections rather than practice the skill incorrectly.

Relapse prevention needs to be addressed early in the treatment plan. Helping the patient expand his or her repertoire of responses to difficult situations assists in meeting treatment goals.

■ = Independent; ▲ = Collaborative

 **Disturbed Thought Processes**

Confusion; Disorientation; Inappropriate Social Behavior; Altered Mood States; Delusions; Impaired Cognitive Processes

NANDA: Disruption in cognitive operations and activities

Cognitive processes include those mental processes by which knowledge is acquired. These mental processes include reality orientation, comprehension, awareness, and judgment. A disruption in these mental processes may lead to inaccurate interpretations of the environment and may result in an inability to evaluate reality accurately. Alterations in thought processes are not limited to any one age group, gender, or clinical problem. The nurse may encounter the patient with a thought disorder in the hospital or community, but patients with significant thought disorders are likely to be hospitalized or housed in extended care facilities until their symptoms can be reduced sufficiently for them to be safe in a community setting. Wherever the patient is encountered, the nurse is responsible for effecting a treatment plan that responds to the specific needs of the patient for structure and safety, as well as effective treatment for the presenting symptoms. This care plan discusses management in the acute phase of the disorder for the hospitalized patient.

Common Related Factors

Organic mental disorders (non–substance-induced):
- Dementia
- Primary degenerative (e.g., Alzheimer's disease, Pick's disease)
- Multiinfarct (e.g., cerebral arteriosclerosis)

Organic mental disorders associated with other physical disorders:
- Huntington's chorea
- Multiple sclerosis
- Parkinson's disease
- Cerebral hypoxia
- Hypertension
- Hepatic disease
- Epilepsy
- Adrenal, thyroid, or parathyroid disorder
- Head trauma
- Central nervous system (CNS) infections (e.g., encephalitis, syphilis, meningitis)
- Intracranial lesions (benign or malignant)
- Sleep deprivation

Organic mental disorders (substance induced):
- Organic mental disorders attributed to the ingestion of alcohol (e.g., alcohol withdrawal; dementia associated with alcoholism)
- Organic mental disorders attributed to the ingestion of drugs or mood-altering substances

Schizophrenic disorders

Personality disorders in which there is evidence of altered thought processes

Affective disorders in which there is evidence of altered thought processes

Defining Characteristics

Disorientation to one or more of the following: time, person, place, situation

Altered behavioral patterns (e.g., regression, poor impulse control)

Altered mood states (e.g., liability, hostility, irritability, inappropriate affect)

Impaired ability to perform self-maintenance activities (e.g., grooming, hygiene, food and fluid intake)

Altered sleep patterns

Altered perceptions of surrounding stimuli caused by impairment in the following cognitive processes:
- Memory
- Judgment
- Comprehension
- Concentration

Ability to reason, problem solve, calculate, and conceptualize

Altered perceptions of surrounding stimuli caused by hallucinations, delusions, confabulation, and ideas of reference

NOC Outcomes

Cognitive Ability; Distorted Thought Control; Safety Behavior: Personal; Mood Equilibrium

NIC Interventions

Delusion Management; Dementia Management; Presence; Behavior Management

■ = Independent; ▲ = Collaborative

Disturbed Thought Processes

 **Disturbed Thought Processes**–cont'd

I. Disorientation

Common Expected Outcomes

Patient experiences reduced disorientation to time, place, person, and situation.
Patient interacts with others appropriately.
Patient is assisted in assuming self-care responsibilities to the limits of his or her ability.

Ongoing Assessment

Actions/Interventions

- Assess degree of disorientation to time, place, person, and situation regularly and frequently.

Rationale

This will determine the amount of reorientation and intervention the patient will need to evaluate reality accurately.

Therapeutic Interventions

Actions/Interventions

- Orient the patient to surroundings and reality as needed:

  - Use the patient's name when speaking to him or her.
  - Speak slowly and clearly. Present information in a matter-of-fact manner.

  - Refer to the time of day, date, and recent events in your interactions with the patient.
  - Encourage the patient to have familiar personal belongings in his or her environment.

  - Be matter-of-fact and respectful when correcting the patient's misperceptions of reality.
- Use the words "you" and "I," instead of "we."

Rationale

Orientation to one's environment increases one's ability to trust others. Increased orientation ensures a greater degree of safety for the patient.

This decreases chances for misinterpretation.

These serve to "ground" the here and now, and provide cues that maintain orientation.

These decrease the sense of alienation that the patient may feel in a strange environment. Familiar personal possessions increase the patient's comfort level.

A nonjudgmental approach is used to enhance self-esteem and maintain orientation.

This increases orientation and encourages the patient to maintain his or her sense of separateness and personal boundary.

II. Altered Behavioral Patterns

Common Expected Outcome

Patient demonstrates socially appropriate behavior, as evidenced by a decrease in suspiciousness, aggression, and provocative behavior.

■ = Independent; ▲ = Collaborative

Ongoing Assessment

Actions/Interventions

- Regularly assess the patient's behavior and social interactions for appropriateness.

- Evaluate the patient's ability and willingness to respond to verbal direction and limits.

- Observe for statements reflecting a desire or fantasy to inflict harm on self or others.

Rationale

Age, gender, cultural, and personal norms may influence an individual's behavior. It is not the nurse's responsibility to generate value judgments on aspects of personal preference. It may be helpful to use considerations of safety when evaluating an individual's behavior.

A patient who has developed a level of trust in a care provider, as well as a relationship with him or her, may be able to accept direction. The patient's ability and/or willingness to respond to verbal direction and/or limits may vary with the patient's mood, perceptions, degree of reality orientation, and environmental stressors.

Confusion, disorientation, impaired judgment, suspiciousness, and loss of social inhibitions all may result in socially inappropriate and/or harmful behavior to self or others.

Therapeutic Interventions

Actions/Interventions

- Maintain routine interactions, activities, and close observation without increasing the patient's suspiciousness.

- Develop an open and honest relationship in which expectations are respectfully and clearly verbalized. Make only those promises that can be kept.
- Verbalize acceptance of the patient despite the inappropriateness of his or her behavior.
- Provide role modeling for the patient through appropriate social and professional interactions with other patients and staff.
- Encourage the patient to assume responsibility for his or her own behavior but verbalize your willingness to assist in maintaining appropriate behavior when the patient appears to need structure.
- Provide situations in which group interactions with other patients allow feedback regarding the patient's behavior.

- Provide positive reinforcement for efforts and appropriate behavior. Confront the patient gently and respectfully when behavior is inappropriate, and withdraw attention that reinforces negative behavior.

Rationale

Patients with impaired judgment and loss of social inhibitions require close observation to discourage inappropriate behavior and prevent harm or injury to self and others.

Keeping promises establishes a sense of trust and reliability between the patient and the care provider.

Honesty, openness, and verbalized acceptance of the patient increase his or her self-respect and esteem.

Role modeling provides the patient with an opportunity to observe socially appropriate behavior.

Encouraging the patient to assume responsibility for his or her own behavior will increase his or her sense of independence; however, the nurse's intervention will provide a feeling of security and reassurance.

It is important for the patient to learn socially appropriate behavior through group interactions. This provides an opportunity for the patient to observe the impact his or her behavior has on others. It also facilitates the development of acceptable social skills.

Consistency in providing feedback supports the patient's efforts to maintain changes in behavior.

> ## Disturbed Thought Processes–cont'd

III. Altered Mood States

Common Expected Outcome

Patient exhibits appropriate affect and decreased lability and hostility.

Ongoing Assessment

Actions/Interventions

- Assess mood and affect regularly.

Rationale

Affect is defined as an emotion that is immediately expressed and observed. Affect is inappropriate when it is not in conjunction with the content of the patient's speech and/or ideation. *Lability* is defined as repeated, abrupt, and rapid changes in affect. *Mood* is defined as a pervasive and sustained emotion. Frequent and regular assessment of the patient's mood and affect will assist in determining the predominance of a particular affect or mood and any deviations. This assessment will also determine the presence of any lability or hostility.

- Assess for environmental and situational factors that may contribute to the change in mood or affect.

It is important to remember that patients with thought disorders may also experience fluctuations in mood and affect based on external stimuli, including environmental and situational factors.

Therapeutic Interventions

Actions/Interventions

- Demonstrate acceptance of the patient as an individual.

Rationale

It is important to communicate to the patient one's acceptance of him or her regardless of his or her behavior.

- Demonstrate tolerance of fluctuations in affect and mood. Address inappropriate affect and mood in a calm, yet firm, manner.

Calmness communicates self-control and tolerance of the patient and his or her affect and mood. Addressing and setting limits for inappropriate behavior communicate clear expectations for the patient.

- Identify environmental stimuli that cause increased restlessness or agitation for the patient. Remove the patient when possible from external stimuli that appear to exacerbate irritable and hostile behavior.

The patient's ability to recognize irritating stimuli and remove himself or herself from the source may be impaired. Removing the patient from external stimuli that exacerbate fluctuations in mood and affect encourages a sense of protection and security for the patient.

- Encourage involvement in group activities as tolerated.

Involvement in group activities is determined by various factors, including the group size, activity level, and the patient's tolerance level. Remain aware that the patient's fluctuations in mood and affect will impact his or her ability to respond appropriately to others and his or her capacity to handle complex and multiple stimuli.

■ = Independent; ▲ = Collaborative

IV. Impaired Ability to Perform Activities of Daily Living

Common Expected Outcome

Patient participates in activities of daily living and self-care measures to the limits of his or her ability.

Ongoing Assessment

Actions/Interventions

■ Regularly assess the patient's ability and motivation to initiate, perform, and maintain self-care activities.

■ Obtain history from the patient, family, and friends regarding the patient's dietary habits.

■ Obtain accurate weight and maintain ongoing records through the patient's length of treatment. Weigh the patient on a scheduled basis (e.g., weekly or monthly).

■ Maintain adequate records of the patient's intake and output, elimination patterns, and any associated concerns verbalized by the patient.

▲ Monitor laboratory values and report any significant changes.

■ Obtain information from the patient's family regarding personal grooming and hygiene habits.

Rationale

Assessment can identify areas of physical care in which the patient needs assistance. These areas of physical care include nutrition, elimination, sleep, rest, exercise, bathing, grooming, and dressing. It is important to distinguish between ability and motivation in the initiation, performance, and maintenance of self-care activities. Patients may have the ability and minimal motivation, or motivation and minimal ability.

Information about the patient's dietary habits is important in determining the presence of food allergies. It can also determine the patient's personal food preferences, cultural dietary restrictions, and ability to verbalize hunger.

Accurate records of the patient's body weight help determine significant fluctuations.

The patient with impaired thought processes may be unable to self-monitor intake, output, and elimination patterns.

Laboratory data provide objective information regarding the adequacy of the patient's nutritional status.

This information will assist in developing a specific plan for grooming and hygiene activities.

Therapeutic Interventions

Actions/Interventions

▲ Obtain dietary consultation and determine the number of calories the patient will require to maintain adequate nutritional intake based on body weight and structure.

■ Encourage adequate fluid intake and physical exercise.

■ Assist patient with bathing, grooming, and dressing as needed.

■ Provide the patient with positive reinforcement for his or her efforts in maintaining self-care activities.

Rationale

The patient with an altered thought process may be impaired in maintaining adequate nutritional intake.

Both ongoing exercise and adequate fluid intake help prevent constipation.

The patient with impaired thought processes may be unable to perform grooming activities.

Positive reinforcement is perceived by the patient as support.

■ = Independent; ▲ = Collaborative

Disturbed Thought Processes–cont'd

V. Altered Sleep

Common Expected Outcome

Patient achieves normal sleep pattern.

Ongoing Assessment

Actions/Interventions

■ Assess how sleep is altered. Establish whether the patient has difficulty falling asleep, awakens during the night or early in the morning, or is experiencing insomnia.

Rationale

It is important to determine an accurate baseline for planning interventions.

Therapeutic Interventions

Actions/Interventions

■ Decrease stimuli before the patient goes to bed by suggesting a warm bath, turning down the television or radio, and dimming the lights.

■ Decrease intake of caffeinated substances (e.g., tea, colas, coffee).

■ Evaluate sedative effects of medications and schedule administration to diminish daytime sedation and promote sleep at night.

■ If the patient is experiencing hypersomnia, discourage sleep during the day. Limit the time the patient spends in his or her room and provide stimulating activities.

Rationale

Sleep and rest will be encouraged when loud stimuli are minimized.

Caffeine stimulates the CNS and may interfere with the patient's ability to rest and sleep.

This discourages sleeping during the day and promotes restful night sleep.

Structured expectations provide a focus for activities; contact also provides opportunity to examine feelings the patient may be avoiding through excessive sleep.

VI. Altered Perceptions of Surrounding Stimuli

Common Expected Outcome

Patient will demonstrate reality-based perceptions as evidenced by decreased verbalizations of hallucinations and delusions and decreased threats to self and others.

Ongoing Assessment

Actions/Interventions

■ Assess and observe the patient's ability to verbalize own needs and trust those around him or her.

■ Assess the patient's memory (recent and remote).

■ Assess and observe the patient's judgment and awareness of safety.

Rationale

Psychotic thought processes often limit a patient's ability to trust others. The person may be dependent on others for basic needs. There may be decreased awareness of body sensations such as hunger, pain, or urge to urinate.

Impaired thinking and disorientation can impair information retrieval from long-term memory.

Distortions of reality and impaired problem solving increases the patient's risk for injury.

■ = Independent; ▲ = Collaborative

Actions/Interventions

- Assess ability to concentrate, follow instructions, and problem solve on an ongoing basis.

- Assess the patient's communication patterns. Observe for the presence of delusions and/or hallucinations.

Rationale

Patients with psychotic thought processes have poor concentration and impaired ability for abstract or logical thinking.

Delusions are false beliefs that have no basis in reality. They may be fixed (persistent) or transient (episodic). *Hallucinations* are perceptions of external stimuli without the actual presence of those stimuli. Hallucinations may be visual, auditory, olfactory, tactile, or gustatory and are perceived by the patient as real.

Therapeutic Interventions

Actions/Interventions

- Encourage the patient to communicate own thoughts and perceptions with significant others in the environment.
- Clarify the patient's misperceptions of events and situations that may result from memory impairment.
- Orient to time, place, person, and situation as needed.

- Minimize situations that provoke anxiety.

- Provide protective supervision.

- If the patient is experiencing delusional thinking, assist him or her in recognizing the delusions. Acknowledge the delusions without agreeing to the content of the delusions.
- If the patient is experiencing hallucinations (e.g., as indicated by inappropriate gestures, laughter, talking to oneself without the presence of others):
  - Communicate verbally with the patient by using concrete and direct words and avoiding gesturing so the patient is not threatened by the care provider.
  - Encourage the patient to inform staff when experiencing hallucinations.

  - Discuss content of the hallucinations to determine appropriate interventions.

  - Determine whether the hallucinations are resulting in thoughts and/or plans to harm himself or herself or others.

Rationale

Validation of the patient's needs, thoughts, and perceptions will encourage trust and openness.

Clarification is necessary and more easily accepted when offered in a respectful manner.

The patient's ability to orient himself or herself may be impaired by memory loss.

Anxiety may impair the patient's ability to communicate, problem solve, and reason.

The patient's safety is a priority. The patient may be unable to accurately assess potentially dangerous items and situations such as wet floors, electrical appliances, and verbal threats from other patients as a result of severe impairment in judgment.

Delusions can be anxiety provoking and distressing for patient. It is important to acknowledge this distress but to convey that one does not accept the delusions as real.

The psychotic person is often more timid and frightened than dangerous.

Contact from the care provider can often distract the patient from the hallucination. This approach can reinforce the patient's ability to remain in control of his or her behavior.

The nurse may be able to take measures that will reduce the frequency of the hallucinations (e.g., leaving the lights on or the door open). If the person is hearing "command" hallucinations, the patient needs to be observed closely to prevent dangerous behavior toward self or others.

This enables the nurse to take protective measures for the safety of the patient and others.

■ = Independent; ▲ = Collaborative

 **Impaired Tissue Integrity**

Tissue Necrosis; Cellulitis

NANDA: Damage to mucous membrane, corneal, integumentary, or subcutaneous tissues

Tissue is a collection of cells with similar structure or function. The four types of tissue are epithelial, connective, muscular, and nervous. Tissue can be damaged by physical trauma, including thermal injury (e.g., frostbite); chemical insult, including reactions to drugs, especially chemotherapeutic drugs; radiation; and ischemia. Inflammation of subcutaneous tissue is called cellulitis. Some damaged tissue is able to regenerate (e.g., skin, mucous membranes) while other damaged tissue may be replaced by connective tissue (e.g., cardiac and smooth muscle cells). If untreated, impaired tissue is at risk for infection and/or necrosis (tissue death) and can lead to systemic infection (e.g., sepsis or septicemia). Persons at risk for impaired tissue integrity include the homeless, individuals undergoing cancer therapy, and individuals with altered sensation.

Common Related Factors

Trauma
Thermal injury
Infection
Altered circulation
Chemical insult

Defining Characteristics

Affected area hot, tender to touch
Skin purplish
Swelling around initial injury
Local pain
Protectiveness toward site

Common Expected Outcome

Condition of impaired tissue improves as evidenced by decreased redness, swelling, and pain.

NOC Outcome

Tissue Integrity: Skin and Mucous Membranes

NIC Interventions

Wound Care; Infection Protection; Teaching: Prescribed Medication

Ongoing Assessment

Actions/Interventions

■ Determine the etiology of tissue damage.

■ Assess condition of tissue.

■ Assess characteristics of the wound, including color, size, drainage, and odor.

■ Assess for elevated body temperature.

Rationale

Information guides design of optimal treatment plan (e.g., infection versus burns).

Redness, swelling, pain, burning, and itching are signs of the body's immune response to localized tissue trauma.

These data provide information on extent of damage. Color of tissue is an indication of tissue viability and oxygenation. Odor may arise from infection present in the wound; it may also arise from necrotic tissue. Wound drainage or exudate is a normal part of wound physiology and must be differentiated from pus, which is an indication of infection. Purulent drainage from the injured area is an indication of infection.

Fever can be an indication of infection unless the patient is immunocompromised.

■ = Independent; ▲ = Collaborative

Nursing Diagnosis Care Plans

Actions/Interventions

- Assess the patient's level of discomfort.
- Identify signs of itching and scratching.

Rationale

Depth of wound may affect pain sensations.

The patient who scratches the skin in attempts to relieve intense itching may open skin lesions and increase risk for infection.

Therapeutic Interventions

Actions/Interventions

- Remove any embedded material (e.g., glass, metal), as needed.
- Cleanse with normal saline or a nontoxic cleanser, as appropriate.
- Provide skin care as needed. For example, cover wound with wet or dry dressing, using topical creams or lubricants, using hydrocolloid dressing (e.g., DuoDerm) or vapor permeable membrane dressing such as Tegaderm. Refer to specific care plans, for example, Burns, Pressure Ulcer, and Impaired Skin Integrity.
- Maintain sterile dressing technique during wound care.
- Premedicate for dressing changes as needed.
- Initiate pressure-relieving devices as needed and improve circulation to painful areas.
- Saturate dressings with sterile normal saline solution before removal.
- ▲ Administer antibiotics as ordered.

- Discourage rubbing and scratching. Provide gloves or clip nails if necessary.
- Encourage diet that meets nutritional needs.

Rationale

This facilitates wound healing and prevention of infection.

This removes debris and pathogens.

Each type of wound is best treated based on its etiology.

This reduces risk for infection.

Manipulation of deeper or extensive wounds may be painful.

These help relieve pressure points and improve circulation to painful areas.

This will ease dressing removal by loosening adherents and decreasing pain, especially with burns.

Wound infections may be treated more easily with topical agents, although intravenous antibiotics may be indicated.

Rubbing and scratching can cause further injury and delay healing.

A high-protein, high-calorie diet may be needed to promote healing.

Education/Continuity of Care

Actions/Interventions

- Teach patient or caregiver about cause of tissue integrity impairment.
- Instruct the patient or caregiver in proper care of wound (i.e., cleansing, dressing, and application of topical medications).
- Teach the patient or caregiver signs and symptoms of infection and when to notify the physician or nurse.
- Teach the patient or caregiver pain control measures (e.g., soaks, use of analgesics, and distraction).

Rationale

Thorough understanding of specific cause is necessary for appropriate follow-through of treatment plan.

Teaching increases the patient's ability to manage therapy independently.

The patient needs to be aware of potential complications to facilitate prompt intervention in the event of a problem.

Information allows the patient to identify when therapy adjustments need to be made.

• RELATED CARE PLANS

Burns, p. 1083
Impaired skin integrity, p.173
Pressure ulcers, p. 1104

Impaired Tissue Integrity

■ = Independent; ▲ = Collaborative

NDx Ineffective Tissue Perfusion: Peripheral, Cardiopulmonary, Cerebral

NANDA: Decrease in oxygen resulting in the failure to nourish the tissues at the capillary level

Reduced arterial blood flow causes decreased nutrition and oxygenation at the cellular level. Management is directed at removing vasoconstricting factors, improving peripheral blood flow, and reducing metabolic demands on the body. Decreased tissue perfusion can be transient with few or minimal consequences to the health of the patient. If the decreased perfusion is acute and protracted, it can have devastating effects on the patient. Diminished tissue perfusion, which is chronic in nature, invariably results in tissue or organ damage or death. This care plan focuses on problems in hospitalized patients.

Common Related Factors

Peripheral:
- Indwelling arterial catheters
- Constricting cast
- Compartment syndrome
- Embolism or thrombus
- Arterial spasm
- Vasoconstriction
- Positioning

Cardiopulmonary:
- Pulmonary embolism
- Low hemoglobin
- Myocardial ischemia
- Vasospasm
- Hypovolemia

Cerebral:
- Increased intracranial pressure (ICP)
- Vasoconstriction
- Intracranial bleeding
- Cerebral edema

Defining Characteristics

Peripheral:
- Weak or absent peripheral pulses
- Edema
- Numbness, pain, ache in extremities
- Cool extremities
- Dependent rubor
- Clammy skin
- Mottling
- Difference in blood pressure (BP) in opposite extremity
- Prolonged capillary refill

Cardiopulmonary:
- Tachycardia
- Dysrhythmias
- Hypotension
- Tachypnea
- Abnormal arterial blood gases (ABGs)
- Angina

Common Expected Outcome

Patient maintains optimal tissue perfusion to vital organs, as evidenced by strong peripheral pulses, normal ABGs, alert level of consciousness (LOC), and absence of chest pain.

NOC Outcomes

Tissue Perfusion: Cardiopulmonary; Tissue Perfusion: Cerebral; Tissue Perfusion: Abdominal Organs; Tissue Perfusion: Peripheral; Fluid Balance; Electrolyte and Acid/Base Balance

NIC Interventions

Circulatory Care; Cardiac Care: Acute; Cerebral Perfusion Promotion

Ongoing Assessment

Actions/Interventions

- Assess for signs of decreased tissue perfusion (see Defining Characteristics above).

Rationale

Specific clusters of signs and symptoms occur with differing etiologies.

■ = Independent; ▲ = Collaborative

Actions/Interventions

- Assess for possible causative factors related to temporarily impaired arterial blood flow.

- Monitor quality of all pulses.

- ▲ Monitor international normalized ratio (INR) and prothrombin time/partial thromboplastin time (PT/PTT) if anticoagulants are used for treatment.

Rationale

Early detection of cause facilitates prompt, effective treatment.

Assessment is needed for ongoing comparisons; loss of peripheral pulses must be reported or treated immediately.

Blood clotting studies are used to determine or ensure that clotting factors remain within therapeutic levels.

Therapeutic Interventions

Actions/Interventions

- Maintain optimal cardiac output.

- ▲ Assist with diagnostic testing, as indicated.

- Anticipate the need for possible embolectomy, heparinization, vasodilator therapy, thrombolytic therapy, and fluid rescue.

Rationale

This ensures adequate perfusion of vital organs. Support may be required to facilitate peripheral circulation (e.g., elevation of affected limb, antiembolism devices).

Doppler flow studies or angiograms may be required for accurate diagnosis.

These facilitate perfusion when obstruction to blood flow exists or when perfusion has dropped to such a dangerous level that ischemic damage would be inevitable without treatment.

Specific Interventions

Actions/Interventions

Rationale

Peripheral

- Do passive range-of-motion exercises to unaffected extremity every 2 to 4 hours.
- Position properly.

- Keep cannulated extremity still. Use soft restraints or arm boards as needed.
- ▲ Prepare for removal of arterial catheter as needed.

- ▲ Anticipate or continue anticoagulation, as ordered.

- ▲ If compartment syndrome is suspected, prepare for surgical intervention (e.g., fasciotomy).

- ▲ If the cast causes altered tissue perfusion, anticipate that the physician will bivalve the cast or remove it.
- ▲ Institute continuous pulse oximetry. Report changes in ABGs (e.g., hypoxemia, metabolic acidosis, hypercapnia). Administer oxygen as needed.

Exercise prevents venous stasis and further circulatory compromise.

This promotes optimal lung ventilation and perfusion. The patient will experience optimal lung expansion in an upright position.

Movement may cause trauma to the artery.

Circulation is potentially compromised with a cannula. It should be removed as soon as is therapeutically safe.

Therapy may range from intravenous heparin, subcutaneous heparin, oral anticoagulants, or antiplatelet drugs.

The fascial covering over muscles is relatively unyielding. Blood flow to tissues can become dangerously reduced as tissues swell in response to trauma from the fracture.

This restores perfusion in the affected extremity.

Oxygen saturates circulating hemoglobin and increases the effectiveness of blood that is reaching the ischemic tissues.

- • RELATED CARE PLAN

Chronic peripheral occlusive arterial disease, p. 353

Ineffective Tissue Perfusion: Peripheral, Cardiopulmonary, Cerebral

■ = Independent; ▲ = Collaborative

Ineffective Tissue Perfusion: Peripheral, Cardiopulmonary, Cerebral–cont'd

Actions/Interventions	Rationale

Cardiovascular

▲ Administer nitroglycerin (NTG) sublingually for complaints of angina. If no relief is obtained, seek medical attention.

NTG improves myocardial perfusion. Up to three tablets can be used (1 tablet every 5 minutes). Chest pain unrelieved by NTG may represent unstable angina or myocardial infarction and should be evaluated immediately.

▲ Administer oxygen as ordered.

Increasing arterial oxygen saturation delivers more oxygen to the myocardium.

> **• RELATED CARE PLANS**
>
> Acute coronary syndromes, p. 215
> Angina pectoris, p. 222

Cerebral

■ Monitor LOC.

Neurological assessment helps in determining diagnosis and response to medication. Change in mentation is an important sign.

■ Monitor BP.

Stable systemic blood pressure is necessary to maintain adequate cerebral perfusion.

▲ Ensure proper functioning of ICP catheter (if present).

A characteristic waveform should be evident; elevated P_2 waves, ICP greater than 10 mm Hg, and wide amplitude waveforms indicate increasing ICP.

■ If ICP is increased, elevate head of bed 30 to 45 degrees.

This promotes venous outflow from the brain and helps reduce pressure.

■ Avoid measures that may trigger increased ICP (e.g., straining, strenuous coughing, positioning with neck in flexion, head flat).

Increased intracranial pressures will further reduce cerebral blood flow.

▲ Administer anticonvulsants as needed.

These reduce risk of seizures, which may result from cerebral edema or ischemia.

■ Reorient to environment as needed.

Decreased cerebral blood flow or cerebral edema may result in changes in the LOC.

Education/Continuity of Care

Actions/Interventions	Rationale

■ Provide information on normal tissue perfusion and possible causes for impairment.

Knowledge of causative factors provides understanding for treatments.

■ Explain all procedures and equipment to the patient.

Explaining expected events and sensations can help reduce anxiety associated with the unknown.

■ Instruct the patient to inform the nurse immediately if symptoms of decreased perfusion persist, increase, or return (see Defining Characteristics in this care plan).

Early assessment facilitates prompt treatment.

> **• RELATED CARE PLANS**
>
> Cerebrovascular accident, p. 559
> Transient ischemic attack, p. 640

(■ = Independent; ▲ = Collaborative)

 **Impaired Urinary Elimination**

Stress Incontinence; Urge Incontinence; Reflex Incontinence; Functional Incontinence; Total Incontinence

NANDA: Disturbance in urine elimination
Stress incontinence: Loss of less than 50 mL of urine occurring with increased abdominal pressure
Urge incontinence: Involuntary passage of urine occurring soon after a strong sense of urgency to void
Reflex incontinence: Involuntary loss of urine at somewhat predictable intervals when a specific bladder volume is reached
Functional incontinence: Inability of usually continent person to reach toilet in time to avoid unintentional loss of urine
Total incontinence: Continuous and unpredictable loss of urine

There are several types of urinary incontinence; all are characterized by the involuntary passage of urine. Urinary incontinence is not a disease, but rather a symptom. Incontinence occurs twice as often in women and the incidence increases with age, although urinary incontinence is not a given with aging. An estimated 12 million people are incontinent; billions of dollars are spent annually in the management of urinary incontinence. Micturition (urination) is a complex physiological function that relies on proper function of the bladder muscles and sphincters responding to spinal nerve impulses (S2, S3, and S4). Urinary incontinence occurs whenever the bladder, sphincter, or the nerves involved in micturition are diseased or damaged. Relaxed pelvic musculature following childbirth, postmenopausal urethral atrophy, central nervous system (CNS) diseases (e.g., Parkinson's and cerebrovascular accident [CVA]), spinal cord lesions or injury, and postoperative injuries can result in urinary incontinence. Careful diagnosis, including urodynamic studies, should precede treatment decisions, although empirical management is common. Urinary incontinence can lead to altered skin integrity, as well as severe psychological disturbances. Incontinent individuals often withdraw from social contact, and urinary incontinence is a major determinant in the institutionalization of older patients. This care plan addresses five types of urinary incontinence: stress, urge, reflex, functional, and total. Education and continuity of care are addressed for each type, as well as for the problem of urinary incontinence as an entity.

I. Stress Incontinence

Common Related Factors

Multiple vaginal deliveries
Pelvic surgery
Hypoestrogenism (aging, menopause)
Diabetic neuropathy
Trauma to pelvic area
Obesity
Radial prostatectomy
Myelomeningocele
Infection

Common Expected Outcome

Patient is continent of urine or verbalizes satisfactory management.

Defining Characteristics

Leakage of urine during exercise
Leakage of urine during coughing, sneezing, laughing, lifting, or exercising

NOC Outcomes
Urinary Continence; Urinary Elimination; Self-Care: Toileting

NIC Intervention
Urinary Habit Training: Urinary Incontinence Care

■ = Independent; ▲ = Collaborative

Impaired Urinary Elimination

➤ Impaired Urinary Elimination—cont'd

Ongoing Assessment

Actions/Interventions

■ Ask whether urine is lost involuntarily during coughing, laughing, sneezing, lifting, or exercising.

■ Examine the perineal area for evidence of pelvic relaxation:
  • Cystourethrocele (sagging bladder or urethra)
  • Rectocele (relaxed, sagging rectal mucosa)
  • Uterine prolapse (relaxed uterus)
■ Determine parity.
■ Explore menstrual history.

■ Ask about previous surgical procedures.

■ Weigh patient.
▲ Culture urine.

Rationale

Whenever intraabdominal pressure increases, a weak sphincter and/or relaxed pelvic floor muscles allow urine to escape involuntarily.

The presence of these conditions can lead to incontinence due to poor muscular control.

Childbirth trauma weakens pelvic muscles.

Postmenopausal hypoestrogenism causes relaxation of the urethra.

In men, transurethral resection of the prostate gland can result in urinary incontinence.

Obesity contributes to increased intraabdominal pressure.

Infection can cause incontinence.

Therapeutic Interventions

Actions/Interventions

■ Encourage weight loss if obese.

▲ Administer or encourage use of medication as ordered:
  • Pseudoephedrine
  • Vaginal estrogen
■ Evaluate effectiveness of behavioral therapies discussed below in Education/Continuity of Care
■ Prepare the patient for surgery as indicated.

■ Prepare the patient for the implantation of an artificial urinary sphincter.

Rationale

Obesity is associated with increased abdominal pressure on the urinary bladder.

These increase sphincter tone and improve muscle tone.

A variety of noninvasive treatments need to be explored before more definitive therapies are initiated.

Many types of procedures are used to control stress incontinence; the most commonly performed are Marshall-Marchetti, Burch's colposuspension, and sling procedures.

This uses a subcutaneous pumping device to deflate or inflate a cuff that controls micturition.

Education/Continuity of Care

Actions/Interventions

■ Instruct the patient to keep a daily "bladder diary" indicating toilet voiding and leaking.

■ Teach the patient to perform Kegel exercises.

Rationale

This allows the nurse to identify patterns in voiding on the toilet or involuntarily and precipitating factors. The information will allow for an individualized treatment plan and regimen.

Kegel exercises are used to strengthen the muscles of the pelvic floor and can be practiced with a minimum of exertion. The repetitious tightening and relaxation of these muscles (10 repetitions four or five times per day) helps some patients regain continence. Kegel exercises may be used in combination with biofeedback to enhance outcome.

■ = Independent; ▲ = Collaborative

Actions/Interventions

- Teach the patient to use transcutaneous electrical nerve stimulation (TENS), as indicated.
- ▲ Teach women patients the use of a vaginal pessary (a device reserved for nonsurgical candidates).
- Refer to stress urinary incontinence website *www.sui.com*.

Rationale

This improves pelvic floor tone and inhibits the micturition reflex.

This works by elevating the bladder neck, thereby increasing urethral resistance.

The site provides additional resources, support, and information.

II. Urge Incontinence

Common Related Factors

Uninhibited bladder contraction
CVA
Spinal cord injury
Parkinsonism
Multiple sclerosis
Benign prostatic hypertrophy
Infections
Psychogenic

Defining Characteristics

Sudden, "unannounced" need to void
Frequent urinary accidents associated with "not getting there in time"
Inability to delay voiding

Common Expected Outcome

Patient is continent of urine or verbalizes management.

NOC Outcomes
Urinary Continence; Urinary Elimination;
  Self-Care: Toileting

NIC Interventions
Urinary Habit Training;
  Urinary Incontinence Care

Ongoing Assessment

Actions/Interventions

- Ask patient to describe episodes of incontinence; note descriptions of feeling the need suddenly to (but being unable to) get to the bathroom in time.
- Consider age.

- ▲ Culture urine.

Rationale

Urge incontinence occurs when the bladder muscle suddenly contracts.

This type of urinary incontinence is the most common type among older patients.

Bladder infection can result in a strong urge to urinate; successful management of a urinary tract infection may eliminate or improve incontinence.

Therapeutic Interventions

Actions/Interventions

- Facilitate access to toileting facilities and teach the patient to make scheduled trips to the bathroom.
- ▲ Administer or encourage use of medications as ordered:
  - Anticholinergics
  - Tricyclic antidepressants

- Prepare the patient for sphincterotomy (surgical correction), as indicated.

Rationale

This allows for frequent bladder emptying.

Anticholinergics reduce or block detrusor contractions, thereby reducing episodes of incontinence. The tricyclics increase serotonin or norepinephrine, which results in relaxation of the bladder wall and greater bladder capacity.

Denervation, resulting in complete incontinence, may be undertaken (rhizotomy). Urinary diversion (ileal conduit) may be performed as a last resort.

■ = Independent; ▲ = Collaborative

Nursing Diagnosis Care Plans

> ## Impaired Urinary Elimination–cont'd

Education/Continuity of Care

Actions/Interventions

■ Instruct the patient to keep a daily bladder diary indicating voiding frequency and patterns.

■ Educate the patient in the use of biofeedback techniques.

Rationale

This allows the nurse to identify patterns in voiding. This information will allow for an individualized treatment plan.

These control pelvic floor musculature.

III. Reflex Incontinence

Common Related Factors

Spinal cord injury
Stimulation of the perineum in the presence of spinal cord injury

Defining Characteristic

Loss of urine without warning

Common Expected Outcome

Patient verbalizes or demonstrates management techniques.

NOC Outcomes
Urinary Continence; Urinary Elimination; Self-Care: Toileting

NIC Interventions
Urinary Catheterization;
    Urinary Catheterization: Intermittent;
    Urinary Habit Training;
    Urinary Incontinence Care

Ongoing Assessment

Actions/Interventions

■ Document history of spinal cord injury, including level. Ask whether the patient feels urgency or sensation of voiding.

Rationale

Spinal cord–injured patients may have damaged sensory fibers, and may not have the sensation of the need to void.

Therapeutic Interventions

Actions/Interventions

■ Consider use of an external catheter.

▲ Use an indwelling catheter as a last resort.

Rationale

An external catheter connected to a gravity drainage device allows the patient to remain dry.

Although the risk of infection is considerable with both external and indwelling catheters, indwelling catheters interfere with clothing, movement, and sexual activity and may result in odor or other embarrassing sensory phenomena.

Education/Continuity of Care

Actions/Interventions

▲ Teach the patient or caregiver (or perform for patient) intermittent (self-) catheterization

Rationale

This empties the bladder at specified intervals.

■ = Independent; ▲ = Collaborative

IV. Functional Incontinence

Common Related Factors

Unavailability of toileting facility
Inability to reach toileting facility
Untimely responses to requests for toileting
Limited physical mobility

Defining Characteristic

Recognizes need to urinate, but is unable to access
toileting facility

Common Expected Outcome

Patient experiences fewer episodes (or no episodes) of
incontinence.

> **NOC Outcomes**
> Urinary Continence; Urinary Elimination;
>   Self-Care: Toileting
>
> **NIC Interventions**
> Urinary Habit Training;
>   Urinary Incontinence Care

Ongoing Assessment

Actions/Interventions

- Assess the patient's recognition of the need to urinate.

- Assess the availability of functional toileting facilities
  (working toilet, bedside commode).

- Assess the patient's ability to reach a toileting facility,
  both independently and with help.

- Assess frequency of the patient's need to urinate.

Rationale

Patients with functional incontinence are incontinent
because they cannot get to an appropriate place to void.
Institutionalized patients are often labeled "incontinent"
because their requests for toileting are unmet. Older
patients with cognitive impairment may recognize the
need to void but may be unable to express the need.

Patients may need a bedside commode if mobility limitations interfere with getting to the bathroom.

This information allows the nurse to plan for assistance
with transfer to a toilet or bedside commode. Functional continence requires that the person is able to
get to a toilet either independently or with assistance.

This is the basis for an individualized toileting program.

Therapeutic Interventions

Actions/Interventions

- Establish a toileting schedule.

- Explore the benefit and safety of placing a bedside
  commode near the patient's bed.

- Encourage use of clothing that can be easily and quickly
  removed.

- Treat any existing perineal skin excoriation with a
  vitamin-enriched cream, followed by a moisture barrier.

Rationale

A toileting schedule assures the patient of a specified time
for voiding and reduces episodes of functional incontinence.

The person needs to accept this alternative toileting facility.
Some people may be embarrassed when using a toilet
in a more open area.

Clothing can be a barrier to functional continence if it
takes time to remove before voiding.

Moisture-barrier ointments are useful in protecting
perineal skin from urine scalds.

Education/Continuity of Care

Actions/Interventions

- Teach the patient or caregiver the rationale behind and
  implementation of a toileting program.

Rationale

Successful functional continence requires consistency in
use of a toileting program.

■ = Independent; ▲ = Collaborative

Nursing Diagnosis Care Plans

> ## Impaired Urinary Elimination–cont'd

V. Total Incontinence

Common Related Factors
Pelvic surgery
Fistulas (iatrogenic, postoperative, and postradiation)
Trauma
Exstrophy of bladder

Defining Characteristic
Continual involuntary loss of urine

Common Expected Outcomes
Patient remains dry and comfortable.
Perineal skin remains intact.

NOC Outcomes
Urinary Continence; Urinary Elimination;
  Self-Care: Toileting
NIC Interventions
Urinary Habit Training;
  Urinary Incontinence Care

Ongoing Assessment

Actions/Interventions

■ Assess amount of urine loss.

■ Assess perineal skin condition.

Rationale

This is a function of assessing intake and output measurements.

The urea in urine converts to ammonia in a short time and is caustic to the skin.

Therapeutic Interventions

Actions/Interventions

■ Encourage use of diapers or external collection devices.

■ Prepare the patient for surgical correction as indicated.

Rationale

Most patients are women with fistulas; indwelling catheters are useless in the presence of vesicovaginal or urethrovaginal fistulas because there is a communication between the bladder or urethra and the vagina.

Information is necessary for the patient to make an educated decision regarding treatment options.

VI. All Types of Incontinence

Education/Continuity of Care

Actions/Interventions

■ Teach the patient or caregiver normal anatomy of genitourinary tract and factors that normally control micturition and maintain continence.

■ Assist the patient in recognizing that any episodes of incontinence that pose a social or hygienic problem deserve investigation so that appropriate therapy can be implemented.

Rationale

This provides a basis of understanding for further teaching and incontinence management techniques.

Many people accept urinary incontinence as an inevitable consequence of aging and may be unaware that therapeutic measures can improve incontinence.

■ = Independent; ▲ = Collaborative

Impaired Urinary Elimination

Actions/Interventions

- Inform the patient of the high incidence of urinary incontinence.

- Assist the patient, through careful interview, to identify possible causes of urinary incontinence.

- Teach the patient the necessity, purpose, and expected results of urodynamic diagnostic evaluation.

- Provide information regarding all available methods of managing urinary incontinence. Methods include the following:
  - Use of absorbent pads or undergarments that accommodate absorbent pads
  - Diapers
  - Linen protectors for bedridden patients
  - External collection devices such as male external catheters and female external catheters
  - Indwelling catheters
  - Intermittent catheterization
  - Surgical procedures
  - Electrical nerve stimulators
  - Pessary
  - Pharmacotherapeutic agents

  - Drugs that may precipitate or worsen incontinence: diuretics, sedatives, hypnotics, anticholinergics, and alcohol
  - Drugs that may be used to treat urinary incontinence:
    - α-Blockers

    - β-Blockers
    - Cholinergics
    - Anticholinergics

    - α-Adrenergics

- Provide information on odor control.

- Familiarize the patient with potential risk of skin breakdown.

- Refer to the American Foundation for Urologic Disease at www.afud.org.

Rationale

This information may decrease feelings of hopelessness and isolation that often accompany urinary incontinence.

This approach will help the patient become an active participant in managing his or her incontinence.

Urodynamic studies evaluate bladder filling and sphincter activity, and are particularly useful in differentiating stress and urge incontinence.

This enables the patient to make an informed decision regarding the best treatment for a specific problem.

Patients need information on drugs used to treat urinary incontinence as well as those used for other problems that may precipitate or worsen incontinence.

These drugs either increase the volume of urine or decrease the patient's ability to sense the need to void.

These increase bladder pressures and decrease outlet pressures.

These increase outlet resistance.

These increase bladder pressure.

These depress smooth muscle activity in the hypertonic bladder.

These increase sphincter tone.

Vinegar and commercially prepared solutions are useful in neutralizing urinary odor.

Urea contained in urine metabolizes to ammonia within minutes and is responsible for "urine burns" or "scalding." Spray or wipe preparations such as Skin Prep and Bard Barrier Film protect the skin from urine.

This organization provides the patient and significant others with information, referrals, and resources.

■ = Independent; ▲ = Collaborative

Urinary Retention

NANDA: Incomplete emptying of the bladder

Urinary retention may occur in conjunction with or independent of urinary incontinence. Urinary retention, the inability to empty the bladder even though urine is present, may occur as a side effect of certain medications, including anesthetic agents, antihypertensives, antihistamines, antispasmodics, and anticholinergics. These drugs interfere with the nerve impulses necessary to cause relaxation of the sphincters, which allow urination. Obstruction of outflow is another cause of urinary retention. Most commonly, this type of obstruction in men is the result of benign prostatic hypertrophy.

Common Related Factors

General anesthesia
Regional anesthesia
High urethral pressures caused by disease, injury, or edema
Pain, fear of pain
Infection
Inadequate intake
Urethral blockage

Defining Characteristics

Decreased (less than 30 mL/hr) or absent urinary output for 2 consecutive hours
Frequency
Hesitancy
Urgency
Lower abdominal distention
Abdominal discomfort
Dribbling

Common Expected Outcome

Patient empties bladder completely.

NOC Outcomes
Urinary Continence; Urinary Elimination; Infection Status

NIC Intervention
Urinary Retention Care

Ongoing Assessment

Actions/Interventions

- Evaluate previous patterns of voiding.
- Visually inspect and palpate lower abdomen for distention.
- Evaluate time intervals between voidings and record the amount voided each time.

▲ Catheterize the patient or use a bladder scan (portable ultrasound instrument) to measure residual urine if incomplete emptying is suspected.

- Assess amount, frequency, and character (e.g., color, odor, and specific gravity) of urine.

Rationale

There is a wide range of "normal" voiding frequency.

The bladder lies below the umbilicus.

Keeping an hourly log for 48 hours gives a clear picture of the patient's voiding pattern and amounts and can help to establish a toileting schedule.

Retention of urine in the bladder predisposes the patient to urinary tract infection and may indicate the need for an intermittent catheterization program.

This allows for assessment of residual urine volumes and risk factors for a urinary tract infection.

= Independent; ▲ = Collaborative

Nursing Diagnosis Care Plans

Actions/Interventions

■ Determine balance between intake and output.

▲ Monitor urinalysis, urine culture, and sensitivity.

■ If an indwelling catheter is in place, assess for patency and kinking.

▲ Monitor blood urea nitrogen and creatinine.

Rationale

Intake greater than output may indicate retention.

Urinary tract infection can cause retention, but it is more likely to cause frequency.

An occluded or kinked catheter may lead to urinary retention in the bladder.

This will differentiate between urinary retention and renal failure.

Therapeutic Interventions

Actions/Interventions

■ Initiate the following methods:

• Encourage fluids.

• Encourage intake of cranberry juice daily.

• Place bedpan, urinal, or bedside commode within reach.

• Position patient upright if possible to facilitate successful voiding.

• Provide privacy.

• Encourage the patient to void at least every 4 hours.

• Have the patient listen to the sound of running water, or place the patient's hands in warm water and/or pour warm water over the perineum.

• Offer fluids before voiding.

• Perform Credé's method over bladder.

▲ Encourage the patient to take bethanechol (Urecholine) as ordered.

▲ Institute intermittent catheterization.

▲ Insert an indwelling (Foley) catheter as ordered:
• Tape the catheter to abdomen (male).
• Tape the catheter to thigh (female).

Rationale

These facilitate voiding.

Unless medically contraindicated, fluid intake should be at least 1500 mL/24 hr.

This keeps urine acidic. This helps prevent infection because cranberry juice metabolizes to hippuric acid, which maintains an acidic urine; acidic urine is less likely to become infected.

An upright position on a commode or in bed on a bedpan increases the patient's voiding success through force of gravity; it also decreases embarrassment of soiling self or bed linens.

Privacy helps the patient relax urinary sphincters.

This stimulates urination.

Sufficient urine volume is needed to stimulate the voiding reflex.

Credé's method (pressing down over the bladder with the hands) increases bladder pressure, which stimulates relaxation of the sphincter to allow voiding.

This stimulates the parasympathetic nervous system to release acetylcholine at nerve endings and to increase tone and amplitude of contractions of smooth muscles of the urinary bladder. Side effects are rare after oral administration of therapeutic dose. In small subcutaneous doses, side effects may include abdominal cramps, sweating, and flushing. In larger doses they may include malaise, headache, diarrhea, nausea, vomiting, asthmatic attacks, bradycardia, lowered blood pressure, atrioventricular block, and cardiac arrest.

Because many causes of urinary retention are self-limited, the decision to leave an indwelling catheter in place should be avoided.

This prevents urethral fistula.

This prevents inadvertent displacement.

■ = Independent; ▲ = Collaborative

Nursing Diagnosis Care Plans

→ Urinary Retention–cont'd

Education/Continuity of Care

Actions/Interventions

▲ Educate the patient or caregiver about the importance of adequate fluid intake (e.g., 8 to 10 glasses of fluids daily).

■ Instruct the patient or caregiver on measures to help voiding (as described on the previous page).

■ Instruct the patient or caregiver on signs and symptoms of overdistended bladder (e.g., decreased or absent urine, frequency, hesitancy, urgency, lower abdominal distention, or discomfort).

■ Instruct the patient or caregiver on signs and symptoms of urinary tract infection (e.g., chills and fever, frequent urination or concentrated urine, and abdominal or back pain).

■ Teach the patient or caregiver to perform meatal care twice daily with soap and water and to dry thoroughly.

■ Teach the patient to achieve an upright position on the toilet if possible.

Rationale

Increased fluid stimulates voiding and decreases the risk for development of urinary tract infections due to flushing of bacteria from the genitourinary tract.

Measures may stimulate voiding.

This allows for early recognition of the condition and treatment.

This allows the patient or caregiver to recognize signs and symptoms, and seek treatment.

This reduces the risk of infection.

This is the natural position for voiding and uses the force of gravity.

→  Dysfunctional Ventilatory Weaning Response

NANDA: Inability to adjust to lowered levels of mechanical ventilator support that interrupts and prolongs the weaning process

A patient is who is reliant on ventilatory support and unable to tolerate the weaning process is experiencing dysfunctional ventilatory weaning response (DVWR). This may result from physiological, psychological, or situational factors. Their influence should be evaluated before weaning and after each unsuccessful weaning attempt. In addition to the listed related factors, physiological factors associated with the inability to wean may include left ventricular failure, use of medications that depress the respiratory drive (e.g., sedative, narcotics) or cause respiratory muscle weakness (neuromuscular blocking agents or aminoglycosides), alterations in metabolic status (hypophosphatemia, hypothyroidism, hypomagnesemia), acid-base imbalances (metabolic acidosis, respiratory alkalosis), respiratory tract infection, overhydration, anemia, significant alterations in vital signs/ara rhythmias, abnormal weaning parameters (negative inspiratory force, tidal volume, vital capacity, minute ventilation, rapid shallow breathing index), and an FIO_2 of greater than 0.50 on the ventilator. Additional psychological factors may include psychological ventilator dependence and agitation associated with intensive care unit psychosis, delirium, increased anxiety, and fear. Inability to wean may also be due to lack of motivation secondary to depression, cognitive impairments, or personality disorders. Unfavorable situational factors such as an inappropriate weaning plan may also contribute to weaning failure. When abnormalities or adverse conditions are identified, the weaning plan should incorporate measures to eliminate them or minimize their effects so the risk of DVWR is reduced. Weaning may be postponed when the patient does not demonstrate readiness to wean. This reduces patient frustration and anxiety and avoids potentially life-threatening situations.

Common Related Factors

Physical:
- Ineffective airway clearance
- Sleep pattern disturbance
- Inadequate nutrition
- Uncontrolled pain or discomfort

Psychological:
- Knowledge deficit of the weaning process or patient role
- Patient-perceived inefficacy about the ability to wean
- Decreased motivation
- Decreased self-esteem
- Anxiety: moderate, severe
- Fear
- Hopelessness
- Powerlessness
- Insufficient trust in the nurse

Situational:
- Uncontrolled episodic energy demand or problems
- Inappropriate pacing of diminished ventilator support
- Inadequate social support
- Adverse environment (e.g., noisy, active environment; negative events in the room; low nurse-patient ratio; extended nurse absence from bedside; unfamiliar nursing staff)
- History of ventilator dependence greater than 1 week
- History of multiple unsuccessful weaning attempts

Defining Characteristics

Mild DVWR:
- Restlessness
- Slight increased respiratory rate (RR) from baseline
- Expressed feelings of increased need for oxygen, breathing discomfort, fatigue, and warmth

Moderate DVWR:
- Slight increase in blood pressure (BP) (less than 20 mm Hg)
- Slight increase in heart rate (HR) (less than 20 beats/min)
- Increase in RR (less than 5 breaths/min)
- Hypervigilance to activities
- Inability to respond to coaching
- Inability to cooperate
- Apprehension
- Diaphoresis
- Pale, slight cyanosis
- "Wide-eyed" look
- Decreased air entry on auscultation
- Slight respiratory accessory muscle use

Severe DVWR:
- Agitation
- Deterioration in arterial blood gases (ABGs) from current baseline
- Increase in BP (greater than 20 mm Hg)
- Increase in HR (greater than 20 beats/min)
- Increase in RR
- Profuse diaphoresis
- Full respiratory accessory muscle use
- Shallow, gasping breaths
- Paradoxical abdominal breathing
- Discoordinated breathing with the ventilator
- Decreased level of consciousness
- Adventitious breath sounds, audible airway secretions
- Cyanosis

Common Expected Outcome

Patient experiences a functional ventilatory weaning response as evidenced by:
- BP, HR, and RR in normal range for patient
- Expressed feelings of comfort
- Being responsive or cooperative to coaching
- ABGs within baseline range
- Effective breathing pattern

NOC Outcomes
Respiratory Status: Ventilation;
Respiratory Status: Gas Exchange

NIC Interventions
Mechanical Ventilatory Weaning;
Mechanical Ventilation

Ongoing Assessment

Actions/Interventions

- Assess for increasing dyspnea, restlessness, apprehension, and agitation.

- Monitor vital signs closely during weaning process, watching for increases in BP, HR, and RR.

Rationale

These are signs of DVWR.

These also are signs of weaning failure.

■ = Independent; ▲ = Collaborative

Dysfunctional Ventilatory Weaning Response–cont'd

Actions/Interventions

- Assess lungs and breath sounds for adventitious sounds.

- Assess skin color and warmth. Assess for presence of cyanosis.

- Assess the patient's ability to cooperate and respond to coaching.

- Monitor for signs of respiratory muscle fatigue (e.g., abrupt rise in $PaCO_2$, rapid shallow ventilation, paradoxical abdominal wall motion) while weaning is in progress.

- Assess for presence of discoordinated breathing with the ventilator.

▲ Continuously monitor pulse oximetry for oxygen saturation. ABGs and capnography should also be evaluated when available.

- For patients with chronic dyspnea, assess usual symptom management.

▲ Before weaning and after each unsuccessful attempt, assess for physiological (e.g., lack of adequate sleep, poor nutrition), psychological (e.g., anxiety, fear), and situational factors that contribute to DVWR.

Rationale

Suctioning may be required to reduce airway resistance and the work of breathing when coarse crackles or sonorous wheezes are present. Proper positioning of endotracheal tubes are usually determined by the presence of bilateral breath sounds.

Cyanosis may occur when 5 g of hemoglobin are desaturated. Cool, pale diaphoretic skin may be due to a compensatory peripheral vasoconstrictive response to hypoxemia.

Cooperation and ability to be coached facilitate implementation of measures used to help patients to control their breathing and anxiety, and remain motivated to perform the work of breathing.

These are signs of DVWR that require resumption of preweaning level of ventilatory support.

This increases the work of breathing, dyspnea, anxiety, and feelings of loss of control over breathing.

These are used to assess the adequacy of oxygenation and ventilation during weaning and the need to resume previous level of ventilatory support.

This may reveal effective strategies for reducing dyspnea during weaning.

Addressing these factors promotes successful weaning and reduces patient frustration and anxiety related to multiple unsuccessful weaning attempts and avoids potentially life-threatening situations.

Therapeutic Interventions

Actions/Interventions

▲ Notify physician and anticipate altering ventilator support depending on the degree of DVWR. When DVWR occurs, greater ventilatory support is needed.

▲ Maintain the prescribed oxygen level and ventilatory settings.

- Suction the airway as needed to maintain patency.

Rationale

Inappropriate settings can increase work of breathing and lead to respiratory muscle fatigue. The respiratory muscles can be rested with appropriate ventilator settings.

Maintain oxygen saturation of 90% or greater so that adequate tissue oxygenation is maintained.

This decreases airflow resistance and minimizes work of breathing.

■ = Independent; ▲ = Collaborative

Actions/Interventions

▲ Individualize the patient's weaning program through collaboration with other health care team members.
  • Method of weaning (e.g., using the SIMV mode to slowly decrease ventilatory support versus use of continuous positive airway pressure and pressure support or short trials of oxygen alone with full suspension of ventilatory support)
  • Provision of adequate rest between weaning trials
  • Scheduled weaning for certain parts of the day

▲ Maintain the patient's feedings. Collaborate with the dietitian to ensure that nutritional replacement is matched to metabolic needs.

▲ Administer pain medications and antianxiety medications, as required.

■ Assist the patient with turning and repositioning during the weaning process. Postpone nonessential physical activities during weaning.

■ Coach the patient through ineffective breathing patterns and episodes of anxiety, assisting him or her to focus on breathing pattern.

■ Give frequent feedback to the patient regarding progress.

■ Establish patient trust with the following measures:
  • Use a calm, empathetic approach.
  • Demonstrate confidence in the patient's abilities.
  • Explain things before doing them.
  • Collaborate with the patient in planning his or her care.
  • Provide individual attention.
  • Answer call light in a timely manner.
  • Do not minimize reports of dyspnea.

■ Determine significant others' effect on the patient during the weaning process. Establish and control visiting times as appropriate.

■ Provide an appropriate environment for weaning: personalized space, a quiet room with a controllable temperature.

■ Assist the patient into a position that is comfortable for breathing (usually semi-Fowler's or Fowler's).

■ Provide the means for communicating (e.g., alphabet board, call light).

Rationale

Patients respond differently to weaning efforts. Tailoring weaning strategies to the patient's needs increases the potential for successful weaning.

Feedings ensure sufficient nutrients to enable weaning. Malnutrition reduces respiratory mass and strength. Overfeeding increases metabolic production of carbon dioxide that increases respiratory drive and respiratory muscle fatigue.

Pain medications are used to relieve uncontrolled pain or discomfort; however, oversedation could prevent the patient from ventilating adequately by blunting the respiratory drive.

This decreases energy expenditure and reduces oxygen demand.

Coaching can reduce anxiety and assist in reestablishment of an effective breathing pattern.

This helps keep the patient working toward weaning.

Patient trust and confidence in the nurse helps motivate the patient in the weaning process and decreases anxiety and fear. Patients who have had previous near-death experiences or feared dying during severe episodes of dyspnea may perceive subsequent occurrences as life or death situations. Failure to respond in an appropriate manner may result in mistrust.

Significant others may be a positive factor and a great support during the weaning process and then should be allowed to remain at the bedside for extended periods; however, some significant others may have a negative effect, causing the patient to become restless and fight the ventilator.

Attention to providing a comfortable environment can reduce some of the stress associated with weaning.

This facilitates lung expansion and minimizes dyspnea.

Frustration, anxiety, fear, panic, and anger can occur when patients cannot communicate their needs. These emotions may increase dyspnea. Communication of breathing difficulties is needed to prevent life-threatening situations.

Dysfunctional Ventilatory Weaning Response

■ = Independent; ▲ = Collaborative

Dysfunctional Ventilatory Weaning Response–cont'd

Education/Continuity of Care

Actions/Interventions

- Discuss with the patient, significant others, or caregiver the individualized weaning plan.

- Discuss with the patient the importance of actively engaging in the work of weaning.

- Reassure the patient that multiple weaning trials are normal and expected.

- Discuss with the patient and significant others or caregiver the importance of setting achievable goals, and explain the probable weaning process, including the potential for setbacks.

- Give positive reinforcement for achievements.

- Avoid instructions to "control your breathing," "relax," or "calm down."

- Before weaning, explain that anxiety and dyspnea may occur during the process, and discuss the measures that may be used to decrease these symptoms (e.g., music, progressive muscle relaxation techniques, imagery, prayer, meditation).

- If the patient is to be removed from ventilator support during weaning attempts, explain that when usual support is reinitiated, there may be some difficulty synchronizing his or her breathing with the ventilator.

Rationale

Increased understanding promotes cooperation with the plan.

Increased understanding promotes cooperation with the plan.

This helps prevent anxiety, frustration, and feelings of hopelessness. Patients fear that they will not be able to be weaned.

Minimizing setbacks may help motivate the patient to try again.

This increases the patient's sense of well-being and motivation to continue the weaning process.

These increase patient frustration and feelings of helplessness because they may not be possible when the patient is dyspneic.

Management of dyspnea and anxiety can prevent premature cessation of weaning trials. Music may increase exercise tolerance in pulmonary patients, decrease heart rate and respiratory rate in ventilator patients, and reduce situational dyspnea.

Prior knowledge decreases fear and anxiety.

■ = Independent; ▲ = Collaborative

Nursing Diagnosis Care Plans

3

Cardiac and Vascular Care Plans

 **Acute Coronary Syndromes**

Unstable Angina; Non–ST-Segment Elevation Myocardial Infarction; Non–Q-Wave Myocardial Infarction; Q-Wave Myocardial Infarction; ST-Segment Elevation Myocardial Infarction; Variant Angina; Prinzmetal's Angina

Acute coronary syndromes (ACS) represent a spectrum of clinical conditions that are associated with acute myocardial ischemia. Clinical conditions included in ACS are unstable angina, variant angina, non–ST-segment elevation myocardial infarction (MI), and ST-segment elevation MI. Evaluation of chest pain related to these disorders is a major cause of emergency department visits and hospitalizations in the United States. The term *ACS* is used prospectively to diagnose patients with chest pain who need to be triaged for treatment of unstable angina or acute MI. Early identification of ACS and intervention to improve myocardial perfusion reduces the risk of sudden cardiac death and acute MI in these patients.

Most patients who experience ACS have atherosclerotic changes in the coronary arteries. The presence of atherosclerotic plaques narrows the lumen of the arteries and contributes to thrombus formation that diminishes blood flow to the myocardium. This imbalance between myocardial oxygen demand and supply is the primary cause of the clinical manifestation in ACS. Other causes of ACS include coronary artery spasm and arterial inflammation. Noncardiac conditions that increase myocardial oxygen demand can precipitate ACS in patients with preexisting coronary artery disease (CAD). These conditions include fever, tachycardia, and hyperthyroidism. Decreased myocardial oxygen supply can occur in noncardiac conditions such as hypotensive states, hypoxemia, and anemia.

Unstable angina is characterized by (1) angina that occurs when the patient is at rest; (2) angina that significantly limits the patient's activity; or (3) previously diagnosed angina that becomes more frequent, lasts longer, and increasingly limits the patient's activity. Patients typically do not have ST-segment elevation and do not release biomarkers indicating myocardial necrosis. Variant (Prinzmetal's) angina is associated with rest pain and reversible ST elevation. Because no myocardial necrosis occurs, cardiac biomarkers are not released. Non–ST-segment elevation MI is distinguished from unstable angina by the presence of cardiac biomarkers (e.g., troponin), indicating myocardial necrosis. Most patients do not develop new Q waves on the electrocardiogram (ECG) and are diagnosed with non–Q-wave MI. ST-segment elevation MI is characterized by release of cardiac markers and the presence of new Q waves on the ECG. This care plan focuses on the assessment of and interventions for patients with non–ST-segment elevation. A care plan on MI with ST-segment elevation is presented later in the chapter.

Acute Coronary Syndromes—cont'd

Nursing Diagnosis

Acute Chest Pain

Common Related Factor	Defining Characteristics
Myocardial ischemia	Angina occurring at rest or with minimal exertion ECG changes: ST-segment depression or elevation, deep symmetrical T-wave inversion in multiple leads, or any transient ECG changes occurring during pain New-onset (less than 2 months) angina Changing pattern of previously stable angina

Common Expected Outcomes

Patient verbalizes relief of pain.
Patient appears relaxed and comfortable.

NOC Outcome
Pain Control

NIC Interventions
Cardiac Care: Acute; Pain Management

Ongoing Assessment

Actions/Interventions

- Assess the following pain characteristics:
  - Quality: as with stable angina (squeezing, tightening, choking, pressure, burning)
  - Location: substernal area; may radiate to extremities (e.g., arms, shoulders)
  - Severity: more intense than stable angina pectoris
  - Duration: persists longer than 20 minutes
  - Onset: with minimal exertion or during rest or sleep
  - Relief: usually does not respond to sublingual nitroglycerin (NTG) or rest; may respond to intravenous (IV) NTG

- Monitor ECG immediately during pain for evidence of myocardial ischemia or injury. See Defining Characteristics above.

- Note time since onset of first episode of chest pain.

▲ Monitor serial myocardial biomarkers (CK-MB, troponin, and myoglobin).

Rationale

Women and patients with diabetes mellitus may present with atypical chest pain. Older patients have atypical symptoms (anginal equivalents) including fatigue, shortness of breath, weakness, syncope, or changes in mental status.

In acute stages, patients with presenting symptoms for unstable angina can have a variety of pain characteristics, making diagnosis difficult. If patients are phoning the health care provider about the pain, they should be advised to seek evaluation in a medical facility. Triage to the appropriate medical setting is a priority task. Patients with significant pain are usually admitted to rule out MI until serial laboratory data provide definitive diagnosis.

If ECG is unchanged, patient is considered low risk and can be managed on an outpatient basis.

If less than 6 hours since first pain occurred and patients have evidence of acute ST-segment elevation or new left bundle branch block on ECG, they may be candidates for IV thrombolytic therapy as in acute MI.

Enzymes and proteins do not elevate with unstable angina or variant angina because cellular death is not occurring. They are used to rule out infarction. Serial enzymes

■ = Independent; ▲ = Collaborative

Actions/Interventions

▲ If biomarkers are negative, anticipate other diagnostic studies:
  • Echocardiography with or without stress testing
  • Exercise stress testing
  • Pharmacological stress testing with dipyridamole, adenosine, or dobutamine and nuclear imaging

Rationale

are needed because cardiac troponins may not be detectable for up to 6 hours after onset of chest pain in some patients.

Exercise and pharmacological stress testing and echocardiography are useful in evaluating ventricular function and myocardial perfusion in patients with ACS. The results of these tests are used to determine the extent of CAD and patient's risk for MI. The test results can be used in making decisions about the need for coronary angiography. Advise patients that they should take nothing by mouth for 2 to 4 hours before the procedure. There is no other special preparation for these procedures. Afterward, the nurse should be alert for changes in blood pressure (BP) and pulse, and for complaints of chest pain or shortness of breath.

Therapeutic Interventions

Actions/Interventions

■ Maintain quiet environment or bed rest.

■ Instruct patient to report pain as soon as it starts.

■ Respond immediately to complaint of pain.

■ Obtain 12-lead ECG during pain episodes.

▲ Administer oxygen as prescribed. Measure oxygen saturation.

▲ Give antiischemic therapy as prescribed, evaluating effectiveness and observing signs or symptoms of untoward reactions:

  • Administer aspirin 160 to 324 mg daily as ordered.

  • Anticipate administration of IV heparin for high-risk patients.

  • Administer NTG drip. Titrate dose until relief of pain as long as BP remains stable.

  • Administer morphine sulfate, 2 to 4 mg intravenously, with increments of 2 to 8 mg IV repeated at 5- to 15-minute intervals.

Rationale

This decreases oxygen demands and may reduce anxiety.

This is important for diagnosis and immediate intervention.

Prompt treatment may decrease myocardial ischemia and prevent damage.

ST segment and T-wave changes help provide definitive diagnosis.

Oxygen improves arterial saturation.

Early, effective treatment aids in salvaging at-risk myocardium.

Aspirin diminishes the platelet aggregation that usually occurs secondary to the disruption of coronary atherosclerotic plaque in unstable angina. Treatment should be started at home or in the emergency department and not delayed until admission.

Heparin is an anticoagulant that reduces frequency of MI when administered during the acute phases of ACS along with aspirin (ASA) administration. Partial thromboplastin time should be maintained at 1.5 to 2.5 times control.

NTG relaxes smooth muscles in vascular system, causing peripheral arterial and venous vasodilation that results in lower BP, lower vascular resistance, and decreased work of the heart. Do not give if systolic BP is less than 90 mm Hg.

Morphine is indicated for patients who continue to have chest pain after three doses of sublingual NTG. In addition to its analgesic properties, morphine produces venous dilation, decreased heart rate (HR), and decreased BP. These effects aid reducing myocardial oxygen demand.

■ = Independent; ▲ = Collaborative

Acute Coronary Syndromes—cont'd

Actions/Interventions

- Administer β-blockers. Anticipate IV administration; observe for side effects: hypotension, bradycardia, congestive heart failure, and bronchospasm.

- Administer calcium channel blockers.

■ Anticipate cardiac catheterization to diagnose and, depending on results, anticipate revascularization by percutaneous transluminal coronary angioplasty with stenting or coronary artery bypass surgery.

Rationale

These drugs decrease myocardial oxygen demand, the magnitude of infarction, and the incidence of associated complications. Do not give in patients with chronic obstructive pulmonary disease, heart block, bradycardia, decompensated left ventricular failure, hypotension, or cocaine toxicity.

These are indicated for patients with significant hypertension, cocaine toxicity, contraindications to β-blocker therapy, or refractory ischemia with coronary spasm.

Definitive diagnosis and early revascularization optimize myocardial perfusion and reduce risk for ischemia, infarction, and related complications.

NDx Nursing Diagnosis

Fear

Common Related Factors

Recurrent anginal attacks
Incomplete relief from pain by usual means (NTG and rest)
Threat of MI
Threat of death
Unfamiliarity of environment
Separation from support system

Defining Characteristics

Restlessness
Increased awareness/tension
Increased questioning
Facial tension or wide-eyed expression
Poor eye contact
Focus on self or repeatedly seeking assurance
Increased HR, BP, respiratory rate
Expressed concern
Trembling
Panic

Common Expected Outcomes

Patient verbalizes fears or concerns.
Patient appears calm and expresses trust in medical management.

NOC Outcomes
Anxiety Self-Control; Fear Self-Control

NIC Interventions
Cardiac Care; Anxiety Reduction; Coping Enhancement

Ongoing Assessment

Actions/Interventions

■ Assess level of fear (mild to severe).

■ Assess cause of fear.

Rationale

Controlling fear and anxiety helps reduce the physiological reactions that can aggravate the condition.

Patient may be afraid of the pain experience itself, of MI, or of dying.

■ = Independent; ▲ = Collaborative

Therapeutic Interventions

Actions/Interventions	Rationale
■ Acknowledge awareness of patient's fear.	Acknowledgment of the patient's feelings validates the feelings and communicates acceptance of those feelings.
■ Maintain confident, assured manner.	The staff's anxiety is easily noticed by the patient. The patient's feeling of stability increases in a calm and nonthreatening atmosphere.
■ Assure patient and significant others of close, continuous monitoring that will ensure prompt intervention.	This provides a measure of safety.
■ Reduce unnecessary external stimuli.	Anxiety may escalate with excessive conversation, noise, and equipment around the patient.
■ Explain all procedures as appropriate, keeping explanations basic.	Information helps allay anxiety. Patients who are anxious may not be able to comprehend anything more than simple, clear, brief instructions.
▲ Administer mild tranquilizer as needed.	Medication may be indicated to reduce stress.
■ Establish rest periods between care and procedures.	Quiet periods assist in relaxation and regaining emotional balance.

NDx Nursing Diagnosis

Deficient Knowledge

Common Related Factor

Unfamiliarity with disease process, treatment, and recovery

Defining Characteristics

Multiple questions or lack of questioning
Verbalized misconceptions

Common Expected Outcome

Patient or significant others verbalize understanding of anatomy and physiology of unstable angina, causes, and appropriate relief measures for pain.

NOC Outcomes

Knowledge: Disease Process;
Knowledge: Treatment Regimen

NIC Interventions

Teaching: Disease Process;
Teaching: Prescribed Medications

Ongoing Assessment

Actions/Interventions	Rationale
■ Assess present level of understanding of "unstable" angina or ACS.	Information provides basis for education.

■ = Independent; ▲ = Collaborative

Cardiac and Vascular Care Plans

 Acute Coronary Syndromes—cont'd

Therapeutic Interventions

Actions/Interventions	Rationale
■ Teach patient or significant others the following:	
• Anatomy and physiology of the coronary condition and atherosclerotic process	Information provides rationale for treatment.
• Angina versus unstable angina versus MI	Information aids the patient in assuming responsibility for care at later time.
• Diagnostic procedures (stress test, echocardiogram, or angiogram)	Information can clarify diagnostic process and reduce anxiety. Ongoing and follow-up testing are common to assess response to medical therapy and evaluate functional capacity.
• Antiischemic medical therapy, as in the following:	Patients are better able to ask questions and seek assistance when they know basic information about prescribed medications.
• Antiplatelet medicines	These drugs reduce the risk of thrombosis formation by inhibiting platelet aggregation.
• Use of NTG if chest pain occurs	These drugs cause vasodilation that reduces myocardial demands. Patients need clear directions on self-administration.
• Use of calcium channel blockers	These drugs are useful if unstable angina has a spasm component or if β-blockers are contraindicated.
• Indicated lifestyle changes (smoking cessation, exercise, diet)	Modification in risk factors can decrease risk of CAD events.
■ Explain that the acute phase of unstable angina is usually over in 4 to 6 weeks.	Unstable angina may progress to infarction as the disease progresses. Discuss proper procedure to follow in case chest pain recurs.
■ Refer to cardiac rehabilitation program as indicated.	These programs can assist with risk factor reduction and provide education and emotional support.

 Nursing Diagnosis

Risk for Decreased Cardiac Output

Common Risk Factor

Prolonged episodes of myocardial ischemia affecting contractility

Common Expected Outcome

Patient maintains optimum cardiac output, as evidenced by HR 60 to 100 beats/min; clear lung sounds; urine output of at least 30 mL/hr; and warm, dry skin.

NOC Outcome
Cardiac Pump Effectiveness

NIC Interventions
Hemodynamic Regulation Cardiac Care: Acute; Dysrhythmia Management

■ = Independent; ▲ = Collaborative

Ongoing Assessment

Actions/Interventions

■ Assess hemodynamic status every hour and especially during episode of pain.

■ Monitor ECG continuously for dysrhythmias, especially during episode of pain.

■ Anticipate pulmonary artery monitoring.

Rationale

The major complications seen in unstable angina include acute heart failure, pulmonary edema, new and worsening mitral regurgitation, cardiogenic shock, ventricular dysrhythmias, and advanced atrioventricular block.

Both tachyarrhythmias and bradyarrhythmias can compromise cardiac output.

Monitoring may be indicated to evaluate left ventricular filling pressures.

Therapeutic Interventions

Actions/Interventions

■ Maintain bed rest or reduced activity.

▲ Anticipate development of life-threatening dysrhythmias.
  • Administer antiarrhythmic agents for ventricular dysrhythmias according to protocol.

  • If high-degree atrioventricular block develops, anticipate atropine, transcutaneous pacing, and/or insertion of temporary pacemaker.

▲ Anticipate treatment by percutaneous transluminal coronary angioplasty (PTCA) or coronary artery bypass graft (CABG) surgery.

▲ Anticipate insertion of implantable cardioverter defibrillator (ICD) if sustained ventricular tachycardia develops.

■ Anticipate intraaortic balloon pump (IABP) management if pain and ischemic changes persist despite maximal medical therapy.

Rationale

This reduces oxygen demands.

Ischemic muscle is electrically unstable and produces arrhythmias. Tachydysrhythmias or bradydysrhythmias may occur. Advanced Cardiac Life Support protocols guide treatment.

These increase HR to improve cardiac output.

PTCA is used to increase the inner lumen of coronary arteries that have been stenosed by CAD to increase coronary blood flow. CABG is used to revascularize multiple coronary lesions that cannot be treated through PTCA or related procedures.

ICDs significantly reduce risk of death.

IABP increases coronary blood flow while reducing work by left ventricle during contraction.

• RELATED CARE PLANS

■ = Independent; ▲ = Collaborative

Angina Pectoris, Stable

Chest Pain

Stable angina pectoris is a clinical syndrome characterized by the abrupt or gradual onset of substernal discomfort (often with radiation to the jaw, shoulder, back or arm) caused by insufficient coronary blood flow and/or inadequate oxygen supply to the myocardial muscle. The patient with stable angina will have episodes of chest pain that are usually predictable. Chest pain will occur in response to or is aggravated by physical exertion or emotional stressors. Situations that increase myocardial oxygen demand or decrease oxygen supply include both cardiac and noncardiac causes. Stable angina usually persists for only a few minutes and subsides with cessation of the precipitating factor, rest, or use of nitroglycerin (NTG). Patients may present in ambulatory settings or during hospitalization for other medical problems. Stable angina usually can be controlled with medications on an outpatient basis. Chronic angina can significantly affect one's quality of life.

NDx Nursing Diagnosis

Acute Chest Pain

Common Related Factors

Myocardial ischemia caused by the following:
- Atherosclerosis and/or coronary spasm
- Less common causes: severe aortic stenosis, cardiomyopathy, mitral valve prolapse, hypothyroidism, hypertension, anxiety, tachyarrhythmias, hyperviscosity of blood

Defining Characteristics

No change in the frequency, duration, time of appearance, or precipitating factors during the previous 60 days
Pain or discomfort characteristics:
- Quality: choking, strangling, pressure, burning, tightness, ache, heaviness, griplike, squeezing
- Location: substernal, may radiate to arms and shoulders, neck, back, jaw
- Severity: scale 1 to 10 (usually not at top of scale)
- Duration: typically minutes in duration
- Onset and aggravating factors: episodic and usually precipitated by physical exertion, emotional stress, smoking, heavy meal, or exposures to temperature extremes
- Relieving factors: rest, use of NTG, or removal of precipitating factor

Common Expected Outcomes

Patient verbalizes relief of chest discomfort.
Patient appears relaxed and comfortable.

NOC Outcome
Pain Level; Medication Response

NIC Interventions
Pain Management; Cardiac Care

■ = Independent; ▲ = Collaborative

Ongoing Assessment

Actions/Interventions

- Assess patient's description of pain. (See Defining Characteristics on the preceding page). Note any exacerbating factors and measures used to relieve the pain.

- Evaluate whether this is a chronic problem (stable angina) or a new presentation.

- Assess for the appropriateness of performing an electrocardiogram (ECG) to evaluate ST-segment and T-wave changes.

- Monitor vital signs during chest pain and after nitrate administration.

- Monitor effectiveness of interventions.

Rationale

The discomfort of angina is often difficult for patients to describe, and many patients do not consider it to be "pain." Older patients, patients with diabetes, and women tend to have more fatigue or shortness of breath as anginal symptoms.

New-onset angina that is severe or frequent (more than three times per day) is considered "unstable" angina/ acute coronary syndrome until proven otherwise. It requires immediate assessment.

Differentiating between angina and myocardial infarction (MI) is important in making decisions about implementing appropriate interventions. Anginal changes are transient, occurring during the actual ischemic episode.

Blood pressure (BP) and heart rate (HR) are usually elevated secondary to sympathetic stimulation during pain; however, nitrates cause vasodilation and a resultant drop in BP. Older patients may experience more significant postural hypotension secondary to decreased responsiveness of the baroreceptors.

Chest pain unresponsive to typical angina treatments requires immediate evaluation.

Therapeutic Interventions

Actions/Interventions

- At first signs of pain or discomfort, instruct patient to relax and/or rest.

- Instruct patient to take sublingual NTG.

- If pain continues after repeating dose every 5 minutes for total of three pills, seek immediate medical attention.

- ▲ If in a medical setting, administer oxygen as ordered.

- Offer assurance and emotional support by explaining all treatments and procedures and by encouraging questions.

Rationale

Decreasing myocardial oxygen demand restores the balance between oxygen supply and demand. When more oxygen is available to the myocardium, ischemia is reversed.

Information allows patient to initiate effective therapy when needed. A stinging or burning in the mouth should occur if tablets are effective.

Patients with chronic disease need to be able to recognize important changes in their condition to avert complications. Chest pain unrelieved by NTG may represent unstable angina or myocardial infarction (MI) and should be evaluated immediately.

Increasing arterial oxygen saturation delivers more oxygen to the myocardium and relieves oxygen supply and demand imbalance.

Anxiety can increase cardiac workload and myocardial oxygen demand through stimulation of the sympathetic nervous system.

■ = Independent; ▲ = Collaborative

Angina Pectoris, Stable—cont'd

 Nursing Diagnosis

Deficient Knowledge

Common Related Factor

Unfamiliarity with disease process and treatment

Defining Characteristics

Overanxiousness or exaggerated behavior
Multiple questions or lack of questioning
Inaccurate follow-through of prescribed treatment

Common Expected Outcomes

Patient or significant others verbalize understanding of angina pectoris, its causes, and appropriate relief measures for pain.
Patient describes own cardiac risk factors and strategies to reduce them.

NOC Outcomes
Knowledge: Disease Process; Knowledge: Treatment Regimen

NIC Interventions
Teaching: Disease Process; Teaching: Medication; Cardiac Care: Rehabilitation

Ongoing Assessment

Actions/Interventions

■ Assess knowledge base regarding the causes of angina, diagnostic procedures, treatment plan, and risk factors for coronary artery disease (CAD).

■ Evaluate compliance with any previously prescribed lifestyle modifications.

Rationale

Information provides starting base for educational sessions.

Smoking, heavy meals, and obesity can easily precipitate anginal attacks. Behavior change is never easy.

Therapeutic Interventions

Actions/Interventions

■ Provide information regarding the following:
  • Anatomy and physiology of coronary circulation

  • Diagnostic tests for evaluating CAD, such as the following:
    • ECG

    • Exercise stress test

Rationale

Patients are better able to ask questions and seek assistance when they have basic knowledge of condition.

Usually ST-segment depression or inverted T wave is present, indicating subendocardial ischemia.

ST-segment changes provide an indirect assessment of coronary artery perfusion. Significant ST depression on stress testing indicates the need for angiography. However, the exercise stress test is not always conclusive for CAD. Women often have false-positive results, and false-negative results can occur if only submaximal exercise is performed. Exercise echocardiograms are often used to evaluate wall motion abnormality present during myocardial ischemia.

■ = Independent; ▲ = Collaborative

Actions/Interventions	**Rationale**
• Pharmacological stress test with nuclear imaging	This test is indicated for subgroups of patients unable to exercise. Two types of agents may be used: coronary vasodilators (adenosine and dipyridamole) and those that increase HR (dobutamine). Scans of the heart identify poorly perfused areas of the myocardium.
• Coronary angiography	This is the gold standard for identifying the extent of the CAD.
• Differentiating angina from noncardiac pain	Patients must have correct information for long-term care.
• Differentiating stable versus unstable angina versus MI	Health care providers are often challenged with differentiating more complex presentations. This information will assist the patient in determining when adjustments need to be made in therapy.
• Need to avoid angina-provoking situations (e.g., heavy meals, physical overexertion, temperature extremes, cigarette smoking, emotional stress, and stimulants such as caffeine or cocaine)	Long-term care is the patient's responsibility; enough information is needed for successful intervention.
• Use of sublingual NTG to relieve attacks, as in the following:	
• Carry pills at all times.	Pills need to be taken immediately at the first sign of pain.
• Keep pills in dark, dry container, away from heat.	NTG is volatile and inactivated by heat, moisture, and light.
• Replace pills every 3 to 4 months.	Once bottle is opened, NTG begins to lose its strength. Tablets that are effective should sting in the mouth.
• Sit or lie down when taking NTG. Put pill under tongue and let dissolve. If pain is not relieved in 5 minutes, take another. If still not relieved, take a third. If this does not relieve pain, call physician or go to emergency department.	NTG causes vasodilation, which can lower BP and cause dizziness.
• Emphasize that NTG is a safe and nonaddicting drug. Use as needed, including prophylactically.	The main side effects are hypotension and headache. Headache can be treated with acetaminophen (Tylenol).
• Use of other medications for long-term management:	
• Long-acting nitrates	These drugs act by producing vasodilation, which increases coronary blood flow and reduces oxygen demands of the heart. They must be used cautiously in older patients who are more susceptible to postural hypotension secondary to reduced response of baroreceptors.
• β-Blockers	These reduce contractility and HR, thereby decreasing myocardial oxygen demand. They must be used cautiously in older patients who have degeneration of the conduction system and who are at risk for bradycardia and conduction heart blocks.
• Calcium channel blockers	These cause vasodilation, which increases coronary blood flow and reduces oxygen demands of the heart.
• Antiplatelet aggregation therapy (aspirin); Plavix if aspirin is contraindicated for high-risk patients (determined by testing).	Aspirin chemically blocks the synthesis of prostaglandins and thromboxane A_2 in platelets. Without prostaglandins, platelets are unable to aggregate and form clots in coronary blood vessels. The effect of aspirin on platelet aggregation is irreversible for the life of the platelet, about 3 to 7 days. Therefore patients who experience chest pain are advised to chew one uncoated adult

■ = Independent; ▲ = Collaborative

> **Angina Pectoris, Stable**—cont'd

Actions/Interventions

- Angiotensin-converting enzyme inhibitors for those with CAD and diabetes and/or left ventricular systolic dysfunction.
- Need to reduce modifiable risk factors for atherosclerosis:
  - Smoking: If patient cannot quit alone, refer to American Heart Association, American Lung Association, or American Cancer Society for support group and interventions.
  - Hypertension: Instruct in need to lower weight, reduce salt intake, initiate an exercise program, and take antihypertensive medications as prescribed.
  - Elevated serum lipid levels: Emphasize need to reduce intake of foods high in saturated fat, cholesterol, or both (e.g., fatty meats, organ meats, lard, butter, egg yolks, dairy products). Arrange for evaluation by dietitian as needed. Include spouse or significant others in meal planning. Treatment usually requires antihyperlipidemic medication.

  - Diabetes: Emphasize control through diet and medication.

  - Obesity

  - Stress: Refer to programs for stress management as appropriate.
  - Physical inactivity: Emphasize benefits of exercise in reducing risk of heart attack. Refer to cardiac rehabilitation program as needed. Keep exercise intensity below angina threshold.
- Therapeutic procedures to relieve angina unresponsive to medications and lifestyle changes:
  - Percutaneous coronary interventions: angioplasty, atherectomy, stent implantation, laser angioplasty

  - Coronary artery bypass graft surgery

  - Enhanced external counterpulsation

  - Surgical laser transmyocardial revascularization

Rationale

aspirin tablet (325 mg) at the onset of pain. Chewing the tablet rather than swallowing it whole enhances the absorption of the drug into the bloodstream.

These decrease afterload, causing vasodilation, and prevent activation of renin-angiotensin-aldosterone system.

Smoking causes vasoconstriction and reduces myocardial oxygen supply. Risk of developing CAD is 2 to 6 times greater in cigarette smokers. Risk is proportional to number of cigarettes smoked.

The stress of constantly elevated BP can increase the rate of atherosclerosis development.

There is a positive correlation between serum lipids (especially low-density lipoprotein [LDL]) and atherosclerosis. Treatment goal for patients with CAD is LDL (bad cholesterol) level less than 100 mg/dL. Newer National Cholesterol Education Program Adult Treatment Panel III guidelines suggest a goal of less than 70 mg/dL as a therapeutic option in patients at high risk for CAD.

Diabetes eliminates the lower incidence of cardiovascular disease in women. Diabetes is associated with a high incidence of silent ischemia. Eighty percent of diabetic patients have cardiovascular disease.

Obesity affects hypertension, diabetes, and cholesterol levels, and attributes to metabolic syndrome, which is highly associated with CAD.

Persistent stress causes the release of catecholamines that contribute to elevated blood pressure and CAD.

Exercise increases high-density lipoprotein levels (good cholesterol), assists with weight loss, lowers hypertension, improves diabetes, and reduces the risk of clot formation (fibrinolytic activity).

These interventions provide a means to nonsurgically improve coronary blood flow and revascularize the myocardium.

This may be recommended for significant left main CAD, triple vessel disease, and disease unresponsive to other treatments.

This technique uses air via cuffs attached to the lower extremities to propel blood back to the heart.

The goal of this intervention is to create a series of transmural endomyocardial channels to improve myocardial revascularization.

■ = Independent; ▲ = Collaborative

Actions/Interventions

- Refer patient to cardiac rehabilitation services for specialized teaching and assistance with recommended lifestyle changes as appropriate.

Rationale

Specialty services may be required to ensure that patients' needs are met and outcomes achieved.

NDx Nursing Diagnosis

Activity Intolerance

Common Related Factors

Occurrence or fear of chest pain
Side effects of prescribed medications
Imbalance between oxygen supply and demand

Defining Characteristics

Chest pain or dyspnea during activity
Fatigue
Abnormal HR or BP response to activity
ECG changes reflecting ischemia or dysrhythmias

Common Expected Outcome

Patient performs activity within limits of ischemic disease, as evidenced by absence of chest pain or discomfort and no ECG changes reflecting ischemia.

NOC Outcome
Knowledge: Prescribed Activity

NIC Intervention
Teaching: Prescribed Activity/Exercise

Ongoing Assessment

Actions/Interventions

- Assess patient's level of physical activity before experiencing angina.
- Assess for defining characteristics before, during, and after activity.
- Assess emotional response to limitations.

Rationale

Sometimes patients have significantly reduced their activity to avoid anginal symptoms.

Information provides basis for treatment.

Depression over inability to perform desired/required activities can be a source of stress and aggravation.

Therapeutic Interventions

Actions/Interventions

- Assist in reviewing required home, work, or leisure activities and in developing an appropriate plan for accomplishing them (e.g., what to do in morning versus afternoon or how to pace tasks throughout the week).
- Evaluate need for additional support at home (e.g., housekeeper, neighbor to shop, family assistance).
- Encourage adequate rest periods between activities.

Rationale

Devising plan that facilitates accomplishment of small, attainable goals can be satisfying.

Coordinated efforts are more meaningful and effective.

Activity should be adequately paced to reduce oxygen demands.

■ = Independent; ▲ = Collaborative

Angina Pectoris, Stable—cont'd

Actions/Interventions

- Remind patient not to work with arms above shoulders for long periods.

- Remind patient to continue taking medications (e.g., β-blockers), despite side effect of fatigue.

- Instruct in prophylactic use of NTG before physical exertion as needed.

- Encourage a program of progressive aerobic exercise. Refer to cardiac rehabilitation as appropriate.

Rationale

Arm activity increases myocardial demands.

Often the body does adjust to the medications after several weeks.

This is an important measure for patients with predictable angina patterns.

Routine exercise can increase functional capacity, making the heart more efficient.

> • RELATED CARE PLANS
>
> Anxiety, p.15
> Cardiac rehabilitation, p. 240
> Health-seeking behaviors, p. 91
> Ineffective coping, p. 51

Aortic Aneurysm

Dissecting Aneurysm; Thoracic Aneurysm; Abdominal Aneurysm; True Aneurysm; False Aneurysm

Aortic aneurysm is a localized circumscribed abnormal dilatation of an artery or a blood-containing tumor connecting directly with the lumen of an artery. True aneurysms involve dilatation of all layers of the vessel wall. There are two types of true aneurysms: (1) saccular—characterized by bulbous outpouching of one side of the artery, resulting in localized thinning and stretching of the arterial wall, and (2) fusiform—characterized by a uniform spindle-shaped dilatation of the entire circumference of a segment of the artery. False aneurysms (pseudoaneurysms) result from rupture or complete tear of all three layers of an arterial wall, with the blood clot retained in an outpouching of tissue from the vessel wall. Dissecting aneurysms occur when the inner layer of the vessel wall tears and splits, creating a false channel and a cavity of blood between the intimal and adventitial layers.

The natural history of an aneurysm is enlargement and rupture. As a rule, the larger the aneurysm, the greater the chance of rupture. Dissection of the aorta is commonly classified according to location. According to the Stanford Classification, type A involves the ascending aorta and its transverse arch, and type B involves the descending aorta. Dissecting aortic aneurysm is the most common catastrophe involving the aorta and has a high mortality rate if not detected early and treated appropriately. It can be treated through surgical intervention or with medical therapy. Aneurysms occur in all arteries, although they are most common in the aorta. Abdominal aortic aneurysms account for about 75% of all aneurysms, and thoracic aneurysms account for about 25%. Aortic aneurysms occur more often in men than in women, in smokers, and in those with a family history of aneurysms. Risk factors for dissection include hypertension, pregnancy, trauma, and Marfan syndrome.

Symptoms depend on size and location of the aneurysm and whether it is intact or ruptured. This care plan focuses on more acute care.

■ = Independent; ▲ = Collaborative

Nursing Diagnosis

Risk for Ineffective Tissue Perfusion/Dissection

Common Risk Factors

Conditions that increase stress on the arterial wall:
- Hypertension
- Pregnancy with hypervolemia
- Coarctation of the aorta

Defect in the vessel wall:
- Marfan syndrome
- Cystic degeneration in the media

Trauma

Iatrogenic causes

Common Expected Outcome

Patient has reduced risk of complications from progressive dissection or rupture as a result of early detection of symptoms and appropriate intervention.

NOC Outcomes

Vital Signs; Circulation Status; Pain Level

NIC Interventions

Vital Sign Monitoring; Circulatory Precautions; Pain Management; Analgesic Administration

Ongoing Assessment

Actions/Interventions

- Obtain a thorough history regarding present complaint.

- Assess and monitor location and characteristics of pain.
  - Abdominal: pain in abdomen or back, flank, or groin caused by pressure on adjacent structures
  - Thoracic: pain in neck, low back pain, shoulders, or abdomen

- Monitor for signs and symptoms indicating progressive dissection.

Rationale

Most patients are asymptomatic until time of dissection or rupture. Symptoms may include awareness of pulsatile mass, severe pain, and shortness of breath. History aids in ruling out cerebrovascular, cardiac, vascular occlusive, and/or renal disease. Aneurysms are commonly secondary to other factors.

Usually pain is not evident until aneurysm is enlarging. Pain may mimic pain patterns associated with other disorders.

A high index of suspicion is key to the treatment to reduce mortality. Clinical signs and symptoms indicate the site and progression of dissection. Acute aortic dissection usually occurs along the thoracic aorta. Pain is severe and may mimic the pain associated with myocardial infarction. Pain may be located both above and below the diaphragm if the dissection is

Aortic Aneurysm

= Independent; ▲ = Collaborative

Actions/Interventions

- Anticipate further diagnostic studies:
  - Chest x-ray (thoracic) study and abdominal or lateral x-ray study of spine (abdominal)
  - Contrast-enhanced computed tomography (CT) scan
  - Magnetic resonance imaging scans
  - Ultrasonography
  - Aortography

For abdominal aneurysms:
- Auscultate for bruit over pulsatile mass (4 to 7 cm in diameter), usually in the upper abdomen, slightly to the left of the midline between the xiphoid process and the umbilicus.

- Monitor urine output.

- Monitor for abnormal bowel function.
- Observe for abdominal distention, diarrhea, or severe abdominal pain and/or fever.

- Assess for gastrointestinal bleeding.
- Assess for lower leg edema.
- Assess lower extremities for signs of peripheral ischemia and insufficiency. These include pain, pallor, pulselessness, paresthesia, poikilothermia (decreased temperature, coolness), and paralysis.
- Observe for retroperitoneal cyanosis.

- Evaluate for sexual dysfunction.

For thoracic aneurysms:
- Monitor blood pressure (BP) for hypertension. Differential arm BP may be present as a result of compression of the subclavian artery.

Rationale

extensive. Changes in level of consciousness and diminished carotid pulses are associated with dissection of the aortic arch. Dissection of the abdominal aorta can cause decreased urine output, diminished motor and sensory function in the lower extremities, abdominal pain, and bloody diarrhea.

Tests are required to confirm diagnosis and delineate anatomy.

This test is the standard for computing size, shape, and location of aneurysms.

Presence of abdominal aortic aneurysm greater than 6 cm in diameter is an indication for elective surgical repair, even when asymptomatic. Surgery for high-risk patients may be deferred until the aneurysm shows progressive enlargement or until it becomes tender or symptomatic.

Reduction may result from compression of the renal arteries from infrarenal abdominal aneurysm, crossclamping of the aorta during surgery, or embolization. However, most aneurysms are located below the renal artery.

This is caused by partial intestinal obstruction.

These rule out embolization or decreased perfusion to the mesenteric artery and rupture into the abdominal cavity.

Bleeding is caused by erosion of the duodenum.

Edema is caused by erosion of the inferior vena cava.

Dissection can cause reduced sensory and motor function in the lower extremities.

Cyanosis is caused by leak or acute rupture of the aneurysm.

This is caused by aortoiliac occlusive disease.

Hypertension is an important risk factor for rupture.

■ = Independent; ▲ = Collaborative

Aortic Aneurysm

Actions/Interventions

- Auscultate for bruits over palpable pulsatile mass.
- Monitor quality of peripheral pulses.

- Assess for dysphagia.
- Assess for hemoptysis.
- Assess for respiratory compromise.

- Observe for upper-extremity and head swelling with cyanosis.

Rationale

Bruit denotes abnormal blood flow.

A suggested grading system is as follows: 0 = absent, 1+ = present, 2+ = strong.

Dysphagia may be caused by esophageal compression.

This results from compression of the trachea or lung.

This is a result of compression of the trachea or bronchus.

These can be caused by superior vena cava obstruction.

Therapeutic Interventions

Actions/Interventions

- Provide nursing measures that alleviate pain:
  - Position of comfort:
    - Place patients exhibiting back pain in a side-lying position.
    - Elevate head of bed for patients who are short of breath.
  - Physical comfort (e.g., hand-holding).
  - Physiological intervention: application of cold towel to forehead
  - Relaxation techniques
- ▲ Administer pain medicines as prescribed.

- ▲ Administer potent vasodilator (e.g., sodium nitroprusside [Nipride]) medication.
- ▲ Administer β-blockers.

- For type A dissections, anticipate surgical treatment and prepare patient.

- For type B dissections, anticipate chronic medical treatment, which consists of the following long-term measures:
  - Decrease or eliminate identified factors that will increase BP and HR.
  - Provide a quiet environment as much as possible.
  - Pace activities (eating, personal hygiene, visitors) appropriately.
  - Administer sedatives as prescribed.

Rationale

Depending on status of the aneurysm, these measures may not be effective.

Persistent pain suggests ongoing dissection or rupture. Surgical intervention may be required to relieve pain.

BP control is imperative for maintaining tissue perfusion. Goal is tomaintain systolic BP less than 120 mm Hg.

These decrease heart rate (HR) and myocardial contractility, thus reducing the stress applied to the arterial walls during each heart beat. The goal is to maintain HR less than 70 beats/min.

The surgical procedure involves replacement of the ascending aorta to prevent aortic rupture or retrograde progression of the dissection.

The major treatment approach for type B involves a pharmacological regimen to control BP. It may require surgical treatment if hypertension is uncontrollable, persistent pain occurs, compromise to major organs occurs, or the aorta ruptures.

■ = Independent; ▲ = Collaborative

Cardiac and Vascular Care Plans

Aortic Aneurysm—cont'd

Nursing Diagnosis

Risk for Decreased Cardiac Output

Common Risk Factors

Side effects of medications
Progressive dissection
Rupture of the aorta

Common Expected Outcome

Patient maintains adequate cardiac output, as evidenced by HR of 60 to 100 beats/min, clear lung sounds, urine output more than 30 mL/hr, and alert mentation.

NOC Outcome
Cardiac Pump Effectiveness
NIC Intervention
Hemodynamic Regulation

Ongoing Assessment

Actions/Interventions

- Assess hemodynamic status. Monitor for signs of decreasing cardiac output, such as tachycardia, decreased urine output, and restlessness.

- Assess for signs of myocardial ischemia: chest pain, tachycardia, or ST-segment and T-wave changes on electrocardiogram (ECG).

Rationale

Patients with dissecting or rupturing aneurysm are hemodynamically compromised. Early evaluation of problem facilitates prompt intervention.

ECG changes help guide timing of interventions.

Therapeutic Interventions

Actions/Interventions

▲ If decreased cardiac output is drug induced, anticipate the following:
  • For sodium nitroprusside:
    • Stop the drug and administer isotonic solution (0.9 normal saline solution) or plasma expanders.
  • For β-blocker:
    • May stop the drug or reduce dose.

▲ If decreased cardiac output is related to further dissection (severe aortic insufficiency) or ruptured aorta, anticipate emergency angiography and surgery:

  • Send blood specimen for type and crossmatch and other routine preoperative blood work.

  • Stay with patient.

Rationale

Fluids are usually required to maintain increased intravascular volume.

β-Blockers have a negative inotropic effect, which can potentiate heart failure. Presence of rales and S_3 indicates heart failure.

Rapid efficient intervention is critical to preserve circulation and life.

Blood replacement therapy may be required to maintain effective blood volume.

Your presence may provide emotional support.

■ = Independent; ▲ = Collaborative

Actions/Interventions

- Administer medications, intravenous fluids, and blood as ordered.
- Prepare patient for surgery according to hospital policy and procedure.

For immediate postoperative course, see **Coronary Bypass/Valve Surgery: Immediate Postoperative Care,** *p. 275.*

Rationale

These maintain adequate cardiac output before surgery.

Knowledge aids in reducing anxiety.

NDx Nursing Diagnosis

Anxiety

Common Related Factors

Sudden onset of illness
Impending surgery
Close monitoring by medical or nursing staff
Fear of death
Multiple tests and procedures

Defining Characteristics

Tense, anxious appearance
Request to have family at bedside all the time
Restlessness
Increased questioning
Constant demands
Glancing about or increased alertness

Common Expected Outcomes

Patient verbalizes reduced anxiety.
Patient demonstrates positive coping method.

NOC Outcome
Anxiety Self-Control

NIC Interventions
Anxiety Reduction;
   Teaching: Procedure/Treatment

Ongoing Assessment

Actions/Interventions

■ Assess anxiety level (mild, severe). Note signs and symptoms, especially nonverbal communication.

Rationale

Aortic dissection/rupture can result in an acute life-threatening situation that will produce high levels of anxiety in the patient as well as in significant others.

Therapeutic Interventions

Actions/Interventions

■ Acknowledge awareness of patient's anxiety.

■ Reduce unnecessary external stimuli.

■ Explain all procedures as appropriate, keeping explanations basic.

■ Provide a quiet, private place for significant others to wait.

Rationale

Acknowledgment of the patient's feelings validates the feelings and communicates acceptance of those feelings.

Anxiety may escalate with excessive conversation, noise, and equipment around patient.

Information helps allay anxiety. Patients who are anxious may not be able to comprehend anything more than simple, clear, brief instructions.

A quiet environment can reduce anxiety.

■ = Independent; ▲ = Collaborative

Aortic Aneurysm—cont'd

 Nursing Diagnosis

Deficient Knowledge: Follow-Up Care

Common Related Factors

New medical problem
Unfamiliarity with surgical procedure and hospital care

Defining Characteristics

Expressed need for information
Multiple questions

Common Expected Outcome

Patient or family verbalizes understanding of disease process, treatment options, and goals of therapy.

NOC Outcomes
Knowledge: Disease Process;
Knowledge: Treatment Regimen

NIC Interventions
Teaching: Disease Process;
Teaching: Procedure/Treatment

Ongoing Assessment

Actions/Interventions

■ Assess knowledge of the disease and treatment options.

Rationale

This provides an important starting point in education.

Therapeutic Interventions

Actions/Interventions

■ Instruct nonsurgical patient about the following:
  • Importance of follow-up CT scanning
  • Goals of therapy (avoid excess BP and strain on the diseased arterial wall)
  • Use of antihypertensive medications as prescribed; importance of compliance
  • Side effects of medicines
  • Signs and symptoms to report
■ Instruct surgical patients about the following:
  • Activity restrictions
  • Wound care

Rationale

Patients treated medically need to maintain goal BP levels and comply with scheduled CT scans to monitor size of the aneurysm. Knowledge of early warning signs facilitates rapid treatment.

Discharge instructions guide patients regarding self-care measures.

■ = Independent; ▲ = Collaborative

Actions/Interventions

- Avoiding activities that are isometric or abruptly raise BP (e.g., lifting and carrying of heavy objects, straining for bowel movement)
- Signs and symptoms to report

Rationale

Heavy lifting of more than 5 to 10 pounds is restricted for 4 to 6 weeks after surgical repair of an aortic aneurysm. These restrictions reduce strain on suture lines until they are completely healed.

• RELATED CARE PLANS

Acute pain, p. 144
Deficient fluid volume, p. 71
Ineffective tissue perfusion, p. 198

Cardiac Catheterization

Coronary Angiography

Cardiac catheterization and coronary angiography are specialized diagnostic procedures in which the internal structure of the heart and coronary arteries can be viewed to determine myocardial function, valvular competency, presence or absence of coronary artery disease (CAD), and location and severity of CAD, as well as to assess the effects of prior percutaneous or surgical interventions. Cardiac catheterization may be an elective or emergency procedure, depending on the patient's clinical status.

NDx Nursing Diagnosis

Deficient Knowledge

Common Related Factor

Unfamiliarity with procedure

Defining Characteristics

Expressed need for information
Multiple questions
Lack of questions
Increase in anxiety level
Statements revealing misconceptions

Common Expected Outcome

Patient verbalizes a basic understanding of heart anatomy, disease, and cardiac catheterization procedure.

NOC Outcome
Knowledge: Treatment Procedure

NIC Interventions
Teaching: Procedure/Treatment; Preparatory Sensory Information

■ = Independent; ▲ = Collaborative

Cardiac Catheterization—cont'd

Ongoing Assessment

Actions/Interventions

■ Assess knowledge of heart disease and catheterization procedure.

Rationale

This provides an important starting point in education.

Therapeutic Interventions

Actions/Interventions

■ Provide information about the specific or suspected heart problem (valve disease, CAD).

■ Encourage patient and family to verbalize concerns.

■ Provide a tour or description of the laboratory environment.

■ Explain the sensations that may be experienced during the procedure:
  • Warm, flushing, nauseous feeling and metallic taste when dye is injected
  • Pressure or skipped heartbeats as the catheter is advanced
  • Slow heart rate (HR) or low blood pressure (BP) due to vasovagal response or injection of contrast medium.
  • Tachycardia and rapid pulse also possible

■ Determine whether patient has allergy to iodine-containing substances.

■ Determine if patient has renal insufficiency.

■ Explain that the patient will be awake during the procedure.

■ Explain that because patients are awake throughout the procedure, they should alert the staff of any needs (e.g., need for blanket, need to urinate, need for back relief from hard table).

■ Inform the patient of precatheterization procedures:
  • Nothing by mouth; clear liquids or a light breakfast may be allowed if the procedure is scheduled for later in the day

Rationale

Information provides rationale for treatment.

Patients are anxious about the procedure and the possible outcomes and may have difficulty asking questions and interpreting information. Even patients who have undergone prior procedures may be fearful of the possible outcome with this procedure. A lower anxiety level will enable patient to cooperate better during the procedure.

This prepares patient for the appearance of the room and complexity of the equipment.

Patients may have less anxiety during the procedure when they know expectations and understand that these sensations are normal.

Patients may be allergic to the contrast dye used during injections and require premedication with antihistamines and/ or steroids. Nonionic contrast agents may be substituted.

Such patients are at high risk for contrast-induced nephropathy and require renal protective interventions such as preprocedure intravenous (IV) fluids, medications such as N-acetylcysteine, and nephrotoxic medications withheld for 24 to 48 hours before and 48 hours after the procedure.

This facilitates any reporting of chest pain and assists in the patient being able to vigorously cough and breathe deeply at designated times to circulate dye, position the catheter, and increase HR and BP.

Patients have a right to comfort measures.

This prevents nausea and aspiration.

■ = Independent; ▲ = Collaborative

Actions/Interventions

- Premedication with antihistamine and/or sedative medicines
- Need to empty bladder
- Intravenous line insertion

■ Explain that the patient will be positioned on a hard x-ray table, and either it or the fluoroscopy camera can be tilted for optimal visualization of the heart.

■ Prepare patient for postcatheterization procedures:

- Frequent vital sign checks
- Assessment of peripheral pulses and dressing
- Mobilization and ambulation procedures

- Importance of drinking fluids

- Monitoring for osmotic diuresis

■ Before discharge, instruct patient to do the following:
- Report any swelling or bleeding at the catheter site or any changes in color, temperature, or sensation in the extremity used for catheterization.
- Report any signs of infection.
- Avoid strenuous activity per physician orders.
- Take acetaminophen or any nonaspirin analgesic for general discomfort.

Rationale

This reduces potential allergic reaction and promotes comfort.

The test may take 2 to 4 hours; the dye has a diuretic effect.

This provides access for medicines and fluids.

Anxiety can be reduced when the patient knows what to anticipate.

Most patients remain in a short-stay unit for 3 to 6 hours after the procedure.

HR and BP provide important hemodynamic information.

It is important to check for occlusion or bleeding.

Most patients require at least 4 hours of bed rest, depending on the type of arterial closure systems used.

Fluids flush dye from the system, reduce risk of renal complications, and promote hydration. Older patients may be more susceptible to the hypovolemic effects of the procedure.

Diuresis can result in hypotension.

Most patients are discharged the same day. Patients need to be aware of potential complications to facilitate prompt intervention in case of an emergency.

NDx Nursing Diagnosis

Risk for Ineffective Peripheral Tissue Perfusion to Catheterized Extremity

Common Risk Factors

Interruption of arterial flow
Thrombus formation

Common Expected Outcome

Patient maintains tissue perfusion in affected extremity as evidenced by baseline pulse quality and warm extremity.

NOC Outcomes
Circulation Status;
  Tissue Perfusion: Peripheral

NIC Interventions
Circulatory Precautions;
  Embolus Precautions

■ = Independent; ▲ = Collaborative

Cardiac and Vascular
Care Plans

> ## Cardiac Catheterization–cont'd

Ongoing Assessment

Actions/Interventions

Before catheterization:

■ Assess and record presence of peripheral pulses; mark pedal pulses with an X. If pulses are markedly decreased, obtain Doppler reading to check for pulse quality or absence.

■ Assess and record skin temperature, color, capillary refill, movement, and sensation of all extremities.

After catheterization:

■ Assess and monitor affected extremities for pulse, skin color, temperature, and sensation according to institutional policy.

■ Check cannulation site for swelling, bruits, and hematoma.

Rationale

More than one site may be needed for cannulation during the procedure. Accurate assessment of baseline is important for comparison. In most procedures, a femoral artery approach is used. The nurse should mark the pedal pulse and posterior tibial pulse locations on both legs.

This provides a baseline for ongoing evaluations.

Decreased peripheral pulse, coolness, mottling, pallor, presence of pain, numbness, and tingling in affected extremity are signs of decreased tissue perfusion.

Severe edema can hinder peripheral circulation by constricting vessels and decrease sensation by compressing nerves. Bruit may indicate arteriovenous fistula or pseudoaneurysm.

Therapeutic Interventions

Actions/Interventions

■ Instruct patient to report signs of reduced tissue perfusion and to follow up with report to physician.

■ Prepare for possible thrombectomy or embolectomy.

▲ Prepare to heparinize if prescribed.

Rationale

Knowledge of potential side effects facilitates prompt interventions in case of complications.

This may be necessary to remove blood clot compromising or obstructing circulation in affected extremity.

Heparin reduces clotting activity.

NDx Nursing Diagnosis

Ineffective Protection

Common Related Factors

Disruption of vessel integrity
Drug therapies

Defining Characteristic

Altered clotting

Common Expected Outcome

Patient experiences no significant bleeding.

NOC Outcome
Blood Coagulation

NIC Interventions
Bleeding Precautions;
    Bleeding Reduction: Wound

(■ = Independent; ▲ = Collaborative)

Ongoing Assessment

Actions/Interventions

- ■ Assess insertion site and dressing for evidence of bleeding.
- ■ Assess for restlessness, apprehension, and change in vital signs.
- ▲ Monitor vital signs, activated clotting time, and hemoglobin level and hematocrit.

Rationale

Bleeding and hematoma formation are common complications.

These are early signs of bleeding.

Changes guide subsequent interventions.

Therapeutic Interventions

Actions/Interventions

- ▲ Maintain bed rest with affected extremity straight for prescribed time. If needed, apply knee immobilizer to affected extremity to remind patient not to move the leg.
- ■ If femoral site is used, do not elevate head of bed greater than 30 degrees.
- ▲ Maintain occlusive pressure dressing.

- ■ Avoid sudden movements of affected extremity.

If bleeding is noted:

- ■ Circle the size of hematoma or amount of drainage on the dressing along with date and time.
- ■ Reinforce dressing; apply pressure and apply sandbag (10 pounds), or mechanical clamp to bleeding site per physician's order.

Rationale

This position minimizes risk of bleeding and allows hemostasis at the cannulation site.

This position reduces risk of bleeding at the insertion site.

A pressure dressing facilitates clot formation and promotes hemostasis. Many types of arterial closure devices are available (e.g., sutures, collagen plugs).

Restricted movement facilitates clot formation and wound closure at the insertion site.

This provides basis for ongoing comparisons.

Control of bleeding is a priority

NDx Nursing Diagnosis

Deficient Fluid Volume

Common Related Factors

Dye-induced diuresis
Restricted intake before procedure

Defining Characteristics

Decrease in urine output
Decrease in BP; increase in HR
Dry mucous membranes
Decreased skin turgor

Common Expected Outcome

Patient maintains adequate fluid volume, as evidenced by balanced intake and output, good skin turgor, and normal BP.

NOC Outcomes

Fluid Balance; Hydration

NIC Interventions

Fluid Monitoring; Fluid Management

■ = Independent; ▲ = Collaborative

Cardiac and Vascular Care Plans

Cardiac Catheterization—cont'd

Ongoing Assessment

Actions/Interventions

- Assess and monitor hydration status: urine output, mental status, skin, and hemodynamic parameters.

- If patient requires nitrates, monitor BP closely, anticipating drop in BP and need for additional fluids secondary to hypovolemic state.

Rationale

The contrast medium acts as a diuretic that can significantly reduce fluid status in high-risk patients.

Hypotension due to hypovolemic states and preload-reducing medication can contribute to impaired tissue perfusion.

Therapeutic Interventions

Actions/Interventions

- Monitor intake and output for several hours after catheterization.

- Anticipate frequent use of urinal/bedpan immediately after catheterization. Keep urinal within reach.

- ▲ Give oral fluids as tolerated; give IV fluids as prescribed.

- Keep water pitcher or juices at bedside.

Rationale

This provides data on fluid status.

Radiographic dye causes osmotic diuresis.

Fluids are needed to maintain hydration status.

Patient has restricted activity.

Cardiac Rehabilitation

Post-Myocardial Infarction; Post–Cardiac Surgery; Post–Percutaneous Transluminal Coronary Angioplasty; Congestive Heart Failure; Activity Progression; Cardiac Education

Cardiac rehabilitation is the process of actively assisting patients with known heart disease to achieve and maintain optimal physical and emotional health and wellness. It has undergone significant evolution, redesigning itself from a primarily exercise-focused intervention into a comprehensive disease management program. Core components of these programs include the following: baseline and follow-up patient assessments; aggressive strategies for reducing modifiable risk factors for cardiovascular disease (CVD; e.g., lipids, hypertension, diabetes, obesity); counseling on heart-healthy nutrition, smoking cessation, and stress management; assistance in adhering to prescribed medications; promotion of lifestyle physical activity; exercise training; and psychosocial and vocational counseling. These integrated services are best provided by a multidisciplinary team composed of physicians, nurses, health educators, exercise physiologists, dietitians, and behavioral medicine specialists. More recently, the nurse has changed from team member to case-manager. Key to providing cost-effective help is the provision of interventions based on each patient's unique needs, interests, and skills.

Cardiac rehabilitation programs typically begin in the hospital setting and progress to supervised (and often electrocardiographically monitored) outpatient programs. However, with shorter hospital stays, little time may be available for adequate instruction regarding lifestyle management and activity progression. Only 11% to 38% of eligible patients reportedly participate in any outpatient programs, usually because of lack of physician referral, lack of insurance coverage, transportation difficulties, gender-related barriers, conflicts with returning to work, and associated medical problems. Therefore newer models are being considered, such as transtelephonic electrocardiogram (ECG) monitoring at home. Many programs also include pulmonary rehabilitation, but that is not discussed in this care plan.

■ = Independent; ▲ = Collaborative

Nursing Diagnosis

Activity Intolerance

Common Related Factors

Imposed activity restrictions secondary to medical condition or high-technology therapies or procedures

Pain (ischemic, postsurgery incisional, related to other underlying conditions or health problems)

Generalized weakness or fatigue (sedentary lifestyle before event, lack of sleep, decreased caloric intake after surgery)

Reduced cardiac output (secondary to myocardial dysfunction, arrhythmias, postural hypotension)

Fear or anxiety (of overexerting heart, of experiencing angina or incisional pain)

Defining Characteristics

Report of fatigue or weakness

Abnormal heart rate (HR) or blood pressure (BP) in response to activity

Exertional dyspnea

Chest pain/other pain

ECG changes reflecting ischemia

Dysrhythmias precipitated by activity

Common Expected Outcomes

Patient verbalizes increased confidence with progressive activity.

Patient participates in prescribed activity programs without complications.

Patient describes readiness to perform activities of daily living (ADLs) and routine home activities.

NOC Outcomes
Circulation Status; Activity Tolerance; Physical Fitness

NIC Interventions
Exercise Promotion; Cardiac Care: Rehabilitation; Teaching: Exercise/Activity

Ongoing Assessment

Actions/Interventions

■ Assess patient's activity tolerance and exercise habits before current illness.

Rationale

This information will serve as a basis for formulating short- or long-term goals. NOTE: Some patients may have participated in regular exercise programs and be quite fit, whereas others may have been incapacitated by chronic angina or congestive heart failure (CHF) or have other health problems that interfere with activity.

■ Assess patient's physical status before initiating activity or exercise session. Note HR, BP, arrhythmia status.

Hospital patients with complications need close observation and may require supplemental oxygen and telemetry monitoring. Outpatients may exhibit hemodynamic changes secondary to changes in prescribed medications or associated illnesses.

■ Assess patient's emotional readiness to increase activity.

Many patients with myocardial infarction (MI) may still be denying they even had a heart attack and may want to do more than prescribed; some post-MI or surgical patients or older patients with CHF can be quite fearful of overexerting their hearts or causing discomfort.

■ = Independent; ▲ = Collaborative

Cardiac Rehabilitation—cont'd

Actions/Interventions

■ Assess health beliefs, motivation level, and interest regarding initiation of outpatient exercise program.

■ Monitor response to progressive activities. Report and modify regimen if the following abnormal responses are noted:
  • Pulse greater than 20 beats/min over baseline, or greater than 120 beats/min (inpatient, phase 1)
  • Chest pain or discomfort; dyspnea
  • Occurrence of or increase in dysrhythmias (inappropriate bradycardia, symptomatic supraventricular tachycardia)
  • Excessive fatigue
  • Decrease of 15 to 20 mm Hg in systolic BP
  • Systolic BP of 200 mm Hg or more, or diastolic BP greater than 110 mm Hg
  • ST-segment displacement, if ECG is monitored

■ For inpatients, monitor oxygen saturation.

■ Assess patient's perception of effort required to perform each activity.

Rationale

Some patients with no prior history of exercise may benefit from more supervised sessions to facilitate adherence. However, other patients may prefer to exercise independently at home, for example, using a stationary bicycle.

Physical activities increase demands on the heart. Close monitoring of the patient's response provides guidelines for optimal activity progression.

A saturation of greater than 90 mm Hg is recommended. Lower values require supplemental oxygen during activity and slower activity progression.

The Borg scale uses ratings from 6 to 20 to determine rating of perceived exertion. A rating of 11 (fairly light) to 13 (somewhat hard) is an acceptable level for most inpatients, whereas 11 to 15 may be appropriate for outpatients.

Therapeutic Interventions

Actions/Interventions

■ Encourage verbalization of feelings regarding exercise or need to increase activity.

■ Inform patient about health benefits and physical effects of activity or exercise.

▲ For inpatients, maintain progression of activities as ordered by cardiac rehabilitation team or physician, and as tolerated by patient. The following cardiac rehabilitation stages are meant only to be a guide. Institutional policies vary regarding the number of stages or steps.

Rationale

An honest relationship facilitates problem solving and successful coping.

Activity prevents complications related to immobilization, improves feelings of well-being, and may improve mortality (with long-term exercise).

Not everyone progresses at the same rate. Some patients progress slowly because of complicated MI, lack of motivation, inadequate sleep, fear of "overexertion," related medical problems, and previous sedentary lifestyle. In contrast, others who experience small infarcts and who had high fitness and activity levels before hospitalization may progress rapidly. Activities are progressed by increasing either distance or time walked, as the patient tolerates or prefers.

Cardiac Rehabilitation Stages:

Stage 1:
  • Perform self-care activities at bedside.
  • Do selected range-of-motion (ROM) exercises in bed.

This promotes feelings of growing independence.

These reduce risk of thromboembolism.

■ = Independent; ▲ = Collaborative

Cardiac Rehabilitation

Actions/Interventions	Rationale
• Dangle lower extremities 15 to 30 minutes at bedside three times daily.	This minimizes occurrences of postural hypotension.
Stage 2:	
• Sit up in chair for 30 to 60 minutes three times daily.	This promotes lung expansion.
• Take partial bath in chair.	
• Continue ROM exercises in chair.	This maintains flexibility. Postsurgical patients are usually afraid to move upper arms because of chest incision; this can result in frozen shoulder.
• Use incentive spirometer and cough and deep breathing exercises, especially after cardiac surgery.	This prevents atelectasis; recommended frequency is 10 times every hour while awake.
Stage 3:	
• Continue with ROM exercises and low-intensity calisthenics.	Exercises should be primarily dynamic, 2 to 3 metabolic equivalents (METs) in intensity.
• Take partial bath at sink.	
• Sit up in room as tolerated.	Chair rest reduces postural hypotension and promotes better lung function.
• Walk 75 to 100 feet in hall two to three times daily.	Repetition helps maintain muscle strength and build confidence.
Stage 4:	
• Continue with calisthenic exercises.	
• Walk in hall 300 feet twice daily.	Increase in distance or speed can be used to increase level of activity.
Stage 5:	
• Continue with calisthenic exercises.	
• Ambulate "ad lib."	
• Climb stairs (5 to 10 steps).	Success in stair climbing promotes confidence before discharge.
• Perform discharge submaximal exercise stress test as prescribed (for most post-MI patients).	This is used to risk-stratify patients.
▲ For patients with neurological or musculoskeletal problems, refer to physical therapy for assessment of ambulatory assistive device.	Assistive aids help reduce energy consumption during physical activity.
■ Encourage adequate rest periods before and after activity.	Rest decreases cardiac workload.
■ Assist and provide emotional support when increasing activity.	Cardiac patients are often afraid of overexerting their hearts.
Before discharge:	
■ Provide written guidelines in activity progression for home exercise programs.	Exercise programs must be individualized, because each patient recovers at his or her own rate. Most patients are not enrolled in outpatient rehabilitation until 2 to 3 weeks after hospital discharge (if at all). Thus patients need to initiate some exercise progression on their own.

■ = Independent; ▲ = Collaborative

Cardiac Rehabilitation—cont'd

Actions/Interventions	Rationale
■ Include MET level guides for determining when to resume various ADLs.	Tables have been developed that indicate the MET level for most ADLs and sports activities. For example, resting in a supine position is 1 MET. Driving a car is about 2.8 METs. Sitting on a bedside commode is about 3 METs, as is walking at 2.5 mph. Walking briskly up stairs is about 7 METs. Shoveling snow is about 8 to 9 METs.
■ Provide instructions for warm-up and cool-down exercises.	Warm-up exercises facilitate the heart and body's transition from rest to physical activity. Cool-down exercises facilitate hemodynamic adjustments and return of HR and BP to near-normal levels.
■ Provide a target HR guide (usually around 20 beats/min above standing resting HR).	Having a target guide aids in monitoring intensity of exercise.
■ Instruct patients regarding whom (e.g., cardiac rehabilitation nurse, physician) to call if any abnormal response to exercise is noted.	Information enables patient to take control of situation.
■ For older patients or patients with significant medical complications, consider referral to a home visiting nurse or physical therapy sessions.	Some patients require more supervision or specialized therapy to regain activity tolerance.

Outpatient programs:

■ Assist patient to set appropriate short- and long-term goals	Some patients are only interested in regaining strength after a cardiac event, whereas others are motivated to improve their functional capacities by beginning new lifelong exercise habits.
■ Determine patient's projected length of time in a supervised program.	Some insurance carriers reimburse for 36 sessions and others for only 6 sessions. Some patients may prefer home exercise rather than the group environment and may attend only a few sessions to get started.
■ Design an individualized plan, including intensity, duration, frequency, and mode of exercise.	Age and fitness level must be considered in designing the exercise prescription. Although the benefits are the same as for younger patients, older patients need more warm-up and cool-down time. Intensity is usually guided by the target HR, which is about 20 beats/min above standing resting HR. For patients who had symptom-limited exercise stress tests, a more individualized and precise target HR can be calculated.
■ Gradually adjust duration and/or intensity of exercise until target HR is reached.	For patients less familiar with exercise or with more complications, it may take several sessions to reach target HR.
■ Provide instruction on appropriate warm-up and cool-down exercises.	Stretching exercises promote flexibility and prepare the muscles and joints for the upcoming stress from exercise. Cool-down is especially important because it helps to pump blood pooled in the primary muscle groups back to the upper part of the body. It also helps prevent muscle soreness. It is especially important for older patients to perform adequate warm-up and cool-down exercises.
■ Instruct in self-monitoring of appropriate and abnormal responses to exercise.	Cardiac patients must be aware of warning signs that warrant cessation of exercise.

■ = Independent; ▲ = Collaborative

Actions/Interventions	Rationale
■ Teach patients how to self-monitor their pulse rate if appropriate.	HR is a guide for monitoring intensity or duration of exercise.
■ Reinforce positive effects of exercise in improving mortality and quality of life.	Studies of cardiac rehabilitation programs have reported significant reduction in mortality in patients with coronary heart disease.
■ Provide positive feedback to patients' efforts.	Ongoing feedback facilitates adherence with a sometimes difficult behavior change.

Nursing Diagnosis

Deficient Knowledge

Common Related Factor

Unfamiliarity with cardiac disease process, treatments, recovery process, follow-up care

Defining Characteristics

Questioning
Verbalized misconceptions
Lack of questions

Common Expected Outcomes

Patient verbalizes understanding of disease state, recovery process, and follow-up care.
Patient identifies available resources for lifestyle changes.
Patient verbalizes reduced fear or anxiety regarding cardiac event and pending discharge.

NOC Outcomes
Knowledge: Disease Process;
    Knowledge: Treatment Regimen

NIC Interventions
Cardiac Care: Rehabilitative; Teaching:
    Disease Process; Teaching: Prescribed
    Medications; Teaching: Prescribed Diet;
    Behavior Modification

Ongoing Assessment

Actions/Interventions	Rationale
■ Assess understanding of disease process, specific cardiac event, treatments, recovery, and follow-up care.	Teaching standardized content that patient already knows wastes valuable time and hinders critical learning.
■ Identify specific learning needs and goals before discharge.	Shortened hospital stays and complex risk factor reduction programs provide challenges to the nurse and patient. Priority needs must be identified and satisfied first.
For outpatients:	
■ Conduct intake interviews regarding prior experiences with risk factor reduction and lifestyle changes that the patient is interested in pursuing.	Coronary atherosclerosis is a chronic disease requiring risk factor modification. Patients may have been told to change their lifestyle at an earlier time. Knowledge of prior behaviors serves to guide management plan.
■ Assess the patient's readiness for and self-efficacy to initiate and maintain recommended behavioral changes.	Lifestyle changes can be extremely difficult to make. Many behavior modification techniques based on social learning theory stress the importance of self-efficacy in initiating change.

■ = Independent; ▲ = Collaborative

> ## Cardiac Rehabilitation—cont'd

Therapeutic Interventions

Actions/Interventions	Rationale
■ Develop a plan for meeting individual goals. Include topics to be covered, format (individual versus group session), frequency (after each exercise session versus monthly), available audiovisual resources (video library, books, Internet, telephone), and specialty personnel (nutritionist, exercise physiologist, others).	Each patient has his or her own learning style, which must be considered when designing a teaching program.
■ Encourage meetings or conferences with family or significant others to discuss home recovery plan.	This approach enhances smooth transition to the home and may help guard against "overprotectedness."
■ Provide information on the following needed topics: • Pathophysiology of cardiac event (MI, CHF, coronary artery disease, percutaneous transluminal coronary angioplasty, valve disease) • Healing process after cardiac event • Incisional pain versus angina versus heart attack • Resumption of ADLs, such as lifting, household chores, driving a car, climbing stairs, social activities, sexual activity, and recreational activity • Return to work	Specific instructions, especially in written form, help reduce the patient's postdischarge fears and reduce risks of either overexertion or "cardiac invalidism."
■ Provide information regarding follow-up medications.	Secondary prevention guidelines recommend that patients should take aspirin (to reduce platelet aggregation), β-blockers (to reduce mortality), lipid-lowering medication (to achieve a low-density lipoprotein level less than 100 mg/dl), and angiotensin-converting enzyme inhibitors (if ejection fraction is less than 40%). Antihypertensive and glucose-lowering medications are added as needed.
■ Provide referral to comprehensive risk reduction programs as indicated: • Lipid management • Hypertension management • Diabetes management • Weight management • Counseling on heart-healthy nutrition • Smoking cessation • Stress management • Immediate treatment for recurrence of chest pain or shortness of breath • Incisional care • Prophylactic antibiotics after valve surgery • Follow-up medical care • Coping mechanisms to help adjustment to new lifestyle	Staff is challenged to individualize services. Programs should focus on increasing awareness of personal risk factors and offer clear directions and strategies for risk reduction.
■ Stress the importance of the patient's own role in maximizing his or her health status.	Patients need to understand that reduction of cardiac risk factors and health maintenance depend on them. Health professionals and family members can only provide information and support.

■ = Independent; ▲ = Collaborative

Actions/Interventions

- Provide information on available educational or support resources: American Heart Association, Mended Hearts Groups, cardiac rehabilitation programs, stress management programs, smoking-cessation programs, and weight management programs.

Rationale

Lifestyle changes may require the assistance of professionals. Support groups provide contact with other individuals "who have been there" and can be beneficial in reducing anxiety and dealing with the impact of a cardiac event.

NDx Nursing Diagnosis

Risk for Ineffective Coping

Common Risk Factors

Recent changes in health status
Perceived change in future health status
Perceived change in social status and lifestyle
Feeling powerless to control disease progression
Unsatisfactory support systems
Inadequate psychological resources

Common Expected Outcomes

Patient identifies own coping behaviors.
Patient identifies available resources for psychological and social support.
Patient implements a positive coping mechanism.
Patient describes positive results from new behaviors.

NOC Outcomes
Coping; Anxiety Self-Control

NIC Interventions
Coping Enhancement; Support System Enhancement; Anxiety Reduction; Teaching: Individual

Ongoing Assessment

Actions/Interventions

- Assess specific stressors.

- Assess available or useful past and present coping mechanisms.

- Evaluate resources or support systems available to patient in hospital and at home.

- Assess the level of understanding and readiness to learn needed lifestyle changes.

Rationale

Accurate appraisal can facilitate development of appropriate coping strategies. A patient's concerns may include fear of overexerting the heart with activity, expectation of becoming a cardiac invalid, inability to resume satisfying sexual activity, or inability to maintain recommended lifestyle changes.

Successful adjustment is influenced by previous coping success. Patients with a history of maladaptive coping may need additional resources.

Women (who manifest cardiac disease at a later age) are often widows living alone with limited support systems. Likewise, older patients with lifelong cardiac disease may have reduced contact with significant others.

This provides an important starting point when intervening with patient.

■ = Independent; ▲ = Collaborative

Cardiac Rehabilitation—cont'd

Therapeutic Interventions

Actions/Interventions

- Encourage verbalization of concerns.

- Encourage patient to seek information that will enhance coping skills.
- Provide information that patient wants or needs. Do not provide more than patient can handle.

- Provide reliable information about future limitations (if any) in physical activity and role performance.

- Provide information about the healing process so that misconceptions can be clarified. Refer to famous people (politicians, athletes, movie stars) who had similar cardiac problems or procedures and are now leading productive lives.
- Explain that patients are often "healthier" after cardiac events.

- Point out signs of positive progress or change.

- Encourage referral to a cardiac rehabilitation program and/or "coronary club."

Rationale

Acknowledging your awareness of the challenges related to recovery from chronic cardiac disease can open doors for ongoing communication.

Patients who are not coping well may need more guidance initially.

With shortened exposure to cardiac rehabilitation services, patients can easily become overwhelmed by the large number of changes that are expected of them in a short time. Lifestyle changes should be considered over a lifelong period.

At least 85% of patients can resume a normal lifestyle. Patients with more complications need guidance in understanding which limitations are temporary during recovery and which may be more permanent.

Examples such as Lyndon Johnson serving as President after a heart attack can provide reassurance and confidence about resuming activities.

Patients' blocked arteries may have been "fixed," they are more knowledgeable of their specific risk factors and treatment plan, and they may be taking medication to improve their health.

Patients who are coping ineffectively may not be able to assess progress.

These programs provide opportunities to discuss fears with specialists and patients experiencing similar concerns.

• RELATED CARE PLANS

Disturbed body image, p. 21
Disturbed sleep pattern, p. 177
Health-seeking behaviors, p. 91
Ineffective sexuality patterns, p. 170

Cardiac Transplantation

Heart Transplant

Cardiac transplantation is a treatment option for persons with end-stage cardiac disease for whom all possible modes of surgical and medical treatment have been exhausted. Transplant candidates must meet certain criteria, including age, adequate liver and renal function, and absence of comorbid conditions that would put the individual at increased risk (e.g., pulmonary hypertension, lung disease, morbid obesity, diabetes with end-stage neuropathy,

■ = Independent; ▲ = Collaborative

malignancy). Additionally, positive social supports and psychological stability are required to maximize the potential for success. The best predictors for a poor (less than 1 year) survival rate without transplantation are an ejection fraction less than 20% and a peak volume of oxygen utilization (Vo_2) less than 14 mL/kg/min. The surgical procedure entails the excision of both donor and recipient hearts and transplantation of the donor heart into the recipient (orthotopically transplanted). With ongoing compliance to medical therapy and adherence to lifestyle changes, the transplant patient can live an active and productive life.

 Nursing Diagnosis

Decreased Cardiac Output

Common Related Factors

Dysrhythmias induced by edema of conductive tissue in the donor heart secondary to manipulation of the nodal tissue at time of transplantation

Dysrhythmias associated with early rejection

Ischemia occurring during transport of donor graft or secondary to surgical procedure

Electrolyte or acid-base imbalance

Defining Characteristics

Cardiac dysrhythmias:
- Atrial fibrillation
- Junctional rhythms
- Symptomatic bradycardia
- Ventricular ectopy

Rapid or slow pulse

Shortness of breath

Dizziness

Change in mental status

Decreased blood pressure (BP)

Cool, clammy skin

Decreased urine output

Common Expected Outcome

Patient maintains optimal cardiac output, as evidenced by regular cardiac rate and rhythm, clear lung sounds, BP within normal limits for patient, adequate urine output, and warm, dry skin.

NOC Outcomes

Circulation Status; Cardiac Pump Effectiveness; Vital Sign Status

NIC Interventions

Hemodynamic Regulation; Dysrhythmia Management; Medication Administration: Parenteral

Ongoing Assessment

Actions/Interventions

■ Monitor electrocardiogram (ECG) continuously, documenting any signs of inadequate heart rate (HR) (e.g., sinus pause, sinus arrest, atrial fibrillation, junctional rhythm, heart blocks, and bradycardias) or ventricular ectopy.

Rationale

The rate and rhythm of the transplanted heart depend on the sinus node impulse in the donor heart. Remnant P waves from the native heart are of no clinical significance because these electrical impulses do not cross the suture line. Junctional rhythms are secondary to suture line edema in the atrium and generally resolve within 2 weeks.

■ = Independent; ▲ = Collaborative

Cardiac and Vascular Care Plans

Cardiac Transplantation—cont'd

Actions/Interventions

■ Assess for signs of decreased cardiac output. See Defining Characteristics on the preceding page.

▲ Monitor electrolyte and acid-base balance.

Rationale

Transplanted hearts are denervated; therefore HR changes gradually in response to altered metabolic needs through circulating catecholamines secreted from the adrenal medulla (i.e., there may be no compensatory tachycardia indicating hypovolemia or pump failure). The resting HR of the denervated heart is higher than normal. The surgical procedure does not allow for restoration of vagus nerve innervation. As a result, the heart does not have the inhibitory neural mechanisms from the vagus nerve.

Hypokalemia and hypomagnesemia are common causes for arrhythmias causing reduced cardiac output.

Therapeutic Interventions

Actions/Interventions

▲ Administer medications as ordered (epinephrine, vaso-pressor, dobutamine, theopylline [Theo-Dur]).

▲ Use temporary epicardial pacing wires to maintain an adequate HR. Check rate, milliamperes, mode, and connections often. If severe ventricular ectopy (ventricular tachycardia) occurs with hemodynamic instability, treat according to Advanced Cardiac Life Support (ACLS) and/or institutional policies.

▲ Give potassium replacement as ordered.

▲ Correct uncompensated metabolic acidosis with sodium bicarbonate, as ordered.

Rationale

These medications increase HR and contractility, which enhance cardiac output. For chronic problems, patients may be discharged on theophylline (Theo-Dur) to "buy time" for decrease in tissue edema.

Temporary atrial pacing is used to support the cardiac rhythm. ACLS guidelines assist in defining dysrhythmia treatment (except for atropine). Atropine, which is a parasympathetic blocker, is ineffective with denervated hearts.

Serum potassium level should be greater than 4 mEq/L. Hypokalemia causes ventricular irritability.

Acidosis precipitates ventricular ectopy.

NDx Nursing Diagnosis

Risk for Decreased Cardiac Output

Common Risk Factors

Right ventricular failure secondary to preexisting pulmonary hypertension
Reperfusion injury of donor heart before transplantation
Rejection

■ = Independent; ▲ = Collaborative

Common Expected Outcome

Patient maintains optimal cardiac output, as evidenced by regular cardiac rate and rhythm, clear lung sounds, BP within normal limits for patient, and warm, dry skin.

NOC Outcome
Cardiac Pump Effectiveness

NIC Interventions
Invasive Hemodynamic Monitoring; Hemodynamic Regulation

Ongoing Assessment

Actions/Interventions	Rationale
▲ Monitor cardiac output by thermodilution on admission and as needed.	This provides information on pump function, guiding pharmacological therapy.
▲ Assess right side of heart performance by documentation of central venous pressure (CVP) and assessment of jugular vein distention, peripheral edema, abdominal distention, nausea, and hepatomegaly.	CVP provides information on filling pressures in the right heart.
▲ Assess left side of heart performance by documentation of pulmonary artery pressure, pulmonary capillary wedge pressure, left atrial pressure, systemic vascular resistance, arterial BP, presence of S_3 and S_4 gallops, and rales.	These provide information on filling pressures and fluid status in the left heart.
■ Monitor intake and output.	This provides evidence of renal perfusion and fluid balance.
■ Assess laboratory values for renal and liver function.	This provides evidence of right- and left-sided congestion or failure.

Therapeutic Interventions

Actions/Interventions	Rationale
▲ Administer parenteral fluids as ordered.	Volume therapy may be required to maintain adequate filling pressures and to optimize cardiac output. Use pulmonary capillary wedge pressure readings to guide therapy.
■ Maintain normothermia and a quiet environment, and place the patient in semi-Fowler's position.	These measures reduce oxygen demands on the heart.
▲ Administer inotropes (dopamine, dobutamine, vasopressin, epinephrine, and milrinone) as ordered.	These increase myocardial contractility. Milrinone also provides some vasodilation.
▲ Administer vasodilators (sodium nitroprusside [Nipride], nitroglycerine, nitric oxide) as ordered.	These control systemic vascular resistance, thereby reducing cardiac workload. Nitric oxide is used to dilate the pulmonary vascular bed in patients with pulmonary hypertension.
▲ Maintain adequate oxygenation.	Oxygen optimizes cardiac function and reduces pulmonary vascular resistance.

■ = Independent; ▲ = Collaborative

Cardiac Transplantation—cont'd

 Nursing Diagnosis

Risk for Injury: Bleeding/Hemorrhage

Common Risk Factors

The pericardial sac is larger than normal after transplant; therefore a small new heart leaves an area that may conceal postoperative bleeding.

Nonsurgical bleeding may be enhanced by preoperative anticoagulation or intraoperative cardiopulmonary bypass and heparinization.

Surgical bleeding may be enhanced by elaborate suture lines and cannulation sites, as well as coagulopathy.

Preoperative hepatomegaly from chronic heart failure may cause clotting deficiencies.

Common Expected Outcome

Patient does not exhibit signs of hemorrhage, as evidenced by stable hemoglobin, hematocrit, BP, or HR within normal limits.

NOC Outcomes
Blood Coagulation; Blood Loss Severity

NIC Intervention
Bleeding Precautions

Ongoing Assessment

Actions/Interventions

■ Assess pulse, BP, hemodynamic measurements.

■ Assess peripheral pulses and capillary refill.

■ Monitor intake and output.

■ Assess mediastinal chest tube drainage for significant cessation (i.e., tamponade) and/or increase (i.e., hemorrhage).

▲ Monitor hemoglobin or hematocrit.

▲ Monitor prothrombin time/partial thromboplastin time and platelet count; check activated clotting time.

Rationale

Hypotension and reduced CVP may signal hypovolemia. HR is not an accurate guide because the denervated heart does not respond to the autonomic nervous system.

As oxygenation and perfusion become impaired, peripheral tissues become cyanotic.

Oliguria is a compensatory response to reduced fluid volume.

Greater than 100 mL/hr for 4 hours or abrupt decrease of drainage is significant.

Drops in hemoglobin or hematocrit must be evaluated as an indication of blood loss, although hematocrit may also decrease as fluids are administered because of dilution.

Deficiencies guide ongoing treatment.

■ = Independent; ▲ = Collaborative

Cardiac Transplantation

Actions/Interventions

- Observe amplitude of ECG configuration.
- Assess heart tones.
- ▲ Evaluate chest x-ray study for widening of mediastinal shadow.

Rationale

Decreased QRS voltage indicates tamponade.

Muffled heart sounds indicate tamponade.

Shadow is seen with cardiac tamponade.

Therapeutic Interventions

Actions/Interventions

- Raise head of bed to 30 degrees and turn patient hourly.
- Milk chest tubes every 30 minutes for 12 hours and then hourly. Note amount and type of drainage (with or without clots); document output.
- ▲ Maintain 20 cm H_2O suction to mediastinal chest tube.
- ▲ Maintain current type and crossmatch to keep 2 units of packed red blood cells available at all times during the intensive care unit (ICU) stay.
- ▲ Use cytomegalovirus (CMV)-negative blood if the recipient is CMV-negative. Use leukocyte-reduced filter for all packed red blood cell transfusions.
- ▲ Replace volume losses with colloids or crystalloids as ordered. Consider autotransfusion. If patient is bleeding rapidly, anticipate return to operating room.

Rationale

This prevents impedance of mediastinal drainage.

Current practice is to not strip chest tubes unless they are clotted.

Suction facilitates drainage.

Being prepared helps ensure early treatment and reduced complications.

These reduce potential complications.

Maintaining an adequate circulating blood volume is a priority. The amount of fluid infused is usually more important than the type.

NDx Nursing Diagnosis

Risk for Infection

Common Risk Factors

Immunosuppressive drug therapy
Disruption of skin and iatrogenic sources of infection
Poor nutrition

Common Expected Outcomes

Patient or family states understanding of need for strict infection control precautions.
Patient/family complies with infection control measures.

NOC Outcomes
Immune Status; Risk Detection; Risk Control

NIC Intervention
Infection Protection

■ = Independent; ▲ = Collaborative

Cardiac Transplantation—cont'd

Ongoing Assessment

Actions/Interventions

■ Observe wound healing process for drainage, wound edge approximation, edema, sensitivity, and temperature of surrounding tissue.

▲ Culture any suspicious drainage from wound sites.

▲ Monitor cultures, sensitivities, and CMV titers of blood, sputum, and urine.

▲ Monitor vital signs routinely. Monitor temperature every 2 hours if elevated.

▲ Monitor white blood cells (WBCs) and cyclosporine levels daily.

Rationale

Infection is the leading cause of death after heart transplantation. Patient is most susceptible during the immediate postoperative period.

Purulent or foul-smelling drainage may indicate infection.

Laboratory cultures determine pathogens present and guide therapy. Bacterial infections are most often encountered.

A temperature greater than 37° C may indicate systemic infection.

Even a slight rise in WBCs may signal an infection because of the patient's impaired immune response. NOTE: Azathioprine (Imuran) causes a decrease in the number of normal WBCs.

Therapeutic Interventions

Actions/Interventions

▲ Keep the patient in a private room with high-efficiency particulate air (HEPA) filter capability throughout hospitalization.

▲ Anticipate prophylactic antiinfective therapy, such as ganciclovir, clotrimazole (Mycelex), or cotrimoxazole (Bactrim).

■ Maintain strict hand washing throughout patient's hospitalization.

■ When patients are transferred to a step-down unit, keep them in private rooms or with a roommate without infections.

■ Exclude personnel and visitors with infectious diseases (e.g., colds, influenza) from patient contact.

■ Control environmental traffic (i.e., limit visitors and staff members in the patient's room).

■ Wash all equipment brought into the patient's room with germicidal detergent (Staphene/hexachlorophene).

■ Change all dressings, ECG patches, and taping (e.g., endotracheal tube) daily.

■ Change all respiratory equipment every 24 hours and encourage aggressive pulmonary toiletry.

Rationale

This further reduces risk for airborne transmission of infection.

Ganciclovir is used to prevent CMV disease when the patient is CMV-negative but the donor is CMV-positive. Bactrim is used to prevent *Pneumocystis carinii* pneumonia (PCP). Mycelex is used for thrush prophylaxis.

The patient's immunosuppression is greatest while in the ICU. The ICU environment is classically known to harbor many bacteria and viruses in light of its patient population.

This prevents cross-contamination and infection. Centers for Disease Control and Prevention (CDC) research does not support the need for protective or modified protective isolation.

Patients' suppressed immune systems put them at risk for infection.

This protects the patient from exposure to potential environmental organisms.

Protective protocols help reduce risk for infection.

This decreases skin irritation and ensures close monitoring of invasive line sites. A primary cause of infection is directly related to interruption of the skin barrier.

The lungs are the most common site of infection. Replacing equipment daily decreases the incidence of contamination.

■ = Independent; ▲ = Collaborative

Cardiac Transplantation

Actions/Interventions

- Change all tubings and intravenous (IV) solutions according to hospital policy. Maintain aseptic technique. Use long-term venous access devices (PICC catheter) for long-term treatment (usually about 6 weeks).

- Ensure adequate diet high in calories and protein.

- Before discharge, warn patients about additional sources of infection, such as from airborne particles (found in large crowds of people, children with colds, visitors with illnesses) and in areas or activities such as gardening, some construction jobs, home remodeling, at construction or renovation sites, and in stagnant water (swimming in lakes).

Rationale

IV lines that are repeatedly accessed provide an entry point for organisms.

Infection risk is greater in patients with end-stage heart disease because of their presurgical debilitated state.

The patient needs education to comanage this challenging diagnosis.

 Nursing Diagnosis

Risk for Ineffective Coping

Common Risk Factors

Fear of dying
Stress of waiting for surgery
Perceived body image changes
Steroid-induced body changes
Sexual dysfunction
Guilt over donor's death
Fear of possibility of heart rejection after transplantation
Loss of role

Common Expected Outcomes

Patient displays feelings appropriate to initial stage of coping.
Patient displays acceptance of the transplant process.
Patient displays beginning signs of effective coping: relaxed appearance, sleeping well, ability to concentrate, interest in surroundings and activities.

NOC Outcomes
Coping; Role Performance; Family Coping

NIC Intervention
Coping Enhancement

Ongoing Assessment

Actions/Interventions

- Assess the patient's feelings about self and body.

- Assess response to changes in appearance.

Rationale

Each individual reacts in a unique way. Perceptions should be assessed, not assumed.

Side effects of cyclosporine and steroid therapy can cause weight gain, increase in body and facial hair, moon face, and fragile skin. Some of these changes are especially troublesome for women.

■ = Independent; ▲ = Collaborative

Cardiac Transplantation—cont'd

Actions/Interventions

- Assess the patient's usual coping mechanisms and their previous effectiveness.

- Assess for signs of ineffective coping such as fears of being alone, insomnia, indifference, lack of concentration, or crying.

Rationale

Successful adjustment is influenced by previous coping success. Patients with history of maladaptive coping may need additional resources. Likewise, previously effective skills may be inadequate in the present situation.

Ineffective coping mechanisms must be identified to promote constructive behaviors.

Therapeutic Interventions

Actions/Interventions

- Encourage patient and family to express feelings.

- Establish open lines of communication, as in the following:
  - Initiate brief visits to patient.
  - Define your role as patient informant and advocate.
  - Understand the grieving process.

- Involve social services and pastoral care for additional and ongoing support resources for the patient and significant others.

- Provide reading materials and resource persons as needed.

- Introduce new information using simple terms, and reinforce instructions or repeat information as necessary.

- Refer to a support group.

Rationale

Verbalization of feelings and sharing of emotions facilitate effective coping.

The nurse is in an ideal position to guide the patient through this stressful period.

The patient and family may have long-term adjustments to make based on the change in the patient's health status. The patient who was chronically ill before transplantation may have difficulty moving from the "sick role" to one of being well. The family may need support adapting to changes in the patient's ability to participate in family responsibilities. The patient and family may have questions about the identity of the donor. They may ask about the age, gender, race, and cause of death of the donor. The patient and family may express a need to contact the donor family to thank the family for allowing the donor heart to be available.

Sometimes it decreases anxiety to have a person who has had a heart transplant talk with the patient or family and answer questions.

Depending on the degree of anxiety, the patient and/or family may not be able to absorb all information at one time.

Relationship with persons with common interests and goals can be beneficial.

■ = Independent; ▲ = Collaborative

Cardiac Transplantation

 Nursing Diagnosis

Ineffective Protection

Common Related Factors

Possibility of acute allograft rejection characterized by perivascular and interstitial mononuclear cell infiltration; progresses to necrosis if untreated
Chronic rejection from vasculopathy

Defining Characteristics

Positive endocardial biopsy
Heart failure symptoms

Common Expected Outcomes

Patient describes early signs of rejection.
Early detection of rejection is achieved.

NOC Outcome
Immune Status

NIC Interventions
Cardiac Care: Acute; Teaching: Disease Process

Ongoing Assessment

Actions/Interventions

■ Assess for increasing malaise and decreasing exercise tolerance.

■ Evaluate ECG for the following:
  • Decreased QRS voltage
  • Atrial dysrhythmias
  • Conduction defects
▲ Monitor cyclosporine trough level (drawn 1 hour before dose).
▲ Monitor WBC and T-lymphocyte counts.

■ Assess for signs of biventricular failure: diaphoresis, reduced urine output, tachycardia, jugular vein distention, ascites, edema, bradycardia, normalized BP, low-grade fever.

Rationale

With routine cyclosporine therapy, there are no dramatic signs of acute rejection. Fatigue can be an important sign.

This may also be seen with conventional immunosuppressants.

These represent signs of rejection.
Nontherapeutic levels increase risk of rejection.

Elevated circulating T-lymphocyte counts detect early rejection.
Early assessment promotes rapid intervention. These can be signs of chronic rejection.

Therapeutic Interventions

Actions/Interventions

▲ Administer immunosuppressive agents daily, as prescribed. These may include cyclosporine, corticosteroids, tacrolimus, azathioprine, muromonab-CD3 (Orthoclone OKT3), antithymocyte preparations, sirolimus, and Zenapax (daclizumab).

Rationale

These agents reduce risk of rejection. Immunosuppression therapy may be started before surgery to aid against acute rejection. A variety of drugs with different mechanism of actions are available.

■ = Independent; ▲ = Collaborative

 **Cardiac Transplantation**—cont'd

Actions/Interventions

- Describe to the patient the procedure for endocardial biopsy, including use of local anesthesia at the biopsy catheter insertion site.

- Teach patient about signs and symptoms of acute rejection. These are increased fatigue, irregular pulse, normalizing or lower than normal BP, increased weight, swelling, and shortness of breath.

Rationale

Routine endocardial biopsies are performed to detect the first signs of rejection. Biopsies are the gold standard and a definitive procedure to confirm rejection.

By the time of patient discharge, it is vital for the patient and family to assume full responsibility for care.

 Nursing Diagnosis

Deficient Knowledge

Common Related Factors

Unfamiliarity with the following:
- Surgical procedure
- Long-term care

Common Expected Outcome

Patient and significant others demonstrate and communicate understanding of disease state, surgical procedures, recovery phase, activities, medications and their side effects, and preventive care by date of discharge.

Defining Characteristics

Questioning
Verbalizing misconceptions
Lack of questioning

NOC Outcomes
Knowledge: Disease Process;
Knowledge: Treatment Regimen

NIC Interventions
Teaching: Preoperative; Teaching: Procedure/Treatment; Teaching: Prescribed Medications; Teaching: Prescribed Diet; Teaching: Prescribed Activity; Teaching: Disease Process

Ongoing Assessment

Actions/Interventions

- Assess the patient's or significant other's understanding of surgical procedure, follow-up care, diet, medications and their side effects, activity progression, special precautions for avoiding infections, and risk factor modification.

Rationale

Preoperative patients are usually critically ill and may have difficulty retaining information. Postoperative patients may be overwhelmed by the amount of important information for which they are responsible (e.g., administering medication, detecting signs of infection).

Therapeutic Interventions

Actions/Interventions

Preoperative:
- Describe the surgical procedure, including the ICU regimen and expected length of stay.

Rationale

Patients are better able to ask questions when they have basic information about what to expect.

___

■ = Independent; ▲ = Collaborative

Actions/Interventions	Rationale
Before discharge:	
▲ Coordinate discharge teaching with dietitian, cardiac rehabilitation staff, occupational and physical therapist, respiratory therapist, social worker, and any other significant departments.	For successful recovery, the patient and family must be knowledgeable of how to provide home care, how to identify potential problems, and what to do when problems arise.
■ Inform the patient and family that the patient will have periodic diagnostic testing, such as endomyocardial biopsy, echocardiogram, and laboratory tests.	These evaluations provide early evidence of heart rejection. Biopsy is an outpatient procedure, the frequency of which tapers from weekly to every 6 months.
■ Instruct patient in cyclosporine regimen by using a flow chart specific for medications to be taken at home:	There is more than one type of cyclosporine available: the standard is Sandimmune or Neoral.
• Advise patient to store cyclosporine capsules in the blister pack in which they are packaged.	Potency of the drug cannot be guaranteed more than 5 days after the package is opened. Cyclosporine is also available in an oil-based solution and is administered in a glass or plastic cup. Do not use polystyrene (Styrofoam), which results in medication adhering to the container wall. Suggest that medication be taken with juice or milk to enhance palatability. Avoid grapefruit juice because it causes elevated blood levels of cyclosporine.
• Instruct that cyclosporine should be given on an empty stomach. Instruct to take at the same time every day, especially when monitoring levels.	NOTE: In contrast, steroids should be given with foods to facilitate its absorption.
■ Instruct regarding side effects of steroids. Caution patients about increased potential for bone brittleness related to steroid use. Recommend calcium supplement or Fosamax as appropriate. Suggest wearing comfortable flat shoes. Instruct patient regarding possibility of glucose intolerance.	Corticosteroids present common problems that patients must be prepared to identify, prevent, and treat.
■ Discuss possibility of emotional lability and mood alteration.	These are partly related to steroids and cyclosporine and partly related to the stress of surgery and recovery phase.
■ Review any additional medications that the patient may be taking.	The patient needs to be aware of administration procedures as well as side effects.
■ Instruct on low-salt and low-fat diets.	Low-salt diet helps decrease amount of steroid-induced fluid retention. Low-fat diet decreases risk of future heart disease.
■ Instruct patient that chest movements associated with coughing, doing housework, climbing stairs, and driving may cause some discomfort for several weeks. This is treated with acetaminophen, not any aspirin-containing product. Instruct not to drive for at least 6 to 8 weeks or as advised by physician. Depending on patient's occupation, returning to work is not suggested for at least 3 to 6 months; sometimes the patient will need to change jobs. Instruct to avoid lifting more than 10 pounds for the first 4 to 6 weeks.	Patients need to balance time for recovery with progressive activity to increase physical conditioning. Patients need appropriate self-monitoring skills to prevent injury.
■ Instruct on importance of practicing good hygiene measures.	Good hygiene decreases incidence of infection from skin irritations and sores.

■ = Independent; ▲ = Collaborative

Cardiac Transplantation—cont'd

Actions/Interventions

- Review signs or symptoms of sternal wound complications, such as dehiscence, wound drainage, redness or swelling, or sternal instability, which may occur up to 1 month after surgery.

- Inform patient that he or she cannot rely on pulse rate to accurately reflect tolerance or effects of activity.

- Discuss modification of cardiac risk factors.

- Discuss primary prevention: cancer screening (mammogram, prostate-specific antigen, colonoscopy), DEXA scans, ophthalmology, and dermatology.

Rationale

Instruction allows for prompt intervention in the event of a complication.

The transplanted heart is denervated, with the resting HR higher than normal.

The patient may continue to be at risk for coronary atherosclerosis and future heart disease.

A variety of conditions can be exacerbated through immunosuppressive drugs and side effects.

> • **RELATED CARE PLANS**
>
> Activity intolerance, p. 7
> Anxiety, p. 15
> Decreased cardiac output, p. 32
> Disturbed body image, p. 21
> Imbalanced nutrition: more than body
>   requirements, p.137
> Powerlessness, p. 153

Chronic Heart Failure

Congestive Heart Failure; Cardiomyopathy; Left-Sided Failure; Right-Sided Failure; Pump Failure; Systolic Dysfunction; Diastolic Dysfunction

Heart failure (HF) is the inability of the heart to pump sufficient blood to meet the oxygen demands of the tissues. It is the only major cardiovascular condition whose incidence continues to rise in the world, including the United States. HF is the final syndrome of a wide spectrum of endothelial and myocardial injuries that produce ventricular systolic dysfunction (poor pumping function) and/or diastolic dysfunction (poor relaxation function). Myocardial ischemia, hypertension, diabetes, and viral infections are the most common etiological factors, although valvular disorders, congenital defects, and pulmonary hypertension can also cause HF. Patients are classified according to the New York Heart Association standards based on severity of symptoms. Class I patients have no symptoms. Class II patients experience slight limitations in their physical activity. They can usually perform most ordinary physical activities without problems; however, they may experience fatigue, palpitations, dyspnea, or angina. Class III patients experience marked limitations of their activity. They are usually fairly comfortable at rest, but less-than-ordinary activity can cause fatigue, palpitations, dyspnea, or anginal pain. Class IV patients experience dyspnea even at rest; activity is extremely limited. The goals of therapy for HF are to improve cardiac output, reduce cardiac workload, prevent complications, recognize early signs of decompensation, decrease mortality, provide patient education to reduce the frequency of readmissions, and improve quality of life.

The basis of medical therapy is neurohormonal inhibition. Angiotensin-converting enzyme (ACE) inhibitors, angiotensin receptor–blocking (ARB) agents, β-blockers (e.g.,

■ = Independent; ▲ = Collaborative

carvedilol), and aldosterone antagonists vasodilate, prevent deterioration, and reduce mortality. These drugs used in conjunction with diuretics are considered "quadruple therapy"—the new cornerstone of treatment. Digoxin is sometimes used in appropriate patients but does not reduce mortality.

A new blood test—B-type natriuretic peptide (BNP) testing—measures a protein that is released from the congested, dilated heart. Elevations of BNP levels aid in diagnosis, are powerful markers for prognosis, and support the functional class symptoms. Newer therapies include the following: nesiritide (Natrecor), a new class of therapeutic peptides that act like vasodilators but with additional unique properties and fewer proarrhythmia effects; cardiac resynchronization therapy (CRT) pacemakers to optimize cardiac output; implantable defibrillators; and ventricular assist devices (VADs) to extend life.

Innovative programs such as cardiac case-managed home care, community-based HF case management, telemanagement, and HF cardiac rehabilitation programs are being developed to reduce the need for acute care or hospital services for this growing population. Because the goal of therapy is to manage the patient outside the hospital, this care plan focuses on patient treatment in an ambulatory care setting.

NDx Nursing Diagnosis

Decreased Cardiac Output

Common Related Factors

Increased or decreased preload
Increased afterload
Decreased contractility
Dysrhythmia
Impaired diastolic function

Defining Characteristics

Low blood pressure (BP)
Increased heart rate (HR)
Decreased urine output
Decreased peripheral pulses
Cold, clammy skin
Crackles
Dyspnea
Fatigue
Edema
Restlessness
Dysrhythmias
Abnormal heart sounds (S_3, S_4)
Decreased activity tolerance or fatigue
Orthopnea or paroxysmal nocturnal dyspnea (PND)

Common Expected Outcome

Patient maintains optimally compensated cardiac output, as evidenced by clear lung sounds, no shortness of breath, and absence of or reduced edema.

NOC Outcomes

Circulation Status; Cardiac Pump Effectiveness

NIC Interventions

Hemodynamic Regulation; Dysrhythmia Management

■ = Independent; ▲ = Collaborative

Chronic Heart Failure—cont'd

Ongoing Assessment

Actions/Interventions	Rationale
■ Assess rate and quality of apical and peripheral pulses.	Most patients have compensatory tachycardia in response to low cardiac output. If dysrhythmias are present (premature atrial contractions, premature ventricular contractions, atrial fibrillation, runs of chronic ventricular tachycardia), the pulse rate will be irregular. Pulsus alternans (alternating strong and weak pulse) is often seen in HF. Peripheral pulses may also be weak.
■ Assess BP. Assess for orthostatic changes.	Most patients have significantly reduced BP secondary to a low cardiac output state, as well as the vasodilating effects of prescribed medications. Typically patients can have systolic BPs in the range of 80 to 100 mm Hg and still be adequately perfusing target organs. However, symptomatic hypotension, systolic BP below 80 mm Hg, or a mean arterial pressure less than 60 mm Hg needs to be reported and further evaluated.
■ Assess heart sounds for presence of S_3 and/or S_4.	S_3 denotes reduced left ventricular ejection and is a classic sign of left ventricular failure. S_4 occurs with reduced compliance of the left ventricle, which impairs diastolic filling.
■ Assess lung sounds. Determine any recent occurrence of PND or orthopnea.	Crackles reflect accumulation of fluid secondary to impaired left ventricular emptying. They are more evident in the dependent areas of the lung. Orthopnea is difficulty breathing when supine. PND is difficulty breathing during the night.
■ Assess for complaints of fatigue and reduced activity tolerance. Determine at what level of activity fatigue or exertional dyspnea occurs.	Fatigue and exertional dyspnea are common problems with low cardiac output states.
■ Assess urine output. Determine how frequently the patient urinates.	Oliguria can reflect decreased renal perfusion. Diuresis is expected with diuretic therapy.
■ Determine any changes in mental status.	Hypoxia and reduced cerebral perfusion are reflected in restlessness, irritability, and difficulty with problem solving.
■ Assess oxygen saturation with pulse oximetry both at rest and after/during ambulation.	Hypoxemia is common, especially with activity.
▲ Monitor serum electrolytes.	Hypokalemia and hypomagnesemia are causative factors for arrhythmias, which can further reduce cardiac output.
▲ Assess BNP.	B-type natriuretic peptide (BNP) is elevated with increased left ventricular filling pressures and serves as a "white count" for HF. It aids in differentiating cardiac from noncardiac causes of dyspnea.

■ = Independent; ▲ = Collaborative

Actions/Interventions

▲ Monitor patient for signs and symptoms of digitalis toxicity. Obtain blood specimens to measure the serum digoxin level.

Rationale

The margin between therapeutic and toxic doses is narrow. The margin is further reduced in older patients and in patients with hypokalemia and renal insufficiency. Patients with digitalis toxicity may develop cardiac dysrhythmias such as sinus bradycardia, atrioventricular blocks, and ventricular tachycardia. Serum drug levels greater than 2.5 ng/mL are associated with toxicity.

Therapeutic Interventions

Actions/Interventions

■ Weigh patient and evaluate trends in weight.

■ Administer or evaluate patient's home compliance with prescribed medications:

• ACE inhibitors (or angiotensin II receptor blockers)

• β-Blockers (e.g., carvedilol)

• Diuretics

• Aldosterone antagonists (e.g., spironolactone).

• Vasodilators (e.g., nitrates, hydralazine)
• Positive inotropes (e.g., digoxin, dopamine, dobutamine, milrinone)

• Antidysrhythmics (e.g., amiodarone, β-blockers, potassium and magnesium supplements)

Rationale

Body weight is a more sensitive indicator of fluid or sodium retention than intake and output. A 2- to 3-pound increase in weight usually indicates a need to adjust diuretic drug therapy.

HF therapy requires administration of several types of medications. The cornerstone of treatment is ACE inhibitors and β-blockers. "Quadruple therapy" adds diuretics and aldosterone antagonists. Polypharmacy is an ongoing challenge for HF patients.

These decrease peripheral vascular resistance and venous tone and suppress aldosterone output. This category of drugs has been shown to increase exercise tolerance and survival in HF patients.

These drugs are used to decrease neurohormonal activity. They have been shown to reduce mortality, slow disease progression, and improve quality of life. Careful titration of starting doses is required because some patients exhibit fatigue, mood disturbances, or dizziness when medication is started or titrated up. These drugs should be given with food and separated from other vasodilators to reduce side effects (e.g., carvedilol with breakfast and dinner, ACE inhibitor with lunch) if side effects are troublesome.

These reduce volume and enhance sodium and water excretion.

These drugs are not given primarily for their diuretic effect, but rather for the beneficial effects on LV remodeling, reduction in sympathetic activity, and improvement in mortality. Patients need to be closely monitored for hyperkalemia.

These reduce preload and afterload.

These improve myocardial contractility. In stable class III to IV patients, intravenous medications may be administered intermittently in the outpatient or home setting.

These correct dysrhythmias such as premature ventricular contractions, ventricular tachycardia, and atrial fibrillation. HF is one of the most arrhythmogenic disorders. Unfortunately, management of dysrhythmias in this population is usually unsuccessful or even

■ = Independent; ▲ = Collaborative

Chronic Heart Failure—cont'd

Actions/Interventions	Rationale
	harmful because some antidysrhythmics have a negative inotropic effect, which may exacerbate HF or actually cause additional dysrhythmias. Atrial fibrillation with its resultant loss of atrial kick can cause significant decompensation. Some dysrhythmias require treatment with pacemakers and/or implantable cardioverters or defibrillators.
• Anticoagulants (e.g., warfarin, clopidogrel, ticlopidine)	Anticoagulation is indicated for patients with chronic HF because of their increased risk for systemic emboli. The risk of embolization increases if the patient also has atrial fibrillation.
▲ Provide oxygen as indicated by the patient's condition and saturation levels (home oxygen through cannula or partial rebreather).	The failing heart may not be able to respond to increased oxygen demand. Oxygen supply may be inadequate when there is fluid accumulation in the lungs. Also, the vasodilating effect of oxygen decreases pulmonary hypertension, thereby reducing the work of the right heart.
▲ If increased preload is a problem, restrict fluids and sodium as ordered.	Restriction decreases extracellular fluid volume and reduces cardiac workload.
▲ If decreased preload is a problem, increase fluids and closely monitor.	Fluids increase extracellular fluid volume to optimize ventricular filling.
■ If the condition does not respond to therapy, consider referral to an acute care setting or hospital for invasive hemodynamic monitoring, more intensive medical therapy, and mechanical assist devices such as intraaortic balloon pump (IABP) and right or left ventricular assist device (VAD).	Hemodynamic monitoring provides information on filling pressures on the right side (central venous pressure) and left side (pulmonary artery diastolic; pulmonary capillary wedge pressure) of the heart. Mechanical assist devices such as the VAD or the IABP provide temporary circulatory support for the failing ventricle. These devices can be used in a variety of patients with chronic HF, including patients waiting for heart transplants, patients with severe ventricular failure after a myocardial infarction, and cardiac surgery patients who cannot be weaned from cardiopulmonary bypass. VAD can be inserted in the right ventricle, the left ventricle, or both ventricles depending on the site of the failure. IABP is used to increase coronary artery perfusion and decrease myocardial work-load. Newer technologies include portable VADs that allow the patient to ambulate. Clinical trials using implantable VADs hold promise for patients to be more mobile.
▲ If chronic life-threatening dysrhythmias are the problem, anticipate treatment with an implantable cardiac defibrillator (ICD).	ICDs are indicated for documented ventricular tachycardia or ventricular fibrillation that puts patients at risk for sudden death.
▲ For patients with intraventricular conduction delay (greater than 0.13 QRS interval), anticipate possible treatment with a biventricular pacemaker.	Research demonstrates improved left ventricular (LV) synchrony and hemodynamics when pacemakers are implanted in both right and left ventricular areas.

■ = Independent; ▲ = Collaborative

Nursing Diagnosis

Excess Fluid Volume

Common Related Factors

Decreased cardiac output causing the following:
- Decreased renal perfusion, which stimulates the renin-angiotensin-aldosterone system and causes release of antidiuretic hormone
- Altered renal hemodynamics (diminished medullary blood flow), which results in decreased capacity of nephron to excrete water

Defining Characteristics

Weight gain
Edema
Crackles
Jugular vein distention
Shortness of breath/orthopnea
Restlessness
Elevated cardiovascular pressure and pulmonary capillary wedge pressure
Ascites/hepatojugular reflux
Decreased urine output

Common Expected Outcome

Patient maintains optimal fluid balance, as evidenced by maintenance of stable weight, absence of or reduction in edema, and clear lung sounds.

NOC Outcome
Fluid Balance

NIC Interventions
Fluid Monitoring; Fluid Management

Ongoing Assessment

Actions/Interventions

- Monitor patient's chart for daily weight, assessing for a significant (greater than 2 pounds) weight change in 1 day or trend over several days. Verify that patient has weighed consistently (e.g., before breakfast, on the same scale, after voiding, in the same amount of clothing, without shoes).

- Evaluate weight in relation to nutritional status.

- Assess for presence of edema by palpating area over tibia, ankles, feet, and sacrum.

- Auscultate lung sounds and assess for labored breathing.

Rationale

Such consistency facilitates accurate measurement and evaluation. Weight gain of 2 to 3 pounds indicates excess fluid volume.

In some HF patients, weight may be a poor indicator of fluid volume status. Poor nutrition and decreased appetite over time result in a decrease in weight, which may be accompanied by fluid retention, although the net weight remains unchanged.

Symmetrical dependent edema is characteristic in HF; it is graded on a trace to 4+ scale. Pitting edema is manifested by a depression that remains after the finger is pressed over an edematous area and then removed.

Elevated pulmonary pressures cause shifting of fluid into interstitial and alveolar spaces.

■ = Independent; ▲ = Collaborative

Cardiac and Vascular Care Plans

→ **Chronic Heart Failure**–cont'd

Actions/Interventions	**Rationale**
■ Assess for jugular vein distention, ascites, nausea, and vomiting.	Right HF causes increased venous pressure and fluid congestion in hepatic and abdominal systems.
■ If the patient is on fluid restriction, review chart of recorded intake.	The patient should be reminded to include items that are liquid at room temperature, such as gelatin, soup, sherbet, and frozen juice bars.
■ Evaluate urine output in response to diuretics.	Focus is on monitoring response to the diuretics, rather than actual amount voided. It is unrealistic to expect patients to measure each void. Therefore recording two voids versus six voids after a diuretic medication may provide more useful information. NOTE: Fluid volume excess in the abdomen may interfere with absorption of oral diuretic medications. Medications may need to be given intravenously by a nurse in the home or outpatient setting.
■ Monitor for excessive response to diuretics: 2-pound weight loss in 1 day, hypotension, weakness, and blood urea nitrogen level elevated out of proportion to serum creatinine level.	Excess fluid loss can stimulate compensatory mechanisms to promote activation of renin-angiotensin-aldosterone system. That can begin the vicious cycle of fluid retention.
▲ Monitor for potential side effects of diuretics: hypokalemia, hyponatremia, hypomagnesemia, elevated serum creatinine level, and hyperuricemia (gout).	The electrolyte and other abnormalities related to diuretic therapy can cause significant problems.

Therapeutic Interventions

Actions/Interventions	**Rationale**
▲ Restrict fluid as prescribed.	Restriction helps decrease extracellular volume. For patients with mild or moderate HF, it may not be necessary to restrict fluid intake. In advanced HF, fluids may be restricted to 1000 mL/day.
■ Provide innovative techniques for monitoring fluid allotment at home. For example, suggest that patient measure out and pour into a large pitcher the prescribed daily fluid allowance (e.g., 1000 mL). Then, every time the patient drinks some fluid, he or she should remove that same amount from the pitcher.	This provides a visual guide for how much fluid is still allowed throughout the day.
▲ Instruct patients to avoid foods and fluids that are high in sodium. Labels on food, drinks, and medication should be accurately read for hidden sodium content.	Patient can begin sodium restriction by eliminating the use of the salt shaker at the table, avoiding obviously salty foods, and not adding salt to food when cooking. A reasonable sodium restriction is less than 2 g/day. Instruct that soups and many ethnic foods contain high amounts of sodium, especially if eaten in restaurants.
▲ Restrict sodium intake as prescribed.	Diets containing 2 to 3 g of sodium are usually prescribed.
■ Instruct patient to avoid medications that may cause fluid retention, such as over-the-counter nonsteroidal antiinflammatory drugs (NSAIDs), certain vasodilators (e.g., calcium channel blockers), and steroids.	These agents can reduce renal blood flow.

■ = Independent; ▲ = Collaborative

Actions/Interventions

▲ Administer or instruct patient to take diuretics as prescribed.

■ Instruct patient to notify health care provider about any significant weight changes, leg swelling, or breathing changes.

▲ For significant fluid volume excess, consider admission to an acute care setting for hemofiltration or ultra-filtration.

Rationale

Diuretic therapy may include several different types of diuretic agents for optimal effect. Patient compliance is often difficult for patients trying to maintain a more normal lifestyle outside the home, who find frequent urination especially troublesome. Some patients prefer taking diuretics later in the day, after their activities. Such creative schedules can increase compliance.

Early recognition and treatment of symptoms at home can help break the cycle of frequent hospital readmission for HF. Patients need to understand their roles in symptom management. Telephone nursing can be initiated to provide for consistent monitoring between office visits.

This is an effective method to draw off excess fluid, but patients should be reminded that compliance with medication regimens and sodium restriction will help keep their conditions stable.

NDx Nursing Diagnosis

Risk for Alteration in Electrolyte Balance

Common Risk Factors

Increased total body fluid (dilutes electrolyte concentration)

Decreased renal perfusion (results in greater reabsorption of sodium and potassium)

Diuretic therapy (enhances renal excretion of total body water and sodium and potassium)

Low-sodium diet

Common Expected Outcomes

Patient maintains electrolytes within normal range when therapy is stable.

Nonacute variation in electrolyte balance is recognized and treated early to prevent complications.

Patient receives medication adjustments as needed if electrolyte imbalance is noted.

NOC Outcome

Electrolyte and Acid/Base Balance

NIC Interventions

Fluid/Electrolyte Management; Electrolyte Management (Specify)

■ = Independent; ▲ = Collaborative

Chronic Heart Failure—cont'd

Ongoing Assessment

Actions/Interventions

▲ Monitor serum electrolyte levels:

- Hyponatremia (sodium less than 136 mEq/L): may be accompanied by headache, confusion, apathy, tachycardia, and generalized weakness.
- Hypokalemia (potassium less than 4 mEq/L): may cause fatigue; gastrointestinal distress; leg cramps; increased sensitivity to digoxin; atrial and ventricular arrhythmia; ST-segment depression; broad, sometimes inverted, progressively flatter T wave; and enlarging U wave.
- Hypomagnesemia (magnesium less than 1.5 mEq/L): may cause lethargy, mood changes, nausea, and paresthesia.
- Hypernatremia (sodium greater than 147 mEq/L): may be accompanied by thirst, dry mucous membranes, fever, and neurological changes if severe.
- Hyperkalemia (potassium greater than 5.1 mEq/L): may be accompanied by muscular weakness, diarrhea, and electrocardiogram (ECG) changes.

■ Monitor fluid losses and gains.

▲ Monitor digoxin level and effects in presence of hypokalemia.

Rationale

This is especially important for patients receiving diuretics, ACE inhibitors, and digoxin, especially in the event of large weight gain or loss or in the presence of renal insufficiency.

In chronic HF, hyponatremia is usually dilutional; it is caused by a greater concentration of water than sodium.

Patients with HF require a higher safety range for "normal" potassium level because they are already prone to ventricular irritability from their dilated hearts. Hypokalemia usually occurs as a side effect of diuretic therapy.

Dysrhythmias and sudden death increase with hypomagnesemia, especially in patients with HF. Hypomagnesemia is usually associated with hypokalemia.

Hypernatremia is commonly caused by large loss of water.

Coadministration of ACE inhibitors, ARBs, or aldosterone blockers can cause significant potassium retention.

Patients with HF have a precarious fluid balance status.

Hypokalemia sensitizes the myocardium to digitalis, thus predisposing the patient to digoxin toxicity.

Therapeutic Interventions

Actions/Interventions

For hyponatremia:

▲ Encourage sodium restriction as prescribed. Provide dietary instruction.

▲ Encourage fluid restriction as indicated. Suggest ice chips, hard candy, or frozen juice bars to quench thirst.

■ Instruct the patient to avoid salt contained in over-the-counter preparations such as antacids (e.g., Alka-Seltzer).

▲ Administer or prescribe diuretics as indicated.

For hypokalemia (commonly caused by prolonged use of thiazide or loop diuretics):

▲ Administer oral or IV potassium supplement as prescribed.

Rationale

Sodium promotes water retention, which can lead to fluid overload.

Restriction of intake reduces the work of the heart and reduces the need for diuretic therapy.

Thorough understanding of hidden salt products is necessary for appropriate self-care.

Diuretics help restore water and sodium balance. Some HF patients are given a sliding scale protocol.

Oral supplements should be given directly after meals or with food to minimize gastrointestinal irritation.

Chronic Heart Failure

Actions/Interventions	Rationale
■ Encourage daily intake of potassium-rich foods (raisins, bananas, cantaloupe, dates, and potatoes).	This will assist in correcting deficiency.
For hypomagnesemia:	
▲ Administer magnesium replacement as indicated.	This may be an oral or IV supplement.
For hypernatremia:	
▲ Carefully replace water orally or intravenously.	HF patients have a precarious fluid balance status.
■ Anticipate reduction in diuretic dosage.	Diuretics are commonly the cause of the large water loss resulting in hypernatremia.
For nonacute hyperkalemia:	
■ Anticipate reduction in potassium supplement.	Some conditions may be easily corrected with reduced supplements.
▲ Provide diet with potassium restriction as prescribed.	Foods with high potassium nutrients can exacerbate the problem.
▲ Discontinue potassium-sparing diuretics as prescribed.	The potassium-sparing class of diuretics is often used to counteract the potassium loss associated with loop or thiazide diuretics. However, they can easily lead to hyperkalemia.
■ Instruct the patient to avoid salt substitutes containing potassium.	All sources of potassium need to be considered.
For acute hyperkalemia (serum potassium greater than 6 mEq/L):	
■ Place patient on ECG monitor.	Common ECG changes may include the following: tall, peaked T waves; widened QRS; prolonged PR interval; decreased amplitude and disappearance of P wave; or ventricular arrhythmia.
▲ Administer the following temporary measures as ordered:	
• Regular IV insulin and hypertonic dextrose	This causes a shift of potassium into the cells. Onset of action is 30 minutes, and duration is several hours.
• Sodium bicarbonate	This causes rapid movement of potassium into the cells. Onset is within 15 minutes, and duration of action is 1 to 2 hours.
• Cation-exchange resins	These resins reduce serum potassium levels slowly but have the advantage of actually removing potassium from the body. They are often given with one of the other measures.
• IV calcium chloride	Duration of action is 1 hour; this immediately antagonizes the cardiac and neuromuscular toxicity of hyperkalemia.
• Dialysis	This is an effective method for removing potassium but is reserved for situations in which more conservative measures fail.
■ Anticipate admission to an acute care setting.	Vigilant monitoring and rapid interventions reduce consequences of hyperkalemia.

■ = Independent; ▲ = Collaborative

Chronic Heart Failure—cont'd

 **Nursing Diagnosis**

Activity Intolerance

Common Related Factors	Defining Characteristics
Decreased cardiac output	Verbal report of fatigue or weakness
Deconditioned state	Inability to perform activity
Sedentary lifestyle	Abnormal physical response to activity
Imbalance between oxygen supply and demand	Exertional discomfort or dyspnea
Insufficient sleep or rest periods	
Lack of motivation or depression	

Common Expected Outcomes

Patient reports improved activity tolerance within capabilities.

Patient reports ability to perform required activity of daily living.

Patient verbalizes and uses energy-conservation techniques.

NOC Outcomes
Activity Tolerance; Energy Conservation

NIC Interventions
Exercise Therapy; Exercise Promotion

Ongoing Assessment

Actions/Interventions

■ Assess patient's current level of activity. Determine reasons for limiting activity.

■ Observe or document response to activity. Have the patient walk in the hall for several minutes as a nurse evaluates HR, BP, and oxygen response to exertion. If the patient is able, evaluate response to stair climbing.

■ Monitor the patient's sleep pattern and amount of sleep achieved during a typical night. Ask the patient and partner whether the patient has periods of apnea or snores.

■ Evaluate the need for oxygen during increased activity.

Rationale

Although newer pharmacological therapies have alleviated many of the disabling symptoms experienced by patients with HF, chronic symptoms of activity intolerance and limited exercise capacity often occur. Changes in functional capacity with chronic HF have a direct impact on the patient's quality of life. The patient may have restricted activity over time to avoid symptoms. Therefore it is important to ask the patient about tolerance for specific activities, such as walking a specific distance (e.g., 100 feet) or climbing a flight of stairs.

HR increases of more than 20 beats/min, BP drop of more than 20 mm Hg, dyspnea, lightheadedness, and fatigue signify abnormal responses to activity. Pulse oximetry provides information on hypoxemia with exertion.

Difficulties sleeping may need to be addressed before activity progression can be achieved. Sleep disorders can cause further deterioration if untreated. If sleep disorders are suspected, they should be reported to the physician for possible sleep study.

Supplemental oxygen may help compensate for the increased oxygen demand.

■ = Independent; ▲ = Collaborative

Therapeutic Interventions

Actions/Interventions	Rationale
■ Establish guidelines and goals of activity with the patient and significant others.	Motivation is enhanced if the patient participates in goal setting. Depending on the classification of HF, some class I or II patients may be able to successfully work outside the home on a part-time or full-time basis. However, other patients may be class III or IV and be relatively homebound.
■ Use slow progression of activity (e.g., walking in a room, walking short distances around the house, and then progressively increasing distances outside of the house (saving energy for return trip).	Slow progression prevents sudden increase in cardiac workload.
■ Teach appropriate use of environmental aids (e.g., bedside commode, chair in bathroom, hall rails).	Appropriate aids enable the patient to achieve optimal independence for self-care.
■ Teach energy conservation techniques, for example: • Sitting to do tasks • Pushing rather than pulling • Sliding rather than lifting • Storing frequently used items within easy reach • Organizing a work-rest-work schedule	These techniques reduce oxygen consumption, allowing for more prolonged activity.
■ Recommend use of light weights (1 to 2 pounds) for upper extremity strengthening.	Strength training can enhance endurance and facilitate performance of activities of daily living; such exercises can be performed while sitting in a chair.
▲ Consult cardiac rehabilitation or physical therapy departments for assistance in increasing activity tolerance.	Specialized therapy or cardiac monitoring may be necessary when initially increasing activity. Some exercises may be provided in the home. A structured program of low-intensity exercise can improve functional capacity, increase self-confidence to exert self, improve quality of life, and provide an environment for early triage of symptoms.
■ Instruct the patient to recognize signs of overexertion.	This promotes awareness of when to reduce activity and provides data for activity progression.
■ Provide emotional support and encouragement while increasing activity levels.	Support reduces feelings of fear and anxiety.

NDx Nursing Diagnosis

Disturbed Sleep Pattern

Common Related Factors	Defining Characteristics
Anxiety/fear Physical discomfort or shortness of breath Medication schedule and effects or side effects	Fatigue Frequent daytime dozing Irritability Inability to concentrate Complaints of difficulty falling asleep Interrupted sleep

■ = Independent; ▲ = Collaborative

→ **Chronic Heart Failure**—cont'd

Common Expected Outcomes

Patient verbalizes improvement in hours and quality of sleep.
Patient appears rested and more alert.
Patient need for daytime napping decreases.

NOC Outcome
Sleep

NIC Intervention
Sleep Enhancement

Ongoing Assessment

Actions/Interventions

■ Assess current sleep pattern and sleep history.

■ Assess for possible deterrents to sleep:
  • Nocturia

  • Volume excess causing dyspnea, orthopnea, and PND

  • Fear of PND

Rationale

Sleep patterns are unique to each individual. Some patients are unaware of their poor sleep patterns, but their significant others report sleeping problems.

Supine position during sleep promotes increased venous return and increased renal blood flow.

When patient is supine, the fluid returning to the heart from the extremities may cause pulmonary congestion.

Patients report this as a significant factor in sleeping difficulties.

Therapeutic Interventions

Actions/Interventions

■ Discourage daytime napping and increase daytime activity.

■ Instruct patient to decrease fluid intake before bedtime.

▲ Plan a medication schedule so that prescribed medications, especially diuretics, are not given during the late evening or night.

■ Encourage patient to follow bedtime rituals and avoid caffeine and smoking

■ Encourage patient to elevate head with two pillows or put head of bed frame on 6-inch blocks.

■ Encourage verbalization of fears.

■ Review measures that the patient can take to prevent or treat PND, chest pain, or palpitations.

■ Review how the patient can summon help during the night.

Rationale

Decreasing daytime sleep will help patient be tired enough to sleep at bedtime.

This measure reduces the need to awaken to void.

This facilitates an undisturbed night, if possible.

These are known to promote relaxation.

Elevating the head of the bed can reduce pulmonary congestion and nighttime dyspnea.

Verbalization may help reduce anxiety and open doors for further problem solving and intervention.

These are common etiologies for disturbed sleep. Prevention is key and may require medication adjustments by the physician.

Information enables the patient to take control.

■ = Independent; ▲ = Collaborative

Nursing Diagnosis

Deficient Knowledge

Common Related Factors

Unfamiliarity with pathology and treatment
Information misinterpretation
New medications
Chronicity of disease
Ineffective teaching or learning in past
Cognitive limitation
Depression

Defining Characteristics

Questioning members of health care team
Denial of need to learn
Verbalizes incorrect or inaccurate information
Development of avoidable complications

Common Expected Outcome

Patient or significant others understand and verbalize causes, treatment, and follow-up care related to chronic HF.

NOC Outcomes

Knowledge: Disease Process;
   Knowledge: Treatment Regimen

NIC Interventions

Teaching: Disease Process;
   Teaching: Prescribed Medications;
      Teaching: Prescribed Diet; Teaching:
         Prescribed Activity/Exercise

Ongoing Assessment

Actions/Interventions

- Assess knowledge of causes, treatment, and follow-up care related to HF.

- Identify existing misconceptions regarding care.

Rationale

Information provides starting base for educational sessions.

Understanding any misconceptions the patient may have about the treatment or side effects will guide future interventions.

Therapeutic Interventions

Actions/Interventions

- Educate patient or significant others about the following:

  • Normal heart and circulation
  • HF disease process

Rationale

Patients are better able to ask questions and seek assistance when they know basic information about disease and treatment.

This is helpful in understanding the disease process.

Knowledge of disease and disease process will promote adherence to suggested medical therapy.

■ = Independent; ▲ = Collaborative

Cardiac and Vascular Care Plans

> ## Chronic Heart Failure—cont'd

Actions/Interventions	Rationale
• Importance of adhering to therapy	HF is the most common reason for readmission, especially in the older population. Strict adherence to therapy aids in reducing symptoms and readmission. Therapy must be simplified as much as possible to facilitate adherence. Patients must be encouraged to follow up closely with health care providers and/or HF nurses.
• Symptoms (e.g., weight gain, edema, fatigue, dyspnea) and when to report them to health care providers	When patients can identify symptoms that require prompt medical attention, complications can be minimized or possibly prevented. Telemanagement, visiting home nurses, and HF case managers can aid in this education and assessment.

• Dietary modification to limit sodium ingestion, including the following:
  • Rationale for restriction
  • Alternative seasonings
  • Foods to generally avoid: canned soups and vegetables, prepared frozen dinners, and fast food meals
  • Ways to recognize hidden sodium: preservatives, labels, and consumer information services
	Understanding the rationale behind dietary restrictions may establish motivation necessary for making this adjustment in lifestyle.

• Activity guidelines	Providing specific information lessens uncertainty and promotes adjustment to recommended activity levels.
• Medications: instruct on action, use, side effects, and administration	Prompt reporting of side effects can prevent drug-related complications. Compliance is improved when patients understand "why" they are expected to take so many medications.
• Psychological aspects of chronic illness	Living with a chronic illness can be depressing, especially for older patients, who may have limited support systems.
• Overall goals of medical therapy	This will help clarify misconceptions and may promote compliance.
• Community resources	Referral may be helpful for financial and emotional support.
■ Encourage questions from the patient or significant others.	This allows verification of understanding of information given. Patients must have correct information to make valid choices in their treatment.

> ## • RELATED CARE PLANS
>
> Cardiac rehabilitation, p. 240
> Imbalanced nutrition: less than body
>   requirements, p. 134
> Impaired gas exchange, p. 78
> Ineffective therapeutic regimen management
>   p. 185
> Powerlessness, p. 153

Coronary Bypass/Valve Surgery: Immediate Postoperative Care

Bypass (Coronary Artery Bypass Grafting [CABG]); Valve Replacement; Minimally Invasive Surgery; Off-Pump CABG (OPCAB)

The surgical approach to myocardial revascularization for coronary artery disease is bypass grafting. An artery from the chest wall (internal mammary) or a vein from the leg (saphenous) is used to supply blood distal to the area of stenosis. Internal mammary arteries have a higher patency rate. Today's CABG patients are older (even octogenarians unresponsive to medical therapy or with failed coronary angioplasties), have poorer left ventricular function, and may have undergone prior sternotomies. Older patients are at higher risk for complications and have a higher mortality rate. Women tend to have CABG surgery performed later in life. They have more complicated recovery courses than men because of the smaller diameter of women's vessels and their associated comorbidity. Women have also been noted to have less favorable outcomes, with more recurrent angina and less return to work. Newer techniques for revascularization are available, such as transmyocardial revascularization with laser and video-assisted thoracoscopy. These techniques use limited incision and reduce the need for cardiopulmonary bypass and related perioperative complications. Surgical procedures for CABG without cardiopulmonary bypass or cardioplegia (off-pump) hold promise for reductions in postoperative morbidity.

Rheumatic fever, infection, calcification, or degeneration can cause the valve to become stenotic (incomplete opening) or regurgitant (incomplete closure), leading to valvular heart surgery. Whenever possible, the native valve is repaired. If the valve is beyond repair, it is replaced. Replacement valves can be tissue or mechanical. Tissue valves have a short life span; mechanical valves can last a lifetime but require long-term anticoagulation. Valve surgery involves intracardiac suture lines; therefore these patients are at high risk for conduction defects and postoperative bleeding. This care plan focuses only on acute care. See Cardiac Rehabilitation care plan presented earlier in this chapter for patient education information.

Nursing Diagnosis

Decreased Cardiac Output

Common Related Factor	Defining Characteristics
Low cardiac output syndrome (occurs to some extent in all patients after extracorporeal circulation [ECC] secondary to reduced ventricular function)	Left ventricular failure (LVF): • Increased left arterial pressure (LAP), pulmonary capillary wedge pressure (PCWP), and pulmonary artery diastolic pressure (PADP) • Tachycardia • Decreased blood pressure (BP) and decreased cardiac output (CO) • Sluggish capillary refill • Diminished peripheral pulses • Changes seen on chest x-ray films • Crackles • Decreased arterial and venous oxygen • Acidosis • Decreasing urine output

■ = Independent; ▲ = Collaborative

→ Coronary Bypass/Valve Surgery: Immediate Postoperative Care—cont'd

Defining Characteristics—cont'd

Right ventricular failure (RVF):

- Increased right arterial pressure (RAP), central venous pressure (CVP), and heart rate (HR)
- Decreased LAP, PCWP, and PADP (unless biventricular failure present)
- Jugular venous distention
- Decreased BP, decreased perfusion, decreased cardiac output

Common Expected Outcome

Patient maintains sufficient cardiac output to maintain vital organ perfusion, as evidenced by strong pulses, urine output greater than 30 mL/hr, adequate BP, and warm, dry skin.

NOC Outcomes

Cardiac Pump Effectiveness; Circulation Status

NIC Interventions

Invasive Hemodynamic Monitoring; Hemodynamic Regulation

Ongoing Assessment

Actions/Interventions	Rationale
■ Document the pump time (ECC) during surgery.	For on-pump procedures, the more prolonged the pump run, the more profound the ventricular dysfunction. The ECC, or the heart-lung machine, is used to divert blood from the heart and lungs, to oxygenate it, and to provide flow to the vital organs while the heart is stopped. Newer surgical techniques are performing CABG without cardiopulmonary bypass (off-pump, or "surgery on the beating heart" to avoid this complication).
■ Assess HR, BP, and pulse pressure. Use direct intra-arterial monitoring as ordered.	Sinus tachycardia and increased arterial BP are seen in early stages to maintain an adequate cardiac output; BP drops as condition deteriorates.
■ Assess peripheral and central pulses, including capillary refill.	Pulses are weak with reduced stroke volume and cardiac output. Capillary refill is slow.
■ Assess for mental status changes.	Early signs of cerebral hypoxia are restlessness and anxiety, with confusion and loss of consciousness occurring in later stages. Older patients are especially susceptible to reduced perfusion to vital organs.
■ Assess respiratory rate, rhythm, and breath sounds.	Rapid shallow respirations and presence of crackles and wheezes are characteristic of decreased cardiac output.
■ Assess urine output with a Foley catheter.	The renal system compensates for low blood pressure by retaining water. Oliguria is a classic sign of inadequate renal perfusion from reduced cardiac output.

■ = Independent; ▲ = Collaborative

Actions/Interventions

■ Assess pulse oximetry and arterial blood gases.

■ If hemodynamic monitoring is in place, assess CVP, pulmonary artery diastolic pressure (PADP), pulmonary capillary wedge pressure (PCWP), and cardiac output/cardiac index (CO/CI).

■ Auscultate lung sounds for signs of RVF versus LVF.

▲ Monitor serial chest x-ray films.

Rationale

Pulse oximetry is a useful tool to detect changes in oxygenation. Oxygen saturation should be kept above 90% or greater. As shock increases, aerobic metabolism ceases and lactic acidosis ensues, raising levels of carbon dioxide and pH.

CVP provides information on filling pressures of the right side of the heart; PADP and PCWP reflect left-sided fluid volumes. Cardiac output provides objective numbers to guide therapy.

Crackles are evident in LVF but not in RVF.

X-ray studies provide information on enlarged heart, increased pulmonary vascular markings, and pulmonary edema.

Therapeutic Interventions

Actions/Interventions

▲ Maintain hemodynamics within set parameters by titration of vasoactive drugs, most commonly:
  • Intravenous (IV) nitroglycerin

  • Sodium nitroprusside (Nipride)

  • Dopamine

  • Dobutamine (Dobutrex)

  • Milrinone

  • Norepinephrine (Levophed)

  • Epinephrine

  • Neosynephrine

  • Vasopressin
  • Nicardipine

▲ Maintain oxygen therapy as prescribed.

■ If patient is unresponsive to usual treatments, anticipate use of mechanical assistance.

Rationale

This drug dilates coronary vasculature, decreases spasm of mammary grafts, and dilates venous system.

This drug lowers systemic vascular resistance and decreases BP. Elevated pressure on new grafts may cause bleeding.

This drug increases contractility, vasopressor effect, and renal blood flow in low doses.

This drug increases contractility without vasopressor effect. This may cause slight vasodilation.

This drug is indicated for RVF; it increases contractility and vasodilation.

This drug increases contractility and HR. This has a vasopressor effect.

This drug causes sympathomimetic (α, β_1, and β_2 receptors) stimulation, causing vasopressor effects and cardiac stimulation.

This drug causes sympathomimetic (α) stimulation, producing vasoconstriction, and is used to increase BP. It resembles epinephrine but has longer action and few cardiac effects.

This drug causes vasoconstriction.

This calcium channel blocker increases cardiac output and decreases peripheral vascular resistance.

Oxygen saturation needs to be greater than 90%.

Mechanical assist devices such as the ventricular assist device or the intraaortic balloon pump provide temporary circulatory support to improve cardiac output. These devices can be used in cardiac surgery patients who cannot be weaned from cardiopulmonary bypass. The intraaortic balloon pump is used to increase coronary artery perfusion and decrease myocardial workload. The nurse needs to follow unit protocols for the management of the patient with a mechanical assist device.

■ = Independent; ▲ = Collaborative

Cardiac and Vascular Care Plans

Coronary Bypass/Valve Surgery: Immediate Postoperative Care—cont'd

Nursing Diagnosis

Deficient Fluid Volume

Common Related Factors

Fluid leaks into extravascular spaces
Diuresis
Blood loss or altered coagulation factors

Defining Characteristics

Decreased filling pressures (CVP, RAP, PADP, PCWP, LAP)
Decreased BP; tachycardia
Decreased cardiac output or cardiac index
Decreased urine output with increased specific gravity
If blood loss occurs:
- Decreased hemoglobin level or hematocrit
- Increased chest tube drainage

Common Expected Outcome

Patient maintains adequate circulating blood volume to meet metabolic demands, as evidenced by normal filling pressures, adequate BP, and urine output at 30 mL/hr.

NOC Outcomes
Circulation Status; Fluid Balance

NIC Interventions
Hemodynamic Regulation; Invasive Hemodynamic Monitoring; Hypovolemia Management

Ongoing Assessment

Actions/Interventions

▲ Assess hemodynamic parameters. See Defining Characteristics above.

■ Monitor fluid status: intake, output, and urine-specific gravity.

▲ Monitor coagulation factors on complete blood count.

▲ Monitor platelets for thrombocytopenia. If platelet count drops below 100,000, or if platelets drop below 50% of preoperative platelet level, check HIPA (heparin-induced platelet antibody).

▲ If HIPA result is positive, stop all heparin products and obtain a hematology consult.

Rationale

Most patients have hypotension and compensatory tachycardia in response to a low fluid volume. Invasive hemodynamic measurements (e.g., CVP, PADP) may be required to determine status and guide therapy.

During ECC, the blood is diluted to prevent sludging in the microcirculation. Total fluid volume may be normal or increased, but because of ECC, changes in membrane integrity cause fluid leaks into extravascular spaces.

Heparin is used with ECC to prevent clots from forming. Clotting derangements and bleeding are common postoperative problems.

Increasing numbers of patients on heparin develop heparin antibodies.

No specific guidelines on positive HIPA are yet defined. Each patient must be evaluated individually. Argatroban is used for anticoagulation in heparin-induced thrombocytopenia.

■ = Independent; ▲ = Collaborative

Actions/Interventions

- Obtain report of blood loss from operating room and type and amount of fluid replacement.

- Assess chest tube drainage and report excess (greater than 100 mL for 3 consecutive hours).

Rationale

These data provide key information on level of fluid balance.

Early intervention facilitates prompt intervention.

Therapeutic Interventions

Actions/Interventions

▲ Administer volume as prescribed (e.g., lactated Ringer's solution).

■ If clots are present, milk chest tubes.
▲ Keep cross-matched blood available.

▲ Administer coagulation drugs as prescribed: vitamin K, protamine.
▲ Administer blood products (packed red blood cells, fresh frozen plasma, platelets, cryoprecipitate).

Rationale

A cell-saver from the ECC is used to replace blood intra-operatively. Further fluid volume replacement is initiated after surgery. These maintain adequate filling pressures.

Clotted tubes may precipitate cardiac tamponade.

In case major bleeding occurs, blood replacement must be immediately available.

Specific drugs work for different etiologies.

Transfusion therapy is used to correct deficiencies.

 Nursing Diagnosis

Risk for Decreased Cardiac Output

Common Risk Factors

Dysrhythmias resulting from the following:
- Ectopy (ischemia, electrolyte imbalance, and mechanical irritation)
- Bradydysrhythmias and heart block (edema or sutures in the area of the specialized conduction system)
- Supraventricular tachyarrhythmias (atrial stretching, mechanical irritability secondary to cannulation, or rebound from preoperative β-blockers)

Common Expected Outcome

Patient maintains normal cardiac output as evidenced by baseline cardiac rhythm, HR between 60 and 100 beats/min, and adequate BP to meet metabolic needs.

NOC Outcomes

Vital Signs; Electrolyte and Acid-Base Balance; Cardiac Pump Effectiveness

NIC Interventions

Dysrhythmia Management; Electrolyte Monitoring; Electrolyte Management (Specify)

■ = Independent; ▲ = Collaborative

Coronary Bypass/Valve Surgery: Immediate Postoperative Care—cont'd

Ongoing Assessment

Actions/Interventions

■ Continuously monitor cardiac rhythm.

▲ Monitor 12-lead electrocardiogram (ECG) as prescribed.

▲ Assess electrolyte levels, especially potassium, magnesium, and calcium.

■ Reassess electrolyte levels if brisk diuresis occurs.

Rationale

Atrial fibrillation is the most common postoperative dysrhythmia.

Besides providing information on dysrhythmias, the ECG may document intraoperative myocardial ischemia that may also affect cardiac output.

Electrolyte imbalances are common causes of dysrhythmias.

Potassium and magnesium loss results from diuresis.

Therapeutic Interventions

Actions/Interventions

■ Maintain temporary pacemaker generator at bedside.

▲ Administer potassium as prescribed to keep serum level at 4 to 5 mEq/L.

▲ Administer magnesium as prescribed to keep level greater than 2 mEq/L.

▲ Administer calcium as prescribed to keep level at 8 to 10 mg/dL.

▲ Treat dysrhythmias according to unit protocol.

▲ If arrhythmias are unresponsive to medical treatment, avoid precordial thump. Use countershock instead.

See also **Dysrhythmias,** *p. 288.*

Rationale

Temporary epicardial pacing wires are often placed prophylactically during surgery for use in overdriving tachydysrhythmias or for backup pacing bradydysrhythmias. Dysrhythmias are common. During the first 24 hours the wires may be connected to a pulse generator kept on standby.

Both hypokalemia and hyperkalemia can initiate cardiac dysrhythmias.

A variety of dysrhythmias can be precipitated by magnesium imbalance.

Although cardiac dysrhythmias are less common with hypocalcemia, they can be dangerous when present.

Amiodarone has become the drug of choice for most dysrhythmias. Pacing through epicardial pacing wires is often ordered.

Avoidance of precordial thump reduces risk of trauma to vascular suture lines.

■ = Independent; ▲ = Collaborative

Nursing Diagnosis

Risk for Injury: Mediastinal or Cardiac Tamponade

Common Risk Factors

Bleeding from cannula sites
Bleeding at suture sites
Persistent coagulopathy

Common Expected Outcomes

Patient experiences no signs of cardiac tamponade.
If tamponade occurs, complications are reduced through early assessment and intervention.

NOC Outcomes

Blood Coagulation; Cardiac Pump Effectiveness

NIC Interventions

Invasive Hemodynamic Monitoring; Hemodynamic Regulation; Fluid Resuscitation

Ongoing Assessment

Actions/Interventions

- Evaluate status of chest tube drainage every hour to ensure patency of tubes.
- ▲ Assess hemodynamic profile using pulmonary artery catheter/LAP. Assess for equalization of pressures.

- Assess for classic signs associated with acute cardiac tamponade:
  - Low arterial BP
  - Tachypnea
  - Pulsus paradoxus (accentuation of normal drop in arterial BP during inspiration)
  - Distant muffled heart sounds
  - Sinus tachycardia caused by compensatory catecholamine release
  - Jugular vein distention
  - Increased pulmonary artery pressures
- ▲ Monitor hemoglobin level, hematocrit, and coagulation factors.
- ▲ Assess chest x-ray study.
- ▲ Assess two-dimensional echocardiogram.

Rationale

A decrease in chest tube drainage with classic hemodynamic signs indicates cardiac tamponade.

The RAP, PADP, and PCWP pressures are all elevated in tamponade and within 2 to 3 mm Hg of each other. These pressures confirm diagnosis.

Symptoms are related to the degree of tamponade. Accumulation of blood in the mediastinum or pericardium applies pressure on the heart and causes tamponade with a resulting decrease in cardiac output.

Excessive bleeding can occur from coagulopathy or inadequate hemostasis.

X-ray studies show widening of the mediastinum.

Changes may show increasing pericardial effusion.

■ = Independent; ▲ = Collaborative

Coronary Bypass/Valve Surgery: Immediate Postoperative Care—cont'd

Therapeutic Interventions

Actions/Interventions	**Rationale**
■ Implement unit protocols to remove clots from chest and/or mediastinal drainage tubes.	Impaired drainage can cause buildup of blood in the pericardial sac or mediastinum, resulting in tamponade.
■ If cardiac tamponade is rapidly developing with cardiovascular decompensation and collapse:	
• Maintain aggressive fluid resuscitation.	Fluids are required to maintain adequate circulating volume as tamponade is evacuated.
• Administer vasopressor agents (dopamine, norepinephrine) as prescribed.	These maximize systemic perfusion pressure to vital organs.
• Assemble open chest tray for bedside intervention; prepare patient for transport to surgery.	Acute tamponade is a life-threatening complication, but immediate prognosis is good with fast, effective treatment.

NDx Nursing Diagnosis

Risk for Ineffective Myocardial Tissue Perfusion

Common Risk Factors

Spasm of native coronary or of internal mammary artery graft
Low flow or thrombosis of vein grafts
Coronary embolus
Perioperative ischemia
Chronic myocardial ischemia

Common Expected Outcome

Risk of perioperative ischemia and/or infarction is reduced through early assessment and treatment.

NOC Outcomes
Circulation Status; Tissue Perfusion: Cardiac

NIC Interventions
Cardiac Care: Acute;
    Hemodynamic Regulation

Ongoing Assessment

Actions/Interventions	**Rationale**
■ Continuously monitor ECG.	Cardiac rhythm changes may occur secondary to myocardial ischemia.
▲ Obtain a 12-lead ECG on admission and as needed. Compare with preoperative ECG. Note any acute changes: T-wave inversions, ST-segment elevation or depression.	Primary nurse must know which vessels were bypassed and must carefully evaluate the corresponding areas on the 12-lead ECG. Patients commonly have chronic myocardial ischemia that is further compromised during surgery, or they may have spasms in specific coronary arteries:

■ = Independent; ▲ = Collaborative

Actions/Interventions

▲ Monitor cardiac markers (CK-MB and troponin) for signs of perioperative ischemia or infarct per institutional policy.

Rationale

- Right coronary artery (RCA): leads II, III, aVF
- Posterior descending: R waves in V_1 and V_2
- Left anterior descending: V_1 to V_4
- Diagonals: V_5 to V_6
- Circumflex, obtuse marginal: I, aVL, and V_5

Patients usually do not express characteristic chest pain because of the effects of general anesthesia during surgery. Laboratory data aid in diagnosis. However, many programs no longer measure these postoperatively, because there are no consistent standards to substantiate normal postoperative levels. New wall motion abnormality on echocardiogram can be used to document changes.

Therapeutic Interventions

Actions/Interventions

▲ Maintain adequate diastolic BP with vasopressors.

▲ Maintain arterial saturation greater than 95%.

▲ If signs of ischemia are noted, administer medications (IV nitroglycerin and/or calcium channel blocker)

▲ Anticipate insertion of intraaortic balloon.

Rationale

Coronary artery flow occurs during diastole. Adequate pressures of at least 40 mm Hg are needed to drive coronary flow and prevent graft thrombosis.

Adequate oxygenation is required for gas exchange.

Nitroglycerin and calcium channel blockers increase coronary perfusion and alleviate possible coronary spasm.

This assist device improves coronary artery blood flow during diastole.

 ## Nursing Diagnosis

Risk for Ineffective Fluid Composition, Electrolyte Imbalance

Common Risk Factors

Fluid shifts
Diuretics

Common Expected Outcome

Patient maintains normal electrolyte balance, as evidenced by sodium level within 130 to 142 mEq/L; potassium, 4 to 5 mEq/L; chloride, 98 to 115 mEq/L; calcium, 9 to 11 mg/dL; and magnesium, 1.7 to 2.4 mEq/L.

NOC Outcomes
Electrolyte and Acid/Base Balance; Fluid Balance

NIC Intervention
Fluid/Electrolyte Management

■ = Independent; ▲ = Collaborative

Coronary Bypass/Valve Surgery: Immediate Postoperative Care—cont'd

Ongoing Assessment

Actions/Interventions	Rationale
▲ Observe and document serial laboratory data: sodium, potassium, chloride, magnesium, and calcium levels.	Hemodilution from ECC and resultant fluid shifts cause changes in fluid composition.
■ Monitor ECG for changes.	Widening QRS, ST changes, arrhythmias, and atrioventricular blocks are seen with electrolyte imbalance.
▲ Monitor for hyperglycemia.	Tight glycemic control significantly reduces the incidence of morbidity and mortality.

Therapeutic Interventions

Actions/Interventions	Rationale
▲ Maintain adequate electrolyte balance by administering desired electrolytes as prescribed.	Hypertonic solutions may be used to correct sodium and chloride deficiencies. Potassium, calcium, and magnesium imbalances may be corrected by IV administration.
▲ Initiate insulin drip per protocol.	The goal is to achieve normal glycemia. Insulin infusion therapy has achieved tighter glycemic control than the standard subcutaneous sliding scale.

NDx Nursing Diagnosis

Risk for Impaired Gas Exchange

Common Risk Factors

Retraction and compression of lungs during surgery
Surgical incision, making coughing difficult
Secretions
Pulmonary vascular congestion

Common Expected Outcome

Patient maintains optimal gas exchange as evidenced by clear lung sounds, normal respiratory pattern, and normal arterial blood gases (ABGs).

NOC Outcomes
Respiratory Status: Gas Exchange; Respiratory Status: Ventilation

NIC Interventions
Respiratory Monitoring; Ventilation Assistance; Airway Management; Endotracheal Extubation

■ = Independent; ▲ = Collaborative

Ongoing Assessment

Actions/Interventions

■ Auscultate lung fields.

▲ Monitor serial ABGs and oxygen saturation for hypoxemia.

■ Assess for restlessness or changes in mental status.

▲ Monitor serial radiographs.

▲ Verify that ventilator settings are maintained as prescribed:
- Tidal volume 10 to 15 mL/kg
- Rate 10 to 14 per minute
- FIO_2 to keep PO_2 greater than 80 mm Hg
- Positive end-expiratory pressure (PEEP) + 5 cm

▲ Monitor rising pulmonary artery pressures and peripheral vascular resistance.

Rationale

Diminished breath sounds are associated with poor ventilation.

Low PO_2 and oxygen saturations are characteristic of hypoxemia.

Hypoxemia results in cerebral hypoxia.

Pleural effusions, pulmonary edema, or infiltrates are contributing factors.

Safety is a priority.

This PEEP parameter is considered physiologically equal to upper airway resistance.

Data provides information on pulmonary hypertension and cor pulmonale.

Therapeutic Interventions

Actions/Interventions

■ Suction as needed.

■ Hyperventilate and hyperoxygenate during suctioning.

▲ Change ventilator settings as ordered.

■ Initiate calming techniques if patient is "fighting" ventilator.

■ Instruct patient or family of rationale and expected sensations associated with use of mechanical ventilation.

▲ Administer sedation as needed:
- Midazolam (Versed): short-acting central nervous system depressant
- Morphine sulfate

▲ Wean from ventilator and extubate as soon as possible.

Rationale

During surgery, the lungs are kept deflated and atelectasis as well as mucous plugs, may result.

These procedures prevent desaturation.

Ongoing titration is expected to maintain ABGs within accepted limits. (NOTE: Patients with preexisting pulmonary dysfunction will have lower PO_2 and higher PCO_2 values.) PEEP may be increased in increments of 2.5 cm to maintain adequate oxygenation on FIO_2 of 50%. Patients can usually tolerate up to 20 cm H_2O of PEEP if they are not hypovolemic or hypotensive.

Patients expend energy when their breathing is asynchronous with the ventilator. Their oxygen demands increase. This breathing pattern may trigger high-pressure alarms on the ventilator.

Adequate educational preparation can reduce anxiety and facilitate adjustment to mechanical ventilation process.

Sedation helps decrease anxiety, which may reduce myocardial oxygen consumption. Patients are usually kept sedated for at least 4 hours to facilitate hemodynamic stability.

Initially the cardiac surgical patient requires mechanical ventilation because of use of general anesthesia. Weaning and extubation occur as soon as the anesthetic agents wear off, after 4 hours in most patients.

■ = Independent; ▲ = Collaborative

Coronary Bypass/Valve Surgery: Immediate Postoperative Care—cont'd

Actions/Interventions	Rationale
■ Encourage coughing and deep breathing. Use a pillow to splint the incision.	Surgical incision may cause chest discomfort and inhibit deep breathing and coughing.
▲ Use pain medications as needed.	Medications decrease incisional discomfort so that patient will cough and breathe deeply.
▲ Provide supplemental oxygen as indicated.	Oxygen saturation needs to be greater than 90%.
■ Instruct in need to use incentive spirometer.	This increases lung volume.
■ Encourage dangling of legs or progressive activity as tolerated.	These activities increase lung volume and ventilation.
■ Consider chest physiotherapy.	Postural drainage and percussion techniques aid in mobilizing respiratory secretions for removal by suctioning or coughing.

 Nursing Diagnosis

Fear

Common Related Factors

Intensive care unit environment
Unfamiliarity with postoperative care
Altered communication secondary to intubation
Threat of pain related to major surgery
Threat of death
Dependence on mechanical equipment

Defining Characteristics

Restlessness
Increased awareness
Glancing about
Trembling/fidgeting
Constant demands
Facial tension
Insomnia
Wide-eyed appearance
Tense appearance

Common Expected Outcomes

Patient appears calm and trusting of medical care.
Patient verbalizes fears and concerns.

NOC Outcomes
Anxiety Self-Control; Coping

NIC Interventions
Anxiety Reduction; Preparatory Sensory Information

Ongoing Assessment

Actions/Interventions	Rationale
■ Recognize patient's level of fear. Note signs and symptoms, especially nonverbal communication.	Controlling fear helps reduce physiological reactions that can aggravate condition and increase oxygen consumption.

■ = Independent; ▲ = Collaborative

Therapeutic Interventions

Actions/Interventions

■ Orient to environment.

■ Display calm, confident manner.

■ Prepare for and explain common postoperative sensations (coldness, fatigue, discomfort, coughing, uncomfortable endotracheal tube). Clarify misconceptions.

■ Explain each procedure before doing it, even if previously described.

■ Avoid unnecessary conversations between team members in front of patients.

▲ Provide pain medication at first sign of discomfort.

■ For intubated patients, provide nonverbal means of communication (slate, paper and pencil, gestures). Be patient with attempts to communicate. Know and anticipate typical patient concerns.

■ Ensure continuity of staff.

■ Encourage visiting by family or significant others.

Rationale

The noise and continuous lighting in the intensive care unit environment increase the amount of sensory stimuli for the patient and add to the level of anxiety. Patient and family need to be aware of the source of noise such as normal sounds from mechanical ventilators, monitoring equipment, and mechanical ventricular assist devices. Because equipment alarms should not be silenced, nurses need to explain each alarm sound and respond to each alarm as quickly as possible to resolve the problem and restore normal function.

This approach increases the patient's feeling of security.

Anticipatory preparation can help reduce anxiety associated with the unknown.

High anxiety levels can reduce attention level and retention of information. Information can promote trust or confidence in medical management. Patients and families also need a basic understanding of the purpose of tubes, monitoring equipment, medication pumps, mechanical ventilators, and other equipment and devices that are part of postoperative care. Misconceptions about the use of the equipment can add to patient's fear of equipment failure and feelings of dependency on machines.

This reduces patient's misconceptions and fear or anxiety.

Effective pain management will reduce discomfort and fear.

Patients' inability to talk can add to their anxiety.

This facilitates communication efforts and provides stability in care.

This promotes a feeling of security; patient does not feel alone.

• RELATED CARE PLANS

Cardiac rehabilitation, p. 240
Dysrhythmias, p. 288
Mechanical ventilation, p. 459

■ = Independent; ▲ = Collaborative

Dysrhythmias

Arrhythmias; Tachycardia; Bradycardia; Atrial Flutter; Atrial Fibrillation; Paroxysmal Supraventricular Tachycardia (PSVT); Heart Block; Pacemakers

Dysrhythmias involve any disturbance in rhythm, rate, or conduction of the heartbeat. They can occur for a variety of reasons. Even the aging process itself causes changes in the function of the cardiac electrical system. The clinical significance of dysrhythmias can range from benign occurrences not requiring treatment to life-threatening situations. For some patients, syncope or even sudden cardiac death is the first occurrence of the dysrhythmia. Evaluation of the etiological factors for and the clinical significance of the dysrhythmia guide the therapeutic management. Treatment usually consists of drug therapy but may also include pacemaker support, electrical cardioversion, radiofrequency catheter ablation, an implantable defibrillator, or cardiopulmonary resuscitation (CPR). The American Heart Association Guidelines for Advanced Cardiac Life Support (ACLS) provide treatment protocols for the management of patients experiencing dysrhythmias. This care plan focuses on acute management in a medical setting.

 Nursing Diagnosis

Risk for Decreased Cardiac Output

Common Risk Factors

Rapid heart rate (HR) or rhythm secondary to the following:
- Myocardial ischemia
- Electrolyte imbalance (especially hypokalemia and hypomagnesemia)
- Anxiety or emotional factors
- Drugs (e.g., aminophylline, isoproterenol, dopamine, digoxin toxicity)
- Substance abuse (e.g., cocaine, alcohol)
- Physical activity
- Heart failure
- Pulmonary embolism
- Thyrotoxicosis
- Hypoxemia
- Stimulant intake (coffee, tea, tobacco)
- Chronic lung disease
- Edema

Slow HR or rhythm secondary to the following:
- Myocardial ischemia
- Drugs (e.g., calcium channel blockers, digoxin toxicity, β-blockers)
- Excessive parasympathetic stimulation (e.g., sensitive carotid sinus artery, inferior wall myocardial infarction)
- Diseases or degeneration of the conduction system

■ = Independent; ▲ = Collaborative

- Cardiomyopathy
- Hypothyroidism
- Increased intracranial pressure

Common Expected Outcome

Patient maintains optimal cardiac output, as evidenced by strong peripheral pulses, blood pressure (BP) within normal limits for patient, skin warm and dry, lungs clear bilaterally, and regular cardiac rhythm.

NOC Outcomes
Vital Signs; Cardiac Pump Effectiveness
NIC Intervention
Dysrhythmia Management

Ongoing Assessment

Actions/Interventions

- Auscultate the heart for tachycardia (rate greater than 100 beats/min), bradycardia (rate less than 60 beats/min), and irregularity.
- Assess for signs of reduced cardiac output: rapid, slow, or weak pulse; hypotension; dizziness; syncope; shortness of breath; chest pain; fatigue; and restlessness.

- Determine acuteness or chronicity of the dysrhythmia.
- Review history and assess for causative factors.

- Evaluate patient's emotional response to the dysrhythmia.

- If the patient is monitored electrocardiographically, determine specific type of dysrhythmia: sinus bradycardia, second- or third-degree heart block, atrial flutter or fibrillation with fast or slow ventricular response, junctional tachycardia, ventricular tachycardia, or paroxysmal supraventricular tachycardia (PSVT).
- Evaluate monitor leads that show the most prominent P waves such as lead II, V_1, or modified chest lead (MCL_1).
- Assess need for parenteral intravenous (IV) line.

- Carefully monitor patient's response to activity.
- Monitor for side effects of medication therapy.

Rationale

Clinical assessment of patient is as important as interpretation of the electrocardiogram (ECG).

Not all patients are symptomatic with each episode. Several factors can influence response to the dysrhythmia (e.g., actual HR, duration, associated medical problems).

These may guide need for and type of therapy.

Dysrhythmias are best suppressed when precipitating factors are eliminated or corrected. Some dysrhythmias such as those caused by heart failure are difficult to eradicate. Lifestyle behaviors such as smoking, caffeine intake, and emotional stress can stimulate some dysrhythmias.

Palpitations or syncope occurring at home can be especially frightening. For patients in whom dysrhythmias are resistant to therapy, chronic episodes of tachycardia can lead to coping difficulties and body image disturbances.

Ability to recognize dysrhythmias is essential to early treatment.

These leads aid in differentiating atrial from ventricular dysrhythmias.

An IV line provides immediate access in case IV medications are prescribed.

Activity may increase or further decrease HR.

Medications prescribed to "treat" dysrhythmias can themselves be proarrhythmogenic.

■ = Independent; ▲ = Collaborative

Cardiac and Vascular Care Plans

Dysrhythmias—cont'd

Therapeutic Interventions

Actions/Interventions	Rationale
■ If the patient is asymptomatic, provide reassurance if the dysrhythmia is not life threatening. Consult physician about further medical treatment.	Assessment of patient's hemodynamic status provides guidance for treatment. The patient, not the dysrhythmia, should be treated. No treatment may be indicated.
▲ Provide oxygen therapy as ordered.	Oxygen decreases tissue irritability and can relieve hypoxia-induced dysrhythmias.
▲ If the patient has acute dysrhythmia, obtain ECG immediately to document it.	ECGs provide the necessary information for diagnosing the type of dysrhythmia. An ECG should be obtained before patient reverts to baseline rhythm.
■ Anticipate need for additional testing.	A variety of tests are available to aid in diagnosis and evaluate treatment (e.g., electrophysiology testing, ambulatory Holter monitoring, signal-averaged ECG, exercise stress testing).
▲ Determine specific type of dysrhythmia.	Knowledge of specific rate or rhythm problem is necessary to accurately anticipate appropriate treatment.

For PSVT (rapid atrial tachycardia, junctional tachycardia, atrial flutter, and atrial fibrillation) with pulses:

• Anticipate use of vagal maneuvers such as carotid sinus massage (compression), the Valsalva maneuver, or the administration of IV adenosine.	These vagal maneuvers stimulate the vagus nerve, which may slow the heart. They may also be used to help diagnose the underlying dysrhythmia. (NOTE: These measures should be avoided in older patients.) Adenosine slows AV node conduction and may facilitate recognition of the origin of the arrhythmia.
• Anticipate or prepare medications to reduce ventricular response: adenosine, calcium channel blockers, β-blockers, amiodarone.	The type of medication to be given and the route of administration (by mouth or intravenously) depends on patient's hemodynamic status, underlying medical condition, acuteness or chronicity of dysrhythmia, and clinical setting. Current guidelines for ACLS provide protocols for management of dysrhythmias, including medications and electrical therapies. Using the ACLS protocols, the nurse can anticipate and prepare for the administration of appropriate medications or electrical therapies based on the progression of the dysrhythmia and the patient's response to each stage of therapeutic intervention.
• If the patient is unresponsive to medications, anticipate treatment with overdrive pacing, especially for atrial fibrillation and atrial flutter after cardiac surgery.	This is pacing the heart for several seconds at a rate about 20% faster than the tachycardia and then stopping the pacemaker to allow the heart's natural rhythm to resume control. It is appropriate when atrial pacing leads are in place.

■ = Independent; ▲ = Collaborative

Actions/Interventions

- If the ventricular rate is greater than 150 beats/min in unstable patients or if dysrhythmia is chronic and unresponsive to medical therapy, anticipate electrical cardioversion.

- For persistent, recurrent PSVT, anticipate use of radiofrequency catheter ablation.

- Instruct patient to avoid intake of stimulants as indicated: caffeine, alcohol, tobacco, and amphetamines.

For sinus bradycardia or second- or third-degree heart block with slow ventricular response:

- Instruct the patient to avoid the Valsalva maneuver (e.g., straining for stool) and vagal stimulating activities (e.g., vomiting).

- If the patient is symptomatic, administer atropine IV push, according to ACLS protocol.

- Anticipate transcutaneous pacing or temporary pacemaker insertion.

- If the patient is unresponsive to atropine, initiate epinephrine or dopamine, according to ACLS protocol.

- Anticipate permanent pacemaker for chronic conditions.

For ventricular tachycardia with a pulse:

- Recognize that this is a potentially life-threatening dysrhythmia.

- Administer medications as ordered, noting effectiveness: amiodarone (IV). Alternative drugs include sotolol and procainamide.

If patient has torsades de pointes:

- Evaluate QT interval on 12-lead ECG. Be especially alert for a 25% or greater increase from the normal QT adjusted for HR and gender.

- Anticipate the need to obtain serum antidysrhythmic drug levels and/or electrolyte levels (potassium, calcium, magnesium).

Rationale

During cardioversion, low levels of energy are used to reset the natural cardiac cycle by electrically interfering with existing dysrhythmia. In nonemergencies, the patient should be sedated before the procedure. Anticoagulation is indicated before cardioversion to reduce the risk of embolization when normal cardiac function is restored.

Radiofrequency current is passed through an endocardial catheter positioned at the site of the dysrhythmia. Heat is created that abolishes the ectopic dysrhythmia.

Stimulants increase the automaticity of the heart, which can precipitate dysrhythmias.

Vagal stimulation reduces HR.

Atropine decreases vagal tone and increases conduction through the atrioventricular node. Repeat doses may be indicated at 3- to 5-minute intervals.

Pacemakers supplement the body's natural pacemaker to maintain a preset HR. Transcutaneous pacemakers can be applied quickly. However, some patients may not tolerate the pacing stimulus to the skin and chest wall.

These medications increase BP and HR. NOTE: Sometimes the hypotension is not a result of the bradycardia but rather of hypovolemia or myocardial dysfunction, and needs to be treated as such.

Several cardiology national associations provide class I indications for permanent pacemaker implantation to improve cardiac output.

Ventricular tachycardia requires immediate attention and efficient treatment. Rapid hemodynamic collapse is possible.

For patients with wide complex tachycardias, ACLS protocols recommend amiodarone as the first-choice drug, followed by procainamide and sotalol.

This is a specific type of multidirectional ventricular tachycardia that alternates in amplitude and direction of electrical activity; the dysrhythmia often requires no immediate intervention but may be life threatening.

Generally this dysrhythmia is associated with a prolonged QT interval on the ECG.

Hypokalemia and hypomagnesemia, or hypocalcemia, along with elevated quinidine, procainamide, or tricyclic levels can precipitate torsades de pointes.

■ = Independent; ▲ = Collaborative

Cardiac and Vascular Care Plans

→ Dysrhythmias—cont'd

Actions/Interventions	Rationale

- Anticipate medical therapies assistive to the treatment of torsades de pointes:
  - Amiodarone

    This drug may be effective for stable polymorphic VT.
  - Magnesium sulfate

    Hypomagnesemia is often the cause of delayed repolarization that precipitates torsades.
  - Overdrive pacing

    ACLS lists overdrive pacing as the treatment of choice to capture/convert the ventricular rhythm.
  - Isoproterenol

    This helps to overdrive the ventricular rate and break the dysrhythmic mechanism.
- Anticipate or prepare for emergency cardioversion or defibrillation, or CPR.

  Being prepared for an emergency helps save life.

For ventricular fibrillation or pulseless ventricular tachycardia:

- Anticipate the use of adjunct therapies, such as CPR and defibrillation by trained personnel.

  Patient with a pulseless dysrhythmia should receive basic cardiac life support measures to support airway, breathing, and circulation, including automatic electrical defibrillation until personnel trained to provide ACLS are on the scene.
- Defibrillate patient.

  ACLS protocols recommend beginning at 200 J for biphasic defibrillator and 360 J for monophasic defibrillator.
- Prepare for airway intubation and oxygen therapy.

  Airway maintenance and supplemental oxygen therapy are needed until cardiac function is restored.
- Prepare for administration of IV medications: epinephrine, vasopressin, amiodarone, lidocaine, magnesium.

  ACLS protocols provide guidelines for appropriate dosages and frequency of administration. Vasopressors are key for their vasoconstricting effects to improve cardiac output and coronary perfusion. If unresponsive to defibrillation shocks, antidysrhythmic medications can be added. Magnesium is used only if the rhythm is torsades.

NDx Nursing Diagnosis

Deficient Knowledge: Cause and Treatment of Dysrhythmia

Common Related Factors	Defining Characteristics
Anxiety	Verbalized knowledge deficit
Misinformation	Verbalized inaccurate information
Lack of information	Questioning of staff about medication and/or management
Misunderstanding of information	Denial of need for information along with inability to describe therapy accurately
	Noncompliance with treatment
	Inappropriate or inaccurate self-treatment

■ = Independent; ▲ = Collaborative

Common Expected Outcome

Patient verbalizes cause of and treatment regimen for dysrhythmia.

NOC Outcomes
Knowledge: Disease Process;
Knowledge: Treatment Regimen

NIC Interventions
Teaching: Disease Process;
Teaching: Prescribed Medications

Ongoing Assessment

Actions/Interventions

- Assess current knowledge of dysrhythmia, diagnostic procedures, and treatments.

Rationale

Information provides basis for educational session.

Therapeutic Interventions

Actions/Interventions

- Instruct patient regarding cause of dysrhythmia if known.

- If patient is having a procedure to diagnose or treat dysrhythmias, show patient equipment and/or procedure room beforehand.

- Instruct patient on the side effects of medications.

- If patient is taking medication that requires maintenance of potassium level (e.g., digoxin), inform patient of foods high in potassium.

- Instruct patient and/or family members of method for checking pulse. State patient's normal rate and rate that should be reported to the physician. Explain any medications that are to be withheld or administered on the basis of pulse rate finding.

- Instruct patient with tachydysrhythmias to avoid stimulant intake: caffeine, tobacco, alcohol, and amphetamines.

▲ By physician's order and hospital protocol, instruct patient of methods to assist with controlling tachydysrhythmias (e.g., Valsalva maneuver, carotid sinus massage).

- Instruct patients with bradydysrhythmias to avoid straining for bowel movements. Provide information on natural laxatives as needed.

- Inform patient of proper procedure to follow in case dysrhythmia recurs (as evidenced by specific signs and symptoms).

Rationale

This may be related to an acute event such as myocardial infarction, cardiac surgery, or electrolyte imbalance. However, it may be a chronic problem secondary to cardiomyopathy or other disorder.

Explanations enhance understanding and reduce anxiety.

Most antidysrhythmics can have significant side effects. If side effects occur, patients need to report immediately so that appropriate therapy can be initiated.

Foods that are sources of potassium include bananas, dried apricots, prune juice, cooked lima or pinto beans, cantaloupe, and winter squash.

Eliciting patient as comanager of care increases self-esteem and ensures more appropriate treatment.

Stimulants increase the automaticity of the heart, which can precipitate dysrhythmias.

These increase patient's sense of control and ensure prompt treatment.

Straining stimulates the vagal nerve, which can further slow the heart rate.

Developing a specific plan of care provides reassurance in ability of the patient to care for self at home.

■ = Independent; ▲ = Collaborative

Dysrhythmias—cont'd

Actions/Interventions

- ▪ Instruct patient that fluid volume deficits caused by gastrointestinal influenza, diarrhea, and dehydration may lead to subsequent electrolyte imbalances and dysrhythmias.

- ▪ Instruct patient's family of sources for learning CPR.

Rationale

Electrolyte abnormalities are major causes for dysrhythmias.

Knowledge of lifesaving skills may reduce anxiety related to "life-threatening" arrhythmias. CPR training saves lives.

NDx Nursing Diagnosis

Risk for Ineffective Coping

Common Risk Factors

Misinterpretation of condition or treatment
Situational crisis
Disturbances in self-concept or body image
Disturbances in lifestyle or role
Inadequate coping methods
Prolonged hospitalization
History of ineffective medical treatments
Perceived personal stress resulting from chronic condition or treatment
Lack of support system

Common Expected Outcomes

Patient verbalizes acceptance of possible chronic medical problem.
Patient describes positive actions he or she can initiate to control or treat dysrhythmia.

NOC Outcomes
Coping; Social Support

NIC Intervention
Coping Enhancement

Cardiac and Vascular Care Plans

Ongoing Assessment

Actions/Interventions

■ Assess for signs of coping difficulties.

■ Assess patient's specific stressors (e.g., difficulty diagnosing cause of dysrhythmia, ineffective therapies, change in self-image related to problem).

■ Evaluate patient's available resources or support systems.

Rationale

Behavioral and physiological responses to life-threatening situations provide clues to level of coping difficulties.

Depending on the cause, a variety of strategies may be required.

An effective support network facilitates coping.

Therapeutic Interventions

Actions/Interventions

■ Encourage the patient and family to verbalize feelings about dysrhythmia, diagnostic procedures and treatment plan, and any lifestyle changes imposed by this medical problem.

■ Explain dysrhythmias, procedures, and medications in a clear and concise manner to the patient and family.

■ Provide opportunities to express concern, fears, feelings, and expectations.

■ Assist patient to evaluate situation accurately.

■ Maintain appropriate level of intensity of action when responding to current dysrhythmia.

■ As necessary, remain with the patient during episodes of dysrhythmia or during treatments.

Rationale

Accurate appraisal can facilitate development of appropriate teaching plan.

Information provides rationale for therapy and aids the patient in understanding treatment and assuming responsibility for ongoing care.

Verbalization may help reduce anxiety and open doors for ongoing communication.

Patient response to acute episode is highly variable, depending on prior experiences and the like. Patient perceptions need to be explored so misinformation can be clarified.

Overreaction or excessive response to a patient's dysrhythmia may encourage or increase feelings of anxiety.

The staff's presence is reassuring to the patient.

→ Femoral-Popliteal Bypass: Immediate Postoperative Care

Revascularization

This is a revascularization procedure of the obstructed arterial segment in the femoral artery by a surgical bypass graft to the popliteal artery. Grafts may consist of native arterial or vein segments or synthetic material such as Dacron or Gore-Tex. Surgery is indicated when medical management is ineffective or when less invasive procedures such as balloon angioplasty, atherectomy, or laser angioplasty have been unsuccessful. Most patients who require arterial bypass surgery have a long history of chronic arterial insufficiency related to atherosclerotic disease. The goals of surgical revascularization are to improve tissue perfusion, prevent tissue necrosis, and delay the need for amputation of the leg.

■ = Independent; ▲ = Collaborative

→ Femoral-Popliteal Bypass: Immediate Postoperative Care—cont'd

 **Nursing Diagnosis**

Risk for Ineffective Peripheral Tissue Perfusion

Common Risk Factors

Graft occlusion
Coagulopathy
Edema
Hypotension
Hematoma or bleeding
Compartment syndrome

Common Expected Outcome

Patient's peripheral circulation is optimized, as evidenced by warm skin on the extremities and adequate arterial pulsation distal to the graft.

NOC Outcome
Circulation Status

NIC Intervention
Circulatory Care

Ongoing Assessment

Actions/Interventions

- Assess the patient's level of pain at the surgical site and distally. Signs of occlusion include the following: burning, itching, pain in tissues distal to site of occlusion, pain aggravated with passive or active movement of limb, numbness or coldness of limb, arterial pulsation weak or absent distal to the occlusion, pallor, or paresthesia.

- Mark distal pulses (pedal and posterior tibial) with skin marker, and check every hour. Use Doppler ultrasound if needed. Note pulse presence and strength, color, temperature, sensation, and movement of extremities. Compare with the side that was not operated on.

- Monitor for sensory and motor function of lower extremities.

- Monitor blood pressure (BP).

- During dressing changes, assess for presence of swelling and/or hematoma. Notify physician immediately if present.

Rationale

Patients with acute arterial occlusion may report pain unrelieved by analgesics. Rapid intervention is critical to preserve circulation to limb.

Graft closure is a high-risk problem in the immediate postoperative period. Distal pulses indicate graft patency.

Compartment syndrome can occur from local swelling in the leg. Signs include severe pain, decreased sensation, and hard, swollen leg.

Hypotension can reduce blood flow to the periphery. An increased BP can cause bleeding or hematoma.

Lymph channels may have been disturbed during surgery, resulting in lymphatic drainage and edema.

■ = Independent; ▲ = Collaborative

Femoral-Popliteal Bypass: Immediate Postoperative Care

Therapeutic Interventions

Actions/Interventions

- Gently reposition patient every 1 to 2 hours. Instruct on importance of keeping affected extremity straight.
- Initiate prescribed activity according to institutional policy and patient's condition.

▲ Maintain fluids and medications as needed.

- Protect toes with lamb's wool, or place cotton between the toes.
- Avoid exposure to cold or excessive heat (e.g., cooling blankets or heating pads).
- Ensure that the surgical site is easily visualized; instruct patient or family to notify staff if bleeding is noted.
- Administer prophylactic anticoagulation therapy as ordered.
- If bleeding is noted, administer intravenous fluids, colloids, and blood products as prescribed.

Rationale

Proper positioning prevents kinking in graft, which may precipitate clot formation or impair blood flow.

Patient is usually on bed rest for 24 hours. The leg is not usually elevated in bed unless limb edema is evident. When the patient is sitting in a chair, elevate the leg to reduce edema. Progressive ambulation is initiated on an individual basis.

These keep BP from becoming hypotensive, which would result in graft occlusion, or hypertensive, which could result in hemorrhage or hematoma formation of the incisional areas and increased edema at the operative site.

Ischemic skin is easily damaged with normal wear and tear.

Cold causes vasoconstriction. Heat increases the risk for skin injury and burns.

Vigilant monitoring helps reduce complications.

Risk for graft occlusion by blood clots is high.

Specific deficiencies guide treatment therapy.

NDx Nursing Diagnosis

Risk for Infection

Common Risk Factors

Surgery
Invasive procedures

Common Expected Outcome

Patient maintains reduced risk of infection as evidenced by afebrile state; no wound drainage, redness, or warmth; and negative cultures.

NOC Outcomes
Wound Healing: Primary Intention;
  Risk Control

NIC Intervention
Infection Protection

■ = Independent; ▲ = Collaborative

Femoral-Popliteal Bypass: Immediate Postoperative Care—cont'd

Ongoing Assessment

Actions/Interventions

- Assess incisional sites for local symptoms of infection: redness, warmth, and drainage.

- Monitor temperature.

▲ Obtain cultures (e.g., of wound or blood) as prescribed.

Rationale

Signs of infection should be reported immediately because delay may cause graft infection. Infection in a synthetic graft requires its removal.

Temperature of up to 38° C for 48 hours after surgery is related to surgical stress; after 48 hours, temperature greater than 37.7° C suggests infection. Temperature spikes that occur and subside are indicative of wound infection.

Culture results determine pathogens present and guide antimicrobial therapy.

Therapeutic Interventions

Actions/Interventions

- Wash hands before and after contact with patient.
▲ Perform dressing changes according to physician's order. Document incision approximation, presence of sutures/staples, and overall appearance. Note presence, amount, and color of drainage.
- Avoid use of cooling mattress.
▲ Administer medications as prescribed for treatment or prevention of infection.

Rationale

Good hygiene decreases risk of nosocomial infection.

Data provide information regarding effectiveness of healing.

Cold may decrease lower extremity perfusion.

Antibiotics may be administered for 3 to 4 days after surgery. Ideally the selection of the drug is based on cultures from the infected area.

NDx Nursing Diagnosis

Acute Pain

Common Related Factors

Incision
Occlusion

Defining Characteristics

Patient reports pain
Guarding behavior, protective self-focusing, and narrowed focus
Facial mask of pain
Alteration in muscle tone (rigid, tense)

Common Expected Outcome

Patient's pain is relieved as evidenced by verbalization of pain relief and relaxed facial expression.

NOC Outcome
Pain Level

NIC Intervention
Pain Management

■ = Independent; ▲ = Collaborative

Ongoing Assessment

Actions/Interventions

■ Assess pain characteristics.

■ Determine techniques that the patient considers helpful in decreasing pain.

■ Observe effectiveness of analgesic and/or therapies used to reduce pain.

Rationale

The description of pain can help differentiate between incisional pain and pain from graft occlusion, which usually has a sudden onset and is severe in intensity.

The patient may have had positive experiences in the past with nonpharmacological pain-reducing methods.

Pain with graft occlusion may not respond to analgesics and requires emergency intervention.

Therapeutic Interventions

Actions/Interventions

▲ Anticipate the need for analgesics and respond immediately to report of pain.

■ Teach use of distraction techniques and nonpharmacological strategies for incisional pain as appropriate.

■ If pain is a result of graft occlusion, anticipate immediate evaluation by the physician or surgeon.

Rationale

Patients have a right to effective pain relief. Patient-controlled analgesia devices may facilitate the patient's sense of control and promote increased comfort. Pain associated with graft occlusion should be reported to the surgeon immediately.

Knowledge about how to implement nonpharmacological pain strategies can help the patient gain maximum pain relief.

Rapid intervention is critical to preserve the limb.

NDx Nursing Diagnosis

Deficient Knowledge

Common Related Factor

New surgical procedure

Defining Characteristics

Multiple questions
Lack of questions
Misconceptions of health status
Request for information
Display of anxiety and/or fear
Noncompliance
Inability to verbalize health maintenance regimen
Development of complications

Common Expected Outcome

Patient or significant others verbalize understanding of surgical procedure and related care.

NOC Outcome
Knowledge: Disease Process

NIC Intervention
Teaching: Disease Process

■ = Independent; ▲ = Collaborative

Femoral-Popliteal Bypass: Immediate Postoperative Care—cont'd

Ongoing Assessment

Actions/Interventions

- Assess knowledge regarding femoral popliteal bypass surgery and postoperative management.

Rationale

Thorough understanding of indications for care related to surgery is necessary for informed consent to be given.

Therapeutic Interventions

Actions/Interventions

- Explain proper leg positioning and reasons for positioning.

- Explain the need for frequent circulatory assessments.

- Instruct the patient to alert the nurse of any change in sensation in lower extremities or any bleeding or swelling.

- Discuss the patient's surgery and its relation to signs or symptoms the patient is experiencing.

- Instruct in the following signs or symptoms to report after discharge:
  - Signs of incisional infection
  - Coolness in leg or foot
  - Pain, discomfort, tingling, or numbness

- Clarify that atherosclerosis is a progressive disease, and although symptoms have been relieved, the disease has not been cured.

- Explain the importance of lifestyle management (e.g., smoking cessation, exercise, diet) as appropriate.

Rationale

Crossing legs may facilitate clot formation and graft closure.

Information relieves the patient's anxiety about the staff's need to be at the bedside often.

This prevents delay in detecting changes in circulation and allows prompt treatment of graft occlusion.

Information may help clarify routine experiences versus significant complications.

Information enables the patient to assume control during recovery.

Living with a chronic disease is challenging. Atherosclerosis is a systemic disease and may likewise affect other vital organs.

Information provides rationale for therapy and aids patient in assuming responsibility for required lifestyle changes.

> **• RELATED CARE PLANS**
>
> Chronic peripheral arterial occlusive disease, p. 353
> Imbalanced nutrition: less than body requirements, p. 134
> Risk for impaired skin integrity, p. 173

Hypertension

High Blood Pressure; Systemic Arterial Hypertension

High blood pressure (BP) is classified according to the level of severity. The following table is from the Seventh Report of the Joint National Committee (JNC-7) on Prevention, Detection, Evaluation, and Treatment of High Blood Pressure (2003).

Classification of BP for adults 18 years of age and older:

	S = Systolic (mm Hg)		D = Diastolic (mm Hg)
Normal:	<120	and	<80
Prehypertension:	120 to 139	or	80 to 89
Hypertension:			
Stage 1:	140 to 159	or	90 to 99
Stage 2:	≥160	or	≥100

Epidemiological studies report that 58 million people in the United States have BPs greater than or equal to 140/90 mm Hg or are taking antihypertensive medications. Age, gender, and ethnic differences are evident. Blacks in the United States have more significantly elevated BP and more target organ disease than whites. Likewise, black women have a higher incidence of hypertension than white women.

Although hypertension can be initiated in childhood, it is most evident in middle life. As the population ages, the prevalence of hypertension will increase unless effective prevention measures are implemented. The category of prehypertension identifies a significant segment of the population who are at twice the risk of developing hypertension than people in the normal category. Preventive efforts in this population are aimed at reducing risk factors through therapeutic lifestyle changes, which are detailed in the JNC-7 guidelines.

This care plan focuses on patients with hypertension in an ambulatory care setting.

NDx Nursing Diagnosis

Deficient Knowledge: Nature of and Complications of Hypertension or Management Regimen

Common Related Factors

Cognitive limitation
Lack of interest
Lack of information

Defining Characteristics

Statement of misconceptions, knowledge gaps
Request for information
Lack of questions

Common Expected Outcomes

Patient verbalizes understanding of the disease and its long-term effects on target organs.
Patient describes self-help activities to be followed.

NOC Outcomes
Knowledge: Disease Process;
Knowledge: Treatment Regimen

NIC Intervention
Teaching: Disease Process

■ = Independent; ▲ = Collaborative

Cardiac and Vascular Care Plans

→ Hypertension—cont'd

Ongoing Assessment

Actions/Interventions

■ Assess knowledge of disease and prescribed management.

Rationale

Patients need to understand that hypertension is a chronic, lifelong disease in which they have a vital role in effective management.

Therapeutic Interventions

Actions/Interventions

■ Encourage questions about hypertension and prescribed treatments.

■ Involve family or significant others.

■ Instruct the patient that hypertension cannot be diagnosed with only one measurement.

■ Instruct the patient to self-measure BP and suggest home monitoring equipment as appropriate.

■ Plan teaching in stages, providing information in the following areas:

• Definition of hypertension, differentiating between systolic and diastolic pressures; prehypertension

• Causes of hypertension

• Risk factors: family history, obesity, diet high in saturated fat and cholesterol, smoking, and stress

• Nature of disease and its effect on target organs (e.g., renal damage, visual impairment, heart disease, stroke)

• Treatment goal: "control" versus "cure"

• Rationale and strategy for weight reduction (if overweight)

Rationale

Knowledge serves to correct faulty ideas.

They can effectively provide support with the treatment regimen. Family members may also need to be screened for hypertension because of its familial tendency.

There are wide variations in "normal" blood pressure over the course of a day or week due to biological and diurnal effects. Thus the JNC-7 states that a diagnosis can be established only with the average of 2 or more BP readings on 2 or more occasions.

This provides the patient with a sense of control and ability to seek prompt medical attention. Many patients have "white coat" hypertension in which BP is elevated during a doctor's office visit because of apprehension or pain. Therefore at least two elevated measurements are required to diagnose hypertension.

Providing information in short sessions over a longer period of time prevents information overload and promotes comprehension.

Patients may falsely believe that only elevated diastolic blood pressure requires treatment, when elevated systolic BP is also associated with high risk. Most patients are not aware of the newest classification of "prehypertension."

Patients need to realize that 90% of hypertension is not related to a primary cause.

Implementing lifestyle changes is the cornerstone of treatment.

There are few signs and symptoms associated with hypertension until target organ damage occurs.

Hypertension is a chronic, lifelong disease. It is treated with medication and lifestyle changes. Treatment should not be stopped because the patient feels better or has problems with medication side effects.

Of all lifestyle changes, weight reduction has most consistently demonstrated BP-lowering effects. Studies show weight reduction lowers BP at all ages and in both genders. A body mass index of 25 or higher is strongly correlated with increased BP. Weight loss of just 10 pounds can lower BP.

■ = Independent; ▲ = Collaborative

Actions/Interventions	Rationale
• Rationale and strategy for adopting the Dietary Approaches to Stop Hypertension (DASH) diet	The DASH diet is high in fruits, vegetables, and low-fat dairy products and low in total and saturated fats. Studies report an average reduction in systolic BP of 8 to 14 mm Hg.
• Rationale and strategies for low-sodium diet	Dietary sodium contributes to fluid retention and elevated BP, although not all patients are "salt sensitive" and lower blood pressure with sodium restriction. Patients find it difficult to adhere to salt reduction. Therefore attention needs to be directed to level of knowledge about fresh versus canned foods versus fast foods, cultural preferences, and financial ability to purchase low-salt foods.
• Common medications: thiazide diuretics, β-blockers, angiotensin II receptor blocker (ARBs), calcium channel blockers, and angiotensin-converting enzyme (ACE) inhibitors	A wide range of medications is available. They are indicated when BP remains above 140/90 mm Hg after lifestyle modification. JNC-7 guidelines recommend a thiazide diuretic for initial therapy. Combination therapies are usually required. Coexisting "compelling conditions" also guide drug selection.
• Establishment of medication routine considering daily activities and sleep habits	This will minimize the chance of error and encourage better compliance with therapy.
• Possible side effects of medications	Warn the patient of possible side effects so that he or she understands what to do if they occur. Explain that not all persons experience side effects. If they do occur and are bothersome (pedal edema, fatigue, hypokalemia, impotence), discuss them with the health care provider before discontinuing medications. Side effects are the most common reason for noncompliance with medications.
• Interaction with over-the-counter drugs such as cough and cold medicines, aspirin compounds, and herbal medications	These drugs have a vasoconstricting effect.
• Rationale and strategy for reduction of alcohol intake	Research indicates that alcohol intake of more than 3 to 4 standard drinks per day is associated with high BP. Limit alcohol consumption to no more than 2 drinks per day for men and 1 drink per day for women.
• Need for potassium-rich foods (e.g., fruit juices, bananas) as appropriate	Some diuretics are potassium wasting; however, most ACE inhibitors and ARBs retain potassium.
• Smoking cessation	Smoking causes vasoconstriction and contributes to reduced tissue oxygenation by reducing oxygen availability.
• Role of physical exercise	Research supports a positive effect of exercise in maintenance of weight loss as well as blood pressure lowering.
• Relaxation techniques to combat stress	These can influence physiological responses that aggravate hypertension.
• Signs and symptoms to report to health care provider: chest pain, shortness of breath, edema, weight gain greater than 2 pounds per day or 5 pounds per week, nosebleeds, changes in vision, headaches, and dizziness	Information enables the patient to take control.

■ = Independent; ▲ = Collaborative

Hypertension—cont'd

Actions/Interventions	Rationale
Observe the following safety measures:	
• Avoid sudden changes in position.	This reduces severity of orthostatic hypotension. This is especially evident in older patients with longstanding hypertension that is reduced too rapidly.
• Avoid hot tubs and saunas.	These cause vasodilation and potential hypotension.
• Avoid prolonged standing; wear support stockings as needed.	Standing can cause venous pooling.
■ Provide information about community resources and support groups (e.g., American Heart Association, weight loss programs, smoking cessation programs).	These can assist and support the patient when lifestyle changes are needed.

 Nursing Diagnosis

Risk for Ineffective Therapeutic Regimen Management

Common Risk Factors

Complexity of therapeutic regimen
Financial costs
Social support deficits
Conflicting health values
Fears about treatment and possible side effects

Common Expected Outcomes

Patient describes system for taking medications.
Patient describes positive effort to lose weight and restrict sodium as appropriate.
Patient verbalizes intention to follow prescribed regimen.
Patient demonstrates ongoing adherence to treatment plan.

NOC Outcomes
Compliance Behavior; Participation: Health Care Decisions

NIC Interventions
Mutual Goal Setting; Support System Enhancement; Teaching: Individual

Ongoing Assessment

Actions/Interventions	Rationale
■ Assess patient's health values and beliefs.	Health behavior models propose that patients compare factors such as perceived susceptibility to and severity of illness or complications with perceived benefits of treatment in making decisions regarding adherence to therapies.
■ Assess previous patterns of adherence.	Long-term therapies provide more opportunity for non-adherence.
■ Assess for risk factors that may negatively affect adherence with regimen.	Knowledge of causative factors provides direction for subsequent interventions.

■ = Independent; ▲ = Collaborative

Therapeutic Interventions

Actions/Interventions	**Rationale**
▲ Simplify drug regimen.	Many patients require three to four BP-lowering medications to achieve treatment goals. Combined medications should be used as available. The more often patients have to take medicines during the day, the greater the risk of noncompliance.
■ Include patient in planning treatment regimen.	Patients who become comanagers of their care have a greater stake in achieving a positive outcome.
■ Instruct in importance of reordering medications 2 to 3 days before running out.	This ensures ongoing therapy but is not easy to accomplish due to many insurance rules.
■ Inform the patient of the benefits of adherence to the prescribed regimen.	Information provides rationale for therapy and aids the patient in assuming responsibility for care.
■ If negative side effects of prescribed treatment are a problem, explain that many side effects can be controlled or eliminated.	Patients need to be aware that adjustments and substitutions can be made to relieve side effects.
■ Instruct patient to self-monitor BP.	This provides the patient with immediate feedback and a sense of control.
■ Include significant others in explanations and teaching.	This encourages support and assistance in reinforcing appropriate behavior and facilitating lifestyle modification.
■ When the patient has inadequate support regarding lifestyle changes, refer him or her to appropriate support groups (e.g., American Heart Association, weight loss programs, smoking cessation programs, stress management classes, social services).	Groups that come together for mutual support can be beneficial.

Mitral Valve Prolapse

Barlow's Disease; Floppy Valve

The mitral valve rests between the left atrium and ventricle. Prolapse of this valve refers to the upward movement of the mitral leaflets back into the left atrium during systole. Primary mitral valve prolapse (MVP) usually results from abnormality in the connective tissue of the leaflets, annulus, or chordae tendineae and occurs in about 5% of the general population. Secondary causes of MVP include rheumatic fever, cardiomyopathy, and ischemic heart disease. Most persons with primary MVP are asymptomatic, although others may experience symptoms associated with mitral regurgitation or chest pain related to tension the prolapsed valve exerts on the papillary muscle. Diagnostic findings include midsystolic click, late systolic murmur, echocardiogram abnormalities, and angiographic findings. MVP is more common in women, noted most often in the fourth decade. This disease is handled in an ambulatory care setting.

■ = Independent; ▲ = Collaborative

Cardiac and Vascular Care Plans

Mitral Valve Prolapse—cont'd

NDx Nursing Diagnosis

Deficient Knowledge

Common Related Factor	Defining Characteristics
New diagnosis	Asking multiple questions Expressing fears Being overly anxious Asking no questions Verbalizing misconceptions

Common Expected Outcome

Patient or significant others verbalize understanding of occurrence of disease, causative factors, physiology of disease, diagnostic procedure, treatment, and possible complications.

NOC Outcome
Knowledge: Disease Process

NIC Interventions
Teaching: Disease Process;
    Risk for Disturbed Body Image

Ongoing Assessment

Actions/Interventions

■ Assess knowledge of MVP: etiological factors, treatment, and prognosis.

Rationale

Assessment provides an important starting point in education. Many misconceptions may be present among the lay public.

Therapeutic Interventions

Actions/Interventions

■ Teach patient about occurrence of disease:
  • Most common form of valvular heart disease
  • Large number of undiagnosed, asymptomatic people in general population
  • Common in women but also diagnosed in men
■ Teach patient about the following causative factors to increase understanding of disease process:
  • Etiological factors usually unknown
  • Can be primary or secondary to previous ischemic heart disease, rheumatic fever, cardiomyopathy, or ruptured chordae tendineae
  • Important to understand that serious heart disease usually is not present, symptoms are more a nuisance than significant, and prognosis is excellent

Rationale

Providing the patient with accurate knowledge about MVP can reduce the anxiety and fear he or she may experience about a diagnosis of heart disease. Knowledge helps the patient participate in decisions about management of this disease.

Thorough understanding of specific causes is necessary for appropriate follow through of the treatment plan.

■ = Independent; ▲ = Collaborative

Actions/Interventions	Rationale
■ Teach patient the physiology of the disease: • Leaflet enlargement causing prolapse of one or both valve leaflets into left atrium	Information provides rationale for therapy.
■ Inform patient of the following typical diagnostic procedures: • Cardiac auscultation for nonejection click and a crescendo murmur that continues to the second heart sound, heard best at the apex • Echocardiogram to evaluate valve motion	Auscultation of characteristic findings may be sufficient for diagnosis. A Doppler echocardiogram is a particularly sensitive means of detecting minor degrees of MVP (abnormal posterior systolic motion of mitral valve leaflets) in apparently healthy adults.
■ Teach patient the following about the treatment of the disease: • Usually no treatment is indicated; patients need reassurance that this is not a severe cardiac condition • Use of exercise to reduce anxiety over condition and increase self-esteem • β-Blocker or calcium channel blocker medication to reduce chest pain and control arrhythmias (if complication); anticoagulant therapy (aspirin or warfarin) may be used if patient has a history of focal neurological events • Self-limitation of activities, foods or drinks, and stresses that precipitate symptoms	A normal lifestyle and regular aerobic exercise are encouraged for patients who are asymptomatic.
■ Teach patient about controversial use of endocarditis prophylaxis.	Antibiotic therapy is indicated if the patient has associated moderate to severe symptoms of mitral insufficiency.
▲ The patient should contact the physician for prophylactic antibiotics before any dental procedures (especially teeth cleaning), gynecological procedures, or other invasive procedures.	It is believed that many common invasive procedures will leave a pathway in which bacteria can travel to the heart, especially the valve leaflets.

NDx Nursing Diagnosis

Risk for Disturbed Body Image

Common Risk Factors

Knowledge of "cardiac" condition
Fatigue secondary to β-blocker medication
Need for prophylactic antibiotics

Common Expected Outcome

Patient verbalizes positive feelings about altered heart function.

NOC Outcomes
Body Image; Coping

NIC Interventions
Body Image Enhancement; Teaching: Disease Process

 = Independent; ▲ = Collaborative

Mitral Valve Prolapse—cont'd

Ongoing Assessment

Actions/Interventions

■ Assess perception of change in body function and meaning of cardiac diagnosis.

■ Note verbal references to heart and related discomfort, as well as any change in lifestyle.

Rationale

A distinction should be made between patients who present without symptoms and who are unintentionally diagnosed during routine examination and patients who sought medical attention because of symptoms.

Symptoms are more common in patients who are told of the prolapse. "Cardiac neurosis" may develop when the condition is brought to the patient's attention.

Therapeutic Interventions

Actions/Interventions

■ Provide accurate information about causes, prognosis, and treatment of condition.

■ Provide reassurance that it is possible to lead a normal life with MVP.

■ For problems with fatigue:
  • Encourage the patient to allow several weeks for adjustment to β-blocker side effects.
  • Encourage appropriate pacing of daily activities.

■ Remind the patient that although risk of bacterial endocarditis is small, appropriate prophylaxis may be warranted.

■ For female patients of childbearing years, instruct that pregnancy is usually not contraindicated.

■ Refer to support group as indicated.

Rationale

Many patients have anxiety when diagnosed with a heart disease about which they know little.

The nurse is in an ideal position to guide the patient through acceptance of the diagnosis.

Information enables the patient to assume some control.

Knowledge of rationale for preventive therapy may reduce anxiety.

Patients are encouraged to live normal lives.

Participation in a support group may allow the patient to realize that others have the same problem; they may use this as a means to help make needed lifestyle alterations.

NDx Nursing Diagnosis

Risk for Chest Pain

Common Risk Factor

Etiological factors of pain are unknown but may be related to excessive stretch of chordae tendineae and papillary muscles or to coronary artery spasm.

Common Expected Outcomes

Patient verbalizes reduced or relieved pain.
Patient appears relaxed and comfortable.

NOC Outcomes
Pain Level; Knowledge: Treatment Regimen

NIC Interventions
Teaching: Disease Process;
Teaching: Medications Prescribed

Ongoing Assessment

Actions/Interventions

■ Assess whether complaints of chest pain are non-anginal in character:
  • May last seconds to several hours
  • Typically left precordial, sharp, stabbing
  • May be substernal or diffuse
  • Usually not specifically related to exertion or stress; may be precipitated by fatigue
  • Usually not relieved by nitroglycerin
  • May present with inverted T waves and ST depression associated with exercise

■ Assess cardiac status during pain occurrence: heart rate, blood pressure, and skin changes.

Rationale

Patients with MVP usually experience atypical chest pain that is not characteristic of angina pectoris. Primary MVP does not involve pathology of coronary arteries. However, some patients with MVP may also have unrelated but additional problem of coronary spasm–causing angina.

Associated symptoms help guide treatment.

Therapeutic Interventions

Actions/Interventions

■ Permit unrestricted activity if the patient is asymptomatic.

■ Encourage rest if pain is exertionally induced.

■ Encourage a nonstressful environment.

■ Provide psychological and emotional support.

▲ Instruct the patient to take medications as prescribed:
  • β-Blockers
  • Calcium channel blockers to provide relief of atypical chest pain

■ Instruct patient about positions that may reduce chest pain
  • Lying down
  • Squatting

Rationale

Because chest pain is not related to "angina," patients are encouraged to participate in regular physical activity.

Warning signs of potential problems need to be emphasized.

Stress has been related to increased occurrence of chest pain.

Support allays fears of the seriousness of this benign disease.

These medications are usually effective in relieving chest pain and associated palpitations.

These positions increase venous return and lessen MVP.

• RELATED CARE PLAN

Disturbed body image, p. 21

■ = Independent; ▲ = Collaborative

Myocardial Infarction: Acute Phase (1 To 3 Days)

Q-Wave Myocardial Infarction; Non–Q-Wave Myocardial Infarction; Thrombolytic Therapy

Acute myocardial infarction (MI) is a destructive process that produces irreversible tissue damage to regions of the heart muscle. It is caused by profound and sustained ischemia related to atherosclerotic narrowing of the coronary artery, subsequent to plaque rupture, endothelial injury, thrombus formation, spasm of the artery, or any combination of these. The increased use of thrombolytic therapy within 6 to 12 hours after the onset of symptoms has significantly decreased the mortality from MI. Of those deaths, about half occur within 1 hour of the onset of symptoms before the patient reaches a hospital emergency department. A significant number of patients who experience MI delay at least 2 hours before seeking medical attention for their symptoms. Some patients, especially women and older persons, may wait 12 hours or longer because they tend to have symptoms that are atypical for MI. Reperfusion therapy with thrombolytics has limited benefit for the patient who delays seeking medical care for more than 12 hours.

Coronary artery disease is the number one killer of both men and women. Women experience coronary artery disease 10 years later than men. Women have higher mortality and reinfarction rates than men. Older patients have more complications from acute MI. These include increased incidence of atrial fibrillation and atrial flutter, ventricular dysrhythmias, complete heart block, congestive heart failure, cardiogenic shock, and myocardial rupture. In light of their increased risks, older patients should also be treated with thrombolytic therapy as indicated. Diabetic patients and patients with heart failure, along with women and older persons, may have atypical chest discomfort or silent symptoms that may go unnoticed, making early treatment challenging.

Acute MI is diagnosed by presenting symptoms, release of serum cardiac biomarkers, and characteristic electrocardiogram (ECG) changes. Some patients may have a permanent Q wave on the ECG as a result of the MI. Therapeutic goals for all patients are to establish reperfusion, to reduce infarct size, to prevent and treat complications, and to provide emotional support and education. This care plan focuses on the acute phase during hospitalization in the coronary care unit. The Cardiac Rehabilitation care plan presented earlier in this chapter addresses specific learning needs.

 Nursing Diagnosis

Acute Chest Pain

Common Related Factors	Defining Characteristics
Myocardial ischemia or MI	Patient verbalizes pain
Reduced coronary blood flow	Restlessness, apprehension
	Facial mask of pain
	Diaphoresis or cold sweat
	Shortness of breath
	Change in vital signs
	Pallor, weakness
	Nausea and vomiting

■ = Independent; ▲ = Collaborative

Myocardial Infarction: Acute Phase (1 To 3 Days)

Common Expected Outcomes

Patient verbalizes relief of pain.
Patient appears comfortable.

NOC Outcome
Pain Control Medication Response

NIC Interventions
Cardiac Care: Acute; Pain Management

Ongoing Assessment

Actions/Interventions	Rationale
■ Assess for characteristics of acute MI pain:	Patients with presenting symptoms for MI can have a variety of pain characteristics, making diagnosis difficult. Older patients, women, diabetic patients, and patients with heart failure often have atypical symptoms for MI. Sudden shortness of breath and fatigue is more common than typical substernal chest pain. Associated diaphoresis may be present. Careful assessment facilitates early or appropriate treatment when time is critical for saving salvageable myocardium.
• Occurs suddenly, usually when patient is at rest	This is due to sudden thrombosis at ruptured atherosclerotic plaque.
• More intense pain than with angina and of longer duration (at least 30 minutes, usually several hours)	Level of pain is not the best discriminator because patients can have silent ischemia during infarction.
• Quality varies: squeezing, aching, heaviness, "vise-like," burning, pressure	Some patients, such as older persons and those with diabetes, experience no pain, but instead have discomfort or shortness of breath.
• Noted along anterior chest, usually substernal; may radiate to shoulder, arms, jaw, neck, and epigastrium	Presentation varies among individuals.
• Not relieved with rest or sublingual nitrates; usually requires narcotic analgesic for relief	This can aid in differentiating angina from MI.
• Not affected by position change or breathing	This aids in differentiating musculoskeletal or pulmonary etiological factors.
• May be associated with nausea, vomiting, dyspnea, anxiety, diaphoresis, and fatigue	This is due to the pain center being in close proximity to the emetic center and to the release of catecholamines.
■ Note time since onset of first episode of chest pain.	If less than 6 hours, patient may be a candidate for thrombolytic therapy.
■ Assess any prior treatments for pain.	The nurse should note treatment that patient received before hospital admission. Patients may have tried several pain relief methods at home, including antacids. Some patients may have taken sublingual nitroglycerin and a single dose of aspirin before contacting emergency medical services.

 **Myocardial Infarction: Acute Phase (1 To 3 Days)**—cont'd

Actions/Interventions

- Monitor heart rate (HR) and blood pressure (BP) during pain episodes and during medication administration.

- Assess baseline ECG for diagnostic signs of MI and during each episode of pain.

- Monitor serial cardiac markers (creatine kinase–MB [CK-MB], troponin, myoglobin).

- Continually reassess patient's chest pain and response to medication. If no relief from optimal dose of medication is achieved, report to physician for evaluation for thrombolytic treatment, angioplasty, cardiac catheterization, or bypass surgery revascularization.

- Assess for contraindications to thrombolytic agents. Patients with *absolute* contraindications include those with the following:
  - Active internal bleeding or bleeding diathesis (excluding menses)
  - History of hemorrhagic stroke or intracranial hemorrhage

- Assess for other *relative* contraindications or warning conditions:
  - Unknown or suspected pregnancy
  - Recent major surgery or trauma within 3 weeks
  - High likelihood of left heart thrombus (seen in dilated cardiomyopathy, left ventricular [LV] aneurysm, mitral stenosis with atrial fibrillation)
  - Current oral anticoagulant use
  - Severe uncontrolled hypertension (systolic BP greater than 180 mm Hg; diastolic BP greater than 110 mm Hg)
  - Traumatic cardiopulmonary resuscitation (greater than 10 minutes), major surgery
  - Known malignant intracranial neoplasm
  - Suspected aortic dissection
  - Significant closed head or facial trauma within 3 months
  - Ischemic stroke within 3 months
  - Recent internal bleeding (within 2 to 4 weeks)
  - Active peptic ulcer
  - For streptokinase/anistreplase medication, prior exposure (e.g., within 5 days to 2 years) or allergic reaction

Rationale

Pain causes increased sympathetic stimulation, which increases oxygen demands on the heart. Tachycardia and increased BP are seen during pain and anxiety; hypotension is seen with nitrate and morphine administration; bradycardia is seen with morphine and β-blocker administration.

MI occurs over several hours. The time course of ST-T wave changes and development of Q waves guide diagnosis and treatment.

CK-MB, troponin, and myoglobin are released into the circulation from necrotic myocardial cells. Their serum levels rise in characteristic patterns over time after an MI. Myoglobin and CK-MB are detectable first, but troponin is more sensitive and specific for myocardial injury, in that it remains elevated for 10 to 14 days.

Ongoing pain can signify prolonged myocardial ischemia that warrants immediate intervention.

Thrombolytic agents do not distinguish a pathological occlusive coronary thrombus from a protective hemostatic clot; therefore patient selection is critical. Guidelines for absolute versus relative contraindications continue to be revised because risk/benefit assessments may change depending on availability of newer treatment modalities.

With the following conditions, the risks of thrombolytic agents must be weighed against the anticipated benefits.

■ = Independent; ▲ = Collaborative

Therapeutic Interventions

Actions/Interventions	Rationale

General

■ Maintain bed rest, at least during periods of pain.

Restricted activity reduces oxygen demands of the heart.

■ Position patient comfortably, preferably in Fowler's position.

This allows for full lung expansion by lowering the diaphragm.

■ Maintain a quiet, relaxed atmosphere; display confident manner.

Physical and emotional rest is promoted in such a setting.

▲ If patient complains of pain, conduct the following:
- Administer oxygen at 4 to 6 L/min.

Goal is to maintain oxygen saturation above 90%.

- Institute medical therapy according to order (see specific interventions).

Specific

▲ Initiate intravenous (IV) nitrates according to unit protocol.

Nitrates cause vasodilation and reduce workload of heart by decreasing venous return. Nitrates also dilate the coronary vessels, thus increasing the blood flow and oxygen supply to the myocardium. Topical and sublingual forms can be used, but IV administration allows for more precise management of treatment and immediate bioavailability.

- Establish baseline BP and HR before beginning medication.

BP should be at least 90 mm Hg systolic.

- Start at low dose, usually 5 to 10 mcg/min through an infusion pump.

Infusion pumps allow close regulation of the drug.

- Titrate dose to relief of pain as long as BP is stable.

Nitrates are both coronary dilators and peripheral vasodilators, causing hypotension.

- If patient complains of headache (common side effect), treat with acetaminophen (Tylenol).

▲ Administer morphine sulfate according to unit protocol.
- Administer IV morphine at increments of 2 to 4 mg over 5 minutes.
- Repeat dose with increments of 2 to 8 mg IV, repeated at 5- to 15-minute intervals.

Morphine sulfate is a narcotic analgesic that reduces the workload on the heart through venodilation. It reduces anxiety and decreases patient's perception of pain. Side effects include hypotension, bradycardia, decreased respirations, and nausea.

▲ Administer IV β-blocker agents according to protocol.

Research reports reduced mortality in acute phase of MI and at 1-year follow-up, as well as chances of reduced reinfarction.

▲ Administer oral aspirin.

Aspirin decreases platelet aggregation and significantly improves mortality and morbidity rates when used within 24 hours of onset of chest pain.

▲ Administer angiotensin-converting enzyme inhibitors.

Research supports use after large transmural MIs, in patients with LV dysfunction, and in patients with diabetes because the risk for recurrent MI and progression to heart failure and death is reduced.

▲ Administer thrombolytic agent according to unit protocol.

Thrombolytic agents are enzymes that convert plasminogen to plasmin, which has potent fibrinolytic activity. These drugs break down fibrin clots and restore perfusion of myocardial tissue through previously blocked coronary arteries. IV therapy is preferred because it is fastest.

■ = Independent; ▲ = Collaborative

Cardiac and Vascular Care Plans

Myocardial Infarction: Acute Phase (1 To 3 Days)—cont'd

Actions/Interventions	Rationale
• Monitor for signs of bleeding: puncture sites, gingiva, and prior cuts.	All agents except tissue plasminogen activator have systemic effects. Most bleeding occurs at vascular access sites. Each thrombolytic agent has a different half-life, so the nurse needs to be aware of the length of time the patient is in a hypocoagulation state.
• Observe for presence of occult or frank blood in urine, stool, emesis, and sputum.	Early signs of bleeding facilitate intervention.
• Assess for intracranial bleeding by frequent monitoring of neurological status.	Changes in mental status, visual disturbances, and headaches are frequent signs of intracranial bleeding.
▲ Administer IV heparin according to unit protocol. Adjust dose to therapeutic partial thromboplastin time, usually 1.5 to 2 times normal.	Heparin maintains patency after vessel is opened with thrombolytic infusion.
▲ If signs of reperfusion are not evident and patient infarction continues, prepare for possible cardiac catheterization, percutaneous transluminal coronary angioplasty, or coronary artery bypass grafting.	Rapid, effective intervention is critical to preserve vital organ function and life.

NDx Nursing Diagnosis

Risk for Decreased Cardiac Output

Common Risk Factors

Electrical instability or dysrhythmias secondary to ischemia or necrosis, sympathetic nervous system stimulation, or electrolyte imbalance (hypokalemia or hypomagnesemia)

Common Expected Outcome

Patient maintains normal cardiac rhythm with adequate cardiac output.

> **NOC Outcome**
> Cardiac Pump Effectiveness
>
> **NIC Interventions**
> Dysrhythmia Management; Hemodynamic Regulation; Cardiac Care: Acute

Ongoing Assessment

Actions/Interventions	Rationale
■ Monitor patient's HR and rhythm continuously.	Most patients experience some dysrhythmias. Early detection may prevent lethal dysrhythmias.
■ Observe for or anticipate the following common dysrhythmias:	All patients may experience premature ventricular contractions (PVCs), ventricular tachycardia, atrial flutter, and atrial fibrillation. Additionally, specific areas of infarct correlate with other expected dysrhythmias.

■ = Independent; ▲ = Collaborative

Actions/Interventions

- With anterior MI: second-degree heart block, complete heart block, right bundle branch block, left anterior hemiblock, left bundle branch block, or bifascicular block
- With inferior MI: sinus bradycardia, sinus pause, and first- and second-degree heart block (Wenckebach phenomenon), and third-degree heart block

■ Assess for signs of decreased cardiac output that accompany dysrhythmias.

■ Monitor PR, QRS, and QT intervals, and note change.

■ Monitor with continuous ECG monitoring in appropriate lead.

- Monitor in lead II, observing for left anterior hemiblock.

- If anterior MI with left anterior hemiblock is already present, monitor in modified chest lead (MCL$_1$) for right bundle branch block.

■ Assess response to treatment.

Rationale

Level of hemodynamic compromise guides treatment.

Many antidysrhythmic drugs also depress the conduction of normal impulses and can cause further dysrhythmias.

Monitoring facilitates prompt detection of conduction problem.

Left anterior hemiblock is characterized by normal QRS width and left axis deviation with deep S waves in leads II, III, and aVF.

Right bundle branch block is characterized by a QRS of greater than 0.12 second and an rSR′ complex in V$_1$ or V$_2$.

Follow-up evaluation guides ongoing treatment.

Therapeutic Interventions

Actions/Interventions

■ Institute treatment as appropriate and according to protocol:
- Potassium or magnesium supplement as guided by serum electrolyte levels
- Lidocaine, amiodarone, or procainamide (Pronestyl) for PVC and ventricular tachycardia
- Atropine sulfate for symptomatic bradycardia; external pacemaker on standby
- Calcium channel blockers, β-blockers, adenosine, and cardioversion for atrial tachydysrhythmias
- Temporary pacemaker for Mobitz type II, new complete heart block, new bifascicular bundle branch block, or left bundle branch block with anterior wall MI
- Implantable cardioverter-defibrillator for recurrent ventricular tachycardia, as indicated
- Defibrillation for ventricular fibrillation
- Cardiopulmonary resuscitation as appropriate

See also **Dysrhythmias,** *p. 288.*

Rationale

Current Advanced Cardiac Life Support guidelines provide protocols for management of dysrhythmias.

Myocardial Infarction: Acute Phase (1 To 3 Days)—cont'd

 Nursing Diagnosis

Risk for Decreased Cardiac Output

Common Risk Factors

Acute MI (especially at anterior site) affecting pumping ability of the heart
Right ventricular infarct (RVI) with reduced right ventricular (RV) pumping
Papillary muscle rupture and mitral insufficiency
Ventricular aneurysm

Common Expected Outcome

Patient maintains adequate cardiac output, as evidenced by strong peripheral pulses, normal BP, clear breath sounds, good capillary refill, adequate urine output, and clear mentation.

NOC Outcomes
Cardiac Pump Effectiveness; Vital Signs; Fluid Balance

NIC Interventions
Invasive Hemodynamic Monitoring; Hemodynamic Regulation

Ongoing Assessment

Actions/Interventions	Rationale
■ Monitor HR and BP.	Sinus tachycardia and increase (compensatory) in arterial BP are early signs of ventricular dysfunction.
■ Assess skin color, temperature, and moisture.	Cool, pale, clammy skin is secondary to compensatory increase in sympathetic nervous system stimulation and low cardiac output and desaturation.
■ Assess peripheral and central pulses, including capillary refill.	Pulses are weak with reduced stroke volume and cardiac output.
■ Assess for mental status changes.	Early signs of cerebral hypoxia are restlessness and anxiety, with confusion and loss of consciousness occurring in later stages. Older patients are especially susceptible to reduced perfusion to vital organs.
■ Assess respiratory rate, rhythm, and breath sounds.	Rapid, shallow respirations and presence of crackles and wheezes are characteristic of reduced cardiac output.
■ Assess urine output with a Foley catheter.	The renal system compensates for low blood pressure by retaining water. Oliguria is a classic sign of inadequate renal perfusion from reduced cardiac output.
■ Auscultate for presence of S_3, S_4, or systolic murmur.	S_3 denotes left ventricular (LV) dysfunction; S_4 is a common finding with MI, usually indicating noncompliance of the ischemic ventricle. Loud holosystolic murmur may be caused by papillary muscle rupture.

■ = Independent; ▲ = Collaborative

Myocardial Infarction: Acute Phase (1 To 3 Days)

Actions/Interventions

- Assess pulse oximetry and arterial blood gases.

- If patient had an inferior MI, evaluate ECG using right precordial leads ($_RV_4 - _RV_6$).

- If patient had inferior MI, assess for signs of RVI and RV failure.

Rationale

Pulse oximetry is a useful tool to detect changes in oxygenation. Oxygen saturation should be kept above 90% or greater. As shock increases, aerobic metabolism ceases and lactic acidosis ensues, raising level of carbon dioxide and pH.

These leads may show ECG changes indicative of RVI.

RVI is seen in 30% to 50% of patients with symptoms for inferior MI. Signs of RV dysfunction include increased central venous pressure, increased jugular venous distention, absence of crackles or rales, and decreased BP.

Therapeutic Interventions

Actions/Interventions

- Anticipate insertion of hemodynamic monitoring catheters.

- Administer IV fluids to keep PCWP at 16 to 18 mm Hg for optimal filling of ventricle.

- If signs of LV failure occur:
  - Administer diuretic and vasodilator medications as prescribed.
  - Administer IV inotropic medications.
  - Initiate oxygen as needed.
- If signs of RV failure occur:
  - Anticipate aggressive fluid resuscitation (3 to 6 L/ 24 hours).
  - Anticipate inotropic and peripheral vasodilator medication.
- Avoid or carefully administer nitrates and morphine sulfate for pain.

Rationale

Pulmonary artery diastolic pressure and pulmonary capillary wedge pressure (PCWP) are excellent guides of filling pressures in the left ventricle; monitoring of central venous pressure and right atrial pressure guides management of RVI.

Too little fluid reduces preload or blood volume and BP; too much fluid can overload the heart and lead to pulmonary edema.

These reduce filling pressures and workload of the infarcted heart, and improve fluid balance.

These improve pumping of the heart.

Oxygen increases arterial saturation.

Fluids may be needed to keep PCWP at 16 to 20 mm Hg to maintain preload and cardiac output.

These improve ventricular contraction and reduce RV and LV afterload, thereby enhancing stroke volume.

They reduce preload and filling pressures, which may compromise cardiac output.

NDx Nursing Diagnosis

Fear

Common Related Factors

Threat to or change in health status
Threat of death
Threat to self-concept
Change in environment

Defining Characteristics

Tense appearance, apprehension; feelings of impending doom
Frightened
Restless or unable to relax
Repeatedly seeking assurance
Increased alertness, wide-eyed appearance
Expressed concern regarding changes in lifestyle
Focus on self

■ = Independent; ▲ = Collaborative

Myocardial Infarction: Acute Phase (1 To 3 Days)—cont'd

Common Expected Outcomes

Patient verbalizes reduced fear.
Patient demonstrates positive coping mechanisms.

NOC Outcomes
Anxiety Self-Control; Coping

NIC Interventions
Anxiety Reduction; Coping Enhancement

Ongoing Assessment

Actions/Interventions

- Assess level of fear. Note all signs and symptoms, especially nonverbal communication.

- Assess coping factors.

Rationale

Controlling fear or anxiety will help reduce sympathetic response that can aggravate condition.

Anxiety and ways of decreasing perceived anxiety are highly individualized. Interventions are most effective when they are consistent with the individual's established coping pattern.

Therapeutic Interventions

Actions/Interventions

- Acknowledge awareness of patient's fears.

- Allow patient to verbalize fears of dying. Reassure patient that most deaths occur before reaching the hospital.

- Offer realistic assurances that recovery is fully anticipated.

- Maintain confident, assured manner.

- Explain in simple terms various aspects of MI, need for cardiac monitoring, and others; identify and clarify misconceptions.

- Assure the patient and significant others of close, continuous monitoring that will ensure prompt intervention.

- Reduce unnecessary external stimuli.

- Explain all procedures as appropriate, keeping explanations basic.

- Provide diversional materials (e.g., newspapers, magazines, music, television).

Rationale

Acknowledgment of the patient's feelings validates the feelings and communicates acceptance of those feelings.

Anxiety can be reduced when patient has accurate knowledge of realistic prognosis; hospital mortality rate is only 5%.

These measures enhance the patient's optimism about recovery.

The staff's anxiety may be easily perceived by the patient. The patient's feeling of stability increases in a calm and nonthreatening atmosphere.

Lack of understanding about purpose and function of monitoring equipment can add to the patient's fear. Normal equipment noise and alarms may increase anxiety, as can the fear that equipment failure will have an adverse effect on the patient's heart.

This provides a measure of safety.

Anxiety may escalate with excessive conversation, noise, and equipment around the patient.

Information helps allay anxiety. Patients who are anxious may not be able to comprehend anything more than simple, clear, brief instructions.

Diversion can be relaxing, decrease anxiety, and prevent feelings of isolation.

■ = Independent; ▲ = Collaborative

Actions/Interventions	Rationale
■ Establish rest periods between care and procedures.	Pacing activities helps the patient relax and regain emotional balance.
■ Refer to other support persons (e.g., clergy, social worker) as appropriate.	Additional specialty expertise may be required.
▲ Administer mild tranquilizers or sedatives as prescribed.	Medication may be required to reduce stress.

 Nursing Diagnosis

Risk for Activity Intolerance

Common Risk Factors

Generalized weakness
Imbalance between oxygen supply and demand

Common Expected Outcomes

Patient tolerates progressive activity, as evidenced by HR and BP within expected range and no complaints of dyspnea or fatigue.
Patient verbalizes realistic expectations for progressive activity.

> **NOC Outcome**
> Activity Tolerance
>
> **NIC Interventions**
> Cardiac Care; Exercise Therapy

Ongoing Assessment

Actions/Interventions	Rationale
■ Assess the patient's respiratory and cardiac status before initiating activity.	Bed rest with bedside commode use is indicated for about the first 12 hours after acute MI. Prolonged bed rest is indicated only for patients who are hemodynamically unstable. If the patient is stable, activity can be gradually progressed after the first 12 hours. Assisted hygiene and ambulation are appropriate to reduce physical deconditioning associated with bed rest.
■ Observe and document response to activity. Signs of abnormal response include the following: • Increased HR of 20 beats/min over resting rate during activity, or 120 beats/min • Increased BP of 20 mm Hg systolic during activity • Decreased BP of more than 10 mm Hg systolic during activity • Chest discomfort • Diaphoresis or pallor • Dyspnea, labored breathing, wheezing • Palpitations/noticeable change in heart rhythm. • Excessive fatigue, weakness • ST segment displacement on ECG	Close monitoring serves as a guide for optimal activity progression.

■ = Independent; ▲ = Collaborative

Myocardial Infarction: Acute Phase (1 To 3 Days)—cont'd

Therapeutic Interventions

Actions/Interventions	Rationale
■ Encourage adequate rest periods, especially before activities (e.g., activities of daily living, visiting hours, meals).	Rest between activities provides time for energy conservation and recovery. Heart rate recovery following activity is greatest at the beginning of the rest period.
■ Provide light meals (i.e., progress from liquids to regular diet as appropriate).	This facilitates digestion and reduces energy needs.
■ Instruct patient not to hold breath while exercising or moving about in bed, and not to strain for bowel movement.	These activities stimulate the Valsalva maneuver, which affects endocardial repolarization and predisposes the patient to ventricular dysrhythmias.
▲ Maintain progression of activity as ordered by the physician and/or cardiac rehabilitation team.	Appropriate progression prevents overexerting the heart while promoting attainment of short-term goals.
• Stage 1: Patient performs self-care activities (washes face, feeds self, performs oral hygiene), does selected range-of-motion (ROM) exercises in bed, dangles lower extremities 15 to 30 minutes at bedside three times daily, and uses bedside commode with assistance.	Commode requires less energy expenditure than bedpan. ROM exercises reduce risk of thromboembolism. Dangling helps reduce occurrence of postural hypertension.
• Stage 2: Patient sits up in chair for 30 to 60 minutes three times daily, takes partial bath in chair, and continues ROM exercises in chair.	Getting out of bed promotes lung expansion.
■ Instruct that further cardiac rehabilitation or activity progression will occur after transfer from the intensive care setting.	Knowledge may enhance positive aspects of recovery.
■ Provide emotional support when increasing activity.	This reduces possible anxiety about overexertion of the heart.

 ## Nursing Diagnosis

Acute Chest Pain

Common Related Factor	Defining Characteristics
Pericarditis secondary to inflammatory response from transmural acute MI	Complaint of pain Pericardial friction rub (transient) ST-segment elevation (concave) in most limb and precordial ECG leads without reciprocal ST-segment depression Fever

■ = Independent; ▲ = Collaborative

Common Expected Outcomes

Patient appears comfortable.
Patient verbalizes relief or reduction in pericardial discomfort.

NOC Outcomes
Pain Control; Knowledge: Disease Process

NIC Interventions
Cardiac Care: Acute; Teaching: Disease
Process; Analgesic Administration

Ongoing Assessment

Actions/Interventions

- Assess characteristics of pericardial pain. It is similar to MI pain, except that pericardial pain does the following:
  - Increases with deep inspiration, movement of upper body, lying down
  - Is relieved by sitting up or leaning forward
  - Is sharp, stabbing, knifelike, and pleuritic
  - Occurs 2 to 3 days after MI
  - May be intermittent or continuous
- Auscultate precordium for presence of pericardial rub.

- Monitor ECG for signs of ST elevation (see Defining Characteristics on the preceding page).
- Monitor temperature.

Rationale

Accurate assessment differentiates the origin of pain and facilitates appropriate treatment.

Pericardial friction rub may be transient or last a few hours.

There is a characteristic pattern of ST changes associated with pericarditis.

Fever accompanies pericarditis secondary to inflammatory response.

Therapeutic Interventions

Actions/Interventions

- Position patient comfortably, preferably sitting up in bed at an angle of 90 degrees or leaning forward propped on a pillow on a side table.
- Offer assurance and emotional support through explanations of pericarditis.

- ▲ Give antiinflammatory medications as prescribed, usually aspirin, steroids, or indomethacin (Indocin). Give medications on full stomach.
- ▲ Administer antipyretics as indicated.

Rationale

These positions effectively reduce discomfort.

Patients fear that this pain is another heart attack and need reassurance that pericarditis is a local pericardial inflammatory response to some infarcts.

Medications reduce inflammation around the heart. Food helps reduce gastric irritation.

Pericarditis is an inflammatory condition that is associated with fever.

■ = Independent; ▲ = Collaborative

Cardiac and Vascular Care Plans

→ **Myocardial Infarction: Acute Phase (1 To 3 Days)**—cont'd

NDx **Nursing Diagnosis**

Deficient Knowledge

Common Related Factor

Unfamiliarity with disease process, treatment, and recovery

Defining Characteristics

Multiple or no questions
Confusion over events
Expressed need for information

Common Expected Outcome

Patient verbalizes understanding of condition, need for observation in critical care unit, diagnosis or treatment of MI, and healing process of MI.

NOC Outcome
Knowledge: Disease Process

NIC Intervention
Teaching: Disease Process

Ongoing Assessment

Actions/Interventions

■ Assess knowledge of acute MI: causes, treatment, and early recovery process.

Rationale

Many patients have been exposed to media information or family and friends experiencing an infarct. Misconceptions may exist.

Therapeutic Interventions

Actions/Interventions

■ Encourage patients to ask questions and verbalize concerns.

■ Provide information on the following (as appropriate), limiting each session to 10 to 15 minutes so that the patient is not overwhelmed:
  • Positive aspects of the critical care unit

  • Diagnosing of MI (e.g., with ECG, blood tests)
  • Healing process

  • Medications: thrombolytics as indicated, anticoagulants (aspirin/heparin) to maintain patency of arteries, pain relievers, and antidysrhythmics
  • Expected return to prior lifestyle (2 to 3 months)

Rationale

The patient needs to be an active partner in follow-up care.

Information provides rationale for treatment during the acute phase.

Information may reduce anxiety and enhance confidence in the health care team.

Explaining expected procedures can help reduce anxiety.

It takes 6 weeks for necrotic tissue to be replaced by scar tissue; progressive activity is required to optimize healing.

Patients may not realize that a clot has caused the MI, thinking instead that cholesterol plaque is the culprit.

More than 85% of patients return to full activity level.

■ = Independent; ▲ = Collaborative

Actions/Interventions

■ Inform patient that more extensive teaching sessions will be instituted after transfer to the medical floor when the next stage of cardiac rehabilitation will be initiated.

Rationale

Readiness for learning is key to effective teaching.

• RELATED CARE PLANS

Cardiac rehabilitation, p. 240
Cardiogenic shock, p. 377
Decreased cardiac output, p. 32
Health-seeking behaviors, p. 91
Ineffective sexuality patterns, p. 170
Powerlessness, p. 153

Pacemaker/Cardioverter-Defibrillator

Implantable (Permanent); External (Temporary); Cardioverter-Defibrillator (Implantable) (ICD)

An implantable, permanent pacemaker delivers an electrical stimulus to the heart muscle when needed. The types of pacemakers currently available are as follows. (1) *Bradycardia pacemaker*—its mode of response is inhibited, triggered, or asynchronous. It is indicated for chronic symptomatic bradydysrhythmias or for second- or third-degree atrioventricular (AV) block. A dual-chamber pacemaker is indicated for bradycardia with competent sinus node to provide AV synchrony and rate variability. (2) *Rate-modulated pacemaker*—this is indicated for patients who can benefit from an increase in pacing rate, either atrial or ventricular, in response to their body's metabolic (physiological) needs or to activity (nonphysiological) for increased cardiac output. (3) *Antitachycardia pacemaker*—this is indicated for pace-terminable conditions: recurrent supraventricular tachycardia (e.g., AV reciprocating tachydysrhythmias [as in Wolff-Parkinson-White], atrial flutter, and other AV tachydysrhythmias). (4) *Cardiac resynchronization pacemakers*—this biventricular pacing system is indicated for severe heart failure and cardiomyopathy patients with intraventricular conduction delays who can benefit from synchronized septal wall motion and improved left ventricular contraction.

An external pacemaker delivers an electrical stimulus to the heart for the acute management of bradyarrhythmias and certain types of tachyarrhythmias and for use in provocative diagnostic cardiac procedures. Transcutaneous cardiac pacing (noninvasive) is rapidly initiated by delivering an electrical current from an external power source through large electrodes applied to the patient's chest. It is an alternative method to transvenous pacing for the initial management of bradyasystolic arrest situations until definitive treatment can be instituted or to overdrive tachyarrhythmias in emergency situations. Transvenous endocardial pacing directly stimulates the myocardial tissue with electrical current pulses through an electrode catheter inserted through a vein into the right atrium or right ventricle. Cardiac resynchronization pacemakers use transvenous pacing electrodes positioned in the right ventricle and in the coronary sinus (to pace left ventricle). Epicardial pacing stimulates the myocardium through one or two pacing electrodes sutured loosely through the epicardial surface of the heart. It is most commonly used after open heart surgery for temporary relief of bradyarrhythmias or for overdrive pacing for tachyarrhythmias.

An implanted cardioverter-defibrillator (ICD) delivers one or more countershocks (depending on device model) directly to the heart after it recognizes a dysrhythmia through rate-detection criteria. It is a life-prolonging therapy for patients with serious

■ = Independent; ▲ = Collaborative

Pacemaker/Cardioverter-Defibrillator—cont'd

ventricular dysrhythmias and is indicated for those (1) who have survived at least one episode of sudden cardiac death caused by tachydysrhythmias not associated with acute myocardial infarction and (2) who have experienced recurrent tachyarrhythmias without cardiac arrest and who can be induced into sustained hypotensive ventricular tachycardia or ventricular fibrillation, or both, despite conventional antidysrhythmic drug therapy. After a preset sensing period in which the system detects a lethal dysrhythmia, the defibrillator mechanism delivers a shock (usually 25 J) to the heart muscle. If needed, repeat shocks are delivered. The shock delivered is often described as a hard thump or as a kick to the chest. The device may be implanted into the left clavicular or left abdominal wall pocket. The sensing lead is implanted transvenously, and the defibrillator lead is implanted either transvenously or subcutaneously in the left axilla area. Models also contain antitachycardia (overdrive) and antibradycardia (backup pacing) pacemakers.

NDx Nursing Diagnosis

Risk for Decreased Cardiac Output

Common Risk Factors

Pacemaker malfunction caused by the following:
- Electrode dislodgment
- Faulty connection between lead and pulse generator
- Faulty lead system (e.g., lead fracture, insulation break)
- Pulse generator circuitry failure
- Battery depletion
- Inadequate pacemaker parameter settings
- Inappropriate type of pacemaker
- Ventricular dysrhythmias caused by irritation from pacing electrode or asynchronous pacing resulting from malsensing problem
- Change in myocardial threshold
- Competitive rhythms

Cardioverter-defibrillator malfunction caused by the following:
- Difficulty determining defibrillation thresholds during electrophysiology study or implant procedure
- Failure to sense and/or emit charge to break tachyarrhythmias
- Failure of myocardium to respond to the charged energy delivered as a result of low-energy output
- Inappropriate sensing of atrial tachyarrhythmias
- Postoperative complications as a result of concomitant cardiac surgery (pericardial effusion, cardiac tamponade)
- Extreme bradycardia or asystole after defibrillation

■ = Independent; ▲ = Collaborative

Common Expected Outcome

Patient maintains adequate cardiac output, as evidenced by strong pulses, blood pressure within normal limits for patient, skin warm and dry, and lungs clear.

NOC Outcomes
Circulation Status;
    Cardiac Pump Effectiveness

NIC Intervention
Dysrhythmia Management

Ongoing Assessment

Actions/Interventions

- Assess apical or radial pulses and hemodynamic status.

- If electrocardiogram (ECG) is monitored:
  - Assess for proper pacemaker function: capture, sensing, firing, and configuration of paced QRS.

  - Assess for pacemaker-induced dysrhythmias.

For Permanent Implantable Pacemaker

Immediately after pacemaker implantation:

▲ Check implant data for the following: type of pacemaker (e.g., single-chamber, dual-chamber, AV sequential, demand, programmable, rate response) and programmed parameters.

▲ Monitor chest x-ray and ECG studies after patient returns from operating room and as prescribed.

- Keep ECG monitor alarms on at all times.
- Record rhythm strips as follows:
  - Routinely according to unit policy
  - If pacemaker malfunction is suspected
  - When pacemaker parameter adjustments are made
▲ If pacemaker malfunction is suspected, conduct the following:
  - Assess hemodynamic stability with spontaneous or competitive rhythm.
  - Obtain 12-lead ECG.

Rationale

Electrical stimulation of the heart does not guarantee effective "pumping" of the heart; hemodynamics need to be assessed.

The nurse's role is to verify proper pacemaker function to reduce risk for malfunction and complications. Each type of pacemaker will have its own configuration for pacing depending on which leads are viewed.

The challenge is to determine the relationship between isolated and pacemaker-induced dysrhythmias.

Certain types of pacemakers have variable functions, which can be difficult to interpret. If using a dual-chamber pacemaker, then preprogrammed, timed intervals and lower and upper rate limits need to be known.

It is necessary to verify correct placement of lead and pacemaker function. Ventricular lead placement is usually in the right ventricular apex; atrial lead placement is in the right atrial appendage.

Safety measures reduce risks.

This provides data for serial comparison.

Not all malfunctions result in hemodynamic compromise. Level of compromise guides level of intervention.

This verifies function of pacemaker and lead placement. Left bundle branch block–paced QRS configuration suggests good right ventricular lead position.

■ = Independent; ▲ = Collaborative

Cardiac and Vascular Care Plans

Actions/Interventions	Rationale
If failure to sense is noted:	Failure to sense occurs when the pacemaker does not recognize spontaneous atrial or ventricular activity and it fires inappropriately.
▲ Monitor chest x-ray films.	These are used to verify placement and status of pacemaker electrode.
■ Observe for phrenic nerve stimulation (hiccups) and intercostal or abdominal muscle twitching.	Stimulation of chest wall and diaphragm indicates possible dislodged pacemaker.
■ Observe for induced ventricular dysrhythmias caused by pacemaker competition.	Pacing stimulus may excite a repolarized cell during the relative refractory period when the heart is at risk of fibrillation; represents an "R on T" phenomenon.
If loss of capture is noted:	Electrical stimulus from pacemaker to myocardium is insufficient to produce an atrial or ventricular beat.
■ Follow the three steps under "failure to sense" above.	
■ Assess for factors that increase myocardial threshold (e.g., ischemia, fibrosis around electrode tip, acidosis, electrolyte imbalance, antidysrhythmic drugs).	Threshold is the minimum amount of electrical energy needed to pace and capture the heart rhythm.
■ If ventricular dysrhythmias occur, assess hemodynamic status.	Level of hemodynamic compromise guides intensity of intervention.
If patient is at home:	
■ Instruct to come to ambulatory care setting.	Pacemaker function must be further evaluated.
■ For repetitive pacemaker problems, consider using transtelephonic monitoring devices.	These devices provide immediate evaluation of cardiac rhythm.
■ Consider registering patients with a 24-hour service.	Such service provides ongoing evaluation as well as a source of support and security for the patient.

For Temporary External Pacemaker

Actions/Interventions	Rationale
▲ Check that the prescribed pacemaker parameters are maintained (rate, pacing output in milliamperes, sensitivity).	Each patient has a different pacing threshold. Also, each type of pacemaker requires different settings (e.g., transvenous uses low milliamperes [2 to 10 mA], whereas transcutaneous may have 40 to 100 mA for capture). Patients with large hearts, large chest muscles, or pleural or pericardial effusions will require more energy.
■ Observe or monitor ECG continuously for appropriate pacemaker function: sensing, capturing, and firing (pacing spikes).	These data verify function and provide early warning for malfunction.
■ Record rhythm strips as follows: • Routinely according to unit policy • When changes in pacing parameters are made • For presence of spontaneous rhythm	This provides data for serial comparison.
■ If pacemaker is on standby, evaluate pacemaker capture daily and as needed.	Capture is represented by a pacing spike followed by ventricular depolarization (QRS).
■ Assess for proper environmental and electrical safety measures.	The pacemaker lead is directly in contact with the myocardium. A small amount of current can initiate fibrillation.
■ If signs of pacemaker malfunction or dysrhythmia occur, assess hemodynamic status until stable.	Level of hemodynamic compromise guides intervention.

■ = Independent; ▲ = Collaborative

Actions/Interventions

- Assess for pacemaker-induced dysrhythmias.

For Implanted Cardioverter-Defibrillator

- Observe or monitor closely for the following:
  - Presence of sustained ventricular dysrhythmias

  - Symptomatic bradycardia or atrial tachydysrhythmias
  - Prolongation of QT interval if patient is receiving antidysrhythmic therapy
- Assess for improper function of implantable defibrillator:
  - Failure to sense ventricular dysrhythmia
  - Failure to emit energy charge
  - Failure to terminate ventricular dysrhythmia
  - Improper sensing of tachydysrhythmias and inappropriate shocks

Rationale

These may be caused by competitive rhythm secondary to asynchronous pacing or tissue excitability.

Such dysrhythmias significantly reduce cardiac output and can be life threatening.

Such dysrhythmias significantly reduce cardiac output.

Prolonged refractory period can precipitate dysrhythmias.

Vigilant monitoring helps reduce consequences of malfunction.

Therapeutic Interventions

Actions/Interventions

For Permanent Implantable Pacemaker

If malfunction is suspected:

- Turn patient on left side (for endocardial pacemaker).

- Notify physician.

- ▲ Call pacemaker specialist to evaluate further pacemaker function and to make changes in parameters if needed through the use of pacemaker programmer.
- ▲ Prepare atropine sulfate, dopamine, epinephrine, and isoproterenol (Isuprel) for standby.

- ▲ Prepare for temporary pacemaker insertion.

- Initiate basic life support measures as needed.

- Anticipate need for medical correction of pacemaker in laboratory.

Rationale

This position facilitates good ventricular wall contact. Malpositioning is a common cause of malfunction, especially in the acute setting.

Pacemaker malfunction can signify a potentially life-threatening condition and warrants immediate intervention.

This is a noninvasive technique of pacemaker programming through radiofrequency signal.

Atropine is an anticholinergic drug that increases cardiac output and HR by blocking vagal stimulation in the heart. Dopamine is an adrenergic stimulator and inotropic drug. Epinephrine and isoproterenol are sympathetic drugs that increase heart rate (HR) and cardiac output by stimulating β-receptors in the heart; these are used to stimulate the ventricles.

Transcutaneous pacing is effective in providing adequate HR and rhythm to patients in emergency situations.

Life-threatening situations warrant immediate attention. Basic cardiopulmonary resuscitation can maintain circulation and perfusion until rhythm is restored.

Depending on the source of the problem, electrode lead system may need to be replaced. For chronically used pacemakers, battery depletion may be the problem.

■ = Independent; ▲ = Collaborative

Pacemaker/Cardioverter-Defibrillator—cont'd

Actions/Interventions	Rationale
For Temporary External Pacemaker	
■ When a transcutaneous pacemaker is used, ensure that a large R wave is obtained on the ECG monitor.	This pacing system reads the signal from the surface ECG, not intracardiac as with the transvenous and epicardial pacemakers.
If failure to sense is noted:	Pacemaker is not sensing spontaneous rhythm, which could lead to dysrhythmias. Pacing stimulus may excite a repolarized cell during a relative refractory period (R-on-T phenomenon).
■ Check that the dial is not on asynchronous pacing (fixed rate).	When the pacer is in asynchronous mode, it does not use the sensing circuit and instead paces at the preset (fixed) rate regardless of underlying cardiac rate and rhythm.
■ Check for loose connections. For transcutaneous pacing, check for adherence of ECG electrodes.	The pacemaker is not picking up cardiac signal when the line of communication is interrupted.
■ Reposition limb of body if lead insertion is through the brachial or femoral vein. If transcutaneous pacing is used, increase size of ECG pattern on monitor, or try a different lead.	Malpositioning can dislodge the pacemaker lead from the wall of the ventricle.
▲ Notify the physician of need to adjust sensitivity dial.	Increasing sensitivity increases the gain of the spontaneous cardiac rhythm signal.
▲ Check position of the endocardial lead by chest x-ray examination. If the problem is not corrected and the patient has adequate rhythm, check with the physician whether the pacemaker should be on standby.	This avoids risk of pacemaker-induced dysrhythmia from competitive rhythms.
▲ If the problem is not corrected and the patient is hemodynamically compromised: with transvenous lead, anticipate use of transcutaneous external pacemaker while awaiting electrode repositioning; with epicardial pacing, anticipate removal of lead and use of transcutaneous external pacemaker or insertion of transvenous pacemaker, depending on patient's status.	Transcutaneous pacing is a rapid, efficient, noninvasive means to restore a cardiac rhythm.
If loss of capture is noted:	The pacemaker fails to depolarize the myocardium.
■ Check all possible connections.	An intact system is required for conducting the cardiac signal.
■ Turn patient on left side (endocardial catheter).	This position facilitates optimal lead placement (right ventricular apex). Capture requires contact between the distal pacing lead and healthy myocardium.
▲ Increase pacing output (milliamperes) and evaluate for good capture.	The pacing threshold may have changed for a variety of reasons and needs to be increased.
■ For transcutaneous pacing, also check for adequate adherence of anterior or posterior electrodes to the patient's skin.	A posterior electrode may have slipped out of position because of diaphoresis.
■ Correct any underlying causes that may reduce myocardial response to electrical stimulation, such as hypoxia or acidosis.	Besides increasing pacing output, treating specific causes for change in threshold optimizes pacemaker function.

■ = Independent; ▲ = Collaborative

Actions/Interventions	Rationale
If loss of pacing spikes is noted:	The pacemaker fails to emit electrical stimulus.
■ Check that the power switch is "on."	This is required to turn on the pacemaker battery.
■ Check whether the needle gauge on the external pacemaker box is fluctuating.	This verifies that the pacemaker senses intrinsic activity.
■ If the needle gauge is not fluctuating, replace batteries in the generator.	Temporary pulse generators use 9-volt batteries. The life of a battery depends on how "pacemaker-dependent" each patient is.
■ Check all possible connections.	An intact system is required for conducting the cardiac signal.
■ Check for electromagnetic interference.	Interference from equipment (e.g., radiation, from cautery, or from imaging resonance) can inhibit pacing output by temporarily turning off the pacemaker.
■ Replace generator as needed.	An effective power source is required for optimal function.
If pacemaker malfunction is noted and not easily corrected by the preceding steps:	
■ Evaluate adequate spontaneous rhythm.	An unreliable escape rhythm will lead to hemodynamic collapse.
■ Monitor vital signs every 15 to 30 minutes.	Treat the patient according to unit protocol and Advanced Cardiac Life Support (ACLS) guidelines.
■ Prepare atropine sulfate, dopamine, epinephrine, and isoproterenol (Isuprel) for standby.	Atropine is an anticholinergic drug that increases cardiac output and HR by blocking vagal stimulation in the heart. Dopamine is an adrenergic stimulator and inotropic drug. Epinephrine and isoproterenol are sympathetic drugs that increase cardiac output and HR by stimulating β-receptors in the ventricle.
If pacemaker-induced dysrhythmia is noted:	
■ Maintain proper environmental and electrical safety measures.	Stray electrical current may enter the heart through the external lead, which can cause dysrhythmia.
■ Ensure that all electrical equipment is properly grounded with three-prong plugs.	Safety measures reduce complications.
▲ Ensure that a biomedical engineer has checked room.	Attention must be directed to ensure a safe environment.
■ Ensure that exposed pacing wire terminals and generator are insulated in a rubber glove or enclosed in a plastic case.	This reduces risk for stray current to travel to heart.
■ Ensure that bed linen and gown are kept dry.	Moisture conducts current.
For Implanted Cardioverter-Defibrillator	
▲ Get information from the electrophysiologist on functions of the implantable defibrillator and how it is programmed. Ask if the device is active (on) or inactive (off).	There are a variety of types and models of ICDs. Each can have variable functions that can be difficult to interpret.
▲ Ensure that a special ring-type magnet is available on the nursing unit.	The magnet is to be used only by qualified personnel to check for proper lead signal (synchronous pulse tone means proper R-wave sensing). Applying the magnet for 30 seconds or more will deactivate the device (constant tone).

■ = Independent; ▲ = Collaborative

Pacemaker/Cardioverter-Defibrillator—cont'd

Actions/Interventions

If ventricular tachycardia or ventricular fibrillation occurs:

▲ Check whether the patient received an internal shock or shocks. If the patient received an internal shock:
  - Notify physician and electrophysiologist.
  - Document total number of shocks that the patient received before conversion.
  - Save rhythm strips in the chart.
  - Check electrolyte level or other factors that predispose to ventricular arrhythmias.

■ If the patient did not receive an internal shock and his or her condition is decompensating:
  - Initiate basic life support measures. Proceed with external defibrillation protocol. Do not wait for the device to emit charges.

  - Apply defibrillation paddles 3 to 4 inches from the pulse generator.

For sustained nonsymptomatic ventricular tachycardia:

■ Notify physician.
▲ Administer antidysrhythmic drug as ordered.
▲ Check potassium and magnesium blood levels or other factors that predispose to ventricular dysrhythmia.
▲ Reevaluate the patient's hemodynamic status for ventricular tachycardia of longer duration.

If implantable defibrillator malfunction is noted:

▲ Notify electrophysiologist at once.
▲ Prepare antidysrhythmic medication.
■ Have emergency cart and defibrillator ready within reach.

▲ If implantable defibrillator exhibits false emission of multiple shocks and is activated:
  - Deactivate the device by applying a magnet over the upper right corner of the device for 30 seconds.
  - Anticipate return to the operating room for possible pulse generator replacement or lead reconfiguration.
  - Document implantable defibrillator malfunction.

Rationale

Most ICD devices have memory and ECG storage capability so the physician or pacemaker nurse can "interrogate" the programmer to determine the sequence or outcome of events.

Prompt intervention is essential to control life-threatening dysrhythmias. Never assume that the internal defibrillator is functioning normally. The magnet can be used over the pulse generator to suppress function during an emergency.

This is to prevent the occurrence of circuit failure and muscle tissue burns. If anterolateral positioning is unsuccessful, try anteroposterior.

The implantable defibrillator does not sense ventricular tachycardia with a rate slower than the programmed cutoff rate (e.g., less than 150 beats/min).

Rapid efficient intervention may be warranted.

ACLS protocols provide guidelines.

Dysrhythmias are best treated by treating the cause.

Patients may be able to sustain ventricular tachycardia only when they are of short duration. Sustained arrhythmia may significantly compromise cardiac output.

ICD malfunction requires specialty intervention.

ACLS protocols provide guidelines.

This will be available for emergency use in case defibrillation is needed to stabilize the patient's rhythm and to support life.

This prevents inappropriate shocks that could worsen arrhythmias and further damage the myocardium. NOTE: When the defibrillator is deactivated, a constant tone is heard instead of a pulse tone (activated).

■ = Independent; ▲ = Collaborative

Actions/Interventions	Rationale
If symptomatic extreme bradycardia or asystole occurs after defibrillation:	
▲ Initiate routine emergency procedure.	Rapid efficient intervention is critical.
▲ Prepare for temporary pacemaker insertion.	This will provide a new source for stimulating cardiac rhythm.
▲ Prepare atropine sulfate, dopamine, epinephrine, and isoproterenol drip. Administer as ordered.	These accelerate the HR and improve cardiac output.
■ Instruct outpatient to do the following:	
• Lie down when device fires.	Each patient needs to understand the plan of care if the ICD discharges inappropriately.
• Report to health care provider any physical symptoms such as chest pain, palpitation, diaphoresis, fainting, dizziness, or other symptoms before receiving shock.	This provides information on degree of hemodynamic compromise associated with specific dysrhythmias.
• Report to staff the delivery of any internal shock or shocks and total number of shocks received.	Protocols vary as to how soon and to whom the patient should report.
• Go to the nearest hospital emergency department if multiple discharges occur in rapid succession and/or if symptomatic.	Safety measures reduce risks and ensure optimal care.

Nursing Diagnosis

Acute Pain/Discomfort

Common Related Factors

Insertion of pacemaker or defibrillator
Self-imposed and imposed activity restriction
Lead displacement
High-pacing energy output
"Frozen" shoulder
Hiccupping (phrenic nerve stimulation); intercostal or pectoral muscle stimulation

Defining Characteristics

Restlessness, irritability
Verbalized discomfort
Splinting of wound with hands
Limited range of motion (ROM) of affected extremity

Common Expected Outcomes

Patient verbalizes relief or reduction in pain or discomfort.
Patient appears relaxed and comfortable.

NOC Outcomes
Pain Level; Pain Control

NIC Intervention
Pain Management

■ = Independent; ▲ = Collaborative

Pacemaker/Cardioverter-Defibrillator—cont'd

Ongoing Assessment

Actions/Interventions

- Assess level of discomfort, source, quality, location, onset, and precipitating and relieving factors.
- Assess for hiccups or muscle twitching.

- Palpate affected site for presence of permanent pulse generator pocket stimulation.

Rationale

Transcutaneous pacing can be especially uncomfortable.

Hiccups occur with phrenic nerve stimulation; muscle twitching occurs with high-energy output.

High pacing output or lead detachment from generator can cause stimulation.

Therapeutic Interventions

Actions/Interventions

- Provide comfort measures (e.g., backrubs, change in position, gentle massage of shoulder on operative side).
- ▲ Administer pain medication as prescribed.

- Instruct patient to report pain and effectiveness of interventions.
- Explain reasons for activity restriction. Emphasize that most are temporary.

- ▲ If hiccups, muscle twitching, or pulse generator pocket stimulation are present, do the following:
  - Notify physician.
  - Obtain chest x-ray film.
  - Obtain ECG.
  - Anticipate return to operating room for lead repositioning.

Rationale

Nonpharmacological measures can promote comfort.

Analgesics or sedatives may be used to reduce painful skeletal muscle contractions with transcutaneous pacing.

Patient comfort is a priority.

Restricted activity and limited ROM can be sources of discomfort in the early postoperative period, but they are required to ensure correct placement of the pacing lead.

These symptoms can indicate dislodged pacemaker.

This provides information on lead status and placement.

This provides information on function of pacemaker.

These discomforts will not be relieved until the lead is repositioned or energy output is reduced.

NDx Nursing Diagnosis

Risk for Impaired Physical Mobility

Common Risk Factors

Imposed activity restriction with transvenous pacemaker
Reluctance to attempt movement because of pain at site of pulse generator/ICD or fear of lead dislodgment

■ = Independent; ▲ = Collaborative

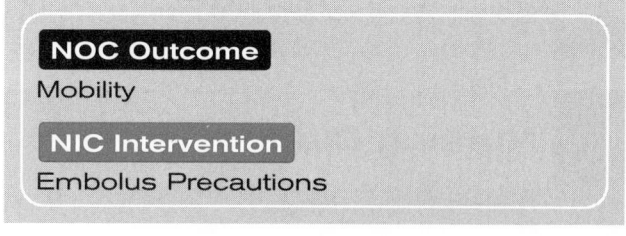

Common Expected Outcomes

Patient engages in activity within prescribed restrictions.
Patient avoids any complications of immobility.

NOC Outcome
Mobility

NIC Intervention
Embolus Precautions

Pacemaker/Cardioverter-Defibrillator

Ongoing Assessment

Actions/Interventions

- Assess whether patient with an implanted pacemaker/ICD is restricting activity because of physician order, discomfort, or fear of malfunction.

- Assess for potential complications related to reduced activity.

- Assess specific activity restrictions for patients with temporary transvenous external pacemakers.

Rationale

Many patients, especially older patients, avoid moving for fear of dislodging the pacemaker/ICD.

Reduced activity can affect peripheral circulation, pulmonary ventilation, ability to sleep, and the gastrointestinal system.

Femoral vein site insertion of pacing leads requires complete bed rest. To prevent dislodging the pacing lead, the affected leg should not be bent. Patients with brachial or internal jugular leads may transfer to a chair with assistance.

Therapeutic Interventions

Actions/Interventions

- Explain the importance of imposed activity restriction (24 to 48 hours after implant).

- Assist in turning every 2 hours. For endocardial pacemaker, avoid turning to right side.

- Assist with active ROM exercises to the nonaffected extremities 3 times daily.

- Assist patient in using affected extremity carefully.

- Provide passive ROM exercise to the shoulder on the operative side.

Rationale

This prevents pacing electrode displacement. Most patients are hospitalized only 24 hours.

The endocardial pacing lead is positioned in the right ventricular apex. Turning to the right side can cause the lead to float or move away from the apex, thereby causing pacemaker malfunction.

This maintains function without compromising pacemaker positioning.

Patient may require assistance with activities of daily living so as not to compromise pacemaker function.

This prevents "frozen" shoulder.

■ = Independent; ▲ = Collaborative

Pacemaker/Cardioverter-Defibrillator—cont'd

 Nursing Diagnosis

Deficient Knowledge

Common Related Factors	Defining Characteristics
Inability to comprehend	Lack of questions
New procedure or equipment	Verbalized misconceptions
Misinterpretation of information	Questioning
Advanced age of patient	

Common Expected Outcomes

Patient and family verbalize understanding about pacemaker or defibrillator.

Patient accepts activity limitation.

Patient understands role in detecting early signs of equipment malfunction or failure.

NOC Outcomes
Knowledge: Disease Process;
Knowledge: Treatment Regimen

NIC Interventions
Teaching: Disease Process;
Teaching: Preoperative;
Teaching: Procedure/Treatment

Ongoing Assessment

Actions/Interventions	Rationale
■ Assess level of understanding about pacemaker and reasons for insertion.	Evaluation provides starting point for educational session.
■ Assess understanding of how to care for pacemaker site, activity prescriptions, and need for follow-up pacemaker checks.	Thorough understanding is necessary for appropriate care and follow-up.

Therapeutic Interventions

Actions/Interventions	Rationale
■ Before surgery, explain the anatomy and physiology of the heart, the pacemaker or defibrillator function and its advantages, and the insertion procedure.	Thorough understanding is necessary for informed consent to be given.
■ After surgery for a permanent pacemaker:	
• Stress importance of bed rest after implantation.	This prevents lead displacement.
• Instruct patient to avoid turning to the right side if endocardial pacemaker was inserted.	Correct positioning ensures good ventricular wall contact.
• Explain importance of notifying the nurse of the following:	
• Any pain or drainage from the insertion site	These are symptoms that require immediate follow-up.
• Complaints of headache, dizziness, confusion, chest pain, shortness of breath, hiccups, or muscle twitching	These may suggest pacemaker malfunction.

■ = Independent; ▲ = Collaborative

Actions/Interventions	Rationale
• Explain the need for chest x-ray evaluation and 12-lead ECG.	These are required to assess pacemaker function.
■ Before discharge and routinely in the ambulatory care setting, teach the patient and reinforce the following for a permanent pacemaker:	
• Need for regular follow-up care	This may be according to routine physician appointment or follow-up at specialized pacemaker clinic or by transtelephonic methods.
• Signs and symptoms of infection; wound care for insertion site	Patients are better able to seek assistance when they know basic information.
• The need to discuss with the physician the types of sports activities in which the patient can participate (avoid contact sports)	Knowledge helps prevent pacemaker complications.
• The need to avoid over-the-head arm motion or overstretching for 1 month	This is necessary to prevent lead displacement because it takes about 1 month for scar tissue to form around the electrode tip.
• The need to carry a pacemaker identification card with the type of pacemaker, brand name, model number, and programmed pacing rate	Pacemakers are becoming more complex. Timely troubleshooting requires knowledge of the specifics of the patient's own pacemaker.
• Signs and symptoms of pacemaker malfunction	Information aids the patient in assuming responsibility for ongoing care.
• How to take and record pulse as needed	Daily pulse checks aid in detecting early battery failure.
• Need to notify physician or pacemaker follow-up office if pulse rate is 5 to 10 beats slower than programmed rate or to inform health care providers of any signs and symptoms of pacemaker malfunction	Vigilant monitoring helps reduce consequences of malfunction.
• Pacemaker longevity and need for pacemaker battery replacement when elective replacement indication time has been reached	Most lithium batteries last 5 to 10 years. Pulse generator replacement (battery) using the same electrode can be done on an outpatient basis.
• Avoidance of strong magnetic field (magnetic resonance, electrocautery equipment, laser, diathermy, lithotripsy, direct radiation, current industrial machinery)	These may cause pulse generator circuitry failure or may cause certain pacemakers to go into backup mode.
• Safety of using newer-model microwave ovens; if dizziness is felt while near the appliance being used, advise patient to move at least 5 to 10 feet away	Pacemaker assumes normal function without permanent effects.
• Need to alert airport personnel, dentist, and others of presence of pacemaker	Newer pacemakers rarely trigger airport screening devices.
■ Before discharge, instruct the patient or family regarding the following for an ICD:	Long-term care will be the patient's responsibility. Enough information is required for successful follow-up.
• Need to carry identification card at all times	
• Need to apply for medical alert identification and wear it at all times	
• Need for regular follow-up care (every 2 to 4 months until the end of life of battery)	
• Procedure for taking pulse	
• How patient can do cough cardiopulmonary resuscitation in case of ICD failure	

Pacemaker/Cardioverter-Defibrillator

■ = Independent; ▲ = Collaborative

Cardiac and Vascular Care Plans

→ **Pacemaker/Cardioverter-Defibrillator—cont'd**

Actions/Interventions	Rationale
• How to enroll family for cardiopulmonary resuscitation course • Chest and abdominal wound care • Signs and symptoms of infection • Signs and symptoms of tachydysrhythmias and implantable defibrillator malfunction • Anticipating shock when symptoms occur • Tingling sensation by person who touches patient being shocked • Avoiding strong magnetic field: diathermy, computed tomography scans, lithotripsy, electrocautery equipment, stimulator, MRI, laser, and current industrial machinery (newer-model microwave ovens have no reported effect); for radiation therapy, device should be shielded • Remembering that the device will emit a beeping noise when near magnetic field • Immediately notifying physician or pacemaker laboratory of shocks received • Alerting dentists or other physicians for presence of implantable defibrillator • Alerting airport personnel regarding implantable defibrillator • Avoiding contact sports like baseball, basketball, football, and other activities • Magnet testing during scheduled follow-up care • Driving restriction	It may cause defibrillator to deactivate or deplete the battery, and defibrillator may become unresponsive. Some states have laws that restrict ICD patients from driving. Others allow driving after a period of no shocks or infrequent shocks. Alternative methods of transportation need to be arranged.

■ Use a variety of teaching materials, as in the following:
  • Video of patients with implantable defibrillators
  • Demonstration model of implantable defibrillator and equipment
  • Handout materials
	Different people take in information in different ways. Match the learning style with the educational approach.

■ Review implantable defibrillator manual with patient and family.	Patients are better able to ask questions and seek assistance when they know basic information about ICDs.
■ Refer to support group.	Support groups provide emotional support and information that may assist patients in coping with pacemaker/ICD devices.

■ = Independent; ▲ = Collaborative

Pacemaker/Cardioverter-Defibrillator

 Nursing Diagnosis

Fear

Common Related Factors

Diagnosis of inducible life-threatening arrhythmia
History of sudden cardiac death, syncope, long history of hospitalization, and multiple diagnostic studies
Anticipation of perceived threat, danger, or death
Insertion of implantable defibrillator
Anticipation of how receiving a shock will feel
Potential for defibrillator system malfunction
Loss of independence caused by change in role functions or routines
Threat or change of socioeconomic status
Interpersonal conflicts

Defining Characteristics

Restlessness, irritability
Insomnia
Increased questioning
Expressed concerns
Expressed feelings of loss of control

Common Expected Outcome

Patient will verbalize his or her fears openly.

NOC Outcomes
Anxiety Self-Control;
    Social Support; Coping

NIC Interventions
Anxiety Reduction;
    Preparatory Sensory Information;
    Teaching: Disease Process/Treatment;
    Support System Enhancement

Ongoing Assessment

Actions/Interventions

■ Assess for source of fear/anxiety.

■ Evaluate past coping mechanisms and their effectiveness.

Rationale

Related factors represent common sources of fear. Accurate assessment of fear guides intervention.

They can serve as a basis for adopting or adapting prior strategies.

Therapeutic Interventions

Actions/Interventions

Inpatient:
■ Encourage patient to talk about fears.

■ Explain electrophysiology and surgical procedures ahead of time.

Rationale

Talking allows ventilation of repressed feelings and promotes nurse-patient relationship. Patients may have heard exaggerated accounts of being shocked.

Answering all concerned questions will reduce the patient's anxiety level. The patient will be able to use problem-solving abilities effectively if anxiety level is low.

■ = Independent; ▲ = Collaborative

Cardiac and Vascular
Care Plans

Pacemaker/Cardioverter-Defibrillator—cont'd

Actions/Interventions	Rationale
■ Institute measures for adequate sleep.	These improve patient's well-being and help patient prepare better for surgery.
▲ Administer medication as prescribed.	This may be indicated for relief of anxiety.
■ Provide emotional support to the patient by expressing concerns in a calm, reassuring manner.	The presence of a trusted person makes the patient feel secure.
■ Rehearse with the patient what it feels like when an ICD device fires.	Talking through the event may help patients cope with their fears. There will be several practice trials with the ICD in the procedure laboratory.
Outpatient:	
■ Assist the patient in developing his or her problem-solving abilities.	Guidance with a less stressful problem-solving situation will provide the base for more complex situations.
■ Assist the patient in providing emotional support to the family.	An ICD shock can be a frightening experience for all family members, especially if the member is touching the patient when the ICD fires. They require assurance that they will not be harmed and that proper firing is a positive experience.
■ Assist the patient with an ICD to understand that not firing does not mean the ICD is defective.	Many patients receive the ICD prophylactically; therefore months or even years may go by without its firing. Periodic laboratory checks will verify accurate function.
■ Encourage use of support groups for patient and family.	Knowing what changes in lifestyle might occur helps to prepare for such situations and facilitates problem solving.

• RELATED CARE PLAN

Disturbed body image, p. 21

Percutaneous Balloon Valvuloplasty

Percutaneous balloon valvuloplasty is a nonsurgical procedure that involves the transluminal dilation of stenotic valvular (mitral valve, aortic valve, pulmonic valve) lesions by using balloon catheters. It is indicated for symptomatic patients who no longer respond to medical therapy and who are not candidates for valve replacement surgery. It is often used for older patients when surgery poses too great a risk. Successful balloon valvuloplasty may improve the patient's hemodynamic state sufficiently to reduce the risks associated with valve replacement surgery. This procedure can be performed in a catheterization laboratory under fluoroscopy and without the use of general anesthesia. A percutaneous retrograde approach through the femoral artery is most commonly used for aortic valves. The femoral vein is used in the antegrade approach across the intraatrial septum to the left atrium for the mitral valve.

■ = Independent; ▲ = Collaborative

Nursing Diagnosis

Deficient Knowledge

Common Related Factor

New procedure

Defining Characteristics

Expressed need for more information
Multiple questions or lack of questions
Anxiousness
Restlessness
Verbalized misconceptions

Common Expected Outcome

Patient or significant others verbalize basic understanding of valvuloplasty and the care associated with it.

NOC Outcomes
Knowledge: Disease Process;
Knowledge: Treatment Procedure

NIC Interventions
Teaching: Disease Process;
Teaching: Procedure

Ongoing Assessment

Actions/Interventions

■ Note baseline level of knowledge of heart anatomy, disease, valvuloplasty procedure, and possible risks or complications.

Rationale

This provides an important starting point for education.

Therapeutic Interventions

Actions/Interventions

■ Provide information about the following:
  • Heart anatomy and physiology

  • Patient's heart problem (mitral or aortic stenosis)

  • Specifics about procedure
    • Sedation
    • Insertion of catheter under fluoroscopy
    • Balloon inflation at several atmospheres of pressure for 12 to 30 seconds; repeated inflations are usually required
    • Monitoring of pressure gradients across valve to verify results

Rationale

Information provides background for understanding the need for the procedure.

Mitral stenosis is associated with fibrous valve leaflets that reduce the valve orifice. Aortic stenosis is associated with thickened, fibrous cusps and valve calcification.

Anxiety can be reduced when the patient knows what to expect.

■ = Independent; ▲ = Collaborative

→ **Percutaneous Balloon Valvuloplasty—cont'd**

Actions/Interventions	Rationale

• Immediate postvalvuloplasty care:
  • Activity restrictions: lying flat with affected site straight until femoral introducer or sheath is removed and usually for 4 to 8 hours after removal
  • Routine vital sign monitoring
  • Increased oral fluid intake
	Patients need to be aware of postprocedure activities so they can participate in care.
	
	Patients are allowed nothing by mouth before the procedure and may experience hypovolemia secondary to dye-induced diuresis.

• Monitoring for complications: bleeding at site, valve tear or rupture, left-to-right shunt
• Recovery:
  • May resume normal activities in 1 week per physician's order
  • Notifying physician of weight gain, dyspnea, edema (signs of valve dysfunction)
  • Medications
	Information enables the patient to reduce risk for or seek help for postprocedure complications.

■ Be in room when physicians discuss risk and complications of procedure so that the patient's subsequent questions can be answered accurately.	Thorough understanding is necessary for informed consent to be given.

NDx Nursing Diagnosis

Risk for Decreased Cardiac Output

Common Risk Factors

Fluid volume deficit related to radiographic dye and restricted oral intake before procedure
Valve tear or rupture leading to valvular insufficiency
Dysrhythmia
Pulmonary artery pressures and pulmonary vascular resistance secondary to left-to-right shunt with transseptal approach

Common Expected Outcome

Patient maintains adequate cardiac output as evidenced by warm, dry skin; normal blood pressure; heart rate 60 to 100 beats/min; absence of rales; and normal pulmonary artery diastolic pressure (PADP) and pulmonary capillary wedge pressure (PCWP).

NOC Outcomes
Cardiac Pump Effectiveness;
  Circulation Status; Fluid Balance

NIC Interventions
Invasive Hemodynamic Monitoring;
  Hemodynamic Regulation;
  Fluid Resuscitation

■ = Independent; ▲ = Collaborative

Ongoing Assessment

Actions/Interventions

■ Assess patient's hemodynamic status closely: obtain vital signs until stable. Note and report changes.

▲ Assess the following parameters as available: PADP, PCWP, central venous pressure, cardiac output, and oxygen saturation.

■ Assess 12-lead electrocardiogram on arrival in the intensive care unit, and monitor each morning.

■ Assess heart sounds for change in murmur.

■ Auscultate lungs. Observe for and report changes in respiratory pattern.

■ Assess fluid balance closely.

■ Monitor voiding or urine output closely. Report if there is no voiding for 8 hours or if urine output is less than 30 mL/hr.

■ Assess for increased restlessness, fatigue, confusion, and disorientation.

▲ Monitor arterial blood gases or pulse oximetry as necessary.

Rationale

The first few hours are crucial to recovery. Declining systolic blood pressure and increasing pulse may indicate decreased cardiac output and decompensation.

PADP and PCWP pressures are elevated with new mitral insufficiency, which is a common complication of the procedure. Venous oxygen saturation will be more than 70% with left-to-right shunt. This shunt may occur secondary to the transseptal approach for mitral valvuloplasty.

Electrocardiography is necessary to assess changes and to monitor potential dysrhythmias.

A blowing high-pitched murmur denotes valvular insufficiency, a complication of the procedure.

This aids in monitoring respiratory status and fluid retention.

Fluid retention is a compensatory mechanism that is activated by decreased cardiac output.

Hypovolemia is a common problem.

Neurological changes can indicate hypoxia due to increased cardiac output. Cerebrovascular accident may occur as a complication.

These provide information on oxygen status.

Therapeutic Interventions

Actions/Interventions

■ If signs of hemodynamic compromise are observed, institute treatment for decreased cardiac output, p. 32.

▲ Administer oxygen therapy.

▲ If cardiac output is decreased secondary to fluid volume deficit, anticipate fluid resuscitation.

▲ If cardiac output is decreased secondary to valve rupture or tear:
  • Administer afterload reducers (sodium nitroprusside).
  • Anticipate emergency open heart surgery for valve replacement.

▲ If cardiac output is decreased secondary to pulmonary hypertension, anticipate use of vasodilators (nitrates, hydralazine).

Rationale

Maintaining an adequate cardiac output is a priority.

It is necessary to increase arterial oxygen saturation above 90%.

Specific deficiencies guide therapy.

Rapid, efficient intervention is critical.

These reduce pulmonary vascular resistance.

■ = Independent; ▲ = Collaborative

Cardiac and Vascular Care Plans

Percutaneous Balloon Valvuloplasty—cont'd

 Nursing Diagnosis

Risk for Ineffective Peripheral Tissue Perfusion

Common Risk Factors

Mechanical obstruction from arterial and venous sheaths
Arterial vasospasm
Thrombus formation
Embolization of calcium debris
Bleeding or hematoma

Common Expected Outcome

Patient maintains peripheral tissue perfusion in affected extremity as evidenced by strong pulse and warm extremity.

NOC Outcomes
Tissue Perfusion: Peripheral;
  Circulation Status

NIC Interventions
Circulatory Care; Bleeding Precautions;
  Embolus Precautions

Ongoing Assessment

Actions/Interventions

Preprocedure:
- Assess and document presence or absence and quality of all distal pulses.

- Obtain Doppler ultrasonic reading for faint, non-palpable pulses. Indicate if pulse check is with Doppler. Mark location of faint pulses with an X.

- Assess and document skin color and temperature, presence or absence of pain, numbness, tingling, movement, and sensation of all extremities.

Postprocedure:
- Assess presence and quality of pulses distal to arterial cannulation site.

- Check cannulation site for swelling and hematoma.

Rationale

This provides baseline for serial assessments.

Marking the pulse site facilitates easier location during postprocedure monitoring.

Knowledge of baseline circulatory status of extremities will assist in monitoring for postprocedure changes.

Embolization from the femoral insertion site may cause distal arterial occlusion.

These may hinder peripheral circulation by constricting vessels and compressing nerves.

Therapeutic Interventions

Actions/Interventions

Postprocedure:
- Ensure safety measures to prevent displacement of arterial and venous sheaths.

Rationale

Significant changes in position cause sheath to bend or move, which fosters potential bleeding and dislodgment.

■ = Independent; ▲ = Collaborative

Actions/Interventions	Rationale

Actions/Interventions

- Maintain bed rest.
- Keep cannulated extremity straight at all times. Apply knee or leg immobilizer or soft restraint.
- Do not elevate head of bed more than 30 degrees.
- Assist with meals, use of bedpan, and position changes appropriate to activity limitations.

▲ Continue prescribed dose of heparin infusion. Check partial thromboplastin time (PTT) and activated clotting time (ACT) 4 hours after start of infusion and after change in dose.

■ Do passive range-of-motion exercises to unaffected extremities every 2 to 4 hours as tolerated.

■ Instruct patient to immediately report presence of pain, numbness, tingling, and decrease or loss of sensation and movement.

■ Immediately report to physician decrease or loss of pulse, change in skin color and temperature, presence of pain, numbness, tingling, delayed capillary refill, and decrease or loss of sensation and motion.

■ If ineffective tissue perfusion is noted, anticipate removal of the catheter sheath.

▲ Prepare for possible embolectomy.

Rationale

PTT is usually kept at 1½ to 2 times control. ACT can assist in determining when the sheath can be removed (ACT less than 150 to 180 sec).

These prevent venous stasis and joint stiffness.

This is important for quick assessment, diagnosis, and treatment of complications.

These may signify ischemia and warrant immediate intervention.

Its presence may obstruct blood flow and cause further complications.

This is indicated to remove a blood clot obstructing or compromising circulation.

NDx Nursing Diagnosis

Ineffective Protection

Common Related Factors

Presence of large catheter sheaths (usually left in place until clotting times are back to normal)
Heparinization
Arterial trauma

Defining Characteristic

Altered clotting

Common Expected Outcomes

Patient does not experience abnormal bleeding at insertion site.
Risk of injury from bleeding is reduced through early assessment and intervention.

NOC Outcome
Blood Coagulation

NIC Interventions
Bleeding Precautions;
  Bleeding Reduction: Wound

■ = Independent; ▲ = Collaborative

Cardiac and Vascular Care Plans

 Percutaneous Balloon Valvuloplasty—cont'd

Ongoing Assessment

Actions/Interventions

■ Assess cannulation site for evidence of bleeding.

■ Assess for signs of retroperitoneal bleeding.

■ Postprocedure, monitor vital signs until stable.

▲ Monitor prothrombin time, PTT, ACT, and platelets.

■ If significant bleeding occurs:
  • Monitor vital signs at least every 15 minutes until bleeding is controlled, and hold pressure above the site until hemostasis.
  • Observe for circulatory compromise in the affected extremity.
■ Note amount of drainage if fresh blood is noted on the dressing. Circle or outline the size of any hematoma.

Rationale

Fresh blood on dressing, oozing, pain, tenderness, swelling, and hematoma are all signs of bleeding.

These may include abdomen, flank, or thigh pain, loss of lower extremity pulse, or drop in hemoglobin level and hematocrit.

Increased heart rate and decreased blood pressure are initial compensatory mechanisms commonly noted with bleeding.

These provide information on coagulation status. Usually PTT is kept at 1½ to 2 times control. Sheaths are usually removed when ACT is less than 150 to 180 seconds.

Vigilant monitoring reduces risk of further complications.

This provides a baseline to assess further bleeding.

Therapeutic Interventions

Actions/Interventions

Before removal of catheter sheaths:

■ Maintain bed rest with patient in supine position with affected extremity straight.
■ Do not elevate head of bed more than 30 degrees. Observe appropriate positioning for meals, bowel and bladder elimination, and position changes.
■ Avoid sudden movement of affected extremity.

■ Instruct patient to apply light pressure on dressing when coughing, sneezing, or raising head off pillow.
■ Instruct patient to notify nurse immediately of signs of bleeding from cannulation site (e.g., feeling of wetness, warmth, "pop" at catheter sheath site, feeling of faintness).
▲ Administer heparin drip through infusion pump.

▲ If significant bleeding occurs:
  • Turn off heparin drip and notify the physician immediately.

Rationale

Length of time for sheath insertion varies according to type of procedure and institutional policy.

This minimizes the risk of bleeding from cannulation site.

Significant changes in position cause catheter to bend or move, which interferes with clot formation and can facilitate bleeding.

This prevents displacement of catheter sheaths (may cause bleeding).

These measures facilitate clot formation.

Educating patients of such interventions can prevent complications from clot being dislodged.

Heparin anticoagulation is initiated during the procedure and for at least 4 to 6 hours afterward to prevent thrombus formation. Institutional policies may vary.

Rapid, efficient intervention is required.

■ = Independent; ▲ = Collaborative

Actions/Interventions	Rationale
• Remove dressing, and apply manual pressure or mechanical clamp directly to bleeding site.	This provides temporary hemostasis.
• Anticipate fluid challenge.	This treats hypotension.
• Administer protamine sulfate as ordered.	This drug reverses effect of heparin.
• Anticipate removal of catheter sheaths.	This facilitates more optimal sealing of insertion site.
After removal of catheter:	When ACT is less than 150 to 180 seconds, ice packs, sandbags, or mechanical clamps may be used to stop any initial bleeding.
▲ Maintain occlusive pressure dressing on cannulation site for 20 to 30 minutes.	Care is guided by institutional protocols.
■ Maintain bed rest in supine position with affected extremity straight for prescribed time.	This promotes clot formation.
■ Avoid sudden movement of affected extremity.	This facilitates clot formation and wound closure at the insertion site.
▲ Resume mobilization and ambulation as prescribed.	Protocols may vary according to institutional policy and type of procedure.

> **• RELATED CARE PLANS**
>
> Anxiety, p. 15
> Deficient fluid volume, p. 71
> Fear, p. 68
> Impaired physical mobility, p. 126

Percutaneous Coronary Intervention: Percutaneous Transluminal Coronary Angioplasty (PTCA), Atherectomy, Stents

Nonsurgical Revascularization; Directional Atherectomy (DCA); Intracoronary Stenting; Intracoronary Radiation; Brachytherapy; Drug-Eluding Stents

These interventions provide a means to nonsurgically improve coronary blood flow and revascularize the myocardium. A variety of procedures have been developed, although percutaneous transluminal coronary angioplasty (PTCA) remains the mainstay. Unfortunately, restenosis remains a critical problem with all techniques. Interventional procedures may be performed in combination with the diagnostic coronary angiogram, electively after diagnostic evaluation, or urgently in the setting of unstable angina or acute myocardial infarction (MI).

PTCA: This procedure uses a balloon-tipped catheter that is positioned at the site of the lesion. Multiple balloon inflations are performed until the artery is satisfactorily dilated. The number of PTCA procedures performed annually continues to rise, especially among the older population, particularly older women, because of the risks associated with coronary artery bypass graft surgery for these patients.

Coronary atherectomy: This term refers to removal of plaque material by excision or ablation. It may be performed in conjunction with PTCA and continues to be applied to a wider patient domain that includes patients with multivessel disease and complex coronary anatomy. Atherectomy may be more effective than PTCA for more calcified lesions. Several types of devices have been developed:

■ = Independent; ▲ = Collaborative

Percutaneous Coronary Intervention: PTCA, Atherectomy, Stents—cont'd

1. *Directional*: has a rotating cutter blade that shaves the plaque. The tissue obtained is collected in a cone for removal. It is indicated for lesions with calcification or thrombus and for those at the ostium of a vessel.
2. *Rotational*: uses a burr at the tip of the catheter, which rotates at high speeds (150,000 to 200,000 rpm) to abrade hard plaque. The removed pulverized microparticles are released into the distal circulation rather than collected as in directional atherectomy.

Intracoronary stents: These metallic coils are inserted after balloon dilation or atherectomy, or they are used alone, to provide structural support ("internal scaffolding") to the vessel. The stent remains in place as the catheter is removed. Because of the thrombogenic nature of the stent, anticoagulation and antiplatelet therapy are indicated for an indefinite period of time. These stents have reduced restenosis rates significantly. The newest models are "drug-eluding" stents that can deliver drugs that inhibit new cell and tissue growth and prevent neointimal hyperplasia and restenosis.

Brachytherapy: This technique uses intracoronary radiation to treat in-stent stenosis. It uses either gamma or beta radiation isotopes.

Coronary laser angioplasty: This technique uses laser energy to treat in-stent stenosis.

 Nursing Diagnosis

Deficient Knowledge

Common Related Factors

Unfamiliarity with procedure
Information misinterpretation
Cognitive limitation

Defining Characteristics

Requests for more information
Statement of misconception
Increase in anxiety level
Lack of questions

Common Expected Outcome

Patient demonstrates basic understanding of heart anatomy and physiology, coronary artery disease (CAD), and anticipated procedure.

NOC Outcomes
Knowledge: Disease Process;
Knowledge: Treatment Procedure

NIC Interventions
Teaching: Disease Process;
Teaching: Procedure or Treatment

Ongoing Assessment

Actions/Interventions

■ Assess patient's knowledge of cardiac anatomy and physiology, CAD, and anticipated procedure.

Rationale

Patients must have correct information to make informed consent. This may be a first-time procedure for some or a repeat procedure for others because of high restenosis rates and the progressive nature of atherosclerosis.

■ = Independent; ▲ = Collaborative

Therapeutic Interventions

Actions/Interventions	Rationale
■ Encourage patient to verbalize questions and concerns.	It is necessary to correct misunderstandings and misconceptions.
■ Provide information about the following:	
• Heart anatomy and physiology; CAD	Information provides rationale for procedure.
• Indications for interventional procedure	Patients with significant obstruction (70% to 100%) in areas reachable by catheterization are the best candidates.
• Type of procedure: PTCA versus atherectomy and use of stents	Some patients want to be involved in decision making regarding the type of procedure to be performed. However, they may lack knowledge regarding technical aspects and complications that guide such decision making.
• Vessels requiring intervention	These may be single lesions or vessels or multiple lesions and vessels.
• Success rate	This is greater than 90% in most cardiac centers.
• Procedure room environment: catheterization laboratory	Anxiety can be reduced when patient knows what to expect.
• Expected length of procedure	This depends on the number of vessels attempted, vessel anatomy, complications, and number of catheters required.
• Postprocedure expectations:	
• Expected discomfort (encourage patient to notify staff when effect wears off)	Local anesthetic is used to reduce discomfort at insertion site. The patient may be uncomfortable when the PTCA balloon is inflated secondary to reduced coronary blood flow. Patients often report discomfort from lying on the hard radiograph table with restricted movement for a prolonged period (1 to 4 hours).
• Possible complications: abrupt closure of artery, acute MI, bleeding, retroperitoneal bleeding, arteriovenous (AV) fistula, stroke, dissection requiring emergency coronary artery bypass graft surgery	Patients need to be aware of potential complications so they can evaluate risk/benefit when making informed consent.
• Immediate postprocedure care as follows:	
• Activity restrictions: lying flat with affected site straight until femoral introducer sheath is removed, vessel has sealed, and hemostasis is achieved	This sheath is usually left in the artery until the activated clotting time (ACT) is within acceptable range (less than 180 seconds) or per institution policy.
• Increased oral fluid intake	Patients are allowed nothing by mouth before the procedure and may experience hypovolemia secondary to dye-induced diuresis and the effects of vasodilator medications.
• Monitoring for complications	These may be bleeding at site and restenosis of vessel.
• Recovery:	
• Avoidance of lifting heavy objects for 1 week	
• Possible return to work within 1 week per physician's discretion	
• When to notify physician (e.g., chest pain, bleeding)	Restenosis of the treated vessel can be a problem. It is usually treated by repeat PTCA.

■ = Independent; ▲ = Collaborative

Percutaneous Coronary Intervention: PTCA, Atherectomy, Stents—cont'd

Actions/Interventions	Rationale
• Medications	A variety of medication regimens are used depending on type of percutaneous coronary intervention performed and whether the procedure was related to an acute coronary syndrome. Medications can include antiplatelets, calcium channel blockers, nitrates, angiotensin-converting enzyme inhibitors, and β-blockers. The primary medication focus postprocedure centers on antiplatelets to prevent restenosis.
■ Include cardiac clinical nurse specialist, catheter laboratory nurse, and coronary care nurses as resource persons.	Specialty expertise may be needed.

See also **Cardiac Catheterization**, *p. 235.*

NDx Nursing Diagnosis

Acute Chest Pain

Common Related Factors

Myocardial ischemia caused by abrupt closure of affected coronary artery, coronary artery spasm, and possible MI
Residual pain from manipulation or dilation of coronary artery

Defining Characteristics

Patient reports pain
Restlessness and apprehension
Facial mask of pain
Diaphoresis
Increased blood pressure (BP) and increased heart rate (HR)
ST-segment and/or T-wave changes

Common Expected Outcomes

Patient is free of pain after procedure.
Patient appears comfortable.

> **NOC Outcome**
> Pain Control
>
> **NIC Interventions**
> Cardiac Care: Acute: Analgesic Administration; Pain Management

Ongoing Assessment

Actions/Interventions	Rationale
■ Assess for characteristics of myocardial ischemia.	Abrupt closure usually has a presenting symptom pattern similar to pain before the interventional procedure.
■ Monitor electrocardiogram for signs of ST-T wave changes reflective of myocardial ischemia or spasm.	ST-segment elevation is commonly seen with abrupt closure of the coronary artery.

■ = Independent; ▲ = Collaborative

Actions/Interventions

■ Assess HR and BP during episode of pain.

■ Obtain serial creatine kinase (CK) and creatine kinase–MB (CK-MB) measurements (6 to 8 hours and 16 to 24 hours postprocedure).

■ Monitor patient response to effectiveness of treatment.

Rationale

Attention to hemodynamic signs may help the nurse in evaluating pain; occurrence of pain after the procedure can be very frightening for the patient.

Elevated CK-MB levels of 5 to 8 times the upper normal limit is considered to be an MI and should be treated as such.

The effects of both oral and intravenous (IV) medications must be monitored. IV medications can be further titrated to relieve pain.

Therapeutic Interventions

Actions/Interventions

■ Instruct the patient to report pain immediately.

■ Notify the physician of chest pain immediately.

▲ Administer medications as ordered:
  • Nitroglycerin
  • Calcium channel blockers
  • Morphine sulfate

  • Antiplatelets and GP IIB/IIIA inhibitors

■ Anticipate the need for possible emergency cardiac catheterization and repeat procedure.

■ Stay with the patient during pain.

Rationale

Abrupt closure results from elastic recoil of the vessel and/or thrombosis. It is important that relief measures be initiated before additional myocardium is jeopardized.

It is important to differentiate expected residual pain from coronary dilation and manipulation from pain related to vessel closure. The physician needs to make the distinction.

This is useful for arterial spasm.

These are useful for arterial spasm.

This is useful for analgesic effect and for reducing myocardial ischemia as by decreasing preload.

These are used to reduce clotting and prevent microembolization.

Abrupt closure occurs most often in the catheter laboratory or during the first 24 hours.

Nursing presence provides emotional support and reassurance.

NDx Nursing Diagnosis

Ineffective Protection

Common Related Factors

Presence of large catheter sheaths (usually left in place until clotting times are back to normal)
Heparinization/antiplatelet agents, especially with stents
Arterial trauma

Defining Characteristic

Altered clotting (bleeding)

■ = Independent; ▲ = Collaborative

Cardiac and Vascular Care Plans

> ## Percutaneous Coronary Intervention: PTCA, Atherectomy, Stents—cont'd

Common Expected Outcomes

Patient does not experience abnormal bleeding at insertion site.

Risk of injury from bleeding is reduced through early assessment and intervention.

NOC Outcome
Blood Coagulation

NIC Interventions
Bleeding Precautions;
Bleeding Reduction: Wound

Ongoing Assessment

Actions/Interventions

- Assess cannulation site for evidence of bleeding.

- Assess for signs of retroperitoneal bleeding.

- After procedure, monitor vital signs until patient's condition is stable.

▲ Monitor prothrombin time, partial thromboplastin time, activated clotting time (ACT), and platelets.

- If significant bleeding occurs:
  - Monitor vital signs at least every 15 minutes until bleeding is controlled.
  - Observe for circulatory compromise in the affected extremity.
  - Hold pressure above the site over the artery until hemostasis is achieved.
- Note amount of drainage if fresh blood is noted on the dressing. Circle or outline the size of any hematoma.

Rationale

Fresh blood on dressing, oozing, pain, tenderness, swelling, and hematoma are all signs of bleeding.

These may include abdominal, flank or thigh pain, loss of lower extremity pulses, or drop in hemoglobin.

Increased HR and decreased BP are initial compensatory mechanisms commonly noted with bleeding.

These provide information on coagulation status. Usually partial thromboplastin time is kept at 1½ to 2 times control. Sheaths can usually be removed when the ACT is less than 150 to 180 seconds.

Vigilant monitoring reduces risk of further complications.

This provides a baseline to assess further bleeding.

Therapeutic Interventions

Actions/Interventions

Before removal of catheter sheaths:

- Maintain bed rest with affected extremity straight.
- Do not elevate head of bed more than 30 degrees. Observe appropriate positioning for meals, bowel and bladder elimination, and position changes.

- Avoid sudden movement of affected extremity.

Rationale

Length of time for sheath insertion varies according to type of procedure (i.e., stents require longer anti-coagulation and longer insertion times) and institutional policy.

This minimizes risk of bleeding from cannulation site.

Significant changes in position cause catheter to bend or move, which interferes with clot formation and can facilitate bleeding. Comfort issues need to be addressed by nursing staff.

This prevents displacement of catheter sheaths (may cause bleeding).

■ = Independent; ▲ = Collaborative

Actions/Interventions	Rationale
■ Instruct patient to apply light pressure on dressing when coughing, sneezing, or raising head off pillow.	These measures facilitate clot formation and prevent dislodgment.
■ Instruct patient to notify nurse immediately of signs of bleeding from cannulation site (e.g., feeling of wetness, warmth, "pop" at catheter sheath site, feeling of faintness).	Educating patients on such intervention can prevent complications from clot being dislodged.
▲ Administer antiplatelet agents.	Antiplatelet therapies are especially required after stent placement. This area is receiving much research because a balance must be achieved between aggressive therapy to reduce restenosis and the risk for bleeding. Current agents include glycoprotein IIB/IIIA receptor inhibitors (e.g., abciximab [ReoPro], tirofiban [Aggrastat], and eptifibatide [Integrilin]). Research has shown these agents to decrease ischemic complications.
▲ If significant bleeding occurs:	
• Notify physician immediately.	Rapid, efficient intervention is required.
• Remove dressing and apply manual pressure or mechanical clamp directly to bleeding site.	This provides temporary hemostasis.
• Anticipate fluid challenge.	This treats hypotension.
• Anticipate removal of catheter sheaths.	This may facilitate more optimal sealing of insertion site.
After removal of catheter sheaths:	
■ Maintain occlusive pressure dressing on cannulation site for 20 to 30 minutes.	Ice packs, sandbags, and mechanical clamps may be used to stop initial bleeding. Common devices include Angio-Seal, Perclose, VasoSeal, and FemoStop. Selection depends on physician preference.
■ Maintain bed rest in supine position with affected extremity straight for prescribed time.	This promotes clot formation.
■ Instruct patient to avoid sudden movement of affected extremity.	This facilitates clot formation and wound closure at the insertion site.
▲ Resume mobilization and ambulation as prescribed.	Protocols may vary according to institutional policy and type of procedure performed.

NDx Nursing Diagnosis

Ineffective Peripheral Tissue Perfusion

Common Related Factors	Defining Characteristics
Mechanical obstruction from arterial and venous sheaths Arterial vasospasm Thrombus formation Embolization Immobility Swelling of tissues Bleeding or hematoma	Decrease or loss of peripheral pulses Decrease in skin temperature of extremity Presence of mottling, pallor, cyanosis, and rubor in skin of distal affected extremity Delayed capillary refill in affected extremity Decrease or loss of sensation and motion

■ = Independent; ▲ = Collaborative

Percutaneous Coronary Intervention: PTCA, Atherectomy, Stents—cont'd

Common Expected Outcome

Patient maintains peripheral tissue perfusion in affected extremity, as evidenced by strong pulse and warm extremity.

NOC Outcomes
Circulatory Care: Arterial Insufficiency; Embolus Precautions
NIC Interventions
Circulation Status; Blood Coagulation

Ongoing Assessment

Actions/Interventions	Rationale
Preprocedure:	
■ Assess and document presence or absence and quality of all distal pulses.	This provides baseline for serial assessments.
■ Obtain Doppler ultrasonic reading for faint, non-palpable pulses. Indicate whether pulse check is with Doppler ultrasound. Mark location of faint pulses with an X.	Marking site of pulse facilitates easier location during postprocedure monitoring.
■ Assess and document skin color and temperature, presence or absence of pain, numbness, tingling, movement, and sensation of all extremities.	Knowledge of baseline circulatory status of extremities will assist in monitoring for postprocedure changes.
Postprocedure:	
■ Assess presence and quality of pulses distal to arterial cannulation site (radial for brachial artery, dorsalis pedis, and/or posterior tibial pulses for femoral artery) until stable.	Arterial thrombosis at puncture site may lead to occlusion of artery or distal thrombosis into extremity.
■ Check cannulation site for swelling and hematoma.	These may hinder peripheral circulation by constricting vessels or compressing nerves. Large hematomas can dissect into the retroperitoneum and be life threatening.
■ Assess for pseudoaneurysm (pulsatile mass, systolic bruit, groin pain).	This is an extraluminal cavity in communication with the adjacent femoral artery. Its presence is best confirmed by Doppler ultrasound.
■ Assess for arteriovenous (AV) fistula (pulsatile mass, groin pain, continuous bruit).	This is a communication between an artery and vein. Its presence is best assessed by Doppler ultrasound.

Therapeutic Interventions

Actions/Interventions	Rationale
Postprocedure:	
■ Ensure safety measures to prevent displacement of arterial and venous sheaths: • Maintain bed rest. • Keep cannulated extremity straight at all times. • Apply knee or leg immobilizer or soft restraint. • Do not elevate head of bed more than 30 degrees.	Significant changes in position cause the sheath to bend or move, which fosters potential bleeding and dislodgment. Researchers continue investigating benefits of early sheath removal and early ambulation.

■ = Independent; ▲ = Collaborative

Actions/Interventions

- Assist with meals, use of bedpan, and position changes appropriate to activity limitations.
- ▲ Continue prescribed dose of antiplatelets. Check clotting times periodically after start of infusion and after change in dose.

- ■ Do passive range-of-motion exercises to unaffected extremities every 2 to 4 hours as tolerated.
- ■ Instruct patient to report presence of pain, numbness, tingling, and decrease or loss of sensation and movement immediately.
- ■ Immediately report to physician decrease or loss of pulse, change in skin color and temperature, presence of pain, numbness, tingling, delayed capillary refill, and decrease or loss of sensation and motion.
- ■ If ineffective tissue perfusion is noted, anticipate removal of catheter sheath.
- ▲ Prepare for possible embolectomy.

Rationale

These medications prevent platelet aggregation, ischemic complications, and systemic clot formation. Patients with stent implantation require more aggressive anticoagulation until endothelialization occurs around the stent.

This prevents venous stasis and joint stiffness.

This is important for quick assessment, diagnosis, and treatment of complications.

These may signify ischemia and warrant immediate intervention.

Its presence may obstruct blood flow and cause further complications.

It is indicated to remove blood clot obstructing or compromising circulation.

• RELATED CARE PLANS

Anxiety, p. 15
Deficient fluid volume, p. 71
Impaired physical mobility, p. 126

Chronic Peripheral Arterial Occlusive Disease

Intermittent Claudication; Arterial Insufficiency; Arteriosclerosis Obliterans; PAD

Chronic peripheral arterial occlusive disease is most commonly caused by atherosclerosis resulting in reduced arterial blood flow to peripheral tissues, causing decreased nutrition and oxygenation at the cellular level. It can be characterized by four stages: asymptomatic, claudication, rest pain, and necrosis. Management is directed at removing vasoconstricting factors, improving peripheral blood flow, and reducing metabolic demands on the body. Because atherosclerosis is a progressive disease, older patients experience an increased incidence of this disease. Diabetes mellitus and tobacco use are significant risk factors in the development of chronic arterial insufficiency. Complications associated with arterial insufficiency include necrotic skin ulcers and progressive amputation of the affected extremity. Peripheral arterial disease (PAD) is a major cause of disability, significantly affecting quality of life. It is also a significant predictor of future cardiac and cerebrovascular events and is considered a cardiovascular disease risk equivalent.

■ = Independent; ▲ = Collaborative

Chronic Peripheral Arterial Occlusive Disease—cont'd

 Nursing Diagnosis

Ineffective Peripheral Tissue Perfusion

Common Related Factors

Atherosclerosis
Vasoconstriction secondary to medications and tobacco
Arterial spasm

Defining Characteristics

Pain, cramping, and ache in extremity
Intermittent claudication (cramping pain or weakness in one or both legs, relieved by rest)
Numbness of toes on walking, relieved by rest
Foot pain at rest
Tenderness, especially at toes
Cool extremities
Pallor of toes or foot when leg is elevated for 30 seconds
Dependent rubor (20 seconds to 2 minutes after leg is lowered)
Decreased capillary refill
Diminished or absent arterial pulses
Shiny skin
Loss of hair
Thickened, discolored nails
Ulcerated areas and gangrene
Edema
Change in skin texture

Common Expected Outcome

Patient maintains optimal tissue perfusion, as evidenced by warm extremities, palpable pulses, reduction in pain, and prevention of ulceration.

NOC Outcomes
Circulation Status;
Tissue Perfusion: Peripheral

NIC Interventions
Circulatory Precautions; Circulatory Care

Ongoing Assessment

Actions/Interventions

- Assess extremities for color, temperature, and texture. See Defining Characteristics above.

- Assess quality of peripheral pulses, noting capillary refill. If no pulses are noted, assess arterial blood flow using Doppler ultrasonic instrumentation.

Rationale

This disease occurs primarily in the legs. The extremities manifest coolness and pallor, with shiny hairless skin.

Arterial occlusions signify reduced peripheral blood flow and diminished or obliterated peripheral pulses. Routine examination should include palpation of femoral, popliteal, posterior tibial, and dorsalis pedis pulses. The posterior tibial pulse is the most sensitive indicator, in that the dorsalis pedis pulse is absent in approximately 10% of healthy people without disease.

■ = Independent; ▲ = Collaborative

Actions/Interventions	**Rationale**
■ Assess for dependent changes.	In advanced disease, the lower extremities become pale when the leg is elevated as a result of reduced capillary blood flow, and they become red (rubor) when placed in a dependent position.
■ Assess pain, numbness, and tingling for causative factors, time of onset, quality, severity, and relieving factors.	Intermittent claudication is the most common symptom of peripheral vascular disease. It is muscle pain that is precipitated by exercise or activity and is relieved with rest. It commonly occurs in the calf muscles or buttocks. Claudication may not be experienced if patients, especially older patients, have limited their physical activity secondary to cardiac or pulmonary disorders or other contributing problems. Pain that occurs at rest signifies more extensive disease requiring immediate attention. Tingling or numbness represents impaired perfusion to nerve tissue cells.
■ Assess segmental limb pressure measurements such as ankle-brachial index (ABI).	Normally the blood pressure (BP) readings in the lower extremities are higher than in the upper extremities. Normal ratio of ankle systolic pressure divided by brachial systolic pressure is 0.9 or greater. An ABI ratio of less than 0.9 in either leg is diagnostic of PAD. A ratio of 0.4 or greater signifies severe disease.
■ Assess for ulcerated areas on the skin.	Ulcers are commonly seen over bony prominences and on the toes and feet. Ulcers develop from chronic ischemia. If not treated, they can lead to gangrene.
▲ Monitor results of diagnostic tests: pulse volume recordings, vascular stress testing, magnetic resonance angiography, conventional arteriography, and digital subtraction angiography.	These are used to identify location and severity of disease; arteriography is useful for patients requiring surgical intervention. Exercise stress testing helps in reproducing claudication and provides data for evaluating the effectiveness of any treatment.

Therapeutic Interventions

Actions/Interventions	**Rationale**
■ Maintain affected extremity in a dependent position.	Gravity can increase peripheral blood flow. However, if edema is present in the lower legs, the feet should be elevated.
■ Keep extremity warm (socks or blankets).	Warmth promotes vasodilation and comfort.
■ Encourage need for progressive activity program, noting claudication.	During exercise, tissues do not receive adequate oxygenation from obstructed arteries and convert to anaerobic metabolism, of which lactic acid is a byproduct. Accumulation of lactic acid causes muscle spasm and discomfort. However, gradual progressive exercise helps promote collateral circulation. Patient should be encouraged to walk to the point of claudication, stop and rest, and continue walking.
■ Provide meticulous foot care.	Cleanliness is important to prevent infection. Minor trauma can result in skin breakdown. Toenails should be trimmed straight across.

■ = Independent; ▲ = Collaborative

Chronic Peripheral Arterial Occlusive Disease—cont'd

Actions/Interventions	Rationale
▲ Administer analgesics as ordered.	The pain caused by chronic PAD is difficult to treat. Analgesics may provide some relief, but antiplatelet and hemorrheologic agents, exercise, and percutaneous or surgical procedures may be more effective.
▲ Provide drug therapy as ordered:	
• Antiplatelets (aspirin, dipyridamole, clopidogrel).	These increase pain-free walking distance, resting limb blood flow, and ABI.
• Cilostazol (Pletal)	This suppresses platelet aggregation, causes arterial dilation, and improves pain-free walking distance. It should not be used in patients with heart failure.
• Pentoxifylline (Trental)	This decreases blood viscosity and reduces platelet aggregation. It has some effect on walking distance, but is less effective than Pletal. Therapeutic response may take months.
■ Explain potential future therapies as indicated: percutaneous transluminal angioplasty, laser-assisted angioplasty, atherectomy, surgical revascularization.	These therapies are appropriate for patients with more advanced disease, especially those with pain at rest.

 Nursing Diagnosis

Deficient Knowledge

Common Related Factors
New condition
Lack of resources
Complexity of lifestyle changes expected

Defining Characteristics
Many questions
Lack of questions
Misconceptions

Common Expected Outcome
Patient verbalizes self-care measures required to treat disease and prevent complications.

NOC Outcomes
Knowledge: Disease Process;
Knowledge: Treatment Regimen

NIC Interventions
Teaching: Disease Process; Teaching:
Prescribed Medication; Teaching:
Prescribed Activity or Exercise

■ = Independent; ▲ = Collaborative

Ongoing Assessment

Actions/Interventions

■ Assess knowledge of physiology of disease and treatment or preventive techniques prescribed.

Rationale

This is a lifelong condition. Patients need to understand the self-care strategies for which they are responsible. Attention should be directed toward both peripheral disease and risk for cardiovascular and cerebrovascular atherosclerosis.

Therapeutic Interventions

Actions/Interventions

■ Instruct on the physiology of blood supply to tissues.

■ Instruct on prescribed diagnostic tests.

■ Instruct on how to prevent progression of disease:

- Smoking:
  - Advise patient to avoid all tobacco.

  - Consider referral to smoking-cessation clinics.

- Dietary modification:
  - Provide diet counseling on need for reduction in fats.

  - If patient is overweight, provide diet counseling regarding attainment of ideal body weight.
  - Instruct patients with diabetes on appropriate diet.
- Hypertension management

■ Provide information on a daily exercise program:

- Walk on flat surface.
- Walk about half a block *after* intermittent claudication is experienced, unless otherwise ordered by the physician.

Rationale

Knowledge helps patient understand rationale for therapies.

Explaining ahead of time reduces anxiety and facilitates appropriate follow through.

The risk factors for atherosclerosis are smoking, hyperlipidemia, hypertension, diabetes mellitus, obesity, sedentary lifestyle, and family history of atherosclerosis. Atherosclerosis is not confined just to the lower extremities; it may occur in the coronary, cerebral, and renal vessels. Risk factor modification early in the disease may slow progression.

Nicotine further decreases already compromised circulation. Nicotine is a vasoconstrictor and increases blood viscosity. Smoking is the single risk factor most commonly implicated in the disease and is said to triple the risk of developing claudication.

Besides providing support for behavior change, adjuncts such as nicotine-replacement therapy or the drug bupropion hydrochloride may be prescribed.

Low-density lipoprotein cholesterol goal is less than 100 mg/dL, because patients with PAD are considered high risk for systemic atherosclerotic disease.

Obesity is a risk factor for PAD and cardiovascular disease.

Control of hypertension can improve systemic tissue perfusion.

Exercise is an essential treatment. It can promote collateral circulation. Consider referral to a vascular rehabilitation program.

Hill climbing/elevations further aggravate calf pain.

Ischemia is the stimulus for collateral circulation.

■ = Independent; ▲ = Collaborative

Chronic Peripheral Arterial Occlusive Disease—cont'd

Actions/Interventions	Rationale
• Stop and rest until all discomfort subsides.	Once the lactic acid clears from the local blood system, pain should subside.
• Repeat same procedure for total of 30 minutes two to three times daily.	Repetition serves to increase progress in improving walking ability.
■ Instruct on prevention of complications:	
• Effects of temperature:	
• Keep extremities warm. Wear stockings to bed.	Warmth promotes vasodilation.
• Keep house or apartment as warm as possible.	
• Wear warm clothes during winter.	
• Never apply hot water bottles or electric heating pads to feet or legs.	Burns may occur secondary to impaired nerve function.
• Avoid local cold applications and cold temperatures.	Cold causes vasoconstriction and reduced blood flow.
• Foot care:	
• Inspect daily.	Patients with diabetes are at increased risk. In addition, patients with diabetic neuropathy may have no perception of pain or injury.
• Wash feet daily with warm soap and water. Dry thoroughly by gentle patting. Never rub dry.	
• File or trim toenails carefully and only after soaking in warm water. File or trim straight across. See podiatrist as needed.	Poor peripheral circulation can result in tissue damage.
• Lubricate skin.	
• Wear clean stockings.	
• Do not walk barefoot.	Ulceration or gangrene of the toe or foot may follow mild trauma. Wearing fleece boots may help prevent injury.
• Wear correctly fitting shoes.	Constriction promotes skin breakdown.
• Inspect feet often for signs of ingrown toenails, sores, blisters, and other concerns.	Early assessment of potential problems reduces complications.
• Discuss available drug treatment.	Currently, antiplatelet and anticoagulant drugs are prescribed. They need to be taken on a long-term basis, thus patient compliance is key to success.
■ Explain that these medicines do not replace other preventive or treatment measures.	Exercise, appropriate positioning, hygienic foot care measures, along with invasive and noninvasive interventions are required for optimal treatment.
■ Provide information on other medical-surgical therapies as indicated:	
• Percutaneous transluminal angioplasty	Nonsurgical procedure uses balloon catheter to dilate obstructed artery.
• Atherectomy	This uses special catheter to "shave" away plaque.
• Surgical revascularization	This bypasses atherosclerotic lesion using autogenous saphenous vein or graft made from synthetic material.
• Amputation	This is required if gangrene is present.

■ = Independent; ▲ = Collaborative

Nursing Diagnosis

Impaired Skin Integrity

Common Related Factors

Pressure over bony prominences
Decreased peripheral tissue perfusion
Trauma to skin

Defining Characteristics

Ulceration over bony prominences, primarily toes and feet
Presence of gangrene
Atrophic skin

Common Expected Outcome

Patient's skin will be intact without signs of ulcers, redness, or infection.

NOC Outcomes

Tissue Integrity: Skin and Mucous Membranes; Wound Healing: Secondary Intention

NIC Interventions

Skin Care: Topical Treatments; Wound Care

Ongoing Assessment

Actions/Interventions

■ Assess lower extremity circulation:
  • Skin temperature and color
  • Pulses and capillary refill
  • Sensation
  • Hair and nail growth patterns

■ Assess skin for signs of redness, open wounds, and vascular ulcers:
  • Location
  • Pain
  • Ulcer characteristics
  • Condition of surrounding tissue

Rationale

Patients with significant arterial insufficiency are at greater risk for the development of skin ulcers. Decreased sensation associated with arterial insufficiency reduces patients' ability to recognize pressure and traumatic injuries. These injuries may go unnoticed until the wound becomes infected.

Arterial ulcers usually develop over bony prominences of toes and feet or any point of trauma. Patient may report pain that is burning or sharp. Ulcers have a well-defined border with a pale tissue bed. Eschar may be present. Ulcers may have drainage if infection is present. Surrounding tissue is usually pale on elevation or may have dependent rubor.

Therapeutic Interventions

Actions/Interventions

■ Protect skin from trauma and prolonged pressure.

■ Cover noninfected wounds with appropriate dressings.

Rationale

The poor peripheral circulation of PAD places the patient at high risk for injury.

A variety of dressing materials are available to protect arterial ulcers during the healing process. Hydrocolloid dressings that can be left in place for several days have the benefit of reducing skin trauma and infection associated with frequent dressing changes. Wound healing process is often prolonged.

■ = Independent; ▲ = Collaborative

Chronic Peripheral Arterial Occlusive Disease—cont'd

Cardiac and Vascular Care Plans

Actions/Interventions

■ Use sterile technique when caring for broken skin or vascular ulcers.

▲ Prepare for debridement of necrotic tissue from ulcer:

• Surgical

• Mechanical

• Pharmacological

▲ Administer antibiotics as prescribed.

■ Measure wound with each dressing change.

Rationale

Patient is at risk for wound infections because of decreased arterial blood flow to the tissue.

Removal of necrotic tissue from the ulcer is necessary to prevent infection and allow for healing of the wound.

Surgical debridement involves use of instruments to manually cut away necrotic tissue. This procedure may be done at the bedside. The patient usually does not experience pain because tissue is dead. However, mild analgesia may be indicated if the patient experiences discomfort. Bleeding will occur when healthy tissue is reached.

Mechanical debridement is usually accomplished with the application of sterile, wet-to-dry dressings. The wet gauze dressing adheres to the wound surface. Necrotic tissue is pulled away from the wound when the dressing is removed several hours after application.

This type of debridement involves the use of enzyme ointments to necrotic tissue in the wound. A sterile dressing is applied.

Antibiotics may be used for infected wounds or to prevent bacteremia. Route of administration may be oral, intravenous, or topical to the wound itself.

Wound should decrease in size as it heals. Regular measurement will aid in evaluating the effectiveness of treatment measures.

> ・ **RELATED CARE PLANS**
>
> Femoral-popliteal bypass, p. 295
> Pressure ulcers, p. 1104

Chronic Venous Insufficiency

Postphlebitic Syndrome; Primary Venous Valve Incompetence; Peripheral Venous Hypertension

Chronic venous insufficiency occurs in patients with incompetence of the venous valves. As many as 50% of patients with a deep vein thrombosis will develop postphlebitic syndrome within 5 to 10 years. Damage to a venous valve during a deep vein thrombosis is responsible for this form of chronic venous insufficiency. When venous valves are incompetent, the pressure from the venous blood column is no longer supported toward the heart. Instead, the pressure is directed as backflow to the ankle area. The increased backflow and pressure cause dilation of the venules of the skin, primarily in the ankle area, with

■ = Independent; ▲ = Collaborative

resulting movement of fluid from the vascular bed to the tissue bed. Because the endothelium of the venules is subjected to higher than normal pressures, red blood cells move across the vessel wall into the interstitial spaces. When these red blood cells break down, they deposit hemosiderin in the tissues. The presence of hemosiderin in the tissues produces the characteristic skin color changes in venous insufficiency. The clinical manifestations of chronic venous insufficiency include leg pain, edema, skin color changes, dermatitis, and ulceration. Once skin ulceration occurs, it is difficult to heal. Ulcers may recur with minimal skin trauma.

 Nursing Diagnosis

Risk for Ineffective Peripheral Tissue Perfusion

Common Risk Factors

Increased venous pressure
Dependent edema

Common Expected Outcome

Patient demonstrates measures to increase venous return and decrease leg edema.

NOC Outcomes
Tissue Perfusion: Peripheral;
    Circulation Status

NIC Intervention
Circulatory Care: Venous Insufficiency

Ongoing Assessment

Actions/Interventions

■ Assess lower extremities for the following:
  • Edema by measuring leg circumference

  • Skin color

  • Pain
  • Skin changes

Rationale

Edema of chronic venous insufficiency may not be relieved with elevation of the extremity.

Skin may have a dark brown discoloration because of deposition of hemosiderin in the tissues. This condition is sometimes referred to as *brawny edema*.

Patient may report a dull aching or heaviness in the legs.

Patient may have areas of induration due to liposclerosis. Areas of skin may be thinned or scarred from previous stasis ulcers.

■ = Independent; ▲ = Collaborative

Chronic Venous Insufficiency—cont'd

Therapeutic Interventions

Actions/Interventions

- Encourage patient to keep legs elevated when not ambulating. Patient may benefit from placement of the foot of the bed on 6-inch blocks to enhance venous return while sleeping.

▲ Apply appropriate venous compression devices such as support hose or pneumatic compression.

- Encourage the patient to avoid standing for prolonged periods.
- Teach the patient to change positions at frequent intervals.

- Teach the patient to avoid crossing legs at the knee when sitting.
- Encourage weight reduction for overweight patients.

- Encourage the patient to begin an exercise program.

▲ Administer prescribed diuretics.

Rationale

Goal of treatment is to reduce venous hypertension and reduce tissue edema. Elevation uses effects of gravity to promote venous return.

Prescription support hose are worn below the knee to support venous return. Hosiery should apply about 40 mm Hg of compression. Above-the-knee hosiery is not needed because the thigh muscle pump is usually adequate. Also, patients are less compliant with thigh-high compression because of difficulty with application and discomfort. Full-leg pneumatic compression devices may be used for short-term management of severe edema.

Standing in one position for a long time without walking will increase venous pressure and edema.

Remaining in one position for more than a couple of hours contributes to venous stasis by compressing veins.

The patient should avoid any position that compresses the veins and limits venous return.

Obesity contributes to venous insufficiency and venous hypertension through compression of the main veins in the pelvic region.

Walking, swimming, and cycling help promote venous return through contraction of the calf and thigh muscles. These muscles act as a pump to compress veins and support the column of blood returning to the heart.

Diuretic therapy may be used as an adjunct treatment to help mobilize fluid and reduce tissue edema.

NDx Nursing Diagnosis

Impaired Skin Integrity

Common Related Factors

Venous stasis ulcers
Stasis dermatitis

Defining Characteristics

Loss of epidermis and dermis in areas of chronic edema around medial malleolus or tibial area
Irregular-bordered ulcer with granulation tissue at base or soft yellow necrosis

■ = Independent; ▲ = Collaborative

Common Expected Outcome

Patient will have intact skin without signs of infection.

NOC Outcomes

Circulation Status; Wound Healing: Secondary Intention; Knowledge: Treatment Regimen

NIC Interventions

Circulatory Care: Venous Insufficiency; Wound Care; Skin Care: Topical Treatments; Teaching: Procedure/ Treatment; Teaching: Prescribed Activity/Exercise

Ongoing Assessment

Actions/Interventions	Rationale
■ Assess ulcer characteristics:	
• Location	Venous stasis ulcers are usually located around the medial malleolus or in the pretibial and laterotibial areas of the ankle.
• Size	Initially a venous stasis ulcer will be small, but it increases in size over time. The borders of venous ulcers tend to be irregular.
• Tissue bed	New ulcers will have a beefy red color consistent with the presence of granulating tissue. Older ulcers may have soft tissue necrosis at the base of the ulcer. This tissue may be yellowish green and have a stringy consistency.
• Surrounding tissue	Tissue surrounding the ulcer will be edematous. Skin may have a dark brown color and may be dry and flaky (chronic stasis dermatitis). Patient may report severe itching.
■ Measure surface of ulcer area at regular intervals; use pictures as appropriate.	Assessment provides data on response to therapy.
■ Monitor for signs of infection.	Many ulcers are already colonized.
▲ Obtain specimens for culture of any wound drainage.	If the ulcer is infected, cultures need to be obtained before appropriate antimicrobial therapy can be started.

Therapeutic Interventions

Actions/Interventions	Rationale
■ Maintain bed rest with leg elevation.	Reducing venous hypertension and edema is important for healing.
■ Cleanse wound using saline or noncytoxic cleanser prior to any dressing change.	Preparation of the wound bed is necessary to promote healing; necrotic tissue may require removal before treatment is started.

■ = Independent; ▲ = Collaborative

Cardiac and Vascular Care Plans

→ **Chronic Venous Insufficiency**—cont'd

Actions/Interventions	Rationale
▲ Apply appropriate dressings to protect ulcer during healing:	These ulcers heal through secondary intention. Use of long-term dressings with compression allows patient to be ambulatory.
• Unna boot	This traditional dressing covers the ulcer and provides compression. It is made of gauze dressing impregnated with zinc oxide, calamine lotion, and glycerin. Once applied, it forms a soft cast from the toes to just below the knee. The boot is covered with an elastic wrap. It can remain in place for 7 days or longer. Disadvantages include discomfort, limitations on bathing, and odor if drainage leaks through the dressing.
• Hydrocolloid (DuoDerm) or vapor-permeable dressing (Op-Site; Tegaderm)	These promote wound debridement and healing. Do not use with heavy exudate-producing wounds.
• Hydrogels (Aqua Skin, Carrasyn V)	These are used for shallow ulcers without exudates. They promote wound debridement and healing.
• Alginates (Kalginate, Kaltostat, Sorbsan)	These are for ulcers with exudates or moderate drainage; avoid in dry or heavily bleeding ulcers.
• Gauze with sodium chloride solution	This maintains a moist environment but requires multiple dressing changes.
▲ If the ulcer is not healing, anticipate surgical intervention.	Nonhealing ulcers may require debridement and skin grafting. For patients with repeated stasis ulcers, removal of veins with incompetent valves may be indicated. In some cases, valve transplantation may be used.
▲ Administer prescribed antibiotics.	Antibiotics are indicated if cellulitis is present in the affected area.
■ Once the ulcer is healed, teach the patient about measures to prevent new ulcer development:	Once the skin integrity has been compromised in venous insufficiency, it is less resistant to trauma. With the slightest trauma, the skin will break. An ulcer forms as a way to relieve pressure in the chronically edematous tissue.
• Continue wearing external compression hosiery as prescribed.	Maintaining compression to reduce venous hypertension is important in preventing new ulcers. Stockings should be applied when first getting up in the morning and removed at bedtime.
• Replace compression hosiery every 3 to 6 months.	Even without signs of wear, the compression effectiveness is lost with long-term use.
• Inspect skin around ankles daily.	Venous stasis ulcers usually develop around the perforator veins in the pretibial and medial malleolar areas of the ankles. The first sign may be a small reddened area that is tender to the touch.
• Keep skin clean and well lubricated.	The patient should avoid moisturizers that contain alcohol because of the drying effect on the skin.
• Exercise care when ambulating.	Even minor trauma to the skin can result in ulcer formation.

■ = Independent; ▲ = Collaborative

Pulmonary Edema, Acute

Pulmonary Congestion; Cardiogenic Pulmonary Edema; Acute Heart Failure

Pulmonary edema is a pathological state in which there is an abnormal accumulation of fluid in the alveoli and interstitial spaces of the lung. This fluid causes impaired gas exchange by interfering with diffusion between the pulmonary capillaries and the alveoli. It is commonly caused by left ventricular failure, altered capillary permeability of the lungs, adult respiratory distress syndrome, neoplasms, overhydration, and hypoalbuminemia. Acute pulmonary edema is considered a medical emergency.

NDx Nursing Diagnosis

Impaired Gas Exchange

Common Related Factors

Pulmonary-venous congestion
Alveolar-capillary membrane changes

Defining Characteristics

Restlessness and apprehension
Irritability
Cough
Pink, frothy sputum
Hypercapnia
Hypoxia
Crackles
Dyspnea
Cyanosis or pallor
Diaphoresis
Tachycardia
Pulmonary capillary wedge pressure (PCWP) greater than 25 to 30 mm Hg (in intensive care unit setting)

Common Expected Outcome

Patient exhibits signs and symptoms of improved ventilation and oxygenation, as evidenced by the following: normal arterial blood gases; oxygen saturation of 90% or greater; decreased crackles and rales and clear lung sounds; respiratory rate of 12 to 16 breaths/min; and relaxed, comfortable appearance.

NOC Outcomes

Respiratory Status: Gas Exchange;
    Respiratory Status: Ventilation

NIC Interventions

Respiratory Monitoring; Ventilation
    Assistance; Medication Administration

■ = Independent; ▲ = Collaborative

 **Pulmonary Edema, Acute**—cont'd

Ongoing Assessment

Actions/Interventions	Rationale
■ Assess respiratory rate and depth, presence of shortness of breath, and use of accessory muscles.	In the early stages, there is mild increase in respiratory rate. As it progresses, severe dyspnea, gurgling respirations, use of accessory muscles, and extreme breathlessness, as if "drowning" in one's own secretions, are noted.
■ Assess secretions.	Frothy, blood-tinged sputum is characteristic of pulmonary edema.
■ Assess lung sounds in all fields, noting aerations and presence of wheezes and crackles in lung bases. Document precise location.	Bubbling wheezes and crackles are easily heard over the entire chest, reflecting fluid-filled airways. The level of fluid ascends as the pulmonary edema worsens.
■ Assess for tachycardia, restlessness, diaphoresis, headache, and confusion.	These are early nonpulmonary signs of hypoxia. Lethargy and somnolence are late signs.
■ Monitor vital signs.	With initial hypoxia and hypercapnia, blood pressure (BP), heart rate (HR), and respiratory rate all rise. As the hypoxia and/or hypercapnia becomes severe, BP and HR will drop and arrhythmias may occur. Respiratory failure may ensue when the patient is unable to maintain the rapid respiratory rate.
▲ Use pulse oximeter to monitor oxygenation.	This tool is useful to detect changes in oxygenation. Oxygen saturation should be maintained at 90% or greater.
▲ Obtain and monitor serial arterial blood gases.	In early stages, there is a decrease in both Po_2 and Pco_2 secondary to hypoxemia and respiratory alkalosis from tachypnea. In later stages, the Po_2 continues to drop while the Pco_2 may increase, reflecting respiratory acidosis.
■ Assess skin, nail beds, and mucous membranes for pallor or cyanosis.	As oxygenation and perfusion become impaired, peripheral tissues become cyanotic.
▲ Monitor chest x-ray films.	As interstitial edema accumulates, the x-ray films show cloudy, white lung fields. Eventually, Kerley B lines appear.

Therapeutic Interventions

Actions/Interventions	Rationale
■ Position patient for optimal breathing patterns (high Fowler's position with feet dangling at bedside).	Upright position allows for increased thoracic capacity and full descent of diaphragm.
■ Encourage slow, deep breaths as appropriate.	This reduces tachypnea and alveolar collapse.
■ Assist with coughing or suctioning as needed.	These remove secretions to maintain patent airway.
▲ Provide oxygen as needed to maintain Po_2 at an acceptable level.	Supplemental oxygen may be required for the patient with pulmonary edema to offset the hypoperfusion.
▲ Anticipate endotracheal intubation and use of mechanical ventilation.	Early intubation and mechanical ventilation are recommended to prevent full decompensation of patient. Bilateral positive airway pressure (BiPAP) may also be indicated.

■ = Independent; ▲ = Collaborative

Pulmonary Edema, Acute

Actions/Interventions

▲ If arterial blood gases are expected to be drawn more often than at four 1-hour intervals, suggest appropriateness of an arterial line.

▲ Administer prescribed medication carefully, as follows:
- Morphine sulfate

- Sodium nitroprusside (Nipride)

- Nitrates
- Diuretics

- Inotropic agents

- Aminophylline

See also **Mechanical Ventilation**, *p. 459.*

Rationale

This is indicated for the patient's comfort and for ease in obtaining necessary arterial blood gases.

This medication reduces preload by vasodilation, decreases respiratory rate, and reduces anxiety.

This reduces afterload and is required if systemic vascular resistance is high.

These reduce preload by dilating venous vessels.

These reduce intravascular fluid volume and decrease preload.

These may be required to support BP and optimize cardiac output.

This dilates bronchioles and dilates venous vessels. However, it is also a cardiac stimulant. Patients must be observed for cardiac dysrhythmias.

Nursing Diagnosis

Decreased Cardiac Output

Common Related Factors	**Defining Characteristics**
Increased preload	Variations in hemodynamic parameters
Increased afterload	Dysrhythmias or electrocardiogram (ECG) changes
Decreased contractility	Weight gain, edema, and ascites
Combined etiological factors	Abnormal heart sounds
	Abnormal lung sounds
	Anxiety and restlessness
	Dizziness, weakness, and fatigue
	Pallor, clammy skin

Common Expected Outcome

Patient maintains cardiac output as evidenced by warm, dry skin; HR of 60 to 100 beats/min; clear breath sounds; good capillary refill; adequate urine output; and normal mentation.

NOC Outcome
Cardiac Pump Effectiveness

NIC Interventions
Invasive Hemodynamic Monitoring; Hemodynamic Regulation

■ = Independent; ▲ = Collaborative

Cardiac and Vascular Care Plans

→ **Pulmonary Edema, Acute—cont'd**

Ongoing Assessment

Actions/Interventions	Rationale
■ Assess skin color, temperature, and moisture.	Cool, pale, clammy skin is secondary to compensatory increase in sympathetic nervous system stimulation and low cardiac output and desaturation.
▲ Assess HR, BP, and pulse pressure. Use direct intra-arterial monitoring as ordered.	Sinus tachycardia and increased arterial BP are seen in early stages to maintain an adequate cardiac output.; BP drops as condition deteriorates. Auscultatory BP may be unreliable secondary to vasoconstriction. Pulse pressure (systolic minus diastolic) decreases in shock. Older patients have a reduced response to catecholamines; thus their response to decreased cardiac output may be blunted, with less increase in HR.
■ Assess peripheral and central pulses, including capillary refill.	Pulses are weak with reduced stroke volume and cardiac output. Capillary refill is slow, sometimes absent.
■ Assess for mental status changes.	Early signs of cerebral hypoxia are restlessness and anxiety, with confusion and loss of consciousness occurring in later stages. Older patients are especially susceptible to reduced perfusion to vital organs.
■ Assess lung sounds.	Crackles, rhonchi, and wheezes develop as fluid overload worsens.
■ Assess fluid balance and weight gain.	Compromised regulatory mechanisms may result in fluid and sodium retention. Body weight is a more sensitive indicator of fluid or sodium retention than intake and output.
■ Assess urine output with a Foley catheter.	The renal system compensates for low BP by retaining water. Oliguria is a classic sign of inadequate renal perfusion from reduced cardiac output.
■ Assess heart sounds.	S_3 denotes reduced left ventricular ejection and is a classic sign of left ventricular failure. S_4 occurs with reduced compliance of the left ventricle, which impairs diastolic filling.
■ Assess cardiac rhythm and ECG.	Cardiac dysrhythmias may occur from low perfusion, acidosis, or hypoxia, as well as from side effects of cardiac medications used to treat this condition. The 12-lead ECG may provide evidence of myocardial ischemia (ST-segment and T-wave changes).
▲ Assess pulse oximetry and arterial blood gases.	Pulse oximetry is a useful tool to detect changes in oxygenation. Oxygen saturation should be kept at 90% or greater. As condition worsens, aerobic metabolism ceases and lactic acidosis ensues, raising the level of carbon dioxide and pH.
▲ If hemodynamic monitoring is in place, assess central venous pressure (CVP), pulmonary artery pressure, pulmonary capillary wedge pressure (PCWP), and cardiac output/cardiac index (CO/CI).	CVP provides information on filling pressures of the right side of the heart; pulmonary artery diastolic pressure and PCWP reflect left-sided fluid volumes. Cardiac output provides an objective number to guide therapy.

■ = Independent; ▲ = Collaborative

Therapeutic Interventions

Actions/Interventions

▲ Anticipate need for hemodynamic monitoring.

■ Position the patient for optimal reduction of preload (high Fowler's position, dangling feet at bedside).

■ Anticipate prescribed medications:
- Positive inotropic agents (e.g., dopamine, dobutamine, milrinone)
- Vasodilators (e.g., nitrates, nitroprusside; angiotensin-converting enzyme inhibitor)
- Diuretics
- Morphine

Rationale

Swan-Ganz catheter provides pulmonary artery and PCWP measurements that guide therapy.

This position reduces preload by pooling blood in the lower extremities and decreasing venous return.

These medications augment myocardial contractility, increase BP, and increase CO/CI.

These reduce preload, reduce afterload, and improve oxygenation.

These reduce intravascular fluid volume and reduce PCWP.

This medicine reduces pulmonary congestion and relieves dyspnea.

NDx Nursing Diagnosis

Anxiety

Common Related Factors

Dyspnea
Excessive monitoring equipment
Increased staff attention
Impact of illness
Threat of death

Defining Characteristics

Sympathetic stimulation
Restlessness
Increased awareness
Increased questioning
Avoidance of looking at equipment
Constant demands and complaints
Uncooperative behavior

Common Expected Outcomes

Patient appears relaxed and comfortable.
Patient verbalizes reduced anxiety.

NOC Outcomes
Anxiety Self-Control; Coping

NIC Interventions
Anxiety Reduction; Calming Technique

Ongoing Assessment

Actions/Interventions

■ Assess anxiety level (mild, severe). Note signs and symptoms, especially nonverbal communication.

■ Assess coping factors.

Rationale

Acute pulmonary edema can result in an acute life-threatening situation that will produce high levels of anxiety in the patient as well as in significant others.

Anxiety and ways of decreasing perceived anxiety are highly individualized. Interventions are most effective when they are consistent with the individual's established coping pattern.

■ = Independent; ▲ = Collaborative

Cardiac and Vascular Care Plans

Pulmonary Edema, Acute–cont'd

Therapeutic Interventions

Actions/Interventions	Rationale
■ Acknowledge awareness of the patient's anxiety.	Acknowledgment of the patient's feelings validates the feelings and communicates acceptance of those feelings.
■ Maintain confident, assured manner.	The staff's anxiety may be easily perceived by the patient. The patient's feeling of stability increases in a calm, nonthreatening atmosphere.
■ Assure the patient and significant others of close, continuous monitoring that will ensure prompt intervention.	This provides a measure of safety.
■ Reduce unnecessary external stimuli.	Anxiety may escalate with excessive conversation, noise, and equipment around the patient.
■ Explain all procedures as appropriate, keeping explanations basic.	Information helps allay anxiety. Patients who are anxious may not be able to comprehend anything more than simple, clear, brief instructions.
■ Provide a quiet, private place for significant others to wait.	A quiet environment can reduce anxiety.
■ Refer to other support persons (e.g., clergy, social worker) as appropriate.	Additional specialty expertise may be required.

> • RELATED CARE PLANS
>
> Disturbed sleep pattern, p. 177
> Dysrhythmias, p. 288
> Excess fluid volume, p. 74
> Ineffective breathing pattern, p. 28

Shock, Anaphylactic

Allergic Reaction; Distributive Shock; Vasogenic Shock

Anaphylactic shock is a potentially life-threatening situation characterized by massive vasodilation and increased capillary permeability. It is the most severe systemic form of hypersensitivity (antigen-antibody interaction); it occurs within 1 to 2 minutes after contact with an antigenic substance and progresses rapidly to respiratory distress, vascular collapse, systemic shock, and possibly death if emergency treatment is not initiated. Causative agents include severe reactions to drugs, insect bites, diagnostic contrast media, transfused blood or blood products, or food.

■ = Independent; ▲ = Collaborative

Nursing Diagnosis

Ineffective Breathing Pattern

Common Related Factors

Facial angioedema
Bronchospasm
Laryngeal edema

Defining Characteristics

Dyspnea
Wheezing
Tachypnea
Stridor
Tightness of chest
Cyanosis
Respiratory distress

Common Expected Outcome

Patient's breathing pattern is restored as evidenced by eupnea, regular respiratory rate or rhythm, and improved lung sounds.

NOC Outcome
Respiratory Status: Ventilation

NIC Interventions
Respiratory Monitoring;
    Ventilation Assistance

Ongoing Assessment

Actions/Interventions

- Monitor respiratory status and observe for changes (e.g., increased shortness of breath, tachypnea, dyspnea, wheezing, stridor, hoarseness, coughing).

- Assess patient for the sensation of a narrowed airway.

- Auscultate lung sounds and report changes.

- Assess presence of angioedema.

Rationale

Histamine is the primary chemical mediator of anaphylaxis. Through stimulation of histamine receptors (H_1), it causes smooth muscle contraction in the bronchi. As the anaphylactic reaction progresses, the patient develops wheezing, dyspnea, and increased pulmonary secretions. Vascular to interstitial fluid shifts contribute to respiratory distress through swelling in the upper airways.

Antigen-antibody reactions result in severe bronchial airway narrowing, edema, and obstruction. As airways narrow, patients demonstrate an increase in respiratory effort.

Wheezing may be heard over the entire chest. However, as the bronchial constriction worsens, audible wheezing will decrease. Therefore it is important to note decreasing air movement, not just adventitious lung sounds.

Angioedema is noticeable in the eyelids, lips, tongue, hands, and feet, resulting from capillary fluid shifts.

■ = Independent; ▲ = Collaborative

Shock, Anaphylactic—cont'd

Actions/Interventions

▲ Assess pulse oximetry and arterial blood gases.

■ Assess level of anxiety.

Rationale

Pulse oximetry is a useful tool to detect changes in oxygenation. Oxygen saturation should be kept at 90% or greater. As shock increases, aerobic metabolism ceases and lactic acidosis ensues, raising the level of carbon dioxide and pH.

Respiratory distress and shock are life-threatening situations that produce high levels of anxiety in the patient and significant others.

Therapeutic Interventions

Actions/Interventions

■ Position the patient upright.

■ Instruct the patient to breathe deeply and slow down respiratory rate.

▲ Administer oxygen as prescribed.

■ Provide reassurance and allay anxiety by staying with the patient during acute distress.

■ Maintain patent airway. Anticipate emergency intubation or tracheostomy if stridor occurs.

▲ Administer medications as ordered.
   • Epinephrine

   • Corticosteroids

   • Antihistamines

   • Bronchodilators
   • Glucagon

▲ Provide intravenous fluids.

■ Maintain a calm, assured manner.

■ Assure the patient and significant others of close, continuous monitoring that will ensure prompt intervention.

Rationale

This provides for optimal lung expansion and ease of breathing.

Focusing on breathing may help calm the patient and facilitate improved gas exchange.

Oxygen increases arterial saturation.

Air hunger can produce an extremely anxious state.

Respiratory distress may progress rapidly. If laryngeal edema is present, endotracheal intubation will be required to maintain a patent airway.

This is the cornerstone of treatment for anaphylaxis. It relaxes pulmonary vessels to improve air exchange and stabilizes cellular permeability.

These stabilize the cell membrane and reduce cellular permeability.

These block the action of histamines and reduce cellular edema.

These reduce bronchospasm and open airways.

This reduces hypotension in patients taking β-blocking medications.

Hypotension due to vasodilation and distributive shock responds to fluid resuscitation.

The staff's anxiety may be easily perceived by the patient. The patient's feeling of stability increases in a calm, nonthreatening environment.

This provides a measure of safety.

■ = Independent; ▲ = Collaborative

Nursing Diagnosis

Decreased Cardiac Output

Common Related Factors

Generalized vasodilation (decreased preload and after-load)

Increased capillary permeability (fluid shifts)

Defining Characteristics

Hypotension

Tachycardia

Decreased central venous pressure (CVP)

Decreased peripheral pulses

Decreased pulmonary pressures

Oliguria

Common Expected Outcome

Patient achieves adequate cardiac output, as evidenced by strong peripheral pulses; normal vital signs; urine output greater than 30 mL/hr; warm, dry skin; and alert, responsive mentation.

NOC Outcomes

Cardiac Pump Effectiveness; Circulation Status; Immune Status

NIC Interventions

Hemodynamic Regulation; Invasive Hemodynamic Monitoring; Allergy Management; Shock Management: Vasogenic

Ongoing Assessment

Actions/Interventions

■ Monitor vital signs with frequent monitoring of blood pressure (BP), specifically direct intraarterial monitoring as ordered.

■ Assess skin temperature and peripheral pulses.

■ Assess for mental status changes.

■ Monitor urine output with a Foley catheter.

■ Monitor cardiac rhythm for dysrhythmias.

Rationale

Auscultatory BP may be unreliable. The intense vasodilation results in severe hypovolemia and hypotension.

The massive vasodilation and increased capillary permeability eventually lead to reduced peripheral blood flow and tissue perfusion. Pulses are weak with reduced stroke volume and cardiac output.

Early signs of cerebral hypoxia are restlessness and anxiety, with confusion and loss of consciousness occurring in later stages. Older patients are especially susceptible to reduced perfusion to vital organs.

The renal system compensates for low BP by retaining water. Oliguria is a classic sign of inadequate renal perfusion.

Cardiac dysrhythmias may occur from the low perfusion state, acidosis, or hypoxia.

■ = Independent; ▲ = Collaborative

Cardiac and Vascular Care Plans

→ Shock, Anaphylactic—cont'd

Actions/Interventions

▲ Assess pulse oximetry.

▲ Monitor arterial blood gas results.

▲ If hemodynamic monitoring is in place, assess CVP, pulmonary artery pressure, pulmonary capillary wedge pressure, and cardiac output/cardiac index.

Rationale

Pulse oximetry is a useful tool to detect changes in oxygenation. Oxygen saturation should be kept at 90% or greater.

In the early compensatory stage of shock, the patient may develop respiratory alkalosis, as indicated by a decreased Pco_2 and an elevated pH. As the shock state progresses, the patient will develop respiratory acidosis as a result of hypoventilation and metabolic acidosis as a result of poor tissue perfusion and lactic acidosis.

CVP provides information on filling pressures of the right side of the heart; pulmonary artery pressure and pulmonary capillary wedge pressure reflect left-sided fluid volumes.

Therapeutic Interventions

Actions/Interventions

▲ Place patient in the physiological position for shock: head of bed flat, with the trunk horizontal and lower extremities elevated 20 to 30 degrees with knees straight.

▲ Administer parenteral fluids using a large-bore needle. Avoid fluid overload in older patients.

▲ Anticipate administration of volume expanders.

▲ Administer medications as prescribed, noting responses:
  • Epinephrine

  • Antihistamine (diphenhydramine)

  • Corticosteroids

  • Glucagon

▲ If transfused blood or blood products are the cause of the reaction, immediately stop the infusion and keep the vein open with normal saline solution; immediately notify the physician.

Rationale

This promotes venous return. Do not use Trendelenburg's (head down) position because it causes pressure against the diaphragm.

Fluids are often required to reverse hypovolemia.

These may be indicated to correct hypovolemia.

This is an endogenous catecholamine with both α- and β-receptor stimulating actions that provide rapid relief of hypersensitivity reactions. It is unknown whether epinephrine prevents mediator release or whether it reverses the action of mediators on target tissues, but its early administration is critical. For prolonged reactions, it may be necessary to repeat the dose.

This reduces circulating histamines and reverses the adverse effects of histamine.

These may be used to suppress immune and inflammatory responses and reduce capillary permeability.

Glucagon reverses hypotension in patients taking β-blocker medications who do not respond to fluid administration and epinephrine.

Safety measures reduce further injury.

■ = Independent; ▲ = Collaborative

Nursing Diagnosis

Risk for Impaired Skin Integrity

Common Risk Factor

Manifestations of allergic reaction

Common Expected Outcome

Patient experiences decrease in urticaria and pruritus, and skin condition returns to normal.

NOC Outcome
Tissue Integrity: Skin and Mucous Membranes

NIC Intervention
Medication Administration

Ongoing Assessment

Actions/Interventions	Rationale
■ Observe for signs of flushing (localized or generalized).	This is due to vasodilation effect.
■ Watch for development of rashes; note character: macules, papules, pustules, petechiae, urticaria.	Rashes occur as a manifestation of the allergic reaction mediated by the release of histamine.
■ Assess for swelling or edema.	This results from capillary fluid shifts.
■ Assess for urticaria and pruritus.	Rash/hives often cause intense itching.

Therapeutic Interventions

Actions/Interventions	Rationale
■ Instruct the patient not to scratch.	Scratching can cause further skin damage, setting up an itch-scratch-itch cycle.
▲ Give medications (e.g., antihistamine) as prescribed.	Administration of antihistamines will relieve the symptoms by blocking the action of histamine.
■ Apply cool washcloths or covered ice.	Cool temperatures soothe irritated, edematous areas.
■ Clip nails if patient is scratching while sleeping.	This reduces skin trauma.
■ Put mittens on hands if necessary.	Mittens prevent excessive scratching.

■ = Independent; ▲ = Collaborative

Cardiac and Vascular Care Plans

 Shock, Anaphylactic—cont'd

 Nursing Diagnosis

Deficient Knowledge: Allergens

Common Related Factors
No previous experience
Misinterpretation of information
Lack of recall

Defining Characteristics
Recurrent allergic reactions
Inability to identify allergens

Common Expected Outcomes
Patient or significant others verbalize understanding of allergic reaction, prevention, and treatment.
Patient and significant others understand need to inform health care providers of allergies, need to wear medical alert bracelet/necklace, and the importance of seeking emergency care.

NOC Outcomes
Knowledge: Disease Process;
Knowledge: Treatment Regimen

NIC Interventions
Allergy Management;
Teaching: Disease Process

Ongoing Assessment

Actions/Interventions

- Assess knowledge of patient's condition and exposure to allergens.

Rationale

Not all allergies occur in youth. Adult-onset experiences may find the patient unaware.

Therapeutic Interventions

Actions/Interventions

- Explain symptoms and interventions.

- Instruct the patient or significant others about factors that can precipitate a recurrence of shock and ways to prevent or avoid these precipitating factors.

- Explain factors that may increase risk of anaphylaxis (e.g., certain drugs, blood products, bee stings, food) and environmental control measures to be instituted.

- Instruct the patient on use of insect sting kits (containing a chewable antihistamine, epinephrine in prefilled syringe, and instructions for use) as appropriate, and indicate how they are to be obtained.

- Discuss the possibility of undergoing desensitization therapy.

- Instruct the patient with known allergies to wear medical alert identification.

Rationale

The patient needs self-help information to prevent anaphylactic shock.

The patient is at high risk for developing anaphylactic shock in the future if exposed to the same antigenic substance.

Information enables the patient to take control and make needed lifestyle modifications.

In situations in which the patient cannot completely avoid exposure to allergens, he or she needs to have access to emergency treatment resources for immediate administration.

Therapy lessens the risk of a life-threatening allergic reaction.

In case of emergency, those providing care will be aware of this significant history.

■ = Independent; ▲ = Collaborative

Actions/Interventions

- Ensure that the patient or significant others are made aware that when giving medical history they should include all allergies (e.g., latex, medications, contrast dyes, blood products).

Rationale

Safety measures reduce potential injury.

Shock, Cardiogenic

Pump Failure; Acute Pulmonary Edema; Intraaortic Balloon Pump; Ventricular Assist Device

Cardiogenic shock is an acute state of decreased tissue perfusion caused by the impaired pumping of the heart. It is usually associated with myocardial infarction, cardiomyopathies, valvular stenosis, massive pulmonary embolism, cardiac surgery, or cardiac tamponade. It is a self-perpetuating condition because coronary blood flow to the myocardium is compromised, causing further ischemia and ventricular dysfunction. Patients with massive myocardial infarctions involving 40% or more of the left ventricular muscle mass are at highest risk for developing cardiogenic shock. The mortality rate for cardiogenic shock often exceeds 80%. This care plan focuses on the care of an unstable patient in a shock state.

 NDx Nursing Diagnosis

Decreased Cardiac Output

Common Related Factors

Mechanical:
- Impaired left ventricular contractility
- Dysrhythmias

Structural:
- Valvular dysfunction
- Septal defects

Defining Characteristics

Mental status changes (restlessness, agitation)
Variations in hemodynamic parameters
Pale, cool, clammy skin
Cyanosis and mottling of extremities
Oliguria and anuria
Sustained hypotension with narrowing of pulse pressure
Pulmonary congestion
Respiratory alkalosis or metabolic acidosis

Common Expected Outcome

Patient achieves adequate cardiac output as evidenced by strong peripheral pulses; normal vital signs; urine output greater than 30 mL/hr; warm, dry skin; and alert, responsive mentation.

NOC Outcomes

Cardiac Pump Effectiveness; Circulation Status; Tissue Perfusion: Cardiac, Renal, Cerebral

NIC Interventions

Invasive Hemodynamic Monitoring; Hemodynamic Regulation; Dysrhythmia Management; Circulatory Care: Mechanical Assist Device; Shock Management: Cardiac

■ = Independent; ▲ = Collaborative

Shock, Cardiogenic—cont'd

Ongoing Assessment

Actions/Interventions	Rationale
■ Assess skin color, temperature, and moisture.	Cool, pale, clammy skin is secondary to compensatory increase in sympathetic nervous system stimulation and low cardiac output and desaturation.
▲ Assess heart rate (HR), blood pressure (BP), and pulse pressure. Use direct intraarterial monitoring as ordered.	Sinus tachycardia and increased arterial BP are seen in early stages to maintain an adequate cardiac output. BP drops as condition deteriorates. Auscultatory BP may be unreliable secondary to vasoconstriction. Pulse pressure (systolic minus diastolic) decreases in shock. Older patients have a reduced response to catecholamines; thus their response to decreased cardiac output may be blunted, with less increase in HR.
■ Assess peripheral and central pulses, including capillary refill.	Pulses are weak with reduced stroke volume and cardiac output. Capillary refill is slow, sometimes absent.
■ Assess for mental status changes.	Early signs of cerebral hypoxia are restlessness and anxiety, with confusion and loss of consciousness occurring in later stages. Older patients are especially susceptible to reduced perfusion to vital organs.
■ Assess respiratory rate, rhythm, and breath sounds.	Rapid, shallow respirations and presence of crackles and wheezes are characteristic of shock.
■ Assess urine output with a Foley catheter.	The renal system compensates for low BP by retaining water. Oliguria is a classic sign of inadequate renal perfusion from reduced cardiac output.
■ Assess fluid balance and weight gain.	Compromised regulatory mechanisms may result in fluid and sodium retention. Body weight is a more sensitive indicator of fluid or sodium retention than intake and output.
■ Assess lung sounds.	Crackles, rhonchi, and wheezes develop as fluid overload worsens.
■ Assess heart sounds.	S_3 denotes reduced left ventricular ejection and is a classic sign of left ventricular failure. S_4 occurs with reduced compliance of the left ventricle, which impairs diastolic filling.
■ Assess cardiac rhythm and electrocardiogram (ECG).	Cardiac dysrhythmias may occur from low perfusion, acidosis, or hypoxia, as well as from side effects of cardiac medications used to treat this condition. The 12-lead ECG may provide evidence of myocardial ischemia (ST-segment and T-wave changes) or pericardial tamponade (decreased voltage of QRS complexes).
▲ Assess pulse oximetry and arterial blood gases.	Pulse oximetry is a useful tool to detect changes in oxygenation. Oxygen saturation should be kept at 90% or greater. As shock increases, aerobic metabolism ceases and lactic acidosis ensues, raising the level of carbon dioxide and pH.
▲ If hemodynamic monitoring is in place, assess central venous pressure (CVP), pulmonary artery pressure, pulmonary capillary wedge pressure (PCWP), and cardiac output/cardiac index (CO/CI).	CVP provides information on filling pressures of the right side of the heart; pulmonary artery diastolic pressure and PCWP reflect left-sided fluid volumes. CO/CI provides an objective number to guide therapy.

■ = Independent; ▲ = Collaborative

Actions/Interventions

■ Assess electrolytes and glucose levels.

Rationale

Moderate hyperglycemia is a normal stress response; electrolytes may reveal hypernatremia/hyponatremia or hyperkalemia/hypokalemia.

Therapeutic Interventions

Actions/Interventions

■ Place patient in optimal position, usually supine with head of bed slightly elevated.

▲ Administer oxygen.

▲ Administer intravenous fluids.

▲ Initiate and titrate drug therapy as ordered:

- Inotropic agents:
  - Dopamine

  - Dobutamine

  - Milrinone
- Vasodilators:
  - Sodium nitroprusside (Nipride)

  - Intravenous nitroglycerin

  - Diuretics

  - Antidysrhythmics

- Vasopressors (e.g., epinephrine, norepinephrine, phenylephrine)

  - Morphine

Rationale

This promotes venous return and facilitates ventilation.

Oxygen may be required to maintain oxygen saturation above 92% or as indicated by order or protocol.

Optimal fluid status ensures effective ventricular filling pressure. Too little fluid reduces circulating blood volume and ventricular filling pressures; too much fluid can cause pulmonary edema in a failing heart. PCWP guides therapy.

Therapy is more effective when initiated early. The goal is to maintain systolic BP greater than 90 to 100 mm Hg.

Positive inotropic and chronotropic effect on the heart improves stroke volume and cardiac output; high dose, however, can cause peripheral vasoconstriction and can be arrhythmogenic.

Positive inotropic effect increases cardiac output and reduces afterload by decreasing peripheral vasoconstriction, also resulting in higher cardiac output.

This increases contractility and vasodilation.

Nitroprusside increases cardiac output by decreasing afterload, and produces peripheral and systemic vasodilation by direct action to the smooth muscles of blood vessels.

This may be used to reduce excess preload contributing to pump failure, and to reduce afterload.

These are used when volume overload is contributing to pump failure.

These are used when cardiac dysrhythmias are further compromising a low-output state.

Vasopressors increase the force of myocardial contraction and constrict arteries and veins. They augment the vasoconstriction that occurs with shock to increase perfusion pressure. They are not routinely used unless aforementioned medications have failed to improve coronary perfusion.

This reduces pulmonary congestion and relieves dyspnea.

■ = Independent; ▲ = Collaborative

Shock, Cardiogenic—cont'd

Actions/Interventions

▲ Provide electrolyte replacement as ordered.

▲ If mechanical assistance by counterpulsation is indicated, institute intraaortic balloon pump (IABP) or ventricular assist device (VAD).

▲ Anticipate need for surgical intervention as needed.

Rationale

Laboratory results guide therapy.

Mechanical assist devices such as VAD or IABP provide temporary circulatory support to improve cardiac output. These devices are used in cardiogenic shock when the patient does not respond to pharmacological interventions. IABP increases myocardial oxygen supply and reduces myocardial workload through increased coronary artery perfusion. The patient's stroke volume increases and thus improves perfusion of vital organs. The nurse needs to follow unit protocols for the management of the patient with a mechanical VAD.

Acute valvular problems or septal defects may require surgical treatment.

NDx Nursing Diagnosis

Impaired Gas Exchange

Common Related Factors

Altered blood flow
Alveolar capillary membrane changes

Defining Characteristics

Fast, labored breathing
May have Cheyne-Stokes respirations
Crackles
Tachycardia
Hypoxia
Hypercapnia
Irritability
Restlessness
Confusion
Headache

Common Expected Outcome

Patient achieves adequate oxygenation, as evidenced by respiratory rate less than 20 beats/min, Po$_2$ greater than 80 mm Hg, and baseline HR for patient.

NOC Outcome
Respiratory Status: Gas Exchange

NIC Interventions
Respiratory Monitoring; Airway Insertion and Stabilization; Airway Management

■ = Independent; ▲ = Collaborative

Ongoing Assessment

Actions/Interventions

■ Assess rate, rhythm, and depth of respiration.

■ Assess lung sounds, noting areas of decreased ventilation and the presence of adventitious sounds.

■ Assess for tachycardia, restlessness, diaphoresis, headache, and confusion.

■ Monitor vital signs.

▲ Use pulse oximeter to monitor oxygenation.

▲ Monitor arterial blood gases and note changes.

■ Assess skin, nail beds, and mucous membranes for pallor or cyanosis.

Rationale

In the early stages of shock, the patient's respiratory rate will be rapid. As shock progresses, the respirations become shallow, and the patient will begin to hypoventilate. Respiratory failure develops as the patient experiences respiratory muscle fatigue and decreased lung compliance.

Moist crackles are caused by increased pulmonary capillary permeability and increased intraalveolar edema.

These are early nonpulmonary signs of hypoxia. Lethargy and somnolence are late signs.

With initial hypoxia and hypercapnia, BP, HR and respiratory rate all increase. As the hypoxia and/or hypercapnia becomes severe, BP and HR will decrease and arrhythmias may occur. Respiratory failure may ensue when the patient is unable to maintain the rapid respiratory rate.

This tool is useful to detect changes in oxygenation. Oxygen saturation should be maintained at 90% or greater.

Increasing $PaCO_2$ and decreasing PaO_2 are signs of respiratory failure. As the patient's condition begins to fail, the respiratory rate will decrease and $PaCO_2$ will begin to increase.

As oxygenation and perfusion become impaired, peripheral tissues become cyanotic.

Therapeutic Interventions

Actions/Interventions

■ Place the patient in optimal position for ventilation.

▲ Initiate oxygen therapy as prescribed.

■ Suction as needed.

▲ Prepare patient for mechanical ventilation if noninvasive oxygen therapy is ineffective:
  • Explain need for mechanical ventilation.
  • Assist in intubation procedure.
  • Institute mechanical ventilation (see p. 459).

Rationale

Slightly elevated head of bed facilitates diaphragmatic movement.

Supplemental oxygen may be required to maintain PO_2 at an acceptable level. The patient in shock has great need for oxygen to offset the hypoperfusion and metabolic state.

Suction removes secretions if the patient is unable to effectively clear the airway.

Early intubation and mechanical ventilation are recommended to prevent full decompensation of patient.

■ = Independent; ▲ = Collaborative

Shock, Cardiogenic—cont'd

 Nursing Diagnosis

Anxiety

Common Related Factors

Guarded prognosis; mortality rate 80%
Fear of death
Unfamiliar environment
Dyspnea
Dependence on IABP or mechanical ventilation

Defining Characteristics

Sympathetic stimulation
Restlessness
Increased awareness
Increased questioning
Uncooperative behavior
Avoids looking at equipment or keeps vigilant watch over equipment

Common Expected Outcomes

Patient appears calm and trusting of medical care.
Patient verbalizes fears and concerns.

NOC Outcomes
Anxiety Self-Control; Coping

NIC Interventions
Anxiety Reduction;
  Support System Enhancement

Ongoing Assessment

Actions/Interventions

■ Assess anxiety level (mild, severe). Note signs and symptoms, especially nonverbal communication.

■ Assess coping factors.

Rationale

Shock can result in an acute life-threatening situation that will produce high levels of anxiety in the patient as well as in significant others.

Anxiety and ways of decreasing perceived anxiety are highly individualized. Interventions are most effective when they are consistent with the individual's established coping pattern.

Therapeutic Interventions

Actions/Interventions

■ Acknowledge awareness of the patient's anxiety.

■ Maintain confident, assured manner.

■ Assure patient and significant others of close, continuous monitoring that will ensure prompt intervention.

Rationale

Acknowledgment of the patient's feelings validates the feelings and communicates acceptance of those feelings.

The staff's anxiety may be easily perceived by the patient. The patient's feeling of stability increases in a calm and nonthreatening atmosphere.

This provides a measure of safety.

■ = Independent; ▲ = Collaborative

Actions/Interventions	Rationale
■ Reduce unnecessary external stimuli.	Anxiety may escalate with excessive conversation, noise, and equipment around the patient.
■ Explain all procedures as appropriate, keeping explanations basic.	Information helps allay anxiety. Patients who are anxious may not be able to comprehend anything more than simple, clear, brief instructions.
■ Provide a quiet, private place for significant others to wait.	A quiet environment can reduce anxiety.
■ Refer to other support persons (e.g., clergy, social worker) as appropriate.	Additional specialty expertise may be required.

> **• RELATED CARE PLANS**
>
> Imbalanced nutrition: less than body
>   requirements, p. 134
> Ineffective coping, p. 51
> Spiritual distress, p. 180

 **Shock, Hypovolemic**

Hypovolemic shock occurs from decreased intravascular fluid volume, resulting from either internal fluid shifts or external fluid loss. This fluid can be whole blood, plasma, or water and electrolytes. Common causes include hemorrhage (external or internal), severe burns, vomiting, and diarrhea. Hemorrhagic shock often occurs after trauma, gastrointestinal bleeding, or rupture of organs or aneurysms. Internal fluid losses occur in clinical conditions associated with increased capillary permeability and resulting shifts in fluid from the vascular compartment to interstitial spaces or other closed fluid compartments (e.g., peritoneal cavity). This third-spacing of fluids in the body is seen in patients with extensive burns or with ascites and leads to hypovolemic shock. Hypovolemic shock can be classified according to the percentage of fluid loss. Mild shock is a 10% to 20% loss, moderate shock is a 20% to 40% loss, and severe shock is a greater than 40% loss. Older patients may exhibit signs of shock with smaller losses of fluid volume because of their compromised ability to compensate for fluid changes.

 Nursing Diagnosis

Deficient Fluid Volume

Common Related Factors	Defining Characteristics
Internal fluid shifts	Mild to moderate anxiety
Internal hemorrhage	Tachycardia
External hemorrhage	Hypotension
Severe dehydration	Capillary refill slow or greater than 3 seconds
Trauma	Tachypnea
	Narrowing pulse pressure

■ = Independent; ▲ = Collaborative

Shock, Hypovolemic—cont'd

Defining Characteristics—cont'd

Urine output may be normal (greater than 30 mL/hr) or as low as 20 mL/hr
Cool, clammy skin
Thirst
Dry mouth
Light-headedness or dizziness

Common Expected Outcome

Patient experiences adequate fluid volume as evidenced by urine output greater than 30 mL/hr, normotensive blood pressure (BP), heart rate (HR) 100 beats/min, and warm, dry skin.

NOC Outcome
Fluid Balance

NIC Interventions
Fluid Monitoring; Invasive Hemodynamic Monitoring; Fluid Resuscitation; Bleeding Precautions; Bleeding Reduction: Gastrointestinal; Shock Management: Volume; Emergency Care

Ongoing Assessment

Actions/Interventions	Rationale
■ Assess for early warning signs of hypovolemia.	Mild to moderate anxiety and tachycardia may be the first signs of impending hypovolemic shock; these may be easily overlooked or attributed to pain, psychological trauma, and fear. BP is not a good indicator of early hypovolemic shock.
▲ Assess HR, BP, and pulse pressure. Use direct intra-arterial monitoring as ordered.	Sinus tachycardia and increased arterial BP are seen in early stages to maintain an adequate cardiac output; BP drops as condition deteriorates. In young adults, compensatory mechanism responses maintain a normal BP until major blood loss occurs.
■ Monitor possible sources of fluid loss: diarrhea, vomiting, profuse diaphoresis, polyuria, burns, ruptured organs, and trauma.	Specific manifestations/etiologies guide therapy.
■ Record and evaluate intake and output.	Accurate measurement is essential in detecting negative fluid balance.
■ If trauma has occurred, evaluate and document extent of patient's injuries; use primary survey (or another consistent survey method) or ABCs: airway with cervical spine control, breathing, circulation.	Primary survey helps identify imminent or potentially life-threatening injuries. This is a quick initial assessment.
■ Perform secondary survey after all life-threatening injuries are ruled out or treated.	Secondary survey uses methodical head-to-toe inspection. Anticipate potential causes of shock state from ongoing assessment.

■ = Independent; ▲ = Collaborative

Actions/Interventions

- ■ If the only visible injury is obvious head injury, look for other causes of hypovolemia (e.g., long-bone fractures, internal bleeding, external bleeding).

- ▲ If hemodynamic monitoring is in place, assess central venous pressure (CVP), pulmonary artery diastolic pressure (PADP), pulmonary capillary wedge pressure (PCWP), and cardiac output/cardiac index (CO/CI).

- ■ If patient is postsurgical, monitor blood loss (weigh dressings to determine fluid loss, monitor chest tube drainage, mark skin area).

- ▲ Obtain spun hematocrit, and reevaluate every 30 minutes to 4 hours, depending on stability.

- ▲ Monitor coagulation studies including prothrombin time, partial thromboplastin time, fibrinogen, fibrin split products, and platelet counts, as appropriate.

Rationale

Hypovolemic shock following trauma usually results from hemorrhage.

CVP provides information on filling pressures of the right side of the heart; pulmonary artery diastolic pressure (PADP) and PCWP reflect left-sided fluid volumes. CO/CI provides an objective number to guide therapy.

It is important to denote expanding hematoma or swelling.

Hematocrit decreases as fluids are administered because of dilution. As a rule of thumb, hematocrit decreases 1% per liter of lactated Ringer's or normal saline solution used. Any other hematocrit decrease must be evaluated as an indication of continued blood loss.

Specific deficiencies guide treatment therapy.

Therapeutic Interventions

Actions/Interventions

- ■ Prevent blood volume loss by controlling source of bleeding. If external, apply direct pressure to the bleeding site.

- ▲ Initiate intravenous (IV) therapy. Start two shorter, large-bore peripheral IV lines. (The amount of volume that can be infused is inversely affected by the length of the IV catheter; it is best to use shorter, large-bore catheters.)

- ▲ Prepare to administer a bolus of 1 to 2 L of IV fluids as ordered. Use crystalloid solutions for adequate fluid and electrolyte balance.

- ■ If hypovolemia is a result of severe burns, calculate fluid replacement according to the extent of the burn and patient's body weight.

Rationale

External bleeding is controlled with firm, direct pressure on the bleeding site, using a thick dry dressing material. Prompt, effective treatment is needed to preserve vital organ function and life.

Maintaining an adequate circulating blood volume is a priority. The amount of fluid infused is usually more important than the type of fluid (crystalloid, colloid, blood).

The patient's response to treatment depends on the extent of blood loss. If blood loss is mild (20%), expected response is a rapid return to normal BP. If IV fluids are slowed, the patient remains normotensive. If the patient has lost 20% to 40% of circulating blood volume or has continued uncontrolled bleeding, fluid bolus may produce normotension, but if fluids are slowed after bolus, BP will deteriorate.

Extreme caution is indicated in fluid replacement in older patients. Aggressive therapy may precipitate left ventricular dysfunction and pulmonary edema.

Formulas such as the Parkland formula, which follows, guide fluid replacement therapy:

% BSA (body surface area) burned × Weight in kg × 4 mL lactated Ringer's = Total fluid to be infused over 24 hours: ½ given intravenously over 8 hours and ½ given over next 16 hours

Shock, Hypovolemic—cont'd

Actions/Interventions	Rationale
▲ Administer blood products (e.g., packed red blood cells, fresh frozen plasma, platelets) as prescribed. Transfuse patient with whole blood–packed red blood cells.	Preparing fully crossmatched blood may take up to 1 hour in some laboratories. Consider using uncrossmatched or type-specific blood until crossmatched blood is available. If type-specific blood is unavailable, type O blood may be used for exsanguinating patients. If available, Rh-negative blood is preferred, especially for women of childbearing age. Autotransfusion may be used when there is massive bleeding in the thoracic cavity.
▲ If hypovolemia is a result of severe diarrhea or vomiting, administer antidiarrheal or antiemetic medications as prescribed, in addition to IV fluids.	Treatment is guided by cause of problem.
■ If bleeding is secondary to surgery, anticipate or prepare for return to surgery.	Surgery may be the only way to correct the problem.
▲ For trauma victims with internal bleeding (e.g., pelvic fracture), military antishock trousers (MAST) or pneumatic antishock garment (PASG) may be used.	These devices are useful to tamponade bleeding. Hypovolemia from long-bone fractures (e.g., femur or pelvic fractures) may be controlled by splinting with air splints. Hare traction splints or MAST/PASG trousers may be used to reduce tissue and vessel damage from manipulation of unstable fractures.

 Nursing Diagnosis

Decreased Cardiac Output

Common Related Factors

Fluid volume loss of 30% or more
Late uncompensated hypovolemic shock

Defining Characteristics

Pulse rate greater than 120 beats/min
Hypotension
Capillary refill greater than 3 seconds
Decreased pulse pressure
Decreased peripheral pulses
Cold, clammy skin
Agitation or confusion
Decreased urinary output (less than 30 mL/hr)
Abnormal arterial blood gases: acidosis and hypoxemia

Common Expected Outcome

Patient achieves adequate cardiac output as evidenced by strong peripheral pulses; normal vital signs; urine output greater than 30 mL/hr; warm, dry skin; and alert, responsive mentation.

NOC Outcome
Cardiac Pump Effectiveness

NIC Interventions
Invasive Hemodynamic Monitoring;
  Hemodynamic Regulation;
  Emergency Care

■ = Independent; ▲ = Collaborative

Therapeutic Interventions

Actions/Interventions	Rationale
■ Assess skin color, temperature, and moisture.	Cool, pale, clammy skin is secondary to compensatory increase in sympathetic nervous system stimulation and low cardiac output and desaturation.
▲ Assess HR, BP, and pulse pressure. Use direct intra-arterial monitoring as ordered.	Sinus tachycardia and increased arterial BP are seen in early stages to maintain an adequate cardiac output. BP drops as condition deteriorates. Auscultatory BP may be unreliable secondary to vasoconstriction. Pulse pressure (systolic minus diastolic) decreases in shock. Older patients have a reduced response to catecholamines; thus their response to decreased cardiac output may be blunted, with less increase in HR.
■ Assess peripheral and central pulses, including capillary refill.	Pulses are weak with reduced stroke volume and cardiac output. Capillary refill is slow, sometimes absent.
■ Assess for mental status changes.	Early signs of cerebral hypoxia are restlessness and anxiety, with confusion and loss of consciousness occurring in later stages. Older patients are especially susceptible to reduced perfusion to vital organs.
■ Assess urine output with a Foley catheter.	The renal system compensates for low BP by retaining water. Oliguria is a classic sign of inadequate renal perfusion from reduced cardiac output.
■ Assess respiratory rate, rhythm, and breath sounds.	Rapid, shallow respirations and presence of crackles and wheezes are characteristic of shock.
▲ Assess pulse oximetry and arterial blood gases.	Pulse oximetry is a useful tool to detect changes in oxygenation. Oxygen saturation should be kept at 90% or greater. As shock increases, aerobic metabolism ceases and lactic acidosis ensues, raising the level of carbon dioxide and pH. The ability of the patient to attain high oxygen delivery parameters correlates with improved chance of survival.
▲ If hemodynamic monitoring is in place, assess central venous pressure (CVP), pulmonary artery pressure, pulmonary capillary wedge pressure (PCWP), and cardiac output/cardiac index (CO/CI).	CVP provides information on filling pressures of the right side of the heart; pulmonary artery diastolic pressure (PADP) and PCWP reflect left-sided fluid volumes. Cardiac output provides an objective number to guide therapy.
■ Assess heart sounds.	S_3 denotes reduced left ventricular ejection and is a classic sign of left ventricular failure. S_4 occurs with reduced compliance of the left ventricle, which impairs diastolic filling.
■ Assess cardiac rhythm and electrocardiogram (ECG).	Cardiac dysrhythmias may occur from low perfusion, acidosis, or hypoxia, as well as from side effects of cardiac medications used to treat this condition.
▲ Administer fluid and blood replacement therapy as described in prior nursing diagnosis, Deficient Fluid Volume.	Maintaining an adequate circulating blood volume is a priority.

■ = Independent; ▲ = Collaborative

Shock, Hypovolemic—cont'd

Actions/Interventions	Rationale
▲ If possible, use a fluid warmer or rapid fluid infuser.	Fluid warmers keep core temperatures warm. Infusion of cold blood is associated with myocardial dysrhythmias and paradoxical hypotension. Macropore filtering IV devices should also be used to remove small clots and debris.
▲ If the patient's condition progressively deteriorates, initiate cardiopulmonary resuscitation or other life-saving measures according to Advanced Cardiac Life Support guidelines, as indicated.	Early assessment and treatment improves outcomes.

NDx Nursing Diagnosis

Anxiety

Common Related Factors

Acute injury
Threat of death
Unfamiliar environment

Defining Characteristics

Restlessness and agitation
Crying
Increased pulse and BP
Increased respirations
Verbalized anxiety
Questioning of patient's condition by patient or significant others

Common Expected Outcomes

Patient appears calm and trusting.
Patient verbalizes reduction in anxiety and expresses concerns.

NOC Outcomes
Anxiety Self-Control; Coping

NIC Intervention
Anxiety Reduction

Ongoing Assessment

Actions/Interventions	Rationale
■ Assess anxiety level (mild, severe). Note signs and symptoms, especially nonverbal communication.	Shock can result in an acute life-threatening situation that will produce high levels of anxiety in the patient as well as in significant others.
■ Assess coping factors.	Anxiety and ways of decreasing perceived anxiety are highly individualized. Interventions are most effective when they are consistent with the individual's established coping pattern.

■ = Independent; ▲ = Collaborative

Therapeutic Interventions

Actions/Interventions	Rationale
■ Acknowledge awareness of the patient's anxiety.	Acknowledgment of the patient's feelings validates the feelings and communicates acceptance of those feelings.
■ Maintain confident, assured manner.	The staff's anxiety may be easily perceived by the patient. The patient's feeling of stability increases in a calm and nonthreatening atmosphere.
■ Assure patient and significant others of close, continuous monitoring that will ensure prompt intervention.	This provides a measure of safety.
■ Reduce unnecessary external stimuli.	Anxiety may escalate with excessive conversation, noise, and equipment around the patient.
■ Explain all procedures as appropriate, keeping explanations basic.	Information helps allay anxiety. Patients who are anxious may not be able to comprehend anything more than simple, clear, brief instructions.
■ Provide a quiet, private place for significant others to wait.	A quiet environment can reduce anxiety.
■ Refer to other support persons (e.g., clergy, social worker) as appropriate.	Additional specialty expertise may be required.

• RELATED CARE PLANS

Acute respiratory distress syndrome, p. 408
Burns, p. 1083
Gastrointestinal bleeding, p. 698
Imbalanced nutrition: less than body
  requirements, p. 134
Impaired gas exchange, p. 78

Shock, Septic

Distributive Shock; Sepsis; Bacteremia; Disseminated Intravascular Coagulation (DIC)

Septic shock is associated with severe infection and occurs after bacteremia of gram-negative bacilli (most common) or gram-positive cocci. Septic shock is mediated by a complex interaction of hormonal and chemical substances through an immune system response to bacterial endotoxins. In the early stages of sepsis, the body responds to infection by the normal inflammatory response. As the infection progresses, sepsis becomes more severe and leads to decreased tissue perfusion and multiple-organ dysfunction. Septic shock occurs as an exaggerated inflammatory response that leads to hypotension even with adequate fluid resuscitation. The primary effects of septic shock are massive vasodilation, maldistribution of blood volume, and myocardial depression. The maldistribution of circulatory volume results in some tissues receiving more than adequate blood flow and other tissues receiving less than adequate blood flow. As shock progresses, disseminated intravascular coagulation (DIC) may occur, resulting in a serious imbalance between clotting and bleeding.

Older patients are at increased risk for septic shock because of factors such as impaired immune response, impaired organ function, chronic debilitating illnesses, impaired mobility that can lead to pneumonia, decubitus ulcers, and loss of bladder control requiring indwelling catheters. The mortality rate from septic shock is high (30% to 50%), especially in older patients. Immunocompromised patients and those with chronic diseases are also at increased risk.

■ = Independent; ▲ = Collaborative

Shock, Septic—cont'd

 Nursing Diagnosis

Infection

Common Related Factors

An infectious process of either gram-negative or gram-positive bacteria

The most common causative organisms and their related factors are as follows:

- *Escherichia coli*: commonly occurs in genitourinary tract, biliary tract, intravenous (IV) catheter, or colon or intraabdominal abscesses
- *Klebsiella*: occurs in the lungs, gastrointestinal tract, IV catheter, urinary tract, or surgical wounds
- *Proteus*: occurs in the genitourinary tract, respiratory tract, abscesses, or biliary tract
- *Bacteroides fragilis*: occurs in the female genital tract, colon, liver abscesses, or decubitus ulcers
- *Pseudomonas aeruginosa*: occurs in the lungs, urinary tract, skin, or IV catheter
- *Candida albicans*: occurs in line-related infections, especially hyperalimentation infusion and pulmonary and urinary abscesses

Defining Characteristics

Changes in level of consciousness: lethargy or confusion

Fever or chills

Ruddy appearance with warm, dry skin

Leukocytosis

Common Expected Outcome

Cause of infection is determined and appropriate treatment initiated.

NOC Outcomes
Vital Signs; Thermoregulation

NIC Interventions
Vital Sign Monitoring; Medication Administration; Temperature Regulation

Ongoing Assessment

Actions/Interventions

■ Monitor heart rate (HR) and blood pressure (BP).

■ Monitor temperature.

■ Assess for presence of chills.

Rationale

Septic shock can present in two phases. During the early, more treatable phase (high-output shock), there is an increase in cardiac output reflected by tachycardia and normal or elevated BP. However, as shock continues and the septic phase ensues, blood vessels dilate, causing hypovolemia and hypotension.

This provides information about the patient's response to invading organisms. Temperature may be higher than 38° C or lower than 36° C.

Chills often precede temperature spikes.

■ = Independent; ▲ = Collaborative

Actions/Interventions	**Rationale**
■ Assess skin turgor, color, temperature, and peripheral pulses.	In early septic shock, warm, dry, flushed skin and bounding pulses are evident as a result of initial vasodilation (warm shock). As shock state continues, skin becomes cool, clammy, and cyanotic with reduced peripheral pulses.
■ Assess level of consciousness or mentation. Use neurological checklist, such as Glasgow Coma Scale.	Altered cerebral tissue perfusion may be the first sign of compensatory response to septic state. The patient may experience fatigue, malaise, anxiety, or confusion. Mild disorientation is common in older adults.
▲ Assess pulse oximetry.	Pulse oximetry is a useful tool to detect changes in oxygenation. Oxygen saturation should be kept at 90% or greater.
▲ Assess arterial blood gases (ABGs). Note presence of respiratory alkalosis from hyperventilation.	Initially, respiratory alkalosis from hyperventilation may be evident. As shock increases, aerobic metabolism ceases and lactic acidosis ensues, raising the level of carbon dioxide and pH.
■ Assess related factors thoroughly: • Lungs: assess lung sounds and presence of sputum, including color, odor, and amount. Note presence of crackles and decreased breath sounds. • Genitourinary: monitor urinalysis reports, assess color and opacity of urine, and assess for presence of drainage or pus around Foley catheter. • Gastrointestinal: check for abdominal distention, and assess for bowel sounds and abdominal tenderness. • IV catheters: assess all insertion sites for redness, swelling, and drainage. • Surgical wounds: assess all wounds for signs of infection, including redness, swelling, and drainage. • Pain: obtain patient's subjective statement of location and description of pain or discomfort. This may help localize a site.	Cause of shock guides treatment plan.
▲ Obtain culture and sensitivity (C&S) samples as ordered.	C&S reports show which antibiotic will be effective against the invading organism.
▲ Draw peak and trough antibiotic titers as needed.	This helps ensure an appropriate level of antibiotic for the patient.
▲ Monitor for toxicity from antibiotic therapy, especially in patients with hepatic and/or renal insufficiency or failure and in older patients.	Aminoglycosides should be followed with urinalysis and serum creatinine levels at least three times per week. Chloramphenicol should be restricted in patients with liver disease.

■ = Independent; ▲ = Collaborative

Shock, Septic—cont'd

Therapeutic Interventions

Actions/Interventions	Rationale
▲ Initiate early administration of antibiotics as prescribed.	Antibiotic therapy is begun with broad-spectrum antibiotics after the C&S is obtained but before the actual C&S report is received. After the C&S report is received, the physician should be notified if the organism is not sensitive to the present antibiotic coverage. The antibiotic may then be changed or supplemented. Common treatment for gram-positive organisms includes vancomycin; for gram-negative organisms, expanded penicillin and aminoglycosides are commonly used.
■ Remove any possible source of infection (e.g., urinary catheter, IV catheter).	These are frequent sites of infection.
▲ Maintain temperature in adequate range: • Administer antipyretics as prescribed. • Apply cooling mattress. • Administer tepid sponge baths. • Limit number of blankets/linens used to cover patients.	Normothermia prevents stress on the cardiovascular system and promotes comfort.
▲ Initiate appropriate isolation measures.	Isolation prevents the spread of infection.
▲ Assist with the incision and drainage of wounds, irrigation, and sterile application of saline-soaked 4 × 4s as indicated.	Early treatment promotes recovery.
▲ Manage the cause of infection, and anticipate surgical consult as necessary.	Surgical treatment may be indicated to drain pus or abscess, resolve obstruction, or repair a perforated organ.
▲ If signs of DIC occur, refer to the nursing care plan for Disseminated Intravascular Coagulation, p. 830.	

 Nursing Diagnosis

Deficient Fluid Volume

Common Related Factors	Defining Characteristics
Early septic shock Decrease in systemic vascular resistance Increased capillary permeability	Hypotension Tachycardia Decreased urine output less than 30 mL/hr Concentrated urine

■ = Independent; ▲ = Collaborative

Common Expected Outcome

Patient experiences adequate fluid volume as evidenced by urine output greater than 30 mL/hour, normotensive BP, and HR less than 100 beats/min.

NOC Outcomes
Fluid Balance; Electrolyte and Acid/Base Balance; Vital Signs

NIC Interventions
Fluid Monitoring; Fluid Resuscitation; Invasive Hemodynamic Monitoring; Hemodynamic Regulation; Shock Management: Vasogenic

Ongoing Assessment

Actions/Interventions

■ Assess for presence of hypotension and tachycardia.

■ Assess urine output with a Foley catheter.

■ Assess fluid balance and weight gain.

▲ If hemodynamic monitoring is in place, assess central venous pressure (CVP), pulmonary artery pressure, pulmonary capillary wedge pressure (PCWP), and cardiac output/cardiac index (CO/CI).

▲ When initiating fluid challenges, closely monitor patient.

Rationale

During the early phase of shock, tachycardia and normal BP are evident, but as shock progresses with subsequent vasodilation, hypotension ensues.

The renal system compensates for low BP by retaining water. Oliguria is a classic sign of inadequate renal perfusion from reduced cardiac output.

Compromised regulatory mechanisms may result in fluid and sodium retention. Body weight is a more sensitive indicator of fluid or sodium retention than intake and output.

CVP provides information on filling pressures of the right side of the heart; pulmonary artery diastolic pressure and PCWP reflect left-sided fluid volumes. CO/CI provides an objective number to guide therapy.

This prevents iatrogenic volume overload.

Therapeutic Interventions

Actions/Interventions

▲ Perform fluid resuscitation aggressively as ordered.

■ Use caution in fluid replacement in older patients.

▲ Adjust fluid as ordered.

▲ If there is poor or no response to fluid resuscitation, administer vasoactive substances, such as dopamine, phenylephrine HCl (Neo-Synephrine), or norepinephrine bitartrate (Levophed) as prescribed.

Rationale

Infusion rates will vary depending on clinical status. Fluid administration is necessary to support tissue perfusion. The fluid needs in septic patients may exceed 8 to 20 L in the first 24 hours.

Older patients may be more prone to congestive heart failure. In these patients, monitor closely for signs of iatrogenic fluid volume overload.

The optimal PCWP is usually 12 mm Hg in the absence of myocardial infarction and 14 to 18 mm Hg if myocardial infarction has occurred.

In early septic shock the cardiac output is high or normal. At this point, the vasoactive agents are administered for their α-adrenergic effect.

■ = Independent; ▲ = Collaborative

Shock, Septic—cont'd

Nursing Diagnosis

Decreased Cardiac Output

Common Related Factors

Late septic shock: a decrease in tissue perfusion leads to increased lactic acid production and systemic acidosis, which causes a decrease in myocardial contractility

Gram-negative infections may cause a direct myocardial toxic effect

Defining Characteristics

Decreased peripheral pulses
Cold, clammy skin
Hypotension
Agitation or confusion
Decreased urinary output less than 30 mL/hr
Abnormal ABGs: acidosis and hypoxemia

Common Expected Outcome

Patient achieves adequate cardiac output, as evidenced by strong peripheral pulses; normal vital signs; urine output greater than 30 mL/hr; warm, dry skin; and alert, responsive mentation.

NOC Outcome
Cardiac Pump Effectiveness

NIC Interventions
Invasive Hemodynamic Monitoring; Hemodynamic Regulation; Acid/Base Management: Metabolic Acidosis; Shock Management: Vasogenic

Ongoing Assessment

Actions/Interventions

■ Assess skin warmth and peripheral pulses.

■ Assess mental status changes.

▲ Assess HR, BP, and pulse pressure. Use direct intra-arterial monitoring as ordered.

Rationale

Compensatory peripheral vasoconstriction in late stages causes cool, pale, diaphoretic skin. Pulses are weak with reduced stroke volume and cardiac output.

Early signs of cerebral hypoxia are restlessness and anxiety, leading to agitation and confusion. The patient may become lethargic and comatose.

Sinus tachycardia and increased arterial BP are seen in early stages to maintain an adequate cardiac output; BP decreases as condition deteriorates. Auscultatory BP may be unreliable secondary to vasoconstriction. Pulse pressure (systolic minus diastolic) decreases in late septic shock. Older patients have a reduced response to catecholamines; thus their response to decreased cardiac output may be blunted, with less increase in HR.

■ = Independent; ▲ = Collaborative

Shock, Septic

Actions/Interventions

■ Assess urine output with a Foley catheter.

■ Monitor for dysrhythmias.

▲ If hemodynamic monitoring is in place, assess CVP, pulmonary artery pressure, PCWP, and CO.

Rationale

The renal system compensates for low blood pressure by retaining water. Oliguria is a classic sign of inadequate renal perfusion from reduced cardiac output.

Cardiac dysrhythmias may occur from the low perfusion state, acidosis, or hypoxia.

CVP provides information on filling pressures of the right side of the heart; pulmonary artery diastolic pressure and PCWP reflect left-sided fluid volumes.

Therapeutic Interventions

Actions/Interventions

▲ Place patient in the physiological position for shock: head of bed flat with trunk horizontal and lower extremities elevated 20 to 30 degrees with knees straight.

▲ Administer inotropic agents: dobutamine HCl (Dobutrex), dopamine, digoxin, or milrinone (Inocor). Continuously monitor their effectiveness. Administer sodium bicarbonate to treat acidosis.

Rationale

This promotes venous return. Do not use Trendelenburg's (head down) position because it causes pressure against the diaphragm.

These improve myocardial contractility and cardiac output.

NDx Nursing Diagnosis

Risk for Ineffective Breathing Pattern

Common Risk Factors

Progressive shock state
Lactic acidosis

Common Expected Outcome

Patient's breathing pattern is maintained, as evidenced by eupnea, regular respiratory rate or pattern, and verbalization of comfort with breathing.

NOC Outcome
Respiratory Status: Ventilation

NIC Interventions
Respiratory Monitoring;
Ventilation Assistance

Ongoing Assessment

Actions/Interventions

■ Assess respiratory rate, rhythm, and depth every hour.

Rationale

Rapid, shallow respirations may occur from hypoxia or from acidosis with sepsis. Development of hypoventilation indicates that immediate ventilator support is needed.

■ = Independent; ▲ = Collaborative

Shock, Septic—cont'd

Actions/Interventions

- Assess for any increase in work of breathing: shortness of breath and use of accessory muscles.
- Assess lung sounds, noting areas of decreased ventilation and the presence of adventitious sounds.

▲ Assess pulse oximetry and ABGs.

Rationale

As septic shock progresses, patients may experience acute respiratory distress syndrome.

Moist crackles are caused by increased pulmonary capillary permeability and increased intraalveolar edema. Older patients, who most commonly experience septic shock, may have difficulty clearing their airways, resulting in atelectasis and pneumonia.

Oxygen saturation should be kept at 90% or greater. As shock increases, aerobic metabolism ceases and lactic acidosis ensues, raising the level of carbon dioxide and pH.

Therapeutic Interventions

Actions/Interventions

- Position the patient with proper body alignment.
- Change position every 2 hours.
- Suction as needed.
- Maintain confident, assured manner.

▲ Maintain oxygen delivery system.

- Anticipate need for intubation and mechanical ventilation.

Rationale

This promotes optimal lung expansion.

This facilitates movement and drainage of secretions.

This promotes patent airway.

The staff's anxiety may be easily perceived by the patient. The patient's feeling of stability increases in a calm and nonthreatening atmosphere.

Oxygen may be required to maintain oxygen saturation at 90% or greater.

Rapid, efficient intervention is critical to preserve vital organ function and life.

 NDx **Nursing Diagnosis**

Deficient Knowledge

Common Related Factor
New condition

Defining Characteristics
Increased frequency of questions posed by patient and significant others
Inability to respond correctly to questions asked

Common Expected Outcome
Patient or significant others demonstrate understanding of disease process and treatment used.

NOC Outcomes
Knowledge: Disease Process;
Knowledge: Infection Control

NIC Interventions
Teaching: Disease Process;
Infection Protection

■ = Independent; ▲ = Collaborative

Ongoing Assessment

Actions/Interventions

■ Evaluate understanding of septic shock and patient's overall condition.

Rationale

Information guides starting point for educational intervention.

Therapeutic Interventions

Actions/Interventions

■ Keep the patient or significant others informed of disease process and present status of the patient.

■ Explain common factors that placed the patient at risk for septic shock:
  • Advanced age with declining immune system
  • Malnourishment/poor hydration
  • Debilitating chronic illnesses
  • Insertion of indwelling catheter
  • Surgical and diagnostic procedure
  • Decubitus ulcer or wounds
  • Cross-contamination or exposure to resistant organisms

■ Instruct regarding general hygiene measures to reduce risk for infection.

Rationale

Septic shock results in a critically ill patient with a tenuous baseline for recovery.

Knowledge is critical, especially in older patients and those who are immunosuppressed and already at greater risk for infection and sepsis.

Practices such as good personal hygiene, hand washing, adequate rest, balanced diet, exercise, and oral care all promote reduced infection risks.

• RELATED CARE PLANS

Acute renal failure, p. 911
Acute respiratory distress syndrome, p. 408
Disseminated intravascular coagulation, p. 830
Fear, p. 68
Imbalanced nutrition: less than body
  requirements, p. 134

Tamponade, Cardiac

Chest Trauma; Cardiac Surgery; Pericardial Effusion

Cardiac tamponade is a life-threatening condition caused by fluid accumulation in the mediastinum or pericardium. As fluid collects, it causes compression of the cardiovascular structures. This impairs cardiac filling and greatly reduces cardiac output. Rapidly accumulating fluid is most often blood and is usually caused by chest trauma or surgery. Chronic effusions are often serous fluid that accumulates gradually secondary to infection (viral, bacterial), inflammation (rheumatoid, uremia, radiation), or neoplastic conditions (primary, metastatic). Rapid recognition and intervention are essential. Treatment modalities include pericardiocentesis, pericardiocentesis with pigtail catheter placement for drainage, open chest drainage, pericardiectomy, and pleuropericardial window.

■ = Independent; ▲ = Collaborative

Cardiac and Vascular
Care Plans

 Tamponade, Cardiac—cont'd

 Nursing Diagnosis

Decreased Cardiac Output

Common Related Factor

External compression of cardiovascular structures causing reduced diastolic filling

Defining Characteristics

Decreased blood pressure (BP)
Narrow pulse pressure
Pulsus paradoxus (systolic pressure decreases 15 mm Hg or more during inspiration)
Tachycardia
Electrical alternans (decreased QRS voltage during inspiration)
Equalization of pressures (central venous pressure [CVP], right ventricular diastolic pressure [RVDP], pulmonary artery diastolic pressure [PADP], pulmonary capillary wedge pressure [PCWP])
Jugular venous distention (JVD)
Chest tubes (if present) suddenly stop draining (suspect clot)
Distant or muffled heart tones
Restlessness, confusion, and anxiety
Decrease in hemoglobin and hematocrit
Cool, clammy skin
Diminished peripheral pulses
Decreased urine output
Decreased arterial and venous oxygen saturation
Acidosis
Beck's triad (distended neck veins, hypotension, muffled heart tones)
Unwillingness to lie supine

Common Expected Outcome

Patient maintains adequate cardiac output as evidenced by the following: BP within normal limits for patient, strong regular pulses, absence of JVD, absence of pulsus paradoxus, skin warm and dry, and clear mentation.

NOC Outcomes

Cardiac Pump Effectiveness; Fluid Balance

NIC Interventions

Hemodynamic Regulation; Invasive Hemodynamic Monitoring; Fluid Resuscitation; Shock Management: Cardiac; Emergency Care

■ = Independent; ▲ = Collaborative

Ongoing Assessment

Actions/Interventions

■ Assess for classic signs associated with acute cardiac tamponade:

• Low arterial BP with narrowed pulse pressure

• Tachycardia
• Distant or muffled heart sounds

• JVD

• Pulsus paradoxus

• Dyspnea
■ Assess mental status.

■ In chest trauma or cardiac surgery patients, monitor chest tube drainage.
▲ Assess 12-lead electrocardiogram (ECG).

▲ Assist with performance of bedside echocardiogram if time permits.

▲ If patient is in an intensive care unit (ICU) setting, assess hemodynamic profile using pulmonary artery catheter; assess for equalization of pressures.
▲ Assess chest x-ray study.

Rationale

Cardiac tamponade is a life-threatening condition. Early assessment of reduced cardiac output facilitates early emergency treatment.

An initial elevation in BP may occur with compensatory vasoconstriction; however, as venous return is compromised from the cardiac compression, a significant decrease in cardiac output occurs.

This is related to compensatory catecholamine release.

These are related to fluid accumulation in the pericardial sac.

The venous pulse (CVP) may rise to 15 to 20 cm H_2O as a result of impedance to diastolic filling by atrial compression.

This is characterized by a drop of more than 10 mm Hg in systolic BP with inspiration.

This is related to fluid backup in the pulmonary system.

Symptoms may range from anxiety to altered level of consciousness in shock.

Sudden cessation of drainage suggests clot.

ECG may reveal ST-segment elevation, nonspecific ST and T-wave changes, and/or electrical alternans (caused by pendulum-like movement of the heart within the pericardial effusion).

This evaluation provides the most helpful diagnostic information. Effusions seen with acute tamponade are usually smaller than with chronic tamponade. However, in light of circulatory collapse, treatment may be indicated before the echocardiogram can be performed.

The CVP, RVDP, PADP, and PCWP are all elevated in tamponade and within 2 to 3 mm Hg of each other. These pressures confirm diagnosis.

X-ray study reveals a widened mediastinum with a normal cardiac silhouette, clear lung fields, and dilation of superior vena cava.

Therapeutic Interventions

Actions/Interventions

If cardiac tamponade is secondary to a slowly developing effusion and the patient's compensatory mechanisms are maintaining temporary cardiovascular stability:
■ Anticipate transfer to the ICU.
▲ Initiate oxygen therapy.
▲ Administer parenteral fluids as ordered.

Rationale

Close monitoring is necessary.

This is needed to maximize oxygen saturation.

Blood products, colloids, and crystalloids may be used to expand circulating volume. Optimal state of hydration will increase venous return and therefore cardiac output.

■ = Independent; ▲ = Collaborative

Tamponade, Cardiac—cont'd

Actions/Interventions	Rationale
▲ Type and crossmatch as ordered. Anticipate blood product replacement.	This is needed to correct any existing alterations in hematology or coagulation factors.
■ Place patient in Fowler's position (unless condition requires supine).	Upright position allows for increased thoracic cavity and full descent of diaphragm.
In the ICU: ▲ Assemble equipment for pericardiocentesis.	Pericardiocentesis may be the emergency treatment of choice. It is indicated when systolic BP is reduced more than 30 mm Hg from baseline. However, if the patient can be stabilized, drainage of fluid should be delayed until surgical or open resection or drainage can be performed. Pericardiocentesis should be performed under sterile conditions. If the blood in the pericardium has already clotted (as is common after cardiac surgery), then pericardiocentesis will not be effective.
▲ Have emergency resuscitative equipment and medications readily available.	Bedside pericardiocentesis can be a high-risk but lifesaving procedure. Complications include pneumothorax and myocardial or coronary artery lacerations.
If cardiac tamponade is rapidly developing (as in trauma or as a complication of cardiac surgery) with cardiovascular decompensation and collapse: ▲ Maintain aggressive fluid resuscitation. Assemble open chest tray for bedside pericardiocentesis (for trauma) and prepare patient for transport to surgery for emergency sternotomy (for postcardiac surgery).	Volume expansion and emergency sternotomy are treatments of choice.
▲ Administer vasopressor and inotropic agents (dopamine hydrochloride, norepinephrine bitartrate [Levophed]) as ordered.	These medications maximize systemic perfusion pressure to vital organs, increase myocardial contraction, and increase cardiac output.
▲ If acute tamponade recurs and repeated pericardiocentesis is ineffective, anticipate surgical pericardiotomy or resection of a portion of the pericardium.	Acute tamponade is a life-threatening complication, but immediate prognosis is good with fast, effective treatment. Open resection and drainage should be performed in a sterile environment.

ND_x Nursing Diagnosis

Anxiety

Common Related Factors	Defining Characteristics
Unfamiliar environment Chest pain Dyspnea Invasive procedures	Sympathetic stimulation Restlessness Increased questioning Uncooperative behavior Avoids looking at equipment or keeps vigilant watch over equipment

■ = Independent; ▲ = Collaborative

Common Expected Outcomes

Patient appears as relaxed as situation warrants.
Patient verbalizes trust in health care providers.

NOC Outcomes
Anxiety Self-Control; Coping

NIC Interventions
Anxiety Reduction; Calming Techniques;
Teaching: Procedure/Treatment;
Active Presence

Ongoing Assessment

Actions/Interventions	Rationale
■ Assess anxiety level (mild, severe). Note signs and symptoms, especially nonverbal communication.	Acute tamponade can result in an acute life-threatening situation that will produce high levels of anxiety in the patient as well as in significant others.
■ Assess coping factors.	Anxiety and ways of decreasing perceived anxiety are highly individualized. Interventions are most effective when they are consistent with the individual's established coping pattern.

Therapeutic Interventions

Actions/Interventions	Rationale
■ Acknowledge awareness of the patient's anxiety.	Acknowledgment of the patient's feelings validates the feelings and communicates acceptance of those feelings.
■ Maintain confident, assured manner.	The staff's anxiety may be easily perceived by the patient. The patient's feeling of stability increases in a calm and nonthreatening atmosphere.
■ Assure patient and significant others of close, continuous monitoring that will ensure prompt intervention.	This provides a measure of safety.
■ Reduce unnecessary external stimuli.	Anxiety may escalate with excessive conversation, noise, and equipment around patient.
■ Explain all procedures as appropriate, keeping explanations basic.	Information helps allay anxiety. Patients who are anxious may not be able to comprehend anything more than simple, clear, brief instructions.
■ Provide a quiet, private place for significant others to wait.	A quiet environment can reduce anxiety.
■ Refer to other support persons (e.g., clergy, social worker) as appropriate.	Additional specialty expertise may be required.

■ = Independent; ▲ = Collaborative

Thrombophlebitis

Deep Vein Thrombosis (DVT); Phlebitis; Phlebothrombosis; Superficial Thrombosis

Thrombophlebitis is the inflammation of the wall of a vein, usually resulting in the formation of a blood clot (thrombosis) that may partially or completely block the flow of blood through the vessel. Venous thrombophlebitis usually occurs in the lower extremities. It may occur in superficial veins, which although painful, is not life threatening and does not require hospitalization, or it may occur in a deep vein, which can be life threatening because clots may break free (embolize) and cause a pulmonary embolism. Superficial thrombophlebitis may occur in response to prolonged intravenous (IV) cannulation or with administration of irritating drugs and solutions. External soft tissue injury may cause vein wall damage and thrombus formation. Three factors contribute to the development of deep vein thrombosis (DVT): venous stasis, hypercoagulability, and endothelial damage to the vein. Prolonged immobility is the primary cause of venous stasis. Hypercoagulability is seen in patients with deficient fluid volume, oral contraceptive use, smoking, and anemia. Venous wall damage may occur secondary to IV infusions, certain medications, fractures, and contrast x-ray studies.

Nursing Diagnosis

Ineffective Peripheral Tissue Perfusion

Common Related Factors

Venous stasis
Injury to vessel wall
Hypercoagulability of blood

Defining Characteristics

Deep vein thrombosis (DVT):
- Usually involves femoral, popliteal, or small calf veins
- Pain
- Edema (unilateral)
- Swelling
- Tenderness
- Pain during palpation of calf muscle
- Positive Homans' sign (not always reliable)
- May be asymptomatic

Superficial thrombophlebitis:
- Usually involves saphenous vein
- Aching and swelling, usually localized into a knot or bump
- A firm mass may be palpable along vein
- Redness
- Warmth
- Tenderness
- May be asymptomatic

Common Expected Outcomes

Patient has adequate blood flow to extremity, as evidenced by warm skin and absence of edema and pain.
Patient does not experience pulmonary embolism, as evidenced by normal breathing, normal heart rate, and absence of chest pain.

NOC Outcomes

Tissue Perfusion: Peripheral;
Blood Coagulation

NIC Interventions

Embolus Care: Peripheral;
Teaching: Disease Process

■ = Independent; ▲ = Collaborative

Ongoing Assessment

Actions/Interventions

- Assess for signs and symptoms of superficial versus deep vein thrombosis (see Defining Characteristics on the preceding page).

- Assess for contributing factors: immobility, leg trauma, intraoperative positioning (especially in older patients), dehydration, smoking, varicose veins, pregnancy, obesity, surgery, malignancy, and use of oral contraceptives.

- With DVT, measure circumference of affected leg with a tape measure.

▲ Monitor results of blood flow studies:

  • Doppler ultrasound

  • Impedance plethysmography

  • Radionuclide scan

  • Venography

▲ Monitor coagulation profile (prothrombin time [PT]/international normalized ratio [INR]/partial thromboplastin time [PTT]).

Rationale

Differentiation is important because treatment goals are different.

Many patients are asymptomatic. Knowledge of high-risk situations aids in early detection. Venous stasis is a leading factor in the development of DVT.

This is to document progression or resolution of swelling. The affected leg will be larger. In some patients, unequal leg circumference may be the only sign of DVT.

These are used to document location of clot and status of affected vein.

Ultrasound uses a Doppler probe to document reduced flow, especially in popliteal and iliofemoral veins.

This uses blood pressure cuffs to record changes in venous flow.

This scan uses radioactive injection (e.g., fibrinogen) followed by scanning to localize areas of obstructed blood flow.

This uses radiopaque contrast media injected through a foot vein to localize thrombi in the deep venous system.

Hospitalized patients with DVT are treated with anticoagulants.

Therapeutic Interventions

Actions/Interventions

For DVT:

- Encourage and maintain bed rest with affected leg elevated.

- Provide warm, moist heat.

▲ Apply elastic stockings as prescribed. Ensure that stockings are of correct size and are applied correctly.

- Maintain adequate hydration.

▲ Administer analgesics as indicated.

Rationale

The goal is prevention of emboli and relief of discomfort.

Bed rest is indicated to reduce the probability of the clot breaking loose. Elevation of the leg will reduce venous pooling and edema.

Heat relieves pain and inflammation.

These promote venous blood flow and decrease venous stagnation. Inaccurately applied stockings can serve as a tourniquet and can facilitate clot formation.

Hydration prevents increased viscosity of blood.

Analgesics relieve pain and promote comfort.

■ = Independent; ▲ = Collaborative

Cardiac and Vascular Care Plans

→ Thrombophlebitis—cont'd

Actions/Interventions

▲ Administer and monitor anticoagulant therapy as ordered (heparin/warfarin [Coumadin]).

■ Use mechanical infusion device.

▲ Anticipate thrombolytic therapy.

▲ If the patient shows no response to conventional therapy or if the patient is not a candidate for anticoagulation, anticipate surgical treatment:
  • Thrombectomy

  • Placement of a vena cava filter

For superficial veins:

■ Explain that hospitalization is not usually required.

■ Instruct the patient on the need for modified bed rest at home with legs elevated until symptoms subside.

■ Instruct patient to apply warm moist heat and/or take warm baths.

■ Explain schedule for nonsteroidal antiinflammatory drugs as ordered.

■ Instruct patient on use of below-the-knee compression stockings.

■ Explain that surgical ligation of the veins may be indicated if therapy attempted is ineffective.

Rationale

Heparin IV is started initially. However, warfarin is added soon after (1 to 2 days) to maximize the achievement of a therapeutic PT or INR before discharge. Therapy will prevent further clot formation by decreasing normal activity of the clotting mechanism. Oral anticoagulant therapy (warfarin) will be initiated while patient is still receiving IV heparin because the onset of action for warfarin can be up to 72 hours. Heparin will be discontinued once the warfarin reaches therapeutic levels.

This ensures accurate dosing and prevention of adverse effects of anticoagulant medications.

Therapy dissolves a massive clot. Lysis carries a higher risk of bleeding than anticoagulation because it dissolves both undesired and therapeutic clots. Therefore use is restricted to patients with severe embolism that significantly compromises blood flow to tissues. Therapy must be initiated soon after the onset of symptoms (within 5 days).

This is a procedure to excise the clot if a major vein is occluded.

This traps any migrating clots and prevents pulmonary embolism.

Goal is symptomatic relief.

This information helps the patient make decisions about therapy.

This may require 2 to 3 days. Then patient can increase activity to promote venous return.

Warm moist heat will relieve pain.

Medications will reduce swelling and promote comfort. Medications should be taken with food.

Stockings will promote venous return and provide comfort.

This information helps the patient make decisions about therapy.

■ = Independent; ▲ = Collaborative

Nursing Diagnosis

Ineffective Protection

Common Related Factor

Anticoagulation therapy for DVT

Defining Characteristic

Altered clotting

Common Expected Outcome

Patient maintains therapeutic blood level of anticoagulant, as evidenced by PTT/PT/INR within desired range.

NOC Outcome
Blood Coagulation

NIC Intervention
Bleeding Precautions

Ongoing Assessment

Actions/Interventions

▲ Monitor for adverse effects of too much anticoagulant:
- Increase in bleeding from sites (e.g., gastrointestinal and genitourinary tracts, IV sites, respiratory tract, wounds).
- Development of new purpura, petechiae, or hematomas
- Bone and joint pain
- Mental status changes
- PTT greater than 2 to 2½ times normal if on heparin; elevated PT/INR if on warfarin (Coumadin)

▲ Monitor for adverse effects of too little anticoagulant:
- Continued evidence of further clot formation (newly developed signs of pulmonary embolus or peripheral thromboemboli)
- PTT below desired level if on heparin; PT/INR low if on warfarin (Coumadin)

▲ Monitor for thrombocytopenia: if platelets drop below 10,000, check for heparin-induced platelet antibody (HIPA).

Rationale

Overanticoagulation promotes bleeding.

These changes may indicate intracranial bleeding.

Undercoagulation promotes blood clotting.

Severe platelet reductions can occur with heparin use, especially unfractionated heparin therapy, and is known as heparin-induced thrombocytopenia (HIT). HIT is less commonly seen with the use of low-molecular-weight heparin.

Therapeutic Interventions

Actions/Interventions

▲ Ensure that infusion is not interrupted (e.g., infiltrated IV line, malfunctioning infusion device).

▲ Reevaluate heparin dose, and administer it as prescribed.

▲ If bleeding occurs, stop heparin infusion as prescribed.

▲ If HIPA is positive, stop all heparin products and anticipate a hematology consult.

Rationale

Correctly maintained infusion device will maintain therapeutic blood level of anticoagulant.

Ineffective anticoagulation increases the risk for clot formation.

Safety measures reduce further complications.

No specific guidelines on positive HIPA are yet defined. Each patient must be evaluated individually.

■ = Independent; ▲ = Collaborative

Cardiac and Vascular Care Plans

 Thrombophlebitis—cont'd

 Nursing Diagnosis

Deficient Knowledge

Common Related Factor

Unfamiliarity with pathology, treatment, and prevention

Defining Characteristics

Multiple questions
Lack of questions
Misconceptions

Common Expected Outcome

Patient and/or significant others verbalize understanding of disease, management, and prevention.

NOC Outcomes
Knowledge: Disease Process;
Knowledge: Treatment Regimen

NIC Interventions
Teaching: Disease Process;
Teaching: Prescribed Medications

Ongoing Assessment

Actions/Interventions

■ Assess understanding of causes, treatment, and prevention plan.

Rationale

This provides an important starting point in education. Patients with superficial thromboses will be treated at home and must understand the treatment plan. Both types of thrombophlebitis may recur.

Therapeutic Interventions

Actions/Interventions

■ Explain the following conditions that place people at risk for blood clots:
- Varicose veins
- Pregnancy
- Obesity
- Surgery (especially pelvic or abdominal)
- Immobility
- Advanced age

■ Explain the rationale for treatment differences between superficial and deep vein thrombosis.

■ Explain the need for bed rest and elevation of leg.

■ Instruct the patient on correct application of compression stockings.

Rationale

Knowledge of causative factors provides direction for subsequent treatment.

Superficial thrombosis is treated at home with supportive care and symptom relief. DVT may be life threatening and require additional treatment with anticoagulation.

Bed rest and elevation of leg prevent embolization with DVT.

Stockings applied incorrectly can act as a tourniquet and facilitate clot formation.

■ = Independent; ▲ = Collaborative

Actions/Interventions

- Instruct the patient to avoid rubbing or massaging calf.

- For patients with DVT, instruct on the following signs of pulmonary embolus:
  - Sudden chest pain
  - Tachypnea
  - Tachycardia
  - Shortness of breath
  - Restlessness

- Discuss the following measures to prevent recurrence:
  - Avoiding staying in one position for long periods

  - Not sitting with legs crossed
  - Maintaining ideal body weight
  - Maintaining adequate fluid status
  - Wearing properly sized, correctly applied compression stockings as prescribed

  - Quitting smoking
  - Participating in an exercise program
  - Avoiding constricting garters or socks with tight bands

Rationale

Avoidance will prevent breaking off clot, which may circulate as embolus.

These can be caused by a clot that breaks off from the original clot in the leg and travels to the lungs.

Avoidance will prevent venous stasis (at home, on train or plane, at desk).

This facilitates blood flow.

This will reduce pressure on legs and venous system.

This prevents hypercoagulability.

Patients with DVT are at high risk for redevelopment and may need to wear stockings over the long term.

Nicotine is a vasoconstrictor that promotes clotting.

Exercise promotes circulation.

Wearing constricting clothing reduces optimal blood flow and promotes clotting.

• RELATED CARE PLAN

Pulmonary thromboembolism, p. 490

Thrombophlebitis

■ = Independent; ▲ = Collaborative

4

Pulmonary Care Plans

 ## Acute Respiratory Distress Syndrome (ARDS)

Shock Lung; Noncardiogenic Pulmonary Edema; Adult Hyaline Membrane Disease; Oxygen Pneumonitis; Posttraumatic Pulmonary Insufficiency; Adult Respiratory Distress Syndrome

Acute respiratory distress syndrome (ARDS) is a form of respiratory failure characterized by noncardiogenic pulmonary edema and a refractory hypoxemia. Although the wet, congested lung condition was known for many years (during World War I the pathology was called *posttraumatic pulmonary insufficiency*, by World War II it was labeled *wet lung* and during the Vietnam War the condition was called *DaNang lung*), it was not until 1967 that Asbaugh first recognized ARDS as a syndrome similar to infant hyaline membrane disease. It is now recognized that the pathology results from damage to the alveolar-capillary membrane. This damage is due to cytokines released by primed neutrophils during a massive immune response (systemic inflammatory response syndrome). These cytokines increase vascular permeability to such an extent that a massive noncardiac pulmonary edema develops. This edema not only interferes with gas exchange but also damages the pulmonary cells that secrete surfactant. Loss of surfactant allows alveoli to collapse and results in very stiff, noncompliant lungs. Fibrin and cell debris build up, forming a membrane (hyaline) and further decreasing gas exchange. The combined edema, loss of surfactant, alveoli collapse, and hyaline membrane formation lead to a progressive refractory hypoxemia and eventually death.

Anyone with a recent history of severe cell damage or sepsis is at risk for developing ARDS. Examples include individuals who have aspirated or who have suffered trauma, burns, multiple fractures, severe head injury, pulmonary contusions, near drowning (salt water aspiration seems to be slightly higher risk than fresh water aspiration), smoke inhalation, carbon monoxide exposure, drug overdose (narcotics, salicylates, tricyclic antidepressants and other sedative drugs, tocolytic agents, hydrochlorothiazide, protamine, interleukin-2), oxygen toxicity, shock, and so on.

Even with outstanding care, the mortality rate for ARDS is 40% to 60%. With such a high mortality rate, it is clear that early detection and prevention are critical as is treatment of any causal factors. Thus careful assessment of all at-risk individuals for early warning signs of developing respiratory distress is a nursing responsibility. Unfortunately, the only early warning sign may be a mild tachypnea. Once ARDS develops, nursing care focuses on maintenance of pulmonary functions. Despite evidence that ARDS is the result of an inflammatory response, antiinflammatory therapy is not effective and, with time, respiratory failure with severe respiratory distress usually results.

This care plan focuses on acute care in the critical care setting where the patient is typically managed with intubation and mechanical ventilation.

Nursing Diagnosis

Ineffective Breathing Pattern

Common Related Factors

Decreased lung compliance:
- Low amounts of surfactant
- Fluid transudation

Fatigue and decreased energy:
- Increased work of breathing
- Primary medical problem
- Buildup of fibrin and cellular debris (hyaline membrane development)

Defining Characteristics

Dyspnea
Shortness of breath
Tachypnea
Abnormal arterial blood gases (ABGs)
Cyanosis
Cough
Use of accessory muscles

Common Expected Outcomes

Patient demonstrates an effective breathing pattern, with normal blood gas results within patient's normal parameters.

Patient verbalizes ability to breathe comfortably without sensation of dyspnea, anxiety, or fear related to a sensation of shortness of breath.

NOC Outcomes

Respiratory Status; Airway Patency; Respiratory Status: Ventilation

NIC Interventions

Respiratory Monitoring; Airway Management

Acute Respiratory Distress Syndrome (ARDS)

Ongoing Assessment

Actions/Interventions

■ Assess respiratory rate and depth.

■ Assess for use of accessory muscles.

■ Assess breath sounds.

Rationale

Breathing pattern is essentially an unconscious response to a perceived threat or to impaired gas exchange. During states of hypoxemia and hypercapnia or hypocapnia, breathing patterns change. Rate and depth of ventilations, controlled by the autonomic nervous system, adjust to maintain homeostasis. With a stiff, noncompliant, wet (pulmonary edema) lung, gas exchange is decreased, leading to hypoxemia, which leads to an increase in the depth and rate of ventilations.

Initially, respiratory rate increases with the decreasing lung compliance. Work of breathing increases greatly as compliance decreases. Moving air in and out of the lungs becomes more and more difficult, and passive ventilation is no longer adequate to meet oxygenation needs. The breathing pattern alters to include use of the accessory muscles to move air into and out of the stiff lungs.

As pulmonary edema increases and fluid moves into the alveoli, adventitious breath sounds (crackles) are heard throughout the lung fields.

Acute Respiratory Distress Syndrome (ARDS)—cont'd

Actions/Interventions	Rationale
■ Assess sensation of dyspnea.	The sensation of dyspnea is associated with hypoxia and may cause anxiety, which leads to increased oxygen demand and may further affect breathing patterns.
■ Assess for cyanosis of tongue, oral mucosa, and skin.	Cyanosis of the tongue, oral mucosa, and skin indicates that the breathing pattern is no longer effective to maintain adequate oxygenation of tissues.
▲ Assess SaO_2 by pulse oximetry; assess ABGs.	Pulse oximetry and ABGs are an objective indication of oxygenation status (and therefore effectiveness of breathing pattern).
■ Assess cough.	Increased pulmonary edema and fibrin buildup stimulate cough reflex.
■ Assess energy level.	As compliance decreases and breathing patterns alter to include use of accessory muscles, the work of breathing increases dramatically, leading to patient fatigue. Energy expenditure increases oxygen demand. Eventually the patient may be incapable of adequately maintaining oxygenation needs.
■ Assess changes in mental status.	Increased restlessness, confusion, and/or irritability can be indicative of insufficient oxygenation and requires further intervention.
▲ Assess electrolyte, complete blood count (CBC) laboratory values, and radiological chest film reports.	Abnormal pH shifts electrolytes, particularly K^+ and Cl^-, which can lead to cardiac dysrhythmias and further compromise oxygenation of the tissues. Decreased hemoglobin and hematocrit further compromises oxygenation (decreased oxygen "carriers"); infection increases inflammatory mediators, which may lead to additional pulmonary insult. As pulmonary edema increases, chest x-rays will reflect increased infiltrates.

Therapeutic Interventions

Actions/Interventions	Rationale
■ Provide reassurance and allay anxiety:	Presence of a trusted person can reduce anxiety. Decreased anxiety will decrease oxygen requirements.
• Have an agreed-on method for calling for assistance (e.g., call light or bell).	The patient will be less anxious if he or she knows the nurse will respond.
• Stay with the patient during episodes of respiratory distress.	Air hunger can cause a patient to be extremely anxious.
■ Position the patient to optimize ventilation: • Although for most ineffective breathing patterns the upright position is most effective because it facilitates lung expansion, for the ARDS patient the prone position may be recommended. Follow physician orders and patient comfort, and observe changes in oxygen saturation levels with position changes. If saturation drops or fails to return promptly to baseline, reposition the patient for optimal oxygenation.	Partial pressure of arterial oxygen may increase in the prone position, possibly because of greater contraction of the diaphragm and increased function of the ventral lung.

■ = Independent; ▲ = Collaborative

Actions/Interventions	Rationale

Actions/Interventions

■ Conserve energy:
  • Bed rest unless otherwise ordered.
  • Organize necessary activity to be least stressful for the patient.
  • Instruct the patient to use diaphragmatic breathing.

▲ Maintain oxygen saturation at or above 90%.

▲ Administer medications as indicated (e.g., steroids, antibiotics, bronchodilators, sedation).

■ Provide suctioning as needed.

■ Keep all team members informed of respiratory status.

▲ Anticipate the need for intubation and mechanical ventilation.

Rationale

Conservation of energy decreases oxygen requirements; diaphragmatic breathing is a more effective breathing pattern.

This breathing technique allows for maximum lung expansion and more efficient exhalation of carbon dioxide.

Oxygen saturation below 90% leads to tissue hypoxia, anaerobic cellular metabolism, acidosis, electrolyte shifts, dysrhythmias, decreased level of consciousness, increasing hypoxia, and ultimately death. Use caution with FIO_2 greater than 40% due to the increased risk of oxygen toxicity.

Steroids may help reduce the inflammation; antibiotics may be indicated in the presence of infection or sepsis to treat the causative organism; the bronchodilators may be useful to provide airway clearance. Sedation increases compliance with ventilation.

Suctioning cleans secretions from pulmonary congestion and reduces the work of breathing.

To be successfully treated, ARDS requires aggressive intervention by multiple team members. The nurse is often the first team member to recognize changes in effective breathing patterns that may require other team members to intervene.

Being prepared for intubation prevents full decompensation of the patient to cardiopulmonary arrest. Early intubation and mechanical ventilation are recommended.

Acute Respiratory Distress Syndrome (ARDS)

NDx Nursing Diagnosis

Impaired Gas Exchange

Common Related Factors

Diffusion defect:
  • Abnormal A-a gradient (greater difficulty for oxygen and carbon dioxide to cross alveolar-capillary membrane) from:
    • Hyaline membrane formation from cellular debris and fibrin
    • Damaged alveolar-capillary membrane
  • Increased shunting leading to an abnormal $\dot{V}/\dot{Q}$ ratio from:
    • Collapsed alveoli
    • Fluid-filled alveoli

Defining Characteristics

Hypoxia resulting in:
  • Restlessness, irritability, and anxiety progressing to somnolence and decreasing level of consciousness
  • Fear of suffocation or death (feeling of "not being able to breathe")
Hypercapnia
Inability to move secretions
Abnormal skin color (pale, dusky)
Tachycardia (effort to increase oxygen delivery to tissues)
Cyanosis

■ = Independent; ▲ = Collaborative

Acute Respiratory Distress Syndrome (ARDS)—cont'd

Common Related Factors—cont'd

- Increased dead space (areas with decreased pulmonary circulation) from:
  - Microembolization in the pulmonary vasculature
  - Increased shunting (shutdown of capillaries to alveoli that are not ventilated)

Common Expected Outcome

Patient maintains optimal gas exchange as evidenced by normal ABGs and alert responsive mentation or no further reduction in mental status.

NOC Outcomes
Respiratory Status: Gas Exchange; Respiratory Status: Ventilation

NIC Interventions
Respiratory Monitoring; Oxygen Therapy; Mechanical Ventilation

Ongoing Assessment

Actions/Interventions	Rationale
■ Assess respirations, noting quality, rate, pattern, depth, and breathing effort.	Abnormality indicates respiratory compromise.
■ Assess for changes in orientation and behavior.	Changes in level of consciousness can indicate development of further hypoxia.
■ Assess lung sounds and note changes.	Adventitious or decreased sounds are indicative of increased pulmonary edema or collapsed alveoli, leading to increased hypoxia.
▲ Use pulse oximetry to monitor oxygen saturation and pulse rate continuously. Keep alarms on at all times.	Pulse oximetry is a useful tool in the clinical setting to detect changes in oxygenation. Oxygen saturation should be maintained at 90% or greater.
▲ Closely monitor ABGs and note changes.	A progressive hypoxemia is apparent on serial ABGs despite increased concentrations of inspired oxygen. Initially, hypocapnia (a decrease in $PaCO_2$) may be present as a result of hyperventilation. However, respiratory acidosis with increase in $PaCO_2$ occurs in later stages as a result of increase in dead space and decrease in lung compliance and alveolar ventilation.
▲ Assess cardiac rhythm for dysrhythmias.	Electrolyte shifts, hypoxia, and mechanical ventilation, especially with positive end-expiratory pressure (PEEP), place patient at risk for cardiac dysrhythmias and decreased cardiac output (see Risk for Decreased Cardiac Output on p. 414).
▲ Monitor chest radiograph reports noting improvement or worsening.	Chest x-ray studies will reflect changing lung status (show bilateral diffuse infiltrates with normal cardiac silhouette to complete whiteout of both lung fields); however, keep in mind that radiographic studies of lung edema lag behind clinical presentation.

■ = Independent; ▲ = Collaborative

Actions/Interventions

▲ Assess pulmonary artery pressure (PAP) and pulmonary capillary wedge pressure (PCWP).

▲ Assess pulmonary function tests.

▲ Assess lactic acid levels.

▲ Assess hydration and electrolytes.

■ Monitor activity level; assess level of fatigue.

■ Assess fear and anxiety.

Therapeutic Interventions

Actions/Interventions

▲ Use a team approach in planning care with the physician, respiratory therapist, family, patient, and other team members.

■ Combine nursing actions (i.e., bath, bed, and dressing changes) and intersperse with rest periods. Temporarily discontinue activity if saturation drops, and make any necessary FIO_2, PEEP, or sedation changes to improve saturation.

■ Change the patient's position every 1 to 2 hours.

■ Elevate head of bed.

■ Institute prone positioning as indicated.

■ Suction as needed.

▲ Administer parenteral fluids and electrolytes as ordered.

■ Measure and record urinary output every hour.

▲ Administer medication as prescribed.

Rationale

Initially PAP will be normal, but with PEEP and continuing deterioration, PAP may increase, leading to further pulmonary edema. Increased capillary blood pressure (BP) forces fluid out of the capillaries and into interstitial spaces and alveoli.

Decreased vital capacity, minute volume, functional residual capacity; decreased pulmonary compliance of greater than 50 mL/cm H_2O; increased shunt fraction greater than 15% to 20% (normal 3% to 4%) are indicative of worsening lung status.

Increasing lactic acid levels are indicative of anaerobic cellular metabolism.

Overhydration or dehydration places the patient at further risk. Tight fluid control is essential to maintain hydration without increasing edema.

Activity can increase the work of breathing and oxygen consumption, leading to fatigue.

Hypoxia and work of breathing decrease available energy and cause feelings of restlessness, anxiety, and fear.

Rationale

Timely and accurate communication of assessments is a must to keep pace with the needed changes: FIO_2, PEEP, calorie requirements, and activity levels.

This minimizes energy expended by the patient and prevents a decreased oxygen saturation.

This facilitates movement and drainage of secretions, increases patient comfort, and maintains skin integrity.

Increasing the head of bed to more than 30 degrees prevents aspiration and ventilator-acquired pneumonia.

Placing patients in the prone position mobilizes blood flow to previously nonperfused (or underperfused) areas of the lungs and can be used to increase oxygenation.

Suctioning clears secretions and increases airway patency to improve gas exchange. Its use should be guided by objective data, not preset time intervals.

These may be required to maintain hydration and electrolyte balance.

Hydration without overhydration is essential. A decrease in urinary output may occur with decreased renal perfusion.

Sedation may be ordered to decrease the patient's energy expenditure during mechanical ventilation and to allow for adequate synchrony of the ventilator so that the

Acute Respiratory Distress Syndrome (ARDS)

■ = Independent; ▲ = Collaborative

Acute Respiratory Distress Syndrome (ARDS)—cont'd

Actions/Interventions

▲ Anticipate the need for intubation and mechanical ventilation with signs of impending respiratory failure.

■ Assist with administration of mechanical ventilation as indicated. Anticipate (assess for) need for PEEP or continuous positive airway pressure (CPAP).

Rationale

patient can be adequately ventilated. Antibiotics may be necessary to treat the underlying cause of the inflammatory response.

Early intubation and mechanical ventilation are recommended to prevent full decompensation of the patient. Mechanical ventilation provides supportive care to maintain adequate oxygenation and ventilation to the patient.

Hypoxemia leads to tissue damage, which leads to increased release of inflammatory mediators, which leads to further lung damage. Mechanical ventilation provides supportive care to maintain adequate oxygenation and ventilation to the patient. Artificial positive pressure (PEEP or CPAP) assists in keeping alveoli open. Treatment with low tidal volumes and increased respiratory rates has been shown to be effective in counteracting decreased lung compliance seen in ARDS. Treatment also needs to focus on the underlying causal factor leading to ARDS (e.g., condition that caused the massive inflammatory response).

NDx Nursing Diagnosis

Risk for Decreased Cardiac Output

Common Risk Factor

Positive pressure ventilation

Common Expected Outcome

Patient achieves adequate cardiac output (CO) as evidenced by strong peripheral pulses, normal vital signs, urine output greater than 30 mL/hr, warm dry skin, no evidence of bowel or cerebral ischemia.

NOC Outcomes

Cardiac Pump Effectiveness; Tissue Perfusion: Peripheral; Tissue Perfusion: Abdominal Organs; Circulation Status

NIC Interventions

Hemodynamic Regulation; Mechanical Ventilation

Pulmonary Care Plans

■ = Independent; ▲ = Collaborative

Ongoing Assessment

Actions/Interventions

▲ Assess vital signs and hemodynamic pressures (central venous pressure, PAP) every hour, and with changes in positive pressure ventilation and inotrope administration.

▲ Obtain CO measurement after positive pressure ventilation changes.

■ Monitor urine output with Foley catheter.

■ Assess skin warmth and quality of peripheral pulses.

Rationale

Changes in BP, pulse, or other pressure monitoring devices are warning signs of decreasing CO and may necessitate changes in PEEP.

Artificial positive pressure (PEEP or CPAP) assists in keeping alveoli open; however, the positive pressure compresses the great vessels returning to the heart, which, in turn, decreases the CO. BP and strong peripheral pulses are one way the nurse can assess CO. The level of consciousness will decrease if CO is severely compromised.

With positive pressure ventilation, pressure from the diaphragm decreases blood flow to the kidneys and the gastrointestinal tract and could result in a drop in urine output and/or an ischemic bowel. The brain is very sensitive to a decrease in blood flow and may respond by releasing antidiuretic hormone (to increase water and sodium retention), further reducing urinary output.

Cold, clammy skin is secondary to compensatory increase in sympathetic nervous system stimulation and low CO and desaturation.

Therapeutic Interventions

Action/Interventions

▲ Administer medications as prescribed, noting response and observing for side effects.

▲ Administer intravenous (IV) fluids, as prescribed.

■ Anticipate need to decrease level of PEEP to a range that facilitates improved CO, if fluid administration and inotropes are not successful.

Rationale

Inotropic medications may be used to increase CO. Sedatives and analgesics are used to relieve pain and agitation. Neuromuscular blocking agents are given to promote synchronous breathing with mechanical ventilation.

This is indicated to maintain optimal fluid balance and increase CO without causing edema.

This helps obtain an "optimal PEEP" level for that individual patient and achieves maximal oxygenation benefits without causing a decrease in CO.

NDx Nursing Diagnosis

Ineffective Protection

Common Related Factors

Positive-pressure ventilation
Decreased pulmonary compliance
Increased secretions

Defining Characteristics

Barotrauma:
- Crepitus
- Subcutaneous emphysema

Acute Respiratory Distress Syndrome (ARDS)

■ = Independent; ▲ = Collaborative

Acute Respiratory Distress Syndrome (ARDS)—cont'd

Defining Characteristics—cont'd

- Altered chest excursion
- Asymmetrical chest
- Abnormal ABGs
- Shift in trachea
- Restlessness
- Evidence of pneumothorax on chest radiograph

Common Expected Outcome

The potential for injury from barotrauma is reduced as a result of ongoing assessment and early intervention.

NOC Outcome
Respiratory Status: Ventilation

NIC Intervention
Mechanical Ventilation

Ongoing Assessment

Actions/Interventions

■ Assess for signs of barotrauma every hour: crepitus, subcutaneous emphysema, altered chest excursion, asymmetrical chest, ABGs, shift in trachea, restlessness, evidence of pneumothorax on chest radiograph.

▲ Notify physician of signs of barotrauma immediately.

▲ Monitor chest radiograph reports daily and obtain a stat portable chest radiograph if barotrauma is suspected.

▲ Monitor plateau pressures with the respiratory therapist.

Rationale

Frequent assessments are needed because barotrauma can occur at any time and the patient will not show signs of dyspnea, shortness of breath, or tachypnea if heavily sedated to maintain ventilation.

Being prepared for an emergency helps prevent further complications.

Vigilant monitoring helps reduce complications.

Elevation of plateau pressures increases both the risk and incidence of barotrauma when a patient is on mechanical ventilation.

Therapeutic Interventions

Actions/Interventions

▲ Use permissive hypercapnia.

▲ Anticipate need for chest tube placement, and prepare as needed.

Rationale

This maintains plateau pressure less than 35 cm H_2O and oxygen saturation of 90% or greater.

If barotrauma is suspected, intervention must follow immediately to prevent tension pneumothorax while the patient is on the ventilator.

■ = Independent; ▲ = Collaborative

Nursing Diagnosis

Impaired Physical Mobility

Common Related Factors

Acute respiratory failure
Monitoring devices
Mechanical ventilation
Medications

Defining Characteristics

Imposed restrictions of movement
Decreased muscle strength
Limited range of motion (ROM)

Common Expected Outcome

Patient's optimal physical mobility is maintained.

NOC Outcome
Mobility Body Positioning: Self-Initiated

NIC Interventions
Positioning; Exercise Therapy:
Joint Mobility

Ongoing Assessment

Actions/Interventions

- Assess for imposed restrictions of movement.

- Assess ROM of extremities and assess muscle strength.

- Assess for orthostatic hypotension.

Rationale

Patients with acute respiratory distress syndrome initially are bedridden and may have multiple IV sites, which, depending on their location, may limit movement. In addition, the patient who is intubated and ventilated is restricted by the ventilator tubing and may need bilateral wrist restraints to prevent dislodgment or self-extubation.

These assessments provide data on extent of physical problem.

Prolonged bed rest, decreased oxygenation, and decreased CO place the patient at risk for orthostatic hypotension.

Therapeutic Interventions

Actions/Interventions

- Turn and reposition the patient every 2 hours.

- Maintain limbs in functional alignment (with pillows). Support feet in the dorsiflexed position.
- Perform or assist with passive ROM exercises to extremities.

Rationale

Frequent position changes help maintain muscular activity.

Proper positioning prevents footdrop.

This prevents contractures, maintains joint mobility, promotes circulation, and decreases dependent edema.

■ = Independent; ▲ = Collaborative

Acute Respiratory Distress Syndrome (ARDS)

Acute Respiratory Distress Syndrome (ARDS)—cont'd

Actions/Interventions

▲ Initiate activity increases (dangling of legs, sitting in chair, ambulation) as condition allows.

Rationale

The pulmonary changes with ARDS may result in activity intolerance, so oxygen saturation through pulse oximetry should be monitored closely with any increase in activity. Increased activity can reduce feelings of helplessness and prevent hazards of immobility such as thrombosis and bone demineralization.

ND𝗑 Nursing Diagnosis

Risk for Impaired Skin Integrity

Common Risk Factors

Prolonged bed rest
Immobility
Altered vasomotor tone
Altered nutritional state
Prolonged intubation
Ischemia

Common Expected Outcome

Patient's skin integrity is maintained as a result of ongoing assessment and early intervention.

NOC Outcomes
Tissue Integrity: Skin and Mucous Membranes; Immobility Consequences: Physiological

NIC Interventions
Skin Surveillance; Pressure Management; Artificial Airway Management

---

Ongoing Assessment

Actions/Interventions

■ Assess bony prominences for signs of threatened or actual breakdown of skin at least once a day.

■ Assess around endotracheal (ET) tube for crusting of secretions, redness, or irritation.

■ Assess for signs of skin breakdown beneath ET-securing tape or device.

Rationale

Early identification of stage I reddened areas allows for intervention to promote resolution and prevent progression to stage II breakdown.

Presence of secretions will increase skin irritation.

This is a common site for skin breakdown and infection.

■ = Independent; ▲ = Collaborative

Therapeutic Interventions

Actions/Interventions	Rationale
■ Turn and reposition the patient every 2 hours.	Frequent pressure changes are needed to relieve pressure sites.
■ Institute prophylactic use of pressure-relieving devices, including air mattress.	Lower-risk patients can use good-quality foam mattress overlay (at least 5 inches thick); higher-risk patients require water mattress, dynamic air mattress, or low-airloss type beds.
■ Consult with physician and dietitian about patient's nutritional intake.	Patients on ventilators may have increased caloric needs but decreased intake of protein and other essential nutrients to support skin integrity.
■ Maintain skin integrity around artificial airway:	
• If the patient is nasally intubated, notify the physician if skin is red or irritated or breakdown is noted.	The tube may need to be moved to the other naris if skin irritation occurs.
• If the patient is orally intubated, the tube should be repositioned from side to side every 24 to 48 hours.	This helps prevent pressure necrosis on the lower lip.
■ Provide mouth care every 2 hours.	Frequent mouth care promotes comfort and decreases bacterial growth in the mouth.
■ Keep ET tube free of crusting of secretions.	This prevents skin irritation.

Nursing Diagnosis

Deficient Knowledge

Common Related Factors

New equipment
New environment
New condition

Defining Characteristics

Increased frequency of questions posed by patient and significant others
Inability to respond correctly to questions

Common Expected Outcome

Patient or significant others demonstrate understanding of serious nature of disease and treatment regimen.

NOC Outcomes

Knowledge: Disease Process;
Knowledge: Treatment Procedures;
Treatment Regimen

NIC Intervention

Teaching: Disease Process

Acute Respiratory Distress Syndrome (ARDS)

■ = Independent; ▲ = Collaborative

Acute Respiratory Distress Syndrome (ARDS)—cont'd

Ongoing Assessment

Actions/Interventions

- Evaluate understanding of ARDS: causal factors and treatment regimen.

▲ Assess level of cognitive function, motivation to learn, barriers to learning, and attitude toward health.

▲ Evaluate critical areas of deficient knowledge for the patient or significant others.

Rationale

This provides an important starting point in teaching.

Learning is most effective if information is presented at the appropriate level and during periods of readiness to learn.

Teaching plan is designed to meet the patient's perception of knowledge needs. Too much information or information given at the wrong time can cause the patient additional anxiety or feelings of being overwhelmed. Give the patient as much control as possible over the learning process.

Therapeutic Interventions

Actions/Interventions

- Keep the patient or significant others informed of current patient status.

Rationale

ARDS is a serious syndrome with a high mortality rate. Significant others must be informed of changes. These patients are typically managed with intubation and mechanical ventilation and require critical care nursing in an acute care setting. Many causal factors are related to ARDS, and the patient or significant others should be informed of the need to treat the underlying cause.

- Orient the patient and significant others to intensive care unit (ICU) surroundings, routines, equipment alarms, and noises.

The ICU is a busy environment that can be very upsetting to the patient or significant others.

- Explain all procedures to the patient before performing them.

This helps decrease the patient's anxiety. Fear of the unknown can make the patient anxious or uncooperative.

> • RELATED CARE PLANS
>
> Acute respiratory failure, p. 508
> Mechanical ventilation, p. 459

Asthma

Bronchial Asthma; Status Asthmaticus

Asthma is a clinical syndrome characterized by an increased responsiveness or reaction of the tracheobronchial tree to a variety of stimuli; hence asthma is often referred to as *reactive airway disease*. Although the stimuli causing a reaction are individually defined, respiratory infection, cold weather, physical exertion, some medications, and allergens are common triggers. When a hypersensitive individual is exposed to a trigger, a rapid inflammatory response with subsequent bronchospasm occurs. Mast cells, signaled by

■ = Independent; ▲ = Collaborative

Pulmonary Care Plans

antibody E, release inflammatory mediators that produce a swelling and spasm of the bronchial tubes. This causes adventitious breath sounds (wheezing), increased mucus production, and feelings of "not being able to breathe." Eosinophils and neutrophils rush to the area and additional cytokines are released, some of which are long acting and result in epithelial damage, late-phase airway edema, continued mucus hypersecretion, and additional hyperresponsiveness of the bronchial smooth muscle. With repeated attacks, remodeling of the airway occurs as scar tissue replaces normal tissue. Status asthmaticus occurs when the asthma attack is refractory to the usual treatment, with clinical manifestations that are more severe, prolonged, and life threatening.

Although this care plan focuses on acute care in the hospital setting, current thinking is to prevent the hypersensitivity reaction and thus keep airway remodeling at a minimum. For this reason, an asthma plan individualized for each patient and for optimal outpatient management is emphasized.

Asthma

NDx Nursing Diagnosis

Ineffective Breathing Pattern

Common Related Factor

Swelling and spasm of the bronchial tubes in response to allergies, drugs, stress, infection, inhaled irritants

Defining Characteristics

Dyspnea
Tachypnea
Cyanosis
Cough
Nasal flaring
Wheezing
Respiratory depth changes
Use of accessory muscles
Prolonged expiratory phase

Common Expected Outcome

Patient maintains optimal breathing pattern, as evidenced by regular respiratory rate or pattern, and eupnea.

NOC Outcomes
Respiratory Status: Ventilation; Vital Signs

NIC Interventions
Respiratory Monitoring; Vital Signs Monitoring; Medical Administration

Ongoing Assessment

Actions/Interventions

■ Assess respiratory rate and depth; monitor breathing pattern.

Rationale

Respiratory rate and rhythm changes can be early warning signs to impending respiratory difficulties.

➤ Asthma–cont'd

Actions/Interventions	Rationale

Actions/Interventions

- ■ Assess relationship of inspiration to expiration.

- ■ Assess for conversational dyspnea.

- ■ Assess for dyspnea, use of accessory muscles, retractions, and flaring of nostrils.
- ■ Assess breath sounds and note wheezes or other adventitious breath sounds.

- ▲ Monitor oxygen saturation by pulse oximetry, maintaining the oxygen saturation at 90% or higher, with oxygen applied as ordered by the physician.
- ▲ Monitor arterial blood gases (ABGs).

- ▲ Monitor peak expiratory flow rates and forced expiratory volumes as obtained by the respiratory therapist.

- ■ Assess level of anxiety.

- ■ Assess for fatigue and the patient's perception of how tired he or she feels.
- ■ Assess the patient's vital signs as needed while in distress.

- ▲ Assess for the presence of pulsus paradoxus of 12 mm Hg or greater.

Rationale

Reactive airways allow air to move into the lungs more easily than out of the lungs. If the patient is gasping and frantically trying to "get air," an intervention to assist the patient develop a more effective breathing pattern may be necessary.

Shortness of breath during normal conversation indicates respiratory distress.

These signify an increase in respiratory effort.

Wheezing occurs as a result of bronchospasm. Adventitious breath sounds may indicate a worsening condition or an additional developing pathology such as pneumonia. Diminishing wheezing and inaudible breath sounds are an ominous finding and indicate impending respiratory failure.

Pulse oximetry is a useful, noninvasive tool to detect early changes in oxygenation.

During a mild to moderate asthma attack, patients may develop a respiratory alkalosis. Hypoxemia leads to increased respiratory rate and depth, and carbon dioxide is blown off. An ominous finding is respiratory acidosis, which usually indicates that respiratory failure is pending and that mechanical ventilation may be necessary.

The severity of the exacerbation can be measured objectively by monitoring these values. The peak expiratory flow rate (PEFR) is the maximum flow rate that can be generated during a forced expiratory maneuver with fully inflated lungs. It is measured in liters per second and requires maximal effort. When done with good effort, it correlates well with forced expiratory volume in 1 second (FEV_1) measured by spirometry and provides a simple reproducible measure of airway obstruction.

Hypoxia and the sensation of being "not able to breathe" is frightening and may cause worsening hypoxia.

Fatigue may indicate increasing distress, leading to respiratory failure.

With initial hypoxia and hypercapnia, blood pressure (BP), heart rate (HR), and respiratory rate increase. As the hypoxia and/or hypercapnia become severe, BP and HR drop and respiratory failure may ensue.

Pulsus paradoxus is an accentuation of the normal drop in systolic arterial BP with inspiration. Normally the difference in systolic BP at expiration and inspiration is less than 10 mm Hg. A pulsus paradoxus of 12 mm Hg or greater with asthma is a predictor of severe airflow obstruction.

■ = Independent; ▲ = Collaborative

Therapeutic Interventions

Actions/Interventions	Rationale
■ Keep head of bed elevated.	This position allows for adequate diaphragm excursion and lung expansion.
■ Encourage slow deep breathing. Instruct the patient to use pursed-lip breathing for exhalation. Instruct the patient to time breathing so that exhalation takes 2 to 3 times as long as inspiration.	Pursed-lip breathing during exhalation produces a positive distending pressure within the bronchioles, which facilitates expiratory airflow by helping to keep the bronchioles open. Prolonged expiration prevents air trapping.
■ Plan activity and rest to maximize the patient's energy.	Fatigue is common with the increased work of breathing from the ineffective breathing pattern. Activity increases metabolic rate and oxygen requirements.
▲ Use β_2-adrenergic agonist drugs by metered-dose inhaler (MDI) or nebulizer (per respiratory therapist) as prescribed.	β_2-Adrenergic agonist drugs relax airway smooth muscle and are the treatment of choice for acute exacerbations of asthma. These short-acting inhaled bronchodilators work quickly to open the air passages, making it easier to breathe and decrease bronchoconstriction.
▲ Administer other medications as ordered.	Corticosteroids are the most effective antiinflammatory drugs for the treatment of reversible airflow obstruction. They may be given parenterally, orally, or inhaled, depending upon the severity of the attack. Inhaled steroids should be administered after β-adrenergic agonists. During severe attacks, anticholinergics (e.g., ipratropium bromide [Atrovent]) may be effective when used in combination with β-adrenergic agonists. They produce bronchodilation by reducing intrinsic vagal tone to the airway and have been found to be synergistic in their effect with β-adrenergic agonists. The gold standard, however, to manage severe attacks continues to be corticosteroids and β-adrenergic agonists.
▲ Use permissive hypercapnia.	This maintains plateau pressure less than 35 cm H_2O and oxygen saturation of 90% or more.
▲ Anticipate the need for alternate therapies if life-threatening bronchospasm continues:	
• Magnesium infusion	Magnesium possesses bronchodilating properties, but the role in acute asthma still remains controversial.
• Heliox (a helium-oxygen mixture)	Helium is less dense than nitrogen and lessens functional resistance when gas flow is turbulent due to bronchospasm. Heliox is not available in all institutions.
• General anesthesia	General anesthesia is used when there is both severe dynamic hyperinflation and profound hypercapnia that cannot be corrected by increasing minute ventilation.

Asthma

■ = Independent; ▲ = Collaborative

Asthma—cont'd

 Nursing Diagnosis

Ineffective Airway Clearance

Common Related Factors	Defining Characteristics
Bronchospasm	Abnormal lung sounds (rhonchi, wheezes)
Excessive mucus production	Changes in respiratory rate or depth
Ineffective cough and fatigue	Cough
	Cyanosis
	Dyspnea
	Abnormal ABGs
	Verbalized chest tightness

Common Expected Outcome	
Patient's airway is maintained free of secretions as evidenced by normal or improved breath sounds and normal ABGs or oxygen saturation of 90% or greater on pulse oximeter.	**NOC Outcomes** Respiratory Status: Airway Patency; Symptom Control **NIC Interventions** Airway Management; Cough Enhancement; Ventilation Assistance; Calming Technique

Ongoing Assessment

Actions/Interventions

- Auscultate lungs with each routine vital sign check.

- Assess secretions, noting color, viscosity, odor, and amount.

- Assess for changes in respiratory rate or depth.

- Assess cough for effectiveness and productivity.

- Note color changes (lips, buccal mucosa, nail beds).

- Monitor pulse oximetry.

Rationale

This allows for early detection and correction of abnormalities.

Thick tenacious secretions increase hypoxia and may be indicative of dehydration. Colored or odorous secretions may indicate bleeding (brown, red) or infections (green, yellow, salmon-colored).

Abnormality indicates respiratory compromise. An increase in respiratory rate may be a compensation for airway obstruction.

Consider possible causes of an ineffective cough: respiratory muscle fatigue, severe bronchospasm, thick tenacious secretions.

Cyanosis occurs when at least 5 g of hemoglobin are desaturated.

Pulse oximetry is a useful tool to detect changes in oxygenation. Oxygen saturation should be maintained at 90% or greater.

■ = Independent; ▲ = Collaborative

Actions/Interventions

▲ Monitor laboratory work as ordered:
- Theophylline level (if on theophylline)

- ABGs

- Complete blood count with special attention to white blood cell (WBC) count
- Serum potassium level

▲ Monitor chest radiograph reports.

Rationale

Results guide further treatment. Theophylline increases anxiety and causes tachycardia. It has a narrow window of therapeutic effectiveness, placing the patient at risk for subtherapeutic levels or toxicity.

Carbon dioxide retention occurs as the patient becomes fatigued from the increased work of breathing caused by the bronchoconstriction. Once the patient is intubated and mechanically ventilated, permissive hypercapnia may be used to maintain plateau pressure less than 35 cm H_2O.

An increased WBC count is associated with infection.

β-Adrenergic agonists cause potassium to shift intracellularly and can result in decline in serum potassium levels.

The chest x-ray provides information about lung hyperinflation, presence of infiltrates, or presence of barotrauma.

Therapeutic Interventions

Actions/Interventions

■ Keep the patient as calm as possible.

■ Pace activities.

▲ Ensure that respiratory treatments are given as prescribed; notify respiratory therapist as the need arises. Obtain PEFR before and after treatments.

■ Encourage the patient to cough, especially after treatments. Teach effective coughing techniques.

▲ Maintain humidified oxygen as prescribed.

▲ Administer medications and intravenous (IV) fluids as prescribed.

■ Anticipate the need for intubation and mechanical ventilation if ABGs begin to deteriorate, work of breathing continues to increase, continued PEFR is less than 30% to 50% of baseline with failure of PEFR to improve after treatment, and patient has subjective feelings of doom and/or decreasing alertness.

■ Encourage increased fluid intake (up to 3000 mL/day) if there are no contraindications such as cardiac or renal disease.

Rationale

Anxiety during an asthma attack can further potentiate the exacerbation.

Fatigue can increase the work of breathing and decrease cough effectiveness.

PEFR is the fastest airflow rate reached at any time during exhalation. It should improve with effective therapy.

Controlled coughing techniques help mobilize secretions from smaller airways to larger airways because the coughing is done more effectively.

This decreases viscosity of secretions.

Mucolytic agents may be used in conjunction with a bronchodilator.

Being prepared for an emergency helps prevent further complications.

Fluids are lost from mouth breathing and oxygen therapy. Mucous membranes dry out. Maintaining hydration increases ciliary action to remove secretions and decreases viscosity of secretions.

Asthma

■ = Independent; ▲ = Collaborative

Pulmonary Care Plans *(vertical sidebar text)*

 Asthma—cont'd

 Nursing Diagnosis

Anxiety

Common Related Factors	Defining Characteristics
Respiratory distress Change in health status Change in environment Hypoxia	Complaints of inability to breathe Uncooperative behavior Restlessness Apprehensiveness Insomnia Increased heart rate Frequent requests for someone to be in room Diaphoresis

Common Expected Outcome

Patient's anxiety is reduced as evidenced by cooperative behavior, calm appearance, and verbalized report of decreased anxiety.

NOC Outcome
Anxiety Self-Control

NIC Interventions
Anxiety Reduction; Calming Technique

Ongoing Assessment

Actions/Interventions

■ Assess anxiety level, including vital signs, respiratory status, irritability, apprehension, and orientation.

▲ Assess oxygen saturation.

▲ Assess theophylline level if the patient is on theophylline.

Rationale

Anxiety increases as breathing becomes more difficult. Also, anxiety can affect respiratory rate and rhythm, causing rapid, shallow breathing.

Anxiety increases with increasing hypoxia and may be an early warning sign that the patient's oxygen levels are decreasing.

Theophylline increases anxiety and causes tachycardia. It has a narrow window of therapeutic effectiveness, placing the patient at risk for subtherapeutic or toxic levels.

Therapeutic Interventions

Actions/Interventions

■ Stay with the patient and encourage slow, deep breathing.

■ Explain all procedures to the patient before starting; be simple and concise.

Rationale

The presence of a trusted person may be helpful during an anxious period.

An informed patient who understands the treatment plan will be more cooperative and less anxious.

■ = Independent; ▲ = Collaborative

Actions/Interventions	Rationale
■ Explain importance of remaining as calm as possible.	Maintaining calmness will decrease oxygen consumption and work of breathing.
▲ Assure the patient and significant others of close, continuous monitoring that will ensure prompt intervention.	This provides a measure of safety.
■ Keep significant others informed of the patient's progress.	Information can help relieve apprehension. Anxiety may be readily transferred to the patient from family members.
■ Avoid excessive reassurance.	Excessive reassurance may actually increase anxiety for many people.
■ Explore coping mechanisms with the patient.	Anxiety-reduction techniques are somewhat patient defined. Music therapy and massage may decrease anxiety for some patients and annoy others. Discussing reasons for the anxious feeling may be effective for some. Interaction with the patient and significant others will help define what works best for the individual.
■ Teach relaxation techniques such as progressive muscle relaxation if the patient's condition permits.	Although anxiety as the result of hypoxia requires correcting the hypoxic condition, some patients will experience anxiety as a learned response to the asthma attack. If this is the case, relaxation techniques may be effective in decreasing the anxiety.

 Nursing Diagnosis

Deficient Knowledge

Common Related Factors
Chronicity of disease
Long-term medical management

Defining Characteristics
Absence of questions
Anxiety
Inability to answer questions properly
Ineffective self-care

Common Expected Outcome
Patient or significant others verbalize knowledge of disease and its management and community resources available to assist the patient in coping with chronic disease.

NOC Outcomes
Knowledge: Health Behaviors; Knowledge: Medication; Asthma Control

NIC Interventions
Teaching Disease Process; Prescribed Medication

Asthma

■ = Independent; ▲ = Collaborative

Asthma–cont'd

Ongoing Assessment

Actions/Interventions	Rationale

■ Assess knowledge of asthma and of asthma medications.
  • Ability to distinguish between rescue medications and stabilizing medications
  • Correct use of MDI
  • Use of spacers with MDI
  • Sequence to use medications
	Short-acting β-agonists are the rescue medication of choice. Long-acting $β_2$-adrenergic agonists take too long to act in an emergency. Antiinflammatory medications, such as mast cell stabilizers or leukotriene-blocking agents, are designed to prevent the release of inflammatory mediators. Once an attack is present, the inflammatory mediators are already at work, and blocking release is not immediately effective. Improper use of MDI will result in the medications not getting deep enough to influence the tracheobronchial tree. $β_2$-adrenergic agonists should be used before inhaled steroids because they open the airways and allow the antiinflammatory medication to reach deeper into the lung fields. Rinsing the mouth after using an inhaled steroid prevents a yeast infection. Increase each medication's effectiveness by correct use of spacers, slow deep inhalation, and breath holding after inhalation.

■ Assess past and present therapies, as well as the patient's response to them.	Evaluation guides subsequent teaching efforts.
■ Evaluate self-care activities: preventive care and home management of acute attack.	The patient is living with a chronic disease and will be required to self-manage the disease.
■ Assess knowledge of care for status asthmaticus, as appropriate.	Assessment guides intervention.
■ Assess tobacco use.	Although assessment of tobacco use is critical for all patients, it is especially important for patients suffering from lung disease. If the patient is a tobacco user, interventions need to be offered.

Therapeutic Interventions

Actions/Interventions	Rationale
■ Explain disease to the patient and significant others.	Thorough understanding facilitates optimal treatment. A common misconception held by patients and families is that asthma attacks can be averted without medication through self-control and discipline.
■ Identify precipitating factors for the patient and instruct patient how to avoid them (e.g., cigarette smoke, aspirin, air pollution, allergens, seasonal variations).	Information enables patient to take control. Environmental trigger control can reduce frequency of attacks and improve patient's quality of life.
■ Instruct in use of peak flow meters and develop an individualized plan on how to adjust medications and when to seek medical advice. Establish the patient's "personal best" PEFR.	This is the standard against which future measurements are evaluated. Use the zone system, individualized to the patient. Personal best is established by having the patient obtain and document peak flow each morning before medication use and in late afternoon for 2 weeks. Personal best in the highest peak flow reading regularly blown, which is then used to calculate the patient's zone.

■ = Independent; ▲ = Collaborative

Actions/Interventions	Rationale
	• GREEN ZONE: 80% to 100% of personal best.
	• YELLOW ZONE: 50% to 80% of personal best; this signals caution, and an acute exacerbation may be present. A temporary increase in medication may be indicated.
	• RED ZONE: Below 50% of personal best; this signals a medical alert. A β_2-adrenergic agonist should be taken, and if there is no improvement in PEFR to yellow or green zones, the physician should be notified.
■ Reinforce need for taking medications as prescribed.	Medications, including antiinflammatory agents and bronchodilators, reduce incidence of full-blown attacks.
■ Review all medications with the patient including review of zones and dosage of each medication in each zone.	Vigilant monitoring helps reduce complications.
■ Teach how to administer MDIs, spacers, dry powder capsules, or diskus with correct technique. Instruct patients to rinse their mouth with water after using inhalants containing a steroid component to avoid oral yeast infection.	Return demonstrations on techniques are necessary to ensure appropriate delivery of the medication.
■ Teach warning signs and symptoms of an asthma attack and importance of early treatment of impending attack. Provide written copy.	Patients need to have their own treatment plan for any situation.
■ Reinforce what to do in an asthma attack: • Home management • When to go to emergency department • Prevention	Information enables the patient to take control and reduce life-threatening situations.
■ Instruct the patient to keep emergency phone numbers by the telephone.	Advance planning avoids delay in securing assistance.
■ Address long-term management issues.	Environmental controls, control of allergens, avoidance of precipitators, controlling air pollutants (avoidance of smoke, perfumes, aerosol sprays, powder, or talc), and good health habits help avoid attacks.
■ Discuss the need for the patient to obtain vaccines for pneumococcal pneumonia and yearly vaccine for influenza.	Regular immunizations decrease occurrence or severity of these diseases.
■ Discuss use of medical alert bracelet or other identification.	These alert others to asthma history.
▲ Refer to support groups, as appropriate.	Community resources can provide support for patients as they learn disease management and appropriate health behavior changes such as smoking cessation.

Asthma

Chest Trauma

Pneumothorax; Tension Pneumothorax; Flail Chest; Fractured Ribs; Pulmonary Contusion; Hemothorax; Myocardial Contusion; Cardiac Tamponade

Chest trauma is a blunt or penetrating injury of the thoracic cavity that can result in a potentially life-threatening situation secondary to hemothorax, pneumothorax, tension pneumothorax, flail chest, pulmonary contusion, myocardial contusion, and/or cardiac tamponade. This care plan focuses on acute care in the hospital setting.

Nursing Diagnosis

Ineffective Breathing Pattern

Common Related Factors

Simple pneumothorax
Tension pneumothorax
Pain
Flail chest
Simple hemothorax (less than 400 mL blood)
Massive hemothorax (1500 mL blood)
Pulmonary contusion

Defining Characteristics

Shortness of breath
Dyspnea
Tachypnea
Chest pain
Decreased breath sounds on affected side
Hyperresonance on affected side to percussion (pneumothorax)
Dullness on affected side to percussion (hemothorax)
Unequal chest expansion
Abnormal arterial blood gases (ABGs)
Anxiety, restlessness
Cyanosis
Jugular venous distention
Tracheal deviation toward unaffected side
Subcutaneous emphysema
Paradoxical chest movements (flail chest)

Common Expected Outcome

Patient experiences effective breathing pattern as evidenced by eupnea, normal skin color, regular respiratory rate or pattern, and normal blood gas values within patient parameters.

NOC Outcome
Respiratory Status: Ventilation

NIC Interventions
Respiratory Monitoring; Airway Management; Ventilation Assistance

Ongoing Assessment

Actions/Interventions

■ Assess airway for patency.
■ Assess for respiratory distress signs and symptoms: breathing patterns, lung sounds (presence or absence),

Rationale

Maintaining airway is always the highest priority.
These allow early detection of deterioration.

■ = Independent; ▲ = Collaborative

Actions/Interventions

use of accessory muscles, changes in orientation, restlessness, skin color, change in ABGs or oxygen saturation through pulse oximetry, and respiratory stridor.

■ Assess chest excursion.

■ Assess for pain quality, location, and severity and whether it increases with inspiration.

■ Assess trachea position.

■ Assess and inspect chest wall for obvious injuries that allow air to enter pleural cavity.

■ Assess wound size and location. Assess for presence of contusions, abrasions, and bruising on chest.

▲ Monitor chest radiographs.

■ Assess for subcutaneous emphysema or crepitus.

■ Assess for tension pneumothorax: respiratory distress, tachycardia, cyanosis, tachypnea, hypotension, paradoxical chest movement, mediastinal shift (toward unaffected side), changes in breath sounds, distant heart sounds, subcutaneous emphysema.

▲ Assess history of traumatic event: what happened, when, pain, and so forth.

Rationale

Paradoxical movement is a sign of flail chest. Decreased chest expansion on affected side is a sign of pneumothorax/hemothorax.

This is a sign of rib fracture.

Deviation from midline is a sign of tension pneumothorax.

Air entering the pleural cavity would cause pneumothorax.

Wound size and location may be the cause of the ineffective breathing pattern. Further injuries may have occurred beneath these integumentary manifestations of trauma (e.g., fractured ribs, pulmonary contusion, myocardial contusion).

The chest radiograph will confirm correct placement of chest tubes, indicate signs of improvement of pneumothorax or hemothorax, and indicate the presence of rib fractures.

This is a sign of air escaping into the subcutaneous tissues.

Tension pneumothorax is a medical emergency. As pressure within the thorax increases, the great vessels and the lung become compressed, resulting in severe cardiovascular and pulmonary compromise that can quickly become fatal. Immediate identification of the problem is essential.

History of traumatic event will assist in alerting the health care team of injury not immediately visible that may be causing the ineffective breathing pattern.

Therapeutic Interventions

Actions/Interventions

■ Suction, as needed.

■ Insert oral or nasal airway as condition warrants.

▲ Provide pain relief.

■ Place in sitting position, if not contraindicated.

▲ Provide oxygen therapy.

■ If flail chest is present, tape flail segment or place manual pressure over the flail segment.

Rationale

Suctioning removes secretions and optimizes gas exchange.

Artificial airways may be indicated to maintain airway patency.

Pain interferes with deep breathing and effective ventilation.

This assists lung expansion.

This maintains oxygen saturation of 90% or greater for adequate oxygenation.

Patients with increasing respiratory distress may require external pressure to stabilize the chest until more definitive treatment (intubation, surgical stabilization) is initiated. This will prevent the outward motion of

Chest Trauma

■ = Independent; ▲ = Collaborative

Pulmonary Care Plans

Actions/Interventions

■ If open pneumothorax is present:
- Cover chest wall defect with 4 × 4 dressing. Tape on three sides with waterproof tape.

▲ If the patient is not in severe respiratory distress, prepare for chest radiograph.

▲ If tension pneumothorax is suspected, prepare for emergency thoracentesis.

▲ If severe respiratory distress or respiratory status is steadily deteriorating, prepare for chest tube placement. Connect the chest tube to water seal drainage to reinflate the lung and remove blood from the pleural space.

▲ Prepare for intubation if the patient's condition warrants.

Rationale

flail chest. The flail segment will still move inward with respirations, but stopping the outward motion will help decrease the pendelluft motion to the mediastinum and great vessels.

An untaped side allows air to escape from the pleural cavity (flutter-valve effect) so that tension does not continue to increase.

The chest radiograph is used to determine pneumothorax or hemothorax size and/or to confirm suspected diagnosis. Patients with small pneumothoraces, hemothoraces, and minimal symptoms may not require a chest tube. However, if the patient's condition deteriorates with the need to be intubated or mechanically ventilated, a chest tube will be required, even with small pneumothoraces, because of the high risk of developing a tension pneumothorax in that circumstance.

This procedure relieves air tension in the pleural space on the affected side.

Larger chest tubes are inserted for hemothorax than for pneumothorax to help alleviate chest tube clotting.

Patients with flail chest may be stable initially because of compensatory mechanisms (e.g., splinting of flail segment and shallow respirations). As these compensatory mechanisms fail, increasing respiratory distress develops. Intubation and positive-pressure ventilation are a means of stabilizing the flail segment by preventing the patient from breathing independently, resulting in inward movement of the flail segment.

NDx Nursing Diagnosis

Deficient Fluid Volume

Common Related Factors	Defining Characteristics
Trauma	Tachycardia
Hemothorax	Hypotension
Chest tube drainage	Cool, clammy skin
	Pallor
	Restlessness
	Anxiety
	Mental status changes
	Decreased urine output

■ = Independent; ▲ = Collaborative

Thirst
Dry mucous membranes
Weakness
Elevated hematocrit

Common Expected Outcome

Patient experiences adequate fluid volume as evidenced by urine output greater than 30 mL/hr, normotensive blood pressure (BP), heart rate less than 100 beats/min, return to baseline skin turgor, and moist mucous membranes.

> **NOC Outcomes**
> Fluid Balance; Blood Loss Severity; Vital Signs; Tissue Integrity: Skin and Mucous Membranes
>
> **NIC Interventions**
> Fluid Monitoring; Fluid Management; Bleeding Reduction; Blood Products Administration; Shock Management: Volume

Ongoing Assessment

Actions/Interventions

■ Assess vital signs until stable. Note heart rate.

▲ Assess central venous pressure (CVP).

■ Assess for jugular venous distention (JVD).

■ Assess anxiety level.

■ Monitor and document intake and output.

▲ Obtain specimens; evaluate laboratory tests for complete blood count (CBC), electrolytes, blood urea nitrogen (BUN), creatinine levels, blood type and cross-match, and urine specific gravity.

■ If chest tube is in place, assess, measure, and document amount of blood in chest tube collection chamber. Monitor chest tube drainage every 10 to 15 minutes until blood loss slows to less than 25 mL/hr.

Rationale

Tachycardia is an early indication of fluid volume deficit. Blood pressure is not a good indicator of early shock.

Changes in CVP will distinguish hypotension caused by hypovolemia (low CVP reading <6 cm H_2O) versus hypotension caused by pericardial tamponade/tension pneumothorax (high CVP reading >10 cm H_2O).

JVD may occur with cardiac tamponade as a result of the increased heart pressures, or with tension pneumothorax from the shifting of the mediastinum toward the unaffected side.

Mild to moderate anxiety may be the first early warning sign before vital sign changes. Anxiety may also indicate pain and/or psychological traumas.

Decreased urine output indicates progressive shock.

Urine output of less than 30 mL/hr may indicate early acute tubular necrosis and acute renal failure secondary to hypovolemia. Increasing urine specific gravity reflects increased urine concentration. Serum sodium, BUN/creatinine ratio, and hematocrit are elevated with decreased fluid volume because they are measures of concentration.

Excessive drainage may indicate hemorrhage.

Chest Trauma

(■ = Independent; ▲ = Collaborative)

→ **Chest Trauma**–cont'd

Actions/Interventions

▲ Establish baseline hematocrit and hemoglobin; monitor and continue to assess.

■ Assess for postural hypotension, muscle cramps, and weakness.

■ Assess daily weight.

Rationale

Deficiencies guide treatment therapy.

Postural hypotension is an early sign of hypovolemia.

Body weight reflects body fluid changes.

Therapeutic Interventions

Actions/Interventions

■ Attempt to control bleeding source by using direct pressure with sterile 4 × 4 dressing.

▲ Insert one to two large-bore peripheral intravenous (IV) lines. Administer crystalloid or colloid fluids as prescribed.

▲ Prepare the patient for transfusions, if prescribed, with typed and crossmatched blood if it is available and time permits.

▲ Prepare the patient for autotransfusion.

■ Prepare the patient for transfer to operating room as condition warrants.

■ Provide oral care as needed.

■ Provide oral fluids as ordered and tolerated.

■ Assist the patient in sitting or standing if orthostatic hypotension is present.

■ Apply meticulous skin care measures.

Rationale

Significant pressure may be required to halt bleeding.

Rule for fluid replacement: infuse 3 mL IV fluid/1 mL blood volume lost.

Type-specific blood may be used if unable to obtain type and crossmatch. Type O-negative blood may be used as last resort.

This procedure is used in cases of blunt or penetrating injuries isolated to the chest area.

An open thoracotomy may be required.

Dry mucous membranes are painful.

Oral fluid replacement is indicated for mild fluid deficit or as a supplement to IV fluids.

This problem is especially evident in older patients.

Deficient fluid volume places the skin at added risk for breakdown.

ND$_x$ Nursing Diagnosis

Decreased Cardiac Output

Common Related Factors

Acute pericardial tamponade
Tension pneumothorax
Severe volume loss

Defining Characteristics

Decreased BP
Narrow pulse pressure
Pulsus paradoxus (systolic pressure falls more than 15 mm Hg during inspiration)
Tachycardia
Electrical alternans (decreased QRS voltage during inspiration)
Equalization of pressures (CVP, pulmonary artery pressure [PAP], and pulmonary capillary wedge pressure [PCWP])

■ = Independent; ▲ = Collaborative

JVD

Widened mediastinum or enlarged heart on chest radiograph

Chest tubes (if present) suddenly stop draining (suspect clot)

Distant or muffled heart tones

Restlessness, confusion, anxiety

Fall in hemoglobin and hematocrit

Cool, clammy skin

Diminished peripheral pulses

Decreased urine output

Decreased arterial or venous oxygen saturation

Acidosis

Common Expected Outcome

Patient maintains adequate cardiac output (CO) as evidenced by BP within normal limits for patient, strong regular pulses, absence of JVD, absence of pulsus paradoxus, warm and dry skin, and clear mentation.

NOC Outcomes
Vital Signs; Cardiac Pump Effectiveness; Circulation Status

NIC Interventions
Vital Sign Monitoring; Invasive Hemodynamic Monitoring; Hemodynamic Regulation

Ongoing Assessment

Actions/Interventions

■ Assess for classic signs associated with acute pericardial tamponade:

• Low arterial BP with narrowing pulse pressure

• Pulsus paradoxus

• Distant or muffled heart sounds
• Sinus tachycardia
• JVD

■ Assess mental status.

Rationale

Pericardial tamponade can decrease CO as the pericardial sac fills with blood to the point that it compresses the myocardium, causing decreased ability of the heart to pump blood out and take blood in.

An initial elevation in BP may occur with compensatory vasoconstriction. However, as venous return is compromised from the cardiac compensation, a significant drop in CO occurs.

This is an accentuation of normal drop in systolic arterial blood pressure with inspiration. Normally the difference in systolic blood pressure at expiration and inspiration is less than 10 mm Hg.

These are caused by distention in pericardial sac.

This is related to compensatory catecholamine release.

The venous pulse (CVP) may rise to 15 to 20 cm H_2O as a result of reducing circulating volume.

Symptoms may range from anxiety to altered level of consciousness in shock.

Chest Trauma

■ = Independent; ▲ = Collaborative

 **Chest Trauma**—cont'd

Actions/Interventions	Rationale
▲ Assess electrocardiogram (ECG) changes.	A slowly developing tamponade may present like heart failure with nonspecific ECG changes. Low voltage is also a common finding.
■ Monitor chest tube drainage for increase or decrease in drainage.	Sudden cessation of drainage suggests a clot.
▲ Assist with performance of echocardiogram if time permits.	This provides the most helpful diagnostic information. Effusions seen with acute tamponade are usually smaller than with chronic tamponade. However, to prevent circulatory collapse, treatment may be indicated before the echocardiogram can be performed.
▲ If the patient is in the intensive care unit, assess the hemodynamic profile using pulmonary artery catheter; assess for equalization of pressure.	The right atrial pressure, right ventricular diastolic pressure, pulmonary artery diastolic pressure, and PCWP are all elevated in tamponade, and are within 2 to 3 mm Hg of each other. These pressures confirm the diagnosis.
▲ Monitor serial chest radiographs.	The chest radiograph is used to evaluate for widened mediastinum or increased heart size.
■ Assess for midline shift of trachea.	Tension pneumothorax will cause a midline shift of the trachea and mediastinum to the opposite side with compression of the great vessels, causing a decrease in CO.

Therapeutic Interventions

Actions/Interventions	Rationale
▲ Initiate oxygen therapy. Maintain oxygen saturation of 90% or greater.	Supplemental oxygen will maximize oxygen saturation.
▲ Establish large-bore intravenous (IV) access.	This provides access for rapid fluid resuscitation and blood administration.
▲ Keep the patient and significant others informed.	With a tamponade, a patient may be feeling well and suddenly develop restlessness and feelings of doom. This can be confusing and frightening for the patients and their loved ones.
▲ Administer parenteral fluids as prescribed.	Optimal hydration state increases venous return.
▲ Type and crossmatch blood as prescribed. Anticipate blood product replacement.	Blood replacement therapy corrects existing hematological or coagulation factor alterations.
■ Place the patient in optimal position to increase venous return dependent on the patient's injuries.	Positioning is guided by the extent of the chest trauma injuries.
■ Have emergency resuscitative equipment and medications readily available.	Pericardiocentesis is the emergency treatment of choice.
▲ Assemble pericardiocentesis tray or open chest tray for bedside intervention of pericardial tamponade, or prepare the patient for transport to surgery.	Bedside pericardiocentesis can be a high-risk life-saving procedure. Complications include pneumothorax and myocardial or coronary artery lacerations. Tamponade must be relieved to improve CO. It is indicated when systolic BP is reduced more than 30 mm Hg from baseline. However, if the patient's condition can be stabilized, drainage of fluid should be delayed until surgical or open resection and drainage can be performed. Pericardiocentesis should be performed under

■ = Independent; ▲ = Collaborative

Chest Trauma

Actions/Interventions

▲ If repeated pericardiocentesis fails to prevent recurrence of acute tamponade, anticipate surgical correction.

▲ Assemble thoracentesis tray or chest tube drainage system for treatment of tension pneumothorax.

▲ Maintain aggressive fluid resuscitation.

▲ Administer vasopressor agents (dopamine, norepinephrine bitartrate [Levophed]), as ordered.

Rationale

sterile conditions. Acute tamponade is a life-threatening complication, but immediate prognosis is good with fast, effective treatment.

Surgical pericardiotomy or resection of a portion of the pericardium may be indicated.

If tension pneumothorax is suspected, intervention must be rapid to lessen the compression of the mediastinum and great vessels, which results in decreased CO and shock.

This may be required to raise venous pressure above pericardial pressure.

These medications maximize systemic perfusion pressure to vital organs.

NDx Nursing Diagnosis

Acute Pain

Common Related Factors

Rib fractures
Chest tube incision
Contusions or abrasions
Penetrating wounds
Pleural irritation

Defining Characteristics

Anxiety
Wincing, grimacing
Shallow respirations to minimize pain
Tachycardia
Agitation
Verbalization of pain
Guarding
Diaphoresis
BP changes

Common Expected Outcome

Patient's pain is reduced or relieved as evidenced by verbalization of pain relief, normotension, and HR less than 100 beats/min.

NOC Outcomes
Comfort Level; Pain Control

NIC Interventions
Pain Management; Analgesic Administration; Distraction

Ongoing Assessment

Actions/Interventions

■ Assess pain level and characteristics.

Rationale

It is important to determine the type of pain the patient is experiencing to aid in the diagnosis and appropriate treatment.

■ = Independent; ▲ = Collaborative

> ### Chest Trauma—cont'd

Actions/Interventions

■ Evaluate effectiveness of all pain management including medication and nonpharmacological interventions.

■ Assess how the patient has successfully dealt with pain in the past.

■ Assess the patient's cultural beliefs about reporting pain.

Rationale

All patients will need some type of pain medication. Unlike other body fractures, rib fractures cannot be casted to reduce pain. The rib cage is in continuous motion; therefore the pain is more difficult to manage. Pain management is easiest if the pain is not allowed to peak but is consistently controlled. If one medication or complementary technique is not effective, other interventions will need to be implemented.

Patient responses to pain are highly varied and must be explored with each patient.

Many factors influence a patient's willingness to report pain. Some are afraid of addiction to pain medications and will need reassurance that addiction is not a problem in treatment of acute pain. Others believe "toughing it out" is the way to handle pain. This knowledge deficit would need to be addressed. Finding out how the patient has dealt with pain in the past gives insight as to how best to effectively relieve current pain.

> ### Therapeutic Interventions

Actions/Interventions

▲ Anticipate the need for analgesics and respond immediately to complaint of pain.

■ Assist the patient in splinting the chest with a pillow.

▲ Give the patient as much control over pain management as the condition allows.

▲ Assist with insertion or maintenance of epidural catheter or intercostal nerve block, as appropriate.

■ Plan care activities for times when the patient is most pain-free, if possible.

■ Use distraction techniques.

■ Teach additional nonpharmacological interventions such as massage therapy, music therapy, heat or cold therapy, imagery, controlled breathing, and so on when pain is relatively controlled.

■ Eliminate additional stressors or sources of discomfort whenever possible.

Rationale

In the midst of painful experiences, a patient's perception of time may become distorted. Prompt responses to complaints may result in decreased anxiety in the patient.

This minimizes discomfort and assists with effective coughing and deep breathing.

The ability to actively participate and control pain management may decrease the patient's fear of pain.

A variety of measures may be used to effectively manage pain.

This facilitates more active participation by the patient.

These heighten one's concentration upon nonpainful stimuli to decrease one's awareness and experience of pain.

Chest trauma results in significant pain. Offering a variety of alternative therapies, such as cutaneous stimulation or cognitive-behavioral strategies, may be useful.

Patients may experience an exaggeration in pain or a decreased ability to tolerate painful stimuli when environmental, intrapersonal, or intrapsychic stressors are present.

■ = Independent; ▲ = Collaborative

Pulmonary Care Plans

Nursing Diagnosis

Anxiety

Common Related Factors	**Defining Characteristics**
Acute injury	Apprehension
Threat of death	Restlessness
Unfamiliar environment	Look of fear
Hypoxia	Crying
	Agitation
	Decreased cognitive function
	Irritability
	Increased blood pressure
	Dry mouth

Common Expected Outcomes

Patient appears calm and trusting.
Patient verbalizes concerns and coping techniques.
Vital signs and cognitive function return to baseline.

NOC Outcomes
Anxiety Self-Control; Coping

NIC Intervention
Anxiety Reduction

Ongoing Assessment

Actions/Interventions	**Rationale**
■ Assess anxiety level (mild, severe). Note signs and symptoms, especially nonverbal communication.	Chest trauma can result in an acute life-threatening injury that will produce high levels of anxiety in the patient as well as in significant others.
■ Assess coping factors.	Anxiety and way of decreasing perceived anxiety are highly individualized. Interventions are most effective when they are consistent with the individual's established coping patterns.

Therapeutic Interventions

Actions/Interventions	**Rationale**
■ Acknowledge awareness of the patient's anxiety; encourage the patient to express fears.	Acknowledgment of the patient's feelings validates the feelings and communicates acceptance of those feelings.
■ Maintain a confident, assured manner.	The staff's anxiety may be easily perceived by the patient. The patient's feeling of stability increases in a calm, nonthreatening atmosphere.
■ Assure the patient and significant others of close, continuous monitoring that will ensure prompt interventions.	This provides reassurance for the patient's safety.

Chest Trauma

■ = Independent; ▲ = Collaborative

Chest Trauma—cont'd

Actions/Interventions

- Reduce unnecessary external stimuli (e.g., clear unnecessary personnel from room; decrease volume of cardiac monitor).

- Reduce the patient's or significant others' anxiety by explaining all procedures and treatment. Keep explanations basic.

- Provide a quiet, private place for significant others to wait.

▲ Refer to other support systems (e.g., clergy, social workers, other family and friends) as appropriate.

Rationale

Anxiety may escalate with excessive conversation, noise, and equipment around the patient.

Information helps allay anxiety. Patients who are anxious may not be able to comprehend anything more than simple, clear, brief instructions.

A quiet environment can reduce anxiety.

Additional specialty expertise may be required.

> • RELATED CARE PLANS
>
> Acute respiratory failure, p. 508
> Impaired gas exchange, p. 78
> Risk for infection, p. 108
> Thoracotomy, p. 520

Chronic Obstructive Pulmonary Disease (COPD)

Chronic Bronchitis; Emphysema; Chronic Airway Limitation

Chronic obstructive pulmonary disease (COPD) refers to a group of diseases, including chronic bronchitis and emphysema, that cause a reduction in expiratory outflow. It is usually a slow, progressive, debilitating disease, affecting those with a history of heavy tobacco abuse and prolonged exposure to respiratory system irritants such as air pollution, noxious gases, and repeated upper respiratory tract infections. It is also regarded as the most common cause of alveolar hypoventilation with associated hypoxemia, chronic hypercapnia, and compensated acidosis. The National Heart, Lung and Blood Institute and the World Health Organization (NHLBI/WHO) reclassified COPD in the Global initiative for chronic Obstruction Lung Disease (GOLD) expert guidelines. These guidelines address the airflow limitation in COPD as progressive, irreversible, and associated with an inflammatory response to harmful inhaled contaminants. This care plan focuses on exacerbation of COPD in the acute care setting, as well as chronic care in the ambulatory setting or chronic care facility.

NDx Nursing Diagnosis

Ineffective Airway Clearance

Common Related Factors

Hyperplasia and hypertrophy of mucus-secreting glands
Increased mucus production in bronchial tubes

Defining Characteristics

"Smoker's cough"
Coarse lung sounds
Persistent cough for months

■ = Independent; ▲ = Collaborative

Decreased ciliary function
Thick secretions
Decreased energy and fatigue
Bronchospasm
Impaired exhalation
Alveolar wall destruction
Smoking

Copious amount of secretions
Wheezing
Loud, prolonged expiratory phase
Dyspnea (air hunger)
Altered arterial blood gases (ABGs) (compensated hypercapnia)
Changes in breathing pattern

Common Expected Outcomes

Patient's airway is free of secretions.
Patient has clear lung sounds after suctioning.
Patient demonstrates effective coughing techniques.
Patient verbalizes strategies to improve health behaviors.

NOC Outcome
Respiratory Status: Airway Patency

NIC Interventions
Cough Enhancement;
Airway Management

Ongoing Assessment

Actions/Interventions

- Auscultate lungs after coughing as needed to note and document significant change in breath sounds:
  - Decreased or absent lung sounds

  - Presence of fine rales (crackles)

  - Wheezing
  - Coarse sounds
- Assess for changes in respiratory rate and depth.

- Assess characteristics of or changes in secretions: consistency, quantity, color, odor.
- Note any color changes in lips, buccal mucosa, or nail beds.
- Assess hydration status: skin turgor, mucous membranes, tongue.
- Monitor daily weights.

▲ Monitor pulse oxygen saturation and ABGs.

- Assess the patient's physical capabilities with activities of daily living (ADLs), including ability to expectorate sputum.

Rationale

Patients with COPD have decreased breath sounds in varying degrees depending on their stage of illness.
These indicate presence of mucous plug or other major airway obstruction.
These may indicate cardiac involvement or secretion trapping.
This indicates increasing airway resistance.
These indicate presence of fluid along larger airways.
Respiratory rate and rhythm changes are early signs of respiratory compromise.
A sign of infection is discolored sputum; an odor may be present.
Cyanosis occurs when at least 5 g of hemoglobin are desaturated.
Airway clearance is impaired with inadequate hydration and subsequent secretion thickening.
Changes in daily weight are a reliable indicator of fluid balance.
Hypoxia can result from increased pulmonary secretions and respiratory fatigue.
Fatigue can limit cough effectiveness.

Chronic Obstructive Pulmonary Disease (COPD)

■ = Independent; ▲ = Collaborative

Chronic Obstructive Pulmonary Disease (COPD)–cont'd

Actions/Interventions	Rationale
▲ Administer β₂-adrenergic agonists (e.g., albuterol) by metered-dose inhaler (MDI) or nebulizer, as prescribed.	These short-acting inhaled bronchodilators work quickly to open the air passages, making it easier to breathe and decreasing bronchoconstriction.
▲ Administer anticholinergics such as ipratropium bromide (Atrovent) by MDI or nebulizer or tiotropium (Spiriva) dry powder inhalation only in conjunction with β₂-adrenergic agonist.	These have been shown to work synergistically with β₂-adrenergic agonists to relieve bronchoconstriction.
▲ Anticipate administration of intravenous (IV) corticosteroids (followed by oral steroids) during the acute exacerbation.	This reduces swelling and inflammation in the airways.
■ Encourage the patient to cough out secretions.	This helps clear the airway.
■ Assist with effective coughing techniques: • Splint chest. • Have patient use abdominal muscles. • Use cough techniques as appropriate (e.g., quad, huff).	This promotes comfort. Cough is more forceful. Controlled cough techniques help mobilize secretions from smaller airways to larger airways because coughing is done more effectively.
▲ Assist in mobilizing secretions to facilitate airway clearance: • Increase room humidification. • Administer mucolytic agents as prescribed. • Perform chest physiotherapy: postural drainage, percussion, and vibration. • Encourage 2 to 3 L of fluid intake unless contraindicated. • Encourage activity and position changes every 2 hours.	Humidity helps liquefy secretions. These help liquefy secretions. This prevents dehydration from increased insensible loss and keeps secretions thin. Activity helps mobilize secretions and prevents pooling in the lungs.
■ Perform nasotracheal suctioning as indicated if the patient is unable to effectively clear secretions. Use a well-lubricated soft catheter.	Suctioning with a lubricated catheter minimizes irritations.
▲ Anticipate intubation and mechanical ventilation, if needed, with transfer to acute care setting.	Early intubation and mechanical ventilation are recommended to prevent full decompensation and a potentially life-threatening situation.

NDx Nursing Diagnosis

Impaired Gas Exchange

Common Related Factors	Defining Characteristics
Increase in dead space caused by the following: • Loss of lung tissue elasticity • Atelectasis • Increased residual volume	Altered inspiratory/expiratory (I/E) ratio (prolonged expiratory phase) Active expiratory phase: use of accessory muscles of breathing

■ = Independent; ▲ = Collaborative

Pulmonary Care Plans

Increased upper and lower airway resistance caused by the following:
- Overproduction of secretions along bronchial tubes
- Bronchoconstriction

Decreased vital capacity (VC)
Increased residual volume (RV)
Hypoxemia/hypercapnia
$PaCO_2$ greater than 55 mm Hg
PaO_2 less than 55 mm Hg
Tachycardia
Restlessness
Diaphoresis
Headache
Lethargy
Confusion
Cyanosis
Increase in rate and depth of respiration
Increase in blood pressure (BP)
Anxiety

Common Expected Outcome

Patient maintains optimal gas exchange, as evidenced by arterial blood gases (ABGs) within baseline for the patient, and alert, responsive mentation or no further reduction in mental status.

NOC Outcomes
Respiratory Status: Gas Exchange; Vital Signs; Knowledge: Treatment Regimen

NIC Interventions
Respiratory Monitoring; Oxygen Therapy; Teaching: Psychomotor Skill

Chronic Obstructive Pulmonary Disease (COPD)

Ongoing Assessment

Actions/Interventions

- Assess for altered breathing patterns:
  - Increased work of breathing
  - Abnormal rate, rhythm, and depth of respiration
  - Abnormal chest excursions
- Assess generalized appearance.

- Assess for restlessness, headache, confusion, dizziness, reduced ability to follow instructions.
- Monitor vital signs.

- Assess level of anxiety and fear.

- Monitor ABGs and oxygen saturation.

Rationale

Patients will adapt their breathing patterns over time to facilitate gas exchange.

Posture, upright positioning and mental alertness cue the nurse to the severity of the COPD exacerbation.

Restlessness is an early sign of hypoxia. Lethargy and somnolence are late signs.

Hypoxia or hypercarbia may cause initial hypertension with restlessness and progress to hypotension and somnolence.

Dyspnea often increases anxiety, and anxiety increases oxygen use by tissues. Anxiety may be an indication of worsening hypoxemia.

Increasing $PaCO_2$ and decreasing PaO_2 are signs of respiratory failure. As the patient's condition begins to fail, the respiratory rate will decrease and $PaCO_2$ will begin to rise. The COPD patient has a significant decrease in pulmonary reserves, and any physiological stress

■ = Independent; ▲ = Collaborative

Chronic Obstructive Pulmonary Disease (COPD)—cont'd

Actions/Interventions	Rationale
	may result in acute respiratory failure. Noninvasive measurement of oxygen saturation by pulse oximetry provides early recognition of impaired oxygenation status.
■ If the patient is on theophylline, monitor for therapeutic and side effects.	It is important to monitor theophylline level to prevent toxic levels and to maintain the level in therapeutic range.
▲ Promote more effective breathing pattern for better gas exchange: • Instruct in positioning for optimal breathing.	Upright and high Fowler's positions favor better lung expansion; the diaphragm is pushed downward. If the patient is bedridden, turning from side to side at least every 2 hours promotes better aeration of all lung lobes, thus minimizing atelectasis.
• Teach the patient pursed-lip breathing.	This encourages more complete exhalation.
• Teach the patient to use abdominal and other accessory muscles.	This assists in a more forceful exhalation.
• Teach the patient to take bronchodilators as prescribed.	These drugs decrease work of breathing by decreasing airway resistance.
▲ Administer low-flow oxygen therapy as indicated (e.g., 2 L/min by nasal cannula). If insufficient, switch to high-flow O_2 apparatus (e.g., Venturi mask) for more accurate oxygen delivery.	COPD patients who chronically retain carbon dioxide depend on "hypoxic drive" as their stimulus to breathe. When applying oxygen, close monitoring is imperative to prevent unsafe increases in the patient's PaO_2, which could result in apnea.
▲ If the PaO_2 level is significantly lower or if the $PaCO_2$ level is higher than the patient's usual baseline (varies from patient to patient), anticipate the following: • Vigorous pulmonary toilet and suctioning • Increase in FiO_2 with use of controlled high-flow system • Use of diuretics • Possible need for intubation and mechanical ventilation with placement in acute care setting	Signs of respiratory failure include increasing $PaCO_2$ and decreasing PaO_2, paradoxical breathing, fatigue, somnolence, and increased respiratory rate.
▲ Use caution in administration of respiratory depressants such as narcotics and tranquilizers.	These reduce respiratory drive.
▲ Plan activity with interspersed rest periods and after bronchodilator treatments. Work with respiratory therapy for best-time sequence of pulmonary treatment.	Pacing activities will help the patient conserve energy.
▲ Administer bronchodilators, expectorants, antiinflammatories (steroids), and antibiotics, as ordered.	These reduce airway resistance, treat infection, and facilitate secretion removal.
▲ Work with the rehabilitation team and patient to establish discharge planning.	COPD is a chronic debilitating disease that requires a multidisciplinary approach to assist the patient maximize quality of life.
▲ Assist the patient in performing spirometry measurements and related procedures and tests (bronchoscopy, pulmonary function tests).	The National Lung Health Education program provides recommendations.

■ = Independent; ▲ = Collaborative

Pulmonary Care Plans

Nursing Diagnosis

Imbalanced Nutrition: Less Than Body Requirements

Common Related Factors

Increased metabolic need caused by increased work of breathing

Poor appetite resulting from fever, dyspnea, and fatigue

Defining Characteristics

Body weight 20% or more below ideal for height and frame

Indifference to food

Caloric intake inadequate for metabolic demands of disease state

Muscle wasting

Abnormal laboratory values (e.g., low serum albumin level)

Common Expected Outcome

Patient's optimal nutritional status is maintained as evidenced by stable body weight and adequate caloric intake; hemoglobin and albumin levels return to normal.

NOC Outcomes

Nutritional Status: Food and Fluid Intake; Knowledge: Diet

NIC Intervention

Nutrition Management

Ongoing Assessment

Actions/Interventions	Rationale
■ Assess for possible cause of poor appetite (see Related Factors above).	Proper assessment guides intervention.
▲ Compile diet history, including preferred foods and dietary habits. Consult with dietitian.	The dietitian can estimate the patient's caloric requirements and daily caloric intake.
▲ Verify ideal body mass index and compare the patient's weight to ideal.	Objective data guides treatment plan.
■ Assess the patient's ability to eat (i.e., energy level).	Work of breathing may allow little energy for other activity including eating.
■ Assess oral cavity.	Dry mucous membranes and poor dentition may contribute to decreased appetite and nutritional status.
▲ Assess laboratory values for serum albumin, total protein, ferritin, transferrin, hemoglobin, hematocrit.	Serum prealbumin and albumin levels reflect protein status, ferritin and transferrin reflect iron status, and hemoglobin and hematocrit reflect oxygen-carrying status. It is not unusual for COPD patients to have elevated hemoglobin and hematocrit. Decreased values may be indicative of poor nutritional status or other pathology.
■ Assess weight weekly.	During aggressive nutritional support, the patient can gain up to 0.5 pound/day.

Chronic Obstructive Pulmonary Disease (COPD)

■ = Independent; ▲ = Collaborative

Chronic Obstructive Pulmonary Disease (COPD)—cont'd

Ongoing Assessment

Actions/Interventions	Rationale
■ Encourage small feedings of nutritionally dense soft food or liquids. Add nutritional supplements as appropriate.	They are easier to digest and require less chewing.
■ Instruct the patient to avoid very spicy foods, gas-producing foods, and carbonated beverages.	Avoidance prevents possible abdominal distention. Cold foods may give less sense of fullness than hot foods.
■ Instruct the patient to eat high-calorie foods first and have favorite foods available.	When anorexia is a problem, these strategies can be useful to maintain nutrition. In addition, adding butter, mayonnaise, margarine, sauces, or gravies to food can add calories.
■ Avoid fluid intake with meals and instead encourage fluids between meals.	This gives less of a sense of fullness with meals.
■ Instruct the patient to plan activities.	Planning activities allows rest before eating.
■ Instruct the patient to eat slowly, use pursed-lip breathing between bites, and use bronchodilators before meals.	These techniques decrease dyspnea.
■ Reinforce the need to substitute nasal prongs for oxygen mask during mealtime.	This will maintain the patient's oxygenation.
■ Stress importance of frequent oral care.	Oral care promotes comfort and appetite.
■ Provide companionship at mealtime.	Attention to the social aspects of eating is important in both the hospital and home settings.
■ Assist with meals as needed (i.e., schedule rest periods before meals and open packages) and cut up food if patients take longer than 1 hour to complete a meal.	This facilitates optimal intake.
■ Have the patient sit up during meals.	This reduces hypoxia and the danger of aspiration.

 ## Nursing Diagnosis

Risk for Infection

Common Risk Factors

Retained secretions (good medium for bacterial growth)
Poor nutrition
Impaired pulmonary defense system secondary to COPD
Use of respiratory equipment
Chronic disease

Common Expected Outcome

Risk for infection is reduced through early assessment and intervention.

NOC Outcomes
Risk Control; Knowledge: Infection Control

NIC Intervention
Infection Protection

■ = Independent; ▲ = Collaborative

Ongoing Assessment

Actions/Interventions

- Auscultate lungs to monitor for significant changes in breath sounds.
- Assess for any of the following significant changes in sputum:
  - Sudden increase in production
  - Change in color (rusty, yellow, greenish)
  - Change in consistency (thick)
- Assess for other signs and symptoms of infection: fever, chills, increase in cough, elevated white blood cell (WBC) count, shortness of breath, nausea, vomitng, diarrhea, anorexia.
- Assess the patient's understanding of techniques to prevent infection, such as careful hand washing, adequate rest and nutrition, and avoidance of crowds.
- Assess vaccination status (flu and pneumococcal vaccines).

Rationale

Bronchial breath sounds and rales (crackles) may indicate pneumonia.

These may indicate presence of infection.

Prompt assessment of infection facilitates early intervention.

Identification of deficient knowledge can allow for early interventions to reduce infection risk.

These prevent some types of infection and are recommended by such organizations as the American Lung Association and the American Thoracic Society.

Therapeutic Interventions

Actions/Interventions

- Encourage an increase in fluid intake, unless contraindicated.

- Ensure that oxygen humidifier is properly maintained. Reinforce not to add new water to old water.
- Minimize retained secretions by encouraging the patient to cough and expectorate secretions frequently. If the patient is unable to cough and expectorate, instruct the patient or caregiver in nasotracheal oropharyngeal suctioning.
- Follow standard precautions, including proper hand washing techniques, to minimize microorganism transmission.

Rationale

Fluid intake maintains good hydration. Insensible loss is markedly increased during infection because of fever and increase in respiratory rate.

Stagnant old water is a medium for bacterial growth.

Retained secretions provide bacterial growth medium.

Friction and running water effectively remove microorganisms from hands.

Chronic Obstructive Pulmonary Disease (COPD)

NDx Nursing Diagnosis

Deficient Knowledge

Common Related Factors

Recent diagnosis
Ineffective past teaching or learning
Unfamiliarity with resources

Defining Characteristics

Display of anxiety or fear
Noncompliance
Inability to verbalize health maintenance regimen
Repeated acute exacerbations
Development of complications

■ = Independent; ▲ = Collaborative

Chronic Obstructive Pulmonary Disease (COPD)—cont'd

Defining Characteristics—cont'd

Misconceptions about health status
Multiple questions or no questions

Common Expected Outcome

Patient verbalizes understanding of disease process and treatment.

NOC Outcomes

Knowledge: Disease Process;
  Knowledge: Health Behaviors;
  Knowledge: Medication;
  Knowledge: Treatment Regimen

NIC Interventions

Teaching: Disease Process;
  Teaching: Prescribed Medications;
  Teaching: Prescribed Activity/Exercise;
  Teaching: Psychomotor Skill

Ongoing Assessment

Actions/Interventions	Rationale
■ Assess knowledge base of COPD.	COPD is a chronic disease in which patients may develop many good techniques as well as integrate misconceptions. New medications and treatments continue to be developed.
■ Assess environmental, social, cultural, and educational factors that may influence the teaching plan.	To be effective, interventions need to be specific to the patient and address individual influences.
■ Assess cognitive function and emotional readiness to learn.	Cognitive impairments need to be assessed so an appropriate teaching plan can be designed.

Therapeutic Interventions

Actions/Interventions	Rationale
■ Allow the patient to identify what is most important to him or her.	This clarifies learner expectations and helps the nurse match the information to be presented to the individual's needs. Adult learning is problem-oriented.
■ Instruct the patient in basic anatomy and physiology of respiratory system, with attention to structure and airflow.	Information helps patients understand the complexities of their airway problems.
■ Discuss the relation of the disease process to signs and symptoms that the patient experiences.	Recognition of key signs prevents delays in seeking help and facilitates appropriate self-management.
■ Discuss purpose and method of administration for each medication.	Return demonstrations on MDI spacers, dry powder capsules, or diskus techniques are necessary to ensure appropriate delivery of the medications. If a steroid component is used, teach the patient to rinse the mouth after use to avoid fungal mouth infections.
■ Instruct patient to avoid central nervous system depressants.	Depressants can depress respiratory drive.
■ Discuss appropriate nutritional habits, including supplements, as appropriate.	COPD patients have increased nutritional needs due to work of breathing.

■ = Independent; ▲ = Collaborative

Actions/Interventions	Rationale
■ Discuss the concept of energy conservation. Encourage resting as needed during activities, avoiding overexertion and fatigue, sitting as much as possible, alternating heavy and light tasks, carrying articles close to the body, organizing all equipment at the beginning of activity, and working slowly.	Patients need to learn self-management skills to reduce dyspnea from fatigue.
■ Discuss signs and symptoms of infection and when to contact the health care provider.	Respiratory infections can increase the work of breathing and precipitate respiratory failure.
■ Discuss common factors that lead to exacerbations of lung problems: smoking, environmental temperature, and humidity.	Chemical irritants and allergens can increase mucus production and bronchospasm.
■ Refer the patient or significant others to smoking cessation support groups as appropriate.	Smoking or chronic exposure to tobacco smoke is the leading cause of COPD. Supportive groups provide emotional support and information.
■ Instruct on indoor or outdoor air quality:	Patients need to learn how to control air quality to promote effective breathing.
• Avoid smoke-filled rooms, sudden changes in temperature, aerosol sprays.	This prevents bronchospasm.
• Use air conditioning in hot weather.	This reduces humidity and allergens.
• Stay indoors when pollen counts are high or when outdoor air quality is poor or during ozone alerts.	This prevents bronchospasm.
• Use scarves or masks over face in cold weather.	This warms inspired air and reduces cold air–induced bronchospasm.

■ Discuss the importance of specific therapeutic measures:
• Breathing exercises
  • Exercise 1—TECHNIQUE:
    1. Lie supine with one hand on chest and one hand on abdomen.
    2. Inhale slowly through mouth, raising abdomen against hand.
    3. Exhale slowly through pursed lips while contracting abdominal muscles and moving abdomen inward.
	This exercise strengthens muscles of respiration.

• Exercise 2—TECHNIQUE :
    1. Walk; stop to take deep breath.
    2. Exhale slowly while walking.
	This exercise develops slowed, controlled breathing.

• Exercise 3—TECHNIQUE :
    1. For pursed-lip breathing, inhale slowly through nose.
    2. Exhale twice as slowly as usual through pursed lips.
	This exercise decreases air trapping and airway collapse.

• Cough: Lean forward; take several deep breaths with pursed-lip method. Take last deep breath, cough with open mouth during expiration, and simultaneously contract abdominal muscles.	Controlled cough techniques help mobilize secretions.
• Chest physiotherapy or pulmonary postural drainage: Demonstrate correct methods for postural drainage: positioning, percussion, vibration.	This facilitates expectoration of secretions and prevents waste of energy.
• Hydration: Discuss importance of maintaining good fluid intake. Recommend 1.5 to 2 L/day.	This decreases viscosity of secretions.
• Humidity: Discuss various forms of humidification.	This prevents drying of secretions.

Chronic Obstructive Pulmonary Disease (COPD)

■ = Independent; ▲ = Collaborative

Chronic Obstructive Pulmonary Disease (COPD)—cont'd

Pulmonary Care Plans

Actions/Interventions

■ Discuss home oxygen therapy:
- Type and use of equipment (compressed O_2 in tanks; liquid O_2; O_2 concentrator):

  - Demonstrate how to start oxygen flow and regulate flowmeter.

  - Discuss flow rate of oxygen at rest, at night, and with activity, as individualized to the patient.

  - Discuss use of portable oxygen system for ambulating in and outside of the home.
  - Discuss use of oxygen-conserving devices, as appropriate.

- Safety precautions:
  - Do not use around a stove or gas space heater.
  - Do not smoke or light matches around cylinder when oxygen is in use.
  - Post "No Smoking" sign and call to visitors' attention.

■ Discuss the need for periodic reevaluation to determine or substantiate oxygen needs.

▲ Discuss available resources:
- Arrange for oxygen delivery or maintenance, as appropriate.
- Arrange for visiting nurse to check patient, as appropriate.
- Refer to local lung association if available for support groups.

▲ Discuss or arrange for the patient to participate in a pulmonary rehabilitation program.

■ Discuss the need for the patient to obtain vaccines for pneumococcal pneumonia and yearly vaccine for influenza.

■ Discuss use of medical alert bracelet or other identification.

■ Provide written instructions and reliable Internet resources.

Rationale

Medicare guidelines for reimbursement for home oxygen require a PaO_2 less than 58 mm Hg and/or oxygen saturation of 88% or less on room air.

Patient or others who are primarily responsible for oxygen therapy at home should be able to demonstrate the process.

Oxygen delivery should be titrated to maintain an oxygen saturation of 90% or more. This will help improve the patient's exercise tolerance and reduce pulmonary hypertension.

This therapy can reduce activity-related hypoxia.

This includes a variety of measures, such as pacing activities, avoiding working with arms raised, or reorganizing home items so that most frequently used ones are within easy reach.

Oxygen is not combustible itself but can feed a fire if one occurs.

Objective data guides ongoing management.

Home care agencies and patient support groups provide patients with resources to maintain compliance with a treatment program.

Pulmonary rehabilitation improves on baseline physical conditioning, increases optimal capabilities, and teaches the patient techniques to control breathing and energy conservation.

Vaccines decrease occurrence or severity of these diseases.

These alert others to COPD history.

These help the patient follow plan and maintain access to current therapies.

• RELATED CARE PLANS

Activity intolerance, p. 7
Disturbed sleep pattern, p. 177
Ineffective therapeutic regimen management, p. 185
Self-care deficit, p. 156

■ = Independent; ▲ = Collaborative

Lung Cancer

Squamous Cell; Small Cell; Non–Small Cell; Adenocarcinoma; Large Cell Tumors

Lung cancer is the second most commonly occurring cancer among men and women, and despite all available therapies, lung cancer remains the most common cancer-related cause of death for men and women. It is also one of the most preventable cancers. The American Lung Association estimates that more than 80% of all lung cancers are directly related to smoking.

Lung cancer occurs most often in persons older than 50 years who have long histories of cigarette smoking. Epidermoid (squamous) carcinomas and adenocarcinomas of the lung are the most commonly identified cell types. Small cell undifferentiated carcinoma is biologically and clinically distinct from the other major histological types and accounts for about 25% of cases. Large cell undifferentiated lung cancer is the least common cell type. Mixed tumors comprise all combinations of major lung cancer types and may represent 10% of all cases. The diagnosis and stage of lung cancer subtype are critical to the determination of appropriate treatment. Non–small cell cancer can be surgically resected in the early stages and treated with chemotherapy if symptomatic disease develops. Small cell cancer is always treated with chemotherapy and radiation therapy.

Prevention is top priority. Providing smoke-free environments, testing for radon, and educational programs remain the most powerful interventions. Smoking cessation interventions are a part of all care plans for patients who smoke.

Although there are currently no effective screening tests for lung cancer, it is hoped that genetic markers will soon be available to help identify people at high risk for developing cancer. Other promising research focuses on making the immune system and chemical messenger more effective. Currently work is being completed in the development of chemical messengers that control and stop abnormal cell growth (antioncogene therapy), the use of monoclonal antibodies that recognize and destroy only abnormal lung cells, and stimulation of the immune system by learning to control cytokines such as interleukin-2 (IL-2) and the interferons.

This care plan focuses on the educational aspects of lung cancer.

NDx Nursing Diagnosis

Deficient Knowledge

Common Related Factors
Unfamiliarity with causes, diagnostic evaluation, and treatment
Lack of readiness to learn

Defining Characteristics
Many questions
Lack of questions
Verbalized misconceptions
Denial of diagnoses

Common Expected Outcomes
Patient describes probable cause of his or her cancer.
Patient describes the diagnostic evaluation for lung cancer.
Patient explains the treatment regimen for own type of lung cancer.
Patient verbalizes resources available for additional information and support.

NOC Outcomes
Knowledge: Disease Process;
Knowledge: Treatment Procedures

NIC Interventions
Teaching: Disease Process;
Teaching: Procedure/Treatment;
Smoking Cessation Assistance

■ = Independent; ▲ = Collaborative

Lung Cancer—cont'd

Ongoing Assessment

Actions/Interventions

- Elicit patient's understanding of causes, diagnostic evaluation, and treatment interventions for lung cancer.
- Assess readiness to learn.

- Assess barriers to learning.

- Assess cognitive functioning, ability to learn, and previous knowledge.

- Assess the family's and significant other's willingness to participate in the teaching and learning process.

Rationale

Many patients are exposed to someone with lung cancer, yet many misconceptions continue to exist.

Some patients are ready to learn soon after they are diagnosed; others cope better by denying or delaying the need for instruction. Learning also requires energy, which patients may not be ready to use.

Physical and emotional pain, grieving, denial, and anger are barriers to learning, and information presented may not be learned.

Educational programs are individualized to meet the patient's level of understanding, ability to learn, and level of previous knowledge.

Often during the acute stages, the family or significant others may require the most teaching. This can assist them in providing support to the patient. Individuals do have a right to refuse educational services.

Therapeutic Interventions

Actions/Interventions

- Involve the patient in developing the teaching plan.

- Involve significant others in development and implementation of the teaching plan.
- Identify and communicate to the patient community resources, websites, and additional sources of information and support.

- Explain possible causes of lung cancer: tobacco use; passive exposure to smoke, radon, asbestos; air pollution containing benzpyrenes and hydrocarbons; and exposure to occupational agents such as petroleum, chromates, and arsenic.
- If the patient is a smoker:
  - Discuss strategies for smoking cessation, such as use of nicotine patch, nicotine gum, behavior modification, and smoking-cessation support groups.

Rationale

Allowing the patient to actively participate in the teaching plan increases motivation and helps ensure that the information most significant to the patient is presented first and in a comfortable format.

Chronic illness and potentially fatal illnesses involve not only the patient but also the patient's loved ones.

The American Lung Association (*www.lungusa.org*), The American Cancer Society (*www.cancer.org*), the National Cancer Institute (1-800-4-CANCER *http://cancernet.nci.nih.gov*), and many other sources have numerous teaching aids available to support and reinforce learning. Support groups can assist in the learning process by reinforcing learning and increasing motivation to learn. Warn the patient about resources that do not provide correct information (i.e., "Dr. Rob's Lung Cancer Cure Website").

The patient may benefit from understanding the broad range of causes for lung cancer.

Continued smoking in the face of a diagnosis of treatable lung cancer may hasten the patient's death. However, the perceived pressure to stop smoking is an added stressor to the patient with newly diagnosed lung cancer.

■ = Independent; ▲ = Collaborative

Actions/Interventions	Rationale

Actions/Interventions

- Communicate information on the risk to children and nonsmokers caused by environmental second-hand tobacco smoke.

■ Discuss evaluation of home for detection of radon and inexpensive removal, if necessary.

■ Discuss the diagnostic evaluation:
  - Chest radiograph

  - Collection of sputum for cytological evaluation

  - Bronchoscopy

  - Percutaneous transthoracic needle aspiration or biopsy under fluoroscopy, and/or computed tomography (CT)

  - Mediastinoscopy

  - Pulmonary function tests

  - Imaging tests

  - Positron emission tomography (PET) scan

  - Blood tests

■ Describe the following tests for patients with small cell cancer:
  - Brain or head CT and magnetic resonance imaging (MRI) scans
  - Liver and abdominal CT scans

  - Bone scan

■ Discuss staging classifications for the following:
  For small cell cancer:
  - Limited stage

Rationale

Secondhand passive smoke is a known carcinogen in individuals with long-term exposure. Children exposed to smoke also have an increased incidence of respiratory complications or disease.

By its own action and by its interaction with cigarette smoking, radon is considered the second leading cause of lung cancer in the United States.

Films are repeated at frequent intervals and may be the initial test performed when new symptoms are reported.

This may help identify tumors that involve the bronchial wall.

Brush biopsies and multiple bronchial washings are performed to obtain a tissue diagnosis. Bronchoscopy is mandatory for small cell cancer.

This is indicated for non–small cell cancer. It is done if bronchoscopy has not yielded an adequate tissue diagnosis or if the lesion is not central and accessible by bronchoscopy.

This is performed if the previous two procedures have not yielded a tissue diagnosis. It is used to sample lymph nodes and is mandatory for staging non–small cell cancer if surgery is being contemplated.

These tests predict whether lung function is sufficient to tolerate a surgical resection. Most patients with lung cancer are long-term smokers with poor lung function.

These tests use x-rays, magnetic fields, sound waves, or radioactive substances to find cancer. Monoclonal antibodies tagged with technetium concentrate in areas of tumor cells and are detected by single-photon emission computed tomography (SPECT).

This test is done to identify mediastinal and distant metastases. It is an option for staging early lung cancer but is recommended in more advanced stages of disease.

These tests are done to determine whether there is liver or bone metastasis.

These procedures determine the presence of brain metastases.

These tests evaluate the liver and adrenals for signs of metastasis.

These tests are done if the patient has bone pain.

Limited usually means one lung and lymph nodes on the same side of the chest that can be encompassed in a single radiation therapy port. *Port* refers to the anatomical location designated to receive radiation therapy.

■ = Independent; ▲ = Collaborative

Lung Cancer

Lung Cancer—cont'd

Actions/Interventions	Rationale

Actions/Interventions

- Extensive stage

For non–small cell cancer:
- Tumor, node, metastasis (TNM) staging classification

■ Explain "Performance Status Assessment."
- Fully ambulatory patients tolerate therapy better and live longer.
- Patients with restricted activities and out of bed more than 50% of the day survive longer than more restricted patients.
- Totally bedridden patients tolerate all forms of therapy poorly and have short survival.

■ Explain treatments for non–small cell cancer.

- Chemotherapy: systemic treatment with platinum-based combination therapy.
- Radiation therapy for regional inoperable tumor.

- Molecular targeted therapy.

- Describe radiation therapy protocol:
  - Carefully mark radiation ports before initiating therapy.
  - Do not remove skin markings.
  - Use gentle soap and water cleansing on skin within ports; avoid perfumed lotions and known skin irritants. Do not use antiperspirants containing aluminum.

  - Follow a treatment schedule, for example, 5 days per week for 6 weeks.
  - Report the following complications: shortness of breath, sore throat, or altered sensation associated with spinal cord damage.

Rationale

This includes all other disease. *Extensive* stage means that cancer has spread to the other lung, to lymph nodes on the other side, or to distant organs.

The clinical diagnostic stage is based on pretreatment scans, radiographs, biopsies, and mediastinoscopy and is used to determine resectability. The postsurgical pathological stage is based on analysis of tissue obtained at thoracotomy and is used to determine prognosis as well as the need for additional treatment. Tumor size, spread to lymph nodes, and metastasis to distant organs are staged from 0 to IV. The lower the number, the less the cancer has spread. Tumor staging classification is helpful to determine the optimal treatment plan.

This probably is the most important prognostic factor for nonresectable cases.

The 5-year survival rate for all newly diagnosed lung cancer patients remains 15%, primarily because the disease has spread beyond the scope of surgical therapy before a diagnosis is made.

Chemotherapy offers palliation of symptoms.

Radiation relieves symptoms in a significant percentage of patients, especially those with superior vena cava syndrome, dyspnea, cough, hemoptysis, and pneumonia secondary to obstruction.

These agents (gefitinib, erlotinib) stop tumor growth by blocking molecules essential to the growth and progression of tumors.

The treatment area must be identified before therapy.

They serve as "landmarks" for therapy doses.

Keeping the skin clean, dry, and free of irritants will promote skin integrity and reduce the risk of wet desquamation. Antiperspirants containing aluminum used in conjunction with radiation therapy will cause severe skin burns.

Each treatment plan is individualized.

Early assessment promotes early intervention.

■ = Independent; ▲ = Collaborative

Actions/Interventions	Rationale
• Address any misconceptions or fears the patient may have about radiation therapy.	Patients may worry about becoming radioactive, being a danger to loved ones, or learning that the treatment is not working.
• Teach use of gentle soap and water for cleansing the skin.	Radiation therapy places the patient at risk for skin breakdown. Mild erythema and dry or moist desquamation are common side effects of radiation therapy.
• Keep skin dry and wear loose-fitting clothing to avoid friction. Do not apply tape to the treatment sites, and do not expose treatment sites to direct sunlight or temperature extremes.	Pressure from tight or irritating clothing will increase skin irritation and the risk of skin breakdown. The skin in the treatment area is more vulnerable to the effects of heat, cold, and ultraviolet light from sunlight or artificial sources.
• In patients with esophagitis, medicated oral suspensions may be prescribed.	These medications reduce discomfort with eating and swallowing.
• Surgery for resectable disease (stages I-IIIA)	Surgical resection offers the best chance for long-term survival. Selection of the type of operation is determined by tumor location and size.
• Pneumonectomy	Removal of the affected lung is reserved for extensive disease that is technically resectable.
• Lobectomy	Lobectomy is performed when the tumor is contained within a lobe and adequate margins can be obtained or when lymph node extension is limited to lobar nodes totally encompassed in the en bloc dissection.
• Wedge resection	This is performed for small (<2 cm) peripheral nodules without lymph node or other extensive involvement.
■ Explain treatments for small cell cancer: • Chemotherapy	Because small cell cancer more often spreads from the primary site and because of its increased sensitivity to chemotherapy, combination chemotherapy is the major treatment and has improved survival fivefold.
• Prophylactic cranial radiation	This is used in patients who have limited disease and those who live for 6 months without relapse.
■ Explain any treatment options or potential clinical trials the physician may feel would be beneficial to the patient and how the patient can get additional information about these other therapies.	Gene therapy, the use of cytokines, and enhanced immune system therapy are topics in the national news. Patients may have questions about the appropriateness of these therapies for their cancer.

Lung Cancer

NDx Nursing Diagnosis

Ineffective Protection

Common Related Factors	Defining Characteristics
Cancer Chemotherapy Radiation Myelosuppression	Paraneoplastic syndromes (see Ongoing Assessment on the next page) Oncological emergencies (see Ongoing Assessment on the next page) Decrease in number of circulating neutrophils, red blood cells, and/or platelets

■ = Independent; ▲ = Collaborative

Lung Cancer—cont'd

Common Expected Outcome

Risk for ineffective protection is reduced by early assessment of complications and appropriate treatment.

NOC Outcomes

Immune Status; Blood Loss Severity; Neurologic Status: Consciousness

NIC Interventions

Surveillance; Bleeding Precautions; Neurologic Monitoring; Electrolyte Monitoring; Respiratory Monitoring

Ongoing Assessment

Actions/Interventions	Rationale

■ Assess for common paraneoplastic syndromes:
 	
Endocrine: caused by secretion of a hormone-like substance by the tumor
 	
Hematological: decreased neutrophils and decreased hematocrit and hemoglobin
 	
Hypercalcemia: most often with squamous cell cancer
• Lethargy, polyuria, nausea, vomiting, abdominal pain, and constipation
• Syndrome of inappropriate antidiuretic hormone (SIADH) with associated hyponatremia
• Ectopic adrenocorticotropic hormone and Cushing's syndrome
 	
Neurological: most common extrathoracic manifestations of lung cancer characterized by the following:
• Weakness of muscles, especially of pelvis and thighs
• Eaton-Lambert syndrome, myasthenic syndrome
• Peripheral neuropathy
• Cerebellar degeneration
• Polymyositis
• Hematological
  • Migratory thrombophlebitis
  • Nonbacterial thrombotic endocarditis
  • Disseminated intravascular coagulation (DIC)
	These are extrapulmonary clinical manifestations of lung cancer that affect multiple body systems.

■ Assess for common oncological emergencies: Neurological: • Headache, vomiting, papilledema • Stroke and seizures Cardiovascular: • Cardiac tamponade: SIGNS: chest pain, apprehension, dyspnea	These can be life threatening and lead to permanent damage. These are caused by increased intracranial pressure. These are caused by central nervous system metastases, infection, or metabolic consequences. This is caused by accumulation of fluid containing tumor cells in the pericardial sac and by encasement of the heart by the tumor.

■ = Independent; ▲ = Collaborative

Actions/Interventions

- Superior vena cava syndrome (SVCS):
  SIGNS: facial and upper extremity edema, tracheal edema, cough, shortness of breath, dizziness, visual changes, hoarseness

Rationale

This is caused by partial or complete obstruction of blood flow through the SVC to the right atrium.

Therapeutic Interventions

Actions/Interventions

▲ Anticipate appropriate treatment for each type of paraneoplastic syndrome:
  - For hypercalcemia: hydration and bisphosphonates
  - For neuromyopathies: first, treatment of the primary tumor; then, steroids and physical therapy
  - For DIC: heparin, cryoprecipitates, platelets, and packed red blood cells

▲ Anticipate treatment for neurological oncological emergencies:
  - Glucocorticoids
  - Brain irradiation
  - For seizures: maintenance of airway, anticonvulsant drug therapy

▲ Anticipate the following treatment for cardiovascular oncological emergencies:
  - For cardiac tamponade: decompression of the heart either surgically or by pericardiocentesis
  - To prevent reaccumulation of effusions:
    - Catheter drainage with instillation of sclerosing agent
    - Radiation therapy
    - Surgical intervention with creation of pericardial window
  - For SVCS: radiation therapy, chemotherapy, surgery, anticoagulation, corticosteroids, diuretics

Rationale

Specific manifestations guide treatment.

Being prepared for an emergency helps prevent further complications.

These are life-threatening problems that require immediate treatment.

Lung Cancer

NDₓ Nursing Diagnosis

Acute Pain

Common Related Factors

Original tumor and metastatic disease
Chemotherapy
Radiation

Defining Characteristics

Complaints of pain
Moaning or crying
Grimacing
Restlessness
Irritability

■ = Independent; ▲ = Collaborative

Lung Cancer—cont'd

Common Expected Outcomes

Patient verbalizes relief of or ability to tolerate pain.
Patient appears relaxed and comfortable.
Patient verbalizes techniques to control pain.

NOC Outcomes
Pain Control; Medication Response

NIC Interventions
Pain Management;
   Analgesic Administration

Ongoing Assessment

Actions/Interventions

- Assess for pain severity using AHCPR 0-10 scale and defining characteristics.
- Assess the patient's expectations for pain relief.

- Monitor effectiveness of pain relief therapies.

- Assess concerns and fears related to pain medication.

- Assess side effects of pain therapies, including constipation.

Rationale

Each individual may exhibit slightly different pain presentation. Bone pain is common.

Some patients may be content to have pain decreased; others may expect complete elimination of pain. This affects their perception of the effectiveness of the treatment modality and their willingness to participate in additional treatment.

Patients have a right to effective pain relief. Use of visual analog scales may provide objective data.

There remain many myths about pain. Some patients fear addiction to medication or incomplete pain relief. These concerns may enhance the perception of pain or decrease the patient's use of safe, effective pain-relieving medications.

Long-term use may result in side effects.

Therapeutic Interventions

Actions/Interventions

▲ Administer prescribed medications as follows (based on WHO analgesic ladder):

- Nonsteroidal antiinflammatory agents

- Short- and long-acting opioid analgesics

- Transdermal opioids

- Morphine and oxygen

Rationale

Various medications may be given by a variety of routes, including patient-controlled analgesia (PCA) in which the patient can control the amount of medication delivered.

These are used to treat muscle spasm associated with progressive tumor spread.

These are most often used with bone metastasis. It is essential to work for pain relief and patient comfort and not fear escalating doses as opioid tolerance develops or patients manifest symptoms of disease progression.

This method of administration may be indicated for patients unable to take oral medications.

These therapies should be considered when other measures are ineffective.

■ = Independent; ▲ = Collaborative

Pulmonary Care Plans

Actions/Interventions

- Teach nonpharmacological interventions for pain relief.

- Consult pain specialist as needed.

Rationale

Massage, distraction, music therapy, and support groups may enhance pharmacological interventions.

Specialty expertise may be required to manage severe chronic or intractable pain.

• RELATED CARE PLANS

Acute pain, p. 144
Anticipatory grieving, p. 82
Cancer chemotherapy, p. 812
Cancer radiation therapy, p. 825
Chronic pain, p. 149
Death and dying, p. 1131
Thoracotomy, p. 520

Mechanical Ventilation

Ventilator; Respirator; Endotracheal Tube; Intubation

Mechanical ventilation can be a temporary or chronic life-saving therapy. Its purpose is to maintain adequate ventilation by delivering preset concentrations of oxygen at an adequate tidal volume while reducing the work of breathing. The patient who requires mechanical ventilation must have an artificial airway (endotracheal [ET] tube) or tracheostomy. It is used most often in patients with hypoxemia and alveolar hypoventilation. While the mechanical ventilator will facilitate movement of gases into and out of the pulmonary system (ventilation), it cannot ensure gas exchange at the pulmonary and tissues levels (respiration). It provides either partial or total ventilatory support for patients with respiratory failure. Mechanical ventilation may be used short-term in the acute care setting (e.g., after surgery; during general anesthesia), or long-term in the subacute, rehabilitation, or home care setting. This care plan focuses on patient care in a hospital setting.

Mechanical Ventilation (side tab)

 ## Nursing Diagnosis

Impaired Spontaneous Ventilation

Common Related Factors	Defining Characteristics
Metabolic factors	pH less than 7.35
Respiratory muscle fatigue	PO_2 less than 50 to 60 mm Hg
Acute respiratory failure	PCO_2 of 50 to 60 mm Hg or greater
	Apprehension
	Increased restlessness
	Dyspnea
	Increased or decreased respiratory rate

■ = Independent; ▲ = Collaborative

Mechanical Ventilation—cont'd

Pulmonary Care Plans

Defining Characteristics—cont'd

Decreased tidal volume
Apnea
Inability to maintain airway (i.e., depressed gag, depressed cough, emesis)
Forced vital capacity less than 10 mL/kg
Rales (crackles), rhonchi, wheezing
Diminished lung sounds
Decreased level of consciousness

Common Expected Outcomes

Patient maintains spontaneous gas exchange resulting in normal arterial blood gases (ABGs) within patient parameters, return to normal pulse oximetry, and decreased dyspnea.
Patient demonstrates no complications from the ventilation.

NOC Outcome

Respiratory Status: Ventilation

NIC Interventions

Respiratory Monitoring; Ventilation Assistance; Airway Insertion and Stabilization; Artificial Airway Management; Mechanical Ventilation

Ongoing Assessment

Actions/Interventions	Rationale
Before intubation:	
■ Assess vital signs.	Hypotension, tachycardia, and tachypnea may result from hypoxia and/or hypercarbia.
■ Assess lung sounds.	These allow early detection of deterioration or improvement.
• Listen closely for rhonchi, rales (crackles), wheezing, and diminished lung sounds in each lobe, assessing side to side.	Changes in lung sounds are important in making an accurate diagnosis.
• Reassess lung sounds after coughing or suctioning.	This determines whether they have improved or cleared.
■ Assess breathing rate, pattern, and depth; note position assumed for breathing.	These help identify early signs of respiratory failure.
▲ Monitor pulse oximetry, as available.	This tool is useful in detecting early changes in oxygenation. Oxygenation must be closely monitored to prevent hypoxemia or hyperoxemia.
■ Monitor ABGs as appropriate.	Increasing $PaCO_2$ and decreasing PaO_2 are signs of respiratory failure. If the patient's condition begins to fail, the respiratory rate decreases and $PaCO_2$ begins to rise.
■ Assess for changes in mental status and level of consciousness.	Signs of hypoxia include anxiety, restlessness, disorientation, somnolence, lethargy, and/or coma.
■ Assess skin color, checking nail beds and lips for cyanosis.	Cyanosis is a late sign of hypoxia because 5 g of hemoglobin must be desaturated for cyanosis to occur.

■ = Independent; ▲ = Collaborative

Actions/Interventions

■ Based on assessments, notify physician immediately of signs of impending respiratory failure.

After intubation:

▲ Assess for ET tube position:
  • Inflate cuff until no audible leaks are heard.

  • Auscultate for bilateral lung sounds while the patient is being manually ventilated by Ambu bag.

  • Observe for abdominal distention.

  • Ensure that chest x-ray evaluation is obtained.
■ Assess ET tube, checking whether it is secure and centimeter markings show placement.
■ Assess ventilator settings and alarm system every hour.

■ Assess patient comfort and ability to cooperate with therapy.

Rationale

Vigilant monitoring reduces risk of further decompensation.

Cuff pressure should not exceed 30 mm Hg. Cuff over-inflation increases incidence of tracheal erosions.

This ensures good ET tube position. If diminished sounds are present over the left lung field, the ET tube is most likely below the carina in the right main stem bronchus and must be pulled back.

This may indicate gastric intubation and can also occur after cardiopulmonary resuscitation when air is inadvertently blown or bagged into the esophagus, as well as the trachea.

This determines ET tube placement.

Securing the ET tube prevents it from accidentally being removed.

This ensures that settings are accurate and alarms are functional.

Patient discomfort may be related to incorrect ventilator settings that result in insufficient oxygenation. Once intubated and breathing on the mechanical ventilator, the patient should be breathing easily and not "fighting the ventilator."

Therapeutic Interventions

Actions/Interventions

Before intubation:

■ Maintain the patient's airway:
  • Encourage the patient to cough and breathe deeply.
  • If coughing and deep breathing are not effective, use nasotracheal suction as needed.
  • Use oral or nasal airway as needed.

  • Provide oxygen therapy as prescribed and indicated.

■ Place the patient in high Fowler's position, if tolerated. Check position often.

Prepare for endotracheal intubation:

▲ Notify respiratory therapist to bring mechanical ventilator.

■ If possible, before intubation, explain to the patient the need for intubation, the steps involved, and the temporary inability to speak because of the ET tube passing through the vocal cords.

Rationale

This facilitates oxygenation.

This is used to clear the airway.

This is used to prevent the tongue from occluding the oropharynx. A patent airway is a priority.

Increasing oxygen tension in the alveoli may result in more oxygen diffusion into the capillaries.

This position promotes lung expansion. Do not let the patient slide down; this causes the abdomen to compress the diaphragm, which would cause respiratory embarrassment.

A variety of types are available, depending on extent and type of the patient's problem. Positive-pressure ventilators are used most frequently.

Preparatory information can reduce anxiety and promote cooperation with intubation.

Mechanical Ventilation

Mechanical Ventilation—cont'd

Actions/Interventions	Rationale

Actions/Interventions

- Prepare equipment:
  - ET tubes of various sizes, noting size used

  - Benzoin and waterproof tape or other methods
  - Syringe

  - Local anesthetic agent (e.g., benzocaine [Cetacaine] spray, cocaine, lidocaine [Xylocaine] spray or jelly, and cotton-tipped applicators)
  - Sedation as prescribed
  - Stylet

  - Laryngoscope and blades
  - Ambu bag and mask connected to oxygen

  - Suction equipment

  - Oral airway if patient is being orally intubated
  - Bilateral soft wrist restraints
- Administer sedation as prescribed.

Assist with intubation:

- Place the patient in supine position, hyperextending neck (if not contraindicated) and aligning the patient's oropharynx, posterior nasopharynx, and trachea.

- ▲ Oxygenate and ventilate the patient as needed before and after each intubation attempt. If intubation is difficult, the physician will stop periodically so that oxygenation is maintained with artificial ventilation by Ambu bag and mask.

- ▲ Apply cricoid pressure as directed by physician.

After intubation:

- Continue with manual Ambu bag ventilation until the ET tube is stabilized. Assist in securing the ET tube once tube placement is confirmed.

- Document ET tube position, noting the centimeter reference marking on ET tube.

- ▲ Institute mechanical ventilation with settings as prescribed.

- Insert oral airway for orally intubated patient.

- Institute aseptic suctioning of airway.

Rationale

Adult sizes range from 7 to 9 mm. Selection is based on size of patient.

These secure the ET tube.

This is used to inflate the balloon after the ET tube is in position.

These suppress the gag reflex and promote general comfort.

This decreases combative resistance to intubation.

This makes the ET tube firmer and gives additional support to direction during intubation.

These provide assisted ventilation with 100% oxygen before intubation.

This maintains a clear airway. Yankauer suction catheter should be available.

This prevents occlusion or biting of ET tube.

These prevent self-extubation of ET tube.

Sedation facilitates comfort and ease of intubation.

This position is necessary to promote visualization of landmarks for accurate tube insertion.

Patent airway and oxygenation are priorities.

This is used to occlude esophagus and allow easier intubation of trachea.

Stabilization is necessary before initiating mechanical ventilation.

Documentation provides a reference for determining possible tube displacement.

Modes for ventilating (assisted versus controlled), tidal volume, rate per minute, fraction of inspired oxygen (FIO_2), peak airway pressure, sighs, and the like must be preset and carefully evaluated for response.

This prevents the patient from biting down on the ET tube.

Suctioning procedures should be based on need rather than preset time intervals to reduce risk for infection.

■ = Independent; ▲ = Collaborative

Actions/Interventions

■ Apply bilateral soft wrist restraints as needed, explaining reason for use.

▲ Administer muscle-paralyzing agents, sedatives, and narcotic analgesics as indicated.

■ Anticipate need for nasogastric/oral gastric suction.

■ Respond to alarms, noting that high-pressure alarms may be from patient resistance or the patient's need for suctioning. A low-pressure alarm may be a ventilator disconnection. If the source of the alarm cannot be located, ventilate the patient with an Ambu bag until assistance arrives.

Rationale

Although all patients do not require restraints to prevent extubation, many do.

These decrease the patient's work of breathing and decrease myocardial work, and may facilitate effective gas exchange.

This prevents abdominal distention. Oral gastric suctioning may reduce the risk of sinusitis.

The key is that the patient receives oxygenation support at all times until mechanical ventilation is no longer required.

 Nursing Diagnosis

Ineffective Protection

Common Related Factors

Dependency on ventilator
Improper ventilator settings
Improper alarm settings
Disconnection of ventilator
Positive-pressure ventilation
Decreased pulmonary compliance

Defining Characteristics

Dyspnea
Apnea
Hypoxia
Hypercapnia
Cyanosis
Pneumonia
Barotrauma:
  • Crepitus
  • Subcutaneous emphysema
  • Altered chest excursion
  • Asymmetrical chest
  • Abnormal ABGs
  • Shift in trachea
  • Restlessness
  • Evidence of pneumothorax on chest radiograph

Common Expected Outcomes

Patient remains free of injury as evidenced by ABGs within normal limits for patient and appropriate ventilator settings.
Potential for injury from ventilator-acquired pneumonia and barotrauma is reduced by ongoing assessment and early intervention.

NOC Outcome
Risk Detection

NIC Intervention
Mechanical Ventilation

Mechanical Ventilation

■ = Independent; ▲ = Collaborative

Mechanical Ventilation—cont'd

Ongoing Assessment

Actions/Interventions	Rationale
▲ Check ventilator settings every hour.	This ensures that the patient is receiving correct mode, rate, tidal volume, FIO_2, continuous positive end-expiratory pressure (PEEP), and pressure support.
• Mode: • Synchronized intermittent mandatory ventilation (SIMV)	This ensures preset rate in synchronization with patient's own spontaneous breathing.
• Controlled mandatory ventilation (CMV)	This ensures preset rate with no sensitivity to patient's respiratory effort. The patient cannot initiate breaths or alter pattern.
• Assist control (AC)	This ensures that the preset rate is sensitive to the patient's inspiratory effort. It delivers a preset tidal volume for each patient-initiated breath.
• Rate of mechanical breaths	Although patient dependent, the usual rate is between 10 and 14 breath/min.
• Tidal volume (TV)	Typical ranges for TV are 10 to 15 mg/kg of body weight. Recent research supports lower standard TVs to reduce barotrauma.
• FIO_2	The amount prescribed depends on patient condition and ABG results.
• Continuous PEEP	PEEP serves to improve gas exchange and prevent atelectasis.
• Pressure support (PS)	This ensures positive airway pressure during the inspiratory cycle of a spontaneous inspiratory effort.
■ Ensure that ventilator alarms are on.	Patient safety is a priority.
▲ Notify respiratory therapist of discrepancy in ventilator settings immediately.	Immediate attention to details can prevent problems.
▲ Monitor oxygen saturation through pulse oximetry and ABGs, as appropriate.	Objective data guide ventilator settings and appropriate intervention.
■ Assess rate or rhythm of respiratory pattern, including work of breathing.	It is important to maintain the patient in synchrony with the ventilator and not permit "fighting" it.
▲ Assess for signs of pulmonary infection.	Nosocomial pneumonias are seen 6 to 21 times more frequently in mechanically ventilated patients. Most ventilator-acquired infections are caused by bacterial pathogens, with gram-negative bacilli being common.
▲ Assess for signs of barotraumas every hour: crepitus, subcutaneous emphysema, altered chest excursion, asymmetrical chest, abnormal ABGs, shift in trachea, restlessness, evidence of pneumothorax on chest radiograph.	Frequent assessments are needed because barotrauma can occur at any time and the patient will not show signs of dyspnea, shortness of breath, or tachypnea if heavily sedated to maintain ventilation.
▲ Monitor chest x-ray reports daily and obtain a stat portable chest radiograph if barotrauma is suspected.	Vigilant monitoring reduces risk of trauma.
▲ Monitor plateau pressures with the respiratory therapist.	Elevation of plateau pressures increases both the risk and incidence of barotrauma when a patient is on mechanical ventilation. There has been less occurrence of barotrauma since guidelines have recommended lower standard tidal volumes.

■ = Independent; ▲ = Collaborative

Actions/Interventions	Rationale
▲ Assess for presence of auto-PEEP with the respiratory therapist.	This is a sign that expiratory time is shorter than the time required to decompress the lungs, which can result in dynamic pulmonary hyperinflation.

Therapeutic Interventions

Actions/Interventions

■ Institute measures to reduce ventilator-acquired pneumonia (VAP).

- Wash hands before and after suctioning, touching ventilator equipment, and/or coming into contact with respiratory secretions.

- Use a continuous subglottic suction ET tube for intubation expected to be longer than 24 hours.

- Keep head of bed elevated to at least 30 degrees unless medically contraindicated.

▲ Listen for alarms. Know the range in which the ventilator will set off the alarm.

- *High peak pressure alarm*
  - If patient is agitated, give sedation as prescribed.
  - Empty water from water traps as appropriate.
  - Auscultate breath sounds; institute suctioning as needed. Notify respiratory therapist and physician if high-pressure alarm persists.
- *Low-pressure alarm*
  - If disconnected, reconnect patient to mechanical ventilator.
  - If malfunctioning, remove patient from mechanical ventilator and use Ambu bag.
  - Notify the respiratory therapist to correct malfunction.
- *Low exhale volume*
  - Reconnect patient to ventilator if disconnected, or reconnect exhale tubing to the ventilator. If the problem is not resolved, notify the physician and respiratory therapist.
  - Check cuff volume by assessing whether the patient can talk or make sounds around the tube or whether exhaled volumes are significantly less than volumes delivered. To correct, slowly reinflate the cuff with air until no leak is detected. Notify the respiratory therapist to check cuff pressure.
- *Apnea alarm*
  - If disconnected, reconnect patient to ventilator.
  - If apnea persists, use Ambu bag to ventilate; notify physician.

▲ Notify physician of signs of barotrauma immediately; anticipate the need for chest tube placement, and prepare the patient as needed.

Rationale

Nosocomial infections are the leading cause of hospital mortality.

An artifical airway bypasses the normal protective mechanisms of the upper airways.

This prevents accumulation of secretions.

Elevation promotes better lung expansion.

The ventilator is a life-sustaining treatment that requires prompt response to alarms.

This indicates bronchospasm, retained secretions, obstruction of ET tube, atelectasis, acute respiratory distress syndrome (ARDS), or pneumothorax, among others.

This indicates possible disconnection or mechanical ventilatory malfunction.

This indicates that the patient is not returning delivered TV (through leak or disconnection).

Cuff pressure should be maintained at 30 mm Hg. Maintenance of low-pressure cuffs prevents many tracheal complications formerly associated with ET tubes. Notify the physician if leak persists. The ET tube cuff may be defective, requiring the physician to change the tube.

Alarm is indicative of disconnection or absence of spontaneous respirations.

If barotrauma is suspected, intervention must follow immediately to prevent tension pneumothorax.

Mechanical Ventilation

Mechanical Ventilation—cont'd

 Nursing Diagnosis

Ineffective Airway Clearance

Common Related Factors

Endotracheal intubation
Increased secretions
Decreased energy

Defining Characteristics

Copious secretions
Cough
Abnormal lung sounds
Dyspnea
Anxiety
Restlessness
Increased peak airway pressure

Common Expected Outcome

Patient's secretions are mobilized and airway remains patent as evidenced by eupnea and clear lung sounds after suctioning.

NOC Outcome
Respiratory Status: Airway Patency

NIC Interventions
Airway Management; Airway Suctioning

Ongoing Assessment

Actions/Interventions

■ Assess lung sounds.

■ Note quantity, color, consistency, and odor of sputum.
▲ Assess ABGs.

■ Assess patient position for optimal airway clearance.

■ Assess the patient's tolerance of suctioning procedure.
■ Assess oxygen saturation before and after the procedure.

Rationale

Diminished lung sounds or the presence of adventitious sounds may indicate an obstructed airway.

Changes in sputum color may indicate infection.

Signs of respiratory failure include decreasing PaO_2 and increasing $PaCO_2$.

Head of bed at 30 to 45 degrees promotes better lung expansion.

Many patients find suctioning to be stressful.

This provides evaluation of effectiveness of therapy.

Therapeutic Interventions

Actions/Interventions

■ Explain suctioning procedure to the patient; give reassurance throughout the procedure.

■ Institute suctioning of airway "as needed" based on the presence of adventitious lung sounds and/or increased ventilatory pressure.

Rationale

Suctioning can be frightening to the patient. Reinforce the need to maintain a patent airway. Provide sedation and pain relief as needed.

Frequency of suctioning should be based on the patient's clinical status, not on a preset routine such as every 2 hours. Oversuctioning can cause hypoxia and injury to bronchial and lung tissue.

■ = Independent; ▲ = Collaborative

Actions/Interventions

■ Avoid saline instillation before suctioning.

■ Use closed in-line suction.

▲ Hyperoxygenate as ordered.

▲ Administer pain medications, as appropriate, before suctioning.

■ Silence ventilator alarms during suctioning.

▲ Administer adequate fluid intake (intravenous [IV] and nasogastric, as appropriate).

■ Turn the patient every 2 hours.

Rationale

Saline instillation before suctioning has an adverse effect on oxygen saturation.

This decreases infection rate, may reduce hypoxia, and is often less expensive. Sterile technique is a priority.

Hyperoxygenation before, during, and after endotracheal suctioning decreases hypoxia and cardiac dysrhythmias related to the suctioning procedure.

These medications decrease peak periods of pain and assist with cough.

This decreases the frequency of false alarms and reduces stressful noise to the patient.

This promotes patient's hydration and keeps secretions liquid.

This mobilizes secretions and helps prevent ventilator-acquired pneumonia.

NDx Nursing Diagnosis

Decreased Cardiac Output

Common Related Factors

Mechanical ventilation
Positive-pressure ventilation

Defining Characteristics

Hypotension
Tachycardia
Dysrhythmias
Anxiety, restlessness
Decreased peripheral pulses
Weight gain
Edema
Cold, clammy skin
Elevated pulmonary artery diastolic pressure
Ejection fraction less than 40%
Decreased cardiac output (CO) measures

Common Expected Outcome

Patient achieves adequate CO as evidenced by strong peripheral pulses, normal vital signs, warm dry skin, and alert responsive mentation.

NOC Outcomes

Cardiac Pump Effectiveness; Circulation Status; Respiratory Status: Ventilation

NIC Interventions

Hemodynamic Regulation; Mechanical Ventilation

Mechanical Ventilation

■ = Independent; ▲ = Collaborative

Mechanical Ventilation—cont'd

Ongoing Assessment

Actions/Interventions

▲ Assess vital signs and hemodynamic parameters, if in place (central venous pressure, pulmonary artery diastolic pressures, CO).

■ Assess peripheral pulses and capillary refill.

■ Assess skin color and temperature.

■ Assess fluid balance through daily weights and measure intake and output.

■ Assess mentation.

■ Monitor for dysrhythmias.

▲ Notify the physician immediately of signs of decrease in CO and anticipate possible ventilator setting changes.

Rationale

Mechanical ventilation can cause decreased venous return to the heart, resulting in decreased CO. This may occur abruptly with ventilator changes: rate, tidal volume, or positive-pressure ventilation. Therefore close monitoring during ventilator changes is imperative.

Pulses are weak and capillary refill prolonged with reduced CO.

Cold, clammy skin is secondary to compensatory increase in sympathetic nervous system stimulation and low CO and desaturation.

After the initial decrease in venous return to the heart, volume receptors in the right atrium signal a decrease in volume, which triggers an increase in the release of antidiuretic hormone from the posterior pituitary and retention of water by the kidneys.

Early signs of cerebral hypoxia are restlessness and anxiety, leading to agitation and confusion.

Cardiac dysrhythmias may result from the low perfusion state, acidosis, or hypoxia.

Vigilant monitoring reduces risk for complications. Hypotension and decreased CO may be related to positive-pressure ventilator itself or use of PEEP mode.

Therapeutic Interventions

Actions/Interventions

▲ Maintain optimal fluid balance.

▲ Administer medications (diuretics, inotropic agents) as ordered.

Rationale

Fluid challenges may initially be used to add volume. However, if pulmonary artery diastolic pressure rises and CO remains low, fluid restriction may be necessary.

Diuretics may be useful to help maintain fluid balance if fluid retention is a problem. Inotropic agents may be useful to increase CO.

See also **Decreased Cardiac Output**, *p. 32.*

NDx **Nursing Diagnosis**

Fear/Anxiety

Common Related Factors

Inability to breathe adequately without support
Inability to maintain adequate gas exchange
Fear of unknown outcome
Inability to communicate verbally

Defining Characteristics

Restlessness
Fear of sleeping at night
Uncooperative behavior
Withdrawal

■ = Independent; ▲ = Collaborative

Indifference
Vigilant watch on equipment
Facial tension
Focus on self

Common Expected Outcomes

Patient demonstrates reduced fear or anxiety as evidenced by calm manner and cooperative behavior.
Patient expresses or demonstrates effective ways to cope with anxiety.

NOC Outcome
Anxiety Self-Control

NIC Intervention
Anxiety Reduction

Ongoing Assessment

Actions/Interventions

- Assess for signs of fear or anxiety.

- Assess specific stressors.

Rationale

Anxiety can affect respiratory rate and rhythm, resulting in rapid, shallow breathing.

Accurate appraisal can facilitate development of appropriate treatment strategies.

Therapeutic Interventions

Actions/Interventions

- Display a confident, calm manner and understanding attitude.
- Inform the patient of alarms on ventilatory system and reassure the patient about close proximity of health care personnel to respond to alarms.
- Be available to the patient or significant others and offer support, as well as explanations of the patient's care and progress.
- Reduce distracting stimuli.

- Encourage visiting by family and friends.

- Encourage sedentary diversional activities (e.g., television, reading, being read to, writing, occupational therapy).
- Provide relaxation techniques (e.g., tapes, imagery, progressive muscle relaxation).
- If impaired communication is the problem, provide the patient with word-and-phrase cards, writing pad and pencil, or picture board.
- ▲ Refer to psychiatric liaison clinical nurse specialist, psychiatrist, or hospital chaplain, as appropriate.

Rationale

The presence of a trusted person may be helpful during periods of anxiety.

An informed patient who understands the treatment plan will be more cooperative.

An ongoing relationship establishes a basis for comfort in communicating anxious feelings.

This provides a quiet environment that enhances rest. Anxiety may escalate with excessive noise, conversation, and equipment around the patient.

The presence of significant others reinforces feelings of security for the patient.

These enhance the patient's quality of life and help pass time.

Using anxiety-reduction techniques enhances the patient's sense of personal mastery and confidence.

This broadens the opportunity for communicating, which may reduce frustration.

Specialty expertise may provide a wider range of treatment options.

Mechanical Ventilation

■ = Independent; ▲ = Collaborative

Mechanical Ventilation—cont'd

 Nursing Diagnosis

Deficient Knowledge

Common Related Factors

New treatment
New environment

Defining Characteristics

Multiple questions
Lack of concern
Anxiety
Cognitive limitation
Lack of interest

Common Expected Outcome

Patient or significant others state basic understanding of mechanical ventilation and care involved.

NOC Outcome
Knowledge: Treatment Procedure

NIC Intervention
Teaching: Individual

Ongoing Assessment

Actions/Interventions

■ Assess the patient's perception and understanding of mechanical ventilation.

■ Assess the patient's readiness and ability to learn.

■ Listen to the patient and significant others.

Rationale

This provides an important starting point in education.

Educational interventions must be designed to meet the learning limitations, motivation, and needs of the patient. Acute care patients may not be able to take in much information due to fatigue, pain, sensory overload, hypoxemia, and the like.

Prioritizing learning material is based on the patient and loved ones' needs.

Therapeutic Interventions

Actions/Interventions

■ Encourage the patient or significant others to express feelings and ask questions.

■ Explain that the patient will not be able to eat or drink while intubated but assure him or her that alternative measures (i.e., IV line, gastric feedings, or hyperalimentation) will be taken to provide nourishment.

Rationale

Knowledge normalizes the process and reduces anxiety.

Risk of aspiration is high if the patient eats or drinks while intubated.

■ = Independent; ▲ = Collaborative

Actions/Interventions

- Explain to the patient the reason for the inability to talk while intubated. Explain alternative efforts for communicating.

- Explain that alarms may periodically sound off, which may be normal, and that the staff will be in close proximity.

- Explain the need for frequent assessments (i.e., vital signs, auscultation of lung sounds, ventilator checks).

- Explain the need for suctioning as needed.

- Explain the weaning process and explain that extubademonstrated adequate respiratory function and a decrease in pulmonary secretions.

- If long-term ventilation is anticipated, discuss or plan for long-term ventilator care management and use appropriate referrals: long-term ventilator care facilities versus home care management.

Rationale

The ET tube passes through the vocal cords, and attempts to talk can cause more trauma to the cords. However, patients must understand how to use supplementary methods for communication (paper, pen, pictures).

Explaining expected events can help reduce anxiety.

This also helps reduce anxiety by providing a basis for actions.

Information can help reduce the anxiety associated with the procedure.

Information aids the patient in maintaining some control.

Continuity of care is facilitated through the use of specialty resources.

• RELATED CARE PLANS

Disturbed sleep pattern, p. 177
Dysfunctional ventilatory weaning response, p. 210
Imbalanced nutrition: less than body requirements, p. 134
Impaired gas exchange, p. 78
Impaired physical mobility, p. 126
Impaired verbal communication, p. 38
Powerlessness, p. 153
Tracheostomy, p. 529

Obstructive Sleep Apnea

(Sleep-Disordered Breathing)

Sleep-disordered breathing (SDB) affects at least 20 million people in the United States and is defined as a cessation of breathing during sleep that is caused by repetitive partial or complete obstruction of the airway and pharyngeal structures. There are two types: the most common form, obstructive sleep apnea (OSA), and central sleep apnea. The prevalence in the general population is 2% to 4%. SDB is strongly linked to cardiovascular diseases—especially hypertension and coronary artery disease, which eventually leads to heart failure—so the prevalence in heart failure patients rises to approximately 50%. Consequences of SDB includes altered alertness, daytime somnolence, cognitive impairment, and increased morbidity and mortality. Common screening methods include pulse oximetry, blood gas analysis, and/or ambulatory airflow measurements, but the diagnosis of SDB is confirmed by overnight sleep laboratory studies.

■ = Independent; ▲ = Collaborative

Obstructive Sleep Apnea—cont'd

Treatment for mild SDB includes conservative measures such as weight loss, abstaining from the use of alcohol and sedatives, avoiding the supine position during sleep, and sometimes oropharyngeal appliances or surgery. However, continuous positive airway pressure (CPAP) is the most consistently effective treatment for clinically significant SDB and appears to substantially improve the condition. Unfortunately, some patients complain that the CPAP mask or nasal device (BiPAP) is uncomfortable, so compliance with the treatment is often low. As technology advances, the treatment of SDB will become more comfortable and less cumbersome. Patients must be encouraged to try different equipment to adapt to their own facial structure, because patients who use CPAP report less fatigue, better blood pressure control, and improved quality of life.

NDx Nursing Diagnosis

Ineffective Breathing Pattern

Common Related Factors

Obesity
Enlarged tonsils and adenoids
Narrowing of respiratory passages
Decreased airway muscle tone during sleep

Defining Characteristics

Snoring
Decreased respiratory rate
Periods of apnea

Common Expected Outcomes

Patient maintains optimal sleep pattern, as evidenced by decreased snoring and apneic episodes and increased sleeping.
Patient adheres to CPAP/BiPAP device regimen as prescribed.

NOC Outcomes
Respiratory Status: Airway Patency;
    Respiratory Status: Ventilation

NIC Interventions
Airway Management;
    Respiratory Monitoring

Ongoing Assessment

Actions/Interventions

- Assess current sleep pattern and sleep history.

- Ask the patient's partner or significant other whether the patient snores or has apneic episode during the night.

- Assess for characteristics of SDB: loud snoring, apneic episodes (5 to 10 per hour), jerky or restless leg movement during sleep, daytime somnolence and fatigue.

Rationale

Periodic changes in sleep pattern need to be differentiated from true obstructive sleep disorder/apnea.

Most patients are unaware of their own snoring and apnea. The partner may have complained about loud snoring followed by stopping breathing and a loud gasp or snort when the patient is aroused by the apnea.

Patients may only be aware of the daytime fatigue and sleepiness.

■ = Independent; ▲ = Collaborative

Actions/Interventions

■ Assess and document nighttime sleeping patterns.

■ Assess for contributing factors to OSA: obesity (body mass index greater than 30), short thick neck circumference, age, large uvula, enlarged tonsils or adenoids, small recessive jaw, oropharyngeal edema, alcohol abuse.

■ Assess physiological effects resulting from OSA: hypoxemia, increased sympathetic activity, hypertension.

■ Assess for comorbidities affected by OSA.

Rationale

Formal sleep studies can be performed as described herein and continue to be the gold standard. Patients can use simpler "screening" techniques such as home sleep monitoring (although it is difficult to maintain equipment during sleep), or overnight pulse oximetry to document drops in oxygen saturation during the apneic periods.

Research has shown that body type affects diagnosis. Excess body weight can result in accumulation of fat on the sides of the upper airway, causing it to become narrow. Increasing neck size has been correlated with severity of apnea. Aging causes loss of muscle mass replaced by fat, again leaving the airway narrow and soft. Anatomical abnormalities affect upper airway musculature. Alcohol use results in excessive relaxation of muscles in the upper airway during sleep.

During sleep apneic periods, there is a fall in PaO_2 levels with a buildup of $PaCO_2$. The immediate "arousal" to breathe causes surges in sympathetic activity that affects many organ systems, especially the cardiovascular system. Hypertension is common in patients with OSA, although the relationship is unclear. The sympathetic stimulation can lead to cardiac arrhythmias, systemic vascular resistance, and reduced cardiac output in compromised heart failure patients.

Research has demonstrated a high prevalence in patients with heart failure, hypertension, coronary artery disease, and stroke, although the exact relationship is unclear. OSA can aggravate conditions such as heart failure because of the increased physiological demands put on the heart during sleep.

Therapeutic Interventions

Actions/Interventions

■ Suggest referral for sleep study if not already performed.

■ In diagnosed patients, explain the mechanisms by which sleep apnea occurs:
- Relaxation of muscles of the soft palate during sleep results in reduced airway size and partial or complete closure.
- This causes cessation of breathing (apnea).
- During the apneic period, the body struggles to breathe and is aroused to awaken, which reopens the airway.

Rationale

Often the hospital night shift nurse may be the one to recognize the disturbed sleep pattern. The most accurate test is the overnight sleep study—polysomnography. Using electrodes, it records the type and depth of sleep, eye movement observations, respiratory effort and movement, oxygen saturation, and muscle movement.

The more the patient understands the condition, the better he or she is able to participate in the treatment plan.

Obstructive Sleep Apnea

■ = Independent; ▲ = Collaborative

Obstructive Sleep Apnea—cont'd

Actions/Interventions	Rationale
• The obstructive periods are associated with reduced oxyhemoglobin saturation.	
• This sleep-apnea-arousal-awaken cycle repeats on an ongoing basis, preventing the patient from reaching the deep stages of rapid eye movement (REM) sleep.	
■ Teach the patient about nonsurgical therapies to treat OSA:	
• Weight loss—indicated for mild sleep apnea.	Weight loss has been shown to improve this condition, although the amount of weight loss required varies among patients.
• Nonsupine positioning—indicated for mild sleep apnea	Supine sleeping causes the most significant relaxation of upper airway muscles. Turning on one's side can reduce episodes of apnea. Suggested techniques include sewing or attaching a sock filled with tennis balls lengthwise down the back of a pajama top. This reminds the patient to stay positioned on the side.
• Oral appliances resembling mouth guards (tongue-retaining or mandibular advance devices)—indicated for mild sleep apnea	Repositioning the muscles may prevent the apneic episode. These devices should be fitted by a specialty dentist. The devices are more appropriate for milder forms of OSA.
• CPAP—indicated for mild to severe apnea. CPAP uses a nasal or facial mask held in place with secure straps. Appropriate mask fitting is key to success. The mask is connected to a small air compressor that delivers preset positive pressure to the upper airway. The mask is usually worn for at least 4 hours during the night's sleep. It should be used daily, although patients with milder levels may need the device only a few days a week. There is a portable unit for travel. Side effects include dry mucous membranes, dermatitis, skin breakdown, nasal congestion, and feelings of claustrophobia.	The positive pressure serves to "stabilize" the airway and maintain patency. Humidification can be added to reduce problems associated with dryness.
• Nasal trumpets—indicated to bypass any nasal, soft palate, or sometimes tongue obstructions and commonly used in postanesthesia settings, but not readily tolerated by patients on a long-term basis	These devices may reduce mucosal trauma.
• BiPAP—a variation of CPAP that delivers a lower amount of positive pressure during exhalation.	Patients often find this device more tolerable than CPAP.
• Supplementary oxygen	This raises oxygen saturation.
■ Emphasize compliance issues, especially related to CPAP.	Patients frequently have difficulty getting masks or nasal devices to fit properly or they may feel claustrophobic while wearing the devices. The CPAP device is only effective while in use, making compliance a key issue. Patients need to take the device with them when they anticipate sleeping away from home, for example, on vacations, for work travel, or on long plane flights, especially if they already have heart failure.

■ = Independent; ▲ = Collaborative

Actions/Interventions

- Instruct patients to bring their CPAP/BiPAP devices to the hospital for personal use while hospitalized. Notify the hospital team, especially the anesthesiologist, of OSA problems so that ventilation needs can be correctly assessed.

- Instruct the patient to reduce or avoid drinking alcohol.

- Instruct the patient regarding possible surgical technique (uvulopalatopharyngoplasty), as indicated.

- Refer to sleep specialist as needed.

Rationale

It is more effective for patients to use their own face mask and devices that have been properly fitted. Use of the positive pressure aids ventilation, maintains tissue oxygen saturation, and reduces the workload of the heart.

Alcohol causes relaxation of the muscles of the upper airway and can aggravate the condition.

This procedure involves removal of part of the soft palate, uvula, and redundant peripharyngeal tissues to eliminate snoring. It does not always prevent the apneic periods. The procedure can be done surgically or with laser assistance. It is indicated for individuals who cannot tolerate CPAP.

Specialists may provide additional treatment strategies.

 Nursing Diagnosis

Sleep Deprivation

Common Related Factors

Cycle of sleep-apnea-arousal-sleep that interferes with REM sleep
Sleep stage shifts
Sleep apnea

Common Expected Outcome

Patient achieves restful, refreshing sleep pattern.

Defining Characteristics

Daytime drowsiness
Decreased ability to function
Tiredness
Irritability
Slowed reaction
Inability to concentrate

NOC Outcomes
Sleep; Rest

NIC Intervention
Sleep Enhancement

Ongoing Assessment

Actions/Interventions

- Assess for complaints of waking up feeling tired or fatigued, and experiencing daytime somnolence.

Rationale

The cycle of interrupted sleep results in reduced REM sleep, which the body requires for rest and to replenish itself. Interrupted sleep results in associated feelings of tiredness and often of complaints of feeling worse upon awakening than when retiring for sleep.

■ = Independent; ▲ = Collaborative

Obstructive Sleep Apnea

Obstructive Sleep Apnea—cont'd

Actions/Interventions

■ Assess for level of wakefulness during the day and ability to stay on task.

■ Assess for safety issues related to alertness, fatigue, or cognitive impairment (e.g., falling asleep during meetings, while driving, while handling heavy machinery).

■ Assess history of automobile accidents.

■ Assess for other factors that contribute to fatigue such as alcohol and medications.

■ For patients with comorbid cardiovascular disease (e.g., heart failure), differentiate between fatigue caused by OSA versus deteriorating heart failure.

■ Assess whether interpersonal relationships and quality of life have been affected by chronic fatigue, irritability, or mood changes.

Rationale

Decreased alertness and impaired concentration during the day can result in lost productivity and places the patient at risk for accidents. Patients are often embarrassed by episodes of falling asleep such as in movie theaters, during work meetings, or while watching television.

Memory and cognitive changes can significantly affect ability to perform activities of daily living and occupational activities.

The "drowsy driver syndrome," which has been linked to frequent automobile accidents, may be caused by OSA and lack of alertness and slowed reflexes while driving.

It is critical that patients with OSA do not aggravate their condition through use of sedatives, analgesics, narcotics, tranquilizers, other prescribed medications, or alcohol that also contribute to reduced alertness and fatigue.

Accurate assessment guides therapy.

Lack of sleep can contribute to irritability and depression, making it difficult to maintain healthy personal relationships. Impotence is also related to OSA and may affect feelings of intimacy.

Therapeutic Interventions

Actions/Interventions

■ Explain the relationship of REM sleep and of feeling refreshed when awakening.

■ Reinforce the importance of adhering to prescribed treatment.

■ Instruct the patient to consider alternative transportation (carpool, public transportation) until achieving a more restful sleep.

■ Refer to social worker as needed for assistance with personal relationships.

Rationale

REM sleep is characterized by rapid eye movements and is essential to waking up feeling refreshed. It is the deepest level of relaxation. This level is not reached when patients are continually being aroused from sleep and restarting their sleep cycles.

Most treatments need to be initiated on a daily basis (weight management, positioning, use of CPAP). Knowledge of the physiological basis for restful sleep may provide the rationale for compliance with treatments.

Daytime somnolence, reduced alertness, impaired concentration, and delayed reaction time place the patient at great risk for injuring self and others. Using alternative modes of travel reduces this risk.

Specialized expertise may be needed to help the patient gain insight into problems.

> • RELATED CARE PLANS
>
> Ineffective therapeutic regimen management,
>   p. 185
> Obesity, p. 714

(■ = Independent; ▲ = Collaborative)

Pneumonia

Pneumonitis; Community-Acquired Pneumonia; Hospital-Acquired Pneumonia

Pneumonia is caused by a bacterial or viral infection that results in an inflammatory process in the lungs. It is an infectious process that is spread by droplets or by contact. It is one of the most common causes of death in older adults. Predisposing factors to the development of pneumonia include upper respiratory infection, excessive alcohol ingestion, central nervous system depression, cardiac failure, any debilitating illness, chronic obstructive pulmonary disease (COPD), endotracheal (ET) intubation, and postoperative effects of general anesthesia. At risk are patients who are bedridden; patients who are immunosuppressed, have a history of smoking, are immobile for prolonged periods, or who are malnourished or dehydrated; and hospitalized patients in whom a superinfection may develop. Older and very young persons are at increased risk as well.

Types of pneumonia include the following:

- Gram-positive pneumonias: pneumococcal pneumonia, staphylococcal pneumonia, streptococcal pneumonia (these account for most community acquired pneumonias)
- Gram-negative pneumonias: *Klebsiella* pneumonia, *Pseudomonas* pneumonia, influenzal pneumonia, legionnaire's disease (these account for most hospital-acquired pneumonias)
- Anaerobic bacterial pneumonias (usually caused by aspiration)
- *Mycoplasma* pneumonia
- Viral pneumonias (most common in infants and children; influenza A is the primary causative viral agent in adults)
- Parasitic pneumonia (opportunistic infection)

This care plan focuses on acute care treatment of pneumonia.

 NDx Nursing Diagnosis

Infection

Common Related Factor	Defining Characteristics
Invading bacterial or viral organisms	Elevated temperature Elevated white blood cell (WBC) count Tachycardia Chills Positive sputum culture report Changing character of sputum

Common Expected Outcomes	
Patient experiences improvement in infection as evidenced by normothermia, normal WBC count, and negative sputum culture report on repeat culture. Patient demonstrates hygiene measures such as hand washing and control of infectious sputum.	**NOC Outcomes** Medication Response; Thermoregulation **NIC Interventions** Infection Protection; Medication Administration

Pneumonia

■ = Independent; ▲ = Collaborative

Pneumonia—cont'd

Ongoing Assessment

Actions/Interventions	Rationale
■ Elicit the patient's description of illness, including onset, chills, chest pain.	Classic signs of pneumonia include chills, fever, pleuritic chest pain, cough, dyspnea, sputum changes.
■ Assess for predisposing risk factors: recent exposure to illness; alcohol, tobacco, or drug abuse; chronic illness; immunosuppressive therapy; malnutrition; prolonged immobility.	Patients are at risk from a variety of sources. Community-acquired pneumonia is more common than nosocomial pneumonia.
■ Assess immunization status.	Preventive measure with pneumococcal vaccine should be assessed.
■ Assess vital signs, closely monitoring temperature fluctuations.	Continued fever may be caused by drug allergy, drug-resistant bacteria, superinfection, or inadequate lung drainage.
▲ Obtain fresh sputum for Gram stain and for culture and sensitivity, as prescribed: <ul><li>Instruct patient to expectorate into a sterile container. Be sure the specimen is coughed up and is not saliva.</li><li>If the patient is unable to cough up a specimen effectively, use sterile nasotracheal suctioning with a sputum trap.</li></ul>	This determines correct antibiotic coverage for the patient. Blood culture obtained before the initial antibiotic is given is an indicator or benchmark used to measure quality of care in hospitals.
▲ Monitor Gram stain, sputum, culture, and sensitivity reports. Watch closely for drug resistance and treat and/or institute isolation precautions, as appropriate.	Vigilant monitoring helps reduce risk of further complications.
■ Monitor lung sounds.	Bronchial breath sounds are evident in areas of lung consolidation. Wheezing is evident if inflammation or narrowing of airways occurs. Crackles are evident if fluid is present in interstitial or alveolar lung areas.
▲ Monitor WBC count.	Rising WBC count indicates the body's efforts to fight pathogens.
▲ Assess hydration.	Water loss is increased with fever.
▲ Monitor pulse oximetry and arterial blood gases (ABGs) as indicated.	These provide information on oxygen and carbon dioxide levels.
▲ Monitor serial chest x-ray reports.	Pneumonia causes increased areas of density on chest radiograph, occurring in an isolated segment, a lobe, unilaterally or bilaterally. Serial changes guide subsequent treatment.
■ Continue to monitor the effectiveness of the prescribed antimicrobial agents.	Parenteral intravenous (IV) antibiotics are usually given for the first few days of acute cases and then changed to oral antibiotics, which may be adequate for milder cases from the first day. To prevent a relapse of pneumonia, the patient needs to complete the course of antibiotics as prescribed. Antiviral drugs (e.g., amantadine, rimantadine) are available for parenteral administration for viral respiratory infections. Antibiotics are not effective against viral pneumonia but may be used when concurrent viral and bacterial pneumonias are present.

■ = Independent; ▲ = Collaborative

Therapeutic Interventions

Actions/Interventions	Rationale

Actions/Interventions

▲ Administer prescribed antimicrobial agents within 4 hours of hospital arrival.

▲ Use appropriate therapy for elevated temperatures: antipyretics, cold therapy.

■ Provide tissues and waste bags for disposal of sputum.

■ Keep the patient away from other patients who are at high risk for developing pneumonia by careful room assignment when patients are in semiprivate rooms.

■ Isolate patients as necessary after review of culture and sensitivity results. If the patient is positive for methicillin-resistant *Staphylococcus aureus* (MRSA), a private room with isolation is required.

Rationale

This is an indicator or benchmark used to measure quality of care in hospitals (see *www.hospitalcompare.hhs.gov*). Ongoing administration needs to be timely to maintain blood levels needed to fight the organism adequately and prevent a relapse or the development of a resistant strain of the organism.

This maintains normothermia and reduces metabolic needs.

These prevent spread of the disease.

Safety measures reduce risk of further infections.

This prevents potential spread of the disease.

 ## Nursing Diagnosis

Ineffective Airway Clearance

Common Related Factors

Increased sputum production in response to respiratory infection
Decreased energy and increased fatigue with predisposing factors present
Aspiration

Defining Characteristics

Abnormal lung sounds (e.g., rhonchi, bronchial lung sounds)
Decreased lung sounds over affected areas
Cough
Dyspnea
Change in respiratory status
Infiltrates seen on chest radiograph
Purulent sputum

Common Expected Outcome

Patient's airway is free of secretions as evidenced by eupnea and clear lung sounds after coughing or suctioning.

NOC Outcomes
Respiratory Status: Airway Patency

NIC Interventions
Airway Management; Cough Enhancement

Pneumonia

■ = Independent; ▲ = Collaborative

Pneumonia—cont'd

Pulmonary Care Plans

Ongoing Assessment

Actions/Interventions

- ■ Assess respiratory movements and use of accessory muscles.
- ■ Assess cough for effectiveness and productivity.

- ■ Observe sputum color, amount, and odor and report significant changes.
- ■ Auscultate lung sounds, noting areas of decreased ventilation and presence of adventitious sounds.

- ▲ Monitor pulse oximetry and ABGs.

- ▲ Monitor chest x-ray reports.

Rationale

Use of accessory muscles to breathe indicates an abnormal increase in work of breathing.

Patients may have ineffective cough due to fatigue or thick tenacious secretions.

A sign of infection is discolored sputum. An odor may be present.

Bronchial lung sounds are commonly heard over areas of lung density or consolidation. Crackles are heard when fluid is present.

Hypoxemia may result from impaired gas exchange from buildup of secretions. ABGs provide data about CO_2 levels in the blood.

These determine progression of disease process (e.g., clearing of infiltrates).

Therapeutic Interventions

Actions/Interventions

- ■ Encourage the patient to cough unless cough is frequent and nonproductive.
- ■ Use optimal positioning; encourage ambulation.

- ■ Assist patient with coughing, deep breathing, and splinting, as necessary.
- ■ Maintain adequate hydration.

- ■ Use humidity (humidified oxygen or humidifier at bedside).
- ■ Assist with oral pharynx suctioning if necessary.

- ■ Assist the patient with use of incentive spirometer.

- ■ For patients with reduced energy, pace activities.

- ■ Provide oral care.

Rationale

Frequent nonproductive coughing can result in hypoxemia.

The sitting position and splinting the abdomen promote more effective coughing by increasing abdominal pressure and upward diaphragmatic movement. Ambulation mobilizes secretions and reduces atelectasis.

This improves productivity of the cough.

Fluids are lost by diaphoresis, fever, and tachypnea and are needed to aid in the mobilization of secretions.

Increasing the humidity of inspired air will loosen secretions.

Coughing is the most helpful way to remove secretions. Nasotracheal suctioning may cause increased hypoxemia, especially without hyperoxygenation before, during, and after suctioning.

Incentive spirometry serves to improve deep breathing and prevent atelectasis.

Effective coughing is hard work and may exhaust an already compromised patient.

Secretions from pneumonia are often foul tasting and smelling. Providing oral care may decrease nausea and vomiting associated with the taste of secretions.

■ = Independent; ▲ = Collaborative

Actions/Interventions	Rationale

▲ Consult the respiratory therapist for chest physiotherapy and nebulizer treatments, as appropriate and as ordered.

Chest physiotherapy includes the techniques of postural drainage and chest percussion to loosen and mobilize secretions in smaller airways that cannot be removed by coughing or suctioning. A nebulizer may be used to humidify the airway to thin secretions to facilitate their removal.

▲ Administer medication such as antibiotics and expectorants for productive coughs and cough suppressants for hacking nonproductive coughs as prescribed, noting effectiveness; administer inhaled bronchodilators and inhaled steroids, as prescribed, to open airway and decrease inflammation.

A variety of medications are available to treat specific problems.

▲ Assist with bronchoscopy and thoracentesis, as appropriate.

Bronchoscopy is done to obtain lavage samples for culture and sensitivity and to remove mucous plugs; thoracentesis is done to drain associated pleural effusions.

▲ Anticipate possible need for intubation if patient's condition deteriorates.

Intubation may be needed to facilitate deep suctioning efforts and to provide source for augmenting oxygenation.

NDx Nursing Diagnosis

Impaired Gas Exchange

Common Related Factors

Collection of mucus in airways
Inflammation of airways and alveoli
Fluid-filled alveoli
Ventilation-perfusion mismatch (especially with bacterial pneumonia)
Lung consolidation with decreased surface area available for gas exchange

Defining Characteristics

Dyspnea
Decreased PaO_2
Increased $PaCO_2$
Cyanosis
Tachypnea
Tachycardia
Decreased activity tolerance
Restlessness
Disorientation or confusion
In older patients, functional decline with or without fever
Loss of appetite
Hypotension

Common Expected Outcome

Patient maintains optimal gas exchange as evidenced by eupnea, normal ABGs, and alert responsive mentation or no further reduction in mental status.

NOC Outcome

Respiratory Status: Gas Exchange

NIC Interventions

Respiratory Monitoring; Oxygen Therapy

Pneumonia

 **Pneumonia**—cont'd

Ongoing Assessment

Actions/Interventions	**Rationale**
■ Assess respirations: note quality, rate, rhythm, depth, dyspnea on exertion, use of accessory muscles, position assumed for easy breathing.	Abnormality indicates respiratory compromise.
■ Monitor for changes in vital signs.	With initial hypoxia and hypercapnia, blood pressure (BP), heart rate (HR), and respiratory rate all rise. As the hypoxia and/or hypercapnia becomes more severe, BP may drop, HR tends to continue to be rapid with dysrhythmias, and respiratory failure may ensue with the patient unable to maintain the rapid respiratory rate.
■ Assess skin color for development of cyanosis.	For cyanosis to be present, 5 g of hemoglobin must desaturate.
■ Assess for changes in orientation and note increasing restlessness.	These can be early signs of hypoxia and/or hypercarbia.
▲ Monitor ABGs or oxygen saturation through pulse oximetry, maintaining oxygen saturation of 90% or greater.	Increasing $PaCO_2$ and decreasing PaO_2 are signs of respiratory failure.

Therapeutic Interventions

Actions/Interventions	**Rationale**
▲ Maintain oxygen administration device as ordered. Avoid high concentrations of oxygen in patients with COPD.	Supplemental oxygen therapy maintains oxygen saturation of 90% or greater to provide for adequate oxygenation. Careful administration of low liter flow oxygen is indicated because hypoxia stimulates the drive to breathe in the patient who chronically retains carbon dioxide.
■ Pace activities to the patient's tolerance.	Activities will increase oxygen consumption and should be planned so the patient does not become hypoxic.
■ Anticipate need for intubation and possibly mechanical ventilation if condition worsens.	Early intubation and mechanical ventilation are recommended to prevent full decompensation of the patient and a potentially life-threatening situation.

NDx Nursing Diagnosis

Acute Pain/Discomfort

Common Related Factors	**Defining Characteristics**
Respiratory distress Coughing	Complaints of discomfort Guarding Withdrawal Moaning Facial grimace

■ = Independent; ▲ = Collaborative

 Pulmonary Care Plans

Irritability
Anxiety
Tachycardia
Increased BP

Common Expected Outcomes

Patient verbalizes relief or reduction in pain.
Patient appears relaxed and comfortable.
Patient verbalizes understanding of nonpharmacological interventions for pain relief.

NOC Outcomes
Pain Control; Medication Response

NIC Interventions
Pain Management; Analgesic Administration

Ongoing Assessment

Actions/Interventions

■ Assess complaints of discomfort: pain or discomfort with breathing, shortness of breath, muscle pains, pain with coughing.

■ Monitor for nonverbal signs of discomfort (e.g., grimacing, irritability, tachycardia, increased BP).

■ Elicit how the patient has effectively dealt with pain in the past.

Rationale

Pain can result in shallow breathing and poor cough effort.

Specific manifestations guide interventions.

This provides opportunity to consider the patient's reactions to and expectations for pain relief.

Therapeutic Interventions

Actions/Interventions

▲ Administer appropriate medications to treat the cough:

• Do not suppress a productive cough; use moderate amounts of analgesics to relieve pleuritic pain.

• Use cough suppressants and humidity for dry, hacking cough.

▲ Administer analgesics as prescribed and as needed. Encourage the patient to take analgesics before discomfort becomes severe. Evaluate medication effectiveness.

■ Use additional measures, including positioning and relaxation techniques.

Rationale

Careful balancing of dosage is needed to prevent reduction in respirations seen with some analgesics.

Coughing is necessary to mobilize secretions. Cough suppression will cause retained secretions and delay the resolution of infection.

An unproductive hacking cough irritates airways and should be suppressed.

Medications allow for pain relief and the ability to deep breathe and cough. Analgesics prevent peak periods of pain.

These facilitate effective respiratory excursion.

Pneumonia

■ = Independent; ▲ = Collaborative

Pneumonia—cont'd

 Nursing Diagnosis

Deficient Knowledge

Common Related Factors

New condition and procedures
Unfamiliarity with disease process and transmission of disease

Defining Characteristics

Questions
Confusion about treatment
Inability to comply with treatment regimen, including appropriate isolation procedures
Lack of questions

Common Expected Outcome

Patient and caregiver demonstrate understanding of disease process and compliance with treatment regimen and isolation procedures.

NOC Outcomes

Knowledge: Disease Process;
Knowledge: Treatment Regimen

NIC Interventions

Teaching: Disease Process; Teaching:
Prescribed Medication; Immunization/
Vaccination Administration

Ongoing Assessment

Actions/Interventions	Rationale
■ Determine understanding of pneumonia complications and treatment.	This provides an important starting point in education.
■ Assess potential home care needs.	Therapy will continue after hospital discharge. Home care needs will depend on availability of supportive persons, the patient's energy level and cognitive level, and the like.

Therapeutic Interventions

Actions/Interventions	Rationale
■ Teach the patient deep breathing exercises and techniques to cough effectively.	Increased knowledge fosters compliance.
■ Discuss with the patient or caregiver the need to complete the full course of antibiotics, as prescribed, and for adequate rest for recuperation.	Full antibiotic course is needed to prevent a relapse or development of a resistant organism. A prolonged period of convalescence may be needed for older patients.
■ Provide information about need to do the following:	These are preventive measures.
• Maintain natural resistance to infection through adequate nutrition, rest, and exercise.	These measures promote a healthy immune system.
• Avoid contact with people with upper respiratory infections.	This reduces reoccurrence of disease.

■ = Independent; ▲ = Collaborative

Pulmonary Care Plans

Actions/Interventions

- Obtain immunizations against influenza for older and chronically ill patients.

Rationale

Pneumococcal vaccine is currently recommended every 5 years.

• RELATED CARE PLANS

Activity intolerance, p. 7
Anxiety, p. 15
Fear, p. 68
Imbalanced nutrition: less than body
  requirements, p. 134
Mechanical ventilation, p. 459

Pneumothorax with Chest Tube

Collapsed Lung

Presence of air in the intrapleural space can cause partial or complete collapse of the lung. Pneumothorax can be iatrogenic, spontaneous, or the result of injury. A chest tube drainage system is used to reestablish negative pressure in the intrapleural space to facilitate lung reexpansion.

 Nursing Diagnosis

Ineffective Breathing Pattern

Common Related Factors

Partially or completely collapsed lung
Pain
Anxiety
Inadequate chest expansion

Defining Characteristics

Shallow respirations
Rapid respirations
Diminished breath sounds on affected side
Dyspnea, shortness of breath
Asymmetrical chest expansion
Use of accessory muscles

Common Expected Outcomes

Patient maintains effective breathing pattern, as evidenced by respiratory rate 12 to 20 breaths/min and clear and equal lung sounds bilaterally.
Chest radiograph shows lungs fully expanded.

NOC Outcomes

Respiratory Status: Ventilation; Pain Level

NIC Interventions

Airway Management; Tube Care: Chest;
  Pain Management

■ = Independent; ▲ = Collaborative

Pneumothorax with Chest Tube

Pneumothorax with Chest Tube—cont'd

Pulmonary Care Plans

Ongoing Assessment

Actions/Interventions

- Assess respiratory rate, depth, and effort.

- Auscultate lungs for area of diminished or absent lung sounds.
- Assess for pain.
- Assess chest tube drainage system for the following:
  - Secure connections

  - Intact water seal
  - Fluctuation (or tidaling) of fluid caused by pressure changes in the intrapleural space during inspiration and expiration
  - Presence of air leak or bubbling in the water seal

  - Amount of fluid in drainage collection chamber
- ▲ Monitor serial chest x-ray films.

Rationale

Respiratory rate and rhythm changes such as an increase in respiratory rate with a decreased tidal volume (rapid shallow respirations) are early warning signs of impending respiratory difficulties.

These may indicate partial or complete collapse of the lung.

Pain can result in shallow breathing.

A loose connection can allow air entry and positive pressure in the intrapleural space, resulting in further lung collapse.

This prevents air entry into the intrapleural space.

Cessation of fluctuating (or tidaling) of fluid can indicate lung reexpansion or, if abrupt, can indicate clogged or kinked tube.

Bubbling indicates air removal from the intrapleural space, especially during expiration or coughing. Cessation of bubbling can indicate lung reexpansion. Continuous bubbling can indicate air leak within the patient's chest or within the system.

Excessive drainage may indicate hemorrhage.

These are used to document lung reexpansion.

Therapeutic Interventions

Actions/Interventions

- Explain the procedure for chest tube insertion.

- Maintain the chest tube drainage system:
  - Secure connections.
  - Maintain proper water levels in water seal and suction control chamber.

  - Secure chest drainage system to an intravenous (IV) pole with wheels. Keep below level of chest.
- Encourage deep breathing and coughing after deep breathing, as needed.
- Instruct the patient in splinting the chest tube site with a pillow during coughing and with movement.

- Assist the patient in repositioning every 2 to 3 hours.

Rationale

This prepares the patient and decreases fear. Chest tubes are required to allow for reexpansion of the collapsed lung by maintaining negative pressure in the intrapleural space.

This prevents dislodgment of tubing.

The amount of suction is determined by the depth of the tubing in the suction control chamber. As water evaporates, additional water is added to each chamber.

This allows mobility while preventing accidental knock-over of the system.

These actions decrease atelectasis and enhance gas exchange.

Providing support to the insertion site will decrease discomfort associated with deep breathing and coughing.

This is for comfort and to promote improved lung expansion.

■ = Independent; ▲ = Collaborative

Actions/Interventions

- Administer pain medication as prescribed before activity: deep breathing, coughing, and physical mobility. Instruct the patient to notify the nurse of pain before it gets severe.
- Offer reassurance.

Rationale

Effective pain management will help the patient's willingness to participate in care.

Anxiety can result in rapid, shallow respirations.

 Nursing Diagnosis

Ineffective Protection

Common Related Factors

Presence of chest tube
Malfunctioning chest tube drainage system
Collapsed lung

Defining Characteristics

Oxygen saturation less than 90%
Abnormal arterial blood gases (ABGs)
Cool, clammy skin
Hypoxia
Hypercapnia
Fever

Common Expected Outcomes

Patient maintains adequate gas exchange as evidenced by normal ABGs for patient, normal skin color, and clear mentation.
Patient remains free of infection.
Oxygen saturation is greater than 92% on room air.

NOC Outcomes
Immune Status; Infection Status

NIC Interventions
Respiratory Monitoring; Tube Care: Chest

Ongoing Assessment

Actions/Interventions

▲ Assess pulse oximetry levels and report if less than 90%.

▲ Assess ABG results for abnormalities and report.

- Assess feelings of dyspnea or shortness of breath.
- Assess vital signs, including temperature.

- Assess mentation for signs of hypoxia and hypercapnia.

- Assess chest drainage system.
- Assess chest tube drainage for increased or purulent drainage.

Rationale

Pulse oximetry is a useful tool to detect early changes in oxygenation. Goal is oxygen saturation levels greater than 92% on room air.

Decreasing PaO_2 and increasing $PaCO_2$ are signs of respiratory failure. As the patient's condition begins to fail, the respiratory rate decreases and the $PaCO_2$ rises.

This may indicate hypoxia.

Tachycardia is common during hypoxia; fever can indicate infection.

Restlessness, inappropriateness, lethargy, and confusion may result with hypoxia and hypercapnia.

An intact system reduces the risk for infection.

This may represent infection and require culturing.

Pneumothorax with Chest Tube

■ = Independent; ▲ = Collaborative

Pneumothorax with Chest Tube—cont'd

Actions/Interventions

■ Assess chest tube insertion site for reddened wound edges.

▲ Assess white blood cell (WBC) count.

Rationale

This may be early sign of infection.

Rising WBC count indicates the body's effort to combat pathogens.

Therapeutic Interventions

Actions/Interventions

▲ Administer supplemental oxygen as prescribed.

■ Elevate head of bed.
■ Use incentive spirometry as needed.

■ Maintain chest tube drainage system; troubleshoot as necessary.
▲ Limit visits of persons with upper respiratory or other infections.

Rationale

This maintains oxygen saturation of 90% or greater for adequate oxygenation.

This enhances lung expansion.

This enhances deep breathing, thereby decreasing potential for atelectasis.

This ensures patency of the drainage tubing.

This reduces the risk of infection transmission.

NDx Nursing Diagnosis

Deficient Knowledge

Common Related Factor

Change in health status

Defining Characteristics

Multiple questions
Lack of questions

Common Expected Outcome

Patient verbalizes understanding of physical condition, reason for chest tube, importance of deep breathing, follow-up care, and signs and symptoms to report.

NOC Outcomes
Knowledge: Disease Process;
Knowledge: Treatment Regimen

NIC Interventions
Teaching: Disease Process;
Teaching: Procedure/Treatment

Ongoing Assessment

Actions/Interventions

■ Assess knowledge of pneumothorax and its treatment.

Rationale

The suddenness of the medical problem may have overwhelmed the patient and served as a barrier to learning.

■ = Independent; ▲ = Collaborative

Actions/Interventions

■ Assess motivation and ability to learn.

Rationale

Adults must see a purpose for learning. Learning also requires energy, which the patient may not be ready to use.

Therapeutic Interventions

Actions/Interventions

■ Encourage questions.

■ Instruct the patient and significant others regarding the following:
  • Pneumothorax (etiology)

  • Purpose of chest tube in lung reexpansion

  • Importance of keeping chest drainage unit below level of chest
  • Chest tube insertion site care.
  • Importance of deep breathing, coughing, and gradually increasing physical activity
  • Pain medication actions and side effects

  • Signs and symptoms to report

▲ Collaborate with physician to determine likelihood of recurrence of pneumothorax. Instruct patient as appropriate.

■ Instruct the patient on use of the Heimlich valve if used for home care.

■ Instruct the patient on the importance of follow-up with a health care provider and the need for a repeat chest x-ray study.

Rationale

Questions facilitate open communication between the patient and health care providers.

Pneumothorax may be iatrogenic, spontaneous, or the result of injury.

This serves to reestablish negative pressure in the intrapleural space to facilitate lung reexpansion.

This prevents backup of drainage or air into intrapleural space.

This decreases incidence of infection.

These enhance lung expansion.

Medications promote comfort, which can enhance effective breathing patterns and early mobilization.

The patient needs to report fever, purulent drainage from insertion site, reddened wound edges, and signs of lung collapse: chest pain, dyspnea, shortness of breath.

In healthy patients who have experienced a spontaneous pneumothorax, recurrence is 10% to 50% for a second incident and 60% for a third incident. The patient needs to be aware of signs and symptoms of recurrence, as well as appropriate emergency medical treatment measures (planned in advance).

The Heimlich valve is a one-way flutter valve that allows air from the pleural space to flow out through the tube with exhalation, but prevents air from flowing into the chest during inhalation.

This confirms lung reexpansion.

• RELATED CARE PLANS

Fear, p. 68
Impaired physical mobility, p. 126
Risk for infection, p. 108

Pneumothorax with Chest Tube

■ = Independent; ▲ = Collaborative

Pulmonary Thromboembolism

Pulmonary Embolus (PE)

Pulmonary thromboembolism occurs when there is an obstruction in the pulmonary vascular bed (pulmonary artery or one of the branches) caused by blood clots (thrombi). It is one of the most common causes of death in hospitalized patients, resulting from a variety of factors that predispose to intravascular clotting. These include postoperative states, trauma to vessel walls, obesity, diabetes mellitus, infection, venous stasis caused by immobility, postpartum state, and other circulatory disorders. The clinical picture varies according to size and location of the embolus. The primary objective when pulmonary embolism (PE) occurs is to prevent recurrence. This care plan focuses on acute care treatment for PE.

NDx Nursing Diagnosis

Ineffective Breathing Pattern

Common Related Factors

Hypoxia (from the ventilation-perfusion disorder caused by the PE)
Pain
Anxiety

Defining Characteristics

Dyspnea
Tachypnea
Cyanosis
Cough
Use of accessory muscles

Common Expected Outcome

Patient's breathing pattern is maintained as evidenced by eupnea, normal skin color, and regular respiratory rate and pattern.

NOC Outcome
Respiratory Status: Ventilation

NIC Interventions
Air Management; Respiratory Monitoring

Ongoing Assessment

Actions/Interventions

■ Assess respiratory rate and depth.

■ Assess for any increase in work of breathing: shortness of breath, use of accessory muscles.

■ Assess lung sounds.

Rationale

Respiratory rate and rhythm changes are early warning signs of impending respiratory difficulties. Tachypnea is a typical finding of PE. The rapid, shallow respirations result from hypoxia. Development of hypoventilation (a slowing of respiratory rate) without improvement in the patient's condition indicates respiratory failure.

Changes in character of respirations may signal deterioration.

This is done to determine the presence of adventitious sounds that may be caused by poor gas exchange.

■ = Independent; ▲ = Collaborative

Actions/Interventions

▲ Monitor arterial blood gases (ABGs) and note changes.

▲ Monitor oxygen saturation through pulse oximetry.

■ Assess characteristics of pain, especially in association with the respiratory cycle.

Rationale

ABGs of the PE patient typically exhibit hypoxemia and respiratory alkalosis from a blowing off of carbon dioxide. Development of respiratory acidosis in this patient indicates respiratory failure, and immediate ventilator support is indicated.

Pulse oximetry is a useful tool to detect early changes in oxygenation. Goal is oxygen saturation levels greater than 92% on room air.

Pain may result in shallow respirations.

Therapeutic Interventions

Action/Interventions

■ Position patient with proper body alignment.

▲ Ensure that the oxygen delivery system is applied to the patient.

■ Provide reassurance and allay anxiety by staying with the patient during acute episodes of respiratory distress.

■ Change position every 2 hours.

■ Assist patient with coughing and deep breathing. Suction as needed.

■ Anticipate the need for intubation and mechanical ventilation.

Rationale

If not contraindicated, a sitting position allows good lung excursion and chest expansion.

The appropriate amount of oxygen is continuously delivered and the patient does not become desaturated.

Air hunger can produce extreme anxiety.

This facilitates movement and drainage of secretions.

This helps keep airways open by clearing secretions.

Intubation and positive-pressure ventilation are a means to stabilize breathing and ventilation.

Pulmonary Thromboembolism

NDx Nursing Diagnosis

Impaired Gas Exchange

Common Related Factors

Decreased perfusion to lung tissues caused by obstruction in pulmonary vascular bed by embolus
Increased alveolar dead space
Increased physiological shunting caused by collapse of alveoli resulting from loss of surfactant

Defining Characteristics

Confusion
Somnolence
Restlessness
Irritability
Hypoxemia
Hypercapnia

Common Expected Outcome

Patient maintains optimal gas exchange as evidenced by normal ABGs, alert responsive mentation, or no further reduction in mental status.

NOC Outcomes
Respiratory Status: Gas Exchange; Tissue Perfusion: Pulmonary

NIC Interventions
Respiratory Monitoring; Oxygen Therapy

■ = Independent; ▲ = Collaborative

➤ **Pulmonary Thromboembolism**—cont'd

Ongoing Assessment

Actions/Interventions	**Rationale**
■ Auscultate lung sounds every shift, noting areas of decreased ventilation and presence of adventitious sounds.	Common clinical findings include rales, tachypnea, and tachycardia.
■ Monitor vital signs, noting any changes.	In initial hypoxia and hypercapnia, blood pressure (BP), heart rate (HR), and respiratory rate all rise. As the hypoxia and/or hypercapnia becomes more severe, BP may drop, HR tends to continue to be rapid and includes dysrhythmias, and respiratory failure may ensue, with the patient unable to maintain the rapid respiratory rate.
■ Assess for signs and symptoms of hypoxemia.	Specific manifestations include tachycardia, restlessness, diaphoresis, headache, lethargy or confusion, and skin color changes.
■ Assess for presence of signs and symptoms of atelectasis.	Specific manifestations include diminished chest expansion, limited diaphragm excursion, bronchial or tubular breath sounds, rales, and tracheal shift to affected side.
■ Assess for presence of signs and symptoms of infarction: cough, hemoptysis, pleuritic pain, consolidation, pleural effusion, bronchial breathing, pleural friction rub, fever.	Hemoptysis occurs as a result of tissue destruction associated with pulmonary infarction.
▲ Monitor ABGs and note changes.	It is important to monitor for signs of respiratory failure (e.g., low PaO_2, elevated $PaCO_2$).
▲ Use pulse oximetry, as available, to continuously monitor oxygen saturation and pulse rate. Keep alarms on at all times.	Pulse oximetry has been found to be a useful tool in the clinical setting to detect changes in oxygenation.
■ Assess for calf tenderness, swelling, redness, and/or hardened area. Assess for presence of Homans' sign.	PE often arises from a deep vein thrombosis and may have been previously overlooked. Homans' sign is characterized by pain when the foot is forcefully dorsiflexed. Homans' sign is neither specific nor sensitive for a deep vein thrombosis.
▲ Assess acid-base balance.	Metabolic acidosis results from lactic acid buildup from tissue hypoxia.

Therapeutic Interventions

Actions/Interventions	**Rationale**
▲ Administer oxygen as needed.	This prevents severe hypoxemia.
■ Position the patient properly.	This promotes optimal lung perfusion. When the patient is positioned on one side, the affected area should not be dependent. Upright and sitting positions optimize diaphragmatic excursions.
■ Pace and schedule activities.	This helps conserve energy.
▲ Anticipate the need to start anticoagulant therapy and, if there is massive thromboembolism, the use of thrombolytic therapy.	Heparin is the first-line drug, unless a massive thrombus is present or the patient is hemodynamically unstable. Then thrombolytic therapy (e.g., urokinase or alteplase) are used to directly lyse or dissolve the clot.
▲ Administer bicarbonate if needed to correct acidosis.	Acidosis has a vasoconstriction effect and will expand the perfusion problem.

■ = Independent; ▲ = Collaborative

Pulmonary Care Plans

Nursing Diagnosis

Risk for Decreased Cardiac Output

Common Risk Factors

Failure of right ventricle of heart resulting from pulmonary hypertension

Failure of left ventricle of heart secondary to reduced preload from right ventricular failure

Common Expected Outcome

Patient achieves adequate cardiac output (CO) as evidenced by strong peripheral pulses; normal vital signs; warm, dry skin; and alert, responsive mentation.

NOC Outcomes
Cardiac Pump Effectiveness; Circulation Status

NIC Interventions
Hemodynamic Regulation; Invasive Hemodynamic Monitoring

Pulmonary Thromboembolism

Ongoing Assessment

Actions/Interventions

■ Assess vital signs, skin warmth, and peripheral pulses.

■ Monitor for dysrhythmias.

▲ If hemodynamic monitoring is in place, assess central venous pressure (CVP), pulmonary artery diastolic pressure, pulmonary capillary wedge pressure (PCWP), and CO.

■ Assess level of consciousness.

■ Monitor weight daily.

■ Observe and document clinical findings that indicate impending or present failure of right side of heart: Accentuated pulmonic component of second heart sound (S_2), splitting of S_2, engorged neck vein, positive hepatojugular reflex, increased CVP readings, palpable liver and spleen, altered coagulation values, electrocardiogram (ECG) changes associated with right atrial hypertrophy, atrial dysrhythmias, pedal edema, weight gain.

■ Auscultate lung and heart sounds every 2 to 4 hours to identify abnormalities indicating impending or present failure of left side of heart, such as the follow-

Rationale

Peripheral vasoconstriction causes cool, pale, diaphoretic skin.

Atrial dysrhythmias are caused by right-sided heart strain and ventricular dysrhythmias are caused by hypoxemia.

CVP provides information on filling pressures of right side of the heart; pulmonary artery diastolic pressure and PCWP reflect left-sided fluid volumes.

Early signs of cerebral hypoxia are restlessness and anxiety, which lead to agitation and confusion.

A gain of 2 to 3 pounds per day is significant for heart failure.

Embolus causes decreased cross-sectional area of pulmonary vascular bed that results in increased pulmonary resistance. This increases the workload of the right side of the heart.

Decreased right ventricular contractility decreases left side blood volume and preload. This decreases left ventricular pumping power if not treated promptly.

■ = Independent; ▲ = Collaborative

Pulmonary Thromboembolism—cont'd

Actions/Interventions

ing: fine rales (bases of the lungs), increased PCWP, presence of S_3, gallop rhythms, frothy secretions, dyspnea, tachycardia, cough, wheezing, orthopnea, hypoxemia, respiratory acidosis, and ECG changes associated with left atrial hypertrophy.

Therapeutic Interventions

Actions/Interventions

▲ Elevate legs or feet, and apply or maintain elastic stockings if cardiac status allows.

▲ For massive pulmonary thromboembolism, anticipate the following:
- Mechanical ventilation
- Insertion of invasive monitoring lines: arterial line and/or Swan-Ganz catheter

- Inotropic agents
- Anticoagulant therapy
- Thrombolytic therapy
- Intracaval filter insertion
- Pulmonary embolectomy (rarely done)

See also **Decreased Cardiac Output,** *p. 32.*

Rationale

This promotes peripheral blood flow and decreases venous stasis. If the cardiac system is failing (congestive heart failure), returning edema to the vascular tree can increase failure.

Ventilatory support is indicated for severe hypoxemia.

Auscultatory BP may be unreliable secondary to vasoconstriction associated with the decreased CO. Swan-Ganz catheter provides information on filling pressures in right and left side of heart.

These improve cardiac output.

This is used to prevent thrombus from enlarging.

This directly lyses or dissolves the blood clots.

This prevents further embolization from thrombophlebitis.

This is the surgical removal of the embolus or emboli from the vascular bed.

ND x Nursing Diagnosis

Ineffective Protection

Common Related Factor

Anticoagulant or thrombolytic therapy

Defining Characteristics

Altered clotting
Bleeding

Common Expected Outcome

Patient's risk for bleeding is reduced through ongoing assessment and early intervention.

NOC Outcomes
Blood Loss Severity; Risk Control

NIC Interventions
Bleeding Precautions; Bleeding Reduction

■ = Independent; ▲ = Collaborative

Ongoing Assessment

Actions/Interventions

- Assess for history of a high-risk bleeding condition: liver disease, kidney disease, severe hypertension, cavitary tuberculosis, bacterial endocarditis, and heparin-induced thrombocytopenia.

▲ Monitor intravenous (IV) dosage and delivery system (tubing or pump).

▲ Monitor activated partial thromboplastin time (aPTT) level. Notify physician immediately if higher or lower than designated range occurs.

▲ Monitor platelets and heparin-induced platelet aggregation (HIPA) status.

- Assess for signs and symptoms of bleeding: petechiae, purpura, hematoma; bleeding from catheter insertion sites; gastrointestinal or genitourinary bleeding; bleeding from respiratory tract; bleeding from mucous membranes; decreased hemoglobin and hematocrit.

Rationale

Because anticoagulation therapy is the hallmark treatment for thromboembolism, prior patient experiences with bleeding or anticoagulants must be assessed before treatment. Risk versus benefit of treatment must be assessed.

This minimizes risk of overcoagulation or undercoagulation.

The aPTT should be maintained at 1.5 to 2 times the normal level in an attempt to prevent further clot formation.

Heparin-induced thrombocytopenia (HIT) is increasingly being identified in the patient population. If the patient is HIPA positive, anticipate consultation with a hematologist.

Early assessment facilitates prompt treatment.

Therapeutic Interventions

Actions/Interventions

▲ Administer anticoagulant therapy as prescribed (continuous IV heparin infusion).

▲ If the patient is HIPA positive, stop all heparin products and consult a hematologist.

▲ If bleeding occurs, anticipate the following:
  • Stop the infusion.
  • Recheck aPTT level stat.
  • Administer protamine sulfate as ordered.
  • Take vital signs often.
  • Reevaluate dose of heparin on basis of aPTT result.
  • Notify blood bank.

▲ Convert from IV anticoagulation to oral anticoagulation after appropriate length of therapy.

  • Monitor international normalized ratio (INR), PT, and aPTT levels.
  • Instruct patients to report signs of bleeding immediately.

Rationale

Heparin is given to prevent further thrombus formation. Argatroban and warfarin (Coumadin) are also used.

Continuation of heparin products further complicates the situation.

Data guide further treatments.

This is a heparin antagonist.

Guide is 1.5 to 2 times normal.

This ensures blood availability if needed.

IV heparin should continue for 5 days of therapeutic anticoagulation before stopping. Administer oral anticoagulant, usually warfarin (Coumadin) for long-term therapy while heparin dose is still administered. Prothrombin time (PT) levels should be in an adequate range for anticoagulation before discontinuing heparin.

Goal INR is 2 to 3.

Early assessment facilitates prompt treatment.

Pulmonary Thromboembolism

■ = Independent; ▲ = Collaborative

Pulmonary Thromboembolism—cont'd

Actions/Interventions	Rationale
▲ Administer thrombolytic therapy as prescribed.	Lytic agents are indicated for patients with massive PE that results in hemodynamic compromise. Be aware of the following contraindications for thrombolytic therapy to minimize complications: recent surgery, recent organ biopsy, paracentesis or thoracentesis, pregnancy, recent stroke, or recent or active internal bleeding.
▲ Institute precautionary measures for thrombolytic therapy:	
• Use only compressible vessels for IV sites.	This facilitates clotting.
• Compress IV sites for at least 10 minutes and arterial sites for 30 minutes.	Pressure helps promote clotting.
• Discontinue anticoagulants and antiplatelet aggregates before thrombolytic therapy.	These medications increase the risk for bleeding.
• Limit physical manipulation of patients.	This reduces risk of trauma and bleeding.
• Provide gentle oral care.	This prevents disruption of formed blood clots.
• Avoid intramuscular injections.	This reduces risk of bleeding.
• Draw all laboratory specimens through an existing line: arterial line or venous heparin-lock line.	Any needle stick is a potential bleeding site.
• Send specimen for type and crossmatch as prescribed.	Blood replacement therapy may be needed to correct abnormalities.
■ Discuss with and provide the patient with a list of what to avoid when taking anticoagulants:	
• Do not use a blade razor (electric razors preferred).	This prevents trauma.
• Do not take new medications without consulting the physician, pharmacist, or nurses.	Many medications interact with Coumadin, altering the anticoagulation effect.
• Do not eat foods high in vitamin K (e.g., dark-green vegetables, cauliflower, cabbage, bananas, tomatoes).	This prevents alteration in anticoagulation control.
• Do not ingest aspirin or other salicylates.	These facilitate bleeding.
• Discuss drug, herb, alcohol, and food interactions with medication. Emphasize that significant diet changes and all over-the-counter medications and complementary therapies need to be discussed with the physician or nurse practitioner before initiation.	These safety measures reduce risk of bleeding.
■ Discuss with and give the patient a list of measures to minimize recurrence of emboli.	
• Take anticoagulants as prescribed.	This ensures appropriate treatment.
• Keep medical checkup and blood test appointments.	This ensures adequate anticoagulation. Each patient has an INR goal.
• Perform leg exercises as advised, especially during long automobile and airplane trips.	This prevents venous stasis.
• Do not cross legs.	Pressure alters circulation and may lead to clotting.
• Use elastic stockings as prescribed.	This prevents venous stasis.
• Maintain adequate hydration.	This prevents increased blood viscosity.

■ = Independent; ▲ = Collaborative

Nursing Diagnosis

Anxiety

Common Related Factors

Threat of death
Change in health status
Overall feeling of intense sickness
Multiple laboratory tests
Increased attention of medical personnel
Increasing respiratory difficulty

Defining Characteristics

Verbalization of anxiety
Restlessness, inability to relax
Multiple questions
Tremors, shakiness
Tense or anxious appearance
Crying
Withdrawal

Common Expected Outcome

Patient experiences reduced anxiety or fear as evidenced by calm and trusting appearance, and verbalized fears and concerns.

NOC Outcome
Anxiety Self-Control

NIC Intervention
Anxiety Reduction

Ongoing Assessment

Actions/Interventions

■ Assess level of anxiety.

Rationale

A patient with a PE experiencing increasing respiratory difficulty and shortness of breath may have a high level of anxiety.

Therapeutic Interventions

Actions/Interventions

■ Reduce the patient's or significant others' anxiety by explaining all procedures or treatment. Keep explanations basic.

■ Maintain a confident, assured manner.

■ Encourage the patient to ventilate feelings of anxiety.

■ Provide adequate rest as follows:
  • Organize activities (e.g., morning care, meals, hospital staff rounds, treatments).
  • Decrease sensory stimulations as follows:
    • Dim lights when appropriate.
    • Remove unnecessary equipment from room.

Rationale

Information helps allay anxiety. Patients who are anxious may not be able to comprehend anything more than simple, clear, brief instruction.

The staff's anxiety may be easily perceived by the patient. The patient's feeling of stability increases in a calm, nonthreatening atmosphere.

Understanding the patient's feelings of anxiety will guide the staff in planning and implementing a care plan to allay individualized anxiety.

Rest improves ability to cope.

Organization of tasks can reduce demands on patient's energy level.

A darkened room can facilitate rest.

This helps maintain more relaxed environment.

Pulmonary Thromboembolism

■ = Independent; ▲ = Collaborative

Pulmonary Thromboembolism—cont'd

Actions/Interventions	Rationale
• Limit visitors and phone calls (to prevent tiring).	Patients feel obligated to entertain, which may be physically and emotionally taxing.
▲ Administer pain medicines or sedatives as indicated.	This assists in allaying anxiety. Anxiety may increase oxygen consumption.
▲ Refer to other support systems (e.g., clergy, social workers, other family or friends), as appropriate.	Specialty expertise may be required.

 ## Nursing Diagnosis

Deficient Knowledge

Common Related Factor
New medical condition

Defining Characteristics
Expresses inaccurate perception of health status
Verbalizes deficiency in knowledge
Multiple questions or none

Common Expected Outcome
Patient understands importance of medications, signs of excessive anticoagulation, and means to reduce risk of bleeding and recurrence of emboli.

NOC Outcomes
Knowledge: Disease Process;
Knowledge: Medication

NIC Interventions
Teaching: Disease Process;
Teaching: Prescribed Medication

Ongoing Assessment

Actions/Interventions	Rationale
■ Assess present knowledge of pulmonary embolus: severity, prognosis, risk factors, therapy.	Most individuals have little experience with this problem.

Therapeutic Interventions

Actions/Interventions	Rationale
■ Provide information on the cause of the problem, effects of PE on body functioning, common risk factors (e.g., immobilization), trauma (e.g., hip fracture, major burns), certain heart conditions, and oral contraceptives.	An informed patient is more likely to avoid common risk factors.
■ Instruct the patient about medications, their actions, dosages, and side effects.	Patients may require anticoagulation for weeks, months, or more, depending on their risks. Accurate knowledge reduces future complications.

■ = Independent; ▲ = Collaborative

Actions/Interventions

- Discuss and give the patient a list of signs and symptoms of excessive anticoagulation: easy bruising, severe nose-bleed, black stools, blood in urine or stools, joint swelling and pain, coughing up of blood, severe headache.
- Inform the patient of the need for routine laboratory testing of PT while on oral anticoagulation.
- Discuss safety or precautionary measures to use while on anticoagulant therapy: need to inform dentist or other caregivers before treatment, use of electric razor, use of soft toothbrush.
- If the patient is HIPA-positive, instruct about the importance of avoiding heparin.

Rationale

Early assessment facilitates prompt treatment.

Continued regular assessment of anticoagulation is necessary.

These measures help prevent bleeding.

Heparin use can result in formation of antiheparin antibodies, which puts the patient at risk.

Radical Neck Surgery

Laryngectomy; Head and Neck Cancer

Radical neck surgery is a surgical procedure for cancer of the larynx. This procedure involves laryngectomy and removal of cervical lymph nodes and lymphatics. Dissection includes fascia, muscle, nerves, salivary glands, and veins in an attempt to eradicate metastatic cancer. This care plan focuses on postoperative care of the patient with radical neck surgery.

Radical Neck Surgery

Nursing Diagnosis

Ineffective Airway Clearance

Common Related Factors

Tracheostomy tube
Thick, copious secretions
Pain
Edema
Fatigue
Refusal to cough

Defining Characteristics

Diminished lung sounds
Coarse lung sounds
Cough
Dyspnea
Tachypnea

Common Expected Outcome

Patient maintains effective airway clearance as evidenced by normal lung sounds, eupnea, and an airway free of secretions with effective cough.

NOC Outcome
Respiratory Status: Airway Patency

NIC Interventions
Airway Management; Cough Enhancement; Airway Suctioning

■ = Independent; ▲ = Collaborative

Radical Neck Surgery—cont'd

Pulmonary Care Plans

Ongoing Assessment

Actions/Interventions

- Assess respiratory rate, rhythm, and effort.

- Assess effectiveness of cough.

- Assess color, consistency, and quantity of secretions.

- Auscultate lungs for normal and abnormal sounds.

- ▲ Assess pulse oximetry and/or arterial blood gases (ABGs).
- Assess color of skin, nail beds, and mucous membranes.
- Assess changes in mental status.

- Assess for pain.

Rationale

Respiratory rate and rhythm changes are early warning signs of impending respiratory difficulties.

Pain may interfere with coughing. Thick, tenacious secretions may be difficult to expectorate.

Abnormalities may be the result of infection, smoking history, or other abnormalities. A sign of infection is discolored sputum.

Changes in lung sounds may be early indicators of complications.

Increasing $PaCO_2$ and decreasing PaO_2 and pulse oximetry readings are signs of respiratory failure.

These are late signs of hypoxemia.

Increasing confusion, restlessness and/or irritability are early signs of cerebral hypoxia.

Postoperative pain can result in shallow breathing and an ineffective cough.

Therapeutic Interventions

Actions/Interventions

- Maintain humidified oxygen through the tracheostomy collar.

- Encourage the patient to deep breathe every 2 hours while awake.
- Encourage effective coughing after taking deep breaths.
- Suction tracheostomy with sterile technique if the patient is unable to clear own secretions.

- Position the patient with the head of bed elevated.

- Encourage and assist the patient to change position every 2 hours and increase activity as tolerated.
- If a disposable inner cannula is used, change the tracheostomy inner cannula every 8 hours; if a non-disposable inner cannula is used, cleanse the inner cannula every 8 hours.
- Maintain secure tracheostomy ties.
- Keep the same size sterile tracheostomy tube at the bedside.
- ▲ Consult respiratory therapy staff as needs arise.

Rationale

This thins secretions for easier expectoration with coughing. With radical neck surgery, a total laryngectomy is done, in which the entire larynx and preepiglottic region are removed and a permanent tracheostomy performed.

This prevents atelectasis and enhances gas exchange.

This approach facilitates more effective coughing.

A patent airway is a priority. Patients with impaired immune systems due to cancer and surgery are at risk for infection.

This decreases surgical edema and increases lung expansion.

This facilitates mobilization of secretions.

Retained secretions can obstruct the airway.

This prevents tracheostomy tube dislodgment.

This is for insertion if dislodgment should occur.

Specialty expertise may be required to guide therapy.

■ = Independent; ▲ = Collaborative

Nursing Diagnosis

Impaired Verbal Communication

Common Related Factor

Laryngectomy (results in permanent loss of voice)

Defining Characteristics

Inability to speak
Frustration
Withdrawal

Common Expected Outcome

Patient effectively communicates needs.

NOC Outcome
Communication: Expressive

NIC Intervention
Communication Enhancement: Speech Deficit

Ongoing Assessment

Actions/Interventions

■ Assess patient's communication ability.

■ Frequently assess the patient's need to communicate.
■ Assess effectiveness of nonverbal communication methods.
■ Assess for additional obstacles to communication (e.g., the patient is hard of hearing, is mentally retarded, or has arthritis of the hands).

Rationale

With laryngectomy, air does not pass over vocal cords, so sound is not produced. Assessment of the best nonverbal method for communication guides subsequent efforts.

This decreases anxiety and helps establish trust.

Each new method needs to be assessed for effectiveness and altered as necessary.

Accurate assessment of the full scope of limitations guides development of optimal treatment plan.

Therapeutic Interventions

Actions/Interventions

■ Keep the call light within reach at all times. Answer the call light promptly.
■ Anticipate the patient's needs.

■ Allow the patient time to communicate needs.

■ Provide emotional support to the patient and significant others.

Rationale

This decreases anxiety and feelings of helplessness.

This decreases frustrations and increases the patient's trust.

The nurse should set aside enough time to attend to all of the details of patient care. Care measures may take longer time to complete in the presence of a communication deficit.

Difficulties communicating are a source of frustration to all involved.

Radical Neck Surgery

■ = Independent; ▲ = Collaborative

Radical Neck Surgery—cont'd

Actions/Interventions

- Instruct the patient and significant others in alternative methods of communication: hand gestures, writing tablet with pen, picture board, word board, electronic communication system, electronic voice box.

▲ Consult the speech therapy staff regarding alternate forms of speech. The following may be used for the patient:
  - Voice prosthesis

  - Electrolarynx

  - Esophageal speech

- Encourage the patient to obtain an audiotape for home use that can be played in an emergency when emergency service is called.

Rationale

This provides the patient with more channels through which information can be communicated, and broadens the group of people with whom the patient can communicate.

The voice prosthesis is inserted into a fistula made between the esophagus and trachea. The prosthesis prevents aspiration, but allows air from the lungs to enter the esophagus and out of the mouth with speech being produced by movement of the tongue and lips.

The electrolarynx is a battery-operated, hand-held device that uses sound waves to create speech while being held against the neck. The pitch is low and is similar to the sound of a robot.

Esophageal speech is a method of swallowing air and "belching" it to create sound.

This promotes security in the home environment.

Nursing Diagnosis

Risk for Ineffective Tissue Perfusion

Common Risk Factors

Tissue edema
Malfunction of wound drainage tubes
Preoperative radiation to surgical area
Extensive surgical dissection of blood vessels
Infection of surgical area

Common Expected Outcome

Patient maintains adequate tissue perfusion, as evidenced by normal incisional healing, gradual decrease in edema, gradual decrease in wound drainage, and no signs and symptoms of infection.

NOC Outcomes
Tissue Perfusion: Peripheral;
    Wound Healing: Primary Intention

NIC Interventions
Wound Care: Closed Drainage;
    Wound Care

■ = Independent; ▲ = Collaborative

Ongoing Assessment

Actions/Interventions

■ Assess surgical wound drainage system for amount and color of drainage.

■ Assess edema at the surgical wound.

■ Assess color of wound and surrounding skin for signs of decreased circulation: pale, blue, or dark in color.

■ Assess wound edges.

■ Monitor body temperature.

Rationale

An abrupt cessation of drainage can indicate a clogged tube. Excessive drainage can indicate a leaking vessel in the area. Purulent drainage can indicate infection.

Excessive edema can impede blood flow to or from the area and result in necrosis or infection.

Changes in perfusion can compromise skin flap integrity.

Wound edges should be proximate (next to each other). Wound edges separate with excessive edema, necrosis, and infection.

Fever is a sign of infection.

Therapeutic Interventions

Actions/Interventions

▲ Gently milk drainage tubes as needed. Maintain suction as prescribed (e.g., Jackson-Pratt drain).

■ Keep head of bed elevated.

■ Perform tracheostomy tube and site cleaning as needed.

■ Promptly change tracheostomy or wound dressings when wet.

Rationale

These procedures maintain patency and prevent buildup of fluid at the surgical site, which would cause excessive edema and possible infection or necrosis.

This decreases local edema.

This keeps respiratory secretions away from the surgical wound.

This prevents maceration of skin.

Radical Neck Surgery

NDx Nursing Diagnosis

Imbalanced Nutrition: Less Than Body Requirements

Common Related Factors

Nothing by mouth (NPO) status
Decreased appetite
Dysphagia
Radiation therapy
Chemotherapy
Edema

Defining Characteristics

Weight loss
Decreased caloric intake

Common Expected Outcome

Patient has adequate caloric intake as evidenced by body weight greater than or equal to admission weight.

NOC Outcomes

Nutritional Status: Biochemical Measures; Nutritional Status: Food and Fluid Intake

NIC Intervention

Nutrition Management

■ = Independent; ▲ = Collaborative

Radical Neck Surgery—cont'd

Ongoing Assessment

Actions/Interventions

- Obtain admission weight. Monitor weight; monitor intake and output.
- ▲ Monitor laboratory test results: serum albumin, protein, electrolytes, glucose.
- Observe the patient during initial oral feeding.

- Assess types of foods that the patient enjoys.

Rationale

This establishes baseline and trends.

These provide data on extent of nutritional deficiency.

Signs of aspiration of food or fluid from tracheostomy, such as choking, may occur when oral feeding is started.

Selection of favorite foods may enhance interest in eating and improve caloric intake.

Therapeutic Interventions

Actions/Interventions

- Instruct the patient on importance of adequate caloric intake.
- ▲ Consult with a dietitian.

- Instruct on need for enteral feedings if prescribed. Instruct on procedure for administration of home enteral feedings if prescribed.
- Assist the patient in performing oral hygiene.

- ▲ Consult speech therapy staff for swallowing evaluation as needed.

- Encourage oral intake of soft foods when allowed, with the tracheostomy cuff inflated.

- Maintain suction setup at bedside for safety. Stay with the patient during initial oral feedings.

Rationale

This promotes incisional healing as well as enhances overall nutritional status.

The dietitian will determine caloric requirements specific to the patient, assess caloric intake, and suggest enteral feedings, as appropriate.

Enteral feedings are initially used postoperatively until suture lines have healed. The feeding tube is put in place during surgery.

Oral hygiene keeps the mouth fresh and promotes interest in eating.

If a total laryngectomy is performed, swallowing should not be a problem because there is no connection between the esophagus and trachea. If a supraglottic laryngectomy is done, swallowing is more difficult because the epiglottis has been removed.

Cuff inflation decreases chances of aspiration. Oral feedings can resume after suture lines are healed (approximately 1 week).

Suction may be needed during or after feedings to keep the airway patent.

■ = Independent; ▲ = Collaborative

Nursing Diagnosis

Disturbed Body Image

Common Related Factors

Visible incision
Facial and neck edema
Tracheostomy
Alteration in verbal communication
Dysphagia
Lifestyle changes
Diagnosis of cancer

Defining Characteristics

Verbalization of negative feelings about body
Preoccupation with change
Refusal to look at face and neck
Withdrawal
Decreased motivation for self-care
Refusal to see visitors

Common Expected Outcome

Patient begins to adjust to body changes as evidenced by planning for discharge, showing interest in learning, and using alternative communication methods.

NOC Outcome
Body Image

NIC Interventions
Body Image Enhancement;
    Support System Enhancement

Ongoing Assessment

Actions/Interventions

■ Assess the patient's mood and behavior for signs of difficulty in coping with changes in body appearance or function.

■ Assess the patient's perception of life changes precipitated by radical neck surgery (i.e., occupational, interpersonal).

Rationale

There is a broad range of behaviors associated with body image disturbance, ranging from totally ignoring the altered structure to preoccupation with it.

This may give some perspective on any perceived misconceptions that could affect recovery.

Therapeutic Interventions

Actions/Interventions

■ Encourage the patient to view the tracheostomy or stoma site.

■ Suggest the use of a loose scarf or shirt over the stoma to camouflage it.

■ Encourage the patient and significant others to communicate fears or concerns regarding diagnosis of cancer treatment.

■ Encourage visits, both in the hospital and at home, from significant others.

Rationale

Looking at the site is often the first indication that the patient is ready to deal with the change in appearance.

This may promote enhanced self-esteem.

Misconceptions may need to be clarified.

Visitors help the patient feel accepted and promote communication and support.

Radical Neck Surgery

■ = Independent; ▲ = Collaborative

Radical Neck Surgery—cont'd

Actions/Interventions	Rationale
■ Refer to support services (e.g., Lost Cords, American Cancer Society, and International Association of Laryngectomies).	Rehabilitation after radical neck surgery is a long process, and support services can have a positive impact on the patient's recovery.
■ Arrange for a visit from a person who has had a laryngectomy.	Lay persons in similar situations offer a different type of support that is perceived as helpful.

NDx Nursing Diagnosis

Deficient Knowledge

Common Related Factors
Postoperative radical neck surgery
New stoma or tracheostomy
Cancer treatment

Defining Characteristics
Anxiety about discharge
Increased questioning
Expressed need for more information

Common Expected Outcomes
Patient and caregiver demonstrate tracheostomy care and suctioning technique.
Patient and caregiver verbalize signs and symptoms of infection and when to report to the health care provider.
Patient and caregiver verbalize understanding of individualized course of postoperative treatment (e.g., radiation therapy).

NOC Outcomes
Knowledge: Disease Process;
Knowledge: Treatment Regimen

NIC Interventions
Teaching: Disease Process;
Teaching: Psychomotor Skill

Ongoing Assessment

Actions/Interventions	Rationale
■ Assess knowledge of postoperative care and follow-up cancer treatment.	This provides an important starting point in education.
■ Assess support systems at home.	Living with a serious disease is challenging and carries an emotional burden. Assessment helps determine home care needs.

Therapeutic Interventions

Actions/Interventions	Rationale
■ Explain postoperative procedures and treatments (e.g., regarding drainage tubes, dressings, feeding tube) to the patient or caregiver.	Adults learn information that is important to them.

■ = Independent; ▲ = Collaborative

Pulmonary Care Plans

Actions/Interventions

- Teach the patient and caregiver as appropriate:
  - Signs and symptoms of infection and when to notify the health care provider.
  - Indications for suctioning

  - Procedure for tracheal suction. Use a mirror for teaching; include return demonstration.
  - Procedure for cleaning inner cannula

  - Procedure for changing and securing tracheal ties

- Once healing has occurred, instruct the patient to use a laryngectomy tube (cleaned in the same manner as the tracheostomy tube) or only the stoma site. The area around the stoma should be washed at least daily.
- Instruct the patient to cover the stoma when coughing to expectorate. The stoma should also be covered to prevent inhalation of foreign materials (e.g., when shaving or applying makeup). Swimming is contraindicated to prevent aspiration of water through the stoma.
- Arrange for a home health nurse care or visit as needed.
- Discuss plans for radiation therapy, including what to expect, probable time schedule for the series, and possible side effects.
- Teach importance of adequate calorie intake.
- Teach exercises after radical neck surgery for strengthening shoulder and neck muscles.
- Discuss medications.

- Discuss the use of a medical alert bracelet or other identification to alert others to the disease process or stoma.

Rationale

Early assessment facilitates prompt treatment.

A patent airway is a priority. Retained secretions can lead to a mucous plug.

Patients may need visual reinforcement to be successful with this procedure.

This decreases the incidence of a clogged tracheostomy tube.

This decreases the incidence of tracheostomy dislodgement.

Washing keeps stoma clean and reduces the risk for infection.

Covering the stoma helps reduce transmission of pathogens. Covering the stoma at other times helps prevent inhalation of foreign materials and reduces aspiration risk.

Continuity of care is facilitated through support services.

Postoperative radiation therapy may be used to control the patient's metastasis.

This facilitates optimal nutritional balance.

Restricted movement affects ability to perform many activities of daily living.

The patient may require follow-up treatment for cancer-related problems.

Patient safety is a priority.

• RELATED CARE PLANS

Anticipatory grieving, p. 82
Anxiety, p. 15
Ineffective coping, p. 51
Risk for aspiration, p. 18
Risk for impaired skin integrity, p. 173

Radical Neck Surgery

■ = Independent; ▲ = Collaborative

Respiratory Failure, Acute

Ventilatory Failure; Oxygenation Failure

Acute respiratory failure is a life-threatening inability to maintain adequate pulmonary gas exchange. Persons with acute respiratory failure cannot carry out its two major functions: delivery of adequate amounts of oxygen into the arterial blood (oxygenation failure) or removal of a corresponding amount of CO_2 from the mixed venous blood (ventilatory function). Respiratory failure can result from obstructive disease (e.g., emphysema, chronic bronchitis, asthma), restrictive disease (e.g., atelectasis, acute respiratory distress syndrome [ARDS], pneumonia, multiple rib fractures, postoperative abdominal or thoracic surgery, central nervous system [CNS] depression), or ventilation-perfusion abnormalities (e.g., pulmonary embolism). This care plan focuses on acute care management of respiratory failure.

NDx Nursing Diagnosis

Impaired Spontaneous Ventilation

Common Related Factors

Metabolic factors
Respiratory muscle fatigue
CNS depression
Drug overdose

Defining Characteristics

Shortness of breath
Increased $PaCO_2$ level
Decreased PaO_2 level
Decreased oxygen saturation level
Increased restlessness and irritability
Tachycardia
Dyspnea
Tachypnea
Cyanosis
Respiratory depth changes
Decrease in level of consciousness (may occur as respiratory insufficiency increases in severity)

Common Expected Outcome

Patient's ventilatory demand is decreased as evidenced by eupnea, no use of accessory muscles, and arterial blood gases (ABGs) normal for patient.

NOC Outcomes

Respiratory Status: Gas Exchange;
Respiratory Status: Ventilation;
Vital Signs

NIC Interventions

Respiratory Monitoring; Ventilation
Assistance; Mechanical Ventilation;
Oxygen Therapy

■ = Independent; ▲ = Collaborative

Ongoing Assessment

Actions/Interventions

■ Observe for changes in patient's respiratory status, including rate, depth, and respiratory effort.

■ Observe for excessive use of accessory muscles.

■ Observe for signs of hypoxia (e.g., dyspnea, tachycardia, tachypnea, restlessness, and cyanosis).

■ Assess for changes in orientation, increased restlessness, anxiety, lethargy, and somnolence.

■ Assess for presence of cough and, if effective, amount expectorated, frequency, and color.

■ Auscultate lungs and assess for adventitious sounds: wheezing, rales (crackles), or rhonchi.

■ Monitor vital signs with frequent monitoring of blood pressure (BP).

■ Monitor for dysrhythmias.

■ Observe for signs of increased $PaCO_2$ (e.g., asterixis or tremors, change in mental status).

▲ Monitor ABGs carefully and notify physician of abnormalities.

Rationale

Respiratory rate and rhythm changes are early warning signs of impending respiratory difficulties.

This is indicative of increased respiratory effort.

Cyanosis is a late sign of hypoxemia because 5 g of hemoglobin must desaturate for cyanosis to occur.

Early signs of cerebral hypoxia are restlessness and anxiety, leading to agitation and confusion. Lethargy and somnolence are late signs of hypoxia.

These may be indicative of an etiology for the alteration in breathing pattern.

Changes in lung sounds may reveal specific problems that guide treatment.

Hypoxia or hypercarbia may cause initial hypertension with restlessness and progress to hypotension and somnolence.

Cardiac dysrhythmias may result from acidosis or hypoxia.

Elevations in $PaCO_2$ result in vasodilation of cerebral blood vessels, increased cerebral blood flow, and increased intracranial pressure.

Increasing $PaCO_2$ and/or decreasing PaO_2 is a sign of respiratory failure. However, ABG values may be acceptable initially and the patient's work of breathing may be too extreme. As the patient's condition begins to fail, respiratory rate will decrease and $PaCO_2$ will begin to rise.

Therapeutic Interventions

Actions/Interventions

■ Position patient with proper body alignment.

■ Maintain adequate airway; position patient.

■ Pace activities. Maintain planned rest periods.

▲ Administer oxygen as needed. For patients with severe chronic obstructive pulmonary disease (COPD), give oxygen cautiously, preferably with a Venturi device.

▲ Discuss with the patient and significant others reversibility of condition, advance directives, and medical power of attorney.

Rationale

This is for optimal chest excursion and breathing pattern.

Airway patency is a priority.

Even simple activities such as bathing can cause fatigue and increase oxygen demands, resulting in dyspnea.

The Venturi device is a high-flow oxygen delivery system with a stable FIO_2 that is unaffected by the patient's respiratory rate or tidal volume. COPD patients who chronically retain carbon dioxide depend on "hypoxic drive" as their stimulus to breathe. When applying oxygen, close monitoring is imperative to prevent unsafe increases in the patient's PaO_2, which could result in apnea.

Patients must make very clear what they want regarding life-sustaining treatments.

Respiratory Failure, Acute

■ = Independent; ▲ = Collaborative

Respiratory Failure, Acute—cont'd

Pulmonary Care Plans

Actions/Interventions

- ◼ Assist with ventilatory support measures as appropriate:
  - • Bilevel positive airway pressure (BiPAP)
  - • When necessary, prepare for intubation and mechanical ventilation:
    - • Position the patient appropriately and have necessary equipment readily available.
    - • Instruct the patient who is awake and alert.

    - • Stay with the patient.

    - • Institute suctioning through an endotracheal (ET) tube as necessary.
    - • After intubation, auscultate lungs for bilateral sounds.
    - • Obtain chest x-ray study after intubation.

Rationale

This is a noninvasive form of positive pressure ventilation.

Early intubation and mechanical ventilation are recommended to prevent full decompensation of the patient.

Proper positioning facilitates alignment for successful intubation.

Explanation is essential to prepare the patient and reduce anxiety.

This allays anxiety and ensures easy observation of the patient.

Airway patency is a priority.

This ensures that the ET tube is not in the right main stem bronchus or the esophagus.

This confirms ET tube placement.

NDx Nursing Diagnosis

Risk for Ineffective Airway Clearance

Common Risk Factors

Inability to cough
Fatigue
Thick secretions
Presence of ET tube

Common Expected Outcomes

Patient's airway is free of secretions.
Patient has clear lung sounds after suctioning.

NOC Outcome
Respiratory Status: Airway Patency

NIC Intervention
Airway Suctioning

Ongoing Assessment

Actions/Interventions

- ◼ Assess for significant alterations in lung sounds (e.g., rhonchi, wheezes).

- ◼ Assess for changes in ventilation rate or depth.

Rationale

Airway obstruction from fluid accumulation produces crackles and rhonchi. Wheezes are caused by bronchospasm.

Respiratory rate and rhythm changes are early warning signs of respiratory problems.

◼ = Independent; ▲ = Collaborative

Actions/Interventions

- Assess secretions: color, consistency amounts.
- Assess the patient's ability to cough, deep breathe, and use incentive spirometer.

Rationale

Changes in sputum color can indicate infection.

This provides basis for nursing interventions and patient education.

Therapeutic Interventions

Actions/Interventions

- Instruct the patient to change position or change the patient's position every 2 hours.
- ▲ Provide humidity (when appropriate) through bedside humidifier or humidified oxygen therapy.
- Instruct the patient to deep breathe adequately, to cough effectively, and to use incentive spirometry, as ordered.
- Use nasotracheal suction for patients who cannot clear secretions before intubation.

After intubation:

- Institute suctioning of airway as needed (not routinely).

Rationale

This mobilizes secretions.

This prevents drying of secretions.

These improve lung capacity and gas exchange.

Patients with a weak cough will need to be suctioned to adequately clear the airway of secretions.

Suctioning should be performed based on presence of adventitious sounds and/or increased ventilatory pressure, not time intervals.

Respiratory Failure, Acute

 Nursing Diagnosis

Risk for Infection

Common Risk Factors

Suctioning of airway
Endotracheal intubation

Common Expected Outcome

Patient's risk of infection is reduced through early assessment and intervention.

NOC Outcomes
Immune Status; Risk Detection; Risk Control

NIC Intervention
Infection Protection

Ongoing Assessment

Actions/Interventions

- Monitor and document temperature and notify physician of temperature higher than 38.5° C (101.3° F).
- ▲ Monitor white blood cell (WBC) count.

Rationale

If the patient is receiving steroid therapy, detecting infections may be more difficult.

Rising WBC count indicates body's efforts to combat pathogens.

■ = Independent; ▲ = Collaborative

Respiratory Failure, Acute—cont'd

Actions/Interventions

- Observe the patient's secretions for color, consistency, quantity, and odor.
- Monitor sputum cultures and sensitivities.

Rationale

Increased amounts of sputum and changes in color may indicate infection.

Identification of the infecting microorganism is important to determine antibiotic coverage.

Therapeutic Interventions

Actions/Interventions

- Practice conscientious bronchial hygiene, good hand washing techniques, and sterile suctioning.
- Administer mouth care (e.g., mouthwash, mouth swabs, mouth spray) every 2 hours and as needed; brush the patient's teeth at least every 12 hours.
- Institute airway suctioning as needed.
- Maintain the patient's personal hygiene, nutrition, and rest.
- Keep head of bed elevated greater than 30 degrees.

Rationale

Many infections are transmitted by hospital personnel.

This helps limit oral bacterial growth and promotes patient comfort.

Accumulation of secretions can lead to invasive process.

This increases natural defenses.

Upright positioning helps prevent ventilator-acquired pneumonia.

NDx Nursing Diagnosis

Anxiety

Common Related Factors

Threat of death
Change in health status
Change in environment
Change in interaction patterns
Inability to speak if intubated
Unmet needs

Defining Characteristics

Restlessness
Diaphoresis
Pointing to throat (possibly unable to speak)
Uncooperative behavior
Withdrawal
Vigilant watch on equipment

Common Expected Outcome

Patient experiences absence or decrease in anxiety, as evidenced by cooperative behavior and calm appearance.

NOC Outcome
Anxiety Self-Control

NIC Intervention
Anxiety Reduction

■ = Independent; ▲ = Collaborative

Ongoing Assessment

Actions/Interventions

■ Assess patient for signs indicating increased anxiety.

Rationale

Respiratory failure is an acute life-threatening condition that will produce high levels of anxiety in the patient as well as significant others.

Therapeutic Interventions

Actions/Interventions

■ If patient is unable to speak because of respiratory status:
  • Provide pencil and pad.

  • Establish some form of nonverbal communication if patient is too sick to write.
■ Anticipate questions. Provide explanations of mechanical ventilation and alarm systems on monitors and ventilators.
■ Display a confident, calm manner and tolerant, understanding attitude.
■ Allow family or significant others to visit; involve them in care.
■ Ensure the patient and significant others of close, continuous monitoring that will ensure prompt interventions. Reassure patient of the staff's presence.
▲ Use other supportive measures (e.g., medications, psychiatric liaison, clergy, social services) as indicated.

Rationale

These provide a channel through which information can be communicated.

Maintaining an avenue of communication is important to alleviate anxiety.

An informed patient who understands the treatment plan will be more cooperative and relaxed.

The staff's anxiety may be easily perceived by the patient.

The presence of significant others may reinforce feelings of security for the patient.

The presence of a trusted health care professional may be helpful during times of anxiety.

Medication and supportive resources may be used if the patient's anxiety continues to escalate.

NDx Nursing Diagnosis

Deficient Knowledge

Common Related Factor

Unfamiliarity with disease process and treatment

Defining Characteristics

Multiple questions
Lack of concern
Anxiety
Noncompliant with medication or health care orders (e.g., smoking)

Common Expected Outcome

Patient verbalizes understanding of disease process, procedures, and treatment.

NOC Outcomes
Knowledge: Disease Process;
  Knowledge: Treatment Regimen

NIC Intervention
Teaching: Disease Process

Respiratory Failure, Acute

■ = Independent; ▲ = Collaborative

Respiratory Failure, Acute—cont'd

Ongoing Assessment

Actions/Interventions

- Evaluate the patient's perception and understanding of the disease process that led to respiratory failure.

- Assess the patient's knowledge of oxygen therapy and deep breathing and coughing techniques.
- Assess the patient's readiness to learn.

Rationale

Hypoxia and the fatigue associated with hypoxia decrease learning ability. Teaching interventions must be designed individually to meet specific patient needs.

This provides an important starting point in education.

The patient may need to focus efforts on effective breathing rather than on the educational session.

Therapeutic Interventions

Actions/Interventions

- Encourage the patient to verbalize feelings and questions.
- Explain the disease process to the patient or significant others and correct misconceptions.

- Include family and significant others in the plan of care.

- Discuss the need for monitoring equipment and frequent assessments.
- Explain all tests and procedures before they occur.
- Explain necessity of oxygen therapy, including its limitations.
- Instruct the patient to deep breathe and cough effectively.
- Instruct the patient in preventive measures as appropriate (e.g., avoidance of exposure to smoke and fumes, cold air, and allergens such as pollens, dust, and dander).
- Provide guidelines for activities and advancement of activities, the need for home oxygen, and timing for follow-up visits with health care providers.

Rationale

Providing information to the patient will increase his or her participation in the treatment plan.

During the acute phase, family or significant others may require the most teaching. This will reduce their feelings of helplessness and assist them in supporting the patient.

Acute respiratory failure is a serious condition; significant others must be informed of the care plan and any changes as they occur.

The patient must be aware that this is an acute episode of respiratory failure.

An informed patient is more cooperative.

Oxygen is used to support arterial saturation.

These techniques facilitate clearance of secretions.

This prevents further respiratory difficulties.

Information aids in the transition from hospital to home.

> • **RELATED CARE PLANS**
>
> Acute respiratory distress syndrome, p. 408
> Asthma, p. 420
> Chest trauma, p. 430
> Chronic obstructive pulmonary disease,
> p. 440
> Mechanical ventilation, p. 459
> Pneumonia, p. 477
> Pulmonary thromboembolism, p. 490

■ = Independent; ▲ = Collaborative

Pulmonary Care Plans

Severe Acute Respiratory Syndrome—SARS

In 2003, severe acute respiratory syndrome (SARS) was identified in humans who had traveled in China, Hong Kong, and Singapore. SARS is a viral respiratory illness that may be confused with influenza. The illness usually begins with an elevated temperature (38° C, or 100.4° F), chills, and possibly other symptoms such as headache, general muscular aches and pains, and in 10% to 20% of cases, diarrhea. Some patients also experience mild respiratory symptoms at the onset. After 2 to 7 days, SARS patients may develop a dry, nonproductive cough that may be accompanied by or progress to hypoxia. Most patients develop pneumonia. Ten percent to 20% of cases will require mechanical ventilation.

SARS is caused by a previously unrecognized coronavirus, called SARS-associated coronavirus (SARS-CoV). Coronaviruses are a common cause of mild upper respiratory illness in humans. The inoculation period for SARS is typically 2 to 7 days, although in some cases it may be as long as 10 days.

SARS appears to spread by close person-to-person contact by respiratory droplets, or when a person touches an object contaminated with infectious droplets and then touches his or her mouth, nose, or eyes. Persons with SARS are more likely to be infectious only when they have symptoms such as fever or cough. According to the Centers for Disease Control and Prevention, they are most infectious the second week of illness. Patients should continue to stay home 10 days after their symptoms are no longer present.

SARS requires strict infection control precautions. A SARS outbreak was brought under control with classic public health techniques of epidemiological investigations, patient isolation, quarantine of exposed persons, and stringent restrictions on travel.

NDx Nursing Diagnosis

Infection

Common Related Factor	Defining Characteristics
Infection with SARS-CoV	Halo or crownlike (corona) appearance of virus when viewed under an electron microscope Exposure to person with SARS Temperature greater than 100.4° F or 38° C for 2 to 3 days Chills, headache, general feeling of discomfort, body aches Mild respiratory symptoms Diarrhea (10% to 20% of cases) Two to 7 days of nonproductive cough Positive diagnostic tests

Severe Acute Respiratory Syndrome—SARS

■ = Independent; ▲ = Collaborative

Severe Acute Respiratory Syndrome–SARS–cont'd

Common Expected Outcomes

Patient exhibits absence of fever and absence of respiratory symptoms.
Risk of spread of infection is reduced.

NOC Outcomes
Community Risk Control:
 Communicable Disease;
 Infection Severity: Risk Control

NIC Interventions
Infection Control; Infection Protection

Ongoing Assessment

Actions/Interventions	Rationale
■ Monitor temperature.	SARS usually begins with a high temperature (>100.4° F) and chills.
■ Monitor for muscular aches and pains.	SARS is commonly associated with headache, generalized aches and pains.
■ Assess for cough.	A dry, nonproductive cough is common.
■ Assess for any signs of respiratory distress.	SARS is a viral respiratory illness that can progress to acute respiratory distress.
■ Monitor lung sounds.	Bronchial lung sounds are evident in areas of lung consolidation. Areas of decreased breath sounds may be noted.
■ Monitor oxygen saturation.	Respiratory compromise results in hypoxia, or oxygen saturation levels less than 90%.
■ Evaluate for predisposing risk factors: • History of recent travel to mainland China, Hong Kong, or Taiwan • Close contact with an ill person with history of recent travel to such areas	The diagnosis of SARS is based on clinical presentation of patients with unexplained pneumonia and with an epidemiological history that raises the suspicion of exposure, such as travel to a SARS-affected area or contact with an ill person.
▲ Collect and monitor diagnostic results. • Radiographic testing (chest computed tomography [CT] scan and chest x-ray).	No specific clinical and laboratory findings can distinguish SARS from other respiratory illnesses rapidly enough to direct treatment. Thus this diagnosis is considered in patients requiring hospitalization for radiographically confirmed pneumonia and who have a suspicious epidemiological history. Chest CT scan provides more rapid interpretation.
• Reverse-transcription polymerase chain reaction test using secretions from nose, blood, and stool	This provides DNA evidence of suspected pathogens and may help rule out alternative diagnoses.

■ = Independent; ▲ = Collaborative

Actions/Interventions

- Serological testing

- Blood and viral cultures

Rationale

This includes testing for presence of antibodies to SARS-CoV. They are more likely detected by the end of the second week of illness.

Small samples of fluid or tissue are placed on a culture medium and checked for presence of SARS virus.

Therapeutic Interventions

Actions/Interventions

- Maintain respiratory isolation.
  - Keep tissues at the patient's bedside.
  - Dispose of secretions properly.
  - Have the patient cover mouth when coughing or sneezing.
  - Use masks (particulate N 95 respirator-type mask is preferred).
  - Have anyone entering the patient's room wear a mask.
  - Keep door closed at all times and place respiratory isolation sign where visible.
  - If the patient is transported out of the room, have him or her wear a mask.
  - Place respiratory stickers on chart, linens, and so on.
  - Assist visitors to follow appropriate isolation techniques.
- Teach the patient to wash hands after coughing.

- Administer antiviral and antiretroviral medications as ordered: lopinavir, ritonavir, and ribavirin.

- Use appropriate therapy for elevated temperature.

- Encourage the patient to cough unless the cough is nonproductive.
- Use humidity as needed.
- Assist in using incentive spirometer.

- For patients with reduced energy, pace activities.

- Consult a respiratory therapist for chest physiotherapy and nebulizer treatments, as ordered.

Rationale

SARS spreads by close contact as do other respiratory illnesses such as colds and influenza. It is spread most rapidly through droplet transmission in which the infected particles are large and can travel only about 3 feet. But the virus can also spread by touching a surface contaminated by the droplets, and then touching one's mouth, nose, or eyes. It is possible that SARS is also transmitted through the broader airborne route.

Friction and running water effectively remove microorganisms.

There is no known treatment directed at the SARS virus. The Centers for Disease Control and Prevention (CDC) recommends similar treatments as for other serious community-acquired atypical pneumonia. Newer antiviral medications have been effective in treating human immunodeficiency virus (HIV) infections and respiratory syncytial virus (RSV).

This maintains normothermia and reduces metabolic needs.

Frequent nonproductive coughing results in hypoxemia.

This may help loosen secretions.

Incentive spirometry serves to improve deep breathing and prevent atelectasis.

Coughing is hard work and may exhaust an already compromised patient.

Chest physiotherapy includes techniques of postural drainage and chest percussion to loosen secretions in smaller airways that cannot be removed by coughing.

Severe Acute Respiratory Syndrome—SARS

Severe Acute Respiratory Syndrome–SARS–cont'd

Actions/Interventions	Rationale
▪ Provide a high-protein, high-calorie, increased fluid diet in small frequent servings.	This maintains optimal nutritional status while reducing risk for nausea and vomiting.
▪ Anticipate possible need for intubation.	Intubation may be required to facilitate deep suctioning efforts and to provide a source for augmenting oxygenation and ventilation. NOTE: The highest transmission rate of SARS to health care workers is during the suctioning before intubation and while assisting with intubation.
▪ Report all confirmed cases to the appropriate health department.	SARS is a reportable illness and is under CDC surveillance.

NDx Nursing Diagnosis

Deficient Knowledge

Common Related Factors

Unfamiliarity with disease transmission information.
Lack of knowledge about SARS.

Defining Characteristics

Many questions
Lack of questions
Unaware of proper prevention methods

Common Expected Outcome

Patient and family verbalize the disease process, transmission, treatment, and complications of SARS.

NOC Outcomes
Knowledge: Disease Process;
Knowledge: Infection Control

NIC Intervention
Teaching: Disease Process

Ongoing Assessment

Actions/Interventions	Rationale
▪ Assess baseline knowledge of disease process, transmission, complications, and treatment.	This provides an important starting point in education. Many misconceptions are common.

▪ = Independent; ▲ = Collaborative

Therapeutic Interventions

Actions/Interventions

- Provide information on disease transmission.
  - SARS is spread predominantly by droplet transmission or when a person touches an object contaminated with infectious droplets and then touches his or her own mouth, nose, or eyes.
  - Persons are infectious mostly when they have symptoms such as fever or cough—most commonly during the second week of illness.
  - According to the CDC, all current laboratory-confirmed SARS cases were acquired after travel to areas where SARS-CoV transmission was occurring (e.g., China, Hong Kong, and Singapore).
- Provide information on diagnostic testing.
  - Reverse-transcription polymerase chain reaction (RT-PCR) test
  - Blood and viral cultures
- Provide information on disease process/complications.
  - The illness usually begins with elevated temperature, chills, and other flulike symptoms.
  - Mild respiratory symptoms (dry, nonproductive cough) predominate and progress to hypoxia and often pneumonia, with some requiring mechanical ventilation.
- Provide information on treatment.
  - Strict respiratory isolation is paramount.
  - Antiviral and antiretroviral mediations are ordered.
  - Supportive care is offered.
  - Intubation and mechanical ventilation may be required.
- Provide information on general protection from SARS.
  - Apply general principles such as frequent hand washing with soap or water or the use of an alcohol-based hand rub.
  - Inform yourself about the latest SARS status of countries being visited.
  - Know ahead of time where you can seek medical care if needed while in a foreign country.

Rationale

The CDC and WHO websites provide updated guidelines on SARS. The incubation period for SARS is typically 2 to 7 days but may be as long as 10 days.

In China, civet cats have been found to carry viruses similar to SARS. If visiting China, avoid visiting the live food markets and avoid wildlife, especially the civet cats sold in these markets.

This includes testing for the presence of antibodies to SARS-associated coronavirus. They are more likely detected by the end of the second week of illness.

Information enables individuals to take control of the situation. The sooner symptoms are recognized, the sooner treatment can begin. According to the CDC, only eight persons in the United States have been confirmed as SARS cases, with no associated deaths.

There is no known treatment directed at the SARS virus. The CDC recommends similar treatments as for other serious community-acquired atypical pneumonia. Newer antiviral medications have been effective in treating HIV infections and respiratory syncytial virus (RSV).

These are effective against the spread of infection.

It is best to get needed shots 4 to 6 weeks before travel. It is worthwhile to purchase coverage for medical evacuation from a country that is having an outbreak of SARS or other infectious disease.

• RELATED CARE PLANS

Acute respiratory distress syndrome, p. 408
Mechanical ventilation. p. 459
Pneumonia, p. 477

Severe Acute Respiratory Syndrome–SARS

■ = Independent; ▲ = Collaborative

 **Thoracotomy**

Chest Surgery; Thoracic Surgery; Lobectomy; Pneumonectomy; Segmental Resection; Wedge Resection

Thoracotomy is a surgical opening into the thorax for biopsy, excision, drainage, and/or correction of defects. The surgical correction may include the following:

- *Lobectomy:* removal of one lobe of the lung; lobectomy is indicated for lung cancer, bronchiectasis, tuberculosis (TB), emphysematous bullae, benign lung tumors, or fungal infections.
- *Segmental resection:* removal of one or more lung segments; segmental resection is indicated for bronchiectasis or TB.
- *Wedge resection:* removal of a small localized lesion that occupies only part of a segment; wedge resection is indicated for excision of nodules or lung biopsy.
- *Endoscopic thoracotomy* (thoracostomy): small incisions, useful for open lung biopsy to determine diagnosis, or for node biopsy.
- *Pneumonectomy:* removal of entire lung; indicated for lung cancer, extensive TB, bronchiectasis, or lung abscess.

This care plan focuses on postoperative care of the thoracotomy patient.

Pulmonary Care Plans

 NDx Nursing Diagnosis

Ineffective Breathing Pattern

Common Related Factors

Positive pressure in pleural space secondary to surgical incision
Collapse of lung on affected side (partial or complete)
Void in thoracic cavity if pneumonectomy performed
Pain
Decreased energy

Defining Characteristics

Dyspnea
Shortness of breath
Tachypnea
Altered chest excursion
Shallow respirations
Asymmetrical chest excursion
Use of accessory muscles for breathing

Common Expected Outcome

Patient's breathing pattern is maintained, as evidenced by normal skin color and regular respiratory rate and pattern.

NOC Outcome
Respiratory Status: Ventilation

NIC Interventions
Tube Care: Chest; Airway Management

Ongoing Assessment

Actions/Interventions

■ Assess respiratory rate and depth by listening to lung sounds.

Rationale

Respiratory rate and rhythm changes such as increase in respiratory rate with decreased tidal volume (rapid shallow respirations) are early warning signs of impending respiratory difficulties.

■ = Independent; ▲ = Collaborative

Actions/Interventions

- ■ Assess pain.
- ▲ Assess skin color and oxygen saturation via pulse oximeter or arterial blood gases (ABGs), if necessary.
- ▲ Perform complete assessment of closed chest drainage system; repeat often:
  - Check the water seal for the following:
    - Correct fluid level
    - Presence or absence of fluctuation
    - Presence of air leaks; document and report to physician

  - Check suction control chamber for correct fluid level as specified.

  - Measure output in the closed chest drainage system. Report drainage of bright red blood of 100 mL/hr for 2 hours consecutively.
- ▲ Monitor postoperative chest x-ray report.

- ■ Assess response to increasing levels of activity.

Therapeutic Interventions

Actions/Interventions

- ■ Position patient appropriately.

- ▲ Ensure that oxygen delivery system is applied to the patient.

- ■ Encourage sustained deep breaths by conducting the following:
  - Demonstration (emphasizing slow inhalation, holding end inspiration for a few seconds, and passive exhalation)
  - Use of incentive spirometer (place close to patient for convenient use)

Rationale

Pain can contribute to shallow breathing.

This determines the degree to which altered breathing pattern is compromising ventilation and oxygenation.

Vigilant monitoring helps reduce complications.

This maintains appropriate closed system.

Absence of fluctuation indicates obstruction or lung reexpansion and must always be investigated.

Bubbling in water seal chamber indicates air leak, which may be present because the lung has not yet expanded or because of a persistent air leak. There may be a leak in the system before the water seal drainage (e.g., loose tubing connection or air leak around entrance site of tube).

Amount of suction (negative pressure) being applied to the pleural space is regulated by the amount of fluid in the suction control chamber, not the amount dialed on Emerson/wall suction.

Excessive drainage may indicate hemorrhage.

This confirms chest tube placement and helps determine whether the lung has reexpanded.

An increase in oxygen consumption and an increase in work of breathing occur as the patient begins to increase activity.

Rationale

This facilitates remaining lung expansion and prevents pooling of secretions. If not contraindicated, a sitting position allows for good lung excursion and chest expansion. After pneumonectomy, position the patient on his or her back or with operative side dependent.

The appropriate amount of oxygen needs to be continuously delivered so that the patient does not become desaturated.

This promotes effective aeration.

Incentive spirometry enhances deep breathing, decreasing the potential for atelectasis.

Thoracotomy

■ = Independent; ▲ = Collaborative

Thoracotomy—cont'd

Actions/Interventions

▲ Maintain chest tube drainage system:

- Position chest drainage system below the patient's chest level.
- Place drainage unit in stand, tape to floor, or hang on bed to prevent tipping of unit.
- Maintain the drainage unit in an upright position.
- Make sure tubing is free of kinks and clots. Milk tubing from insertion site downward.
- Set suction correctly to maintain a constant gentle bubbling in the suction control chamber.

▲ Maintain tubing or connections:
- Anchor the chest tube catheter to the patient's chest wall with waterproof tape.
- Secure drainage tubing connection sites with bands or tape.

▲ Do not clamp chest tubes unless:
- The physician has prescribed clamping
- Closed chest drainage system is being changed to new system
- System becomes disconnected or water seal is disrupted

■ Assist the patient as activity level increases.

Rationale

NOTE: Postpneumonectomy patients generally do not have chest tubes. The space gradually fills with serosanguineous fluid.

Gravity will aid in drainage and prevent backflow into chest.

This maintains integrity of system and prevents tube dislodgment.

This ensures patency for drainage.

This promotes tube drainage.

Vigorous bubbling does not produce additional suction (the water level determines the amount of suction), but it would be a "noisy" irritant to the patient and would cause earlier evaporation of the water level, with a need to refill the chamber to the correct level.

This prevents dislodgment of the tubing.

This prevents dislodgment of the tubing.

Clamping chest tubes is dangerous because a tension pneumothorax may occur.

Mobilizing the patient postoperatively can help prevent pulmonary and circulatory complications.

NDx Nursing Diagnosis

Ineffective Airway Clearance

Common Related Factors	Defining Characteristics
Thoracic surgery	Complaint of pain
Incisional pain	Refusal to cough
	Diminished lung sounds
	Abnormal lung sounds (e.g., rhonchi, wheezes)
	Splinting of respirations
	Dyspnea
	Fever

■ = Independent; ▲ = Collaborative

Common Expected Outcome

Patient's secretions are mobilized and airway is maintained free of secretions as evidenced by clear lung sounds, eupnea, and ability to cough up secretions effectively after deep breaths.

NOC Outcome
Respiratory Status: Airway Patency
NIC Interventions
Cough Enhancement; Airway Suctioning

Ongoing Assessment

Actions/Interventions

■ Auscultate lung sounds every shift, noting areas of decreased ventilation and presence of adventitious sounds.
■ Assess cough effectiveness and productivity.

■ Assess the patient for subjective complaints of discomfort or pain.

■ Assess temperature.

Rationale

Large forced vital capacity reductions follow thoracic surgery.

Several factors can interfere with effective coughing, such as fatigue, pain, malpositioning, and thick, tenacious secretions.
Postoperative pain can prevent the patient from taking deep breaths and from coughing effectively to clear the airway.
Fever may develop in response to retained secretions or atelectasis.

Therapeutic Interventions

Actions/Interventions

▲ Administer humidified oxygen as prescribed.

▲ Assist the patient in performing coughing and breathing maneuvers every hour.
■ Instruct the patient in the following:
  • Use of pillow or hand splints when coughing

  • Use of incentive spirometry

  • Importance of early ambulation and/or frequent position changes

■ Use suctioning as needed to clear airway. Avoid deep tracheal suctioning in the postpneumonectomy patient.
▲ Administer pain medication as needed, offering it before the patient asks for it.
■ Assist the patient with ambulation or position changes.

Rationale

Humidity prevents drying of secretions and facilitates movement.
The patient may be unable to perform independently. These maneuvers keep airways open by clearing secretions.

Providing support, especially to insertion site, will reduce discomfort with deep breathing and coughing.
This facilitates deep breathing. The patient needs a visual marker as to expected goal.
These methods help the patient maintain adequate lung expansion, thus preventing buildup of secretions or atelectasis.
This decreases the risk of bronchial stump suture line rupture.
This prevents peak periods of pain and helps the patient participate in pulmonary therapy measures.
The patient with pneumonectomy should never be positioned with remaining lung in dependent position; this would compromise respiratory excursion of the remaining lung.

Thoracotomy

■ = Independent; ▲ = Collaborative

Thoracotomy—cont'd

 Nursing Diagnosis

Risk for Impaired Gas Exchange

Common Risk Factors

Malfunctioning chest tube drainage system
Mediastinal shift

Common Expected Outcome

Patient's optimal gas exchange is maintained through early assessment and intervention.

NOC Outcome
Respiratory Status: Gas Exchange

NIC Interventions
Respiratory Monitoring; Tube Care: Chest

Ongoing Assessment

Actions/Interventions	Rationale
■ Monitor lung sounds.	Absent or adventitious breath sounds are signs of poor gas exchange or movement.
■ Assess for restlessness and changes in level of consciousness.	Altered mentation can indicate development of hypoxia.
■ Assess for presence of tachypnea and tachycardia.	These may indicate increased work of breathing and hypoxia.
■ Assess for tracheal deviation.	Tracheal deviation is a sign of mediastinal shift, which occurs from increase in intrathoracic pressure on the affected side. The presence of tachypnea and tachycardia is an emergency that requires immediate intervention.
■ Assess patency of chest tube drainage system.	See Ineffective Breathing Pattern diagnosis on p. 520.
■ Assess around chest tube insertion site for crepitus or subcutaneous emphysema.	This signifies air in the tissue.
■ Mark the presence of subcutaneous emphysema and monitor closely for any increase.	This could signify a malfunction in chest tube drainage and/or a continued air leak.
▲ Monitor oxygen saturation through pulse oximeter or ABGs as necessary.	Pulse oximetry is a useful tool to detect early changes in oxygenation. For CO_2 levels, ABGs would need to be obtained.
▲ Monitor serial radiograph reports.	Chest radiographs are done to monitor reexpansion of the lung.

Pulmonary Care Plans

■ = Independent; ▲ = Collaborative

Therapeutic Interventions

Actions/Interventions

- Maintain occlusive dressing around chest tube insertion site, using petroleum jelly (Vaseline) gauze dressing as needed.

- Maintain patency of chest tube drainage system; troubleshoot as necessary.

- Position pneumonectomy patient (with no chest tubes) on operated side.

▲ If tracheal deviation is present with signs of respiratory distress, prepare for additional chest tube insertion, needle aspiration, or emergency thoracentesis.

Rationale

This prevents air leakage into the tissues.

This ensures patency of the drainage tubing system. (See Ineffective Breathing Pattern diagnosis on p. 520.)

Pooling and consolidation on the operated side are desired outcomes; dependent position facilitates this process while enhancing the remaining lung function.

Tracheal deviation may indicate presence of a tension pneumothorax.

NDx Nursing Diagnosis

Acute Pain

Common Related Factor

Incisional pain

Defining Characteristics

Report of pain
Guarding behavior
Relief or distraction behavior (moaning, crying, restlessness, irritability, alteration in sleep pattern)
Facial mask of pain
Autonomic responses not seen in chronic stable pain (e.g., diaphoresis, change in blood pressure [BP], increased pulse rate, pupillary dilation, increased or decreased respiratory rate, pallor)

Common Expected Outcome

Patient's pain is relieved, as evidenced by verbalization of pain relief and relaxed facial expression.

NOC Outcomes
Pain Control; Medication Response

NIC Interventions
Pain Management;
   Analgesia Administration

Thoracotomy

Ongoing Assessment

Actions/Interventions

- Assess pain level and characteristics.

Rationale

Joint Commission on Accreditation of Healthcare Organizations mandates frequent and regular assessment of pain.

■ = Independent; ▲ = Collaborative

Thoracotomy—cont'd

Actions/Interventions

- Solicit techniques that the patient considers useful in pain prevention or relief.
- Assess the degree to which pain interferes with the treatment plan.

Rationale

The patient may have prior experiences with pain that can be useful in this situation.

Assessment guides level of treatment.

Therapeutic Interventions

Actions/Interventions

- Anticipate the need for pain medications.

▲ Respond immediately to complaints of pain by administering analgesics as prescribed and evaluating effectiveness.

▲ Assist the patient as needed with patient-controlled analgesia (PCA) and assess its effectiveness.

- Use nonpharmacological methods of pain management (e.g., positioning, distraction, touch).
- Reinforce techniques to support the incision during movement and breathing or coughing.
- Provide scheduled rest periods.

Rationale

Effective pain management facilitates ambulation and breathing exercises. Postoperative thoracotomy pain can be severe with the continued movement of respiratory muscles needed to maintain ventilation.

Patients have a right to pain relief.

The patient may be hesitant to use PCA effectively for fear of drug overdose. Likewise, the patient may not have full cognitive or manual ability to use PCA correctly.

This can promote comfort alone or in combination with medications.

This may promote comfort and reduce pain.

This promotes comfort, sleep, and relaxation.

NDx Nursing Diagnosis

Impaired Physical Mobility: Arm on Affected Side

Common Related Factors

Incisional pain and/or edema
Decreased strength

Defining Characteristics

Limited range of motion (ROM)
Reluctance to attempt movement

Common Expected Outcome

Patient experiences full ROM in affected extremity.

NOC Outcome
Joint Movement: Shoulder

NIC Intervention
Exercise Promotion: Stretching

■ = Independent; ▲ = Collaborative

Ongoing Assessment

Actions/Interventions

- Ask the patient to raise arm on affected side laterally, assessing degree of ROM present.

- Assess pain.
- Assess fear of further injury.

Rationale

During thoracotomy, muscles are incised in the chest, resulting in the patient's reluctance to move the shoulder and arm on the surgical side.

Gathering information guides treatment choices.

Fear that additional injury will result with use of affected side will decrease spontaneous use of the arm.

Therapeutic Interventions

Actions/Interventions

- Encourage movement of affected arm with activities of daily living (ADLs) (e.g., combing hair).
- Instruct the patient to perform arm circles, with the arm moving in a 360-degree arc.
- Instruct the patient to continue exercises at home.

Rationale

Arm movement or exercising helps maintain muscle tone and function.

Exercise helps maintain mobility and strength of the arm on the affected side.

This promotes optimal physical mobility.

 Nursing Diagnosis

Deficient Knowledge

Common Related Factor

Unfamiliarity with postoperative thoracotomy care

Defining Characteristics

Multiple questions
Lack of questions
Verbalized misconceptions

Common Expected Outcome

Patient or significant others verbalize understanding of postoperative thoracotomy care.

NOC Outcomes

Knowledge: Disease Process;
Knowledge: Treatment Regimen

NIC Interventions

Teaching: Disease Process;
Support System Enhancement

Ongoing Assessment

Actions/Interventions

- Determine understanding of postoperative care and home recovery.
- Determine knowledge of etiological factors of disease and need for behavior modification.

Rationale

Postoperative patients may be overwhelmed by the amount of information for which they are responsible.

This protects remaining lung (e.g., avoidance of smoke, pollutants, inhalants).

Thoracotomy

■ = Independent; ▲ = Collaborative

> ## Thoracotomy—cont'd

Pulmonary Care Plans

Actions/Interventions

■ Assess support system and knowledge of additional resources.

Rationale

Specialized services may be required to meet specific needs.

> ## Therapeutic Interventions

Actions/Interventions

▲ Collaborate with the physician and reinforce post-operative surgical routine, expected recovery, and explanations.

▲ Instruct the patient or caregiver to have the patient resume normal activities gradually (e.g., begin with short walks rather then stair climbing) as approved by physician.

■ Instruct the patient in administration and potential side effects of medications and/or home oxygen.

■ Instruct on use of Heimlich valve if used for home care.

■ Instruct the patient or significant others to seek professional advice for dyspnea, fever, chills, unusual wound drainage, change in wound appearance, loss of appetite, or unintentional weight loss.

■ Refer the patient or significant others to smoking cessation groups or support groups as appropriate.

■ Reinforce the need for or encourage compliance with recommended follow-up therapies and appointments.

■ If surgery was treatment for lung cancer:
  • Instruct the patient or significant others about known causes of lung cancer: cigarette smoking, air pollution, industrial pollutants.
  • Stress importance of avoiding these.

  • Refer the patient to the American Cancer Society for informational support.

Rationale

Information enables the patient to assume some control over events and enhance cooperation.

An informed patient is more cooperative and successful.

Patient safety is a priority.

The Heimlich valve is a one-way flutter valve that allows air from the pleural space to flow out through the tube with exhalation but prevents air from flowing into the chest during inhalation.

The patient needs to know when to seek health care advice for possible problems.

Groups that come together for mutual support and information can be beneficial.

Ongoing monitoring facilitates optimal recovery.

This helps in understanding environmental etiologies.

This protects remaining lung and improves oxygenation. Respiratory irritants can cause bronchoconstriction with resultant irritating cough and rapid, shallow respiratory rate.

Patients may be unaware of services available for questions or problem resolution.

> ## • RELATED CARE PLANS
>

■ = Independent; ▲ = Collaborative

Tracheostomy

Artificial Airway; Tracheotomy

Tracheostomy is a surgical opening into the trachea that is used to prevent or relieve airway obstruction and/or to serve as an access for suctioning and for mechanical ventilation. A tracheostomy can facilitate weaning from mechanical ventilation by reducing dead space and lowering airway resistance. It also improves patient comfort by removing the endotracheal (ET) tube from the mouth or nose. Methods can be instituted for the patient to eat and speak, as well. This care plan focuses on tracheostomy in the acute care setting, as well as the patient in a chronic care facility or with home care.

NDx Nursing Diagnosis

Ineffective Airway Clearance

Common Related Factors

Copious secretions
Thick secretions
Fatigue; weakness
Uncooperativeness
Confusion
Tracheostomy

Defining Characteristics

Increasing restlessness and irritability
Change in mental status
Pallor, cyanosis
Diaphoresis
Tachypnea
Increased breathing effort: use of accessory muscles, intercostal retractions, nasal flaring

Common Expected Outcome

Patient's airway remains patent as evidenced by eupnea, clear lung sounds, and normal skin color.

NOC Outcome
Respiratory Status: Airway Patency

NIC Interventions
Airway Management; Cough Enhancement; Airway Suctioning; Artificial Airway Management

Tracheostomy

Ongoing Assessment

Actions/Interventions

- Assess for tachypnea, nasal flaring, and increased use of accessory muscles of respiration.
- Assess vital signs.

Rationale

These signs indicate increased breathing effort.

With initial hypoxia and hypercapnia, blood pressure (BP), heart rate (HR), and respiratory rate all rise. As the hypoxia and/or hypercapnia become severe, BP and HR drop.

■ = Independent; ▲ = Collaborative

Pulmonary Care Plans

Actions/Interventions

■ Auscultate chest for normal and adventitious sounds.

■ Assess for changes in mental status.

■ Record amount, color, and consistency of secretions.

Rationale

Decreased or absent breath sounds may indicate the presence of a mucous plug or other airway obstruction; wheezing may indicate partial airway obstruction or narrowing; coarse crackles may indicate presence of secretions along larger airways.

Increasing confusion, restlessness, and/or irritability can be early signs of cerebral hypoxia.

Abnormalities may be a result of infection, bronchitis, long-term smoking, or other conditions. A sign of infection is discolored sputum.

Therapeutic Interventions

Actions/Interventions

■ Keep suction equipment and Ambu bag at bedside.

▲ Provide warm, humidified air.

▲ Administer oxygen as needed.

■ Encourage the patient to cough out secretions.

■ Institute suctioning of airway as needed.

■ Provide stoma care:
  • Clean area around stoma and under phalanges of tube with a swab of half-strength hydrogen peroxide.
  • If applicable, clean inner cannula with hydrogen peroxide; rinse with sterile water or saline solution. If disposable inner cannula is used, dispose of used inner cannula and replace with a new inner cannula of the correct size.
  • Keep stoma clean and dry by using a sterile gauze dressing around tracheostomy site.
  • Secure tracheostomy tube with twill tape, using a square knot on the side of the neck or specially designed foam tracheostomy ties.

■ Keep spare tracheostomy tube of same size and brand at bedside.

■ Keep tracheal obturator taped at head of bed for emergency use.

■ Maintain inflated tracheostomy cuff:
  • Immediately after operation
  • If patient is on mechanical ventilation
  • If patient is prone to regurgitate and aspirate; cuff should be deflated at other times to prevent tracheal erosion

Rationale

Being prepared for an emergency helps prevent further complications.

A tracheostomy bypasses the nose, which is the body area that humidifies and warms inspired air. A decrease in the humidity of the inspired air will cause secretions to thicken. Also, cool air may decrease ciliary function. Providing humidification of inspired air will prevent drying and crusting of secretions.

This provides for adequate tissue oxygenation.

This facilitates patent airway.

This removes secretions if the patient is unable to effectively clear the airway.

Frequent stoma care is required for postoperative patients. Care for patients with long-term stoma placement is based on need.

Twill tape will not fray and produce loose threads, which could be inhaled into the tracheostomy opening.

Being prepared for an emergency helps prevent future complications.

The tracheal obturator is used to reinsert the tracheostomy.

Inflated cuff protects the airway.

■ = Independent; ▲ = Collaborative

Actions/Interventions

- Transport the patient with portable oxygen, Ambu bag, suction equipment, and extra tracheostomy tube.

Rationale

Being prepared for an emergency helps prevent future complications.

 Nursing Diagnosis

Risk for Impaired Gas Exchange

Common Risk Factors

Superimposed infection
Copious tracheal secretions
Tracheostomy leak
Pneumothorax (during insertion, apices of lungs are at risk for damage)
Aspiration
Restricted lung expansion from immobility
Preexisting medical conditions
Inability to cough and deep breathe

Common Expected Outcome

Patient's gas exchange is maintained as evidenced by normal arterial blood gases (ABGs), alert responsive mentation, or no further reduction in mental status.

NOC Outcome
Respiratory Status: Gas Exchange
NIC Interventions
Respiratory Monitoring; Oxygen Therapy

Ongoing Assessment

Actions/Interventions

- Monitor respirations, pulse, and temperature and assess changes.

- Assess for headache, dizziness, lethargy, reduced ability to follow instructions, disorientation.
- Auscultate lung sounds, assessing for decreased or adventitious sounds.
- ▲ Use pulse oximetry as appropriate to monitor oxygen saturation. Monitor ABGs and note changes.

- ▲ Monitor effectiveness of tracheostomy cuff. Collaborate with the respiratory therapist, as needed, to determine cuff pressure.

Rationale

Tachypnea and tachycardia are associated with increased work of breathing or hypoxia. Fever may develop in response to retained secretions or atelectasis.

These are signs of hypercapnia.

Changes in lung sounds may reveal the etiology of impaired gas exchange.

Pulse oximetry is a useful tool to detect changes in oxygenation. Oxygen saturation should be maintained at 90% or greater. Increasing $PaCO_2$ and decreasing PaO_2 are signs of respiratory failure.

Maximum recommended levels range from 20 to 25 mm Hg (27 to 33 cm H_2O) or less, if the trachea can be sealed with less. If a leak is present, try to reinflate the cuff, checking the pilot tube and valve for leaks. If unsuccessful, notify the physician. If the patient is being mechanically ventilated and is losing a large portion of the tidal volume because of a cuff leak, the tracheostomy tube will need to be replaced.

■ = Independent; ▲ = Collaborative

Tracheostomy

Tracheostomy—cont'd

Pulmonary Care Plans

Actions/Interventions

■ Assess for development of signs of impaired gas exchange: shortness of breath, tachypnea, increased breathing effort, diaphoresis, pallor. Notify the physician if these occur.

Rationale

Hypoxia is associated with signs of increased breathing effort.

Therapeutic Interventions

Actions/Interventions

■ Stay with the patient during episodes of respiratory distress to allay anxiety.

■ Maintain adequate airway. If obstruction is suspected, troubleshoot as appropriate:
  • Move head and neck.
  • Attempt to deflate cuff.

  • Try to pass a suction catheter.
  • Remove inner cannula and replace with backup inner cannula.
  • Remove and replace tracheostomy tube if all else is unsuccessful.

■ Place the patient in semi-Fowler's to high-Fowler's position.

▲ Administer humidified oxygen as needed.

■ If lung sounds are abnormal, use tracheal suction as needed.

■ Ensure that smoke, aerosol spray, dust, whiskers, and so forth do not enter the trachea.

▲ If pneumothorax is present, set up chest tube placement.

Rationale

Anxiety can increase dyspnea and work of breathing.

A patent airway is a priority.

This corrects any kinking of the tube.

This is important if there is a possibility of a herniated cuff.

This is an attempt to aspirate a mucous plug.

A mucous plug can become lodged in the tube and obstruct the patient's airway.

A new tube can restore airway patency.

This promotes full lung expansion and improved air exchange.

This maintains oxygenation and prevents drying of mucosal membranes.

Suctioning is indicated when patients are unable to remove secretions from airway by coughing because of weakness, thick mucous plugs or excessive or tenacious mucus production.

Chemical irritants and allergens can increase mucus production and bronchospasm.

This evacuates air from the pleural cavity and reexpands the collapsed lung.

NDx Nursing Diagnosis

Risk for Infection

Common Risk Factors

Surgical incision of tracheostomy
Increased secretions

■ = Independent; ▲ = Collaborative

Common Expected Outcome

Patient's risk for infection is reduced as a result of ongoing assessment and early intervention.

NOC Outcomes
Immune Status; Risk Control; Tissue Integrity: Skin and Mucous Membranes

NIC Interventions
Infection Protection; Wound Care; Skin Surveillance

Ongoing Assessment

Actions/Interventions	Rationale
▲ Observe the stoma for erythema, exudates, odor, and crusting lesions. If present, culture stoma and notify the physician.	Culture and sensitivity reports guide antibiotic selection.
■ Assess skin integrity under tracheal ties.	This is a common site for infection.
▲ Monitor white blood cell (WBC) count and differential count.	Rising WBC count indicates the body's efforts to combat pathogens.
■ Assess for fever.	Fever may be a manifestation of an infection or inflammatory process.

Therapeutic Interventions

Actions/Interventions	Rationale
■ Provide routine tracheostomy care as needed.	This prevents airway obstruction and infection.
■ Do not allow secretions to pool around the stoma. Suction the area or wipe with aseptic technique.	This keeps the stoma clean and dry.
■ Keep skin under tracheostomy ties clean and dry.	This prevents skin irritation.
■ Use a hydrocolloid dressing (e.g., Reston foam or DuoDerm) under tracheostomy ties.	This prevents breakdown if redness is present.
▲ If signs of infection are present, apply topical anti-fungal or antibacterial agent, as ordered.	These agents are either toxic to the pathogen or retard their growth.

Tracheostomy

NDx Nursing Diagnosis

Impaired Verbal Communication

Common Related Factor

Tracheostomy

Defining Characteristics

Difficulty in making self understood
Withdrawal
Restlessness
Frustration

■ = Independent; ▲ = Collaborative

Tracheostomy—cont'd

Common Expected Outcome

Patient uses alternative methods of communication to effectively express self.

NOC Outcome
Communication: Expressive

NIC Intervention
Communication Enhancement: Speech Deficit

Ongoing Assessment

Actions/Interventions

- Assess the patient's ability to express ideas.

- Assess anxiety and fear of not being able to communicate needs.
- Assess ability to read and use alternate forms of communication if possible before tracheostomy placement.

Rationale

Standard tracheostomy tubes allow the vocal cords to move, but no airflow passes over them; therefore phonation is not possible.

The inability to communicate enhances a patient's sense of isolation and may promote a sense of helplessness.

Such knowledge builds on prior strengths.

Therapeutic Interventions

Actions/Interventions

- Provide a call light within easy reach at all times.
- Place patient in a room close to the nurse's station.

- Provide patient with pad and pencil. Use picture or alphabet board for patients who are unable to write.

- Provide the patient with reassurance and patience.
- ▲ Collaborate with the physician and speech therapist on possible use of "talking" tracheostomy tube (as appropriate).
- ▲ If the patient no longer requires mechanical ventilation, consider use of a Passy-Muir valve or fenestrated tracheostomy tube.

Rationale

Patient safety is a priority.

This ensures easy observation of the patient by nursing staff.

This provides the patient with more channels through which information can be communicated. This can be especially helpful for tracheal patients.

This allays frustration.

The "talking" tracheostomy tube provides a port for compressed gas to flow in above the tracheostomy tube, allowing air for phonation.

This facilitates talking.

Pulmonary Care Plans

■ = Independent; ▲ = Collaborative

Nursing Diagnosis

Deficient Knowledge

Common Related Factor

New procedure or intervention in hospital

Defining Characteristics

Anxiety
Lack of questioning
Increased questioning
Expressed need for more information

Common Expected Outcome

Patient or caregiver demonstrates skills appropriate for tracheostomy care.

NOC Outcomes
Knowledge: Treatment Procedure;
Knowledge: Treatment Regimen

NIC Interventions
Teaching: Disease Process;
Teaching: Psychomotor Skill

Ongoing Assessment

Actions/Interventions	Rationale
■ Assess knowledge of the purpose and care of a tracheostomy.	This provides an important starting point in education.
■ Assess ability to provide adequate home health care.	Both cognitive and technical skills are required for managing tracheostomy tubes.
■ Assess ability to respond to emergency situations.	This is especially important, because lack of airway patency is a life-threatening problem.

Therapeutic Interventions

Actions/Interventions	Rationale
■ Discuss the patient's need of tracheostomy and its particular purpose.	Adults learn information that is important to them.
■ Begin teaching skills one at a time and reinforce daily.	The patient or caregiver can begin to acquire skills at a pace that is not overwhelming.
■ Provide instruction on sterile tracheostomy care and suctioning; include step-by-step care guidelines on the following: • How to suction • Use of twill tape and/or loop-and-pile fasteners • Cleaning of tracheostomy with or without disposable inner cannula • Cleaning around tracheostomy site	Information enables the patient to take control of his or her life.

Tracheostomy

■ = Independent; ▲ = Collaborative

→ **Tracheostomy—cont'd**

Actions/Interventions

- Provide information on reinsertion of tracheostomy tube.

  - Need to call health care provider if amount of secretions increases or change in color or characteristic occurs

- Discuss the weaning process, as appropriate, with the use of fenestrated tracheostomy tubes, tracheostomy buttons, or progressively smaller tubes.

- Reinforce knowledge of the following emergency techniques:
  - Tracheostomy reinsertion (as appropriate)
  - Emergency phone numbers

▲ Use a case manager or social worker as appropriate to attain equipment and arrange for visiting nurses.

- Explain the process of decannulation, as appropriate.

- Explain home care as follows:
  - Stoma should be covered.

  - Swimming is contraindicated.
  - A loose scarf or shirt may be used over the tracheostomy site.

Rationale

The first tube change is done by the physician usually at 7 days after the tracheostomy, because reinsertion may be difficult if the stoma is not mature or healed. Thereafter, the patient or caregiver should be taught step-by-step reinsertion instructions and should complete a return demonstration.

This could signify the presence of an infection.

Preparation and explanation helps reduce anxiety.

Preparing ahead of time can reduce distress and complications. Correct techniques and procedures need to be reinforced.

Continuity of care is facilitated through the use of appropriate resources.

When the patient's tracheostomy remains capped with the patient effectively maintaining own respirations and airway clearance, the tracheostomy tube can be removed. With removal, the stoma site is covered with a folded 4 × 4 bandage and tape. The opening will close in a few days. Until the site is healed, the patient should be instructed to cover the site with two fingers while attempting to cough or talk to prevent outward airflow through the stoma site.

This prevents inhalation of foreign materials (e.g., shaving, makeup).

Aspiration is possible if water gets into the stoma.

This camouflages the area.

• RELATED CARE PLANS

Disturbed body image, p. 21
Imbalanced nutrition: less than body
  requirements, p. 134
Impaired verbal communication, p. 38
Pneumothorax with chest tube, p. 485
Risk for aspiration, p. 18

■ = Independent; ▲ = Collaborative

Tuberculosis, Active

TB; Mycobacterium Tuberculosis

Patients infected with *Mycobacterium tuberculosis* (MTB) develop either latent TB infections or TB disease. Among adults, TB disease is usually confined to the respiratory tract. Everyone with TB disease needs antimicrobial therapy, as do people with latent TB infections who are at high risk of progressing to TB disease. Pulmonary TB disease is contagious, spread by airborne droplet nuclei that are produced when an infected person coughs or sneezes. Those at higher risk for development of clinical disease include the immunosuppressed (patients receiving cancer chemotherapy, patients infected with human immunodeficiency virus [HIV], patients with diabetes mellitus, adolescents, and patients younger than 2 years of age). Patients with latent TB infections may progress to TB disease. A reactivation can occur later in patients with decreased resistance, concomitant diseases, and immunosuppression. There has been a recent resurgence of TB related to the emergence of multidrug-resistant strains and because of dramatic increase in incidence in patients with HIV infection. The following groups are more likely to be infected with TB: close contacts of a person with TB disease; persons from areas where TB is common (e.g., Asia, Africa, and Latin America); medically underserved persons; low-income persons, including high-risk racial and ethnic groups; and older persons. This care plan focuses on both acute care and home management.

Nursing Diagnosis

Infection

Common Related Factor	Defining Characteristics
Pulmonary TB disease	Purulent or bloody expectoration Temperature spikes Positive culture report Night sweats and chills Cough, possibly nonproductive Fatigue Weight loss Loss of appetite

Common Expected Outcomes

Patient's infection is effectively treated as evidenced by negative culture report on reexamination and absence of fever.
Risk of spread of infection is reduced.

NOC Outcomes
Infection Status; Medication Response

NIC Interventions
Infection Control;
    Medication Administration

Tuberculosis, Active

■ = Independent; ▲ = Collaborative

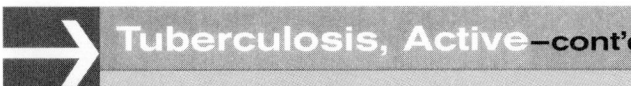

Tuberculosis, Active—cont'd

Ongoing Assessment

Actions/Interventions

■ Check amount, color, and consistency of sputum.

■ Monitor temperature.

▲ Monitor sputum cultures.

Rationale

Yellow or yellow-green sputum is indicative of respiratory infection. Hemoptysis can be a sign of TB.

Fever suggests infection. Night sweats may accompany fever.

Sputum cultures are repeated throughout treatment to determine whether antimicrobial drugs are effective.

Therapeutic Interventions

Actions/Interventions

▲ Induce sputum with heated aerosol if needed to expedite diagnosis and start early treatment.

■ Maintain respiratory isolation.

• Keep tissues and sputum cups at bedside; dispose of secretions properly.

• Have patient cover mouth when coughing or sneezing.
• Use masks. Have anyone entering the patient's room wear a mask.
• If the patient is transported out of room for any reason, have the patient wear a mask.
• Keep the door to the patient's room closed at all times and post an isolation sign where visible. Place respiratory isolation sticker on chart.
• Assist visitors to follow appropriate isolation techniques.

■ Teach patient hand washing techniques to use after handling sputum.

■ Provide a high-protein, high-calorie, increased-fluid diet.

■ Refer patient contacts to be assessed for possible infection and for chemoprophylactic treatment.

Rationale

Precautions to prevent airborne transmission are important during and after procedures that stimulate coughing (e.g., sputum collection, bronchoscopy). These procedures need to be carried out in rooms designated for this with appropriate ventilation.

Respiratory isolation is indicated until the patient responds to the medication (days to weeks). Follow Occupational Safety and Health Act guidelines for fitting and using high-frequency personal respirators for health care workers.

Droplet spread can happen when droplets from the cough or sneeze are propelled in the air and deposited on nearby persons.

This decreases airborne contaminants.

To be effective, the masks need to be designed to filter out droplet nuclei. Other masks are of limited value.

Private respiratory isolation rooms should be maintained with negative pressure to avoid spreading infected particles outward.

This prevents spread of infection.

Friction and running water effectively remove microorganisms from hands.

This maintains optimal nutritional status.

This prevents spread or development of infection. The area of induration of a Mantoux TB skin test that indicates a positive result depends on the patient's age, immune status, injection drug use, and HIV co-infection. Isoniazid (INH) prophylaxis is recommended for preventive TB therapy.

■ = Independent; ▲ = Collaborative

Pulmonary Care Plans

Actions/Interventions	**Rationale**

▲ Administer medications as ordered. The primary drugs used are isoniazid (INH), rifampin (RIF), pyrazinamide (PZA), and ethambutol (EMB).

Anti-TB drug treatment should be promptly initiated for patients with TB disease. For patients taking anti-HIV drugs, rifabutin and rifapentine should replace rifampin.

▲ Monitor for side effects:

Treatment of active disease usually consists of a combination therapy of these drugs in an attempt to increase the therapeutic effectiveness and decrease the development of resistant strains. Combination medications, such as Rifamate (isoniazid and rifampin) or Rifater (isoniazid, rifampin, and pyrazinamide) may improve adherence to therapy, but they make side effects and drug interactions more difficult to evaluate. Patients on anti-TB therapy should be monitored monthly for drug side effects, for infectiousness, and for clinical and bacteriological response to therapy.

1. Isoniazid
   • Monitor baseline measurements of hepatic enzymes and repeat measurements if baseline results are abnormal or if symptoms of adverse reactions occur.

Potential adverse reactions for these drugs include hepatic enzyme elevation, hepatitis, peripheral neuropathy, mild effects on central nervous system, and drug interactions. Hepatitis risk increases with age and alcohol consumption. Pyridoxine can prevent peripheral neuropathy.

2. Rifampin
   • Monitor baseline complete blood count, platelets, and hepatic enzymes. Repeat measurements if baseline is abnormal or if symptoms of adverse reaction occur.

Potential adverse reactions for these drugs include gastrointestinal upset, drug interactions, hepatitis, bleeding problems, influenza-like symptoms, and rash. This drug colors body fluids orange and may permanently discolor soft contact lenses. There are interactions associated with oral contraceptives, which may be rendered ineffective by accelerating estrogen metabolism.

3. Pyrazinamide
   • Monitor baseline uric acid and hepatic enzymes. Repeat measurements if baseline is abnormal or if symptoms of adverse reaction occur. Ask about joint pain.

Adverse reactions include hepatitis, rash, gastrointestinal upset, joint aches, hyperuricemia, and gout.

4. Ethambutol
   • Monitor baseline and monthly tests for visual acuity and color vision.

Adverse reactions include optic neuritis.

▲ Monitor interactions with the patient's other medications.

Older patients are more susceptible to drug interactions due to decreased liver function and chronic conditions. People treated for HIV infection need careful monitoring to manage drug interactions.

■ Report all confirmed TB cases to the health department.

This is for coordination of follow-up care and contact investigation to facilitate prophylaxis for patient contacts.

Tuberculosis, Active

Tuberculosis, Active—cont'd

 Nursing Diagnosis

Ineffective Breathing Pattern

Common Related Factors

Decreased lung volumes
Increased metabolism as result of high fever
Frequent productive cough and hemoptysis
Nervousness, fear of suffocation

Defining Characteristics

Increased work of breathing: tachypnea, use of accessory muscles, retractions, diaphoresis, tachycardia
Purulent or bloody expectoration

Common Expected Outcome

Patient's breathing pattern is maintained as evidenced by eupnea and regular respiratory rate or pattern.

NOC Outcome
Respiratory Status: Ventilation

NIC Intervention
Respiratory Monitoring

Ongoing Assessment

Actions/Interventions

■ Assess respiratory status. Note depth, rate, and character of breathing. Check for increased work of breathing.

■ Assess cough (productive, weak, or hard).

■ Assess nature of secretions: color, amount, consistency.
■ Auscultate lungs for presence of normal and abnormal lung sounds.
■ Monitor vital signs. Note time of temperature spikes.
▲ Monitor oxygen saturation through pulse oximetry or arterial blood gases (ABGs) as indicated.

Rationale

Symptoms may be masked by chronic respiratory conditions common among older adults.

The cough typically becomes frequent and productive; it may be accompanied by chest pain during coughing.
Hemoptysis may be present in advanced cases.
Bronchial breath sounds and crackles may be present.

Low-grade fever occurs, especially in the afternoon.
Decreased oxygen saturation and increased $PaCO_2$ are signs of hypoxia and respiratory compromise.

Therapeutic Interventions

Actions/Interventions

▲ Administer oxygen as ordered.
■ Push fluids and promote hydration.
■ Maintain semi-Fowler's position.
■ Assist the patient to cough, change position, and deep breathe.
■ Provide frequent rest periods.

Rationale

This decreases the work of breathing.
This liquefies secretions for easy expectoration.
This facilitates ease in breathing.
These improve productivity of the cough.

This helps mobilize energy for more effective breathing and coughing efforts.

■ = Independent; ▲ = Collaborative

Pulmonary Care Plans

Nursing Diagnosis

Ineffective Therapeutic Regimen Management

Common Related Factors

Patient value system: health and spiritual beliefs, cultural beliefs, and cultural influences
Long-term therapy
Lack of knowledge of disease process
Lack of motivation
Inadequate follow-up care
Patient and provider relationship
Incomplete knowledge of available resources
Financial difficulty
Language barriers

Defining Characteristics

TB reactivation shown on chest x-ray and sputum examination
Poor nutritional status: signs of malnutrition, not feeling well
Drug-resistant organism seen in culture and sensitivity
Verbal cue by patient or significant others of noncompliance

Common Expected Outcome

Patient displays optimal adherence to treatment regimen, as evidenced by regular medication schedule, reduced coughing, and weight gain or no loss.

NOC Outcomes
Compliance Behavior;
    Knowledge: Treatment Regimen;
    Adherence Behavior

NIC Interventions
Health System Guidance; Surveillance;
    Teaching: Disease Process

Ongoing Assessment

Actions/Interventions

■ Assess the patient for evidence of noncompliance: weight loss; increased coughing; thick, green-gray purulent sputum; drug-resistant organism on culture and sensitivity.

■ Identify the cause of noncompliance, including understanding of treatment; importance of compliance; and financial, emotional, and language barriers.

■ Conduct pill counts.

■ Review laboratory results for expected changes associated with medication side effects.

■ Monitor for expected signs and symptoms, such as orange-stained urine associated with certain medication side effects.

Rationale

These are potential clues suggesting lack of improvement in condition that could be related to noncompliance.

To be effective, interventions need to be patient specific and address individual concerns. Language barriers and cultural influences may be strong among foreign-born patients.

This provides some objective evidence of drug compliance.

Specific manifestations may alert health care providers to drug noncompliance.

This provides some objective evidence of drug compliance for specific medications.

Tuberculosis, Active

■ = Independent; ▲ = Collaborative

→ **Tuberculosis, Active**—cont'd

Therapeutic Interventions

Actions/Interventions	Rationale
■ Teach the patient the following:	A patient with knowledge of disease will be more likely to be compliant with the treatment regimen.
• Detection, transmission, signs or symptoms of relapse	Individuals may experience relapse and so should be taught to recognize the possible recurrence of TB and to seek immediate medical attention.
• Treatment and length of therapy	Patients may require drugs for 6 months or longer.
• Prevention of spread of infection to others	Persons most susceptible are those in close contact during the infectious period. After 2 to 3 weeks of effective medication therapy, patients showing signs of clinical improvement may no longer be infectious.
• Importance of compliance with therapy	Compliance is key to halt progression of disease and promote suppression of infection.
• Health regimen to follow after discharge: clinic appointments, sources of free medication, resource telephone numbers	Long-term follow-up is required.
■ Discuss importance of following therapeutic regimen.	Most treatment failures result from patients prematurely stopping the medication, taking the medication irregularly, or failing to take the medication at all. If the patient cannot adhere to a medication regimen, a responsible person should be designated to administer the medication. The patient should be instructed of the likelihood of developing a "multiple drug-resistant" strain of TB if medications are not taken as prescribed.
■ Suggest formulations that combine two to three medications to decrease pill burden.	Compliance often declines near the end of treatment.
■ Refer noncompliant patients for directly observed therapy programs.	This may be required as a means to enhance adherence and optimal management of TB.
■ Review potential side effects of treatment: • Drug side effects: nausea; loss of appetite; vomiting; persistent, dark urine; yellow skin; malaise; unexplained fever for more then 3 days; or abdominal tenderness.	All patients taking isoniazid, rifampin, or pyrazinamide need to report immediately any symptoms suggesting hepatitis.
• The need to abstain from alcohol while on isoniazid.	Alcohol increases the incidence of hepatitis.
• The need to obtain an eye examination monthly while on ethambutol.	The major side effect is reduced visual acuity.
• Rifampin may accelerate the clearance of drugs metabolized by the liver, including methadone, warfarin sodium (Coumadin), glucocorticoids, estrogens, oral hypoglycemic agents, digitalis, anticonvulsants, ketoconazole, fluconazole, a cyclosporine, and anti-HIV medications, especially protease inhibitors.	Persons co-infected with HIV may need alternative treatments or dosage adjustments of anti-TB and anti-HIV medications.
• Women taking rifampin should use an alternative birth control method other than oral contraceptives or contraceptive implants.	Rifampin may render oral contraceptives ineffective by accelerating estrogen metabolism.

■ = Independent; ▲ = Collaborative

Actions/Interventions

- Rifabutin and rifapentine cause harmless orange-stained tears, saliva, and urine.

■ Adapt respiratory isolation techniques to home environment:

- Have the patient cover mouth when coughing or sneezing.
- Teach appropriate use of tissues and to dispose of secretions properly.
- Teach the patient to wash hands after coughing or sneezing.

■ Explain the importance of good nutrition while taking TB medications.

■ Review possible individual risk factors that may reactivate TB (e.g., malnutrition, alcoholism, immunosuppression, diabetes mellitus, and cancer).

■ Encourage the patient to abstain from smoking.

■ Provide smoking cessation resources.

▲ Arrange for social service involvement for the patient and family.

> **• RELATED CARE PLANS**
>
> Activity intolerance, p. 7
> Imbalanced nutrition: less than body
>   requirements, p. 134

Rationale

Most family members at home have been exposed; however, respiratory safeguards are indicated until medication therapy suppresses the infectious phase.

This decreases airborne contaminants.

Meeting the patient's metabolic needs will decrease fatigue and help the patient build resistance.

Any conditions that lower one's immune defenses can result in reactivation of the disease.

Smoking would increase the possibility of bronchitis and respiratory dysfunction.

Continued smoking in the face of significant respiratory infection and disease may hasten the patient's death. There are numerous resources and supports to assist the patient in quitting smoking.

Continuity of care is facilitated through the use of these services.

Tuberculosis, Active

■ = Independent; ▲ = Collaborative

5

Neurological Care Plans

Alzheimer's Disease/Dementia

Multi-Infarct Dementia (MID); Dementia of the Alzheimer Type (DAT)

Dementia is characterized by a progressive impairment of cognitive function, personality, and behavior. The person with dementia experiences loss of memory, orientation, language skills, concentration, and judgment. In advanced stages, the person experiences behavior and personality changes such as aggressiveness, mood swings, wandering, and confusion. These changes interfere with the person's ability to carry out role responsibilities and activities of daily living. The causes of dementia are numerous and include degenerative disorders of the nervous system, vascular disorders, and autoimmune disorders.

Alzheimer's disease is an irreversible disease of the central nervous system that manifests as a cognitive disorder. Onset is usually between 50 and 60 years and is characterized by progressive deterioration of memory and cognitive function. Disease progression begins with memory impairment, speech and motor difficulties, disorientation of time and place, impaired judgment, memory loss, forgetfulness, and inappropriate affect (lasts 2 to 4 years), followed by loss of independence, complete disorientation, wandering, hoarding, communication difficulties, complete memory loss (lasts up to 7 years), and the final stage with blank expression, irritability, seizures, emaciation, and absolute dependence (in the last year) until death. The estimated total duration of the disease is 14 years.

Although the cause is unknown, research suggests genetic predisposition, along with viral infection and immune dysfunction. Drug therapy for Alzheimer's disease includes cholinesterase inhibitors and NMDA (N-methyl-D-aspartate) antagonists. These drugs have been shown to delay the progression of cognitive impairment in the patient. Some patients may experience improved memory function with these drugs.

This care plan addresses needs for patients with a wide variety of dementia, of which Alzheimer's is a type. Focus is on the home care setting.

NDx Nursing Diagnosis

Risk for Violence: Self-Directed or Other-Directed

Common Risk Factors

Impaired perception of reality
Impaired frustration tolerance
Decreased self-esteem

| (■ = Independent; ▲ = Collaborative)

Perceived threat to self
Alteration in sleep or rest pattern
Impaired self-expression (verbal and nonverbal)
Anxiety
Impaired coping skills
Decreased sense of personal boundaries
Drug intoxication or idiosyncratic reaction
Physical discomfort
Overstimulation

Common Expected Outcomes

Early manifestations of violence are detected and interventional techniques applied to prevent escalation.
Patient avoids physical harm.
Caregiver avoids physical harm.

NOC Outcomes

Aggression Control; Cognitive Ability;
Mood Equilibrium; Risk Control

NIC Interventions

Mood Enhancement; Environmental
Management: Violence Prevention

Ongoing Assessment

Actions/Interventions

- Assess cognitive factors that may contribute to development of violent behaviors, including the following:
  - Decreased ability to solve problems
  - Alteration in sensory and perceptual capacities
  - Impairment in judgment
  - Psychotic or delusional thought patterns
  - Impaired concentration or decreased response to redirection

- Assess physical factors that may foster violence: physical discomfort, such as being wet or cold, and sensory overload (overstimulation), such as noise.

- Assess emotional factors that can lead to violence: inability to cope with frustrating situations, expressions of low self-esteem, noncompliance with treatment plan, and history of aggressive behaviors as a means of coping with stress.

Rationale

Factors may indicate decline in cognitive condition. The patient may become overresponsive to environmental stimuli, leading to agitation and combativeness.

Correcting physical factors will decrease stimulation and may decrease confusion.

Thorough assessment of precipitating factors is needed so that preventive measures can be instituted.

Therapeutic Interventions

Actions/Interventions

- Involve the patient on a cognitive level as much as possible. Instruct the caregiver in the following techniques. Begin with least restrictive measures and progress to most restrictive measures.

Rationale

This allows the patient some measure of control over the environment. This may increase compliance.

Alzheimer's Disease/Dementia

■ = Independent; ▲ = Collaborative

Alzheimer's Disease/Dementia—cont'd

Actions/Interventions	**Rationale**
Level I:	
Nonaggressive behaviors: may include wandering or pacing, restlessness or increased motor activity, climbing out of bed, changing clothes or disrobing, hand wringing or hand washing.	
■ Give verbal feedback and institute interpersonal approaches.	At this level of dementia, the patient may still have insight about the losses he or she is experiencing.
■ Consider environmental measures to be taken.	Sensory stimulation needs to be reduced.
■ Evaluate impact of medication regimen on behaviors in terms of contribution to agitation. Consider use of medications prescribed for agitation.	Neuroleptics (e.g., loxapine) and antipsychotics (e.g., haloperidol) may cause extrapyramidal side effects, manifested as restlessness.
■ Speak in slow, clear, soothing tones. Make comments brief and to the point. Repeat as needed.	Attention to technique helps avoid communication conflicts. The patient may have declines in short-term memory that require frequent repetition of new information.
■ Use distraction	Impaired short-term memory may allow introduction of new stimuli to calm agitated behavior.
Level II:	
Verbally aggressive behaviors: may include cursing, yelling, screaming, unintelligible or repetitious speech, and threats or accusations.	
■ Attempt verbal control; attempt feedback about behavior (for less cognitively impaired), distraction (for cognitively impaired), or limit setting (although this may increase agitation at times).	These techniques can decrease sensory stimuli. Asking the patient questions may help identify unmet needs that prompted the behavior.
■ If feasible, allow the patient more personal space.	If the patient's memory span is short, leaving the room briefly may decrease his or her agitation.
■ Acknowledge fear of loss of control; evaluate use of touch and hand holding.	Touch may be calming to some and aggravating to others.
■ If the patient wanders or paces, consider the need to provide visual supervision, especially if the patient expresses the need to leave.	Providing for safety is a priority. The patient needs to be dressed appropriately and needs to wear identification.
■ Provide diversional activity (e.g., folding towels, handling worry beads, walking with the patient).	These activities may assist in increasing the patient's feelings of self-worth and meet his or her need for activity.
Level III:	
Physically aggressive behaviors: may include hitting, kicking, spitting or biting, throwing objects, pushing or pulling others, and fighting.	
■ Permit verbalization of feelings associated with agitation.	This may diffuse aggressive behavior.
■ Offer acceptable alternatives to unacceptable behaviors, such as undressing in public, by allowing the patient to select his or her own clothing.	This allows the patient some control over the environment.
■ If the patient poses a potential threat of injury to self or others, consider use of soft physical restraints, such as cloth wrist, hand, leg, belt, or vest type restraints.	As initial measures become ineffective, more extreme measures may be indicated to ensure safety of the patient or caregiver.

■ = Independent; ▲ = Collaborative

Actions/Interventions

- Use pharmaceutical restraints, such as antidepressants (amitriptyline) or antipsychotics (haloperidol), only if agitation has reached a point where soft restraints are inadequate to protect the patient from injury.

Rationale

Medication may be indicated to decrease potential risk of injury.

NDx Nursing Diagnosis

Self-Care Deficit: Bathing, Grooming, Feeding

Common Related Factor

Alteration in cognition, including impaired memory, disorientation, memory deficits, impaired judgment, impaired sense of social self

Defining Characteristics

Requires assistance with at least one of the following: bathing, oral hygiene, dressing or grooming, feeding

Denies need for personal hygiene measures

Refuses to change clothes or wears more than one set of clothing

Unable to assist in personal care because of motor deficits or confusion

Common Expected Outcome

Patient participates in self-care activities, as evidenced by dressing, bathing, and feeding self.

NOC Outcome

Self-Care: Bathing, Grooming, Eating

NIC Intervention

Self-Care Assistance: Bathing, Grooming, Feeding

Ongoing Assessment

Actions/Interventions

- Assess cognitive deficits or behaviors that would create difficulty in bathing self, performing oral hygiene, selecting and putting on appropriate clothing, choosing food menu items, and feeding self.
- Assess level of independence in completing self-care.

- Assess need for supervision or redirection during self-care.

Rationale

In the early stages of the disease, the patient may have problems with forgetfulness, information processing, and the retrieval of information necessary to make decisions about self-care activities.

The patient with impaired thought processes is unable to self-monitor personal grooming, hygiene, and nutrition needs adequately.

The patient's ability to perform self-care activities may change often over the course of the disease. The nurse needs to reassess the patient's self-care ability at regular intervals to provide assistance for the patient and caregivers.

Alzheimer's Disease/Dementia

■ = Independent; ▲ = Collaborative

Alzheimer's Disease/Dementia—cont'd

Therapeutic Interventions

Actions/Interventions	Rationale
Instruct the caregiver to do the following:	
■ Stay with the patient during self-care activities if his or her judgment is impaired.	This approach promotes safety and provides necessary redirection.
■ Allow enough time in quiet environment; limit distractions.	Rushing promotes frustration and failure.
■ Follow established routines for self-care, if possible, or develop a routine that is consistently followed.	An established routine becomes rote and requires less decision making.
■ Provide a simple, easy-to-read, large-print list of self-care activities to complete each day (e.g., brush teeth, comb hair).	Reminders may enhance functional abilities.
■ Assist, as needed, with perineal care each morning and evening (or after each episode of incontinence).	This prevents skin breakdown.
■ Assist, as needed, in selecting clothing. Allow the patient to choose if possible (e.g., put out two or three sets of clothing and allow a choice).	This gives the patient some control over the environment.
■ Encourage the patient to dress as independently as possible. Provide easy-to-wear clothes (elastic waistbands, snaps, large buttons, loop-and-pile closures).	It is important for the patient to maintain functional ability for as long as possible.
■ Assist in selecting nutritious, high-bulk foods. Allow the patient to choose foods he or she prefers, if possible.	These measures promote adequate intake.
■ Assist in setup of meal as needed (e.g., open containers, cut food).	Easy access promotes better nutritional intake.
■ If judgment is impaired, cool down hot liquids to palatable temperatures before serving.	This is necessary to avoid injury.
■ Limit number of choices of food on plate or tray.	It is important to reduce the number of decisions that the patient is required to make.
■ Provide easy-to-eat finger foods if motor coordination is impaired.	This approach promotes meeting the patient's nutritional needs.
■ Provide nutritious between-meal snacks if nutritional intake is inadequate.	This does not usually become a problem until late stage or if psychotic symptoms develop.
■ If the patient refuses a task, use distraction techniques; break the task into smaller steps; use calm, unhurried voice to offer praise and encouragement.	The patient's limited short-term memory makes it harder to concentrate on complex tasks.

NDx Nursing Diagnosis

Impaired Social Interaction

Common Related Factor	Defining Characteristic
Alteration in cognition, including impaired sense of social self, memory deficits, impaired judgment, disorientation, social isolation	Change in patterns of social interaction, including language or behaviors inappropriate to social situations, lack of relationships with others

■ = Independent; ▲ = Collaborative

Common Expected Outcome

Patient engages in social interaction as evidenced by positive contacts with caregiver or significant others.

NOC Outcome
Social Involvement

NIC Intervention
Socialization Enhancement

Ongoing Assessment

Actions/Interventions

■ Assess cognitive deficits or behaviors that interfere with forming relationships with others.

■ Assess previous patterns of interaction.

■ Assess potential to interact in a community day care situation.

Rationale

As disease progresses, ability to maintain attention and memory deteriorates. Behavior may be socially unacceptable.

Ability and/or willingness to interact may vary with the patient's mood, perceptions, and reality orientation.

Confusion, disorientation, and loss of social inhibitions may result in socially inappropriate and/or harmful behavior to self or others. Programs vary in capacity for handling patients in late stages of dementia of Alzheimer's type (DAT).

Therapeutic Interventions

Actions/Interventions

■ Within the context of the nurse-patient relationship, provide regular opportunity for frequent, brief contacts.

■ Discuss subjects in which the patient is interested but which do not require extensive recall.

■ When discussing past experiences, assist the patient in connecting them with here-and-now.

■ Identify where the patient is currently living and with whom.

■ Assist the caregiver to do the following:
  • Support participation in social activities appropriate to the patient's level of cognitive functioning, such as small family parties.

  • Redirect the patient when behaviors become socially embarrassing.

  • If the patient expresses delusional ideas, focus on reality-based interactions.

  • Do not correct the patient's ideas or confront them as delusional.

Rationale

Being present demonstrates caring and provides the patient with an opportunity for social interaction.

Short-term recall becomes more and more difficult and frustrating.

Past coping strategies may assist with current situations. Reminiscence promotes long-term memory skills and can relieve depression.

This is necessary to determine the degree of isolation.

Large gatherings become more problematic as symptoms intensify. The patient may not be able to tolerate excessive stimuli in large gatherings.

Decreased short-term memory may help the patient respond to more calming stimuli.

The patient's short-term memory loss allows the nurse to redirect the patient's thinking and promote reality orientation.

Confrontation can increase the patient's agitation.

Alzheimer's Disease/Dementia

■ = Independent; ▲ = Collaborative

Alzheimer's Disease/Dementia—cont'd

Actions/Interventions

- Consider impact of environment on social inter-action. Avoid an overstimulating environment (noise, lights, activity).

- Involve the patient in developing a daily schedule that includes time for social activity, as well as quiet time. Consider the patient's talents, interests, and abilities when developing a daily program. Post a schedule.

- ■ Provide information on community daycare programs that will help the patient maintain social interaction.

Rationale

Sensory overload aggravates cognitive thinking.

Patient participation improves compliance. A schedule that includes activities interspersed with rest periods can limit episodes of wandering.

Involvement with group activities is determined by various factors, including group size, activity level, and the patient's tolerance level. Fluctuations in mood and affect may influence ability to respond appropriately to others. Adult daycare also provides needed respite for the caregiver.

NDx Nursing Diagnosis

Impaired Home Maintenance

Common Related Factor

Alteration in cognition: impaired memory, disorientation, memory deficits

Defining Characteristics

Disorientation in familiar surroundings
Need for supervision in potentially hazardous situations
Family caregiver concerns about caring for the patient at home

Common Expected Outcomes

Caregiver or family provides safe home environment.
Caregiver or family describes nursing or community resources available for home care.

NOC Outcomes
Family Functioning; Safety Behavior: Home Physical Environment; Self-Care: Instrumental Activities of Daily Living

NIC Interventions
Family Support; Self-Care Assistance; Home Maintenance Assistance

Ongoing Assessment

Actions/Interventions

- ■ Assess motor, sensory, and cognitive deficits to deter-mine safety needs.

Rationale

Impaired judgment can limit the patient's ability to live without supervision.

■ = Independent; ▲ = Collaborative

Actions/Interventions

- Assess ability to recognize danger (smoke, fire).

- Assess frequency of disorientation, wandering, becoming lost in familiar surroundings.

- Assess the family's or caregiver's understanding of the patient's needs or deficits, resources to provide adequate supervision and behavior management, the family's ability to cope, and internal or external support systems.

- Determine adequacy of the home environment.

Rationale

Cognitive impairment limits the patient's ability to perceive potential threats in the environment.

These behaviors are the most frequent reason given by family members for placing the patient in a closely supervised care setting.

Thorough assessment is needed to determine potential problems and complications.

Social services agencies can provide help in determining whether patients can live in their home safely.

Therapeutic Interventions

Actions/Interventions

- Involve the patient, family, or caregiver in all home planning.

- Discuss need to wear identification bracelet at all times.

- Assist in developing a daily schedule that allows rest and activity periods.

- Suggest daily supervised exercise or a walking program.

- Provide information about home security devices, such as keyed door locks and audible alarms.

- Recommend procedures for getting help (e.g., calling police, notifying neighbors) in case the patient becomes lost.

- Identify and encourage correction of obstacles and hazards in the home.

- Help the family identify and mobilize available support networks.

- Discuss available home health and community services, such as church groups and senior citizens organizations.

- Provide information about support groups available to family members.

- Provide literature and references related to caring for cognitively impaired persons in the home.

- Discuss available home health and community services.

Rationale

In initial stages, the patient will be able to contribute to care decisions and should not be excluded from home planning.

This approach allows patients to be identified quickly if they become lost.

Fatigue makes coping difficult for the patient.

Structured activity may decrease wandering behavior and meet the patient's need for exercise.

Attention to security measures may decrease wandering behavior.

Caregivers need to have up-to-date photographs and physical description information readily available for people who will search for the lost patient.

Ensuring environmental safety is a priority.

A network of family members, friends, and community resources can facilitate home patient care.

This serves to promote independence and reduce caregiver burden.

Support groups often have the best practical tips and suggestions.

The Alzheimer Association has a broad range of resources to help families and caregivers.

These may be required to assist the caregiver with day-to-day tasks.

Alzheimer's Disease/Dementia

■ = Independent; ▲ = Collaborative

Alzheimer's Disease/Dementia—cont'd

 Nursing Diagnosis

Caregiver Role Strain

Common Related Factors

Knowledge deficit regarding management of care
Personal and social life disrupted by demands of care-giving
Multiple competing roles
No respite from caregiver demands
Unaware of available community resources
Reluctant to use community resources
Community resources not available
Community resources not affordable

Defining Characteristics

Expresses difficulty in performing patient care
Verbalizes anger with responsibility of patient care
States that formal and informal support systems are inadequate
Expresses problems in coping with patient's behavior
Expresses negative feeling about patient or relationship
Neglects patient care

Common Expected Outcomes

Caregiver demonstrates competence and confidence in performing the caregiver role by meeting care recipient's physical and psychosocial needs.
Caregiver verbalizes positive feelings about care recipient and their relationship.
Caregiver reports that formal and informal support systems are adequate and helpful.

NOC Outcomes
Caregiver Well-Being;
  Caregiver-Patient Relationship

NIC Intervention
Caregiver Support

Ongoing Assessment

Actions/Interventions

- Assess relationship between caregiver and patient.

- Assess family communication pattern.

- Assess family resources and support systems.

- Determine the caregiver's knowledge and ability to provide patient care, including bathing, skin care, safety, intake and output measurement, medications, and diet management.

Rationale

Caregiver anger or illness may be reflected in their relationship.

Open communication among all family members creates a positive environment, whereas concealing feelings creates problems for the caregiver and care recipient.

Family and social support is related positively to coping effectiveness of caregiver.

Basic instruction may reduce caregiver anxiety and improve the relationship. Caregiver frustration can lead to anger directed toward the patient. These emotions may result in verbal or physical abuse or neglect of the patient.

Neurological Care Plans

Therapeutic Interventions

Actions/Interventions

- Provide information on disease process and management strategies.

- Encourage the caregiver to identify available family and friends who can assist with care giving.

- Suggest that the caregiver use available community resources such as respite, home health care, adult daycare, Alzheimer's Disease and Related Disorders Association (ADRDA), 70 East Lake St., Chicago, IL, 60601.

- ▲ Consult a social worker for referral for community resources and/or financial aid, if needed.

- Encourage the caregiver to set aside time for self.

- Acknowledge to the caregiver his or her role and its value.

Rationale

Accurate information increases understanding of the care recipient's condition and behavior, including the knowledge that regardless of the quality of care, the disease will progress and care requirements will continually increase. Families need to understand the importance of consistency when caring for the person with dementia.

Respite care helps family members cope with the burden of care. As the patient's cognitive function declines, they require more hours of direct supervision. Nighttime wandering may keep family members from getting adequate sleep.

Resources such as adult daycare may allow family members to continue job responsibilities and other family activities.

The family may need guidance in planning for long-term care, estate planning, powers of attorney, and living wills for the patient.

Simple activities such as a relaxing bath or reading a book help to maintain physical and mental well-being.

The patient may not be able to express this himself or herself.

> • RELATED CARE PLANS
>
> Disturbed sleep pattern, p. 177
> Ineffective coping, p. 51

Cerebral Artery Aneurysm: Preoperative/Unclipped

Subarachnoid Hemorrhage [SAH]; Intraparenchymal Hemorrhage; Intracranial Aneurysm

Aneurysms are saccular or berry-shaped, thin-walled blisters, 2 mm to 3 cm in size. Small aneurysms in the internal carotid artery rupture easily. Aneurysms of the middle cerebral artery and posterior circulation may grow to 5 to 8 mm before rupturing. They protrude from the arteries of the circle of Willis or its major branches, located predominantly at the bifurcation of vessels; 85% of subarachnoid hemorrhages (SAHs) are in the circle of Willis. Intracranial aneurysm may be congenital, traumatic, arteriosclerotic, or septic in origin. Approximately 90% are congenital. They are presumed to be the result of developmental defects in the media and elastica. The intima bulges outward, covered only by adventitia, and eventually rupture may occur. SAH occurs in about 15,000 Americans per year and in females more often than in males. On admission to the hospital, most patients are classified according to Hunt and Hess's graded scale based on clinical status as follows: (I) asymptomatic, minimal headache, slight/mild nuchal rigidity; (II) moderate-severe headache, nuchal rigidity, no neurological deficit other than

Cerebral Artery Aneurysm: Preoperative/Unclipped

■ = Independent; ▲ = Collaborative

Cerebral Artery Aneurysm: Preoperative/ Unclipped—cont'd

third nerve palsy; (III) drowsiness, confusion, mild focal deficit; (IV) stupor, moderately severe hemiparesis; (V) coma. After subarachnoid hemorrhage, patients are at risk for rebleeding, vasospasm (stroke), and hydrocephalus. This care plan focuses on the acute care of the preoperative patient with an aneurysm.

NDx Nursing Diagnosis

Ineffective Cerebral Tissue Perfusion

Common Related Factors

Subarachnoid or intracerebral hemorrhage
Ruptured aneurysm
Vasospasm (ischemia)
Cerebral edema
Increased intracranial pressure (ICP)
Hydrocephalus

Defining Characteristics

Severe headache (unlike any experienced before)
Unconsciousness: transitory or lasting
Nuchal rigidity
Mental confusion, drowsiness
Seizures
Transitory or fixed neurological signs (numbness, speech disturbance, paresis)
Hypertension, which may accentuate or aggravate any vascular weakness, although not necessarily a causative factor in aneurysm development or rupture

Common Expected Outcomes

Patient maintains optimal cerebral perfusion as evidenced by intact orientation (Glasgow Coma Scale [GCS] score >13).
Potential complications related to SAH are detected early, allowing prompt medical and surgical intervention.

NOC Outcomes

Tissue Perfusion: Cerebral; Blood Coagulation; Vital Signs

NIC Interventions

Neurological Monitoring; Medication Administration; Vital Sign Monitoring

Ongoing Assessment

Actions/Interventions

■ Complete an initial assessment of the patient's symptoms.

■ Complete baseline assessment of neurological status and deficits, with attention to level of consciousness (LOC), mental status, pupils, speech and motor function. Use GCS. Record serial assessments, monitoring for signs of ischemia (stroke): impaired mental status, change in LOC, focal abnormalities, speech difficulties, motor deficit, headache, fever.

Rationale

Time of onset is important in assessing time of initial bleed and subsequent hemorrhage, and it may influence timing of surgery.

After SAH, stroke resulting from vasospasm is the most important cause of death or disability. The more severe the hemorrhage, the greater the risk. The usual onset is 3 to 10 days after hemorrhage, lasting for at least 2 weeks. The patient will have signs of increased ICP.

■ = Independent; ▲ = Collaborative

Actions/Interventions

- Assess for seizure activity.

- Assess for meningeal signs: nuchal rigidity, photophobia.
- Monitor vital signs. Closely monitor blood pressure (BP). Report if systolic BP is less than 100 or greater than 150 mm Hg; if diastolic BP is less than 60 or greater than 90 mm Hg; if mean BP is less than 90 or greater than 100 mm Hg.
- ▲ Monitor arterial blood gases.

- ▲ Monitor closely serum electrolytes, blood urea nitrogen (BUN), creatinine, serum osmolarity, urine specific gravity, and input and output for signs of dehydration.

Rationale

Anticonvulsants are given prophylactically to prevent seizures caused by cerebral irritation.

Pronounced signs indicate a more severe aneurysm.

Hypertension may accentuate or aggravate any vascular weakness. Hypotension will decrease cerebral perfusion.

Hypoxia and/or hypercapnia can cause increased blood flow and ICP.

Dehydration is thought to aggravate vasculature and induce vasospasm.

Therapeutic Interventions

Actions/Interventions

- Place the patient on bed rest in a private room, if possible; limit visitors.
- Keep lighting subdued.
- ▲ Administer anticonvulsants as ordered:
  - Dilantin (phenytoin): By mouth or intravenously (IV). Give slow IV push (not faster than 50 mg/min); cannot be given in D_5W (precipitation occurs).
  - Valium: Give slow IV infusion, no faster than 10 mg/min. Also monitor heart rate and BP.
  - Phenobarbital: 100 to 200 mg PO, IV, or IM daily in divided doses; may cause drowsiness.
- ▲ Administer antihypertensive agents.

- ▲ Administer IV fluids and encourage liquid intake if cardiovascular status and electrolytes are within normal limits.
- ▲ Administer nimodipine (Nimotop).

- Anticipate surgical repair.

- ▲ Administer antifibrinolytic agents as prescribed.

Rationale

A quiet environment and noise control may decrease BP and prevent rebleeding.

Photophobia is associated with subarachnoid hemorrhage.

Anticonvulsants are used to prevent and control seizure activity. The presence of blood on the surface of the brain causes irritation and is a stimulus for seizures.

Slow administration prevents respiratory arrest. Sedation will promote rest and help prevent increased ICP.

This drug helps with seizure management and sedation.

These medications decrease the risk of rebleeding associated with hypertension. Sodium nitroprusside may be used initially. Changing to oral antihypertensives requires caution (possibility of sudden hypotension with methyldopa or clonidine therapy).

Dehydration has an adverse effect on cerebral vasospasm.

This calcium channel blocker is given to prevent or minimize cerebral vasospasm. Initial dose is given as soon as possible after the initial bleed.

If repair is within 2 to 3 days, the risks of vasospasm and rebleeding are significantly decreased. Repair is typically done on relatively stable grade I, II, and III aneurysms.

In patients who cannot tolerate or refuse early surgery to clip or wrap the aneurysm, epsilon aminocaproic acid (Amicar) may be given to inhibit fibrinolysis, prevent clot degradation, and avoid potential rebleeding.

Cerebral Artery Aneurysm: Preoperative/Unclipped

■ = Independent; ▲ = Collaborative

Cerebral Artery Aneurysm: Preoperative/ Unclipped—cont'd

ND x Nursing Diagnosis

Acute Pain

Common Related Factor	Defining Characteristics
Meningeal irritation	Headache Nuchal rigidity Photophobia Restlessness Increased BP and heart rate Complaint of pain, stiffness, tenderness

Common Expected Outcome

Patient verbalizes acceptable level of comfort.

> **NOC Outcome**
> Pain Control
>
> **NIC Intervention**
> Pain Management

Ongoing Assessment

Actions/Interventions

- Assess for defining characteristics.

- Determine the patient's perspective on level of pain or discomfort using a 1- to 10-point scale.

Rationale

Each patient's perception of pain is unique. Headache may be the only symptom of aneurysm rupture in some patients. Patients may describe the pain as the worst headache they have ever experienced. They may also complain of pain over or behind their eyes. Nuchal rigidity and upper back pain may occur with grade II aneurysms.

A 10-point scale promotes objective pain measurement.

Therapeutic Interventions

Actions/Interventions

- Assist the patient into a comfortable position. Raise head of bed, and support head and neck with pillows.
- Encourage use of relaxation methods.

- Decrease environmental stimulation.

Rationale

This promotes patient comfort and reduces pain.

Nonpharmacological measures will not mask neurological changes associated with vasospasm or rebleeding.

A quiet environment reduces meningeal irritation and promotes pain control.

■ = Independent; ▲ = Collaborative

Neurological Care Plans

Actions/Interventions

▲ Administer analgesics.

Rationale

Acetaminophen may be effective alone, or stronger drug therapy may be needed (codeine with a mild sedative) depending on the severity of the aneurysm and the patient's perception of pain. Selection of analgesics is based on promoting comfort without masking changes in neurological status.

NDx Nursing Diagnosis

Ineffective Protection

Common Related Factor

Complications of antifibrinolytic therapy

Defining Characteristics

Nausea
Cramps
Diarrhea
Dizziness
Headache
Rash
Deep vein thrombosis (DVT)
Pulmonary emboli

Common Expected Outcome

Risk of complications of antifibrinolytic therapy is reduced through early assessment and treatment.

NOC Outcomes
Blood Coagulation; Medication Response; Tissue Perfusion: Peripheral/ Pulmonary

NIC Interventions
Embolus Care: Pulmonary/Peripheral; Medication Administration

Ongoing Assessment

Actions/Interventions

■ Monitor the patient for side effects of antifibrinolytic therapy. See Defining Characteristics above.

▲ Monitor electrolytes, BUN, creatinine, serum osmolarity, central venous pressure (CVP), and pulmonary capillary wedge pressure carefully during hydration.

■ Monitor for signs and symptoms of the following:
  • Deep vein thrombosis: pain in lower extremities, positive Homans' sign, increased extremity circumference, increased temperature

Rationale

Antifibrinolytic therapy is used to prevent clot degradation and avoid potential rebleeding.

Changes in renal function and hemodynamic parameters allow early identification of overhydration, dehydration, and electrolyte imbalances.

Early assessment allows for titration of antifibrinolytic therapy and prevents development of further symptoms.

Cerebral Artery Aneurysm: Preoperative/Unclipped

■ = Independent; ▲ = Collaborative

Cerebral Artery Aneurysm: Preoperative/ Unclipped—cont'd

Actions/Interventions

- Pulmonary emboli: dyspnea, tachycardia, wheezing, chest pain, hemoptysis, right axis deviation on electrocardiogram
- If pulmonary infarct occurs: pleural effusion, friction rub, fever
- Dehydration: decreased CVP (<5 cm H_2O), poor skin turgor, dry mucous membranes

Rationale

Pulmonary embolism is a serious complication that can be life threatening.

Dehydration causes hemoconcentration and increases risk of DVT and pulmonary emboli.

Therapeutic Interventions

Actions/Interventions

▲ Apply antiembolic stockings and sequential compression devices to lower extremities, as ordered.

▲ Ensure correct dosage and administration of aminocaproic acid (Amicar).

▲ Administer IV fluids. Hourly rate may be greater than 125 mL/hr. This prevents dehydration.

■ Explain possible side effects of drug to patient or significant others: nausea, cramps, diarrhea, dizziness, headache, rash, DVT, pulmonary emboli.

Rationale

This promotes venous return and decreases risk of DVT.

This drug inhibits fibrinolysis, thereby reducing bleeding. It must be given carefully to avoid further complications.

This prevents dehydration.

Drug therapy will be maintained until surgical correction can be achieved.

NDx Nursing Diagnosis

Deficient Knowledge

Common Related Factor

Unfamiliar diagnosis

Defining Characteristics

Multiple questions
Lack of questions
Misconceptions

Common Expected Outcome

Patient verbalizes understanding of extent and cause of bleed; potential for rebleeding, vasospasm (stroke), and elevated ICP; diagnostic testing; and treatment.

NOC Outcomes
Knowledge: Disease Process;
Knowledge: Treatment Regimen

NIC Intervention
Teaching: Disease Process

Ongoing Assessment

Actions/Interventions

■ Assess level of understanding of diagnosis, treatment, and possible complications.

Rationale

This is important in order to provide necessary information.

■ = Independent; ▲ = Collaborative

Therapeutic Interventions

Actions/Interventions	Rationale
■ Explain possible causes of intracranial hemorrhage and/or aneurysmal rupture. Explain potential complications (rebleeding, vasospasms [stroke], and increased ICP secondary to hydrocephalus or cerebral edema).	It is important to clarify the patient's current knowledge of the disease process.
■ Explain rationale for limitation of length and frequency of visits by family members and friends.	This provides a quiet and restful environment to prevent excitement or stimulation associated with changes in BP and ICP.
■ Explain necessity to avoid Valsalva maneuver. Stress importance of exhaling when pulled up in bed and avoiding coughing and straining at stool.	This prevents increase in BP and ICP.
▲ Provide stool softener if necessary.	Preventing straining with bowel movements reduces risk of performing Valsalva maneuver.
■ Discuss ordered tests or studies (e.g., computed tomography [CT], cerebral angiography, cerebral blood flow).	These tests are done to pinpoint the position and size of the aneurysm and to assist the surgeon in determining the surgical treatment plan.
■ When possible, coordinate time for the patient or family to ask the neurosurgeon questions about the patient's condition, treatment plan, and surgery.	In many cases the patient's condition does not allow for a great deal of time before surgical intervention is necessary. Discussion with the patient and family will help decrease anxiety and increase understanding.
■ When the patient is ready during hospitalization, begin teaching about smoking, diet, stress, and other risk factors associated with aneurysm and stroke.	These new health-related behaviors are important after discharge.
▲ Involve a social worker or case manager.	Referrals are indicated if prolonged hospitalization, need for rehabilitation, or need for assistance to obtain medications (nimodipine is expensive) is anticipated.

Cerebrovascular Accident (CVA)

Brain Attack; Thrombotic Stroke; Embolic Stroke; Hemorrhagic Stroke

Cerebrovascular accident (CVA) is a sudden neurological incident related to impaired cerebral blood supply, which may be caused by hemorrhage, embolism, or thrombosis, resulting in ischemia to the brain. Stroke is the leading cause of serious, long-term disability in the United States and Canada. It is the third leading cause of death in the United States; 72% of those affected are older than 65 years of age. The risk increases until 75 years of age. It is more prevalent in older persons because of atherosclerosis and in African Americans as a result of hypertension. Stroke also occurs in younger patients as a result of aneurysm, hypertension, the use of some birth control pills, and drug abuse (cocaine in particular). The clinical manifestations of stroke and outcomes for the patient vary, depending on the area of the brain affected. A stroke in the nondominant hemisphere often causes spatial-perceptual deficits, changes in judgment and behavior, and unilateral neglect. A stroke in the dominant right hemisphere typically causes dysphasia, dysarthria, left-sided sensory loss and homonymous hemianopsia, a decreased awareness of the left side of the body, left-sided paralysis and/or paresis, apraxia, impaired judgment, increased emotional lability, and deficits in handling new spatial information. A stroke in the dominant left hemisphere can cause repetitive or expressive dysphasia, dysarthria,

■ = Independent; ▲ = Collaborative

Cerebrovascular Accident (CVA)—cont'd

right-sided sensory loss and homonymous hemianopsia, right-sided paralysis and/or paresis, increased emotional lability, and a deficit in handling new language information. There is typically intact judgment, infrequent apraxia, and usually a normal awareness of both sides of the body. This care plan focuses on acute care, maintenance of vital functions, prevention of complications, and the initiation of rehabilitation in the hospital.

ND Nursing Diagnosis

Impaired Physical Mobility

Common Related Factors

Intracranial hemorrhage
Ischemic (embolism or thrombosis)

Defining Characteristics

Headache
Vertigo
Visual changes
Dizziness
Ataxia
Motor deficits
Paresthesias
Hemorrhage: rapid onset, occurs during activity
- Seizure activity
- Coma
- Bloody cerebrospinal fluid (CSF) (unless intra-cerebral)
- Positive radiological findings

Thrombosis: gradual onset, occurs at rest
- Conscious
- Seizures rare
- Normal CSF
- Positive radiological findings

Embolus: sudden onset, unrelated to activity
- Conscious
- Seizures, rare
- Normal CSF
- Negative radiological findings

Common Expected Outcome

Cerebral perfusion pressure will be maintained.

NOC Outcomes

Tissue Perfusion: Cerebral; Neurological Status; Blood Coagulation; Medication Response

NIC Interventions

Cerebral Perfusion Promotion; Neurological Monitoring; Medication Administration

■ = Independent; ▲ = Collaborative

Ongoing Assessment

Actions/Interventions	Rationale
■ Monitor and record neurological status (serially) using Glasgow Coma Scale.	This information is used to determine the effects of stroke and prevent life-threatening complications such as severe hypertension and increased intracranial pressure (ICP). Specific neurological changes can help identify the specific location of the stroke.
■ Assess past history of systemic problems: previous cardiac disease, hypertension, smoking, previous pulmonary disease.	Cardiac workup is warranted if stroke is embolic; atrial fibrillation is a major cause of embolic stroke. Hypertension seems to be related to hemorrhagic stroke. Atherosclerosis and transient ischemic attacks are associated with thrombotic stroke.
■ Monitor vital signs as needed.	Frequent assessment of blood pressure (BP) is essential. A normotensive state is desired to promote effective cerebral perfusion pressure.
▲ Monitor baseline electrocardiogram and observe for changes.	Stroke can produce cardiac electrical changes and dysrhythmias.
■ Monitor intake and output and urine specific gravity.	Because of cerebral edema, fluid balance must be regulated. Fluids may be restricted if the patient has significant increase in ICP, or volume expanders may be used if the patient is hypotensive with decreased cerebral perfusion.
▲ Monitor arterial blood gases and/or pulse oximetry.	Pulse oximetry should be 90% or greater for adequate cerebral oxygenation.

Therapeutic Interventions

Actions/Interventions	Rationale
■ Raise head of bed no higher than 30 degrees.	Current evidence suggests that elevating the head of bed reduces ICP. This position may also reduce cerebral perfusion and contribute to increased risk for cerebral infarction.
■ Keep the patient's head and neck in neutral position.	This position promotes venous drainage from the brain and decreases ICP.
■ Avoid unnecessary care activities.	Frequent stimulation of the patient increases brain activity and ICP. Clustering care activities in a short period of time also increases ICP.
▲ Control body temperature: administer antipyretics, initiate topical cooling methods, administer hypothalamic depressants, as prescribed.	Controlling fever reduces metabolic demands of the brain. Fever may be a result of hypothalamic irritation or infection (bladder or respiratory).
▲ Maintain volume status by replacing or restricting fluids, as prescribed.	Fluid balance will be adjusted to reduce cerebral edema and prevent a hypercoagulable state.
▲ Administer the following medications:	
• Hyperosmotics	These decrease ICP.
• Antihypertensives	These control severe hypertension and reduce risk for further bleeding in hemorrhagic stroke.
• Corticosteroids	These control intracranial inflammation.
• Anticoagulants and/or thrombolytics	These decrease risk of further stroke. Tissue plasminogen factor is the first drug of choice in acute ischemic stroke. The use of heparin is not recommended for acute stroke.

Cerebrovascular Accident (CVA)

■ = Independent; ▲ = Collaborative

Cerebrovascular Accident (CVA)—cont'd

 Nursing Diagnosis

Risk for Ineffective Airway Clearance

Common Risk Factors

Neurological dysfunction
Obstruction
Secretions

Common Expected Outcome

Patient maintains patent airway as evidenced by respiratory rate, rhythm, and lung sounds within normal limits.

NOC Outcome
Respiratory Status: Airway Patency

NIC Intervention
Airway Management

Ongoing Assessment

Actions/Interventions

- Monitor respiratory rate and rhythm, lung sounds, and ability to handle secretions.
- Check presence of gag reflex.

- Observe for evidence of respiratory distress that may result from pulmonary edema: patient complaints, cyanosis, restlessness, shortness of breath.

Rationale

A stroke in evolution may cause neurological deterioration, including respiratory dysfunction.

Brainstem strokes may diminish cranial nerve function. Oral feeding should not be attempted if gag reflex is absent to prevent aspiration and obstruction of the airway. When the patient is able to participate, consult speech or occupational therapist to initiate "swallow" exercises.

The use of volume expanders to promote cerebral perfusion can also cause pulmonary edema.

Therapeutic Interventions

Actions/Interventions

- Position the patient upright. Monitor ICP and BP during position changes.
- If the patient is comatose, use an oropharyngeal airway.

- Change position of patient every 2 to 4 hours. Encourage deep breathing, coughing, and use of incentive spirometer (if able); add humidity to environment.

Rationale

This reduces the work of breathing.

This keeps the tongue from obstructing the airway. Cranial nerve involvement (hypoglossal nerve) may cause unilateral weakness and tongue deviation.

Positioning prevents pooling of secretions. Older persons are most susceptible to atelectasis and pneumonia.

Neurological Care Plans

■ = Independent; ▲ = Collaborative

Actions/Interventions

▲ Provide respiratory support:
- Administer supplemental oxygen.

- Provide endotracheal or tracheal care if warranted.

- Avoid respiratory measures that increase ICP, such as frequent suctioning, but keep in mind that a patent airway is first priority.

Rationale

This reduces hypoxemia, which can cause cerebral vasodilation and increased ICP.

The patient in a coma after 48 hours may require intubation.

Frequent airway suctioning can decrease oxygen saturation and increase ICP.

NDx Nursing Diagnosis

Impaired Physical Mobility

Common Related Factors

Paresis or paralysis
Loss of balance and coordination
Increased muscle tone

Defining Characteristics

Inability to move purposefully within physical environment
Limited range of motion
Decreased muscle strength, control, and/or mass

Common Expected Outcome

Patient maintains maximum level of function and risk of complications is reduced.

NOC Outcomes
Mobility; Body Positioning: Self-Initiated; Transfer Performance; Ambulation

NIC Intervention
Exercise Therapy: Muscle Control

Ongoing Assessment

Actions/Interventions

■ Assess degree of weakness in both upper and lower extremities.
■ Assess ability: to move and change position, to transfer and walk, for fine muscle movement, and for gross muscle movements.
■ Determine active and passive range-of-motion (ROM) capabilities.
■ Observe for activities or situations that increase or decrease tone.
■ Monitor skin integrity for areas of blanching or redness as signs of potential breakdown.

Rationale

There may be differing degrees of involvement on the affected side.

Paralysis, paresis, and sensory loss are contralateral to the side of the brain affected by the stroke.

Initially muscles demonstrate hyporeflexia, which later progresses to hyperreflexia.

Activities that cause spastic response can be postponed until later in recovery.

Impaired mobility increases the risk for skin breakdown.

Cerebrovascular Accident (CVA)

■ = Independent; ▲ = Collaborative

Cerebrovascular Accident (CVA)—cont'd

Therapeutic Interventions

Actions/Interventions	Rationale
■ Change position of patient at least every 2 hours, keeping track of position changes with a turning schedule.	Patients may not feel increases in pressure or have the ability to adjust position. Loss of motor control can contribute to abnormal posturing.
■ Perform active and passive ROM exercises in all extremities several times daily.	This preserves muscle strength and prevents contractures, especially in spastic extremities.
■ Increase functional activities as strength improves and the patient is medically stable.	Early mobilization and ROM exercises should begin as soon as the patient is stable and no longer requires intensive care.
■ Teach the patient and family exercises and transfer techniques.	Once medically stable, the patient may have continuing deficits such as altered perception and motor strength. Exercise will increase strength, promote use of the affected side, and promote transfer safety.
■ Use pressure-relieving devices on the bed and chair.	This decreases risk of pressure ulcer development.
■ Initiate rehabilitation techniques in the hospital setting as soon as medically possible.	This prevents further systemic deterioration and facilitates transition to rehabilitation.

For balance and coordination problems:

Actions/Interventions	Rationale
■ Assist the patient in performing movements or tasks. Begin with tasks that require a small range of movements and encourage control (e.g., sitting upright and maintaining balance).	Tremors make fine motor control more difficult.
■ Encourage focusing on proximal muscle control initially and then distal muscle control, such as beginning with limb positioning and progressing to self-feeding and writing.	Larger muscle groups are easier to focus on and control.
■ Ensure that the center of gravity is over the pelvis or equally distributed over stance for sitting and standing activities; provide a safe environment for these activities.	Patients may have impaired righting reflexes and wide base stance. Spatial deficits make it difficult for patients to determine their position in space.
■ Teach the patient and family exercises and techniques to improve balance and coordination.	Support from significant others will encourage compliance and success.
■ Reinforce safety precautions with the patient and family.	Spatial deficits, impaired judgment, and loss of motor function increase the patient's risk for falls, perceptual accidents (bumping into things), wandering, and impulsive behavior.

For increased muscle tone (spasticity):

Actions/Interventions	Rationale
■ Perform activities in a quiet environment with few distractions.	Impaired cognitive function that occurs with stroke may decrease the patient's attention span and concentration. The patient may be easily distracted.
■ Apply heat or cold to the extremities.	This is an effort to reduce tone before initiating movement.
■ Perform muscle stretching activities in gentle, rhythmical motions.	These provide input into the central nervous system.
▲ Apply splinting devices to spastic extremities as prescribed, with ongoing assessment for increasing tone.	Devices are used to prevent muscle shortening that occurs with chronic flexion.

■ = Independent; ▲ = Collaborative

Neurological Care Plans

Actions/Interventions

- Instruct the family in concepts of spasticity and ways to reduce tone.

Rationale

Spasticity is a sign of improvement. Muscles that remain flaccid are not likely to recover. Spasticity will gradually diminish as control of muscles is regained. As spasticity decreases, a phenomenon known as *synergy* often occurs. This is the *involuntary* movement of part of an extremity after an initial *voluntary* movement of the whole extremity.

NDx Nursing Diagnosis

Risk for Impaired Verbal Communication

Common Risk Factor

Left brain hemisphere stroke

Common Expected Outcomes

Patient effectively communicates basic needs.
Patient maximizes remaining communication ability.
Patient and family verbalize understanding of communication impairment.
Patient and family are involved in measures to promote communication.

NOC Outcome
Communication Ability

NIC Intervention
Communication Enhancement: Speech Deficit

Ongoing Assessment

Actions/Interventions

- Assess speech-language history: determine primary language; ability to read, write, and understand spoken language; level of education.
- Assess speech-language function: automatic speech, auditory comprehension, comprehension of written language, expressive ability, ability to write.

Rationale

These data provide a baseline for developing an individualized teaching plan.

Depending on the area of brain involvement, patients may experience dysphasia (receptive or expressive), dysarthria, or both. Receptive dysphasics cannot understand the spoken word. Expressive dysphasics cannot use written symbols.

Therapeutic Interventions

Actions/Interventions

- Approach the patient as an adult.
- Enhance the environment.

Rationale

Inability to express needs or feelings is most distressing to patients. The staff needs to be sensitive to the dignity of the patient.

Communication can be facilitated and distractions minimized by turning off the television or radio, or by closing the door.

Cerebrovascular Accident (CVA)

■ = Independent; ▲ = Collaborative

Cerebrovascular Accident (CVA)—cont'd

Actions/Interventions	Rationale
■ Provide clear, simple directions.	The patient with dysphasia requires directions to be repeated frequently. Tasks need to be explained in very simple steps and presented one at a time.
■ Incorporate multimodality input, such as music, song, and visual demonstration.	These enhance function in intact speech-language areas.
■ Use written materials (if appropriate).	These supplement auditory input (e.g., communication board with pictures, numbers, words, and/or alphabet). If the patient has homonymous hemianopsia, place material in the unaffected field of vision. Homonymous hemianopsia affects the field of vision in both eyes, opposite the side of the brain affected by stroke.
■ Use prompting cues, such as gestures or holding an object that is being discussed.	Visual cueing can enhance the patient's understanding of verbal messages.
■ Allow adequate time for patient response.	If the patient feels rushed, communication problems are worsened. The patient needs more time to cognitively process information and formulate a verbal response.
■ Provide opportunities for spontaneous conversation.	This provides the patient a chance to talk without the expectation of a desired outcome (decreases anxiety about abilities).
■ Anticipate the patient's needs until alternative means of communication can be established.	The nurse should plan enough time to attend to all the details of patient care. Care measures may take longer to complete in the presence of a communication deficit.
■ Provide reality orientation and focus attention, but avoid constantly correcting errors.	Constant correction increases frustration, anxiety, and anger.
▲ Collaborate with a speech-language pathologist.	A comprehensive multidisciplinary plan of care may be required.
■ Encourage the family to attempt communication with the patient; explain type of dysphasia and methods of communication that can be tried.	Consistency of approach by professional caregivers and family members promotes more effective communication for the patient.
■ Demonstrate to the patient any progress made.	This increases confidence and facilitates ongoing efforts.

NDx Nursing Diagnosis

Risk for Disturbed Sensory Perception (Tactile)

Common Risk Factor

Stroke within the sensory transmission and/or integration pathways of the brain

Common Expected Outcomes

Patient and family demonstrate skill in therapeutic interventions.

Patient's skin remains free of injuries, including pressure ulcers.

NOC Outcomes
Risk Detection; Risk Control

NIC Intervention
Peripheral Sensation Management

Ongoing Assessment

Actions/Interventions

- Assess the patient's ability to sense light touch, pinprick, and temperature. Touch skin lightly with a pin, cotton ball, or hot/cold object and ask him or her to describe the sensation and point to where the touch occurred.

- Using the patient's toes or fingers, assess position sense (ability to sense whether the joint is moved in an upward or downward position).

Rationale

This determines the level of alteration and identifies specific areas of risk. Tactile deficits increase risk for injury related to the patient's inability to sense pain or temperature.

Loss of position sense occurs in patients with strokes affecting the anterior cerebral artery, basilar artery, and posterior cerebral artery. Spatial-perceptual deficits increase the patient's risk for injury.

Therapeutic Interventions

Actions/Interventions

- Perform regular skin inspections and instruct the patient in techniques to do the same. Explain consequences of prolonged pressure on the skin.

- Provide tactile stimulation to affected limbs using rough cloth or hand, and instruct the patient or family in methods used.

- Explain how a stimulus might feel (e.g., cool water, soft flannel).

- Teach the patient to check temperature of water with unaffected side before using water (thermal screening).

- Instruct the patient to regularly move affected limbs.

- Enhance the immediate and home environments.

▲ Facilitate referral to a rehabilitation or occupational therapist to learn compensatory skills.

Rationale

Pressure on the affected side should last no longer than 30 minutes. Inability to sense pressure increases risk for skin breakdown.

This helps patients learn to recognize sensations.

This improves patient understanding.

Diminished temperature sensation, especially for heat, increases the risk for accidental burn injury.

Movement promotes circulation. Impaired sensitivity to pain or numbness increases the likelihood of prolonged stationary positioning.

Optimal safety can be achieved by modification in the environment, by regulating the temperature setting on the hot water heater, by moving sharp-edged furniture, and by lighting hallways.

Patients and caregivers need to learn adaptive skills to reduce risk for injury.

Cerebrovascular Accident (CVA)

■ = Independent; ▲ = Collaborative

Cerebrovascular Accident (CVA)—cont'd

 Nursing Diagnosis

Risk for Unilateral Neglect

Common Risk Factor

Stroke in the nondominant hemisphere or the dominant right side

Common Expected Outcomes

Patient incurs no injuries as a result of deficit.
Patient can cross midline with eyes and unaffected arm.
Patient observes and touches affected side during ADLs.
Patient begins to wash, dress, and eat with attention to both sides.
Patient and family verbalize cognitive awareness of deficit.

NOC Outcomes
Body Positioning: Self-Initiated; Self-Care: Activities of Daily Living (ADL); Safety Behavior: Personal

NIC Intervention
Unilateral Neglect Management

Ongoing Assessment

Actions/Interventions	Rationale
■ Conduct sensory assessment.	This determines the actual level of sensation for comparison with how the patient uses the senses on the affected side. Use may be different from actual ability.
■ Perform visual fields confrontation test.	The patient may not be able to see on the affected side (hemianopsia). The patient who complains of diplopia may benefit from patching one eye.
■ Observe the patient's performance of ADLs.	This provides information on the patient's recognition of the affected side. The patient may not, for example, bathe the affected side, forgetting that it is there.
■ Assess for distorted spatial relationships.	Impaired spatial awareness and proprioception interferes with the patient's awareness of the affected side of the body.
■ Observe for remark of denial of body parts (anosognosia).	Anosognosia occurs with injury to the parietal lobe in the nondominant hemisphere. The patient is unable to recognize the contralateral side of the body, even if visual fields are intact.
■ Have the patient point to various body parts (somatagnosia).	The patient may not recognize body parts on the affected side.

Therapeutic Interventions

Actions/Interventions	Rationale
■ Approach the patient from the unaffected side when the patient initially regains consciousness.	This decreases anxiety and fear while the patient is unable to interpret the whole environment.

■ = Independent; ▲ = Collaborative

Neurological Care Plans

Actions/Interventions	**Rationale**
■ As the patient becomes more alert, approach from the affected side while calling the patient's name during the rehabilitation phase.	This will encourage the patient to use the affected side of the body.
■ Ensure a safe environment by placing a call bell on the patient's unaffected side.	Hemianopsia limits the patient's ability to see objects in the affected visual field. If the patient cannot find the call light, he or she may attempt to get up without assistance. This behavior increases the risk for falls.
■ Provide tactile stimulation to the affected side.	This stimulates short-term memory of sensation.
■ Place all food in small quantities, arranged simply on a plate.	This approach diminishes spatial/visual deficits. Small quantities make it easier to delineate foods because of the space between food items.
■ Attach a watch or bright bracelet to the affected arm.	This draws the patient's attention to the affected side.
■ Encourage the patient to wash the affected side of the body and to dress the affected side of the body first.	This approach to ADLs increases the patient's awareness of the affected side of the body. Increased tactile and visual awareness of the affected side promotes neural perception and integration of external stimuli.
■ Practice drawing and copying figures with the patient.	This helps develop fine motor skills and relearn spatial relationships.
■ Draw a bright mark on the sides of a newspaper or book when the patient is reading.	This cues the end of a line and the return for next line.
■ Teach compensatory strategies such as visual scanning (turning head in order to visualize entire area).	This reduces chance of injury and increases visual awareness of entire field of vision.
▲ Initiate physical therapy or occupational therapy consults.	Physical and occupational therapists can help the patient learn adaptive skills to promote increased self-care and decrease risk for injury.

NDx Nursing Diagnosis

Deficient Knowledge

Common Related Factors
Unfamiliar with diagnosis
Unfamiliar with risk factors
Required rehabilitation

Defining Characteristics
Questions about diagnosis and outcomes
Concerns about follow-up

Common Expected Outcome
Patient and/or caregivers verbalize understanding of disease process and potential outcomes.

NOC Outcomes
Knowledge: Disease Process; Knowledge: Treatment Regimen; Knowledge: Medication; Knowledge: Personal Safety

NIC Intervention
Teaching: Disease Process, Prescribed Activity/Exercise

Cerebrovascular Accident (CVA)

■ = Independent; ▲ = Collaborative

 **Cerebrovascular Accident (CVA)—cont'd**

Ongoing Assessment

Actions/Interventions

- Determine stroke-related deficits that may affect learning: emotional lability, loss of self-control, communication deficits, and cognitive changes.

- Assess the patient's perception of the diagnosis and care needs.

- Determine readiness and ability to learn.

- Prepare the patient and family for possible changes in patient behavior and judgment.

- Determine counseling and social service needs.

Rationale

Each stroke patient has different deficits and must be treated as an individual.

Patients are more receptive to learning if their own identified needs and goals are being met.

The teaching plan will be individualized based on the patient's ability to comprehend and remember new information.

These occur more often in stroke of the nondominant hemisphere. Patients may experience mood changes and depression within 6 months of the initial stroke injury. Emotional lability may continue for several months.

Some patients may not be ready to accept disability and will not want to learn. Further counseling may be necessary, as may be social services involvement to help facilitate care outside the hospital.

Therapeutic Interventions

Actions/Interventions

- Discuss type of stroke, progress, treatments, and preventive measures.

- Include the caregiver in the rehabilitation process to learn and assist with care, as well as to provide emotional support for the patient's efforts.

- Assist the spouse or family in obtaining the support they need.

- List risk factors for repeated stroke, including mechanism and possible preventive measures. Risk factors include hypertension, heart disease, smoking, polycythemia, alcohol use, obesity, hypercholesterolemia, diabetes mellitus, and sedentary lifestyle.

- Teach strategies for handling ADLs, safety, and swallowing difficulties.

- Provide education concerning long-term medication use, such as of aspirin or warfarin therapy.

Rationale

Explaining physical and mental changes that occur with stroke helps reduce anxiety and limit the onset of depression. Knowing what to expect during stroke recovery promotes effective coping and the motivation to participate in the rehabilitation process.

Almost all stroke victims will have some degree of disability and will require assistance and emotional support. Family members need to understand how a stroke may influence their social and personal roles and activities.

Stroke victims are often older persons whose disabilities may be overwhelming to an equally elderly or frail spouse. The responsibility of caregiving can increase fear and stress for the family member.

Knowing the risk factors is the first step in controlling them and decreasing the chance of further stroke.

These encourage independence and reduce frustration.

This increases knowledge and prevents potential over-the-counter medication errors.

■ = Independent; ▲ = Collaborative

Actions/Interventions

■ Encourage the use of community resources and support groups.

Rationale

The family needs information about how community resources can promote effective coping and decrease feelings of caregiving as a burden.

> **• RELATED CARE PLANS**
>
> Anxiety, p. 15
> Constipation, p. 46
> Decreased intracranial adaptive capacity, p. 112
> Disturbed thought processes, p. 189
> Imbalanced nutrition: less than body requirements, p. 134
> Ineffective coping, p. 51
> Ineffective sexuality patterns, p. 170
> Risk for aspiration, p. 18
> Risk for impaired skin integrity, p. 173
> Self-care deficit, p. 156
> Situational low self-esteem, p. 161

Craniotomy

Craniectomy; Burr Hole; Cranioplasty

Craniotomy is the surgical opening of the cranium to gain access to disease or injury affecting the brain, ventricles, or intracranial blood vessels. Craniectomy is removal of part of the cranium to treat compound fractures, infection, or decompression. Burr holes are drilled in the cranium and used for clot evacuation and decompression of fluid beneath the dura or in preparation for craniotomy. Cranioplasty is the application of artificial material to repair the skull to improve integrity and shape. Cranial surgery is either supratentorial—above the tentorium, involving the cerebellum; or infratentorial—below the tentorium, involving the brainstem or cerebrum. Care decisions are often based on surgical location.

 Nursing Diagnosis

Decreased Intracranial Adaptive Capacity

Common Related Factors	Defining Characteristics
Brain injury	Changed level of consciousness (LOC)
Cerebral edema, intracranial bleeding	Changed pupillary size, reaction to light, deviation
Cerebral ischemia or infarction	Focal or generalized motor weakness
Increased intracranial pressure (ICP)	Presence of pathological reflexes (Babinski)
Metabolic abnormalities	Seizures
Hydrocephalus	Increased blood pressure (BP) and bradycardia
Systemic hypotension	Changed respiratory pattern

Craniotomy

■ = Independent; ▲ = Collaborative

Craniotomy—cont'd

Defining Characteristics—cont'd

Repeated increases in ICP greater than 10 mm Hg for longer than 5 minutes
Disproportionate increase in ICP after a nursing activity
Elevated P_2 ICP waveform
Baseline ICP greater than 10 mm Hg
Wide amplitude ICP waveform

Common Expected Outcome

Optimal cerebral perfusion is maintained, as evidenced by Glasgow Coma Scale (GCS) score greater than 13, absence of new neurological deficit, and ICP of 10 mm Hg or less.

NOC Outcomes
Fluid Balance; Neurological Status; Electrolyte and Acid-Base Balance

NIC Interventions
ICP Monitoring; Neurological Monitoring; Cerebral Edema Management

Ongoing Assessment

Actions/Interventions

- Assess and document baseline level of consciousness: pupillary size, symmetry, reaction to light; motor movement and strength of limbs; and vital signs.

- Use the GCS to compare serial assessments. Report any deviations.

- Evaluate contributing factors to change in responsiveness; reevaluate in 5 to 10 minutes to see whether change persists.

- Check head dressing for presence of drains.

- Evaluate function of catheter used to monitor ICP. Analyze monitored values.

▲ Monitor serum glucose, osmolarity, complete blood count (CBC), electrolytes, and arterial blood gases. Report the following:
  • PO_2 less than 80 mm Hg

Rationale

Early detection of changes is necessary to prevent permanent neurological dysfunction. Cerebral edema occurs for 24 to 72 hours postoperatively.

Worrisome early signs include change in LOC, pupillary asymmetry, blurred vision, diplopia, new focal deficits, respiratory changes, speech changes, increased complaint of headache, yawning, or hiccuping. Increased BP, one fixed and dilated pupil, and bradycardia are late signs usually associated with medullary ischemia or compression. Herniation will occur if edema is not managed.

Factors such as anesthesia, medications, awakening from sound sleep, or not understanding a question can affect responsiveness.

Intraventricular drains and self-contained bulb suction and drainage systems are most commonly used. All drains and catheters should be secured to the patient or bed to prevent falls to floor, negative-gravity suctioning, and increased risk of bleeding or dislodging the drain.

An ICP monitor is usually in place for 24 to 72 hours postoperatively. Elevated P_2 waves, ICP greater than 10 mm Hg, and wide-amplitude waveforms indicate increasing ICP.

Fluid and electrolyte management is essential to maintaining cerebral perfusion. As part of the autoregulatory response, if PO_2 falls, PCO_2 increases and acidosis occurs, both causing vasodilation and increasing ICP.

■ = Independent; ▲ = Collaborative

Neurological Care Plans

Actions/Interventions

- PCO_2 greater than 45 mm Hg
- CBC: hematocrit less than 30%
- Electrolytes: sodium less than 130 or greater than 150 mEq/L
- Glucose less than 80 or greater than 200 mg/dL
- Osmolarities less than 185 or greater than 310 mOsm/L
- Report temperature greater than 39° C (102.2° F)

Rationale

Decreasing serum osmolarity indicates increasing edema. Additional signs such as anxiety; moist respirations; cold, clammy skin; cyanosis; or mucus or blood expectoration are indicative of neurogenic pulmonary edema. This life-threatening complication is a pressor response to sudden severe increase in ICP.

Therapeutic Interventions

Actions/Interventions

▲ Apply tepid sponge in bath or antipyretics (use acetaminophen, not aspirin, to avoid gastric irritation and bleeding) or hypothermia blanket as ordered. Turn blanket off at temperature of less than 38° C rectally (100° F).

■ Maintain head of bed (HOB) at 30 degrees unless contraindicated (e.g., if patient is hemodynamically unstable, following insertion of ventricle-peritoneal shunt, following drainage of chronic subdural hematoma, or following infratentorial surgery).

■ Turn the patient onto nonoperative side, with head supported in neutral alignment, every 2 hours. Avoid neck flexion or rotation.

■ Reorient the patient to the environment as needed.

■ Limit direct care activities.

▲ Administer artificial tears (methyl-cellulose drops) every 2 hours. Cover the patient's eyes or tape eyelids closed.

▲ Administer osmotic diuretic and/or corticosteroids, if ordered. Maintain Foley catheter for accurate measurement.

Rationale

This maintains normothermia. Fever may be related to expected postoperative response; dehydration; infection; or surgery near the third and fourth ventricles, hypothalamus, or pons. Shivering will increase metabolic demands, which can affect ICP.

This improves venous drainage and reduces ICP. Keeping the HOB flat will decrease risk of new or recurrent subdural hemorrhage, dizziness, and orthostatic hypotension. The HOB should be raised gradually over 24 hours. Patients who have supratentorial surgery will have the HOB elevated. The bed may be kept flat for a patient who had infratentorial surgery.

This prevents venous outflow obstruction and increased ICP.

Reality orientation reduces anxiety. Increased anxiety can cause increased ICP.

Unnecessary nursing care activities (e.g., routine linen changes, bathing) contribute to increased ICP.

This protects the exposed cornea and prevents dryness. The unconscious patient may have difficulty closing the eyes (cranial nerve VII palsy).

These actions reduce ICP.

NDx Nursing Diagnosis

Risk for Deficient Fluid Volume

Common Risk Factors

Neurogenic diabetes insipidus (DI)
Dehydration secondary to use of hyperosmotic agents, profuse diaphoresis, fluid restriction.

Craniotomy

(■ = Independent; ▲ = Collaborative)

Craniotomy—cont'd

Common Expected Outcome

Optimal fluid volume is maintained as evidenced by normal serum sodium and osmolarity, and urine specific gravity less than 1.025.

NOC Outcomes
Fluid Balance; Medication Response

NIC Interventions
Fluid/Electrolyte Management; Medication Administration

Ongoing Assessment

Actions/Interventions

■ Monitor intake and output with specific attention to fluid volume infused over output. Report urine output greater than 200 mL/hr for 2 consecutive hours.

■ Check urine specific gravity.

▲ Monitor serum and urine electrolytes and osmolality.

■ Assess for signs of dehydration (tachycardia, hypotension, poor skin turgor).

■ Weigh daily if possible.

Rationale

DI occurs when the renal tubules are unable to conserve water. Disruption of the neurohypophyseal system during surgery decreases production and release of antidiuretic hormone (ADH).

Specific gravity is decreased to less than 1.005 with DI. Supratentorial surgery (near the pituitary fossa) can cause temporary DI. A decrease in ADH secretion seems to be a common response to irritation at this site.

DI results in hypernatremia (>135 mEq/L), increased serum osmolality (>295 mOsm/kg), decreased urine sodium, and decreased urine osmolality (<400 mOsm/kg).

The patient with DI will complain of unquenchable thirst and a preference for ice water or other cold beverages. Decreased circulatory volume causes hypotension and a compensatory tachycardia.

DI causes weight loss because of fluid loss.

Therapeutic Interventions

Actions/Interventions

▲ Replace fluid output as directed.

▲ Administer vasopressin as prescribed.

■ Monitor for signs of myocardial ischemia.

Rationale

The patient who is alert can respond to thirst and increase oral fluid intake. Intravenous (IV) fluids may be indicated to replace fluids lost with polyuria and to prevent dehydration.

Vasopressin is ADH replacement. The drug is administered intravenously or subcutaneously. The onset of action is within 1 to 2 hours with duration of 3 to 6 hours.

Vasopressin can have vasopressor effects that increase risk for myocardial ischemia as an adverse reaction.

■ = Independent; ▲ = Collaborative

Neurological Care Plans

Nursing Diagnosis

Risk for Excess Fluid Volume

Common Risk Factor

Syndrome of inappropriate antidiuretic hormone secretion (SIADH)

Common Expected Outcome

Patient maintains optimal fluid balance, as evidenced by normal serum sodium, normal osmolarity, and urine specific gravity greater than 1.005.

NOC Outcomes
Fluid Balance; Electrolyte and Acid-Base Balance

NIC Intervention
Fluid/Electrolyte Management

Ongoing Assessment

Actions/Interventions

▲ Monitor serum and urine electrolytes and osmolarity (at least every 6 hours if IV saline is being administered).

■ Monitor intake and output, daily weight.

■ Assess for signs of confusion, headache, fatigue, vomiting, muscle twitching, or seizures.

Rationale

These tests provide information on fluid volume excess (usually determined by hyponatremia and lowering of serum osmolarity). SIADH occurs from persistently high levels of circulating ADH. The secretion of ADH is no longer regulated by changes in plasma osmolality.

Urine output will be significantly less than fluid intake. Urine volume may be less than 30 to 40 mL/hr. Weight gain occurs in SIADH without signs of peripheral edema.

These clinical manifestations are associated with hyponatremia. SIADH may cause cerebral edema and increased ICP.

Therapeutic Interventions

Actions/Interventions

▲ Restrict oral or IV fluids as ordered. In a patient with a nasogastric tube and feedings, normal saline solution can be used for flush after feedings.

▲ If fluid restriction fails to correct hyponatremia, anticipate orders for a 3% IV saline solution with the concurrent use of potassium and IV furosemide (Lasix).

Rationale

Fluid restriction of 1 to 1.2 L/day usually corrects hyponatremia associated with SIADH. Intravenous D_5W is inappropriate because of excess free water and should not be used for piggyback medications.

Administration of a hypertonic solution may cause cardiac problems from further fluid overload. Furosemide promotes diuresis. Potassium supplementation corrects diuretic-induced potassium excretion. Rapid administration of hypertonic saline may cause demyelination of the pons with permanent brainstem dysfunction.

Craniotomy

■ = Independent; ▲ = Collaborative

Craniotomy—cont'd

 Nursing Diagnosis

Risk for Injury: Seizures

Common Risk Factors

Intracranial bleeding
Infarction
Tumor
Trauma

Common Expected Outcomes

Patient's risk for seizures is reduced as a result of prophylaxis.
Risk of injury during seizures is reduced due to maintenance of seizure precautions.

> **NOC Outcomes**
> Risk Control; Risk Detection;
>   Safety Status: Physical Injury;
>   Medication Response
>
> **NIC Intervention**
> Seizure Precautions/Management

Ongoing Assessment

Actions/Interventions

■ Observe for seizure activity. Record and report the following observations:
  • Note time and signs of seizures.
  • Observe body parts involved: order of involvement and character of movement.
  • Check deviation of eyes; note change in pupillary size.
  • Assess for incontinence.
  • Note duration of seizure.
  • Note tonic-clonic stages.
  • Assess postictal state (e.g., loss of consciousness, loss of airway).

■ Monitor for signs of airway obstruction.

Rationale

A record of activity will determine seizure type. Postoperative seizure activity may occur as a result of neuronal injury from decreased cerebral perfusion pressure. Hyponatremia from SIADH may precipitate seizure activity.

Loss of motor control during a seizure can compromise the airway if the tongue falls back into the upper airway.

Therapeutic Interventions

Actions/Interventions

▲ Administer anticonvulsants preoperatively.

Rationale

These drugs are given to patients considered at high risk for seizures, such as those with lesions near the motor cortex.

■ = Independent; ▲ = Collaborative

Actions/Interventions

- Keep bed in low position.
- Keep padded side rails up.

- Maintain minimal environmental stimuli: noise reduction, curtains closed, private room (when available or advisable), dim lights.
- If seizure occurs, remain with patient, do not attempt to introduce anything into the mouth during the seizure. Maintain airway. Turn patient on side, suction, and administer oxygen if needed.
- ▲ Administer anticonvulsants as indicated.

Rationale

This maintains patient safety.

This measure reduces risk of injury during tonic-clonic seizure activity.

During the postictal phase of a seizure, the patient may be disoriented.

Inserting objects could result in increased risk of aspiration, broken teeth, or soft tissue injury.

When phenytoin is given intravenously it should be administered in normal saline. It will precipitate in any dextrose solution. Infuse no faster than 50 mg/min to prevent hypotension. IV diazepam (Valium) is often used to control recurrent seizures and should not be administered any faster than 10 mg/min to prevent respiratory compromise. Valium is short-acting.

NDx Nursing Diagnosis

Deficient Knowledge

Common Related Factor

New procedure and treatments

Common Expected Outcome

Patient and significant others verbalize understanding of diagnosis, surgical procedure, and expected results.

Defining Characteristic

Patient and significant others verbalize questions and concerns.

NOC Outcomes
Knowledge: Disease Process;
Knowledge: Treatment Regimen

NIC Intervention
Teaching: Procedure/Treatment

Ongoing Assessment

Actions/Interventions

- Assess the patient's or significant others' knowledge regarding surgery and postoperative expectations.

Rationale

The patient may have cognitive impairment that limits his or her ability to understand explanations. The family may need more detailed explanations. They may have misperceptions about the outcomes of surgery.

Craniotomy

■ = Independent; ▲ = Collaborative

Craniotomy—cont'd

Actions/Interventions

■ Assess readiness for learning.

Rationale

The patient's and caregiver's readiness will be affected by the situation. A planned surgical intervention can usually allow for more structured patient preparation as compared with an emergent surgical event following a trauma.

Therapeutic Interventions

Actions/Interventions

■ Discuss care issues with the patient and family. Include the following:
  • Deep breathing
  • Need for monitoring equipment and frequent assessments

  • Change in body image related to head dressing, loss, and regrowth of hair at the surgical site, potential for and duration of facial edema

  • Wound care after the dressing is removed: antiseptic cleanser and antibiotic ointment
  • Long-term medications such as corticosteroids, anticonvulsants, antibiotics
■ Encourage caregivers to participate in patient reorientation postoperatively.
■ Before discharge, discuss protecting the scalp and head from cold, sun, and injury.

▲ Obtain social work and/or case management assistance in transitioning the patient to a rehabilitation facility or home.

Rationale

Information helps the patient and family cooperate with the treatment plan.

Knowledge about equipment used postoperatively can reduce anxiety.

The edema usually peaks about 3 days after surgery and then gradually diminishes. Patients and families need information about the short-term duration of most of these changes.

These prevent wound infection.

These reduce or prevent edema, seizure, and infection.

Family participation in postoperative care can reduce patient anxiety.

Protective garments should be worn until completely healed and hair has regrown. If the patient has had only burr holes, these will heal relatively quickly with the bone regenerating and filling in the holes. A patient who has had a craniectomy (removal of a piece of the skull) will need greater protection from injury to the uncovered area of brain. Large pieces of the skull will not sufficiently regenerate. Plastic surgery can be done in many cases (depending on the primary diagnosis) to restructure the shape of the skull after craniectomy.

Depending on the patient's age, primary diagnosis, and level of function postoperatively, the patient may require rehabilitation or home care services.

> • RELATED CARE PLANS
>
> Diabetes insipidus (see the **Evolve** website)
> Syndrome of inappropriate antidiuretic
>   hormone, p. 1072

■ = Independent; ▲ = Collaborative

Neurological Care Plans

Head Trauma

Blunt Trauma; Closed Trauma; Skull Fracture; Subdural Hematoma; Concussion

Head injury (craniocerebral trauma) is the leading cause of death in the United States for persons 1 to 42 years of age. An estimated 3 million people suffer head injuries every year. About two thirds of all severe head injuries result from motor vehicle crashes. Death and injury rates are increasing as a result of firearm usage. The severity of the head injury is defined by the traumatic coma data bank on the basis of the Glasgow Coma Scale (GCS): Severe head injury = GCS of 8 or less; moderate head injury = GCS of 9 to 12. Most head injuries are blunt (closed) trauma to the brain. Damage to the scalp, skull, meninges, and brain runs the gamut of skull fracture with loss of consciousness, concussion, and/or extracerebral or intracerebral pathological conditions. Patients with moderate to severe head trauma are usually observed in a critical care unit where immediate intervention can be achieved. Most deaths occur in the first few hours after head trauma as a result of internal bleeding or worsening cerebral edema. Patients with minor head trauma (scalp laceration or concussion) are most often treated and released to be observed at home with instructions to call or return if symptoms worsen. Older persons are most often affected with postconcussion syndrome, characterized by decreased neurological function 2 weeks to 2 months after the initial injury and often caused by a slow subdural bleed. This care plan focuses on moderate-to-severe head trauma in the acute care setting.

Nursing Diagnosis

Decreased Intracranial Adaptive Capacity

Common Related Factors

Cerebral edema
Increased intracranial pressure (ICP)
Decreased cerebral perfusion pressure (CPP)
Impaired autoregulation
Cortical laceration
Intracranial hemorrhage

Defining Characteristics

Decreased level of consciousness (confusion, agitation, inappropriate affect, disorientation, somnolence, lethargy, coma)
Headache
Vomiting
Pupillary asymmetry
Changes in pupillary reaction
ICP greater than 15 mm Hg
CPP less than 60 mm Hg

Common Expected Outcome

Patient maintains optimal cerebral tissue perfusion, as evidenced by GCS greater than 13 and absence of secondary neurological deficit (cerebral ischemia, herniation, hypoxemia).

NOC Outcomes
Fluid Balance; Neurological Status

NIC Interventions
Cerebral Edema Management; Neurological Monitoring; ICP Monitoring

Head Trauma

■ = Independent; ▲ = Collaborative

→ **Head Trauma**—cont'd

Ongoing Assessment

Actions/Interventions	Rationale

Actions/Interventions

- Serially assess and document neurological status as follows:

  - Level of consciousness
  - Orientation to person, place, and time
  - Motor signs: drift, decreased movement, abnormal or absent movement, increased reflexes
  - Pupil size, symmetry, and reaction to light

  - Extraocular movement, deviation

  - Speech, thought processes, and memory changes

- Report deteriorating neurological status immediately.
- Assess for rhinorrhea (cerebrospinal fluid [CSF] drainage from nose), otorrhea (CSF drainage from ear), battle sign (ecchymosis over the mastoid process), raccoon eyes (periorbital ecchymosis).

- Evaluate presence or absence of protective reflexes: corneal, gag, blink, cough, startle, grab, Babinski.

- Monitor vital signs.

▲ Monitor ICP through cranial catheter device. Report ICP greater than 15 mm Hg sustained for more than 5 minutes.
- Calculate the CPP (CPP = Mean systemic arterial pressure – ICP).
▲ Monitor oxygen and carbon dioxide levels through arterial blood gases (ABGs) and/or pulse oximetry.

- Monitor intake and output. Assess urine specific gravity and urine glucose.

Rationale

Consider the patient's age; older adults tend to have more intracranial space, which affects the timing and severity of neurological symptoms.

A GCS score of less than 13 indicates neurological dysfunction and possible damage.

Focal signs of neurological dysfunction suggest structural versus metabolic abnormality.

Pupillary changes indicate an increase in intracranial pressure.

Changes in eye movement and gaze occur with cranial nerve injury.

Impaired cognitive function indicates injury to the cerebral cortex.

Surgical intervention may be necessary.

These signs may indicate frontal, orbital, or basal skull fractures.

These are an indication of increased ICP. Absence of these reflexes indicates disruption of the brainstem. Loss of protective reflexes increases the patient's risk for injury.

Increased blood pressure associated with bradycardia is a late sign of increased ICP that suggests medullary ischemia or compression. Increase in core body temperature in the absence of infection usually indicates hypothalamic damage. Hyperthermia increases metabolic demands and contributes to increased ICP. Changes in breathing patterns occur as compensation for increased ICP or in response to specific patterns of brain injury.

Normal ICP should be below 15 mm Hg with the patient at rest.

CPP should be 80 to 100 mm Hg. There is little or no perfusion if CPP is less than 60 mm Hg.

Normal levels are PO_2 greater than 80 mm Hg and PCO_2 less than 35 mm Hg. Goal of hyperventilation is PCO_2 = 25 mm Hg to 30 mm Hg. Secondary insults such as hypoxia, hypercapnia, and hypotension are significant causes of mortality and morbidity in head injury patients.

The use of hyperosmotics will alter hydration and electrolytes.

■ = Independent; ▲ = Collaborative

Neurological Care Plans

Actions/Interventions

▲ Monitor serum electrolytes, blood urea nitrogen, creatinine, osmolarity, glucose, and hemoglobin and hematocrit.

■ Assess for pain, fever, and shivering.

■ Monitor closely when initiating and titrating treatment.

Rationale

Be aware that hemoconcentration will cause false "normal" hemoglobin levels and hematocrit.

These symptoms increase cerebral blood flow and ICP.

Changes in fluid administration or medication dosages can cause sudden shifts in ICP.

Therapeutic Interventions

Actions/Interventions

■ If ICP is above 15 mm Hg, postpone nursing care activities that can be deferred (e.g., routine care, invasive procedures).

■ Elevate head of bed (HOB) 30 degrees.

■ Position head in neutral position.

■ If patient is intubated, ensure that neck tapes securing the endotracheal (ET) tube are not too tight.

▲ Assist with diagnostic testing (radiograph, computed tomography [CT], and magnetic resonance imaging [MRI]).

■ If restraints are needed, position the patient on the side.

■ Reorient the patient to the environment, and provide familiar objects and pictures.

▲ Administer hyperosmotic agents such as mannitol, as ordered. Infuse mannitol through a filter. Insert a Foley catheter.

■ If neuromuscular blocking agents are used (pancuronium [Pavulon]), remember that cerebration is still intact and that pain is perceived.

■ Avoid neck and hip flexion.

■ Prevent constipation

■ Hyperventilate and hyperoxygenate before suctioning ET tube or trachea.

Rationale

These prevent further ICP increases. Clustering of care in a short period of time is associated with increased ICP.

Raising the HOB minimizes cerebral edema by promoting venous blood flow from the brain.

This promotes venous drainage.

Tight tape impedes jugular venous outflow.

This ensures safe head positioning, continued monitoring, and maintenance of stable ICP. Diagnostic evaluation is necessary to determine the exact location of brain injury.

Restraints should be used judiciously, because they may increase agitation and anxiety, which will increase ICP. Restraints should be used only if continuous observation is not available to prevent the patient from removing therapeutic equipment such as airways and ICP monitoring lines.

These measures decrease anxiety and help maintain stable ICP levels.

Urinary catheterization allows for accurate measurement of diuretic response (20 to 30 minutes after infusion). Hyperosmotic diuretics reduce cerebral edema.

These drugs may be used to control response to noxious stimuli (e.g., intubation and suctioning) to reduce effect on ICP.

This prevents venous obstruction and decreases cerebral edema.

This prevents increased ICP caused by Valsalva maneuver.

This avoids hypoxemia, hypercapnia, and hypotension.

Head Trauma

■ = Independent; ▲ = Collaborative

 Head Trauma—cont'd

 Nursing Diagnosis

Risk for Deficient Fluid Volume

Common Risk Factors

Diabetes insipidus (DI)
Administration of hyperosmotic agents such as mannitol
  or high-protein tube feedings
High temperature
Profuse diaphoresis
Vomiting

Common Expected Outcome

Patient maintains optimal fluid volume, as evidenced
  by normal skin turgor and urine specific gravity
  between 1.005 and 1.025.

NOC Outcomes
Fluid Balance; Electrolyte and Acid-Base
  Balance

NIC Intervention
Fluid/Electrolyte Management

Ongoing Assessment

Actions/Interventions

■ Monitor intake and output every hour. Keep accurate
  records of all fluid losses (blood draws, vomiting). Notify
  physician of urine output greater than 200 mL/hr for
  2 consecutive hours.

■ Assess urine specific gravity every 2 to 4 hours. Notify
  physician of urine specific gravity less than 1.005.

▲ Monitor serum and urine electrolytes and osmolarity.

■ Monitor for signs of dehydration (decreased skin turgor,
  weight loss, increased heart rate, decreased blood
  pressure).

■ Assess urine for glucose if intravenous (IV) glucose is
  being infused. Notify physician of positive glucose
  finding.

■ Monitor daily weights.

Rationale

These assessments allow for early diagnosis of DI.

DI is a common complication of head trauma as a result
  of injury to the hypothalamus and will result in a
  decrease in urine specific gravity and excretion of large
  volumes of urine.

DI causes hypernatremia, increased serum osmolality,
  and decreased urine osmolality and urine sodium
  concentration.

Polyuria causes decreased circulatory blood volume and
  weight loss.

Glucosuria causes an osmotic diuresis, which may lead
  to dehydration and increased urine output, worsening
  the effects of or mimicking DI.

Changes in daily weight are reliable indicators of changes
  in fluid balance. Polyuria causes weight loss.

■ = Independent; ▲ = Collaborative

Neurological Care Plans

Therapeutic Interventions

Actions/Interventions	Rationale
■ Maintain an indwelling Foley catheter.	This provides accurate assessment of urine output.
▲ Control nausea and vomiting with antiemetics, as ordered.	These symptoms often occur as a result of cerebral irritation.
■ Replace fluid output as directed.	The patient with DI has intense thirst. Oral intake in response to thirst may correct the problem. IV fluid administration may be needed if the patient is unable to maintain fluid intake in response to thirst.
▲ Administer vasopressin as ordered.	Vasopressin is a synthetic antidiuretic hormone that will reduce urine concentration and decrease urine output. Careful monitoring of the urine output and serum sodium and osmolarity is mandatory when vasopressin is administered.

NDx Nursing Diagnosis

Risk for Excess Fluid Volume

Common Risk Factors

Free water excess
Syndrome of inappropriate secretion of antidiuretic hormone (SIADH) (seen in 5% of head injury patients)

Common Expected Outcome

Patient maintains optimal fluid balance, as evidenced by normal serum sodium, normal osmolarity, and urine specific gravity between 1.005 and 1.025.

NOC Outcomes
Fluid Balance; Electrolyte Balance

NIC Intervention
Fluid/Electrolyte Management

Ongoing Assessment

Actions/Interventions	Rationale
■ Assess intake and output, and monitor weight.	Decreased output and weight gain (without edema) are first signs of SIADH. Urine output may be less than 30 to 40 mL/hr.
▲ Assess serum and urine electrolytes and osmolality.	Serum sodium levels and osmolality decline as a result of hemodilution.
■ Monitor vital signs and neurological status.	Excess circulating fluid can cause further cerebral edema.

Head Trauma

■ = Independent; ▲ = Collaborative

Head Trauma—cont'd

Therapeutic Interventions

Actions/Interventions

▲ Restrict fluid intake as directed (usually 1 L/day combined with oral, IV, or nasogastric [NG] tube liquids).

▲ Limit free water intake. Use 0.9% normal saline for medication piggyback or NG tube irrigation.

▲ If fluid restriction fails to correct hyponatremia, anticipate order for 3% saline solution infusion given with potassium and furosemide (Lasix).

Rationale

This is needed to maintain fluid balance.

This is done to limit electrolyte loss.

Furosemide promotes diuresis. Potassium is lost with the fluid and must be replaced.

NDx Nursing Diagnosis

Risk for Ineffective Airway Clearance

Common Risk Factors

Decreased level of consciousness (LOC)
Possible mechanical obstruction resulting from facial trauma
Facial edema
Use of neuromuscular paralytic agents
Concomitant cervical/high thoracic spinal cord injury

Common Expected Outcome

Patient maintains patent airway, as evidenced by clear lung sounds, normal respiratory rate, normal ABGs, and normal cardiac rate and rhythm.

NOC Outcome
Respiratory Status: Airway Patency

NIC Intervention
Airway Management

Ongoing Assessment

Actions/Interventions

■ Assess rate and quality of respirations.
■ Monitor breath sounds.

▲ Monitor ABGs and/or pulse oximetry as needed.

■ Assess ability to cough and swallow without gurgling. Check for gag reflex.

Rationale

This establishes pulmonary function baseline.
Diminished breath sounds may indicate airway obstruction.

Airway obstruction impairs effective gas exchange. The patient may exhibit signs of hypoxemia.

Neurological damage and traumatic injury may have affected normal function. Loss of airway protective reflexes increase the risk of aspiration.

■ = Independent; ▲ = Collaborative

Therapeutic Interventions

Actions/Interventions

■ Suction oral secretions as needed.

Rationale

Nasotracheal suctioning is contraindicated with head trauma resulting from possible basilar skull fracture. This could result in the introduction of the catheter tip into the brain.

■ Turn the patient frequently side to side.

This prevents consolidation of lung secretions.

▲ Administer oxygen as directed.

Supplemental oxygen corrects hypoxemia and prevents increased ICP.

■ If the patient is at risk for increased ICP or if ICP is elevated above baseline, hyperoxygenate and hyperventilate before and after suctioning.

Hyperventilation reduces risk for increasing ICP when suctioning the patient. Prolonged and frequent suctioning contributes to hypoxemia and an increase in ICP.

NDx Nursing Diagnosis

Risk for Seizures

Common Risk Factors

Cortical laceration
Temporal lobe contusion
Acute intracranial bleeding
Hyponatremia or hypoglycemia
Hypoxia
Multiple contusions
Penetrating injuries to brain
Seizure activity within the first week of head injury

Common Expected Outcome

Patient's risk for additional injury is decreased due to maintenance of appropriate seizure precautions.

NOC Outcomes
Safety Behavior: Physical Injury;
Risk Detection; Risk Control;
Medication Response

NIC Intervention
Seizure Precautions/Management

Ongoing Assessment

Actions/Interventions

■ Observe for seizure activity. Record and report the following observations:
  • Length of seizure
  • Body part involved; pattern and order of movement

Rationale

Any cerebral irritation puts the patient at risk for seizure activity. Seizures occur in about 5% of patients with nonpenetrating head trauma; the risk is greater with penetrating injuries. Seizures increase cerebral metabo-

Head Trauma

■ = Independent; ▲ = Collaborative

Head Trauma—cont'd

Actions/Interventions

- Preictal activity
- Direction of eye deviation and change in pupil size
- Airway and respiratory pattern
- Length of postictal state and characteristics
- Incontinence
- Effect on ICP

Rationale

lism and oxygen demand. Ischemic injury from the primary trauma can be aggravated by seizure-induced hypoxia. Careful documentation of seizure activity helps in diagnosing the specific type of seizure. Generalized tonic-clonic seizures are more likely to occur with increased ICP.

Therapeutic Interventions

Actions/Interventions

- Implement seizure precautions: side rails up and padded, bed in low position, head protection if needed.

- Administer anticonvulsants as directed. Observe for hypotension during the administration and administer phenytoin IV 50 mg/min.

- If seizure occurs, protect the head and body from injury. Do not attempt to put anything in the patient's mouth.

- Turn the patient's head to the side and suction secretions as necessary.

Rationale

Patient safety is a priority.

Phenytoin (Dilantin) can only be mixed in normal saline. Precipitation will be noted when mixed with D_5W. Drug may also be given prophylactically. Lorazepam (Ativan) and fosphenytoin may be used as part of pharmacological management.

Inserting objects will often cause more harm, such as dislodged teeth, causing lacerations and obstructing the airway.

This is done to maintain airway patency during the postictal state.

NDx Nursing Diagnosis

Risk for Imbalanced Nutrition: Less Than Body Requirements

Common Risk Factors

Facial trauma
Restriction of intake
Physical immobility
Impaired LOC
Multisystem trauma

Common Expected Outcome

Patient maintains optimal nutritional status, as evidenced by good skin turgor, normal electrolyte levels, and appropriate weight gain.

NOC Outcome
Nutritional Status: Nutrient Intake

NIC Intervention
Nutrition Management

Neurological Care Plans

Ongoing Assessment

Actions/Interventions	Rationale
▲ Monitor albumin, protein, glucose, and electrolytes.	These are indicative of general nutritional states.
■ Assess skin color, turgor, and muscle mass.	Dry, flaky skin; tenting; and decreased muscle mass indicate decreased nutritional intake.
■ Assess rate and quality of wound healing.	Extra calories are needed to maintain basic metabolism plus wound healing.
■ Observe for general signs of infection and local infection at cranial catheter insertion site, if present.	Immunocompetence depends on good nutrition.
■ Monitor daily weights.	Changes in weight will occur with nutritional changes. Daily fluctuations occur with shifts in fluid balance. Sustained changes over a week are reflections of nutritional status.
▲ Consult with speech therapist to evaluate for dysphagia.	Swallowing and gag reflexes may be impaired as a result of head trauma. Evaluation of swallowing needs to be done before initiating oral intake. This assessment is done to reduce risk of aspiration with oral intake.
■ Measure gastric residual volumes at regular intervals.	Delayed gastric emptying increases risk of aspiration.

Therapeutic Interventions

Actions/Interventions	Rationale
■ Administer tube feedings.	Patients with head injury need about 2000 kcal/day. Patients with multiple trauma may need 2 to 3 times that (or more). The enteral route of nutritional support is preferred over the IV route. IV nutritional support requires placement of a central venous catheter. The central line increases the risk for infection. Hyperglycemia is a complication of total parenteral nutrition that requires frequent blood glucose monitoring and insulin administration.
■ Maintain HOB at 30 degrees.	This prevents risk of aspiration.
■ Verify placement of gastric tube before initiation of feedings. Avoid insertion of feeding tube through the nose in a patient with head injury unless the possibility of a basal skull fracture has been excluded.	Basilar fractures often traverse the paranasal sinuses. A feeding tube could penetrate brain tissue through the fracture site.

 Nursing Diagnosis

Deficient Knowledge

Common Related Factor	Defining Characteristics
Lack of prior experience with head injury	Questioning members of health care team or other family members Verbalization of incorrect information Withdrawal from environment Frustration with health care and family members

Head Trauma

■ = Independent; ▲ = Collaborative

Head Trauma–cont'd

Common Expected Outcome

Patient or family describes the type of head injury, treatment, and expected outcome.

NOC Outcomes
Knowledge: Disease Process;
  Knowledge: Treatment Regimen

NIC Interventions
Teaching: Disease Process; Teaching:
  Procedure/Treatment

Ongoing Assessment

Actions/Interventions

■ Assess knowledge of injury, treatment, and expected outcome.

■ Assess the patient's cognitive function.

Rationale

Knowledge will reduce the fear of the unknown. Because most head trauma occurs as an unexpected accident, the patient and family have no previous experience with this type of injury.

Head trauma can cause impaired short-term memory, decreased attention span, and decreased concentration. These changes can limit learning new information.

Therapeutic Interventions

Actions/Interventions

■ Prepare the family for the intensive care unit (ICU) environment.

■ Explain treatments or procedures and equipment used, such as the following:
  • ICP monitor
  • IV lines and medications
  • Cardiopulmonary and oximetry monitors
  • Feeding tubes and pumps
  • Mechanical ventilation

■ Reinforce information given to the patient or family about the following:
  • Type of head injury, where the injury is in the brain, and what brain functions will be affected by the injury
  • Results of CT scan, radiographs, MRI

Rationale

Head trauma can result in life-threatening injury that will produce high levels of anxiety. In addition, the ICU environment may be stressful at first visit. The presence of "high-tech" equipment is a source of anxiety to most patients and families. A brief explanation of the positive features of these monitoring devices and treatments may reduce their anxiety.

The patient with cognitive impairment may have distorted perceptions of therapeutic equipment. The patient who is disoriented may perceive the equipment as threatening and attempt to remove it. Frequent explanations in simple terms may calm anxiety and promote reality orientation.

Repetition may be beneficial in retaining new information. Daily updates and explanations can help the patient and family cope with the uncertainty they experience with the long-term rehabilitation.

■ = Independent; ▲ = Collaborative

Actions/Interventions	**Rationale**
• Care plan and changes in condition	The care plan varies depending on the type and extent of skull and brain injury. A patient with a mild contusion, nondisplaced skull fracture, and mild concussion can likely expect a full recovery. The plan will focus on reestablishing physical and mental function. A patient with a depressed skull fracture and severe brain injury may require long-term care as a result of permanent neurological deficits. The care plan will focus on prevention of complications resulting from chronic mobility, communication, and sensory and cognitive deficits.
■ If the patient has impaired LOC, instruct the family and significant others to avoid discussions at the bedside that they would not want the patient to hear.	Although the patient may be unresponsive, ability to hear may be intact.
■ Encourage the family or significant others to bring in pictures, tapes of favorite music, or messages from children and friends.	These provide familiar environmental stimuli.
■ Keep the family up-to-date with any new changes in condition.	Regular conferences with family caregivers help them become members of the rehabilitation team. They can provide insights about the patient's personality and behavior before the injury.
■ Discuss the role of physical, occupational, or speech therapist.	Specialized service may be required for recovery.
■ Discuss the need for rehabilitation and home care support, if necessary.	Parents or spouses often become the primary caregivers when the patient is discharged from the rehabilitation setting. They need ongoing support to adapt to the changes in roles and responsibilities.
■ Prepare the patient and family for changes in personality and behavior.	It may take months for the patient to recover; some personality changes may be permanent.
■ Provide the family with names and numbers of local support groups, if available.	Groups that come together for mutual support can be beneficial.
■ Refer the family to social services or financial counselors, as appropriate.	The patient and family may need ongoing support for decisions about financial resources, guardianship, powers of attorney, and living wills. Resources for respite care may help families cope more effectively with responsibilities for patient care.
■ Obtain pastoral care if desired.	Ethical and religious questions may need to be addressed if the patient's survival is questionable or debatable.

• RELATED CARE PLAN

Self-care deficit, p. 156

Head Trauma

■ = Independent; ▲ = Collaborative

Herniated Intervertebral Disk

Slipped Disk; Ruptured Disk; Sciatica; Laminectomy

Herniated cervical and lumbar intervertebral disks are the most common cause of severe back pain. Thoracic herniations are rare. Age of onset is typically between 30 and 50 years of age, with men affected more often than women. Etiological factors include trauma (50%), degenerative diseases (e.g., osteoarthritis and ankylosing spondylitis), and congenital defects (e.g., scoliosis). In many cases the disk is spontaneously reduced or reabsorbed without treatment, but more often the problem becomes chronic with pain and disability depending on the location and severity of the herniation. The amount of disk pulposus herniated into the spinal canal affects the narrowing of the space and the degree of compression on the cervical, lumbar, or sacral spinal roots. Spinal cord compression may occur in cervical herniation because of already limited space in this section of the spinal column. Conservative management (rest, heat or ice, and nonsteroidal antiinflammatory drugs [NSAIDs]) is usually accomplished in the ambulatory setting and is the focus of this care plan.

 Nursing Diagnosis

Acute Pain

Common Related Factors

Trauma
Muscle spasm
Nerve root compression

Defining Characteristics

Verbalized complaint of the following:
- Mild to excruciating lower back pain (lumbar)
- Radiating pain to buttock or leg (lumbar)
- Shoulder, neck, arm pain (cervical)
- Forearm and finger pain (cervical)
- Guarding behavior
- Change in sleep pattern
- Physical and social withdrawal

Common Expected Outcome

Patient describes relief from pain and improvement in sensorimotor function.

NOC Outcomes
Pain Control; Medication Response

NIC Interventions
Pain Management; Positioning; Medication Management

Ongoing Assessment

Actions/Interventions

■ Identify the following changes in sensorimotor function:
Lumbar
- Absent lumbar lordosis
- Lumbar scoliosis

Rationale

Decrease in motor function is often a guarding behavior, a protective action or inaction to control pain. The lumbar and cervical spine are affected most often because they are the most flexible segments of the

■ = Independent; ▲ = Collaborative

Actions/Interventions

- Limited movement or flexion
- Slight motor weakness
- Decreased knee and ankle reflexes
- Paresthesia or numbness
- Changes in bowel or bladder function

Cervical
- Paresthesia or numbness of forearm and fingers
- Biceps weakness
- Decreased reflexes in biceps or supinator or triceps
- Decreased neck movement

▲ Facilitate diagnostic testing, if needed: spinal x-ray, computed tomography, magnetic resonance imaging, lumbar puncture for cerebrospinal fluid (protein will be high with normal cell count), myelogram, and/or nerve conduction studies.

■ Obtain detailed pain history, including the following:
- Location and onset of pain
- Presence of radiating pain
- Recurrent (duration and frequency) or continuous pain
- Precipitating factors
- Relief factors (preference for standing or lying down)
- Aggravating factors (sitting, jarring movements)

■ Evaluate effectiveness of previous treatments.

Rationale

spine. A herniated disk can press against adjacent nerves causing pain and paresthesias. The specific level of injury will determine the symptoms experienced by the patient. Alterations in gait and posture may represent nerve injury or adaptation to chronic pain.

Serial testing may be done to determine progression of herniation. While clinical signs clearly point to lumbar disk herniation, diagnostic testing is more accurate in determining cervical herniation.

Remission and exacerbation of pain in the patient with a lumbar herniation often occur due to decreased edema and root compression, as well as spontaneous reduction of the disk into its normal position and reabsorption of disk exudate. Lumbar disk disease may cause pain that radiates along the path of the sciatic nerve into the leg. Muscle weakness may occur with the pain.

Patients may have tried multiple home remedies for pain relief before seeking professional care.

Therapeutic Interventions

Actions/Interventions

■ Implement conservative treatment plan.

■ Instruct the patient to do the following:
- Begin bed rest on a firm mattress.
- Use a pillow under the knees (lumbar).
- Use small pillow at nape of neck (cervical).

▲ Initiate drug therapy, possibly including analgesics, muscle relaxants, antiinflammatory drugs, and/or sedatives as ordered.

Rationale

Duration of treatment depends on location of herniation and severity of symptoms. Conservative treatment can be accomplished in the home. Hospitalization is necessary only if pain and sensorimotor deficits are incapacitating or if cervical herniation threatens respiratory function.

A firm mattress provides back support. A board can be placed underneath a soft mattress for support.

Most patients find positioning in a semi-Fowler's position with knees flexed reduces pressure on nerve roots and promotes muscle relaxation. A supine position may aggravate pain. The use of appropriate sleep aids for body positioning will promote comfort and decrease stress on nerve roots.

These drugs reduce inflammation and muscle spasm. Medications and dosage depend on patient symptoms and amount of relief.

Herniated Intervertebral Disk

■ = Independent; ▲ = Collaborative

Herniated Intervertebral Disk—cont'd

Actions/Interventions	Rationale
▲ Refer the patient for a physical therapy consult.	The physical therapist can provide guidance for garment selection and fitting and for physiotherapy, including ultrasound and thermal treatments. The physical therapist can help the patient learn exercises to strengthen back muscles and prevent further injury.
■ Instruct the patient in traction therapy (pelvic belt or head halter).	Traction does not seem to have a direct effect on disk placement, but does provide relief from spasms and decreases pressure on nerve roots, thereby providing pain relief.
■ Assist the patient in using additional pain control modalities, such as heat and cold applications, relaxation therapy, imagery, and anxiety reduction.	Nonpharmacological pain interventions will contribute to effective pain management. These strategies may reduce the development of problems associated with overuse of opioid analgesics.

 Nursing Diagnosis

Risk for Ineffective Breathing Pattern

Common Risk Factors

Cervical nerve root compression
Cervical spinal cord compression

Common Expected Outcome

Patient maintains breathing pattern within normal limits.

> **NOC Outcome**
> Respiratory Status: Ventilation
>
> **NIC Intervention**
> Respiratory Monitoring

Ongoing Assessment

Actions/Interventions	Rationale
■ Assess respiratory rate, rhythm, depth, and dyspnea.	Cord compression at C3 to C5 impedes the phrenic nerve, which innervates the diaphragm.
■ Determine history of respiratory deficits or disease.	Other respiratory disorders can mimic symptoms of cervical cord compression.
■ Report deteriorating respiratory signs immediately.	Prompt surgical intervention may be necessary to relieve cord compression and maintain respiratory function.

■ = Independent; ▲ = Collaborative

Neurological Care Plans

Therapeutic Interventions

Actions/Interventions

- Instruct the patient to report respiratory difficulties immediately.

- Explain consequences of ignoring symptoms.

- Provide emergency phone numbers.

Rationale

Alteration in respiratory function may occur quickly.

Cervical cord compression is potentially life threatening and can result in respiratory failure.

Patients and family members may not remember phone numbers in an emergency situation.

NDx Nursing Diagnosis

Deficient Knowledge

Common Related Factors

Unfamiliar diagnosis
New treatments

Defining Characteristics

Verbalized lack of understanding
Multiple questions
Noncompliance

Common Expected Outcome

Patient verbalizes understanding of treatment program and demonstrates skills necessary for protecting vertebrae.

NOC Outcomes

Knowledge: Disease Process;
Knowledge: Treatment Regimen

NIC Interventions

Teaching: Disease Process; Teaching:
Prescribed Activity/Exercise

Ongoing Assessment

Actions/Interventions

- Assess the patient's understanding of the diagnosis and treatment plan.

- Determine readiness for learning.

Rationale

Pain inhibits ability to concentrate and learn.

Optimal learning occurs when the patient is ready to learn new information.

Therapeutic Interventions

Actions/Interventions

- Design a teaching plan specific to the patient's needs and treatment plan.

Rationale

The patient needs information about treatment options to guide decision making. The long-term effectiveness of nonsurgical and surgical approaches to treatment is similar for patients with mild to moderate disease. Surgical therapy is associated with better outcomes for patients with moderate to severe disease.

Herniated Intervertebral Disk

■ = Independent; ▲ = Collaborative

Herniated Intervertebral Disk—cont'd

Actions/Interventions	Rationale
Conservative treatment plan	
• Discuss remission and exacerbation	Patients experience periods of improvement and exacerbation of symptoms because of changes in the amount of inflammation at the level of herniation until the area is healed.
• Exercise program: muscle strengthening exercise is prescribed	Exercise helps support the spinal column.
• Proper body mechanics: instruction on proper lifting and avoidance of repetitive motion and body movements	Improper body mechanics can aggravate weakened disks.
• Medications: analgesics, NSAIDs, muscle relaxants	These medications reduce pain associated with edema.
• Application and use of support garments and traction equipment	These minimize injury and relieve nerve root compression.
Surgical intervention	
• Type of surgery:	Surgery may be required for patients who suffer severe herniation resulting in cord compression, loss of function, and unrelenting pain. Laminectomy may also be done after poor response to conservative treatment.
• Diskectomy—partial removal of lamina	
• Laminectomy—excision of posterior arch of vertebra (lamina)	
• Spinal infusion—fusion of vertebrae with bone grafts, rods, plates, or screws	
• Pain: immediately postoperative (spasms, incisional)	Patients who have experienced long-term radiating pain and paresthesias may continue to have these symptoms for several postoperative weeks.
• Postoperative expectations: initial immobility, relearning how to move	Physical therapy will be required in the home and as an outpatient to strengthen muscles, to learn to move, and to protect the spine.
• Lifestyle modifications: weight control, body mechanics, posture, stress management, medications	Lifestyle modifications are necessary to prevent reinjury of the spine.
• Recurrent herniation: may occur near site of original herniation or at another location	Degenerative or other changes may predispose the patient to repeat herniation and repeat laminectomy, despite following prescribed treatment plan.

• RELATED CARE PLANS

Chronic pain, p. 149
Disturbed body image, p. 21
Impaired physical mobility, p. 126
Ineffective coping, p. 51

Intracranial Infection

Encephalitis; Brain Abscess, Central Nervous System Infection; Meningitis; Ventriculitis; Empyema

Intracranial infection may be the result of meningitis, encephalitis, ventriculitis, brain abscess, or empyema. *Meningitis* is an inflammation or infection of the membranes of the brain or spinal cord caused by bacteria, viruses, or other organisms. Pneumococcal meningitis is often secondary to pneumonia, sinusitis, alcoholism, and trauma (such as a basal skull fracture). Meningococcal meningitis is more common in children and young adults.

■ = Independent; ▲ = Collaborative

Epidemics are seen in winter and spring months. Immunizations are available for both forms of meningitis. Antibiotic therapy is required. *Viral* illnesses are treated symptomatically. Viral meningitis is more likely to occur in summer months. Hydrocephalus often occurs secondary to viral meningitis. *Encephalitis* is an inflammation/infection of the brain and meninges. The highest mortality rate is caused by herpes simplex virus (HSV) and is the most common form. *Ventriculitis* is an infection that establishes itself in the ventricular system. An abscess is a localized purulent collection in the brain. *Empyema* is a type of brain abscess that forms in a preexisting space such as the subdural space of the brain, requiring surgical drainage and injection of antibiotics. Causes may be direct or indirect. Direct causes are a result of extension of infections from the ear, tooth, mastoid, or sinus. Indirect causes include bacterial endocarditis, skull fracture, or nonsterile procedures. Empyema may also form in the epidural space of the spine. Hospitalization is usually required for differential diagnosis, neurological monitoring, and treatment.

 Nursing Diagnosis

Infection

Common Related Factors	Defining Characteristics
Brain infection Encephalitis Brain abscess	Temperature greater than 39° C (102° F) Increased white blood cell (WBC) count Nuchal rigidity Altered level of consciousness (LOC) Irritability Motor- sensory abnormalities Chills Malaise Headache Localized redness and swelling (e.g., along a suture line or area of injury)

Common Expected Outcome
Source of infection is determined and treated.

NOC Outcomes
Thermoregulation; Medication Response

NIC Interventions
Fever Treatment;
   Medication Administration, Parenteral

Ongoing Assessment

Actions/Interventions

■ Monitor temperature.

Rationale

This provides information about the patient's response to invading organisms. Fever is a classic manifestation of meningitis. Fever is not common with a brain abscess.

Intracranial Infection

■ = Independent; ▲ = Collaborative

Intracranial Infection—cont'd

Actions/Interventions

▲ Monitor WBC count.

■ Evaluate LOC.

■ Evaluate motor-sensory status.

■ Evaluate for signs of cerebrospinal fluid (CSF) otor-rhea/rhinorrhea.

▲ Monitor peak or trough levels of antibiotics as prescribed.

■ Assess for headache.

Rationale

Elevated WBC counts occur in both bacterial and viral infections.

Symptoms provide a clinical picture upon which treatment will be based. Alterations in LOC occur in most patients with intracranial infections. Changes may range from drowsiness to coma.

Changes in nerve function are common manifestations of intracranial infections. Meningeal or cerebral inflammation can produce nuchal rigidity, Brudzinski's sign (flexion of neck onto chest causes flexion of both legs and thighs), and Kernig's sign (resistance to extension of the leg at the knee with the hip flexed).

After basal skull fracture, CSF leakage may lead to intracranial infection.

These levels provide means to monitor effectiveness and prevent toxicity of medication.

Headache may be the only manifestation of a brain abscess. The pain may intensify with exertion.

Therapeutic Interventions

Actions/Interventions

▲ Administer antibiotics on a strict administration schedule.

▲ Administer antipyretics as prescribed; document patient response.

▲ Administer intravenous (IV) fluids as ordered.

■ Administer tepid sponge baths as needed.

■ Apply cooling blanket for temperature greater than 39.5° C (103.1° F).

Rationale

Consistent timing is required to maintain therapeutic blood levels, reduce virulence, eradicate pathogens, and prevent swings in antibiotic blood levels.

Fever increases cerebral metabolic demand.

Fluids prevent dehydration.

Baths reduce fever and provide physical comfort.

High temperatures can add to neurological damage.

 Nursing Diagnosis

Risk for Injury: Seizures

Common Risk Factors

Cerebral irritation
Focal edema
Cerebritis
Ventriculitis

Neurological Care Plans

Common Expected Outcomes

Patient does not experience seizure activity.
If patient experiences seizure, early assessment and treatment are initiated to prevent injury.

NOC Outcomes
Risk Detection; Risk Control;
  Safety Behavior: Physical Injury

NIC Intervention
Seizure Precautions/Management

Ongoing Assessment

Actions/Interventions	Rationale
■ Monitor LOC.	Deterioration in alertness, orientation, verbal response, eye opening, or motor response indicates deteriorating neurological status and an increased likelihood of seizure development.
■ Monitor for seizure activity.	Seizures may exhibit as involuntary repetitive motor or sensory movement and spasticity, or repetitive psychomotor activity.
■ Document seizure pattern and frequency of occurrence. Notify physician of seizure activity.	First seizure, repetitive seizures, or a seizure pattern that varies may indicate a need for anticonvulsant medications, reevaluation, and/or further neurological evaluation. Seizures usually occur before intracranial pressure (ICP) increases. Adequate treatment of infection will alleviate further deterioration.
▲ Monitor anticonvulsant drug levels.	Anticonvulsants are ordered both prophylactically and as a treatment. Therapy involves keeping blood levels adequate to prevent seizure activity.
■ During a seizure, evaluate patency of airway.	The tongue may obstruct the airway.

Therapeutic Interventions

Actions/Interventions	Rationale
▲ Administer anticonvulsants as ordered.	Anticonvulsants are administered intravenously to interrupt seizure activity. Long-term oral administration is given to prevent seizures.
■ Institute seizure precautions for high-risk patients, such as keeping side rails raised at all times, padding rails, and making frequent observations.	Safety measures are implemented to prevent injury. Early recognition of seizure activity allows the nurse to initiate treatment as soon as possible.
■ If seizure occurs, roll the patient to the side or to a semiprone position after motor activity has ceased.	This promotes gravity drainage of secretions and maintains airway patency.
■ Suction as needed.	Patients are at risk for aspiration of oral secretions during the ictal and post-ictal phases.

See also **Seizure Activity,** *p. 626.*

Intracranial Infection

■ = Independent; ▲ = Collaborative

Intracranial Infection–cont'd

Nursing Diagnosis

Risk for Ineffective Cerebral Tissue Perfusion

Common Risk Factors

Cerebral edema
Increased ICP
Hydrocephalus

Common Expected Outcome

Patient maintains optimal tissue perfusion, as evidenced by alertness, normal pupillary reaction, absence of seizures, Glasgow Coma Scale (GCS) score greater than 13, and absence of meningeal signs.

NOC Outcome
Neurological Status

NIC Intervention
Neurological Monitoring

Ongoing Assessment

Actions/Interventions	**Rationale**
■ Assess LOC (include seizure activity and vital signs) and GCS. Record serially.	GCS less than 13 indicates a deterioration of brain function. Neurological assessment helps in determining diagnosis and response to treatment.
■ Monitor pupillary size and reaction to light.	Changes in pupil size and reactivity occur with some forms of meningitis. These changes are associated with involvement of cranial nerves III, IV, and VI.
■ Report persistent deterioration in LOC.	If LOC decreases, treatment may need to be changed, new treatment instituted, or additional tests obtained. Change in mentation, seizures, increased blood pressure (BP), bradycardia, or respiratory abnormalities may indicate increasing ICP with decreased cerebral perfusion pressure.
■ Monitor motor strength and coordination.	Sensorimotor function is often within normal limits in meningitis, but abnormal in encephalitis.
■ Assess ability to follow simple or complex commands.	Impaired cognitive function occurs with cerebral hemisphere involvement.
■ Evaluate presence or absence of protective reflexes: swallow, gag, blink, cough.	Absence of reflexes is a late sign indicative of increasing ICP.
■ Assess for meningeal signs: nuchal rigidity, headache, photophobia, Brudzinski's sign, Kernig's sign.	Symptoms provide a clinical picture upon which further diagnosis and treatment are based. Meningeal signs are a result of meningeal and spinal root inflammation, and/or pooling of infectious exudate.

■ = Independent; ▲ = Collaborative

Neurological Care Plans

Therapeutic Interventions

Actions/Interventions

■ Elevate head of bed (HOB) to 30 to 45 degrees with the patient's head in neutral alignment.

■ Reorient the patient to the environment, as needed.

▲ Administer hyperosmotics if ordered.

▲ Assist with diagnostic testing:
  • Lumbar puncture for CSF

  • Magnetic resonance imaging (MRI), computed tomography (CT), or ventriculogram

  • Electroencephalogram

Rationale

If there is actual or potential increased ICP, positioning with elevated HOB will promote venous outflow from the brain and help decrease ICP.

Frequent reality orientation is needed to promote cognitive function.

Osmotic diuretics decrease cerebral edema.

This diagnostic procedure is done to determine cerebral pressure and presence of infectious organisms.

It is important to identify structural changes caused by abscess.

Changes in brain wave patterns can help identify the localization of lesions in the brain.

NDx Nursing Diagnosis

Acute Pain

Common Related Factors

Meningeal irritation
Increased ICP

Common Expected Outcomes

Patient verbalizes relief from pain or discomfort.
Patient appears comfortable.

Defining Characteristics

Headache
Photophobia
Nuchal rigidity
Irritability

NOC Outcomes
Pain Control; Medication Response

NIC Interventions
Analgesic Administration;
  Environmental Management: Comfort

Ongoing Assessment

Actions/Interventions

■ Assess for headache, photophobia, restlessness, irritability.

Rationale

Severe headache is the most common early symptom of intracranial infection. Headache is due to irritation of dura and tension on vascular structures. The location of the headache helps determine the source of the infection. Headaches are usually intensified by movement or exertion.

Intracranial Infection

■ = Independent; ▲ = Collaborative

Intracranial Infection–cont'd

Therapeutic Interventions

Actions/Interventions	Rationale
■ Decrease external stimuli, such as restricting visitors as appropriate and reducing noise in the environment.	Stimulation can increase ICP, thereby aggravating pain.
■ Keep the patient's room darkened or have the patient wear sunglasses.	Reducing visual stimuli can minimize effects of photophobia.
▲ Administer analgesics as prescribed.	NSAIDs are usually effective in managing pain.
■ Discourage the Valsalva maneuver (e.g., instruct the patient to exhale when moving up in bed; provide stool softeners).	Straining can cause increased cerebral blood flow and increased ICP.
■ Explain that treatment of infection will also decrease pain.	Antibiotic and corticosteroid therapy reduce acute inflammation and thereby reduce pain.

NDx Nursing Diagnosis

Risk for Deficient Fluid Volume

Common Risk Factors

Reduced LOC
Lack of oral intake
Fever
Vomiting
Diarrhea

Common Expected Outcome

The patient maintains optimal fluid volume, as evidenced by good skin turgor and normal specific gravity, serum sodium, and osmolality.

NOC Outcome
Fluid Balance

NIC Intervention
Fluid/Electrolyte Management

Ongoing Assessment

Actions/Interventions	Rationale
■ Monitor intake and output. Evaluate for causes of fluid deficit.	Antibiotics may cause diarrhea. Vomiting results from pressure on brainstem.
■ Assess skin turgor.	Loss of interstitial fluid causes loss of skin elasticity.
■ Monitor weight.	Changes may reflect fluid volume changes.
▲ Monitor and record serum electrolytes, urine specific gravity, and blood urea nitrogen (BUN) and creatinine.	Results that reflect dehydration include urine specific gravity greater than 1.025, serum sodium greater than 150 mEq/L, serum osmolality greater than 310 mOsm/kg, BUN greater than 18 mg/dL, creatinine greater than 0.4 mg/dL.

■ = Independent; ▲ = Collaborative

Actions/Interventions

■ Document and report changes in BP and heart rate (HR).

Rationale

Reduction in circulating blood volume can cause hypotension and tachycardia.

Therapeutic Interventions

Actions/Interventions

■ Encourage fluid intake as appropriate.

■ Provide oral care and lubrication to lips.

Rationale

Patient may require IV or nasogastric feedings to ensure hydration. Average daily fluid loss is approximately 1500 mL in urine, 200 mL in stool, and 700 to 1300 mL in perspiration, respiration, and insensible water loss.

These measures promote comfort.

NDx Nursing Diagnosis

Deficient Knowledge

Common Related Factors

Unfamiliarity with disease process
New treatment (possible surgical drainage)

Common Expected Outcome

Patient or significant others can discuss current infection, possible causes, tests, treatment, and follow-up care.

Defining Characteristics

Patient or significant others verbalize questions or concerns
Incorrect or inaccurate information is conveyed

NOC Outcomes
Knowledge: Disease Process;
Knowledge: Treatment Regimen

NIC Interventions
Teaching: Prescribed Medication;
Teaching: Disease Process

Ongoing Assessment

Actions/Interventions

■ Assess the patient's or significant others' knowledge base about current central nervous system infection, treatment, and follow-up care.

■ Assess the patient's mental status (orientation, thought processes, memory, insight, judgment).

Rationale

Intracranial infection is frequently an unfamiliar diagnosis. Assessing actual learning needs will provide guidance in designing a teaching plan.

Altered mental status is a barrier to learning; the family or significant others will need to be more actively involved.

Intracranial Infection

■ = Independent; ▲ = Collaborative

→ **Intracranial Infection**–cont'd

Therapeutic Interventions

Actions/Interventions

- Provide explanations of disease process, cause if known, and diagnostic testing (e.g., CT, MRI, lumbar puncture).
- Instruct the patient or significant others in principles of antibiotic therapy, effects and possible side effects, maintenance of therapeutic levels, and duration of treatment. Involve the patient and significant others.
- Discuss the projected length of convalescence.

- If the patient is to be discharged on medications (e.g., antibiotics, anticonvulsants), instruct in dose, frequency, route, and possible side effects. It is best to provide written instructions for reference at home.
- Provide information about adjunct treatments that may be indicated: physical and occupational therapy, and speech therapy.

- Provide information about appropriate immunizations.

Rationale

Information helps the patient and family become part of the health care team.

Instruction decreases anxiety and increases accuracy in learning.

Convalescence after an intracranial infection usually takes several weeks.

Compliance with pharmacological therapy is necessary to promote effective outcomes and prevent reinfections.

Physical and occupational therapy can assist in overcoming residual muscle rigidity from lengthy bed rest and to retrain in activities of daily living if infection caused memory loss or neurological dysfunction. Speech therapy may be necessary to assist with swallowing and articulation problems. Therapy required depends on diagnosis, promptness of treatment, and resultant recovery or disability.

Vaccines for meningitis are recommended for high-risk patients such as children, college students living in dormitories, and older adults.

> • RELATED CARE PLANS
>
> Acute pain, p. 144
> Decreased intracranial adaptive capacity,
>   p. 112
> Deficient fluid volume, p. 71
> Imbalanced nutrition: less than body
>   requirements, p. 134

→ **Lyme Disease**

Lyme disease (LD) is primarily a vector-borne infection. In the United States, Lyme disease is localized to states in the northeast, mid-Atlantic, upper north central regions, and several counties in northwest California. The causative agent is *Borrelia burgdorferi*, which is a bacteria transmitted to humans by the bite of an infected deer tick. Diagnosis of LD is based primarily on clinical findings and is often treated based on early objective signs and a known exposure. Testing for LD via enzyme-linked immunoassay (ELISA) should be performed to confirm diagnosis. Infection often presents with a characteristic "bull's-eye" rash (erythema migrans) in 60% to 80% of cases. It is often accompanied by nonspecific symptoms such as fever, malaise, fatigue, headache, muscle aches (myalgia), and joint pain (arthralgia). The time period from infection to onset of symptoms is usually 7 to 14 days.

(■ = Independent; ▲ = Collaborative)

Some individuals are asymptomatic or only manifest nonspecific symptoms like fever, headache, or myalgia. These individuals may delay treatment until the disease becomes disseminated or latent. Nearly all patients can be successfully treated with antibiotics. Oral amoxicillin or doxycycline is the preferred antibiotic for treatment. LD treated in the early, localized stage is generally curable. Patients whose diagnosis is made in the latent stage of LD usually require longer therapy with oral or intravenous antibiotics. In these cases, the severity of LD symptoms may be reduced, but the disease remains indefinitely.

 Nursing Diagnosis

Deficient Knowledge

Common Related Factors
Unfamiliarity with disease process and treatment
Lack of knowledge about Lyme disease

Common Expected Outcome
Patient and family verbalize the disease process, transmission, treatment, and complications of Lyme disease.

Defining Characteristics
Many questions
Lack of questions
Unaware of proper prevention methods

NOC Outcomes
Knowledge: Infection Control;
Knowledge: Treatment Regimen;
Knowledge: Disease Process

NIC Interventions
Teaching: Disease Process;
Teaching: Prescribed Medication

Ongoing Assessment

Actions/Interventions

■ Determine understanding of disease process, transmission, complications, and treatment.

Rationale

This provides an important starting point for education. Many misconceptions are common.

Therapeutic Interventions

Actions/Interventions

■ Provide information on disease transmission.
  • LD is spread by the bite of an infected deer tick (arbovirus).
  • Persons most likely at risk live or work in areas surrounded by tick-infested woods or overgrown brush, or participate in outdoor activities in those areas.
  • LD is not transmitted from person to person, nor from casual contact like touching or kissing someone with LD.

Rationale

The Centers for Disease Control and Prevention (CDC) provides updated guidelines on LD.

Lyme Disease

■ = Independent; ▲ = Collaborative

Lyme Disease—cont'd

Actions/Interventions

- Provide information on disease process/complications.
  - Early symptoms are localized to rash and muscle stiffness and pain. If untreated, symptoms may progress weeks later to cardiac and neurological manifestations.
  - If not treated early enough, arthritis-type manifestations and memory problems may occur later and may be permanent.
- Provide information on treatment.
  - Early symptoms are treated with antibiotics.
  - Later complications may not respond to treatment.

- Provide information on strategies to prevent reinfection.
  - Avoid grassy and wooded areas with thick brush.
  - Use insect repellants containing DEET (*N, N*-diethyl-*m*-toluamide). Follow instructions on the package. Spray clothing so ticks do not bite through.
  - Wear long sleeves, pants, and stockings, as well as closed shoes and a hat.
  - Wear light-colored clothing outdoors to help visualization of ticks.
  - Perform tick checks during and after outdoor activity. Ticks are about the size of a pinhead.
  - Remove any tick with a tweezer or finger. Dispose of the tick carefully to prevent spread of infection.
  - Report any early symptoms such as rash or flulike symptoms.

Rationale

Information enables individuals to take control of situation. The sooner symptoms are recognized, the sooner treatment can begin.

Persons with increased risk factors or who have the rash (erythema migrans), fever, myalgia, or other nonspecific symptoms must be treated with oral antibiotics immediately.

Prevention of tick bites is the best way to avoid LD. Persons with LD can be reinfected.

NDx Nursing Diagnosis

Infection

Common Related Factor	Defining Characteristics
B. burgdorferi spirochete	Early: erythema migrans, fatigue, headache, chills/fever, myalgia, arthralgia, enlarged lymph nodes Disseminated: infection spreads affecting other body systems, numbness or pain in arms and legs, paralysis of facial muscles, meningitis, cardiac arrhythmia (rare) Late (chronic infection, weeks to years after infection): chronic arthritis affecting more than one joint; nervous system problems including memory loss and poor concentration; chronic pain; insomnia

■ = Independent; ▲ = Collaborative

Neurological Care Plans

Common Expected Outcome

Patient has no signs of infection following completion of antibiotic therapy.

NOC Outcomes

Treatment Behavior: Illness or Injury; Infection Severity

NIC Intervention

Infection Control Surveillance

Ongoing Assessment

Actions/Interventions

■ Monitor for characteristic "bull's-eye" rash.

■ Monitor temperature and for headache or joint aches.

■ Monitor for common manifestations of later disseminated stages of LD.

■ Monitor for late changes and signs of chronic arthritis, especially in large weight-bearing joints.

▲ Monitor results of laboratory testing:
  • ELISA
  • Indirect fluorescent antibody test

Rationale

This rash (erythema migrans) is the most common early sign. It develops within days to weeks after the bite.

Fever, headache, and muscle aches are predominant early symptoms of LD.

As the infection spreads to other body systems (nervous system, musculoskeletal, or the heart), there may be signs of pain or numbness in extremities, paralysis of facial muscles, or meningitis.

The severe cases of LD present weeks to years after infection with chronic arthritis affecting more than one joint along with nervous system problems.

Diagnosis of LD can be made based on clinical findings and known exposure. Laboratory testing provides the confirmatory diagnosis.

Therapeutic Interventions

Actions/Interventions

▲ Administer antibiotics for prescribed period:
  • Doxycycline or amoxicillin for 3 to 4 weeks for early stages
  • IV ceftriaxone or penicillin for 4 weeks for late stages

▲ Administer antipyretic and analgesic medications as ordered.

▲ Encourage oral and IV fluids as ordered.

▲ Administer medications for chronic arthralgia:
  • Analgesics
  • NSAIDs
  • Corticosteroids

Rationale

LD is easily treatable once the diagnosis is made. The sooner therapy is started, the faster and more complete the recovery.

Treatment in milder cases involves treating flulike symptoms by reducing fever and relieving headache and body aches.

Fluids are lost by fever and diaphoresis. Increasing fluid intake during fever prevents dehydration and helps in actual fever reduction.

Early in disease process, complaints of migrating pain in muscles, joints, bursae, or tendons are reported. In latent disease, complaints of intermittent or chronic arthritis-type symptoms are reported, primarily in large joints. These complaints usually occur over several years.

Lyme Disease

■ = Independent; ▲ = Collaborative

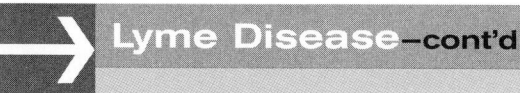

Lyme Disease—cont'd

Actions/Interventions

- Report confirmed cases to local health department and/or the CDC.

Rationale

LD is a reportable illness and is under CDC surveillance. It is still a relatively new disease, so data continue to be gathered.

Migraine Headache

Headache is defined as pain in the head or face, either "primary" or "secondary" in origin. Migraine and muscular headaches are classified as primary, without pathological cause. Secondary headaches are a result of a known pathology, such as cranial tumor or aneurysm. Migraine headache is a benign, recurring headache that can be unilateral or bilateral. Migraine headache is the most common type of vascular headache. Women are affected three times more often than men. Migraines may occur with an aura or without. The aura is a collection of neurological symptoms that precede the onset of pain by 10 to 30 minutes. These symptoms include changes in level of consciousness, vision, behavior, and motor or sensory function. A variety of precipitating events trigger migraine headaches, including stress, foods high in tyramine, hunger, sleep disturbances, and for women, alterations in reproductive hormone levels. Manifestations are associated with autonomic nervous system dysfunction. Migraines may begin in early childhood and adolescence, and 65% of patients with migraine headaches have a family history of migraine headache. It was once thought that pain was associated with vasodilation and increased blood flow. Evidence now suggests that neurological, vascular, and chemical factors are involved. The neurotransmitter serotonin plays a role in pain progression. The neurogenic model implies that the trigeminovascular system is stimulated, causing vasodilation and resulting in headache. This care plan focuses on the classic migraine, which is believed to be a dysfunction of the hypothalamic and upper brainstem areas. Diagnosis, treatment, and follow-up care are usually accomplished in an outpatient setting.

NDx Nursing Diagnosis

Deficient Knowledge

Common Related Factor

Unfamiliar with diagnosis and treatment plan

Defining Characteristics

Verbalized lack of understanding
Questions
Noncompliance

■ = Independent; ▲ = Collaborative

Common Expected Outcomes

Patient will verbalize understanding of migraine headache etiological factors and treatment.

Patient will verbalize understanding of prevention protocol for recurrent headaches and successful prevention of recurrent headaches.

NOC Outcomes
Knowledge: Disease Process;
Knowledge: Medication

NIC Interventions
Teaching: Disease Process;
Teaching: Prescribed Medications

Ongoing Assessment

Actions/Interventions

■ Determine patient's level of pain and readiness for learning. Use a 10-point scale.

■ Assess the patient's current understanding of the cause of headache, prevention, and treatment.

Rationale

Pain needs to be controlled before the patient will be able to participate. A 10-point scale provides objective measurement of pain.

An individualized teaching plan is based on the patient's level of understanding, current knowledge, and need for new information.

Therapeutic Interventions

Actions/Interventions

■ Explain etiological factors of migraine headache:
  • The central pain mechanism in the brain is regulated by serotonin and norepinephrine level, usually in excess, that cause vasodilation and pain.
  • Serotonergic cells are hyperactive during migraine (can be seen on positive emission tomography [PET]) and serotonin levels are more easily manipulated than other neurotransmitters.

▲ Explain and facilitate diagnostic testing (may include a computed tomography, PET scan, magnetic resonance imaging scan, and/or electroencephalogram).

■ Discuss avoidance of foods known to precipitate migraine, such as caffeinated drinks, chocolate, most alcohol (especially red wine), citrus fruits or drinks, pickled or cured foods, some cheeses, and monosodium glutamate.

■ Help the patient recognize and prevent situations that seem to cause headache, such as exhaustion, fatigue, stress, fever, or bright lights.

■ Ensure thorough understanding of prescribed medication therapy for prophylaxis and frequent headache. Prescriptive choices include the following:

Rationale

Knowledge may reduce anxiety and clear up common misconceptions.

These tests are done to rule out other possible diagnoses; results should be negative.

Migraine headaches may or may not have a precipitating event. For those that do, knowledge of one's individual "stressor" may guide treatment. Foods high in the amino acid tyramine are known to trigger migraine headaches. Tyramine stimulates release of epinephrine and norepinephrine.

Changing lifestyle and behavior is usually the most difficult aspect of the treatment plan for migraine sufferers.

Preventive medications are prescribed for patients who experience frequent or incapacitating headaches that are not controlled with acute pain management.

Migraine Headache

■ = Independent; ▲ = Collaborative

Migraine Headache—cont'd

Actions/Interventions	Rationale
• Amitriptyline hydrochloride (Elavil) 50 to 75 mg/day	This blocks uptake of serotonin and catecholamines; often used for migraines associated with muscle contraction.
• Clonidine hydrochloride (Catapres) 0.1 mg three times daily	This decreases response to vasodilation and vasoconstriction; used for migraines associated with food reactions.
• Propranolol hydrochloride (Inderal) 20 to 40 mg three times daily	This inhibits serotonin uptake and prevents vasodilation.
• Methysergide maleate (Sansert) 2 mg three times daily with meals for 5 months	The dose may be adjusted to avoid rebound; prevents serotonin release from platelets.
• Sumatriptan succinate (Imitrex) orally, as a nasal spray, or by subcutaneous injection; dosage varies with route of administration	This drug causes vasoconstriction of cerebral vessels and therefore relieves migraine pain. It provides best relief when taken at the onset of migraine symptoms.
■ Discuss treatment plan to relieve pain (abortive therapy); see the following nursing diagnosis, Acute Pain.	Knowledge of the goals of treatment helps the patient make appropriate decisions about headache management.
■ Provide printed guidelines.	Guidelines assist the patient in complying with the plan and preventing pain.
■ Provide support group information: • National Headache Foundation (800)-843-2256 • American Council for Headache Education (800)-255-ACHE	These resources provide additional information about coping with headaches.

 NDx Nursing Diagnosis

Acute Pain

Common Related Factor
Cerebral artery vasoconstriction causing increased serotonin levels, followed by vasodilation

Defining Characteristics
Aura (30% of sufferers)
Premonition
Unilateral (60%) or bilateral headache
Nausea, vomiting
Scalp tenderness
Scalp and neck muscle contraction
Throbbing pain with activity
Exhaustion

Common Expected Outcome
Patient verbalizes relief of pain.

NOC Outcomes
Pain Control; Medication Response

NIC Intervention
Analgesic Administration

■ = Independent; ▲ = Collaborative

Ongoing Assessment

Actions/Interventions	**Rationale**
■ Perform or assist with complete physical examination.	Headache may be attributed to a particular source such as head injury, sinus or dental infection, hypertension, eye problems, seizures, arthritis, or allergies.
■ Obtain thorough medical history and family history.	Migraines tend to occur in family members and can be related to stress or the physical environment.
■ Obtain detailed headache history, including the following:	Each individual may exhibit a slightly different presentation with a headache.
• Age of onset, frequency, and duration	Migraine headache pain may reach peak intensity an hour after onset. The pain may continue for several hours or even days.
• Typical location	The pain may begin on one side of the head and spread to include both sides.
• Type of pain	Patients may describe the pain as deep, steady, throbbing, or stabbing.
• Precipitating factors (foods, weather, menstruation)	Identifying headache triggers is important in developing a plan for prevention.
• Aggravating factors	Bright lights and noise may intensify headache pain.
• Associated symptoms (nausea, vomiting, numbness, visual disturbances, vertigo, sensitivity to odors and weather changes)	These associated symptoms may occur before, during, or after the headache.
• Relief measures	Patients may have tried a variety of treatments to cope with headache pain. Those measures that have been successful should be included in the individualized care plan.
• Effect on activities of daily living	For some patients, migraine headaches are incapacitating. Headache episodes can disrupt the patient's ability to work and participate in family or social activities.
■ Review headache calendar or diary, if available.	Detailed information is necessary to differentiate from other serious neurological problems, and to determine etiological factors and type of headache before a specific treatment protocol can be designed.
■ Assess for depression and suicide risk.	Many patients experience anxiety and depression with recurrent and disabling headaches. The treatment plan needs to include a holistic approach to support effective coping strategies.

Therapeutic Interventions

Actions/Interventions	**Rationale**
■ Encourage the patient to lie down in a quiet dark room.	Darkness diminishes photophobia and quiet decreases neural stimulation.
■ Provide gentle head massage if tolerated.	Massage may promote relaxation of scalp muscles and reduce pain intensity.
■ Apply cold packs.	Application of cold therapy to the forehead, temples, or back of the neck may decrease headache intensity.
■ Support head and neck with pillows.	This reduces muscle tension, which aggravates pain.

Migraine Headache

■ = Independent; ▲ = Collaborative

Migraine Headache—cont'd

Actions/Interventions

▲ Administer medication: Begin with aspirin, acetaminophen, or a nonsteroidal antiinflammatory agent. If ineffective, a narcotic (codeine, meperidine) may be used to stop pain. An ergot preparation or sumatriptan (Imitrex) may be added.

▲ Administer abortive therapy ergot preparations such as ergotamine tartrate, dihydroergotamine mesylate, and ergotamine with caffeine (Cafergot).

■ Discuss medication use and precautions:
- Take at earliest sign of impending headache (aura or prodromal signs from history).
- Repeat dose as prescribed. Do not overdose; it causes rebound headache.
- Do not use for more than 2 days consecutively.
- Take antiemetic if prescribed.

■ Provide information on ergotism, which results from too frequent use.

▲ Identify adjunct medications that may be helpful: analgesics, nonsteroidal antiinflammatory drugs, diuretics, antihistamines, and calcium channel blockers.

■ Provide information on additional pain or stress-relieving measures, including relaxation techniques, physical therapy, exercise, and biofeedback.

Rationale

Sumatriptan functions like ergot preparations in diminishing serotonin levels. This drug should not be used within 24 hours of receiving an ergot preparation or by patients with cardiovascular disorders or who are pregnant.

Ergot alkaloids cause cerebral vasoconstriction; they can be taken orally, intramuscularly, or by rectal suppository. Contraindications to ergot use are diabetes mellitus, sepsis, liver or renal disease, vascular disorders, hypertension, and pregnancy.

The earlier a migraine headache is treated, the easier it is to control.

Overuse of medications can cause rebound headache pain.

For some patients, an antiemetic alone, such as prochlorperazine (Compazine), is effective in relieving migraine pain.

Drug has cumulative effect. Side effects include finger and toe numbness and tingling, weakness, myalgia, gangrene, and blindness.

Some success has been achieved with other treatments such as ergot with phenobarbital and belladonna.

Patients can decrease the frequency of migraine headaches by avoiding precipitating events that trigger pain episodes. Regular sleep patterns, exercise, and stress management activities can reduce headache frequency.

> ### • RELATED CARE PLAN
> Ineffective coping, p. 51

Multiple Sclerosis

Disseminated Sclerosis; Demyelinating Disease

Multiple sclerosis (MS) is a chronic progressive and degenerative nervous system disease characterized by scattered patches of demyelination and glial tissue overgrowth in the white matter of the brain and spinal cord, which leads to decreased nerve conduction. As the inflammation or edema diminishes, some remyelination may occur, and nerve conduction returns. Among the clinical symptoms associated with MS are extremity weakness, visual disturbances, ataxia, tremor, incoordination, sphincter impairment, and impaired position sense. Remissions and exacerbations are associated with the disease. While cause is unknown, etiological hypotheses include environmental, viral, and genetic factors. An autoimmune response to an environmental stimulus begins the inflammatory process that causes demyelination. Loss of myelin disrupts nerve conduction. MS lesions are found in the cerebral white matter, optic nerves, brainstem, cerebellum, and cervical spinal cord. MS is considered the disease of young adults. Onset is typically between 15 and 50 years of age. Women are affected more often than men. This care plan focuses on maintenance care in the ambulatory care setting.

NDx Nursing Diagnosis

Deficient Knowledge

Common Related Factor

Unfamiliarity with the disease process and management

Defining Characteristics

Verbalization of misconceptions
Questioning

Common Expected Outcome

Patient or significant others discuss disease process, medications used, adverse effects, follow-up care.

NOC Outcomes
Knowledge: Disease Process;
Knowledge: Treatment Regimen

NIC Interventions
Teaching: Disease Process;
Teaching: Procedures/Treatment;
Teaching: Prescribed Medications

Ongoing Assessment

Actions/Interventions

■ Assess knowledge of disease, exacerbations, remissions, medical regimen, and resources.

Rationale

Lack of knowledge about MS and its progressive nature can compromise the patient's ability to care for self and cope effectively.

Therapeutic Interventions

Actions/Interventions

■ Discuss disease process in simple, straightforward manner, as follows:

• MS is a chronic, slowly progressive nervous system disease that affects nerve conduction.

• There is no definitive diagnostic test, but some tests are used in conjunction with a careful history and physical examination, such as computed tomography or magnetic resonance imaging to detect sclerotic plaques; brainstem-evoked response to detect delayed response; cerebrospinal fluid analysis to detect increased immunoglobulin G, lymphocytes, and monocytes that are indicative of MS.

Rationale

This reduces anxiety and allows the patient to comprehend the disease process. The patient and family members need to understand the disease process in order to make informed decisions concerning financial resources, long-term care, power of attorney, and living wills.

The patient needs to provide a detailed history to assist in accurate diagnosis of MS. Patients may experience symptoms for many months before a diagnosis is made.

Multiple Sclerosis

■ = Independent; ▲ = Collaborative

Multiple Sclerosis—cont'd

Actions/Interventions	Rationale

Actions/Interventions

- There is no specific cure. Newest treatments include β-interferon administration to decrease the number of exacerbations and Copolymer I administration, a synthetic myelin basis protein, to replace the lost myelin.

- MS can result in weakness, visual disturbance, walking unsteadiness, and sometimes urine or bowel problems.

■ Instruct the patient or significant others when to contact the health care team (e.g., urinary symptoms; motor, sensory, visual disturbances; exacerbations).

■ Instruct the patient or significant others about steroid therapy:
  - Side effects (e.g., sodium retention, fluid retention, pedal edema, hypertension, gastric irritation).
  - Measures to control side effects (e.g., low-sodium diet, daily weighing, leg elevation, support hose, blood pressure monitoring, antacids, adequate rest, and avoidance of contact with persons with infectious disease).

■ Explain all other medications that may be prescribed: muscle relaxants, antidepressants, and immunosuppressants.

■ Instruct on the following:
  - Importance of maintaining the most normal activity level possible
  - Avoidance of hot baths
  - Sleeping in a prone position
  - Need to inspect areas of impaired sensation for serious injuries
  - Need to use energy conservation techniques

■ Instruct the patient to avoid potentially exacerbating activities: emotional stress, physical stress or fatigue, infection, pregnancy, physically "run down" condition.

■ Facilitate involvement with support groups and/or counseling, as desired.

Rationale

The cost of treatment may be covered by the patient's health insurance.

The patient and family need to plan strategies for management of exacerbations of MS.

Prompt treatment of exacerbations can be initiated when the patient and family know what to report.

Steroid therapy decreases edema and acute inflammatory response within evolving plaque. Prednisone and adrenocorticotropic hormone are used most often for acute exacerbations.

These measures reduce fluid retention and the risk for infection and gastric ulcers.

A range of medications can be used for management of MS. Biological response modifiers delay and decrease the exacerbations of MS. Immunosuppressants are effective in reducing neurological disability from MS. Muscle spasticity can be managed with muscle relaxants. Other symptoms are treated with specific medications. Drugs may be used for short-term or long-term therapy.

When the patient can have a normal activity pattern, it helps maintain functional limits and improve body image.

Heat increases metabolic demands and may increase weakness.

Good positioning during sleep decreases flexion spasms.

Careful attention to these areas decreases risk for injury. Patients may have decreased temperature sensation that increases risk for burns.

The fatigue in MS is from nerve demyelination not muscle fatigue. A balance of daily rest and exercise is indicated. Drugs such as amantadine or pemoline are helpful in treating fatigue.

Young female patients may choose to become pregnant. Symptoms of MS diminish during pregnancy, but exacerbation is common and sometimes severe during the postpartum period. Stress is the most common cause of exacerbations.

Support groups can assist with issues such as family process, work, parenting, and sexuality. Developmentally, this age group is typically in its most productive years, therefore MS has the potential for causing major life cycle alterations. Depression and cognitive impairment are common problems for the patient with MS.

Neurological Care Plans

■ = Independent; ▲ = Collaborative

Nursing Diagnosis

Impaired Physical Mobility

Common Related Factors

Motor weakness
Tremors
Spasticity

Defining Characteristics

Unsteady gait
Limited range of motion (ROM)
Lack of coordination
Inability to move purposefully
Reluctance to attempt movement

Common Expected Outcomes

Patient verbalizes ability to move appropriately within limits of disease.
Patient uses adaptive techniques to maximize mobility.

NOC Outcomes
Ambulation; Mobility

NIC Interventions
Environmental Management; Teaching: Prescribed Activity/Exercise; Exercise Therapy: Stretching/Muscle Control

---

Ongoing Assessment

Actions/Interventions

- Assess the patient's gait, muscle strength, weakness, coordination, and balance.

- Assess endurance level and stamina (e.g., number of stairs the patient can climb, distance the patient can walk, ability to work, ability to perform activities of daily living [ADLs] independently).

- Determine the patient's perception of muscle strength and ability to use assistive devices (cane, walker) and adaptive techniques (using larger muscle groups).

- Inquire about falls.

Rationale

These are a gauge to assess progression and remission.

Motor dysfunction contributes to weakness with MS. Cerebellar dysfunction causes tremors, poor coordination, and ataxia. These symptoms can interfere with ADLs and mobility. Fatigue and reduced functional ability may be more pronounced in the evening.

Proper use of assistive devices can promote activity and reduce risk of falls.

Determining the etiology for falls (e.g., weakness, cluttered environment) guides the treatment plan.

Therapeutic Interventions

Actions/Interventions

- Encourage self-care as tolerated and to seek assistance when necessary; arrange for home care when needed.

- Suggest placing frequently needed items (cooking material, personal care items, cleaning supplies) within easy reach.

Rationale

Exacerbations become more frequent and longer in duration as the disease progresses.

Home modifications can help the patient maintain a desired level of functional independence and reduce fatigue with activity.

Multiple Sclerosis

■ = Independent; ▲ = Collaborative

Multiple Sclerosis—cont'd

Actions/Interventions	Rationale
■ Suggest scheduled rest periods.	Exercises and early ambulation require much energy. Rest periods help reduce the level of fatigue.
▲ Consult a physical therapist and occupational therapist for use of assistive or ambulatory devices and ADL evaluation.	Home environment evaluation may be necessary.
■ Instruct the patient in use of adaptive techniques and equipment. These may include wrist weights, adaptive equipment such as stabilized plates and nonspilling cups, stabilization of extremity, and training patient to use trunk and head.	Aids can compensate for impaired function and increase the level of activity. The goal for using adaptive devices is to promote safety, increase mobility, prevent falls, and conserve energy.
■ Encourage stretching exercises and ROM daily.	These promote venous return, prevent flexion contractures, and maintain muscle strength and endurance.
■ Explain use of antispasmodics as prescribed.	Decreased spasticity will help improve muscle control.
■ Encourage ambulation with assistance or supervision.	This exercise keeps the patient as functionally active as possible.

NDx Nursing Diagnosis

Disturbed Sensory Perception: Visual

Common Risk Factor

Optic nerve demyelination

Common Expected Outcome

Patient uses adaptive techniques to cope with visual impairment.

NOC Outcomes
Risk Control: Visual Impairment;
    Vision Compensation Behavior

NIC Intervention
Communication Enhancement: Visual
    Deficit

Ongoing Assessment

Actions/Interventions	Rationale
■ Assess for visual impairment.	Common symptoms include diplopia, blurred vision, nystagmus, visual loss, scotomas (blind spots), and impaired color perception.
■ Assess the patient's ability to perform ADLs.	Restricted vision affects the ability to perform many ADLs. Assessment can determine the level of assistance that is necessary.

■ = Independent; ▲ = Collaborative

Neurological Care Plans

Therapeutic Interventions

Actions/Interventions

- Encourage the patient to ask for orientation to new environments, such as location of bathrooms, stairs, and other features in unfamiliar homes, restaurants, and businesses.
- Encourage the patient and family to place objects within reach. Do not change familiar home environments without informing the patient.
- Provide an eye patch for diplopia; encourage alternating the patch from eye to eye.

- Instruct the patient to rest eyes when fatigued.
- Advise the patient of the availability of large-type reading materials and talking books.
- If the patient is hospitalized, place the call light within reach with side rails up and bed in low position to prevent injury.
- Teach the patient to turn head from side to side when entering an unfamiliar environment.

Rationale

The patient may be embarrassed or hesitant to ask for assistance.

Consistent placement of belongings enhances independence.

Alternating patches alleviates diplopia. Using adaptive techniques can help the patient cope with visual changes. Corrective lenses may be beneficial for changes in visual acuity.

Fatigue can aggravate visual problems.

These resources allow the patient to retain desired activity for work and leisure.

Patient safety is a priority.

Visual scanning will help the patient who has decreased peripheral vision. This technique promotes safety in a new environment.

NDx Nursing Diagnosis

Risk for Urinary Retention/Incontinence

Common Risk Factor

Neurogenic bladder

Common Expected Outcomes

The patient maintains residual urine of less than 100 mL/hr.
The patient does not experience urinary tract infection (UTI).

NOC Outcomes
Urinary Continence; Urinary Elimination

NIC Interventions
Urinary Retention;
  Urinary Incontinence Care

Ongoing Assessment

Actions/Interventions

- Inquire about symptoms of urinary retention, frequency, urgency, pain, and abdominal distention.

- Assess for signs of UTI.

Rationale

Patients may experience either a spastic bladder characterized by frequency and dribbling, or a flaccid bladder, in which an absence of sensation to void results in urine retention.

Retention predisposes to infection. Infection can trigger an exacerbation of MS.

■ = Independent; ▲ = Collaborative

Multiple Sclerosis

→ Multiple Sclerosis—cont'd

Therapeutic Interventions

Actions/Interventions

- Initiate individualized bladder training program. Instruct the patient about the Credé method and intermittent catheterization for residual urine if signs of retention are present.

- Encourage the patient to drink 2 to 3 liters of fluid daily.

- Instruct the patient about signs and symptoms of UTI.

- Explain prescribed medications.

- Recommend vitamin C and liberal intake of cranberry juice.

See also **Impaired Urinary Elimination,** *p. 201,* *and* **Urinary Retention,** *p. 208.*

Rationale

Residual urine greater than 100 mL predisposes the patient to UTIs. Bladder Credé methods stimulate complete emptying of the bladder.

Increased fluid intake increases urine output and reduces the risk of infection.

Patients need to be able to recognize symptoms of UTI so that treatment can be started as soon as possible.

Cholinergic drugs are indicated for flaccid bladder, and anticholinergic drugs are indicated for spastic bladder

These acidify urine and reduce bacterial growth.

NDx Nursing Diagnosis

Risk for Impaired Skin Integrity

Common Risk Factors

Sensory changes
Immobility

Common Expected Outcome

Patient maintains intact skin as evidenced by absence of breakdown, burns, or pressure ulcer formation.

NOC Outcome
Tissue Integrity: Skin and Mucous Membranes

NIC Intervention
Skin Surveillance

Ongoing Assessment

Actions/Interventions

- Assess skin integrity and areas of body with decreased sensation.

Rationale

Sensory changes may result in hypoalgesia, paresthesia, and loss of position sense, which can lead to trauma, injury, and skin integrity changes.

■ = Independent; ▲ = Collaborative

Neurological Care Plans

Therapeutic Interventions

Actions/Interventions	Rationale
■ Instruct the patient to avoid extremes in heat and cold (water and environmental), and prolonged physical pressure.	The patient needs knowledge to prevent thermal and pressure injury to the skin.
■ Instruct the patient to test bath water with unaffected extremity.	Decreased temperature sensation increases risk for burns.
■ Instruct the patient to notice foot placement when ambulating.	This compensates for decreased position sense.
■ Instruct the patient to change position every 2 hours, even when watching television or working at a desk.	Normal protective mechanisms are absent, so a conscious decision must be made to change position.

See also **Risk for Impaired Skin Integrity,** *p. 173.*

NDx Nursing Diagnosis

Disturbed Body Image

Common Related Factors

Physical body changes
Psychosocial changes
Negative feelings about self
Negative feelings about body
Change in social involvement
Feelings of hopelessness, powerlessness

Defining Characteristics

Poor eye contact
Refusal to participate in care or treatment
Negative verbalizations about self

Common Expected Outcomes

Patient verbalizes positive coping mechanisms.
Patient expresses positive attitude about self.

NOC Outcomes
Body Image; Social Support

NIC Interventions
Body Image Enhancement;
 Coping Enhancement;
 Support System Enhancement

Ongoing Assessment

Actions/Interventions	Rationale
■ Assess quality and quantity of verbalizations about body and self-image.	There is a broad range of normal behaviors associated with body image disturbance, from denial to preoccupation.
■ Inquire about physical dysfunction, and any new symptoms that may affect lifestyle or function (sexual, urinary, bowel problems). Determine what the patient thinks may help alleviate problems.	Patients with chronic diseases may have a unique perspective on what interventions may be most effective for them.

Multiple Sclerosis

■ = Independent; ▲ = Collaborative

Multiple Sclerosis—cont'd

Actions/Interventions

- Observe for changes in behavior and/or level of functioning.

- Inquire about coping skills used before illness, but consider that even successful coping skills in the past may become ineffective as the disease state deteriorates over time.

Rationale

Patients with MS may also experience cognitive changes, depression, anger, and emotional lability. In later stages, memory deficits, confusion, and disorientation may occur.

Successful adjustment is influenced by previous coping success. However, additional resources may be required.

Therapeutic Interventions

Actions/Interventions

- Provide opportunity at each visit to ask questions and talk about feelings.
- Include the patient in decisions regarding long-term care.
- Support the patient's efforts to maintain independence.

- ▲ Use referral sources (psychiatry service) when appropriate.
- Refer to support groups.

Rationale

Verbalization provides an outlet for concerns.

This fosters positive self-concept or body image.

Functional independence can support stress management and reduce exacerbations.

Additional resources may facilitate the patient's attempts at coping.

Groups that come together for mutual goals and information exchange can provide valuable education and emotional support in dealing with life-changing effects of the disease process.

> • RELATED CARE PLANS
>
> Anticipatory grieving, p. 82
> Constipation, p. 46
> Ineffective sexuality patterns, p. 170
> Powerlessness, p. 153
> Self-care deficit, p. 156

Parkinson's Disease

Paralysis Agitans, Parkinsonism

Parkinson's disease (PD) is a movement disorder associated with dopamine deficiency in the brain. Other neurotransmitter alterations may also contribute to the disease process. This chronic neurological disorder affects the extrapyramidal system of the brain responsible for control and regulation of movement. The four characteristic signs are tremor at rest, rigidity, postural instability, and slowness of movement. Other clinical manifestations include shuffling gait, masklike facial expressions, and muscle weakness affecting writing, speaking, eating, chewing, and swallowing. Onset is usually around 60 years of age; however, a significant number of young adults have Parkinsonism. Secondary Parkinsonism is associated with other nervous system disorders; however, most cases are idiopathic. Etiological hypotheses include exposure to environmental toxins and age-related degeneration of brain neurons. Some theories suggest gene mutation may play a role in the development of PD. Free radical formation has also been considered as a contributing factor. Patient care is usually managed in the outpatient setting.

■ = Independent; ▲ = Collaborative

Nursing Diagnosis

Impaired Physical Mobility

Common Related Factors	**Defining Characteristics**
Neuromuscular impairment Decreased strength and endurance	Tremors Muscle rigidity Decreased ability to initiate movements (akinesis) Impaired coordination of movement Limited range of motion (ROM) Impaired ability to carry out activities of daily living (ADLs) Postural disturbances

Common Expected Outcome	
Patient achieves optimal level of functioning as evidenced by ability to safely ambulate and perform ADLs.	**NOC Outcomes** Ambulation; Mobility **NIC Interventions** Teaching: Prescribed Activity or Exercise; Environmental Management

Ongoing Assessment

Actions/Interventions	**Rationale**
■ Assess for rigidity:	Rigidity may be unilateral or bilateral
• Cogwheel	Cogwheel rigidity is an interrupted but rhythmic muscle movement.
• Plastic	Plastic rigidity represents more resistance to movement.
• Lead pipe	This type of rigidity is complete resistance to movement.
■ Assess extent of tremors.	Typically they are more prominent at rest and are aggravated by emotional stress. Hand tremors may present as a "pill-rolling" movement at rest. Tremors occur as a result of unopposed acetylcholine activity from the dopamine deficiency.
■ Assess posture, coordination, and ambulation.	Clinical manifestations may range from only a slight limp to the typical shuffling, propulsive gait with rigidity. These changes are more common in advanced PD.
■ Assess for bradykinesia.	The patient with PD will have difficulty initiating movement or change direction of movement. This results from poor coordination of opposing muscle groups. The patient's movements will be slow and hesitant.

Parkinson's Disease

■ = Independent; ▲ = Collaborative

Parkinson's Disease—cont'd

Therapeutic Interventions

Actions/Interventions	Rationale
■ Encourage patient to perform ROM to all joints daily.	Exercise reduces muscle rigidity, maintains joint mobility, and prevents muscle atrophy.
■ Provide tips for getting in and out of chair. Use sturdy, high-seated chair with arms.	This type of chair provides more support and reduces risk of falls with changes in position.
■ Reinforce need for regular activity and ambulation.	Activity is important to reduce hazards of immobility. Some patients have shown improvement with rhythmic exercise programs such as yoga or tai chi.
■ Encourage the family to supervise and assist with ambulation as needed.	Safety with ambulation is an important concern to prevent falls. The use of mobility aids such as canes and walkers promotes stability and reduces the risk of falls.
■ Encourage the patient to lift feet and take large steps while walking.	A broad-based gait helps improve balance and reduces shuffling.
■ Discuss the need for removing environmental barriers in the home.	Maintaining patient safety is a priority.
■ Instruct the family to allow sufficient time for ADLs.	The family often wants to perform the task rather than enabling the patient to do it.
▲ Consult physical and occupational therapists about aids to facilitate ADLs and safe ambulation and to promote muscle strengthening.	Aids can increase mobility and allow the patient some control over the environment.

 NDx Nursing Diagnosis

Imbalanced Nutrition: Less Than Body Requirements

Common Related Factors
Difficulty swallowing and dysphagia
Choking spells
Drooling
Regurgitation of food or fluids through nares

Defining Characteristics
Documented intake below required caloric level
Malnutrition
Weight loss
Constipation

Common Expected Outcome
Patient maintains optimal nutritional status, as evidenced by adequate oral intake, weight gain, weight within normal limits for height and age, and absence of constipation.

NOC Outcomes
Nutritional Status: Nutrient Intake;
Respiratory Status: Airway Patency

NIC Interventions
Nutrition Management;
Aspiration Precautions

■ = Independent; ▲ = Collaborative

Neurological Care Plans

Ongoing Assessment

Actions/Interventions

- Assess degree of swallowing difficulty with fluids, solids, and/or medications.

- Inquire about episodes of choking and nasal regurgitations.
- Assess for episodes of vomiting.
- Assess overall nutritional status.

- Monitor weight at each visit. Encourage the patient or family to keep a weight and/or diet log.

Rationale

Swallowing difficulty accompanied by fatigue and fine motor impairment causes diminished appetite and poor nutritional intake. Swallowing problems are associated with the later stages of the disease.

These provide data on the patient's level of impairment and risk for aspiration.

This is a common side effect of medication therapies.

Bradykinesia, tremors, and rigidity may interfere with feeding self-care, chewing, and swallowing.

This provides data on nutritional status. Weight loss is usually the result of decreased intake.

Therapeutic Interventions

Actions/Interventions

- Reinforce the need for high Fowler's position for eating and drinking.
- Elicit family supervision during meals. Avoid distractions.
- Stress importance of allowing adequate time for meals; avoid rushing the patient.

- Suggest high-calorie, low-volume supplements between meals.
- Suggest the patient take small bites of food. Encourage the patient to swallow two to three times after taking a bite of food.
- Suggest appetizing foods that are easily chewed and fluids that are thickened rather than watery fluids.
- Suggest four to five small meals per day and at least 2000 mL of fluids (if fluids are not restricted for another health reason).
- Encourage oral hygiene after meals.

- ▲ Consult a dietitian for needed changes in food consistency, for caloric counts, and for diet suggestions to help avoid constipation.
- ▲ If swallowing difficulties worsen, consult the speech therapist.
- ▲ Consult a physical therapist for wrist or hand brace.

Rationale

This reduces the risk of aspiration.

The patient needs to focus on swallowing.

It may be difficult for patients to swallow under pressure. Bradykinesia may require more time for feeding self-care.

Additional caloric intake may be required for optimal nutrition.

Smaller bites may be easier to swallow.

Fluids are more difficult to control when swallowing.

These may be tolerated with greater success than three meals daily.

This is useful in removing residual and pocketed food that can be aspirated later.

The dietitian can recommend alterations in food selection to promote adequate calorie and nutrient intake.

A specialist may be needed to design plans to improve the patient's ability to swallow.

Braces help control tremors and improve ability to feed self.

Parkinson's Disease

■ = Independent; ▲ = Collaborative

Parkinson's Disease—cont'd

 Nursing Diagnosis

Impaired Verbal Communication

Common Related Factor	**Defining Characteristics**
Dysarthria	Difficulty in articulating words Monotonous voice tones Slow, slurred speech Stammered speech

Common Expected Outcomes

Patient communicates needs adequately.
Patient uses alternative methods of communication as indicated.

> **NOC Outcome**
> Communication Ability
>
> **NIC Intervention**
> Communication Enhancement: Speech Deficit

Ongoing Assessment

Actions/Interventions

- Evaluate the patient's ability to speak, as well as to understand spoken words, written words, and pictures.

- Assess for echolalia.

- Assess voice quality.

Rationale

As the disease progresses, cognitive abilities diminish. The patient with PD may have slurred speech as a result of dysarthria.

The patient may automatically repeat words or phrases spoken by another person.

As PD progresses, the patient's voice may become lower-pitched and softer.

Therapeutic Interventions

Actions/Interventions

- Maintain eye contact when speaking.
- Allow patient time to articulate.

- Encourage face and tongue exercises.

- Encourage the patient to practice reading aloud or singing.
- Avoid speaking loudly unless the patient is hard of hearing.
- ▲ Consult a speech therapist if indicated.

- Provide alternative communication aids as needed, such as picture or word boards.

Rationale

This promotes patient focus and attention.

The patient may be discouraged and give up if rushed. The patient needs time to organize thoughts before speaking.

Regular exercise can reduce rigidity and facilitate muscle relaxation.

Activities that involve the affected muscles help the patient practice muscle control.

Loud talking does not improve the patient's ability to understand.

The speech therapist can evaluate the patient's need of adaptive devices such as voice synthesizers or computers.

These aids reduce communication frustration.

■ = Independent; ▲ = Collaborative

Nursing Diagnosis

Chronic Low Self-Esteem

Common Related Factors

Changes in body image, especially drooling, tremors, gait, slurred speech
Dependence on others

Defining Characteristics

Minimal eye contact
Self-deprecating statements
Anger
Expression of shame
Rejection of positive feedback

Common Expected Outcome

Patient recognizes self-maligning statements and begins to verbalize positive expression of self-worth.

NOC Outcomes
Body Image; Self-Esteem

NIC Interventions
Body Image Enhancement; Self-Esteem Enhancement

Ongoing Assessment

Actions/Interventions

- Assess the patient's perception of self. Note verbalizations regarding self.

- Assess the degree to which the patient feels loved and respected by others.

- Evaluate the patient's support system.

Rationale

Patients may attempt to hide tremors. Over time, they may withdraw from social interactions because they are embarrassed by their symptoms.

The manner in which one is treated by others influences self-esteem. Feeling loved and respected despite disabilities implies that one is valued by others and supports self-esteem.

A positive social network can promote effective coping with the changes of PD.

Therapeutic Interventions

Actions/Interventions

- Encourage the patient to verbalize fears and concerns. Listen attentively.

- Discuss feelings about symptoms: tremors, drooling of saliva, slurred speech.
- Discuss the impact of alteration in health status on self-esteem.

- Instruct the family to avoid overprotection of the individual; promote social interaction as appropriate.

Rationale

Verbalization of actual or perceived threats can help reduce anxiety. Patients may express concern about increasing dependency on others for mobility and ADLs.

Patients may be ashamed about changes in their appearance and their inability to control symptoms.

Disturbances in self-esteem are natural responses to significant changes. Reconstruction of the individual's self-esteem occurs after grieving has taken place and acceptance has followed.

Patients should not be forced into uncomfortable situations. Overprotection by family members may reinforce the patient's feelings of unworthiness.

Parkinson's Disease

■ = Independent; ▲ = Collaborative

Parkinson's Disease—cont'd

Actions/Interventions

- Instruct the family to provide privacy, if desired, especially when performing ADLs and eating.

- Explore strengths and resources with the patient.

- Teach the patient necessary self-care measures related to the disease.

- Advise of the realistic need for additional support in coping with lifelong illness.

- Refer to support groups.

- Refer to the American Parkinson's Disease Association.

Rationale

The patient may be embarrassed about eating in public places because of swallowing difficulties; family meals should be encouraged.

Attention to the patient's strengths will reinforce a more positive self-esteem.

Each success will reinforce positive self-esteem.

As this disease progresses, self-care and home care issues become more evident, especially for older persons who may live alone or with an equally elderly or frail spouse.

Use of lay support groups or individuals may help the patient recognize positives even in the face of disease.

Local chapters of the organization provide information and resources such as support groups.

NDx Nursing Diagnosis

Deficient Knowledge

Common Related Factor

Uncertainty about cause of disease and its treatment

Common Expected Outcome

Patient or caregiver verbalizes disability and special needs with regard to disease process, activity, exercises, ambulation, medication, diet, and elimination.

Defining Characteristics

Multiple questions
Lack of questions
Apparent confusion over condition

NOC Outcomes

Knowledge: Disease Process;
    Knowledge: Treatment Regimen

NIC Interventions

Teaching: Disease Process;
    Teaching: Prescribed Medication;
    Teaching: Activity/Exercise

Ongoing Assessment

Actions/Interventions

- Evaluate the patient's and caregiver's understanding of the disease process, diagnostic tests, treatments, and outcomes.

Rationale

An individualized teaching plan is based on the patient's previous knowledge and desire for additional information.

■ = Independent; ▲ = Collaborative

Therapeutic Interventions

Actions/Interventions	Rationale
■ Reinforce explanation of the disease and treatment: • Disease: has a gradual onset and progression; has no known cure. • Treatment: therapy aimed at relieving symptoms and preventing complications.	Knowledge of the disease process and treatment may assist with the patient's coping skills. Information helps the patient and family make decisions about long-term care, financial resources, living arrangements, power of attorney, and living wills.
■ Discuss potential surgical interventions: • Stereotactic pallidotomy	Stereotactic pallidotomy involves the use of electrical stimulation of selected neuron centers to diminish rigidity or tremors by creating permanent lesions.
• Stereotactic thalamotomy to relieve tremors and rigidity	Stereotactic thalamotomy uses thermal coagulation of neuron centers to reduce tremors.
• Neurotransplantation of dopamine-producing cells and stem cell research	Transplantation of dopamine-producing cells from fetal tissue is considered an experimental procedure. Sources of fetal tissue are either human or porcine. The procedure is considered high risk but many patients demonstrate symptomatic improvement.
• Deep brain stimulation	Deep brain stimulation using an implanted pulse generator, similar to a cardiac pacemaker, provides control of tremors in patients whose drug therapy has been unsuccessful.
■ Encourage independence and avoid overprotection by encouraging the patient to do things for self: feeding, dressing, ambulation.	In early stages and with medication therapy, most ADLs can be continued (driving, working), but as the disease progresses, assistance will be required.
■ Discuss with the patient, family, and caregiver the use and the potential side effects of the following:	Dosage of medication may need to be adjusted.
• Anticholinergics: benztropine mesylate (Cogentin), procyclidine (Kemadrin), cycrimine (Pagitane), trihexyphenidyl (Artane)	These drugs decrease tremors by blocking acetylcholine activity. Side effects include constipation, dry mouth, confusion, blurred vision.
• Dopaminergic drugs • Dopamine precursors: levodopa, carbidopa/levodopa (Sinemet)	These drugs cross the blood-brain barrier where they are converted to dopamine. The addition of carbidopa decreases peripheral conversion of levodopa and makes more of the drug available to the brain. Side effects include nausea, hypotension, confusion, and dyskinesia. The patient may develop a tolerance to these drugs, producing an "on-off" phenomenon. The primary management for this condition is to reduce the dosage or give the patient a 7- to 10-day drug holiday.
• Dopamine agonists: bromocriptine (Parlodel), ropinirole (Requip), pergolide (Permax)	This class of drugs mimics the activity of dopamine on postsynaptic receptors. They are used in combination with carbidopa/levodopa. Side effects are increased sleepiness, confusion, and hypotension.
• Monoamine oxidase B inhibitor: selegiline (Deprenyl)	This drug potentiates the effect of carbidopa/levodopa. Patients may experience sleep problems as a side effect. Adverse interactions with meperidine have been reported.

Parkinson's Disease

■ = Independent; ▲ = Collaborative

Parkinson's Disease—cont'd

Actions/Interventions	Rationale
• Indirect agonist: amantadine (Symmetrel)	This antiviral medication has both anticholinergic and dopaminergic effects in patients with PD. It also reduces the development of dyskinesia from other PD drugs. Side effects may include dry mouth, ankle swelling, and a reddish-blue mottling of the skin (livedo reticularis)
• Catechol-O-methyl-transferase inhibitor (COMT): tolcapone (Tasmar), entacapone (Comtan)	These drugs block peripheral conversion of levodopa, making more of the drug available to cross the blood-brain barrier. They decrease the development tolerance to levodopa. Liver toxicity is associated with the use of these drugs.

■ Discuss activity recommendations:
  - Encourage the family and significant others to participate in physical therapy exercises of stretching and massaging muscles.

As the disease progresses, muscles and joints become stiff. Exercise improves strength and decreases rigidity.

  - Encourage daily ambulation outdoors but avoidance of extreme hot and cold weather.

Extremes in temperature exacerbate symptoms in the patient with PD and are not generally well tolerated by older persons whose physiological responses are impaired.

  - Encourage the patient to practice lifting feet while walking, using heel-toe gait, and swinging arms deliberately while walking.

A wide base of support is best for balance.

  - Encourage the patient to dress daily, avoiding clothing with buttons (use zippers or loop-and-pile fasteners instead) and shoes with laces or snaps.

These actions may increase the patient's self-esteem.

  - Prevent falls by clearing walkways of furniture and throw rugs and provide side rails on stairs.

Environmental modifications will facilitate patient safety.

• RELATED CARE PLANS

Activity intolerance, p. 7
Caregiver role strain, p. 35
Constipation, p. 46
Diarrhea, p. 54
Risk for aspiration, p. 18
Self-care deficit, p. 156

Seizure Activity

Convulsion; Epilepsy; Seizure Disorder

A seizure is an occasional, excessive disorderly discharge of neuronal activity from the cerebral cortex causing behavioral and physical disturbances. Recurrent seizures (epilepsy) may be classified as partial, generalized, or partial complex. Etiological factors include fever, cerebral lesions, biochemical disorders (hyponatremia), trauma, and idiopathic disease. Onset is usually before 20 years of age, and there seems to be a genetic predisposition to idiopathic epilepsy. Seizure activity has three distinct phases. The preictal phase is that time before the actual seizure. The patient may experience symptoms that warn of an

■ = Independent; ▲ = Collaborative

impending seizure. This is called an *aura*. During the ictal phase, the patient experiences a progression of neuromuscular changes as a result of the disorganized neuron activity. The postictal phase is the period immediately following seizure activity. This phase represents brain recovery and return to baseline status. A patient with new onset of seizures will require hospitalization for diagnosis and initiation of treatment. Follow-up care is in the outpatient setting. This care plan focuses on self-care in the ambulatory setting.

NDx Nursing Diagnosis

Deficient Knowledge

Common Related Factors

Lack of exposure
Information misinterpretation
Unfamiliarity with information resources

Common Expected Outcome

Patient discusses the disease process, treatment, and safety measures.

Defining Characteristics

Verbalization of problem
Request for information
Statement of misconception

NOC Outcomes

Knowledge: Disease Process;
Knowledge: Treatment Regimen;
Safety Behavior: Physical Injury

NIC Interventions

Seizure Precautions/Management;
Teaching: Disease Process;
Teaching: Treatment/Procedures

Ongoing Assessment

Actions/Interventions

- Assess knowledge concerning the disorder and treatment plan.

- Assess frequency, duration, and type of seizure activity. Ask the patient and family about seizure history, if precipitating factors are involved, such as odors, visual stimulation, fatigue, stress, febrile illness, menstruation, or alcohol consumption.

- Inquire about warnings before seizure (aura, prodromal signs).

- Determine physical effects of prior seizures, such as change in level of consciousness preceding seizure activity, body part in which seizure started, epileptic cry, automatism, length of seizure, head and eye turning, pupillary reaction, associated falls, oral secretions, urinary or fecal incontinence, cyanosis, postictal state, any post-seizure focal abnormality (Todd's paralysis that can last for up to 24 hours).

Rationale

This information provides a baseline upon which to design an individualized teaching plan.

This is necessary for planning appropriate treatments.

Each individual may present with his or her own pattern. Understanding this can facilitate treatment.

Knowledge of changes that occur with each phase of seizure activity may help the patient and family plan appropriate care to prevent seizures and prevent injury during a seizure.

Seizure Activity

■ = Independent; ▲ = Collaborative

Seizure Activity–cont'd

Actions/Interventions

- Assess readiness for learning.

- Evaluate barriers that may interfere with the patient's ability to obtain medication or return for follow-up checkups.

Rationale

Information is presented when comprehension will be optimal.

Knowledge of causative factors provides direction for subsequent intervention.

Therapeutic Interventions

Actions/Interventions

- Provide information specific to patient needs, as related to severity of disorder and seizure control.

- Discuss the disease process, including aura and prodrome.

- Teach the patient and family about specific antiepilepsy medications.

  - Hydantoins: phenytoin (Dilantin), fosphenytoin (Cerebyx)

  - Iminostilbenes: carbamazepine (Tegretol), oxcarbazepine (Trileptal)

  - Phenobarbital

  - Valproates: valproic acid (Depakene), divalproex sodium (Depakote)

Rationale

Generalized seizures affect the entire brain and are bilateral and symmetrical. There is usually no aura, but there is loss of consciousness. Generalized seizures range from staring spells to the stiffening (tonic) and jerking (clonic) of extremities seen in grand mal seizures. Partial seizures, or focal onset seizures, affect a specific region of the cerebral cortex with physical effects depending on where the seizure originated. Partial (simple) seizures are typically just motor or sensory and do not cause loss of consciousness. Partial (complex) seizures are psychomotor like partial simple seizures, but also involve changes in consciousness such as confusion and memory loss. This seizure can spread through the cerebrum and culminate in a generalized seizure.

Knowledge of warnings facilitates use of safety measures that can be implemented, such as sitting or lying down or pulling over if driving.

Drug therapy is the primary approach to management of seizure activity. Patients may need to take a combination of medications to achieve effective seizure control.

This class of drugs is a mainstay of drug therapy for seizures. Patients need to implement routine dental care to decrease the development of gingival hyperplasia. This side effect occurs with long-term use of these drugs.

These drugs are used for partial complex and generalized seizures. The side effects of these drugs include nausea, diplopia, hepatic toxicity, and leukopenia. The patient may need periodic blood work done to monitor for drug side effects.

This drug is a long-acting barbiturate. It is used in combination with hydantoins in the management of partial complex and generalized seizures. The drug is a class IV controlled substance. Dependency can develop with long-term use.

These drugs are used in the management of partial, partial complex, and generalized seizures. With long-term use the patient may develop weight gain, alopecia, hepatic toxicity, and thrombocytopenia. Periodic blood work needs to be done to monitor for side effects. The patient needs to implement safety precautions to prevent bleeding.

■ = Independent; ▲ = Collaborative

Neurological Care Plans

Actions/Interventions

- Review need for medication and optimal schedule. Discuss danger of seizure activity with abrupt withdrawal.

- Discuss the need for periodic follow-up check on anticonvulsant blood levels and possible complete blood count check. Instruct the patient to discuss frequency and time intervals with the physician.

- Provide information for patients undergoing continuous video electroencephalogram (EEG) monitoring.

▲ Reinforce information about surgical therapy for seizure management.

- Explain to the patient, caregiver, or significant others what to do during a seizure:
  - If the patient is on the floor, remove furniture or other potentially harmful objects from the area.
  - Do not restrain the patient during seizure. Loosen clothing.
  - Allow the seizure to run its course. Do not place a tongue blade or other objects in the patient's mouth.
  - If the airway is occluded, open the airway, then insert an oral airway.
  - Roll the patient to the side after cessation of muscle twitching.
- If seizures persist longer than 30 to 60 seconds or are incessantly repetitive, instruct the caregiver or patient to call 911.
- Educate about safety measures:
  - Driving

  - Home safety—The patient should have someone else present when cooking and bathing, for example, to reduce the risk of injury
  - Work safety—Avoid construction work, ladder climbing, heavy equipment operation
  - Personal safety—Dive or swim with a companion; wear medical alert identification; be aware of the effect of alcohol and drugs
▲ Refer the patient to a dietitian if a ketogenic diet is prescribed.

Rationale

Patients sometimes believe they no longer need medication because they have not experienced a seizure in some time. Abrupt discontinuation of anticonvulsants may trigger seizure activity.

Anemia and other blood dyscrasias occur with anticonvulsant therapy.

This assessment technique is used for patients who have new-onset seizures or seizures that do not respond to drug therapy. Documentation of the brain location of seizure activity and type of seizure will guide decisions about drug therapy and other treatment. The patient may be hospitalized for several days until a seizure is documented.

Patients who do not respond to drug therapy may be candidates for surgical intervention. Procedures range from destruction of a single seizure focus to a hemispherectomy. Surgery may be curative or palliative.

This prevents injury.

Physical restraint applied during seizure activity can cause pathogenic trauma.

Inserting objects often causes more harm, such as dislodging teeth, causing lacerations, and obstructing the airway.

Airway patency is a priority.

Positioning is important to prevent aspiration.

The patient may require intravenous phenytoin, phenobarbital, diazepam, or lorazepam to stop status epilepticus.

Laws vary from state to state; in most states, the patient must be seizure-free for 6 months to 2 years.

Most states have laws prohibiting workplace discrimination for people with epilepsy.

There is an increased risk of seizures produced by interaction of alcohol with anticonvulsant drugs.

This intense diet therapy is usually attempted only for severe, unrelenting seizure disorders. The diet is a high-fat, low-carbohydrate, low-protein diet, divided into several small meals per day. The diet is complex and requires education about careful selection of foods.

Seizure Activity

■ = Independent; ▲ = Collaborative

Seizure Activity—cont'd

Actions/Interventions	Rationale
■ Refer to the Epilepsy Foundation of America.	This organization provides information and resources to support effective coping and seizure management.
■ Provide information, as appropriate, about specially trained animals for epileptics.	Some dogs are able to detect a seizure prodrome and warn the patient so safety measures can be implemented before the seizure begins.

 Nursing Diagnosis

Risk for Chronic Low Self-Esteem

Common Risk Factors

Seizure activity
Dependence on medications
Social isolation
Discrimination
Misperceptions

Common Expected Outcome

Patient verbalizes positive statements about self in relation to living with a seizure disorder.

NOC Outcome
Self-Esteem

NIC Intervention
Self-Esteem Enhancement

Ongoing Assessment

Actions/Interventions	Rationale
■ Assess feelings about self, disorder, and long-term therapy.	Patients may express frustration, anxiety, and unrealistic expectations because of the unpredictability of their seizures. Many patients begin to identify themselves as chronically ill and express feelings of loss of independence.
■ Assess perceived implications of the disorder and its effect on socialization.	Patients may have a fear of or have experienced actual discrimination in jobs and schooling, as well as a fear of loss of control and embarrassment in public.

Therapeutic Interventions

Actions/Interventions	Rationale
■ Encourage ventilation of feelings.	Talking about feelings can support effective coping and improved insight.
■ Incorporate the family and significant others in the care plan.	This may be helpful in providing support.

■ = Independent; ▲ = Collaborative

Neurological Care Plans

Actions/Interventions	**Rationale**
■ Assist the patient and others in understanding the nature of the disorder.	The patient may require a medical statement for a driver's license, work, or school issues.
■ Dispel common myths and fears about convulsive disorders.	Historically, epilepsy has been seen as a mental disorder with negative connotations, but with good health habits and maintenance of a medication schedule, most seizure disorders are controllable and have no relationship to mental capabilities or intellect.
■ Refer to support group if possible.	These groups provide practical assistance in dealing with social and personal issues.
▲ Consult a social worker to assist with financial and vocational issues.	Human rights organizations and/or labor relations departments may need to be contacted if job security or discrimination is evident.
▲ Consult a psychologist if anxiety, depression, and lifestyle changes become troublesome.	The patient may benefit from talk therapy to promote effective coping and support positive self-esteem.

> **• RELATED CARE PLANS**
>
> Impaired home maintenance, p. 99
> Risk for aspiration, p. 18

Spinal Cord Injury

Quadriplegia; Paraplegia; Neurogenic Shock; Spinal Shock

Spinal cord injury (SCI) is damage to the spinal cord at any level from C1 to L1 or L2, where the spinal cord ends. Injury may result in (1) concussion (transient loss of function), (2) complete cord lesion (no preservation of motor and sensory function below the level of injury; irreversible damage), (3) incomplete lesion (can be a partial transection); residual and mixed motor/sensory function below level of injury with some potential for improvement in function. Complete cord injury above C7 results in tetraplegia (formerly called quadriplegia); injury from C7 to L1 causes paraplegia.

Neurogenic (or spinal) shock often follows cervical and high thoracic SCI. Spinal shock can last for 7 to 10 days to weeks or months after injury. It temporarily results in (1) total loss of all motor and sensory function below the injury; (2) sympathetic disruption, resulting in loss of vasoconstriction and leaving parasympathetics unopposed, leading to bradycardia and hypotension; (3) loss of all reflexes below the injury; (4) inability to control body temperature, secondary to the inability to sweat, shiver, or vasoconstrict below the level of injury; (5) ileus; and (6) urinary retention. When neurogenic shock resolves, it is followed by a stage of spasticity.

Primary causes of SCI are motor vehicle accidents, followed by sporting accidents, falls, and penetrating injuries (gunshot or knife wounds). Approximately 10,000 new SCIs occur per year; about 80% occur in men younger than 40 years of age. This care plan focuses on the acute care of an SCI victim.

Spinal Cord Injury

Spinal Cord Injury—cont'd

 Nursing Diagnosis

Risk for Ineffective Breathing Pattern

Common Risk Factor

High cervical SCI with neuromuscular impairment

Common Expected Outcome

Patient maintains adequate ventilation, within limits, as evidenced by PO_2 greater than 80 mm Hg, PCO_2 less than 45 mm Hg, and oxygen saturation greater than 95%.

NOC Outcomes

Respiratory Status: Airway Patency; Respiratory Status: Ventilation

NIC Interventions

Respiratory Monitoring; Airway Stabilization and Management

Ongoing Assessment

Actions/Interventions	**Rationale**
■ Monitor respiratory rate, depth, effort.	Injury at C4 or above causes paralysis of the diaphragm, necessitating intubation. All patients with tetraplegia will have some degree of respiratory insufficiency as a result of intercostal muscle weakness or paralysis.
■ Assess the patient's ability to speak and swallow.	These determine if the airway is patent and if the patient is able to swallow secretions.
■ Assess the patient's ability to cough.	If the patient has a C5 to T6 cord injury, abdominal and intercostal muscle innervation will be absent/diminished and the patient will be unable to take deep breaths and cough. This situation increases the patient's risk for respiratory infection.
■ Auscultate lungs and note lung sounds.	Hypoventilation occurs with diaphragmatic respirations as a result of decreased vital capacity and tidal volume. Lung sounds will be diminished.
▲ Monitor serial arterial blood gases (PO_2, PCO_2) and/or pulse oximetry.	Spinal cord edema (even with an incomplete lesion at or below C4) and hemorrhage can affect phrenic nerve function and cause respiratory insufficiency. The patient may have a chronically low PaO_2 level and elevated $PaCO_2$ level.
■ Observe for additional chest, neck, or facial injuries that may contribute to ineffective breathing.	Because of the traumatic nature of SCI, other injuries are often present.
▲ Monitor central venous pressure, pulmonary artery pressure, and pulmonary capillary wedge pressure if invasive hemodynamic lines are in place.	Hemodynamic monitoring will aid in recognition of ventilation/perfusion mismatch.

Neurological Care Plans

■ = Independent; ▲ = Collaborative

Therapeutic Interventions

Actions/Interventions

▲ Administer oxygen as needed.

▲ Assist with intubation and ventilatory support, if indicated.

■ Suction the patient as needed. When stabilized, implement respiratory toilet.

■ Avoid neck movement when positioning the patient.

■ Teach an assisted cough technique.

■ Encourage use of an incentive spirometer.

Rationale

Initially, supplemental oxygen is necessary to maintain a high PaO$_2$ level.

Patients with high cervical cord injury (above C4 or C5) are at greatest risk for apnea and respiratory arrest. Blind nasotracheal intubation or fiberoptic endotracheal intubation without neck involvement will be performed. Duration of intubation depends on extent of spinal cord damage. Mechanical ventilation may be needed for the tetraplegic patient who cannot maintain spontaneous respirations.

These measures help prevent pneumonia or atelectasis.

If the patient has an unstable fracture, it is important to prevent further injury and loss of function.

The low tetraplegic and the paraplegic patient can use a coughing technique that employs manual abdominal pressure to support air movement with coughing.

This device promotes deep breathing.

NDx Nursing Diagnosis

Risk for Decreased Cardiac Output

Common Risk Factor

Neurogenic shock (traumatic sympathectomy) as a result of spinal cord injury at T5 or above

Common Expected Outcome

Patient maintains heart rate of 60 to 100 beats/min and systolic blood pressure (BP) greater than 90 mm Hg.

NOC Outcomes
Circulation Status; Vital Signs

NIC Interventions
Hemodynamic Regulation; Invasive Hemodynamic Monitoring

Ongoing Assessment

Actions/Interventions

■ Assess heart rate and BP closely.

■ Assess mental status.

Rationale

Loss of sympathetic innervation results in bradycardia and vasodilation of vessels below the injury resulting from an unopposed parasympathetic nervous system. The patient will be hypotensive.

Restlessness is an early sign of hypoxia.

Spinal Cord Injury

■ = Independent; ▲ = Collaborative

Spinal Cord Injury—cont'd

Actions/Interventions

- Assess peripheral pulses and capillary refill.

- Monitor intake and output.

▲ Assist with measurement of vital capacity and other lung volumes.

Rationale

Peripheral vasodilatation decreases venous return, further decreasing cardiac output and blood pressure.

Changes in intake and urine output are an indication of fluid balance.

The respiratory therapist can evaluate changes in lung volumes that indicate respiratory insufficiency.

Therapeutic Interventions

Actions/Interventions

- Administer intravenous (IV) fluids as ordered to maintain BP.

- Avoid elevating head of bed.

▲ Administer vasopressors if needed.

▲ Apply military antishock trouser suit (MAST) or sequential compression boots (SCBs).

▲ Administer anticoagulants as prescribed.

Rationale

Because of abnormal autonomic hemodynamics, overhydration may lead to pulmonary edema. Ascending edema can cause respiratory insufficiency.

Because of sympathetic disruption and resultant loss of vasoconstrictor tone below the injury, head elevation will result in further drop of BP.

These drugs are titrated to maintain a mean arterial pressure of 80 mm Hg or higher.

These help compensate for lost muscle tone and decreases venous pooling. During the acute phase, the patient is at risk for deep vein thrombosis (DVT).

Subcutaneous administration of low-dose or low-molecular-weight heparin may be indicated to reduce the risk of DVT.

NDx Nursing Diagnosis

Impaired Physical Mobility

Common Related Factors

SCI
Neurogenic (spinal) shock
Imposed immobilization by traction

Defining Characteristics

Inability to move purposely within environment
Limited range of motion (ROM)
Decreased muscle strength

Common Expected Outcomes

Patient's neurological status is stabilized as evidenced by no further deterioration of neurological function.
Early signs of deterioration are detected and treated appropriately.
Patient maintains full ROM as evidenced by absence of contractures and absence of footdrop.

NOC Outcomes

Mobility; Ambulation: Wheelchair; Immobility Consequences: Physiological

NIC Interventions

Positioning; Traction/Immobilization Care; Neurological Monitoring

Neurological Care Plans

■ = Independent; ▲ = Collaborative

Ongoing Assessment

Actions/Interventions

- Perform neurological assessment to estimate level of injury.
  - Evaluate movement of major muscle groups in upper and lower extremities: at toes, ankles, knees, hips, fingers, elbows, and shoulders.
  - Assess motor strength, checking for level of progression, symmetry and asymmetry, ascending and descending paralysis, paresthesia.
  - Evaluate sensation to pinprick (spinothalamic tract). Start at toes and ascend gradually up to face. If sensation changes, mark skin.
  - Assess light touch (anterior spinothalamic track). Start at toes and ascend as described.
  - Check for proprioception (joint position sense that reflects posterior columns). Ask the patient to close eyes. Move the toes and fingers up and down slowly to determine whether the patient can perceive motion.
  - Evaluate deep tendon reflexes: biceps, triceps, knee, ankle.
- Serially monitor the patient for any deviation from initial baseline examination, noting signs of complete or incomplete injury.

Rationale

This provides baseline for future comparison.

The patient's functional ability will depend on the level of injury.

Injury to the corticospinal tracts results in loss of motor strength.

The spinothalamic tracts transmit sensations of pain and temperature.

The anterior spinothalamic tracks transmit sensations of light touch.

Changes in proprioception are the result of injury to the dorsal column spinal tracts.

Changes in reflexes will be related to the level of injury.

If the patient has a worsening deficit or higher evolving sensory deficit, additional studies such as magnetic resonance imaging or myelography are indicated. A change from flaccid to spastic paralysis indicates resolution of spinal shock.

Therapeutic Interventions

Actions/Interventions

- Apply a low–air loss mattress to bed before the patient is placed in bed. Immobilize the patient. Maintain the patient in a collar and on a backboard.

- ▲ Insert nasogastric tube if appropriate.

- If the patient requires traction to stabilize or reduce a fracture or subluxation, keep the weights off the bed and floor and hanging freely
- Once all studies are completed and the patient is stabilized, remove the backboard.
- If the spine is stable, log roll and reposition the patient at least every 2 hours.
- Begin ROM exercises.

- Provide support to feet.

Rationale

Immobilization is necessary to prevent active or passive movements of the spine. Special mattresses promote even distribution of pressure to reduce risk for skin breakdown.

This prevents vomiting and aspiration. Paralytic ileus is common after SCI. Vomiting will cause jerking movements that can further spinal injury. The immobilization of head and neck prevents the patient from protecting his airway if vomiting occurs.

Traction devices are used to stabilize the spine to prevent further injury.

Early removal of the backboard reduces potential for pressure ulcer formation.

Frequent turning relieves pressure and reduces risk for skin breakdown.

These reduce potential for contractures, which may occur once neurogenic shock advances to the next stage of spasticity.

A high-top sneaker or special device may be helpful to prevent footdrop.

Spinal Cord Injury

■ = Independent; ▲ = Collaborative

Spinal Cord Injury—cont'd

Actions/Interventions

▲ Administer methylprednisolone as prescribed.

▲ Consult and work with physical and occupational therapists.

■ Prepare the patient and family for possible surgical intervention.

Rationale

Methylprednisolone seems to decrease spinal cord ischemia, improves impulse conduction, represses release of free fatty acids from the spinal cord, and restores extracellular calcium. Current evidence suggests that the use of IV steroids in the immediate postinjury period is not associated with improved outcomes to reduce cord damage. Recent studies suggest that risks with this therapy outweigh the benefits.

An interdisciplinary approach needs to be initiated early in the patient's care to promote effective mobility in the rehabilitation phase of care. Splints and braces may be used to maintain joints and extremities in a position of anatomical function.

Decompression, realignment, and/or stabilization can be accomplished with traction or surgery depending on the site and extent of damage. Early surgery to remove bone fragments, relieve cord compression, and repair open wounds improves chances for good recovery.

NDx Nursing Diagnosis

Risk for Impaired Skin Integrity

Common Risk Factors

Impaired physical mobility
Complete bed rest
Sensory disturbance

Common Expected Outcome

Patient maintains intact skin as evidenced by no signs of pressure breakdown or infection.

NOC Outcome
Tissue Integrity: Skin and Mucous Membranes

NIC Intervention
Skin Surveillance

Ongoing Assessment

Actions/Interventions

■ Assess skin integrity, noting color, moisture, texture, and temperature, especially at pressure points.

Rationale

Pressure ulcers are a common complication of spinal cord injury.

■ = Independent; ▲ = Collaborative

Neurological Care Plans

Actions/Interventions

■ If the patient is in traction, check pin and tong sites for signs of infection or tissue breakdown.

Rationale

Pin site infections can progress to osteomyelitis.

Therapeutic Interventions

Actions/Interventions

■ Keep skin clean and dry.

■ Apply thin dressing of DuoDerm or similar product to bony prominences.

■ Keep skin lubricated.

■ Turn the patient every 2 hours. Use lift sheets when repositioning patient.

■ Provide appropriate prophylactic use of pressure-relieving devices.

■ Instruct the patient in a wheelchair to shift position every 20 to 30 minutes.

■ Provide adequate nutritional intake.

■ Teach the patient and caregivers to inspect skin daily. Provide a long-handled, angled mirror.

Rationale

This prevents skin maceration from moisture accumulation.

A variety of dressings are available to protect and maintain intact skin.

Dry skin is more susceptible to injury and breakdown.

Because of sensory disturbance, the patient will be unable to detect painful pressure. Lift sheets reduce shear forces, which further contribute to skin breakdown.

The use of pressure-relief devices helps prevent skin breakdown. These devices should be used on the patient's bed and wheelchair.

Frequent position changes prevent pressure areas from developing.

A high-protein, high-carbohydrate, and high-calorie diet is needed to counteract catabolic effects of injury and maintain healthy, intact skin. Enteral feedings may be necessary.

Skin breakdown is an ongoing, lifetime concern for the patient with a spinal cord injury. Use of a mirror allows the patient independence in doing skin inspection.

See also **Risk for Impaired Skin Integrity**, *p. 173.*

NDx **Nursing Diagnosis**

Disturbed Body Image

Common Related Factor

Paralysis secondary to SCI

Defining Characteristics

Verbalization of functional alteration of body part
Denial of injury outcome or refusal to look at body
Withdrawal, isolation
Focused behavior or verbal preoccupation with body part or function

Spinal Cord Injury

■ = Independent; ▲ = Collaborative

Spinal Cord Injury—cont'd

Common Expected Outcomes

Patient discusses feelings about injury and possible disabilities.
Patient identifies/uses positive coping mechanisms.

NOC Outcomes
Body Image; Self-Esteem

NIC Interventions
Coping Enhancement;
 Body Image Enhancement

Ongoing Assessment

Actions/Interventions

- Assess perception of dysfunction.

- Assess perceived impact on activities of daily living (ADLs), personal relationships, and occupational activity.

- Inquire about coping skills used before injury.

- Assess the patient's social support system.

Rationale

The patient may perceive changes that are not present or real. The effects of neurogenic shock will seem permanent to the patient, even if the injury is an incomplete lesion.

Help the patient understand that decisions about relationships and occupation need not be made immediately because prior knowledge and beliefs about disability may change.

Previous coping skills may not be sufficient or appropriate to help the patient adjust to the dramatic life changes from SCI.

The patient will have a new level of dependency. A strong social support network can help the patient achieve an appropriate level of functional independence that promotes self-esteem.

Therapeutic Interventions

Actions/Interventions

- Acknowledge normality of emotional response to change in body function. Allow the patient to grieve.

- Help the patient verbalize feelings regarding impairment.
- Help the patient identify helpful coping mechanisms (prayer, communication, perseverance, distraction).
- Encourage interaction with family and friends to enhance self-worth.

- ▲ Refer for counseling as needed.

Rationale

Stages of grief over loss of body function are normal (e.g., losing the function of one's legs is like a "death" of the body part as well as the "death" of future plans). The grieving process may take years.

Expression of feelings supports coping and the development of insights about the impact of the injury.

As a result of the overwhelming nature of SCI, prior coping skills may not be effective.

Family and friends will provide feedback as the patient integrates the impact of injury into a new perception of self.

Both the patient and caregivers may benefit from professional help in developing effective coping and adjustment.

■ = Independent; ▲ = Collaborative

Neurological Care Plans

Nursing Diagnosis

Deficient Knowledge

Common Related Factors
Lack of exposure
New injury
Misperceptions
Cognitive limitation

Defining Characteristics
Verbalized lack of knowledge
Request for information
Statement of misconception

Common Expected Outcome
Patient and caregivers are able to discuss the injury, prognosis, ongoing care measures, and rehabilitation expectations.

NOC Outcomes
Knowledge: Disease Process;
Knowledge: Treatment Regimen

NIC Interventions
Teaching: Disease Process;
Teaching: Treatment/Procedures;
Discharge Planning

Ongoing Assessment

Actions/Interventions

■ Assess the patient's knowledge of injury and prognosis.

■ Assess readiness for learning.

■ Assess understanding of treatment and rehabilitation process.

Rationale

An understanding of the prognosis is necessary to progress to rehabilitation. The patient must understand the need for and participate in therapy.

A patient or caregiver in denial may be unable to accept information or participate in patient care.

An effective teaching plan will build on previous knowledge of treatment.

Therapeutic Interventions

Actions/Interventions

■ Explain what is happening as care/tests (ventilatory support, radiographs, laboratory tests) are performed.

■ Explain spinal cord function and effects of injury on body functions (respiration, mobility bowel, and bladder function). Expect to see a grieving process. Wait until the patient is ready for more information.

Rationale

Knowledge is power. This will assist with eventual coping once the situation has stabilized. Many patients are young and may have no previous experience with illness or hospitalization.

The patient and family need to develop realistic expectations about the patient's long-term needs for assistance with self-care activities and ADLs.

Spinal Cord Injury

■ = Independent; ▲ = Collaborative

→ **Spinal Cord Injury**—cont'd

Actions/Interventions

■ Encourage the patient and caregiver to participate in care while the patient is hospitalized. Explain about positioning, skin care, ulcer prevention, bowel and bladder management, nutrition, and medications.

■ Initiate discussion concerning the caregiver's ability to provide long-term home care, especially if the patient requires mechanical ventilation, and if special equipment or transportation is required.

▲ Provide social service referral.

■ Encourage participation in support groups.

Rationale

Patients and caregivers need time to develop new skills for meeting ADLs and other dimensions of SCI care.

Family members need to learn to balance their desire to help the patient and the patient's need to achieve functional independence. The demands of supportive care may be perceived by family members as an overwhelming burden.

Although care at home is less costly, many third-party payers may not cover special equipment, supplies, home alterations, or utility costs. The patient and family may need help with financial resources to support long-term care.

Support groups assist the patient to cope with the disability.

• RELATED CARE PLANS

Anxiety, p. 15
Bowel incontinence, p. 25
Caregiver role strain, p. 35
Hopelessness, p. 101
Ineffective coping, p. 51
Ineffective sexuality patterns, p. 170
Risk for infection, p. 108
Self-care deficit, p. 156
Urinary retention, p. 208

→  **Transient Ischemic Attack**

Transient Ischemic Attack (TIA); Carotid Endarterectomy

A transient ischemic attack (TIA) is a cerebrovascular disorder that produces temporary neurological deficits. Atherosclerosis in the cerebral vessels is the primary cause of TIA. Emboli that originate in blood vessels outside the cerebral circulation also contribute to the occurrence of TIAs. A TIA is considered an early warning of the risk for an impending stroke. Clinical manifestations of a TIA depend on the location of the ischemia in the brain. Symptoms usually resolve within 24 hours of onset. The patient will not have any residual neurological deficits. Treatment of TIA includes measures to promote cerebral blood flow and manage risk factors for stroke. Long-term drug therapy to control coagulation is an important part of the treatment. A carotid endarterectomy is done to remove atherosclerotic plaques in the carotid arteries and improve blood flow to the brain.

■ = Independent; ▲ = Collaborative

Nursing Diagnosis

Deficient Knowledge

Common Related Factors

Unfamiliarity with disease process and treatment
Lack of exposure to information

Defining Characteristics

Lack of questions about problem
Multiple questions about problem
Misinformation about disease and its treatment

Common Expected Outcome

Patient verbalizes accurate knowledge about TIAs and
their treatment.

NOC Outcomes

Knowledge: Disease Process;
 Knowledge: Medication;
  Knowledge: Treatment Procedure

NIC Interventions

Teaching: Disease Process;
 Teaching: Prescribed Medication;
  Teaching: Procedure/Treatment

Ongoing Assessment

Actions/Interventions

■ Assess the patient's knowledge of TIAs, anticoagulant
therapy, surgical procedures, and risk factors for stroke.

■ Determine the patient's preferred learning style.

Rationale

Patient education is based on the person's knowledge of
the disorder. The patient needs to understand the cause
of a TIA and the importance of risk factor management
to prevent a stroke.

The teaching plan is individualized to include teaching
methods that are consistent with the patient's preferred
learning style.

Therapeutic Interventions

Actions/Interventions

■ Provide the patient and family with information about
cerebrovascular disease and TIAs.

■ Teach the patient and family about managing risk
factors for stroke.

Rationale

The patient and family need to understand the relationship
between atherosclerosis, cerebrovascular disease, and
TIAs to make appropriate decisions about risk factor
management. Compliance with medical and surgical
therapies will be enhanced if the patient and family
have appropriate knowledge.

Risk factors for TIA and stroke include poorly controlled
hypertension, diabetes mellitus, obesity, smoking, and
atrial fibrillation. Cardiac dysrhythmias such as atrial
fibrillation are associated with the formation of atrial
thrombi that can embolize to the carotid arteries and
cerebral blood vessels.

Transient Ischemic Attack

■ = Independent; ▲ = Collaborative

Transient Ischemic Attack–cont'd

Actions/Interventions

- Teach the patient about the use of medications to control coagulation.

  - Low-dose aspirin

  - Platelet aggregation inhibitors

- Provide the patient and family with information about surgical procedures.

Rationale

Medications to reduce the formation of thrombi and embolizations of existing thrombi are given to decrease the risk of stroke.

Administration of a single daily dose of aspirin (81 to 325 mg) is effective in reducing thrombus formation and embolization because of its antiplatelet activity.

Dipyridamole (Persantine) decreases platelet aggregation. Ticlopidine (Ticlid) and clopidogrel (Plavix) are platelet aggregation inhibitors that have been shown to be as effective as aspirin in reducing thrombus formation.

Carotid endarterectomy involves removal of atherosclerotic plaques from the carotid arteries. The procedure has a high rate of success in restoring blood flow through narrowed carotid arteries. Complications include bleeding at the operative site and neurological deficits.

NDx Nursing Diagnosis

Risk for Ineffective Cerebral Tissue Perfusion

Common Risk Factors

Edema from carotid endarterectomy
Clot formation
Hemorrhage
Hematoma formation
Hypotension
Increased intracranial pressure

Common Expected Outcome

Patient's optimal cerebral perfusion is maintained as evidenced by alert responsive mentation or no further reduction in mental status, and absence of progression of neurological deficits.

NOC Outcome
Tissue Perfusion: Cerebral

NIC Intervention
Cerebral Perfusion Promotion

Ongoing Assessment

Actions/Interventions

- Assess responsiveness or level of consciousness as indicated.

Rationale

Serious neurological complications are associated with carotid endarterectomy as a result of embolization and reduced cerebral perfusion during surgery, from clotting at the incision site, and from increased intracranial pressure from intracranial bleeding.

■ = Independent; ▲ = Collaborative

Neurological Care Plans

Actions/Interventions

- Assess speech, symmetry of face, visual ability, and intellectual ability as compared with baseline (assessing for impairment of mental ability); motor responses (noting for weakness, paresis of an extremity); and pupillary reaction.

- Monitor blood pressure (BP).

- Check for symmetry of neck. Check behind neck of supine patient.

- Assess function of the cranial nerves.

- Assess quality of the pulse proximal and distal to the incision.

Rationale

The blood supply of the brain may be altered from a decrease in carotid blood flow that can occur from excessive edema, hematoma of the operative site, or from embolization. The changes could result in neurological deficits (stroke).

Stable systemic BP is necessary to maintain adequate cerebral perfusion.

Blood may pool; hematoma formation posteriorly from the incision line is possible. Respiratory distress can occur from a hematoma compressing the trachea.

Cranial nerve damage may be temporary or last for months.

This ensures adequate blood flow distally.

Therapeutic Interventions

Actions/Interventions

- Report sudden or progressive deterioration in neurological status.

- ▲ Administer antihypertensives as ordered to prevent extreme elevations in BP. Keep BP at 120 to 150 mm Hg systolic and 70 to 90 mm Hg diastolic, or 86 to 110 mm Hg mean arterial pressure. Notify physician if BP is out of this range.

Rationale

This minimizes damage from inadequate cerebral blood flow.

Hypertension could result in increased edema at the operative site, hemorrhage of the incisional area, or even carotid artery disruption. However, avoid hypotension to prevent cerebral ischemia and thrombosis.

NDx Nursing Diagnosis

Ineffective Breathing Pattern

Common Related Factors

Edema
Hematoma formation
Postoperative carotid endarterectomy

Defining Characteristics

Tachypnea
Change in depth of breathing
Complaint of shortness of breath
Use of accessory muscles

Common Expected Outcome

Patient's optimal breathing pattern is maintained as evidence by eupnea, regular respiratory rate/pattern, and verbalization of comfort with breathing.

NOC Outcomes
Respiratory Monitoring;
  Ventilation Assistance

NIC Interventions
Respiratory Monitoring;
  Ventilation Assistance

Transient Ischemic Attack

 = Independent; ▲ = Collaborative

Transient Ischemic Attack—cont'd

Ongoing Assessment

Actions/Interventions	Rationale
■ Assess respiratory rate, rhythm, and depth.	Changes in breathing patterns can occur with hemispheric injury or brainstem injury.
■ Assess for any increase in work of breathing such as shortness of breath and use of accessory muscles.	It is important to determine adequacy of respiratory excursion.
■ Auscultate lungs for character of lung sounds.	Routine assessment of lung sounds allows for early detection and correction of abnormalities.
■ Assess trachea for midline position and assess neck for symmetry.	Swelling or hematoma can obstruct the airway.

Therapeutic Interventions

Actions/Interventions	Rationale
■ Elevate head of bed 30 to 40 degrees.	A semi-Fowler's position can help reduce neck edema and promote effective lung expansion.
■ Maintain the patient's head in a straight position.	Positioning is important to decrease stress or pulling of the operative site.
■ Change the patient's position every 2 hours.	This facilitates movement and drainage of secretions.
■ Suction airway as needed.	Suctioning removes accumulated secretions.
■ Provide reassurance and allay anxiety by staying with the patient during acute episodes of respiratory distress.	Air hunger can produce extreme anxiety.
■ Maintain oxygen delivery system.	This is to ensure that the appropriate amount of oxygen is applied continuously and the patient's condition does not desaturate.
■ Notify the physician immediately of any abnormalities.	An expanding hematoma in the neck can be a life-threatening emergency.

West Nile Virus

West Nile virus (WNV) is an arboviral infection that is spread to humans through infected mosquitoes and birds. Wild birds are the host/reservoir, and the mosquito is the vector. The causative agent in WNV infection is a single-stranded RNA virus. Before 1999, WNV existed only in the Eastern hemisphere with wide distribution in Africa, Asia, the Middle East, and Europe. Human infection was infrequent. However, in 1999, several cases of encephalitis in the United States were isolated as WNV infection. Since 1999, there have been many more cases of WNV, including WNV encephalitis in the United States.

The WNV is a potentially serious illness that affects the central nervous system. Diagnosis relies on a high index of suspicion; confirmation is made through laboratory testing. Symptoms vary, with 80% of infected persons exhibiting no symptoms, and about 20% exhibiting mild flulike symptoms. Symptoms can last 3 to 6 days and are treated with supportive therapy for pain and fever. Less than 1% of cases result in severe neurological disease caused by meningitis or encephalitis. Although there is no specific treatment for WNV infection, persons with the more severe disease require hospitalization and supportive care with intravenous (IV) fluids, airway management, respiratory support, and prevention of secondary infection.

 Nursing Diagnosis

Deficient Knowledge

Common Related Factors

Unfamiliarity with disease process and treatment
Lack of knowledge about WNV

Defining Characteristics

Many questions
Lack of questions
Unaware of proper prevention methods

Common Expected Outcome

Patient verbalizes knowledge of disease process, mode of transmission, prevention, complications, and treatment.

NOC Outcomes
Knowledge: Disease Process;
Knowledge: Infection Control

NIC Interventions
Teaching: Disease Process;
Teaching: Prescribed Medication

Ongoing Assessment

Actions/Interventions

■ Determine understanding of the disease process, transmission, complications, and treatment.

Rationale

This provides an important starting point for education. Many misconceptions are common.

Therapeutic Interventions

Actions/Interventions

■ Provide information on disease transmission.
  • WNV is spread by the bite of an infected mosquito (arbovirus). Mosquitoes are the carriers that themselves get infected when they feed on infected birds.
  • WNV is not transmitted from person to person. It is not spread through casual contact such as touching or kissing a person with the virus.
  • According to the CDC, in rare cases the virus has been transmitted through blood transfusion, organ transplants, breast-feeding, and even during pregnancy from mother to baby.
  • The incubation period of WNV is 2 to 15 days.

Rationale

The Centers for Disease Control and Prevention (CDC) provides updated guidelines on WNV. The CDC recommends using standard precautions when handling infectious materials.

West Nile Virus

■ = Independent; ▲ = Collaborative

West Nile Virus—cont'd

Actions/Interventions	Rationale
■ Provide information on the disease process and complications.	Information enables individuals to take control. Persons in whom a high temperature develops should contact their health care provider.

- Most persons (about 80%) infected with WNV are asymptomatic.
- West Nile fever, which lasts from a few days to weeks, develops in about 20% of those infected. Symptoms include fever, headache and body aches, nausea, vomiting, and sometimes swollen lymph glands or skin rash.
- About 1 in 150 cases results in severe neurological disease caused by meningitis or encephalitis. Symptoms include high temperature, headache, stiff neck, disorientation, tremors, convulsions, coma, muscle weakness, vision loss, and paralysis. Symptoms may last for weeks or be permanent.
- WNV is detected in all age groups; however, older or immunosuppressed individuals are at increased risk for neurological disease after infection.

■ Provide information on treatment.

Early assessment of symptoms facilitates prompt interventions.

- Most individuals have asymptomatic presentations and do not require treatment.
- Patients with West Nile fever require supportive treatment with antipyretics and analgesic medications.
- Patients with more severe disease require hospitalization and supportive treatment with IV fluids, respiratory support, and prevention of secondary infections. Most common residual symptoms include memory deficit, weakness, and arthralgias.

■ Provide information on strategies to prevent reinfection.

Prevention of mosquito breeding grounds and bites is the best way to avoid WNV.

- Use insect repellants containing DEET (*N,N*-diethyl-*m*-toluamide). Follow instructions on the package. Spray clothing so mosquitoes do not bite through.
- Wear long sleeves, pants, and stockings at dusk and dawn when mosquitoes are most active.
- Wear light-colored clothing to help visualization of mosquitoes.
- Maintain integrity of window and door screens to keep mosquitoes out.
- Remove standing water from flower pots, catch basins, gardening equipment, and the like. Change water in birdbaths at least weekly. Avoid stagnant water in children's swimming pools.

■ = Independent; ▲ = Collaborative

Nursing Diagnosis

Infection

Common Related Factors

WNV RNA
WNV encephalitis or meningitis

Defining Characteristics

Malaise, myalgia, rash, headache, eye pain, sudden onset of fever
Lethargy, mental status changes, or focal neurological deficit—more specific to encephalitis or meningitis

Common Expected Outcome

Patient's infection is treated with supportive therapy to maintain comfort and prevent further complication.

NOC Outcome
Infection Severity

NIC Interventions
Infection Control; Surveillance

Ongoing Assessment

Actions/Interventions

- Monitor temperature and for headache or body aches.

- Monitor for common manifestations of milder forms of WNV.
- Monitor for mental status changes, and signs of meningitis or encephalitis.

- Monitor oxygenation and respiratory effort.

▲ Monitor results of laboratory testing:
  • Enzyme-linked immunoassay (ELISA) for WNV
  • Virus-specific IgM antibody in serum or cerebrospinal fluid

Rationale

Fever and headache are predominant milder symptoms in most cases of WNV infection.

These may include rash, nausea, vomiting, and sometimes lymph node swelling.

The severe cases of WNV are associated with meningitis or encephalitis, and patients present with headache, stiff neck, high temperature, disorientation, stupor, coma, tremors, convulsions, muscle weakness, or paralysis.

Acute onset of muscle weakness can occur in absence of sensory loss. Involvement of respiratory muscles can lead to respiratory failure.

Laboratory testing provides the confirmatory diagnosis of WNV.

Therapeutic Interventions

Actions/Interventions

▲ Administer antipyretic and analgesic medications as ordered.

▲ Encourage oral and IV fluids as ordered.

Rationale

Treatment in milder cases involves treating flulike symptoms by reducing fever and relieving headache and body aches.

Fluids are lost by fever and diaphoresis. Increasing fluid intake during fever prevents dehydration and helps in actual fever reduction.

West Nile Virus

■ = Independent; ▲ = Collaborative

West Nile Virus—cont'd

Actions/Interventions	Rationale
▲ Provide respiratory support as needed: oxygen, airway management, ventilator.	A patent airway and respiratory support are priorities.
▲ Administer antibiotics as ordered.	WNV infection is a viral syndrome; hence antibiotic therapy is only introduced for secondary infections seen in more complicated cases.
■ Report confirmed cases to the local health department and/or CDC.	WNV is a reportable illness and is under CDC surveillance. It is still a relatively new disease in the United States. Data are being gathered and research is ongoing in hopes of developing new treatment recommendations.

Neurological Care Plans

■ = Independent; ▲ = Collaborative

6

Gastrointestinal and Digestive Care Plans

Abdominal Surgery

Gastrectomy; Splenectomy; Pancreatectomy; Cholecystectomy; Prostatectomy; Cystectomy; Appendectomy; Hysterectomy; Nephrectomy; Abdominal Aortic Aneurysm Resection; Bowel Resection; Exploratory Laparotomy

Open surgery of the abdomen may be done for the following: gastrectomy (removal of all or part of the stomach); splenectomy (removal of the spleen); pancreatectomy (partial or total removal of the pancreas); liver resection; cholecystectomy (removal of the gallbladder); removal of biliary stones or resection of biliary structures; prostatectomy (removal of the prostate gland); cystectomy (removal of the bladder); appendectomy (removal of the appendix); hysterectomy (removal of the uterus); nephrectomy (removal of a kidney); resection or repair of abdominal aortic aneurysms; small and large bowel resection; or repair of trauma to any abdominal structure resulting from blunt or penetrating trauma, commonly referred to as an exploratory laparotomy. Nursing care interventions are similar for all patients having abdominal surgery, regardless of the type. This care plan addresses the major common diagnoses associated with open abdominal surgical procedures. Although most postoperative abdominal surgical patients remain in the hospital for 3 to 7 days, shorter stays (<24 hours) are becoming more common. As laparoscopic techniques and instrumentation continue to develop, less open abdominal surgery is being performed.

NDx Nursing Diagnosis

Deficient Knowledge: Preoperative

Common Related Factors	Defining Characteristics
Proposed surgical experience	Questions
Lack of previous similar surgical procedure	Lack of questions
Fear	Verbalized misconceptions
Anxiety	

Gastrointestinal and Digestive Care Plans

Abdominal Surgery—cont'd

Common Expected Outcomes

Patient verbalizes understanding of proposed surgical procedure and realistic expectations for the postoperative course.

Patient demonstrates the ability to cough, deep breathe, use the incentive spirometer, and perform leg exercises.

> **NOC Outcome**
> Knowledge: Treatment Procedure(s)
>
> **NIC Intervention**
> Teaching: Preoperative

Ongoing Assessment

Actions/Interventions

- Assess the patient's knowledge of proposed surgical procedure

- Assess any factors that would affect the patient's ability to learn.
- Assess the patient's previous experience with surgery.

Rationale

The patient should be aware of the nature of the surgical procedure, as well as risks and benefits of the surgical procedure, the reason it is being done, location of the surgical incision, and expected length of recovery.

The patient should have information provided for understanding of surgical procedure and postoperative care.

Patients who have had surgery in the past may have negative feelings related to side effects of anesthesia and postoperative pain; they may recall longer hospitalizations than today's typical shorter stays.

Therapeutic Interventions

Actions/Interventions

- Explain and reinforce the surgeon's explanations regarding the proposed surgical procedure.
- Prepare patients having open abdominal surgery to expect the following:
  - An incision in the abdomen, either stapled or sutured closed, with a dressing in place
  - Surgical drains near the surgical incision

  - Intravenous (IV) lines
  - Nasogastric (NG) tube

  - Early ambulation, usually out of bed the first postoperative day
  - Postoperative leg exercises

  - Antiembolic stockings or sequential compression devices for patients who remain on bed rest for more than 12 hours

Rationale

The patient has knowledge of and can verbalize about the surgical procedure.

Size and location depend on the nature of the surgical procedure.

Surgical drains promote drainage of fluid from the incisional site, decrease pressure on healing tissue, and reduce abscess formation.

These provide fluid, electrolytes, and emergency IV access.

This keeps the stomach free of fluid and prevents distention, nausea, and vomiting. The NG tube is discontinued when normal peristaltic activity resumes, which is indicated by the patient having audible bowel sounds and passing flatus.

This helps prevent pulmonary atelectasis, deep vein thrombosis, and other complications of immobility.

Leg exercises help promote venous return and decrease the incidence of deep vein thrombosis.

These prevent deep vein thrombosis.

■ = Independent; ▲ = Collaborative

Actions/Interventions

- Need for dynamic turning, coughing, deep-breathing exercises, and incentive spirometry; give opportunities for return demonstration
- Need for pain management

Rationale

This helps prevent pulmonary atelectasis and stasis of secretions, which could lead to pneumonia.

Adequate pain management allows patients having abdominal surgery to participate actively in their care, to ambulate, and to breathe effectively. The patient has a right to be involved in selecting the type of pain management used.

NDx Nursing Diagnosis

Ineffective Breathing Pattern

Common Related Factors

Abdominal incision pain
Abdominal distention compromising lung expansion
Sedation
Lack of knowledge

Defining Characteristics

Poor coughing effort
Shallow breathing
Splinting respirations
Refusal/inability to use incentive spirometer

Common Expected Outcome

Patient maintains an effective breathing pattern as evidenced by a respiratory rate of 12 to 20 breaths/min, nonlabored deep respirations, ability to use incentive spirometer correctly, and clear lung sounds.

NOC Outcomes

Respiratory Status: Airway Patency;
Respiratory Status: Ventilation

NIC Interventions

Respiratory Monitoring;
Cough Enhancement

Ongoing Assessment

Actions/Interventions

- Assess rate and depth of respirations.

- Auscultate lung sounds at least every 4 hours for the first 48 hours postoperatively.
- Observe for splinting.

- Assess ability to use incentive spirometer.

Rationale

Respirations are typically shallow, because the least amount of excursion is less painful when an abdominal incision is present. Also, the higher the incision, the more the breathing is affected.

The bases of the lungs are least likely to be ventilated; therefore lung sounds may be diminished over the bases.

Splinting refers to the conscious minimization of an inspiration to reduce the amount of discomfort caused by full expansion.

In incentive spirometry, the patient takes and holds a deep breath for a few seconds. Incentive spirometry encourages deep breathing, and holding the breath allows for full expansion of alveoli.

■ = Independent; ▲ = Collaborative

Abdominal Surgery—cont'd

Actions/Interventions

- Assess for abdominal distention.

- Assess vital signs according to postoperative policy, then every 4 hours.
- Assess the amount and characteristic of sputum.

Rationale

Distention can impair thoracic excursion and result in an ineffective breathing pattern.

Elevated temperature may indicate atelectasis, which can lead to pneumonia.

Increased amounts of sputum, as well as changes in color and a thicker consistency, may indicate pneumonia.

Therapeutic Interventions

Actions/Interventions

▲ Manage pain using whatever plan for pain management has been prescribed.

- Position patient with head of bed (HOB) elevated 30 degrees.
- Encourage or assist the patient to turn side to side every 2 hours; position with pillows or positioning devices as needed.
- Encourage the patient to do deep-breathing exercises a minimum of 10 times every hour.
- Encourage coughing every hour.
- Help the patient splint the abdominal incision by using hands or a pillow.
- Encourage use of incentive spirometer every 1 to 2 hours.

- Encourage ambulation as tolerated.

- Promote hydration.

▲ Administer oxygen as prescribed.

Rationale

Patients using patient-controlled analgesia (PCA) may need reinstruction or reminders to push the button during the early postoperative phase until they are fully recovered from anesthesia.

This position puts the least strain on abdominal muscles and enhances diaphragmatic excursion.

These actions mobilize secretions by using gravity to increase drainage.

Deep breathing keeps alveoli from collapsing.

This clears the bronchial tree of secretions.

Splinting the incision eases the discomfort of coughing and taking deep breaths.

Incentive spirometry encourages deep breathing, and holding one's breath allows for the full expansion of alveoli.

Breathing effectiveness and mobilization of secretions are enhanced by position change and an upright position.

Respiratory secretions will be thinner and more easily expectorated if the patient is hydrated.

Promoting lung expansion and oxygenation of the tissues is a goal of the patient with atelectasis.

NDx Nursing Diagnosis

Acute Pain

Common Related Factors

Abdominal incision
Presence of drains, tubes

Defining Characteristics

Subjective complaint of pain
Guarded movement
Expressive behavior of pain

■ = Independent; ▲ = Collaborative

Common Expected Outcomes

Patient requests pain medications or demonstrates effective use of alternative pain control measures.

Patient verbalizes relief of pain using a pain rating scale.

Patient has a relaxed posture and facial expression.

NOC Outcomes
Comfort Level; Pain Control; Pain Level

NIC Interventions
Analgesic Administration; Pain Management; Patient-Controlled Analgesia (PCA) Assistance; Positioning

Ongoing Assessment

Actions/Interventions

- Assess the nature of pain (location, quality, onset, frequency, radiation, and duration). Have the patient rate pain intensity on a scale (1 to 10 or Faces).

- Monitor change in the patient's perception of pain associated with abdominal distention.

- Check abdomen for rigidity (hard, boardlike abdomen) and rebound tenderness (pain elicited when pressure is applied and then released on the abdomen).

- Ensure function of suction machines.

Rationale

Some pain is expected after abdominal surgery; appropriate pain management will provide comfort and enable the patient to move and rest.

Distention of the abdomen by accumulation of gas and fluid occurs postoperatively because normal peristalsis does not return until the third or fourth day after surgery; distention stresses suture lines and causes pain.

Either of these may indicate peritonitis, a serious inflammation of the lining of the peritoneum that can result from intraabdominal leakage of organ secretions or visceral contents after abdominal surgery.

Accumulation of gastric secretions and gas will cause tension on suture lines and aggravate abdominal discomfort.

Therapeutic Interventions

Actions/Interventions

- Assist the patient to a comfortable position.

- Use nonpharmacological treatment measures (e.g., distraction, music relaxation).

▲ Administer analgesics or assist the patient in using PCA before pain becomes too severe.

▲ Administer pain medication before painful procedures (e.g., dressing changes, ambulation).

- Document the patient's response to pain-relieving measures.

▲ Collaborate with the physician for patient's optimal pain management.

Rationale

A semi-Fowler's position is usually most comfortable, because stress on the suture line is relieved.

These measures reduce perception and sensation of pain.

It is more difficult to control pain once it becomes severe.

This maximizes the patient's ability to tolerate or participate in procedures.

Patients have individualized pain-tolerance levels, and all patients will not be made comfortable with standard doses.

Individualizing the pain-relieving regimen recognizes individual differences in pain perception and provides for more effective control. Nonsteroidal antiinflammatory drugs are used alone for mild pain and in combination with opioids for moderate or severe pain.

See also **Acute Pain,** *p. 144.*

■ = Independent; ▲ = Collaborative

→ Abdominal Surgery—cont'd

 Nursing Diagnosis

Risk for Deficient Fluid Volume

Common Risk Factors

Nasogastric suctioning
Loss of fluid from intestinal or interstitial space drains
Wound drainage
Blood loss in surgery or postoperative bleeding
NPO (nothing by mouth) status
Vomiting

Common Expected Outcome

Patient maintains normal fluid volume balance, as evidenced by stable blood pressure (BP) at or above 90/60 mm Hg or patient's baseline, heart rate of 60 to 100 beats/min, urine output of at least 30 mL/hr, specific gravity less than 1.030, and good skin turgor.

NOC Outcomes
Fluid Balance; Hydration

NIC Interventions
Fluid/Electrolyte Management; Surveillance

Ongoing Assessment

Actions/Interventions	Rationale
■ Monitor and report any postoperative bleeding:	
• Intraabdominal	This may occur from any vessel in the dissected area; usually seen as increased bloody drainage on dressing.
• Intraluminal	Usually from anastomosis, this is seen as increased bloody drainage from tubes.
• Incisional	Usually from subcutaneous tissue, this is seen as increased bloody drainage on dressings.
■ Mark extension of drainage from incisions.	Outlining the stain on the surface of the dressing and indicating the time of the assessment allows staff to quantify the amount of drainage and severity of bleeding later.
■ Assess hydration status:	
• Monitor BP and heart rate.	Hypotension and/or tachycardia may indicate fluid volume deficit.
• Check mucous membranes, skin turgor, and thirst.	Increasing thirst and a coated tongue occur with fluid volume deficit.
• Monitor urine output.	Output of 30 mL/hr indicates adequate hydration.
• Monitor, record, and report output of emesis, NG tube output, output from surgical drains (check for drainage around drains also), and incisional drainage.	Wound drainage, tube drainage, and emesis can be sources of fluid loss from the body.

Gastrointestinal and Digestive Care Plans

Abdominal Surgery

Actions/Interventions

- If available, check central venous pressure (CVP).
- Weigh patient daily at the same time, using the same scale.
▲ Monitor hemoglobin (Hgb) and hematocrit (Hct).
▲ Monitor coagulation profile.

▲ Monitor electrolytes.

Rationale

CVP is an indication of circulating blood volume.

Changes in the patient's body weight can be an indicator of fluid balance changes.

Dropping Hgb and Hct may indicate internal bleeding.

Excessive postoperative bleeding may result from coagulopathy.

Electrolytes are measured with a focus on sodium and potassium levels.

Therapeutic Interventions

Actions/Interventions

▲ Administer IV fluid as ordered; be prepared to increase fluids if signs of fluid volume deficit appear.
▲ Provide oral fluids of patient's choice, as allowed.

■ Provide oral hygiene every 4 hours.

Rationale

IV fluids are often prescribed to correct fluid volume deficit and maintain fluid balance postoperatively.

Oral fluids are usually restricted until peristalsis returns (typically 72 to 96 hours) and NG tube is removed, because swallowed fluids will be sucked out by the NG tube along with electrolytes; this puts the patient at risk for electrolyte imbalance, especially hypokalemia. However, patients may be allowed ice chips or small sips of clear fluids.

NPO status and/or fluid volume deficit will cause a dry, sticky mouth.

NDx Nursing Diagnosis

Risk for Infection

Common Risk Factors

Abdominal incision
Respiratory complications such as bronchitis, atelectasis, and pneumonia.
Indwelling urinary catheter
Venous access devices
Presence of tubes and drains
Invasion of pathogens through inadvertent interruption of closed drainage systems
Obesity
Smoking history
Immunosuppression
Poor nutritional status
Diabetes

■ = Independent; ▲ = Collaborative

Abdominal Surgery—cont'd

Common Expected Outcomes

Patient is free of infection, as evidenced by the following:
- Healing wound/incision that is clean, dry, well approximated, and free of redness, swelling, purulent discharge, and pain
- Normal body temperature within 72 hours postoperatively
- Venous access sites free of redness and purulent drainage
- Clear breath sounds without cough or sputum production

NOC Outcomes
Risk Detection; Wound Healing: Primary Intention

NIC Interventions
Infection Control; Tube Care; Tube Care: Urinary; Wound Care; Wound Care: Closed Drainage

Ongoing Assessment

Actions/Interventions	Rationale
■ Monitor temperature.	For the first 48 to 72 hours postoperatively, temperatures of up to 38.5° C (101.3° F) are expected as a normal stress response after major surgery. Beyond 72 hours, temperature should return to patient's baseline. Temperature spikes, usually occurring in the later afternoon or night, are often indications of infection.
▲ Monitor white blood cell (WBC) count.	Elevated WBC count is typically an indication of infection; however, in older patients, infection may be present without an increase in WBC count because of normal changes in the immune system.
■ Assess incision and wound for redness, drainage, swelling, and increased pain: • Closed wounds or incisions	Incisions that have been closed with sutures or staples should be free of redness, swelling, and drainage. Some incisional discomfort is expected. These incisions are usually kept covered by a dry dressing for 24 to 48 hours; beyond 48 hours there is no need for a dressing if the incision is not draining.
• Open wounds	Wounds left open to heal by secondary intention should appear pink/red and moist and should have minimal serosanguineous drainage. These wounds are usually packed with sterile gauze moistened with sterile saline. Discomfort is expected upon packing.
■ Assess all peripheral and central IV sites for redness, swelling, warmth, purulent drainage, and pain.	Continual monitoring for signs of inflammation or infection is essential.
■ Assess color, clarity, and odor of urine.	Cloudy, foul-smelling urine is an indication of urinary tract infection, which can occur as the result of an indwelling catheter.
▲ Obtain culture of cloudy, foul-smelling urine.	This determines which pathogens are present.

■ = Independent; ▲ = Collaborative

Actions/Interventions

- Assess quality of breath sounds, cough, and sputum production.
- Assess stability of tubes and drains.

- ▲ Obtain culture of any unusual drainage from wound, incision, tubes, or drains.

Rationale

Adventitious breath sounds can indicate a respiratory infection.

In-and-out motion of improperly secured tubes and drains allows access by pathogens through stab wounds where tubes and drains are placed.

This determines the presence of pathogens.

Therapeutic Interventions

Actions/Interventions

- Wash hands before contact with the postoperative patient.
- Use aseptic technique during dressing change, wound care, or handling or manipulation of tubes and drains.
- Ensure that closed drainage systems (urinary catheter, surgical tubes and drains) are not inadvertently interrupted (opened).
- Tape connectors and pin extension or drainage tubing securely to the patient's gown. Prevent kinking of drain tubing.
- Provide aseptic site care to all peripheral and central venous access devices according to hospital policy.
- Provide meticulous meatal care daily.

- Encourage adequate nutritional intake.

- Educate the patient and family on the signs and symptoms of infection: elevated temperature, redness, swelling of the incisional area, and purulent or foul-smelling wound drainage.
- ▲ Irrigate tubes and drains only by physician prescription; use aseptic technique and sterile irrigant.
- ▲ Administer antibiotics and antipyretics as prescribed.

Rationale

Hand washing remains the most effective method of infection control.

Aseptic technique for dressing changes and wound care limits the introduction of pathogens.

Opening of sterile systems allows access by pathogens and puts the patient at risk for infection.

This minimizes tension on tubes and connection. Kinking of tubing prevents drainage of urine or wound exudate. Stasis contributes to the development of infection.

Aseptic technique prevents transmission of bacterial infections.

This reduces the number of pathogens around the urinary catheter entrance site.

Adequate intake of protein, vitamins, and minerals is essential to promote tissue and wound healing.

Educating the patient and family assists in early recognition of adverse signs and symptoms. It promotes their sense of control and minimizes anxiety and fear.

Intraabdominal infection can result from introduction of pathogens into interrupted systems.

This prevents or treats infections and the fever usually associated with infection.

NDx Nursing Diagnosis

Risk for Impaired Tissue Integrity

Common Risk Factors

Delayed wound healing
Infection
Presence of seroma or hematoma
Increased intraabdominal pressure
Mechanical force (e.g., stress, tension against wound)

 = Independent; ▲ = Collaborative

Abdominal Surgery—cont'd

Common Expected Outcome

Patient has an intact wound or has complications such as dehiscence, evisceration, or fistulization recognized and treated promptly.

NOC Outcomes

Wound Healing: Primary Intention; Tissue Integrity: Skin and Mucous Membranes

NIC Interventions

Skin Surveillance; Wound Care; Positioning

Ongoing Assessment

Actions/Interventions

- Assess wound for hematoma (collection of bloody drainage beneath the skin) or seroma (collection of serous fluid beneath the skin).

- Assess wound for intactness:

  • Closed wounds

  • Open wounds

- Assess condition of stitches or staples and retention sutures, if present; report any closures that appear to have loosened or fallen out.

- Assess open wounds for evidence of evisceration (protrusion of abdominal contents).

- Assess wounds and dressings for suspicious drainage.

Rationale

Presence of either predisposes the wound to separation and infection.

Wound dehiscence (separation of the suture line or wound) occurs with excessive stress on a new incision.

Wound edges should remain approximated, without tension, puckering, or open gaps between stitches or staples.

Wounds left open to heal by secondary intention are open only as deep as the subcutaneous tissue is deep; the fascia, muscle, and peritoneum have usually been closed. The deepest portion of the wound will come together, with the presence of tissue beneath being visible.

This is especially important during the first 48 hours, before wound strength begins to develop. Retention sutures (large sutures placed in addition to routine closures) are used when obesity, extreme abdominal distention, intraabdominal infection, poor nutritional status, and/or a history of wound evisceration is present.

Evisceration of a surgical wound is a serious complication. The wound should be covered immediately with a sterile dressing moistened with normal saline.

The presence of yellow, green, or brown fluid or material with an acrid or fecal odor indicates the presence of a fistula, a communication between some portion of the bowel and the incision or open wound.

Therapeutic Interventions

Actions/Interventions

- Prevent strain on the abdominal incision or wound:
  • Keep HOB elevated 30 degrees.

Rationale

Elevation relaxes abdominal muscles and reduces tension on the incision.

■ = Independent; ▲ = Collaborative

Abdominal Surgery

Actions/Interventions

- Encourage patient to splint with pillow or hands before coughing.
- Ensure proper functioning of suction machine.

▲ If dehiscence or evisceration occurs or is suspected (i.e., wound edges are separated and/or abdominal viscera are visible and protruding through the abdominal wound):
- Place the patient in Fowler's position.

- Cover area with saline solution–soaked sterile gauze.

- Notify the physician of the need for wound evaluation.

▲ If a fistula is suspected, protect wound edges with petrolatum-based ointment or hydrocolloid.

Rationale

Excessive coughing and straining of abdominal muscles and skin can predispose the wound to dehiscence.

Malfunction of NG suctioning can cause nausea, which may lead to retching and increased strain of abdominal muscles.

Positioning promotes relaxation of abdominal muscles and reduces strain on the incision.

Keeping viscera moist increases viability and reduces risk for infection.

This situation usually requires a return to surgery for repair.

Intestinal contents can be highly corrosive to skin, denuding it in a matter of hours; this causes pain and may interfere with later attempts to close or pouch the fistula.

NDx Nursing Diagnosis

Risk for Ineffective Tissue Perfusion: Peripheral

Common Risk Factors

Prolonged time in operating room (OR)
Position in OR
Decreased postoperative activity
Dehydration
Decreased vascular tone

Common Expected Outcome

Patient remains free of thrombophlebitis and deep vein thrombosis, as evidenced by bilaterally equal calves and absence of calf pain.

NOC Outcome
Tissue Perfusion: Peripheral

NIC Intervention
Circulatory Care: Venous Insufficiency

Ongoing Assessment

Actions/Interventions

■ Assess legs for swelling; compare right leg to left leg.

■ Assess for presence of distended leg veins.

Rationale

Except for minor differences, calves should have the same approximate circumference. Unilateral swelling could indicate thrombophlebitis or deep vein thrombosis.

This may indicate venous congestion and poor venous circulation.

■ = Independent; ▲ = Collaborative

Abdominal Surgery—cont'd

Actions/Interventions

- Assess for bluish discoloration of legs.
- Assess for pain on compression of calf and calf pain on dorsiflexion of foot.
- Assess for normal skin color and temperature. Palpate peripheral pulses.

Rationale

This may also indicate venous congestion.

Either is an indication of thrombophlebitis or deep vein thrombosis.

These are indicators of adequate tissue perfusion.

Therapeutic Interventions

Actions/Interventions

- Reinforce or encourage leg exercises taught preoperatively; strive for 10 repetitions each hour until fully ambulatory.
- ▲ Use antiembolic stockings or sequential compression devices while the patient is in bed.
- Discourage gatching of the bed at the knee. Encourage the patient not to cross legs at the knee or ankle while in bed.
- ▲ Encourage ambulation by the patient as soon as possible according to physician's prescription.

- ▲ Administer prophylactic anticoagulant therapy as prescribed.
- ▲ Administer IV fluids; encourage fluid intake as prescribed.
- Before discharge, instruct the patient and family about guidelines for resuming normal activity.

Rationale

Contracting the leg muscles decreases venous stasis and encourages good venous return; both decrease the opportunity of thromboembolic developments.

Both are useful in improving venous return.

This contributes to venous pooling in the legs and decreased venous return.

Being fully upright is preferable to "dangling" or sitting in a chair because contracted muscles push against the leg vessels and improve venous return most effectively when the patient is upright and legs are straight.

Low-dose anticoagulants are used to prevent thrombus formation.

This reduces hemoconcentration, which contributes to deep vein thrombosis.

Providing guidelines promotes the return of activity at an appropriate level, which will help reduce the complications of immobility and promote a sense of well-being.

NDx Nursing Diagnosis

Deficient Knowledge

Common Related Factors

Lack of previous experience with abdominal surgery
Need for home management

Defining Characteristics

Multiple questions
Lack of questions
Inability to provide self-care on discharge

■ = Independent; ▲ = Collaborative

Common Expected Outcome

Patient verbalizes understanding of and demonstrates ability to provide wound care, advance diet as tolerated, limit activities as appropriate, recognize signs and symptoms of wound infection or other surgical complications, and return for follow-up care with physician.

NOC Outcomes

Knowledge: Diet; Knowledge: Treatment Regimen; Knowledge: Prescribed Activity

NIC Interventions

Teaching: Disease Process; Teaching: Prescribed Diet; Teaching: Prescribed Activity/Exercise; Teaching: Psychomotor Skill

Ongoing Assessment

Actions/Interventions

■ Assess the patient's ability to perform wound care, verbalize appropriate activity, and verbalize appropriate diet.

■ Assess the patient's understanding of the need for further therapy, if necessary.

■ Assess the patient's understanding of the need for close follow-up observation.

Rationale

The patient's participation in self-care will provide a sense of purpose, accomplishment, and control.

Patients who have had abdominal surgery for malignancies may require further therapy, such as chemotherapy, irradiation, or immunotherapy.

Patients who leave the hospital with sutures, staples, or drains in place need to return for their removal or arrange to have a home health caregiver remove them.

Therapeutic Interventions

Actions/Interventions

■ Teach the patient to perform appropriate wound care:
Closed abdominal incision
• Staples or sutures and dressings are usually removed by the time of discharge, and Steri-Strips have been placed.
Open abdominal wounds
• Wounds require twice-daily wet-to-dry saline solution packings until the wound has granulated in enough to close.

■ Teach the patient appropriate activity:
• No lifting more than 10 pounds for 6 weeks
• Mild exercise (e.g., walking)
• Showering

• No driving until anterior abdominal wound has healed

Rationale

These maintain wound approximation. Steri-Strips should be left in place until they fall off.

The primary purpose of a wet-to-dry dressing is to mechanically debride a wound. The moistened layer of the dressing increases the absorptive ability of the dressing to collect exudates and wound debris. As the dressing dries, it adheres to the wound and debrides the wound of the tissue when the dressing is removed.

This minimizes risk of loss of wound integrity.

Exercise increases stamina and improves circulation.

When there is an open wound, which may take up to 8 weeks to heal completely, use of a hand-held shower head is a good way to clean the wound.

Operating foot pedals while driving, especially the brake, increases abdominal pressure and muscle straining.

■ = Independent; ▲ = Collaborative

Abdominal Surgery—cont'd

Actions/Interventions

- Teach the patient that a well-balanced, high-calorie, high-protein diet is desirable for healing that continues over a period of weeks.

- Teach the patient the importance of any further cancer therapy planned (e.g., chemotherapy, radiation therapy, immunotherapy).

- Teach the patient that bowel function will return to preoperative baseline in 2 to 3 weeks.

- Instruct the patient to seek medical attention for any of the following: temperature of 38° C (100.4° F) or higher, foul-smelling wound drainage, redness or unusual pain in any incision, or absence of bowel movement.

Rationale

Patients who have undergone gastrectomy should be taught to eat small, frequent meals, because they no longer have the same preoperative gastric capacity. Small, frequent meals are less likely to cause "dumping syndrome," which results from too large an osmotic load.

These therapies are typically offered if the pathology report indicates that the tumor was not confined to the bowel or bowel wall.

This is usually after the patient has returned to a normal schedule and diet.

The patient needs to report and receive prompt treatment for postoperative complications such as infection or possible bowel obstruction.

Bowel Diversion Surgery: Ostomy, Postoperative Care

Colostomy; Ileostomy; Fecal Diversion; Stoma

This surgical procedure results in an opening into the small or large intestine for the purpose of diverting the fecal stream past an area of obstruction or disease, protecting a distal surgical anastomosis, or providing an outlet for stool in the absence of a functioning intact rectum. Bowel diversion surgery may be performed to promote wound healing of an ulcer on the perineum. Diverted fecal material is directed away from the wound to promote wound healing. Depending on the purpose of the surgery and the integrity and function of anatomical structures, stomas may be temporary or permanent. Peristomal irritation, adaptation, and knowledge deficit are important nursing concerns. This care plan focuses primarily on the person with a new stoma who is being cared for in the hospital environment.

NDx Nursing Diagnosis

Deficient Knowledge

Common Related Factors

Lack of previous similar experience
Need for additional information
Previous contact with poorly rehabilitated ostomate

Defining Characteristics

Verbalized need for information
Verbalized misinformation/misconceptions
Multiple questions
Lack of questions

■ = Independent; ▲ = Collaborative

Common Expected Outcomes

Patient describes alteration in normal gastrointestinal (GI) anatomy and physiology requiring surgical creation of the stoma.

Patient verbalizes that loss or bypass of anal sphincter will result in the need to wear a pouch.

NOC Outcomes
Knowledge: Treatment Regimen; Knowledge: Treatment Procedures

NIC Interventions
Teaching: Procedures/Treatment; Teaching: Preoperative

Ongoing Assessment

Actions/Interventions

- Inquire regarding information from surgeon about ostomy formation (e.g., purpose, site). Ascertain (from chart, physician) whether stoma will be permanent or temporary.

- Explore previous contact that the patient has had with persons with a stoma.

- Identify and dispel any misinformation and misconceptions the patient has about the ostomy.

Rationale

Learning readiness/adaptation is often delayed in patients with temporary stomas; individuals with temporary stomas may often feel that learning ostomy management is not necessary.

Previous experience, whether positive or negative, will have an impact on the patient's expectations and fears regarding this surgery.

Providing factual information can ease the patient's anxiety.

Therapeutic Interventions

Actions/Interventions

- Reinforce and reexplain the proposed procedure.

- Use diagrams, pictures, and audiovisual equipment to explain anatomy and physiology of GI tract, pathophysiology necessitating ostomy, and proposed location of stoma.

- Explain need for a pouch in terms of loss of sphincter.

- Show the patient the actual pouch or one similar to the one that the patient will wear after surgery.

- Offer a visit from a rehabilitated ostomate.

Rationale

Preoperative anxiety often makes it necessary to repeat instructions or explanations several times before patients are able to comprehend.

Ileostomy stomas are located in the right lower quadrant; colostomy stomas may be in the upper right quadrant, midabdomen at waistline, or left upper or lower quadrant.

Patients should be told that preoperative bowel habits may return after surgery but that control of defecation is lost, and therefore a pouch is necessary to collect or contain stool and gas. The location of the stoma in the GI tract determines stool frequency and consistency. Output from a sigmoid colostomy is soft to solid, frequency is similar to preoperative patterns, and output may be regulated by irrigation. With a transverse colostomy, the output is mushy, occurs after meals, and cannot be regulated. Output from an ileostomy is liquid.

Understanding the purpose and need for a pouch encourages the patient to participate in ostomy management.

Often, contact with another individual who has undergone the same procedure is more beneficial than factual information from health care personnel.

■ = Independent; ▲ = Collaborative

Gastrointestinal and Digestive Care Plans

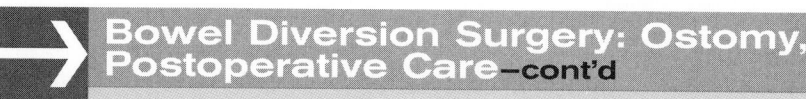

Bowel Diversion Surgery: Ostomy, Postoperative Care—cont'd

ND× Nursing Diagnosis

Risk for Self-Care Deficit: Toileting

Common Risk Factors

Presence of new stoma
Presence of poorly placed stoma
Presence of pouch
Poor hand-eye coordination

Common Expected Outcome

Patient performs self-care needs (emptying and changing pouch) independently or with assistance depending on specific situation.

NOC Outcome
Self-Care: Toileting

NIC Intervention
Ostomy Care

Ongoing Assessment

Actions/Interventions

■ Assess for the following: presence of old abdominal scars, presence of bony prominences on the anterior abdomen, presence of creases or skinfolds on the abdomen, extreme obesity, scaphoid abdomen, pendulous breasts, and ability to see and handle equipment.

Rationale

Stoma placement is easier for a patient who has a flat abdomen with no scars, bony prominences, or extremes of weight. The stoma should be placed in a site that is visible and easily reached by the patient.

Therapeutic Interventions

Actions/Interventions

▲ Consult an enterostomal therapy (ET) nurse or surgeon to indelibly mark the proposed stoma site that the patient can easily see and reach; scars, bony prominences, and skinfolds are avoided; hip flexion should not change contour.

■ If possible, have the patient wear a pouch over the proposed site; evaluate effectiveness 12 to 24 hours after applying the pouch.

Rationale

Stoma location is a key factor in self-care. A poorly located stoma can delay or preclude self-care. ET nurses are commonly asked by surgeons to preoperatively mark stoma areas.

Stoma site selection is facilitated by observing the appliance faceplate on the person's body under normal wearing conditions (e.g., dressed in normal clothing, moving about).

■ = Independent; ▲ = Collaborative

Nursing Diagnosis

Risk for Ineffective Stoma Tissue Perfusion

Common Risk Factors

Surgical manipulation of bowel
Postoperative edema
Tightly fitted faceplate
Pressure from rod or other support device

Common Expected Outcome

Patient's stoma remains pink and moist.

NOC Outcome
Tissue Perfusion: Abdominal Organs

NIC Interventions
Ostomy Care; Surveillance

Ongoing Assessment

Actions/Interventions

■ Assess the following at least every 4 hours for the first
24 hours and notify the physician of changes:

• Color of stoma

• Moist appearance of stoma

• Stomal edema

• Presence of rods or support devices

• Correctly fitted faceplate

Rationale

The stoma (a piece of intestine) should be pink and
moist, indicating good perfusion and adequate venous
drainage. Dusky or blue appearance may indicate
venous congestion or poor blood supply, either of
which could result in a necrotic stoma.

Healthy intestine continuously secretes mucus, which
maintains the moisture of the stoma.

Edema is either caused by preoperative pathology or by
manipulation of the bowel during surgery; the stoma
can be quite swollen.

Transverse or loop stomas are often supported by a rod
or other support device, which usually is removed on
the seventh to tenth postoperative day; patients may
be discharged with the support device in place.

The opening of the ostomy appliance should be ⅛-inch
larger than the stoma itself. A faceplate that is too
tight can constrict the venous return of the stomal
circulation and result in edema or damage to the stoma.

Therapeutic Interventions

Actions/Interventions

■ Fit the patient with a correctly sized faceplate.

Rationale

Proper fit protects the surrounding skin from contact
with drainage.

■ = Independent; ▲ = Collaborative

Bowel Diversion Surgery: Ostomy, Postoperative Care–cont'd

Actions/Interventions	Rationale
■ Anticipate and prepare the patient for possible surgical stoma revision if signs or symptoms of compromised circulation are present.	Necrosis extending to the fascia may represent a surgical emergency due to threat of perforation and peritonitis.
■ Examine the abdomen for distention.	Abdominal distention may decrease blood flow to the distal bowel and stoma.

 Nursing Diagnosis

Impaired Skin Integrity

Common Related Factor

Continuous contact of bowel secretions with skin

Defining Characteristics

Patient complains of burning and itching
Skin is red and tender
Skin is excoriated

Common Expected Outcome

Patient's skin is free of irritation caused by contact with fecal output from ostomy.

NOC Outcomes
Tissue Integrity: Skin and Mucous Membranes; Bowel Continence

NIC Interventions
Skin Care: Topical Treatments; Ostomy Care

Ongoing Assessment

Actions/Interventions	Rationale
■ Assess peristomal skin for redness, excoriation, tenderness, vesicles, papular rashes, or drainage.	Loss of peristomal skin integrity is associated with allergies, mechanical trauma, chemical reactions, and infection. Small bowel effluent contains proteolytic enzymes. Exposure of the skin to the effluent can cause skin irritation within hours. *Candida albicans* is a common cause of peristomal skin infection.

Therapeutic Interventions

Actions/Interventions	Rationale
■ Maintain intact peristomal skin using the pouch method. • Choose appropriate pouch by evaluating skin condition (pouch adhesives will not adhere to wet or moist skin), size and shape of abdomen, presence of current or recent sutures, stoma site, and characteristics of ostomy effluent.	The pouch opening should be no more than $\frac{1}{8}$-inch larger in diameter than the stoma.

■ = Independent; ▲ = Collaborative

Actions/Interventions

- Clean and prepare skin with mild soap and water.

- Prepare pattern as a guide to customize the fit of the pouch; apply hydrocolloid skin barrier.
- Fashion pouch; apply over skin barrier.

- Keep the pouch emptied routinely. Change the skin barrier every 3 to 4 days.

Rationale

Skin preparation is the most important step in pouching the stoma to prevent leakage.

A correctly fitted pouch used with a skin barrier will promote skin integrity.

The skin barrier is protected and the pouch will last longer if drainage is channeled from the skin seal.

More frequent changes of the skin barrier can cause mechanical trauma to the skin. Emptying the pouch when it is $1/3$ to $1/2$ full reduces the risk of leakage and odor.

NDx Nursing Diagnosis

Risk for Disturbed Body Image

Common Risk Factors

Presence of stoma
Loss of fecal continence
Presence of pouch
Fear of offensive odor
Fear of appearing "different"
Primary disease (after cancer)

Common Expected Outcome

Patient begins to verbalize feelings about the stoma and body image.

NOC Outcomes
Body Image; Psychosocial Adjustment; Life Change

NIC Interventions
Ostomy Management; Body Image Enhancement

Ongoing Assessment

Actions/Interventions

- Assess the patient's perception of change in body structure and function.

- Assess the patient's perceived impact of change.

- Note verbal and nonverbal references to the stoma.

Rationale

The patient may experience a period of grief about the loss of normal bowel elimination. The patient needs to recognize feelings before they can be dealt with effectively.

The patient's response to real or perceived changes in body structure and/or function is related to the importance that the patient places on the structure or function (e.g., a very fastidious person may experience the visual presence of a stool-filled pouch on the anterior abdomen as intolerable).

Patients often "name" stomas as an attempt to separate the stoma from themselves. Others may look away or totally deny the presence of the stoma until they are able to cope.

■ = Independent; ▲ = Collaborative

Bowel Diversion Surgery: Ostomy, Postoperative Care—cont'd

Actions/Interventions	**Rationale**
■ Note the patient's ability and readiness to look at, touch, and care for the stoma and ostomy equipment.	Looking at the stoma is often the first indication that the patient is ready to participate in stoma care.

Therapeutic Interventions

Actions/Interventions	**Rationale**
■ Acknowledge appropriateness of emotional response to perceived change in body structure and function.	Because control of elimination is a skill/task of early childhood and is a socially private function, loss of control precipitates body image change and possible self-concept change. The patient needs to understand that grief is a normal response.
■ Assist the patient in looking at, touching, and caring for the stoma when ready.	The patient's readiness to learn may be judged by willingness to look at the stoma and ask questions. Some patients acknowledge the stoma with minimal emotional difficulty, whereas others have a more difficult time adjusting.
■ Assist the patient in identifying specific actions that could be helpful in managing the perceived loss or problems related to the stoma.	The most common concern is odor; helping patients gain control over odor will facilitate an acceptable body image (see Deficient Knowledge care plan below).

NDx Nursing Diagnosis

Deficient Knowledge

Common Related Factors	**Defining Characteristics**
Presence of new stoma Lack of similar experience	Demonstrated inability to empty and change pouch Verbalized need for information about diet, odor, activity, hygiene, clothing, interpersonal relationships, equipment purchase, or financial concerns

Common Expected Outcome	
Patient or significant other is capable of ostomy care on discharge.	**NOC Outcomes** Knowledge: Treatment Regimen; Knowledge: Prescribed Diet; Knowledge: Health Resources **NIC Interventions** Ostomy Management; Teaching: Psychomotor Skill; Teaching: Prescribed Diet

■ = Independent; ▲ = Collaborative

Ongoing Assessment

Actions/Interventions

■ Assess the patient's ability to empty and change the pouch.

■ Assess the patient's ability to care for peristomal skin and identify problems.

■ Assess knowledge of the following:
  • Diet

  • Activity

  • Hygiene

  • Clothing

Rationale

Most patients will be independent in emptying the pouch by time of discharge; some may still need assistance with pouch change and may require outpatient follow-up care by a home health care nurse.

This prevents fecal material from coming into contact with the skin and causing breakdown.

The postoperative patient should consume a high-protein, high-carbohydrate diet to facilitate healing. The patient must understand that not eating to minimize fecal output is detrimental and that the stoma will have output regardless.

The patient should understand that activity should not be altered by the presence of the stoma or pouch.

Normal bathing or showering is acceptable; the patient should be prepared for the possibility that small amounts of stool may pass during bathing and showering. Some patients purchase small, disposable pouches for bathing and showering; others prefer removing the pouch for bathing and showering.

No special clothing or alterations in existing clothing should be required by the presence of the stoma or pouch.

Therapeutic Interventions

Actions/Interventions

■ Provide psychomotor teaching during first and subsequent applications of the pouch.

■ Include at least one caregiver as approved or desired by the patient.

■ Gradually transfer responsibility for pouch emptying and changing to the patient.

■ Allow at least one opportunity for supervised return demonstration of pouch change before discharge.

■ Teach the patient the following regarding diet:
  • For ileostomy: eat a balanced diet; use special care in chewing high-fiber foods (e.g., popcorn, peanuts, coconut, vegetables, string beans, olives); increase fluid intake during hot weather or vigorous exercise.
  • For colostomy: eat a balanced diet; no foods are specifically contraindicated; certain foods (e.g., eggs, fish, green onions, cheese, asparagus, broccoli, leafy vegetables, carbonated beverages) may increase flatus and fecal odor.

Rationale

Even before patients are able to participate actively, they can observe and discuss ostomy care.

It is beneficial to teach others alongside the patient, as long as all realize that the goal is for the patient to become independent in ostomy self-care.

Repeated practice by the patient with positive feedback from the nurse will help the patient gain confidence in self-care ability.

Ostomy care requires both cognitive and psychomotor skills. Postoperatively, learning ability may be decreased, requiring repetition and need for return demonstrations.

Dietary intake will influence the consistency and frequency of fecal output from the stoma. Patients need to learn individual responses to foods.

■ = Independent; ▲ = Collaborative

Bowel Diversion Surgery: Ostomy, Postoperative Care—cont'd

Actions/Interventions

■ Discuss odor control and acknowledge that odor (or fear of odor) can impair social functioning.

■ Discuss availability of ostomy support groups (e.g., United Ostomy Association, National Foundation for Ileitis and Colitis).

■ Instruct the patient to maintain contact with an ET nurse.

Rationale

Odor control is best achieved by eliminating odor-causing foods from the diet. Green leafy vegetables, eggs, fish, and onions are primary odor-causing foods. Oral deodorants and pouch deodorants may also help. Pouch filters help muffle sounds and deodorize flatus.

Contact with other people who have ostomies increases the perception of the colostomy being manageable and enhancing the patient's sense of control.

This provides an opportunity for follow-up and problem solving.

> • RELATED CARE PLAN
>
> Risk for infection, p. 108

Cholecystectomy: Laparoscopic/Open, Postoperative Care

Cholecystitis is an inflammation of the gallbladder. Most patients who develop cholecystitis have cholelithiasis or gallstones. Right upper quadrant pain that occurs after eating a high-fat meal is the most common manifestation of acute cholecystitis. Although eating a fat-free diet will decrease the patient's symptoms temporarily, surgical removal of the gallbladder and gallstones is usually recommended. A laparoscopic surgical technique is the preferred method for cholecystectomy. Laparoscopic surgery uses small abdominal incisions in combination with telescopic visualization of the abdominal cavity. The abdominal cavity is inflated with carbon dioxide to facilitate visualization of the abdominal organs generally and the gallbladder specifically. Once the gallbladder is dissected away from surrounding tissue, it is removed through one of the puncture wounds. The carbon dioxide is evacuated, and the multiple puncture wounds are closed. If the surgeon is not able to successfully remove the gallbladder using a laparoscopic approach, a larger open incision is made in the right upper quadrant for direct visualization and removal of the gallbladder.

 ## Nursing Diagnosis

Risk for Infection

Common Risk Factors

Abdominal incisions
Presence of tubes and drains

> ■ = Independent; ▲ = Collaborative

Common Expected Outcome

Patient remains free of infection as evidenced by healing wound or incision that is free of redness, swelling, purulent discharge, and pain, and by normal body temperature within 48 hours postoperatively.

NOC Outcomes
Knowledge: Infection Control; Tissue Integrity: Skin and Mucous Membranes; Wound Healing: Primary Intention

NIC Interventions
Infection Control; Teaching: Prescribed Medication; Wound Care

Ongoing Assessment

Actions/Interventions

■ Monitor temperature.

■ Assess incisions for redness, drainage, swelling, and increased pain.

■ Assess stability of tubes and drains.

Rationale

For the first 48 to 72 hours postoperatively, temperatures of up to 38.5° C (101.3° F) are expected as a normal stress response to surgery. Beyond 72 hours, temperature should return to the patient's baseline. Temperature spikes, usually occurring in late afternoon or at night, are often indications of infection.

Incisions that have been closed with sutures or staples should be free of redness, swelling, and drainage. Some incisional discomfort is expected. These incisions are usually kept covered by a large adhesive bandage for 24 to 48 hours; beyond 48 hours, there is no need for a dressing.

In-and-out motion of improperly secured tubes and drains allows access by pathogens through stab wounds where tubes and drains are placed. If an open cholecystectomy was performed, a wound drain may be placed and removed before discharge.

Therapeutic Interventions

Actions/Interventions

■ Instruct the patient and caregiver to wash hands before contact with the postoperative patient.

■ Teach use of aseptic technique during dressing change, wound care, or handling or manipulating of tubes and drains.

■ Ensure that surgical tubes and drains are not inadvertently interrupted (opened). Securely tape connectors and pin extension or drainage tubing to the patient's clothing.

■ Instruct the patient and caregiver in administration of antibiotics and antipyretics as prescribed.

Rationale

Hand washing remains the most effective method of infection control.

Aseptic technique prevents transmission of bacterial infections to the area.

Opening sterile systems allows access by pathogens and puts the patient at risk for infection.

Drains may be left in place until the first return visit to the surgeon (about 7 days), if not removed at the time of discharge.

Antibiotics are necessary for the treatment of abscess and infection. Antipyretics will reduce fever and promote comfort.

■ = Independent; ▲ = Collaborative

Cholecystectomy: Laparoscopic/Open, Postoperative Care—cont'd

NDx Nursing Diagnosis

Risk for Ineffective Breathing Pattern

Common Risk Factors

Right upper quadrant abdominal incision
Presence of pain

Common Expected Outcome

Patient maintains effective breathing pattern as evidenced by respiratory rate of 12 to 20 breaths/min, nonlabored clear respirations, ability to use the incentive spirometer correctly, and clear lung sounds.

NOC Outcomes
Respiratory Status: Ventilation;
   Comfort Level

NIC Interventions
Respiratory Monitoring; Pain Management;
   Cough Enhancement

Ongoing Assessment

Actions/Interventions

■ Monitor respiratory rate, depth, and chest wall excursion.

■ Monitor pain level and use of analgesics.

Rationale

The right upper quadrant incision and pain may limit the patient's ability to take a deep breath. Shallow breathing puts the patient at risk for atelectasis and pneumonia.

Pain inhibits the ability to cough and deep breathe and use the incentive spirometer correctly.

Therapeutic Interventions

Actions/Interventions

■ Encourage deep breathing, coughing, and use of incentive spirometer every hour while the patient is awake.

■ Encourage the patient to splint the incision area when coughing and deep breathing.

▲ Administer analgesics at regular intervals.

Rationale

Increasing deep breathing will expand the alveoli and decrease the development of atelectasis.

Providing external support to the operative site will decrease discomfort associated with increased respiratory effort.

Controlling pain will help the patient feel more comfortable with deep breathing.

■ = Independent; ▲ = Collaborative

Nursing Diagnosis

Deficient Knowledge

Common Related Factors	Defining Characteristics
Lack of previous experience with laparoscopic surgery Need for home management	Multiple questions Lack of questions Inability to provide self-care on discharge

Common Expected Outcome

Patient verbalizes understanding of and demonstrates ability to perform postoperative care after discharge.

NOC Outcomes

Knowledge: Treatment Regimen;
Knowledge: Prescribed Activity

NIC Interventions

Wound Care; Teaching: Prescribed
Activity; Teaching: Psychomotor Skills

Ongoing Assessment

Actions/Interventions

■ Assess the patient's ability to perform wound care, verbalize appropriate activity, and describe appropriate diet.

■ Assess the patient's understanding of the need for close follow-up observation.

Rationale

This information is the foundation for an individualized teaching plan.

Patients who leave the hospital with sutures, staples, or drains in place need to return for removal, usually about 1 week after surgery.

Therapeutic Interventions

Actions/Interventions

■ Teach the patient to perform appropriate wound care:
  • Abdominal incisions

  • Dressings

■ Provide the patient with a measuring receptacle and chart or flow sheet for recording drain output.
■ Teach the patient to empty drainage collection devices.

■ Teach the patient appropriate activity: no lifting more than 10 pounds for 6 weeks, return to work in 3 or 4 days, showering and bathing are acceptable.
■ Teach the patient the following about diet: eat a well-balanced, high-calorie, high-protein diet.

Rationale

Staples or sutures and dressings may be present at the time of discharge.
Dressings are usually adhesive bandages, which should be changed daily and after showering.
Drains are left in place until drainage is less than 30 mL/ 24 hours; this usually occurs 3 to 7 days postoperatively.
Patients should prepare a clean surface (e.g., clean paper towels) to work on and should wash hands under running water before emptying the collection device. These measures reduce risk of infection.
Activity restrictions reduce strain on abdominal muscles and promote healing. This reduces the risk of wound dehiscence.
Such a diet promotes healing. A high-fat meal may result in diarrhea because of the reduced availability of bile for fat digestion.

■ = Independent; ▲ = Collaborative

Cholecystectomy: Laparoscopic/Open, Postoperative Care—cont'd

Actions/Interventions	**Rationale**
■ Teach the patient that bowel function will return to preoperative baseline in 2 to 3 days.	Bowel sounds will be hypoactive initially but should return to normal within the first 2 to 3 days postoperatively. The presence of flatus or stool signals the return of peristalsis.
■ Instruct the patient to seek medical attention for any of the following: temperature higher than 38° C (100.4° F), foul-smelling wound drainage, redness or unusual pain in any incision, or absence of bowel movement.	Signs and symptoms of infection should be reported to the physician.
■ Teach the patient that minor abdominal pain and shoulder pain are expected after laparoscopic surgery and should be managed with oral analgesic agents.	During abdominal laparoscopic surgery, the peritoneal cavity is filled with carbon dioxide; this facilitates visualization of structures by the surgeon. Until the gas is completely absorbed, some discomfort is typical in the shoulder area; this referred pain is caused by irritation of the nerves by the unabsorbed carbon dioxide gas.

Cirrhosis

Laënnec's Cirrhosis; Hepatic Encephalopathy; Ascites; Liver Failure

Cirrhosis is an inflammatory disease of the liver. The inflammatory process results in irreversible fibrosis and scarring of hepatic tissue. Alcohol abuse is the primary cause of cirrhosis. Other causes include biliary obstruction, hepatitis B and C, and metabolic defects such as alpha-1 antitrypsin deficiency. The incidence of cirrhosis is highest in men between 40 and 60 years old. The development of cirrhosis occurs over many years before the person presents with characteristic symptoms. Malnutrition contributes to the development of cirrhosis in people who abuse alcohol. The disruption of hepatic function in cirrhosis can lead to the development of ascites, portal hypertension, hepatic encephalopathy, and liver failure.

NDx Nursing Diagnosis

Imbalanced Nutrition: Less Than Body Requirements

Common Related Factors	**Defining Characteristics**
Poor eating habits	Documented inadequate dietary intake
Excess alcohol intake	Weight loss
Lack of financial means	Muscle wasting, especially in extremities
Altered hepatic metabolic function	Skin changes consistent with vitamin deficiency (flaking, loss of elasticity)
Inadequate bile production	Coagulopathies
Nausea, vomiting, anorexia	Dark urine
	Pale or clay-colored stool

■ = Independent; ▲ = Collaborative

Common Expected Outcome

Patient achieves adequate nutrient intake as evidenced by consumption of 3000 kcal/day and by weight stabilization.

NOC Outcomes

Nutritional Status: Nutrient Intake; Knowledge: Diet

NIC Interventions

Nutrition Therapy; Nutrition Monitoring; Teaching: Prescribed Diet

Ongoing Assessment

Actions/Interventions

■ Assess for changes in body weight and muscle mass.

■ Document intake.

▲ Monitor serum electrolyte levels and albumin/protein levels.

▲ Monitor glucose levels.

▲ Monitor coagulation profile.

Rationale

Actual weight may remain steady while muscle mass deteriorates and ascitic fluid accumulates. Muscle wasting and weight loss are common in advancing cirrhosis.

A diary kept by the patient or caregiver may facilitate nutritional assessment in the home.

Hypokalemia (K^+ less than 3.5 mEq/L) is common in cirrhosis as a result of increased aldosterone levels, which increase K^+ excretion. Serum protein levels are decreased secondary to decreased hepatic production of protein and loss of protein molecules to the peritoneal space.

Patients with cirrhosis may be hypoglycemic, because the liver fails to perform glycolysis (breakdown of stored glycogen) and gluconeogenesis (formation of glucose from amino acids).

Several coagulation factors made by the liver require adequate amounts of vitamin K. Patients with cirrhosis commonly have hypovitaminosis that is severe enough to precipitate coagulopathy.

Therapeutic Interventions

Actions/Interventions

■ Instruct the patient in the need for a diet high in calories from carbohydrate sources. Instruct the patient to limit proteins in the diet.

■ Suggest small, frequent meals and assistance with meals as needed.

▲ Provide dietary or pharmacological vitamin supplementation.

▲ Provide enteral or parenteral nutritional support as ordered, using carbohydrates as the calorie source.

Rationale

Aberrant protein metabolism in the failing liver can cause hepatic encephalopathy because ammonia, which is normally metabolized into urea (which can be excreted), passes through the damaged liver unchanged and goes on to become a cerebral toxin.

Fatigue is a common symptom in cirrhosis that can limit energy for eating. Meals should be planned for times when the person is least fatigued.

If bile production is impaired, absorption of fat-soluble vitamins A, D, E, and K will be inadequate.

Nutritional support is typically provided during advanced stages of cirrhosis or if bleeding complications make the gut unsuitable for enteral nutrition.

■ = Independent; ▲ = Collaborative

Cirrhosis—cont'd

Actions/Interventions

▲ Administer prescribed medications:
  • Acid-suppressing agents
  • Antiemetics

Rationale

Medications alleviate gastric distress and promote increased appetite and food intake.

 Nursing Diagnosis

Excess Fluid Volume, Extravascular (Ascites)

Common Related Factors

Increased portal venous pressure
Hypoalbuminemia
Low serum oncotic pressure
Aldosterone imbalance

Defining Characteristics

Increasing abdominal girth
Ballottement
Taut abdomen, dull to percussion
Dehydration

Common Expected Outcomes

Patient experiences a decrease in ascites formation and accumulation as evidenced by decreased abdominal girth.
Patient remains hydrated.

NOC Outcomes

Fluid Balance; Knowledge: Treatment Regimen; Nutrition Status: Food and Fluid Intake

NIC Interventions

Fluid Monitoring; Fluid/Electrolyte Management

Ongoing Assessment

Actions/Interventions

■ Assess for presence of ascites:

  • Measure abdominal girth, taking care to measure at the same point consistently.

  • Check the abdomen for dullness on percussion.

▲ Monitor serum albumin, serum protein, and globulin levels.

■ Assess for signs of portal hypertension: history of upper gastrointestinal (GI) bleeding, and spider nevi.

Rationale

Ascites is the collection of protein-rich fluid in the peritoneal cavity. Its volume may be so severe as to impair respiratory and digestive functions, as well as mobility.

Measuring changes in abdominal girth can help assess the progression of ascites.

Fluid in the peritoneal cavity will produce a dull percussion sound.

Protein molecules act as fluid "magnets" that help maintain body fluid in correct compartments; low protein level allows shift of fluid to extravascular space.

Portal hypertension is high blood pressure within the vascular bed, which is usually a high-flow, low-resistance vascular system. As cirrhosis progresses, normally distensible hepatic tissue is replaced by nonelastic scar tissue; blood flowing through the hepatic vasculature is subjected to higher pressures, called portal hypertension.

■ = Independent; ▲ = Collaborative

Actions/Interventions

- Monitor intake and output.

- Assess breathing patterns.

Rationale

Although overall intake of fluid may be adequate, shifting of fluid out of the intravascular to the extravascular spaces may result in dehydration. The risk of this occurring increases when diuretics are given. Patients may use diaries for home assessment.

Ascites may limit excursion of the diaphragm on inspiration. The patient may hypoventilate in a supine position.

Therapeutic Interventions

Actions/Interventions

- Instruct the patient and caregiver to:
  - Restrict fluid and sodium intake as ordered.

  - Take or administer spironolactone as prescribed.

  - Take or administer diuretics cautiously.

▲ For patients unresponsive to the aforementioned measures, assist with paracentesis as needed.

- For patients with a peritoneovenous shunt (LaVeen shunt, Denver shunt):

  - Apply abdominal binder.
  - Encourage use of incentive spirometer.

Rationale

Increased aldosterone levels contribute to aggressive sodium reabsorption, which enhances accumulation of ascitic fluid.

Spironolactone, a diuretic, antagonizes aldosterone. It causes excretion of sodium and water but spares potassium.

Excess fluid is extravascular; aggressive diuresis can lead to dehydration and acute tubular necrosis or hepatorenal syndrome.

Rapid removal of ascitic fluid may be necessary to improve breathing, appetite, mobility, and comfort; reaccumulation of the fluid is common.

Although paracentesis (removal of peritoneal fluid by needle) effectively removes ascitic fluid, it also wastes protein and is only a temporary measure. Peritoneovenous shunting returns ascitic fluid to the vascular space.

Inspiring against resistance and the use of an abdominal binder increase intraperitoneal pressures, causing the valve in the shunt to open and allowing ascitic fluid to shunt into vascular space.

NDx Nursing Diagnosis

Risk for Deficient Fluid Volume

Common Risk Factors

Overly aggressive diuresis
GI bleeding
Coagulopathies

Defining Characteristics

Increasing abdominal girth
Ballottement
Taut abdomen, dull to percussion
Dehydration

Common Expected Outcome

Patient maintains normal fluid volume as evidenced by stable vital signs, urine specific gravity less than 1.030, urinary output greater than 30 mL/hr, and moist mucous membranes.

NOC Outcomes
Fluid Balance; Hydration

NIC Interventions
Fluid Monitoring; Hypovolemia Management

■ = Independent; ▲ = Collaborative

> ## Cirrhosis—cont'd

Ongoing Assessment

Actions/Interventions

- Monitor blood pressure and heart rate; check for orthostatic changes.

- Measure urine specific gravity, amount, and color.

- Check moisture of mucous membranes.
- Assess for hematemesis (vomited blood), hematochezia (bright red blood per rectum), and melena (dark, tarry stool). Test any emesis, gastric aspirate, or stool for blood.

Rationale

Changes from the patient's baseline vital signs can indicate shifts in fluid balance. Decreased blood pressure and elevated heart rate may occur with decreased circulatory blood volume.

Decreased fluid volume is associated with decreased urine volume, increased specific gravity, and darker urine color.

Dry mucous membranes indicate dehydration.

As portal hypertension worsens and possible coagulopathies develop, patients with cirrhosis are at risk for bleeding. Esophageal varices, because of the close proximity of the hepatic vasculature and the venous drainage of the esophagus, are common among cirrhotic patients.

Therapeutic Interventions

Actions/Interventions

▲ For signs of fluid volume deficit:
- Hold diuretics
- Administer intravenous (IV) fluids as prescribed.

▲ If GI bleeding occurs, administer IV fluids, blood products, or volume expanders.

Rationale

These may deplete intravascular volume.

This may be administered at home, or patient may require hospital admission for severe dehydration.

These expand intravascular fluid volume and prevent complications of hypovolemia (e.g., acute tubular necrosis, shock). If bleeding occurs, transfusion with blood products may be necessary.

Nursing Diagnosis

Risk for Disturbed Sensory Perception

Common Risk Factors

Hepatic encephalopathy
Delirium tremens
Acute intoxication
Hepatic metabolic insufficiency

Common Expected Outcome

Patient remains arousable, oriented, able to follow directions, and free from injury caused by neurosensory changes.

> **NOC Outcomes**
> Cognitive Orientation; Neurological Status
>
> **NIC Interventions**
> Surveillance: Safety; Medication Administration; Delusion Management

> ■ = Independent; ▲ = Collaborative

Ongoing Assessment

Actions/Interventions

■ Monitor or instruct caregiver to monitor for the following signs and symptoms: altered attention span; inability to give accurate history; inability to follow commands; disorientation to person, place, and/or time; delusions; inappropriate behavior; self-directed or other-directed violence; and inappropriate affect.

▲ For patients requiring hospitalization, monitor blood alcohol level on admission.

■ Note time since last ingestion of alcohol.

▲ Monitor blood ammonia levels; evaluate factors that may increase cerebral sensitivity to ammonia (infections, acid-base imbalances).

■ Assess for signs and symptoms of hepatic encephalopathy; note stage:
  • Stage I: mild confusion, mood changes, inability to concentrate, sleep disturbances, and mild asterixis (rapid wrist flapping or liver flap)
  • Stage II: confusion, apathy, aberrant behavior, asterixis, and apraxia (loss of ability to carry out familiar, purposeful movements)
  • Stage III: severe confusion, incoherence, diminished responsiveness to verbal stimuli, and hyperactive deep tendon reflexes
  • Stage IV: no reaction to stimuli, no corneal reflex, dilated pupils, and flexion or extension posturing

Rationale

All may be caused by alcohol intoxication, delirium tremens, or hepatic encephalopathy. Hepatic encephalopathy typically occurs in end-stage disease. Accumulation of ammonia and other neurological toxins can impair thinking and neuromuscular function.

It is important to determine whether changes in mentation are related to acute alcohol intoxication or to hepatic encephalopathy.

Delirium tremens can occur up to 7 days after last alcohol intake.

Normally, ammonia is produced in the colon by the interaction of amino acids and colonic bacteria, metabolized by the liver, and excreted. Cirrhotic patients may lack the hepatic ability to metabolize ammonia, which accumulates and acts as a cerebral toxin.

In the early stages, hepatic encephalopathy can be reversed with early intervention. Symptoms of encephalopathy may progress slowly. The patient may fluctuate among the four stages.

Therapeutic Interventions

Actions/Interventions

▲ Protect the patient from physical harm:
  • Pad side rails.
  • Keep bed in low position.
  • Assist patient with ambulation.
  • Restrain patient if necessary.
  • Administer sedatives (nonhepatic metabolism) as prescribed, document effectiveness, and notify physician if dosage needs adjustment.
  • Orient patient to time, place, and person; place calendar and clock in room, provide environmental stimulation (television, radio, newspaper, visitors).
  • Provide emotional support by reassuring patient of physiological cause of confusion.

▲ Decrease intestinal bacteria content:
  • Administer nonabsorbable antibiotics (neomycin, kanamycin) as prescribed.

Rationale

Impaired sensory perception increases the patient's risk for injury and falls. Physical restraints and sedatives should be used only when all other interventions prove ineffective. Overmedication may precipitate coma.

Because ammonia is produced by the interaction of the colonic bacteria and amino acids, reduction of the bacteria colonies normally present in the colon will result in reduced production of ammonia.

■ = Independent; ▲ = Collaborative

Gastrointestinal and Digestive Care Plans

Cirrhosis—cont'd

Actions/Interventions

- Administer lactulose as prescribed.

Rationale

This alters colonic pH and stimulates evacuation. An acidic pH in the colon inhibits bacteria production; evacuation of colonic contents reduce the absorption of ammonia into the bloodstream and therefore improves encephalopathic states.

▲ Decrease sources of dietary ammonia: order low-protein diet (0 to 40 g/day). Limit ammonia-containing foods such as gelatin, onions, and string beans.

Protein makes amino acids available in the colon, which in turn enhances production of ammonia.

 Nursing Diagnosis

Risk for Impaired Skin Integrity (Itching)

Common Risk Factors

Jaundice
Elevated bilirubin levels

Common Expected Outcomes

Patient has intact skin.
Patient verbalizes decreased itching or ability to tolerate itching without scratching.

NOC Outcomes
Tissue Integrity: Skin and Mucous Membranes; Self-Care: Hygiene

NIC Interventions
Skin Care: Topical Treatments; Medication Administration

Ongoing Assessment

Actions/Interventions

■ Assess for jaundice (yellow staining of skin by bilirubin).

Rationale

14 to 16 g of bilirubin are released into the bloodstream each day as red blood cells die and disintegrate. In normal hepatic function, bilirubin is conjugated and excreted through the urine and stool. In hepatic failure, bilirubin is not rendered soluble, cannot be excreted, and accumulates as more and more bilirubin is released.

▲ Monitor findings of liver function tests, especially bilirubin levels.

Unexcreted bilirubin moves by diffusion into subcutaneous and cutaneous structures and irritates the tissue, causing histamine release and itching.

■ Assess itchiness and scratching.

As bilirubin levels drop, skin irritation and itchiness are resolved.

■ = Independent; ▲ = Collaborative

Therapeutic Interventions

Actions/Interventions	Rationale

■ Emphasize importance of keeping skin clean and well moisturized.
  • Use tepid water.
  • Avoid alkaline soaps.
  • Apply emollient lotions.
	Keeping the skin clean and moisturized reduces drying that can contribute to itching.

■ Discourage scratching; keep nails short. Suggest that the patient wear hand mitts if scratching cannot be discouraged by other means.	Nails can introduce pathogens and cause localized infection. Long fingernails may cause skin trauma from repeated scratching.
■ Keep room temperature cool. Encourage patient to wear loose-fitting, soft cotton clothing.	Cotton clothing allows for evaporation of perspiration and adds to the patient's comfort.
▲ Administer antihistamines as ordered.	These medications can reduce itching.

NDx Nursing Diagnosis

Ineffective Health Maintenance

Common Related Factors

Lack of material resources
Ineffective coping
Perceptual/cognitive impairment
Inability to make thoughtful judgments

Defining Characteristics

Demonstrated lack of knowledge regarding basic health practices
Observed inability to take responsibility for health
Reported lack of resources

Common Expected Outcomes

Patient follows prescribed treatment regimen.
Patient identifies and uses available resources as appropriate.
Patient participates in alcohol treatment program as feasible or appropriate.

NOC Outcomes

Health-Promoting Behavior; Knowledge: Treatment Regimen; Self-Direction of Care; Symptom Control

NIC Intervention

Teaching: Disease Process

Ongoing Assessment

Actions/Interventions	Rationale
■ Assess available support systems.	Maintaining health behavior change is more successful if the person has a network of social support.
■ Assess resources and ability to provide housing, food, and medical care.	Alcoholic persons commonly have difficulty holding steady jobs or may use money to buy alcohol instead of necessities such as food and medication. Many homeless individuals abuse alcohol.
■ Assess need for or readiness for alcohol rehabilitation.	Success in alcohol rehabilitation requires readiness of the patient.

■ = Independent; ▲ = Collaborative

Gastrointestinal and Digestive Care Plans

Cirrhosis—cont'd

Therapeutic Interventions

Actions/Interventions	Rationale

■ Teach the effects of alcohol intake and abstinence, and the need for high-calorie, low-protein diet.

Such a diet facilitates regeneration of damaged liver cells.

■ Teach the signs and symptoms of complications of cirrhosis: abdominal pain; vomiting; anorexia; loss of blood from GI tract; generalized bleeding (from gums, skin, genitourinary tract); changes in level of consciousness.

Early identification of complications can limit their impact on the patient's long-term health.

■ Teach dose, administration schedule, expected actions, and possible side effects of prescribed medications.

Knowledge of the details of the treatment plan can increase the patient's willingness and ability to manage care at home.

■ Teach the importance of rest periods.

Rest is important to promote healing of liver tissue.

■ Refer to alcohol rehabilitation program, if appropriate.

Spouses, family members, and other caregivers may also benefit from referrals to support groups.

> • RELATED CARE PLANS
>
> Disturbed body image, p. 21
> Disturbed thought processes, p. 189

Colorectal Cancer

Large Bowel Cancer; Rectal Cancer; Bowel Resection; Hemicolectomy; Colectomy

Colorectal cancer is the second most common cancer death in the United States. Risk factors of colorectal cancer include familial polyposis, family history of colorectal cancer, a personal history of colorectal cancer, colorectal polyps or chronic bowel inflammatory disease. Other risk factors include physical inactivity, obesity, and a diet that is high in fat and low in fiber, smoking, and alcohol consumption. Over all, men and women are affected about equally. Early colorectal cancer often has no symptoms, which is why screening is so important. Most colorectal cancers begin as a polyp, a small growth in the wall of the colon. However over time, some polyps grow and become malignant. Signs of colorectal cancer include bleeding from the rectum, blood in the stool or in the toilet after having a bowel movement, a change in the shape of the stool, cramping pain in the lower stomach, and a feeling of discomfort or an urge to have a bowel movement when there is no need to have one. The TNM staging system, which indicates tumor depth, nodal metastasis, and presence of tumor metastasis has been shown to be the most significant variables in determining the prognosis of colon cancer. Surgical removal is the preferred treatment for colorectal cancer, although irradiation may be used preoperatively. Postoperative chemotherapy has proven beneficial in treatment of colon cancer. Irradiation and immunotherapy are used, but with limited success. This care plan addresses the preoperative stage, care of the patient who has undergone colon resection, and self-care teaching. Patients are usually hospitalized for up to a week.

Nursing Diagnosis

Deficient Knowledge

Common Related Factors
New disease
Preoperative preparation

Defining Characteristics
Questions
Lack of questions
Verbalized misconceptions
Inability to participate in making treatment decisions

Common Expected Outcomes
Patient verbalizes understanding of disease process.
Patient verbalizes understanding of proposed procedures.

NOC Outcomes
Knowledge: Disease Process;
    Knowledge: Treatment Procedure(s)

NIC Interventions
Teaching: Disease Process; Teaching:
    Preoperative; Teaching: Procedure/
    Treatment

Ongoing Assessment

Actions/Interventions

■ Assess knowledge of common signs/symptoms of colon cancer.

■ Assess knowledge of necessary diagnostic procedures.

■ Assess knowledge of proposed method of treatment and possible outcomes.

Rationale

Because many colon cancers are advanced by the time of diagnosis, patients may feel guilty about not having sought treatment sooner.

The patient may have had multiple diagnostic examinations at this point and may not understand the importance of repeating procedures or undergoing further diagnostic studies.

As with other cancers, patients may feel hopeless that "nothing can be done."

Therapeutic Interventions

Actions/Interventions

■ Teach patient the following about colon cancer:
  • Risk factors

  • Signs and symptoms

Rationale

Family history and a personal history of colorectal cancer, colorectal polyps, or chronic inflammatory bowel disease is the greatest risk for cancer. Other risk factors include the American diet (high calorie, high fat, low fiber) and history of other cancers, especially breast cancer in women.

Because the right side of the colon is distensible, tumors on the right side are usually asymptomatic until the disease is widespread. Symptoms at that time include weight loss, anemia, weakness, and fatigue. Tumors on the left side of the colon usually result in bleeding,

■ = Independent; ▲ = Collaborative

Colorectal Cancer—cont'd

Actions/Interventions	Rationale
	constipation and/or diarrhea, increased abdominal cramping, decreased caliber of the stool (i.e., pencil or ribbon shaped), a feeling of incomplete evacuation, and sometimes complete obstruction.
• Method of spread and relationship to treatment	Colon cancer spreads by direct extension into surrounding tissue, by lymphatic channels, and by seeding into the peritoneal cavity. Excision of the tumor and surrounding tissue is the only curative treatment, although radiation therapy, chemotherapy, and immunotherapy may help reduce the tumor and check the spread. Biopsies done by colonoscopy may indicate stage of a colon tumor, although only at operation will the full extent of the disease be known.
■ Teach the patient about the following diagnostic procedures, as appropriate:	
• Colonoscopy with biopsy of lesions to confirm a diagnosis	Colonoscopy is a procedure that uses a flexible scope instrument to visualize the entire colon directly. Although a tumor may have been identified by digital examination, the entire colon should be examined before surgery; the presence of more than one tumor is possible.
• Carcinoembryonic antigen (CEA)	CEA is a blood test that gives an indication of ongoing cancer activity. Blood is drawn preoperatively so that progress can be monitored postoperatively.
• Chest x-ray examination	A preoperative chest x-ray study is done to evaluate the lung for evidence of metastatic disease.
• Computed tomography (CT) scans	CT scans are done to determine distant metastatic spread. This information helps the surgeon decide how extensive a procedure is necessary.
• Complete blood count (CBC)	CBC is determined to assess for anemia. Colon tumors, particularly advanced colon tumors, bleed; bleeding may result in significant anemia, which is corrected before surgery.
• Endoscopic ultrasound	This identifies lesions within the layers of the bowel wall and distinguishes involved lymph nodes.
• Types of surgical treatment	The type of surgery will be determined by the location of the tumor and whether or not there is metastasis. Right or left hemicolectomy (removal of the right or left half of the colon or large intestine) is done to remove tumors of the ascending, transverse, descending, and sigmoid colon. Tumors that are too close to the anus are treated with abdominoperineal resection (resection of a portion of the colon, along with the rectum); this procedure results in a permanent colostomy because the rectum is gone. Tumors that are in the lower rectosigmoid colon or in the rectum may be treated with a low anterior resection, in which the tumor and surrounding colon are removed and the colon is then anastomosed (no colostomy).

■ = Independent; ▲ = Collaborative

Actions/Interventions	Rationale
■ Teach the patient about steps taken to prepare the bowel for surgery:	
• Clear liquid diet	This reduces the residue in the bowel.
• Antibiotics	These reduce bacteria normally present in the colon to prevent postoperative peritonitis.
• Colyte, GoLYTELY, and/or other osmotic agents	These induce diarrhea and clean bowel before surgery; these may also be used before colonoscopy. Bowel prep is done universally, but is not supported by the literature.
■ Prepare the patient for what to expect after surgery:	
• Incisions, drains	After colectomy, most patients have one midline incision. Patients who have had an abdominoperineal resection have an anterior midline incision, a perineal incision where the rectum was removed, and a colostomy. Anterior incisions are typically sutured or stapled closed; perineal incisions may be closed or may be packed and left to heal by secondary intention. All patients have small drains in the lower abdomen to drain lymphatic fluid from the operative area.
• Intravenous (IV) lines	Patients resume oral feedings 72 to 96 hours postoperatively when peristalsis resumes; therefore administration of IV fluids is necessary and continues until the patient can tolerate oral fluids.
• Activity	Patients should expect to get out of bed on the first postoperative day to prevent complications of immobility (e.g., deep vein thrombosis, atelectasis).
• Pain management	Patients should be involved in choice of postoperative pain management. Options include traditional intramuscular medications given as needed, medications given via patient-controlled analgesia, or bolus or continuous-infusion epidural analgesics.
• Thromboembolism precaution	Patients undergoing colon resection for cancer have a high incidence of venous thromboembolism, including deep vein thrombosis and pulmonary embolism. There is strong evidence that the use of low-molecular-weight heparin (e.g., Lovenox) reduces the risk. Intermittent pneumatic calf compression has been shown to be effective in reducing the risk of thromboembolism. Whether there is an additive effect by using more than one mode of prophylaxis for patients undergoing colonic resection is yet to be determined.

ND x Nursing Diagnosis

Altered Bowel Elimination: Postoperative Ileus

Common Related Factors	Defining Characteristics
General anesthesia	Abdomen silent on auscultation
Manipulation of bowel during surgery	No stooling

■ = Independent; ▲ = Collaborative

Colorectal Cancer—cont'd

Defining Characteristics—cont'd

Report of bloated feeling
Nausea
Abdominal distention
No flatus

Common Expected Outcome

Patient has bowel sounds within 48 to 72 hours post-operatively.

NOC Outcome
Bowel Elimination

NIC Interventions
Flatulence Reduction;
  Bowel Management

Ongoing Assessment

Actions/Interventions

■ Assess for bowel sounds, abdominal distention, presence of flatus or stool, and abdominal fullness every shift.

■ Note passage of first flatus and stool.
■ Assess for distention or subjective complaints of nausea.

Rationale

Bowel sounds will be hypoactive initially, but should return to normal 48 to 72 hours after surgery. The presence of flatus or stool indicates the return of peristalsis. Abdominal distention and fullness, and the absence of bowel sounds, flatus, and stool may indicate a post-operative paralytic ileus.

This signals returning gastrointestinal motility.

Both may occur if bowel contents accumulate in the absence of peristalsis.

Therapeutic Interventions

Actions/Interventions

■ Maintain NPO (nothing by mouth) status until bowel sounds return and patient begins to pass flatus. Fluids will be administered intravenously.

■ Ensure patency of nasogastric tube and provide good oral care.

■ Encourage and assist with ambulation beginning the first postoperative day.

■ Assist the patient with initial food and fluid selection.

Rationale

Until peristaltic activity returns, oral intake puts the patient at risk for nausea and vomiting.

This keeps the stomach empty and reduces the risk of nausea, vomiting, and aspiration.

This hastens resolution of ileus by stimulating peristalsis.

This minimizes gaseous distention. Low-fiber foods and easily digestible foods produce less gas and distention.

■ = Independent; ▲ = Collaborative

Colorectal Cancer

 Nursing Diagnosis

Imbalanced Nutrition: Less Than Body Requirements

Common Related Factors	Defining Characteristics
Increased metabolic demands (stress of surgery) NPO for more than 4 days Primary diagnosis (cancer) Fever Decreased gastrointestinal motility	Weight loss Poor wound healing Low serum albumin (<3.5 g/dL)

Common Expected Outcome

Patient returns to general diet within 5 to 7 days after surgery.

NOC Outcome
Nutritional Status: Nutrient Intake

NIC Intervention
Nutritional Monitoring

Ongoing Assessment

Actions/Interventions	Rationale
■ Assess postoperative weight; compare to preoperative weight.	The weight is compared to the patient's baseline weight to determine the severity of malnutrition.
■ Remain cognizant of length of NPO status.	If patient experiences prolonged postoperative ileus, additional days of IV therapy may be required to achieve protein sparing. In the absence of calorie intake, the body begins to break down lean muscle mass for necessary energy needs.
▲ Monitor serum albumin level.	Serum albumin less than 3.5 g/dL is an indication of inadequate visceral protein levels and indicates postoperative starvation.
■ Monitor wound healing.	Delayed wound healing is a sign of imbalanced nutrition and protein deficiency.
■ Monitor temperature.	For each degree Fahrenheit above normal body temperature, metabolic need for calories increases by 7%.

Therapeutic Interventions

Actions/Interventions	Rationale
▲ Administer IV fluids as ordered.	One liter of 5% dextrose provides approximately 200 kcal, which may achieve protein sparing.
▲ If poor nutritional status and ileus have not resolved, consider peripheral or central hyperalimentation.	Nutritional supplement may be given intravenously to maintain anabolic state.
▲ Administer antipyretics if temperature is above 38.3° C (101° F).	This class of drugs is given to control fever, which increases metabolic needs.

See also **Imbalanced Nutrition: Less Than Body Requirements**, *p. 134.*

■ = Independent; ▲ = Collaborative

Gastrointestinal and Digestive Care Plans

 Colorectal Cancer—cont'd

 Nursing Diagnosis

Risk for Infection

Common Risk Factors

Length of procedure
Intraoperative leakage of bowel contents
Insertion of circular staple gun through rectum to abdominal cavity
Postoperative wound contamination

Common Expected Outcome

Patient remains free of infection as evidenced by temperature less than 38.5° C (101.3° F) and by a clean, dry, healing wound.

NOC Outcomes
Risk Control; Wound Healing: Primary Intention

NIC Interventions
Infection Control; Wound Care

Ongoing Assessment

Actions/Interventions

- Assess length of surgical procedure.

- Assess wound for redness, warmth, drainage, pain, swelling, or dehiscence.
▲ Obtain culture of suspicious drainage.
- Monitor temperature.

▲ Monitor white blood cell (WBC) count.

Rationale

The longer the patient is in surgery, the greater the risk for postoperative infection.
These are signs of wound infection.

Normal drainage is clear, yellow, and odorless.
Temperature above 38.5° C (101.3° F) should arouse suspicion of infection.
An elevated WBC count is an indication of infection.

Therapeutic Interventions

Actions/Interventions

- Wash hands on entering room.

- Use aseptic technique for dressing changes.

▲ Administer antibiotics and antipyretics as prescribed.

- If stoma is present, maintain good skin seal.

See also **Risk for Infection**, *p. 108.*

Rationale

Hand washing remains the most effective means of infection control.
Aseptic technique prevents transmission of bacterial infections to the surgical wound.
This prevents or treats infections and the fever associated with infections.
This isolates fecal drainage.

■ = Independent; ▲ = Collaborative

Nursing Diagnosis

Deficient Knowledge

Common Related Factors

Lack of previous experience with colon surgery
Need for home management
Need for long-term follow-up care

Common Expected Outcome

Patient or caregiver verbalizes knowledge and demonstrates ability to perform wound care, select appropriate diet, plan activity, report complications, and receive necessary follow-up care.

Defining Characteristics

Multiple questions
Lack of questions
Inability to provide self-care on discharge

NOC Outcomes

Knowledge: Diet; Knowledge: Disease Process; Knowledge: Treatment Regimen

NIC Interventions

Teaching: Disease Process; Teaching: Psychomotor Skill; Teaching: Prescribed Activity/Exercise; Teaching: Prescribed Diet

Ongoing Assessment

Actions/Interventions	Rationale
■ Assess ability to perform wound care, verbalize appropriate activity, and describe appropriate diet.	Adults learn best when they are active participants. Active participation also facilitates changes needed to allow for discharge.
■ Assess understanding of need for further cancer therapy.	Patients who have abdominal surgery for malignancies may require further therapy such as chemotherapy, irradiation, or immunotherapy.
■ Assess understanding of need for close follow-up care.	Ongoing surveillance is needed to detect recurrence of cancer.
■ Assess understanding of expected bowel function.	Patient should understand that usual bowel pattern might not return until 2 to 3 weeks postoperatively.

Therapeutic Interventions

Actions/Interventions	Rationale
■ Teach patient or caregiver to perform appropriate wound care:	
• Anterior abdominal wound	Staples or sutures and dressings usually have been removed by the time of discharge, and Steri-Strips have been placed to maintain wound approximation. Steri-Strips should be left in place until they fall off.
• Perineal wound	The patient can take sitz baths twice daily for cleansing and comfort, after which the wound is repacked with saline solution-moistened gauze. Usually clean technique (hands washed; clean but not sterile gloves) is used.

■ = Independent; ▲ = Collaborative

Colorectal Cancer—cont'd

Actions/Interventions	Rationale
■ If patient has a colostomy: • Teach patient or caregiver how to apply skin barrier around stoma.	This promotes peristomal skin integrity and prevents irritation of skin from fecal output.
• Inform patient or caregiver that the barrier can remain on the skin for 3 to 4 days. It should be removed after the fourth day, and the skin around the stoma should be inspected.	Skin infections, irritation, and allergic reactions to barrier material can occur around the stoma.
• Clean the skin with warm water and mild soap. Dry the skin completely before applying a new barrier.	These measures promote skin integrity and reduce infection.
• Apply a clean collection bag (appliance) and empty the bag when it is about half full of stool.	Emptying the bag before it gets too full reduces the risk of leakage of fecal material and odor.
• Note amount, color, and consistency of stool.	Changes in the diet and infections can produce changes in the fecal output from the stoma.
• If there is no stool from the colostomy, check stoma with a gloved, lubricated finger. If there is still no stool or flatus, notify the physician.	An absence of colostomy output may be a sign of intestinal obstruction.
■ Teach the patient that bowel function may not return to preoperative baseline for several weeks.	The more colon that is resected, the longer the period of adaptation. During this time stool may be loose and stooling more frequent.
■ Teach patient appropriate activity guidelines: • No lifting more than 10 pounds for 6 weeks	This reduces strain on abdominal muscles and the risk for stoma prolapse.
• Mild exercise (e.g., walking)	Exercise increases stamina and prevents deep vein thrombosis and pneumonia.
• Showering	The patient can usually shower once the incisions have healed.
• Bathing unless open perineal wound exists	It may take up to 8 weeks to heal completely. Using a hand-held shower head is a good way to clean the wound.
• No driving until anterior abdominal wound has healed	Operating foot pedals while driving, especially the brake pedal, increases strain on abdominal muscles.
■ Teach the patient the following about diet: • A well-balanced, high-calorie, high-protein diet is desirable for healing.	This type of diet should continue over a period of weeks to promote effective healing.
• Fiber should be added to the diet.	Because the patient has already had colon cancer, the risk for future tumors is high. A high-fiber diet is associated with more frequent bowel movements and less time for suspected carcinogenic food by-products to be in contact with the colonic mucosa. Foods high in fiber include grains, fruits, and vegetables.
■ Teach the patient the rationale for any further cancer therapy planned (e.g., chemotherapy, radiation therapy, immunotherapy).	These therapies are typically offered if the pathology report indicates that the tumor was not confined to the bowel or bowel wall.
■ Teach the patient the importance of follow-up colonoscopies.	These allow early detection of any recurrent tumors. They are usually scheduled every 6 months for persons with a history of colon cancer.

■ = Independent; ▲ = Collaborative

Actions/Interventions

- Discuss family risk with patients.

- Teach patients who have had removal of the rectum that phantom rectum sensations and a feeling of needing to have a normal bowel movement are normal and will subside over time.

- Instruct the patient to seek medical attention for any of the following: temperature higher than 38°C (100.4° F), foul-smelling wound drainage, redness or unusual pain in any incision, or absence of bowel movement.

Rationale

Parents, siblings, and adult children older than 40 years should be screened yearly for colon cancer.

These situations are related to remaining nerve fibers in the perineum.

These signs and symptoms are indicative of an infection or possible bowel obstruction.

> • **RELATED CARE PLANS**
>
> Acute pain, p. 144
> Anticipatory grieving, p. 82

Enteral Tube Feeding

Enteral Hyperalimentation; G-Tube; Jejunostomy; Duodenostomy; PEG Tube; Duboff

This method of providing nutrition uses a nasogastric tube, a gastrostomy tube, or a tube placed in the duodenum or jejunum. Tubes may be inserted through the external nares or may be placed through a small incision into the stomach. Enteral tube feedings are indicated for patients who have a functional gastrointestinal system but are unable to maintain adequate nutritional intake. Enteral tube feedings can be more cost effective than total parenteral nutrition (TPN). Critically ill patients receiving enteral tube feedings tend to have better outcomes and fewer complications. The problems associated with the administration of enteral tube feedings include pulmonary aspiration of feeding formula, diarrhea, and fluid and electrolyte imbalances. Feedings may be continuous or intermittent (bolus). Enteral feeding may occur in the hospital, in long-term care, or in home care. The focus of this care plan is the prevention of problems commonly associated with enteral feeding.

NDx Nursing Diagnosis

Imbalanced Nutrition: Less Than Body Requirements

Common Related Factor	Defining Characteristics
Mechanical problems during feedings, such as clogged tube, inaccurate flow rate, stiffening of tube, pump malfunction	Continued weight loss Failure to gain weight Weakness

> ■ = Independent; ▲ = Collaborative

Gastrointestinal and Digestive Care Plans

> **Enteral Tube Feeding**–cont'd

Common Expected Outcome

Patient's nutritional status improves as evidenced by gradual weight gain or stable weight and increased physical strength.

NOC Outcomes

Nutritional Status: Nutrient Intake; Weight Control

NIC Interventions

Nutritional Monitoring; Enteral Tube Feeding; Gastrointestinal Intubation

---

Ongoing Assessment

Actions/Interventions

- Assess tubing for patency and free flow of enteral feeding.

- Assess equipment (pump) used for administration; ensure that proper flow rate is indicated and that pump is delivering enteral feeding at appropriate rate.

- Assess weight every other day or as ordered.

- Assess physical strength of patient; note improvement or deterioration.

Rationale

A clogged feeding tube decreases the delivery of nutrients.

A feeding pump regulates formula delivery at a continuous rate. This method causes less diarrhea than with intermittent feedings.

Weight gain is an indicator of improved nutritional status; however sudden gain of more than 2 pounds in a 24-hour period usually indicates fluid retention. Most commercially available tube feeding preparations contain 1 kcal/mL. An adult of average size and weight requires 1800 to 2400 kcal/24 hours.

Improved muscle strength and activity tolerance are indicators of sufficient calories.

Therapeutic Interventions

Actions/Interventions

- Instruct caregiver to:
  - Flush tubing with 20 mL of water after medication administration and any time the flow of solution is interrupted.

  - Crush medications and dilute with water.

  - Keep pump alarms on.
- ▲ Consult dietitian.

- In case flow is interrupted for more than 1 hour, instruct the caregiver how to recalculate amount to be given over 8 hours and reset the administration rate.

Rationale

Flushing the tube is important to reduce the risk of clogging. Clogging of a feeding tube may require replacement of the tube. Any delay in the administration of the feeding formula decreases the patient's nutrient intake.

Whenever possible, liquid forms of medication should be administered through a feeding tube to reduce the risk of clogging. Pills should be crushed to the finest consistency possible and mixed with water before being administered through the feeding tube.

Any interruption in the flow of solution is noted early.

This ensures that ongoing nutritional needs are being met as the patient's condition or situation changes.

Rapid administration to "catch up" can precipitate a hyperglycemic crisis because the pancreas may not be able to produce adequate insulin for the increased carbohydrate load. The risk of diarrhea also increases when the rate is suddenly increased.

■ = Independent; ▲ = Collaborative

Enteral Tube Feeding

 Nursing Diagnosis

Risk for Aspiration

Common Risk Factors

Lack of gag reflex
Poor positioning of tube at placement
Migration of the tube
Supine positioning of patient as feeding is administered
Overfeeding

Common Expected Outcome

Patient maintains a patent airway as evidenced by clear lung sounds, absence of coughing, no shortness of breath, and no aspiration.

NOC Outcomes
Risk Control; Risk Detection; Respiratory Status: Ventilation; Knowledge: Treatment Procedure(s)

NIC Interventions
Aspiration Precautions; Enteral Tube Feeding

Ongoing Assessment

Actions/Interventions

▲ Obtain an x-ray study immediately after tube insertion.

■ Assess correct position of tube before initiation of feeding by aspirating fluid from the tube and checking the color and pH of the fluid.

■ Assess level of consciousness (LOC) and gag reflex before administration of feeding.

■ Monitor respiratory status throughout feeding.

■ Assess for residual volume before feeding. If the patient is on continuous feedings, check residual every 4 hours.

Rationale

Radiological confirmation of the feeding tube position should be obtained after placement of a nasoenteric access tube.

pH readings of 0 to 5 usually indicate gastric placement of the tube. The color of the gastric fluid varies from off-white to grassy green or brown. Intestinal fluid is golden yellow to brownish green and has a pH of 6 or higher. A pH of 6 or higher in watery yellow fluid may indicate respiratory placement of the tube. This is especially important for gastrostomy tubes because the potential for reflux is increased; duodenostomy and jejunostomy tubes carry somewhat less risk. Also, smaller-diameter, more flexible feeding tubes can easily enter the trachea during insertion.

High-risk patients are comatose, have decreased gag reflex, or cannot tolerate the head of bed (HOB) elevated. Nasoduodenal or gastroduodenal feeding tubes are preferred for high-risk patients.

Coughing and shortness of breath may indicate aspiration.

Feedings are held if residual volume is greater than 50% of the amount to be delivered in 1 hour. Gastric residuals should be checked frequently when feedings are initiated, and feedings should be held if residual volumes exceed 200 mL.

■ = Independent; ▲ = Collaborative

Gastrointestinal and Digestive Care Plans

→ Enteral Tube Feeding—cont'd

Therapeutic Interventions

Actions/Interventions

- Elevate HOB to 30 degrees during and for 1 hour after each feeding.

- If the patient has an endotracheal or tracheostomy tube, keep the cuff inflated during feedings and for 1 hour after feedings.

- In case of aspiration:
  - Stop the feeding.
  - Keep the HOB elevated.
  - Suction airway as necessary.
  - Document time feeding was stopped, patient's appearance, and change in respiratory status.
  - Document adventitious lung sounds.

See also **Risk for Aspiration**, *p. 18.*

Rationale

This facilitates gravity flow of feeding past the gastroduodenal sphincter and reduces the risk of aspiration.

This protects the airway from inadvertent entry of feedings into the trachea.

Respiratory aspiration requires immediate action by the caregiver to maintain the airway and promote effective breathing and gas exchange.

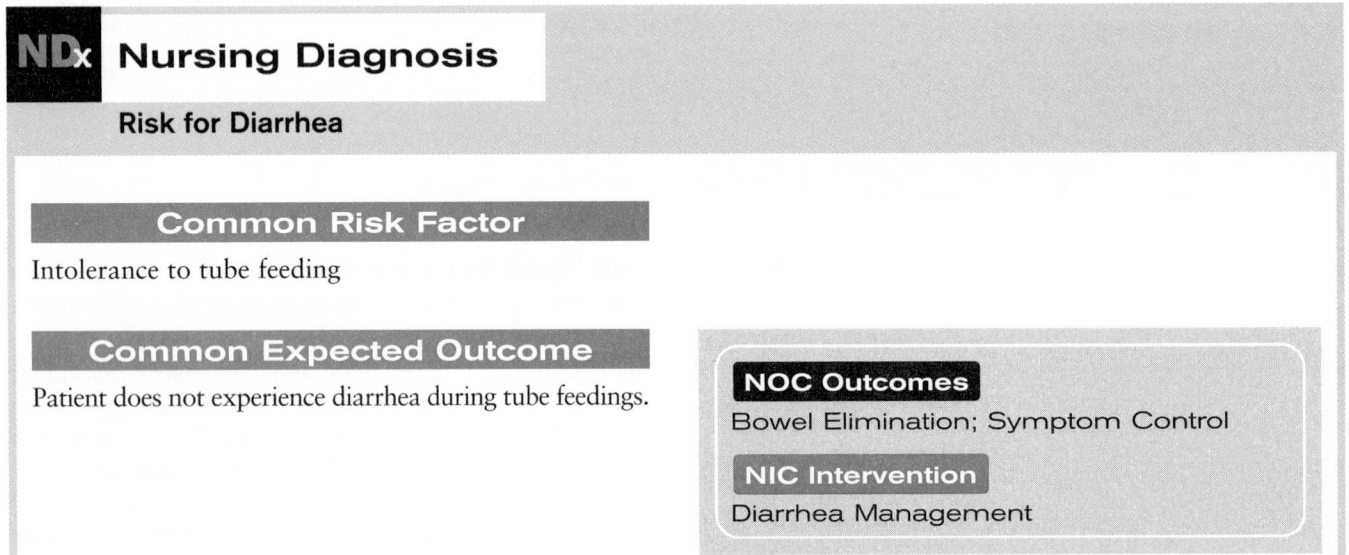

NDx Nursing Diagnosis

Risk for Diarrhea

Common Risk Factor

Intolerance to tube feeding

Common Expected Outcome

Patient does not experience diarrhea during tube feedings.

NOC Outcomes
Bowel Elimination; Symptom Control

NIC Intervention
Diarrhea Management

Ongoing Assessment

Actions/Interventions

- Assess bowel sounds, abdominal distention, or cramping.

- Assess number and character of stools.

Rationale

Diarrhea is typically accompanied by hyperactive bowel sounds.

A patient diary can be useful for gathering data. Many factors contribute to the development of diarrhea in tube-fed patients. Sorbitol-based elixirs for liquid forms of medications may increase the incidence of diarrhea. *Clostridium difficile* has been found to occur more often in tube-fed hospitalized patients than in non–tube-fed patients.

■ = Independent; ▲ = Collaborative

Actions/Interventions	Rationale
■ Monitor intake and output.	Intake and output are indicators of fluid volume excess or deficit.
■ Note osmolarity and fiber content of the feeding.	Hyperosmolar or high-fiber feedings draw fluid into the bowel and can cause diarrhea. Isotonic feedings are preferred.
■ Note history of lactose intolerance.	Milk-based feedings contain lactose, which is not tolerated by individuals with lactase deficiency.

Therapeutic Interventions

Actions/Interventions	Rationale
■ Begin feedings slowly; consider a dilute solution.	Large amounts of concentrated solutions may stimulate osmotic diarrhea. Gradual increase in rate will allow time for the gastrointestinal system to adapt to the increased volume and solutes.
■ Instruct the caregiver to increase both rate and strength to prescribed amounts, but not at the same time.	High-rate feeding combined with high osmolality may precipitate diarrhea.
■ Administer feedings at room temperature.	Cold stimulates peristalsis.
■ Do not allow formula to hang longer than 8 hours at room temperature.	This minimizes risk of bacterial contamination.
■ Change setup daily.	This minimizes risk of bacterial contaminations.
■ Encourage light activity 30 minutes after feeding.	This facilitates digestion by increasing peristalsis.

NDx Nursing Diagnosis

Impaired Oral Mucous Membrane

Common Related Factors
Dry mucous membranes
Presence of tube

Defining Characteristics
Dry, cracked lips
Swallowing difficulty
Verbalized discomfort

Common Expected Outcome
The patient remains comfortable, as evidenced by moist oral cavity and ease in swallowing.

NOC Outcomes
Oral health; Tissue Integrity: Skin and Mucous Membranes

NIC Intervention
Oral Health Maintenance

Ongoing Assessment

Actions/Interventions	Rationale
■ Assess mucous membranes.	The presence of a nasally inserted tube will cause mouth breathing. This contributes to dry, cracked mouth and lips.

■ = Independent; ▲ = Collaborative

Enteral Tube Feeding—cont'd

Actions/Interventions

■ Assess discomfort on swallowing.

Rationale

Dry oral and nasopharyngeal mucosa make swallowing difficult.

Therapeutic Interventions

Actions/Interventions

■ Provide or instruct the caregiver to provide mouth care. Avoid lemon-glycerin swabs.

■ Allow ice chips, hard candy, or gum if permissible.

▲ Provide anesthetic mouthwash as ordered.

Rationale

Lemon-glycerin can lead to further drying.

These stimulate salivary secretion.

This numbs throat and eases pain.

NDx Nursing Diagnosis

Risk for Deficient Fluid Volume

Common Risk Factors

Osmolarity of feedings
Glucose content of feedings

Common Expected Outcome

Patient maintains normal fluid volume, as evidenced by moist mucous membranes, good skin turgor, baseline mental status, and normal blood glucose level.

NOC Outcomes
Fluid Balance; Hydration

NIC Intervention
Fluid Management

Ongoing Assessment

Actions/Interventions

■ Monitor intake and output.

■ Assess for change in mental status.

▲ Monitor blood glucose levels by glucometer.

Rationale

Intake and output are indicators of fluid volume excess or deficit.

Changes in mental status or LOC may be early signs of dehydration or hyperosmolar coma.

High glucose levels cause fluid shift resulting in dehydration. Patients who are unable to metabolize glucose are at risk.

Therapeutic Interventions

Actions/Interventions

■ Recommend keeping a pitcher of water at the bedside.

Rationale

Availability of free water reduces the risk of fluid volume deficit by allowing the patient to respond readily to thirst, an early sign of fluid volume deficit or hyperosmolarity.

■ = Independent; ▲ = Collaborative

Actions/Interventions

▲ Administer or encourage the patient to take antihyperglycemic agents as prescribed.

See also **Deficient Fluid Volume,** *p. 71.*

Rationale

Blood glucose should be monitored frequently upon initiation of feedings, after any change in insulin, and until measurements are stable.

Nursing Diagnosis

Deficient Knowledge

Common Related Factor

New procedure and treatment

Defining Characteristics

Verbalized inaccurate information
Inappropriate behavior
Questions

Common Expected Outcomes

Patient or caregiver verbalizes reasons for tube feedings and begins to participate in care.
Patient or caregiver demonstrates independence in enteral feeding administration.

NOC Outcome
Knowledge: Treatment Procedure(s)

NIC Interventions
Teaching: Psychomotor Skill;
Teaching: Procedure/Treatment

Ongoing Assessment

Actions/Interventions

■ Assess patient's or caregiver's knowledge of:
  • Tube feeding purpose, expected length of therapy, and expected benefits.
  • Ability to administer own feedings.
  • Ability to use equipment related to feeding: measuring devices, feeding pump, and tubing.
  • Ability to minimize complications related to tube feedings: checking for residual volume, assuming sitting position, and maintaining a bacteria-free feeding.

Rationale

Many patients require feedings well beyond hospitalization and can administer feedings to self. Teaching the patient and caregiver is based on their knowledge and ability to manage the equipment and minimize complications. Assessment of their understanding is the foundation for an individualized teaching plan.

Therapeutic Interventions

Actions/Interventions

■ Demonstrate feedings and tube care. Allow return demonstration.

■ Arrange for visiting nurse if the patient is unable to feed self.

Rationale

Necessary alteration in teaching plan can be undertaken.

Community resources provide support for the patient and caregiver as they learn new skills.

■ = Independent; ▲ = Collaborative

 **Gastrointestinal Bleeding**

Lower Gastrointestinal Bleed; Upper Gastrointestinal Bleed; Esophageal Varices; Ulcers

Loss of blood from the gastrointestinal (GI) tract is most often the result of erosion or ulceration of the mucosa, but it may also be the result of arteriovenous (AV) malformation or malignancies, increased pressure in the portal venous bed, or direct trauma to the GI tract. Alcohol abuse is a major etiological factor in GI bleeding. Varices, usually located in the distal third of the submucosal tissue of the esophagus or the fundus of the stomach, can also cause life-threatening GI hemorrhage. Treatment may be medical or surgical or may involve mechanical tamponade. Acute GI bleeding may be life threatening without prompt treatment. In patients with GI bleeding, stabilization of blood pressure and restoration of intravascular volume is the highest priority. The focus of this care plan is the acute hospital management phase of an active GI bleeder.

 Nursing Diagnosis

Deficient Fluid Volume

Common Related Factors

Upper GI bleeding (mouth, esophagus, stomach, duodenum) caused by gastric ulcer, duodenal ulcer, gastritis, esophageal varices, Mallory-Weiss tear, blunt or penetration trauma, cancer

Lower GI bleeding (small or large intestine, rectum, anus) caused by tumors, inflammatory bowel disease (diverticular disease, Crohn's disease, ulcerative colitis), AV malformations, blunt or penetrating trauma, hemorrhoids

Generalized GI bleeding: systemic coagulopathies; radiation therapy; chemotherapy; family history of GI bleeding; history of recent violent retching; history of alcohol use or abuse; altered coagulation profile; history of aspirin, anticoagulant therapy, steroid, nonsteroid, or ibuprofen use or abuse

Defining Characteristics

Hematemesis (observed or reported)
Melena
Hematochezia (bright red blood per rectum)
Coffee ground emesis (indicates slower upper GI bleed)
Orthostatic changes
Tachycardia
Hypotension
Change in level of consciousness (LOC)
Thirst
Dry mucous membranes
Weakness
Pallor

Common Expected Outcome

Patient maintains normal fluid volume as evidenced by showing no signs of active bleeding, urine output greater than 30 mL/hr, stable blood pressure (BP) and heart rate, and moist mucous membranes.

NOC Outcomes
Blood Coagulation; Fluid Balance

NIC Interventions
Bleeding Reduction: Gastrointestinal; Hypovolemia Management; Shock Management; Volume

■ = Independent; ▲ = Collaborative

Ongoing Assessment

Actions/Interventions

- Monitor color and consistency of hematemesis, melena, or rectal bleeding; encourage patient to describe unwitnessed blood loss accurately using common household measures (e.g., a cupful, a spoonful, a pint).

- Obtain history of use or abuse of substances known to predispose to GI bleeding: aspirin, aspirin-containing drugs, nonsteroidal antiinflammatory drugs, alcohol, steroids.

- Monitor BP for orthostatic changes (from patient lying prone to high-Fowler's). Note orthostatic hypotension significance.

- Assess for tachycardia.

- Monitor coagulation profile, hemoglobin (Hgb), and hematocrit (Hct).

- Obtain diet history.

- Monitor urine output.

Rationale

Careful assessment of GI bleeding can help determine the exact site of the bleeding.

Drugs that cause ulceration of the GI mucosa contribute to the development of bleeding.

A drop in BP greater than 10 mm Hg indicates that circulating blood volume is decreased by 20%. A drop in BP greater than 20 to 30 mm Hg indicates that circulating blood volume is decreased by 40%.

An increase in pulse rate indicates hypovolemia. This change in pulse is a compensatory mechanism to maintain cardiac output.

Many individuals with GI bleeding have longstanding nutritional deficits that result in an altered coagulation profile because of the liver's inability to produce adequate amounts of vitamin K, a precursor to many coagulation factors. Hgb and Hct are monitored as indicators of both blood loss and hydration status. Initially, Hgb and Hct will drop because of blood loss; as fluid resuscitation proceeds, hemodilution will result in further drop in Hgb and Hct.

A history of inadequate or sporadically adequate nutrition is important in understanding hemopoietic capability.

Urine output of at least 30 mL/hr is an indication of adequate renal perfusion.

Therapeutic Interventions

Actions/Interventions

- For active bleeding, start one or more large-bore intravenous (IV) lines.

- Insert nasogastric (NG) tube for stomach lavage.

- Lavage stomach until clots are no longer present and return is clear; use room-temperature saline solution.
- Provide volume resuscitation with crystalloids or blood products as ordered.

- Monitor cardiopulmonary response to volume expansion.

Rationale

Rapid volume expansion is necessary to prevent or treat hypovolemia complications; IV medication and/or blood component administration is likely.

The NG tube provides a way to monitor continuing blood loss closely and for medication administration.

Iced saline solution may cause undesirable ischemic changes in gastric mucosa.

Crystalloids are more commonly used, whereas blood products are selectively used to replace specific coagulation factors (e.g., platelets only, fresh-frozen plasma).

Patients with history of alcohol abuse may have alcohol-related cardiomyopathies. Elderly patients may experience cardiovascular difficulty with rapid fluid volume resuscitation because of diminished cardiac function, a normal phenomenon of aging. Amount of fluid administered will depend on rate of bleeding and patient's hemodynamic status.

■ = Independent; ▲ = Collaborative

Gastrointestinal Bleeding—cont'd

Actions/Interventions	Rationale
▲ Assist with or coordinate diagnostic procedures performed to identify bleeding site:	
• Endoscopy	This provides direct visualization of the esophagus, stomach, and duodenum. The procedure must precede radiographs requiring barium ingestion to maximize visualization by the endoscopist.
• Sigmoidoscopy, proctoscopy, and colonoscopy	These provide direct visualization of the rectum and colon.
• Barium studies:	
• Barium swallow	This is an indirect visualization of the esophagus, stomach, and small intestine.
• Barium enema	This is an indirect visualization of colon.
• Small bowel follow-through	This is an indirect visualization of the small intestine.
• Angiography	This may be diagnostic or performed for arterial line placement to infuse vasoconstrictive medications locally. Conclusive diagnosis is made only if bleeding is more than 0.5 mL/min.
• After angiography: dress the site with pressure dressing; connect arterial line to pressure or flush system.	
▲ Administer vasopressin drip as ordered. May be given IV continuous drip, piggyback bolus, or intraarterially if a line was placed during an angiographic procedure to a specific area (e.g., celiac artery for esophageal bleeding).	A potent vasoconstrictive agent is typically ordered after diagnosis of esophageal bleeding.
▲ Administer vitamin K as ordered.	This allows coagulation factor production.
▲ Administer antacids and H_2-receptor antagonists (e.g., cimetidine, Zantac).	This suppresses gastric and duodenal secretions.
■ Guard against administration of drugs that may potentiate further bleeding, such as aspirin-containing compounds and anticoagulants.	Drugs that interfere with the coagulation mechanisms increase the risk for bleeding.
▲ For the patient who is bleeding from esophageal or gastric varices and who is in a critical care area, prepare for insertion of a Sengstaken-Blakemore tube.	The Sengstaken-Blakemore tube has balloons that inflate in the esophagus and upper portion of the stomach to provide tamponade (pressure) against the vessels that are bleeding.
▲ Assist with preparation of the patient for surgical procedures such as sclerotherapy, endoscopic varicose ligation, or thermal coagulation.	If esophageal varices are the source of the bleeding, surgical measures may be used to control the bleeding.

NDx Nursing Diagnosis

Risk for Pain/Discomfort

Common Risk Factors

Invasive therapies
Diagnostic procedures
Vomiting
Diarrhea

■ = Independent; ▲ = Collaborative

Common Expected Outcomes

Patient verbalizes absence of pain or tolerable levels of pain.

Patient is comfortable.

NOC Outcomes
Comfort Level; Pain Control

NIC Interventions
Environmental Management: Comfort; Perineal Care

Ongoing Assessment

Actions/Interventions

- Assess for evidence of discomfort: verbalizing pain or discomfort, facial grimacing, and restlessness.
- Assess specific sources of discomfort.

- Ask patient what measures he or she believes might provide comfort.

Rationale

Verbal and behavioral cues help the nurse determine the patient's experience of discomfort.

Patients with GI bleeding have several potential sources of discomfort including presence of IV lines, tubes for lavage or tamponade, invasive diagnostic procedures such as scope procedures, nausea, and diarrhea.

Knowledge of the patient's preferences is the foundation for an individualized approach to promoting comfort.

Therapeutic Interventions

Actions/Interventions

- Tape or stabilize all tubes, drains, and catheters.

- Provide frequent oral hygiene.

- Provide meticulous perineal care after all bowel movements.
- For patients with any indwelling NG tube, moisten external nares with water-soluble lubricant at least once per shift to reduce adherence of mucus.
- For patient with traction helmet for stabilization of Sengstaken-Blakemore tube, pad parts contacting the skin.
- Change linens as necessary.

- ▲ Use analgesics with caution.

See also **Acute Pain,** *p. 144.*

Rationale

This minimizes movement of tubes that may cause discomfort.

This removes blood and emesis and moistens mucous membranes.

This reduces the possibility of painful perineal excoriation.

Presence of NG tube can dry nares and cause irritation.

This minimizes occurrence of skin friction and/or ischemia.

This minimizes discomfort and reduces unpleasant melenic odor.

Analgesics may mask LOC changes related to fluid volume deficit.

■ = Independent; ▲ = Collaborative

Gastrointestinal and Digestive Care Plans

Gastrointestinal Bleeding—cont'd

 Nursing Diagnosis

Risk for Impaired Skin Integrity

Common Risk Factors

Bed rest
Frequent stooling
Hypovolemia leading to skin ischemia
Poor nutritional status

Common Expected Outcome

Skin remains intact.

> **NOC Outcomes**
> Risk Control; Tissue Integrity: Skin and
>   Mucous Membranes
>
> **NIC Interventions**
> Perineal Care; Skin Care: Topical
>   Treatments

Ongoing Assessment

Actions/Interventions

■ Assess condition of skin for redness or irritation.

Rationale

An area of redness is the first sign of impaired skin integrity.

Therapeutic Interventions

Actions/Interventions

■ Turn the patient side to side as hemodynamic status allows.

■ Place pressure-relief devices beneath patient.

■ Do not allow the patient to sit on the bedpan for long periods.

■ Clean perianal skin with soap and water after each bowel movement; dry well.

■ Apply liquid film barrier to perianal area.

■ Minimize use of plastic linen protectors.

Rationale

Hemodynamically unstable patients may have a drop in blood pressure when turned side to side.

Pressure relief over bony prominences reduces the risk of skin breakdown.

The bedpan can be a source of pressure.

Clean, dry skin is more resistant to breakdown.

This avoids direct skin contact with stool.

These harbor moisture and enhance macerations.

■ = Independent; ▲ = Collaborative

Nursing Diagnosis

Risk for Ineffective Protection

Common Risk Factor

Vasopressin (pitressin) therapy

Common Expected Outcome

Patient is free of complications related to vasopressin therapy as evidenced by stable vital signs, normal sinus rhythm, and no nausea or vomiting.

NOC Outcome
Medication Response

NIC Interventions
Surveillance; Medication Management

Ongoing Assessment

Actions/Interventions

■ Assess for side effects of vasopressin.

■ Monitor BP.

Rationale

Side effects of vasopressin may include anginal pain, ST-segment changes on electrocardiogram, sinus brady-cardia, tremors, sweating, vertigo, pounding in head, abdominal cramps, circumoral pallor, nausea and vomiting, flatus, urticaria, and fluid retention.

Elevated BP can be the result of vasoconstriction from vasopressin.

Therapeutic Interventions

Actions/Interventions

▲ Administer vasopressin as ordered.

▲ If side effects occur:
  • Stop infusion of vasopressin drip.

  • Have atropine on hand for decreased heart rate.

■ Provide comfort measures such as massage, cognitive distraction, and imagery.

Rationale

Vasopressin is a commercial preparation of antidiuretic hormone that promotes vasoconstriction and reduces bleeding.

IV vasopressin preparation is short acting; cessation of administration diminishes adverse effects rapidly.

Atropine will increase the heart rate.

These measures reduce restlessness, which increases oxygen consumption.

■ = Independent; ▲ = Collaborative

> **Gastrointestinal Bleeding**—cont'd

 Nursing Diagnosis

Deficient Knowledge

Common Related Factors	**Defining Characteristics**
First GI bleed Unfamiliar environment	Multiple questions Lack of questions Verbalized misconceptions

Common Expected Outcome

Patient or significant other verbalizes understanding of causes and management of GI bleeding.

NOC Outcomes

Knowledge: Treatment Regimen;
Knowledge: Treatment Procedures

NIC Interventions

Teaching: Procedures/Treatment;
Teaching: Prescribed Medication;
Substance Use Treatment

Ongoing Assessment

Actions/Interventions

- Assess understanding of the cause and treatment of GI bleeding.

- Assess understanding of the need for long-term follow-up, observation, and possible lifestyle changes.

Rationale

A teaching plan is based on the patient's previous knowledge.

Prevention of recurrence of bleeding may require health behavior changes by the patient.

Therapeutic Interventions

Actions/Interventions

- Explain procedures necessary for diagnosis and/or treatment before they are performed.

- Encourage or stress importance of avoidance of substances containing aspirin, alcohol, nonsteroidal antiinflammatory drugs, ibuprofen, and steroids.
- Teach the patient the dose, administration schedule, expected actions, and possible adverse effects of medications that may be prescribed for long periods.

- Refer the patient to alcohol rehabilitation if indicated.

Rationale

Understanding the need for unpleasant procedures may help the patient comply or participate in and increase the yield or effectiveness of treatment or procedure.

Use of these products is known to damage the mucosal barrier and predispose to bleeding.

Drugs given to decrease gastric acid production may be prescribed indefinitely; patients must understand that cessation of bleeding or other symptoms does not mean the need for medication has ended.

Not all GI bleeding is the result of alcohol use or abuse.

• RELATED CARE PLANS

Fear, p. 68
Ineffective therapeutic regimen management, p. 185

■ = Independent; ▲ = Collaborative

Hepatitis

Serum Hepatitis; Infectious Hepatitis; Viral Hepatitis

Hepatitis is inflammation of the liver, usually caused by a virus. Hepatitis may also result from adverse drug reactions or other chemical ingestion; this type is noninfectious, whereas all types of viral hepatitis are infectious. Viral hepatitis types A and E are transmitted via the fecal-oral route or through poor sanitation; person-to-person contact; or consumption of contaminated food, water, or shellfish. Hepatitis E infections are associated with contaminated water and occur most commonly in developing countries. Cases of hepatitis E in the United States are seen in patients who have traveled to areas that are endemic for the virus. There is no specific treatment for this form of hepatitis, and immune globulin is not useful in prophylaxis after exposure. Types B and C (formerly called non-A, non-B) are transmitted by blood, semen, and vaginal secretions; they can be transmitted via contaminated needles and renal dialysis (parenterally) or through intimate contact with carriers. Hepatitis D occurs only in the presence of hepatitis B. Hepatitis D develops as a coinfection or superimposed infection with hepatitis B. A co-infection with hepatitis D tends to increase the severity of the hepatitis B infection. Vaccine for the prevention of hepatitis B is widely available; the Occupational Safety and Health Administration (OSHA) requires that employers offer the hepatitis B vaccine to health care workers who are at risk for all types of hepatitis. A vaccine is also available for hepatitis A, although its use is not as widespread as hepatitis B vaccine. Some cases of hepatitis remain subclinical, and most are managed in the home. Fulminant hepatitis can result in massive destruction of liver tissue and can be fatal. This care plan addresses nursing concerns that may be managed in the hospital or at home.

Nursing Diagnosis

Deficient Knowledge

Common Related Factors

New condition
Unfamiliarity with disease course and treatment

Defining Characteristics

Lack of questions
Many questions
Noncompliance with infection control procedures

Common Expected Outcome

Patient or caregiver verbalizes and demonstrates knowledge of and compliance with treatment regimen and infection control procedures.

NOC Outcomes

Knowledge: Disease Process;
Knowledge: Treatment Regimen

NIC Interventions

Teaching: Disease Process;
Teaching: Procedures/Treatment

■ = Independent; ▲ = Collaborative

Hepatitis—cont'd

Ongoing Assessment

Actions/Interventions

- Determine the patient's understanding of the disease process, disease transmission, complications, treatment, and signs of relapse.

Rationale

Noncompliance may be related to incomplete understanding of disease transmission and/or the treatment regimen.

Therapeutic Interventions

Actions/Interventions

- Teach the patient or caregiver about disease transmission:
  - Hepatitis A

  - Hepatitis B

  - Hepatitis C

- Teach about treatment.

- Teach about infection control procedures.

- Discuss future need to avoid blood donation.

- Teach about possible complications and long-term sequelae of hepatitis.

Rationale

Fecal-oral transmission occurs as a result of crowded living conditions; poor personal hygiene; contaminated food, water, milk, or raw shellfish.

Percutaneous and permucosal transmission occurs from needles, blood products, sex, and birth.

Percutaneous transmission occurs from blood products and needles.

Adequate rest, nutrition, and prevention of complications are the mainstay of therapy for all types of hepatitis. Because the disease is typically viral, medications are not helpful.

Hand washing is the most effective method of preventing the transmission of type A. Patients usually do not need to be isolated unless they are incapable of or unwilling to participate in infection control measures. Personal care items (e.g., razors, toothbrushes) should not be shared because the risk of parenteral exposure exists. Safe sex should be discussed and encouraged.

Even after patients with hepatitis are well, they may carry the virus and should refrain from blood donation to prevent risk of disease transmission.

Hepatitis can lead to chronic hepatitis and/or fulminant hepatitis if liver cells do not regenerate. Chronic hepatitis can result in cirrhosis and liver failure.

NDx Nursing Diagnosis

Activity Intolerance

Common Related Factors	Defining Characteristics
Decreased metabolism of nutrients Increased basal metabolic rate caused by viral infection	Fatigue Inability to initiate activity Weakness Dyspnea associated with activity Tachycardia and elevated blood pressure (BP) associated with activity

■ = Independent; ▲ = Collaborative

Common Expected Outcomes

Patient avoids fatigue or exhaustion by alternating activity with periods of rest.

Patient is able to perform desired activities of daily living (ADLs).

NOC Outcomes
Activity Tolerance; Energy Conservation; Self-Care: Activities of Daily Living

NIC Intervention
Energy Management

Ongoing Assessment

Actions/Interventions

■ Assess general energy levels and activity tolerance; note specific trends.

■ Assess need for assistive devices.

▲ Monitor liver enzyme levels.

Rationale

Some patients have peak energy levels early in the day or after naps; personal care, household activities, and nursing care (as required) should be scheduled accordingly to prevent exhaustion.

The use of assistive devices can decrease exertion.

Elevations in hepatic enzyme levels indicate damage or death of liver cells; new elevations or failure of enzyme levels to trend toward normal indicates continuing damage, which could result from premature activity or overexertion.

Therapeutic Interventions

Actions/Interventions

■ Maintain or encourage bed rest until enzyme levels begin to normalize. Provide for long, uninterrupted periods of rest and relaxation.

■ Encourage bathroom use or provide a bedside commode.

■ Provide or encourage a quiet environment and promote rest using strategies that the patient identifies as helpful (e.g., music, reading, dim lights).

■ Provide information on energy-conservation techniques.

■ Assist the patient in identifying realistic goals for engaging in activity.

■ Assist the patient in planning the day.

Rationale

Healing damaged liver cells and generating new ones requires metabolic expenditure; maintaining bed rest reduces the energy required for movement and increases the energy available for healing.

Use of a bedpan requires more energy expenditure than getting up to use the bathroom or commode.

The patient needs to be included in creating an environment that promotes effective rest.

Fatigue is often the most profound manifestation of hepatitis. Setting priorities for activity and keeping frequently used objects within easy reach help conserve energy. Patients need to learn to delegate tasks to others during recovery.

The patient may need assistance in balancing the desire for activities with the reality of a need for rest and of the activity intolerance imposed by the disease process.

Activities should be planned to coincide with the patient's peak energy level. If the patient attempts activities but is too exhausted to participate meaningfully, then the patient may experience increased frustration about activity intolerance.

■ = Independent; ▲ = Collaborative

Hepatitis—cont'd

 Nursing Diagnosis

Risk for Imbalanced Nutrition: Less Than Body Requirements

Common Risk Factors

Alteration in nutrient absorption
Alteration in nutrient metabolism
Decreased nutrient intake
Anorexia
Nausea and vomiting
Diarrhea

Common Expected Outcome

Patient maintains adequate nutritional status as evidenced by stable weight or by weight gain.

NOC Outcomes
Nutritional Status: Nutrient Intake;
  Knowledge: Prescribed Diet

NIC Interventions
Nutrition Management; Teaching:
  Prescribed Diet; TPN Administration

Ongoing Assessment

Actions/Interventions

■ Document the patient's actual weight and encourage the patient to weigh self weekly.

■ Obtain nutritional history.

▲ Monitor laboratory values indicative of nutritional status:
  • Serum albumin level
  • Hemoglobin (Hgb) level

  • Cellular immune response skin test

Rationale

A decrease in body weight over time is an indication of inadequate caloric intake.

A complete nutritional history provides information about the patient's weight loss history, food likes and dislikes, food intolerances, and food allergies. Anorexia is a major problem in hepatitis. Patients may experience aversion to specific foods such as meat.

This is an indication of visceral protein reserve.

This is an important component of red blood cells; Hgb level determines the ability of blood to carry adequate amounts of oxygen.

This is an overall indicator of nutritional well-being; a patient who is anergic (has no response to the injection of intradermal antigens) is severely nutritionally compromised.

■ = Independent; ▲ = Collaborative

Therapeutic Interventions

Actions/Interventions	Rationale
▲ Administer or teach use of antiemetics as prescribed before meals.	These decrease nausea, increase food tolerance, and maximize intake.
▲ Consult dietitian as indicated.	Diet should be high in calories to provide a source for energy; high in carbohydrates because carbohydrates are easily metabolized and stored by the liver; and limited in fats, which may trigger nausea.
■ Provide or encourage small meals with frequent snacks.	This increases daily intake because less energy is required to eat smaller meals.
■ Provide or encourage largest meal at breakfast.	Anorexia tends to worsen later in the day.
■ Discourage the use of alcoholic beverages.	Alcohol damages liver cells and provides "empty calories" (calories without nutritional value).
▲ Administer or teach use of vitamin supplement as prescribed.	Liver damage may limit adsorption and metabolism of fat-soluble vitamins.
▲ Administer or teach the patient or caregiver to administer total parenteral nutrition (TPN) (see p. 723) as ordered.	This provides nourishment for patients unable to maintain adequate oral intake or nutrients.

Inflammatory Bowel Disease

Crohn's Disease; Ulcerative Colitis; Diverticulitis

Inflammatory bowel disease (IBD) refers to a cluster of specific bowel abnormalities whose symptoms are often so similar as to make diagnosis difficult and treatment empirical. Crohn's disease is associated with involvement of all four layers of the bowel and may occur anywhere in the gastrointestinal (GI) tract, although it is most common in the small bowel at the terminal ileum. Ulcerative colitis involves the mucosa and submucosa only and occurs only in the colon. Cause is unknown for both diseases. Incidence is usually in the 15- to 30-year-old age group. Systemic manifestations can involve the liver, joints, skin, and eyes. Diverticular disease often occurs in persons older than 40 years of age; it seems to be etiologically related to high-fat, low-fiber diets and occurs almost exclusively in the colon. IBD is treated medically. If medical management fails or if complications occur, surgical resection and, possibly, fecal diversion are undertaken. This care plan focuses on chronic, ambulatory care.

 Nursing Diagnosis

Abdominal Pain, Joint Pain

Common Related Factors	Defining Characteristics
Bowel inflammation and contractions of diseased bowel or colon	Reports of intermittent colicky abdominal pain associated with diarrhea
Systemic manifestations of IBD	Abdominal rebound tenderness

■ = Independent; ▲ = Collaborative

Inflammatory Bowel Disease—cont'd

Defining Characteristics—cont'd

Hyperactive bowel sounds
Abdominal distention
Pain and cramps associated with eating
Chronic joint pain

Common Expected Outcome

Patient verbalizes adequate relief from pain.

> **NOC Outcomes**
> Comfort Level; Medication Response;
>   Symptom Control
>
> **NIC Interventions**
> Medication Administration: Oral;
>   Medication Administration: Topical;
>   Pain Management

Ongoing Assessment

Actions/Interventions	Rationale
■ Assess pain: intermittent, colicky abdominal pain; abdominal pain and cramping associated with eating; joint pain.	Although the exact mechanism is unclear, a strong auto-immune etiology is believed to exist in Crohn's disease and ulcerative colitis; systemic manifestations often include arthritis-like symptoms. Changes in the severity and nature of the abdominal pain may indicate a life-threatening condition such as perforation of the GI tract.
■ Auscultate bowel sounds.	Hyperactive bowel sounds are typical.
■ Evaluate patient's perception of dietary impact on abdominal pain.	Many patients with IBD cannot tolerate dairy products and may not tolerate many other foods.
■ Assess presence of changes in bowel habits, such as diarrhea.	Cramping abdominal pain often increases with diarrhea.
■ Determine measures the patient has successfully used to control pain.	This information can be helpful in developing an effective pain management program.
■ Evaluate and document effectiveness of therapeutic interventions; observe for signs of untoward effects of medications.	The goal of medical treatment is to induce clinical remission while avoiding toxic medications. Medications such as mesalamine (Asacol, Pentasa), olsalazine (Dipentum), and sulfasalazine (Azulfidine) are often used to maintain remission. If patients do not respond to these medications, corticosteroids are initiated.

Therapeutic Interventions

Actions/Interventions	Rationale
▲ Instruct patient to take medications as prescribed.	Sulfasalazine (Azulfidine), which contains aspirin, and corticosteroids, which decrease inflammation, are typically used to bring the disease to remission. Topical

■ = Independent; ▲ = Collaborative

Actions/Interventions	Rationale
	preparations of corticosteroids (e.g., enemas, rectal foam) may also relieve pain and discomfort. In the most severe cases, immunosuppressive drugs (e.g., Imuran) may be given.
■ Encourage patient to engage in usual diversional activities, hobbies, relaxation techniques, and psychosocial support systems as tolerated.	These facilitate comfort and relaxation.
■ Recommend necessary alterations in diet.	Small frequent meals tend to be better tolerated and cause less gastrointestinal distress. Bowel rest is not necessary to achieve clinical remission in patients with exacerbation of inflammatory bowel disease.

NDx Nursing Diagnosis

Imbalanced Nutrition: Less Than Body Requirements

Common Related Factors

Malabsorption and diarrhea
Increase nitrogen loss with diarrhea
Decreased intake
Poor appetite and nausea

Defining Characteristics

Body weight more than 10% to 20% below ideal
Decreased serum calcium, potassium, vitamins K and B$_{12}$, folic acid, and zinc
Muscle wasting
Pedal edema
Skin lesions
Poor wound healing

Common Expected Outcome

Patient's nutritional status improves, as evidenced by weight gain or stabilization of weight; controlled diarrhea; and normal serum electrolyte, vitamin, and mineral profiles.

NOC Outcome
Nutritional Status: Nutrient Intake

NIC Interventions
Nutrition Monitoring;
   Nutrition Management

Ongoing Assessment

Actions/Interventions	Rationale
■ Document patient's actual weight (do not estimate).	Decreased body weight is a sign of poor nutrition.
■ Obtain nutritional history; monitor dietary intake.	This provides the basis for initiating diet therapy.
■ Assess for skin lesions, skin breaks, tears, decreased skin integrity, and edema of extremities.	Protein malnutrition causes impaired skin integrity and tissue edema.
▲ Assess serum electrolytes, calcium, vitamins K and B$_{12}$, folic acid, and zinc levels to determine actual or potential deficiencies.	Patients may experience deficiencies related to altered food intake and/or inability of the bowel mucosa to absorb nutrients.
■ Assess patterns of elimination: color, amount, consistency, frequency, odor, and presence of steatorrhea (stools high in undigested fat).	Diarrhea and steatorrhea are indications of nutrient malabsorption.

■ = Independent; ▲ = Collaborative

→ Inflammatory Bowel Disease—cont'd

Therapeutic Interventions

Actions/Interventions

▲ Consult dietitian to review nutritional history, how to perform calorie count, and to assist in menu selection.

■ Encourage patient or caregiver to evaluate factors that enhance appetite, and adjust environment accordingly.

▲ Encourage use of vitamin and mineral supplements as ordered.

▲ Anticipate need for total parenteral nutrition as prescribed.

▲ Administer or instruct the patient to take medications to control diarrhea.

Rationale

High-calorie, high-protein, low-residue diets are recommended to maximize calorie absorption.

This will enhance intake.

These compensate for deficiencies.

This is for patients who cannot tolerate oral intake and/or require bowel rest during an acute exacerbation of the disease.

Loperamide can reduce loose stools, urgency, and fecal soiling.

NDx Nursing Diagnosis

Risk for Deficient Fluid Volume

Common Risk Factors

Presence of excessive diarrhea or nausea and vomiting
Blood loss from inflamed bowel mucosa
Poor oral intake

Common Expected Outcome

Patient remains adequately hydrated as evidenced by good skin turgor, urine output greater than 30 mL/hr, and moist mucous membranes.

NOC Outcomes
Fluid Balance; Coagulation Status

NIC Interventions
Bleeding Reduction: Gastrointestinal;
    Fluid Monitoring

Ongoing Assessment

Actions/Interventions

■ Assess hydration status: skin turgor, mucous membranes, intake and output, weight, blood pressure, and heart rate.

■ Document Hemoccult-positive stools or obvious presence of bloody diarrhea.

▲ Monitor hemoglobin and hematocrit if the patient is bleeding.

Rationale

Tenting of the skin, dry mucous membranes, reduced urine output, weight loss, increased heart rate, and hypotension are signs of fluid deficit.

Blood loss is typically most severe in patients with ulcerative colitis, but patients with Crohn's disease also may have bloody diarrhea.

Decreased hemoglobin and hematocrit occur with bleeding.

■ = Independent; ▲ = Collaborative

Actions/Interventions

■ Monitor urine output and specific gravity.

Rationale

Concentrated urine is an indication of fluid volume deficit.

Therapeutic Interventions

Actions/Interventions

■ Maintain fluid intake that equals output.

■ Instruct and encourage patient to take medications as ordered, noting possible reactions.

▲ Anticipate need for intravenous therapy.

See also **Deficient Fluid Volume,** *p. 71.*

Rationale

Intake and output are indicators of fluid volume excess or deficits.

Azulfidine affects inflammatory response; corticosteroids may be used for both antiinflammatory and immuno-suppressive benefits.

This is used if patient's oral intake is inadequate to maintain normal fluid volume status.

NDx Nursing Diagnosis

Deficient Knowledge

Common Related Factors

Need for continuous and long-term management of chronic disease
Change in health care needs related to remission or exacerbation of disease

Defining Characteristics

Multiple questions by patient or caregivers related to disease process and management
Noncompliance with therapy

Common Expected Outcome

Patient or caregiver verbalizes understanding of disease and management.

NOC Outcomes
Knowledge: Disease Process; Knowledge: Treatment Regimen

NIC Interventions
Teaching: Disease Process;
Teaching: Prescribed Diet;
Teaching: Prescribed Medication

Ongoing Assessment

Actions/Interventions

■ Assess patient's understanding of IBD and necessary management.

Rationale

Patients need to understand that IBD differs from individual to individual; some cases are managed successfully throughout the course of the disease on medications alone, whereas others progress to needing surgical intervention.

■ = Independent; ▲ = Collaborative

Inflammatory Bowel Disease

Inflammatory Bowel Disease—cont'd

Therapeutic Interventions

Actions/Interventions	**Rationale**
■ Discuss the disease process and its management. Explain that IBD is characterized by remissions and exacerbations.	The chronic nature of IBD requires that the patient understand that remissions and exacerbations are the expected course of the disease; as such, medication and dietary management are typically ongoing, although adjustments may be required, depending on the stage of the disease. Careful medical management may eliminate or postpone the need for surgical intervention.
■ Make appropriate referrals: dietary, psychiatric counseling, National Foundation for Colitis and Ileitis.	Community resources provide the patient and caregiver with ongoing support and information.
■ Discuss the need for follow-up to detect changes or problems.	Patients with long-term disease may be at risk for colon cancer.

> • RELATED CARE PLANS
>
> Risk for impaired skin integrity, p. 173
> Total parenteral nutrition, p. 723

Obesity

Overweight

Overweight and obesity are common health problems in the United States, and their prevalence is growing globally. About 97 million adults in the United States are overweight or obese. Recent reports from the National Institutes of Health (1998) estimate that one in two adults in the United States is overweight or obese. Overweight is defined as a body mass index (BMI) of 25 to 29.9 kg/m², and obesity is defined as a BMI of 30 kg/m² or more. Obesity is now classified as follows: class 1, BMI of 30 to 34.9 kg/m²; class 2, BMI of 35 to 39.9 kg/m², and class 3 (extreme obesity), BMI of 40 kg/m² or more. Excess weight accounts for significant health problems including cardiovascular disease, type 2 diabetes mellitus, hypertension, stroke, dyslipidemia, osteoarthritis, respiratory problems, sleep disorders, and some cancers. Women are more likely to be obese than men. Obesity tends to coincide with age (older adults are more likely to be obese than younger adults), and obesity is more prevalent among African-American and Hispanic individuals than among Caucasians. Genetics are also believed to play a role in obesity. A sedentary lifestyle; physiological factors involved in appetite, satiety, and metabolism; and emotional factors associated with overeating all contribute to the complexity of obesity, which is best managed using a multifocused approach. Simple nutritional management, exercise, behavior modification, use of medications, and surgical procedures are all possible methods for managing obesity. The focus of this care plan is on the obese individual in the outpatient setting.

Nursing Diagnosis

Deficient Knowledge

Obesity

Common Related Factors

Lack of familiarity with options to address obesity
Emotional state affecting learning (anxiety, denial)

Defining Characteristics

Lack of knowledge regarding nutritional needs for height and frame
Lack of knowledge regarding food selection and preparation
Demonstrated inability to correctly read labels on food products
Lack of knowledge regarding role of exercise in weight management
Demonstrated inappropriate food selections
Demonstrated inability to plan an appropriate menu
Continued weight gain
Lack of knowledge regarding complications of unmanaged obesity

Common Expected Outcomes

Patient verbalizes measures necessary to achieve weight-reduction goals.
Patient demonstrates appropriate selection of meals or menu planning toward the goal of weight reduction.
Patient begins an appropriate program of exercise.
Patient verbalizes other measures (medications, surgery, behavior-modification programs) to consider if conservative management fails to achieve desired weight loss.
Patient verbalizes health consequences of continued obesity.

NOC Outcomes

Knowledge: Diet; Knowledge: Prescribed Activity

NIC Interventions

Health Education; Teaching: Prescribed Activity/Exercise; Teaching: Prescribed Diet

Ongoing Assessment

Actions/Interventions

- Assess knowledge regarding nutritional needs for height and level of activity or other factors (e.g., pregnancy).
- Assess ability to read food labels.

- Assess ability to plan a menu, making appropriate food selections.
- Assess ability to accurately identify appropriate food portions.

Rationale

Obese individuals may underestimate their calorie intake and overestimate their activity level.

Food labels contain information necessary in making appropriate selections but can be misleading. Patients need to understand that "low-fat" or "fat-free" does not mean that a food item is calorie free. Serving sizes must also be understood to limit intake according to a planned diet.

Unplanned, impulsive eating can lead to overeating.

Obese people often underestimate portion sizes.

■ = Independent; ▲ = Collaborative

Obesity—cont'd

Actions/Interventions

■ Assess usual activity level.

■ Assess or explore with the patient how social situations may contribute to overeating.

Rationale

Patients may confuse routine activity with exercise necessary to enhance and maintain weight loss.

Overeating may be triggered by environmental cues unrelated to physiological hunger sensations.

Therapeutic Interventions

Actions/Interventions

■ Include the family, caregiver, and food preparer in nutrition counseling.

■ Review and reinforce basic nutrition information:
  • Four food groups or the food pyramid
  • Proper serving sizes (may need to teach use of gram scale)
  • Caloric content of food
  • Methods of preparation to avoid additional calories

■ Teach the patient to read food labels.

■ Teach the patient to plan a menu incorporating nutritional needs and food preferences.

■ Encourage the patient to see a physician before beginning an aggressive exercise program.

▲ Refer the patient to commercial weight-loss program as appropriate.

■ Inform the patient about less conservative methods of weight reduction, and encourage medical supervision:
  • Pharmacological agents: appetite suppressants (amphetamines and serotonergic drugs)

  • Surgery: removal of fat (lipectomy, liposuction), reduction of the ability to absorb nutrients (bypass procedures), and restriction of gastric capacity (gastric banding, gastric balloons)

Rationale

Research has demonstrated that men whose wives diet with them are more likely to achieve goals than those for whom "special food" is prepared.

The key principle of obesity therapy is to eat fewer calories than are expended in order to consume fat stores as fuel.

Baking, boiling, broiling, poaching, and grilling are preferable to frying in oil.

Portion size in relation to calories is important in food selection and meal planning.

Compliance with a diet is enhanced when the patient's preferences are incorporated into the planned diet.

Overexertion should be avoided. Low-impact exercise, such as walking, is a good initial exercise plan.

Some individuals require the regimented approach or ongoing support during weight loss, whereas others are able to (and may prefer to) manage a weight-loss program independently.

These drugs act by chemically altering the patient's desire to eat. Side effects of the amphetamines include agitation, palpitations, and restlessness. Because drugs do nothing to permanently alter eating behaviors, use of drugs for weight management often fails when the patient stops taking the medication.

Options depend on the patient's appropriateness for a procedure and usually according to extensive criteria, such as extent of obesity, existing complications of obesity, and likelihood of postprocedure compliance. Patients should be referred to their physicians to discuss the appropriateness of such procedures.

■ = Independent; ▲ = Collaborative

NDx Nursing Diagnosis

Imbalanced Nutrition: More Than Body Requirements

Common Related Factors

Lack of knowledge regarding weight-control measures
Poor dietary habits
Use of food as a coping mechanism
Metabolic disorders
Diabetes
Sedentary lifestyle
Inadequate exercise

Defining Characteristics

Weight 20% or more over ideal body weight for height and frame
Reported or observed dysfunctional eating patterns
Reported or observed noncompliance with recommended diet or exercise plan

Common Expected Outcome

Patient demonstrates understanding of and participates in planned dietary and exercise treatment program.

NOC Outcomes

Weight Control; Nutritional Status: Nutrient Intake

NIC Interventions

Nutritional Monitoring; Weight-Reduction Assistance; Self-Responsibility Facilitation

Obesity

Ongoing Assessment

Actions/Interventions	Rationale
■ Obtain baseline weight and weigh weekly.	Daily weights are not recommended. Slight variations may unnecessarily encourage or discourage a patient; minor variations occur as the result of time of day.
■ Determine BMI.	BMI describes relative weight for height and is significantly correlated with total body fat content. BMI should be used to assess the degree of overweight and obesity and to monitor changes in body weight. BMI is calculated as weight (in kilograms) divided by height squared (in square meters). Convenient conversion tables of heights and weights resulting in selected BMI units are commonly used in clinical practice.
■ Record weight history.	It is helpful to use milestones to help patients recall the history of their weight gain. Questions such as, "How much did you weigh in high school?" How much did you weigh when you got married?" "How much did you weigh after your first child was born?" may help establish when obesity became a problem. This information may also be helpful in identifying psychosocial or emotional factors in the development of obesity.
■ Perform a nutritional assessment.	This should include types and amount of foods eaten, how food is prepared, and the pattern of intake (time of day, frequency, and other activities the patient is engaged in while eating).

■ = Independent; ▲ = Collaborative

Actions/Interventions

- Assess the patient's activity patterns, including regular exercise program.
- Assess compliance with recommended diet and exercise plan.
- Explore the importance and meaning of food with the patient.

Rationale

Increasing activity levels may need to begin at a slow pace if the person has a very sedentary lifestyle.

This will depend on the accuracy and honesty of the patient's reporting, as well as observation.

When food is used as a coping mechanism or as self-reward, the emotional needs being met by intake of food will need to be addressed as part of the overall plan for weight reduction.

Therapeutic Interventions

Actions/Interventions

- Encourage the patient to keep a diet diary.

▲ Arrange for consultation with a dietitian.

- Help the patient plan how to avoid or manage social situations that result in overeating.
- Encourage the patient to be more aware of nutritional habits that may contribute to or prevent overeating:
  - To realize the time needed for eating

  - To focus on eating and avoid other diversional activities (e.g., reading, watching television, talking on the telephone)
  - To observe for cues that lead to eating (e.g., time of day, boredom, depression)
  - To eat in a designated place (e.g., at the table rather than in front of the television or standing in front of the refrigerator)
  - To recognize actual hunger versus desire to eat

- Encourage the patient to set realistic goals for beginning an exercise program.

- Encourage successes; assist the patient to cope with setbacks.

Rationale

A food intake record provides a means for objectively discussing actual versus perceived intake.

This will assist the patient in selecting appropriate types and amounts of foods, discussing food preparation, and planning nutritious meals.

The patient needs to learn new strategies to cope with settings that trigger overeating.

Hurried eating may result in overeating because satiety is not realized until 15 to 20 minutes after ingestion of food.

Distractions at mealtime contribute to overeating.

Awareness and recognition of cues can help the person substitute other activities for eating.

Limiting eating to a designated place can help reduce snacking and other impulse eating.

Eating when not hungry is a commonly recognized symptom among overeaters.

A balanced, reasonable diet and a modest exercise program will provide weight reduction for a great many patients. Remind patients that missing a day of planned exercise or occasional dietary indiscretion will inevitably happen and should not be construed as failure.

Social support is important in successful weight loss and long-term weight management.

■ = Independent; ▲ = Collaborative

Nursing Diagnosis

Disturbed Body Image

Obesity

Common Related Factors

Recent or longstanding change in appearance
Loss of social status

Defining Characteristics

Verbalized discontent with size and appearance
Withdrawal from social contact

Common Expected Outcomes

Patient demonstrates enhanced body image and self-esteem as evidenced by ability to discuss the role weight plays in body image disturbance.
Patient verbalizes satisfaction with ability to begin managing obesity.

NOC Outcomes
Body Image; Self-Esteem

NIC Interventions
Body Image Enhancement;
   Weight-Reduction Assistance

Ongoing Assessment

Actions/Interventions

■ Assess the patient's perception of the impact of being overweight.

■ Assess the degree to which body image disturbance is affecting the patient's overall self-esteem.

Rationale

These perceptions often include exclusion from social activities, being passed over for jobs or promotions, inability to find and purchase attractive clothing, and general disdain by a public that cherishes a "fit-and-trim" look. Research has shown that the morbidly obese (i.e., those 100% above ideal body weight) are subject to certain types of job discrimination.

Body image is a major component of self-esteem; as such, body image disturbance can and often does result in self-esteem disturbance, which can affect the person's overall ability to function.

Therapeutic Interventions

Actions/Interventions

■ Acknowledge normalcy of feelings related to being overweight; encourage verbalization about the same.

■ Demonstrate empathy and empower the patient to participate in a corrective plan.

■ Engage the patient in realistic goal setting.

■ Include significant others and caregivers in planning and goal setting.

Rationale

Guilt about feelings can contribute to overeating.

Self-esteem is enhanced when the patient feels a sense of control.

Patients are easily discouraged when they cannot meet unrealistic goals. This sense of failure can lead to overeating.

These people will be important sources of ongoing support for the patient facing a long-term weight-reduction plan.

■ = Independent; ▲ = Collaborative

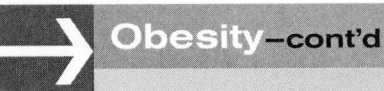

Obesity—cont'd

Actions/Interventions

■ Refer the patient to support groups, if desired.

Rationale

Support groups can provide companionship, enhance motivation for weight loss, and decrease loneliness. Sharing may provide solutions to common problems.

> **• RELATED CARE PLANS**
>
> Activity intolerance, p. 7
> Ineffective breathing pattern, p. 28
> Noncompliance, p. 131
> Powerlessness, p. 153
> Self-care deficit, p. 156

Pancreatitis, Acute

Pancreatitis is an inflammatory disorder of the pancreas that results in the self-destruction of the pancreas by its own enzymes; this causes edema, necrosis, and hemorrhage. The two most common causes are alcohol abuse and biliary obstruction. In severe cases, pancreatitis can be complicated by acute respiratory distress syndrome (ARDS). The focus of this care plan is the care of the acutely ill person with pancreatitis.

NDx Nursing Diagnosis

Acute Pain

Common Related Factors

Inflammation of pancreas and surrounding tissue
Biliary tract disease
Biliary obstruction
Excessive alcohol intake
Abdominal trauma or surgery
Infectious process
Heavy metal poisoning

Defining Characteristics

Verbalized pain
Guarding behavior
Moaning
Facial mask of pain

Common Expected Outcome

Patient verbalizes relief of pain or adequate pain management.

> **NOC Outcomes**
> Pain Control; Comfort Level; Symptom Control
>
> **NIC Interventions**
> Medication Administration; Pain Management; Positioning

■ = Independent; ▲ = Collaborative

Pancreatitis, Acute

Ongoing Assessment

Actions/Interventions

- Assess pain characteristics.

- Assess history of previous attacks.
- Assess precipitating factors.

- Observe for increased abdominal distention; auscultate abdomen for bowel sounds; report decrease or absence of bowel sounds.

Rationale

Epigastric pain or umbilical pain radiating to the back and/or shoulders, increasing pain in the supine position, abdominal distention with rebound tenderness, extreme restlessness, and pain aggravated by food intake are typical pain complaints related to pancreatitis.

Pancreatitis may be a chronic, relapsing disease.

Often a bout of pancreatitis is precipitated by an alcoholic binge or consumption of a large meal that is high in fat content.

Extravasation of pancreatic enzymes causes paralytic ileus.

Therapeutic Interventions

Actions/Interventions

- ▲ Reduce pancreatic stimulus by maintaining patient NPO (nothing by mouth) or with nasogastric tube to low suction as ordered.

- Anticipate need for pain medication.

- ▲ Administer medication, such as anticholinergic drugs.

- ▲ Avoid morphine derivatives.

- Use repositioning, massage, and other nonpharmacological measures.

Rationale

Oral intake causes vagally stimulated pancreatic secretion; the escape of pancreatic secretions into the pancreas causes pain and damage by autodigestion.

Pain management is most effective when pain is treated before it becomes severe. Narcotics are used for pain management.

These mimic sympathetic stimulation and quiet pancreatic secretion.

These may cause spasms of Oddi's sphincter, increasing pain.

These provide comfort.

Nursing Diagnosis

Risk for Deficient Fluid Volume

Common Risk Factors

Vomiting
Decreased intake
Shifting of fluids to extravascular space
Hemorrhage
Ileus

■ = Independent; ▲ = Collaborative

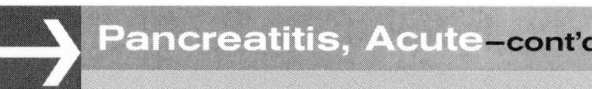

Pancreatitis, Acute—cont'd

Common Expected Outcome

Patient maintains normal fluid volume as evidenced by urine output greater than 30 mL/hr, good skin turgor, and stable blood pressure (BP) and heart rate.

> **NOC Outcomes**
> Fluid Balance; Electrolyte and Acid-Base Balance
>
> **NIC Interventions**
> Fluid Monitoring; Fluid and Electrolyte Management

Ongoing Assessment

Actions/Interventions

- Monitor BP and heart rate.

- Assess hydration status, including skin turgor, daily weight, and hemodynamic parameters.
- Observe for complications of dehydration.

▲ Monitor serum and urine amylase.

▲ Monitor serum calcium levels.

Rationale

Fluid volume deficit occurs rapidly in pancreatitis; BP decreases and heart rate increases. Subtle vital sign changes may indicate profound fluid volume deficit.

The single most important element in preventing multiple organ failure is maintaining fluid balance.

Oliguria and impaired renal function can occur rapidly as a result of the severity of fluid volume deficit.

Both are typically elevated and are an indication of the severity of the pancreatitis.

Although total body calcium is not affected, calcium can be trapped in the edematous tissue of the inflamed pancreas and thus not be available to the circulation.

Therapeutic Interventions

Actions/Interventions

▲ Maintain circulatory volume; administer intravenous fluid as prescribed.

▲ Administer volume expanders or blood transfusion as prescribed.

See also **Deficient Fluid Volume,** *p. 71.*

Rationale

In acute pancreatitis, a patient may require several liters of fluid over the first 24 hours. Fluid resuscitation is essential to maintain hemodynamic stability.

Blood transfusions may be required to correct fluid loss from hemorrhage.

NDx Nursing Diagnosis

Deficient Knowledge

Common Related Factor

Unfamiliarity with disease process

Defining Characteristics

Multiple questions
Misconceptions
Repeat admissions to hospital with recurrent bouts of pancreatitis

 ■ = Independent; ▲ = Collaborative

Common Expected Outcome

Patient verbalizes understanding of causative factors for pancreatitis.

NOC Outcomes
Knowledge: Disease Process;
    Knowledge: Substance Use Control

NIC Intervention
Teaching: Disease Process

Ongoing Assessment

Actions/Interventions	Rationale
■ Assess the patient's understanding of the disease process, particularly potentially controllable behaviors that may trigger episodes of pancreatitis.	Continuation of precipitating behaviors can lead to a chronic form of pancreatitis.

Therapeutic Interventions

Actions/Interventions	Rationale
■ Teach about the relationship of alcohol consumption to pancreatitis.	Eliminating alcohol use can reduce episodes of pancreatitis.
■ Teach about relationship of biliary (gallbladder) disease to pancreatitis.	Patients with pancreatitis secondary to gallstones should undergo cholecystectomy during the same hospitalization.
■ Teach about the recurrent nature of pancreatitis.	This is particularly evident after an alcohol binge.
■ Teach the patient that certain foods may precipitate a bout of pancreatitis.	Many patients with chronic pancreatitis tolerate fatty and spicy foods poorly, although other patients are intolerant to other foods best identified by the individual.

Total Parenteral Nutrition

Intravenous (IV) Hyperalimentation

Total parenteral nutrition (TPN) is the administration of nutrients consisting of concentrated glucose and amino acid solutions via a central catheter or large-diameter peripheral vein. TPN therapy is necessary when the gastrointestinal (GI) tract cannot be used or is not used to meet the patient's nutritional needs. TPN solutions may contain 20% to 60% glucose and 3.5% to 10% protein (in the form of amino acids), in addition to various amounts of electrolytes, vitamins, minerals, and trace elements. These solutions can be modified, depending on the presence of organ system impairment and/or the specific nutritional needs of the patient. Fluid and electrolyte status require frequent monitoring while receiving TPN. To provide necessary amounts of fat and the fat-soluble vitamins (A, D, E, and K), intralipids are often administered two or three times per week along with TPN. TPN is often used in-hospital, long-term, and in subacute care, but it is also commonly used in the home care setting. This care plan addresses nursing care needs that may occur in any of these settings.

■ = Independent; ▲ = Collaborative

Total Parenteral Nutrition—cont'd

 Nursing Diagnosis

Imbalanced Nutrition: Less Than Body Requirements

Common Related Factors

Prolonged NPO (nothing by mouth) status

Alternations in GI tract function (e.g., GI surgery, fistulas, bowel obstruction, esophageal injury or disease, dysphagia, stomatitis, nausea, vomiting, or diarrhea)

Increased metabolic rate or other conditions necessitating increased intake (e.g., sepsis, burns, or chemotherapy)

Psychological reasons for refusal to eat

Defining Characteristics

Caloric intake less than body requirements

Weight loss (or weight 20% below ideal)

Poor skin turgor and wound healing

Decreased muscle mass

Decreased serum albumin, total protein, and transferrin levels

Electrolyte imbalances

Common Expected Outcome

Patient achieves an adequate nutritional status as evidenced by stable weight or weight gain and by improved albumin levels.

NOC Outcome
Nutritional Status: Nutrient Intake

NIC Intervention
Nutritional Monitoring: TPN Administration

Ongoing Assessment

Actions/Interventions

■ Perform a comprehensive baseline nutritional assessment before TPN initiation and periodically thereafter; document findings.

■ Obtain accurate intake and output, daily weights and calorie counts, including calories provided by TPN.

▲ Assess response to nutritional support (e.g., daily weights initially, weekly thereafter; laboratory results: electrolyte, glucose, albumin levels; wound healing; skin condition).

Rationale

The composition of TPN is based on the individual's calculated needs.

Changes in fluid balance, weight, and caloric intake are used to monitor the effectiveness of TPN.

Daily weights are necessary to determine if nutritional goals are being met. Weight is also used to assess fluid volume status. Weight gain of more than $^1/_2$-pound per day may indicate fluid retention.

Therapeutic Interventions

Actions/Interventions

■ Assist with insertion and maintenance of central venous or peripherally inserted central venous lines.

▲ Administer prescribed rate of TPN solution via infusion pump.

Rationale

The osmolality of TPN solutions requires infusion into a large central vein with high-volume blood flow.

Falling behind on TPN administration deprives the patient of needed nutrition; boluses (or too-rapid administration) can precipitate a hyperglycemic crisis because the hormonal response (i.e., insulin) may not be available to allow use of the increased glucose load.

■ = Independent; ▲ = Collaborative

Actions/Interventions

- Familiarize the patient and caregiver with additive content of TPN solution (glucose, amino acids, electrolytes, insulin, vitamins, and trace minerals).

- Assist with or encourage oral intake if indicated.

▲ Refer to or collaborate with appropriate resources: nutritional support team, dietitian, pharmacy, home health nurse.

Rationale

Alterations in laboratory profile will be considered against TPN contents and adjustments made accordingly.

Unless complete bowel rest is indicated, patients may be fed orally in addition to TPN to maximize nutritional support.

The risk of most complications that occur in the hospital is decreased when the administration of parenteral nutrition is supervised by an experienced nutritional support team.

NDx Nursing Diagnosis

Risk for Deficient Fluid Volume

Common Risk Factors

Hyperglycemia
Inability to respond to thirst mechanisms because of NPO status
Low serum protein level

Common Expected Outcome

Patient maintains normal fluid volume as evidenced by good skin turgor, balanced intake and output, and urine output of at least 30 mL/hr.

NOC Outcome
Fluid Balance

NIC Interventions
Fluid Monitoring; TPN Administration

Ongoing Assessment

Actions/Interventions

- Assess for signs and symptoms of fluid volume deficit: decreased blood pressure, increased heart rate, elevated body temperature, skin dryness, loss of turgor, high urine specific gravity.
- Monitor intake and output.

▲ Monitor blood glucose levels.

▲ Monitor serum protein levels according to protocol, usually every 3 to 7 days.

Rationale

Early identification of changes in fluid balance facilitates prompt interventions.

An intake consistently lower than output indicates fluid volume deficit and need for additional fluid to prevent dehydration. An intake higher than output may indicate fluid overload and result in pulmonary complications.

Hyperglycemia, caused by infusion of glucose in the TPN solution, can lead to hyperosmolar, nonketotic coma with subsequent dehydration secondary to osmotic diuresis.

Low serum protein level may lead to loss of fluids from intravascular spaces, secondary to low colloidal pressures.

■ = Independent; ▲ = Collaborative

Total Parenteral Nutrition—cont'd

Actions/Interventions

■ During the first week of TPN administration, weigh patient daily and record weight; weigh weekly thereafter.

Rationale

Daily weights are necessary to determine if nutritional goals are being met. Weight is also used to assess fluid volume status. Weight gain of more the ½-pound per day may indicate fluid retention.

Therapeutic Interventions

Actions/Interventions

▲ Administer TPN at prescribed, constant rate; if infusion is interrupted, infuse 10% dextrose in water until TPN infusion is restarted.

▲ Encourage oral intake of fluids unless contraindicated. Administer maintenance or bolus fluids as prescribed, in addition to TPN.

Rationale

This provides needed fluid in addition to protecting the patient from sudden hypoglycemia; hypoglycemia can result when the high glucose concentration to which the patient has metabolically adjusted is suddenly withdrawn.

Patients who are NPO and only receiving TPN may not be receiving adequate amounts of fluids, especially because TPN is initiated in low administration rates; therefore additional fluid may be required.

NDx Nursing Diagnosis

Risk for Excess Fluid Volume

Common Risk Factors

Overinfusion of TPN
Inability to tolerate increased vascular load

Common Expected Outcome

Patient maintains normal fluid volume as evidenced by balanced intake and output, absence of edema, and absence of excessive weight gain.

NOC Outcome
Fluid Balance

NIC Interventions
Fluid Monitoring; TPN Administration

Ongoing Assessment

Actions/Interventions

■ Assess for signs and symptoms of fluid volume excess:
  • Edema

Rationale

This occurs when fluid accumulates in the extravascular spaces. Edema usually begins in the fingers, facial area, and presacral area. Generalized edema, called anasarca, occurs later and involves the entire body. Weight gain in excess of 1 pound per day is an indication of fluid volume excess.

■ = Independent; ▲ = Collaborative

Actions/Interventions

- Intake greater than output

- Shortness of breath and crackles
- Jugular venous distention
▲ Monitor serum sodium level.

Rationale

An intake greater than output may indicate fluid overload.

These are caused by accumulation of fluid in the lungs.

This is caused by elevated central venous pressure.

Hypernatremia may cause or aggravate edema by holding fluid in the extravascular spaces.

Therapeutic Interventions

Actions/Interventions

▲ If signs and symptoms of fluid volume excess occur, administer diuretics as prescribed.

■ Position the patient in a semi-Fowler's or high Fowler's position.

■ Handle edematous extremities with caution.

Rationale

Diuretics aid in the excretion of excess body fluids.

Elevating the head of the bed allows for ease in breathing. This position promotes pooling of fluid in the bases and makes more lung tissue available for gas exchange.

Edematous skin is more susceptible to injury and breakdown.

NDx Nursing Diagnosis

Risk for Altered Body Composition

Common Risk Factors

Electrolyte imbalances:
- Hypokalemia (K^+ <3.5 mEq/L)
- Hyponatremia (Na <115 mEq/L)
- Hypocalcemia (Ca <6.8 mg/dL)
- Hypomagnesemia (Mg <1.5 mg/dL)
- Hypophosphatemia (PO_4 <2.5 mg/dL)
Essential fatty acid deficiency (EFAD)
Hyperglycemia (glucose >200 mg/dL)
Hypoglycemia (glucose <60 mg/dL)

Common Expected Outcomes

Patient maintains normal serum electrolyte levels.
Patient has normal blood glucose level.

NOC Outcome
Electrolyte and Acid-Base Balance

NIC Intervention
Electrolyte Monitoring

■ = Independent; ▲ = Collaborative

Total Parenteral Nutrition—cont'd

Ongoing Assessment

Actions/Interventions

▲ Assess for signs and symptoms of electrolyte imbalance:
- Hypokalemia
  - Alteration in muscle function (e.g., weakness, cramping)
  - Electrocardiogram changes (e.g., ventricular dysrhythmias, ST-segment depression, or U-wave)
  - Mental status changes (e.g., confusion, lethargy)
  - Abdominal distention and loss of bowel sounds
- Hyponatremia
  - Decreased skin turgor, weakness, tremors or seizures, lethargy, confusion, nausea, vomiting
- Hypocalcemia
  - Paresthesias, tetany, seizures, positive Chvostek's sign, irregular heart rate
- Hypomagnesemia
  - Muscle weakness, cramping, twitching, tetany, seizures, irregular heart rate
- Hypophosphatemia
  - Muscle weakness, mental status changes

■ Assess for signs and symptoms of essential fatty acid deficiency.

- Alopecia
- Tendency to bruise and thrombocytopenia

- Dry, scaly skin
- Poor wound healing

▲ Monitor serum triglyceride level twice weekly if patient is receiving intralipids.

■ For patients receiving intralipid therapy, monitor for signs and symptoms of adverse reactions: dyspnea, cyanosis, headache, flushing.

▲ Assess for hyperglycemia or hypoglycemia signs and symptoms; notify physician.
- Hypoglycemia
  - Glucose level less than 60 mg/dL
  - Weakness, agitation, clammy skin, tremors
- Hyperglycemia
  - Glucose level greater than 200 mg/dL
  - Glycosuria
  - Thirst, polyuria, confusion

Rationale

When patients are receiving TPN and no other nutrition, there is a risk, especially early in TPN therapy, that all electrolyte needs may not be met. As physiological condition changes, patients may have altered needs for electrolytes and will require adjustment of the TPN solution.

TPN solutions contain no fat; fat is a nutritional requirement that allows essential fat-soluble vitamins A, D, E, and K to be absorbed. Patients commonly receive intralipid (intravenous [IV] fat) solutions at the same time as TPN.

These are caused by coagulopathy secondary to inadequate vitamin K levels.

This relates to vitamin D and E deficiencies.

This relates to vitamin A and E deficiencies.

Patients receiving an intravenous fat emulsion should have serum triglyceride monitored until levels are stable and when changes are made in the amount of fat administered.

Fat embolism is a rare but serious complication of intralipid therapy.

Blood glucose should be monitored frequently upon initiation of TPN, after any changes in insulin dose, and untill measurements are stable.

■ = Independent; ▲ = Collaborative

Therapeutic Interventions

Actions/Interventions

▲ Administer electrolyte replacement therapy as prescribed.

▲ Administer 10% or 20% intralipids as ordered:

- Piggyback intralipids into the most proximal part of the TPN tubing after preparing the port aseptically. Do not infuse intralipids through a filter. Secure tubing with tape to prevent dislodgment.

■ When discontinuing TPN therapy, taper rate over 2 to 4 hours.

▲ Use corrective actions if TPN solution stops or must be stopped suddenly:
- For clotted catheter or if subsequent TPN bags are not available, hang 10% dextrose and water at the rate of TPN infusion.
- For hyperglycemia, administer insulin as prescribed.
- For emergency or cardiac arrest situations, stop TPN infusion; administer bolus doses of 50% dextrose.

Rationale

Electrolytes are supplied based on the patient's calculated need.

It is recommended that patients who are NPO and/or receiving only TPN for more than 2 weeks receive IV fat emulsions or intralipids. Intralipids can also be given in absence of EFAD to provide extra calories.

Intralipids are used to prevent essential fatty acid deficiency.

This prevents hypoglycemic episode caused by abrupt TPN withdrawal.

This solution provides a higher concentration of glucose to prevent sudden hypoglycemia.

This facilitates metabolic use of glucose.

This prevents hypoglycemia during resuscitation.

> ● RELATED CARE PLAN
>
> Risk for infection, p. 108

Total Parenteral Nutrition

■ = Independent; ▲ = Collaborative

7

Musculoskeletal Care Plans

→ 🕴 **Amputation, Surgical**

Surgical amputation is the term used to reflect the surgical removal of a part from the body. The portion of the limb that remains intact after the surgery is referred to as the *residual limb* or *stump* and may be fitted with an artificial device called a *prosthesis* that is used to take the place of the severed limb. The level of the amputation depends on the amount of affected tissue, the ability of the blood supply to promote healing, and the prognosis for fitting a functional prosthesis. Generally there are about 11 lower limb amputations for every upper limb amputation performed. The leading cause of amputation is vascular disease, with an equal prevalence rate in men and women, who are usually in the 61- to 70-year-old age range. Clinical conditions that predispose the patient to amputation include peripheral vascular disease, diabetes, arterial sclerosis, and Buerger's disease. Another cause for amputation is trauma, the second leading cause of amputation, in which the accident itself may sever the limb or in which the limb is so damaged that it must be removed after the accident. Primary bone tumors occur in 4.5% of all amputations, and about 33% of these occur in the 16- to 20-year-old age range. The surgical procedure for an uncomplicated amputation rarely requires hospitalization for more than 5 days, but often the clinical situations surrounding amputation make these patients medically unstable. Under those circumstances, the hospital course may be longer. The vast majority of recovery takes place out of the hospital, either in a rehabilitation center or on an outpatient basis. This care plan primarily covers information about patient care before and immediately after lower extremity surgery. Because nurses will encounter patients in various stages of recovery and rehabilitation, references are made about posthospitalization rehabilitation.

ND_x Nursing Diagnosis

Impaired Skin Integrity

Common Related Factors	Defining Characteristics
Surgical incision	Redness
Skin breakdown caused by immobility	Pain
Abnormal wound healing	Edema
Surgical drain	Drainage/discharge
	Incomplete closure of skin flap

Common Expected Outcome

Patient manifests signs of optimal wound healing, as evidenced by intact skin, absence of skin breakdown, and a properly fitting prosthesis.

NOC Outcomes

Tissue Integrity: Skin and Mucous Membranes; Wound Healing: Primary Intention

NIC Interventions

Amputation Care; Incision Site Care; Skin Surveillance

Ongoing Assessment

Actions/Interventions	Rationale
■ Assess wound for: • Normal healing	Wound should be clean and dry, with edges of incision approximated and intact. Diabetics and patients with poor circulation, such as the elderly, may face considerable obstacles in healing, and the course of wound healing may be anything but normal.
• Bleeding and hemorrhage	As with other surgical dressings, there should be no frank bleeding from the incisional site. Keep a tourniquet at the bedside in case hemorrhage develops. A small amount of oozing from the incision is normal. Documentation of drainage characteristics helps other care givers assess status change. Initially most postamputation dressings are pressure or pressure cast dressings. A surgical drain may be placed to remove fluid or blood that might interfere with granulation.
• Proper fit of postsurgical cast or pressure dressing	A rigid dressing or a cast may be applied to the residual limb immediately after the surgery and will remain in place for 7 to 10 days, until the sutures are removed. After removal of the sutures, a new cast or rigid dressing may be applied. Occasionally these casts are fit with a primitive prosthetic device that allows for early ambulation.
■ Monitor the residual limb every hour for the first 24 hours; observe for symptoms indicative of infection.	Signs of inflammation may be present. Edema, redness, pain, and tenderness should decrease over the next 3 to 5 postoperative days.
■ Check residual limb for signs of impaired circulation. Check pulses above the amputation site.	The residual limb should be warm and dry with no discoloration reflective of impaired circulation. Remember that many patients experienced circulatory compromise before the amputation; this problem may continue to represent a threat to the residual and unaffected limb. Preserving the health in the residual limb is of utmost importance. Adaptation to a properly fitting prosthesis is dependent on having an adequate residual limb remaining for a good prosthetic fit and stability of the joints above the residual limb.
■ Assess for prolonged pressure on tissues associated with immobility.	Early ambulation is of great psychological benefit to the patient. It will also prevent development of pressure sores and contractures from prolonged inactivity.

Amputation, Surgical

■ = Independent; ▲ = Collaborative

→ **Amputation, Surgical**—cont'd

Actions/Interventions	**Rationale**
■ Monitor and report complaints of unusual pain.	This may reflect the development of postoperative infection.
■ Monitor vital signs, including temperature, according to postoperative protocol.	Tachycardia, tachypnea, and fever are early signs of infection. It is normal for the temperature and heart rate to be elevated in the first few days after surgery. Temperature should not exceed 38.3° C (101° F), and the heart rate should not exceed 120 beats/min.

Therapeutic Interventions

Actions/Interventions	**Rationale**
■ Elevate the residual limb for the first 24 hours.	Elevation of the residual limb for the first 24 hours reduces edema and promotes venous return.
■ Reinforce or change the dressing as needed; use aseptic technique. Note drainage. If a rigid dressing is not used, remove bandage on residual limb, cleanse wound frequently, and reapply dressings using a smooth figure-eight wrap.	Daily cleansing helps prevent infection. The proper application of Ace bandages in the figure eight helps reduce edema and helps shape the residual limb.
■ Protect the residual limb from contamination. If the patient is incontinent, protect the limb with a plastic covering.	Exposing the residual limb to microorganisms increases the risk of infection.
■ Instruct the patient on how to wrap the residual limb with compression bandages.	Compression bandages aid in shaping the residual limb in preparation for prosthesis fitting. Wrapping the compression dressing around the waist seems to be essential in keeping the bandage firmly in place, and compressing the medial thigh encourages the residual limb to shrink in a fashion that will promote good interface with the prosthetic socket.
■ Assist the patient with wrapping the residual limb; use an elastic bandage and when indicated a residual limb shrinker if wrapping is too difficult.	Patients may need time to adjust to seeing their residual limb and may balk at assuming responsibility for its care until they are ready.
■ Instruct the patient to report slippage of the cast, rigid dressing, or compression dressing.	Slippage of the cast or rigid dressing may reflect underlying pathology such as infection or incomplete closure of skin flap, which would interrupt healing.
■ Discuss weight-bearing limitations and their importance.	These restrictions prevent skin breakdown and facilitate proper wound healing. The patient's limb may be non–weight bearing for 4 to 6 weeks after surgery; other patients will begin partial weight bearing on he residual limb soon after the surgery. Factors that influence how soon weight bearing takes place include the indications for the amputation, the level and the type of the amputation, and the repair/preparation of the residual limb.
■ Teach signs and symptoms of residual limb breakdown.	Early detection of residual limb breakdown allows for prompt treatment. Complications may jeopardize the patient's rehabilitation plan and make further amputation necessary.

■ = Independent; ▲ = Collaborative

Nursing Diagnosis

Impaired Physical Mobility

Common Related Factors

Activity limitations caused by loss of body part
Change in center of gravity creating balance problems
Postoperative protocol
Difficulty in using assistive devices
Pain on mobility
Fatigue

Defining Characteristics

Inability to move purposefully within environment
Reluctance to attempt movement
Limited range of motion (ROM)

Common Expected Outcomes

Patient maintains functional alignment of all extremities and avoids contractures.
Patient begins the process of learning to perform activities of daily living.
Patient achieves optimal level of mobility (walking with prosthesis, crutches; use of wheelchair).

NOC Outcomes

Mobility; Ambulation: Wheelchair; Coordinated Movement: Transfer Performance

NIC Interventions

Exercise Therapy: Ambulation; Energy Management; Exercise Therapy: Balance

Ongoing Assessment

Actions/Interventions

■ Assess positioning and transfer skills.

■ Assess nutritional status.

■ Assess activity tolerance.

■ Assess understanding of postoperative activity and exercise program.

■ Assess the patient's knowledge of ambulating and moving with assistive devices.

Rationale

Learning transfer techniques helps reestablish the patient's independence and promotes a feeling of security when moving in bed and ambulating.

Adequate calories and protein are needed for healing and energy for ambulation and transfer techniques. Performing transfer techniques and performing activities with a prosthetic device consume more calories and take a greater physical effort than normal ambulation.

A patient who had normal activity tolerance before the amputation may find crutch walking and walking with a prosthesis more tiring and requiring strengthening of certain muscle groups to support movement.

Postoperatively, ROM exercises will be encouraged in all unaffected extremities. Some patients will begin to ambulate soon after surgery. Other patients will remain non–weight bearing until the temporary prosthesis is made 4 to 6 weeks after surgery. At that time physical therapists will implement a program of functional training with the patient and the prosthesis.

Patients may already know how to crutch walk, but balance is significantly affected after an amputation. Attention must be paid to developing an awareness of new physical boundaries after the amputation.

■ = Independent; ▲ = Collaborative

Amputation, Surgical

Amputation, Surgical—cont'd

Musculoskeletal Care Plans

Actions/Interventions

▲ Assess whether patient is a candidate for a prosthesis.

■ Assess the impact of the loss of sensory information that was perceived via the amputated part.

Rationale

This decision involves consideration of type and level of amputation, age and strength of the patient, the type of function the patient is attempting to regain, and perhaps most of all the motivation of the patient. Elderly or debilitated patients may not be able to handle a prosthesis; a wheelchair may be more appropriate. On the other hand, no assumptions should be made about older patients being too old to adapt to a prosthesis.

The lack of sensory feedback may be more important for an upper extremity loss than for a lower extremity loss. The lack of sensory feedback may be the major limiting factor in the effective use of artificial hands and hooks. Other factors that may exaggerate the effect of the sensory loss are the age of the patient and the existence of other sensory deficits (e.g., vision or hearing deficits, bilateral amputations).

Therapeutic Interventions

Actions/Interventions

■ Reinforce and teach prevention of postoperative complications (flexion, abduction, and external rotation of hip): avoid sitting for long periods; avoid use of pillows under residual limb; maintain proper alignment; avoid flexing residual limb while sitting or lying.

■ Reinforce and teach proper positioning:
  • Have the patient lie on his or her back, keeping the pelvis level and the hip joint extended.

  • Maintain neutral rotation. Use or teach the patient to use a trochanter roll to prevent external rotation.

  • Have the patient lie prone with lower extremity in extension for 30 minutes three or four times a day.

■ Instruct the patient to perform ROM exercises:
  • Adduction exercises of lower extremity 10 times every 4 hours after the first 24 hours
  • Hamstring tightening exercises in prone position 10 times every 4 hours after the first 24 hours

Rationale

Patients often develop contractures of the affected extremity, which complicates rehabilitation and the recovery period.

This positioning prevents contractions.

The residual limb will have the tendency to externally rotate.

This prevents positioning deformities (flexion contraction).

Exercise therapy maintains and strengthens muscle groups. ROM exercises are directed toward maintaining normal joint mobility. Disuse can cause permanent shortening of the muscle, resulting in contractures. Quadriceps settings are performed for above- and below-the-knee amputations. Straight leg raises are performed with the knee fully extended for below-the-knee amputations. Hip adductions are done for above-the-knee amputations. Biceps and triceps strengthening is done for below-elbow amputations.

Patients will need to continue the muscle-strengthening program throughout the rehabilitation program and beyond. Optimal muscle strength is required to maintain balance while using assistive devices such as crutches, a walker, and a prosthesis.

Actions/Interventions	Rationale
■ Instruct patient to be sitting up in chair two to three times a day after the first 24 hours	This activity helps the patient develop skill with transfer techniques.
■ Encourage early ambulation with assistive devices. The patient may use a walker, crutches, or wheelchair as appropriate. The patient should be able to stand within 48 hours. Ambulate with crutches at least three times daily.	Early ambulation promotes confidence about regaining independence.
■ Teach crutch walking to patients with no previous experience with crutches. Instruct patients on the use of wheelchairs, walkers, support bars, and a trapeze.	Learning correct technique with assistive devices promotes safety and reduces the risk of falls.
■ Do not allow the knee to bend over the bed or edge of the chair if the patient had a below-the-knee amputation.	Allowing the residual limb to hang in a dependent position decreases venous return and increases edema. Flexion contractures may occur if the residual limb remains bent.
■ Provide a trapeze bar in bed.	A trapeze increases mobility in bed and allows the patient to be more independent.
■ Assist the patient with transfers and ambulation until able to perform safely. Encourage the patient to ask for needed assistance.	Assistance may be required to prevent new injuries that would complicate recovery. Muscle weakness and impaired balance after a lower extremity amputation may result in an injury.
■ Teach the patient to perform activities of daily living (ADLs) to foster independence. If the patient is not a candidate for a prosthesis, instruct in self-care activities from a wheelchair.	The nurse will coordinate activities of different disciplines to maximize the patient's return to optimal function. The disciplines involved will include (but not be limited to) occupational therapy and job training, rehabilitation and physical therapy, work of the prosthetic maker, ongoing medical care and psychological support services, and financial assistance programs.
■ Instruct the patient awaiting a prosthesis regarding the need for a long-term functional training program.	It may take as long as 6 to 12 months for a lower extremity to reach a point where a final device may be fitted. This period allows for the patient to adapt progressively to wearing a prosthesis and to work toward regaining function of the remaining limb. Generally, lower extremity prosthetics replace function much better than upper extremity prosthetics, but upper extremity devices can be applied earlier.

Amputation, Surgical

NDx Nursing Diagnosis

Disturbed Body Image

Common Related Factors	Defining Characteristics
Loss of body part	Verbal preoccupation with changed body part
Loss of independence	Refusal to discuss change
Inability to maintain prior lifestyle	Actual change in function
	Change in social behavior

■ = Independent; ▲ = Collaborative

→ **Amputation, Surgical**–cont'd

Common Expected Outcomes

Patient demonstrates increasing comfort with body changes, as evidenced by ability to look at residual limb and talk about amputation and the ability to provide self-care to the residual limb (as appropriate).

Patient reports increased independence in the performance of activities.

Patient reports to be resuming aspects of his or her life or role that may have necessitated relearning after the amputation.

NOC Outcomes

Acceptance: Health Status; Body Image; Grief Resolution

NIC Interventions

Amputation Care; Body Image Enhancement; Grief Work Facilitation

Ongoing Assessment

Actions/Interventions

■ Assess the patient's ability to adjust to loss of body part.

■ Assess the patient's feelings about using a mechanical part to replace or substitute for a missing body part.

■ Assess the patient's ability to use effective coping mechanisms.

■ Assess the patient's perception of the impact of the amputation on his or her ability to perform self-care measures and on his or her social behavior, personal relationships, and occupational activities.

■ Assess the need for a support group.

Rationale

The acute (versus chronic) nature of the factors requiring amputation, the patient's prior health and age, the feelings and responses of the significant others, and the patient's lifestyle and work impact the adjustment to amputation.

Artificial limbs are clearly mechanical devices that never feel or perform like a real body part. There is always some loss of function, and sensory changes are massive and may include some low-level noise that may draw further attention to the operation of the prosthesis. Patients may be dependent on a prosthesis, but they may also despise the experience of wearing and using one.

At the heart of the grief process for the patient with an amputation is the need to accept the loss of the limb and to realize that the loss is permanent. Patients will express a wide range of feelings in response to their loss, including anger, rage, sadness, helplessness, and hopelessness. Patients will be likely to fall back on known coping skills, including humor, denial, distraction, and expression of thoughts and feelings in talk and writing.

For some patients who have undergone an amputation, the psychological and social aspects of amputation are experienced as far greater consequences of the surgical procedure.

Support groups are usually a component of most formal rehabilitation programs; however, patients may require this kind of intervention earlier, in the immediate postoperative period.

Therapeutic Interventions

Actions/Interventions

■ Encourage verbalization of feelings.

Rationale

Loss of a limb requires significant psychological adjustment.

■ = Independent; ▲ = Collaborative

Actions/Interventions	Rationale
■ Allow the patient time to work through grief stages.	Patients will do this at their own pace and in their own way. Accommodation to amputation is a lifetime process for some patients.
■ Listen and support verbalized feelings about body and lifestyle changes.	These changes will be massive. There is no way to prepare patients for the impact this will have on their lives. It is important that the health care provider not minimize or negate the patient's experiences.
■ Encourage the patient to participate fully in design of the therapeutic regimen.	This fosters a sense of still being in control of one's own life.
■ Encourage family members to support the patient and allow independence.	A grieving family may have a need to take care of the patient, but this response may feed into an unhealthy dependence, setting a precedent that is difficult to disrupt later in the recovery period and that communicates the concept of the patient as damaged.
■ Encourage the patient to participate in the care of the residual limb when able.	Such activity promotes independence and helps the patient's adjustment to a new body image.
■ Allow the patient sufficient time to perform ADLs.	Amputees experience an overall increase in fatigue as they perform even normal activities. In addition to this, conscious attention must be paid to functions that one carried out on a fairly autonomic level when the neuromuscular system was intact. Attention to this level of detail is exhausting and limits the number of activities that can be carried out at the same time. This tends to be especially true for patients with upper level amputations.
■ Encourage use of clothing to enhance appearance.	Amputation is a very public disability. It may be the first thing people notice about an individual, especially if the amputation was of an upper limb. Shock and embarrassment are often initial responses of the public to seeing an individual with an amputation. Attractive clothing can enhance a patient's self-image and confidence.
■ Discuss use of a prosthesis for both cosmetic and functional purposes.	Both are equally acceptable reasons to use a prosthesis. Some people have more than one device, one for cosmetic use and one for functional use. This is especially true for the individual whose amputation was of an upper limb.
▲ Consult social services for support groups.	Persons who have themselves experienced an amputation can offer a unique type of support that is perceived as helpful by patients. It is often possible to match up individuals by age, sex, and education; in some situations, career matches can be made.

NDx Nursing Diagnosis

Acute Pain and Chronic Pain

Common Related Factors	Defining Characteristics
Phantom sensation	Verbal complaints
Phantom pain	Facial expressions of discomfort

■ = Independent; ▲ = Collaborative

Amputation, Surgical—cont'd

Common Related Factors—cont'd

Surgical procedure
Decreased mobility
Prosthesis fit

Defining Characteristics—cont'd

Protection of residual limb
Refusal to be mobile
Refusal to participate in rehabilitation
Crying, moaning
Restlessness
Withdrawal, irritability

Common Expected Outcomes

Patient verbalizes that postoperative discomfort is adequately relieved.
Patient verbalizes understanding of phantom limb sensation.
Patient verbalizes that phantom pain is adequately relieved.

NOC Outcomes
Pain Control; Medication Response

NIC Interventions
Analgesic Administration;
  Pain Management

Ongoing Assessment

Actions/Interventions

- Assess the patient's description of pain. Have the patient rate the pain on the pain scale.

- Assess for nonverbal signs of pain. Observe for tense posture, tightening fists, diaphoresis, and increased pulse rate.

- Assess the degree of relief the patient is receiving from the prescribed medications.

- Assess the patient's understanding of the occurrence and management of phantom limb sensations.

- Assess understanding of phantom pain.

Rationale

Thorough assessment of pain characteristics will assist the nurse in differentiating phantom limb sensation from incision pain. The nurse needs to understand the type of pain the patient is experiencing in order to select appropriate pain management interventions. Pain is what the patient states it is. Early detection and intervention promote patient comfort.

Behavioral pain responses may be the only indication of acute pain.

Patients receiving oral analgesics or intramuscular injections could benefit from analgesics delivered via the epidural route or through intravenous patient-controlled analgesia.

Phantom limb sensations are the painless awareness of the presence of the amputated part and are often experienced as a tingling sensation caused by nerve stimulation proximal to the level of amputation, but perceived as coming from the amputated limb. These sensations are frequently experienced as incomplete. Sensations in the hand will be experienced more than the arm and the thumb more than the other fingers. In a lower limb amputation, sensations in the foot will be experienced more strongly than the leg and the great toe more strongly than the other toes.

When phantom sensations become disagreeable and painful, they are called *phantom pain*. Phantom pain may be continuous or occasional, with a wide range in

Musculoskeletal Care Plans

Actions/Interventions

■ Assess the fit of the prosthesis to determine whether the fit is resulting in the development of pressure points.

Rationale

the intensity experienced by the patient. Patients may experience the pain as a cramping or squeezing sensation; a burning sensation; or a sharp, shooting pain. Phantom pain tends to disappear over time, but phantom sensation tends to remain indefinitely.

A properly fitting prosthetic device is almost always experienced as uncomfortable by the patient. Furthermore, prosthetic devices are fitted over tissues that would not normally bear weight. Patients will experience significant discomfort until these tissues become adjusted. Assessments as to the fit of the device should be made by the device maker.

Therapeutic Interventions

Actions/Interventions

▲ Provide medications as prescribed for surgical pain relief; evaluate effectiveness and modify doses as needed.

▲ Use additional comfort measures as appropriate to relieve phantom sensations: diversional activities; relaxation techniques; position change, exercise; ROM of residual limb; application of pressure to residual limb; and transcutaneous electrical nerve stimulation.

Rationale

Patients have a right to adequate pain relief. Bone surgery is extremely painful and generally requires higher levels of narcotic relief. Phantom pain is real pain, and the patient requires appropriate analgesics as part of a total pain management program.

Long-term management of phantom sensations includes the use of nonpharmacological measures. Current research indicates that these measures are effective.

Amputation, Surgical

ND_x Nursing Diagnosis

Deficient Knowledge

Common Related Factor

New condition

Defining Characteristics

Expressed concerns about home management
Questions about medications/treatment
Questions about rehabilitation/prosthesis management

Common Expected Outcomes

Patient verbalizes understanding of residual limb care.
Patient verbalizes understanding of the rehabilitation program.
Patient describes course of prosthetic fitting.

NOC Outcomes

Knowledge: Disease Process;
Knowledge: Treatment Regimen

NIC Interventions

Teaching: Disease Process;
Teaching: Psychomotor Skills

■ = Independent; ▲ = Collaborative

Amputation, Surgical—cont'd

Ongoing Assessment

Actions/Interventions

■ Assess knowledge of the following: care of residual limb, phantom limb pain management, signs and symptoms of circulatory problems, prosthetic care, follow-up appointments, and community resources.

Rationale

Accurate understanding of self-care issues facilitates smooth transition from hospital to home.

Therapeutic Interventions

Actions/Interventions

■ Inform of discharge medications, exercises, and follow-up appointments.

■ Reinforce teaching for care of residual limb (e.g., wrapping the residual limb, skin care, and weight-bearing limitations).

■ Provide information for phantom limb pain or sensation management.

■ Discuss signs and symptoms of circulatory problems. Reinforce the need for the patient to protect the residual limb from infection and circulatory compromise or damage.

■ Reinforce teaching about care of prosthesis if applicable.

▲ Coordinate social services, physical therapy, and occupational therapy.

▲ Contact social services for information about community resources and support groups (e.g., visiting nurses, homemakers, outpatient therapy).

Rationale

This information promotes effective self-care by the patient.

Accurate self-care measures promote optimal rehabilitation.

Phantom limb sensations may continue for several months or longer.

Signs of infection, circulatory compromise, or skin breakdown should be reported to the physician immediately.

The patient needs to understand how to maintain the prosthesis in proper working order.

Such services enhance adequate discharge planning and home treatments after discharge.

Special assistance may be necessary to help the patient accept and adapt to the amputation.

Arthritis, Rheumatoid

Rheumatoid arthritis (RA) is a chronic, systemic, inflammatory disease that usually presents as symmetrical synovitis primarily of the small joints of the body. Extraarticular manifestations may include rheumatoid nodules, pericarditis, scleritis, and arteritis. RA is characterized by periods of remission and prolonged exacerbation of the disease, during which the joints can become damaged. In the initial phase of RA, the synovial membrane becomes inflamed and thickens, associated with an increased production of synovial fluid. As this tissue develops, it causes erosion and destruction of the joint capsule and subchondral bone. These processes result in decreased joint motion, deformity, and finally ankylosis, or joint immobilization. Anyone can develop RA, including children and older adults, but it usually strikes people in the young to middle years. RA strikes women at a 3:1 ratio compared with men and occurs in all ethnic groups worldwide. The specific cause of RA is unknown, but the tendency to develop it may be inherited. The gene that seems to control RA is one of the genes that controls the immune system, but not everyone who has this gene goes on to develop RA. The disease behaves differently in each person who contracts it. In some people the joint inflammation that marks RA will be mild with long periods of remission between "exacerbations," or increased periods

■ = Independent; ▲ = Collaborative

of disease activity. For others the activity of the disease may seem continuously active and worsening as time passes. The goals of treatment are to relieve pain and inflammation and to reduce joint damage. The long-term goal of treatment is to maintain or restore use in the joints damaged by RA. This care plan focuses on the outpatient management of patients who are affected by RA.

 Nursing Diagnosis

Deficient Knowledge

Common Related Factors

New disease/procedures
Unfamiliarity with treatment regimen
Lack of interest/denial

Defining Characteristics

Multiple questions
Lack of questions
Verbalized misconceptions
Verbalized lack of knowledge
Inaccurate follow-through of previous instructions

Common Expected Outcome

Patient verbalizes understanding of the disease and treatment.

NOC Outcomes
Knowledge: Disease Process;
    Knowledge: Medication;
        Knowledge: Treatment Regimen

NIC Interventions
Teaching: Disease Process;
    Teaching: Prescribed Medications

Ongoing Assessment

Actions/Interventions

■ Assess the patient's level of knowledge of RA and its treatment.

Rationale

Patients will be responsible for evaluating their condition on a daily basis to make determinations about exercise, the use of analgesics, and seeking medical intervention.

Therapeutic Interventions

Actions/Interventions

■ Introduce or reinforce disease process information: unknown cause, chronicity of RA, process of inflammation, joint and other organ involvement, remissions and exacerbations, and control versus cure.

Initial Presentation with Symptoms of Joint Inflammation
- Patients may feel systemically ill with additional symptoms of fever, chills, loss of appetite, decreased energy, and weight loss.
- The synovial lining of the joints and tendons becomes inflamed, with a progressive proliferation of the synovium within and outside of the joint capsule itself (pannus formation).

Rationale

Patients must have a comprehensive understanding of the disease to actively participate in their own care.

This inflammatory process is not limited to the joints; progressive changes occur in the heart, with pericarditis, congestive heart failure, and cardiomyopathies developing; in the skin; in the kidneys, with chronic renal failure developing; and in the lungs, with chronic restrictive pulmonary disease and repeated infections occurring.

Arthritis, Rheumatoid

■ = Independent; ▲ = Collaborative

Arthritis, Rheumatoid—cont'd

Musculoskeletal Care Plans

Actions/Interventions

- Joint inflammation may affect more than one joint at a time, and usually the inflammation affects the same joint bilaterally.
- Cartilage eventually becomes involved; the inflammatory process erodes the surface between the bone ends, leaving the surfaces exposed.
- Further inflammation results in the development of bone fissures, cysts on the bones, spurs, fibrosis, and shortening of the tendons.

Diagnosis

- Laboratory tests:
  - Rheumatoid factor (or the RA antibody)

  - Hemoglobin and hematocrit

  - Serum complement
  - Erythrocyte sedimentation rate (ESR)
  - C-reactive protein

  - Liver function tests and kidney function tests

- X-rays of the hands, feet, and chest are recommended initially, and x-rays of the feet and hands should be repeated annually for the first 3 years of the disease.

General Treatment/Management Guidelines

- Adequate sleep, at least 8 to 10 hours each night with periods of rest during the day
- Rest of the affected joints

- Application of hot and cold

- Physical therapy especially designed for the individual patient

- Relearning how to perform activities of daily living (ADLs) and professional roles within the limitations of the disease (may require the help of an occupational therapist)

Rationale

It is important to note that not all people with RA will have a positive antibody titer. No single laboratory test is capable of ruling out RA.

Anemia may be present, and there will be an elevation in the erythrocyte sedimentation rate.

This is decreased during periods of exacerbation.

Laboratory tests should include acute phase reactors (ESR and C-reactive protein). These two tests are good indicators of the inflammatory activity of the disease.

These tests help facilitate rheumatoid arthritis monitoring, early detection of disease complications, and side effects of treatments.

X-rays should be examined for the presence of bony erosion, which are more frequent at the beginning of the disease process. Erosions of the hands or feet develop in about 70% of patients by the end of the first 2 to 3 years. Their presence and the speed of onset are associated with poorer outcomes. A chest x-ray is recommended for initial evaluation and to identify the appearance of possible problems during the course of the disease and its treatment.

Sleep enhances immune system function to reduce inflammation. Fatigue contributes to increased joint pain.

Splinting is sometimes helpful in protecting joints, which can become overused during the course of daily activities.

Alternating use of hot and cold may reduce the local inflammatory process.

This provides a balance between maintaining function in a threatened joint while respecting the inflammatory nature of the disease.

As joint deformity progresses and joint mobility decreases, the patient may benefit from using assistive devices to complete ADLs, such as using long-handled eating utensils. The occupational therapist can evaluate the patient's needs and provide devices that can be adjusted to fit the individual patient.

■ = Independent; ▲ = Collaborative

Actions/Interventions	Rationale
• Prescribed medications	Patients may be taking many drugs and need to understand the different methods of administration and the potential side effects.
A. Acetaminophen	Simple analgesics such as acetaminophen should be used first. They relieve pain but have no effect on inflammation.
B. Salicylates: aspirin, salsalate, magnesium salicylate, choline salicylate, and combination salicylate	These drugs relieve pain in the mild to moderate range and have an antiinflammatory effect. Side effects include gastrointestinal (GI) disturbances, increased risk of bleeding, and tinnitus.
C. Nonsteroidal antiinflammatory drugs (NSAIDs): phenylacetic acid, oxicam, indole, propionic acid, and pyrazolone derivatives	NSAIDs are recommended at disease onset, when a new DMARD (disease-modifying antirheumatic drug) is introduced, and when uncontrolled isolated symptoms persist despite good response to antirheumatic drugs. Patients should be aware of the risks and benefits of using NSAIDs. Potential complications include GI and cardiovascular risks. NSAIDs relieve pain and reduce minor inflammation, but they are not strong enough to alter the long-term damaging effects of rheumatoid arthritis on the joints.
D. Selective NSAIDs, COX-2 inhibitors (celecoxib)	These drugs act by binding prostaglandin synthesis via inhibition of cyclooxygenase-2.
	People who have a history of coronary artery disease, angina, a stroke, or are at a higher than average risk for these diseases and who are not taking aspirin may want to avoid the COX-2 inhibitors until more information is available on the safety of this class of drugs.
E. Corticosteroids: cortisone, hydrocortisone, prednisone, triamcinolone, methylprednisolone, dexamethasone, and betamethasone	Corticosteroids should be used when NSAIDs are contraindicated or have a high risk of adverse side effects, as bridge therapy until the onset of disease-modifying antirheumatic drugs therapy, or when NSAIDs do not adequately control inflammation. Steroids have strong antiinflammatory effects. Steroids may be taken orally, be administered intravenously, or be injected directly into a joint. Steroids promptly improve symptoms of RA such as pain and stiffness, and they decrease joint tenderness and swelling. However, if used alone, steroids have only a modest effect on decreasing arthritis damage.
F. DMARDs: hydroxychloroquine (Plaquenil), methotrexate (Rheumatrex), gold salts (Ridaura, Solganal), D-penicillamine (Depen, Cuprimine), sulfasalazine (Azulfidine), azathioprine (Imuran), leflunomide (Arava), and cyclosporine (Sandimmune, Neoral)	These drugs substantially reduce inflammation of rheumatoid arthritis, although DMARDs act slowly when compared with steroids. Studies suggest that DMARDs can reduce or prevent joint damage, preserve structure and function, and enable a person to continue his or her daily activities. Several weeks to months of treatment are often necessary before the effects of DMARDs become evident.
	Because of its efficacy and toxicity profile, methotrexate is the recommended initial treatment in all patients who have not previously received DMARDs.

Arthritis, Rheumatoid

■ = Independent; ▲ = Collaborative

Arthritis, Rheumatoid—cont'd

Actions/Interventions

G. Biological response modifiers: etanercept (Enbrel), adalimumab (Humira), and infliximab (Remicade)

■ Stress the importance of long-term follow-up.

■ Encourage the patient to discuss new or over-the-counter treatments with health care workers.

■ Inform the patient of resources such as the Arthritis Foundation.

■ Suggest referral to an arthritis specialist for optimal treatment.

Rationale

This class of drugs treats RA by interfering with signaling pathways involved in inflammation. The onset of action of these medications is more rapid than that of DMARDs. Because of the cost of these medications and uncertainty about their long-term effects, they are often reserved for people who have not responded fully to DMARDs and for people who cannot tolerate DMARDs in doses large enough to control inflammation.

These drugs interfere with the ability to fight infection; these should not be used in people with serious infections such as kidney infection or pneumonia.

Patients with RA should be monitored for an indefinite period of time. Patients in complete remission should be seen every 6 months or yearly; patients with recent disease onset, frequent exacerbations, or persistent activity should be seen on demand (in general every 1 to 2 months) depending on the treatment used and disease activity until control is achieved. Aging may alter hepatic function, thus decreasing the metabolization of drugs that are broken down in the liver. The possibility of adverse effects and drug interactions should be monitored in older patients.

The patient may be vulnerable to fads or advertisements claiming curative effects of high-dose vitamins, special health foods, or copper bracelets.

This is a comprehensive resource center for patients suffering with RA.

This practitioner may be in the best position to understand the nuances of an individual's disease, because so much of it is seen within the practice. In addition, the rheumatologist will be aware of the latest treatment regimens.

 Nursing Diagnosis

Joint Pain

Common Related Factors

Inflammation associated with increased disease activity
Degenerative changes secondary to longstanding inflammation

Defining Characteristics

Patient report of pain
Guarding on motion of affected joints
Facial mask of pain
Moaning or other sounds associated with pain and movement

■ = Independent; ▲ = Collaborative

Common Expected Outcomes

Patient verbalizes a decrease in pain.
Patient is able to participate in self-care activities.

NOC Outcomes
Pain Control; Medication Response

NIC Interventions
Pain Management;
  Analgesic Administration

Ongoing Assessment

Actions/Interventions

- Assess for signs of joint inflammation (redness, warmth, swelling, decreased motion).
- Evaluate location and description of pain.

- Assess interference with lifestyle.

Rationale

Local signs of inflammation may be the first to manifest.

Pain occurs primarily in small joints, such as hands, wrists, fingers, and ankles.
Joint pain and decreased range of motion (ROM) can limit the fine motor and gross motor movements required for completing ADLs.

Therapeutic Interventions

Actions/Interventions

- Instruct the patient to take antiinflammatory medication as prescribed.

▲ Suggest the use of nonnarcotic analgesic as necessary.

- Encourage the patient to monitor position and to always maintain anatomically correct alignment of the body.
- Instruct to:
  - Not use knee gatch or pillows to prop knees.

  - Use small flat pillow under head.

  - Wear splints as prescribed.

- Recommend use of hot (e.g., heating pad) or cold packs on painful, inflamed joints.

- Encourage use of ambulation aids when pain is related to weight bearing.

- Suggest that the patient apply a bed cradle.

- Encourage use of alternative methods of pain control such as relaxation, guided imagery, or distraction.

Rationale

Antiinflammatory drugs should not be taken on an empty stomach (they can irritate the stomach lining and lead to ulcer disease).
Central-acting analgesics such as narcotics are not as effective in relieving inflammatory pain.
Muscle spasms can result from nonfunctional body alignment and result in pain and predispose to deformity formation.

Prolonged knee flexion can lead to decreased ROM and increased pain.
It is important not to increase the flexion of the neck, which could lead to further deformity and neck strain.
Splints provide rest to inflamed joints and may reduce muscle spasm.
Alternating use of hot and cold is sometimes helpful in reducing the inflammatory response in the joints. Individual patients may prefer heat over cold or vice versa. Suggest trying what works best at the time.
Some of the weight normally transferred to the affected extremity can be shifted to the ambulation device; the device may also improve balance.
Protective devices keep pressure of bed covers off inflamed lower extremities and prevent the development of contractures.
These measures may augment other medications to diminish pain.

= Independent; ▲ = Collaborative

Arthritis, Rheumatoid

Arthritis, Rheumatoid—cont'd

 Nursing Diagnosis

Joint Stiffness

Common Related Factors

Inflammation associated with increased disease activity
Degenerative changes secondary to longstanding inflammation

Defining Characteristics

Patient's complaint of joint stiffness
Guarding on motion of affected joints
Refusal to participate in usual self-care activities
Decreased functional ability

Common Expected Outcomes

Patient verbalizes decrease in stiffness.
Patient is able to participate in self-care activities.

NOC Outcomes
Pain Control; Coordinated Movement

NIC Interventions
Pain Management; Heat Therapy

Ongoing Assessment

Actions/Interventions

■ Assess the patient's description of stiffness:
  • Location: What specific joints are affected?

  • Timing (morning, night, all day)

  • Length of time the stiffness persists

  • Relationship to activities (aggravate or alleviate stiffness)

  • Measures used to alleviate stiffness

■ Assess how pain interferes with lifestyle.

Rationale

Stiffness may rotate among various joints involved in RA.

Stiffness characteristically occurs on awaking in the morning.

This usually lasts 30 minutes; it may last longer as the disease progresses.

Stiffness is usually aggravated by prolonged inactivity; it may be precipitated by joint motion.

Most patients will have rituals that they perform to reduce pain (e.g., taking a warm bath, foot soaks).

RA is a chronic disease with periods of remission and exacerbation.

Therapeutic Interventions

Actions/Interventions

■ Encourage the patient to take a 15-minute warm shower or bath on arising. Localized heat (hand soaking) is also useful. Encourage the patient to perform ROM exercises after the shower or bath, two repetitions per joint.

■ Suggest that the patient plan sufficient time for performing activities.

Rationale

Warm water reduces stiffness and relieves pain and muscle spasms. ROM is important to maintain joint mobility.

Performing tasks while in pain depletes energy, because the functional capacity of the joints may be reduced. Performing simple tasks may take longer.

■ = Independent; ▲ = Collaborative

Actions/Interventions

- Suggest that the patient avoid scheduling tasks or therapy when stiffness is present.
- Instruct the patient to take antiinflammatory medications in the morning. Remind the patient that antiinflammatory drugs should not be given on an empty stomach.

- Suggest use of elastic gloves (e.g., Isotoner) at night.
- Remind the patient to avoid prolonged periods of inactivity.

Rationale

Excessive movement at these times may increase the inflammatory response.

The first dose of the day should be taken as early in the morning as possible, with a small snack. The sooner the patient takes the medication, the sooner stiffness will abate. Many patients prefer to take these medications as early as 6 or 7 AM. Antiinflammatory agents are caustic to the gastric mucosa.

Supportive gloves may decrease hand stiffness.

Muscle activity must be balanced with rest, or the joint will become frozen and muscles will atrophy.

NDx Nursing Diagnosis

Fatigue

Common Related Factors

Increased disease activity
Anemia secondary to chronic disease or the medications administered

Defining Characteristics

Patient describes lack of energy, exhaustion, listlessness
Excessive sleeping
Decreased attention span
Facial expressions: yawning, sadness
Decreased functional capacity

Common Expected Outcomes

Patient verbalizes a higher level of energy and appears rested.
Patient maintains optimal mobility within limitations (e.g., sitting, transferring, ambulation).

NOC Outcomes
Endurance; Energy Conservation

NIC Intervention
Energy Management

Arthritis, Rheumatoid

Ongoing Assessment

Actions/Interventions

- Assess the patient's description of fatigue: timing (afternoon or all day), relationship, activities, and aggravating and alleviating factors.
- Determine nighttime sleep pattern.
- Determine whether fatigue is related to psychological factors (e.g., stress, depression).

Rationale

Specific information about the patient's experience of fatigue can help the nurse develop an individualized approach.
Pain may interfere with achieving a restful sleep.
Depression is common in patients suffering from chronic pain.

Therapeutic Interventions

Actions/Interventions

- Provide periods of uninterrupted rest throughout day (30 minutes one to two times a day)

Rationale

Patients often have limited energy reserve. Fatigue may cause exacerbation of disease.

■ = Independent; ▲ = Collaborative

Arthritis, Rheumatoid—cont'd

Musculoskeletal Care Plans

Actions/Interventions

- Reinforce principles of energy conservation:
  - Pacing activities (alternating activity with rest)

  - Adequate rest periods (throughout day and at night)
  - Organization of activities and environment

  - Proper use of assistive and adaptive devices; ensure that the patient is properly trained in the use of assistive devices
- If fatigue is related to interrupted sleep, encourage warm shower or bath immediately before bedtime.
- Instruct the patient to take nighttime analgesic or long-acting antiinflammatory drug before retiring for the night.
- Encourage gentle ROM exercises (after shower or bath).

- Determine whether the patient is adhering to prescribed mobility restrictions and guidelines.

Rationale

Patient often uses more energy than others to complete the same tasks.

Objects commonly used should be accessible; environments should be free of stairs and objects that could result in patient falls or injury.

There are effective ways to use assistive devices that do not demand more energy expenditure on the part of the patient.

Warm water relaxes muscles, facilitating total body relaxation.

This optimizes the likelihood that the patient will sleep through the night.

The patient needs to maintain strength in unaffected joints, which is critical for successful rehabilitation.

Disease exacerbations may be related to the patient exceeding mobility guidelines.

NDx Nursing Diagnosis

Impaired Physical Mobility

Common Related Factors

Pain
Stiffness
Fatigue
Psychosocial factors
Altered joint function
Muscle weakness

Defining Characteristics

Patient's description of difficulty with purposeful movement
Decreased ability to transfer and ambulate
Reluctance to attempt movement
Decreased muscle strength
Decreased ROM

Common Expected Outcomes

Patient verbalizes or demonstrates increased ability to move purposefully.
Patient participates in self-care activities.

NOC Outcomes
Ambulation; Self-Care: ADLs

NIC Interventions
Exercise Therapy: Ambulation; Self-Care Assistance

■ = Independent; ▲ = Collaborative

Ongoing Assessment

Actions/Interventions

- Assess the patient's description of what type of movement aggravates or alleviates the condition and to what degree these things interfere with lifestyle.
- Observe the patient's ability to ambulate and to move all joints functionally.
- Assess the need for analgesics before activity.

- Observe the patient's ability to bathe, carry out personal hygiene, dress, toilet, and eat.
- Assess the impact of self-care deficit on lifestyle.

- Determine the need for assistive or adaptive devices to use in self-care activities.
- Assess the need for home health care during exacerbations.

Rationale

Symptoms will change as the disease progresses.

Pain may cause progressive loss of function.

Pain may be dealt with effectively by preventing or reducing it.

Joint pain and stiffness interfere with performing ADLs.

Some patients have successfully adjusted their routines and complete required tasks. Other patients may be unable to care for themselves.

The patient may not have knowledge of newly available assistive devices.

Home health care services can help the patient remain in the home setting as the disease progresses.

Therapeutic Interventions

Actions/Interventions

- Reinforce the need for adequate time to perform activities.
- Reinforce proper use of ambulation devices as taught by the physical therapist.

- Encourage the patient to wear proper footwear (properly fitting, with good support and nonskid bottoms) when ambulating, and to avoid wearing house slippers.
- Assist with ambulation as necessary.

- Reinforce techniques of therapeutic exercise taught by the physical therapist.

- Instruct the patient to avoid excessive exercise during acute inflammatory exacerbations.
- Reinforce principles of joint protection taught by the occupational therapist.
- Reinforce proper body alignment when sitting, standing, walking, and lying down.
- Encourage family members to promote independence by:
  - Assisting the patient only as necessary

  - Providing necessary adaptive equipment (e.g., raised toilet seat, dressing aids, eating aids).

Rationale

The patient may need more time than others to complete same tasks.

Proper use conserves energy and provides more protection and support to the patient. It also reduces the load on joints.

Patients may select floppy shoes because of pain or because of deformities in the foot. It is important for the patient's safety that footwear fit correctly and be properly supportive.

The first few minutes of weight bearing may be difficult on a joint; support to the standing or sitting position may be helpful to the patient.

ROM, muscle strengthening, and endurance exercise within a prescribed regimen promote joint function and increase physical stamina.

Exercise during this time may exaggerate the inflammatory process.

Joint protection preserves joint mobility and prevents injury that increases inflammation.

Improper body alignment can lead to unnecessary pain and contracture.

During times of exacerbations, patients need more assistance than at other times; the family needs to be sensitive to this.

Such aids promote independence and may enhance safety.

Arthritis, Rheumatoid

■ = Independent; ▲ = Collaborative

Arthritis, Rheumatoid—cont'd

Actions/Interventions	Rationale
• Providing enough time for the patient to complete tasks.	The patient's self-image improves when he or she can perform personal care independently.

Arthroplasty/Replacement: Total Hip, Knee, Shoulder

Hip Hemiarthroplasty; Total Hip Surface Arthroplasty; Cup/Mold Arthroplasty; Knee Hemiarthroplasty; Shoulder Hemiarthroplasty

Total hip arthroplasty/replacement is a total joint replacement by surgical removal of the diseased hip joint, including the femoral neck and head, as well as the acetabulum. The femoral canal is reamed to accept a metal component placed into the femoral shaft, which replaces the femoral head and neck. A polyethylene cup replaces the reamed acetabulum. The prosthesis is either cemented into place or a porous coated prosthesis is used, which allows bio-ingrowth, resulting in retention and stability of the joint. Some arthroplasty procedures are done using a minimally invasive approach. These techniques use multiple small incisions compared to the more traditional approach that uses a single, long incision. Evidence suggests that a less invasive surgical technique for joint arthroplasty is associated with earlier ambulation, decreased incidence of joint dislocation, and shorter length of stay postoperatively.

Other variations of this surgical procedure include the following:

- Hip hemiarthroplasty: Surgical removal of the femoral head and neck and replacement with metal component.
- Total hip surface arthroplasty: Reaming out of the acetabulum and implantation of an acetabular cup while the femoral head is only reamed down to accept a metal femoral head.
- Cup/mold arthroplasty: The acetabulum and head of the femur are reamed down to an untraumatized surface, and an appropriate-size metal cup is fitted over the head of the femur. This surgery provides the patient with increased (although not complete) mobility and pain-free joint movement. However, there has been insufficient time to study the long-term questions of implant longevity, wear, and the long-term response of bone to the prosthesis to make this a real alternative for the patient younger than 60 years who will retain the device for an extended time. Therefore, the ideal candidate for this surgery is the elderly patient whose disability and pain have reached a point where these debilitating factors outweigh the decreased function and mobility that remain after successful surgery. Conditions that predispose the patient to requiring a total hip arthroplasty include osteoarthritis (the most common cause), injury, loss of blood supply to the hip, and rheumatoid arthritis. Patients may require additional care in a rehabilitation setting.

Knee hemiarthroplasty is replacement of deteriorated femoral, tibial, and patellar articular surfaces with prosthetic metal and plastic components. The prosthetic devices are held in place through the use of cement or the device is porous, allowing for bio-ingrowth, which eventually secures the replacement. Total knee replacement is the preferred treatment for the older patient with advanced osteoarthritis and for the young and elderly with rheumatoid arthritis. Although knee implants are thought to be durable over time and result in a degree of predictable pain relief, which makes them desirable for all patients, younger patients will almost certainly require revision at some point after the device becomes worn. The hospitalization for total knee replacement rarely exceeds 5 days,

■ = Independent; ▲ = Collaborative

with rehabilitation and recovery expected to take from 6 weeks to 3 months. Elderly patients may require additional care in a rehabilitation setting.

Shoulder hemiarthroplasty is the surgical removal of the head of the humerus with replacement by a prosthesis. Total shoulder arthroplasty is the surgical removal of the head of the humerus and the glenoid cavity of the scapula, with replacement by an articulating prosthesis. A metallic humerus is inserted into the shaft, and a high-density polyethylene cup is cemented into place. Patients most likely to undergo this procedure (many of whom are older) have experienced joint damage and functional limitations secondary to osteoarthritis or rheumatoid arthritis. Many arthropathies are bilateral, necessitating the eventual replacement of both shoulder joints. Full recovery takes 3 to 6 months for optimal movement (70 to 90 degrees of abduction is usual, but the quality of postsurgical joint function is directly linked to the strength of the muscles that will move the implant).

 Nursing Diagnosis

Acute Pain

Common Related Factors

Bones and soft tissue trauma caused by surgery
Intense physical therapy or rehabilitation program
Restricted mobility

Defining Characteristics

Complaint of pain
Facial grimaces, guarding behavior, crying
Withdrawal, restlessness, irritability
Altered vital signs
Refusal to participate in a physical therapy or rehabilitation program

Common Expected Outcomes

Patient verbalizes relief or acceptable reduction in pain.
Patient appears comfortable.

NOC Outcomes

Pain Control; Medication Response; Self-Care: Parenteral Medication

NIC Interventions

Pain Management; Analgesic Management; Patient-Controlled Analgesia

Ongoing Assessment

Actions/Interventions

■ Assess the patient's description of pain.

Rationale

The first step in alleviating pain is assessing location, severity, and degree of both physical and emotional pain. Postoperative pain is usually localized to the affected joint. It will be acute and sharp. The pain should decrease in intensity over the 5 days after surgery. Intense pain that persists or pain that returns to previous levels of intensity may indicate a developing complication such as infection or compartment syndrome. Compartment syndrome is a condition that

Arthroplasty/Replacement: Total Hip, Knee, Shoulder

> ## Arthroplasty/Replacement: Total Hip, Knee, Shoulder—cont'd

Actions/Interventions

- Assess mental and physical ability to use patient-controlled analgesia (PCA) versus intramuscular or oral analgesics.
- Assess effectiveness of pain-relieving interventions.

Rationale

results from the unyielding nature of fascial coverings over muscles. The inflammatory process, which is the result of injured tissues (tissues traumatized by surgery), increases venous pressure, reduces venous return, and subsequently decreases arterial inflow. If tissue ischemia persists for longer than 6 hours, permanent tissue damage may result.

Successful use of PCA requires the patient to have knowledge of its use and the manual dexterity to operate it.

Patients have a right to effective pain relief. Pain relief is not determined to be effective until the patient indicates that it is acceptable.

Therapeutic Interventions

Actions/Interventions

- Explain analgesic therapy, including medication and schedule. If the patient is a candidate for PCA, explain the concept and routine.

- ▲ Administer narcotic analgesics every 3 to 4 hours around the clock for the first 24 hours.

- Instruct the patient to request pain medication before the pain becomes severe.
- Encourage use of analgesics 30 to 45 minutes before physical therapy.
- Change position (within hip precautions) every 2 hours or more often for comfort.
- ▲ Apply ice packs as ordered.
- Provide comfort measures (frequent repositioning, back rubs, diversional activities). Encourage stress management techniques (guided imagery, progressive relaxation).
- Maintain proper position of the operated extremity.

- Investigate reports of sudden severe joint pain with muscle spasms and changes in joint mobility, and of sudden severe chest pain with dyspnea and restlessness.

Rationale

Care providers often assume that the patient will request pain medication when needed. The patient may be waiting for the nurse to offer it when it is available and may think it is his or her duty or responsibility to tolerate pain until it can no longer be tolerated.

There is a massive amount of manipulation, nerve trauma, and tissue damage done during the surgical procedure. Assume that the patient requires analgesia. The patient's ability to fall asleep between checks is not a good indicator of the patient's level of comfort.

If pain is too severe before analgesics or therapy is instituted, relief takes longer.

Unrelieved pain hinders the rehabilitative progress.

The patient's inability to move freely and independently may result in pressure and pain on bony prominences.

Cold therapy may decrease edema and enhance comfort.

These measures reduce muscle tension, refocus attention, promote a sense of control, and may enhance coping abilities in relation to pain.

This reduces muscle spasm and undue tension on the new prosthesis and surrounding tissue.

Early recognition of developing problems such as dislocation of prosthesis or pulmonary emboli provide for prompt intervention and treatment of more serious complications.

(■ = Independent; ▲ = Collaborative)

Nursing Diagnosis

Impaired Physical Mobility

Common Related Factors

Surgical procedure
Discomfort
Pain

Defining Characteristic

Limited ability to ambulate or move in bed

Common Expected Outcomes

Patient maintains optimal mobility within limitations (sitting, transferring, ambulation).
Patient maintains strength in unaffected joints.
Patient adheres to prescribed mobility restrictions and guidelines.
Patient participates in an ongoing program of rehabilitation and physical therapy.

NOC Outcomes

Bone Healing; Ambulation; Coordinated Movement

NIC Interventions

Positioning; Exercise Therapy: Joint Mobility; Exercise Therapy: Ambulation

Ongoing Assessment

Actions/Interventions

- Assess fear and anxiety of transferring or ambulating.

- Assess the level of understanding of postoperative restriction.

- Assess postoperative range of motion (ROM); document improvement and failure to progress compared to preoperative status.

Rationale

The patient may be fearful of injuring the joint replacement. Allaying anxiety or fear will allow the patient to concentrate on correct techniques.

Precautions must be maintained at all times to prevent dislocation.

ROM exercises of unaffected joints must be maintained during periods of decreased activity. Arthritic joints lose function more rapidly when activity is restricted.

Therapeutic Interventions

Actions/Interventions: Hip

- Encourage ROM in bed with all unaffected extremities.

- Encourage exercise as prescribed to affected joint.

- Encourage use of analgesic before position changes.

- Use trapeze in bed to assist in mobility.
- Instruct the patient on maintaining total hip arthroplasty precautions during position changes.
- Have the patient sit on the side of the bed for several minutes before getting out of bed.
- Maintain weight-bearing status on the affected extremity as prescribed.

Rationale

Bed rest results in the loss of muscle tone in all muscle groups.

Such exercise aids in increasing muscle strength and tone in the affected extremity.

Decreased or controlled pain allows better performance during therapy.

This device facilitates movement in bed.

These precautions prevent hip dislocation.

This prevents orthostatic hypotension.

Excessive weight bearing on the new hip will be discouraged until the hip has healed. Patients will begin physical therapy immediately after surgery.

Arthroplasty/Replacement: Total Hip, Knee, Shoulder

■ = Independent; ▲ = Collaborative

> ## Arthroplasty/Replacement: Total Hip, Knee, Shoulder—cont'd

Actions/Interventions: Knee

- If prescribed, apply continuous passive motion (CPM) machine to affected leg at prescribed degrees.

- ▲ Maintain proper position in CPM: maintain leg in neutral position; adjust CPM so knee joint corresponds to bend in CPM machine; adjust foot plate so foot is in a neutral position in the boot; instruct patient to keep opposite leg away from machine.

- Assist and encourage the patient to perform quad sets, gluteal sets, and ROM to both legs.

- ▲ Reinforce muscle-strengthening exercises taught by the physical therapist.

- Elevate leg on a pillow when not in CPM. Place pillow under calf.

- Encourage and assist the patient to sit in a chair on first and second postoperative days. Instruct to sit with legs dependent several times a day. Initiate weight bearing as prescribed.

- Encourage ambulation with walker or canes after initiated by the physical therapist.

- Maintain arm in shoulder immobilizer for 1 to 2 days or as prescribed. After the immobilizer is removed, maintain the patient's arm in a sling.

- Begin active or passive ROM exercises (extension, abduction, flexion) of all extremities.

- Reinforce instructions for rehabilitative activities as prescribed.

- Encourage and assist the patient in performing basic ADLs: self-feeding, brushing teeth, and combing hair. Provide extra time for the performance of these activities.

Rationale

CPM facilitates joint ROM, promotes wound healing, maintains mobility of knee, and prevents formation of adhesions to operative knee.

Proper positioning is imperative to prevent injury from moving parts.

These exercises increase muscle strength and tone.

These exercises optimize return of full knee extension.

This position promotes full leg extension.

Patients will progress from a walker to crutches and finally to a cane. Weight bearing progresses with each advancement.

Progressive daily ambulation promotes the patient's return to increased physical activity and self-care.

The immobilizer may consist of a sling or a sling and a strap that is applied around the body to restrain the arm and maintain proper body alignment.

Maintenance of optimal function in all unaffected joints is critical to overall recovery, because collateral extremities will be performing all activities of daily living (ADLs) until recovery is completed.

Achieving increasing mobility is one of the primary goals of surgery, along with elimination of pain.

The patient may be performing ADLs using the non-dominant arm, because the surgical site is most likely located in the dominant arm.

NDx Nursing Diagnosis

Risk for Ineffective Tissue Perfusion

Common Risk Factors

Surgical procedure
Immobility

■ = Independent; ▲ = Collaborative

Common Expected Outcomes

Patient maintains adequate tissue perfusion, as evidenced by warm extremities, good color, good capillary refill, absence of pain and numbness, and bilaterally equal pulses.

Patient is free of signs and symptoms of deep vein thrombosis (DVT), pulmonary embolus (PE), and fat embolism, as evidenced by negative Homans' sign, normal respiratory status, stable vital signs, and normal arterial blood gases (ABGs).

NOC Outcome
Tissue Perfusion: Peripheral

NIC Interventions
Circulatory Care; Circulatory Precautions

Ongoing Assessment

Actions/Interventions

■ Assess and compare neurovascular status of affected limb preoperatively and postoperatively.

■ Assess affected extremity every 1 to 2 hours as ordered using the 8-point check for signs of neurovascular compromise and damage:
  • Temperature of affected tissue

  • Capillary refill of nail beds

  • Color of surgical site and surrounding tissues

  • Edema
  • Sensory function

  • ROM

  • Pain

  • Evaluation of tissues, comparing affected and unaffected tissues
▲ Check sequential compression device and thromboembolic disease support (TED) stocking for extreme tightness.
■ Assess for signs and symptoms of DVT:

  • Positive Homans' sign

Rationale

Assessment must include unaffected and affected extremity to establish baseline and monitor for change in neurovascular status.

Injured tissues are usually cooler than on the nonoperative side. Normal temperature indicates adequate perfusion.

Normal refill is 2 to 4 seconds. In the first hours after surgery, capillary refill may be sluggish, but refill that exceeds 4 to 6 seconds should be reported to the physician.

Color should be pink, not pale or white. The affected extremity may be paler than the unaffected extremity.

Severe swelling may indicate venous stasis.

Complaints of numbness, tingling, or "pins and needles" feeling may indicate pressure on nerves.

This indicates the amount and degree of limitations. Injured tissues will have decreased ROM.

This indicates injury, trauma, or pressure. Surgical site will normally be painful. Monitor and report excessive complaints of pain as a possible harbinger of compartment syndrome.

This allows comparison and perception of patient's own "normal" presurgical status.

Excessive compression may result in neurovascular compromise.

DVT is a serious complication after joint replacement surgery.

The examiner dorsiflexes the patient's foot toward the tibia, and the patient experiences pain in the calf muscles.

Arthroplasty/Replacement: Total Hip, Knee, Shoulder

■ = Independent; ▲ = Collaborative

Actions/Interventions

- Swelling, tenderness, redness in calf; palpable cords

- Abnormal blood flow study findings (if prescribed)

■ Assess for signs and symptoms of PE: tachypnea, chest pain, dyspnea, tachycardia, hemoptysis, cyanosis, anxiety, abnormal ABGs, and abnormal ventilation-perfusion scan result.

■ Assess for signs and symptoms of fat embolism: pulmonary (dyspnea, tachypnea, cyanosis); cerebral (headache, irritability, delirium, coma); cardiac (tachycardia, decreased blood pressure, petechial hemorrhage of upper chest, axillae, and conjunctivae); fat globules in urine.

■ Observe for a normal inflammatory process at surgical site.

Rationale

Redness, swelling, and tenderness in the calf region may be indicative of a DVT. Further studies are indicated.

A Doppler ultrasound may be performed to diagnose a DVT.

Onset of symptoms can be sudden and overwhelming and can constitute an immediate threat to the life of the patient.

Fat embolism is usually seen the second day after surgery. Symptoms may be sudden and precipitous and represent an immediate threat to the patient's life.

Expect signs of inflammation to decrease within 2 to 3 days after surgery.

Therapeutic Interventions

Actions/Interventions

▲ Notify the physician immediately if signs of compartment syndrome are noted.

■ Encourage leg exercises, including quad sets, gluteal sets, and active ankle ROM.

■ Encourage incentive spirometry every hour while the patient is awake.

▲ Institute antiembolic devices as prescribed (sequential compression device or TED hose).

▲ Administer thrombolytic and anticoagulant agents as ordered.

■ Encourage the patient to be out of bed as soon as prescribed.

Rationale

Venous pressures in the interstitial area surrounding an operative site can be measured through a small catheter inserted into the compartment. A surgical fasciotomy can be performed, which would release constriction and increase arterial inflow, restoring adequate circulation. The best indicators of developing compartment syndrome are patient complaint of excessive pain, peripheral pulses becoming weaker or absent, and an increase in pain on passive movement of the distal part to the surgery.

Venous stasis may predispose the patient to circulatory compromise.

Deep breathing exercises increase lung expansion and prevent atelectasis, hypoxemia, and pneumonia.

Antiembolic devices increase venous blood flow to the heart and decrease venous stasis, thereby decreasing the risk of DVT and PE.

Thrombolytics dissolve blood clots rapidly, thus preventing complications related to DVT and PE. Prophylactic anticoagulants reduce the risk of thrombophlebitis or thromboembolism. The patient must be monitored closely because these medications may cause bleeding.

Mobility restores normal circulatory function and decrease the risk of venous stasis.

■ = Independent; ▲ = Collaborative

Nursing Diagnosis

Deficient Knowledge

Common Related Factors

New condition
Unfamiliarity with discharge and rehabilitation plan

Defining Characteristics

Lack of or multitude of questions
Expressed confusion about arthroplasty precautions
Inability to follow mobility instructions

Common Expected Outcome

Patient expresses understanding of discharge instructions and follow-up rehabilitation regimen.

NOC Outcomes
Knowledge: Disease Process;
 Knowledge: Treatment Regimen;
 Knowledge: Prescribed Activity

NIC Interventions
Teaching: Disease Process; Teaching:
 Prescribed Activity/Exercise

(side tab) Arthroplasty/Replacement: Total Hip, Knee, Shoulder

Ongoing Assessment

Actions/Interventions

- Assess understanding of discharge instructions and follow-up regimen.
- Assess home and support systems.

Rationale

An individualized teaching plan is based on the patient's understanding of the treatment plan.

These assessments ensure that the environment is safe and supportive to the recovering patient.

Therapeutic Interventions

Actions/Interventions

- Review total hip arthroplasty precautions:
  - Maintain abduction with abductor device when at rest.
  - Always keep legs externally or neutrally rotated.
  - Avoid hip flexion of greater than 90 degrees.
  - Avoid bending from waist.
  - Lie flat in bed at least 1 to 2 hours per day.
  - Do not cross legs.
  - Ambulate (weight bearing as instructed) with assistive device (walker or crutches).
  - Call the physician immediately if sharp pain or "popping" is felt in the affected extremity or if there is a feeling of the hip being "out of socket."
  - Instruct the patient not to drive for 6 weeks until directed by physician.

Rationale

The patient needs to understand how to prevent hip dislocation. Extremes of joint flexion and adduction during the healing process increase the risk of dislocation.

Bending causes hip flexion of greater than 90 degrees.

This prevents hip flexion contracture.

This causes adduction, which can lead to dislocation.

Protected ambulation promotes healing of the affected hip.

Dislocation of the prosthesis requires immediate attention and possible surgical intervention.

Muscle contraction and joint movement associated with operating the accelerator and brake pedals puts stress on the healing prosthetic joint.

■ = Independent; ▲ = Collaborative

Arthroplasty/Replacement: Total Hip, Knee, Shoulder—cont'd

Actions/Interventions	Rationale
■ Review knee arthroplasty precautions:	
• Use walker or crutches to ambulate with prescribed weight bearing on the operative knee.	Assistive devices reduce stress on the affected joint during the healing process.
• Maintain proper body weight.	Weight gain increases stress on the prosthesis.
• Do not participate in sports until the physician indicates that it is permissible.	The patient needs to limit activities that put stress on the affected joint during healing.
• Notify the physician of knee pain that returns to a previous level of discomfort, excessive swelling, leaking of fluid from incision, chest pain, shortness of breath, or pain and swelling in the calf of either leg.	These symptoms indicate complications of joint replacement and require immediate attention.
■ Review shoulder arthroplasty precautions:	Gradual increase in ROM and weight bearing as necessary allows healing of the affected joint and prevents dislocation of the prosthesis.
• Initially, perform only passive ROM exercises, gradually adding active exercises as instructed.	
• Avoid using affected arm for heavy lifting (greater than 5 pounds), pulling, or pushing. Follow weight-bearing precautions as instructed.	
• Avoid activities that involve exaggerated external rotation and abduction of the affected shoulder.	
■ Reinforce the need to continue prescribed ROM exercises. May require home physical therapy.	Physical therapy at home helps the patient gain strength in muscle groups to support the integrity of the prosthetic joint.
■ Emphasize importance of removing environmental hazards (e.g., throw rugs, low tables, pets, electrical cords, toys).	The patient needs to understand how to maintain a safe home environment to promote progressive ambulation and prevent falls.

Arthroscopy

Arthroscopy is the direct visualization of a joint interior using a rigid fiberoptic endoscope. The procedure can be done for diagnostic evaluation and/or surgical repair of a joint. Arthroscopy is used when joint problems cannot be identified by noninvasive techniques such as x-ray examination. The procedure has wide application in the diagnosis and management of joint problems associated with sports injuries, degenerative disorders, and acute or chronic inflammatory disorders. Most arthroscopic procedures are done to evaluate and correct injuries to the knee. Problems related to the meniscus, cartilage, and ligaments of the knee can be repaired with arthroscopy. There is increasing use of the technique with other joints in the body such as for rotator cuff injuries of the shoulder. Joint arthroscopy may be used in patients with rheumatoid arthritis to remove joint debris and thereby reduce joint pain. Advantages of this procedure for the patient include decreased surgical risks and fewer complications because it can be done using smaller incisions and usually with local or regional anesthesia. Complications of arthroscopy are not common but include infection, neurovascular damage, hemarthrosis (bleeding into the joint), and joint injury. The majority of arthroscopic procedures are done on an outpatient basis.

■ = Independent; ▲ = Collaborative

Nursing Diagnosis

Deficient Knowledge

Common Related Factor	**Defining Characteristics**
Unfamiliarity with procedure	Multiple questions about procedure and follow-up care Verbalized lack of knowledge about procedure

Common Expected Outcome

Patient verbalizes understanding of the procedure and postprocedure home care.

NOC Outcome
Knowledge: Treatment Procedure

NIC Interventions
Teaching: Preoperative;
    Teaching: Procedure/Treatment

Ongoing Assessment

Actions/Interventions

■ Assess the patient's understanding of arthroscopy.

■ Assess the patient's level of knowledge about home care after the procedure.

■ Determine the patient's readiness to learn and learning preferences.

Rationale

Patients will be able to cooperate during the procedure if they understand what is going to occur. Patients' anxiety level may be decreased if they know what to expect.

Patients will be responsible for monitoring their status after the procedure and implementing care to prevent complications.

Patient teaching will be more effective when it is individualized to the learning needs and preferences of the patient.

Therapeutic Interventions

Actions/Interventions

■ Introduce or reinforce information about the arthroscopic procedure.
  • The patient may need to be NPO (nothing by mouth) for at least 8 hours before the procedure.

  • The hair around the joint will be shaved before the procedure.

Rationale

Restriction of food and fluids before the procedure will depend on the type of anesthesia. For patients receiving general anesthesia, fasting from solid foods before the procedure reduces the risk of vomiting and respiratory aspiration. Some patients may be allowed clear liquids up to 2 hours before the procedure to maintain hydration. Patients may be able to take certain prescription medications with small sips of water before the procedure.

Hair is usually removed in an area 6 inches above and below the affected joint.

Arthroscopy

■ = Independent; ▲ = Collaborative

→ Arthroscopy—cont'd

Actions/Interventions

- An intravenous infusion will be started to facilitate administration of sedatives and other medications for anesthesia during the procedure.

- The procedure will be started after an appropriate level of anesthesia has been achieved.

- The patient may experience transient sensations of joint pressure during the procedure when local or regional anesthesia is used.

- A tourniquet or compression bandage may be applied to the affected extremity.

■ Introduce or reinforce information concerning home care after the procedure.
  - Pain management
  - Use of joint immobilizers
  - Activity and weight bearing
  - Care of incisions
  - Signs and symptoms to report to the physician

Rationale

The surgeon and anesthesia care provider will determine the type of anesthesia required for the procedure. The choice of local or general anesthesia will be based on the extent of the procedure.

Patients need to be assured that they will not feel pain during the procedure, if they are to be awake and a local or regional anesthesia is used.

Informing patients about sensory experiences during the procedure may reduce their anxiety.

These measures are used to control bleeding during the procedure.

Discharge teaching done before the procedure may need to be repeated at the time of discharge. Written instructions given to the patient and family members will reinforce verbal instructions and allow them to review the material as needed.

NDx Nursing Diagnosis

Acute Pain

Common Related Factors

Bone and soft tissue trauma caused by the procedure
Swelling of affected joint

Defining Characteristics

Verbal report of pain
Irritability
Restlessness
Protective behavior of joint
Positioning of joint to avoid pain

Common Expected Outcome

Patient verbalizes a satisfactory level of comfort and pain control.

NOC Outcomes
Pain Control; Pain Level

NIC Interventions
Analgesic Administration;
  Pain Management

Musculoskeletal Care Plans

Ongoing Assessment

Actions/Interventions

■ Assess the patient's description of pain.

Rationale

The first step in effective pain management is assessing the location, severity, and quantity of pain experienced by the patient. Postprocedure pain is usually restricted to the affected joint. The patient may describe the pain as acute, sharp, or throbbing. The pain should decrease in intensity during the first 5 to 7 days after the procedure. Pain levels that persist or increase after 5 days may be indications of infection or joint injury.

■ Assess the patient's expectations and goals for pain relief.

Pain management is not effective until the patient is satisfied with the level of comfort achieved.

Therapeutic Interventions

Actions/Interventions

■ Teach the patient about using analgesic medications.

Rationale

The patient will be responsible for pain management and needs information to support decision making. After arthroscopy, most patients require mild analgesics for effective pain relief.

• Take medications before the pain becomes severe.

If the patient waits until the pain is severe before taking analgesics, it takes longer to obtain effective relief.

• Take medications at regular intervals.

Regular dosing with analgesics achieves stable serum drug levels that provide effective pain management.

■ Apply ice packs to the affected joint.

Cold therapy produces vasoconstriction and reduces swelling. Release of pain-causing chemicals and conduction of pain impulses are decreased with cold therapy.

■ Maintain joint immobilizers applied after the procedure.

Immobilization of the joint after arthroscopy reduces unnecessary movement that causes pain and further joint injury.

Arthroscopy

NDx Nursing Diagnosis

Risk for Infection

Common Risk Factors

Invasive procedure
Lack of knowledge about infection prevention
Surgical incisions

Common Expected Outcome

Patient will be free of infection.

NOC Outcomes
Infection Status; Knowledge: Infection Control

NIC Interventions
Infection Control; Infection Protection

■ = Independent; ▲ = Collaborative

Arthroscopy—cont'd

Ongoing Assessment

Actions/Interventions

- Assess the patient's knowledge of signs and symptoms of infection.
- Assess the patient's ability to implement wound care procedures.

Rationale

The patient will assume responsibility for monitoring the affected joint for signs of infection.

The patient will need to provide wound care using techniques that reduce the chance of infection. After arthroscopy, wounds are closed with single sutures or Steri-Strips. A sterile dressing may be applied and the area wrapped with an elastic bandage.

Therapeutic Interventions

Actions/Interventions

- Teach the patient to report signs of infection.

- Teach the patient appropriate wound care.
  - Wash hands before touching the wounds.
  - Clean the wounds with mild soap and water. Dry thoroughly.
  - Apply antibiotic ointment as ordered and a clean dressing.

Rationale

The patient should be alert for fever; joint swelling, redness, warmth, and swelling at the incision site; and increased joint pain. These signs should be reported to the physician as soon as possible.

If Steri-Strips are used for wound closure, the patient may be instructed to leave them in place until they fall off on their own. Adhesive bandages may be used to cover wounds and prevent irritation from joint immobilizers. Skin sutures are usually removed in 7 days.

NDx Nursing Diagnosis

Impaired Physical Mobility

Common Related Factors

Prescribed activity restrictions for joint movement and weight bearing
Pain

Defining Characteristics

Limited ROM of affected joint
Reluctance to move
Presence of joint immobilizer

Common Expected Outcomes

Patient maintains mobility level within limits of prescribed restrictions.
Patient uses assistive devices for mobility utilizing proper technique.

NOC Outcomes
Mobility Level; Coordinated Movement:
Knowledge: Prescribed Activity

NIC Interventions
Teaching: Prescribed Activity/Exercise;
Exercise Therapy: Joint Mobility

■ = Independent; ▲ = Collaborative

Ongoing Assessment

Actions/Interventions

- Assess ROM in unaffected and affected joints.

- Assess muscle strength, coordination, and ability to use mobility aids. Refer to physical therapist.

Rationale

After arthroscopy, the affected joint may be immobilized with slings, splints, or commercially made immobilizers. The type of immobilizer used and the length of time the joint will be immobilized depend on the extent of the procedure.

The patient's overall strength and coordination will determine the type of mobility aids needed after arthroscopy. A physical therapist can provide expert evaluation of the patient's ability and make recommendations.

Therapeutic Interventions

Actions/Interventions

- Instruct the patient in proper application and use of the prescribed immobilizer.

- Teach the patient about activity and weight-bearing restrictions.

- Instruct the patient in use of mobility aids.

Rationale

The immobilizer maintains the joint in anatomical alignment and protects the joint from unnecessary movement during the healing process. Such movements can lead to increased pain and joint injury.

The degree of mobility restrictions depends on the extent of the procedure. Most patients with diagnostic arthroscopy can resume weight bearing. Activity and excessive use of the joint may be limited for several days after the procedure. The patient is often referred to a physical therapist for progressive ROM and joint-strengthening exercises.

Crutches, canes, or walkers may be provided to assist the patient with mobility until activity restrictions are no longer needed.

Fractures: Extremity, Pelvic (Stable/Unstable)

 # Fractures: Extremity, Pelvic (Stable/Unstable)

Closed Reduction; Open Reduction; Internal Fixation; External Fixation

A fracture is a break or disruption in the continuity of a bone. Fractures occur when a bone is subjected to more stress than it can absorb. Fractures are treated by one or a combination of the following: closed reduction—alignment of bone fragments by manual manipulation without surgery; open reduction—alignment of bone fragments by surgery; internal fixation—immobilization of fracture site during surgery with rods, pins, plates, screws, wires, or other hardware or immobilization through use of casts, splints, traction, or posterior molds; external fixation—immobilization of bone fragments with the use of rods and pins that extend from the incision externally and are fixed. This care plan covers the management of patients with fractures and cast immobilization, and contains occasional references to more complicated fractures.

■ = Independent; ▲ = Collaborative

Fractures: Extremity, Pelvic (Stable/Unstable)—cont'd

 Nursing Diagnosis

Acute Pain

Common Related Factors

Fracture
Soft tissue injury

Defining Characteristics

Complaints of pain or discomfort
Guarding behavior
Increased muscle spasm
Increased pulse rate
Increased blood pressure (BP)
Crying, moaning
Grimacing
Anxiety
Restlessness
Withdrawal
Irritability

Common Expected Outcomes

Patient verbalizes pain relief or an acceptable reduction in pain.
Patient appears comfortable.

NOC Outcomes
Pain Control; Medication Response

NIC Interventions
Pain Management;
    Analgesic Administration

Ongoing Assessment

Actions/Interventions	Rationale
■ Assess for pain or discomfort.	Immediately after the fracture, there may be a period of 15 to 20 minutes in which no pain is apparent. This period of transient anesthesia may be related to the immediate response of nerves that are damaged by the trauma of the fracture. Eventually, sensation is returned and the traumatized area becomes painful enough for the patient to guard the affected area.
■ Assess the patient's description of pain.	Intense pain that persists or pain that returns to previous levels of intensity may indicate a developing complication such as infection or compartment syndrome. Patients with pelvic fractures may have intense pain from secondary injuries associated with the fracture. These injuries include trauma to pelvic blood vessels, the intestines, or the urinary bladder.

■ = Independent; ▲ = Collaborative

Actions/Interventions

- Assess mental and physical ability to use patient-controlled analgesia (PCA) versus intramuscular or oral analgesics.

- Assess effectiveness of pain-relieving interventions.

Rationale

Successful use of PCA requires the patient to have knowledge of its use and the manual dexterity to operate it.

Patients have a right to effective pain relief. Pain relief is not determined to be effective until the patient indicates that it is acceptable.

Therapeutic Interventions

Actions/Interventions

- Explain analgesic therapy, including medication and schedule; instruct the patient to take pain medications as needed.

- If the patient is a candidate for PCA (inpatients only), explain its concept and use.

- ▲ Administer narcotic analgesics every 3 to 4 hours around the clock for the first 24 hours after surgical reduction or pin placement.

- Instruct the patient to request pain medication before the pain becomes severe.

- Encourage use of analgesics 30 to 45 minutes before physical therapy.

- Encourage the patient to change position every 2 hours or more often for comfort.

- Maintain immobilization and support of affected part.

- Reposition and support the unaffected parts as permitted.

- Elevate the affected extremity.

- Apply cold for 20 to 30 minutes every 1 to 2 hours.

- Teach relaxation techniques.

- ▲ Administer muscle relaxants as necessary.

Rationale

Discomfort will be directly related to the type of fracture and the amount of soft tissue damage. Patients with simple fractures may only experience mild discomfort after the fracture has been immobilized, and pain may be effectively managed with ibuprofen or aspirin. Pain related to more serious fractures with complicated types of tissue damage and need for surgical reduction requires stronger medication. Care providers often assume that the patient will request pain medication when needed. The patient may think it is his or her duty or responsibility to tolerate pain until it can no longer be tolerated and may be waiting for the nurse to offer pain medication when it is available.

PCA refers to a method that allows the patient to control pain by using an intravenous drug delivery system. This method allows the patient to self-administer a prescribed narcotic analgesic in controlled doses at a frequency necessary to effectively manage the pain.

Manipulation, nerve trauma, and tissue damage result from the fracture and the surgical procedure. Assume that the patient requires analgesia. The patient's ability to fall asleep between checks is not a good indicator of the patient's level of comfort.

If pain is too severe before analgesics or therapy is instituted, relief takes longer.

Unrelieved pain hinders rehabilitative progress.

Repositioning reduces pressure and pain on bony prominences.

Immobility prevents further tissue damage and muscle spasm.

These techniques promote general comfort and maintain good body alignment.

Elevation decreases vasocongestion and edema.

Cold therapy decreases swelling (first 24 to 48 hours).

Complementary therapies can enhance the effects of analgesic agents.

These medications prevent muscle spasms, which may be painful.

Fractures: Extremity, Pelvic (Stable/Unstable)

Fractures: Extremity, Pelvic (Stable/Unstable)—cont'd

NDx Nursing Diagnosis

Impaired Physical Mobility

Common Related Factors

Cast
Fixation device
Immobilizer device
Pain
Surgical procedure

Defining Characteristics

Reluctance to attempt movement
Limited range of motion (ROM)
Mechanical restriction of movement
Decreased muscle strength and/or control
Impaired coordination
Inability to move purposefully within physical environment (bed, mobility, transfer, ambulation)

Common Expected Outcome

Patient maintains maximum mobility within prescribed restrictions.

NOC Outcomes
Ambulation; Mobility; Balance; Bone Healing

NIC Interventions
Exercise Therapy: Joint Mobility; Exercise: Ambulation

Ongoing Assessment

Actions/Interventions

- Assess ROM of unaffected parts proximal and distal to the immobilization device.

- Determine the type of mobility supports the patient will require in anticipation of discharge.

- Assess muscle strength in all extremities.

Rationale

Optimal ROM is critical for movement and necessary for rehabilitation.

Patients may require a cane, walker, or crutches to enhance ambulation.

The rehabilitation program will be geared toward maximizing strength in the unaffected extremities and maintaining as much strength as possible in the affected or immobilized extremity.

Therapeutic Interventions

Actions/Interventions

- Encourage isometric, active, and resistive ROM exercises to all unaffected joints on a schedule consistent with the rehabilitation program and as tolerated.

- Perform flexion and extension exercises to proximal and distal joints of the affected extremity, when indicated.

- ▲ Apply splint to support foot in neutral position (applied to lower extremity frames and traction).

Rationale

Exercise prevents muscle atrophy and maintains adequate muscle strength required for mobility.

These exercises serve to maintain mobility.

A splint prevents footdrop in patients immobilized in traction and in external fixation devices.

■ = Independent; ▲ = Collaborative

Actions/Interventions

- Assist the patient up to chair when ordered; teach transfer technique. Lift extremity by external fixation frame if stable; avoid handling of injured soft tissue.
- Reinforce crutch ambulation taught by physical therapist, using appropriate weight-bearing techniques as prescribed.
- Assist with gait belt until gait is stable.

▲ Obtain occupational therapy consultation as indicated.

Rationale

Early mobility reduces the complication of immobility. Learning the correct way to transfer is important to maintain optimal mobility and patient safety.

Some patients will have limited or no weight bearing on the affected extremity to allow the fracture adequate time to begin healing.

The belt enhances the patient's balance and sense of security.

Referral may be indicated to evaluate the patient's need for skill retraining.

NDx Nursing Diagnosis

Risk for Ineffective Tissue Perfusion

Common Risk Factors

Fracture
Manipulation
Inflammatory process and edema
Mobilization of a fat embolism
Immobility

Common Expected Outcome

Patient maintains adequate tissue perfusion, as evidenced by warm extremities, good color, good capillary refill, absence of pain and numbness, and bilaterally equal pulses.

NOC Outcomes
Tissue Perfusion: Peripheral; Risk Control; Risk Detection

NIC Interventions
Circulatory Care; Circulatory Precautions

Fractures: Extremity, Pelvic (Stable/Unstable)

Ongoing Assessment

Actions/Interventions

- Assess and compare neurovascular status of all extremities before and after the application of the cast.
- Assess the affected extremity every 1 to 2 hours as ordered using the 8-point check for signs of neurovascular compromise and damage:
  - Temperature of affected tissue

  - Capillary refill of nail beds

  - Color of injury or surgical site and surrounding tissues

Rationale

Assessment must include unaffected and affected extremity to establish baseline and monitor for change in neurovascular status.

Injured tissues are usually cooler than on the nonaffected side. Normal temperature indicates adequate perfusion.

Normal refill is 2 to 4 seconds. In the first hours after injury, capillary refill may be sluggish, but refill that exceeds 4 to 6 seconds should be reported to the physician.

Color should be pink, not pale or white. The affected area may be paler than the unaffected area.

■ = Independent; ▲ = Collaborative

Fractures: Extremity, Pelvic (Stable/Unstable)—cont'd

Musculoskeletal Care Plans

Actions/Interventions

- Edema

- Sensory function

- ROM

- Pain

- Evaluation of tissues, comparing affected and unaffected tissues
- ■ Observe normal inflammatory process at surgical site if an open reduction of the fracture was performed or pins were inserted.
- ▲ Administer anticoagulants as ordered

- ▲ Apply antiembolic hose or sequential compression devices as indicated.
- ▲ Monitor results of lung scans, chest films, and films of extremity fracture.

- ■ Assess for symptoms of fat embolism.

- ■ Assess vital signs, auscultate lung sounds, and monitor blood gases.

Rationale

Swelling at the injured site may be apparent, but severe swelling may indicate venous stasis. All peripheral pulses will be felt; however, the posterior tibialis and the dorsalis pedis in the lower extremities and the radial and ulnar pulses in the upper extremities may be weaker than in the unaffected area.

Complaints of numbness, tingling, or "pins and needles" feeling may indicate pressure on nerves and should be investigated.

This indicates the amount and degree of limitation. Injured tissues will have decreased ROM. Opposite side should have normal ROM.

This indicates injury, trauma, or pressure. The surgical site will normally be painful. Monitor and report excessive complaints of pain as a possible harbinger of compartment syndrome.

This allows comparison and perception of the patient's own "normal" preinjury status.

Expect signs of inflammation to decrease within 2 to 3 days of surgery.

These may be given prophylactically to reduce threat of deep vein thrombosis.

These decrease venous pooling and may enhance venous return, thereby reducing the risk of thrombus formation.

These tests may be used to identify a nonhealing fracture or respiratory complications, such as a pulmonary embolus or a fat embolus.

The patient may experience a sense of impending doom; chest pain; and signs and symptoms of shock, including tachypnea, tachycardia, hypoxia confusion, or disorientation. The patient may manifest a rash over the chest from below the nipple line up to the neck (may also include the conjunctivae).

Thorough assessment is needed to determine the extent of oxygenation in the presence of fat embolism.

Therapeutic Interventions

Actions/Interventions

- ■ Notify the physician immediately if signs of altered circulation are noted.

Rationale

Venous pressures in the interstitial area surrounding an operative site can be measured through a small catheter inserted into the compartment. A surgical fasciotomy can be performed, which would release constriction and increase arterial inflow, restoring adequate circulation. The best indicators of developing compartment syndrome are patient complaints of excessive pain, peripheral pulses becoming weaker or

■ = Independent; ▲ = Collaborative

Actions/Interventions	Rationale
	absent, and an increase in pain on passive movement of the distal part.
▲ Split or bivalve cast as needed.	This may be done on an emergency basis to reduce restriction and improve impaired circulation resulting from compression and edema of the injured extremity.
■ Instruct the patient on the symptoms of fat embolism.	This complication occurs most often within 2 to 4 days after long bone or pelvic fractures. It may occur because fat molecules are mobilized into general circulation from the bone marrow during a fracture. Fat emboli represent a fatal risk to patients as much as 40% of the time and must be regarded as a potential life-threatening risk.
▲ Implement emergency measures in the presence of symptoms of pulmonary edema or fat embolism:	
• Monitor oxygen saturation and administer oxygen to keep saturation level greater than 92%.	Impaired gas exchange is a priority concern. Supplemental oxygen will improve gas exchange and promote effective breathing.
• Titrate intravenous fluids closely.	Fluid overload can lead to pulmonary edema.
• Administer antianxiety medications.	Anxiety can interfere with effective breathing.
• Place patient on ventilator.	Mechanical ventilation may be required to enhance oxygenation.
• Transfer patient to intensive care unit.	Significantly compromised or unstable patients require critical care management.

Fractures: Extremity, Pelvic (Stable/Unstable)

NDx Nursing Diagnosis

Deficient Knowledge

Common Related Factors

New procedures or treatment
New condition
Home care needs

Defining Characteristics

Verbalizes inadequate knowledge of care or use of immobilization device, mobility limitations, complications, and follow-up care
Expresses concerns about ability to manage independently at home
Confusion; asking multiple questions
Lack of questions
Inaccurate follow-through of instruction

Common Expected Outcome

Patient or caregiver verbalizes understanding of treatment, possible complications, and follow-up care.

NOC Outcomes

Knowledge: Treatment Regimen; Safety Behavior: Home Physical Environment

NIC Interventions

Cast Care: Maintenance; Teaching: Psychomotor Skill; Teaching: Prescribed Activity/Exercise

■ = Independent; ▲ = Collaborative

Fractures: Extremity, Pelvic (Stable/Unstable)—cont'd

Musculoskeletal Care Plans

Ongoing Assessment

Actions/Interventions

- Assess the patient's understanding of the factors that facilitate bone healing:
  - The bone ends and/or fragments must be brought into anatomical alignment.
  - Fracture site is immobilized.
  - Weight bearing is reduced or prohibited.
  - Joints above and below the injury may be immobilized to prevent movement that might dislodge bone ends.

- Assess current understanding of treatment, follow-up care, and readiness and ability to assume self-care and activities of daily living (ADLs).

- Determine whether hazards exist in the home that will compromise the patient's ability to be effectively mobile at home.

- Assess the availability of people on whom the patient may rely for support and assistance while mobility is impaired.

Rationale

Knowledge about fractures and the treatment procedures can help the patient be an active participant in making decisions about his or her care. The patient needs to understand that limited weight bearing on the affected extremity is a necessary component of the healing process for a fracture.

Effective discharge planning is based on a clear understanding of the needs of the patient and family members who will assume caregiver roles. Referral to a home care agency may be necessary to support a safe transition from hospital to home for the patient and family caregivers.

Stairs, areas rugs, and so on can limit the patient's progressive mobility and increase the risk for falls.

A social support network can help the patient cooperate with mobility restrictions during the healing process.

Therapeutic Interventions

Actions/Interventions

- Instruct patient/caregiver to:
  - Perform prescribed exercises several times a day.

  - Use appropriate assistive device (walker, crutches) and maintain prescribed weight-bearing status.
  - Identify and report to the physician signs of neurovascular compromise of the extremity: pain, numbness, tingling, burning, swelling, or discoloration.
  - Use pain-relief measures as ordered.

  - Obtain proper nutrition.

  - Keep all follow-up and physical therapy appointments.

- Instruct the patient in cast care:
  - To keep the cast clean and dry; tub bathe only if the cast is protected, not immersed
  - To inspect skin around cast edges for irritation

  - Not to put anything under the cast, poke under the cast, or put powder or lotion under the cast

Rationale

Regular exercise is necessary to maintain muscle tone and promote bone healing.

Assistive devices help the patient maintain mobility.

Early assessment reduces the risk of injury or complications.

Knowledge helps the patient make decisions about measures to achieve effective pain management.

This promotes bone and wound healing, and prevents constipation.

The rehabilitation program will be modified regularly as the fracture heals.

Moisture can break down the cast and limits the cast's ability to stabilize the fracture during healing.

Rough edges of the cast can lead to skin irritation and breakdown.

These actions may abrade skin and cause infection.

■ = Independent; ▲ = Collaborative

Actions/Interventions

- • To notify the physician if the cast cracks or breaks, of foul odor under the cast, of fresh drainage through the cast, if anything gets inside the cast, of areas of skin breakdown around the cast, of pain or burning inside the cast, or of warm areas on the cast

- ■ Instruct the patient with a surgical incision to observe for signs of infection and to notify the physician if they develop.

- ■ Instruct the patient with an external fixation device to perform pin care, perform wound care, and observe for loosening of pins.

- ■ Involve the patient or caregiver in procedures. Supervise those performing procedures and teach proper technique.

- ■ Provide the patient with medical supplies and assistive devices as needed.

Rationale

The cast may need to be removed and reapplied if infection or skin breakdown occurs.

Prompt treatment of infection is necessary to prevent osteomyelitis.

A strong knowledge base optimizes the patient's sense of independence and sense of mastery over the ability to perform self-care.

Ability to perform self-care procedures decreases risk of infection and optimizes therapeutic effect in the home care environment.

Efforts to enhance self-care abilities promote successful transition and accommodation to home environment.

NDx Nursing Diagnosis

Risk for Deficient Fluid Volume

Common Risk Factors

Blood vessel damage
Organ damage
Multiple fractures

Common Expected Outcome

Patient maintains adequate blood and fluid volume, as evidenced by normal heart rate; warm, dry skin; good capillary refill; and normal BP.

NOC Outcomes
Blood Coagulation; Fluid Balance

NIC Interventions
Bleeding Reduction; Hemorrhage Control

Ongoing Assessment

Actions/Interventions

- ■ Assess degree of pelvic fracture.

- ■ Assess amount of any blood loss.

Rationale

Because pelvic fractures are generally associated with high-energy forces, multiple injuries should be anticipated and systematically evaluated. Hemorrhage continues to be the primary cause of early mortality after an unstable pelvic fracture. The bladder (especially if it was full at the time of impact) may rupture. There may be tears in the gut, ureters, or urethra. Women who may have been pregnant at the time of impact may suffer perinatal loss with massive hemorrhage.

Hemoglobin and hematocrit values are the best indicators of blood loss.

Fractures: Extremity, Pelvic (Stable/Unstable)

■ = Independent; ▲ = Collaborative

Fractures: Extremity, Pelvic (Stable/Unstable)—cont'd

Musculoskeletal Care Plans

Actions/Interventions

■ Assess for signs of hypovolemia: weak, rapid pulse; decreased BP; rapid, shallow respiration; cold, clammy skin; sluggish capillary refill; cyanosis; decreased urinary output; change in level of consciousness.

Rationale

Early recognition of hypovolemia allows for prompt initiation of fluid replacement therapy.

Therapeutic Interventions

Actions/Interventions

■ Apply pressure to bleeding areas.

▲ Administer intravenous fluids and blood products or expanders, as prescribed.

Rationale

Direct pressure can be applied until surgical repair can be done to stabilize bleeding and repair tissue and organ damage.

These are required to replace lost circulating fluid volume.

NDx Nursing Diagnosis

Risk for Impaired Skin Integrity

Common Risk Factors

Physical immobility
Presence and contact with immobilization device

Common Expected Outcomes

Patient maintains intact skin.
Risk of further breakdown is reduced through ongoing assessment and early intervention.

NOC Outcome
Tissue Integrity: Skin and Mucous Membranes

NIC Interventions
Pressure Management; Pressure Ulcer Prevention

Ongoing Assessment

Actions/Interventions

■ Assess skin for color, texture, moisture, redness, or breakdown.

Rationale

Early recognition of areas of skin breakdown allows for prompt interventions to restore skin integrity.

Therapeutic Interventions

Actions/Interventions

■ Turn and position the patient every 2 hours if not contraindicated.

Rationale

Shifting body weight off bony prominences is necessary to prevent pressure areas from developing and to prevent tissue from breaking down.

■ = Independent; ▲ = Collaborative

Actions/Interventions

- Apply pressure-relief device to bed (e.g., flotation devices, air mattress, foam or eggcrate mattress), as appropriate.
- Maintain protective padding under immobilization device.
- Keep area as clean and dry as possible if patient is unable to control bowel or bladder function.
- Keep bed linens free of wrinkles and foreign matter.

- Lift patient as necessary. Do not allow friction of skin when placing or removing bedpan. Do not drag or pull patient to position.
- Apply overhead frame and trapeze. Keep heels of bed at all times. Apply heel and elbow protectors as needed.
- Maintain adequate nutritional status.

Rationale

Such devices assist in preventing the development of pressure areas.

This prevents device from rubbing on underlying tissues.

Moisture, urine, or fecal material contribute to skin breakdown.

This prevents pressure areas, which may progress to ulcerations.

Friction may traumatize tissues.

A trapeze enables the patient to move in bed more freely. Foot care is needed to prevent the development of pressure areas.

Ischemia and progressive tissue deterioration are more likely to appear in malnourished persons who are in negative nitrogen balance.

See also **Risk for Impaired Skin Integrity,** *p. 173.*

NDx Nursing Diagnosis

Risk for Impaired Urinary Elimination

Common Risk Factors

Urinary tract injuries (e.g., urethral tear secondary to high-velocity trauma)
Bladder rupture secondary to punctures from bony fragments
Immobility
Presence of catheter
Infection

Common Expected Outcome

Patient maintains adequate urine output (>30 mL/hr) without complications.

NOC Outcome
Urinary Elimination

NIC Interventions
Urinary Retention Care; Urinary Catheterization

Ongoing Assessment

Actions/Interventions

- Assess frequency, amount, and character of urine and for any signs of incontinence.

Rationale

Bladder trauma may occur with pelvic fractures and result in changes in urinary elimination.

■ = Independent; ▲ = Collaborative

Fractures: Extremity, Pelvic (Stable/Unstable)—cont'd

Actions/Interventions

- Observe for gross hematuria, pelvic hematoma, and edematous and ecchymotic scrotum.

- Record intake and output.

- Monitor for urine retention: decreased urine output, bladder distention, suprapubic pain.

- Assess for signs and symptoms of urinary tract infection: frequency, burning on urination, elevated temperature, and elevated white blood cell count.

Rationale

Blood-tinged urine may reflect trauma or damage of the urinary tract system. These symptoms may indicate damage to the structures indicated.

This enables the care provider to determine adequate fluid balance. Hourly output should not fall below 30 mL/hr. A Foley catheter may be required to assess output.

This may indicate edema or nerve damage secondary to the trauma. Pelvic injuries frequently cause internal injury to the urinary tract; intravenous pyelogram cystogram, and a kidney and ureter bladder examination may be required for diagnosis.

Urinary tract infection may be a complication of bladder trauma.

Therapeutic Interventions

Actions/Interventions

- Encourage fluids and juices.

- ▲ Insert Foley catheter or institute intermittent catheterization using aseptic technique, as prescribed.
- ▲ Administer antibiotics, as prescribed.

- Notify the physician immediately of any abnormalities in the urine or the process of voiding.

Rationale

If the urine is kept dilute, calcium particles are less likely to precipitate and stasis with resultant infection is less likely.

Catheterization prevents bladder distention and further trauma to bladder.

Antibiotics may be given to reduce the risk of urinary tract infection from bladder trauma.

Bladder trauma may not be immediately apparent after pelvic fracture.

NDx Nursing Diagnosis

Risk for Injury

Common Risk Factors

Improper positioning of immobilization device—sling, traction, external fixator
If cast is in place, loss of continuity of cast

Common Expected Outcomes

Patient maintains correct body position and alignment.
Patient maintains intact cast.

NOC Outcomes
Risk Control; Risk Detection; Bone Healing

NIC Interventions
Cast Care: Wet; Cast Care: Maintenance; Traction/Immobilization Care

■ = Independent; ▲ = Collaborative

Musculoskeletal Care Plans

Ongoing Assessment

Actions/Interventions

Rationale

■ Assess immobilization device periodically for weights, knots, and ropes.

For traction to be effective, the device must be properly applied. The patient's own movement or the movement of others within the patient's room may result in subtle changes in the apparatus, which can result in malalignment. This would result in patient discomfort and poor healing of the fracture.

■ Assess the patient's position in the immobilization apparatus.

The patient should be in an anatomically correct body alignment. If not, painful muscle spasms, muscle fatigue, and malalignment of the healing pelvic bones can occur.

■ Assess that bed linens are not interfering with the immobilization device.

Ropes and pulleys that become tangled in bed linen interrupt the pull or stretching forces that keep the body in alignment and that must be constant to be therapeutically effective.

■ Assess the cast for cracks; weakened, softened, or wet areas; indentations; or odors.

A weakened cast cannot adequately hold the patient's limbs in the positions necessary for correct healing. It may also indicate that there is bleeding or an infective process going on within the cast.

Therapeutic Interventions

Actions/Interventions

Rationale

Traction:

■ Maintain proper alignment of the pelvis and of the affected extremity.

Only in this position will it be possible for the fracture to be reduced (the edge of the fracture will be properly aligned and juxtaposed).

▲ Maintain continuous traction at all times.

The weight and the position of the patient's body to apply countertraction against the traction are essential and increase the overall effectiveness of the therapy.

■ Maintain mechanics of traction at all times.

Traction may be indirectly applied to the bones by exerting pull to the skin. This is called skin traction. Skeletal traction is applied directly to the affected bone through the placement of pins or wires. Pelvic fractures are usually reduced through the use of a pelvic sling when there is separation of the symphysis bone in a fracture of the innominate bones.

■ Maintain the foot of the bed in gatch position.

This position enhances circulation and relieves back strain while in a pelvic sling, if not contraindicated.

▲ Verify with the physician how much lifting and turning the patient is allowed.

Activity limitations are necessary to enhance healing and recovery.

Cast:

■ Leave the cast open to air until completely dry. Do not cover with blankets or sheets or balance on the edge of a hard surface.

Coverings may retain moisture and prevent the proper drying of the cast. Resting the cast on the edge of a hard surface will cause indentation.

■ Prevent indenting of the wet cast by moving and supporting it with the palms of your hands.

Indentations will contribute to skin irritation under the cast.

■ Reposition the patient in a cast every 2 hours.

Changing position allows for complete drying.

Fractures: Extremity, Pelvic (Stable/Unstable)

■ = Independent; ▲ = Collaborative

Fractures: Extremity, Pelvic (Stable/Unstable)—cont'd

Actions/Interventions

■ Instruct the patient not to insert anything into the cast (such as an object that might be used to scratch an itch).

■ Petal the edges of the cast.

Rationale

Objects may damage the underlying tissue and result in infection or may become trapped within the cast and cause constriction and nerve damage.

This procedure reduces or prevents tissue trauma to the skin underlying the edges of the cast.

NDx **Nursing Diagnosis**

Risk for Ineffective Coping

Common Risk Factors

Posttraumatic response
Restricted activity
Dependence
Self-care deficit

Common Expected Outcomes

Patient begins to verbalize positive expressions, feelings, and reactions about self and situation.
Patient identifies available resources and support.

NOC Outcomes
Coping; Decision Making; Social Support

NIC Interventions
Coping Enhancement; Support System Enhancement; Distraction

Ongoing Assessment

Actions/Interventions

■ Assess psychosocial status before hospitalization—lifestyle, physical capabilities, body image, attitudes.

■ Assess how the patient is responding to the need to be more dependent on others.

■ Assess for excessive and extreme dependency.

■ Assess for signs of behavior change and level of acceptance of injury and treatment.

Rationale

This will provide a baseline for understanding needs during hospitalization or period of prolonged activity limitations.

Responses are individual. Some patients adapt to this enforced dependency better than others.

This may indicate the development of a potentially debilitating response to injury and hospitalization.

Most patients will begin to accommodate to their recovery. Early identification of those who will require additional support will be helpful in overall recovery.

Therapeutic Interventions

Actions/Interventions

■ Provide time for listening to the patient's concerns.

Rationale

Consider that because the accidents that cause unstable pelvic fractures are major ones, signs of posttraumatic stress disorder may be exhibited.

■ = Independent; ▲ = Collaborative

Musculoskeletal Care Plans

Actions/Interventions	Rationale
■ Provide diversionary activities as allowed by the patient's condition.	No individual can remain bedfast for an extended period without some consideration being given to mental stimulation.
■ Explain procedures and treatment.	Preparatory information regarding treatments can alleviate anxiety and enhance a sense of autonomy.
■ Encourage the patient to plan and participate in care activities. Adapt care to the patient's routines and needs.	This increases the patient's sense of control over decisions that affect him or her.
■ Provide opportunities for independent activities.	Independence facilitates coping.
■ Arrange the patient's environment to promote independent use of materials needed for activities of daily living.	The patient and significant others must be allowed to participate actively in rehabilitation to promote positive self-esteem.
▲ Initiate social service and/or psychiatry referrals as needed.	Depression is a frequent consequence of long hospital stays and debilitating diseases.

See also **Ineffective Coping**, *p. 51.*

• RELATED CARE PLANS

Deficient diversional activity, p. 57
Disturbed body image, p. 21

 Osteoarthritis

Osteoarthritis (OA) is the most common kind of arthritis and generally is a disease of older adults. This disorder was formerly known as degenerative joint disease (DJD). In patients younger than 45 years of age, it most commonly affects men, whereas in patients older than 55 years of age, women are more frequently affected. After 75 years of age, it is found in some degree in almost all patients. OA is characterized by a progressive degeneration of the cartilage in a joint—usually a weight-bearing joint, but any joint can be affected. In younger adults, OA develops as a result of repeated stress and injury to weight-bearing joints. In this group of patients, OA is associated more often with work-related or sports-related joint stress. Cartilage becomes thin, rough, and uneven with areas that soften, eventually allowing bone ends to come closer together. Microfragments of the cartilage may float about freely within the joint space, and as a result inflammation occurs. True to the progressive nature of the disease, the cartilage continues to degenerate, and bone spurs called osteophytes develop at the joint margins and at the attachment sites of the tendons and ligaments. Over time they have an effect on the mobility and size of the joint. As joint cartilage becomes fissured, synovial fluid leaks out of the subchondral bone and cysts develop on the bone. Treatment is aimed at relieving pain, maintaining optimal joint function, and preventing progressive disability. This care plan focuses on the outpatient nursing management for this group of patients.

Osteoarthritis–cont'd

 Nursing Diagnosis

Acute Pain

Common Related Factors	**Defining Characteristics**
Joint degeneration	Reports of pain, spasm, tingling, numbness
Muscle spasm	Reports of a decreased ability to perform activities of
Physical activity	daily living because of discomfort
Bone deformities	Facial grimaces
	Crying
	Protective, guarded behavior
	Restlessness
	Withdrawal
	Irritability
	Refusal or inability to participate in ongoing exercise
	or rehabilitation program

Common Expected Outcomes

Patient verbalizes reduction in or relief of pain.
Patient verbalizes ability to cope with chronic pain.

NOC Outcomes
Pain Control; Medication Response

NIC Interventions
Medication Administration;
Analgesic Administration

Ongoing Assessment

Actions/Interventions

- Assess the patient's description of pain:
  - Pain is usually provoked by activity and relieved by rest; joint pain and aching may also be present when the patient is at rest.
  - Pain may manifest as an ache, progressing to sharp pain when the affected area is brought to full weight bearing or full range of motion (ROM).
  - Sharp, painful muscle spasms may be present.
  - Tingling or numbness may be present.

- Identify factors or activities that seem to precipitate acute episodes or aggravate a chronic condition.

- Assess previous experiences with pain and pain relief.

- Determine the patient's emotional reaction to chronic pain.

Rationale

The patient may manifest any or part of the defining characteristics, so focused assessment is important. The patient may report pain in fingers, hips, knees, lower lumbar spine, and cervical vertebrae.

Pain may be associated with specific movements, especially repetitive movements.

The patient may have a tried-and-true plan to implement when OA becomes exacerbated. Consideration should be given to implementing this plan, with modifications if necessary, when pain becomes acute.

The patient may find coping with a progressive, debilitating disease difficult.

■ = Independent; ▲ = Collaborative

Musculoskeletal Care Plans

Actions/Interventions

- Determine whether the patient is reporting all of the pain he or she is experiencing.

Rationale

Patients who have become accustomed to living with chronic pain may learn to tolerate basal levels of discomfort and only report those discomforts that exceed these "normal levels." The care provider is not getting an accurate picture of patient status if this pain is not reported. The nurse may need to be sensitive to nonverbal cues that pain is present (see Defining Characteristics on the previous page).

Therapeutic Interventions

Actions/Interventions

- Develop a pain-relief regimen based on the patient's identified aggravating and relieving factors. Instruct the patient to do the following:
  - Change positions frequently while maintaining functional alignment.
  - Support joints in slightly flexed position through the use of pillows, rolls, and towels
  - Apply hot or cold pack.

  - Provide for adequate rest periods.
  - Use adaptive equipment (e.g., cane, walker), as necessary.
  - Medicate for pain before activity and exercise therapy.

  - Eliminate additional stressors.

- Take prescribed analgesics and/or anti-inflammatory medication.
- Provide instruction in important side effects.
  A. Acetaminophen

  B. Salicylates: aspirin, salsalate, magnesium salicylate, choline salicylate, and combination salicylate

  C. Nonsteroidal antiinflammatory drugs (NSAIDs): phenylacetic acid, oxicam, indole, propionic acid, and pyrazolone derivatives

  D. Selective NSAIDs, COX-2 inhibitors (celecoxib)

Rationale

Muscle spasms may result from poor body alignment, resulting in increased discomfort.

Flexion of the joint may reduce muscle spasms and other discomforts.

Some patients prefer hot therapy over cold therapy to provide comfort.

Fatigue impairs ability to cope with discomfort.

These aids assist in ambulation and reduce joint stress.

Exercise is necessary to maintain joint mobility, but patients may be reluctant to participate in exercise if they are in too much pain.

Chronic pain takes an enormous emotional toll on its victims. Reducing other factors that cause stress may make it possible for the patient to have greater reserves of emotional energy for effective coping.

Simple analgesics such as acetaminophen should be used first. They relieve pain but have no effect on inflammation.

These drugs relieve pain in the mild to moderate range and have an antiinflammatory effect. Side effects include GI disturbances, risk for bleeding, and tinnitus.

These drugs are antiinflammatory, antipyretic, and analgesic agents. They are usually used for their antiinflammatory action to relieve mild to moderate pain. Side effects include mild GI disturbances and fluid retention.

This class of drugs acts by binding prostaglandin synthesis via inhibition of cyclooxygenase-2. These drugs are used with caution in people with a history of gastric ulcers, liver disease, stroke, or cardiovascular disease. Ongoing research is being conducted to evaluate the safety of these drugs for long-term use.

■ = Independent; ▲ = Collaborative

Osteoarthritis

→ **Osteoarthritis—cont'd**

Actions/Interventions

E. Corticosteroids: cortisone, hydrocortisone, prednisone, triamcinolone, methylprednisolone, dexamethasone, and betamethasone

F. Central-acting muscle relaxants: diazepam, baclofen, orphenadrine citrate, carisoprodol, chlorzoxazone, cyclobenzaprine, methocarbamol, and metaxalone

See also **Acute Pain**, *p. 144.*

Rationale

These drugs are antiinflammatory and usually used over a short period of time for the treatment of acute episodes of musculoskeletal pain disorders. In long-term therapy (exceeding 1 week), a vast array of symptoms may be seen, including sodium retention and edema, weight gain, glaucoma, psychosis, Cushing-like syndrome, and altered adrenal function.

These drugs may relax painful muscle spasms. These drugs may cause drowsiness and may exaggerate the CNS depressive effects of alcohol and other drugs.

ND× Nursing Diagnosis

Impaired Physical Mobility

Common Related Factors

Pain
Stiffness
Fatigue
Restricted joint movement
Muscle weakness

Defining Characteristics

Reluctance to move
Limited ROM
Decreased muscle strength
Decreased ability/refusal to transfer and ambulate or perform activities of daily living (ADLs)

Common Expected Outcome

Patient verbalizes and demonstrates ability to move purposefully.

NOC Outcomes
Ambulation; Knowledge: Prescribed Activity

NIC Interventions
Exercise Therapy: Joint Mobility; Exercise Therapy: Ambulation; Teaching: Prescribed Activity/Exercise

Ongoing Assessment

Actions/Interventions

■ Assess ROM in all joints. Assess the patient's range, comparing passive and active ROM in all joints.

■ Assess posture and gait.

Rationale

Pain on motion or joint deformity may cause progressive loss of range.

It is important to assess for indicators of decreased ability to ambulate and move purposefully: shorter steps, making gait appear unstable; uneven weight bearing; an observable limp; or a rounding of the back or hunching of the shoulders.

■ = Independent; ▲ = Collaborative

Actions/Interventions

■ Assess ability to perform ADLs. Determine what adaptive measures the patient has already taken to be able to perform self-care measures.

■ Assess the patient's comfort with and knowledge of how to use assistive devices.

■ Assess weight.

■ Assess the patient's vital signs after physical activity.

▲ Consult with the physician to determine whether joint degeneration has reached the point where surgical replacement is required.

Rationale

Spouse may assist in buttoning clothes or picking up dropped objects. The patient may have had assistive devices installed in the shower or near the toilet (e.g., handlebars, raised toilet seat). Knowing this gives the nurse a sense of the measures the patient has had to take to remain functional.

Some patients refuse to use assistive devices because they attract attention to their disability.

Excessive weight may be additionally stressing painful joints.

Elevations in heart rate, respiratory rate, and blood pressure may be a function of increased effort and discomfort during the performance of tasks.

Surgical replacement of the joint will resolve pain and most flexibility and movement issues.

Therapeutic Interventions

Actions/Interventions

■ Instruct the patient on how to perform isometric, and active and passive ROM exercises to all extremities.

■ Encourage the patient to increase activity as indicated.

▲ Consult physical therapy staff to prescribe an exercise program.

■ Encourage the patient to ambulate with assistive devices (e.g., crutches, walker, cane).

■ Encourage sitting in a chair with a raised seat and firm support.

■ Encourage the patient to rest between activities that are tiring. Suggest strategies for getting out of bed, rising from chairs, and picking up objects from the floor to conserve energy.

■ Stress the importance of the patient taking adequate time for activities.

■ Discuss environmental barriers to mobility.

■ Provide the patient with access to and support during weight-reduction programs.

Rationale

Muscular exertion through exercise promotes circulation and free joint mobility, strengthens muscle tone, develops coordination, and prevents nonfunctional contracture.

Home exercise can be effective in maintaining joint function and independence. A balance must exist between the patient performing enough exercise to keep joints mobile and not taxing the joint too much.

The physical therapist can evaluate the patient's need for an individualized program.

Using mobility aids reduces the load on the joint and promotes safety.

This facilitates getting in and out of a chair.

Rest periods are necessary to conserve energy. The patient must learn to respect the limitations of his or her joints; pushing beyond the point of pain will only increase the stress on the joint.

The patient will need to recognize and accept the limitations of his or her joints. Rushing is likely to be frustrating and self-defeating, and may result in unsafe conditions for the patient.

It may no longer be reasonable for the patient to continue to live in a home or apartment with multiple flights of stairs or to continue to try to take care of a large home. If the patient is using a cane or walker, carpets must be tacked down or removed. Items that are used often should be kept within reach.

Weight reduction results in decreased trauma to bones, muscles, and joints.

Osteoarthritis

■ = Independent; ▲ = Collaborative

Osteoarthritis—cont'd

Actions/Interventions

- Suggest referral to community resources such as the Arthritis Foundation.

- Provide written information for the patient and family on living with osteoarthritis.

Rationale

Community resources can provide the patient with peer support and additional information about resources (e.g., assistive devices)

Accurate knowledge can assist them in understanding this disorder and its impact on their lives.

• RELATED CARE PLANS

Chronic pain, 149
Disturbed body image, p. 21
Self-care deficit, p. 156

Osteomyelitis

Bone Infection

Osteomyelitis is an infection of the bone that occurs as a result of direct or indirect invasion of an infective agent. Direct entry of the infective agent occurs after fracture or surgical intervention. Indirect entry (also called hematogenous) occurs as a result of a blood-borne infection with seeding of the infective organism, usually in the metaphyseal of the bone. The most common site for the infection is in the long bones of the leg, although any bone can be affected. Older adults who are at greatest risk for developing osteomyelitis via the indirect route commonly have a debilitating disease such as diabetes, sickle cell disease, peripheral vascular disease, or trauma to the specific bone. The most common infective agent is *Staphylococcus aureus*, which accounts for more than 90% of osteomyelitis infections; other organisms identified include *Neisseria gonorrhoeae, Escherichia coli, Clostridium perfringens,* and *Pseudomonas aeruginosa.* Osteomyelitis may be acute (<1 month's duration) or chronic (>1 month's duration or unresponsive to one course of adequate antibiotic treatment). Traditionally, patients with osteomyelitis are treated in the hospital over extended periods. The bone infection is stabilized with intravenous (IV) antibiotics. Surgical debridement may be performed to infective areas on the bone. The patient is discharged home on IV antibiotics. Today, with the overall length of inpatient stays down, the length of hospitalization for the patient with osteomyelitis is also reduced. Patients are often discharged with IV access devices that allow them to continue aggressive antibiotic therapy at home, and home care nurses monitor patients' progress and coordinate the activities of other agencies including social services and physical therapy. Complications of this disease include pathological fracture and the development of a systemic infection, which can be fatal. Infections can become chronic if treatment is unresponsive or not effective.

Nursing Diagnosis

Infection

Common Related Factors

Infection of a bone resulting from an infective organism that enters through an open wound

Infection that has migrated to bone tissue from another source

Defining Characteristics

Local inflammation over the site of the involved bone characterized by edema, tenderness, redness, and warmth with or without a palpable mass over the site

Wound drainage

Common Expected Outcome

Patient responds to antibiotic therapy, as evidenced by normal white blood cell (WBC) count and negative wound culture findings.

NOC Outcomes

Medication Response; Knowledge: Infection Control; Wound Healing: Primary Intention; Wound Healing: Secondary Intention

NIC Interventions

Infection Precautions; Wound Care; Medication Administration: Parenteral

Ongoing Assessment

Actions/Interventions

■ Assess affected area for signs and symptoms of infection.

▲ Assess laboratory values, especially WBC count and erythrocyte sedimentation rate (ESR).

▲ Assess x-ray and bone scan findings.

▲ Obtain appropriate culture and sensitivity specimens.

Rationale

Symptoms of inflammation as listed above in Defining Characteristics may be noted. Other symptoms might include malaise, chills, fever, diaphoresis, headache, and nausea.

WBC values will be extremely elevated; they may exceed 30,000. The sedimentation rate also will be elevated. The degree of elevation of the erythrocyte sedimentation rate relates to the extent of the infection.

Early x-rays may be negative for as long as 2 weeks. Later, bone in the infected area will show destruction and decalcification. Later still, the bone will appear moth-eaten, and the dead bone may be surrounded by an area of sequestration where the infection has been sealed off and is impervious to the effects of antibiotics. Eventually new areas of infection will be apparent proximal to the original infection. Computed tomography (CT) scans may be more useful in the early days of the infection, because they can reflect more subtle changes. CT scans can also reveal the spread of the infection to soft tissues.

Aspirate from the affected bone will reflect the causative organism. Blood cultures will rule out bacteremia or septicemia. Blood cultures may reveal infecting organisms when the infection has become systemic.

■ = Independent; ▲ = Collaborative

Osteomyelitis

Osteomyelitis—cont'd

Therapeutic Interventions

Actions/Interventions	Rationale
▲ Administer IV antibiotics as ordered.	Aggressive antibiotic treatment is the primary therapy. Type and dosage of the medications ordered are specific for the patient with consideration of the patient's age and weight and the identified organism.
▲ Administer antipyretics and provide fluids.	These prevent dehydration while the patient is in a febrile state. Temperatures may reach as high as 40° C (104° F).
■ Use specialized cooling blankets or mattresses.	These devices are used to reduce fever.
■ Ensure sterile technique during dressing changes.	Proper technique prevents cross-contamination and the introduction of additional organisms into the wound.
■ Provide nutritional supplementation, increased levels of protein, and vitamins A, B, and C.	Adequate nutrition enhances cellular healing.
▲ For patients with chronic osteomyelitis, prepare for surgical debridement.	Surgery may be necessary to remove infected tissue and bone. Anticipate constant wound irrigation with antibiotics. Sepsis and unsuccessful antibiotic therapy are major complications.

NDx Nursing Diagnosis

Impaired Physical Mobility

Common Related Factors

Surgical procedure
Discomfort

Defining Characteristic

Limited ability to ambulate or move in bed

Common Expected Outcomes

Patient maintains optimal mobility within limitations (sitting, transferring, ambulation).
Patient maintains strength in unaffected joints.
Patient adheres to prescribed mobility restrictions and guidelines.
Patient participates in an ongoing program of rehabilitation and physical therapy.

NOC Outcomes
Coordinated Movement; Body Positioning: Self-Initiated; Bone Healing

NIC Interventions
Positioning; Exercise Therapy: Joint Mobility

Ongoing Assessment

Actions/Interventions	Rationale
■ Assess the patient's overall muscle strength and ability to perform range of motion (ROM) and movement of all joints.	The patient may not be able to perform full-range movements in the affected extremity. It is critical that optimal movement and muscle strength and flexibility

■ = Independent; ▲ = Collaborative

Actions/Interventions

Rationale

be maintained in all muscle groups on the unaffected extremity to support body movement, maintain as much independence as possible, and promote eventual rehabilitation.

■ Assess the patient's weight-bearing capacity on the affected extremity.

Some patients may be maintained in external fixation devices and have little or no weight-bearing capacity on the affected side until the bone has healed sufficiently so that a pathological fracture is no longer a threat.

■ Assess the patient's previous level of physical activity.

This may be the therapeutic set-point for functional return after rehabilitation has been completed.

■ Assess the degree to which pain influences the patient's ability to move, change positions, and perform activities of daily living.

Patients may experience intense pain on movement of the affected extremity. Splints and slings are sometimes helpful in maintaining functional alignment of the affected body part. Splinting may also decrease the amount of movement allowed in the affected joint or extremity, thus decreasing the amount of pain the patient experiences.

▲ Assess for signs and symptoms of deep vein thrombosis (DVT):
  • Positive Homans' sign

DVT is a serious complication of long-term bed rest.

The examiner dorsiflexes the patient's foot toward the tibia, and the patient experiences pain in the calf muscles.

  • Swelling, tenderness, redness in calf; palpable cords

These may be indicative of a DVT and require further studies.

  • Abnormal blood flow study findings (if prescribed)

A Doppler ultrasound may be performed to diagnose a DVT.

Therapeutic Interventions

Actions/Interventions

Rationale

▲ Maintain traction and support devices as ordered (cast, splint, fixator).

Immobilization and external support devices decrease pain and assist in the healing of fractures by protecting the infected bone from excessive stress.

■ Provide gentle passive and active ROM exercises to the affected extremity within prescribed therapeutic limits and limits of the patient's tolerance.

These exercises prevent loss of muscle tone and maintain flexibility.

■ Encourage active ROM in all unaffected extremities.

Active movement exercises increase muscle strength and tone.

■ Encourage the patient to sit at the side of the bed for several minutes before changing positions.

This procedure prevents orthostatic hypotension and provides opportunity to plan transfer and movement.

■ Reassure the patient regarding safety in transferring and ambulating.

The patient may be fearful of injuring the affected side. Allaying anxiety and fear will allow the patient to concentrate on correct techniques.

▲ Reinforce the physical therapist's instructions for exercises, ambulation technique, and the use of assistive devices.

Consistent instructions from interdisciplinary team members promote safe, secure rehabilitation environment.

■ Maintain weight-bearing status on the affected extremity, as prescribed.

Excessive weight bearing on the affected limb before sufficient new bone growth takes place may result in pathological fracture of the extremity.

Osteomyelitis

■ = Independent; ▲ = Collaborative

Osteomyelitis—cont'd

 Nursing Diagnosis

Risk for Ineffective Tissue Perfusion

Common Risk Factors

Immobility
Poor circulation in the affected extremity
Infection
Surgical procedure

Common Expected Outcomes

Patient maintains adequate tissue perfusion, as evidenced by warm extremities, good color, good capillary refill, absence of pain and numbness, and bilaterally equal pulses.
Patient is free of signs and symptoms of DVT, pulmonary embolus (PE), and fat embolism, as evidenced by negative Homans' sign, normal respiratory status, stable vital signs, and normal arterial blood gases (ABGs).

NOC Outcomes
Tissue Perfusion: Peripheral;
Tissue Perfusion: Pulmonary

NIC Interventions
Circulatory Care; Circulatory Precautions

Ongoing Assessment

Actions/Interventions

■ Assess and compare neurovascular status of all extremities.

■ Assess affected extremity every 1 to 2 hours or as ordered using the 8-point check for signs of neurovascular compromise and damage:
  • Temperature of affected tissue

  • Capillary refill of nail beds

  • Color of surgical site and surrounding tissues

  • Edema

Rationale

Assessment must include both unaffected and affected extremities to establish baseline and monitor for change in neurovascular status.

Injured tissues are usually cooler than the noninjured or operative side. Normal temperature indicates adequate perfusion.

Normal refill is 2 to 4 seconds. In the first hours after surgery, capillary refill may be sluggish, but refill that exceeds 4 to 6 seconds should be reported to the physician.

Color should be pink, not pale or white. The area over the infection may appear red, inflamed, and swollen; a mass may be present over the affected bone; if there is an open wound, drainage may be apparent.

Swelling in the surgical or injury site may be apparent, but severe swelling may indicate venous stasis. All peripheral pulses will be felt; however, the posterior tibialis and the dorsalis pedis pulses for lower extremity

---

■ = Independent; ▲ = Collaborative

Actions/Interventions

- Sensory function

- ROM

- Pain

- Evaluation of tissues, comparing affected and unaffected tissues
- ■ Check sequential compression device or thromboembolic disease support (TED) stocking or external fixation devices for extreme tightness.
- ■ Assess for signs and symptoms of pulmonary embolus: tachypnea, chest pain, dyspnea, tachycardia, hemoptysis, cyanosis, anxiety, abnormal ABGs, and abnormal ventilation-perfusion scan.
- ■ Assess for signs and symptoms of fat embolism: pulmonary (dyspnea, tachypnea, cyanosis); cerebral (headache, irritability, delirium, coma); cardiac (tachycardia, decreased blood pressure, petechial hemorrhage of upper chest, axillae, and conjunctivae); fat globules in urine.
- ■ Observe for normal inflammatory process at the surgical or infection site.

Therapeutic Interventions

Actions/Interventions

- ■ Notify the physician immediately if signs of altered circulation are noted.

- ■ Encourage leg exercises, including quad sets, gluteal sets, and active ankle ROM.
- ■ Encourage the patient to be out of bed as soon as prescribed.
- ■ Encourage incentive spirometry every hour while the patient is awake.

Rationale

involvement or the radial and the ulnar pulses if an upper extremity is involved may be weaker than in the unaffected part.

Complaints of numbness, tingling, or "pins and needles" feeling may indicate pressure on nerves.

This indicates the immediate amount and degree of limitations. Injured tissues will have decreased ROM. The other extremities will have normal ROM.

This indicates injury, trauma, or pressure. The entire extremity will normally be painful, but stronger pain may be felt immediately over the affected bone. Monitor and report excessive complaints of pain as a possible harbinger of compartment syndrome.

This allows comparison and perception of the patient's own "normal" presurgical status.

Excessive compression may result in neurovascular compromise.

Onset of symptoms can be sudden and overwhelming and can constitute an immediate threat to the life of the patient.

Fat embolism is usually seen the second day after surgery. Symptoms may be sudden and precipitous and represent an immediate threat to the patient's life.

Expect signs of inflammation to decrease within 2 to 3 days after implementation of an IV antibiotic regimen.

Rationale

Venous pressures in the interstitial area surrounding the injury or surgical or infection site can be measured through a small catheter inserted into the compartment. A surgical fasciotomy can be performed, which would release constriction and increase arterial inflow, restoring adequate circulation. The best indicators of developing compartment syndrome are patient complaint of excessive pain, peripheral pulses becoming weaker or absent, and an increase in pain on passive movement of the distal part to the surgery.

Venous stasis may predispose the patient to circulatory compromise.

Mobility restores normal circulatory function and decreases the risk of venous stasis.

These exercises increase lung expansion and prevent atelectasis, hypoxemia, and pneumonia.

■ = Independent; ▲ = Collaborative

Osteomyelitis—cont'd

Actions/Interventions

▲ Institute antiembolic devices as prescribed (sequential compression device or TED hose).

▲ Administer thrombolytic agents as ordered.

Rationale

Antiembolic devices increase venous blood flow to the heart and decrease venous stasis, thereby decreasing the risk of DVT and PE.

These medications dissolve blood clots rapidly, thus preventing complications related to DVT and PE.

NDx Nursing Diagnosis

Acute Pain

Common Related Factors

Fractured limb
Skeletal pins (pain at insertion site)
Muscle spasms
Bone and soft tissue trauma caused by surgery or infection
Intense physical therapy or rehabilitation program
Restricted mobility

Defining Characteristics

Verbalized pain
Irritability
Restlessness
Crying, moaning
Facial grimaces
Altered vital signs; increased pulse, increased blood pressure, increased respirations
Withdrawal
Unwillingness to change position
Inability to sleep

Common Expected Outcomes

Patient expresses acceptable relief of or reduction in pain.
Patient appears comfortable.

NOC Outcomes
Pain Control; Medication Response; Self-Care: Parenteral Medication

NIC Interventions
Pain Management; Analgesic Management; Patient-Controlled Analgesia; Positioning; Splinting

Ongoing Assessment

Actions/Interventions

■ Assess the patient's description of pain.

Rationale

A careful analysis of the pain is essential to adequately treat it. Postoperative pain is usually localized to the surgical area. It will be acute and sharp. The pain should decrease in intensity over the 5 days after surgery. Intense pain that persists or pain that returns to previous levels of intensity may indicate a developing complication such as infection or compartment syndrome. Pain related to the infective process and the muscle spasms caused by osteomyelitis may be acute in the infective area until antibiotics sufficiently diminish the infective process.

■ = Independent; ▲ = Collaborative

Actions/Interventions

- Assess for correct positioning and alignment of affected extremity.
- Identify the types of activity or positions that increase pain.
- Assess the patient's past experience with pain and pain-relief measures.
- Assess the patient's mental and physical ability to use patient-controlled analgesia (PCA) versus intramuscular or oral analgesics.
- Assess effectiveness of present pain-relief measures.

Rationale

Incorrect positioning and malalignment can result in muscle spasms, which may be painful.

Measures may be taken to avoid precipitating factors.

Patients who have had experience with chronic pain may have high tolerances for first line analgesics.

Successful use of PCA requires the patient to have knowledge of its use and the manual dexterity to operate it.

Patients may know that their pain is effectively managed by a specific medication and dosage. This knowledge should be integrated into the nursing plan for pain management.

Therapeutic Interventions

Actions/Interventions

- Elevate and support the affected extremity.

- Explain analgesic therapy, including medication and schedule. If the patient is a candidate for PCA, explain its concept and routine.

- ▲ Administer narcotic analgesics and nonsteroidal anti-inflammatory drugs as ordered and carefully monitor their effectiveness. Monitor for adverse side effects.

- Instruct the patient to request pain medication before the pain becomes severe.
- Encourage use of analgesics 30 to 45 minutes before physical therapy.
- Change or assist the patient in changing position every 2 hours or more often for comfort.
- Eliminate additional stressors or sources of pain and discomfort by providing comfort measures: relaxation techniques, diversionary activity (e.g., books, games, television, sewing, radio), heat or cold application, position changes, and touch (e.g., backrubs).
- If indicated, explain that immobilization devices such as splints and external fixation devices may decrease muscle spasms and abrupt movement of the affected extremity, thereby helping to reduce pain.

Rationale

Elevation of the affected extremity promotes venous return to reduce inflammatory edema. Supportive positioning protects against muscle strain and spasm.

Care providers often assume that the patient will request pain medication when needed. The patient may think it is his or her duty or responsibility to tolerate pain until it can no longer be tolerated and may be waiting for the nurse to offer it when it is available.

There is a massive amount of manipulation, nerve trauma, and tissue damage as a result of the infective process. Assume that the patient requires analgesia. The patient's ability to fall asleep between checks is not a good indicator of the patient's level of comfort.

If pain is too severe before analgesics or therapy is instituted, relief takes longer.

Unrelieved pain hinders the patient's ability to participate in the rehabilitative progress.

The patient's inability to move freely and independently may result in pressure and pain on bony prominences.

Directing attention away from pain or to other body areas decreases perception of pain.

Information about the purpose of immobilization devices can reduce the patient's anxiety, which may aggravate pain.

> **• RELATED CARE PLANS**
>
> Deficient diversional activity, p. 57
> Ineffective coping, p. 51
> Self-care deficit, p. 156

Osteomyelitis

■ = Independent; ▲ = Collaborative

Osteoporosis

Brittle Bone

Osteoporosis is a metabolic bone disease characterized by a decrease in bone mass, resulting in porosity and brittleness. Ultimately, bone resorption is more efficient than the process of bone deposition. Primary causes are a decrease in dietary intake of calcium or a decrease in calcium absorption and estrogen deficiency. Secondary causes may include steroid use, tobacco and alcohol use, and endocrine and liver diseases. Osteoporosis occurs most commonly in women who are menopausal, although it may also be present in women who exercise to such an extent that menstruation and resultant estrogen production are suppressed. Men and African-American women have denser bones than white women. These factors together with a decrease in physical activity and weight-bearing activities result in bones that are brittle and fragile. Even normal physical activity can result in fracture. Common fractures include compression fractures of the vertebrae and fractures of the femur, hip, and forearm. Estrogen has been demonstrated to have a protective effect against the development and progression of bone changes that result in osteoporosis. Adequate calcium and vitamin D intake are fundamental to all prevention and treatment programs for postmenopausal osteoporosis. Bisphosphonates (Fosamax, Actonel), salmon calcitonin, and raloxifene are medications used to prevent and treat osteoporosis. They act by reducing bone resorption.

Estrogen has traditionally been considered first line therapy for prevention of osteoporosis, but if the only reason estrogen therapy has been prescribed is for osteoporosis prevention, then other therapies should be considered. A program of moderate exercise has been demonstrated to arrest the progression of osteoporosis and reverse some of the effects of the disease. This care plan focuses on early identification and prevention of the disease.

NDx Nursing Diagnosis

Deficient Knowledge

Common Related Factors

Lack of information about calcium-rich foods
Lack of information about prevention
Newly diagnosed with osteoporosis
Unfamiliarity with treatment regimen
Lifestyle places patient at risk for osteoporosis

Defining Characteristics

Patient verbalizes questions
Patient expresses misconceptions
Request for help

Common Expected Outcomes

Patient verbalizes an understanding of prevention measures.
Patient verbalizes understanding of the disease and treatment.

NOC Outcomes

Knowledge: Disease Process;
Knowledge: Medication; Knowledge: Diet;
Safety Behavior: Fall Prevention

NIC Interventions

Teaching: Disease Process;
Teaching: Prescribed Diet; Teaching:
Prescribed Medication

■ = Independent; ▲ = Collaborative

Ongoing Assessment

Actions/Interventions

- Assess the patient's knowledge of osteoporosis and treatment.

- Assess whether the patient maintains a balanced, calcium-rich diet.
- Obtain history of calcium supplementation.
- Assess whether the patient is postmenopausal or has had hysterectomy with bilateral oophorectomy.
- Assess tobacco, alcohol, and exercise history.

- Assess whether the patient is taking medications that decrease calcium absorption: cortisone, antacids, tetracycline, and laxatives.
- ▲ Monitor calcium levels.

Rationale

As people live longer, the risk for osteoporosis increases. However, many women do not believe that they are susceptible to it, do not understand the life-threatening injuries that may occur secondary to it, and do not realize that it can be prevented.

Daily dietary intake of 1000 to 1200 mg of calcium is necessary.

This is necessary if dietary intake is inadequate.

Reabsorption of bone is accelerated with natural or surgically induced menopause.

Smoking, drinking alcohol, and having only minimal weight-bearing exercise are risk factors for the development of osteoporosis.

This information is necessary for developing an individualized teaching plan.

Elevated calcium levels indicate calcium malabsorption. This may indicate the need for vitamin D supplementation to aid in calcium absorption. The usual dose is 200 to 400 international units daily.

Therapeutic Interventions

Actions/Interventions

- Instruct or reinforce regarding risk factors for osteoporosis:
  - Estrogen deficiency is the primary risk factor. Other risk factors are an inadequate dietary calcium intake, family history, red or blonde hair, white or Asian heritage, and an inactive lifestyle. Also at risk are people who use cigarettes, caffeine, and alcohol and are older than 45 years, with or without endocrine disease.
- Describe diagnostic tests available:
  - Dual-energy x-ray absorptiometry (DEXA)

  - Quantitative computed tomography (QCT)
  - Qualitative ultrasound

  - Biochemical assessment

- Reinforce dietary teaching about increased calcium intake. Encourage increased intake of calcium-rich foods: skim milk, cheeses, yogurt, ice cream; whole-grain cereals; green leafy vegetables; almonds and hazelnuts.

Rationale

This knowledge allows the patient to make decisions about lifestyle modifications to delay development of osteoporosis.

This is used for early detection of the disease. Dual photons are used to measure bone density. This type of screening can be done for the hip, wrist, or spinal column. Patients at risk for osteoporosis should begin bone density screening in their 40s.

QCT measures the density of bone.

Ultrasound measures of bone density of the heel have been found to reliably detect osteoporosis and risk for subsequent fractures of the hip.

Tests such as serum osteocalcin provide information on osteoblastic activity. Low levels of alkaline phosphatase are present in patients with osteoporosis.

Natural sources of calcium may provide more elemental or useful forms.

Osteoporosis

■ = Independent; ▲ = Collaborative

> **Osteoporosis**—cont'd

Actions/Interventions

▲ Consult a dietitian when appropriate. Reinforce meal planning taught by the dietitian.

▲ Instruct the patient on taking calcium supplementation therapy as ordered.

■ Introduce or reinforce self-management techniques:
- Physical activity, at least 30 minutes most days of the week

- Use of assistive devices (e.g., canes, walkers)

- Protection from injury and falls

■ Introduce or reinforce information on medications:
- Bisphosphonate, given in conjunction with calcitonin

- Calcitonin injection or nasal spray for patients who are unable or choose not to take estrogen

- Estrogen therapy

Rationale

A registered dietitian can provide specific dietary guidelines for calcium intake based on analysis of the patient's dietary history.

The patient needs to understand that calcium supplements are available as calcium compounds. Calcium carbonate has the highest concentration of elemental calcium. This compound is often the least expensive. The patient should read labels and look for the word "purified" or "USP" (United States Pharmacopeia). Supplements without these words may be less reliable and may contain high levels of lead. Calcium supplements are better absorbed when taken with meals. If flatulence or constipation occurs with taking calcium supplements, the patient can increase his or her fluid and dietary fiber intake. However, eating large amounts of dietary fiber can interfere with calcium absorption. Foods high in oxalates such as spinach may also interfere with calcium absorption.

Weight-bearing exercise at a moderate level, such as walking, running, dancing, skipping rope, or circuit-resistance training, aids in development and maintenance of bone mass.

These devices assist in balance and take up partial weight bearing.

Until bone density is enhanced and stabilized, falls will constitute a grave risk to the patient manifesting symptoms of osteoporosis. Severe hip fractures can be fatal in certain debilitated populations.

These compounds inhibit bone breakdown and slow bone removal. Bisphosphonates increase bone density and decrease the risk of fractures. Alendronate (Fosamax) is a bisphosphonate approved by the Food and Drug Administration (FDA) to treat osteoporosis in postmenopausal women.

Calcitonin is a naturally occurring hormone involved in calcium regulation and bone metabolism. Calcitonin prevents further bone loss by slowing the removal of bone and may be helpful in relieving the pain associated with osteoporosis.

Women who are currently taking menopausal hormone therapy should reconsider whether they should continue. Estrogen is given as pills or patches. It should be started soon after menopause to be effective. Estrogen replacement therapy is controversial because it may lead to increased risk of endometrial and breast cancer.

■ = Independent; ▲ = Collaborative

Actions/Interventions

- Selective estrogen receptor modulators (SERMs)

- Recombinant human parathyroid hormone

- Drugs under investigation, including vitamin D metabolites and new forms of bisphosphonates

Rationale

SERMs activate estrogen receptors in target organs to produce effects on estrogen-responsive tissues. Raloxifene (Evista) has been approved by the FDA for prevention and treatment of postmenopausal osteoporosis.

The FDA has approved teriparatide for the treatment of postmenopausal osteoporosis and in men with idiopathic or hypogonadal osteoporosis who are at high risk for fractures or who failed or are intolerant to prior osteoporosis therapy.

NOTE: These drugs are often used in conjunction with each other in an approach to osteoporosis treatment and prevention called coherence therapy, or ADFR:
- A = activate osteoblasts
- D = depress the activity of the osteoclasts
- F = free up the osteoblasts to create new bone
- R = repeat the treatment, and continue to do so until therapeutic effect has taken place

NDx Nursing Diagnosis

Risk for Impaired Physical Mobility

Common Risk Factors

Deformities
Fractures
Pain

Common Expected Outcomes

Patient verbalizes or demonstrates increased ability to move.
Patient is free of falls.
Patient identifies or implements safe environment practices at home.

NOC Outcomes
Ambulation; Fall Prevention Behavior

NIC Interventions
Exercise Therapy: Ambulation; Exercise Therapy: Joint Mobility; Environmental Management

Ongoing Assessment

Actions/Interventions

- Assess the patient's description of aggravating and alleviating factors, joint and bone pain and stiffness, and interference with lifestyle.
- Observe the patient's ability to ambulate and to move all body parts functionally.

Rationale

Because fractures can occur spontaneously with normal activity, protective measures must be taken until bone density has increased sufficiently to tolerate exercise.

Walking or getting up from a chair or bed may present difficulty to the patient because of pain, balance, or gait problems.

■ = Independent; ▲ = Collaborative

Osteoporosis—cont'd

Actions/Interventions

■ Assess the environment for safety.

Rationale

A safe environment reduces the risk for falls and potential fractures.

Therapeutic Interventions

Actions/Interventions

■ Promote mobility through physical therapy and exercise. Suggest moderate weight-bearing exercise (e.g., walking, bicycling, dancing) for 30 minutes three times a week.

▲ Reinforce techniques of therapeutic exercise (range of motion and muscle strengthening) taught by a physical therapist.

■ Encourage the patient to request assistance with ambulation as necessary. Recommend low, comfortable shoes for walking.

■ Provide adaptive equipment (e.g., cane, walker) as necessary.

■ Teach the patient to create a safe environment at home: remove or tack down throw rugs, wear firm-soled shoes, install grab bars in bathroom, do not carry heavy objects.

■ If a patient is hospitalized, provide a safe environment: bed rails up, bed in down position, necessary items (e.g., telephone, call light, walker, cane) within reach, adequate lighting, grab bars in bathroom (if available).

Rationale

Weight bearing stimulates osteoblastic activity and new bone growth.

An exercise program will require modification on an ongoing basis as the patient's condition improves and bone strength is enhanced.

Pathological fractures are a complication of falls.

These devices promote increased ambulation.

A safe home environment is necessary to prevent falls and potential fractures.

These measures may decrease the risk of falls.

NDx Nursing Diagnosis

Disturbed Body Image

Common Related Factors

Deformities
Fractures
Use of assistive devices

Defining Characteristics

Verbalization of negative feelings about altered structure and function of body part or use of assistive devices
Preoccupation with altered body part or function
Refusal to use assistive devices

Common Expected Outcomes

Patient verbalizes positive aspects of body and self.
Patient is able to use protective devices as needed.

NOC Outcomes
Body Image; Acceptance: Health Status

NIC Interventions
Body Image Enhancement; Self-Awareness Enhancement; Support Group

---

■ = Independent; ▲ = Collaborative

Ongoing Assessment

Actions/Interventions

- Assess perception of change in body part structure and function.

- Assess perception of how physical changes associated with osteoporosis change the patient's ability to perform activities of daily living, interact with others, and continue to be involved in occupational and diversional activities.

Rationale

Bone loss causes loss of height and appearance of humped back (dowager's hump). Kyphosis and lordosis are deformities often found in osteoporosis.

The patient may isolate self for fear of falling, difficulty in getting around, or self-consciousness about changed appearance.

Therapeutic Interventions

Actions/Interventions

- Acknowledge the emotional response to actual or perceived change in body structure and function.

- Encourage a positive attitude that some of the physical disabilities experienced will respond to adequate treatment and be abolished, reduced, or controlled.

- Remind the patient to allow adequate time for self-care activities.

- ▲ Reinforce self-care techniques taught by an occupational therapist.

- Provide the patient with community resources that can be helpful in supporting special needs in the home.

- Encourage participation in support groups.

Rationale

Once these changes have been acknowledged, ways can be found to reenter social life, interpersonal relationships, and occupational activities while still respecting actual limitations.

The therapeutic regimen can be effective in reversing some of the early changes of osteoporosis.

The patient's self-image improves when he or she can perform personal care independently.

Patients can learn new ways to perform self-care activities; this increases their sense of independence.

Such resources can increase independence and foster enhanced self-image.

This allows for open, nonthreatening discussion of feelings with others with similar experiences. Groups can give a realistic picture of the condition and suggestions for problem solving and coping.

Osteoporosis

NDx Nursing Diagnosis

Risk for Pain

Common Risk Factors

Fracture
Deformities

Common Expected Outcome

Patient verbalizes an absence of pain or a tolerable level of pain.

NOC Outcomes
Pain Control; Medication Response; Treatment Behavior: Illness or Injury

NIC Interventions
Analgesic Administration; Heat/Cold Application; Pain Management

■ = Independent; ▲ = Collaborative

Osteoporosis—cont'd

Ongoing Assessment

Actions/Interventions

■ Assess the patient's description of pain.

■ Assess the patient's response to pain medication or therapeutics aimed at abolishing or relieving pain. Modify plan as needed.

■ Determine to what degree pain is a limiting factor in mobility.

Rationale

The patient may report burning pain or aching in the neck and back, hips, and wrists. The patient may manifest a facial mask of pain when extremities are moved or body is palpated.

Patients are entitled to adequate pain relief.

The patient must have reached a certain level of pain relief before he or she can participate in an exercise program. Exercise is an essential aspect of the therapeutic regimen.

Therapeutic Interventions

Actions/Interventions

▲ Administer or instruct the patient on the use of pain medications as necessary and as prescribed.

■ Apply heat and cold as required.

■ Encourage use of ambulation aids for pain related to weight bearing.

See also **Acute Pain**, *p. 144.*

Rationale

Traditional analgesics and antiinflammatory agents are helpful in reducing the pain until bone density is enhanced.

These therapies reduce local inflammation and discomfort.

Assistive devices can help support body weight that otherwise could add to pain in fractures of weight-bearing joints and bones.

> **• RELATED CARE PLANS**
>
> Ineffective coping, p. 51
> Risk for falls, p. 59
> Self-care deficit, p. 156

Traction

Skeletal Traction; Skin Traction

Traction is the application of a pulling force to an area of the body or to an extremity. Skeletal traction is applied directly through the bone via pins or wires. It is commonly used for the reduction of fractures of the cervical spine, femur, tibia, and humerus. Traction can also be applied through the use of balanced suspension or skin traction. Skin traction may be intermittent or continuous and is often used to relieve muscle spasms and pain. Certain types of traction can be performed at home or in a rehabilitation facility or physical therapy department; others require inpatient hospitalization. This care plan addresses some of the general care principles governing nursing management of traction patients.

■ = Independent; ▲ = Collaborative

Musculoskeletal Care Plans

Nursing Diagnosis

Deficient Knowledge

Common Related Factor

Lack of experience with traction

Defining Characteristics

High anxiety level
Multitude of questions
Lack of questions
Expressed questions regarding traction

Common Expected Outcome

Patient verbalizes understanding of purpose and application of traction.

NOC Outcomes
Bone Healing; Knowledge: Treatment Procedure

NIC Interventions
Teaching: Procedures/Treatment; Traction/Immobilization Care

Ongoing Assessment

Actions/Interventions

■ Assess the patient's knowledge of traction.

Rationale

Patients will need to understand the type of traction prescribed for them and how traction will be applied. They may be responsible for applying the traction themselves under certain circumstances. In addition, they can be helpful in identifying when tractions is not properly balanced.

Therapeutic Interventions

Actions/Interventions

■ Explain the purpose of the traction device as it relates to the patient's injury or illness and healing process. General information might include the following:
  • Skin traction

  • Skeletal traction

Rationale

Skin traction is used for injuries that are less severe and that are associated with limited or fewer soft tissue injuries. Application may be intermittent. There may be planned intervals of rest during which traction is removed and skin care is provided. The amount of weight used ranges from very little for older patients to as much as 10 pounds for younger patients.

Skeletal traction is used in the treatment of more severe injuries that are often associated with more soft tissue damage. The amount of weight used ranges from 10 to 30 pounds and is maintained continuously. Treatment lengths range from 1 to 2 weeks or longer when indicated.

■ = Independent; ▲ = Collaborative

Traction—cont'd

Actions/Interventions	Rationale
■ Teach indicators that may suggest that the device requires adjustment:	
• The patient reports feeling like he or she is being pulled out of bed.	This indicates that the apparatus may be improperly applied. Provide the patient with a foot plate or a wrist splint to maintain proper position of the affected extremity.
• The patient complains of tingling or "pins and needles."	This may indicate nerve compression caused by improper application or fit of the device.
• The patient complains of itching, especially under the traction device.	This may indicate an allergic reaction to the material used to make the apparatus.
■ Instruct the caregiver to avoid elevating the head of bed more than 30 degrees.	Higher levels of elevation decrease the countertraction produced by the patient's body, thereby diminishing the effectiveness of the traction.

NDx **Nursing Diagnosis**

Acute Pain

Common Related Factors

Fractured limb
Skeletal pins (pain at insertion site)
Muscle spasms
Bone and soft tissue trauma caused by surgery
Intense physical therapy or rehabilitation program
Restricted mobility

Defining Characteristics

Verbalized pain
Irritability
Restlessness
Crying, moaning
Facial grimaces
Altered vital signs: increased pulse, increased blood pressure, increased respirations
Withdrawal
Unwillingness to change position
Inability to sleep

Common Expected Outcomes

Patient expresses acceptable relief of or reduction in pain.
Patient appears comfortable.

NOC Outcomes

Pain Control; Medication Response

NIC Interventions

Pain Management; Analgesic Management; Patient-Controlled Analgesia

■ = Independent; ▲ = Collaborative

Ongoing Assessment

Actions/Interventions

■ Assess the patient's description of pain.

Rationale

Careful analysis of the pain is essential to adequately treat it. Pain caused by malaligned traction will not be responsive to analgesia; it will be resolved only when the traction is rebalanced. Postoperative pain is usually localized. It will be acute and sharp. The pain should decrease in intensity over the 5 days after surgery. Intense pain that persists or pain that returns to previous levels of intensity may indicate a developing complication such as infection or compartment syndrome. Compartment syndrome is a condition that results from the unyielding nature of fascial covering over muscles. The inflammatory process, which is the result of injured tissues (tissues traumatized by surgery), increases venous pressure and decreases venous return, with a subsequent decrease in arterial inflow. If tissue ischemia persists for longer than 6 hours, permanent tissue damage may result.

■ Assess for correct positioning of traction and alignment of affected extremity

Incorrect positioning and malalignment can result in muscle spasms, which may be painful.

■ Identify the types of activity or positions that increase pain.

Measures may be taken to avoid precipitating factors.

■ Assess the patient's past experience with pain and pain-relief measures.

Patients who have had experience with chronic pain may have high tolerances for first line analgesics.

■ Assess effectiveness of current pain-relieving interventions.

Patients have a right to effective pain relief. Pain relief is not determined to be effective until the patient indicates that it is acceptable.

■ Assess the patient's mental and physical ability to use patient-controlled analgesia (PCA) versus intramuscular or oral analgesics.

Successful use of PCA requires patients to have knowledge of its use and the manual dexterity to operate it.

Therapeutic Interventions

Actions/Interventions

■ Explain that traction decreases muscle spasms and will gradually help lessen pain.

■ Explain analgesic therapy, including medication and schedule. If the patient is a candidate for PCA, explain its concept and routine.

Rationale

The patient needs to understand how traction can promote pain relief.

Care providers often assume that the patient will request pain medication when needed. The patient may think it is his or her duty or responsibility to tolerate pain until it can no longer be tolerated and may be waiting for the nurse to offer it when it is available.

▲ Administer narcotic analgesics every 3 to 4 hours around the clock for the first 24 hours after traction is applied.

There is a massive amount of manipulation, nerve trauma, and tissue damage during the surgical or manual reduction of a fracture. Assume that the patient requires analgesia. The patient's ability to fall asleep between checks is not a good indicator of the patient's level of comfort.

■ Instruct the patient to request pain medication before pain becomes severe.

If pain is too severe before analgesics or therapy is instituted, relief takes longer.

■ Encourage use of analgesics 30 to 45 minutes before physical therapy.

Unrelieved pain hinders rehabilitative progress.

■ = Independent; ▲ = Collaborative

Traction

Traction—cont'd

Actions/Interventions

- Change position (within precautions) every 2 hours or more often for comfort.
- Eliminate additional stressors or sources of pain and discomfort by providing comfort measures: relaxation techniques, diversionary activity (e.g., books, games, television, sewing, radio), heat or cold application, position changes, and touch (e.g., backrubs).

Rationale

The patient's inability to move freely and independently may result in pressure and pain on bony prominences.

Directing attention away from pain or to other body areas decreases perception of pain.

NDx Nursing Diagnosis

Impaired Physical Mobility

Common Related Factors

Fracture
Imposed restrictions related to traction and injury
Surgical or manual reduction of fracture
Discomfort

Defining Characteristics

Reluctance to move
Inability to move
Limited range of motion (ROM) and muscle strength

Common Expected Outcomes

Patient maintains optimal mobility within limitations (sitting, transferring, ambulation).
Patient maintains strength in unaffected joints.
Patient adheres to prescribed mobility restrictions and guidelines.
Patient participates in an ongoing program of rehabilitation and physical therapy.

NOC Outcome
Immobility Consequences: Physiological

NIC Interventions
Positioning; Exercise Therapy: Joint Mobility

Ongoing Assessment

Actions/Interventions

- Assess the patient's understanding of and ability to perform ROM exercises of the affected and unaffected extremity.

- Assess the patient's fear and anxiety of transferring or ambulating.

Rationale

It is important to preserve as much strength as possible in the unaffected extremity. This will enhance the patient's ability to function independently and aid in rehabilitation of the affected extremity.

The patient may be fearful of reinjuring the extremity. Allaying anxiety and fear will allow the patient to concentrate on correct techniques.

Therapeutic Interventions

Actions/Interventions

- Encourage ROM in bed with all unaffected extremities.

Rationale

Bed rest results in the loss of muscle tone in all muscle groups. Maximum muscle strength will be needed in

■ = Independent; ▲ = Collaborative

Actions/Interventions

- Instruct in use of assistive devices such as overhead trapeze and side rails.

- Teach strengthening exercises of the affected extremities as appropriate: quad sets, ankle pumps, straight leg raises, gluteal sets, push-ups, heel slides, and abductor sets.

- Elevate head of the bed no more than 30 degrees for meals and bedpan use.

- ▲ Reinforce the physical therapist's instructions for exercises, positioning, and ambulation.

Rationale

the unaffected muscle groups to support movement and positioning in bed. The patient may be fearful of reinjuring the extremity.

Use of these devices promotes active movement within the limits imposed by traction.

These exercises help prevent development of stiff joints and muscle atrophy.

Greater elevations decrease the countertraction that the patient's body produces, defeating the effectiveness of the traction device.

Consistent instructions from interdisciplinary team members promote a safe, secure rehabilitation environment.

NDx Nursing Diagnosis

Risk for Ineffective Tissue Perfusion

Common Risk Factors

Application of traction devices
Surgical procedure
Immobility

Common Expected Outcomes

Patient maintains adequate tissue perfusion, as evidenced by warm extremities, good color, good capillary refill, absence of pain and numbness, and bilaterally equal pulses.

Patient is free of signs and symptoms of deep vein thrombosis (DVT), pulmonary embolus (PE), and fat embolism as evidenced by negative Homans' sign, normal respiratory status, stable vital signs, and normal arterial blood gases (ABGs).

NOC Outcomes
Tissue Perfusion: Peripheral; Circulation Status

NIC Interventions
Circulatory Care; Circulatory Precautions

Ongoing Assessment

Actions/Interventions

- Assess and compare neurovascular status of both lower extremities preoperatively and postoperatively.

- Assess affected extremity every 1 to 2 hours as ordered using the 8-point check for signs of neurovascular compromise and damage:
  - Temperature of affected tissues

Rationale

Assessment must include unaffected and affected extremity to establish baseline and monitor for change in neurovascular status.

Injured tissues are usually cooler than on the nonoperative side. Normal temperature indicates adequate perfusion.

■ = Independent; ▲ = Collaborative

Actions/Interventions	Rationale
• Capillary refill of nail beds	Normal refill is 2 to 4 seconds. In the first hours after surgery, capillary refill may be sluggish, but refill that exceeds 4 to 6 seconds should be reported to the physician.
• Color of surgical site and surrounding tissues	Color should be pink, not pale or white. The affected side may be paler than the collateral side immediately after surgery or injury.
• Edema	Swelling of the injured area will be apparent, but severe swelling may indicate venous stasis. All peripheral pulses will be felt; however, the posterior tibialis and the dorsalis pedis pulses for the lower extremities or the radial and ulnar pulses for the upper extremities may be weaker than in the unaffected extremity immediately after surgery or injury.
• Sensory function	Complaints of numbness, tingling, or "pins and needles" feeling may indicate pressure on nerves from the cast or traction device.
• ROM	This indicates the amount and degree of limitation. Injured tissues will have decreased ROM. Unaffected extremity and muscle groups will have normal ROM.
• Pain	This indicates injury, trauma, or pressure. The surgical site will normally be painful. Monitor and report excessive complaints of pain as a possible harbinger of compartment syndrome.
• Evaluation of tissues, comparing affected and unaffected tissues	This allows comparison and perception of the patient's own "normal" presurgical status.
■ Check sequential compression device, thromboembolic disease (TED) support stocking, traction, or cast for extreme tightness.	Excessive compression may result in neurovascular compromise.
■ Observe for normal inflammatory process at the surgical site.	Expect signs of inflammation to decrease within 2 to 3 days after surgery.
■ Assess for signs and symptoms of DVT:	
• Increased leg circumference	Increased leg circumference occurs with swelling and may be the only indication of DVT.
• Positive Homans' sign	The examiner dorsiflexes the patient's foot toward the tibia, and the patient experiences pain in the calf muscles.
■ Assess for signs and symptoms of PE: tachypnea, chest pain, dyspnea, tachycardia, hemoptysis, cyanosis, anxiety, abnormal ABGs, and abnormal ventilation-perfusion scan.	Onset of symptoms can be sudden and overwhelming and can constitute an immediate threat to the life of the patient.
■ Assess for signs and symptoms of fat embolism: pulmonary (dyspnea, tachypnea, cyanosis); cerebral (headache, irritability, delirium, coma); cardiac (tachycardia, decreased blood pressure, petechial hemorrhage of upper chest, axillae, and conjunctivae); and fat globules in urine.	The manifestations of PE and fat embolism are similar. These syndromes can be life threatening and require immediate recognition and intervention.

■ = Independent; ▲ = Collaborative

Therapeutic Interventions

Actions/Interventions	Rationale
▲ Notify the physician immediately if signs of altered circulation are noted.	Venous pressures in the interstitial area surrounding an operative site can be measured through a small catheter inserted into the compartment. A surgical fasciotomy can be performed, which would release constriction and increase arterial inflow, restoring adequate circulation. The best indicators of developing compartment syndrome are patient complaint of excessive pain, peripheral pulses becoming weaker or absent, and an increase in pain on passive movement of the distal part to the surgery.
■ Encourage leg exercises, including quad sets, gluteal sets, and active ankle ROM.	Venous stasis may predispose the patient to circulatory compromise.
■ Encourage incentive spirometry every hour while the patient is awake.	Deep breathing exercises increase lung expansion and prevent atelectasis, hypoxemia, and pneumonia.
▲ Institute antiembolic devices as prescribed (sequential compression device or TED hose).	Antiembolic devices increase venous blood flow to the heart and decrease venous stasis, thereby decreasing the risk of DVT and PE.
▲ Administer thrombolytic agents as ordered.	These medications dissolve blood clots rapidly, thus preventing complications related to DVT and PE.
■ Encourage the patient to be out of bed as soon as prescribed.	Mobility restores normal circulatory function and decreases the risk of venous stasis.

Nursing Diagnosis

Risk for Infection: Pin Sites/Open Wounds

Common Risk Factors

Interrupted first line of defense
Interruption of bone structure
Insertion of retaining pins or wires into bones

Common Expected Outcome

Patient manifests no signs of infection, as evidenced by a normal thermal state, normal white blood cell (WBC) count, and no redness or drainage at the pin or wound site.

NOC Outcomes
Risk Control; Risk Detection; Tissue Integrity: Skin and Mucous Membrane

NIC Interventions
Infection Protection; Surveillance; Wound Care

Traction

■ = Independent; ▲ = Collaborative

 Traction—cont'd

Ongoing Assessment

Actions/Interventions

- Assess pin sites and open wounds for signs of infection.

- Assess for drainage at incision and pin sites.

- Assess vital signs, especially heart rate and temperature.

▲ Monitor laboratory values (WBC count).

Rationale

Early signs of infection or bone necrosis must be identified and treated so that risk of further complications can be reduced.

After the insertion of pins or wires into bone, there may be serosanguineous drainage for as long as 3 days. If drainage increases or becomes thick or cloudy, bone necrosis or infection may be developing.

Report heart rates above 100 beats/min or temperatures above 38.3° C (101° F), because these may be signs of developing infection.

Elevated WBC counts are present during an infective process.

Therapeutic Interventions

Actions/Interventions

▲ Perform wound and pin care every 8 hours or as prescribed:
  • Use sterile technique.

  • Clean area; remove dried secretions.

  • Reapply dressings as needed.
  • Cover the ends of retaining pins with tape or cork.
▲ Administer antibiotics as prescribed.

- Encourage foods high in protein and vitamin C.

Rationale

Protocols for pin site care may vary in terms of solutions used and frequency.

Cleaning the pin site reduces the risk of infection. Pin site infection can lead to osteomyelitis.

These measures prevent dislodgment of the pins.

Because of the amount of manipulation required to reduce a fracture or insert pins and wires, prophylactic antibiotics are often prescribed.

Adequate nutrition facilitates wound healing.

NDx Nursing Diagnosis

Risk for Impaired Skin Integrity

Common Risk Factors

Immobility
Prolonged bed rest
Contact with traction apparatus
Countertraction (patient's body weight)

■ = Independent; ▲ = Collaborative

Common Expected Outcome

Patient maintains intact skin.

NOC Outcome
Tissue Integrity: Skin and Mucous
    Membranes

NIC Intervention
Traction Care

Ongoing Assessment

Actions/Interventions

- Inspect the skin at least every 4 hours (especially of the affected extremity maintained in traction).
- Assess for preexisting risk factors for skin breakdown.

Rationale

Redness is the first sign of the effects of prolonged pressure.

Factors such as physical health, increasing age, altered mental state, and immobility increase potential for breakdown. Because these patients face a greater risk of developing problems, proactive measures to prevent infection and skin compromise must be taken.

Therapeutic Interventions

Actions/Interventions

- Clean, dry, and moisturize skin daily. Remove traction boot if possible.
- Massage bony prominences. Never massage reddened areas.
- Maintain correct padding for affected extremity in traction.
- Keep bed linen dry and free of wrinkles.

- Apply prophylactic pressure-relieving mattress to bed if needed.
- Encourage adequate hydration and teach importance of balanced diet.

Rationale

These measures maintain skin integrity.

Massage enhances circulation.

Pressure areas and skin irritation can develop under or at the edge of traction device and/or other equipment.

Sheets bunched under the patient or apparatus can apply pressure and compromise the integrity of sensitive skin.

Pressure-reduction devices can aid in the prevention of skin breakdown.

This is critical in maximizing overall health and healing. Patients who are malnourished are less likely to resist infection and other types of compromise.

• RELATED CARE PLANS

Constipation, p. 46
Deficient diversional activity, p. 57
Impaired urinary elimination, p. 201
Ineffective breathing pattern, p. 28
Ineffective coping, p. 51

Traction

■ = Independent; ▲ = Collaborative

Hematolymphatic, Immunological, and Oncological Care Plans

 Anemia

Iron Deficiency; Cobalamin Deficiency; Aplastic Anemia; Pernicious Anemia

Anemia is a general diagnostic term that refers to a decrease in the total number and/or function of erythrocytes (red blood cells [RBCs]). Anemias can be classified according to the etiology of the changes in erythrocytes. Anemias associated with decreased erythrocyte production include nutritional deficiency anemias (iron, cobalamin vitamin [B_{12}], folic acid), aplastic anemia, and the anemias that occur with other chronic diseases. Pernicious anemia is characterized by a lack of vitamin B_{12} absorption resulting from an absence of intrinsic factor in the stomach. Anemia can occur as the result of acute or chronic blood loss. Increased erythrocyte destruction is the cause of anemias that occur with sickle cell disease, enzyme deficiencies, and transfusion reactions. Aplastic anemia is a disease of diverse causes characterized by a decrease in precursor cells in the bone marrow and replacement of the marrow with fat. Aplastic anemia is characterized by pancytopenia, depression of all blood elements: white blood cells (WBCs) (leukopenia), RBCs (anemia), and platelets (thrombocytopenia). The underlying cause of aplastic anemia remains unknown. Possible pathophysiological mechanisms include certain infections, toxic dosages of chemicals and drugs, radiation damage, and impairment of cellular interactions necessary to sustain hematopoiesis. Advances in bone marrow transplantation and immunosuppressive therapy have significantly improved outcomes. This care plan focuses on ongoing care in the ambulatory care setting.

 NDx Nursing Diagnosis

Deficient Knowledge

Common Related Factors	Defining Characteristics
Unfamiliarity with disease	Many questions
Lack of resources	Verbalized misconceptions
	Lack of questions

Common Expected Outcome

Patient describes known facts about own disease and treatment plan.

NOC Outcomes
Knowledge: Disease Process;
   Knowledge: Treatment Procedures

NIC Interventions
Teaching: Disease Process;
   Teaching: Procedure/Treatment

Ongoing Assessment

Actions/Interventions

- Assess understanding of new medical vocabulary.

- Assess current knowledge of diagnosis, possible causative factors, disease process, and treatment.

Rationale

Most persons have little exposure to hematological diseases and therefore have not heard or do not understand terms commonly used by health professionals.

Appropriate and individualized teaching can begin only after the patient's current knowledge and perceptions are determined. Patients may have a general understanding of anemia related to iron deficiency but lack knowledge of other types of anemia.

Therapeutic Interventions

Actions/Interventions

- Explain hematological vocabulary and functions of blood elements, such as RBCs, WBCs, and platelets.
- Instruct the patient to avoid causative factor if known (e.g., certain chemicals).
- Explain the necessity for diagnostic procedures including bone marrow aspiration.

Rationale

Patients commonly have only a basic understanding of the hematological system.

The anemia may be acute or chronic, depending on the etiology.

Diagnosis of anemia is based on characteristic changes in RBC indexes and bone marrow. For example, in aplastic anemia, RBC indexes are normal (normochromic, normocytic), but the bone marrow is hypocellular. The patient with iron deficiency anemia has hypochromic, microcytic RBCs, and the bone marrow will indicate erythroid hyperplasia. Cobalamin deficiency and folic acid deficiency anemias have macrocytic RBCs with giant myeloid forms of megaloblasts in the bone marrow. Serum levels of iron, vitamin B_{12}, and folate are measured as part of the diagnosis of anemia. Gastric analysis to detect decreased hydrochloric acid is part of the diagnosis of cobalamin deficiency anemia.

For nutritional deficiency anemias:

- Explain the use of diet therapy and medications.
  - Teach the patient and family about food sources of iron, folic acid, and vitamin B_{12}.

A balanced diet that includes a variety of foods from each food group usually contains adequate nutrients to support RBC formation. In particular, patients need to have adequate intake of dark-green, leafy vegetables; meat; eggs; and whole grain, enriched, and fortified breads and cereals.

Anemia

■ = Independent; ▲ = Collaborative

Anemia—cont'd

Actions/Interventions	Rationale
• Teach the patient and family about replacement therapy with iron and folic acid.	Dietary replacement may not be sufficient to correct nutritional deficiency anemia. Supplementation is often necessary to support the formation of normal RBCs. The dosage and frequency of administration will depend on the severity of the anemia. Folic acid is given orally. Iron supplements may be given orally with meals to reduce gastric irritation. Stool discoloration is common with oral supplementation. Feces may have a dark greenish or black color and a tarry consistency. Intramuscular injections of iron may be given using the Z-track method to prevent leakage of the solution into subcutaneous tissue along the needle track.
• Explain the need for vitamin B_{12} replacement.	Vitamin B_{12} injections are the primary therapy for this vitamin deficiency. These injections may need to be given monthly for the remainder of the patient's life. High doses of oral vitamin B_{12} have been shown to be effective in overcoming impaired vitamin absorption resulting from a lack of intrinsic factor.

For blood loss anemia:

■ Instruct the patient regarding medications that may stimulate RBC production in the bone marrow.	Recombinant human erythropoietin, a hematological growth factor, increases hemoglobin and decreases the need for RBC transfusions.
■ Explain that a transfusion of packed RBCs may be needed.	The use of packed RBCs will replace volume and cellular components.

For aplastic anemia:

■ Explain the need for rapid human leukocyte antigen (HLA) typing.	This is performed to identify possible marrow donors.
■ Explain that allogeneic bone marrow transplantation is the recommended treatment for patients younger than 40 years of age and who have HLA-identical related donors.	This treatment has a very high success rate.
■ Explain that blood transfusions from prospective marrow donors should be avoided.	Histocompatibility antigens could lead to rejection of donor marrow.
■ Explain that immunosuppressive therapy is the treatment of choice in patients without HLA-matched donors and/or older than 40 years of age.	
• Immunosuppressive therapy includes antithymocyte globulin, cyclophosphamide, antilymphocyte globulin, granulocyte-macrophage colony-stimulating factor, and cyclosporine.	These have become standard therapy for patients who do not have an HLA-identical donor. Autologous transplantation is not an option, because the patient's own marrow is defective. Marrow must be transferred from an identically matched donor who is healthy (i.e., allogeneic transplantation with identical HLA-matched donor).
• Drug administration requires continuous monitoring of heart rate and blood pressure.	These medications are not without significant side effects.
• Emergency resuscitation equipment must be immediately available.	Patient safety is a priority. Because of the risk of severe anaphylaxis, some centers admit patients to the critical care unit for drug administration.

■ = Independent; ▲ = Collaborative

Actions/Interventions

- Complications:
  - Rejection of donor marrow

  - Acute graft-versus-host disease (GVHD)

  - Chronic GVHD

Rationale

Rejection results from sensitization to histocompatibility antigens acquired during previous blood transfusions and carries a high mortality rate. Conditioning regimens using cyclophosphamide (Cytoxan) and total lymphoid irradiation show a reduction in the risk of graft failure.

A red maculopapular rash within 3 months after transplantation signals acute GVHD and carries a 20% to 40% mortality rate.

This can be manifested by many symptoms. Mucosal degeneration leading to guaiac-positive diarrhea, vomiting, and malnutrition is one manifestation.

NDx Nursing Diagnosis

Fatigue

Common Related Factor

Reduced oxygen-carrying capacity of blood from decreased number of RBCs

Common Expected Outcome

Patient achieves adequate activity tolerance, as evidenced by ability to perform activities of daily living (ADLs) and verbalization of return to normal or near-normal activity levels.

Defining Characteristics

Report of weakness or fatigue
Exertional discomfort or dyspnea
Inability to maintain usual routine
Decreased performance

NOC Outcomes
Endurance Energy Conservation;
  Activity Tolerance

NIC Intervention
Energy Management

Ongoing Assessment

Actions/Interventions

- Assess current activity level.

- Assess specific cause of fatigue.

▲ Monitor hemoglobin, hematocrit, and RBC counts.

Rationale

Fatigue and exertional dyspnea are characteristic symptoms of anemia.

Besides tissue hypoxia from normocytic anemia, the patient may have associated depression or related medical problems that can compromise activity tolerance.

Adjustment to treatments may be needed. Decreased RBC indexes are associated with decreased oxygen-carrying capacity of the blood.

Anemia

■ = Independent; ▲ = Collaborative

Anemia—cont'd

Therapeutic Interventions

Actions/Interventions

■ Teach energy-conservation principles.

■ Assist the patient in planning ADLs. Guide in prioritizing activities for the day.

■ Stress the importance of frequent rest periods.

▲ Refer the patient and family to an occupational therapist.

■ Instruct regarding medications that may stimulate RBC production in the bone marrow.

▲ Anticipate the need for transfusion of packed RBCs.

▲ Institute supplemental oxygen therapy, as needed.

Rationale

Patients and caregivers may need to learn skills for delegating tasks to others, setting priorities, and clustering care to use available energy to complete desired activities.

Not all self-care and hygiene activities need to be completed in the morning. Likewise, not all housework needs to be completed in 1 day.

Energy reserves may be depleted unless the patient respects the body's need for increased rest.

The occupational therapist can teach the patient about using assistive devices. The therapist also can help the patient and family evaluate the need for additional energy conservation measures in the home setting.

Recombinant human erythropoietin, a hematological growth factor, increases hemoglobin and decreases the need for RBC transfusions.

These increase oxygen-carrying capacity of the blood.

This relieves dyspnea, or shortness of breath.

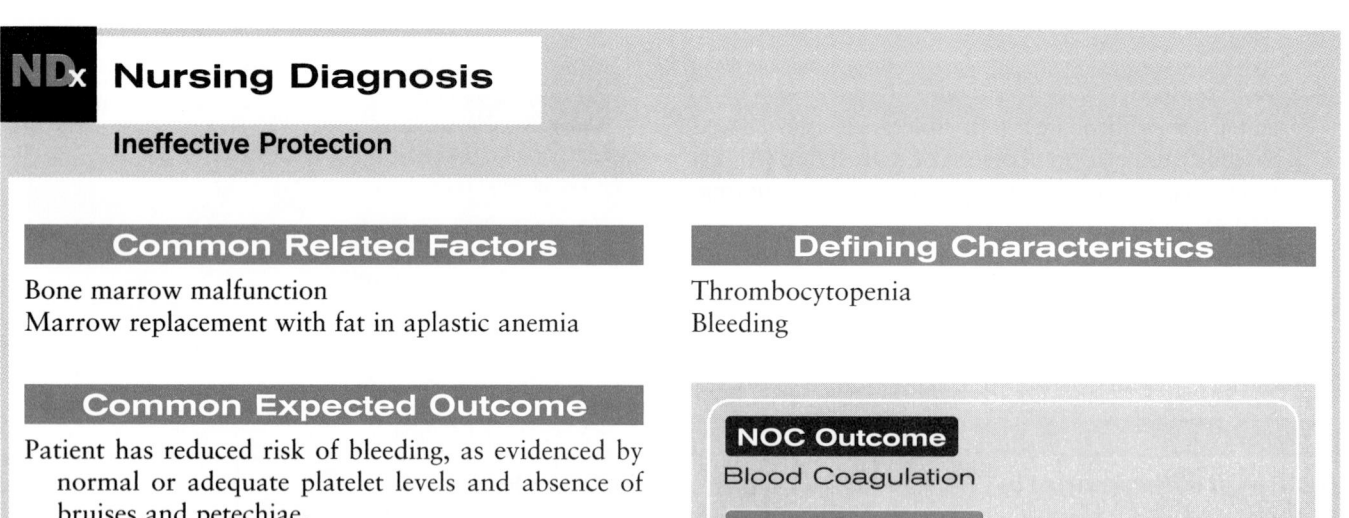

NDx Nursing Diagnosis

Ineffective Protection

Common Related Factors

Bone marrow malfunction
Marrow replacement with fat in aplastic anemia

Common Expected Outcome

Patient has reduced risk of bleeding, as evidenced by normal or adequate platelet levels and absence of bruises and petechiae.

Defining Characteristics

Thrombocytopenia
Bleeding

NOC Outcome
Blood Coagulation

NIC Intervention
Bleeding Precautions

Ongoing Assessment

Actions/Interventions

▲ Monitor platelet count.

Rationale

Thrombocytopenia is caused by bone marrow malfunction. Risk of bleeding is increased as platelet counts are decreased.

■ = Independent; ▲ = Collaborative

Hematolymphatic, Immunological, and Oncological Care Plans

Actions/Interventions

- Assess skin for evidence of petechiae or bruising.

- Assess for frank bleeding from nose, gums, vagina, or urinary or gastrointestinal tract.

- Monitor stool (guaiac) and urine (Hemastix) for occult blood.

Rationale

These are usually seen when platelet count falls below 20,000/mm^3.

Early assessment facilitates prompt treatment. These sites are most common for spontaneous bleeding.

These help identify the site of bleeding.

Therapeutic Interventions

Actions/Interventions

- Consolidate laboratory blood sampling tests.

- Instruct the patient regarding bleeding precautions.

- Avoid rectal procedures such as enemas, suppositories, and temperature readings. Also avoid douching, sexual intercourse, vaginal suppositories, and tampons.

- Instruct the patient to shave with an electric razor and to use a soft toothbrush.

- Instruct on the need for appropriate fall precautions, especially for older patients.

- ▲ If platelet counts are very low, anticipate the need for platelet transfusions and premedication with anti-pyretics and antihistamines.

Rationale

This reduces the number of venipunctures and optimizes blood volume.

Precautions are necessary when platelet count falls below 50,000/mm^3.

These can stimulate bleeding.

Trauma should be avoided to reduce risk of bleeding.

Proper attention to prevention may avoid trauma.

Premedication may reduce transfusion reaction effects.

NDx Nursing Diagnosis

Risk for Infection

Common Risk Factors

Bone marrow malfunction
Marrow replacement with fat in aplastic anemia

Common Expected Outcome

Patient has reduced risk of infection, as evidenced by normal WBC count, absence of fever, and implementation of preventive measures.

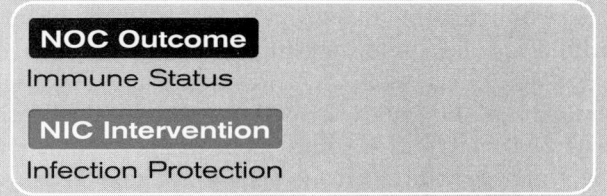

NOC Outcome
Immune Status

NIC Intervention
Infection Protection

Ongoing Assessment

Actions/Interventions

- ▲ Monitor WBC and differential.

- Assess for local or systemic signs of infection, such as fever, chills, malaise, swelling, and pain.

Rationale

Leukopenia is a decrease in the number of circulating WBCs.

Early assessment facilitates effective treatment.

■ = Independent; ▲ = Collaborative

Anemia

Anemia–cont'd

Therapeutic Interventions

Actions/Interventions	Rationale
■ Stress the importance of vigilant hand washing by the patient and caregiver.	Meticulous hand washing is a priority in both the hospital and the outpatient or home setting to prevent transmission of pathogens.
■ Reinforce the need for daily hygiene, mouth care, and perineal care.	These prevent skin breakdown and reduce the risk for infection.
■ Instruct the patient to avoid contact with persons with colds or infections.	These are sources of infection for the compromised patient. Children 12 years of age or younger put the patient at particular risk because they can be "carriers" of infection, especially upper respiratory infections.
■ Instruct the patient to avoid eating raw fruits and vegetables and uncooked meat.	These can harbor bacteria.
▲ Administer WBC growth factor to stimulate production of neutrophils.	Granulocyte colony stimulating factor (G-CSF) and long-acting pegfilgrastim are effective as mobilizers of peripheral blood progenitor cells.
■ Instruct the patient to report signs and symptoms of infection immediately.	Early assessment facilitates prompt treatment. Antibiotics may be indicated.
▲ Anticipate the need for antibiotic, antifungal, and antiviral intravenous agents.	These counteract opportunistic infections.
■ If the patient is hospitalized, provide a private room for protective isolation.	Protective isolation may be necessary if absolute neutrophil count is less than 500/mm³. These patients are at significant risk for infection.

> • RELATED CARE PLAN
>
> Hematopoietic stem cell transplantation, p. 837

Cancer Chemotherapy

Cancer chemotherapy is the administration of cytotoxic drugs by various routes for the purpose of destroying malignant cells. Chemotherapeutic drugs are commonly classified according to their antineoplastic action: alkylating agents, antitumor antibiotics, antimetabolites, vinca alkaloids, and hormonal agents. Another way of classifying cancer chemotherapeutic agents is based on where in the cancer cell's life cycle the drug has its effect. Cell cycle–specific drugs exert their cytotoxic effect at a specific point in the cell cycle. Drugs that affect the cancer cell at any point in its cycle are called cell cycle–nonspecific drugs. These drugs are dose dependent in their therapeutic effect. Typically a combination of chemotherapeutic agents is administered to destroy the greatest number of tumor cells at different stages of cell replication. Cancer chemotherapy may be administered in the hospital, ambulatory care, or even home setting by a qualified chemotherapy-certified nurse. The goal of chemotherapy is cure, control, or symptom relief. It is often used as an adjunct to surgery and radiation. Because these drugs are highly toxic and are given systemically, they affect normal cells as well as cancer cells. Most of the side effects of cancer chemotherapy are the result of the drugs' effects on rapidly dividing normal cells in the hair follicles, the gastrointestinal tract, and the bone marrow.

■ = Independent; ▲ = Collaborative

Nursing Diagnosis

Deficient Knowledge

Common Related Factors

Unfamiliarity with proposed treatment plan and procedures
Misinterpretations of information
Unfamiliarity with discharge and follow-up care

Defining Characteristics

Verbalized lack of knowledge
Expressed need for information
Multiple questions
Lack of questions
Verbalized misconceptions
Verbalized confusion over events

Common Expected Outcome

Patient or caregiver verbalizes understanding of chemotherapy treatment, including rationale for treatment, self-management of interventions to prevent or control side effects, and follow-up care.

NOC Outcome
Knowledge: Treatment Procedure

NIC Interventions
Teaching: Procedure/Treatment; Chemotherapy Management

Ongoing Assessment

Actions/Interventions

■ Assess understanding of diagnosis, rationale for chemotherapy, goal of treatment, chemotherapeutic agents to be used, rationale for occurrence of side effects, strategies (including interventions for self-management) aimed at prevention or control of adverse side effects, method of chemotherapy administration, potential problems experienced during chemotherapy administration, schedule of overall treatment plan, anticipated length and number of hospitalizations and clinic or office visits, and follow-up care.

Rationale

The patient and family need information based on their understanding of the treatment plan using chemotherapeutic agents. A successful treatment plan requires the cooperation of the patient and support of the patient's family members.

Therapeutic Interventions

Actions/Interventions

■ Instruct the patient and caregiver as needed:

Treatment plan:

• Need and schedule for laboratory tests before and during treatment

• Chemotherapy agents to be used

Rationale

Regular laboratory tests are done to assess for electrolyte and metabolic changes; cardiac, pulmonary, and renal alterations; bone marrow function; the need for blood component transfusions; and the presence of infection.

Single agents are rarely used. Instead, combination therapies are used for their synergistic effects and to capitalize on their different mechanisms of action and side effect profiles. Many chemotherapy agents in combination with monoclonal antibody regimens are approved and are in wide use.

■ = Independent; ▲ = Collaborative

Cancer Chemotherapy

Cancer Chemotherapy—cont'd

Actions/Interventions	**Rationale**
• Method of administration	Oral and intravenous (IV) routes are most common, although regional delivery directly to the tumor site may be selected.
• Schedule of administration	Each drug protocol has a preferred time for administration followed by a rest period. Therapy is usually given in cycles.
• Site for administration	Although therapy may be initially started in the hospital setting, the trend is to provide comprehensive yet less costly treatment in the outpatient setting.
Chemotherapy:	
• Potential short- and long-term side effects and toxicities	A variety of serious and distressing side effects occur with aggressive chemotherapy.
• Period of anticipated side effects and toxicities	Patients need to be informed of the side effect profile for their specific agents.
• Preventive measures to minimize or alleviate potential side effects and toxicities	Patients need to be informed that most side effects can be managed to some degree.
Discharge planning and teaching:	
• Catheter care (central venous, arterial, intraperitoneal catheters and devices)	Ongoing care is an important responsibility. Refer to the care plan for **Central Venous Access Devices** on the **Evolve** website.
• Signs and symptoms to report to health care professionals (e.g., bleeding, fever, shortness of breath, intractable nausea and vomiting, inability to eat or drink, diarrhea)	Patients and family caregivers need to be able to recognize early indications of drug side effects. Early interventions to control side effects can minimize the impact on the patient's daily routines.
• Measures to prevent infection	The patient's immune function is often impaired by chemotherapy-induced bone marrow suppression.
• Importance of balanced diet and adequate fluid intake	The patient and family caregivers need to understand how adequate nutrition can promote improvement in the patient's quality of life, but patients should not be forced to eat.
• Dietary and medication restrictions if indicated	Information can enhance compliance.
• Medications after discharge	Patients will be assuming responsibility for care.
• Activities of daily living	Fatigue, neutropenia, and common side effects will determine the patient's rate of return to activities of daily living.
• Follow-up care	Periodic evaluation of the patient's response to therapy will need to be closely monitored.
• Community resources and support systems	Advocates are available for information, support, and even caregiving.

■ = Independent; ▲ = Collaborative

Nursing Diagnosis

Imbalanced Nutrition: Less Than Body Requirements

Common Related Factors

Treatment effects:
- Side effects of chemotherapy (inability to taste and smell foods, loss of appetite, nausea, vomiting, mucositis, dry mouth, diarrhea)
- Medications (e.g., narcotics, antibiotics, vitamins, iron, digitalis)

Disease effects:
- Primary malignancy or metastasis to central nervous system
- Increased intracranial pressure resulting from tumor, intracranial bleeding
- Obstruction of gastrointestinal (GI) tract by tumor
- Tumor waste products
- Renal dysfunction
- Electrolyte imbalances (e.g., hypercalcemia, hyponatremia)
- Pain

Psychogenic effects:
- Conditioning to adverse stimuli (e.g., anticipatory nausea and vomiting; tension, anxiety, stress)
- Depression

Defining Characteristics

Weight loss
Documented inadequate caloric intake
Weakness, fatigue
Poor skin turgor
Dry, shiny oral mucous membranes
Thick, scanty saliva
Muscle wasting

Common Expected Outcome

Patient maintains optimal nutritional status, as evidenced by caloric intake adequate to meet body requirements, balanced intake and output, weight gain or reduced loss, absence of nausea and vomiting, and good skin turgor.

NOC Outcomes

Medication Response; Nutritional Status; Food and Fluid Intake

NIC Interventions

Chemotherapy Management; Nutrition Therapy; Oral Health Maintenance; Medication Administration

Ongoing Assessment

Actions/Interventions

- Obtain history of previous patterns of nausea and vomiting and any treatment measures effective in the past.

- Assess the patient's description of nausea and vomiting pattern.

Rationale

The patient may have had adverse side effects in the past. However, newer antiemetic medications have improved this condition for many patients. These side effects can significantly affect the quality of one's life. Nausea and vomiting are the most distressing side effects for patients and families.

Patient responses are individualized, depending on type and dosage of chemotherapy. Nausea and vomiting may be acute, delayed, and for some patients even "prior to" (anticipatory) the chemotherapy treatment.

Cancer Chemotherapy

■ = Independent; ▲ = Collaborative

 **Cancer Chemotherapy**—cont'd

Actions/Interventions

- Evaluate the effectiveness of the antiemetic and comfort measure regimens.

- Observe the patient for potential complications of prolonged nausea and vomiting: fluid and electrolyte imbalance (e.g., dehydration, hypokalemia, decreased sodium and chlorine), weight loss, decreased activity level, weakness, lethargy, apathy, anxiety, aspiration pneumonia, esophageal trauma, and tenderness or pain in the abdomen and chest.

- Weigh the patient weekly or twice weekly at the same time and with the same scale. If the patient is at home, stress the importance of maintaining a log.

- Encourage the patient to record any food intake using a daily log.

- ▲ Monitor appropriate laboratory values (e.g., complete blood count and differential, electrolytes, serum iron, total iron-binding capacity, total protein, albumin).

Rationale

Patient responses to antiemetic medications are highly variable and must be explored with each patient.

Chemotherapeutic drugs produce nausea and vomiting as a side effect by stimulating central receptors in the chemoreceptor trigger zone in the medulla or in the cerebral cortex. Some of the drugs stimulate peripheral receptors in the GI tract to cause nausea and vomiting.

Consistent weighing ensures accuracy. Without monitoring, the patient may be unaware of actual weight loss.

Determination of type, amount, and pattern of food intake (if any) is facilitated by accurate documentation, which provides data as to whether oral intake meets daily nutritional requirements.

These reflect nutritional, fluid, and electrolyte status.

Therapeutic Interventions

Actions/Interventions

- ▲ Administer antiemetics according to protocol.

- ▲ Administer antiemetic around the clock rather than as needed during periods of high incidence of nausea and vomiting.

- ▲ Titrate dosage and frequency of antiemetic within prescribed parameters as needed until effective therapeutic levels are achieved.

- Institute or teach measures to reduce or prevent nausea and vomiting:

Rationale

Newer agents are much more effective in reducing the incidence and severity of emesis. Treatment protocols using a combination of antiemetic medications are most effective in controlling the nausea and vomiting associated with chemotherapy. This approach uses drugs that block nausea receptors at different sites and through different mechanisms of action. A typical combination protocol may include administration of a 5HT3 (serotonin) receptor antagonist such as ondansetron and dexamethasone before chemotherapy. For delayed nausea, the protocol may include administration of dexamethasone and metoclopramide. New agents currently approved for acute and delayed nausea and vomiting include aprepitant and palonosetron. Other classes of drugs used to control nausea and vomiting include phenothiazines, butyrophenones, cannabinoids, and benzodiazepines.

Effectiveness of antiemetic therapy is increased when adequate plasma levels are maintained.

Each patient has his or her own threshold for relief.

Behavioral and dietary interventions seem to be most effective in the management of anticipatory nausea and vomiting. This pattern of nausea and vomiting is

■ = Independent; ▲ = Collaborative

Actions/Interventions	Rationale
	related to classical conditioning. The patient develops nausea and vomiting in response to stimuli associated with administration of chemotherapeutic drugs. Patients may try a variety of interventions to find those that best control this type of nausea and vomiting before drug administration. Antiemetic medications are less effective in the management of anticipatory nausea and vomiting. However, antianxiety medications suchas lorazepam may be effective.
• Small dietary intake before treatments	Limited intake reduces gastric overstimulation.
• Foods with low potential to cause nausea and vomiting (e.g., dry toast, crackers, ginger ale, cola, Popsicles, gelatin, baked or boiled potatoes, fresh and canned fruit)	These foods are easily digested and provide a measure of success to augment nutrition.
• Avoidance of spices, gravy, greasy foods, and foods with strong odors	These foods can stimulate gastric motility.
• Modifications in diet (e.g., choice of bland foods)	Bland foods may be better tolerated.
• Small, frequent nutritious meals	Eating small amounts prevents gastric distention from stimulating vomiting.
• Meals at room temperature	Hot foods can stimulate peristalsis.
• Avoidance of coaxing, bribing, or threatening in relation to intake (help family to avoid being "food pushers")	Such behaviors tend to only aggravate the situation.
• Rest periods before and after meals	This provides needed energy for eating and digestion.
• Sucking on hard candy while receiving chemotherapeutic drugs with "metallic taste" (e.g., Cytoxan, dacarbazine [DTIC], cisplatin, actinomycin D, Mustargen, methotrexate)	Hard candies can reduce metallic or bitter taste.
• Minimal physical activity and no sudden rapid movement during times of increased nausea	Activity may potentiate nausea and vomiting.
• Quiet, restful, cool, well-ventilated environment	Relaxation reduces peristalsis.
• Relaxation and distraction techniques, guided imagery	These techniques can be helpful if used before nausea occurs or increases.
• Antiemetic half an hour before meals as prescribed	Antiemetics relieve nausea and vomiting.
■ Identify and provide the patient's favorite foods; avoid serving these during nausea and vomiting.	The patient may develop an aversion.
■ Explain measures to increase sensitivity of taste buds: perform mouth care before and after meals; change seasoning to compensate for altered sweet/sour threshold; increase use of sweeteners and flavorings in foods.	These strategies may improve ability to tolerate foods.
■ Serve foods cold if odors cause aversions.	The smell of cooking foods may aggravate feelings of nausea.
■ Offer meat dishes in the morning.	Aversions tend to increase during the day; chicken, cheese, and eggs are usually well-tolerated protein sources.
■ Serve supplements between meals; have the patient sip slowly.	These prevent bloating, nausea, vomiting, and diarrhea.
■ Explain measures to provide moisture in the oral cavity if indicated:	These may improve the patient's ability to tolerate food.
• Frequent intake of nonirritating fluids (e.g., grape or apple juice)	

Cancer Chemotherapy

■ = Independent; ▲ = Collaborative

Cancer Chemotherapy—cont'd

Actions/Interventions	Rationale
• Sucking on smooth, flat substances (e.g., ice chips; lozenges; tart, sugar-free candy) to increase saliva flow	
• Use of artificial saliva	
• Liquids sipped with meals	
• Foods moistened with sauces or liquids	
• Strict oral hygiene before and after meals; avoidance of alcohol-containing commercial mouthwashes or lemon-glycerin swabs that dry oral mucosa	
• Lips moistened with balm, water-soluble lubricating jelly, lanolin, or cocoa butter	
• Humidified air environment via vaporizer or pan of water near heat	Humidity should be used cautiously when the patient is leukopenic because of risk of *Pseudomonas* infection.
■ If reduced oral intake is secondary to mucositis, see Impaired Oral Mucous Membrane, p. 141.	Patients undergoing chemotherapy commonly develop some degree of soreness in the mucous membranes.
■ Place the patient in Fowler's position or a side-lying position during vomiting episode.	This decreases aspiration risk.

NDx Nursing Diagnosis

Ineffective Protection

Common Related Factors

Bone marrow toxicity of chemotherapy
Disease of bone marrow
Invasion of bone marrow by malignant cells
Genetically transmitted platelet deficiency coagulopathies (tumor related or other)
Abnormal hepatic or renal function
Exposure to toxic substances (e.g., benzene, antibiotics)
Nutritional deficiencies (e.g., decreased vitamin K, folic acid, vitamin B_{12}, iron intake absorption or use)

Defining Characteristics

Thrombocytopenia
Bleeding
Anemia

Common Expected Outcomes

Patient has reduced risk of bleeding, as evidenced by platelets within acceptable limits, coagulation and fibrinogen within acceptable limits, and absence of overt and occult bleeding.
Patient is free of anemia, as evidenced by heart rate and blood pressure (BP) within normal limits, hemoglobin (Hgb) and hematocrit (Hct) within normal limits, and ability to perform activities of daily living (ADLs).

NOC Outcome
Blood Coagulation

NIC Interventions
Bleeding Precautions; Chemotherapy Management; Blood Product Administration

Hematolymphatic, Immunological, and Oncological Care Plans

Ongoing Assessment

Actions/Interventions

▲ Monitor platelets daily.

Rationale

Risk of bleeding increases as platelet count drops:
- $<20,000/mm^3$ = Severe risk
- $20,000$ to $50,000/mm^3$ = Moderate risk; may note prolonged bleeding at invasive sites
- $50,000$ to $100,000/mm^3$ = Mild risk; does not usually require treatment
- $>100,000/mm^3$ = No significant risk

■ Anticipate platelet count nadir.

Nadir is when platelets are at lowest point.

▲ Monitor coagulation parameters (fibrinogen, thrombin time, bleeding time, fibrin degradation products) if indicated.

Changes in coagulation profile may be marked by ecchymosis, hematomas, petechiae, blood in body excretions, bleeding from body orifices, and change in neurological status.

■ Evaluate for any medications that can interfere with hemostasis (e.g., salicylates, anticoagulants, nonsteroidal antiinflammatory drugs).

Drugs that interfere with clotting mechanisms or platelet activity increase risk for bleeding.

■ Inspect patient regularly for evidence of the following:
- Spontaneous petechiae (all skin surfaces, including oral mucosa)
- Prolonged bleeding or new areas of ecchymoses or hematoma from invasive procedures (venipuncture, injection, and bone marrow sites)
- Oozing of blood from nose or gums
- Rectal bleeding, vaginal bleeding, and/or increased menstruation

Early assessment facilitates prompt treatment and reduced risk for complications.

▲ If any significant bleeding occurs, monitor vital signs closely until bleeding is controlled.

Patient safety is a priority.

For risk of anemia:

■ Assess for signs of anemia secondary to bone marrow toxicity of chemotherapy or radiation therapy: tiredness, weakness, lethargy, fatigue; pallor (skin, nail beds, conjunctivae, circumoral); dyspnea on exertion, palpitations or chest pain on exertion; dizziness or syncope; hypersensitivity to cold; increased pulse, decreased BP.

Although anemia may not signify a life-threatening problem such as infection or bleeding, it can significantly impact the quality of one's life.

▲ Monitor Hgb/Hct daily.

Low hemoglobin affects the oxygen-carrying capacity of the blood.

■ Assess for orthostatic changes secondary to reduced blood volume.

Assessment may be more significant in older patients.

■ Determine nadir and anticipated recovery of bone marrow after chemotherapy administration.

These help in planning nursing measures.

Therapeutic Interventions

Actions/Interventions

■ Instruct patient or significant others of relationship between platelets and bleeding:
- Platelet function
- Normal platelet count
- Effects of chemotherapy on bone marrow function and platelet count

Rationale

A successful treatment plan requires the knowledge and cooperation of the patient and family members.

Cancer Chemotherapy

■ = Independent; ▲ = Collaborative

Cancer Chemotherapy—cont'd

Actions/Interventions	Rationale
▲ Implement bleeding precautions for a platelet count of less than 50,000/mm³.	At this level, spontaneous bleeding can occur.
■ Avoid nonessential invasive procedures, punctures, and injections.	This reduces bleeding at vascular access sites.
■ Avoid rectal thermometers, suppositories, and enemas.	Use increases the chance of rectal bleeding.
■ Maintain appropriate fall precautions.	This reduces risk of trauma.
▲ Communicate the anticipated need for platelet support to a transfusion center.	It is important to have platelets available when needed (e.g., when platelets are less than 20,000/mm³ or in the presence of active bleeding). Prophylactic platelet transfusions may be administered.
▲ Transfuse single or random donor platelets, as ordered.	Transfusions may be needed to maintain adequate platelet count.
▲ Administer fresh frozen plasma or coagulation factors, as prescribed.	These replace needed clotting factors.
■ Emphasize to the patient and/or significant others the importance of consistent practice of measures to prevent bleeding and prompt reporting of all signs and symptoms of suspected or actual bleeding.	Early assessment facilitates prompt, often lifesaving intervention.
■ For bleeding precautions and nursing interventions, see also Leukemia, p. 858.	

For risk of anemia:

■ Estimate energy expenditures of ADLs; prioritize activities accordingly.	A plan that balances periods of activity with periods of rest can help the patient complete desired activities without increased fatigue.
■ Plan or promote rest periods.	Rest lowers the body's oxygen requirement and decreases cardiopulmonary strain.
■ Provide warm clothing, blankets, and a comfortable environment; avoid drafts.	These promote comfort.
■ Instruct the patient to change position slowly.	This method allows for circulatory compensation to prevent dizziness and possible injury.
▲ Administer erythropoietin agent as ordered (e.g., epoetin alfa, darbepoetin alfa).	These agents correct anemia by stimulating production of red blood cells (RBCs) in the same way as endogenous human erythropoietin.
▲ Maintain a current blood sample for "type and screen" in the transfusion center.	This ensures availability and readiness of packed RBCs when needed.
▲ Transfuse packed RBCs, as ordered.	This may be required to restore Hgb/Hct to levels at which the patient experiences minimal symptoms.
▲ Administer iron supplement therapy as ordered.	Administer with meals to maximize absorption.

See also **Anemia,** *p. 806.*

Hematolymphatic, Immunological, and Oncological Care Plans

Nursing Diagnosis

Risk for Injury

Common Risk Factors

Hypersensitivity to drugs
Potential side effects and toxicities of drugs
Extravasation
Infiltration of drug from vein

Common Expected Outcome

Patient has reduced risk of injury from drug therapy, as evidenced by normal vital signs, absence of reaction, no pain at infusion site, adequate blood return from IV catheter, and prompt reporting of adverse signs and symptoms.

NOC Outcomes
Blood Circulation; Medication Response; Risk Control; Risk Detection

NIC Interventions
Allergy Management; Medication Administration; Emergency Care; IV Therapy; Venous Access Device Management

---

Ongoing Assessment

Actions/Interventions

■ Note allergy history.

■ Monitor for potential hypersensitivity, side effects, or toxicities to chemotherapeutic drugs: restlessness, facial edema and flushing, wheezes, bronchospasms, tachycardia, hypotension or hypertension, diaphoresis, fever, increased uric acid levels, runny nose, skin rash, temporomandibular joint pain, frontal sinusitis, ileus, diarrhea.

■ Monitor for hypersensitivity, side effects, or toxicities to common antiemetic drugs: agitation and restlessness, hypotension, tachycardia, irritability, facial flushing, extrapyramidal reactions, dry mouth, sedation, blurred vision, drowsiness, dizziness, headache, diarrhea, urine retention.

▲ Monitor relevant laboratory data.

■ Assess IV insertion site at frequent intervals according to established hospital policy and procedure: blood return, patency of vein and catheter, signs of infiltration.

▲ Check for blood return frequently with IV push vesicant chemotherapy and every 4 hours with continuous infusion chemotherapy.

Rationale

Patient safety is a priority.

A variety of responses to chemotherapy are possible. Patients, family, and staff need to be vigilant when the patient is starting any new agent, as well as monitoring effects for prolonged periods.

Antiemetic medications meant to be helpful also exhibit their own side effects.

Complete blood count, differential, platelets, and electrocardiogram provide baseline and response data.

Defective or malpositioned indwelling central venous catheter or access device can cause extravasation into local subcutaneous tissue surrounding the administration site.

Chemotherapy can cause tissue damage if it leaks outside the vein. Refer to hospital policy and procedure manual for guidelines.

Cancer Chemotherapy

■ = Independent; ▲ = Collaborative

Cancer Chemotherapy—cont'd

Actions/Interventions	Rationale
■ Determine whether the chemotherapeutic agent has vesicant properties. Observe injection or infusion site closely during chemotherapy administration.	Not all agents have the same likelihood of causing tissue damage if infiltrated (vesicant).

Therapeutic Interventions

Actions/Interventions	Rationale
■ Verify written order with another RN for specific drug name, dose, route, time, and frequency of antiemetic or chemotherapy drugs to be administered.	Patient safety is a priority.
■ Know immediate and delayed side effects of drugs to be administered.	Each nurse has a responsibility to be familiar with potential side effects or complications associated with each agent being administered, whether a standard or experimental drug treatment.
■ Inform the patient or significant others to report adverse effects. Delineate which changes indicate emergencies that must be reported immediately.	Changes that a patient perceives as "minor" may be highly significant.
■ Maintain or restore adequate fluid balance.	Fluid therapy reduces potential drug toxicity in that fluids help clear the body of accumulated metabolic by-products. Older patients with reduced blood volumes and functional deterioration are especially at risk.
▲ For drugs associated with a high risk for anaphylaxis: • Administer the first dose in a hospital setting. • Stay with the patient while the drug is being administered. • Keep emergency drugs (IV Benadryl, hydrocortisone, epinephrine 1:1000) readily available.	Patient safety is a priority.
▲ When an adverse drug reaction is suspected, stop infusion; administer emergency drugs as prescribed; notify physician; take and record vital signs; maintain patent IV with normal saline solution; reassure patient.	Prompt treatment reduces complications and provides reassurance to the patient.
■ Select veins most suitable for administration of chemotherapeutic agents.	These are the cephalic, median brachial, and basilic veins in the mid-forearm area. Venous access devices may also be used. NOTE: Only specially trained and certified nurses can administer chemotherapy.
■ Avoid veins in the antecubital fossa, near the wrist, or on the dorsal surface of the hand.	Damage to underlying tendons and nerves may occur in the event of drug extravasation.
■ Instruct the patient to report tenderness, stinging, burning, or other unusual sensation at the IV site immediately.	Pain is the most frequent complaint.
■ Evaluate patient complaints of "painful infusion"; rule out source extravasation versus other causes of pain (which may include chemical composition of drug, venous spasm, phlebitis, and/or psychogenic factors).	Accurate assessment guides treatment.
▲ Keep extravasation kit accessible.	Contents vary according to hospital policy. Kits and procedures for treating extravasation must also be available in the home if chemotherapy is being administered in that setting. Chemotherapy "spill kits" should also be available in the home.

■ = Independent; ▲ = Collaborative

Actions/Interventions

▲ When drug extravasation is suspected, stop infusion, initiate extravasation management appropriate for the chemotherapeutic drug being infiltrated, notify the physician, reassure the patient, and document the incident according to institutional policy and procedure.

Rationale

Management of the site after extravasation remains a controversial issue in chemotherapy administration. However, most hospitals and agencies have developed care standards in management of extravasation of drugs classified as "vesicants." These agents potentially cause cellular damage, ulceration, and tissue necrosis. A plastic surgeon may be consulted for debridement or skin grafting, depending on the extent of injury.

 Nursing Diagnosis

Disturbed Body Image

Common Related Factors

Loss of hair (scalp, eyebrows, eyelashes, pubic and body hair)
Discoloration of fingernails, veins
Breakage or loss of fingernails
Changes in skin color and texture
Generalized "wasting"
Presence of externalized or implanted venous access device
Concurrent surgical changes (mastectomy, colostomy)

Defining Characteristics

Self-deprecating remarks
Refusal to look at self in mirror
Crying
Anger
Decreased attention to grooming
Verbalized ambivalence
Compensatory use of makeup, concealing makeup, clothing, devices
Decreased social interaction

Common Expected Outcomes

Patient verbalizes understanding of temporary nature of side effects.
Patient verbalizes positive remarks about self.

NOC Outcome
Body Image

NIC Interventions
Body Image Enhancement;
  Hope Installation

Ongoing Assessment

Actions/Interventions

■ Assess for presence of defining characteristics.

■ Observe for verbal and nonverbal cues to note image alteration.

Rationale

Extent of losses or changes is individual and depends on type, dosage, and duration of chemotherapy.

Attention to a range of behaviors may help in accurate assessment.

Therapeutic Interventions

Actions/Interventions

■ Acknowledge normalcy of emotional response to the actual or perceived changes in physical appearance.

■ Encourage verbalization of feelings; listen to concerns.

Rationale

For some patients, the fear of treatment side effects can feel worse than the disease.

This may open lines of communication and help relieve anxiety.

(■ = Independent; ▲ = Collaborative)

Cancer Chemotherapy

Cancer Chemotherapy—cont'd

Actions/Interventions

- Convey feelings of acceptance and understanding.

- Provide anticipatory guidance on hair alternatives for alopecia (e.g., suggest purchase of a wig or turbans before chemotherapy), on makeup and skin care for changes in skin color and texture, and on clothing to camouflage venous access device.

- Offer realistic assurance of temporary nature of some physical changes.

- Refer to support group.

Rationale

The nurse is in an ideal position to promote acceptance of the situation.

Patients need to understand that hair loss may occur over a short period of time. Some patients begin wearing wigs, scarves, or other types of head coverings before the hair loss occurs. This approach decreases the dramatic changes in their appearance.

It is important that the patient understand that hair and nails will regrow, usually within 1 to 2 months after chemotherapy and that external or implanted venous access devices will eventually be removed.

Groups that come together for mutual support and information can be a valuable resource. Although family and friends can be great allies, often a formal support group or communication with a cancer survivor is most helpful.

See also **Disturbed Body Image,** *p. 21.*

NDx Nursing Diagnosis

Risk for Injury

Common Risk Factor

Improper handling or disposal of waste material in the home

Common Expected Outcome

Nurse, patient, or caregiver maintains safe handling and disposal of waste material according to institutional procedures and policies.

NOC Outcome
Safe Home Environment

NIC Interventions
Surveillance: Safety;
Home Maintenance Assistance

Ongoing Assessment

Actions/Interventions

If chemotherapy is administered in the home:

- Determine that chemotherapy medications are clearly labeled and safely transported to the home.

- Determine that an adequate area is available for the safe preparation of the medication.

Rationale

Safety is a priority.

This area should be at a bathroom or kitchen counter but away from food items that could become contaminated.

■ = Independent; ▲ = Collaborative

Actions/Interventions

■ Ensure that waste materials are disposed of in accordance with established policies (e.g., not flushing unused medication or fluids down the toilet; always placing contaminated needles, tubing, and syringes in biohazard containers).

Rationale

Waste materials are usually returned to the health care facility for appropriate disposal.

Therapeutic Interventions

Actions/Interventions

■ Instruct the family and caregiver to avoid contact with the patient's excreta.

■ If a spill occurs, institute safety precautions according to established procedures (e.g., use of gloves, gown, goggles, plastic disposal bags).

Rationale

The patient may need to use a private bathroom. Contaminated linen should be cared for according to established procedure.

These measures should be rehearsed in the home environment.

> • RELATED CARE PLANS
>
> Anxiety, p. 15
> Deficient fluid volume, p. 71
> Diarrhea, p. 54
> Fear, p. 68
> Hematopoietic stem cell collection (see the **Evolve** website)
> Neutropenia, p. 890
> Risk for infection, p. 108

→ Cancer Radiation Therapy

External Beam; Brachytherapy; Teletherapy

Radiation therapy is the use of ionizing radiation delivered in prescribed doses to a malignancy. Ionizing radiation interacts with the atoms and molecules of malignant cells, interfering with mitotic activity, thereby causing DNA damage. This damage interferes with the malignant cell's ability to reproduce. Adjacent healthy cells experience the same detrimental effects, however, resulting in untoward side effects to radiation therapy. Radiation therapy may be curative of some cancers, or it may be used as a palliative treatment to reduce the pain and pressure from large tumors. Radiation may be used alone or in combination with other treatment modalities such as surgery and chemotherapy.

Radiation therapy can be divided into two broad categories: external radiation, also known as *teletherapy*, and internal radiation, commonly known as *brachytherapy*. Teletherapy administers a prescribed dosage of radiation at a distance from the patient using a linear accelerator. Brachytherapy is the implantation of either sealed (solid) or unsealed (fluid) radioactive sources. The sealed radioactive implant may be contained within an applicator, needle, or seed, and is placed in or near the malignancy. The unsealed radioactive isotope can be administered through the intravenous or oral route or by instillation into a specific body cavity.

The radiation oncologist prescribes the treatment modality and amount of treatment necessary. This treatment plan is based on the location, size, and biological characteristics of the malignancy. The patient's health history and current health status are taken into consideration in treatment planning. All health care providers need to implement principles of radiation safety when caring for patients undergoing radiation therapy.

Cancer Radiation Therapy

■ = Independent; ▲ = Collaborative

Cancer Radiation Therapy—cont'd

 Nursing Diagnosis

Deficient Knowledge

Common Related Factors

Unfamiliarity with treatment protocols
Misinformation about radiation therapy

Defining Characteristics

Verbalizes anxiety about therapy
Asks many questions about treatment
Lack of questions about treatment

Common Expected Outcome

Patient verbalizes accurate knowledge about radiation therapy.

NOC Outcomes

Knowledge: Treatment Procedure;
 Anxiety Self-Control

NIC Interventions

Teaching: Procedure/Treatment;
 Radiation Therapy Management;
 Anxiety Reduction

Ongoing Assessment

Actions/Interventions

■ Assess the patient's knowledge of and previous experience with radiation therapy.

■ Assess any fears, myths, or misconceptions that the patient has about radiation therapy.

Rationale

Appropriate and individualized teaching is based on the patient's current knowledge and perceptions.

Patients and families may have anxiety and fear about the radioactivity of the patient during therapy. These misconceptions need to be clarified and corrected to promote the patient's cooperation with the treatment plan.

Therapeutic Interventions

Actions/Interventions

■ Explain the purpose of radiation therapy.

■ Teach the patient and family what to expect during the treatment procedure:
  • Planning simulation
  • External beam treatment
  • Insertion of internal radiation

Rationale

The patient and family need to understand the role that radiation therapy has in the treatment of the patient's cancer. They need to understand whether the treatment goal is curative or palliative and how it may work with other treatment procedures.

The process of preparation for therapy can be more anxiety producing than the actual procedure itself. Patients having external beam therapy will undergo an extensive and time-consuming planning process that includes a simulation of the treatment. During this

■ = Independent; ▲ = Collaborative

Actions/Interventions	Rationale
	simulation, the treatment area is located and marked on the skin. Adjacent tissue areas that will be shielded or blocked during therapy are identified. The procedure for implanting internal radiation will depend on the location of the malignancy.
■ Explain all site-specific care to the patient and family.	For the patient with external beam therapy, maintaining skin integrity and reporting side effects will facilitate prompt intervention and reduce complications. The generalized side effects associated with radiation therapy are fatigue and anorexia.
■ Correct any misconceptions the patient and family have about radioactivity.	The patient undergoing external beam therapy is never radioactive. The patient and family do not need to take any special safety precautions. The patient with a temporary implant emits radioactivity during the time the implant is in place. These patients are usually hospitalized and specific precautions are taken to reduce radiation exposure to staff and visitors. The patient with a permanent sealed implant has a low level of radiation outside the body and the risk to others is minimal. The patient and family will be taught specific precautions to be taken at home depending on the location of the implant and the half-life of the isotope.
■ Provide information about common side effects.	Fatigue and skin reactions are commonly experienced during radiation to any site. Fatigue can be debilitating. Site-specific side effects may include dry mouth, difficulty swallowing, and bone changes.

NDx Nursing Diagnosis

Risk for Impaired Skin Integrity

Common Risk Factor

External beam radiation

Common Expected Outcome

The patient's skin will remain intact.

NOC Outcome
Tissue Integrity: Skin and Mucous Membranes

NIC Interventions
Skin Surveillance; Radiation Therapy Management; Skin Care: Topical Treatments

Cancer Radiation Therapy

■ = Independent; ▲ = Collaborative

→ **Cancer Radiation Therapy—cont'd**

Ongoing Assessment

Actions/Interventions

■ Assess the patient's skin in the treatment area for signs of radiation effects.

• Erythema and darkening

• Dry desquamation

• Wet desquamation

■ Assess the skin for long-term effects of radiation therapy.

Rationale

Every effort is made in planning external beam treatment to implement skin-sparing approaches to minimize the effect on healthy skin.

Redness of skin may develop within the first 24 hours after the first treatment. As the melanocytes in the skin are stimulated during treatment, the skin may appear darker.

When basal cells of the epidermis are affected by radiation, they begin to shed from the skin and allow new cells to develop.

If the rate of epidermal cell sloughing exceeds the rate of new cell replacement, the skin becomes moist and begins to break down.

Long-term changes in the skin are related to the total amount of radiation the patient received during therapy. The epidermis may be thinner, with less hair and fewer sweat glands in the treatment area. The skin will be less resistant to trauma and may take longer to heal. Fibrosis of the dermis and hyperplasia of the blood vessels may lead to development of telangiectasia and spider veins.

Therapeutic Interventions

Actions/Interventions

■ Clean the skin in the treatment area with a mild, nonperfumed soap and tepid water. Use a soft cloth and avoid rubbing the skin. Dry thoroughly.

■ Apply lubricating lotions or creams that do not contain metals, alcohol, fragrances, or additives that irritate the skin. This includes antiperspirants containing aluminum.

■ Teach the patient to avoid scratching dry, itchy skin.

■ Teach the patient to avoid exposing the skin to pressure, sunlight, rough clothing, shaving, and extremes of temperature.

Rationale

Any markings used as treatment guidelines should not be removed from the skin until therapy is completed. Keeping the skin clean, dry, and free of irritants will promote skin integrity and reduce the risk of wet desquamation.

Intervention protocols may vary among treatment centers. The radiation oncologist may recommend particular brands of moisturizers to relieve dry skin.

Scratching increases skin trauma in the treatment area. Cornstarch, sprinkled on the skin, may provide some relief from itching.

Pressure from tight or irritating clothing will increase skin irritation and the risk of skin breakdown in the treatment area. Lightweight cotton clothing is best. The skin in the treatment area is more vulnerable to the effects of heat, cold, and ultraviolet light from sunlight or artificial sources such as tanning lamps. Use of protective clothing and sunscreens is recommended for the treatment area even after therapy is completed.

■ = Independent; ▲ = Collaborative

Actions/Interventions

▲ Implement skin care protocol for wet desquamation.

Rationale

Treatment of wet desquamation varies among treatment centers. A standard treatment protocol may include irrigation of the area with a solution of one part hydrogen peroxide with three parts normal saline. Dry the area thoroughly and leave open to air. If drainage is present or if the area comes in contact with clothing, a nonadherent dressing may be applied. Use nontape methods to secure the dressing.

Nursing Diagnosis

Risk for Injury (Radiation Exposure)

Common Risk Factors

Internal radiation
Dislodged radiation implant
Lack of knowledge of radiation safety principles

Common Expected Outcome

Health care providers and visitors will have minimal radiation exposure.

NOC Outcomes
Knowledge: Personal Safety;
    Risk Control; Risk Detection

NIC Interventions
Radiation Therapy Management;
    Environment Management;
    Worker Safety

Ongoing Assessment

Actions/Interventions

■ Review the radiation treatment plan:
  • Type of radiation
  • Isotope half-life
  • Method of delivery
  • Duration of treatment

Rationale

Implementation of radiation safety precautions will depend on the amount of energy emitted by the isotope, the half-life of the isotope, and the method used to deliver the radiation. With a sealed implant, the patient's excreta are not radioactive, but the actual implant is. If a systemic unsealed delivery method is used, the patient's secretions and excretions will be radioactive for a time based on the isotope's half-life.

Therapeutic Interventions

Actions/Interventions

■ Provide the patient with a private room and a private bathroom.

Rationale

This type of room placement reduces the risk of radiation exposure to other patients.

Cancer Radiation Therapy

■ = Independent; ▲ = Collaborative

Cancer Radiation Therapy—cont'd

Actions/Interventions

▲ Consult with the hospital's radiation safety officer about appropriate radiation safety protocols.

■ Post signs outside the patient's room.

■ Provide film badges to staff members who are responsible for direct care of the patient.

■ For patients with encapsulated forms of internal radiation, keep appropriate lead-lined containers in the patient's room.

■ Implement all direct patient care activities using principles of time and distance.
- Organize care activities to minimize the amount of time at the patient's bedside.
- Provide only essential care to promote patient comfort.
- Prepare meal trays outside the room.
- Keep bedside tables, call lights, and personal care items within easy reach of the patient at all times to reduce return trips to the bedside.

Rationale

The radiation safety officer will provide appropriate safety guidelines based on the type of internal radiation to be used.

Health care providers and visitors at risk to the effects of radiation need to be warned before entering the patient's room. The signs should indicate precautions to be used when entering the patient's room. Women who are pregnant should avoid all direct contact with the patient until radiation treatment is completed.

Film badges record the amount of exposure to a radiation source. The badge should be worn outside the clothing during all direct contact activities with the patient. The radiation safety officer will periodically review all film badges and quantify the staff member's amount of radiation exposure.

When an implanted radiation source becomes dislodged, most institutions require nurses *not* to touch the source but to call a radiation safety officer to handle the source. The nurse should never pick up a radiation source with bare hands.

Radiation exposure is based on the law of inverse squares. The amount of radiation exposure is inversely related to the square of the distance from the radiation source. A nurse standing 2 feet from the patient has $\frac{1}{4}$ the exposure of someone standing next to the patient ($2^2 = 4$; the inverse of 4 is $\frac{1}{4}$).

> **• RELATED CARE PLAN**
>
> Fatigue, p. 65

Disseminated Intravascular Coagulation (DIC)

Coagulopathy; Defibrination Syndrome

Disseminated intravascular coagulation (DIC) is a coagulation disorder that prompts overstimulation of the normal clotting cascade and results in simultaneous thrombosis and hemorrhage. The formation of microclots affects tissue perfusion in the major organs, causing hypoxia, ischemia, and tissue damage. Coagulation occurs in two different pathways: intrinsic and extrinsic. These pathways are responsible for formation of fibrin clots and blood clotting, which maintains hemostasis. In the intrinsic pathway, endothelial cell damage commonly occurs due to sepsis or infection. The extrinsic pathway is initiated

■ = Independent; ▲ = Collaborative

by tissue injury such as from malignancy, trauma, or obstetrical complications. The medical management of DIC is primarily aimed at (1) treating the underlying cause, (2) managing complications from both primary and secondary causes, (3) supporting organ function, and (4) stopping abnormal coagulation and controlling bleeding.

NDx Nursing Diagnosis

Ineffective Protection

Common Related Factors

Depleted coagulation factors
Adverse effects of heparin

Common Expected Outcomes

Patient experiences reduced episodes of bleeding and hematomas.
Patient's side effects of medication therapy (e.g., heparin, aspirin, warfarin, and nonsteroidal antiinflammatory drugs) are reduced through ongoing assessment and early intervention.
Patient maintains optimal fluid balance, as evidenced by normotensive blood pressure (BP) and urine output greater than 30 mL/hr.

Defining Characteristics

Active bleeding
Abnormal clotting times

NOC Outcomes
Blood Coagulation; Circulation Status

NIC Interventions
Bleeding Precautions;
  Bleeding Reduction;
  Blood Product Administration;
  Medication Administration

Ongoing Assessment

Actions/Interventions

▲ Assess for underlying cause of DIC.

▲ Monitor serial coagulation profiles.

▲ Monitor hematocrit (Hct) and hemoglobin (Hgb).

■ Examine skin surface for signs of bleeding. Note petechiae; purpura; hematomas; oozing of blood from intravenous (IV) sites, drains, and wounds; and bleeding from mucous membranes.

Rationale

DIC is not a primary disease but occurs in response to a precipitating factor such as infection or tumor. Successful treatment of DIC includes management of the underlying disorder.

Initially, accelerated clotting is noted. As the clotting then stimulates the fibrinolytic system, clotting factors become depleted. Common laboratory values in DIC are prothrombin time (PT) greater than 15 seconds, partial thromboplastin time (PTT) greater than 60 to 90 seconds, hypofibrinogenemia, thrombocytopenia, elevated fibrin split products (FSPs), elevated D-dimers (a type of FSP), and prolonged bleeding time. All put the patient at risk for increased bleeding. Specific deficiencies guide treatment therapy.

Decreased Hgb and Hct levels are associated with bleeding from DIC.

Prolonged oozing of blood from injection sites or venipuncture sites could be the first indication of DIC.

Disseminated Intravascular Coagulation (DIC)

■ = Independent; ▲ = Collaborative

Disseminated Intravascular Coagulation (DIC)—cont'd

Actions/Interventions

- Observe for signs of external bleeding from gastro-intestinal (GI) and genitourinary (GU) tracts.

- Note any hemoptysis or blood obtained during suctioning.
- Observe for signs of internal bleeding, such as pain or changes in mental status. Institute neurological checklist.
- Monitor heart rate and BP.

- Observe for signs of orthostatic hypotension (drop of more than 15 mm Hg when changing from supine to sitting position).
- ▲ If heparin therapy is initiated, observe for:
  - Any increase in bleeding from IV sites, GI/GU tracts, respiratory tract, or wounds
  - New purpura, petechiae, or hematomas

Rationale

One of the diagnostic hallmarks of acute DIC can be manifested as bleeding simultaneously from at least three unrelated sites associated with shock, respiratory failure, or renal failure. For example, the patient may have increased skin bruising, hemoptysis, and hematuria.

These are common manifestations of acute DIC.

Mental status changes may occur with the decreased fluid volume or with decreasing Hgb.

Tachycardia and hypotension are signs of decreased cardiac output.

This indicates reduced circulating fluids.

Heparin aborts clotting process by blocking thrombin production.

Therapeutic Interventions

Actions/Interventions

- Institute precautionary measures:

  - Avoid unnecessary venipunctures; draw all laboratory specimens through an existing line: arterial line or venous heparin lock line.
  - Use only compressible vessels for IV sites.
  - Apply pressure to any oozing site.
  - Avoid intramuscular injections.
  - Prevent trauma to the catheters and tubes by proper taping; minimize pulling.
  - Minimize number of cuff BPs.
  - Maintain integrity of arterial line.
  - Use gentle suctioning.
  - Use gentle chest physiotherapy, such as turning, repositioning, coughing, deep breathing, percussion, and vibration.
  - Provide gentle oral care, using saline and water rinses instead of toothbrushes.
  - Use electric rather than safety razor for shaving.
  - If the patient is confused or agitated, pad the side rails.
- ▲ Administer blood products as prescribed: red blood cells (RBCs), fresh frozen plasma (FFP), cryoprecipitate, and platelets.

Rationale

Nursing interventions should be planned and implemented to eliminate potential sources of bleeding and to control the amount of potential bleeding and tissue injury.

This reduces the potential for bleeding from new puncture sites.

This aids in controlling bleeding.

Direct constant pressure prevents excess blood loss.

Any needle stick is a potential bleeding site.

Use of adhesive tape increases the risk of skin trauma.

Cuff inflation can traumatize fragile blood vessels.

This prevents trauma to respiratory mucosa.

This reduces the risk of trauma.

This reduces the risk of bleeding.

This reduces the risk of bleeding.

Safety measures reduce risk of trauma and subsequent bleeding.

RBCs increase oxygen-carrying capacity; FFP replaces clotting factors and inhibitors.

■ = Independent; ▲ = Collaborative

Actions/Interventions

▲ Administer heparin therapy as prescribed. Dose may be titrated based on laboratory values and clinical situation.
  • If bleeding is increased, notify the physician of the possible need to decrease the IV drip

▲ Administer parenteral fluids as prescribed. Anticipate the need for an IV fluid challenge with immediate infusion of fluids for patients with hypotension.

▲ Administer additional medications or investigational drugs as ordered:
  • Amicar (epsilon aminocaproic acid)

  • Antithrombin III concentration

  • Hirudin

Rationale

Heparin inhibits the action of thrombin, which interrupts the clotting cycle and conversion of fibrinogen to fibrin. It also blocks the intrinsic and extrinsic pathways by inhibiting factor X, which slows clot formation.

As the clinical situation improves, the need for heparin decreases. The challenge lies in differentiating the blood loss as an untoward effect of heparin therapy from a worsening of DIC.

Maintenance of an adequate blood volume is vital.

This inhibits fibrinolysis. It is used as an adjunct to heparin. However, its use can lead to organ failure from large vessel thrombosis, and thus its use is controversial.

This is a cofactor of heparin that is used alone or with heparin on a limited basis.

This is a thrombin inhibitor and neutralizer; there is limited clinical experience with this drug.

NDx Nursing Diagnosis

Impaired Gas Exchange

Common Related Factors

Inappropriate coagulation resulting in blood loss with decreased available hemoglobin
Generalized systemic microvascular clot formation

Defining Characteristics

Confusion
Somnolence
Restlessness
Irritability
Hypercapnia
Hypoxia

Common Expected Outcome

Patient maintains optimal gas exchange, as evidenced by normal arterial blood gases (ABGs), and alert, responsive mentation or no further reduction in mental status.

NOC Outcome
Respiratory Status: Gas Exchange

NIC Interventions
Respiratory Monitoring;
  Ventilation Assistance

Ongoing Assessment

Actions/Interventions

■ Assess respiratory rate, rhythm, and depth.

Rationale

Rapid, shallow respirations may result from hypoxia or from the acidosis with the shock state. Development of hypoventilation indicates that immediate ventilator support is needed.

Disseminated Intravascular Coagulation (DIC)

■ = Independent; ▲ = Collaborative

Disseminated Intravascular Coagulation (DIC)—cont'd

Actions/Interventions

- Assess for shortness of breath, use of accessory muscles.
- Assess lung sounds. Assess cough for signs of bloody sputum.
- Assess for changes in orientation and behavior.

- ▲ Monitor pulse oximeter and ABGs.

Rationale

These signify an increased work of breathing.

Hemoptysis is an indication of bleeding in the respiratory tract.

Early signs of cerebral hypoxia are restlessness and anxiety, which lead to agitation and confusion.

Pulse oximetry is a useful tool to detect early changes in O_2. However, for CO_2 levels, ABGs need to be obtained.

Therapeutic Interventions

Actions/Interventions

- Position the patient in high Fowler's position (if hemodynamically stable).
- Change the patient's position every 2 hours and perform chest physiotherapy.
- Suction as needed.
- Provide reassurance and allay anxiety by staying with the patient during acute episodes of respiratory distress.
- ▲ Maintain oxygen delivery system.

- ▲ Anticipate the need for intubation and mechanical ventilation.

See also **Mechanical Ventilation,** *p. 459, and* **Acute Respiratory Distress Syndrome,** *p. 408.*

Rationale

This promotes optimal lung expansion.

This facilitates movement and drainage of secretions.

This clears secretions.

Air hunger can produce an extremely anxious state.

The appropriate amount of oxygen must be delivered continuously so that the patient does not become desaturated.

The ventilator is a life-sustaining treatment.

NDx Nursing Diagnosis

Risk for Ineffective Peripheral, Cardiopulmonary, Cerebral, and Renal Tissue Perfusion

Common Risk Factors

DIC with peripheral thromboembolus formation in capillaries and arterioles resulting in possible interruption of arterial flow

Hypovolemia and blood loss

■ = Independent; ▲ = Collaborative

Common Expected Outcome

Patient's systemic and peripheral circulation is optimized through ongoing assessment and early intervention.

NOC Outcomes

Circulatory Status; Tissue Perfusion: Cardiopulmonary, Cerebral, Peripheral, and Renal

NIC Interventions

Circulatory Precautions; Circulatory Care; Medication Administration

Ongoing Assessment

Actions/Interventions

- Assess color, warmth, movement, and sensation of extremities.
- Assess peripheral pulses and mark with skin marker if diminished. Use Doppler ultrasound as needed to assess for presence of pulses. Notify the physician immediately of signs of decreasing perfusion to an extremity.
- Assess for signs of pulmonary embolus.

- Assess mental status.

- Monitor urine output.
- Assess for any sites of pain.

Rationale

Acute occlusion results in a numb, cold limb, with pain aggravated by movement of the limb.

Although signs of thrombosis are less evident than bleeding in DIC, clots can form in blood vessels of any size in the body. Clots can lead to obstruction of blood flow, with resulting tissue and organ ischemia and infarction.

Intravascular coagulation is part of the pathophysiology of DIC.

Restlessness and anxiety are early signs of reduced cerebral blood flow.

Decreased urine volume suggests reduced renal perfusion.

Obstruction of vessels can occur throughout the body, which can cause pain and physiological complications, such as vasoconstriction and tachycardia. Severe abdominal pain is common due to small bowel infarction from an embolus, partial necrosis of the gut, or hemorrhage into the retroperitoneal space. Other areas to monitor include joints.

Therapeutic Interventions

Actions/Interventions

- Elevate extremities.

▲ Maintain fluids as needed to prevent hypotension.

▲ Administer medications such as heparin, as prescribed.

Rationale

This promotes venous return and prevents edema formation. Edema formation could further add to a decrease in peripheral perfusion.

Hypotension will lead to a further decrease in systemic and peripheral perfusion.

Heparin inhibits formation of microemboli and facilitates perfusion to vital organs.

Disseminated Intravascular Coagulation (DIC)

■ = Independent; ▲ = Collaborative

→ Disseminated Intravascular Coagulation (DIC)—cont'd

NDx Nursing Diagnosis

Deficient Knowledge

Common Related Factors	Defining Characteristics
Lack of familiarity with procedures Unfamiliar environment	Increased questioning Lack of questions

Common Expected Outcome

Patient/significant others verbalize basic understanding of DIC and its management.

NOC Outcomes
Knowledge: Disease Process;
Knowledge: Treatment Procedures

NIC Interventions
Teaching: Disease Process;
Bleeding Precautions

Ongoing Assessment

Actions/Interventions

■ Assess present knowledge of DIC.

Rationale

DIC usually occurs acutely, so the patient and family have no prior knowledge of it.

Therapeutic Interventions

Actions/Interventions

■ Carefully explain the underlying etiology that precipitated DIC.

■ Instruct the patient or significant others to notify the nurse of new bleeding from wounds or IV sites.

■ Explain the purpose of drug and transfusion therapy.

■ Instruct the patient to try to avoid trauma.

Rationale

The causative factor of DIC stimulates the clotting mechanism until it is depleted, and bleeding results. Treatment is aimed first at alleviating the primary cause.

This can aid in achieving early intervention at bleeding sites. However, any new episodes of bleeding may have a traumatic impact on the patient and family.

The controversial nature of treatment may be difficult for the patient or significant others to understand in the acute setting. In addition, frequent use of blood components may also cause fear regarding transmission of infectious diseases such as hepatitis or human immunodeficiency virus.

Trauma may precipitate further bleeding.

• RELATED CARE PLANS

Acute pain, p. 144
Anxiety, p. 15
Deficient fluid volume, p. 71

■ = Independent; ▲ = Collaborative

Hematolymphatic, Immunological, and Oncological Care Plans

Hematopoietic Stem Cell Transplantation (HSCT)

Bone Marrow Transplant; Peripheral Blood Stem Cell Transplant

Bone marrow transplantation (BMT) and peripheral blood stem cell transplantation (PBSCT) are terms that now more commonly fall under the umbrella term of *hematopoietic stem cell transplantation*. The indications for HSCT are expanding; it is used as both a curative and investigational treatment for both malignant and nonmalignant conditions. HSCT should not be confused with the controversial field of embryonic stem cells. Embryonic stem cells, derived from fertilized embryos, are undifferentiated cells that have the ability to form any adult cell. Hematopoietic stem cells are the "mother" cells that differentiate only into the cells of the blood system (e.g., white blood cells [WBCs], red blood cells [RBCs], platelets).

HSCT is used to replace diseased bone marrow, as a hematopoietic rescue after high-dose therapy (radiation and/or chemotherapy), as a form of immunotherapy, and as a vehicle for gene therapy.

There are three major types of transplants:

- *Autologous:* self
- *Syngeneic:* donor from an identical twin
- *Allogeneic:* can be related (from a matched sibling), or unrelated (from a volunteer in the National Marrow Donor Pool [NMDP]). This is also referred to as a MUD (matched unrelated donor) transplant.

There are three sources of hematopoietic stem cells:

- *Bone marrow:* These cells are collected from the pelvic bones through a series of aspirations. Bone marrow harvesting is a surgical procedure done under general anesthesia.
- *Peripheral blood:* The stem cells that normally reside in the bone marrow can be moved or mobilized into the bloodstream (peripheral circulation) and collected in an outpatient procedure via a cell separator or apheresis machine. This procedure does not require anesthesia. The majority of all transplants performed today (>95%) use peripheral blood stem cells rather than bone marrow stem cells.
- *Umbilical cord, placental:* This is a rich source of stem cells that are collected at the time of delivery from tissue that is normally discarded.

There is one other classification of transplant based on the amount and type of pretransplant therapy that is administered. Standard transplants use strong treatment (chemotherapy and/or radiation therapy) administered before transplantation to destroy the host's diseased cells and suppress the host's immune system. This therapy is referred to as *ablative therapy*, because it eliminates all host blood and immune cells. Reduced-intensity transplants—also called *nonmyeloablative transplants* or *minitransplants*—is a transplant that uses less intense treatment to prepare for transplantation than a standard transplant does. Thus the doses of chemotherapy given before transplantation are much lower and do not necessarily eliminate all diseased cells. This type of transplant is only used in the allogeneic setting, because this method relies on the donor's immune cells to fight disease. This care plan focuses on inpatient care. Emotional issues related to HSCT are not addressed here.

Hematopoietic Stem Cell Transplantation (HSCT)

■ = Independent; ▲ = Collaborative

Hematopoietic Stem Cell Transplantation (HSCT)—cont'd

NDx Nursing Diagnosis

Deficient Knowledge

Common Related Factors

Unfamiliarity with procedures and treatments in HSCT
Unfamiliarity with overall schedule of events
Unfamiliarity with possible side effects
Unfamiliarity with discharge and follow-up care

Defining Characteristics

Verbalized lack of knowledge
Expressed need for information
Multiple questions
Lack of questions
Verbalized misconceptions

Common Expected Outcome

Patient or significant others verbalize understanding of procedures, treatments, possible complications, and follow-up care.

NOC Outcomes

Knowledge: Disease Process;
Knowledge: Treatment Procedure

NIC Interventions

Teaching: Disease Process;
Teaching: Preoperative;
Teaching: Prescribed Medications;
Teaching: Procedure/Treatment

Ongoing Assessment

Actions/Interventions

■ Assess the patient's and significant others' understanding of procedures, treatment protocol, potential side effects and complications, schedule of overall treatment plan, and follow-up care after discharge.

Rationale

The patient and family need information based on their understanding of the treatment care plan. A successful treatment plan requires the cooperation of the patient and support of the patient's family.

Therapeutic Interventions

Actions/Interventions

■ Share with the patient a written calendar or schedule of the overall treatment plan.

■ Instruct the patient (significant others as needed) about central venous access device if not already in place.

■ Explain bone marrow or peripheral stem cell collection, storage, and potential complications.

Rationale

The transplantation process includes several phases (i.e., mobilization, collection of HSC, conditioning, infusion, engraftment) depending on the type of transplant.

It is used for administration of chemotherapy, collection of peripheral blood stem cells, stem cell infusion, antibiotic treatment, blood draws, blood component replacement, and total parenteral nutrition (TPN) as appropriate. These catheters may remain in place for several months or longer.

If bone marrow is used, the patient will require preoperative and postoperative teaching. If peripheral blood stem cells are used, the patient will require

■ = Independent; ▲ = Collaborative

Actions/Interventions

Rationale

mobilization therapy with chemotherapy and/or growth factors, and collection of peripheral blood stem cells via apheresis (see **Hematopoietic Stem Cell Collection** care plan on the **Evolve** website).

■ Discuss preparative or conditioning regimen, potential short- and long-term side effects, and preventive measures to minimize or alleviate toxicities (e.g., antiemetic, oral regimens, pain control).

The conditioning regimen can be ablative (high-dose) or nonmyeloablative (reduced-intensity). Potential side effects will vary (e.g., nausea and vomiting and loss of appetite are generally less with the nonmyeloablative conditioning protocols).

■ Discuss the HSCT procedure for bone marrow and peripheral stem cell infusion and potential complications, and discuss the time frame for marrow engraftment.

The procedure and potential complications for stem cell infusion depend on whether the stem cell product is fresh or frozen. Allogeneic transplants generally mean that the stem cell product is collected from the donor and infused to the recipient on the same day (i.e., "fresh"). In this case, the stem cell infusion is similar to a blood transfusion. Autologous transplants use frozen stem cells, in that stem cells from the donor (i.e., the patient) have been collected and stored ahead of time. Infusion of frozen or cryopreserved stem cells is more involved, with more potential complications related to infusion of the cryopreservative (DMSO), which can cause side effects in the recipient.

■ Discuss the time frame for marrow engulfment.

After infusion, stem cells travel to the bone marrow and stimulate production of new blood cells (RBCs, WBCs, and platelets). This process is referred to as *engraftment*. The time after transplantation until engraftment depends upon the source of cells: for peripheral blood stem cells, engraftment occurs as early as 7 to 10 days, but can take up to 21 days. Cord blood transplants take longer to engraft (21 to 35 days). Full recovery of function may take up to several months or longer (1 to 2 years) depending on the type of transplant.

■ Discuss administration of neutrophil growth factors (i.e., granulocyte colony-stimulating factor [G-CSF]).

Growth factors are administered after stem cell infusion to accelerate engraftment.

■ Discuss blood component transfusions (i.e., packed RBCs and platelets). Encourage the patient and significant others to participate in blood component donor accrual to fulfill transfusion requirements as needed.

These transfusions constitute adjunct management of anemia, and thrombocytopenia. The widespread adoption of peripheral blood as the stem cell source has resulted in a reduced period of pancytopenia and a subsequent reduced need for transfusion support. Many patients get through the peritransplant phase without ever needing an RBC or platelet transfusion. However, families can still be encouraged to donate blood products, although this is not required specifically for family members.

■ Discuss the need to maintain a protective environment (e.g., private room, laminar airflow room). Provide information about isolation techniques and procedures.

Environmental changes protect the patient from contagions during the myelosuppression period.

■ Discuss antibacterial, antifungal, and antiviral therapy to prevent and treat infections.

Infections can be caused by bacteria, viruses, or fungi. Patients are given drugs to prevent infection even if they do not have any signs of such.

■ Discuss dietary modifications, which may include a low-bacterial diet (no fresh fruits or vegetables; "well-cooked" food items).

This decreases bacterial contamination of the alimentary tract.

Hematopoietic Stem Cell Transplantation (HSCT)

(■ = Independent; ▲ = Collaborative)

Hematopoietic Stem Cell Transplantation (HSCT)—cont'd

Actions/Interventions	Rationale
■ Explain the need for frequent blood sampling.	Sampling is indicated to assess for electrolyte and metabolic changes; cardiac, pulmonary, and renal alterations; bone marrow function; the need for blood component transfusions; and the presence of infection.
■ Explain the need for frequent inspection and culturing of all orifices and potential infection sites.	This is required for surveillance of opportunistic microorganisms, early detection, and prompt treatment of infection.
■ Discuss discharge planning and teaching:	
• Timing of discharge	Timing depends on type of transplant and course of postengraftment period. Length of stay averages 14 to 21 days. Discharge criteria include absolute granulocyte count above 500 to 1000/mm³, oral intake of at least 1000 kcal/day, no evidence of infection or bleeding, and psychological readiness to return home.
• Importance of follow-up visits for blood studies and monitoring for potential complications	Information aids the patient in assuming responsibility for ongoing care.
• Activities of daily living	The patient should gradually resume activities, because fatigue and reduced endurance will be a problem.
• Medications after discharge	Patients are better able to ask questions and seek assistance when they know basic information about all medications prescribed.
• Importance of balanced diet/adequate fluid intake	Information provides rationale for therapy.
• Central venous catheter care (e.g., Hickman, Perma-Cath)	Risk of complications is associated with long-term use. Aseptic techniques need to be taught.
• Measures to prevent infection (e.g., avoiding children with infections or who have recently been immunized, avoiding crowds)	The patient's immune function is not fully restored until about 6 to 12 months after transplantation; many patients are fearful of leaving the hospital's "protective isolation" environment.
• Recognition and reporting of signs and symptoms of bleeding, low RBC count, and infection	Early assessment facilitates prompt treatment.
• Sexual relations and contraception	Libido may be decreased. Women may need vaginal lubrication.
• Return to work or school	Timing for return is related to risk for infection.

NDx Nursing Diagnosis

Risk for Infection

Common Risk Factors

Immunosuppression secondary to high-dose chemotherapy or radiation therapy
Antimicrobial therapy (i.e., superimposed infection)
Prolonged bone marrow regeneration
Failure of bone marrow graft
Cytomegalovirus (CMV)/herpes simplex virus seropositivity

■ = Independent; ▲ = Collaborative

Common Expected Outcome

Patient is at reduced risk of local and systemic infection, as evidenced by negative blood surveillance culture findings, compliance with preventive measures, normal chest radiograph, intact mucous membranes and skin, and prompt reporting of early signs of infection.

NOC Outcomes
Infection Status; Medication Response

NIC Interventions
Infection Protection; Chemotherapy Management; Medication Administration; Teaching: Individual

Ongoing Assessment

Actions/Interventions

- Inspect body sites with high potential for infection (mouth, throat, axilla, perineum, rectum).

- Inspect peripheral intravenous and/or catheter sites for redness and tenderness.

- Observe closely for fever and chills.

- Auscultate lung field.
- Assess risk factors predisposing to CMV infection: allogeneic BMT, CMV seropositivity, total body irradiation, acute graft-versus-host disease (GVHD).

▲ Monitor WBC count with differential and absolute neutrophil count daily for evidence of rising or falling counts.

▲ Monitor cultures and sensitivities and CMV titers of blood, sputum, and urine.

Rationale

Early detection facilitates prompt treatment.

These are frequent sites of infection.

A temperature greater than 37° C (98.6° f) may indicate systemic infection. These may be the initial presentation of infection because, in the absence of granulocytes, the locus of infection may develop without characteristic inflammation or pus formation at the site.

Pneumonia can be fatal in this population.

Infections are common posttransplant.

Neutropenia puts patients at increased risk, especially before engraftment. Even a slight rise in WBC count may signal an infection due to the patient's impaired immune system.

Cultures provide data on which microorganisms are causing infection and antibiotic drug sensitivity.

Therapeutic Interventions

Actions/Interventions

▲ Place the patient in protective isolation according to transplant protocol.

- Ensure thorough hand washing (using vigorous friction) by the staff and visitors before physical contact with the patient.

Rationale

Protective isolation precautions may include placing the patient in a private room, limiting visitors, and having all people who come in contact with the patient use masks, gloves, and gowns. Some hospitals may place patients in special sterile laminar airflow rooms. These precautions reduce the risk of patient exposure to opportunistic infections.

Hand washing removes transient and resident bacteria from hands, thus minimizing or preventing transmission to the patient.

Hematopoietic Stem Cell Transplantation (HSCT)

■ = Independent; ▲ = Collaborative

Hematopoietic Stem Cell Transplantation (HSCT)—cont'd

Actions/Interventions	Rationale
■ Teach or provide meticulous total body hygiene with special attention to frequent sites of infection (e.g., anal area, breast folds, skin folds, groin).	The perineal area is a source of many pathogens and frequent portal of entry for microorganisms.
■ Implement a meticulous oral hygiene regimen.	This is important in prevention of periodontal disease as a locus of infection.
▲ Institute a low-bacterial diet.	This protects the patient from exposure to pathogens from foods at a time when host defenses are greatly compromised.
▲ Administer antiinfective drugs for prophylaxis or treatment, as prescribed.	Medications may be given before and after transplant as well as to treat infection. Prophylactic administration of acyclovir, trimethoprim-sulfamethoxazole (Bactrim), and/or penicillin is routine until immune function is restored. Ganciclovir can effectively treat CMV viremia.
■ Explain the effects of chemotherapy and radiation therapy on the immune system.	Information provides basis for ongoing education.

■ Explain to the patient or significant others the role of WBCs in infection prevention
• Normal range of WBC
• Function of leukocytes and neutrophils
• Meaning or importance of absolute neutrophil count (ANC):
  • >2000/mm^3 = No risk
  • 1500-2000/mm^3 = Mild risk
  • 1000-1499/mm^3 = Moderate risk
  • 500-999/mm^3 = High risk
  • <500/mm^3 = Life-threatening risk
	Patients need to be comanagers of their treatment plan. Adequate knowledge is necessary for ongoing monitoring of potential complications.

■ Teach the patient or significant others measures to prevent infection after discharge until immune function is fully restored (about 9 to 12 months after transplantation): • Avoid crowds or contact with persons with known infections. • Avoid contact with cat litter boxes, fish tanks, bird cages, and dog and human excreta. • Avoid swimming in private or public pools for at least a year. • Avoid construction sites and home remodeling. • Avoid sweeping and vacuuming. • Practice meticulous oral and body hygiene, including frequent hand washing, especially before handling food. • Use aseptic technique when caring for a central venous catheter. • Maintain a balanced diet with sufficient protein, calories, vitamins, minerals, and fluids.	Patients and family members are more likely to implement infection control measures at home when they understand the risks and benefits to the patient. Animal excreta, soil, and people with known infections are sources of opportunistic infections for the immune-compromised patient after transplantation.

Hematolymphatic, Immunological, and Oncological Care Plans

■ = Independent; ▲ = Collaborative

Nursing Diagnosis

Ineffective Protection

Common Related Factors

Bone marrow suppression secondary to chemotherapy and radiation therapy
Prolonged bone marrow regeneration
Failure of bone marrow graft
Invasion of bone marrow by malignant cells
Venoocclusive disease (VOD)
GVHD
Drug injury (chemotherapy or antimicrobial therapy)
Hepatic malignancy
Immunosuppressive therapy (e.g., cyclosporine, methotrexate, steroids, antithymocyte globulins)
Drug or transfusion reactions

Defining Characteristics

Pancytopenia: reduced platelets, reduced RBCs, reduced WBCs
Liver dysfunction or failure
Renal dysfunction
Facial edema and flushing
Wheezing
Skin rashes

Common Expected Outcomes

Patient maintains reduced risk of bleeding, as evidenced by normal platelet count, absence of signs of bleeding, and early report of any signs of bleeding.
Patient maintains optimal liver function, as evidenced by serum and urine laboratory values within normal limits, absence of ascites, balanced intake and output (I&O), and normal weight for patient.
Patient maintains optimal renal function, as evidenced by balanced I&O, weight within normal limits, normal vital signs, and alert mentation.
Patient maintains optimal skin integrity.
Patient is free of injury from drug or blood therapy as evidenced by normal vital signs, absence of pain, and absence of nausea and vomiting.

NOC Outcomes

Circulation Status; Blood Coagulation; Vital Signs

NIC Interventions

Chemotherapy Management; Bleeding Precautions; Hemodynamic Regulation; Vital Sign Monitoring

Ongoing Assessment

Actions/Interventions

For risk of bleeding:

■ Assess for any signs of bleeding.

■ Monitor vital signs as needed.

▲ Monitor platelets, RBCs, hemoglobin (Hgb), and hematocrit (Hct) daily.

Rationale

These are most commonly seen during the first 4 weeks after BMT. Signs may be obvious (e.g., epistaxis, bleeding gums, hematemesis, hemoptysis, retinal hemorrhages, melena, hematuria, vaginal bleeding) or occult (e.g., neurological changes, dizziness).

Increased heart rate and orthostatic blood pressure changes accompany bleeding.

Engraftment (recovery) of bone marrow stem cells begins in 1 to 2 weeks. Normal values from successful engraftment may be seen in 2 to 3 months.

Hematopoietic Stem Cell Transplantation (HSCT)

■ = Independent; ▲ = Collaborative

Hematopoietic Stem Cell Transplantation (HSCT)—cont'd

Actions/Interventions

For risk of liver dysfunction:

- Assess for risk factors predisposing to development of VOD:
  - Intense toxic conditioning regimen
  - Total body irradiation
  - Liver abnormalities before transplantation (hepatitis)
  - Allogeneic BMT
  - Patients with malignant diseases (leukemia, lymphoma, solid tumors)
  - Second BMT

- Assess for signs of liver dysfunction: sudden weight gain, enlarged liver, right upper quadrant pain, ascites, jaundice, tea-colored urine, labored and shallow respirations, dyspnea, confusion, and lethargy and fatigue.

- ▲ Monitor laboratory values daily for:
  - Increased alkaline phosphatase, bilirubin, serum aspartate aminotransferase, alanine aminotransferase, lactic dehydrogenase, and ammonia levels
  - Decreased serum albumin level
  - Electrolyte imbalance
  - Abnormal coagulation profile

For risk of renal dysfunction:

- Monitor urine output. Measure urine volume for a single nursing shift and compare with volume for previous shift.

- ▲ Monitor laboratory data: sodium, potassium, blood urea nitrogen (BUN), creatinine, osmolality.

- Monitor fluid balance (I&O, weight).

- Observe for presence of peripheral and/or dependent edema.

- Monitor for changes in mental status.

- Monitor drug profile for medications potentially contributing to renal insufficiency and/or mental status changes.

For risk from drug or transfusion reactions:

- Assess for reaction from chemotherapeutic drugs: restlessness, facial edema and flushing, wheezing, skin rash, tachycardia, hypotension, hematuria (Cytoxan), and increased uric acid levels.

- Test urine for blood.

Rationale

Chemotherapy or radiation therapy can cause deposits of fibrous materials to form in the small veins of the liver, obstructing blood flow from it. VOD is the occlusion of these vessels. There is no proven preventive therapy for VOD.

Classic signs of VOD include weight gain, ascites, hepatomegaly. Typically, symptoms develop 1 to 4 weeks after transplantation. Patients usually present with some but not all of these symptoms.

Specific deficiencies guide treatment.

Decreased urine volume less than 30 mL/hr suggests renal insufficiency.

Increased potassium, BUN, and creatinine are associated with decreased renal function. Chemotherapy, radiation therapy, antibiotics, and immunosuppressive drugs may cause renal failure.

Close monitoring of fluid balance is necessary to determine adequate replacement needs and to prevent excessive administration of oral or IV fluids during decreased renal function.

These changes reflect fluid imbalance.

BUN and other waste products can build up in the blood and can cause uremic encephalopathy.

Drug dosage adjustment or discontinuation may be necessary to prevent toxic side effects of poorly excreted drugs.

Careful monitoring for potential adverse effects is required both during and after administration.

Hematuria may be caused by irritation of the bladder lining secondary to metabolites from Cytoxan therapy. High urine flow, alkalinization of urine, and frequent voiding help prevent concentration of Cytoxan metabolites in the bladder, thus reducing risk of hemorrhagic cystitis.

■ = Independent; ▲ = Collaborative

Hematolymphatic, Immunological, and Oncological Care Plans

Actions/Interventions

■ Assess for reactions from immunoglobulins: urticaria, pain (local erythema), headache, muscle stiffness, fever and malaise, nephrotic syndrome, angioedema, and anaphylaxis.

■ Assess for reactions to immunosuppressive therapy: mucositis, nausea and vomiting, bone marrow suppression, fluid retention, hypertension, headache, hypomagnesemia, renal toxicity, tingling in extremities, tremors, and anaphylaxis-like reactions.

For risk from GVHD:

■ Assess risk factors predisposing to development of GVHD: older age, sex-mismatched donor, human leukocyte antigen–mismatched donor.

■ Assess for signs of acute GVHD: skin rash or scaling, elevated bilirubin levels, gastrointestinal (GI) changes (diarrhea, abdominal cramps).

Rationale

Reactions can be serious and even life threatening.

A variety of reactions may occur depending on the agent administered.

GVHD is one of the most serious complications of allogeneic HSCT. It occurs when T cells from the donated marrow (the "graft") identify the recipient body (the "host") as foreign and attack it. However, the presence of some level of GVHD does indicate adequate or successful engraftment.

GVHD can affect skin, GI tract, and liver.

Therapeutic Interventions

Actions/Interventions

For risk of bleeding:

▲ Implement bleeding precautions for platelet count less than 50,000/mm³:

  • Avoid nonessential invasive procedures, punctures, and injections.

  • Avoid rectal thermometers, suppositories, and enemas.

  • Maintain appropriate fall precautions.

▲ Communicate anticipated need for platelet support to transfusion center.

▲ Transfuse platelets as prescribed.

▲ Maintain a current blood sample for "type and screen" in the transfusion center.

▲ If a significant drop in Hgb and Hct is noted, transfuse packed RBCs as prescribed.

For risk for liver dysfunction:

▲ Restrict fluids and sodium as prescribed.

▲ Consult a dietitian about dietary modifications in enteral or parenteral nutrition.

Rationale

At this level, spontaneous bleeding can occur.

This reduces bleeding at vascular access sites.

This reduces mucosal injury.

Safety measures reduce risk of trauma.

This ensures availability and readiness of platelets.

Platelet transfusion is indicated for counts less than or equal to 10,000/mm³ unless the patient is actively bleeding; this decreases the risk for the patient becoming refractory to platelet transfusions.

This ensures availability and readiness of packed RBCs.

These are used to restore Hgb and Hct to levels where the patient experiences minimal symptoms (check whether blood components were irradiated before transfusion).

Restrictions reduce fluid buildup. Fluid management is key.

Oral protein may need to be restricted; TPN solutions may need to be concentrated.

Hematopoietic Stem Cell Transplantation (HSCT)

■ = Independent; ▲ = Collaborative

Hematopoietic Stem Cell Transplantation (HSCT)—cont'd

Actions/Interventions	Rationale
▲ Administer Actigall as ordered.	This medication is used routinely for patients at high risk of VOD or those exhibiting signs and symptoms of potential VOD.
▲ Administer IV medications with minimal amount of solution. Consult a pharmacist.	This decreases unnecessary fluids.
▲ Administer diuretics as prescribed.	These decrease the amount of ascites and helps maintain adequate renal perfusion.
▲ Transfuse packed RBCs as prescribed.	Packed RBCs maintain intravascular fluid volume. The goal of hypertransfusion of packed RBCs is to attain an Hct of 40 or greater, which helps maintain high osmotic pressure within the vascular space. This in turn draws extravascular interstitial fluid back into the vessels.
▲ Administer analgesics as prescribed.	These are used for patient discomfort with ascites and related problems. Narcotics and sedatives with shorter half-lives and fewer metabolites given in reduced doses should be considered to prevent compounding of hepatic encephalopathy.

For risk of renal dysfunction:

▲ Administer IV fluids and diuretics as prescribed.	These are used to correct vascular volume disequilibrium.
▲ Administer electrolytes in IV fluids.	This is necessary to match calculated loss and correct any deficit.
▲ Administer low-dose ("renal dose") dopamine.	This is indicated to maintain urine flow.
▲ Consult a dietitian about dietary modifications in enteral or parenteral nutrition.	Specialty expertise may be needed.

For risk from drug or blood reactions:

▲ Keep emergency drugs (IV Benadryl, hydrocortisone, epinephrine 1:1000) readily available.	Patient safety is a priority. Being prepared reduces complications.
▲ Administer IV fluids and diuretics before, during, and after Cytoxan therapy, as prescribed.	These are used to maintain good urine output and counteract antidiuretic effect of Cytoxan. As chemotherapy destroys tumor cells, uric acid is liberated and accumulates in blood. High urine flow prevents uric acid deposits in kidneys.
▲ Premedicate patient with antiemetic and antihistamine as prescribed before infusion.	These are used to reduce incidence of nausea and vomiting and of allergic reactions. Allergic reactions, including shortness of breath, are possibly the result of liberation of histamines from broken marrow cells.
■ Provide warm blankets if chills occur during reinfusion.	Chills usually are secondary to cool temperature of thawed marrow or peripheral stem cell concentrate.
▲ Do the following when drug or transfusion reaction is suspected: stop infusion, notify physician, administer emergency drugs as prescribed, and reassure the patient.	Rapid, efficient intervention is critical to saving life.

For GVHD:

▲ Administer immunosuppressive drugs as prescribed.	These are used to prevent or treat acute GVHD (drugs include cyclosporine, tacrolimus, methotrexate, steroids, immunoglobulins). GVHD results when the T lymphocytes in the transplanted donor bone marrow

■ = Independent; ▲ = Collaborative

Actions/Interventions

Rationale

recognize the marrow recipient as "foreign" and mount an immunological "attack" against the "host." GVHD generally is seen in patients receiving allogeneic BMT. It remains one of the major causes of transplantation-related mortality.

▲ Implement the following once signs of GVHD skin changes are present:

- Use mild soap and oatmeal bath preparation daily.

These soothe dry, flaky, irritated skin.

- Administer antipruritic medications (i.e., antihistamines).

Systemic agents can be effective in relieving itching and promoting comfort.

- Trim the patient's nails and discourage him or her from scratching; consider use of mittens.

This reduces skin trauma.

- Lubricate skin well with frequent applications of a mixture of half-and-half mineral oil and ointment.

This provides relief.

NDx Nursing Diagnosis

Diarrhea

Common Related Factors

Intestinal GVHD
Side effects of high-dose chemotherapy or radiation therapy
Oral magnesium
Antacids
Antibiotic therapy
Infection

Defining Characteristics

Abdominal pain
Cramping
Frequency of stools
Loose or liquid stools
Urgency
Hyperactive bowel sounds and sensations

Common Expected Outcome

Patient passes soft, formed stool no more than three times per day.

NOC Outcomes
Bowel Elimination; Medication Response

NIC Interventions
Diarrhea Management; Nutrition Therapy; Medication Administration; Perineal Care

Ongoing Assessment

Actions/Interventions

Rationale

■ Check bowel sounds; observe for abdominal distention, rigidity, and discomfort.

Hyperactive bowel sounds and abdominal pain and cramping are associated with diarrhea.

■ Observe stool pattern; record frequency, character, and volume.

Diarrhea can be the first manifestation of GVHD; it is usually high volume (500 to 1500 mL/day) and watery green, and contains mucus strands, protein, and cellular debris.

■ = Independent; ▲ = Collaborative

Hematopoietic Stem Cell Transplantation (HSCT)

Hematopoietic Stem Cell Transplantation (HSCT)—cont'd

Actions/Interventions

▲ Obtain stool specimen for culture and sensitivity, as prescribed.

■ Hematest all watery stools.

Rationale

Specimen provides evidence of causative organism, such as *Clostridium difficile*.

This aids in detecting possible GI mucosal sloughing caused by chemotherapy or radiation therapy or by GVHD-related mucosal injury.

Therapeutic Interventions

Actions/Interventions

▲ Administer antidiarrheal, antispasmodic medication as prescribed; document effectiveness.

▲ Administer IV analgesics.

■ Implement meticulous perianal care regimen.

▲ Administer parenteral nutrition as prescribed.

▲ Consult a dietitian for diet specifications.

Rationale

Most antidiarrheal drugs suppress GI motility, thus allowing for more fluid absorption.

These relieve abdominal pain and cramping.

This prevents mucosal irritation/breakdown.

Optimal nutritional support is important in view of inadequate oral intake and decreased absorption secondary to diarrhea and intestinal GVHD.

Specialist may be able to tailor an optimal meal plan for the patient.

NDx Nursing Diagnosis

Risk for Imbalanced Nutrition: Less Than Body Requirements

Common Risk Factors

Side effects of chemotherapy or radiation therapy (inability to taste and smell foods, loss of appetite, nausea and vomiting, mucositis, mouth and throat lesions, xerostomia, diarrhea)

Intestinal GVHD: abdominal cramping, diarrhea, and malabsorption of nutrients

Increased metabolic rate secondary to fever or infection and other metabolic alterations

Common Expected Outcome

Patient maintains optimal nutritional status and protein stores as evidenced by caloric intake adequate to meet body requirements, balanced I&O, and absence of nausea and vomiting or other GI symptoms.

NOC Outcomes

Nutritional Status: Food and Fluid Intake; Nutritional Status: Nutrient Intake

NIC Interventions

Nutrition Therapy; Total Parenteral Nutrition; Chemotherapy Management

Hematolymphatic, Immunological, and Oncological Care Plans

Ongoing Assessment

Actions/Interventions	**Rationale**

■ Determine specific cause or causes for imbalanced nutrition. See Common Risk Factors on the previous page.

Specific cause guides treatment plan.

■ Obtain history of side effects of previous chemotherapy or radiation therapy and treatment measures used in the past.

Patients may have had adverse side effects in the past. However, newer antiemetic agents have improved the management of nausea and vomiting for many patients.

■ Review the patient's description of current nausea and vomiting pattern, if present.

Pattern may guide treatment because not all patients experience the same response.

■ Evaluate the effectiveness of the current antiemetic regimen.

Ongoing nausea and vomiting can significantly affect the quality of one's life. Newer antiemetics may be effective.

■ Monitor daily calorie counts and I&O.

These are important to determine whether the patient's oral intake meets daily nutritional requirements.

■ Weigh the patient daily on the same scale and at the same time.

This ensures accuracy of weight. The patient may be unaware of small weight changes.

▲ Monitor laboratory values: complete blood count with differential; electrolytes; serum iron, total iron-binding capacity, total protein, and albumin.

These provide information on nutritional, fluid, and electrolyte status.

■ If on TPN, monitor closely for tolerance to TPN solution and for any potential adverse complications.

Common problems include hyperglycemia or hypoglycemia, hypophosphatemia, electrolyte disorders, hyperosmolarity, dislodgment of catheter or infiltration, and catheter sepsis.

Therapeutic Interventions

Actions/Interventions	**Rationale**

■ Identify and provide favorite foods; avoid serving them during periods of nausea and vomiting.

The patient may develop an aversion to specific foods as a result of drug side effects.

▲ Administer supplemental feedings or fluids, as prescribed.

Such supplements can be used to increase calories and protein.

■ Implement appropriate GVHD diet or NPO (nothing by mouth) status ("gut rest") in the presence of abdominal cramps, pain, or diarrhea.

These symptoms generally indicate injury to intestinal mucosal surfaces, resulting in nutrient malabsorption and making TPN support necessary.

■ Teach methods to minimize or prevent nausea and vomiting and maintain adequate nutritional intake:

Modifications in dietary intake may reduce the stimulus for nausea and vomiting. Interventions to stimulate appetite and reduce noxious environmental stimuli may enhance nutrient intake.

• Small dietary intake before treatments

Limited intake reduces gastric overdistention.

• Foods with low potential for nausea (e.g., dry toast, crackers, ginger ale, cola, Popsicles, gelatin, baked or boiled potatoes)

These foods are easily digested and provide a measure of success to augment nutrition.

• Avoidance of spices, gravy, greasy foods, and foods with strong odors

These foods can stimulate gastric motility.

• Modification of food consistency or type, as needed

Bland foods may be better tolerated.

• Rest periods before and after meals

This provides needed energy for eating and digestion.

• Quiet, restful environment

Relaxation reduces peristalsis.

Hematopoietic Stem Cell Transplantation (HSCT)

■ = Independent; ▲ = Collaborative

Hematopoietic Stem Cell Transplantation (HSCT)—cont'd

Actions/Interventions

- Oral hygiene measures before, after, and between meals
- Antiemetic half an hour before meals, as prescribed
- Relaxation therapy, guided imagery

▲ Administer antiemetic around the clock rather than as needed. Schedule before, during, and after chemotherapy or radiation therapy.

Rationale

Nausea is often associated with anorexia and increased salivation. Oral hygiene will help promote comfort.

Antiemetics relieve nausea and vomiting.

These techniques can be helpful if used before nausea occurs or increases.

This is important to maintain adequate blood levels.

> **• RELATED CARE PLANS**
>
> Central venous access devices (see the **Evolve** website)
> Leukemia, p. 858
> Neutropenia, p. 890

Human Immunodeficiency Virus (HIV)

Acquired Immunodeficiency Syndrome (AIDS)

Human immunodeficiency virus (HIV) causes acquired immunodeficiency syndrome (AIDS). Transmission of HIV occurs in situations that allow contact with body fluids that are infected with the virus. The primary body fluids associated with transmission are blood, vaginal secretions, semen, and breast milk. Transmission of HIV can occur during sexual intercourse with an infected partner. Transmission through blood and blood product administration occurred early in the history of HIV in the United States. With current methods for screening blood donors and testing donated blood before transfusion, this is no longer considered a route of infection transmission. However, contact with infected blood through shared intravenous equipment and accidental needle sticks is still possible. Perinatal transmission of the virus from mother to baby is thought to occur during pregnancy, during delivery, or through breast-feeding. Most of the early victims of the syndrome were homosexual men; however, in many cities today, infected intravenous (IV) drug users, their sexual partners, and their children outnumber infected homosexual men. HIV is spreading most rapidly in the Hispanic and African-American communities, and among people older than 50 years of age.

The first signs of HIV infection occur when the body produces HIV antibodies. Flulike signs and symptoms that may last 1 to 2 weeks characterize this stage of the infection. After this stage, the patient may be asymptomatic for acute infection, depending on his or her general state of health. This asymptomatic stage can last 10 years or longer. When the immune system begins to fail, the patient exhibits signs of immune system incompetence. The patient begins to develop clinical conditions such as cancers and opportunistic infections. When the patient's CD4 lymphocyte count falls below 200, AIDS is diagnosed. Patients present at various stages of the disease. Treatment regimens are changing rapidly. Patients are treated in hospital, ambulatory care, and home care settings. People may receive prophylactic antiretroviral therapy following high-risk, unprotected sexual or injection drug exposures. The nursing diagnosis list of problems for various stages of HIV/AIDS is extensive. Some are highlighted here.

■ = Independent; ▲ = Collaborative

Nursing Diagnosis

Deficient Knowledge: Disease and Transmission

Common Related Factors

New condition
Fear of AIDS

Defining Characteristics

Multiple questions
Lack of questions
Confusion about disease, complications

Common Expected Outcome

Patient verbalizes understanding of disease process, transmission, complications, and treatment modalities.

NOC Outcomes

Knowledge: Disease Process;
Knowledge: Infection Control;
Knowledge: Sexual Functioning

NIC Interventions

Teaching: Disease Process;
Teaching: Prescribed Medications;
Teaching: Safe Sex; Teaching: Individual;
Infection Protection

Ongoing Assessment

Actions/Interventions

- Assess the patient's knowledge of the disease process, routes of transmission, complications, and treatment modalities.

- Determine the patient's or significant others' concerns about HIV infection.

- Determine at-risk behaviors, including sexual activities and IV drug use.

Rationale

Because of the chronic nature of HIV infection, the patient needs information about the disease and its treatment to make appropriate decisions about his or her health behaviors.

Patients, family members, and significant others may have fear of rejection or retaliation when disclosing a patient's HIV infection. Lack of accurate information about the disease and its transmission may interfere with interpersonal relationships and social support for the patient.

HIV is spread primarily through unprotected sexual activity and by sharing contaminated needles and syringes for IV drug use.

Therapeutic Interventions

Actions/Interventions

- Instruct the patient about a schedule of appointments and treatments.
- Instruct the patient on the signs and symptoms of disease, opportunistic infections, and neoplasms, as well as the person to whom information should be reported.

Rationale

Information enables the patient to take some control of situation.

Collaborative management of this disease focuses on monitoring for progression of disease, effectiveness of drug therapy, side effects experienced, and occurrence of complications. This requires an ongoing relationship with the health care provider.

Human Immunodeficiency
Virus (HIV)

■ = Independent; ▲ = Collaborative

Human Immunodeficiency Virus (HIV)—cont'd

Actions/Interventions

■ Instruct the patient regarding interventions to prevent opportunistic infections:
  - Vaccines

  - Medications

  - Other
    - Avoid raw vegetables, raw fish, milk, and raw meat.
    - Avoid changing the cat's litter box.

■ Instruct the patient in methods of preventing HIV transmission sexually:
  - Safe sex: kissing, touching, mutual masturbation
  - Probably safe: vaginal or anal intercourse with latex condom and spermicidal lubricant
  - Possibly safe: oral intercourse between man and woman, two men, or two women.
  - Unsafe: vaginal or anal intercourse without condom; sexual activities that cause bleeding

■ Explore ways to express physical intimacy that do not lead to infection.

■ Explore the patient's sexual partner's perception of personal risk of HIV infection.

■ Role-play to practice new behaviors (e.g., saying "no" or negotiating condom use) in situations that may lead to transmission.

■ Explore the benefits and drawbacks of HIV testing of sexual partners and needle-sharing partners.

■ Instruct the patient and partners to prevent pregnancy. Instruct in birth control methods, including condom use.

■ Counsel pregnant women at high risk for HIV infection to be tested for HIV.

Rationale

Appropriate prophylaxis can reduce morbidity and mortality.

Vaccines may include hepatitis B virus (HBV) vaccine, as well as annual influenza and pneumococcal vaccines.

Patients with a lymphocyte count of less than 200 CD4 cells need medications to prevent PCP (*Pneumocystis carinii* pneumonia). Patients with a lymphocyte count of less than 100 CD4 cells who are infected with *Toxoplasma gondii* need medication to prevent reactivation. Patients with a lymphocyte count of less than 50 CD4 cells need medication to prevent *Mycobacterium avium* complex (MAC) infection. Patients with a history of cryptococcal meningitis or end-organ cytomegalovirus disease need ongoing medication to prevent recurrence. Patients with tuberculosis (TB) skin test results that indicate latent TB infection need treatment to prevent progression to TB.

These foods harbor bacteria and protozoa that may cause infection in severely compromised people.

Toxoplasma gondii may be transmitted from the stool of an infected cat.

Activities in which there is no contact with a partner's blood, semen, or vaginal secretions are safe. When properly used, latex condoms reduce the risk of HIV transmission for both partners. Both male and female condoms are available.

Patients need to have open communication with their sexual partners to negotiate risk-reduction methods.

It is important to assess knowledge rather than make assumptions.

Practice instills confidence to perform desired behavior. Older adults may be reluctant to use condoms because they are past childbearing age.

If the test is positive, benefits include initiation of antiviral therapy; drawbacks include possible discrimination and emotional depression.

Without treatment, approximately 15% to 50% of infants of HIV-infected mothers are infected. Zidovudine (AZT) administered to the mother during pregnancy and to the infant after birth reduces the infant's risk of becoming infected with HIV.

Only through early diagnosis can both mother and baby reduce their risk.

■ = Independent; ▲ = Collaborative

Actions/Interventions

- Encourage use of clean IV equipment when recreational drugs are used. Refer patients to drug rehabilitation programs as appropriate.
- Explain the importance of the following:
  - Refraining from donating blood, semen, or organs
  - Cleaning blood or excreta containing blood with 10% hypochlorite solution

- Instruct the patient to avoid exposure to infectious diseases:
  - Avoid sexual practice that leads to sexually transmitted infections (STIs).
  - Avoid contact with people who have infectious diseases.

Rationale

HIV is quickly killed by 10% hypochlorite solution. Flush syringe and needles with household bleach diluted ninefold with water; rinse with tap water.

These are established modes of transmission.

HIV is not spread casually; thus it is not necessary to use bleach to wash the patient's dishes, clothes, or personal items.

Used properly, condoms can help prevent STIs spread during vaginal or anal intercourse. Immunocompromised people are especially vulnerable to viral infections (e.g., herpes or genital warts). Syphilis is more difficult to diagnose and treat in HIV-infected persons and progresses more rapidly. Normally nonpathogenic intestinal flora may cause disease in HIV-infected persons; therefore, such persons should refrain from anal-oral sexual activities.

 Nursing Diagnosis

Infection

Common Related Factor

HIV infection

Defining Characteristics

Decreased number of CD4 cells
Altered CD4 cell function
Altered cellular immune response
Altered humoral immune response
Decreased response to antigens in skin testing
Positive HIV antibody with confirmatory Western blot
Detectable HIV viral load (HIV RNA)

Common Expected Outcomes

Patient does not experience opportunistic infections.
The number of CD4 cells stabilizes or increases.
Viral load decreases or becomes undetectable.

NOC Outcomes
Medication Response; Infection Status

NIC Interventions
Infection Protection;
    Medication Administration

Ongoing Assessment

Actions/Interventions

- Assess for presence of defining characteristics.

Rationale

Patients need to have regular laboratory testing of CD4 levels and viral load to monitor the status of HIV. Decreasing CD4 levels and increasing viral load indicate progression of the infection and increasing risk for opportunistic infections.

Human Immunodeficiency Virus (HIV)

■ = Independent; ▲ = Collaborative

Human Immunodeficiency Virus (HIV)—cont'd

Therapeutic Interventions

Actions/Interventions	Rationale
■ Instruct on the terminology commonly used in treatments. • CD4 cell count	CD4 cells (T cells) are white blood cells that fight infection.
• Viral load	Viral load is the amount of HIV in a sample of blood.
• Antiretroviral	Antiretrovirals are medications that interfere with the replication of retroviruses such as HIV.
■ Instruct regarding types of and complexities in selecting antiretroviral drugs for treatment along with potential side effects to monitor.	According to the Food and Drug Administration, more than 20 anti-HIV medications have been approved to date. These medications interfere with HIV enzymes (reverse transcriptase, protease, or integrase) needed for replication of infectious virions. Antiretrovirals are usually used in combination to stall the emergence of drug-resistant HIV. Guidelines from the U.S. Department of Health and Human Services (DHHS) recommend combining three or more medications in a regimen called highly active antiretroviral therapy (HAART). However, each regimen needs to be tailored to the individual patient. Rising viral loads may indicate resistance and a need to change therapy. Choice of medication may depend on chronic conditions such as renal failure, hepatic dysfunction, diabetes, TB, pregnancy, or cardiovascular disease.
Nucleoside reverse-transcriptase inhibitors (NRTIs)	According to the DHHS, NRTIs are "faulty versions of building blocks that HIV needs to make more copies of itself." Its use stalls reproduction of the HIV virus.
• Abacavir (Ziagen): Monitor for skin rash (potentially fatal) and lactic acidosis with hepatic steatosis (rare but life threatening).	This drug may also cause headaches, fatigue, nausea, vomiting, diarrhea, fever, cough, or shortness of breath. Report rash immediately.
• Didanosine (ddI, Videx, or Videx EC): Advise to take on an empty stomach and to abstain from alcohol.	This may cause diarrhea, peripheral neuropathy, or pancreatitis (pancreatitis is more likely with a history of alcohol abuse or while the patient is receiving IV pentamidine or IV ganciclovir). Medication decreases the absorption of dapsone, ketoconazole, or quinolones and tetracycline if given simultaneously.
• Emtricitabine (Emtriva): Monitor for lactic acidosis with hepatic steatosis (rare but life threatening).	This drug may also cause cough, diarrhea, dizziness, nausea, vomiting, headaches, difficulty sleeping, runny nose, skin discoloration, or rash.
• Lamivudine (3TC or Epivir): Monitor for neutropenia and anemia.	This may cause headache, fatigue, nausea, peripheral neuropathy, or diarrhea.
• Stavudine (d4T or Zerit): Monitor complete blood count (CBC) for neutropenia, and monitor liver function tests for elevated alanine aminotransferase.	This may cause peripheral neuropathy.
• Tenofovir (Viread, TDF): Monitor renal function. Monitor for signs of exacerbation of chronic hepatitis B after discontinuation of medicine among people co-infected with HBV and HIV. Monitor for lactic acidosis with hepatic steatosis.	Absorption is improved when administered with a high-fat meal. The drug may also cause rash, headaches, fatigue, nausea, diarrhea, and flatulence.

■ = Independent; ▲ = Collaborative

Actions/Interventions	Rationale

Actions/Interventions

- Zalcitabine (ddC or Hivid): Monitor for signs of peripheral neuropathy and pancreatitis.
- Zidovudine (AZT, ZDV, or Retrovir): Advise to take with food to mitigate gastrointestinal upset. Monitor CBC for neutropenia and anemia.

- Combivir: This drug contains fixed doses of zidovudine and lamivudine.
- Trizivir: This drug contains fixed doses of abacavir, lamivudine, and zidovudine.

Nonnucleoside reverse transcriptase inhibitors (NNRTIs)

- Delavirdine (Rescriptor): Monitor liver function tests.

- Efavirenz (Sustiva, EFV): Monitor for disturbed thinking, hallucinations, and nightmares. Monitor liver function tests.

- Nevirapine (Viramune, NVP): Monitor liver function tests.

Protease inhibitors (PIs)

- Amprenavir (Agenerase, APV): Monitor liver function tests, lipids, and glucose. Monitor for bleeding in hemophiliacs.
- Atazanavir (Reyataz, ATV): Monitor liver function, bilirubin, lipids, and glucose. Monitor for bleeding in hemophiliacs.

- Fosamprenavir (Lexiva, FPV): Monitor lipids, liver function, and glucose. Monitor for bleeding in hemophiliacs.
- Indinavir (Crixivan, IDV): Monitor for signs of kidney stones—flank pain and hematuria; advise patient to maintain good hydration.

- Lopinavir, ritonavir (Kaletra, LPV/r): Monitor liver, lipids, and glucose. Monitor for pancreatitis. Monitor for bleeding in hemophiliacs.

- Nelfinavir (Viracept, NFV)

- Ritonavir (Norvir, RTV): Monitor serum triglycerides and cholesterol. If coadministered with ddI, separate dose by 2.5 hours.

Rationale

This drug may cause pancreatitis, peripheral neuropathy, stomatitis, or aphthous ulcers.

This drug may also cause headaches, depression, insomnia, fatigue, and muscle inflammation. Some patients may require blood transfusions or therapy with erythropoietin to correct anemia.

These medications bind to and disable reverse transcriptase, a protein that HIV needs to make more copies of itself.

This drug may cause rash, nausea, diarrhea, fatigue, or headache.

This drug may cause rash, dizziness, insomnia, and difficulty concentrating. Laboratory test results may be falsely positive for marijuana.

This drug may cause rash, fever, headache, or nausea.

PIs disable protease, a protein that HIV needs to make more copies of itself.

This drug may cause gastrointestinal intolerance, headaches, oral paresthesia, rash, fat redistribution, lipid abnormalities, and hyperglycemia.

Absorption is improved when given with food. Do not break, chew, or crush capsule. Drug may cause gastrointestinal intolerance, drowsiness, hyperbilirubinemia, hyperglycemia, lipid abnormalities, fat redistribution, or cardiac arrhythmias.

This drug may cause gastrointestinal intolerance, rash, oral paresthesia, hyperglycemia, lipid abnormalities, or fat redistribution.

This drug is better absorbed on an empty stomach and may cause abdominal pain, nausea, headache, or insomnia. Hydration may prevent kidney stones. Because rifampin reduces indinavir concentrations, do not coadminister. If coadministered with ddI, separate dose by 2.5 hours.

Absorption is improved with food. Liquid and capsules must be refrigerated. This drug may also cause gastrointestinal intolerance, asthenia, fat redistribution, lipid abnormalities, and hyperglycemia.

Absorption is improved with food. This drug may cause diarrhea that resolves over time.

Absorption of capsules is increased with food and decreased with tobacco use. Capsules must remain refrigerated. This drug may cause nausea, diarrhea, vomiting, asthenia, or circumoral paresthesia. Most side effects abate in 1 to 2 months. Oral contraceptives with ethenyl may be ineffective.

Human Immunodeficiency Virus (HIV)

■ = Independent; ▲ = Collaborative

Human Immunodeficiency Virus (HIV)—cont'd

Actions/Interventions	Rationale
• Saquinavir (Fortovase, SQV, Invirase)	Absorption is improved when administered with a high-fat meal. This drug may cause diarrhea, nausea, or abdominal pain.
Fusion inhibitors	Fusion inhibitors prevent HIV entry into cells.
• Enfuvirtide (Fuzeon, T-20): Monitor severity of injection site reaction. Monitor for signs of a serious allergic reaction.	Administer subcutaneously following the manufacturer's instructions. This drug usually causes mild to moderate injection site reactions. It may also cause insomnia, weakness, constipation, depression, muscle pain, loss of appetite, and pain and numbness in the lower extremities.
■ Review the entire medication profile for potential drug interactions. Consult a pharmacist as needed.	All PIs and NNRTIs are metabolized by the cytochrome P450 (CYP) system, which leads to drug interactions. Double check with a pharmacist about contraindicated medications or therapeutic drug monitoring. Older patients and others with chronic conditions may experience more drug interactions or require more frequent therapeutic drug monitoring.
■ Encourage adherence to therapy, and avoid interruptions of therapy.	Strict adherence is needed to stall the emergence of drug-resistant HIV. Antiretrovirals are taken throughout the course of infection unless the toxicities outweigh the potential benefits.
▲ Follow local regulations for obtaining a separate consent to be tested for HIV and for reporting results to the health department.	Pregnant women may be required to be tested because of local or state regulations.

NDx Nursing Diagnosis

Imbalanced Nutrition: Less Than Body Requirements

Common Related Factors	Defining Characteristics
Loss of appetite	Weight loss
Fatigue	Caloric intake inadequate to meet metabolic requirements
Oral or esophageal candidiasis	Loss of fat and muscle
Cryptosporidiosis	Decreased body mass index (BMI)
Enteric cytomegalovirus disease	
MAC (cultured from blood, bone marrow, or lymph node biopsy)	
Increased nutritional needs	
Nausea and vomiting	
Malabsorption	

■ = Independent; ▲ = Collaborative

Common Expected Outcomes

Patient regains weight or does not lose additional weight.

Patient verbalizes understanding of necessary caloric intake.

NOC Outcomes
Nutritional Status: Food and Fluid Intake; Nutrient Intake

NIC Interventions
Nutrition Monitoring: Nutrition Therapy; Medication Administration; Total Parenteral Nutrition; Oral Health Restoration

---

Ongoing Assessment

Actions/Interventions	Rationale
■ Assess changes in weight.	HIV wasting syndrome is one of the clinical conditions that occur with AIDS. This condition is defined as an involuntary loss of more than 10% of total body weight. Persistent diarrhea and recurrent fevers are associated with the syndrome. Other factors contributing to weight loss in the patient with HIV infection include reduced food intake from anorexia, oral or esophageal lesions from candidiasis, and drug side effects. Inflammatory bowel disease from HIV may lead to malabsorption syndromes. Chronic HIV infection increases metabolic demands.
■ Obtain nutritional history: intake, difficulty in swallowing, weight loss.	Attention to individual factors helps in designing an appropriate plan.
■ Inspect mouth for candidal infection.	This infection causes difficulty in swallowing.
■ Evaluate for possible adverse reactions to medications.	Many drugs used to treat HIV can cause anorexia, nausea and vomiting, and weight loss.
▲ If the patient receives total parenteral nutrition (TPN), monitor serum glucose and electrolyte levels.	The high glucose content of TPN solutions can cause short-term hyperglycemia that may require insulin administration.

Therapeutic Interventions

Actions/Interventions	Rationale
■ Provide dietary planning to encourage intake of high-calorie, high-protein foods and dietary supplements.	Patients may not easily understand what is involved in a special dietary plan.
▲ Provide antiemetics before meals.	Antiemetics can reduce nausea and improve intake.
■ Assist with meals as needed.	Fatigue and weakness may prevent the patient from eating.
■ Encourage exercise as tolerated.	Metabolism and utilization of nutrients are enhanced by activity.
▲ Administer dietary supplements or TPN, as ordered.	Despite supplements, HIV may cause wasting syndrome.
▲ Administer antimonilial medication, as prescribed.	Oral and esophageal candidiasis can cause sore throat, which may cause lack of appetite.
▲ Administer megestrol acetate (Megace), as prescribed.	Dose will be individualized to degree of wasting and patient's response. The drug increases body weight by increasing appetite. Side effects include carpal tunnel syndrome, thrombophlebitis, alopecia, reduced sex drive, and impotence.

Human Immunodeficiency Virus (HIV)

■ = Independent; ▲ = Collaborative

Human Immunodeficiency Virus (HIV)—cont'd

Actions/Interventions	Rationale
▲ Administer anabolic steroids or testosterone supplements, as ordered.	These can enhance appetite but are not without their own side effects. Monitor for edema and jaundice.
▲ Administer human growth hormones, as ordered. Monitor for hyperglycemia and hypertriglyceridemia.	Hormones may cause arthralgia, joint stiffness, or carpal tunnel syndrome.
▲ Administer dronabinol (THC, Marinol) as ordered.	This can increase appetite. It may cause restlessness, insomnia, dizziness, loss of coordination, and clouded sensorium or euphoria.
▲ Administer medications for opportunistic pathogens affecting the gastrointestinal tract.	Bowel inflammation from opportunistic infections causes malabsorption of nutrients.
▲ Administer clarithromycin (Biaxin), rifabutin (Mycobutin), or azithromycin (Zithromax).	These help prevent MAC in patients with advanced disease.

> ● **RELATED CARE PLANS**
>
> Compromised family coping, p. 49
> Diarrhea, p. 54
> Fatigue, p. 65
> Ineffective coping, p. 51
> Ineffective therapeutic regimen management, p. 185
> Spiritual distress, p. 180

Leukemia

Acute Lymphocytic Leukemia; Acute Myelocytic Leukemia; Chronic Lymphocytic Leukemia; Lymphocytic Leukemia; Chronic Myelocytic Leukemia; Nonlymphocytic Leukemia; Myelogenous Leukemia; Granulocytic Leukemia

Leukemia is a malignant disorder of the blood-forming system, including the bone marrow and spleen. The proliferation of immature white blood cells (WBCs) interferes with the production and function of the red blood cells (RBCs) and platelets. Leukemia can be characterized by identification of the type of leukocyte involved: myelogenous or lymphocytic. In acute lymphocytic leukemia there is a proliferation of lymphoblasts (most commonly seen in children); in acute myelocytic leukemia (most common after 60 years of age), there is a proliferation of myeloblasts. In chronic lymphocytic leukemia, there are increased lymphocytes (more common in men, especially after 50 years of age); in chronic myelocytic leukemia, granulocytes are increased (common in middle age).

Depending on the type of leukemia, therapeutic management may consist of combined chemotherapeutic agents, radiation therapy, and/or bone marrow transplantation. Chemotherapeutic treatment consists of several stages: induction therapy, intensification, consolidation therapy, and maintenance therapy. The goals of nursing care are to prevent complications and to provide educational and emotional support. This care plan addresses ongoing care of a patient in an ambulatory setting receiving maintenance therapy.

■ = Independent; ▲ = Collaborative

Nursing Diagnosis

Deficient Knowledge

Common Related Factors
New disease
Lack of information resources

Common Expected Outcome
Patient verbalizes understanding of diagnosis, treatment strategies, and prognosis.

Defining Characteristics
Many questions
Lack of questions
Misconceptions

> **NOC Outcomes**
> Knowledge: Disease Process;
> Knowledge: Treatment Procedures
>
> **NIC Intervention**
> Teaching: Disease Process

Ongoing Assessment

Actions/Interventions

■ Assess knowledge of disease, treatment strategies, and prognosis.

Rationale

Several types of leukemia occur, which can be confusing. Each has its own treatment approach and prognosis.

Therapeutic Interventions

Actions/Interventions

■ Describe the etiology of leukemia:
  • Not well understood; probably multifactorial
  • May be related to exposure to radiation or chemical agents, genetic factors, congenital abnormalities, viruses, immunological deficiencies, or antineoplastic drugs
■ Explain the blood-forming changes that occur with all types of leukemia:
  • Bone marrow failure; leukemic infiltrates
  • Granulocytopenia from reduced number of WBCs
  • Anemia from reduced RBC production
  • Thrombocytopenia from decreased platelet production
■ Clarify the difference between acute and chronic leukemia:
  • Acute leukemia is abnormal proliferation of *immature* leukocytes or blasts with rapid onset of symptoms.
  • Chronic leukemia is characterized by disease of *mature* WBCs with a progressive, gradual onset of symptoms.
■ Describe the patient's specific type of leukemia.

Rationale

The exact cause of leukemia in human beings is unknown. Many causative factors seem to play a role in the development of both the acute and chronic forms of the disease. A group of preleukemic or myelodysplastic syndromes has been identified as significant in the development of leukemia in older adults.

Most people are unfamiliar with the various components of normal blood and marrow and the respective functions of the different blood cells.

Leukemias may be further classified as lymphocytic or myelocytic according to the type of WBC that is involved in the disease.

Four major types of leukemia are known, as described in the introductory paragraph. Distinguishing specific subtypes is important to guide appropriate therapy.

Leukemia

■ = Independent; ▲ = Collaborative

Leukemia–cont'd

Actions/Interventions	Rationale
■ Explain the diagnostic process:	
• Peripheral blood evaluation	This is necessary to detect immature blood cells.
• Bone marrow examination	This is the key diagnostic tool.
• Lumbar puncture and computed tomography scan	These are done to determine the presence of leukemic cells throughout the body.
■ Describe common approaches to treatment:	Treatment is guided by current research findings and definitive protocols for specific types of leukemia. Initial chemotherapy doses may be given in the hospital. However, follow-up courses may be administered in an outpatient or even in a home setting.
• Combination chemotherapy	This is the primary treatment. It has reduced side effects and improved response. A variety of drugs are available depending on leukemia type.
• Radiation therapy	This may be used as an adjunct to chemotherapy.
• Bone marrow and stem cell transplantation, especially with acute myelocytic leukemia	Bone marrow transplantation is a standard treatment for leukemia.
• Targeted therapies	Monoclonal antibody targeted therapies have recently been approved by the Food and Drug Administration for treatment in some cancers.
■ Explain common complaints:	
• Bleeding	This is from decreased platelet production.
• Infection	This is from immature WBC production.
• Anemia	This is from decreased circulating hemoglobin and RBCs.
■ Discuss prognosis:	
• The prognosis is hopeful, with the treatment goal being a curative attempt, although at times the treatment may only result in prolonged remission.	The patient's adjustment to any form of leukemia and its treatment requires understanding of the expected course of exacerbations and remissions.
• Patients may be in remission for a long time, especially with chronic leukemia.	

ND_x Nursing Diagnosis

Risk for Ineffective Coping

Common Risk Factors

Situational crisis
Inadequate support system
Inadequate coping methods

■ = Independent; ▲ = Collaborative

Common Expected Outcome

Patient demonstrates positive coping strategies, as evidenced by expression of feelings, fears, and hopes; realistic goal setting for future; and use of available resources and support systems.

NOC Outcomes
Coping; Social Support; Family Coping

NIC Interventions
Coping Enhancement; Hope Instillation; Grief Work Facilitation

Ongoing Assessment

Actions/Interventions

- Assess the patient's knowledge of disease and treatment plan.
- Assess for coping mechanisms used in previous illnesses and hospitalization experiences.
- Evaluate resources and support systems available to the patient in the home and community.

- Assess financial resources required for expensive long-term therapy.

Rationale

Because leukemia is cancer, patients may expect to die. Realistic but positive information may be indicated.

Successful coping is influenced by previous success.

Leukemia treatment may include months and years of ongoing chemotherapy, depending on the length of remission. Availability of support systems may change over time.

The financial aspects of acute care and long-term follow-up can be overwhelming, especially when the patient is dealing with a new diagnosis.

Therapeutic Interventions

Actions/Interventions

- Establish open lines of communication; define your role as patient informant and advocate.

- Provide opportunities for the patient and significant others to openly express feelings, fears, and concerns. Provide reassurance and hope.
- Assist the patient and significant others in redefining hopes and components of individuality (e.g., roles, values, and attitudes).
- Encourage the patient to seek information that will improve coping skills.
- Introduce new information about disease treatment as available.
- Assist the patient to become involved as a comanager of the treatment plan.

Rationale

The nurse may be the first source of support for the patient and family. The unpredictable nature of leukemia adds to the stress of the patient's daily activities. Even in remission, the patient and family may live with the fear of a relapse of the disease at any time. The demands of managing therapy and preventing complications in the home setting can disrupt the lives of both the patient and the family members.

Verbalization of actual or perceived threats can help reduce anxiety.

Emphasizing the patient's intrinsic worth and viewing the immediate situation as manageable in time may provide support.

Patients who are not coping well may need more guidance.

At this time there is no cure for leukemia. However, remission is possible and long-term survival is feasible.

This helps the patient regain control over the situation. Many patients become educated about their chemotherapeutic agents, using abbreviations fluently (e.g., MOPP, COAP). Others become knowledgeable about blood components and vigilantly record daily or weekly laboratory results.

Leukemia

■ = Independent; ▲ = Collaborative

Leukemia—cont'd

Actions/Interventions

■ Describe community resources available to meet the unique demands of leukemia, its treatment, and survival (e.g., Leukemia Society of America, American Cancer Society, National Coalition for Cancer Survivorship).

▲ Refer to a social worker for financial assistance, as indicated.

■ Assist in the development of an alternative support system, as indicated. Encourage participation in self-help groups as available.

■ Assist the patient to grieve and work through the losses from life-threatening illness and change in body function.

Rationale

It is helpful for patients to have more than one resource for helping them in this process. Reliable websites may likewise offer information and support.

The social worker can assist the patient and family with decisions about finances, living arrangements, wills, advance directives, and power of attorney.

Relationships with persons with common interests and goals can be beneficial. Participation in support groups may allow the individual to realize that others have the same problem, and they may use this as an aid for coping.

Grief is a universal experience; people who have successfully undergone grief over loss can be enormously helpful to others undergoing the same feelings.

NDx Nursing Diagnosis

Risk for Infection

Common Risk Factors

Altered immunological responses related to disease process
Immunosuppression secondary to chemotherapy or radiation therapy

Common Expected Outcome

Patient has reduced risk of local or systemic infection, as evidenced by afebrile state, compliance with preventive measures, and prompt reporting of early signs of infection.

NOC Outcomes
Immune Status; Knowledge: Infection Control

NIC Interventions
Infection Protection; Teaching: Disease Process; Oral Health Maintenance

Ongoing Assessment

Actions/Interventions

■ Auscultate lung fields for crackles, rhonchi, and decreased lung sounds.
■ Observe the patient for coughing spells and character of sputum.

Rationale

Pulmonary infections are common.

Increased sputum production and change in color from clear or white to yellow or green may indicate respiratory infection.

■ = Independent; ▲ = Collaborative

Actions/Interventions

- Inspect body sites with high infection potential (mouth, throat, axilla, perineum, rectum).

- Inspect intravenous or central catheter site for redness, tenderness, pain, and itching.

- Observe for changes in color, character, and frequency of urine and stool.

- Monitor temperature as indicated. Report temperature higher than 38° C (100.4° F).

- ▲ Obtain cultures as indicated.

Rationale

Many infections that occur in patients with leukemia are opportunistic due to the patients' immunocompromised status.

In absence of granulocytes, site of infection may develop without characteristic pus formation.

These observations provides data on possible urinary tract infection or intestinal infection.

Fever may be the only sign of infection. Patients need to be instructed to record serial temperatures at home.

These are required to determine antibiotic sensitivity and presence of fungi.

Therapeutic Interventions

Actions/Interventions

- Explain the cause and effects of leukopenia.

- Instruct the patient to maintain personal hygiene, especially at home:
  - To bathe with chlorhexidine (Hibiclens)

  - To wash hands well before eating and after using bathroom

  - To wipe perineal area from front to back

- Instruct the patient to brush teeth with a soft toothbrush four times a day and as necessary, to remove dentures at night, and to rinse mouth after each emesis or when expectorating phlegm.

- Teach the patient to inspect the oropharyngeal area daily for white patches in the mouth, coated or encrusted oral ulcerations, swollen and erythematous tongue with white or brown coating, infected throat and pain on swallowing, debris on teeth, ill-fitting dentures, amount and viscosity of saliva, and changes in vocal tone.

- Teach the patient to avoid mouthwashes that contain alcohol and to avoid irritating foods and acidic drinks.

- Teach the patient to use prescribed topical medications (e.g., nystatin [Nilstat] and lidocaine [Xylocaine]).

- Instruct the patient and caregiver to maintain strict aseptic technique when changing dressings and to avoid wetting central catheter dressings.

- Instruct the patient to observe for fever spikes and flulike symptoms (e.g., malaise, weakness, myalgia) and to notify the nurse or physician if they occur.

- Instruct the patient and caregiver regarding the importance of eliminating potential sources of infection at home (especially when neutrophil counts are low):
  - Avoidance of contact with visitors and family, especially children with colds or infections

Rationale

Leukemic cells replace normal cells. Also, chemotherapy causes bone marrow suppression and reduced number of neutrophils needed to fight infection.

This is useful for removing skin surface bacteria that may play a role in secondary infection.

This removes transient and resident bacteria from hands.

The perineal area is a source of pathogens and a frequent entry port for microorganisms.

Keeping oral mucous membranes intact reduces a possible site for opportunistic infection to develop.

Candidiasis is a common opportunistic infection in the immunocompromised patient.

Alcohol has a drying effect on mucous membranes.

These agents may require specific instruction.

These measures help prevent bacterial growth.

Early assessment facilitates prompt treatment.

Patients must understand strategies and measures by which they can protect themselves during times of compromised defense.

Leukemia

= Independent; ▲ = Collaborative

Leukemia—cont'd

Actions/Interventions

- Avoidance of shared drinking and eating utensils
- Avoidance of contact with cat litter boxes, fish tanks, and human or animal excreta
- Avoidance of swimming in private or public pools
- Restricting contact with live plants

■ Instruct the patient regarding "protective isolation" if laboratory results indicate neutropenia (WBC count less than 500 to 1000/mm³):
- Implement thorough hand washing for staff and visitors before physical contact with the patient.
- Wear a face mask.

■ Instruct the patient to take prescribed antibiotic, antifungal, or antiviral drugs on time.

■ Explain the importance of regular medical and dental checkups.

▲ Refer the patient to a dietitian for instructions on maintenance of a well-balanced diet.

Rationale

Institutional protocols may vary.

This removes transient and resident bacteria from hands, thus minimizing or preventing transmission to patient.

A regular schedule is needed to maintain therapeutic drug levels.

Early identification of problems reduces subsequent complications.

A specialist may provide additional help.

NDx Nursing Diagnosis

Ineffective Protection

Common Related Factors

Bone marrow depression secondary to chemotherapy
Proliferation of leukemic cells

Defining Characteristics

Altered clotting
Bleeding

Common Expected Outcome

Patient's risk for bleeding is reduced, as evidenced by platelet count within acceptable limits, compliance with preventive measures, and prompt reporting of early signs and symptoms.

NOC Outcomes

Blood Coagulation;
Knowledge: Treatment Regimen

NIC Interventions

Bleeding Precautions;
Teaching: Disease Process

Ongoing Assessment

Actions/Interventions

 Monitor platelet count.

Rationale

Data determine risk for bleeding:
- Mild thrombocytopenia: platelets 50,000 to 100,000/mm³
- Moderately severe: platelets 20,000 to 50,000/mm³
- Severe: platelets 20,000/mm³ or less
- Transfusion threshold: platelet count less than 10,000/mm³ or signs of active bleeding

■ = Independent; ▲ = Collaborative

Actions/Interventions	Rationale
■ Assess for signs and symptoms of bleeding.	These may include petechiae and bruising; hemoptysis; epistaxis; bleeding in oral mucosa; hematemesis; hematochezia; melena; vaginal bleeding; dizziness; orthostatic changes; decreased blood pressure (BP); headaches; changes in mental and visual acuity; and increased pulse rate.
■ Note bleeding from any recent puncture site (e.g., venipuncture, bone marrow aspiration site).	Prolonged oozing of blood from puncture sites may be the first sign of a coagulation problem.

Therapeutic Interventions

Actions/Interventions	Rationale
■ Explain to the patient and significant others the symptoms of thrombocytopenia and the functions of platelets: • Normal range of platelet count • Effects of thrombocytopenia • Rationale of bleeding precautions	Most individuals are not familiar with the complexities of the hematological system.
■ Instruct the patient in precautionary measures. Initiate bleeding precautions for platelet count less than 50,000/mm^3:	Understanding of precautionary measures reduces risk of bleeding.
• Use soft toothbrush and nonabrasive toothpaste.	This reduces risk of bleeding.
• Inspect gums for oozing.	This can be an early sign of bleeding.
• Avoid use of toothpicks and dental floss.	It is important to reduce mucosal trauma.
• Avoid rectal suppositories, thermometers, enemas, vaginal douches, and tampons.	This reduces mucosal trauma.
• Avoid aspirin or aspirin-containing products, nonsteroidal antiinflammatory drugs (NSAIDs), and anticoagulants.	These interfere with platelet function.
• Avoid straining with bowel movements, forceful nose blowing, coughing, or sneezing.	This reduces the risk of bleeding.
• Count used sanitary pads during menstruation. Report menstrual cycle changes.	This provides data on bleeding status.
• Use electric razor for shaving (not razor blades).	This reduces risk for injury.
• Avoid sharp objects such as scissors and knives.	It is important to prevent cuts, which would not only bleed but also become portals of entry for microorganisms, leading to infection in the presence of neutropenia.
• Lubricate nostrils with saline solution drops as necessary.	This prevents drying and cracking.
• Lubricate lips with petroleum jelly as needed.	This prevents drying and cracking.
• Practice gentle sex; use water-based lubricant before sexual intercourse.	This prevents mucosal trauma.
• Protect self from injury and trauma (e.g., falls, bumps, strenuous exercise, contact sports).	Patient safety is a priority.

In the health care setting:

Actions/Interventions	Rationale
■ Avoid finger sticks if possible. Coordinate laboratory work so all tests are done at one time.	This reduces bleeding potential.
■ Avoid intramuscular and subcutaneous injections. If necessary, use small-bore needles for injections and apply ice to the injection site for 5 minutes. Observe the site for oozing.	These measures reduce bleeding potential.

Leukemia

■ = Independent; ▲ = Collaborative

Leukemia—cont'd

Actions/Interventions	Rationale
■ Inflate BP cuff as little as possible while monitoring pressure.	Overinflation can cause bruising.
■ Apply pressure, dressing, or sandbag to the bone marrow aspiration site.	This prevents excessive pressure when compressing soft tissues and deeper structures of the arm, because this may lead to bruising or hematomas.
■ Give the patient and family at least two telephone numbers to call in case of bleeding.	This facilitates early treatment.
▲ Apply ice or topical thrombin promptly as prescribed for bleeding mucous membranes.	These promote clot formation.
■ Instruct the patient to take antacids as prescribed when taking steroids, NSAIDs, and/or aspirin.	This reduces gastric irritation.
■ Discuss the possibility of platelet transfusions. Teach the patient the purpose and possible reactions to transfusions.	Knowledge reduces anxiety.
▲ Ensure availability and readiness of platelets for transfusion.	This prevents spontaneous or excessive bleeding (generally for platelet count less than 10,000/mm³, unless active bleeding is present, or according to institutional protocol).

NDx Nursing Diagnosis

Fatigue

Common Related Factors
Side effects of chemotherapy or radiation therapy
Reduced oxygen-carrying capacity of blood from reduced number of red blood cells

Defining Characteristics
Report of weakness or fatigue
Inability to maintain usual routine
Exertional discomfort or dyspnea
Decreased performance

Common Expected Outcomes
Patient achieves adequate activity tolerance, as evidenced by ability to perform activities of daily living (ADLs) and verbalization of return to normal or near-normal activity levels.
Patient establishes a pattern of sleep and rest that facilitates optimal performance of required or desired activities.

NOC Outcomes
Energy Conservation; Activity Tolerance

NIC Interventions
Energy Management; Risk for Impaired Individual Coping

Ongoing Assessment

Actions/Interventions	Rationale
■ Assess specific cause of fatigue.	Fatigue is a characteristic side effect of leukemia treatment. The extent will vary depending on whether the patient is in remission or relapse. However, patients

■ = Independent; ▲ = Collaborative

Actions/Interventions

■ Assess current and desired activity level.

Rationale

may also exhibit lack of interest in performing activities because of associated depression, sleeping difficulties, or other personal problems.

These provide basis for development of treatment plan.

Therapeutic Interventions

Actions/Interventions

■ Assist patient in planning ADLs. Guide in prioritizing activities for the day.

■ Stress importance of frequent rest periods.

■ Teach energy-conservation principles.

▲ Anticipate need for transfusion of packed red cells.

▲ Refer the patient and family to an occupational therapist.

Rationale

Not all self-care activities need to be completed in the morning. Likewise, not all housework needs to be completed in 1 day.

Energy reserves may be depleted unless the patient respects the body's need for increased rest.

Patients and caregivers may need to learn skills for delegation of tasks to others, setting priorities, and clustering care to use available energy to complete desired activities.

These increase oxygen-carrying capacity of the blood.

The occupational therapist can teach the patient about using assistive devices. The therapist also can help the patient and family evaluate the need for additional energy conservation measures in the home setting.

NDx Nursing Diagnosis

Imbalanced Nutrition: Less Than Body Requirements

Common Related Factors

Treatment effects:
- Side effects of chemotherapy (inability to taste and smell foods, loss of appetite, nausea, vomiting, mucositis, dry mouth, diarrhea)
- Medications (e.g., narcotics, antibiotics, vitamins)

Disease effects:
- Primary malignancy or metastasis
- Tumor waste products
- Renal dysfunction
- Electrolyte imbalances (e.g., hypercalcemia, hyponatremia)
- Pain

Psychogenic effects:
- Conditioning to adversive stimuli (e.g., anticipatory nausea and vomiting, tension, anxiety, stress)
- Depression

Defining Characteristics

Weight loss
Documented inadequate caloric intake
Weakness, fatigue
Poor skin turgor
Dry, shiny oral mucous membranes
Thick, scanty saliva
Muscle wasting

Leukemia

■ = Independent; ▲ = Collaborative

Leukemia—cont'd

Common Expected Outcome

Patient maintains optimal nutritional status, as evidenced by caloric intake adequate to meet body requirements, balanced intake and output, weight gain or reduced loss, absence of nausea and vomiting, and good skin turgor.

NOC Outcomes
Nutritional Status: Food and Fluid Intake; Nutritional Status: Nutrient Intake

NIC Interventions
Chemotherapy Management; Nutrition Therapy; Oral Health Maintenance; Medication Administration

Ongoing Assessment

Actions/Interventions

- Obtain history of previous patterns of nausea and vomiting and treatment measures effective in the past.

- Assess the patient's description of nausea and vomiting pattern.

- Evaluate the effectiveness of the antiemetic and comfort measures regimens.

- Observe the patient for potential complications of prolonged nausea and vomiting: fluid and electrolyte imbalance (e.g., dehydration, hypokalemia, decreased sodium and chlorine), weight loss, decreased activity level, weakness, lethargy, apathy, anxiety, aspiration pneumonia, esophageal trauma, and tenderness or pain in the abdomen and chest.

- Weigh the patient daily at the same time and with the same scale. If the patient is at home, stress the importance of maintaining a daily log.

- Encourage the patient to record any food intake using a daily log.

- ▲ Monitor appropriate laboratory values (e.g., complete blood count and differential, electrolytes, serum iron, total iron-binding capacity, total protein, albumin).

Rationale

The patient may have adverse side effects in the past. However, newer antiemetic medications have improved this condition for many patients. These side effects can significantly affect the quality of one's life. Nausea and vomiting are the most distressing side effects for patients and families.

Patient responses are individualized, depending on type and dosage of chemotherapy. Nausea and vomiting may be acute, delayed, and for some patients even "prior to" (anticipatory) the chemotherapy treatment.

Patient response to antiemetic and comfort medications is highly variable and must be explored with each patient.

Chemotherapeutic drugs produce nausea and vomiting as a side effect by stimulating central receptors in the chemoreceptor trigger zone in the medulla or in the cerebral cortex. Some of the drugs stimulate peripheral receptors in the gastrointestinal tract to cause nausea and vomiting.

Consistent weighing is important to ensure accuracy. Without monitoring, the patient may be unaware of small changes in weight.

Determination of type, amount, and pattern of food intake (if any) is facilitated by accurate documentation, which provides information as to whether oral intake meets daily nutritional requirements.

These reflect nutritional and fluid electrolyte status.

Therapeutic Interventions

Actions/Interventions

▲ Administer antiemetics according to protocol.

▲ Administer antiemetic around the clock rather than as needed during periods of high incidence of nausea and vomiting.

▲ Titrate the dosage and frequency of the antiemetic within prescribed parameters as needed until effective therapeutic levels are achieved.

■ Institute or teach measures to reduce or prevent nausea and vomiting:

- Small dietary intake before treatment
- Foods with low potential to cause nausea and vomiting (e.g., dry toast, crackers, ginger ale, cola, Popsicles, gelatin, baked or boiled potatoes, fresh or canned fruit)
- Avoidance of spices, gravy, greasy foods, and foods with strong odors
- Modifications in diet (e.g., choice of bland foods)
- Small, frequent nutritious meals

- Meals at room temperature
- Avoidance of coaxing, bribing, or threatening in relation to intake (help family avoid being "food pushers")
- Rest periods before and after meals
- Sucking on hard candy while receiving chemotherapeutic drugs with "metallic taste"

Rationale

Newer agents are much more affective in reducing the incidence and severity of emesis. Treatment protocols using a combination of antiemetic medications are most effective in controlling nausea and vomiting associated with chemotherapy. This approach uses drugs that block nausea receptors at different sites and through different mechanisms of action. A typical combination protocol may include administration of a 5HT3 (serotonin) receptor antagonist such as ondansetron and dexamethasone before chemotherapy. For delayed nausea, the protocol may include administration of dexamethasone and metoclopramide. Other classes of drugs used to control nausea and vomiting include phenothiazines, butyrophenones, cannabinoids, and benzodiazepines.

Effectiveness of antiemetic therapy is increased when adequate plasma levels are maintained.

Each patient has his or her own threshold for relief.

Behavioral and dietary interventions seem to be most effective in the management of anticipatory nausea and vomiting. This pattern of nausea and vomiting is related to classic conditioning. The patient develops nausea and vomiting in response to stimuli associated with administration of chemotherapeutic drugs. Patients may try a variety of interventions to find those that best control this type of nausea and vomiting before drug administration. Antiemetic medications have been found to be less effective in managing anticipatory nausea and vomiting. However, antianxiety medications such as lorazepam may be effective.

Limited intake reduces gastric overstimulation.

These foods provide a measure of success to augment nutrition.

These foods can stimulate gastric motility.

Bland foods may be better tolerated.

Eating small amounts prevents gastric distention from stimulating vomiting.

Hot foods can stimulate peristalsis.

Such behaviors tend to only aggravate the situation.

This provides needed energy for eating and digestion.

Hard candies can reduce metallic or bitter taste.

Leukemia

■ = Independent; ▲ = Collaborative

Leukemia—cont'd

Actions/Interventions

- Minimal physical activity and no sudden rapid movement during times of increased nausea

- Quiet, restful, cool, well-ventilated environment

- Relaxation and distraction techniques; guided imagery

- Antiemetic half an hour before meals as prescribed

- ■ Identify and provide favorite foods; avoid serving during nausea and vomiting.

- ■ Explain measures to increase sensitivity of taste buds: perform mouth care before and after meals; change seasonings to compensate for altered sweet and sour threshold; increase use of sweeteners and flavorings in foods; warm foods to increase aroma.

- ■ Serve foods cold if odors cause aversions.

- ■ Offer meat dishes in the morning.

- ■ Serve supplements between meals; have the patient sip slowly.

- ■ Explain measures to provide moisture in oral cavity, if indicated:
  - Frequent intake of nonirritating fluids (e.g., grape or apple juice)
  - Sucking on smooth, flat substances (e.g., ice chips; lozenges; tart, sugar-free candy) to increase saliva flow
  - Use of artificial saliva
  - Liquids sipped with meals
  - Foods moistened with sauces and liquids
  - Strict oral hygiene before and after meals; avoidance of alcohol-containing commercial mouthwashes or lemon-glycerin swabs that are drying to oral mucosa
  - Lips moistened with balm, water-soluble lubricating jelly, lanolin, or cocoa butter
  - Humidified air environment via vaporizer or pan of water near heat

- ■ If reduced oral intake is secondary to mucositis, see Impaired Oral Mucous Membrane, p. 141.

- ■ Position the patient in a Fowler's position or side-lying position during vomiting episode.

Rationale

Activity may potentiate nausea and vomiting.

Relaxation reduces peristalsis.

These techniques can be helpful if used before nausea occurs or increases.

Antiemetics relieve nausea and vomiting.

The patient may develop an aversion.

These may improve ability to tolerate foods.

The smell of cooking food may aggravate feelings of nausea.

Aversions tend to increase during the day: chicken, cheese, eggs, and fish are usually well-tolerated protein sources.

These prevent bloating, nausea, vomiting, and diarrhea.

These can facilitate swallowing.

Humidity should be used cautiously when the patient is leukopenic because of risk of *Pseudomonas* infection.

Patients undergoing chemotherapy commonly develop some degree of soreness in the mucous membranes.

This decreases aspiration risk.

> ### • RELATED CARE PLANS
>
> Anxiety, p. 15
> Cancer chemotherapy, p. 812
> Cancer radiation therapy, p. 825
> Caregiver role strain, p. 35
> Deficient fluid volume, p. 71
> Disturbed body image, p. 21
> Fear, p. 68
> Hematopoietic stem cell transplantation, p. 837

■ = Independent; ▲ = Collaborative

Lymphoma: Hodgkin's Disease; Non-Hodgkin's Lymphoma

Lymphoma is a malignant disorder of the lymph nodes, spleen, and other lymphoid tissue. Lymphomas include a number of related diseases with a variety of symptoms, treatment options, and outcomes depending on the lymphocyte type and stage of disease. Lymphomas are classified as either Hodgkin's disease or non-Hodgkin's lymphoma. A specific etiology has not been identified, although associations with viral disease such as Epstein-Barr and mononucleosis and environmental exposure to toxins have been noted. The Centers for Disease Control and Prevention has included lymphoma in the list of clinical conditions that are part of the case definition for AIDS.

Hodgkin's disease is a disorder of the lymph nodes, usually presenting with node enlargement. It is seen more frequently in men than women, first between the ages of 20 and 40, and then again after 60 years of age. Non-Hodgkin's lymphoma is a disorder of the lymphocytes that involves many different histological variations. It is seen more frequently in middle-age men.

Depending on the type of lymphoma, therapeutic management may consist of combination chemotherapy, radiation therapy, and/or bone marrow and peripheral stem cell transplantation. The prognosis is usually poorer for non-Hodgkin's lymphoma because of its later stage at diagnosis.

The goals of nursing care are to provide educational and emotional support and to prevent complications. This care plan addresses ongoing care of a patient in an ambulatory setting receiving maintenance therapy.

NDx Nursing Diagnosis

Deficient Knowledge

Common Related Factors

New disease
Lack of information resources

Defining Characteristics

Many questions
Lack of questions
Misconceptions

Common Expected Outcome

Patient verbalizes understanding of diagnosis, treatment
  strategies, and prognosis.

NOC Outcomes

Knowledge: Disease Process;
  Knowledge: Treatment Procedures

NIC Interventions

Teaching: Disease Process;
  Teaching: Procedures/Treatment

■ = Independent; ▲ = Collaborative

> ## Lymphoma: Hodgkin's Disease; Non-Hodgkin's Lymphoma—cont'd

Ongoing Assessment

Actions/Interventions

- Assess knowledge of disease, treatment strategies, and prognosis.

Rationale

Several types of lymphoma occur, each with its own treatment approach and prognosis; this can be confusing.

Therapeutic Interventions

Actions/Interventions

- Describe the function of the lymphatic system and the abnormalities associated with lymphoma.

- Clarify the diagnostic process:
  - Peripheral blood analysis

  - Lymph node biopsy

  - Bone marrow biopsy
  - Lymphangiogram

  - X-ray study
  - Computed tomography scan

- Clarify the similarities and differences between Hodgkin's disease and non-Hodgkin's lymphoma.
  - Common presenting symptoms include fever, weight loss, night sweats, pruritus, nontender enlarged lymph nodes, and possibly enlarged spleen and liver.
- Discuss common treatment approaches:
  - Radiation therapy

  - Combined chemotherapy

Rationale

Most individuals are not familiar with the complexities of the hematological system unless an illness strikes.

Analysis may reveal a microcytic hypochromic anemia, lymphopenia (neutrophilic leukocytosis), and elevated platelet count.

This provides tissue for histological examination that is needed in diagnosing cell type and staging the disease. The presence of Reed-Sternberg cells confirms Hodgkin's disease. Knowing the stage of the disease determines treatment and aids in estimation of prognosis. Biopsy may be performed either as open biopsy (in operating room) or a closed needle biopsy (at bedside or as outpatient).

This can assist with staging of disease.

This uses x-ray and special dye injected to outline the lymph nodes and vessels.

This is used to detect additional sites of disease.

This is used to assess abdominal lymph nodes and liver, spleen, bone, and brain infiltrates.

Although both have similar presenting symptoms and treatment approaches, significant differences in actual treatment therapies and response to therapy do exist. Non-Hodgkin's lymphoma has a poorer prognosis because of its later stage at diagnosis.

This is indicated for stages 1 and 2 in Hodgkin's disease and for localized non-Hodgkin's disease.

This is common for stages 3 and 4 in Hodgkin's disease and may include ABVD (Adriamycin, bleomycin, vincristine, and dacarbazine) and MOPP (mechlorethamine = nitrogen mustard, Oncovin = vincristine, procarbazine, and prednisone). Chemotherapy is also indicated for generalized non-Hodgkin's lymphoma. Many protocols exist depending on the type of lymphoma (e.g., COPP, CHOP, BACOP, M-BACOP). NOTE: Older patients have significant problems dealing with the adverse side effects of these aggressive treatments. Initial chemotherapy is performed in the hospital. However, follow-up courses may be administered in an outpatient or sometimes a home setting.

Actions/Interventions

- Biological response modifier therapy

- Bone marrow and peripheral stem cell transplantation

■ Explain common complications of the therapy.

■ Discuss prognosis.

Rationale

Investigational and clinical trials for biological therapy of non-Hodgkin's lymphoma include the use of interferon, interleukin, and tumor necrosis factor. Rituximab (Rituxan) is a monoclonal antibody that binds to the lymphoma cells and allows the patient's own immune system to recognize and destroy malignant cells.

Transplantation is indicated when patients have not shown remission with radiation and/or chemotherapy, or have relapsed after chemotherapy. Autologous (patient is donor) bone marrow transplantations are most frequently used. Allogenic (matched donor) transplantation is used if the disease has spread to the bone marrow.

These include pancytopenia from radiation and chemotherapy (anemia, bleeding, infection); nausea and vomiting from chemotherapy; fatigue and weakness.

Prognosis depends on type of disease, stage at which diagnosis was made, and response to treatment plan. Generally complete remissions are possible in about 80% of patients with Hodgkin's disease. Patients with non-Hodgkin's lymphoma usually have a poorer prognosis because of later stage at diagnosis.

NDx Nursing Diagnosis

Fatigue

Common Related Factors

Side effects of chemotherapy or radiation therapy
Reduced oxygen-carrying capacity of blood from reduced number of red blood cells (RBCs)

Defining Characteristics

Report of weakness or fatigue
Inability to maintain usual routine
Exertional discomfort or dyspnea
Decreased performance

Common Expected Outcomes

Patient achieves adequate activity tolerance, as evidenced by ability to perform activities of daily living (ADLs) and verbalization of return to normal or near-normal activity levels.
Patient establishes a pattern of sleep and rest that facilitates optimal performance of required or desired activities.

NOC Outcomes
Energy Conservation; Activity Tolerance

NIC Interventions
Energy Management; Risk for Impaired Individual Coping

Lymphoma: Hodgkin's Disease; Non-Hodgkin's Lymphoma

■ = Independent; ▲ = Collaborative

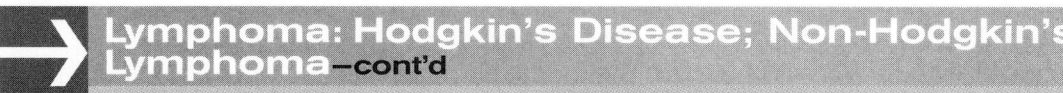

Lymphoma: Hodgkin's Disease; Non-Hodgkin's Lymphoma—cont'd

Ongoing Assessment

Actions/Interventions

- Assess specific cause of fatigue.

- Assess current and desired activity level.

Rationale

Fatigue is a characteristic side effect of lymphoma treatment. The extent will vary depending on whether the patient is in remission or relapse. However, patients may also exhibit lack of interest in performing activities because of associated depression, sleeping difficulties, or other personal problems.

These provide basis for development of treatment plan.

Therapeutic Interventions

Actions/Interventions

- Assist patient in planning ADLs. Guide in prioritizing activities for the day.

- Stress importance of frequent rest periods.

- Teach energy-conservation principles.

▲ Anticipate need for transfusion of packed RBCs.
▲ Refer the patient and family to an occupational therapist.

Rationale

Not all self-care activities need to be completed in the morning. Likewise, not all housework needs to be completed in 1 day.

Energy reserves may be depleted unless the patient respects the body's need for increased rest.

Patients and caregivers may need to learn skills for delegation of tasks to others, setting priorities, and clustering care to use available energy to complete desired activities.

These increase oxygen-carrying capacity of the blood.

The occupational therapist can teach the patient about using assistive devices. The therapist also can help the patient and family evaluate the need for additional energy conservation measures in the home setting.

NDx Nursing Diagnosis

Risk for Ineffective Coping

Common Risk Factors

Situational crisis
Inadequate support system
Inadequate coping methods

Common Expected Outcome

Patient demonstrates positive coping strategies, as evidenced by expression of feelings and hopes, realistic goal setting for future, and use of available resources and support systems.

NOC Outcomes
Coping; Social Support; Family Coping

NIC Interventions
Coping Enhancement; Hope Installation; Grief Work Facilitation; Support System Enhancement

Hematolymphatic, Immunological, and Oncological Care Plans

■ = Independent; ▲ = Collaborative

Ongoing Assessment

Actions/Interventions

■ Assess patient's knowledge of disease and treatment plan.

■ Assess for coping mechanisms used in previous illnesses or prior hospitalizations.

■ Evaluate resources and support systems available to the patient at home and in the community.

Rationale

Because lymphoma is a cancer, the patient may expect to die. Realistic but positive information may be indicated.

Successful coping is influenced by previous successes.

Lymphoma treatment may require months and years of ongoing chemotherapy, depending on length of remission. Available support systems may change over time.

Therapeutic Interventions

Actions/Interventions

■ Establish open lines of communication; define your role as a patient informant and advocate.

■ Provide opportunities for the patient and significant others to openly express feelings, fears, and concerns. Provide reassurance and hope as indicated.

■ Assist the patient to grieve and work through the losses associated with life-threatening illness, if appropriate.

■ Assist the patient and significant others in redefining hopes and components of individuality (e.g., roles, values, and attitudes).

■ Introduce new information about disease treatment, as available.

■ Assist the patient to become involved as a comanager of the treatment plan.

■ Assist in the development of an alternative support system. Encourage participation in self-help groups as available.

■ Describe community resources available to meet unique demands of lymphoma, its treatment, and survival.

Rationale

The nurse may be the first person the patient and family turn to as a source of support. The uncertain prognosis for non-Hodgkin's lymphoma adds to the burden of illness for the patient and family. Managing ongoing treatment and side effects in the home setting can be stressful for the patient and family.

Verbalization of actual or perceived threats can help reduce anxiety.

Grief is a universal experience; people who have successfully undergone grief over a loss can be enormously helpful to others undergoing the same feelings.

Emphasizing the patient's intrinsic worth and viewing the immediate situation as manageable in time may provide support.

Chemotherapy agents may change. The patient may become a candidate for bone marrow transplantation. Clinical trials are also available for these patients.

This helps the patient regain control over the situation. Many patients become educated about their chemotherapeutic agents and possible side effects.

Relationships with persons with common interests and goals can be beneficial. Participation in support groups may allow the individual to realize that others have the same problem, and they may use this as an aid for coping.

It is helpful for patients to have more than one resource for assisting them in this process.

Lymphoma: Hodgkin's Disease; Non-Hodgkin's Lymphoma

■ = Independent; ▲ = Collaborative

Lymphoma: Hodgkin's Disease; Non-Hodgkin's Lymphoma—cont'd

Nursing Diagnosis

Risk for Infection

Common Risk Factors

Altered immunological responses related to disease process

Immunosuppression secondary to chemotherapy and radiation therapy

Common Expected Outcome

Patient has reduced risk of local or systemic infection, as evidenced by afebrile state, compliance with preventive measures, and prompt reporting of early signs of infection.

NOC Outcomes

Immune Status; Knowledge: Infection Control; Tissue Integrity: Skin and Mucous Membranes

NIC Interventions

Infection Protection; Teaching: Disease Process; Oral Health Maintenance

Ongoing Assessment

Actions/Interventions	Rationale
■ Auscultate lung fields for crackles, rhonchi, and decreased lung sounds.	Pulmonary infections are common.
■ Observe patient for coughing spells and character of sputum.	Increase in the amount of sputum and changes in color from clear or white to yellow or green may indicate a respiratory infection.
■ Inspect body sites with high infection potential (mouth, throat, axilla, perineum, rectum).	Opportunistic infections of the mucous membrane surfaces of the body are often the first type of infection to develop in the immunocompromised patient.
■ Inspect intravenous central catheter sites for redness, tenderness, pain, and itching.	In the absence of granulocytes, site of infection may develop without characteristic pus formation.
■ Observe for changes in color, character, and frequency of urine and stool.	These provide data on possible urinary tract infection or intestinal infection.
▲ Monitor temperature as indicated. Report if higher than 38° C (100.4° F).	Fever may be the only sign of infection. Patients need to be instructed to record serial temperatures at home.
▲ Obtain cultures as indicated.	These are required to determine antibiotic sensitivity and presence of fungi.

Therapeutic Interventions

Actions/Interventions	Rationale
■ Explain the cause and effects of leukopenia.	Leukemic cells replace normal cells. Also, chemotherapy causes bone marrow suppression and reduced number of neutrophils needed to fight infection.
■ Instruct the patient to maintain personal hygiene, especially at home: • To bathe with a mild antiseptic soap • To wash hands well before eating and after using bathroom • To wipe perineal area from front to back	This is useful for removing skin surface bacteria that may play a role in secondary infection. The perineal area is a source of pathogens and a frequent entry port for microorganisms.
■ Instruct the patient to brush teeth with a soft tooth-brush four times a day and as necessary, to remove dentures at night, and to rinse mouth after each emesis or when expectorating phlegm.	Intact oral mucous membranes are the first line of defense in controlling development of oral infections.
■ Teach the patient to inspect the oropharyngeal area daily for white patches in the mouth, coated or encrusted oral ulcerations, swollen and erythematous tongue with white or brown coating, infected throat and pain on swallowing, debris on teeth, ill-fitting dentures, amount and viscosity of saliva, and changes in vocal tone.	Candidiasis is a common opportunistic infection of the oral and esophageal mucous membranes.
■ Teach the patient to avoid mouthwashes that contain alcohol and to avoid irritating foods and acidic drinks.	Alcohol has a drying effect on mucous membranes.
■ Teach the patient to use prescribed topical medications (e.g., nystatin [Nilstat] and lidocaine [Xylocaine]).	These agents may require specific instructions.
■ Instruct the patient and caregiver to maintain strict aseptic technique when changing dressings and to avoid wetting central catheter dressings.	These measures help prevent bacterial growth.
■ Instruct the patient to observe for fever spikes and flulike symptoms (e.g., malaise, weakness, myalgia) and to notify the nurse or physician if they occur.	Early assessment facilitates prompt treatment.
■ Instruct the patient and caregiver regarding the importance of eliminating potential sources of infection at home (especially when neutrophil counts are low): • Avoid contact with visitors or family, especially children with colds or infections and/or who attend daycare, preschool, or elementary school. • Avoid shared drinking and eating utensils. • Avoid contact with cat litter boxes, fish tanks, and human or animal excreta. • Avoid swimming in private or public pools. • Restrict contact with live plants.	Patients must understand strategies/measures by which they can protect themselves during times of compromised defense.
■ Instruct the patient regarding "protective isolation" if laboratory results indicate neutropenia (absolute neutrophil count [ANC] less than 500 to 1000/mm³). • Implement thorough hand washing for staff and visitors before physical contact with the patient. • Wear a face mask.	Institutional protocols may vary. Hand washing removes transient and resident bacteria from hands, thus minimizing or preventing transmission to the patient.
■ Instruct the patient to take prescribed antibiotic, antifungal, or antiviral drugs on time.	A regular schedule is needed to maintain therapeutic drug levels.

Lymphoma: Hodgkin's Disease; Non-Hodgkin's Lymphoma

■ = Independent; ▲ = Collaborative

Lymphoma: Hodgkin's Disease; Non-Hodgkin's Lymphoma—cont'd

Actions/Interventions	Rationale
■ Explain importance of regular medical and dental checkups.	Early identification of problems reduces subsequent complications.
■ Refer the patient to a dietitian for instructions on maintenance of a well-balanced diet.	A specialist may provide additional help.

 Nursing Diagnosis

Ineffective Protection

Common Related Factor
Bone marrow depression secondary to chemotherapy or radiation therapy

Defining Characteristics
Altered clotting
Bleeding

Common Expected Outcome
Patient's risk for bleeding is reduced, as evidenced by platelet count within acceptable limits, compliance with preventive measures, and prompt reporting of early signs and symptoms.

NOC Outcomes
Blood Coagulation; Knowledge: Disease Process

NIC Interventions
Bleeding Precautions; Teaching: Disease Process

Ongoing Assessment

Actions/Interventions	Rationale
▲ Monitor platelet count.	Data determine risk for bleeding: • Mild thrombocytopenia: platelets 50,000 to 100,000/mm³ • Moderately severe: platelets 20,000 to 50,000/mm³ • Severe: platelets 20,000/mm³ or less • Transfusion threshold: platelet count less than 10,000/mm³ or signs of active bleeding
■ Assess for signs and symptoms of bleeding.	These may include petechiae and bruising; hemoptysis; epistaxis; bleeding in oral mucosa; hematemesis; hematochezia; melena; vaginal bleeding; dizziness; orthostatic changes; decreased blood pressure (BP); headaches; changes in mental and visual acuity; and increased pulse rate.
■ Note bleeding from any recent puncture site (e.g., venipuncture, bone marrow aspiration site).	Prolonged oozing from puncture sites may be the first sign of bleeding problems.

■ = Independent; ▲ = Collaborative

Hematolymphatic, Immunological, and Oncological Care Plans

Therapeutic Interventions

Actions/Interventions	Rationale
■ Explain to the patient and significant others the symptoms of thrombocytopenia and the functions of platelets: • Normal range of platelet count • Effects of thrombocytopenia • Rationale of bleeding precautions	Most individuals are not familiar with the complexities of the hematological system.
■ Instruct the patient in precautionary measures. Initiate bleeding precautions for platelet count less than 50,000/mm³:	Understanding of precautionary measures reduces risk of bleeding.
• Use soft toothbrush and nonabrasive toothpaste.	This reduces risk of bleeding.
• Inspect gums for oozing.	This can be an early sign of bleeding.
• Avoid use of toothpicks and dental floss.	These stimulate bleeding.
• Avoid rectal suppositories, thermometers, enemas, vaginal douches, and tampons.	This reduces mucosal trauma.
• Avoid aspirin or aspirin-containing products, nonsteroidal antiinflammatory drugs (NSAIDs), and anticoagulants.	These interfere with platelet function.
• Avoid straining with bowel movements, forceful nose blowing, coughing, or sneezing.	This reduces the risk of bleeding.
• Count used sanitary pads during menstruation. Report menstrual cycle changes.	This provides data on bleeding status.
• Use electric razor for shaving (not razor blades).	This reduces risk for injury.
• Avoid sharp objects such as scissors and knives.	It is important to prevent cuts, which would not only bleed but also become portals of entry for microorganisms, leading to infection in the presence of neutropenia.
• Lubricate nostrils with saline solution drops as necessary.	This prevents drying and cracking.
• Lubricate lips with petroleum jelly as needed.	This prevents drying and cracking.
• Practice gentle sex; use water-based lubricant before sexual intercourse.	This prevents mucosal trauma.
• Protect self from injury and trauma (e.g., falls, bumps, strenuous exercise, contact sports).	Patient safety is a priority.

In the health care setting:

Actions/Interventions	Rationale
■ Avoid finger-sticks if possible. Coordinate laboratory work so all tests are done at one time.	This reduces bleeding risk.
■ Avoid intramuscular and subcutaneous injections. If necessary, use small-bore needles for injections and apply ice to the injection site for 5 minutes. Observe the site for oozing.	These measures reduce bleeding potential.
■ Inflate BP cuff as little as possible while monitoring pressure.	Overinflation can cause bruising.
■ Apply pressure, dressing, or sandbag to the bone marrow aspiration site.	This prevents excessive pressure when compressing soft tissues and deeper structures of the arm, because this may lead to bruising or hematomas.
■ Give the patient and family at least two telephone numbers to call in case of bleeding.	This facilitates early treatment.
▲ Apply ice or topical thrombin promptly as prescribed for bleeding mucous membranes.	These promote clot formation.

Lymphoma: Hodgkin's Disease;
Non-Hodgkin's Lymphoma

■ = Independent; ▲ = Collaborative

Lymphoma: Hodgkin's Disease; Non-Hodgkin's Lymphoma—cont'd

Actions/Interventions

■ Instruct the patient to take antacids as prescribed when taking steroids, NSAIDs, and/or aspirin.

■ Discuss the possibility of platelet transfusions. Teach the patient the purpose and possible reactions to transfusions.

▲ Ensure availability and readiness of platelets for transfusion.

Rationale

This reduces gastric irritation.

Knowledge reduces anxiety.

This prevents spontaneous or excessive bleeding (generally for platelet count less than 20,000/mm^3, or according to institutional protocol).

 Nursing Diagnosis

Imbalanced Nutrition: Less Than Body Requirements

Common Related Factors

Treatment effects:
- Side effects of chemotherapy (inability to taste and smell foods, loss of appetite, nausea, vomiting, mucositis, dry mouth, diarrhea)
- Medications (e.g., narcotics, antibiotics, vitamins)

Disease effects:
- Primary malignancy or metastasis
- Tumor waste products
- Renal dysfunction
- Electrolyte imbalance (e.g., hypercalcemia, hyponatremia)
- Pain

Psychogenic effects:
- Conditioning to adversive stimuli (e.g., anticipatory nausea and vomiting, tension, anxiety, stress)
- Depression

Defining Characteristics

Weight loss
Documented inadequate caloric intake
Weakness, fatigue
Poor skin turgor
Dry, shiny oral mucous membranes
Thick, scanty saliva
Muscle wasting

Common Expected Outcome

Patient maintains optimal nutritional status, as evidenced by caloric intake adequate to meet body requirements, balanced intake and output, weight gain or reduced loss, absence of nausea and vomiting, and good skin turgor.

NOC Outcomes

Nutritional Status: Food and Fluid Intake; Nutritional Status: Nutrient Intake

NIC Interventions

Chemotherapy Management; Nutrition Therapy; Oral Health Maintenance; Medication Administration

Hematolymphatic, Immunological, and Oncological Care Plans

Ongoing Assessment

Actions/Interventions

- Obtain history of previous patterns of nausea and vomiting and treatment measures effective in the past.

- Assess the patient's description of nausea and vomiting pattern.

- Evaluate the effectiveness of the antiemetic and comfort measures regimens.

- Observe the patient for potential complications of prolonged nausea and vomiting: fluid and electrolyte imbalance (e.g., dehydration, hypokalemia, decreased sodium and chlorine), weight loss, decreased activity level, weakness, lethargy, apathy, anxiety, aspiration pneumonia, esophageal trauma, and tenderness or pain in the abdomen and chest.

- Weigh the patient daily at the same time and with the same scale. If the patient is at home, stress the importance of maintaining a daily log.

- Encourage the patient to record any food intake using a daily log.

▲ Monitor appropriate laboratory values (e.g., complete blood count and differential, electrolytes, serum iron, total iron-binding capacity, total protein, albumin).

Rationale

The patient may have adverse side effects in the past. However, newer antiemetic medications have improved this condition for many patients. These side effects can significantly affect the quality of one's life. Nausea and vomiting are the most distressing side effects for patients and families.

Patient responses are individualized, depending on type and dosage of chemotherapy. Nausea and vomiting may be acute, delayed, and for some patients even "prior to" (anticipatory) the chemotherapy treatment.

Patient response to antiemetic and comfort medications is highly variable and must be explored with each patient.

Chemotherapeutic drugs produce nausea and vomiting as a side effect by stimulating central receptors in the chemoreceptor trigger zone in the medulla or in the cerebral cortex. Some of the drugs stimulate peripheral receptors in the gastrointestinal tract to cause nausea and vomiting.

Consistent weighing is important to ensure accuracy. Without monitoring, the patient may be unaware of small changes in weight.

Determination of type, amount, and pattern of food intake (if any) is facilitated by accurate documentation, which provides information as to whether oral intake meets daily nutritional requirements.

These reflect nutritional and fluid electrolyte status.

Therapeutic Interventions

Actions/Interventions

▲ Administer antiemetics according to protocol.

▲ Administer antiemetic around-the-clock rather than as needed during periods of high incidence of nausea and vomiting.

Rationale

Newer agents are much more affective in reducing the incidence and severity of emesis. Treatment protocols using a combination of antiemetic medications are most effective in controlling nausea and vomiting associated with chemotherapy. This approach uses drugs that block nausea receptors at different sites and through different mechanisms of action. A typical combination protocol may include administration of a 5HT3 (serotonin) receptor antagonist such as ondansetron and dexamethasone before chemotherapy. For delayed nausea, the protocol may include administration of dexamethasone and metoclopramide. Other classes of drugs used to control nausea and vomiting include phenothiazines, butyrophenones, cannabinoids, and benzodiazepines.

Effectiveness of antiemetic therapy is increased when adequate plasma levels are maintained.

Lymphoma: Hodgkin's Disease; Non-Hodgkin's Lymphoma

■ = Independent; ▲ = Collaborative

→ **Lymphoma: Hodgkin's Disease; Non-Hodgkin's Lymphoma**—cont'd

Actions/Interventions	Rationale
▲ Titrate the dosage and frequency of the antiemetic within prescribed parameters as needed until effective therapeutic levels are achieved.	Each patient has his or her own threshold for relief.
■ Institute or teach measures to reduce or prevent nausea and vomiting:	Behavioral and dietary interventions seem to be most effective in the management of anticipatory nausea and vomiting. This pattern of nausea and vomiting is related to classical conditioning. The patient develops nausea and vomiting in response to stimuli associated with administration of chemotherapeutic drugs. Patients may try a variety of interventions to find those that best control this type of nausea and vomiting before drug administration. Antiemetic medications have been found to be less effective in the management of anticipatory nausea and vomiting. However, antianxiety medications such as lorazepam may be effective.
• Small dietary intake before treatment	Limited intake reduces gastric overstimulation.
• Foods with low potential to cause nausea and vomiting (e.g., dry toast, crackers, ginger ale, cola, Popsicles, gelatin, baked or boiled potatoes, fresh or canned fruit)	These foods are easily digested and provide a measure of success to augment nutrition.
• Avoidance of spices, gravy, greasy foods, and foods with strong odors	These foods can stimulate gastric motility.
• Modifications in diet (e.g., choice of bland foods)	Bland foods may be better tolerated.
• Small, frequent nutritious meals	Eating small amounts prevents gastric distention from stimulating vomiting.
• Meals at room temperature	Hot foods can stimulate peristalsis.
• Avoidance of coaxing, bribing, or threatening in relation to intake (help family avoid being "food pushers")	Such behaviors tend to only aggravate the situation.
• Rest periods before and after meals	This provides needed energy for eating and digestion.
• Sucking on hard candy while receiving chemotherapeutic drugs with "metallic taste"	Hard candies can reduce metallic or bitter taste.
• Minimal physical activity and no sudden rapid movement during times of increased nausea	Activity may potentiate nausea and vomiting.
• Quiet, restful, cool, well-ventilated environment	Relaxation reduces peristalsis.
• Relaxation and distraction techniques; guided imagery	These techniques can be helpful if used before nausea occurs of increases.
• Antiemetic half an hour before meals as prescribed	Antiemetics relieve nausea and vomiting.
■ Identify and provide favorite foods; avoid serving during nausea and vomiting.	The patient may develop an aversion.
■ Explain measures to increase sensitivity of taste buds: perform mouth care before and after meals; change seasonings to compensate for altered sweet and sour threshold; increase use of sweeteners and flavorings in foods; warm foods to increase aroma.	These may improve ability to tolerate foods.

■ = Independent; ▲ = Collaborative

Actions/Interventions	Rationale
■ Serve foods cold if odors cause aversions.	The smell of cooking foods may aggravate feelings of nausea.
■ Offer meat dishes in the morning.	Aversions tend to increase during the day: chicken, cheese, eggs, and fish are usually well-tolerated protein sources.
■ Serve supplements between meals; have the patient sip slowly.	These prevent bloating, nausea, vomiting, and diarrhea.
■ Explain measures to provide moisture in oral cavity, if indicated:	These can facilitate swallowing.

■ Explain measures to provide moisture in oral cavity, if indicated:
- Frequent intake of nonirritating fluids (e.g., grape or apple juice, iced or hot tea)
- Sucking on smooth, flat substances (e.g., ice chips; lozenges; tart, sugar-free candy) to increase saliva flow
- Use of artificial saliva
- Liquids sipped with meals
- Foods moistened with sauces and liquids
- Strict oral hygiene before and after meals; avoidance of alcohol-containing commercial mouthwashes or lemon-glycerin swabs that dry oral mucosa
- Lips moistened with balm, water-soluble lubricating jelly, lanolin, or cocoa butter
- Humidified air environment via vaporizer or pan of water near heat

Humidity should be used cautiously when the patient is leukopenic because of risk of *Pseudomonas* infection.

■ If reduced oral intake is secondary to mucositis, see Impaired Oral Mucous Membrane, p. 141.

Patients undergoing chemotherapy commonly develop some degree of soreness in the mucous membranes.

■ Position the patient in a Fowler's position or side-lying position during vomiting episode.

This decreases aspiration risk.

• **RELATED CARE PLANS**

Anxiety, p. 15
Cancer chemotherapy, p. 812
Cancer radiation therapy, p. 825
Caregiver role strain, p. 35
Deficient fluid volume, p. 71
Disturbed body image, p. 21
Fear, p. 68
Hematopoietic stem cell transplantation, p. 837

Multiple Myeloma

Plasmacytoma; Myelomatosis; Plasma Cell Myeloma

Multiple myeloma is the second most common hematologic malignancy. It is a plasma B-cell malignancy that is characterized by the overproduction of immunoglobulins. This pathophysiology results in disruption of normal red blood cells, leukocytes, and platelets, resulting in anemia, infection, and bleeding problems. The cause of multiple myeloma is unknown. Clinically, it may present itself as destruction of bone, infiltration of bone marrow, the presence of immunoglobulins in the urine or serum, or symptoms of renal failure. This disease affects the elderly, with a median age at diagnosis of 65 years. It is twice as common in African-Americans as whites, and twice as frequent in men as in women.

Multiple Myeloma

Multiple Myeloma–cont'd

 Nursing Diagnosis

Deficient Knowledge

Common Related Factors
New diagnosis
Unfamiliarity with disease process, treatment, and discharge and follow-up care

Defining Characteristics
Questions
Lack of questions
Confusion over disease and outcome

Common Expected Outcome
Patient and significant others describe diagnosis and treatment plan, side effects of medications, and follow-up care.

NOC Outcomes
Knowledge: Disease Process;
Knowledge: Treatment Procedures

NIC Interventions
Teaching: Disease Process;
Support System Enhancement

Ongoing Assessment

Actions/Interventions

- Assess knowledge of disease, treatment plan, and prognosis.

Rationale

This type of cancer is less publicized in the media than lung, breast, and colon cancers, with which patients may be quite familiar.

Therapeutic Interventions

Actions/Interventions

- Provide information on the following:
  - Nature of disease

  - Diagnosis
    - Bone marrow analysis
    - Computed tomography bone scans and skeletal survey
    - Laboratory studies (chemistry, complete blood count, serum protein electrophoresis)

  - Treatment plan—medical treatment of signs and symptoms: calcitonin to reduce hypercalcemia; alkylating chemotherapeutic agents; newer therapies such as proteasome inhibitors, thalidomide and arsenic trioxide; corticosteroids; high-dose chemo-

Rationale

Malignant plasma cells infiltrate the bone marrow and disrupt blood cells.

Large numbers of immature plasma cells are noted.

This test shows demineralization and osteoporosis.

An abnormal globulin (Bence Jones protein) is seen in serum and urine; increased serum calcium is noted. Because of the increased number of plasma cells producing immunoglobulins, plasma electrophoresis is performed to quantitate amounts.

Treatment is focused on managing both disease and its symptoms.

■ = Independent; ▲ = Collaborative

Actions/Interventions

therapy; palliative radiation therapy to treat bone pain; or bone marrow transplantation.

- Pain management strategies
- Diet and fluid therapy

- Importance of mobility
- Safety precautions

■ Refer to the U.S. Department of Health and Human Services (for information on multiple myeloma) and the American Cancer Society.

■ Involve the family and caregivers so they can effectively provide support in the home environment.

Rationale

Analgesic combination is often required for relief.

Therapy is required to prevent or treat hypercalcemia, hyperuricemia, and renal impairment.

Weight bearing prevents further bone demineralization.

Great care must be placed on preventing falls and pathological fractures in this high-risk population.

New treatments continue to be studied.

Because more patients are older, a variety of support services may be required.

NDx Nursing Diagnosis

Acute Pain

Common Related Factors

Invasion of marrow and bone by plasma cells
Pathological fractures

Defining Characteristics

Constant, severe bone pain on movement
Low back pain
Abdominal pain
Swelling, tenderness
Guarding behavior
Decreased physical activity
Moaning, crying
Pacing, restlessness, irritability, altered sleep pattern

Common Expected Outcomes

Patient reports reduction in or relief of pain.
Patient appears comfortable.

NOC Outcome
Pain Control

NIC Interventions
Pain Management; Analgesic Administration; Distraction

Ongoing Assessment

Actions/Interventions

■ Assess pain characteristics.

■ Assess effectiveness of relief measures.

Rationale

Skeletal pain, especially in the lower back and ribs, occurs most commonly and is often the presenting symptom.

During terminal stages, pain management is extremely challenging.

Multiple Myeloma

■ = Independent; ▲ = Collaborative

Multiple Myeloma—cont'd

Therapeutic Interventions

| **Actions/Interventions** | **Rationale** |

Actions/Interventions

▲ Provide analgesics in dosage, route, and frequency best suited to the individual patient. Consider around-the-clock schedule, continuous infusion, fentanyl (Duragesic) patch, or patient-controlled analgesia.

▲ Consider combination analgesics.

■ Instruct the patient to take analgesics early and regularly to prevent severe pain. Schedule pain-inducing procedures and activities during peak analgesic effect.

■ Suggest nonpharmacological measures for comfort: decreased noise and activity, relaxation and distraction techniques, good body alignment, additional rest and sleep periods, and ambulation unless contraindicated (e.g., because of spinal lesions).

■ Notify the physician if pain medications are ineffective.

Rationale

The patient with multiple myeloma responds to a combination of interventions for effective pain management. Drug therapy that combines nonsteroidal antiinflammatory drugs with low doses of opioid analgesics is often more effective in decreasing bone pain.

Combinations such as acetaminophen-opioids may be helpful.

Timing of administration is crucial to prevent peak pain periods. Each patient must be evaluated individually as to the optimal regimen.

Patients may not be aware of the effectiveness of nonpharmacological therapies. A trial-and-error period may be required to match therapy to patient preference. Immobilization of painful areas with braces and splints may enhance pain relief.

Pain service may need to be consulted. Radiation therapy may be required to decrease the size of lesions causing pain.

NDx Nursing Diagnosis

Impaired Physical Mobility

Common Related Factors

Bone weakness and osteoporosis
Generalized weakness caused by chemotherapy
Pain

Defining Characteristics

Inability to move purposefully within physical environment
Decrease in activities of daily living (ADLs)
Reluctance to attempt movement
Limited range of motion (ROM)
Decreased muscle strength or control
Restricted movement and impaired coordination

Common Expected Outcome

Patient maintains optimal state of mobility, as evidenced by participation in ADLs within ability and by necessary lifestyle adaptations.

NOC Outcomes
Ambulation; Mobility

NIC Interventions
Exercise Therapy: Joint Mobility;
    Exercise Therapy: Muscle Control;
    Exercise Therapy: Ambulation

Hematolymphatic, Immunological, and Oncological Care Plans

■ = Independent; ▲ = Collaborative

Ongoing Assessment

Actions/Interventions

■ Assess ability to carry out ADLs.

■ Assess ROM and muscle strength.

Rationale

Osteoporosis, progressive weakness, skeletal muscle pain, and malaise are common symptoms of this disease and reduce mobility.

Decreases in ROM and muscle strength occur as a result of decreased mobility.

Therapeutic Interventions

Actions/Interventions

■ Instruct regarding the importance of ambulation.

■ Stress the importance of maintaining an uncluttered environment.

■ Encourage the patient to perform ROM exercises.

■ Instruct the patient to change position every 1 to 2 hours and to get up in a chair as tolerated.

■ Encourage caregivers to assist the patient with ADLs as indicated.

■ Provide assistive devices (e.g., walker, cane, back brace) as needed.

■ Stress the importance of rest periods after ambulation.

Rationale

Weight bearing stimulates reabsorption and helps prevent further bone demineralization.

This prevents falls and bumping into objects. Bone weakening can readily result in fractures.

This prevents contractures of upper and lower extremities.

Activity and movement reduce risk of pneumonia, a complication of immobility, especially in older patients.

Help may be required for safety and comfort, but it needs to be balanced with not making the patient unnecessarily dependent.

These enhance patient safety.

Rest optimizes energy balance.

NDx Nursing Diagnosis

Risk for Impaired Urinary Elimination

Common Risk Factors

Immunoglobulin precipitates
Hypercalcemia, hypercalciuria
Hyperuricemia
Pyelonephritis
Myeloma kidney
Renal vein thrombosis
Spinal cord compression

Common Expected Outcome

Patient maintains optimal renal function, as evidenced by serum and urine laboratory values within normal limits, balanced intake and output, and normal blood pressure.

NOC Outcome
Electrolyte and Acid-Base Balance

NIC Interventions
Electrolyte Management: Hypercalcemia; Fluid Management

Multiple Myeloma

■ = Independent; ▲ = Collaborative

Multiple Myeloma—cont'd

Ongoing Assessment

Actions/Interventions

▲ Monitor serum laboratory values.

■ Assess for signs of hypercalcemia: nausea, vomiting, anorexia, confusion, weakness, constipation, ileus, or abdominal pain.

■ Monitor for signs of decreased urine output related to impaired renal function.

■ Assess for signs of fluid overload: dyspnea, tachycardia, crackles, distended neck veins, and peripheral edema.

▲ Monitor urine for specific gravity, pH, color, odor, and blood.

■ Assess for bladder distention.

Rationale

Hypercalcemia and increased uric acid levels occur from bone destruction. Crystallization leads to renal impairment as seen by increased blood urea nitrogen and creatinine levels.

Gastrointestinal and neurological changes are common manifestations.

Hyperuricemia may cause renal tubular obstruction and interstitial nephritis from uric acid buildup.

Hydration is used to counterbalance effects of calcium and protein buildup. Overhydration needs to be prevented.

These tests provide data on fluid balance, as well as evidence of bleeding.

This may indicate spinal cord compression from bone damage.

Therapeutic Interventions

Actions/Interventions

■ Promote calcium excretion; prevent dehydration.

▲ If hypercalcemia is present, increase fluids to 2500 to 3000 mL/day as prescribed.

▲ Provide low-calcium, low-purine diet, if prescribed.

▲ Administer medications: Didronel, Aredia, Mithracin, calcitonin, Ganite.

NOTE: Some are given intravenously and require aggressive intravenous hydration with 0.9% normal saline; allopurinol is given for hyperuricemia; oral phosphates are given for hypophosphatemia.

■ If the patient is confused secondary to increased calcium, provide a safe environment.

▲ Prepare for dialysis or plasmapheresis for ongoing renal problems.

Rationale

The effects of hypercalcemia are reduced when urine output is maintained at a level of 1.5 to 2 L per 24 hours.

Hydration dilutes calcium and prevents renal tubular obstruction from protein buildup.

Hypercalcemia is a clinical manifestation of multiple myeloma.

These may be used for hypercalcemia to inhibit resorption of bone.

Safety is a priority.

These therapies may be indicated to prevent or treat impending renal failure.

■ = Independent; ▲ = Collaborative

Nursing Diagnosis

Ineffective Protection

Common Related Factors

Bone marrow depression or failure
Replacement or invasion of bone marrow by neoplastic plasma cells
Decrease in synthesis of immunoglobulin by plasma cells secondary to decrease in normal circulating antibodies
Decreased autoimmune response
Chemotherapy
Bone marrow transplantation

Defining Characteristics

Bleeding
Thrombocytopenia
Anemia
Infection

Common Expected Outcomes

Patient maintains hemoglobin (Hgb), hematocrit (Hct), and platelets within normal limits.
Patient's risk of infection is reduced or prevented, as evidenced by normal temperature and absence of active infection.

NOC Outcomes
Immune Status; Blood Coagulation; Infection Status

NIC Interventions
Chemotherapy Management; Bleeding Precautions; Infection Protection

Ongoing Assessment

Actions/Interventions	Rationale
▲ Monitor Hgb, Hct, red blood cells, and platelet count.	Impaired bone marrow function caused by infiltration by plasma cells can predispose the patient to bleeding.
■ If on chemotherapy, evaluate regimens for potential myelosuppression.	This may aggravate an already existing problem.
▲ If the patient is a candidate for bone marrow transplant, monitor closely for signs of anemia, bleeding, and infection.	Pretreatment with high-dose chemotherapy to eradicate disease may cause significant problems.
■ Observe for signs and symptoms of bleeding.	Abnormal platelet production increases risk for bleeding.
■ Monitor for signs of infection.	Infection is a frequent complication secondary to deficient antibody production and reduced granulocytes from bone marrow depression.
■ Observe for coughing (productive and nonproductive) and changes in color and odor of sputum.	Bronchopneumonia is a common complication.
■ Review medications.	The patient taking steroids may not have overt infection symptoms.
▲ Obtain urine, sputum, and blood for culture and sensitivity testing and x-ray study if temperature exceeds 37.7° C (100° F).	Culture and sensitivity results guide antibiotic therapy.

Multiple Myeloma

■ = Independent; ▲ = Collaborative

Multiple Myeloma—cont'd

Therapeutic Interventions

Actions/Interventions	**Rationale**
■ Instruct the patient to avoid unnecessary trauma.	Platelet abnormalities increase risk of bleeding.
▲ Avoid unnecessary intravenous or intramuscular (IM) injections; if necessary, use smallest needle possible; apply direct pressure for 3 to 5 minutes after IM injection, venipuncture, and bone marrow aspiration.	This reduces the potential for bleeding.
■ Instruct the patient to:	
• Prevent constipation by increasing oral fluid, increasing fiber intake, and using stool softeners, as prescribed.	Straining causes breakage of small blood vessels around the anus.
• Use soft toothbrushes.	This reduces risk of bleeding.
• Use electric razor, not blades.	This reduces risk of injury.
• Avoid rectal temperatures and enemas.	These can traumatize the intestinal mucosa.
■ Instruct the patient to avoid aspirin and aspirin-containing compounds.	These drugs interfere with hemostatic platelet function.
▲ Administer hormones (steroids and androgens) and erythropoietin agents as ordered (e.g., epoetin alfa).	These stimulate red blood cell production.
▲ Consider platelet and packed red blood cell transfusion for platelet count below 20,000/mm^3, Hgb below 10, or Hct below 30%.	Replacement therapy is indicated to correct deficiencies.
■ Discourage exposure to visitors and friends with current or recent infection (e.g., a family member with an upper respiratory infection should wear a mask).	Multiple myeloma weakens the immune system.
▲ If granulocyte counts are low, institute low-bacteria, no-fresh-fruit diet. Avoid contact with living plants.	This reduces exposure to microbes in food and the environment, which could colonize and increase risk of infection.
▲ Maintain normal or near-normal body temperature with medications as prescribed, tepid bath, cooling blanket, and ice packs.	Normothermia prevents stress on the body and promotes comfort.

> • **RELATED CARE PLANS**
>
> Anticipatory grieving, p. 82
> Anxiety, p. 15
> Cancer chemotherapy, p. 812
> Ineffective coping, p. 51

Neutropenia

Granulocytopenia

Neutropenia is a deficiency in granulocytes, a type of white blood cell (WBC). There are three types of granulocytes: basophils, eosinophils, and neutrophils. Neutropenia and its complications center around the neutrophilic granulocyte. Neutropenia is a below-normal number of circulating neutrophils that may result in overwhelming, potentially

■ = Independent; ▲ = Collaborative

life-threatening infection. Neutrophils constitute 60% to 70% of all WBCs. Their primary function is phagocytosis, the digestion and subsequent destruction of microorganisms; as such, they are one of the body's most powerful first lines of defense against infection. The chance of developing a serious infection is related not only to the absolute level of circulating neutrophils but also to the length of time the patient is neutropenic. Prolonged duration predisposes the patient to a higher risk of infection. Neutropenia not only predisposes one to infection but also causes it to be more severe when an infection occurs. This care plan focuses on outpatient management.

NDx Nursing Diagnosis

Risk for Infection

Common Risk Factors

Neutropenia, secondary to:
- Radiation therapy
- Chemotherapy
- Hypersplenism
- Bone marrow depression or failure
- Autoimmune responses

Common Expected Outcome

Patient is at reduced risk of local or systemic infection, as evidenced by normal temperature and vital signs, chest radiograph result within normal limits, negative results of blood and surveillance cultures, and prompt reporting of early signs of infection.

> **NOC Outcomes**
> Infection Status; Risk Control
>
> **NIC Interventions**
> Infection Protection; Infection Control; Self-Care Assistance; Home Maintenance Assistance; Support System Enhancement

Ongoing Assessment

Actions/Interventions

▲ Monitor WBC with differential count (especially neutrophils and bands).

Rationale

This is used to determine relative risk of bacterial infections associated with absolute neutrophil count (ANC):
- 2000-1500/mm³ = Mild risk
- 1000-1499/mm³ Moderate risk
- 500-999/mm³ Severe risk
- <500/mm³ = Life-threatening risk

The ANC can be calculated by using the following formula:

$$ANC = Total\ WBC \times \frac{\%\ Neutrophils}{100}$$

or

$$ANC = Total\ WBC \times \frac{(\%\ Segs + Bands)}{100}$$

Neutropenia

■ = Independent; ▲ = Collaborative

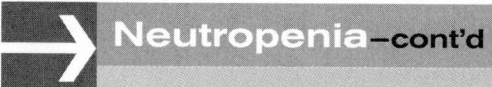

Neutropenia—cont'd

Actions/Interventions

- Identify sources of low WBC count.

- Inspect body sites with high potential for infection (e.g., orifices, catheter sites, skinfolds).
- Note abnormalities in color and character of sputum, urine, and stool that might indicate presence of infection.
- Monitor for increased temperature, tachycardia, tachypnea, and hypotension.
- Observe closely for fever and chills.

- Assess for local or systemic infection signs and symptoms (e.g., fever, chills, diaphoresis, local redness, warmth, pain, tenderness, excessive malaise, sore throat, dysphagia, retrosternal burning, cellulitis).
- Identify medication that the patient may have taken that would mask infection signs and symptoms (e.g., steroids, antipyretics).
- ▲ Send and evaluate cultures as prescribed for temperature higher than 38.5° C (101.3° F).

Rationale

Several cytotoxic and immunosuppressive medications and therapies can potentially cause neutropenia (e.g., Tegretol, propylthiouracil, methimazole, Bactrim, Indocin, gold injections for rheumatoid arthritis, neoplastic agents).

These are frequent sites for infection.

Early detection facilitates prompt intervention for what could be a life-threatening infection.

Signs and symptoms are often subtle, with fever being the predominant warning sign.

These may be the initial presentation of infection because in absence of granulocytes, locus of infection may develop without characteristic inflammation or pus formation.

Inflammation and exudate may be absent because of decrease or lack of neutrophils necessary for an inflammatory reaction. Lack of physical signs and symptoms does not exclude the possibility of infection.

Knowledge may lead to more aggressive assessments.

These are required to determine the organism causing the infection and antibiotic sensitivity.

Therapeutic Interventions

Actions/Interventions

- Wash hands thoroughly with antimicrobial cleanser before physical contact with the patient.

- Encourage daily shower. Explain the need for perineal care (with soap and water) after urination and defecation.
- Apply lotion to body after bath and as needed.

- Encourage meticulous oral hygiene before and after each meal and at bedtime.

Rationale

Meticulous hand washing is a priority both in the hospital and in the home or ambulatory care setting. Hand washing removes transient and residual bacteria from hands and prevents transmission to the high-risk patient. Because microorganisms can also be transmitted from one site of infection to other portals of entry, thorough hand washing is also important between patient care activities (e.g., central line dressing change, mouth care, perineal care).

The perineal area is a source of many pathogens and frequent portal of entry for microorganisms.

The skin and mucous membranes are the first line of defense for the body; when this barrier is weakened or interrupted (e.g., dryness, cracking, abrasions), the site becomes a potential portal of entry for microorganisms and a source of infection.

This is important in prevention of periodontal disease as a locus of infection.

■ = Independent; ▲ = Collaborative

Actions/Interventions

■ Encourage oral fluids.

▲ Initiate low-bacterial diet (e.g., no fresh fruits or vegetables, only well-cooked foods).

▲ Assist the patient in selection of high-protein, high-vitamin, high-calorie diet (refer to dietitian as needed).

▲ Administer stool softeners and high-fiber foods.

■ Avoid rectal temperatures, suppositories, and enemas.

■ Encourage women to use sanitary napkins instead of tampons.

■ Use sterile technique with dressing changes and catheter care.

▲ Observe neutropenic protocol.

■ Restrict contact with live plants.

■ Limit visitors. Discourage anyone with a current or recent infection from visiting either in the hospital or the home. Avoid contact with children of school age.

■ If hospitalized, avoid unnecessary invasive procedures. Limit intramuscular and subcutaneous injections.

■ Initiate measures for fever control (e.g., cool sponge bath, cooling blanket, light covers, antipyretics).

▲ Initiate intravenous broad-spectrum antibiotic therapy as prescribed.

■ Instruct the patient regarding possible addition of granulocyte colony-stimulating factor (G-CSF) and granulocyte-macrophage colony-stimulating factor (GM-CSF) to the medical regimen.

Rationale

Fluids assist in meeting hydration requirements (particularly during fever episodes).

This reduces the microbial level in foods, which could colonize and infect the gastrointestinal tract.

This is for maintenance of optimal health status, which promotes improvement of host resistance and provides nutrients necessary to meet energy demands for bone marrow recovery and tissue repair.

These prevent constipation, which could traumatize the intestinal mucosa and increase the risk of perirectal abscess or fistula formation.

These can traumatize the intestinal mucosa.

Napkins avoid trauma to vaginal mucosa.

This also applies to home health nurses and caregivers.

This protects the patient from exposure to environmental contagions.

Plants could harbor infective organisms.

Children are commonly exposed to sick playmates.

This minimizes risk of infection.

Such measures promote comfort.

Therapy prevents early dissemination of suspected infection. Once the infection-causing organism is determined, antimicrobial therapy may be adjusted to the type of organism and infection and to the clinical response.

These factors can enhance granulocyte recovery secondary to chemotherapy and potentiate the phagocytic activity of neutrophils. Pegfilgrastim is a newer agent with a longer half-life, stimulating neutrophil activity for up to 14 days.

NDx Nursing Diagnosis

Deficient Knowledge

Common Related Factor	Defining Characteristics
Unfamiliarity with nature and treatment of condition.	Multiple questions Lack of questions Misconceptions Request for information

Neutropenia

(■ = Independent; ▲ = Collaborative)

Neutropenia—cont'd

Common Expected Outcome

Patient or caregiver verbalizes understanding of medical diagnosis, treatment plan, safety measures, and follow-up care.

NOC Outcomes
Knowledge: Disease Process;
Knowledge: Infection Control

NIC Interventions
Teaching: Disease Process;
Teaching: Prescribed Medication;
Infection Protection

Ongoing Assessment

Actions/Interventions	Rationale
■ Assess knowledge of neutropenia.	Understanding may vary among patients exhibiting their first episode versus patients who experience this side effect more routinely.

Therapeutic Interventions

Actions/Interventions	Rationale
■ Explain factors that contribute to low neutrophil count (e.g., chemotherapy, drug sensitivity).	Information enables the patient to understand the cause of the problem.
■ Explain that low neutrophil counts produce high susceptibility to infection.	Infection and sepsis in a neutropenic patient can be fatal. Patients must understand the significance of these counts and their own role in prevention.
■ Explain signs and symptoms of infection; instruct the patient to contact the appropriate health team member immediately if any signs or symptoms occur or is suspected.	Vigilant monitoring helps reduce consequences of infection.
■ Instruct the patient regarding: • Use of prescribed medications (indications, dosages, side effects), which may include:	
• G-CSF (filgrastim)	This stimulates the bone marrow to produce granulocytes.
• Acyclovir	This prevents or treats viral infection.
• Diflucan	This prevents or treats fungal infection.
• Bactrim	This prevents bacterial infections.
• Need for frequent blood draws	These are required to monitor neutrophil WBC status.
■ Instruct the patient regarding: • Importance of good hand washing • Importance of meticulous body and oral hygiene • Avoidance of shared drinking and eating utensils; need to wash food well • Avoidance of crowds and persons with current or recent infection	Patients must understand strategies and measures by which they can protect themselves during times of compromised defense. Most infections result from organisms residing in the local environment.
• Avoidance of contact with cat litter boxes, fish tanks, and human and animal excreta	These are possible sources of parasites that can cause infection in the immune compromised person.

■ = Independent; ▲ = Collaborative

Actions/Interventions	Rationale
■ Instruct the patient regarding:	
• Avoidance of activities that may result in trauma to mucosa	Trauma sites can easily become infected.
• Alternatives where appropriate (e.g., oral and axillary temperatures instead of rectal, electric razors instead of razor blades, sanitary napkins instead of tampons, tooth sponge instead of toothbrush); limited sexual intercourse if WBCs and platelets are low	These measures reduce the risk for injury and infection.
■ Instruct the patient to make routine dental visits when WBC counts are not compromised (e.g., before starting chemotherapy treatment or bone marrow transplantation).	Dental care reduces the opportunity for infection to begin in the oral cavity.

> • RELATED CARE PLAN
>
> Impaired oral mucous membrane, p. 141

Sickle Cell Disease (Crisis and Maintenance)

Vasoocclusive Crisis

Sickle cell disease is a severe genetic hemolytic anemia caused by a defective hemoglobin molecule (HbS). This disease is found in Africans, African-Americans, and people from Mediterranean countries. The formation of sickle cells is increased by low oxygen partial pressure. Factors associated with sickling include hypoxia, dehydration, infection, acidosis, cold exposure, and exertion. This chronic disease can cause impaired renal, pulmonary, nervous system, and spleen function; increased susceptibility to infection; and ultimately decreased life span. Sickle cell pain crisis is defined as pain of sufficient severity to require medical attention and hospitalization. The severe pain, usually in the extremities, is caused by the occlusion of small blood vessels by sickle-shaped red blood cells. Research continues in identifying effective antisickling agents and possible gene therapy to correct this defect. This care plan focuses on the physical and emotional aspects of sickle cell disease.

NDx Nursing Diagnosis

Risk for Ineffective Therapeutic Regimen Management

Common Risk Factors

Social support deficits
Family patterns of health care
Excessive demands on individual or family
Knowledge deficit
Decisional conflicts
Perceived powerlessness

■ = Independent; ▲ = Collaborative

Sickle Cell Disease
(Crisis and Maintenance)

Sickle Cell Disease (Crisis and Maintenance)—cont'd

Common Expected Outcomes

Patient verbalizes understanding of sickle cell disease, prevention of crisis, and appropriate treatment.
Patient identifies appropriate resources.
Patient describes intention to follow prescribed regimen.

NOC Outcomes
Knowledge: Disease Process;
Knowledge: Health Behaviors

NIC Interventions
Teaching: Individual; Teaching Disease Process; Support System Enhancement; Genetic Counseling

Ongoing Assessment

Actions/Interventions

- Assess pattern of crisis episodes and compliance with treatment plan.

- Assess for related factors that may negatively affect success in following the regimen.

- Assess the individual's perception of the health problem.

- Assess ability to learn desired regimen.

Rationale

Crises may occur frequently or only sporadically. Treatment is supportive. There is no cure.

Knowledge of causative factors provides direction for subsequent intervention.

The patient may not understand the chronicity of this disease or his or her ability to control some of the precipitating factors.

Cognitive impairments need to be identified so an appropriate alternative plan can be implemented.

Therapeutic Interventions

Actions/Interventions

- Explain causes of sickle cell disease and the pain of crisis.

- Inform the patient of the benefits of adhering to the prescribed lifestyle.

- Instruct the patient on preventable and treatable situations that can precipitate crisis: decreased fluid intake, infection, strenuous exertion, emotional stress, smoking, alcohol ingestion, extreme fatigue, cold exposure, hypoxia, high altitudes, and trauma.

- Instruct the patient on the importance of the following:
  - Drinking at least 4 to 6 L of fluid daily
  - Dressing appropriately in severe cold weather
  - Taking prescribed medications such as folic acid
  - Keeping follow-up appointments

Rationale

Hypoxia is the primary stimulus for an acute pain crisis in sickle cell disease. With hypoxia, the erythrocyte containing the HbS hemoglobin changes shape from a biconcave disk to an elongated or crescent-shaped cell. The abnormally shaped erythrocyte can obstruct capillaries and contribute to hypoxemia, tissue ischemia, and pain.

Benefits may involve significantly less hospitalization and pain.

Patients with sickle cell disease can reduce the number of acute crisis episodes by avoiding situations that contribute to the development of hypoxia.

This reduces blood viscosity.

Cold causes vasoconstriction and reduced blood flow.

These replace depleted folic acid stores in the bone marrow.

Sickle cell disease is a chronic condition.

■ = Independent; ▲ = Collaborative

Hematolymphatic, Immunological, and Oncological Care Plans

Actions/Interventions

■ Instruct the patient on the necessity of contacting a health care provider at the first sign of infection.

■ Inform the patient of high risk for leg ulcers, which are commonly seen around the ankle and shin area.

■ Refer to support groups.

■ Inform the patient of the need for genetic counseling in family planning.

Rationale

Sickle cell patients have functional asplenia (no spleen), which interferes with phagocytosis. Early assessment facilitates prompt treatment.

Because of altered circulation to the area, these lesions are difficult to treat and often become infected.

Groups that meet for mutual information can be beneficial.

Pregnancy has increased risks for women with sickle cell disease. Also, the sickle cell trait is genetically transmitted.

NDx Nursing Diagnosis

Acute Pain

Common Related Factors

Vasoocclusive crisis hypoxia, which causes cells to become rigid and elongated, thus forming crescent shape
Stasis of red blood cells (RBCs)

Defining Characteristics

Complaint of generalized or localized pain
Tenderness on palpation
Inability to move affected joint
Swelling of area
Deformity to joint
Warmth, redness

Common Expected Outcomes

Patient verbalizes relief from pain.
Patient appears relaxed and comfortable.

NOC Outcomes
Medication Response; Pain Control

NIC Interventions
Pain Management; Analgesic Administration; Distraction

Ongoing Assessment

Actions/Interventions

■ Assess for pain characteristics:

• Severity (use 1 to 10 scale)

• Location

• Type
• Duration

Rationale

Pain of sickle cell crisis can be severe, requiring large doses of medication.

The lack of objective criteria by which sickle cell disease and even occurrence of crises can be judged makes evaluation difficult. However, the patient's report of pain should be believed and treated appropriately.

This is usually described as bone or joint pain, less often as muscle pain. This may include abdominal or back pain.

This may be reported as tenderness or inability to move.

Pain may persist for 4 to 6 days.

■ = Independent; ▲ = Collaborative

Sickle Cell Disease (Crisis and Maintenance)—cont'd

Actions/Interventions

▲ Monitor laboratory values (e.g., hemoglobin [Hgb], electrophoresis for amount of sickling, and RBC count).

Rationale

A severe decrease in functioning RBCs may indicate the need for replacement transfusion of packed RBCs.

Therapeutic Interventions

Actions/Interventions

▲ Administer pain medications as prescribed:

- Morphine sulfate, Dilaudid, or fentanyl by IV injection or via PCA pump
- Nonsteroidal antiinflammatory drugs (NSAIDs) with narcotics

▲ As pain control is achieved, begin titration of medication, as prescribed.

▲ Administer prescribed oral or IV fluids (6 to 8 L/day).

▲ Initiate transfusion or exchange transfusion of packed RBCs, as ordered.

■ Use additional comfort measures such as positioning devices and splints for joint discomfort.

■ Use foam overlay mattresses. Use moist heat or massage if preferred.

■ Use distraction devices such as television or movies, as well as relaxation techniques.

■ Provide rest periods.

▲ Administer oxygen as indicated.

Rationale

Initial sickle cell pain crisis requires parenteral intravenous (IV) administration on an around-the-clock schedule. Undertreatment of pain by health care providers is a common problem for patients with sickle cell pain crisis. Patients with sickle cell pain crisis have been shown to metabolize opioid and analgesics at a faster than normal rate. Larger than usual doses of analgesics may be needed to control the pain. The use of IV patient-controlled analgesia (PCA) may diminish the patient's need to make frequent requests for analgesics. Patients may develop opioid tolerance and physical dependence with prolonged use of these analgesics.

Morphine is the drug of choice. Medications should be given intravenously on a routine basis for acute pain.

Oral doses are indicated for milder pain.

Both oral narcotics and NSAIDs may be prescribed for home care.

Fluids promote hemodilution, which reverses agglutination of sickled cells within the microcirculation. Hydration and reversal of viscous blood flow in small blood vessels work to reestablish blood flow so that tissue necrosis does not occur.

Transfusion of packed RBCs can restore the oxygen-carrying capacity or blood volume. Exchange transfusion can be used in emergencies and in chronic transfusions because of improved viscosity effects and to reduce iron overload potential.

Adjunct therapies can promote comfort.

Heat and massage increase circulation to the area.

These can facilitate pain control.

Rest reduces tissue oxygen demand and helps reduce pain.

Hypoxia aggravates sickle cell disease.

■ = Independent; ▲ = Collaborative

Nursing Diagnosis

Risk for Ineffective Coping

Common Risk Factors

Chronicity of disease
Inadequate psychological resources (e.g., self-esteem)
Personal vulnerability
Situational crises
Unsatisfactory support system
Inadequate coping method

Common Expected Outcomes

Patient identifies own maladaptive coping behaviors.
Patient identifies available resources and support systems.
Patient initiates alternative coping strategies.

NOC Outcomes
Coping; Social Support

NIC Interventions
Coping Enhancement; Support System Enhancement

Ongoing Assessment

Actions/Interventions

■ Assess the patient's ability to openly express feelings about disease.

■ Assess the family's and significant others' support for disease management.

■ Assess how often the patient goes to the emergency department for crisis management.

■ Assess the frequency of hospital admissions.

■ Assess for level of fatigue secondary to anemia.

Rationale

Patients may need assistance in sharing feelings, especially if they sense that health care providers are judging them or doubt the severity of their pain.

Although family and friends can be great allies, they sometimes may have trouble dealing with chronic illnesses.

This provides information on the patient's ability to follow the prevention and treatment plan.

Patients frequently need to escalate their "controlling" behaviors to gain attention by health care providers, who may see the patient as "only seeking medication."

This may compromise effective coping.

Therapeutic Interventions

Actions/Interventions

■ Set aside time to talk with the patient when the pain is controlled.

■ Assist the patient in understanding the chronicity of this disease and the need to follow the suggested treatment plan.

■ Provide information on coping strategies.

Rationale

During crisis, the patient is distracted by the pain and may not be receptive to counseling.

The patient may not understand his or her ability to control some of the precipitating factors.

Strategies that have worked in the past may no longer be effective.

Sickle Cell Disease (Crisis and Maintenance)

Sickle Cell Disease (Crisis and Maintenance)—cont'd

Actions/Interventions

- Establish a working relationship with the patient through continuity of care.

▲ Involve social services, psychiatric liaison support groups, and/or pastoral care as additional and ongoing support resources.

- Avoid placing the patient in crisis in the same hospital room with another crisis patient.

- Inform the patient of community resources such as the National Association of Sickle Cell Anemia.

Rationale

An ongoing relationship facilitates trust, and can assist with problem solving and successful coping.

The patient or family may need additional help to deal with chronic problems. Participation in support groups may allow the individual to realize that others have the same problem and they may use this as a means to find alternative coping mechanisms.

Contact with similar patients may only intensify behavior if the crisis is precipitated by maladaptive behavior.

Relationships with persons with common interests and goals can be beneficial.

> **· RELATED CARE PLANS**
>
> Activity intolerance, p. 7
> Risk for impaired skin integrity, p. 173
> Risk for infection, p. 108

Systemic Lupus Erythematosus

SLE; Lupus

Systemic lupus erythematosus (SLE) is a chronic, autoimmune disease that causes a systemic inflammatory response in various parts of the body. The cause of SLE is unknown, but genetics and hormonal and environmental factors are involved. Under normal circumstances the body's immune system produces antibodies against invading disease antigens to protect itself. In individuals with SLE the body loses its ability to discriminate between antigens and its own cells and tissues. It produces antibodies against itself, called *autoantibodies*, and these antibodies react with the antigens and result in the development of immune complexes. Immune complexes proliferate in the tissues of the patient with SLE and result in inflammation, tissue damage, and pain. Mild disease can affect joints and skin. More severe disease can affect kidneys, heart, lung, blood vessels, central nervous system (CNS), joints, and skin.

There are three type of lupus. The discoid type is limited to the skin and only rarely involves other organs. Systemic lupus is more common and usually more severe than discoid; it can affect any organ system in the body. With systemic lupus there may be periods of remission and flares. The third type of lupus is drug induced. The drugs most commonly implicated in precipitating this condition are hydralazine, procainamide, and some antiseizure drugs. The symptoms are usually abolished when the drugs are discontinued.

Women are affected by SLE eight times more often than men, most commonly between 15 and 40 years of age. That the symptoms occur more frequently in women, especially before menstrual periods and during pregnancy, may indicate that hormonal factors influence development and progression of the disease. For some individuals, the disease remains mild and affects only a few organ systems; for others, the disease can cause life-threatening complications that can result in death. This care plan addresses the nursing management of patients with systemic lupus in an ambulatory setting.

■ = Independent; ▲ = Collaborative

Nursing Diagnosis

Deficient Knowledge

Common Related Factors

New diagnosis
Unfamiliarity with treatment regimen

Defining Characteristics

Multiple questions
Lack of questions
Verbalized misconceptions
Request for information
Inaccurate follow-through on instructions

Common Expected Outcome

Patient verbalizes increased awareness of disease process and its treatment.

NOC Outcomes
Knowledge: Disease Process;
Knowledge: Medication; Knowledge:
Treatment Regimen

NIC Interventions
Teaching: Disease Process;
Teaching: Prescribed Medications;
Circulatory Precautions

Ongoing Assessment

Actions/Interventions

- Assess knowledge of SLE and its treatment.

Rationale

Lack of knowledge about SLE and its chronic and progressive nature can compromise the patient's ability to care for self and cope effectively.

Therapeutic Interventions

Actions/Interventions

- Schedule educational sessions when the patient is most comfortable.

- Introduce or reinforce disease process information: unknown cause, chronicity of SLE, processes of inflammation and fibrosis, remissions and exacerbations, control versus cure.

- Discuss common diagnostic tests.

- Introduce or reinforce information on drug therapy. Instruct the patient on potential effects of steroids, immunosuppressant medication, and other drugs used to treat SLE.

Rationale

Pain and discomfort will distract the patient and may lead to inability to absorb new information.

The goal of treatment is to reduce inflammation, minimize symptoms, and maintain normal body functions. The incidence of flares can be reduced by maintaining good nutrition and engaging in exercise habits.

A variety of immunological-based tests may be performed (e.g., antinuclear antibody [ANA], erythrocyte sedimentation rate [ESR], serum protein electrophoresis, rheumatoid factor, serum complement). Tests may also be indicated to assess for major organ or systemic involvement.

Negative effects of drugs are related to long-term use or high-dose regimens.

Systemic Lupus Erythematosus

■ = Independent; ▲ = Collaborative

Systemic Lupus Erythematosus—cont'd

Actions/Interventions	Rationale
• Nonsteroidal antiinflammatory drugs and COX-2 inhibitors	These are used for their antiinflammatory actions. These agents should never be administered on an empty stomach. Side effects include gastrointestinal distress.
• Antimalarials (hydroxychloroquine, chloroquine)	These medications are used in the treatment of skin and joint symptoms of SLE. Side effects are rare, but patients are cautioned to see their eye physician several times a year to rule out the development of irreversible retinopathy. Patients may also experience mild gastrointestinal disturbances.
• Steroids	This classification of drugs is used for their antiinflammatory and immunoregulatory properties (they suppress the activity of the immune system). The dose is regulated to secure maximum benefits from the drug's administration with minimal side effects. Topical preparations are effective for skin problems. Oral-dose prednisone may be indicated for minor disease effects. Use lowest dose possible. Common side effects include facial puffiness, buffalo hump, diabetes mellitus, osteoporosis, avascular necrosis of the hip, increased appetite, increased infection risk, cataracts, and increased risk of infection.
• Stress to the patient the importance of not altering the steroid dose or suddenly stopping the medication.	Steroids must be tapered slowly after high-dose or long-terms use. The body produces the hormone cortisol in adrenal glands. After high-dose or long-term use of exogenous forms of steroids, the body no longer produces adequate cortisol levels. Increased cortisol levels are needed in times of stress. Without supplementation, a steroid-dependent person will enter addisonian crisis. The nurse must stress the importance of wearing a medical alert tag at all times that states the patient uses steroids and immunosuppressants.
• Immunosuppressants (azathioprine, cyclophosphamide)	This classification of drug is used to suppress the activity of the immune system, thereby decreasing the proliferation of the disease, especially during severe flare and in renal or CNS involvement. Side effects include increased infection risk caused by bone marrow suppression, nausea and vomiting, sterility, hemorrhagic cystitis, and cancer.
■ Instruct the patient to monitor for signs of fever.	Fever is a common manifestation of SLE in the active phase of the disease. Patients should also report accompanying chills, shaking, and diaphoresis. Patients taking aspirin as an antipyretic should have frequent liver studies performed, because aspirin use by patients with SLE has been demonstrated to cause transient liver toxicity.

■ = Independent; ▲ = Collaborative

Actions/Interventions	Rationale
■ Instruct the patient about the possibility of developing organ system involvement:	
• Renal involvement	About 50% of patients develop some type of glomerulonephritis. This is the most common cause of death.
• Instruct the patient to report changes in urinary output, the presence of edema, elevations in blood pressure (BP), or sudden weight changes.	It is important to report subtle changes in an effort to prevent progression of renal damage through early identification of changing conditions.
• Cardiac involvement • Instruct the patient to report tachycardia, shortness of breath, and chest pain.	Pericarditis, endocarditis, and myocarditis may occur, although sometimes without any manifestations. Accelerated atherosclerosis may also develop secondary to long-term steroid use.
• Raynaud's phenomenon • Instruct patients to protect extremities from cold exposure, including using oven mitts or mittens when removing food from the refrigerator and or avoiding placing feet on a cold floor. • Suggest that the patient wear multiple layers of clothing in a cold environment.	Diminished blood flow to the fingers and toes in response to cold results in color changes that follow a prescribed pattern: blanching or white phase, cyanosis or blue phase, and erythema or red phase.
• CNS involvement	Headache, transient ischemic attack, stroke, and depression may occur. Changes in mentation have been reported in the early active stages of aggressive SLE. These changes are often accompanied by an increase in the activity of the disease in other organ systems.
• Pulmonary involvement	Pleuritis or pleural effusion may occur.
■ Instruct the patient or family to report severe, throbbing headaches (may be accompanied by seizure or organic brain syndrome); seizures (most often grand mal); impaired judgment; inappropriate speech; disorganized behavior; disorientation; decreased attention; or hallucinations (organic psychosis may be caused by high-dose corticosteroids).	Early assessment facilitates prompt treatment.
■ Instruct the patient to avoid sulfa antibiotics and to use oral contraceptives cautiously.	These drugs can induce exacerbations.

NDx Nursing Diagnosis

Impaired Skin Integrity

Common Related Factors	Defining Characteristics
Inflammation Vasoconstriction	Redness Pain and tenderness Itching Skin breakdown Oral and nasal ulcers Skin rash

Systemic Lupus Erythematosus

■ = Independent; ▲ = Collaborative

Systemic Lupus Erythematosus—cont'd

Common Expected Outcomes

Patient maintains optimal skin integrity, as evidenced by absence of rashes and skin lesions.

Skin lesions are identified early so that treatment can be implemented.

NOC Outcome

Tissue Integrity: Skin and Mucous Membranes

NIC Interventions

Teaching: Disease Process; Skin Care: Topical Treatments; Skin Surveillance

Ongoing Assessment

Actions/Interventions

- Assess for erythematous rash, which may be present on the face, neck, or extremities.

- Assess skin for integrity.

- Assess for photosensitivity.

- Assess the patient's description of pain.

Rationale

The classic "butterfly" rash may appear across the bridge of the nose and on the cheeks and is characteristically displayed in the configuration of a butterfly.

Small lesions may appear on the oral and nasal mucous membranes. Disk-like lesions that appear as a dense maculopapular rash may occur on the patient's face or chest.

Patients may respond violently to ultraviolet light or to sunlight. Disease flares or outbreaks of severe rash may occur in response to exposure.

Gathering information about pain can guide treatment. Each individual may exhibit slightly different presentations.

Therapeutic Interventions

Actions/Interventions

- Instruct the patient to clean, dry, and moisturize intact skin; use warm (not hot) water, especially over bony prominences; use unscented lotion (e.g., Eucerin or Lubriderm).

- Encourage adequate nutrition and hydration.

- Recommend prophylactic pressure-relieving devices (e.g., special mattress, elbow pads).

- Instruct the patient to avoid contact with harsh chemicals (e.g., household cleaners, detergents) and to wear appropriate protective gloves, as needed.

For skin rash:

- Instruct the patient to:
  - Avoid ultraviolet light.
  - Wear maximum protection sunscreen (SPF 15 or above) in the sun. Sunbathing is contraindicated.
  - Wear a wide-brimmed hat and carry an umbrella.
  - Wear protective eyewear.

Rationale

Scented lotions may contain alcohol, which dries skin.

These promote healthy skin and healing in the presence of wounds.

Such devices aid in the prevention of skin breakdown.

Chemicals aggravate this condition.

The sun can exacerbate skin rash or precipitate a disease flare. Special lotions, glasses, and other items may be required to protect skin from exposure to sunlight.

■ = Independent; ▲ = Collaborative

Actions/Interventions

■ Introduce or reinforce information about use of hydroxychloroquine sulfate (Plaquenil Sulfate).

■ Inform the patient of the availability of special makeup (at large department stores) to cover rashes, especially facial rash (e.g., Covermark [Lydia O'Leary], Dermablend, Marilyn Miglin).

For oral ulcers:

■ Instruct the patient to rinse mouth with half-strength hydrogen peroxide three times a day.

■ Instruct the patient to avoid spicy or citric foods.

■ Instruct the patient to keep ulcerated skin clean and dry. Apply dressings as needed.

■ Instruct the patient to apply topical ointments as prescribed.

Rationale

This antimalarial drug is a slow-acting medicine used to relieve or reduce inflammation and rash. It may take 8 to 12 weeks for effect. A potential side effect is retinal toxicity. The patient must follow up with an ophthalmologist every 6 months. Topical cortisone medication may likewise be used.

These preparations are especially formulated to completely cover rashes, birthmarks, and darkly pigmented areas. This will help the patient who is having problems adjusting to body image changes.

Hydrogen peroxide helps keep oral ulcers clean.

These might irritate fissures or ulcers in mucous membranes.

It is necessary to prevent infection and promote healing.

Vitamins A and E may be useful in maintaining skin health.

 Nursing Diagnosis

Impaired Skin Integrity: Alopecia (Scalp Hair Loss)

Common Related Factors

Inflammation
Exacerbation of disease process
High-dose corticosteroid use
Use of immunosuppressant drugs

Defining Characteristics

Diffuse areas of hair loss
Loss of discrete patches of scalp hair
Scalp hair loss possibly accompanied by lesions, scarring, or dry scaling skin tissue

Common Expected Outcomes

Patient verbalizes ability to cope with hair loss.
Patient identifies ways to conceal scalp loss as required by personal preference.

NOC Outcomes
Knowledge: Treatment Regimen; Body Image

NIC Interventions
Teaching: Disease Process; Skin Surveillance; Skin Care: Topical Treatments; Body Image Enhancement

Systemic Lupus Erythematosus

Ongoing Assessment

Actions/Interventions

■ Assess amount and distribution of scalp hair loss. Note scarring in areas of scalp hair loss.

Rationale

Patient may experience total or patchy hair loss. Hair may regrow after disease exacerbation is abated.

■ = Independent; ▲ = Collaborative

Systemic Lupus Erythematosus—cont'd

Actions/Interventions

■ Assess degree to which symptom interferes with patient's lifestyle and self-image.

Rationale

There is a broad range of behaviors associated with body image changes, ranging from totally ignoring the change to preoccupation with it.

Therapeutic Interventions

Actions/Interventions

■ Instruct the patient to avoid scalp contact with harsh chemicals (e.g., hair dye, permanent solution, curl relaxers).

■ Instruct the patient to use mild shampoo and decrease frequency of shampooing.

■ Instruct the patient that scalp hair loss occurs during exacerbation of disease activity.

■ Explain that regrown hair may have a different texture and is often finer; hair will not regrow in areas of scarring.

■ Instruct the patient that scalp hair loss may be caused by high-dose corticosteroids (prednisone) and/or immunosuppressant drugs.

■ Encourage the patient to investigate ways (e.g., scarves, hats, wigs) to conceal scalp hair loss.

Rationale

These aggravate the condition.

These measures reduce drying of the scalp and maintain skin integrity.

Scalp hair loss may be the first sign of impending disease exacerbation. Scalp hair loss may not be permanent. As disease activity subsides, scalp hair begins to regrow.

Prevention of infection in scalp lesions is critical if one is attempting to promote long-term hair regrowth.

Hair will regrow as dose decreases.

Hair loss may interfere with lifestyle and self-image.

NDx Nursing Diagnosis

Joint Pain

Common Related Factor

Inflammation

Defining Characteristics

Pain
Guarding on motion of affected joints
Facial mask of pain
Moaning or other pain-associated sounds

Common Expected Outcome

Patient verbalizes a reduction in pain.

NOC Outcomes
Pain Control; Medication Response

NIC Interventions
Analgesic Administration;
    Pain Management

Hematolymphatic, Immunological, and Oncological Care Plans

(■ = Independent; ▲ = Collaborative)

Ongoing Assessment

Actions/Interventions

■ Assess for signs of joint inflammation (redness, warmth, swelling, decreased motion).

■ Assess description of pain.

■ Determine past measures used to alleviate pain.

■ Assess the impact of pain on the patient's ability to perform interpersonally, socially, and professionally.

Rationale

Usual signs of inflammation may not be present with this disease.

Patients with SLE often experience arthralgias of many joints with morning stiffness. Arthritis is present in nearly all patients and tends to migrate from joint to joint.

Patients may not know of or may not have tried all currently available treatments. Pain management is directed at resolution of discomfort as it is presenting at that specific moment in time, because relief measures may change with the joints affected.

Strategies may have to be developed so that the patient is able to maintain a maximum level of function in each of these areas. Strategies must be integrated into a flexible plan.

Therapeutic Interventions

Actions/Interventions

▲ Instruct the patient to take antiinflammatory medication as prescribed. Explain the need for taking the first dose of the day as early in the morning as possible with a small snack.

▲ Suggest nonnarcotic analgesics as necessary.

■ Encourage the patient to assume an anatomically correct position with all joints. Suggest that the patient use a small flat pillow under the head and not use a knee gatch or pillow to prop the knee.

■ Encourage use of ambulation aids when pain is related to weight bearing.

■ Suggest using a bed cradle.

▲ Consult an occupational therapist for proper splinting of affected joints.

▲ Encourage the patient to wear splints, as ordered.

■ Encourage use of alternative methods of pain control such as relaxation, guided imagery, or distraction.

Rationale

Antiinflammatory drugs should not be given on an empty stomach (can be irritating to stomach lining and lead to ulcer disease).

Narcotic analgesia appears to work better on mechanical pain and is not particularly effective in dealing with pain associated with inflammation. Narcotics can be habit forming.

Such measures assist in preventing development of contractures.

Crutches, walkers, and canes can be used to absorb some of the weight from the inflamed extremity.

Such devices keep pressure of bed covers off inflamed lower extremities.

Specialty expertise may be required.

Splints provide rest to inflamed joints.

These measures may augment other medications used to diminish pain.

Systemic Lupus Erythematosus

■ = Independent; ▲ = Collaborative

Systemic Lupus Erythematosus—cont'd

 Nursing Diagnosis

Joint Stiffness

Common Related Factor	Defining Characteristic
Inflammation	Verbalized complaint of joint stiffness

Common Expected Outcomes

Patient verbalizes reduction in stiffness.
Patient uses strategies to reduce stiffness.
Patient demonstrates ability to perform required activities of daily living.

NOC Outcomes
Pain Control; Mobility

NIC Interventions
Analgesic Administration; Pain Management; Exercise: Joint Mobility

Ongoing Assessment

Actions/Interventions

- Evaluate description of stiffness:
  - Location: generalized or localized
  - Timing
  - Length of stiffness
  - Relationship to activities

- Assess to what effect stiffness has on the patient's interpersonal relationships, social activities, and professional occupation.

Rationale

Joint stiffness associated with SLE is often migratory.

Most often stiffness is present in the morning.

Stiffness may last longer as disease progresses.

Joint stiffness related to SLE may not be related to activity or overuse; it is instead a response to immune complexes proliferating and setting up an inflammatory response in that particular body part. Patients with SLE may also have arthritis; thus stiffness and discomfort are multifactorial.

SLE-related arthritis usually does not result in deformity as in rheumatoid arthritis, but physical activity may still be severely limited at times.

Therapeutic Interventions

Actions/Interventions

- Encourage the patient to take a 15-minute warm shower or bath on arising.

- Encourage the patient to perform range-of-motion exercises after the shower or bath, two repetitions per joint.

- Remind the patient to allow sufficient time for all activities.

Rationale

Warmth reduces stiffness and relieves pain. Water should be warm. Excessive heat may promote skin breakdown.

These exercises help reduce stiffness and maintain joint mobility.

Performing even simple activities in the presence of significant joint stiffness can take longer.

■ = Independent; ▲ = Collaborative

Actions/Interventions

▲ Instruct the patient to take antiinflammatory medication as prescribed.

■ If the patient is hospitalized, ask about the normal home medication schedule and try to continue it.

■ Remind the patient to avoid prolonged periods of inactivity.

Rationale

The sooner the patient takes medication, the sooner stiffness will abate. Many patients prefer to take medications as early as 6 to 7 AM. Antiinflammatory drugs should not be taken on an empty stomach.

Patients often develop effective regimens for dealing with their disease, and this should be respected.

Activity is required to prevent further stiffness and to prevent joints from freezing and muscles from becoming atrophied.

NDx Nursing Diagnosis

Fatigue

Common Related Factors

Increased disease activity
Anemia of chronic disease

Defining Characteristics

Lack of energy, exhaustion, listlessness
Excessive sleeping
Decreased attention span
Facial expressions: yawning, sadness
Decreased functional capacity

Common Expected Outcomes

Patient verbalizes reduction in fatigue level.
Patient demonstrates use of energy-conservation principles.

NOC Outcomes
Activity Tolerance; Endurance;
    Energy Conservation; Sleep

NIC Interventions
Energy Management; Simple Relaxation
    Therapy; Exercise Therapy: Joint
    Mobility

Ongoing Assessment

Actions/Interventions

■ Assess the patient's description of fatigue: timing (afternoon or all day), relationship to activities, and aggravating and alleviating factors.

■ Determine nighttime sleep pattern.

■ Determine whether fatigue is related to psychological factors (e.g., stress, depression).

Rationale

This may be helpful in developing and organizing patterns of activity that optimize the times when the patient has the greatest energy reserve.

The discomfort associated with SLE may obstruct sleep.

Depression is a common problem for people suffering from chronic disease, especially when discomfort is an accompanying problem. Medications are available that are successful in treating clinical depression.

Systemic Lupus Erythematosus

■ = Independent; ▲ = Collaborative

Systemic Lupus Erythematosus—cont'd

Therapeutic Interventions

Actions/Interventions	Rationale
◼ Reinforce energy conservation principles:	
• Pacing of activities (alternating activity with rest)	The patient often needs more energy than others to complete the same tasks.
• Adequate rest periods (throughout day and night)	Energy reserves may be depleted unless the patient respects the body's need for increased rest.
• Organization of activities and environment	Organization can help the patient conserve energy and reduce fatigue.
• Proper use of assistive and adaptive devices	Adequately used, these devices can support movement and activity, resulting in conservation of energy.
If fatigue is related to interrupted sleep:	
◼ Encourage a warm shower or bath immediately before bedtime.	Warm water relaxes muscles, facilitating total body relaxation; excessive heat may promote skin breakdown.
◼ Encourage gentle range-of-motion exercises (after shower or bath).	These exercises maximize the muscle-relaxing benefits of the warm shower or bath.
◼ Encourage the patient to sleep in an anatomically correct position and not to prop up affected joints.	Good body alignment will result in muscle relaxation and comfort.
◼ Encourage the patient to change position frequently during the night.	Repositioning promotes comfort.
◼ Instruct the patient to avoid stimulating foods (caffeine) or activities before bedtime.	Environmental stimuli can inhibit relaxation, interrupt sleep, and contribute to fatigue.
◼ Encourage the use of progressive muscle-relaxation techniques.	These promote relaxation and rest.
▲ Suggest nighttime analgesic and/or long-acting anti-inflammatory drug as ordered.	Relief of pain can facilitate rest and sleep.

• RELATED CARE PLANS

Acute pain, p. 144
Anticipatory grieving, p. 82
Chronic pain, p. 149
Disturbed body image, p. 21
Disturbed sleep pattern, p. 177
Ineffective coping, p. 51
Self-care deficit, p. 156

◼ = Independent; ▲ = Collaborative

Renal and Urinary Tract Care Plans

 **Acute Renal Failure**

Acute Tubular Necrosis (ATN); Renal Insufficiency

In acute renal failure (ARF), the kidneys are incapable of clearing the blood of the waste products of metabolism. This may occur as a single acute event, with return of normal renal function, or may result in chronic kidney disease or kidney failure. During the period of loss of renal function, hemodialysis, peritoneal dialysis, or continuous renal replacement therapy may be required to clear the accumulated toxins from the blood. Ultrafiltration may also be used to increase fluid removal. Renal failure can be divided into three major types: prerenal failure (resulting from a decrease in renal blood flow); postrenal failure (caused by an obstruction); and intrarenal failure (caused by a problem within the vascular system, the glomeruli, the interstitium, or the tubules). Hospital-acquired renal failure is most likely a result of acute tubular necrosis (ATN), which results from nephrotoxins or an ischemic episode. Due to normal declines in renal function related to age, older patients are more at risk when receiving nephrotoxic agents such as intravenous (IV) contrast media or certain medications. This care plan focuses on the patient with ARF during hospitalization. After discharge, home convalescence may require 3 to 12 months.

 Nursing Diagnosis

Impaired Urinary Elimination

Common Related Factors	Defining Characteristics
Severe renal ischemia secondary to sepsis, shock, or severe hypovolemia with hypotension (usually after surgery or trauma) Nephrotoxic drugs (including antibiotics such as amphotericin B or aminoglycosides) Renal vascular occlusion Hemolytic blood transfusion reaction	Increased blood urea nitrogen (BUN) and serum creatinine Reduced creatinine clearance Urine specific gravity fixed at or near 1.010 Hematuria, proteinuria Urine output less than 400 mL/24 hours (in absence of inadequate fluid intake or fluid losses by other route) Weight gain Hyperkalemia, hyperphosphatemia, hypocalcemia, metabolic acidosis, hyponatremia, and hypermagnesemia

Renal and Urinary Tract Care Plans

→ **Acute Renal Failure—cont'd**

Common Expected Outcome

Patient achieves optimal urinary elimination, as evidenced by the following: urine output greater than 30 mL/hr; electrolytes, BUN within or near normal levels; and normal specific gravity.

NOC Outcomes
Urinary Elimination; Fluid Balance; Vital Signs

NIC Interventions
Urinary Elimination Management; Fluid/Electrolyte Management

Ongoing Assessment

Actions/Interventions

■ Monitor and record intake and output; include all fluid losses (e.g., stool, emesis, and wound drainage). Report output less than 30 mL/hr.

■ Monitor urine specific gravity.

■ Palpate bladder for distention.

▲ Monitor blood and urine laboratory tests as prescribed:
  • Sodium

  • Potassium

  • Calcium, phosphate

  • Magnesium

  • pH

  • Urinalysis (especially for protein and blood), urine electrolytes, creatinine clearance

Rationale

Renal patients may exhibit oliguria (<400 mL/day) or anuria (<100 mL/day). Their fluid status also changes as they move from an oliguric to diuretic phase. In the diuretic phase the patient is at risk for dehydration and hypokalemia.

Specific gravity measures the ability of the kidneys to concentrate urine. The ability to concentrate urine is lost in intrarenal failure and remains low at 1.010.

Bladder distention indicates that the flow of urine is blocked. Urine backs up into the renal pelvis, resulting in hydronephrosis and anuria.

Hyponatremia is caused by the dilutional effect of hypervolemia because water excretion is impaired.

Levels rise in ARF because the kidneys are unable to excrete potassium.

In ARF, the ability to excrete phosphate and to activate vitamin D needed for calcium absorption in the gut is impaired. The serum calcium level falls to less than 8.5 mg/100 mL and serum phosphate is increased to greater than 4.5 mg/100 mL.

Hypermagnesemia occurs as a result of decreased excretion of magnesium due to the damage of the kidney.

Metabolic acidosis develops because acid cannot be excreted, and the production of bicarbonate and ammonia (to correct the acidosis) is decreased.

The presence of protein or blood indicates an abnormal state. The 24-hour creatinine clearance test or outpatient spot urine testing provides evidence of the kidney's ability to clear creatinine. Older patients will normally have a somewhat reduced clearance. A creatinine clearance of less than 10 mL/min indicates kidney failure. Urine sodium concentrations are high with renal damage, yet low with prerenal causes.

■ = Independent; ▲ = Collaborative

Actions/Interventions

- BUN, creatinine

- Monitor daily weights.

- Monitor for signs and symptoms of excess fluid volume:
  - Edema (degree and location)

  - Neck vein distention

  - Hypertension

  - Lung crackles upon auscultation

  - Increased respiratory rate

Rationale

Both BUN and creatinine are elevated in renal failure; however, creatinine is more specific and reliable because it is not affected by diet, blood in the gut, or metabolism.

Sudden weight gains indicate fluid retention and not true weight gains.

When water excretion is impaired, fluid is retained and moves from the vascular space into interstitial spaces.

Engorgement of neck veins with the head of the bed at 30 to 45 degrees indicates excess fluid volume.

Excess circulatory volume contributes to an increase in blood pressure (BP).

Movement of fluid from pulmonary circulation into alveolar spaces causes adventitious lung sounds.

Presence of fluid in the alveoli impairs gas exchange.

Therapeutic Interventions

Actions/Interventions

▲ Evaluate the cause of the renal failure: prerenal, intrarenal, postrenal.

▲ Administer fluids and diuretics as prescribed.

▲ Maintain patency of Foley catheter. If urine output decreases, irrigate catheter with sterile saline solution to ensure patency.

▲ When administering medications (e.g., antibiotics) metabolized by kidneys, remember that excretion of these drugs may be altered. Dosages, frequency, or both may require adjustment.

▲ Anticipate renal replacement therapy if conservative management is ineffective.

Rationale

Medical therapy is determined by the cause of renal failure.

The kidney's ability to regulate fluid balance is lost in ARF, and hypervolemia can easily occur. Close fluid management is important. Volume replacement may be especially important in prerenal causes.

Maintaining catheter patency excludes low urinary tract obstruction as a cause of decreased urine output.

Drug excretion will be affected by impaired renal function, and increased drug levels and toxicity can occur. Hemodialysis may accelerate drug clearance, and dosages should be administered after dialysis treatments and levels monitored closely.

Hemodialysis is the most commonly used renal replacement therapy for the patient with ARF. Continuous renal replacement therapies are growing in availability for the hemodynamically unstable patient not able to withstand conventional hemodialysis.

NDx Nursing Diagnosis

Excess Fluid Volume

Common Related Factors

Compromised regulatory mechanisms
Excess fluid intake
Excess sodium intake

Defining Characteristics

Increased central venous pressure (CVP), jugular vein distention (JVD)
Increased BP
Tachycardia

■ = Independent; ▲ = Collaborative

Renal and Urinary Tract Care Plans

→ Acute Renal Failure–cont'd

Common Expected Outcome

Patient experiences optimal fluid balance as evidenced by stable weight, vital signs within normal range, and clear lung sounds.

NOC Outcome
Fluid Balance
NIC Intervention
Fluid/Electrolyte Management

Ongoing Assessment

Actions/Interventions

- Weigh the patient daily.
- Monitor and record intake and output. Include all stools, emesis, and drainage.

- Assess for signs of circulatory overload.

- Monitor heart rate, BP, CVP, and respiratory rate.

- Auscultate lung sounds and heart sounds for signs of fluid overload (e.g., crackles, presence of S_3 gallop).

Rationale

Patient weights are a good indicator of fluid status.

Close monitoring of all fluid losses and urine output is necessary to determine adequate replacement needs and to prevent excessive administration of oral or IV fluids during decreased renal function.

Signs of circulatory overload include increased CVP, increased BP, tachycardia, weight gain, edema, JVD, crackles, and dyspnea.

Edematous patients may actually be intravascularly depleted; similarly, when fluids begin to shift, overload can occur quickly, requiring management adjustments. Central venous lines may be helpful in determining fluid balance.

The kidney's ability to regulate fluid balance is lost in ARF, and hypervolemia can easily occur, resulting in heart failure.

Therapeutic Interventions

Actions/Interventions

▲ Administer IV medications in least amount of fluid possible.

▲ Administer oral and IV fluids as prescribed.

Rationale

This minimizes fluid intake during periods of decreased renal function.

This is to replace sensible and insensible losses. Not all patients enter the oliguria phase of renal failure. If urine output remains high, volume replacement needs can be considerable. The diuretic phase of renal failure requires fluid replacement as well as close monitoring of sodium and potassium levels. With tubular patency partially

---

■ = Independent; ▲ = Collaborative

Actions/Interventions	Rationale
	restored, sodium and potassium losses may occur. The patient may still require renal replacement therapy during this phase for clearance of solutes and toxins.
▲ Administer medications (e.g., diuretics) as prescribed.	Diuretic therapy requires close supervision because reduced blood volume can result in inadequate renal perfusion.
■ If peripheral edema is present, move the patient gently and reposition often.	Edematous skin is more susceptible to breakdown.
▲ Prepare the patient for renal replacement therapy if indicated.	Therapy clears the body of excess fluid and waste products. Even when the patient reaches the diuretic phase of renal failure, renal replacement therapy may be needed to clear solutes, and dehydration should be treated.

(side tab) Acute Renal Failure

NDx Nursing Diagnosis

Risk for Decreased Cardiac Output

Common Risk Factors

Dysrhythmias caused by electrolyte imbalance from ARF:
- Hyperkalemia
  - Decreased renal elimination of electrolytes: potassium, phosphate, magnesium, sodium
  - Metabolic acidosis (present with ARF): exacerbates hyperkalemia by causing cellular shift of hydrogen and potassium; excess hydrogen ions are traded intracellularly with potassium ions, causing increased extracellular potassium
- Hyponatremia: results from excessive intracellular fluid (dilutional effect), edema, and restricted IV or dietary intake
- Hypocalcemia: may also occur; exact cause is unknown

Volume overload leading to heart failure
Pericarditis or pericardial effusion
Dehydration resulting from the diuretic stage of ARF

Common Expected Outcome

Patient maintains adequate cardiac output (CO) as evidenced by strong regular pulses, hemodynamically stable cardiac rhythm, and BP within normal limits for patient.

NOC Outcomes
Circulation Status; Vital Signs; Electrolyte and Acid-Base Balance

NIC Interventions
Hemodynamic Regulation; Electrolyte Management

■ = Independent; ▲ = Collaborative

Ongoing Assessment

Actions/Interventions	Rationale
■ Assess for signs of decreased CO: change in BP, heart rate, CVP, peripheral pulses; JVD; decreased urine output; abnormal heart sounds; dysrhythmias; anxiety or restlessness.	These signs may indicate decreased CO.

▲ Monitor serum electrolytes as prescribed, assessing for electrolyte disturbances:
 	
Hyperkalemia (potassium >5.5 mEq/L):
• Electrocardiogram changes:
  • Increased T waves
  • Widened QRS segment
  • Prolonged PR interval
• Bradycardic dysrhythmias
 	
Hyponatremia (sodium <115 mEq/L):
• Nausea and vomiting
• Lethargy, weakness
• Seizures (with severe deficit)
 	
Hypocalcemia (calcium <6 mg/100 mL):
• Perioral paresthesia
• Twitching, tetany, seizures
• Cardiac dysrhythmias
	Electrolyte imbalances can be caused by very high ultra-filtration rates seen in continuous renal replacement therapies (CRRTs). High clearances of small molecules such as sodium, potassium, and bicarbonate occur as a result. Inadequate replacement of fluids and electrolytes during CRRT may also contribute to electrolyte imbalances.

■ Monitor cardiac rhythm. Determine the patient's hemodynamic response to any dysrhythmias.	Hyperkalemia and hypocalcemia can cause life-threatening dysrhythmias.
■ Auscultate heart sounds for the presence of a third heart sound (indicating heart failure) or a pericardial friction rub (indicating uremic pericarditis).	If either is present, the patient may require prompt renal replacement therapy. Pericarditis can occur with ARF and develop into a pericardial effusion and even result in cardiac tamponade. Pericarditis is thought to be caused by the presence of uremic toxins in the pericardial fluid.
▲ Monitor chest x-ray reports.	Evaluate the cardiac silhouette for early detection of any cardiac enlargement.
▲ Monitor for signs and symptoms of metabolic acidosis: • Arterial blood pH less than 7.4 • Altered PaCO₂ levels	In ARF, acidosis can be severe and may occur in conjunction with diabetic ketoacidosis, lactic acidosis, or septic catabolism.
• Plasma bicarbonate levels less than 22 mEq/L	Acid production in ARF results in a significant decrease in serum bicarbonate. The renal tubular cells are unable to reabsorb bicarbonate ions.
• Increased respiratory rate and depth, dyspnea	The lungs increase the excretion of carbon dioxide in an attempt to decrease the levels of bicarbonate present in body fluids. This mechanism represents respiratory compensation for metabolic acidosis.
• Tachycardia, initially progressing to bradycardia as the acidosis worsens	Electrolyte imbalances such as hyperkalemia that occur with acidosis can contribute to cardiac dysrhythmias.
• Hypotension	At a pH of 7.2 or less, myocardial depression and vasodilation may produce hypotension.
• Decreased level of consciousness	Changes in cerebral blood flow in acidosis can alter neurotransmission.

■ = Independent; ▲ = Collaborative

Acute Renal Failure

Actions/Interventions	Rationale
• Fatigue and malaise	Acidosis increases cellular resistance to insulin and decreases energy metabolism.
• Nausea and vomiting	

Therapeutic Interventions

Actions/Interventions	Rationale
▲ Administer medications as prescribed:	These diminish electrolyte disturbances.
• Sodium bicarbonate	This corrects acidosis or hyperkalemia. Sodium bicarbonate will temporarily shift potassium back into the cell; however, it can result in elevation of sodium and water retention from the sodium load.
• Calcium salts	Calcium salts treat hypocalcemia. Calcium salts may also be given to stabilize the cell membrane from depolarization in the hyperkalemic state.
• Glucose and/or insulin drip	These drive potassium into the cell. Insulin is able to shift potassium back into the cells, and the glucose is administered to prevent hypoglycemia from the effect of insulin.
• Potassium exchange resins	Resins exchange potassium for sodium in the gastrointestinal tract, thereby decreasing serum potassium levels. The bound potassium is then excreted in the bowel movement.
▲ Prepare the patient for renal replacement therapy when indicated.	Therapy corrects electrolyte imbalances. CRRT slowly removes water, electrolytes, and uremic toxins and is indicated for hemodynamically unstable patients not able to tolerate conventional hemodialysis.
▲ If dysrhythmias occur, treat as appropriate.	Treating dysrhythmias helps reduce risk for decreased cardiac output.
▲ Notify the physician of presence of pericardial friction rub.	If pericarditis is present, the patient will need to be started on steroids or nonsteroidal antiinflammatory drugs to reduce inflammation and discomfort. Also, heparin use should be limited to decrease the potential of bleeding into the pericardial space.
▲ If signs of decreased CO are noted:	
• Administer oral and IV fluids as prescribed. Note effects.	Administration of fluids will help increase CO by increasing circulating blood volume.
• Administer inotropic agent (e.g., digoxin) as prescribed.	An increase in myocardial contractility will help increase CO through an increase in stroke volume.

NDx Nursing Diagnosis

Imbalanced Nutrition: Less Than Body Requirements

Common Related Factors	Defining Characteristics
Stomatitis	Loss of weight
Anorexia, decreased appetite	Documented inadequate caloric intake
Nausea, vomiting	Caloric intake inadequate to keep pace with abnormal disease or metabolic state
Diarrhea	
Constipation	
Melena, hematemesis	

■ = Independent; ▲ = Collaborative

Acute Renal Failure—cont'd

Common Expected Outcome

Patient's nutritional state is maximized as evidenced by maintenance of weight and adequate caloric intake.

NOC Outcome
Nutritional Status: Nutrient Intake

NIC Intervention
Nutrition Management

Ongoing Assessment

Actions/Interventions

- Assess for possible cause of decreased appetite or gastrointestinal discomfort (e.g., stomatitis, anorexia, nausea and vomiting, diarrhea, constipation, melena, or hematemesis).

- Assess actual oral intake; obtain calorie counts as necessary.
- ▲ Monitor serum laboratory values (e.g., electrolytes, albumin level).

- Assess weight gain pattern.

Rationale

Uremia manifestations include gastrointestinal disturbances related to the accumulation of toxins and altered motility (increased or decreased).

This provides accurate measurement of nutritional intake.

Serum albumin indicates degree of protein depletion (3.8 to 4.5 g/100 mL is normal).

Weight gain is often related to fluid retention. A weight increase of $^1/_2$ to 1 pound a week is associated with increased nutritional intake.

Therapeutic Interventions

Actions/Interventions

- Administer small, frequent feedings as tolerated.

- Make meals look appetizing; try to eliminate other procedures at mealtime if possible and focus on eating.

- Provide frequent oral hygiene.

- Offer ice chips or hard candy if not contraindicated.
- ▲ Consult a dietitian.

- ▲ Adjust potassium restriction as indicated.

- ▲ Administer enteral or parenteral feedings as prescribed.

- ▲ Offer antiemetics as prescribed.
- ▲ Administer antacids and H$_2$-receptor blocking agents.

Rationale

The patient with gastrointestinal symptoms will better tolerate small meals, over large meals.

Decreasing distractions at mealtime allows the patient to focus attention on eating. The patient needs to use available energy to increase nutritional intake.

Frequent oral hygiene will keep oral mucous membranes moist and stimulate saliva production, which can help increase the patient's oral intake.

These decrease the discomfort of thirst.

In general, a diet high in carbohydrates and low in protein is used to reduce catabolism and prevent additional elevations of BUN.

In ARF, the kidney is unable to excrete potassium. Dietary restriction is needed to keep serum levels within normal limits.

These help maintain optimal nourishment; however, patients are at increased risk for fluid volume overload.

These reduce nausea.

These reduce gastric acidity and prevent mucosal ulceration. Antacids should not contain magnesium because the patient with ARF cannot excrete magnesium, and hypermagnesemia would develop.

■ = Independent; ▲ = Collaborative

Actions/Interventions	Rationale
▲ Provide renal replacement therapy as ordered.	Therapy removes uremic toxins and prevents the gastrointestinal complications that result from accumulation of uremic toxins.

NDx Nursing Diagnosis

Risk for Injury: Anemia

Common Risk Factors

Bone marrow suppression secondary to insufficient renal production of erythropoietic factor

Increased hemolysis leading to decreased life span of red blood cells secondary to abnormal chemical environment in plasma

Common Expected Outcome

Patient's risk of injury from anemia is reduced through ongoing assessment and early intervention.

NOC Outcomes
Blood Coagulation; Medication Response

NIC Intervention
Bleeding Precautions

Ongoing Assessment

Actions/Interventions	Rationale
■ Observe and document signs of fatigue, pallor, and weakness.	Early signs of anemia are the result of the decreased oxygen-carrying capacity of the blood.
▲ Monitor results of laboratory studies (hemoglobin and hematocrit).	Hemoglobin and hematocrit are decreased in the presence of anemia.
■ Check for occult blood in all stools and emesis.	Gastrointestinal bleeding is a potential problem with ARF and can lead to an increase in mortality.
▲ Monitor BUN.	BUN increases with internal bleeding and may be an additional clue to the presence of internal bleeding.
▲ Monitor coagulation status of the patient undergoing renal replacement therapy.	Heparin is used during renal replacement therapy to prevent coagulation in the extracorporeal circuit. Coagulation in the dialyzer can contribute to anemia. Overheparinization may lead to bleeding.

Therapeutic Interventions

Actions/Interventions	Rationale
▲ Administer oxygen as prescribed.	Supplemental oxygen therapy is indicated to maintain arterial oxygen saturation.
▲ Administer blood transfusions as prescribed.	Transfusion therapy may be necessary to replace blood loss.

■ = Independent; ▲ = Collaborative

 **Acute Renal Failure**–cont'd

Actions/Interventions

▲ Administer epoetin alfa (Epogen), as prescribed.

▲ Administer iron supplements or folic acid as indicated.

Rationale

Exogenous erythropoietin stimulates the bone marrow to produce more red blood cells. It takes 10 to 14 days for a response to be seen; therefore this may not be of benefit in acute anemia.

Dietary supplements help replace functional iron stores and support the development of mature red blood cells.

ND× Nursing Diagnosis

Risk for Infection

Common Risk Factors

Uremia resulting in decreased immune response
Debilitated state with poor nutrition
Use of indwelling catheters, dual-lumen venous catheters, peripherally inserted central catheters, Foley catheters, and endotracheal (ET) tubes

Common Expected Outcome

Patient's risk of systemic or local infection is reduced through ongoing assessment and early intervention.

NOC Outcomes
Risk Control; Risk Detection; Immune Status

NIC Intervention
Infection Protection

Ongoing Assessment

Actions/Interventions

■ Assess for potential sites of infection: urinary, pulmonary, wound, or IV line.

■ Monitor temperature.

▲ Monitor white blood cell (WBC) count.

■ Note signs of localized or systemic infection; report promptly.

▲ If infection is suspected, obtain specimens of blood, urine, and sputum for culture and sensitivity, as prescribed.

Rationale

Infection must be monitored closely because there is a tendency for development of infection with ARF. Infection increases the mortality associated with ARF, especially in older patients.

Because of a decreased immune response, an elevated temperature may not be present with infection.

The patient's WBC count will increase in the presence of infection.

Infection is the leading cause of death in ARF.

Identifying the source of the infection is necessary to plan appropriate therapy.

■ = Independent; ▲ = Collaborative

Therapeutic Interventions

Actions/Interventions

■ Provide meticulous skin care.

■ Use aseptic technique during dressing changes, wound irrigations, catheter care, and suctioning.

■ Avoid use of indwelling catheters or IV lines whenever possible.

■ Protect the patient from exposure to other infected people.

▲ If infection is present, administer antibiotics, as prescribed.

Rationale

Skin is the first line of defense against infection. Skin that is clean, dry, and free of prolonged pressure is resistant to breakdown and possible infection.

This decreases risk for infection.

This minimizes the patient's exposure to infectious agents.

Visitors, family members, and other patients with obvious infections pose an infection risk to the patient in renal failure who may be immune compromised.

Treatment of any infection with antibiotics is necessary to prevent further complications associated with infections.

NDx Nursing Diagnosis

Deficient Knowledge

Common Related Factor

New condition

Common Expected Outcome

Patient and significant others verbalize understanding of ARF and associated treatments.

Defining Characteristics

Verbalized confusion about treatment
Lack of questions
Request for information

NOC Outcome
Knowledge: Disease Process

NIC Intervention
Teaching: Disease Process

Ongoing Assessment

Actions/Interventions

■ Assess knowledge and understanding of ARF.

Rationale

ARF occurs with an acute decline in renal function, and most patients have no prior exposure to or experience with the cause, treatment, or outcomes of ARF.

Therapeutic Interventions

Actions/Interventions

■ Encourage the patient and family to ask questions.

Rationale

Patient education begins with responses to the questions asked by the patient and family.

■ = Independent; ▲ = Collaborative

Acute Renal Failure—cont'd

Actions/Interventions	Rationale
■ Explain all tests and procedures before they occur. Use terms the patient can understand; be clear and direct.	Patients are more likely to cooperate with care and experience less anxiety when they understand what is happening during tests and procedures.
■ Explain the purpose of fluid restrictions.	As the patient moves from the oliguric to diuretic phase, fluid allowances will vary.
■ Discuss the need for a reduced-protein diet.	The reduced protein diet helps prevent excessive elevations in BUN.
■ Explain the need for renal replacement therapy as appropriate and what to expect during the procedure.	This may involve ultrafiltration, peritoneal dialysis, hemodialysis, or CRRT.
■ Discuss the need for follow-up visits after discharge.	Return of renal function may occur over a 12-month period, necessitating changes in medications, diet, and fluid restriction, as well as close medical supervision. Occasionally, renal function does not return and instead deteriorates to chronic renal failure.
▲ Encourage family conferences with members of the patient's health care team (e.g., physician, nurses, rehabilitation personnel, dietitians, social workers), as necessary.	This facilitates family involvement in multidisciplinary planning. The patient may recover renal function or may need chronic dialysis if there is no return of kidney function.
▲ Consult appropriate resource persons (e.g., rehabilitation personnel, physicians, social workers, psychologists, clergy, occupational therapists, dietitians, clinical specialists), as needed.	Management of a patient with renal failure requires a multidisciplinary approach.

> ● RELATED CARE PLANS
>
> End-stage renal disease, p. 922
> Ineffective coping, p. 51
> Peritoneal dialysis, p. 939
> Vascular access for hemodialysis (see the **Evolve** website)

End-Stage Renal Disease

Chronic Renal Failure; Dialysis; Uremia

End-stage renal disease (ESRD) is defined as irreversible kidney disease, causing chronic abnormalities in the body's homeostasis and necessitating treatment with dialysis or renal transplantation for survival. African Americans have a higher incidence of ESRD than whites. Diabetes and hypertension are the most common causes. Uremia, or uremic syndrome, consists of the signs, symptoms, and physiological changes that occur in renal failure. These changes involve all body systems and are related to fluid and electrolyte abnormalities, accumulation of uremic toxins that cause physiological changes and altered function of various organs, and regulatory function disorders (e.g., hypertension, renal osteodystrophy, anemia, and metastatic calcifications). Patients with ESRD may be limited in their ability to carry out normal activities. This care plan may be used for the patient with ESRD in inpatient, outpatient, or at-home settings.

■ = Independent; ▲ = Collaborative

Nursing Diagnosis

Excess Fluid Volume

Common Related Factors

Excess fluid intake
Excess sodium intake
Compromised regulatory mechanisms

Defining Characteristics

Edema
Blood pressure (BP) elevated (above patient's normal BP) before dialysis
Weight gain
Distended neck veins
Orthopnea
Tachycardia
Restlessness

Common Expected Outcome

Patient experiences optimal fluid balance as evidenced by normotensive BP, weight gain less than 2 to 3 pounds between hemodialysis treatments, and eupnea.

NOC Outcomes

Fluid Balance; Electrolyte and Acid-Base Balance

NIC Intervention

Fluid/Electrolyte Management

Ongoing Assessment

Actions/Interventions

- Assess for signs of fluid volume excess: elevated BP, tachycardia, tachypnea, edema, weight gain, distended neck veins, and orthopnea.
- Assess respiratory pattern and work of breathing.
- Auscultate for crackles.
- Assess the amount of peripheral edema by palpating area over the tibia, ankles, sacrum, and back; and by assessing appearance of the face.
- Assess the patient's compliance with dietary and fluid restrictions at home.
- Assess weight at every visit before and after dialysis (weight gain not to exceed 2 to 3 pounds between visits).

Rationale

The signs of fluid volume excess are the result of sodium retention and increased intracellular fluid volume.

Kussmaul's respiration and dyspnea may be evident.
Crackles signify the presence of fluid in the small airways.
Dependent areas often exhibit signs of edema formation.

Excess fluid and/or sodium intake can lead to fluid volume excess in the ESRD patient.
Changes in weight are a reliable measure of fluid gains and losses.

Therapeutic Interventions

Actions/Interventions

- Have the patient sit up if he or she complains of shortness of breath.
- Advise the patient to elevate his or her feet when sitting down.

Rationale

This maintains optimal positioning for air exchange.

This prevents fluid accumulation in the lower extremities.

■ = Independent; ▲ = Collaborative

End-Stage Renal Disease—cont'd

Actions/Interventions	Rationale
■ Instruct in administration of antihypertensive medications if prescribed.	Common medications include calcium channel blockers and angiotensin-converting enzyme inhibitors. As a rule, hypertension management can be difficult in this population.
■ Instruct the patient regarding restricting fluid intake as required by the patient's condition.	Patients on dialysis need to understand the importance of maintaining fluid balance between treatments.
■ Instruct the patient regarding restricting dietary sodium.	Sodium intake produces a feeling of thirst. By restricting sodium intake, the amount of fluid a patient drinks can be reduced.
■ Instruct the patient in methods to relieve dry mouth and maintain fluid restriction:	
• Suggest taking ice chips, as needed.	One cup of ice equals only $1/2$ cup of water. Sucking a cup of ice takes much longer than drinking a $1/2$ cup of water; patient can attain more satisfaction.
• Suggest keeping sugar-free hard candy on hand.	This alleviates dry mouth (stimulates secretion of saliva).
• Suggest frequent mouth rinses using $1/2$ cup of mouthwash mixed with $1/2$ cup of ice water.	Rinses can produce freshness in the mouth and temporarily alleviate thirst.
▲ Adjust dialysis therapy as indicated.	This maintains fluid balance.

 Nursing Diagnosis

Risk for Decreased Cardiac Output

Common Risk Factors

Fluid volume excess
Electrolyte imbalances
Accumulated toxins
Pericarditis

Common Expected Outcome

Patient achieves adequate cardiac output as evidenced by strong peripheral pulses, normal vital signs, warm dry skin, alert responsive mentation, and no further reduction in mental status.

NOC Outcomes
Circulation Status; Electrolyte and Acid-Base Balance

NIC Interventions
Hemodynamic Regulation; Hemodialysis Therapy; Electrolyte Management

■ = Independent; ▲ = Collaborative

Ongoing Assessment

Actions/Interventions

■ Monitor vital signs with frequent monitoring of BP.

■ Assess skin warmth and peripheral pulses.

■ Assess level of consciousness.

■ Monitor for dysrhythmias and irregular heart beat.

▲ Monitor laboratory study findings for serum potassium, blood urea nitrogen (BUN), and creatinine.

■ Auscultate heart sounds for the presence of a third heart sound (indicating heart failure), for a pericardial friction rub (indicating uremic pericarditis), and for jugular venous distention, distant or muffled heart sounds, and hypotension (indicating cardiac tamponade).

Rationale

Hypertension is experienced by the majority of patients with renal failure.

Peripheral vasoconstriction causes cool, pale, diaphoretic skin.

Early signs of cerebral hypoxia are restlessness and anxiety, leading to agitation and confusion.

Cardiac dysrhythmias may result from the low perfusion state, acidosis, hypoxia, hyperkalemia, or hypocalcemia.

These tests provide data on electrolyte imbalances and accumulated toxins. The BUN may also be increased from nonrenal causes such as dehydration; however, in those situations the creatinine will not be elevated. Hyperkalemia can cause the most serious life-threatening dysrhythmias.

Chronic renal failure patients on dialysis are at high risk for development of pericarditis, increasing the risk for pericardial effusion and pericardial tamponade. Pericarditis is thought to be caused by the presence of uremic toxins in the pericardial fluid. Pericarditis can develop into a pericardial effusion and even result in cardiac tamponade.

Therapeutic Interventions

Actions/Interventions

▲ Administer oral and intravenous (IV) fluids as prescribed. Use fluid restriction as appropriate.

▲ Administer medications as prescribed:

• Sodium bicarbonate

• Glucose and insulin drip

• Potassium-exchange resins (e.g., sodium polystyrene sulfonate [Kayexalate]).

• Calcium salts

▲ Administer oxygen as needed.

▲ Treat dysrhythmias as appropriate.

Rationale

Optimal fluid balance improves cardiac output.

These temporarily equilibrate electrolyte disturbances and reduce the risk for dysrhythmias.

This corrects acidosis or hyperkalemia. Sodium bicarbonate will temporarily shift potassium back into the cell; however, it can result in elevation of sodium and water retention from the sodium load.

Insulin shifts potassium back into the cells, and glucose is administered to prevent hypoglycemia from the effect of insulin.

Kayexalate exchanges potassium for sodium in the gastrointestinal tract, thereby decreasing serum potassium levels. Kayexalate can be administered orally or rectally, usually 1 mEq of sodium for 1 mEq of potassium. The bound potassium is then excreted in the bowel movement.

Calcium salts treat hypocalcemia. They may also be given to stabilize the cell membrane from depolarization in the hyperkalemic state.

Oxygen improves arterial saturation.

Untreated dysrhythmias contribute to decreased cardiac output.

■ = Independent; ▲ = Collaborative

End-Stage Renal Disease—cont'd

Actions/Interventions	Rationale
▲ Observe for signs of decreased cardiac output; administer inotropic agents (e.g., dobutamine, dopamine, digoxin, or amrinone), as prescribed.	These increase myocardial contractility.
▲ Prepare the patient for dialysis when indicated.	Providing information allows the patient to ask questions, discuss fears and concerns, and develop a basic understanding of the treatment process and procedure.

NDx Nursing Diagnosis

Ineffective Protection: Hypocalcemia

Common Related Factors

Phosphorus retention (level greater than 5 mg/100 mL)
Bone resorption of calcium (demineralization)
Increased parathyroid hormone
Inadequate calcium absorption

Common Expected Outcomes

Patient's risk for hypocalcemia is diminished through ongoing assessment and early intervention.
Patient follows appropriate ambulation and safety measures.

Defining Characteristics

Calcium less than 8 mg/100 mL
Bone demineralization
Metastatic calcifications
Bone pain or joint swelling

NOC Outcomes
Electrolyte and Acid-Base Balance;
   Medication Response

NIC Interventions
Electrolyte Management: Hypocalcemia;
   Electrolyte Management:
   Hyperphosphatemia

Ongoing Assessment

Actions/Interventions	Rationale
■ Assess for signs and symptoms of hypocalcemia: tingling sensations at the ends of fingers or around the mouth, muscle cramps and carpopedal spasms, tetany, convulsion.	The inability of the kidneys to excrete phosphorus leads to hyperphosphatemia with resultant hypocalcemia.
▲ Monitor calcium and phosphorus levels regularly to determine whether the patient is at risk of metastatic calcification from high-calcium replacement and high-phosphate level.	Hypercalcemia can result from the calcium binders used to decrease phosphate levels. Metastatic calcifications occur from calcium phosphate deposits in soft tissues of the body (e.g., blood vessels, joints, lungs, muscles, myocardium, and eyes).
■ Assess for signs or symptoms of extremity pain and joint swelling.	Calcium phosphate deposits can be painful.
■ Observe the patient's gait, ambulation, and movement of extremities.	Hypocalcemia can lead to bone pain and altered mobility.

■ = Independent; ▲ = Collaborative

Actions/Interventions

■ Assess for history of tendency to fracture easily.

Rationale

The decreased blood calcium level causes a demineralization of the bones that makes them brittle, porous, painful, and thinner.

Therapeutic Interventions

Actions/Interventions

■ Instruct the patient in the need to restrict dietary phosphorus intake.

▲ Administer or instruct the patient to take phosphate-binding medications (e.g., calcium acetate, sevelamer hydrochloride, calcium carbonate) as prescribed. Avoid magnesium antacids that may not be excreted by the impaired kidneys.

▲ Evaluate the need for or instruct the patient to take vitamin D analogs as ordered.

■ Apply or instruct the patient to use lotion for itching; recommend use of a scratcher rather than fingernails.

■ Discuss needed safety measures: uncluttered room, orientation to surroundings, proper lighting.

▲ Refer to rehabilitation medicine or physical therapy as indicated for instruction in use of crutches, transport from wheelchair to chair or vice versa.

Rationale

Phosphorus and calcium have an inverse relationship. Hyperphosphatemia worsens hypocalcemia.

The phosphate-binding medication acts to keep ingested phosphorus from being absorbed; instead, phosphorus can bind with medication and be excreted through bowel movement.

There are several vitamin D analogs that promote calcium absorption.

Sharp fingernails may lead to skin excoriation.

Bones become so fragile that they break easily, even from mild trauma.

This helps promote safety in ambulation and transfer to reduce the risk of injury.

 Nursing Diagnosis

Ineffective Protection: Anemia/Thrombocytopenia

Common Related Factors

Bone marrow suppression secondary to insufficient renal production of erythropoietic factor

Increased hemolysis leading to decreased life span of red blood cells secondary to abnormal chemical environment in plasma

Nutritional deficiencies

Bleeding tendencies: decreased platelets and defective platelet cohesion, inhibition of certain clotting factors

Defining Characteristics

Decreased hemoglobin (Hgb) and hematocrit (Hct)
Fatigue or pallor
Decreased platelet count
Increase in coagulation times
Bruising tendencies

Common Expected Outcome

Patient maintains near-normal Hgb and Hct levels and adequate platelet counts.

NOC Outcome
Blood Coagulation

NIC Interventions
Bleeding Precautions; Surveillance

■ = Independent; ▲ = Collaborative

→ **End-Stage Renal Disease—cont'd**

Ongoing Assessment

Actions/Interventions

- Observe for signs of anemia: fatigue, pallor, decreased activity tolerance.

- Observe for signs of thrombocytopenia: bruising tendencies, bleeding from puncture sites and incisions.

▲ Monitor results of laboratory studies (Hgb, Hct, platelets, coagulation studies), as prescribed.

- Instruct the patient in the signs and symptoms of gastrointestinal bleeding.

- Test stools and emesis for blood if Hct and Hgb drops.

Rationale

Anemia is associated with decreased oxygen-carrying capacity of red blood cells.

Uremia leads to coagulopathies and increases the patient's risk of bleeding.

The Hct may be as low as 20% to 22% from the reduced secretion of erythropoietin by the kidney.

The patient needs to be alert for signs of bright red blood per rectum or for a change in feces to a black, tarry color and consistency. These changes are associated with gastrointestinal bleeding.

Gastrointestinal bleeding may be identified by testing for the presence of occult blood.

Therapeutic Interventions

Actions/Interventions

▲ Administer or instruct the patient in administration of epoetin alfa (Epogen), as prescribed.

▲ Instruct the patient to take iron supplements as ordered.

▲ Instruct the patient in the need for folic acid, as prescribed.

▲ Administer oxygen as prescribed.

▲ Anticipate or administer blood transfusions if Hct falls below 20%.

- For patients with thrombocytopenia, institute precautionary measures for patients with a tendency to bleed: avoid intramuscular injections and monitor heparin administration closely.

- Draw all laboratory specimens through an existing arterial or venous access line.

- Instruct the patient in the use of soft toothbrush and electric razor and in avoiding constipation, forceful blowing of the nose, and contact sports.

- Instruct the patient to avoid aspirin products.

- Instruct the patient in the importance of wearing a medical alert bracelet.

Rationale

This decreases the effects of the anemia and helps reduce the need for frequent blood transfusions by maintaining Hgb and Hct.

Even with the use of epoetin alfa, functional iron stores may be low.

This corrects iron deficiency. Folic acid is lost during dialysis and must be given after treatments.

This maintains tissue oxygenation.

With recent advances in medical therapy (e.g., Epogen), blood transfusions are only required for severely compromised patients.

Any needle stick is a potential bleeding site. Heparin is used to decrease the risk of clotting in the extracorporeal circuit during hemodialysis. In patients at risk for bleeding, heparin doses may need to be reduced or discontinued.

Bleeding can occur easily because of platelet abnormalities. Precautionary measures need to be implemented.

These reduce the risk of bleeding.

These prolong bleeding time.

This will alert community members and health care workers of the patient's medical condition in case of emergency.

■ = Independent; ▲ = Collaborative

Nursing Diagnosis

Risk for Situational Low Self-Esteem

Common Risk Factors

Change in perceptions as autonomous and productive individual
Loss of organ function
Dependence on outpatient dialysis
Financial strain due to disability status or need to seek a less physically demanding job
Body image changes

Common Expected Outcome

Patient manifests more positive self-esteem as evidenced by verbalization of positive feelings about self.

NOC Outcomes
Self-Esteem; Coping

NIC Interventions
Self-Esteem Enhancement; Counseling; Support System Enhancement

Ongoing Assessment

Actions/Interventions

■ Assess for signs of low self-esteem: self-negating verbalizations, depression, expressed anger, withdrawal, expressions of shame or guilt, or evaluation of self as unable to deal with events.

Rationale

The long-term dialysis patient is faced with long-term changes in lifestyle, occupation, and financial status. The patient's future depends on medications, dietary restrictions, and dialysis. The patient may grieve this loss of autonomy.

Therapeutic Interventions

Actions/Interventions

■ Assist the patient in identifying the major areas of concern related to altered self-esteem. Use a problem-solving technique with the patient.

■ Assist the patient in incorporating changes in health status into activities of daily living (ADLs), social life, interpersonal relationships, and occupational activities.

■ Talk with the patient, caregivers, and friends, if possible, about expectations regarding chronic outpatient dialysis or renal transplantation.

■ Allow the patient time to voice concerns and express anger related to having a chronic condition.

■ Encourage an attitude of realistic hope.

▲ Use case managers and social workers as necessary.

Rationale

The nurse-patient relationship can provide a strong basis for implementing other strategies to assist the patient and family with adaptation.

As the patient's condition worsens with ESRD, it is more difficult to engage in even routine activities.

Survival depends on such treatments. The patient may resent such dependence.

Denial and anger are anticipated responses to the diagnosis of a chronic illness.

Hope provides a way of dealing with negative feelings.

They can provide psychological support and assist in financial arrangements.

■ = Independent; ▲ = Collaborative

End-Stage Renal Disease—cont'd

Actions/Interventions	Rationale
▲ Refer to psychiatric consultant as necessary.	Most dialysis patients experience some degree of emotional imbalance. With professional psychiatric consultation, most patients can gradually accept changed self-esteem.
■ Provide or encourage discussions with other patients with ESRD.	Such patients can share their responses to illness.
■ Encourage use of support groups.	Groups that come together for mutual goals can be most helpful.

 ## Nursing Diagnosis

Risk for Impaired Skin Integrity

Common Risk Factors

Edema related to ESRD
Peripheral neuropathy from ESRD

Common Expected Outcomes

Patient's optimal skin integrity is maintained as evidenced by the absence of breakdown.
Patient demonstrates self-care measures to reduce or treat pruritus.

NOC Outcome
Tissue Integrity: Skin and Mucous Membranes

NIC Interventions
Skin Surveillance; Skin Care: Topical Treatments

Ongoing Assessment

Actions/Interventions	Rationale
■ Assess skin integrity for pitting of extremities on manipulation, and demarcation of clothing and shoes on the patient's body.	Chronic fluid excess can result in skin breakdown.
■ Assess for the presence of peripheral neuropathy.	This results in changes in sensation such as paresthesias (burning), weakness, and twitching.
■ Assess for dry, scaling skin.	Uremic skin does not have the usual amount of oil because of decreased sweat and oil glands.
■ Assess for pruritus.	Pruritus can be caused by dry skin and/or calcium phosphate precipitation.

■ = Independent; ▲ = Collaborative

Therapeutic Interventions

Actions/Interventions

- Instruct the patient to wear loose-fitting clothing when edema is present.
- Teach factors important to skin integrity: nutrition, mobility, hygiene, early recognition of skin breakdown.

- Instruct the patient regarding dangers when heating or cooling devices are used.
- ▲ Encourage the patient to take prescribed medications to reduce altered phosphorus levels (phosphate binders).
- Stress the importance of not scratching skin and of keeping fingernails short.
- Suggest skin lotions or emollients for dry, scaling skin.

- Suggest use of tepid water for bathing.
- ▲ Instruct the patient to take medications to reduce pruritus (antihistamines) as instructed by the dialysis staff.

Rationale

Restrictive clothing can increase risk of skin breakdown.

Each factor plays a role in preventing skin breakdown or contributes to successful skin healing if breakdown has occurred.

The peripheral neuropathy can impair sensation, especially in the lower extremities.

Elevated phosphorus levels lead to pruritus and excoriation of the skin due to scratching.

Scratching can cause lesions and open sores.

Lotions and emollients can provide lubrication and lipids to the skin and provide comfort.

Increased warmth can increase the itch.

Antihistamines can relieve itching.

NDx Nursing Diagnosis

Risk for Ineffective Therapeutic Regimen Management

Common Risk Factors

Knowledge deficit
Lack of resources
Side effects of treatment, diet, and medications
Poor relationship with health care team
Denial of full extent of disease process and treatment needed

Common Expected Outcome

Patient demonstrates adherence to therapy as evidenced by attendance at appointments, laboratory values within normal range, and verbalization of compliance with therapy.

NOC Outcomes
Compliance Behavior; Participation: Health Care Decisions

NIC Intervention
Self-Modification Assistance

■ = Independent; ▲ = Collaborative

Renal and Urinary Tract Care Plans

→ **End-Stage Renal Disease**—cont'd

Ongoing Assessment

Actions/Interventions

- Assess for signs of noncompliance: missed appointments, excessive fluid gains between dialysis treatments, unused medications, abnormal laboratory values, acknowledgment of noncompliance, and early treatment termination.

- Elicit the patient's understanding of the treatment regimen, including dialysis and diet.

- Explore with the patient his or her feelings about illness and treatment.

- Determine additional factors that may contribute to noncompliance: coping difficulties, medication side effects, financial limitations, transportation problems.

Rationale

The presence of these factors indicate the patient is not following the therapeutic regimen.

This determines whether an added knowledge base will help decrease the noncompliance.

According to the Health Belief Model, the patient's perceived susceptibility to and perceived seriousness and threat of disease affect compliance.

Knowledge of causative factors provides direction for subsequent intervention.

Therapeutic Interventions

Actions/Interventions

- Promote decision making and management of ADLs; use social support systems.

▲ Explore alternatives with the health care team.

- Contract with the patient for behavioral changes by establishing goals with the patient.

- If the patient lacks adequate support in following the treatment plan, initiate referral to a support group.

Rationale

Social support has been closely linked to compliance with dialysis; it is necessary to manage the role demands of daily living, and it is especially important in coping with stressful life events and transitions.

Collaborative planning that includes the patient and family with other members of the health care team can increase the patient's ability to follow a treatment program.

This will help encourage cooperation and willingness to follow the established program.

Groups that come together for mutual support and information can be beneficial.

NDx Nursing Diagnosis

Sexual Dysfunction

Common Related Factors

Effects of uremia on the endocrine system: amenorrhea, failure to ovulate, and decreased libido in females; azoospermia, atrophy of testicles, impotence, decreased libido, and gynecomastia in males
Psychosocial effects of renal failure and its treatment

Defining Characteristics

Verbalization of concern about altered or reduced sexual function
Expressed decrease in sexual satisfaction
Reported change in relationship with partner

■ = Independent; ▲ = Collaborative

Common Expected Outcome

Patient's sexual functioning is enhanced as evidenced by ability to discuss concerns and verbalization of improved sexual outlook.

NOC Outcomes
Sexual Functioning; Self-Esteem

NIC Intervention
Sexual Counseling

Ongoing Assessment

Actions/Interventions

- Assess the patient's perception of change in or lack of sexual function.
- Assess the impact of changes in sexual function on the patient.
- Explore the meaning of sexuality with the patient.
- Assess the need for counseling related to birth control and the need for contraception.

Rationale

Both genders characteristically experience infertility and a decreased libido.

Changes in sexual function can lead to depression, low self-esteem, and impaired interpersonal relationships.

This determines a realistic approach to care planning.

With the use of Epogen and with improvement in the female patient's Hgb and Hct levels, menses is often restored and the possibility of pregnancy increases.

Therapeutic Interventions

Actions/Interventions

- Encourage the patient to verbalize feelings about the change in or lack of sexual function.

- Discuss alternate methods of sexual expression with the patient or significant others. Emphasize the importance of giving and receiving love and affection, as opposed to "performing."
- ▲ Confer with the physician about medical treatments and procedures that may alleviate some sexual dysfunction. Discuss the possibility of a penile implant or medications. If the patient has low zinc levels, discuss possible replacement therapy for male patients.

Rationale

Respecting the patient and treating his or her concerns as normal and important may foster greater self-acceptance.

Patients need to understand that intercourse is not the only method for a satisfying sexual relationship.

Patients may experience restoration of sexual function through use of a variety of therapeutic methods.

NDx Nursing Diagnosis

Deficient Knowledge

Common Related Factors

Lack of interest in learning
Unfamiliarity with disease process or treatment
Information misinterpretation

Defining Characteristics

Questions
Request for information
Verbalized confusion about treatment

 = Independent; ▲ = Collaborative

→ End-Stage Renal Disease—cont'd

Common Expected Outcome

The patient verbalizes a general understanding of chronic renal failure, prevention of complications, medication therapy, and necessary dietary restrictions.

NOC Outcomes

Knowledge: Disease Process;
Knowledge: Treatment Regimen

NIC Interventions

Teaching: Disease Process;
Teaching: Prescribed Diet

Ongoing Assessment

Actions/Interventions	**Rationale**
■ Assess understanding of ESRD.	An understanding of ESRD will help with compliance with the needed treatment.
■ Determine who will be the learner: patient, family, or caregiver.	Many older or terminally ill patients may view themselves as dependent on their caregiver and therefore may not want to be part of the educational process.

Therapeutic Interventions

Actions/Interventions	**Rationale**
■ Discuss end-stage renal failure with the patient, including the need for dialysis or renal transplantation for survival.	Patients need information about treatment options in order to make informed decisions.
■ Instruct the patient in dietary restrictions.	Diet needs to be individualized according to the impairment of renal function. In general, diets are high in carbohydrates (unless contraindicated by the diagnosis of diabetes mellitus), and within allotted sodium, potassium, phosphorus, and protein limits. Actual daily requirements depend on the type of dialysis treatment used (hemodialysis versus peritoneal dialysis).
■ Involve significant others in instruction sessions on special diets and fluid restrictions.	Significant others may be the people who buy and/or prepare the patient's food.
■ Discuss the need for reading food labels for sodium, potassium, and other mineral content before using.	Many processed foods contain high levels of sodium. The sodium may be in forms other than salt or sodium chloride.
■ Discuss the importance of taking prescribed medications. Discuss thoroughly dosages and side effects.	Patients are better able to manage the complexity of their medications with sufficient knowledge.
■ Instruct the patient to notify health care personnel of any questions or concerns regarding over-the-counter medications and food or herbal supplements.	This helps prevent complications from medications or other substances used inappropriately.

■ = Independent; ▲ = Collaborative

Actions/Interventions

■ Instruct the patient in recognition of complications such as fluid volume excess and electrolyte imbalances.

Rationale

Changes in fluid and electrolyte balance may indicate the need for adjustments in the treatment plan. The patient and caregivers at home need to know early signs and symptoms to report to their health care provider such as headache, swelling of the hands and feet, or paresthesias.

> **• RELATED CARE PLANS**
>
> Activity intolerance, p. 7
> Anticipatory grieving, p. 82
> Disturbed body image, p. 21
> Interrupted family processes, p. 63
> Powerlessness, p. 153
> Risk for infection, p. 108

 ## Glomerulonephritis

Acute Poststreptococcal Glomerulonephritis; Acute Glomerulonephritis; Rapidly Progressive Glomerulonephritis

Glomerulonephritis, or inflammation of the glomeruli, is caused by an immune response to bacterial or viral infection, drugs or other chemicals, immunizations, or systemic disease such as systemic lupus erythematosus (SLE) and scleroderma. It is an autoimmune disease with either antiglomerular basement membrane antibodies or nonglomerular antigens reacting with antibodies and resulting in an immune reaction complement that becomes trapped with antibodies and antigens in the glomerular basement membrane. An inflammatory response occurs, resulting in decreased metabolic waste filtration and increased membrane permeability to large protein molecules. Tubular, interstitial, and vascular changes also occur. Another form of glomerulonephritis is rapidly progressive glomerulonephritis (RPGN). This form of the disease is precipitated by infection and chemicals; and by Goodpasture's syndrome, an autoimmune disease that results in destruction of lung and renal tissue. RPGN is characterized by a sudden onset with rapid deterioration. In most cases, treatment requires dialysis and renal transplantation. Renal failure and chronic glomerulonephritis develop in about 50% of patients with RPGN. Chronic glomerulonephritis, which is often asymptomatic and undetected, can also result in renal failure and progress to end-stage renal disease. The more common acute glomerulonephritis (AGN) and acute poststreptococcal glomerulonephritis (APSGN) have less incidence in patients with renal failure (<1%) or chronic glomerulonephritis (5% to 15%), with complete recovery occurring in most patients.

 ## Nursing Diagnosis

Excess Fluid Volume

Common Related Factors

Compromised regulatory mechanism (diminished glomerular filtration)
Increased sodium retention

Defining Characteristics

Periorbital edema
Facial puffiness
Generalized edema

> ■ = Independent; ▲ = Collaborative

Glomerulonephritis–cont'd

Defining Characteristics–cont'd

Dark urine, dysuria
Decreased output, oliguria
Hematuria
Proteinuria
Specific gravity greater than 1.020
Increased blood urea nitrogen (BUN) and creatinine
Serum electrolytes within normal limits
Anorexia
Mild or moderate hypertension

Common Expected Outcome

Patient maintains fluid volume within normal limits as
    evidenced by absence of edema and increased urinary
    output.

NOC Outcomes

Fluid Balance; Electrolyte and Acid-Base
    Balance

NIC Interventions

Fluid/Electrolyte Management;
    Vital Sign Monitoring

Ongoing Assessment

Actions/Interventions

- Determine history of illness:
  - When symptoms were first noticed
  - Exposure to drugs, recent immunizations
  - Exposure to other chemicals (hydrocarbons)
  - Exposure to or recent infection (viral or bacterial)
  - Known chronic diseases (SLE or scleroderma)

- Assess for edema.

- Measure intake and output.

- Evaluate pulse, respiration, and blood pressure (BP).

- Weigh daily.

- Evaluate laboratory results: urinalysis, serum electrolytes, BUN, creatinine, erythrocyte sedimentation
  rate (ESR), and antistreptolysin O (ASO) titer.

Rationale

Known precipitants need to be treated or controlled.

Facial and periorbital edema occurs in the morning,
    whereas generalized edema appears later in the day
    and late in the course of the disease.

The patient may become oliguric; persistent anuria or
    oliguria may indicate acute renal failure. A slight
    increase in output usually indicates increasing kidney
    function, with diuresis following in 3 to 4 days.

Moderate hypertension is expected; severe hypertension
    must be treated with antihypertensives. Changes in
    pulse and respiration may indicate cardiac decom-
    pensation.

Rapid weight increase with associated oliguria indicates
    diminishing renal function.

Urinalysis may reveal 3+ to 4+ hematuria and proteinuria
    with increasing specific gravity. Serum electrolyte,
    especially sodium and potassium, and BUN or creati-
    nine abnormalities reflect altered renal function. ESR

■ = Independent; ▲ = Collaborative

Actions/Interventions

▲ Review test results: magnetic resonance imaging, ultrasound, computed tomography, and/or possible renal biopsy.

▲ Assess for hyperlipidemia, hypoalbuminemia, massive proteinuria, and fatty casts in the urine.

Rationale

reflects acute inflammation and can be used to follow the disease course. ASO titer can be used to detect streptococcal antibodies 4 to 6 weeks after infection.

Tests differentiate or confirm diagnosis. Renal biopsy is not always necessary with good quality radiography.

Presence indicates development of nephrotic syndrome, seen in approximately 20% of adult cases of glomerulonephritis.

Therapeutic Interventions

Actions/Interventions

▲ Restrict fluid intake to equal urinary and insensible loss.

■ Provide a no-added-salt diet.

■ Restrict potassium only if the patient is oliguric.

▲ Restrict protein if BUN is elevated, indicating increase in circulating nitrogenous wastes.

▲ Administer antihypertensives and, in severe cases, loop diuretics such as furosemide (Lasix), bumetanide (Bumex), or ethacrynic acid (Edecrin).

■ Keep the patient on bed rest until hypertension, proteinuria, and hematuria are resolved.

▲ Administer corticosteroids if prescribed.

▲ Prepare the patient for possible dialysis.

Rationale

This minimizes risks of pulmonary edema, hypertension, and cardiac failure.

Increased sodium will increase fluid retention.

Potassium is retained if the patient is oliguric. Hyperkalemia can cause cardiac dysrhythmias.

This poses risk for metabolic acidosis, especially if the patient is oliguric and not excreting protein in urine. Because of anorexia, dietary restrictions are seldom needed.

These control blood pressure and fluid volume.

Bed rest decreases metabolic demand and enhances diuresis.

Although not usually used in the treatment of acute glomerulonephritis, corticosteroids may have a positive antiinflammatory effect in rapidly progressive glomerulonephritis.

Patients at risk for significant complications and renal failure can benefit from early initiation of dialysis.

NDx Nursing Diagnosis

Infection

Common Related Factors	Defining Characteristics
Pharyngitis	Fever
Impetigo	Pain
Upper respiratory infection	Redness
Scarlet fever	Skin rash
	Lethargy
	Positive culture result, group A β-hemolytic streptococci

■ = Independent; ▲ = Collaborative

Glomerulonephritis—cont'd

Common Expected Outcome

Patient is infection-free as evidenced by negative culture, resolution of symptoms, and temperature within normal limits.

NOC Outcomes
Medication Response; Infection Status

NIC Intervention
Medication Management

Ongoing Assessment

Actions/Interventions

■ Assess for physical evidence of infection.

▲ Review results of specimen cultures.

■ Obtain a recent history for signs and symptoms of infection or exposure to infected individuals.

Rationale

Infections must be treated to stop the immune response and glomerular inflammation.

Identification of specific microorganisms will guide selection of appropriate antimicrobial drugs.

Symptoms of acute glomerulonephritis appear 10 to 14 days after initial streptococcal illness. In Goodpasture's syndrome, respiratory illness with possible pulmonary hemorrhage may occur weeks or months before onset of rapidly progressive glomerulonephritis.

Therapeutic Interventions

Actions/Interventions

■ Implement appropriate measures to protect the patient from potential infection sources.
▲ Administer antibiotics for positive culture findings.

Rationale

Hand washing by all people in contact with the patient is the primary method to reduce the risk of infection.

Viral infection does not respond to antibiotic therapy. To decrease the risk of development of bacterial strains resistant to antibiotics, drug therapy should be based on specific culture and sensitivity results.

NDx Nursing Diagnosis

Deficient Knowledge

Common Related Factors

New diagnosis
Hospitalization
Treatment regimen

Defining Characteristics

Stated lack of understanding
Many questions
Appearance of confusion

■ = Independent; ▲ = Collaborative

Common Expected Outcome

Patient verbalizes understanding of the disease process, treatment regimen, and follow-up care required.

NOC Outcomes
Knowledge: Disease Process;
   Knowledge: Treatment Regimen

NIC Interventions
Teaching: Disease Process;
   Teaching: Treatments, Procedures

Ongoing Assessment

Actions/Interventions

- Assess for knowledge of disease process and current status.

Rationale

Most patients have no prior experience with glomerulonephritis.

Therapeutic Interventions

Actions/Interventions

- Provide information about the course of disease and all treatments and procedures.

- Explain home care measures: intake and output, BP measurement.

- Explain the need for follow-up care.

Rationale

This allows the patient to make informed decisions regarding care. Patients need to understand the importance of dietary and fluid restrictions as part of the treatment plan.

Once stabilized, patients are discharged from the hospital to recuperate at home. Consider a home care nurse if renal status needs close monitoring.

Although most patients (70%) recover completely, there may be persistent hematuria and above-average BUN for some weeks. A small percentage of patients may progress to chronic glomerulonephritis or acute renal failure.

• RELATED CARE PLANS

Acute renal failure, p. 911
Fatigue, p. 65

Peritoneal Dialysis

Intermittent Peritoneal Dialysis; Continuous Ambulatory Peritoneal Dialysis; Continuous Cyclic Peritoneal Dialysis

Peritoneal dialysis, hemodialysis, or transplantation is necessary to maintain life in patients with absence of kidney function. Peritoneal dialysis is indicated for patients with kidney failure who have vascular access problems, who cannot tolerate the hemodynamic alterations of hemodialysis, or who prefer the independence of managing their own therapy in their home environment. A peritoneal catheter is placed through the anterior abdominal wall to achieve access. During peritoneal dialysis, the peritoneum functions as the membrane by which molecules flow from the side of higher concentration to the side of lower concentration. This procedure removes excess fluid and waste products from the body. Peritoneal dialysis may be performed as intermittent peritoneal dialysis (IPD), continuous ambulatory peritoneal dialysis (CAPD), or continuous cyclic peritoneal dialysis (CCPD).

■ = Independent; ▲ = Collaborative

> ## Peritoneal Dialysis—cont'd

Peritoneal dialysis provides more gradual physiological changes than hemodialysis and is appropriate for the older adult patient with diabetes and cardiovascular disease. It is contraindicated in patients with peritonitis, recent abdominal surgery, or respiratory insufficiency because the fluid in the peritoneum decreases lung volume. This care plan focuses on peritoneal dialysis in the acute care setting with teaching for the ambulatory and home care setting.

NDx Nursing Diagnosis

Excess Fluid Volume

Common Related Factors

Renal insufficiency
Increased peritoneal permeability to glucose, water, and protein

Defining Characteristics

Acute weight gain
Elevated blood pressure (BP)
Peripheral edema
Shortness of breath
Orthopnea
Crackles

Common Expected Outcome

Patient's fluid volume excess is reduced as evidenced by vital signs within normal limits, clear lung sounds, absence or reduction in edema, and stable weight.

NOC Outcomes

Fluid Balance; Systemic Toxin Clearance: Dialysis

NIC Interventions

Fluid Management; Peritoneal Dialysis Therapy

Ongoing Assessment

Actions/Interventions	Rationale
■ Obtain baseline weight when peritoneal cavity is empty, then every day.	Weight gain can be caused by dialysate reabsorption or fluid excess.
■ Measure inflow and outflow of dialysate with each exchange, checking that the outflow is greater than or equal to inflow, and maintain a record of cumulative fluid balance.	The concentration of the dialysate fluid determines the rate and amount of fluid removal. An acutely ill hospitalized patient may receive 12 to 24 exchanges in 24 hours, whereas with CAPD the patient may only have four exchanges daily, with dwell times ranging from 4 to 10 hours.
■ Monitor BP and pulse.	BP and pulse can provide indication of fluid status.
■ Check catheter for kinks, fibrin, or clots.	These could obstruct outflow of fluid from the catheter, resulting in retained fluid in the abdomen.

■ = Independent; ▲ = Collaborative

Actions/Interventions

- Assess work of breathing and for presence of orthopnea.

- Monitor patient for tachypnea, retractions, or nasal flaring.

- Auscultate lung sounds.

- Check for sacral and peripheral edema from fluid excess or protein depletion from dialysis, especially with more hypertonic dialysates.

- ▲ Monitor serum glucose.

- ▲ Monitor serum magnesium, potassium, and calcium levels.

Rationale

Patients already fluid-overloaded, who receive 1 to 2 L of additional fluid in the peritoneal space, may be significantly compromised.

If dialysate fluid is retained in the abdomen, it may cause pressure on the diaphragm, resulting in a decrease in lung expansion and possible respiratory distress.

Increased fluid absorption can lead to pulmonary congestion.

Edema may develop if adequate fluid volumes are not removed by the dialysis exchanges or the exchanges are resulting in removing protein that the patient is not nutritionally replacing.

Glucose absorption may occur from the dialysate. This is especially critical in diabetic patients.

Electrolyte imbalances may occur if a balanced concentration of dialysate is not used.

Therapeutic Interventions

Actions/Interventions

- Instruct the patient to change position frequently. Elevate head of bed at 45 degrees and turn patient from side to side.

- ▲ Institute fluid restrictions as appropriate.

- ▲ Administer intravenous (IV) fluids via an infusion pump, if possible.
- Elevate edematous extremities.
- Instruct the patient in deep breathing exercises.

- ▲ Notify the physician if electrolyte imbalance is present.

- ▲ In the acute care setting, notify the physician and change the dialysate concentration when the patient reaches dry weight.
- Stop dialysis if drainage is less than infusion.

- Ensure proper functioning if using automatic cycler for the peritoneal dialysis exchanges.

- For home or ambulatory care: instruct on maintenance of fluid restriction and maintenance of a diary monitoring the cumulative record of dialysate inflow or outflow exchange. Also, instruct to obtain daily weights (dry weights) at the same time daily.

Rationale

Position changes facilitate drainage and help prevent pulmonary complications by preventing an upward displacement of the diaphragm, which can result from inadequate drainage.

Fluid restrictions are individualized for peritoneal dialysis patients.

This ensures accurate delivery.

This increases venous return and, in turn, lessens edema.

Atelectasis may occur from upward displacement of the diaphragm and a decrease in lung expansion. Repositioning and deep breathing exercises may help prevent this.

Early intervention can reduce adverse effects from electrolyte imbalances.

This prevents dehydrating the patient by removing too much fluid.

Overinfusion causes pain, dyspnea, nausea, and electrolyte imbalance.

The cycler may be used to deliver CCPD, IPD, or nightly peritoneal dialysis. For nightly peritoneal dialysis, the machine cycles 4 to 8 exchanges per night with alarms built into the system to make it safe for the patient to sleep at home.

These assist in monitoring fluid balance.

→ **Peritoneal Dialysis**—cont'd

 Nursing Diagnosis

Risk for Infection

Common Risk Factor

Possible contamination of peritoneal catheter entry site

Common Expected Outcome

Patient's risk for infection is reduced through ongoing assessment and early intervention.

NOC Outcomes
Infection Status; Risk Control

NIC Interventions
Infection Protection; Peritoneal Dialysis Therapy

Ongoing Assessment

Actions/Interventions

- Assess and instruct the patient to watch for signs or symptoms of infection: fever; generalized malaise; complaints of abdominal pain, tenderness, warm feeling, or chills; rigid abdominal wall; peritoneal catheter site reddened with discharge; cloudy returned dialysate; positive culture and sensitivity results; nausea; vomiting; or diarrhea.

- Assess and instruct the patient to assess peritoneal fluid drainage (normal is clear):
  - Cloudiness
  - Volume

  - Fibrin

▲ If infection is suspected, collect effluent as appropriate for the following:
  - White blood cell (WBC) count with differential

  - Culture or sensitivity with Gram stain

▲ Assess area around the catheter site. Evaluate purulent drainage by culture and sensitivity.

- Assess the patient for complaint of abdominal tenderness.

- Palpate the abdomen for rebound tenderness and pain along the catheter tunnel tract.

Rationale

Peritonitis carries a great risk of infection, and repeated occurrences may necessitate catheter removal with need for hemodialysis.

This indicates increased white blood cell (WBC) count.

Decreased volume is noted with increased peritoneal permeability.

Increased production is noted with peritonitis.

WBC count of 100 cells/mm^3 with 50% polymorphonucleocytes indicates peritonitis.

These indicate need for appropriate antibiotic. Gram stain may reveal fungus, which takes 5 to 7 days to grow.

Area should be clean with no signs of inflammation.

Abdominal tenderness may indicate inflammation.

This indicates inflammation.

■ = Independent; ▲ = Collaborative

Actions/Interventions

- Auscultate the abdomen for bowel sounds.

- Assess vital signs, including temperature.
- Ask the patient to describe how he or she feels during exchanges.
- Instruct the patient of the need to notify the nephrologist, dialysis staff, or home health nurse for any signs of infection.

Rationale

Absent bowel sounds may indicate ileus from bacterial toxins that lead to infection.

An elevated temperature occurs with infection processes.

Early detection and treatment of infection minimizes complications of infection.

Treatment can be instituted quickly and more serious complications can be prevented.

Therapeutic Interventions

Actions/Interventions

- Use strict aseptic technique and apply a mask to the patient and each person in the room when setting up dialysis and connecting the patient.

- Maintain drainage receptacle below the level of the peritoneum.
- Ensure aseptic handling of the peritoneal catheter and connections.
- Anchor connections and tubing securely.

- ▲ If peritonitis is suspected:
  - Obtain cultures *before* beginning antibiotic therapy.
  - Administer antibiotics intraperitoneally as prescribed, using shortened dwell periods for the first 24 hours.

- ▲ If aminoglycosides are administered, obtain blood levels after 48 hours as prescribed.
- ▲ Perform exit site care according to unit or agency protocol.

Rationale

Poor hygiene and improper technique during connection can lead to catheter site infection, the most common complication of peritoneal dialysis. It is critical to maintain aseptic technique in peritoneal dialysis. The patient should be thoroughly instructed in this technique for home use. Tubing connection devices are commercially available to help maintain an aseptic system.

This prevents backflow of dialysate.

This decreases the risk for "touch-contamination" of the catheter and connections.

This prevents inadvertent disconnection and risk of infection. This also prevents pulling and pressure on the catheter exit site, which can cause skin breakdown and predispose to infection.

This ensures accurate culture results.

This places medications at the source of infection. Shortened dwell periods are used so that dialysate reabsorption is decreased.

Ototoxicity can occur with prolonged use.

Exit sites are a potential source of infection. Cleansing the area and dressing changes at regular intervals reduce the risk of infection. Each unit has an established site care protocol.

 Nursing Diagnosis

Risk for Pain

Common Risk Factors

Length of procedure
Actual infusion of dialysate
Rapid infusion of dialysate

■ = Independent; ▲ = Collaborative

Peritoneal Dialysis—cont'd

Common Risk Factors—cont'd

Distended abdomen
Peritonitis
Infusion of cold dialysate

Common Expected Outcomes

Patient verbalizes relief or absence of pain.
Patient appears comfortable.

> **NOC Outcome**
> Pain Control
>
> **NIC Interventions**
> Pain Management; Peritoneal Dialysis
>   Therapy

Ongoing Assessment

Actions/Interventions	Rationale
■ Assess for signs of discomfort.	Infusion of larger amounts of dialysate, especially at a rapid rate, can cause abdominal pressure and discomfort or back discomfort from the additional weight. Fortunately, the use of newer cycling systems has significantly reduced this problem.
■ Assess for pain in the scapula region.	Referred pain to the scapula occurs when air is inadvertently infused into the peritoneal cavity.

Therapeutic Interventions

Actions/Interventions	Rationale
■ For hospitalized patients, remain at the bedside during initiation of dialysis. Do not allow air inflow with the exchange; always use warm fluids.	Cool fluids can cause cramping.
■ Change the patient's position.	This relieves discomfort during inflow.
■ If the patient experiences scapula pain, allow adequate drain time and position the patient on his or her side with knees to chest.	This assists in removal of any air from the peritoneal cavity.
■ Explain reasons for inflow pain.	Fluid with a lower pH than the body's causes discomfort until equilibration occurs; air in cavity causes discomfort; pressure on organs and diaphragm causes discomfort until the patient becomes accustomed to the procedure; cold or hot solution may be uncomfortable.
■ Discuss with the patient appropriate steps to prevent air inflow and to maintain the appropriate temperature of the dialysate.	Hot or cold dialysate solution and air ingress may lead to discomfort and pain.
■ If discomfort is associated with flow rate, reduce rate as appropriate.	Rapid infusion rates may lead to abdominal cramping or pain.
▲ Provide mild analgesics as indicated.	Lidocaine can be added to the dialysate solution as needed.

■ = Independent; ▲ = Collaborative

Peritoneal Dialysis

Actions/Interventions

■ If lower back pain is the problem, suggest use of an orthopedic binder and regular low back exercises.

▲ If peritonitis is the cause of pain, administer antibiotics as prescribed.

■ Provide diversional activities.

Rationale

These support back muscles.

Antibiotics are required to treat the infectious process. Antibiotics will be adjusted based upon peritoneal fluid cultures.

This directs focus away from pain or procedure.

 Nursing Diagnosis

Deficient Knowledge

Common Related Factor

Unfamiliarity with peritoneal dialysis technique and its complications

Defining Characteristics

Verbalizes inaccurate information
Requests information
Expresses frustration and confusion when performing task
Performs task incorrectly
Acknowledges noncompliance

Common Expected Outcomes

Patient or caregiver becomes proficient at performing peritoneal dialysis.
Patient or caregiver is able to verbalize signs and symptoms indicating when to contact health care personnel.

NOC Outcome
Knowledge: Treatment Regimen

NIC Interventions
Teaching: Procedure/Treatment;
Peritoneal Dialysis Therapy;
Teaching: Psychomotor Skill

Ongoing Assessment

Actions/Interventions

■ Assess knowledge of the purpose or goals of peritoneal dialysis.

■ Assess understanding of the types of peritoneal dialysis available for the home setting.

■ Assess ability to perform tasks related to peritoneal dialysis.

Rationale

Knowledge of the goals of therapy is the basis for training on procedural steps, complications, and fluid management goals.

Automated cycler machines are most often used while the patient is sleeping at night. Ambulatory techniques requiring manual exchanges (CAPD) are also an option for independent patients.

The advantage of peritoneal dialysis over hemodialysis is the greater independence and greater mobility, especially during dialysis with CAPD. The major disadvantage is the possibility of developing peritonitis. The patient or a trained family member needs to be capable of performing the tasks of peritoneal dialysis to be allowed to do home dialysis.

■ = Independent; ▲ = Collaborative

Peritoneal Dialysis—cont'd

Therapeutic Interventions

Actions/Interventions	Rationale
■ Review patient diagnosis and need for peritoneal dialysis.	An understanding of the importance of performing the procedure as prescribed may increase patient compliance.
■ Discuss dietary or fluid requirements and restrictions: low sodium, low potassium, adequate protein, high calories. Fluids are generally not restricted, but intake should not be excessive. Arrange dietary consultation if necessary.	As a rule, peritoneal dialysis patients have more liberal dietary allowances than hemodialysis patients because of the continuous nature of peritoneal dialysis.
■ Demonstrate and request return demonstration of peritoneal catheter care.	Catheter-related infection puts patient at great risk.

■ Demonstrate and have patient perform repeat demonstration of dialysis procedure. Emphasize how to adapt techniques to home environment:
• Appropriate hand washing techniques
• Steps to peritoneal dialysis:
  • Ensuring a clean work area
  • Using appropriate supplies
  • Checking dialysate for expiration date, dextrose concentration, correct volume, pinhole leaks, and foreign particles
  • Wearing mask during the procedure
  • Clamping tubing; using sterile technique when spiking or unspiking from dialysate
	Supervised practice of skills and positive feedback from the nurse will add to the patient's confidence about managing peritoneal dialysis at home.

■ When instructing in CAPD, review the use of commercially available devices that help maintain the sterility of the system during tubing connections.	It is of critical importance to maintain sterile technique to prevent infection.
■ Work collaboratively with the patient to fine-tune the length of dialysis, diet regulations, pain management, and diversion needs.	Careful planning helps the patient achieve optimum benefit of the treatment.
■ Provide information on securing materials for traveling and vacations.	Patients must plan ahead when scheduled to be away from home. Supplies may need to be shipped to the destination before travel.
■ Describe signs and symptoms of infection or peritonitis, including basis of occurrence and when to call the health care provider.	Early detection and treatment preserves peritoneal membrane functionality and decreases the loss of membrane surface area and function.
■ Discuss return appointments, follow-up care, and emergency numbers.	Ongoing care on an outpatient basis allows for laboratory monitoring, physical examination, and treatment management discussions.
■ Arrange for a home health nurse or a peritoneal dialysis training nurse visit, as appropriate.	Home care visits allow for assessment of procedures in the home environment and offers support in the environment where the procedure is conducted.
▲ Arrange a social service consultation, if necessary.	Patients may have financial needs related to long-term dialysis that can be addressed.

> **• RELATED CARE PLAN**
>
> Ineffective therapeutic regimen management, p. 185

■ = Independent; ▲ = Collaborative

Renal Calculi

Kidney Stones; Urolithiasis; Nephrolithiasis; Staghorn Calculi

Renal stones are a common problem, affecting men more frequently than women, and whites more commonly than African Americans. People in warmer climates are more commonly affected, probably indicating that dehydration is a factor. Stones may form anywhere in the urinary tract but most often form in the kidney; they commonly move to other parts of the urinary tract, causing pain, infection, and obstruction. Approximately 90% of stones pass spontaneously. Stones may be treated medically, mechanically (by nephroscopic technique or by lithotripsy [use of shock waves to crush the stones]), or surgically (by pyelolithotomy or nephrolithotomy). Renal stones may be made up of calcium phosphate, calcium oxalate, uric acid, cystine, magnesium ammonium phosphate (so-called struvite stones), or combinations of these substances. Calculi develop in situations associated with decreased urine flow, urinary tract injury, and metabolic disorders that alter calcium balance. Changes in urine pH and side effects of some drugs may also contribute to stone formation. Staghorn calculi are large stones that fill and obstruct the renal pelvis. Recurrence of stones is a problem; patients face lifelong need for preventive management. This care plan addresses management of the patient hospitalized with kidney stones; it also addresses postoperative and postlithotripsy care.

NDx Nursing Diagnosis

Deficient Knowledge

Common Related Factors

Unfamiliarity with factors related to development of urolithiasis
Unfamiliarity with potential courses of management
Need for long-term management
Need for prevention of recurrence of renal calculi

Common Expected Outcome

Patient verbalizes understanding of factors related to development and recurrence of renal calculi, and verbalizes understanding of treatment options.

Defining Characteristics

Multiple questions
Lack of questions
Anxiety about management
Recurrence of urolithiasis

NOC Outcomes

Knowledge: Disease Process;
Knowledge: Treatment Regimen

NIC Interventions

Teaching: Disease Process;
Teaching: Prescribed Diet;
Teaching: Prescribed Medication;
Teaching: Procedure/Treatment

■ = Independent; ▲ = Collaborative

Renal and Urinary Tract Care Plans

 Renal Calculi—cont'd

Ongoing Assessment

Actions/Interventions

- Assess history of renal stone formation.

- Assess for family history of kidney stones.

- Assess understanding about relationship of diet to development or recurrence of renal stones.

- Assess knowledge of relationship between development of renal stones and climate or fluid intake.

- Assess understanding of relationship between activity and development of renal stones.

- Assess understanding of medical factors that predispose to formation of renal stones.

Rationale

Recurrence may indicate knowledge deficit regarding prevention.

Incidence of stones is higher among individuals with positive family history.

Intake of foods high in purine, calcium, and oxalate is associated with development of urolithiasis.

Persons in the southeastern and southwestern United States are more likely to develop calculi; this is believed to be a result of warmer weather, higher chance for dehydration, and more concentrated urine.

Persons who have a sedentary lifestyle or limited mobility are at higher risk for development of calculi, because of calcium loss from bones combined with urinary stasis.

Medical conditions including hyperparathyroidism; Paget's disease; breast, lung, and prostate cancer; and Cushing's disease, resulting in stasis of urine, are associated with development of urolithiasis.

Therapeutic Interventions

Actions/Interventions

- Teach the patient the following regarding diet:
  For patients with stones related to hypercalciuria:
  - Calcium intake should be limited.

  - Vitamin D intake should be limited.

  For patients with stones related to oxalate:
  - Foods containing oxalate should be restricted.

  For patients with stones related to uric acid:
  - An alkaline-ash diet should be followed.

  For patients with struvite stones:
  - An acid-ash diet is recommended.

- Teach the patient the importance of maintaining a fluid intake of 3000 to 4000 mL/day.
- Teach the patient about medications used to prevent the recurrence of renal calculi:
  - Sodium cellulose phosphate

Rationale

This includes limiting dairy products, beans, nuts, and chocolate. Phosphorus intake also may be limited.

Vitamin D intake enhances calcium uptake from the gastrointestinal tract.

These include green leafy vegetables, coffee, tea, chocolate, colas, peanuts, and peanut butter.

Foods encouraged on an alkaline-ash diet include dairy products; fruits, except cranberries, plums, and prunes; vegetables, especially beans; and meats.

Foods encouraged on an acid-ash diet include meat, eggs, poultry, fish, cereals, and most fruits and vegetables.

This maintains high-flow, low-solute (dilute) urine and prevents stasis.

This binds calcium so that gastrointestinal absorption of calcium is decreased.

■ = Independent; ▲ = Collaborative

Actions/Interventions	Rationale
• Diuretic agents (thiazide)	These increase tubular reabsorption of calcium, making it less available for calculi formation in the urinary tract.
• Cholestyramine	This binds oxalate and enhances gastrointestinal excretion.
• Allopurinol	This reduces uric acid production.
• Antibiotics	These are used long-term to prevent chronic urinary tract infections that can be precursors to renal calculus formation.
■ Teach patients to increase activity.	This prevents stasis of urine in the bladder. In men, prostatic hyperplasia and resulting urine stasis may contribute to stone formation.
■ Teach the patient the following about possible courses of treatment:	
• Medical management	Ninety percent of stones pass spontaneously; there may be considerable pain, nausea, and vomiting. If it is thought that the stone is moving and will pass, management will consist of fluid therapy, pain management, and antibiotics to prevent or treat infection caused by stasis of urine and/or obstruction caused by the stone.
• Mechanical intervention	Percutaneous catheters may be used to instill chemicals to dissolve the stone. Nephroscopic procedures using a basket to catch and crush the stone may be used. Use of shock waves, either passed through percutaneous catheters or transmitted through a fluid medium from outside the body (extracorporeal shockwave lithotripsy), may be used to pulverize stones so that the fragments can pass.
• Surgical intervention	Surgical procedures include ureterolithotomy (an incision into a ureter to remove a stone), pyelolithotomy (incision into the renal pelvis to remove a stone), and nephrolithotomy (incision into the calyx of the kidney to remove a stone). Partial or complete nephrectomy may be done if damage or infection from the stone is severe.
■ Teach postoperative patients about care of incisions:	
• Incisions should be cleaned using clean technique and dressed with sterile gauze or vapor-permeable membrane dressings.	Vapor-permeable membrane dressings (Op-Site, Tegaderm) allow showering and bathing without risk of infection.
■ Teach the patient to report signs of infection:	Early recognition of infection allows for prompt treatment.
• Pain not relieved by medication	
• Fever accompanied by nausea, vomiting, chills	
• Changes in appearance or odor of urine	
■ Teach patients to strain urine.	Stone fragments may continue to pass for weeks after stone crushing or lithotripsy.

Renal Calculi

■ = Independent; ▲ = Collaborative

Renal Calculi–cont'd

NDx Nursing Diagnosis

Acute Pain

Common Related Factors

Irritation by presence of, obstruction by, or movement of the stone
Obstruction of flow of urine caused by the stone

Defining Characteristics

Verbal reports of pain, usually severe
Restlessness
Grimacing
Sleeplessness

Common Expected Outcome

Patient verbalizes relief of pain or ability to tolerate pain.

NOC Outcome
Pain Control

NIC Interventions
Pain Management;
   Analgesic Administration

Ongoing Assessment

Actions/Interventions

■ Assess location and duration of pain. Use a quantitative rating scale (1 to 10) to assess pain intensity.

■ Assess symptoms related to severe pain.

■ Assess patency of drains or catheters in postoperative patients.

Rationale

Pain associated with kidney stones is typically located in the flank region and may radiate to the pelvic or abdominal area. Pain subsides when and if the stone passes into the bladder.

Pain related to kidney stone obstruction or movement is commonly severe and may be associated with profuse diaphoresis, nausea, and vomiting.

Obstructed flow of urine results in increased renal pressure and causes or intensifies pain.

Therapeutic Interventions

Actions/Interventions

▲ Administer analgesics as prescribed; evaluate effectiveness.

■ Explore and use nonpharmacological pain management methods that have been successful for the patient in the past.

■ Minimize gross motor movement.

Rationale

This prevents peak periods of pain.

Positioning, distraction, and application of heat may relieve or ease pain and reduce amount of analgesic required.

Patients with renal calculi typically assume a crouched, still position; motion may be associated with increased pain.

See also **Acute Pain**, *p. 144.*

■ = Independent; ▲ = Collaborative

Renal Calculi

 Nursing Diagnosis

Risk for Infection

Common Risk Factors

Obstructed flow of urine
Stasis
Instrumentation of urinary tract
Percutaneous punctures communicating with renal
    pelvis
Long-term use of collection devices
Incisions
Presence of gravel

Common Expected Outcome

Patient remains free of infection as evidenced by normal
    temperature, normal white blood cell (WBC) count,
    and clear urine.

NOC Outcomes
Infection Status; Risk Control;
    Risk Detection

NIC Interventions
Infection Protection; Tube Care: Urinary;
    Incision Site Care

Ongoing Assessment

Actions/Interventions	Rationale
■ Monitor urine output.	Desired urine output is 2000 to 3000 mL/24 hours. The more dilute and the higher the flow of urine, the less stasis there is; this lessens the possibility of further stone formation and increases the possibility that the stone will pass spontaneously.
■ Monitor urine for hematuria, cloudiness, and odor.	Hematuria results from trauma to the urinary tract as the stone moves. Changes in urine characteristics are signs of infection.
■ Observe for the following changes in elimination pattern: • Dysuria • Frequency • Hesitancy • Retention	These symptoms are usually indicative of a urinary tract infection.
■ Monitor temperature.	Urinary tract infection can result in very high fever.
▲ Monitor WBC count.	Elevated WBC count is a sign of infection.
Postprocedure:	
■ Observe percutaneous sites and/or incisions for redness, swelling, and pain.	These may indicate infection.
▲ Obtain a culture of urine and drainage from around catheters (meatal or percutaneous).	This determines the presence of pathogens. Antibiotic therapy will be based on the specific microorganism causing the infection.

■ = Independent; ▲ = Collaborative

Renal Calculi—cont'd

Actions/Interventions

■ Check pH of urine.

Rationale

Urine with a pH of 6.0 or greater (i.e., alkaline urine) is more susceptible to infection than acidic urine.

Therapeutic Interventions

Actions/Interventions

■ Strain all urine.

Rationale

This detects passage of stone, stone fragments, or gravel. If the type of stone (i.e., composition) is unknown, the stone may be sent to a laboratory for analysis. This assists in planning therapy to prevent the recurrence of stones and for diet modification.

■ Encourage fluid intake of 3000 to 4000 mL of fluid daily.

This keeps urine diluted and the flow of urine high.

■ Clean and/or replace leg bags, gravity collection bags, and any other collection system daily.

This prevents accumulation of pathogens.

■ Teach and encourage meatal care every 8 hours for patients with indwelling catheters.

This reduces pathogens around catheter.

■ Encourage measures to acidify urine. Recommend vitamin C (ascorbic acid) 500 to 1000 mg/day; and cranberry juice, four to six 8-ounce glasses per day.

Acidic urine inhibits the growth of pathogenic bacteria. Cranberry juice yields hippuric acid as it metabolizes and is excreted.

▲ Administer antibiotics as prescribed.

Specific antibiotics will reduce pathogens and resolve infection.

■ If a catheter is removed, encourage the patient to continue drinking fluids; instruct the patient to notify the physician if the patient has not voided 6 hours after catheter removal.

Maintaining urine output is essential to prevent infection, even after the catheter is removed.

■ Instruct the patient to report changes in pain, fever, or chills.

These are indications of infection.

■ Following surgical procedures, teach the patient or caregiver to change dressings over percutaneous nephrostomy tubes and incisions as prescribed, using good hand washing and aseptic technique.

Patients and their caregivers can prevent infection through use of appropriate hygiene measures at home.

Renal Transplantation, Postoperative

Kidney Transplantation

Renal transplantation is the surgical implantation of a renal allograft from either a cadaver or a live donor into a patient with kidney failure. Most cadaver kidneys are procured from trauma accident patients who have been pronounced dead, with surgical removal of the kidney occurring before discontinuing ventilation and fluids necessary to perfuse and oxygenate the organ. Most commonly, transplant candidates are on hemodialysis or peritoneal dialysis, exhibiting symptoms of azotemia, anemia, fluid overload, and oliguria. The number of transplants continues to grow as a result of the government funding of such procedures, and with improved survival rates from advances in surgical

■ = Independent; ▲ = Collaborative

techniques and immunosuppression therapy. Survival rates at 1 year are at least 95%. All potential donors must be matched for ABO blood and HLA (human leukocyte antigen) typing. Living related donors are usually siblings, parents, or children. Due to advances in immunosuppressive therapy, living nonrelated transplantations are being performed with growing success. The transplant experience is a planned, usually elective surgery. In contrast, patients on waiting lists for cadaver kidneys may have a long, difficult wait. This care plan addresses the immediate postoperative care of the renal transplant patient.

NDx Nursing Diagnosis

Risk for Deficient/Excess Fluid Volume

Common Risk Factors

Variable time for initiating renal function:
- Immediately after renal transplantation, patient may vacillate between fluid depletion and fluid overload.
- Prolonged transport time may cause acute tubular necrosis (ATN).

Rejection

Bleeding from surgical site

Common Expected Outcome

Patient's risk for development of fluid volume deficit or excess is reduced through ongoing assessment and early intervention.

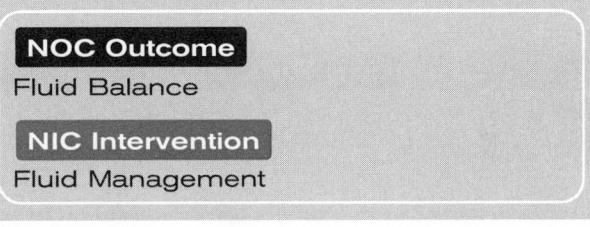

NOC Outcome
Fluid Balance

NIC Intervention
Fluid Management

Ongoing Assessment

Actions/Interventions	Rationale
■ Monitor for signs and symptoms of fluid volume deficit: polyuria, weight loss, dry mucous membranes, weakness, and thirst.	Transplanted kidney may have experienced prolonged ischemia resulting in ATN that may progress to diuretic phase during recovery.
■ Monitor for signs and symptoms of fluid volume excess: edema, weight gain, reduced urine output, shortness of breath, crackles, elevated blood pressure.	Acute rejection is evidenced by reduced renal function.
■ Weigh the patient daily using the same scale.	This prevents discrepancies due to measuring device.
■ Monitor intake and output. Notify the physician if urine output is less than 30 mL/hr.	Urine output less than 30 mL/hr is considered oliguria.

■ = Independent; ▲ = Collaborative

Renal and Urinary Tract Care Plans

 Renal Transplantation, Postoperative—cont'd

Therapeutic Interventions

Actions/Interventions

▲ Replace fluids milliliter for milliliter plus 30 mL/hr.

▲ For fluid overload, conduct the following:
  • Administer diuretics and restrict fluids as indicated.
  • Begin progressive ambulation.

▲ If there is no urine production, prepare for hemodialysis, as necessary, until the transplanted kidney is functioning.

Rationale

This amount of fluid replacement accounts for insensible loss. Unit protocol may vary among institutions. ATN patients may have diuresis several days after surgery, exceeding 200 to 400 mL/hr. Living related transplant recipients have greater urine volumes in the early postoperative period (may exceed 400 to 600 mL/hr). Fluid replacement must match output so the patient does not become dehydrated.

These measures reduce fluid excess.

This facilitates adequate tissue perfusion to edematous body areas, mobilizes fluids, and decreases edema.

Occasionally the new kidney does not produce urine immediately and the patient must be dialyzed until adequate renal function occurs.

NDx Nursing Diagnosis

Risk for Urinary Retention

Common Risk Factors

Obstructed Foley catheter
Anastomosis leak

Common Expected Outcome

Patient's risk of urinary retention is decreased as evidenced by patency of Foley catheter or patient request to void every 1 to 2 hours.

NOC Outcome
Urinary Elimination

NIC Intervention
Urinary Elimination Management

Ongoing Assessment

Actions/Interventions

■ Obtain preoperative history of the patient's pattern of urinating.

■ Assess urine for color, amount, sediment, and presence of clots.

■ Assess for abdominal or bladder distention resulting from a clotted Foley catheter or anastomosis leak.

Rationale

If patient was oliguric, the urinary bladder may be atrophied and/or reduced in size.

Depending on the volume of urine, the bladder capacity, muscle tone, and the degree of hematuria, the indwelling catheter will remain in place for approximately 3 days.

Distention of the lower abdomen just above the pubic bone may be the first sign of urinary retention.

■ = Independent; ▲ = Collaborative

Renal Transplantation, Postoperative

Actions/Interventions

- Record intake and output.

- After discontinuing the Foley catheter, assess the amount, color, clarity, sediment, and blood in the voided urine.

Rationale

A decreased urine output that is less than fluid intake may indicate urinary retention.

Hematuria and signs of infection must be assessed and treated immediately.

Therapeutic Interventions

Actions/Interventions

- Maintain Foley catheter drainage, preventing kinks.
- ▲ If gross hematuria is evident, strain urine for clots. Irrigate the Foley catheter with physician approval.
- After discontinuing the Foley catheter, ask the patient to void every 1 to 2 hours.

- Instruct the patient to record daily urine output and notify the transplantation team if output decreases or if color, clarity, or consistency changes.

Rationale

These would obstruct flow.

Bleeding from the anastomosis can cause a clotted Foley catheter.

Voiding at regular intervals prevents urinary retention and urinary bladder overdistention. If bladder capacity is significantly compromised, the patient will need to empty the bladder more often. A full bladder causes additional strain on the ureteral anastomosis.

Decreased urine volume and changes in urine characteristics indicate postoperative complications that can compromise the healing of the transplanted kidney.

NDx Nursing Diagnosis

Risk for Infection

Common Risk Factors

Immunosuppression with antirejection medications
Disruption of skin and iatrogenic sources of infection

Common Expected Outcomes

Patient's risk of infection is reduced through ongoing assessment and early intervention.
Patient or family states understanding of need for strict infection control measures.

NOC Outcomes
Infection Status; Risk Control

NIC Intervention
Infection Protection

Ongoing Assessment

Actions/Interventions

- Monitor temperature.
- ▲ Monitor white blood cell (WBC) count.

- Inspect wound for local erythema, purulent drainage, or dehiscence; notify the transplant physician if they occur.

Rationale

A low-grade fever may be a sign of infection or rejection.

Even a slight rise in WBC count may signal an infection because of the patient's impaired immune response (i.e., decreased circulating lymphocytes and ability to fight infectious organism).

Wound infections can delay healing and contribute to more serious complications.

■ = Independent; ▲ = Collaborative

> ## Renal Transplantation, Postoperative—cont'd

Actions/Interventions

▲ Culture the wound for aerobic organisms if drainage is purulent, green, or foul-smelling. Culture urine if the patient is febrile or dysuric, or if urine turns cloudy.

▲ Monitor all culture reports.

■ Assess the patient's respiratory rate and rhythm, and assess for signs of increased work of breathing: use of accessory muscles.

■ Assess lungs for development of adventitious sounds.

Rationale

The results of cultures provide a guideline for selecting appropriate antimicrobial medications to treat infections.

Bacterial infections are most commonly encountered.

Increased respiratory effort occurs with infection.

Respiratory infections are common and serious in the immunocompromised patient.

Therapeutic Interventions

Actions/Interventions

■ Wash hands before and after touching the patient.

▲ When transferred to a step-down unit, obtain a private room for the patient or place the patient with a roommate without infections. Restrict visitors and flowers at the transplantation team's discretion.

■ Encourage deep breathing, coughing, and turning.

■ Encourage postoperative use of incentive spirometry.

▲ Administer antibiotics as prescribed.

■ Encourage diet high in calories and protein (as kidney function allows).

■ Teach the patient or significant others about avoidance of infectious crowds, importance of good hygiene, and signs or symptoms of infection.

Rationale

Bacteria, viruses, fungi, and protozoa indigenous in non-transplantation populations may be infectious in the immunosuppressed transplantation patient. The hospital environment is known to harbor many bacteria and viruses.

This prevents cross contamination. These patients do not require isolation.

These prevent associated respiratory complications. Preventing a pulmonary infection is important to facilitate the recovery process.

A respiratory infection can result in postoperative mortality when maximum doses of immunosuppressive drugs are being given. Respiratory infections are the most common cause of death from infection.

Antibiotic therapy should be based on culture and sensitivity results to decrease development of drug-resistant microorganisms.

Infection risk is greater in patients with end-stage renal disease who have debilitated presurgical states.

The patient must understand the increased infection risk and the importance of calling the transplantation team about signs of infection.

NDx Nursing Diagnosis

Risk for Ineffective Coping

Common Risk Factors

Threat of rejection or infection
Postoperative need for dialysis

■ = Independent; ▲ = Collaborative

Concern over donor
Concern over lifetime immunosuppression therapy
Perceived body image changes
Change in role functioning

Common Expected Outcomes

Patient displays acceptance of transplant process.
Patient displays beginning signs of effective coping as
evidenced by cooperative behavior, calm appearance,
and interest in surroundings.

NOC Outcomes
Coping; Anxiety Self-Control

NIC Interventions
Coping Enhancement; Anxiety Reduction

Ongoing Assessment

Actions/Interventions

■ Assess for signs of ineffective coping: apprehension, feelings of inadequacy, facial tension, restlessness, worry.

■ Assess available support systems and functional coping mechanisms.

■ Assess the patient's ability to accept self-care responsibility.

■ Assess the impact of the patient's life situation on roles and relationships.

■ As the patient recovers, assess his or her response to changes in appearance.

Rationale

Occasionally the patient must be dialyzed postoperatively until the transplanted kidney begins functioning. This can be anxiety-provoking for the patient. The patient should be reassured that this is not uncommon. Patients may also respond negatively to the fear of possible rejection.

Strategies useful in the past may or may not be useful.

This is important because the patient must take immunosuppressive medications for the rest of his or her life to prevent rejection of the kidney.

Changes in roles that occurred with illness may change again after successful transplantation. Family members may have new expectations of the patient and his or her role in the family.

Side effects of cyclosporine and steroid therapy can cause weight gain, increase in body and facial hair, moon face, and fragile skin. Some of these are especially troublesome for women.

Therapeutic Interventions

Actions/Interventions

■ Allow the patient time to ventilate fears and anxiety.

■ Assist with identifying available support systems such as a support group or a transplant patient to talk with regarding all of the changes affecting the patient's life.
■ Offer emotional support.

Rationale

After surgery, the transplant patient must maintain health and cannot rely on the dialysis staff. This independence is often frightening, especially with the potential for rejection or infection.

Relationships with persons with common experiences and goals can be beneficial.

The patient may be anxious about the need for postoperative dialysis; he or she may need to be reassured that this is not uncommon (especially with cadaver-donated kidneys).

■ = Independent; ▲ = Collaborative

> ## Renal Transplantation, Postoperative—cont'd

Nursing Diagnosis

Deficient Knowledge

Common Related Factors	Defining Characteristics
New condition Long-term management plan	Verbalized confusion about treatment Lack of questions Request for information

Common Expected Outcome

Patient or caregiver states an understanding of renal transplantation, including postoperative self-care.

NOC Outcomes
Knowledge: Disease Process;
Knowledge: Treatment Regimen

NIC Interventions
Teaching: Disease Process;
Teaching: Prescribed Medications

Ongoing Assessment

Actions/Interventions	Rationale
■ Assess the patient's and family's understanding of transplant surgery, postoperative course, medications and their side effects, and potential lifestyle changes.	Postoperatively, patients may be overwhelmed by the amount of important information they are responsible for (e.g., medications, detecting signs of infection).

Therapeutic Interventions

Actions/Interventions	Rationale
■ Instruct the patient or caregiver as follows regarding medication therapy:	
• Instruct to take immunosuppressive medication every day for life:	Immunosuppressive medications must be taken daily—as long as the patient has a kidney transplant—to prevent rejection. These immunosuppressive agents put the patient at increased risk for infection and for the development of malignancies caused by the altered immune system, such as lymphoma.
• Cyclosporine	This interferes with the production, release, and action of T cells but does not interfere with normal inflammatory response.
• Steroids	Antiinflammatory action helps stabilize cell membranes to prevent T-cell infiltration.
• Muromonab-CD3 (Orthoclone OKT)	Blocks the function of CD3 molecules in the membrane of human T cells, helping to prevent rejection.

■ = Independent; ▲ = Collaborative

Actions/Interventions	Rationale

Actions/Interventions

- Mycophenolate mofetil (CellCept)

- Tacrolimus (Prograf)

- Sirolimus (Rapamune)

- Instruct in specific regimen for each medication (e.g., take cyclosporine on empty stomach; take steroids with food).
- Instruct regarding side effects of medications (e.g., hypertension, brittle bones, mood alteration).

■ Instruct regarding signs or symptoms of local and systemic infection.

■ Instruct regarding signs or symptoms of graft rejection: fever; weight gain; decreased urine output, increased blood pressure; swollen, tender transplant site; increased serum creatinine; increased blood urea nitrogen.

■ Ensure that the patient knows what to do or whom to call for suspected rejection or infection.

■ Instruct regarding prescribed diet.

■ Instruct on importance of practicing good hygiene measures.

■ Instruct the patient to wear medical alert bracelet stating that he or she uses antirejection medications and is a transplant patient.

Rationale

This is used to reduce the incidence of acute organ rejection in patients receiving allogenic renal transplants; it is usually given in combination with cyclosporine and corticosteroids.

This drug inhibits T-lymphocyte activation and is used in combination with corticosteroids to prevent rejection of allogenic renal transplants. Use in African-American patients is associated with improved graft survival.

This drug inhibits T-lymphocyte activation and proliferation and is used in combination with cyclosporine and corticosteroids as prophylaxis for organ rejection in allogenic renal transplants. Significant side effects of this medication are increased serum cholesterol and triglyceride levels.

Medication compliance is critical to the ongoing success of the transplant, so medication regimen and side effects should be discussed.

Transplant recipients are at increased risk for developing infection because of immunosuppressive therapy.

Most patients will experience some type of acute rejection that responds to therapy. Chronic rejection comes on more gradually and may result in a nonfunctioning kidney. Acute rejection is treated with high-dose steroids, polyclonal antibodies such as antithymocytic globulin (ATG) and antilymphocyte globulin (ALG), or monoclonal antibodies such as OKT3.

Being prepared for an emergency helps prevent further complications.

Patients with transplants no longer need to follow the strict renal diets. However, it is important that they maintain reduced levels of sodium (to offset fluid retention from steroids) and increased levels of protein (steroids break down protein).

This decreases incidence of infection.

In case of emergency, this alerts the community members and health care professionals of the medical condition.

• RELATED CARE PLANS

Acute pain, p. 144
Disturbed body image, p. 21

■ = Independent; ▲ = Collaborative

Urinary Diversion

Bladder Cancer; Urostomy; Ileal Conduit; Ileal Reservoir; Koch Pouch; Neobladder; Nephrostomy; Sigmoidostomy; Ureterostomy; Vesicostomy

Urinary diversion is the surgical diversion of urinary flow from its usual path through the urinary tract. Urinary diversion procedures may be performed as a result of obstruction of the urinary tract; destruction of normal urinary structures by trauma; neurogenic bladder caused by disease or injury; and cancer, usually of the bladder. Bladder cancer occurs more often in older men than in women. When the tumors are superficial in the bladder wall, a variety of surgical procedures can be performed to remove the tumor and maintain normal urinary tract function. These procedures include transurethral resection, laser photocoagulation, and segmental cystectomy. If the bladder tumor is invasive and involves the trigone area, the preferred treatment is total cystectomy with a urinary diversion to maintain outflow of urine. Some procedures result in incontinence and necessitate the wearing of a collection system or pouch. Other procedures reroute the urinary flow to another structure (e.g., a surgically created internal reservoir, colon) from which the urine is eventually excreted (often called continent procedures). Nephrostomy may be performed under fluoroscopic control as an outpatient procedure. Other diversions require open abdominal surgery, and the patient is typically hospitalized for 4 to 7 days. This care plan addresses those procedures that result in urinary incontinence and that can be used for newly postoperative patients, as well as for individuals who have undergone urinary diversion at some point in the past.

NDx Nursing Diagnosis

Deficient Knowledge: Preoperative

Common Related Factor

Lack of previous surgical experience

Common Expected Outcome

Patient verbalizes understanding of proposed surgical procedure, including permanent loss of urinary continence and postoperative need for a collection system.

Defining Characteristics

Questions
Lack of questions
Verbalized misconceptions

NOC Outcome
Knowledge: Treatment Procedures

NIC Interventions
Teaching: Preoperative;
    Teaching: Procedure/Treatment

Ongoing Assessment

Actions/Interventions

- Assess the patient's understanding of the proposed surgical procedure:

Rationale

Options depend on the nature of disease or disorder that makes the urinary diversion necessary.

■ = Independent; ▲ = Collaborative

Actions/Interventions	**Rationale**
• Ileal conduit (or ileal loop)	This is the most common type of urinary diversion performed. It uses a piece ("loop") of small intestine as a conduit to which the ureters are attached. One end of the conduit is brought to the anterior abdominal surface as a stoma, over which a pouch must always be worn. An ileal conduit is usually done with cystectomy (removal of the bladder) for bladder cancer.
• Nephrostomy	Percutaneous catheterization of one or both kidneys is usually done when the urinary path is obstructed distally. Nephrostomy may be performed when the patient is not a candidate (e.g., a terminally ill cancer patient or a very poor surgical risk) for more permanent diversion. This necessitates wearing one or two leg bags for collection of urine.
• Sigmoidostomy	The ureters are anastomosed to the sigmoid colon. Urine is excreted with bowel elimination. The patient may experience bowel incontinence. The patient will not have an abdominal stoma.
• Ureterostomy (unilateral or bilateral)	This is implantation of one or both ureters to the anterior abdominal wall as small stomas and is usually done when reestablishment of normal urinary flow is anticipated.
• Vesicostomy	This is usually a temporary urinary diversion performed when the lower urinary tract must be bypassed (e.g., in urethral trauma). An opening is made into the bladder wall, which is attached to the lower anterior abdomen. A pouch must be worn over the vesicostomy stoma to collect the urine. This procedure may also be used to create a continent diversion by using a valve to prevent urine leakage at the stoma.
• Continent urinary diversions (e.g., Koch, Mainz, Indiana, or Florida pouch)	A continent urinary diversion uses a portion of the bowel to surgically create a reservoir that collects urine within the abdominal cavity. A stoma is created on the surface of the abdominal wall. The patient inserts a catheter through the stoma to drain urine from the reservoir.
■ Assess the patient's understanding of the proposed surgical procedure and its relationship to urinary continence.	It is important that the patient understand that the proposed surgical procedure will make him or her incontinent of urine. This incontinence necessitates wearing and maintaining an external collection device. Postoperative adaptation will require management of the collection system and incorporation of the altered function and the collection system into the body image or self-concept of the person.
■ Assess the patient's knowledge about whether the urinary diversion proposed is temporary or permanent.	The patient's ability to cope with changes in activities of daily living necessitated by wearing an external collection device is facilitated when the patient understands that the diversion is permanent. Patients having temporary diversion may decline involvement in self-care and defer care to a family member or outside caregiver.
■ Ask whether the patient has had contact with another person who has a urinary diversion.	Previous contact, either positive or negative, influences the patient's perception of what his or her experience will be.

■ = Independent; ▲ = Collaborative

Urinary Diversion—cont'd

Therapeutic Interventions

Actions/Interventions	Rationale
■ Reinforce and reexplain the proposed procedure.	Preoperative anxiety often makes it necessary to repeat instructions or explanations several times for the patient to comprehend.
■ Use diagrams, pictures, and models to explain anatomy and physiology of the genitourinary tract, pathophysiology necessitating urinary diversion, and proposed location of stoma:	Teaching methods need to be adapted to the patient's learning preferences.
• Ileal conduit	This is usually located in the lower right quadrant of the abdomen.
• Nephrostomy	Tubes exit on one or both flanks, just below the costal margin.
• Ureterostomy	This is anywhere on the anterior abdominal surface, preferably below the waistline.
• Vesicostomy	This is on the anterior abdomen, suprapubic area.
■ Show the patient the pouch or collection system that will be used postoperatively.	Allowing the patient to wear the pouch or collection device is also helpful and may identify the need for relocation of the proposed stoma.
■ Offer the patient a visit with a rehabilitated ostomate.	Sometimes contact with another individual who has experience with the condition is more beneficial than factual information given by a health professional.

ND_x Nursing Diagnosis

Risk for Toileting Self-Care Deficit

Common Risk Factors

Presence of poorly placed stoma
Presence of pouch
Poor hand-eye coordination

Common Expected Outcome

Patient performs self-care (emptying or changing pouch) independently.

NOC Outcome
Self-Care: Toileting

NIC Intervention
Ostomy Care

Ongoing Assessment

Actions/Interventions

■ Assess for the following: presence of old abdominal scars, presence of bony prominences on anterior abdomen, presence of creases or skinfolds on abdomen, extreme obesity, scaphoid abdomen, pendulous breasts, ability to see and handle equipment.

Rationale

Stoma placement is facilitated by a flat abdomen that has no scars, bony prominences, or extremes of weight. When these factors are present, the stoma site selection may need to be altered to locate the stoma where the patient can see and reach it and where a relatively flat surface for pouching exists.

Therapeutic Interventions

Actions/Interventions

▲ Consult an enterostomal therapy nurse or surgeon to mark the proposed stoma site indelibly in an area that the patient can easily see and reach; where scars, bony prominences, and skinfolds are avoided; and where hip flexion does not change contour.

■ If possible, have the patient wear a collection device over the proposed site; evaluate effectiveness in terms of the patient's ability to see and handle equipment and to wear normal clothing.

Rationale

It is best to determine site selection with the patient in a sitting position.

Stoma location is a key factor in self-care. A poorly located stoma can delay or preclude self-care abilities. The patient can be shown how the collection bag works and how it can be covered by clothing.

NDx Nursing Diagnosis

Risk for Disturbed Body Image

Common Risk Factors

Presence of stoma
Presence of pouch or collection system
Loss of urinary continence
Fear of offensive odor or leakage
Fear of appearing different

Common Expected Outcome

Patient begins to express feelings about stoma and body image.

NOC Outcomes
Body Image; Self-Esteem; Coping

NIC Intervention
Body Image Enhancement

Ongoing Assessment

Actions/Interventions

■ Assess the perceived impact of change in body structure and function.

Rationale

The patient's response to real or perceived changes in body structure and/or function is related to the importance the patient places on the structure or function (e.g., a fastidious person may experience the presence of a

■ = Independent; ▲ = Collaborative

Urinary Diversion—cont'd

Actions/Interventions

- Note verbal and nonverbal references to the stoma.

- Note the patient's ability or readiness to look at, touch, and care for the stoma and ostomy equipment.

Rationale

urine-filled pouch on the anterior abdomen as intolerable, or a person who works out or swims may find the presence of visible tubes protruding from flanks as intolerable). However, some patients will express that such changes are "a small price to pay" for absence of disease.

Patients often "name" stomas as an attempt to separate the stoma from themselves. Others may look away or totally deny the presence of the stoma until they are able to cope.

Often the first sign of a patient's readiness to participate in stoma care is when he or she looks at the stoma.

Therapeutic Interventions

Actions/Interventions

- Acknowledge the appropriateness of the emotional response to actual and perceived changes in body structure and function.

- Assist the patient in looking at, touching, and caring for the stoma when ready.

- Assist patients in identifying specific actions that could be helpful in managing their perceived loss or problems related to their stoma.

Rationale

Because control of elimination is a skill or task of early childhood and a socially private function, loss of control precipitates a body image change and possible self-concept change.

Patients look for reactions, both positive and negative, from caregivers. Positive reactions by the nurse, such as, "The stoma looks pink and healthy," or "The urine is clear and yellow, as it should be," helps the patient develop a sense of normalcy about the change in his or her elimination.

Leakage of contents from the pouch, with resultant embarrassment about odor and loss of control, is a major concern. Emptying the collection device when it is about half full reduces the risk of the device leaking. A full device can pull away from the stoma because of the weight of the urine. Assuring the patient that skill will develop and that accidents are preventable will go a long way in helping him or her adapt to the altered structure or function.

NDx Nursing Diagnosis

Risk for Ineffective Gastrointestinal or Urinary Tract Tissue Perfusion

Common Risk Factors

Surgical manipulation of small intestine (ileal conduit), bladder (vesicostomy), ureters (ureterostomy)
Poorly fitting faceplate

■ = Independent; ▲ = Collaborative

Common Expected Outcome

Patient's stoma remains pink and moist.

NOC Outcomes
Tissue Perfusion: Gastrointestinal;
Tissue Perfusion: Peripheral

NIC Interventions
Surveillance; Ostomy Care

Ongoing Assessment

Actions/Interventions

- Assess the stoma for adequate arterial tissue perfusion at least every 4 hours for the first 24 hours postoperatively:
  - Color of ileal conduit stoma

  - Appearance of ureterostomy stoma

  - Vesicostomy stoma

- Assess the stoma for edema at least every 4 hours for the first 24 hours postoperatively.

Rationale

The ileal conduit stoma is a piece of rerouted small intestine with attached mesentery (blood supply). It should appear pink and moist if perfusion is adequate.

Because the ureters have a small diameter, manipulation at surgery or edema of surrounding tissue can compress the ureters at the skin line and compromise perfusion. Ureteral stomas should appear pink and moist if perfusion is adequate.

This stoma is constructed of inverted bladder that has been surgically sewn to abdominal skin; normal appearance is pink and moist. This stoma is least susceptible to impaired tissue perfusion.

Some postoperative edema is expected and will subside over a period of 2 to 6 weeks. When edema becomes severe, venous congestion, evidenced by a purplish discoloration of the stoma, may occur.

Therapeutic Interventions

Actions/Interventions

- Ensure that the faceplate of the pouch is correctly fitted.

- Remove the faceplate and notify the surgeon immediately if the stoma appears dusky blue, black, or dry.

Rationale

A faceplate that is tightly fitted to the stoma can reduce blood flow to the stoma and impede venous drainage, resulting in further edema and increasing the risk of ischemia.

A stoma that is dusky blue, black, or dry is receiving inadequate blood supply; usually the patient returns to surgery for stoma revision. Although this is primarily a concern during the first 24 to 48 hours postoperatively, patients should be taught to examine stoma color each time they perform a pouch change.

■ = Independent; ▲ = Collaborative

Renal and Urinary Tract Care Plans

→ Urinary Diversion—cont'd

 Nursing Diagnosis

Risk for Infection

Common Risk Factors

Surgical incision
Small bowel anastomosis (ileal conduit)
Anastomosis of ureters to small bowel (ileal conduit),
    abdominal wall (ureterostomy)
Percutaneous access to renal pelvis (nephrostomy)
Direct opening into bladder (vesicostomy)

Common Expected Outcome

Patient remains free of infection as evidenced by normal
temperature, normal white blood cell (WBC) count,
absence of signs of local wound infection, and absence
of purulent drainage from around nephrostomy tubes
and all incision sites.

NOC Outcomes
Infection Status; Wound Healing: Primary
    Intention

NIC Interventions
Wound Care; Tube Care: Urinary;
    Ostomy Care; Infection Protection

Ongoing Assessment

Actions/Interventions

- Assess surgical incisions and areas around percutaneous nephrostomies for redness, swelling, and suspicious drainage.

- Monitor temperature. Assess for signs of infection.
  Possible sites of infection in patients who have had
  urinary diversion surgeries include the following:
  • Incision

  • Anastomosis of ureters to small bowel

  • Area where ureters are attached to the abdomen
  • Percutaneous puncture sites
  • Bladder

- Monitor urine output.

▲ Send any suspicious drainage from surgically placed
  drains to the laboratory.

Rationale

These indicate wound infection.

Temperature above 38.5°C (101.3°F) after the third postoperative day is an indication of infection.

As the ileal conduit is fashioned, ureters are anastomosed
into the segment of small bowel designated for the conduit; breakdown of these anastomoses results in peritonitis because urine spills into the peritoneal cavity instead
of traveling to the conduit and out through the stoma.

These are where nephrostomy tubes have been placed.

In patients with a vesicostomy, the bladder communicates
with the outside.

Diminishing amounts of urine output in patients with an
ileal conduit may indicate spillage of urine into the
peritoneal cavity.

Drainage is analyzed to determine internal urine leak.

■ = Independent; ▲ = Collaborative

Urinary Diversion

Actions/Interventions

▲ Monitor WBCs.
▲ Obtain culture of urine.

■ Check pH of urine.

Rationale

Elevated WBC count is a sign of infection.

Laboratory culture determines pathogens present and guides antimicrobial therapy.

Urine with a pH above 6.0 (i.e., alkaline urine) is more susceptible to infection than acidic urine.

Therapeutic Interventions

Actions/Interventions

▲ Provide wound care to incisions and areas around percutaneous sites, vesicostomy outlet, and ureterostomies, as prescribed, using aseptic technique.
■ Wash hands before handling any tubes or drains.
■ Maintain closed drainage systems and change leg bags, gravity collection bags, and any other collection systems to prevent accumulation of pathogens.

▲ Encourage measures to acidify urine:
 • Vitamin C (ascorbic acid) 500 to 1000 mg/day
 • Cranberry juice, four to six 8-ounce glasses per day

▲ Encourage fluid intake of 3000 to 4000 mL of fluid daily.
■ Instruct the patient to report pain, fever, and chills.
▲ Administer antibiotics and antipyretics as prescribed.

Rationale

Appropriate hygiene measures with dressing changes reduce the risk of wound infections.

This reduces pathogens.

Most patients can expect to wear a single collection device for up to 5 days; keeping the system closed reduces the risk of contamination. Collection devices should be emptied at least every 8 hours to prevent urine being reintroduced into the stoma.

Acidic urine inhibits the growth of pathogenic bacteria.

Cranberry juice yields hippuric acid as it metabolizes and is excreted.

This keeps urine diluted and flushes out bacteria.

These are signs of infection.

These eliminate infection and lower fever.

NDx Nursing Diagnosis

Risk for Impaired Home Maintenance

Common Risk Factors

Presence of new stoma
Presence of ureterostomy
Presence of percutaneous nephrostomy
Presence of vesicostomy

Common Expected Outcome

Patient demonstrates ability to provide care for ostomy, nephrostomy tubes, and/or skin.

NOC Outcomes
Coping; Knowledge: Treatment Regimen; Social Support

NIC Interventions
Home Maintenance Assistance; Teaching: Psychomotor Skill; Support System Enhancement; Ostomy Care

■ = Independent; ▲ = Collaborative

Urinary Diversion—cont'd

Ongoing Assessment

Actions/Interventions	**Rationale**
■ Assess the patient's perception of ability to care for self at time of discharge.	Preexisting poor eyesight or lack of manual dexterity can be real problems for patients providing self-care.
■ Assess resources (family member, friend, other caregiver) who may be available and willing to assist the patient with care after discharge.	With shorter hospitalizations and same-day surgeries, patients often do not have adequate time for learning and returning demonstration before assuming full responsibility for self-care. Also, concerned others, in addition to assisting with or providing care, are often comforted by being able "to help somehow."
■ Assess the patient's ability to empty and change pouch (ileal conduit, vesicostomy).	Some patients will be independent in emptying their pouch by time of discharge; many will still need assistance and may require outpatient follow-up or in-home care.
■ Assess the patient's ability to care for peristomal skin.	Care of peristomal skin is important to promote skin integrity and reduce the risk of fungal skin infections.
■ Assess the patient's ability to identify peristomal skin problems:	
• Excoriation	This appears as a sore, reddened area, most typically the result of a poorly fitted faceplate that allows urine to contact the skin; of too frequent changing of the pouch; or the result of frequent accidents in which urine comes into contact with the skin.
• Crystal formation	This appears as a collection of white crystals around the stoma or on skin around the stoma or tubes; it forms when urine is highly alkaline.
• Yeast infection	This acts as an abrasive, resulting in excoriation, and appears as a beefy-red, itchy area around the stoma or tubes. Infection tends to spread by "satellite," small round extensions at the perimeter of the main area of redness.
• Contact dermatitis	This is usually the result of allergy to some product in use around the stoma or tubes and appears as a continuous reddened area; it may itch and feel painful. Contact dermatitis can develop even after years of successful use of products. It is characterized by its size and shape, which approximate the area of contact with the offending product.
■ Assess the patient's knowledge about the following:	
• Diet	Patients with urinary diversion are instructed to drink 3000 to 4000 mL of fluid per day to prevent stasis and infection. This amount may need to be adjusted for persons with diminished cardiovascular, renal, or pulmonary function.
• Activity	Patients may bathe or shower with the pouch on or off; patients with nephrostomy tubes should always cover gauze dressings with waterproof dressing (e.g., Op-Site, Tegaderm) or with waterproof tape. Other activities are governed by the patient's desire and energy level. Patients may be afraid to engage in usual activities, such

■ = Independent; ▲ = Collaborative

Rationale

as sports or sex. The lack of confidence in abilities usually diminishes as the patient gains control over management of the urinary diversion and fear of an "accident" diminishes.

Therapeutic Interventions

Actions/Interventions

- Provide teaching during the first and subsequent pouch changes, or during opportunities to care for nephrostomy tubes.

- Include one or more caregivers as appropriate or desired by the patient.

- Gradually transfer responsibility for care to the patient or family.

- Allow at least one opportunity for supervised return demonstration of a pouch change before discharge from the hospital or arrange for home nursing care.

- Teach the patient how to care for peristomal skin or skin around the nephrostomy tube:
  - Wash and dry skin around the stoma and tubes using soap and water.
  - Apply a liquid barrier film (Bard Protective Barrier Film, Skin Prep).
  - Change the pouch every 3 to 6 days.

- Discuss odor control and acknowledge that odor (or fear of odor) can impair social functioning.

- Discuss availability of ostomy support groups.
- Instruct the patient to maintain contact with an enterostomal therapy nurse.
- For patients who travel, provide local enterostomal therapy resources and phone numbers.

- Assist patients in keeping receipts organized.

Rationale

Even before patients are able to participate actively, they can observe and discuss ostomy care.

It is beneficial to teach others alongside the patient, as long as all realize that the goal is for the patient to become independent in self-ostomy care. Patients with nephrostomy tubes cannot reach the flank and will need to rely on another person to provide care.

The patient and caregivers need to gain confidence in their ability to care for the urinary diversion before discharge.

Self-ostomy care requires both cognitive and psychomotor skills; postoperatively, learning ability may be decreased, requiring repetition and opportunity for return demonstration. Teaching in the patient's home setting helps the patient fit the routine and equipment management into his or her own setting. Problem-solving small but important issues assists the patient toward adaptation.

Initial cleaning of the skin removes pathogens and skin oils that can reduce adherence of pouching adhesives.

This protects skin from moisture and any adhesives used in the area.

More frequent changing strips away epithelial cells and can led to excoriation.

Odor control is best achieved by attention to pouch hygiene; urinary equipment can be rinsed with a half-and-half solution of water and vinegar to reduce urinary odor. Certain foods (e.g., asparagus, coffee) cause a disagreeable urinary odor and can be eliminated from the diet to control odor. Patients should not be given "absolutes," but rather assisted in deciding what is worth eliminating versus what is really important or enjoyed.

These are for ongoing peer support.

These contacts help the patient with follow-up care and problem solving.

Travel away from home poses special concerns in terms of buying equipment, managing emergencies, and adjusting to different surroundings. Having a resource to call upon often eases these concerns.

These are required for insurance benefits.

(■ = Independent; ▲ = Collaborative)

Urinary Tract Infection

UTI; Pyelonephritis; Cystitis; Urethritis; Nephritis

Urinary tract infection (UTI) is an invasion of all or part of the urinary tract (kidneys, bladder, urethra) by pathogens. UTIs are usually caused by bacteria, most typically *Escherichia coli*, although viral and fungal organisms may also cause UTI. UTIs may begin as pathogens from the perineum and ascend through the urethra to the urinary bladder. UTIs are common nosocomial infections and often result following instrumentation (e.g., catheterization or diagnostic procedures of the genitourinary tract). UTIs are more common in women than men, particularly in sexually active, younger women. UTIs, which can be chronic and recurring, can lead to systemic infection such as urosepsis, which can be life-threatening. In older patients, diagnosis and treatment of UTIs may be delayed because UTI may be asymptomatic or accompanied by only subtle cognitive changes and urinary incontinence rather than the typical complaints of urgency, frequency, burning, and pain upon urination. If infections of the urinary tract are not treated effectively, renal damage and loss of renal function can occur. The focus of this care plan is care of any individual with a UTI in any setting.

Nursing Diagnosis

Infection

Common Related Factors

Instrumentation or catheterization
Indwelling catheter
Improper toileting
Pregnancy
Chronically alkaline urine
Stasis (urinary retention)

Defining Characteristics

Burning on urination
Frequency of urination
Foul-smelling urine
Fever
Suprapubic tenderness
Elevated white blood cell (WBC) count
Hematuria
Bacteriuria
Chills
Low back pain or flank pain
Fatigue
Anorexia
Cognitive changes (elderly)

Common Expected Outcome

Patient is free of UTI as evidenced by clear, non–foul-smelling urine; pain-free urination; normal WBC count; and absence of fever, chills, flank pain, and/or suprapubic pain.

NOC Outcomes

Infection Status; Medication Response; Urinary Elimination

NIC Interventions

Urinary Elimination Management; Teaching: Prescribed Medication; Fluid Management

■ = Independent; ▲ = Collaborative

Ongoing Assessment

Actions/Interventions

■ Assess for any history that would predispose the person to UTI.

■ Assess for signs and symptoms of UTI: frequency and burning or pain on urination, cloudy or bloody urine, complaints of lower abdominal pain or suprapubic pain. Assess for signs that kidneys are involved: flank or back pain.

▲ Assess laboratory data:
- Urinalysis: hematuria (presence of blood in the urine), pyuria (presence of pus [WBCs] in the urine)

- Bacteria count in urine

- Urine culture: causative organism

- WBC count

Rationale

History of UTIs, instrumentation, sexual activity, history of signs of sexually transmitted infections, previous surgeries of the genitourinary tract that may have resulted in scarring, and/or recent antibiotic therapy may all place the individual at increased risk for developing UTI.

It is important to note that patients with UTI may be asymptomatic, especially those with recurrent infection; in older patients who may not be cognitively capable of describing symptoms, a general change in behavior or decline in overall functional ability often heralds a UTI. Confusion and incontinence are often the only signs of UTI in the older adult.

These are signs of UTI.

Bacterial counts of 10^5 are usually considered diagnostic for UTI, although lower counts may also indicate UTI.

Identification of the causative organism is necessary for selecting the most effective antibiotic.

Presence of WBCs in the urine is an indication of UTI.

Therapeutic Interventions

Actions/Interventions

■ Encourage the patient to drink extra fluid.

■ Instruct the patient to void often (every 2 to 3 hours during the day) and to empty the bladder completely.

■ Suggest cranberry or prune juice, or vitamin C, 500 mg to 1000 mg/day.

■ Encourage the patient to finish all prescribed antibiotics; note effectiveness.

Rationale

Fluid promotes renal blood flow and flushes bacteria from the urinary tract; minimum fluid intake is 2 to 3 L/day.

This enhances bacterial clearance, reduces urine stasis, and prevents reinfection; voiding in an upright position can facilitate bladder emptying.

This acidifies urine; bacteria grow poorly in an acidic environment. Ideal urine pH is around 5. Cranberry juice has been shown to decrease bacterial adherence to the bladder wall. The juice may take several weeks to produce a therapeutic result.

Drugs may be used in combination (i.e., more than one antimicrobial at a time) to reduce development of resistance. The usual length of antibiotic therapy is 5 to 10 days; patients with pyelonephritis typically require a 3- or 4-day course of parenteral antibiotics to prevent bacteremia and sepsis. Long-term antibiotic therapy may be prescribed for patients with chronic UTIs.

■ = Independent; ▲ = Collaborative

Urinary Tract Infection—cont'd

 ## Nursing Diagnosis

Acute Pain

Common Related Factor	Defining Characteristics
Infection	Burning on urination Cramps or spasm in lower back and bladder area Facial mask of pain Guarding behavior Protective decreased physical activity

Common Expected Outcome	
Patient verbalizes relief of discomfort and pain or ability to tolerate pain.	**NOC Outcome** Pain Control **NIC Interventions** Heat/Cold Application; Pain Management

Ongoing Assessment

Actions/Interventions

■ Assess the patient's description of pain. Inquire as to the quality, nature, and severity of pain.

Rationale

Typically, pain associated with UTI is described as burning on urination. Patients may also experience lower abdominal or suprapubic pain. Patients with renal involvement (i.e., pyelonephritis) will have back or flank pain. Some patients are asymptomatic.

Therapeutic Interventions

Actions/Interventions

■ Apply a heating pad to the lower back.

■ Instruct the patient in use of a sitz bath.

▲ Encourage use of analgesics (e.g., acetaminophen) and/or antispasmodics (e.g., phenazopyridine), as prescribed.

■ Use distractions and relaxation techniques whenever appropriate.

See also **Acute Pain,** *p. 144.*

Rationale

This relieves back pain.

Sitz baths may reduce perineal itching and pain.

These relieve pain and spasms caused by UTI.

Complementary and alternative therapies provide non-pharmacological approaches to pain management.

■ = Independent; ▲ = Collaborative

Nursing Diagnosis

Risk for Ineffective Therapeutic Regimen Management

Common Risk Factor

Unfamiliarity with nature and treatment of UTI

Common Expected Outcome

Patient verbalizes knowledge of causes and treatment of UTI, controls risk factors, and completes medical treatment of UTI.

NOC Outcome
Knowledge: Treatment Regimen

NIC Interventions
Teaching: Disease Process;
Teaching: Prescribed Medication

Ongoing Assessment

Actions/Interventions

■ Assess knowledge of nature of UTI.

■ Assess factors the patient feels may interfere with compliance.

Rationale

Frequent recurrences of UTI may indicate that the patient does not understand risk factors or medical management of UTI.

Identifying barriers to the patient's ability to follow the treatment program allows for individualizing the plan of care.

Therapeutic Interventions

Actions/Interventions

■ Provide health teaching. Teach the patient:
  • Need for follow-up urine cultures
  • Need for frequent bladder emptying

  • Hygienic measures; showering is preferable to tub bathing
  • Wiping from front to back

  • Need to void immediately after sexual intercourse
  • Need for changing underpants daily and wearing well-ventilated clothing (e.g., cotton underpants, cotton-crotched pantyhose) and avoidance of tight or constricting underwear or pants.
■ Encourage patients on long-term antimicrobial therapy to take medications before bedtime.
■ Encourage reporting of signs and symptoms of recurrence.

Rationale

This reduces recurrence of infection.

These determine effectiveness of the antimicrobial therapy.

Voiding at first urge prevents stasis of urine in the bladder and minimizes the opportunity for bacterial growth.

This decreases concentration of pathogens.

This prevents the introduction of enteric pathogens into the urethra.

Voiding clears urethra of pathogens.

Synthetic materials harbor moisture and provide a medium for perineal bacterial growth.

This ensures overnight concentration of drug.

One to 2 weeks after completion of a course of antimicrobial therapy is a common time frame for signs and symptoms to recur.

■ = Independent; ▲ = Collaborative

10

Men's Health Care Plans

Benign prostatic hyperplasia (BPH) is a common urologic disorder in men, and its incidence is age related. The prevalence rises from approximately 20% in men 41 to 50 years of age to 50% in men 51 to 60 years of age, then to more than 90% in men 80 years of age and older. BPH is an overgrowth of muscle and connective tissue (hyperplasia) of the prostate gland. As the glandular tissue enlarges, it causes obstruction of the urethra. Severity of symptoms may be ranked according to the American Urological Symptom Index. Early diagnosis and staging have improved with the availability of prostate ultrasound technology. Treatment options include medications that cause either regression of overgrown tissue or relaxation of the urethral muscle tissue; nonsurgical treatment including direct heat application, dilatation, laser, or placement of stents to allow drainage; and surgical treatment to remove prostate tissue. The focus of this care plan is the patient with newly diagnosed BPH.

NDx Nursing Diagnosis

Urinary Retention

Common Related Factor

Urethral blockage

Defining Characteristics

Sensation of bladder fullness
Frequency
Incomplete bladder emptying
Dribbling at the end of a void

Common Expected Outcome

Patient has unobstructed flow of urine, either by medications, catheterization, after medical or noninvasive therapies, or after surgical removal of hyperplastic prostatic tissue.

NOC Outcome
Urinary Elimination

NIC Interventions
Urinary Catheterization;
    Urinary Elimination Management

Ongoing Assessment

Actions/Interventions

- Assess urinary elimination; inquire about symptoms, which include difficulty starting a stream, dribbling at the end of a void, nocturia, frequency, straining to void, and feeling of incomplete emptying of the bladder.
- Assess history of urinary tract infections (UTIs).

- Assess the effects of BPH according to the American Urological Association's Symptom Score for BPH (Table 10-1).
- Assess pain discomfort.

- Palpate the abdomen for distended bladder.
- Assess postvoid residual urine.

- Assess intake and output, noting the amount and frequency of voids.
- Assess for hematuria.

- ▲ Review radiographs or ultrasound findings.

Rationale

The male urethra is surrounded by the prostate gland. When the prostate gland is enlarged as a result of prostatic hyperplasia, the urethra is compressed; symptoms are a result of the decreased caliber of the urethra.

Because the flow of urine is chronically obstructed, stasis of urine occurs and infections are common.

This tool provides serial objective measurements of symptom severity.

Pain may be related to concurrent urinary tract infection, residual urine, or bladder distention.

Urinary retention is a key symptom.

Data aid in detection of urinary stasis and impaired detrusor function.

Data give clues to completion of bladder emptying.

Hematuria can result from distention of the bladder with resultant rupture of small blood vessels.

Hydroureters (distended ureters) and hydronephrosis (enlarged, overdistended kidneys) may result from longstanding obstruction caused by prostatic disease.

Therapeutic Interventions

Actions/Interventions

- Encourage oral fluids for adequate hydration, but do not push fluids or overhydrate.

- ▲ Prepare the patient for the possible need for an indwelling catheter to restore flow of urine. NOTE: Special catheters with curved or firm tips may be needed to accomplish catheterization in the patient with an enlarged prostate.
- Encourage the patient to take antibiotics as prescribed.

- Encourage the patient to take medications to reduce prostate size and improve urinary flow.

Rationale

Rapid filling of the bladder can precipitate complete urinary retention. Overhydration can aggravate problem of residual urine and bladder distention.

Indwelling catheterization is used to allow free drainage of the bladder. Chronic urinary obstruction can result in severe damage to the kidneys and, ultimately, renal failure.

Medication may be indicated to treat or prevent UTI resulting from obstruction and stasis.

Prostate size can be reduced with a 5α-reductase inhibitor such as finasteride and dutasteride. These drugs inhibit production of the hormone dihydrotestosterone (DHT), which enhances prostate growth. A class of α-blocking agents—terazosin, doxazosin, tamsulosin, and alfuzosin—all relax musculature within the bladder neck and improve urinary flow. Using both classes of drugs together alleviates more symptoms and prevents the progression of BPH.

Benign Prostatic Hyperplasia (BPH)

■ = Independent; ▲ = Collaborative

Benign Prostatic Hyperplasia (BPH)—cont'd

Table 10-1. The American Urological Association's Symptom Score for Benign Prostatic Hyperplasia (BPH)*

	Not at all	Less than 1 time in 5 times	Less than half of the time	About half of the time	More than half of the time	Almost always
During the past month or so, how often did you have the feeling of not having completely emptied your bladder after urinating?	0	1	2	3	4	5
During the past month or so, how often did you have to urinate again less than 2 hours after you finished urinating?	0	1	2	3	4	5
During the past month or so, how often did you have to stop and start the urinary stream several times while urinating?	0	1	2	3	4	5
During the past month or so, how often did you find it difficult to delay urination?	0	1	2	3	4	5
During the past month or so, how often did you find that your urinary stream was weak?	0	1	2	3	4	5
During the past month or so, how often did you have to push or strain to begin urinating?	0	1	2	3	4	5
Frequency of Waking Up to Urinate						
During the past month or so, how often did you typically get up to urinate between going to bed in the evening and waking up in the morning?	0	1 (one time)	2 (two times)	3 (three times)	4 (four times)	5 (five times or more)

Modified from Barry MJ, Fowler FJ, O'Leary MP, et al. The American Urological Association Symptom Index for benign prostatic hyperplasia. *J Urol* 148:1549, 1992.
* 0 = Not at all; 1 = less than 1 time in 5 times; 2 = less than half of the time; 3 = about half of the time; 4 = more than half of the time; 5 = almost always.
Score key:
Mild = 0 to 7 points; moderate = 8 to 9 points; severe = 20 to 35 points.

NDx Nursing Diagnosis

Deficient Knowledge

Common Related Factor	**Defining Characteristics**
Newly diagnosed prostate disorder	Multiple questions Lack of questions Stated misconceptions or confusion regarding diagnosis and treatment options

■ = Independent; ▲ = Collaborative

Common Expected Outcome

Patient is able to verbalize understanding of diagnostic procedures and treatment options for BPH.

NOC Outcomes
Knowledge: Disease Process;
Knowledge: Treatment Regimen

NIC Interventions
Teaching: Disease Process;
Teaching: Procedures/Treatment

Ongoing Assessment

Actions/Interventions

■ Assess the patient's understanding of prostate disorders and the following commonly performed diagnostic procedures for prostate disorders:

• Digital rectal examination (DRE)

• Uroflowmetry

• Cystourethroscopy

• Urinalysis

• Laboratory studies: blood urea nitrogen (BUN) and creatinine; prostate-specific antigen (PSA)

• Prostate ultrasound

■ Assess the patient's understanding of the following treatment options for prostate disorders:
Medical management:
• Medications

Minimally invasive therapies for BPH:

• Dilatation of the urethra

Rationale

Men are often embarrassed or hesitant to discuss prostate problems and often delay seeking attention for symptoms for which onset is typically gradual.

The American Urological Association recommends that men older than 50 years of age should have an annual DRE for the purpose of prostate palpation.

Urodynamic flow studies include determination of flow rate and evaluation of residual urine.

Visualization of the bladder and urethra through a fiber-optic scope allows the physician to see the extent of enlargement and consequent obstruction.

Examination of the urine for presence of blood, white blood cells (WBCs), and/or bacteria is useful in the identification of UTI, which often accompanies obstruction that causes stasis of urine.

BUN and creatinine determine renal function, which can be impaired as a result of longstanding obstructive uropathy. PSA is used to differentiate BPH from prostate enlargement due to cancer.

This ultrasound is performed rectally using a wand-type ultrasound before examining the prostate gland for enlargement.

These may include hormone manipulation or use of smooth muscle relaxers that relax the prostatic urethra. Drugs that block androgens (e.g., finasteride [Proscar]) and α-adrenergic blockers, which relax the urethra (e.g., doxazosin [Cardura] and terazosin [Hytrin]), may be used. The most recent drug advances (e.g., tamsulosin [Flomax]) block α-receptors, which are localized in the prostate and bladder neck; these result in an increase in urinary flow with fewer side effects.

Newer minimally invasive procedures are available; however, no long-term data are available as yet for some of them.

Dilatation enhances urine flow.

Benign Prostatic Hyperplasia (BPH)

■ = Independent; ▲ = Collaborative

Benign Prostatic Hyperplasia (BPH)—cont'd

Actions/Interventions	Rationale
• Placement of urethral stents	These small tubes allow for drainage of urine by pushing back the prostatic urethra. They are used for poor operative-risk patients.
• Transurethral vaporization of the prostate	This vaporization procedure has reduced bleeding complications.
• Transurethral microwave therapy	Several techniques can be employed to heat and destroy excess prostatic tissue and reduce compression of the urethra.
• Transurethral needle ablation	Low-level radio frequency energy using needles is delivered to burn away designated areas of the enlarged prostate.
Surgical management for BPH:	Several surgical approaches are available.
• Transurethral resection of the prostate (TURP)	This "closed" procedure is widely used to treat BPH and remains the gold standard for evaluating newer therapies. The surgeon removes the prostate by inserting a resectoscope through the urethra to remove obstructing tissue. The TURP is significantly less traumatic than open forms of surgery.
• Suprapubic prostatectomy • Retropubic prostatectomy • Perineal prostatectomy	These three procedures are "open" surgical procedures using a variety of approaches. They are used when the prostatic tissue is very enlarged, or when the bladder needs repair.
• Laser-assisted surgery	This newer procedure uses a laser to make the incision into the prostate.

Therapeutic Interventions

Actions/Interventions	Rationale
■ Discuss with the patient the advantages and disadvantages of medical and surgical treatment options.	Many factors affect selection of optimal treatment, including severity of symptoms, ability to tolerate medication side effects, medical contraindications to surgery, and concern for postoperative erectile dysfunction.
■ Provide the patient with postprocedure instructions about signs and symptoms to be reported, including:	Early assessment of complications facilitates prompt treatment.
• Hematuria	In the first few weeks after TURP, some bleeding is expected. However, thick red urine or clots must be reported.
• Infection	Urinary instrumentation and surgical incisions carry risk of sepsis.
• Unresolved incontinence or retention	Temporary incontinence is common until healing has occurred. Retention is also common after urethral catheterization.
■ Discuss PSA testing.	Controversies exist over routine PSA testing due to the number of false-positive results. Rising levels of PSA can be an indication of an enlarging prostate or prostate cancer.
■ Teach about the need for annual prostate examination.	Existing prostatic tissue could become cancerous. One treatment does not reduce future risk for prostate disease.

■ = Independent; ▲ = Collaborative

Actions/Interventions

- Teach about behavioral methods to reduce symptom severity or reduce occurrence or aggravation of symptoms.
  - Limit fluid intake after dinner.
  - Avoid medications known to worsen urinary symptoms such as cold preparations, diuretics, antispasmodics, antihistamines, and some antidepressants.
- Discuss any prior experience in taking over-the-counter herbs such as saw palmetto extract to relieve symptoms.

- Provide Internet resources for further education.

Rationale

This can help avoid nocturia and interrupted sleep

These may precipitate acute urinary retention or worsen existing symptoms.

This extract has the most evidence to date for use in treating symptoms in men with mild disease. Further research is ongoing.

The National Cancer Institute and the National Kidney and Urologic Disease Information Clearing House offer excellent materials.

NDx Nursing Diagnosis

Risk for Deficient Fluid Volume

Common Risk Factor

Postoperative hemorrhage from transurethral resection of the prostate

Common Expected Outcome

Patient maintains normal fluid volume as evidenced by stable blood pressure (BP), heart rate (HR), and absence of gross hematuria.

NOC Outcomes
Urinary Elimination; Fluid Balance

NIC Interventions
Bladder Irrigation; Bleeding Reduction; Tube Care: Urinary

Benign Prostatic Hyperplasia (BPH)

Ongoing Assessment

Actions/Interventions

- Monitor for decreased BP, orthostatic BP, and increased HR.
- Monitor amount and severity of hematuria and clots in the urine.

- Monitor intake and output.

 Monitor hemoglobin and hematocrit.

Rationale

Changes can alert to fluid deficit.

Bright red blood in the urine is expected over the first 24 hours after transurethral resection but should irrigate to clear pink without clots during that period.

Intake and output should include careful record of any irrigation fluid instilled.

Decreases indicate significant blood loss.

■ = Independent; ▲ = Collaborative

Benign Prostatic Hyperplasia (BPH)—cont'd

Therapeutic Interventions

Actions/Interventions

▲ Perform closed bladder irrigation (continuous or intermittent) as prescribed.

■ Position tubing and collection system in a gravity-dependent fashion.

▲ If catheter obstruction is suspected, irrigate the catheter manually with a small amount of normal saline solution as prescribed; do not irrigate against resistance.

▲ If bleeding occurs, administer intravenous (IV) fluids as prescribed.

■ Encourage oral fluids as prescribed or tolerated by the patient.

Rationale

Irrigation of the bladder through an indwelling catheter using normal saline solution is done postoperatively to remove clots and to wash away debris that has been resected. Irrigation is necessary until urine is clear and debris is absent, usually 24 to 72 hours postoperatively.

This ensures drainage away from the patient and prevents clotting; clots in the bladder can predispose to further hemorrhage.

The surgeon should be notified to assess the level of obstruction.

Fluid therapy restores fluid balance.

Fluid therapy restores fluid balance.

> **• RELATED CARE PLANS**
>
> Disturbed sleep pattern, p. 177
> Impaired urinary elimination, p. 201
> Ineffective sexuality patterns, p. 170
> Risk for infection, p. 108

Prostate Cancer

Radical Prostatectomy

Prostate cancer is the most common non–skin cancer among males in the United States. There has been a significant increase in prostate cancer findings since the introduction of the recommended blood screening of prostate-specific antigen (PSA). More than 75% of prostate cancers are diagnosed in men older than 65 years of age. With prostate cancer, the patient is generally asymptomatic until obstructive symptoms of the urinary tract appear. Medical and surgical options depend on the stage of the cancer, symptoms, and response to other therapies. Treatment may include a radical prostatectomy, orchiectomy (surgical removal of the testes because prostate cancer grows more rapidly in the presence of the male hormone androgen), radiation, drug therapy, and newer laparoscopic radical prostatectomy procedures. There are three approaches for a radical prostatectomy for cancer: suprapubic, retropubic, and perineal. The approach depends on several factors, such as coexisting bladder abnormalities, size of the prostate, and degree of risk of the surgical candidate. Each procedure has its advantages and disadvantages. The focus of this care plan is for the patient undergoing a radical prostatectomy.

■ = Independent; ▲ = Collaborative

NDx Nursing Diagnosis

Anxiety

Common Related Factor

Lack of knowledge about diagnosis, treatment, and prognosis

Defining Characteristics

Fearfulness
Feelings of helplessness
Restlessness
Worried behavior
Expressed concerns

Common Expected Outcome

Patient demonstrates positive coping mechanisms.

NOC Outcomes

Anxiety Self-Control; Coping

NIC Interventions

Anxiety Reduction; Presence; Calming Techniques; Emotional Support

Prostate Cancer

Ongoing Assessment

Actions/Interventions	Rationale
■ Assess level of anxiety as mild, moderate, or severe.	The threat to health, life, and role function resulting from cancer can predispose the patient to anxiety.
■ Determine factors affecting anxiety.	Many misconceptions exist regarding prognosis, treatments, and potential complications such as sexual dysfunction. Accurate assessment data about the source of the patient's concern guide appropriate treatments and supportive coping strategies.
■ Determine the patient's support systems.	In some cases, there may be no readily available resources. Evaluation of supportive persons from the past may provide the assistance required at this time.
■ Determine the patient's coping methods.	These determine the effectiveness of coping strategies currently used by the patient.

Therapeutic Interventions

Actions/Interventions	Rationale
■ Give the patient opportunity to ask questions or verbalize concerns.	Men's concerns may include fear of death, feelings of loss of control, questions regarding determination of appropriate treatment, and how diagnosis and treatment may affect relationships with significant other.
■ Provide education about diagnosis and treatment plan.	Education decreases anxiety and promotes cooperation.
■ Provide information about institutional and community resources for coping with the diagnosis.	The increased public awareness of prostate cancer has resulted in a variety of lay and professional books and Internet sites for information. Social services, support groups, and community agencies can help the patient cope with his illness and treatments.

■ = Independent; ▲ = Collaborative

Prostate Cancer—cont'd

Actions/Interventions

▲ Administer pharmacological agents to decrease anxiety.

Rationale

Medication may be used if anxiety becomes disabling.

NDx Nursing Diagnosis

Risk for Infection

Common Risk Factors

Surgical resection
Instrumentation
Open incision
Indwelling catheter
Bladder irrigation
Wound drains (e.g., Penrose, Jackson-Pratt)
Altered immune system secondary to malignancy

Common Expected Outcome

Patient remains free of infection as evidenced by normal temperature; clear urine; and clean, dry, healing incisions.

NOC Outcome
Infection Status

NIC Interventions
Infection Protection; Tube Care: Urinary

Ongoing Assessment

Actions/Interventions

■ Assess the patient's understanding of the following surgical interventions for cancer of the prostate:
  • Suprapubic resection

  • Retropubic resection

  • Perineal resection

  • Orchiectomy

■ Assess incision for redness, swelling, pain, and purulent drainage.

Rationale

Each procedure carries its own risk for infection.

An abdominal incision that extends through the bladder is used to remove the prostate gland completely.

This is the most commonly performed procedure. A low abdominal incision is made, but the bladder is not opened. The prostate gland is completely removed; this approach also allows for removal of lymph nodes, if necessary. It reduces risk for erectile dysfunction.

An incision is made in the perineum; the prostate gland is removed through the perineal incision. It is associated with a reduced risk for urinary incontinence.

The testes are surgically removed to eliminate the production of androgens, upon which prostate cancer is dependent for growth.

These are signs of local wound infection.

■ = Independent; ▲ = Collaborative

Men's Health Care Plans

Actions/Interventions

■ Monitor color and odor of urine.

▲ Obtain culture of cloudy, foul-smelling urine.

▲ Monitor urinalysis for presence of white blood cells (WBCs).

■ Monitor temperature.

Rationale

Cloudy, foul-smelling urine may be infected.

Culture determines which pathogens are present and guides antimicrobial therapy.

This is an indication of urinary tract infection.

A temperature of up to 38.5°C (101.3°F) for 48 to 72 hours postprocedure is expected. A higher temperature may indicate infection.

Therapeutic Interventions

Actions/Interventions

■ Maintain sterile, closed urinary drainage or irrigation system.

■ Change dressings using aseptic technique.

■ Provide and encourage intake of high-protein, high-calorie diet.

■ Provide meatal care every shift.

▲ Administer antibiotics and antipyretics as prescribed.

Rationale

This prevents bacterial invasion of compromised urinary tract.

Dressings reduce pathogens at the surgical incision.

This promotes healing.

This reduces pathogens at the site of the catheter entrance.

Medications reduce pathogen growth and reduce fever.

NDx Nursing Diagnosis

Acute Pain

Common Related Factors

Bladder spasm
Surgical incision
Surgical drains

Common Expected Outcome

Patient verbalizes absence of pain or spasms, or ability to tolerate discomfort.

Defining Characteristics

Verbal reports of pain or spasm
Facial grimacing
Escape of urine from around catheter
Pulling or tugging at catheter

NOC Outcomes
Pain Control; Pain Level

NIC Interventions
Pain Management; Tube Care: Urinary

Ongoing Assessment

Actions/Interventions

■ Assess severity, location, and quality of pain.

Rationale

The most severe pain after prostate surgery is caused by spasm of the bladder, which the patient is usually able to differentiate from incisional pain; spasms are typically described as intense suprapubic squeezing discomfort.

■ = Independent; ▲ = Collaborative

Prostate Cancer

Prostate Cancer—cont'd

Actions/Interventions

■ Assess concurrence of spasms or pain with irrigation or catheter care.

Rationale

Manipulation of catheter or activity by the patient can stimulate painful bladder spasms.

Therapeutic Interventions

Actions/Interventions

▲ Anticipate the need for analgesics and antispasmodics (e.g., belladonna and opium suppositories).

■ Maintain traction on the catheter.

■ Teach and encourage use of splinting the incision.

■ Stabilize other tubes or drains, such as Penrose or other space drains.

Rationale

One can most effectively deal with pain by preventing it. Early intervention may prevent peak pain periods.

Traction prevents movement that can stimulate spasm. Traction can be accomplished by taping the catheter securely to the patient's upper thigh, or by using commercially available catheter straps.

This minimizes incisional pain during movement and coughing.

This minimizes inadvertent movement.

 Nursing Diagnosis

Risk for Sexual Dysfunction

Common Risk Factors

Injury to perineal nerves during surgery
Presence of indwelling urinary catheter
Incontinence following removal of catheter

Common Expected Outcome

Patient or significant other is able to discuss concerns about sexual functioning.

NOC Outcome
Sexual Functioning

NIC Intervention
Sexual Counseling

Ongoing Assessment

Actions/Interventions

■ Assess the patient's and significant other's expectations for sexual function.

■ Assess the patient's and significant other's understanding of the potential impact that surgery may have had on sexual functioning.

Rationale

Although many men undergoing prostatectomy are older, do not assume that sexual functioning is unimportant.

A discussion of the possible negative impact of prostatectomy on sexual functioning should occur preoperatively, but often the patient is too anxious or preoccupied with other information (e.g., fear about

■ = Independent; ▲ = Collaborative

Actions/Interventions

Rationale

surgery, prognosis with cancer diagnosis) to comprehend fully. If this is the case, the patient may benefit
from postoperative discussion. Not all patients who
have had prostatectomy have sexual dysfunction.
Perineal resection carries the highest risk for sexual
dysfunction. Orchiectomy renders the patient sterile,
but not necessarily impotent. Newer nerve-sparing
surgical procedures are becoming available and may
be an option for some men.

■ Assess whether the patient and significant other need
or want information during the postoperative period
or if they prefer to wait a few weeks.

Timing of patient readiness to learn should guide the
teaching plan. At a minimum, written materials can
be given to the patient.

■ Assess for urinary incontinence after removal of the
catheter.

The psychological impact of urinary incontinence can
negatively impact the patient's perceived ability to
perform sexually. Dribbling may occur for as long as
a few months after prostatectomy and catheter removal.

Therapeutic Interventions

Actions/Interventions

Rationale

■ Teach the patient which nerves are necessary for erection
and ejaculation; distinguish between sterility and impotence. Clarify all language; use diagrams and models
as needed, depending on the patient's learning style.

Patients may be embarrassed to ask questions that highlight a limited knowledge base; however, many misconceptions may exist.

■ Offer the patient and significant other suggestions for
alternatives to usual sexual practices during the postoperative period.

Usual sexual activity can be resumed 4 to 6 weeks after
surgery. Medications such as 5-phosphodiesterase
(5PDE, such as sildenafil) or intraurethral alprostadil
may be given to maintain blood flow to the corpora
cavernosa during recovery.

■ Inform the patient that retrograde ejaculation often
occurs after prostatectomy.

Retrograde ejaculation means that ejaculate goes into
the bladder rather than into the urethra; this is harmless and results in a cloudy discoloration of the urine.
This is of no consequence in terms of sexual performance or satisfaction.

■ Discuss urinary incontinence as a consequence of prostatectomy; teach Kegel exercises.

Dribbling may occur for months and then resolve. Kegel
exercises will increase sphincter tone needed to achieve
continence. They should be performed at each time of
urination and several times throughout the day. Occasionally, incontinence after prostatectomy is permanent.

▲ Refer for sexual counseling as indicated.

Specialty therapy may be indicated for some patients

NDx Nursing Diagnosis

Deficient Knowledge, Postoperative

Common Related Factors

Need for home management
Lack of previous experience with prostate surgery

Defining Characteristics

Questions
Lack of questions
Verbalized misconceptions

■ = Independent; ▲ = Collaborative

Prostate Cancer

Prostate Cancer–cont'd

Common Expected Outcome

Patient verbalizes understanding of need for follow-up care, wound care, and management of incontinence and/or erectile dysfunction.

NOC Outcomes
Knowledge: Disease Process;
Knowledge: Treatment Procedures

NIC Interventions
Wound Care; Teaching: Disease Process

Ongoing Assessment

Actions/Interventions

- Assess understanding of need for follow-up care:
  - Patients who have had incomplete prostatectomy remain at risk for developing prostate cancer.

  - Further treatment (e.g., chemotherapy, radiation therapy) may be needed in patients who have had surgery to remove prostatic cancer, who have had orchiectomy to remove prostatic cancer, or who have had orchiectomy to remove the glands that produce hormones on which prostatic cancers are dependent.
- Assess ability to care for surgical wounds.
- Assess understanding of potential dribbling and methods for improving and dealing with incontinence.
- Assess knowledge of resources for erectile dysfunction (ED).

Rationale

This is because management of benign prostatic hyperplasia does not alter the possibility of later development of cancer of the prostate.

These treatments are part of the overall management to eliminate cancer cells that were not removed at surgery.

Infection is a common complication.

The extent of the problem depends on the type of resection performed.

ED may occur as a complication of prostate surgery. ED may not have been a problem in the past; thus the patient may be unaware of available resources.

Therapeutic Interventions

Actions/Interventions

- Teach wound care:
  - Suprapubic and retropubic wounds

  - Perineal wounds

- Teach the patient the following about incontinence:
  - Remind the patient that urinary incontinence may resolve up to 1 year postoperatively.

Rationale

Stitches or staples are usually removed 7 to 10 days postoperatively. Daily cleaning of the wounds with soap and water is sufficient.

Stitches or staples are usually removed 7 to 10 days postoperatively; these wounds, however, remain tender longer than abdominal wounds because of their location. They are also at higher risk for infection because of proximity to the anus. Warm sitz baths or tub baths once or twice daily are recommended until the wound has healed completely and soreness is gone.

This knowledge may reduce anxiety and may help the patient with decision making about management of urinary elimination.

■ = Independent; ▲ = Collaborative

Actions/Interventions	**Rationale**
• Encourage use of Kegel exercises.	These exercises improve perineal musculature and control over the urinary stream. They need to be performed several times throughout the day.
• Refer the patient to a self-help incontinence group if incontinence is a problem.	Relationships with persons with common issues can be beneficial.
• Instruct the patient regarding self-care and temporary use of an indwelling catheter, if needed.	Some patients are discharged with an indwelling catheter still in place.
■ Teach the patient to report any of the following:	Early assessment facilitates prompt treatment.
• Signs of infection: fever; unusual drainage from incisions; unusual drainage from the urethra, especially in patients having transurethral resection	
• Signs of urinary tract infection (cloudy, foul-smelling urine; frequency)	
• Hematuria	
• Unresolved incontinence	
• Bone pain	Bone pain may indicate metastatic cancer in patients with prostate cancer.
■ Encourage the patient to seek help for erectile dysfunction, as appropriate.	Change in sexual function may have an adverse effect on the couple's relationship. Specialists are needed for complex situations.

> **• RELATED CARE PLANS**
>
> Erectile dysfunction (see the **Evolve** website)
> Impaired urinary elimination, p. 201

Sexually Transmitted Infections (STIs)

Sexually transmitted infections (STIs) are infections that occur as a result of contact with an infected person. Although most cases of STI are associated with sexual activity, some can be transmitted through contact with infected blood. The incidence of specific STIs has changed over time. Some infections have reached epidemic proportions among specific cohorts of the population. Many factors have contributed to the rise in types of STIs and the number of people infected in the United States. These contributing factors include ease of travel, increased population mobility, changes in cultural and social norms about sexual activity and marriage, changes in women's roles, more explicit sexual content in the popular media, and decreased use of barrier methods of contraception, such as condoms. Research indicates a strong correlation between the incidence of STI and drug abuse. Many drug abusers, especially women, trade sex for drugs. Many times, STIs occur with other STIs. That is, when a patient presents with one STI, there is a higher risk that he or she will have others. This care plan describes the most common STIs: chlamydia, gonorrhea, syphilis, genital herpes, and genital warts, along with trichomoniasis and chancroid.

Sexually Transmitted Infections (STIs)

■ = Independent; ▲ = Collaborative

Sexually Transmitted Infections (STIs)—cont'd

 Nursing Diagnosis

Deficient Knowledge

Common Related Factors

New diagnosis of STI
Information, misinformation, or misinterpretation of diagnosis
Lack of exposure
Fear of AIDS (acquired immunodeficiency syndrome)
Embarrassment about topic

Defining Characteristics

Multiple questions
Lack of questions
Inaccurate follow-through of previous instruction
Inappropriate or exaggerated behaviors (e.g., hysteria, hostility, agitation, or apathy)

Common Expected Outcome

Patient verbalizes understanding of the disease process, transmission, complications, and treatment modalities.

NOC Outcomes
Knowledge: Disease Process;
Knowledge: Treatment Regimen

NIC Interventions
Crisis Intervention; Learning Facilitation;
Teaching: Individual

Ongoing Assessment

Actions/Interventions

■ Assess the patient's readiness to learn about the specific STI.

■ Assess barriers to learning.

■ Determine the patient's previous knowledge of the disease process, routes of transmission, complications, and treatment modalities.

■ Determine the patient's understanding of medical terminology as well as slang or lay terms.

Rationale

Some patients are ready to learn immediately after receiving the diagnosis; others cope by delaying the need for instruction.

While patients may have their own personal barriers (e.g., guilt, embarrassment), health care professionals may themselves be uncomfortable in eliciting key information or in providing required information.

Information is assimilated into previous assumptions and facts. Patients may have misconceptions about disease transmission and treatment. Patients may not be knowledgeable about the long-term risks and effects of STIs.

It is important to speak in terms the patient understands. Accurate information about sex and STIs is not always easily available to younger patients. Material must be presented at the educational and developmental level of each individual.

■ = Independent; ▲ = Collaborative

Actions/Interventions

- Determine sexual orientation, number of sexual partners, and recent sexual activities in a non-judgmental manner.

Rationale

STIs are spread during homosexual and heterosexual activity. Risks increase with the number of lifetime sexual partners. Judgmental attitudes may preclude patients from following through with a treatment plan.

Therapeutic Interventions

Actions/Interventions

- Teach the medication regimen to include the name of the drug, dosage, administration, side effects, and action of the prescribed medication.

- Review basic hygiene before topical administration of drugs (e.g., wash lesions with soap and water, keep area dry, wear loose-fitting cotton undergarments).

- Discuss the importance of notifying all sexual partners.

- Instruct the patient about scheduling appointments and treatments.

- Instruct the female patient regarding the importance of yearly gynecological examinations with Papanicolaou (Pap) smears.

- Instruct patients in safe methods of preventing STI transmission:
  - Kissing
  - Touching
  - Mutual masturbation
  - Oral sex with latex condom

- Instruct in use of latex male condom.

- Discuss the benefits of monogamous relationships.

Rationale

Effective treatment requires that the patient complete prescribed medications to prevent reinfection.

Basic hygiene of lesions helps prevent further contamination. Cotton products decrease perspiration.

This decreases the chance of reinfection and of further spread of the disease. In most states, STIs are reportable diseases. Public health workers will contact sexual partners for testing and treatment.

Follow-up testing is necessary to prove eradication of certain STIs.

These are excellent screening tools.

These methods are considered "safe" in preventing STIs because there is no exchange of infected body fluids between sexual partners.

Latex male condoms, when used consistently and correctly, can reduce the risk of transmission of most STIs.

The surest way to avoid transmission of STIs is to abstain from sexual contact, or to be in a long-term mutually monogamous relationship with a partner who has been tested and is known to be uninfected.

Sexually Transmitted Infections (STIs)

NDx Nursing Diagnosis

Infection

Common Related Factors	Defining Characteristics
Inadequate primary defenses	Urethral discharge
Tissue destruction	Genital lesions
Extension of infection	Fever
Sexual exposure	Malaise
Insufficient knowledge to avoid exposure	Dysuria
	Enlarged lymph nodes

■ = Independent; ▲ = Collaborative

Sexually Transmitted Infections (STIs)—cont'd

Common Expected Outcome

Patient has a decrease in or complete resolution of symptoms of infection.

NOC Outcome
Infection Status

NIC Interventions
Infection Control; Infection Protection

Ongoing Assessment

Actions/Interventions

- Assess for signs and symptoms associated with specific STIs:
  - Vaginal or penile discharge
  - Dysuria
  - Genital lesions
  - Abdominal pain

- Assess for general signs and symptoms of infection:
  - Fever
  - Malaise
  - Lymphadenopathy
- Identify those at risk (e.g., sexual partners, persons who share drug needles).
- Assess individual risk factors for reactivation of disease process.

Rationale

Urethral inflammation is a common symptom in men with STI. The discharge may be purulent. Men will often complain of pain and burning with urination. In women, yeast infections such as trichomoniasis usually present with malodorous vaginal discharge and vulvar itching. The characteristics of genital lesions vary with specific STIs.

Some STIs, such as genital herpes, may be associated with general symptoms of infection. Enlarged lymph nodes may occur in the inguinal area in many of the STIs.

Those exposed may require treatment to prevent the spread or development of the infection.

Recurrence of genital warts or genital herpes is common.

Therapeutic Interventions

Actions/Interventions

- Provide information about the pertinent STI.
  - *Chlamydia trachomatis* infection is the most common STI. Symptoms range from none to dysuria, to purulent vaginal or penile discharge, to pelvic inflammatory disease (PID) in women. Treatment includes course of antibiotic therapy. Latex male condoms may prevent transmission. Sexual partners must be notified and treated. This is a mandatory reportable STI.
  - Gonorrhea is caused by the *Neisseria gonorrhoeae* organism, which produces vaginal discharge, abnormal uterine bleeding, and PID. If the infection is acquired during menstruation, the risk of dissemination increases. It can affect joints and skin, causing arthralgias and skin lesions. Treatment includes a course of antibiotics, partner notification with treatment, as well as mandatory reporting to the state. Prevention may be acquired through consistent and correct condom usage.

Rationale

There is a wide range of STIs that can confuse the public. Each has its own infective organism and pattern of symptoms. Diagnosis varies depending on the specific STI. Diagnostic aids include history, physical examination, Pap smears, serology testing, and tissue cultures and stains. For many infections the definitive diagnostic test has yet to be developed. Treatment is based on Centers for Disease Control and Prevention (CDC) guidelines.

■ = Independent; ▲ = Collaborative

Men's Health Care Plans

Actions/Interventions	**Rationale**

- Syphilis is caused by *Treponema pallidum*. Sexual transmission occurs only in the presence of muco-cutaneous lesions. Syphilis is easy to cure in its early stages, with penicillin being the treatment of choice.
- Genital herpes is an incurable and recurrent viral infection caused by the herpes simplex virus (HSV). HSV causes painful genital lesions that start as papules or vesicles. Treatment includes systemic antiviral therapy, which may control the signs and symptoms but does not cure the disease. Genital herpes may be transmitted even when no lesions are present, contrary to previously held beliefs. Even though condoms may help prevent some disease transmission, they are not fail-safe due to the location of the lesions.
- Genital warts are caused by human papillomavirus (HPV) infection. There are many strains of HPV, some of which are associated with cervical dysplasia. Visible genital warts are dominated by HPV strains 6 and 11. Clinically, genital warts are nonpainful and asymptomatic. Treatment consists of using anti-mitotic gels or immune-enhancing cream for removal. Even though treatments may eliminate the warts, it does not erase infectivity.
- Although trichomoniasis occurs in both men and women, it is one of the most common STIs in women, characterized by malodorous vaginal discharge and vulvar irritation and/or itching. The offending organism is *Trichomonas vaginalis*, which responds to treatment with oral metronidazole. Persons taking this drug must be cautioned against alcohol intake during and several days after treatment. In men, symptoms range from asymptomatic carriers to urethritis to prostatitis.
- Chancroid is an acute ulcerative disease caused by *Haemophilus ducreyi*, a gram-negative bacillus. Some patients with chancroid are also infected with *T. pallidum* or HSV. These infections are associated with an increased rate of human immunodeficiency virus (HIV) transmission. Recommended treatment is with azithromycin or ceftriaxone.

■ Teach about use of antiinfective agents as indicated:

Extended therapy may be indicated for reactivation of disease process, or in the presence of other medical diseases such as HIV infection. The reader is referred to the CDC website for the most current treatment guidelines for STIs.

- Acyclovir, famciclovir, valacyclovir

These antivirals are the primary treatment for genital herpes. They may be given orally or be used topically for mild disease. Intravenous administration is recommended for severe disease and recurrent lesions. Long-term use at lower dosages is suggested to reduce transmission to partners.

Sexually Transmitted Infections (STIs)

■ = Independent; ▲ = Collaborative

Sexually Transmitted Infections (STIs)—cont'd

Actions/Interventions	Rationale
• Penicillin	Penicillin is the treatment of choice for syphilis. It can be given as a single intramuscular injection in the early stages of the disease. In the later stages, multiple injections may be used, or the drug may be given intravenously.
• Doxycycline, erythromycin, and tetracycline	These antimicrobials are used in the treatment of syphilis for patients allergic to penicillin. They are also used alone or in combination for the treatment of chancroid, chlamydia, and gonorrhea.
• Ceftriaxone	This drug is the treatment of choice for gonorrhea and chancroid. Doxycycline is often given in combination because many patients with gonorrhea are also infected with chlamydia.
• Azithromycin	This drug is used for the treatment of chancroid and chlamydia.
• Metronidazole	This drug is the treatment of choice for trichomoniasis.
• Antimitotic gels or immune-enhancing cream	These agents are effective in treating genital warts.
■ Teach the patient to complete the prescribed treatment and take all medications.	Recurrence and transmission of infection can occur if the patient does not take all of the medication. Patients often stop treatment prematurely when symptoms disappear.
■ Teach about recurrence and/or reinfection.	Have the patient abstain from sexual activity during treatment and for the prescribed number of days afterward. Partners should be evaluated and treated to prevent reinfection of the patient. Persons with herpes should abstain from sexual activity with unaffected partners when lesions or other symptoms of herpes are present.
■ Provide the patient with information and education obtained from the latest guidelines.	The National Guideline Clearinghouse and the CDC are two excellent Internet resources.
■ Notify the local health department.	In most states, STIs must be reported to local health departments for case finding. Laws and regulations regarding which STIs are reportable vary by state.

NDx Nursing Diagnosis

Disturbed Body Image

Common Related Factors	Defining Characteristics
Lesions	Verbalizes fear, anger, anxiety
Urethral discharge	Discusses feelings of inadequacy and self-worth
Odiferous discharge	Discusses difficulty with coping with diagnosis of STI
Topical medications	

■ = Independent; ▲ = Collaborative

Common Expected Outcome

Patient demonstrates enhanced body image and self-esteem as evidenced by the ability to look at, talk about, and care for the altered body part.

NOC Outcomes
Body Image; Self-Esteem

NIC Intervention
Self-Esteem Enhancement

Ongoing Assessment

Actions/Interventions

- Assess and validate feelings about changes in appearance and body function.
- Note the patient's withdrawal from social situations.

- Assess the impact of body image disturbance in relation to patient's developmental stage.

- Assess coping mechanisms that the patient has used in the past.

Rationale

The value or importance the patient places on the body part is more important than its actual value.

STIs are associated with a social stigma. Withdrawal may indicate feelings of social isolation or fear of rejection by others.

Early experience with STIs and its "social stigma" may affect developmental changes at a time when fostering social and intimate relationships is particularly important.

Previous coping strategies may not be adequate to support patient adjustment.

Therapeutic Interventions

Actions/Interventions

- Encourage verbalization of positive or negative feelings about body changes.

- Assist the patient to identify the extent of changes in appearance.
- Provide hope within the parameters of the disease process. Do not give false reassurance.
- Encourage the patient and significant other to interact.

- Refer to support groups.

▲ Refer for sexual counseling to help cope with sexuality issues.

Rationale

It is worthwhile to encourage the patient to separate feelings about changes in the body from feelings of self-worth.

This helps begin the process of looking toward the future and how sexual activity will be different.

Hope promotes a positive attitude and provides an opportunity to plan for the future. Many STIs can be cured.

This maintains an open line of communication. One's partner has a key role in treatment and follow-up.

Lay persons in similar situations offer a different type of support, which is perceived as helpful.

The patient may need professional assistance to deal with issues and accept self.

Testicular Cancer

Malignant tumors of the testes are rare, with approximately two to three new cases per 100,000 males reported in the United States each year. Testicular cancer is slightly more common on the right side, which parallels the increased incidence of cryptorchidism (undescended testes) on the same side. Although the cause of testicular cancer is unknown, both congenital and acquired factors are associated with tumor development.

■ = Independent; ▲ = Collaborative

Testicular Cancer

→ Testicular Cancer—cont'd

The strongest association has been with cryptorchidism. In patients who have a history of cryptorchidism, approximately 7% to 10% develop testicular tumors. Orchiopexy (repair of an undescended testicle) does not seem to alter the malignancy potential, but it does facilitate examination and tumor detection.

Classification by histological types of tumors as well as clinical staging determines the treatment. Classification by histology is divided into two major divisions: (1) seminoma and (2) nonseminomatous germ tumors, which include embryonal, teratoma, choriocarcinoma, and mixed tumors. Seminoma accounts for approximately 35% of testicular cancers and is most common in men in their 40s. Embryonal cell carcinoma, which accounts for 20%, is divided into adult type and infantile type. The infantile type is the most common testicular tumor in infants and children. When diagnosed in adults, it is generally seen as a mixed histological type. Teratoma accounts for approximately 5% of testicular cancers and is seen in both children and adults. Approximately 40% of testicular cancer is a category of mixed cell types. The majority are teratocarcinomas, a combination of teratoma and embryonal cell carcinomas.

The most common clinical staging system categorizes testicular cancer as stage I, a lesion confined to the testes. Stage II involves regional lymph node spread, and stage III is spread beyond the retroperitoneal lymph nodes. Reflecting the improvement and refinement of combination chemotherapy, survival in testicular cancer has dramatically improved, with a cure rate of more than 90% in all stages combined according to the American Cancer Society.

NDx Nursing Diagnosis

Health-Seeking Behaviors: Technique for Monthly Testicular Self-Examination (TSE)

Common Related Factors

Lack of knowledge about regular testicular self-examination (TSE)
TSE used as screening technique for men 15 to 40 years of age

Defining Characteristics

Questions or statements of misconception
Failure to do TSE

Common Expected Outcome

Patient correctly performs TSE.

NOC Outcome
Knowledge: Health Promotion

NIC Interventions
Self-Modification Assistance;
    Health Education: TSE

Ongoing Assessment

Actions/Interventions

■ Assess the patient's understanding, ability, and desire to learn.

Rationale

It is necessary to create an individual instruction plan based on the patient's readiness to learn.

■ = Independent; ▲ = Collaborative

Actions/Interventions	Rationale
■ Be alert to signs of avoidance (e.g., changing the subject or becoming withdrawn).	Denial is a defense mechanism that can block learning and the assimilation of information.

Therapeutic Interventions

Actions/Interventions	Rationale
■ Present method of TSE using audiovisual aids or tapes, then allow for question-and-answer period.	Multiple learning methods may enhance retention of the TSE information.
■ Provide information in written form for the patient to take home.	Written instructions may be a helpful resource when the patient is alone. Many Internet sites offer printable material.
■ Identify known risk factors: • Family history of testicular cancer • Cryptorchid testes • Exogenous estrogen exposure	Testicular cancer is generally diagnosed in white males 15 to 40 years of age. An increased incidence is linked to maternal exposure to diethylstilbestrol (DES) and use of oral contraceptives during pregnancy.
■ Instruct on warning signs of testicular cancer: • Lump on testes that is small, hard, and painless • Pain in the testes • Heaviness in testes or scrotum • Discomfort in lower abdomen or groin • Breast enlargement or nipple tenderness	Malignant tumors of the testes are rare but are the most common malignancy in males 15 to 40 years of age.
■ Instruct in procedure of TSE: • Examine testicles monthly immediately after a shower or bath.	The warmth from the water relaxes the scrotal sac.
• Examine each testicle separately by gently rolling it between thumb and fingers.	Testicular tumors tend to appear deep in the center of the testicle.
• Report any lump or swelling or any changes in size, shape, or consistency of the testes to the health care provider as soon as possible.	Early detection of changes facilitates treatment and can affect the cure.

Nursing Diagnosis

Deficient Knowledge

Common Related Factors

New condition
Unfamiliarity with diagnostic procedure and/or treatments

Defining Characteristics

Asks questions about causes, diagnosis, and treatment
Verbalizes inaccurate information
Lack of questions

Common Expected Outcome

Patient demonstrates an understanding of the risk for and causes of testicular cancer, common diagnostic procedures, and treatment options.

NOC Outcomes

Knowledge: Disease Process;
Knowledge: Treatment Regimen

NIC Interventions

Teaching: Disease Process;
Teaching: Preoperative;
Teaching: Procedure/Treatment

Testicular Cancer

■ = Independent; ▲ = Collaborative

→ Testicular Cancer—cont'd

Ongoing Assessment

Actions/Interventions

■ Assess knowledge of the diagnosis and treatment options.

Rationale

This topic is difficult for many men to discuss. Men may not realize how curable testicular cancer has become.

Therapeutic Interventions

Actions/Interventions

■ Encourage questions about the diagnosis of testicular cancer and proposed treatment regimen:

■ Provide information on diagnostic testing.
  • Review of TSE results

  • Physical examination of testes, lymph nodes, and abdomen

  • Laboratory tests: tumor markers such as alpha feto-protein (AFP) and human chorionic gonadotropin (hCG).

  • Diagnostic tests:
    • Ultrasound

    • Computed tomography and magnetic resonance imaging
    • Chest radiograph and bone scan
    • Radical orchiectomy (surgical removal of one or both testes)

■ Provide preoperative teaching about orchiectomy:
  • The procedure may be a same-day surgery or may require an overnight hospital stay.
  • The patient will have an inguinal incision. The surgical site may be closed with staples or Steri-Strips.
  • Serosanguineous fluid may ooze from the surgical site for up to 24 hours.
  • Report any excessive bleeding or wound separation immediately to the urologist.
  • Apply ice for 24 hours.
  • Wear scrotal support at all times until the incision is well healed.
  • Follow-up appointments are made 7 to 10 days after surgery.
  • Contact the urologist if temperature is greater than 38.3° C (101° F), or if chills, excessive weakness, or scrotal edema occur.

■ Provide preoperative teaching about retroperitoneal lymph node dissection (RPLND):
  • RPLND is generally performed as laparoscopic surgery, or it may be an open-abdominal surgery.

Rationale

Often patients are embarrassed about asking questions and may need permission to ask them.

Most commonly men note a lump that is painless but uncomfortable, or they may note swelling.

Testes are evaluated for lumps and swelling. Other organs are evaluated for potential metastatic disease.

These markers are used to diagnose types of cancer as well as response to treatment.

This aids in determining solid versus fluid-filled masses and benign versus malignant tumor.

These detect metastatic lesions.

These detect metastatic lesions.

This is used both for biopsy diagnosis and for treatment. The interval between discovery of a scrotal lump in the testes and radical orchiectomy is often within 1 week.

This is a relatively uncomplicated procedure.

These will remain in place for 7 to 10 days.

Patients should be prepared for routine drainage after surgery.

It is important to seek immediate attention because the wound may have dehiscence.

Ice prevents edema.

Support alleviates discomfort and prevents edema.

Appointments may relate to postoperative recovery and/or further cancer therapy.

Complications can be caused by infection of wound or bleeding from the spermatic cord stump.

Lymph node dissection is used for tumor staging. Treatment modalities depend on this staging process. RPLND is more commonly seen with embryonic cancer due to its high rate of metastasis.

(■ = Independent; ▲ = Collaborative)

Actions/Interventions	**Rationale**
• Pain management may be provided by epidural or patient-controlled analgesia pump.	
• The patient may receive prophylactic antibiotics.	
• There are potential complications, such as infection, ileus, and pneumonia.	
■ Instruct on potential for semen storage.	The patient may feel secure knowing there is the potential for future access to his sperm.
■ Explain the need to consult with both an oncologist and radiologist regarding chemotherapy and/or radiation therapy.	Both radiation and chemotherapy are generally coordinated by the medical oncologist. The nurse serves as the advocate by offering support, providing information, and coordinating follow-up appointments with the urologist.
■ Provide information on follow-up therapy:	Men must realize that testicular cancer is not a death sentence. Many modalities are available to treat advanced disease.
• Chemotherapy	Chemotherapy is indicated for nonseminomatous tumors or for metastatic disease. Many effective therapies are available, including cisplatin, ifosfamide, etoposide, vinblastine, and bleomycin.
• Radiation therapy	Radiation beam therapy is indicated for patients with pure seminoma, because this tumor is radiosensitive.
■ Provide written materials and videotapes.	These reinforce verbal information presented by the health care team.
■ Provide referral to the National Cancer Institute, the American Cancer Society, or the Lance Armstrong Foundation.	This provides the patient and family with additional helpful resources including support groups.

Testicular Cancer

NDx Nursing Diagnosis

Ineffective Sexuality Patterns

Common Related Factors
Acute illness
Pain
Recent orchiectomy
Hormonal change
Infertility

Defining Characteristics
Verbalizes concerns regarding sexual functioning
Actual or perceived limitations secondary to orchiectomy
Reports changes in previously established sexual patterns

Common Expected Outcome
Patient or couple verbalizes satisfaction with the way they express physical intimacy.

NOC Outcomes
Sexual Identity: Acceptance; Self-Esteem

NIC Interventions
Sexual Counseling: Anticipatory Guidance; Teaching: Sexuality

■ = Independent; ▲ = Collaborative

Testicular Cancer–cont'd

Ongoing Assessment

Actions/Interventions

- Assess level of understanding regarding human sexuality and functioning.
- Explore current and past sexual patterns, practices, and degree of satisfaction.
- Identify level of comfort in discussion of patient and/or significant other.

- Assess the patient's or couple's prior plans for conceiving children.

Rationale

Many people have misconceptions about facts of sexual intimacy.

This aids in developing a realistic approach to care planning.

It is important for the nurse to create an environment wherein the patient and/or couple feel safe and comfortable in discussing their feelings.

Inability to conceive after surgery or treatment (unless sperm was banked) can affect the individual or couple in many ways, threatening their self-esteem, gender roles, and interactions.

Therapeutic Interventions

Actions/Interventions

- Explore awareness of and comfort with a range of sexual expression and activities (not just sexual intercourse).
- Discuss the effect of an orchiectomy on future fertility.

- ▲ Refer to a reproductive specialist about sperm banking.

- Encourage discussion of feelings regarding alternative methods for reproduction.

- Refer to support groups.

Rationale

The patient may be unaware of potential options.

Failure to conceive can affect the individual or couple in many ways, threatening their self-esteem, gender roles, and sexual interactions.

If fathering a child is an important role for the patient, and sperm banking was not an option, discuss other options such as donor insemination and adoption.

Removing one testicle does not affect fertility or sexual function. Newer "nerve-sparing" surgical procedures are improving fertility rates.

Support and self-help groups are unique sources of information and empathy. With the high cure rate among patients with advanced disease, a growing number of survivors are serving as role models and political advocates.

NDx Nursing Diagnosis

Disturbed Body Image

Common Related Factor

Orchiectomy

Defining Characteristics

Expressions of negative feelings about the body
Focusing behavior on changed body part or function
Refusal to look at, touch, or care for scrotal sac
Change in social behavior (withdrawal or isolation

■ = Independent; ▲ = Collaborative

Common Expected Outcome

Patient demonstrates enhanced body image as evidenced by the ability to look at, care for, and talk about the altered appearance of the scrotal sac.

NOC Outcomes
Body Image; Self-Esteem
NIC Interventions
Body Image Enhancement; Grief Work Facilitation; Coping Enhancement

Ongoing Assessment

Actions/Interventions

- Assess and validate feelings about changes in appearance.

- Assess perceived impact on social behavior or personal relationships.

- Assess previous coping strategies.

Rationale

The extent of the response is related more to the value or importance the patient places on the body part than to the actual value or importance.

Young adult men may be particularly affected by changes in the structure or function of their bodies at a time when they are developing social and intimate relationships.

Help the patient identify ways of coping that were successful in the past, although prior coping skills may not be adequate at this time.

Therapeutic Interventions

Actions/Interventions

- Teach the patient self-care activities related to body image.
- Reinforce any attempts to care for the scrotum.

- Acknowledge normalcy of emotional response to actual or perceived change in body structure and function.
- Provide information about institutional, Internet-based, political, and community resources for coping with testicular cancer.

Rationale

These enable adaptation to the changes in body image.

Positive reinforcement allows the patient to feel good about accomplishments and gain confidence.

Acknowledging the patient's emotional response enables the patient to move through the grieving process.

Social services, support groups, and community agencies can help the patient cope with this illness and treatments. As more men are being cured of this cancer, there is a growing body of "survivors" serving as role models and advocates, for example—The Lance Armstrong Foundation.

• RELATED CARE PLANS

Cancer chemotherapy, p. 812
Cancer radiation therapy, p. 825

Testicular Cancer

■ = Independent; ▲ = Collaborative

11

Women's Health Care Plans

 Breast Cancer/Mastectomy and Lumpectomy

Breast cancer is the most commonly occurring cancer in American women, accounting for approximately 31% of all cancer cases. It is the second leading cause of cancer death in women; lung cancer remains the most fatal of all cancers for both men and women. A woman has a one-in-eight lifetime risk of developing this highly treatable disease. Despite its common occurrence, most women with breast cancer will not succumb to the disease; the 5-year survival rate is about 88%. Complete sequencing of the human genome has lead to the identification of two genes associated with the development of breast cancer and ovarian cancer. Women who carry a mutation in the BRCA1 and BRCA2 gene are known to be at increased risk for the development of breast cancer, and these cancers often develop at a much younger age than usual (age 45 or younger). The lifetime breast cancer risk for women with hereditary cancer (defined as having an inherited mutation in the BRCA1 or BRCA2 gene) is 56% to 85%. Hereditary breast cancer, however, accounts for only 5% to 10% of all breast cancer cases. The remainder of all breast cancers (85%) do not have an identified hereditary component. In other words, most women who get breast cancer have a noninherited form. In these women the incidence of the disease increases with age, with most occurring in women over 65 years of age.

Two other risk factors are associated with an increased risk of breast cancer: exposure to radiation (e.g., women exposed during the atomic bomb blasts in Japan or women who have received chest irradiation as prior treatment for other malignancies such as Hodgkin's disease) and the period of time that the body makes estrogen. The earlier a woman begins to menstruate and the later she has her first pregnancy, or following prolonged hormone replacement therapy, the higher her risk for breast cancer. The later menopause occurs, the higher is her postmenopausal risk for breast pancer. Another significant risk factor is cigarette smoking. Research suggests that some women have a slow-acting form of a liver enzyme that normally detoxifies carcinogens, permitting the carcinogens present in tobacco to remain in the body longer.

With the use of breast self-examination and screening mammography, most breast cancer is successfully diagnosed at an early stage. Treatment recommendations are made according to the disease stage and may include surgery, radiation, and/or chemotherapy. Prognosis is related to the stage and type of tumor. Adjuvant chemohormonal therapy has decreased recurrence and has improved survival rates in most subgroups of patients. Even though the treatment modalities have lengthened the survival time for metastatic breast cancer, stage IV or metastatic disease is not curable.

Surgical management of breast cancer includes two major approaches: (1) breast conservation therapy, often referred to as a lumpectomy, or (2) removal of the entire breast, which is called a modified radical or radical mastectomy. Both of these surgical approaches may also include examination of the axillary lymph nodes for evidence of micrometastatic disease. The presence or absence of disease in the lymph nodes determines prognosis (and subsequent treatment) and is referred to as nodal status. Women with node-negative disease generally have a better prognosis than women with node-positive disease. Women undergoing mastectomy have several options for breast reconstruction, including immediate or delayed reconstruction. This care plan does not address the management of women who have received mastectomy with immediate reconstruction. Breast-conserving therapy (lumpectomy) with adjuvant chemotherapy and/or radiation therapy is considered a treatment that is medically equivalent to mastectomy.

Specialized breast cancer treatment centers are available, providing a multidisciplinary treatment approach (e.g., medical and surgical oncologists, gynecologists, radiation oncologists, clinical nurse specialists, nurses, and social workers). This care plan addresses the surgical management of breast cancer. Follow-up care and adjunct treatment would be performed in the ambulatory care setting.

ND_x Nursing Diagnosis

Deficient Knowledge: Preoperative

Common Related Factors

Unfamiliarity with proposed treatment plan and procedures
Uncertainty about treatment options
Misinterpretation of information
Decisional conflict

Defining Characteristics

Asks questions about diagnostic tests and treatment options
Makes statements indicating misinformation

Common Expected Outcome

Patient verbalizes understanding of breast cancer, its diagnosis, treatment options, and prognosis.

NOC Outcomes
Knowledge: Disease Process;
  Knowledge: Treatment Regimen

NIC Interventions
Teaching: Disease Process;
  Teaching: Procedures/Treatment

Ongoing Assessment

Actions/Interventions

- Assess understanding of diagnostic testing.

- Assess understanding of relationship between disease stage and prognosis and treatment.
- Assess understanding of treatment modalities:
  - Surgery
  - Radiation
  - Chemotherapy
  - Hormonal therapy

Rationale

Thorough understanding of indications for testing is necessary for informed consent to be given.

Treatment depends on stage and extent of disease.

Most women want a collaborative relationship in disease management and require information about treatment rationales. They may have a preference for specific treatment plan, but decision-making capacity may be challenged due to stress of disease.

Breast Cancer/Mastectomy and Lumpectomy

■ = Independent; ▲ = Collaborative

Breast Cancer/Mastectomy and Lumpectomy—cont'd

Therapeutic Interventions

Actions/Interventions	Rationale

■ Explain rationale for diagnostic procedures:

• Clinical examination of breast

Lesion (lump) usually occurs in the upper outer quadrant of the breast. It is typically hard, irregularly shaped, nonmobile, and poorly delineated.

• Mammography

This is used to locate the position and extent of a known tumor and to screen for the presence of other abnormalities not detected by clinical examination.

• Breast biopsy

This is performed via fine-needle aspiration, needle core biopsy, excisional biopsy or lumpectomy, or needle localization for microscopic examination to confirm benign or malignant tissue diagnosis.

• Ultrasonography

Lesions larger than 1 cm can be evaluated. The ultrasound can determine whether the lesion is solid or cystic (fluid-filled).

• Tumor tissue testing (hormone receptor assays, DNA, and protein markers with diagnostic and prognostic value)

Estrogen and progesterone are female hormones affecting breast and other cancer tissues. The level of hormone receptors present in the tumor indicates the tumor's dependence on these hormones. Tumors are classified as estrogen receptor or progesterone receptor (ER/PR) positive or negative according to the amount of receptor protein present. This classification suggests tumor growth and treatment options. Tumors with positive receptors (more prevalent in postmenopausal women) are associated with better prognosis and longer survival.

• Complete physical examination

It is important to screen for signs of cancer in other locations.

• Liver function tests and scans

These tests aid in identifying possible liver metastasis.

• Genetic markers (e.g., HER2/neu)

This aids in determining prognosis and monitoring the course of disease. The HER2/neu gene is associated with breast cancer; an overexpression gives the patient a poorer prognosis. The best prognosis is ER/PR-positive, H_2-negative; the worst prognosis is ER/PR-negative, H_2-positive.

• Bone scan

This is used in ruling out bone metastasis.

• Computed tomography (CT) scan/magnetic resonance imaging (MRI)

This is used in evaluating for tumors and distant sites of metastasis.

■ Explain rationale for suggested treatment based on site, type, and stage of tumor:

• The TNM classification system

This system is used to stage breast cancer according to the extent of the primary tumor (T), regional lymph node metastasis (N), distant metastasis (M).

• Clinical stages
  • Stage 0: Treated by lumpectomy with radiation or mastectomy
  • Stages I and II: Treated with lumpectomy or mastectomy, with or without surgical axillary staging. The use of adjuvant radiation, chemotherapy, or

The clinical stages range from stage 0 to IV. Stage 0 implies in situ (localized) cancer; stage IV implies extensive metastasis.

■ = Independent; ▲ = Collaborative

Actions/Interventions	Rationale
hormonal or biological therapy is dependent on a number of prognostic indicators (e.g., tumor size, nodal status, hormone receptor status, age, menopausal status)	
• Stages III and IV: Mastectomy and systemic chemotherapy; other adjuvant therapies (radiation, hormonal or biological therapy) are dependent on prognostic indicators as listed previously	
• Chemoprevention	This is the prophylactic use of antiestrogen agents (e.g., tamoxifen) in women at high risk for development of breast cancer.
■ Explain and clarify misconceptions about treatment approaches:	
• Hormonal therapy	ER/PR-positive tumors respond to hormonal treatment with antiestrogens. A number of different antiestrogen therapies are available depending on the menopausal status of the woman, including tamoxifen and anastrozole.
• Biological (Herceptin)	Trastuzumab (Herceptin) is a monoclonal antibody that targets the HER2/neu protein expressed on the surface of breast cells. Approximately 25% of all women with breast cancer overexpress this protein, which leads to unregulated cell growth. The use of Herceptin can slow the growth of cancer cells.
■ Provide teaching materials (e.g., videos, slides, reliable internet websites, and printed information). Contact the National Cancer Institute in Bethesda, MD (1-[800]-4-CANCER) for additional materials.	Providing the patient with information in different formats allows her to choose the format that best suits her learning style and needs.

NDx Nursing Diagnosis

Acute Pain

Common Related Factors

Contraction of tissue resulting from surgery and healing process
Intraoperative arm position
Possible injury to brachial plexus
Lymphedema
Infection and phlebitis

Defining Characteristics

Complaints of pain and discomfort
Guarding behavior
Restlessness and irritability
Appearance of discomfort

Common Expected Outcomes

Patient verbalizes reduced pain and discomfort.
Patient appears comfortable.
Patient performs range-of-motion (ROM) exercises with minimal discomfort.

NOC Outcomes
Circulation Status; Pain Level; Pain Control

NIC Interventions
Circulatory Precautions; Circulatory Care; Pain Management; Positioning

Breast Cancer/Mastectomy and Lumpectomy

■ = Independent; ▲ = Collaborative

Breast Cancer/Mastectomy and Lumpectomy—cont'd

Ongoing Assessment

Actions/Interventions	Rationale
■ Note subjective reports of pain and discomfort.	Pain assessment is the basis for an individualized approach to pain management.
■ Assess neurovascular status of affected arm immediately after surgery and at regular intervals.	This assessment detects possible brachial plexus injury.
■ Measure biceps 2 inches above elbow of affected arm immediately after surgery and every shift.	An increase in arm circumference may indicate impaired lymphatic drainage.
■ Evaluate ROM of affected arm.	Woman may refrain from certain movements to reduce pain.
■ Assess for signs of infection or phlebitis in the affected arm (e.g., pain, redness, warmth, and swelling).	Early identification of complications allows for early intervention.

Therapeutic Interventions

Actions/Interventions	Rationale
■ Keep arm elevated on two pillows while the patient is in bed (mastectomy).	This decreases edema and promotes lymph drainage.
■ Avoid constriction of the affected arm.	This prevents circulatory impairment.
■ Protect affected arm from injury. Ensure that no procedures are performed on the affected arm (e.g., blood pressure, blood drawing, intravenous injections). Post notice at the bedside.	Mastectomy procedures remove lymph nodes and lymphatic vessels that drain the arm on the involved side of the body, increasing the risk of injury and infection in the involved arm.
■ Instruct regarding postoperative exercises: • Straight extension and abduction • Straight elbow raises • Wall climbing • Repeated 5 to 10 times per hour as tolerated	These increase ROM progressively in the affected arm.
■ Administer analgesics for pain as required (e.g., before ROM exercises are performed).	Patients have a right to effective pain relief.

NDx Nursing Diagnosis

Risk for Injury: Seroma

Common Risk Factors

Altered lymph drainage (in mastectomy patients)
Drain malfunction

■ = Independent; ▲ = Collaborative

Women's Health Care Plans

Common Expected Outcome

Patient is at reduced risk for injury as evidenced by the absence of postoperative complications such as drain malfunction and lymphatic stasis.

> ### NOC Outcome
> Wound Healing: Primary Intention
>
> ### NIC Interventions
> Wound Care: Closed Drainage;
> Wound Care

Ongoing Assessment

Actions/Interventions

- Check wound drain for suction pressure, clots, air leaks, and drainage output at regular intervals after surgery.
- Document amount of output from the drain.

- Assess for tenderness or presence of fluid accumulation beneath flap.

Rationale

Seroma formation is a common complication after mastectomy.

Wound drainage will normally decrease in volume the first 48 to 72 hours after surgery.

Fluid accumulation can be a source of infection.

Therapeutic Interventions

Actions/Interventions

- Milk or strip the drain tubing every hour.
- Notify the physician of drain malfunctions or fluid accumulation beneath the flap.

Rationale

This helps to maintain patency.

Wound drainage malfunction requires immediate intervention.

NDx Nursing Diagnosis

Risk for Situational Low Self-Esteem/Disturbed Body Image

Common Risk Factors

Excision of breast and adjacent tissue
Beginning scar tissue
Asymmetrical breasts caused by implant or prosthesis fit or by lumpectomy
Diagnosis of cancer
History of sexual problems

Common Expected Outcome

Patient adjusts to changes in body image as evidenced by use of positive coping strategies, use of available resources, and absence of or decreased number of self-deprecating remarks.

> ### NOC Outcomes
> Body Image; Self-Esteem; Social Support
>
> ### NIC Interventions
> Body Image Enhancement;
> Self-Esteem Enhancement;
> Support System Enhancement

Breast Cancer/Mastectomy and Lumpectomy

 = Independent; ▲ = Collaborative

Breast Cancer/Mastectomy and Lumpectomy—cont'd

Ongoing Assessment

Actions/Interventions

- Assess for previous problems with self-esteem, body image, or sexual relations.

- Assess for changes in the patient's self-perceptions following surgery (e.g., preoccupation with altered body part, concerns about loss of femininity and sexual identity, and negative feelings about body image).

Rationale

Professional counseling may aid women with prior negative experiences associated with divorce, unsatisfactory intimate relationships, or widowhood.

The psychological impact of surgery may be devastating to self-esteem. Cultural and societal values about a woman's breast will influence the patient's response to surgery.

Therapeutic Interventions

Actions/Interventions

- Encourage the patient to look at the wound and help care for it.
- Encourage the patient to verbalize feelings about effects of surgery on the ability to function as a woman, a sexual partner, and a worker.
- Assist the patient with wearing a prosthetic insert at discharge.
- Provide information on shops specializing in prostheses; arrange an in-hospital consult if possible.
- Encourage the family (especially significant others) to provide positive input (i.e., feelings of being loved and needed).
- Refer the patient to community support resources (e.g., Reach-to-Recovery).

- Provide the patient with information about reconstructive options.

Rationale

Looking at the wound is often the first indication that the patient is ready to participate in self-care.

It is worthwhile to encourage women to separate feelings about changes in body structures and/or function from feelings about self-worth.

Wearing a prosthesis can provide a feeling of normalcy.

Community resources provide support for the woman who is adjusting to changes in her body.

Limited or impaired social supports cause adjustment difficulties.

Interactions with women who have successfully dealt with breast surgery can help with adjustment to the changed body.

Increased effectiveness of reconstructive surgical techniques can restore body contours in women who do not want to wear external prostheses. Include information about various types of surgical techniques and external prostheses.

NDx Nursing Diagnosis

Risk for Anxiety/Fear

Common Risk Factors

Diagnosis of cancer
Uncertain prognosis

■ = Independent; ▲ = Collaborative

Common Expected Outcome

Patient or family demonstrates reduced levels of anxiety as evidenced by use of positive coping strategies and decreased number or absence of verbalized fears, feelings of helplessness, or other self-defeating statements.

NOC Outcomes
Anxiety Self-Control; Social Support

NIC Interventions
Anxiety Reduction; Support System Enhancement

Ongoing Assessment

Actions/Interventions

■ Assess for signs of anxiety or fear (e.g., withdrawal, crying, restlessness, or inability to focus).

■ Assess previous successful coping strategies.

Rationale

The threats accompanying a diagnosis of cancer can cause anxiety about health and continued productivity.

These may be useful in dealing with the current crisis.

Therapeutic Interventions

Actions/Interventions

■ Encourage verbalizations about feelings of grief, anger, fear, and anxiety.

■ Reassure the patient that these feelings are normal.

■ Provide accurate information about the future with breast cancer.

■ Assist in use of previously successful coping measures.

▲ Work collaboratively with other health care providers as indicated:
  • Social worker
  • Psychologist
  • Chaplain

■ Support realistic assessment; avoid false reassurances.

▲ Administer antianxiety medications as ordered and indicated.

Rationale

Verbalization of actual or perceived threats can help reduce anxiety. Initial focus may be on the threat of dying rather than on reactions to the mastectomy.

Stages of fear and grief over change or loss of a body part are normal.

Most women have experience with women who have died of breast cancer. Misinformation should be corrected, and new treatment options and prognosis explained.

Modification may be necessary for this specific problem.

An interdisciplinary approach to patient care provides the patient with diverse support and resources.

This assists the patient in dealing with the current crisis and in gaining control over the situation.

These may facilitate ability to cope.

NDx Nursing Diagnosis

Deficient Knowledge: Postoperative

Common Related Factors

Lack of previous experience
Unfamiliarity with existing informational resources
Information misinterpretation

Defining Characteristics

Verbalizes knowledge deficits
Demonstrates lack of awareness of existing resources
Asks questions

Breast Cancer/Mastectomy and Lumpectomy

■ = Independent; ▲ = Collaborative

Breast Cancer/Mastectomy and Lumpectomy—cont'd

Common Expected Outcome

Patient verbalizes importance of follow-up care and proper wound care.

NOC Outcomes
Knowledge: Disease Process;
Knowledge: Treatment Regimen

NIC Interventions
Teaching: Disease Process;
Teaching: Procedures/Treatment

Ongoing Assessment

Actions/Interventions

- Assess knowledge level of home care and required health maintenance.

Rationale

The patient may be unaware of important self-care procedures.

Therapeutic Interventions

Actions/Interventions

- Educate about wound care and arm care (if applicable):

  - The arm will be stiff and uncomfortable.

  - Continue ROM exercises for at least 1 month.

  - Notify the health care provider regarding fever, swelling, wound drainage, or injury.
  - Protect the arm from injury or infection.

  - Use an electric razor when shaving, gloves when gardening or doing dishes, and mitts when handling hot dishes.
  - Avoid blood draws, intravenous lines, and injections or blood pressure measurement in the operative arm during subsequent medical treatments.
  - Carry heavy packages or handbags with the opposite arm.
  - Massage the incision site gently with cocoa butter and vitamin E cream.
  - Wear temporary prosthesis or brassiere at least occasionally.
- Instruct about activity guidelines:
  - Resume all routine activities as tolerated (e.g., driving).
  - Resume sexual activity as tolerated

Rationale

Information enables the woman to take control during recovery.

Exercise decrease stiffness, but numbness may remain for a prolonged time if nodes were dissected.

Exercise eases tension in the arm and shoulder, maintains muscle tone, and improves lymph and blood circulation on the affected side.

Prompt assessment facilitates early intervention.

The operative arm will remain vulnerable to lymphedema after axillary lymph node dissection.

The woman needs to learn to protect the operative arm from any type of injury for the rest of her life.

These measures reduce the risk for injury to the blood and lymphatic vessels in the operative arm.

This measure reduces the risk of muscle and joint strain in the operative arm.

These promote healing and skin softness, and minimize scar formation.

These help adjustment to recent loss of breast.

Each woman will progress at her own rate.

■ = Independent; ▲ = Collaborative

Women's Health Care Plans

Actions/Interventions	Rationale
■ Instruct about required follow-up care:	
• Monthly breast self-examination (BSE)	Women may hesitate to perform BSE due to difficulty viewing or touching the surgical site on the chest or fear of finding another lump.
• Annual mammogram (or more often)	There is increased risk of cancer in the opposite breast. Mammography can identify breast tumors before they are palpable.
• Reconstructive surgery (if desired)	Reconstructive surgery does not influence survival rates but may improve the quality of life. It may be contra-indicated in locally advanced, progressively metastatic, or inflammatory cancer.
• Importance of large-breasted women to be fitted with weighted prosthesis as soon as possible	This provides balance for proper posture.
■ Instruct about possible family needs:	
• All women older than 20 years of age should perform monthly BSE.	Risk is increased in daughters or sisters of women with breast cancer, and is further increased in daughters or sisters of women with premenopausal bilateral breast cancer or if more than one relative has cancer.
• Women older than 40 years of age should have an annual mammogram.	
■ Instruct on follow-up consultations with medical and radiation specialists if required due to nodal status.	Ongoing evaluation is necessary for the development of lymphedema, metastasis, and recurrence of cancer.
■ Provide appropriate educational materials from the American Cancer Society, the National Cancer Institute, the Susan G. Komen Breast Cancer Foundation, or YWCA's ENCORE program.	Information from specialty organizations can enhance learning and compliance.

> **• RELATED CARE PLANS**
>
> Ineffective peripheral tissue perfusion, p. 198
> Ineffective sexuality patterns, p. 170

Cervical Cancer

Cancer of the cervix is one of the most common cancers affecting women's reproductive organs, occurring between 35 and 55 years of age. It is more commonly seen in the African-American and Hispanic populations. Several factors increase one's risk for cervical cancer, including many sexual partners, early sexual activity, history of sexually transmitted infections, weakened immune systems, and smoking habit. At least 95% of the cases are reported to be related to sexual exposure to the human papillomavirus (HPV). A vaccine approved by the Food and Drug Administration for HPV is recommended for girls as young as 9 to 12 years of age and for women 13 to 26 years of age.

The death rate from cervical cancer has significantly dropped due to Papanicolaou (Pap) smear screening. When diagnosed at an early, preinvasive stage, the survival rate is nearly 100%. According to the American Cancer Society, invasive cancer that is diagnosed while still confined to the cervix has a 5-year survival rate of around 91%. Treatment options depend on the tumor stage at diagnosis. Treatment may consist of conization, LEEP (loop electrosurgical excision procedure), cryosurgery, cauterization, laser surgery, hysterectomy, radiation, chemotherapy, or biological therapy.

> ## Cervical Cancer—cont'd

Nursing Diagnosis

Deficient Knowledge

Common Related Factor	Defining Characteristics
Unfamiliarity with disease and treatment	Multiple questions Lack of questions Verbalizes misinformation

Common Expected Outcome

Patient verbalizes understanding of the risk factors, and diagnosis and treatment procedures for cervical cancer.

NOC Outcomes

Knowledge: Disease Process;
Knowledge: Treatment Regimen

NIC Interventions

Teaching: Disease Process;
Teaching: Procedure/Treatment

Ongoing Assessment

Actions/Interventions

■ Assess understanding of cervical cancer.

Rationale

Women may have misinformation about types of female cancers and their causes, treatments, and prognoses. Previous experience with other women being treated for cancer or who have died of cancer will influence beliefs; some of these may be negative or incorrect.

Therapeutic Interventions

Actions/Interventions

■ Explain that the cause of cervical cancer is unknown, although several risk factors have been identified:
  • Exposure to HPV and other sexually transmitted infections
  • Many sexual partners
  • Early sexual activity (before 18 years of age)
  • Smoking history
  • Chronic cervical infections
  • Weakened immune systems

Rationale

Various strains of the sexually transmitted HPV account for 95% of diagnosed cases. Sexually transmitted infection (STI) viruses have been linked to atypical cell transformations that eventually convert to cancerous cells. However, not all women with HPV infections develop cancer. Studies have demonstrated higher incidences in women who have early and varied sexual habits. The mechanism between cigarette smoking and cervical cancer is unclear, although it is proposed that smoking affects the immune system's ability to respond to strains of viruses. Its effects increase with the number of cigarettes smoked daily and with pack-years of smoking. Women with weakened immune systems from human immunodeficiency virus (HIV) or immunosuppressant agents are also at higher risk.

■ = Independent; ▲ = Collaborative

Women's Health Care Plans

Actions/Interventions	Rationale
■ Explain signs and symptoms of cervical cancer.	Early cancer usually has no specific signs and is not identified without a screening Pap test. However, as the cancer progresses, abnormal bleeding is the major sign (e.g., from the vagina after intercourse, between periods, or after menopause). An increased watery, bloody vaginal discharge may also be noted.
■ Discuss common diagnostic procedures:	
• Pelvic examination and Pap test	The Pap test allows for detection of abnormal cells. It is only a screening test, not for diagnosis. Newer Pap smear collection procedures have enhanced diagnostic ability. Women should avoid douching or using spermicidal foams or creams for about 2 days before testing to avoid altering any abnormal cells.
• Colposcopy	Colposcopy uses a lighted magnifying instrument to examine the vagina and cervix for epithelial abnormalities.
• Biopsy	Biopsy may include a simple "punch" technique using forceps to pinch off a small piece of tissue. Another method is termed *LEEP* (loop electrosurgical excision procedure), in which an electric wire loop slices off a thin, round area of tissue. These biopsies are performed under local anesthesia.
• Conization (cone biopsy)	Conization is surgery to remove a cone-shaped piece of tissue from the cervix as well as the cervical canal. It can be used for diagnosis as well as treatment.
■ Discuss the treatment options for precancerous and cancerous conditions. *Precancerous* • LEEP • Conization • Cryosurgery (freezing) • Laser • Surgery (hysterectomy)	Many factors determine the optimal treatment for precancerous lesions. These depend on the severity of the lesion (grade), whether the woman wants to have children in the future, the age of the woman, and her general health. Hysterectomy may be indicated if abnormal cells are found inside the cervical opening and the woman is not interested in having children.
Cancer of cervix • Surgery (hysterectomy) • Radiation therapy • Chemotherapy • Biological therapy	Treatment often requires a radical hysterectomy or radiation therapy or both. If the tumor is small, surgery may be sufficient treatment. Radiation is more effective for larger tumors or for tumors that have spread outside the cervical area but are confined to the pelvic area. The radiation may come from external sources or from an internal implant. Platinum-based chemotherapy with concurrent radiation is recommended for systemic treatment. Chemotherapy involves systemic treatment. Biological therapy uses substances to boost the body's immune system (e.g., interferon). Most women will benefit from seeking a second opinion to guide optimal therapy.
■ Discuss common side effects related to treatments.	Minor surgery causes pelvic cramping, bleeding, or a watery discharge. Hysterectomy involves pain in the lower abdomen, some difficulty voiding or having bowel movements, and fatigue. If the uterus was removed, women will no longer have menstrual

Cervical Cancer

■ = Independent; ▲ = Collaborative

Cervical Cancer–cont'd

Rationale

periods and may experience a change in their sexuality. Patients having external radiation therapy may experience local hair loss and drying and reddening of skin. Patients with internal implants must avoid intercourse. Both types of radiation can cause diarrhea and uncomfortable voiding. Chemotherapy effects vary with the agent used and the patient's response to it.

NDx Nursing Diagnosis

Risk for Ineffective Coping

Common Risk Factors

Threat of malignancy
Situational crisis
Inadequate support system
Inadequate coping methods
Lack of knowledge related to disease process

Common Expected Outcome

Patient demonstrates positive coping strategies as evidenced by expression of feelings and hopes, realistic goal-setting for future, and use of available resources and support systems.

NOC Outcomes
Coping; Anxiety Self-Control; Decision Making

NIC Interventions
Coping Enhancement; Decision-Making Support; Anxiety Reduction; Emotional Support

Ongoing Assessment

Actions/Interventions

■ Assess patient's knowledge of disease and treatment.

■ Assess for coping mechanisms used in previous illnesses or prior personal problems.

■ Evaluate resources and support systems available to the patient at home and in the community.

Rationale

Patients may hear the word "cancer" or even the words "precancerous tumor" and expect to die. Realistic information about the high survival rates with cervical cancer needs to be conveyed.

Successful coping is influenced by previous successes. Patients with a history of maladaptive coping may need additional resources. Likewise, previously successful coping skills may be inadequate in the present situation.

With diagnosis of a precancerous tumor, the patient may need only short-term support to get through the initial diagnosis and treatment period. For women with

■ = Independent; ▲ = Collaborative

Rationale

advanced disease requiring more radical surgery, radiation, or chemotherapy treatment, ongoing support will be required. Available support systems may change over time.

Therapeutic Interventions

Actions/Interventions	**Rationale**
■ Establish open lines of communication.	An ongoing relationship establishes trust, reduces the feeling of isolation, and may facilitate coping.
■ Define your role as patient informant and advocate.	The nurse is in an ideal position to guide women through this stressful period.
■ Provide opportunities for the patient or significant other to openly express feelings, fears, and concerns. Provide reassurance and hope as indicated.	Verbalization of actual or perceived threats can help reduce anxiety. Patients receiving radiation implant therapy may express a sense of social isolation while hospitalized, especially with staff required to limit presence in the room and restrict visitors.
■ Assist the patient to become involved as comanager of her treatment plan.	This provides a way for the patient to gain some control over the situation. Many patients with advanced disease become quite educated about their treatment plan and possible side effects.
■ Provide information the patient wants and needs. Do not provide more than the patient can handle.	People who are coping ineffectively have reduced ability to assimilate information.
■ Encourage the patient to communicate feelings with significant others.	Unexpressed feelings can increase stress.
■ Encourage participation in self-help groups as available.	Relationships with women with common interests and experiences can be beneficial. Women need to help spread the word that this cancer is easily treated if diagnosed early.

> #### • RELATED CARE PLANS
>
> Acute pain, p. 144
> Cancer chemotherapy, p. 812
> Cancer radiation therapy, p. 825
> Disturbed body image, p. 21
> Hysterectomy, p. 1013
> Ineffective sexuality patterns, p. 170

 ## Hysterectomy

Salpingectomy; Oophorectomy; Total Abdominal Hysterectomy; Cervical Cancer

This is a surgical procedure that involves the removal of the uterus with or without removal of the cervix. The surgery may also include removal of the ovaries (oophorectomy) and the fallopian tubes (salpingectomy). Indications for the surgery include endometriosis, uterine fibroids, cancer, elective sterilization, uterine dysfunction or bleeding, and ectopic pregnancy. Approximately 600,000 hysterectomies are performed each year in the United States, with women 40 to 44 years of age being the most likely to have the procedure. Hysterectomy with oophorectomy results in surgically induced menopause. The woman may experience symptoms of menopause more severely than normal menopause because of the sudden loss of hormones.

Hysterectomy

■ = Independent; ▲ = Collaborative

Hysterectomy—cont'd

Every attempt is usually undertaken to retain the reproductive function of women who are still of childbearing age; however, certain clinical situations, such as aggressive forms of cancer, may require aggressive surgery. A hysterectomy can be performed using an abdominal, vaginal, or laparoscopic approach. The surgical approach used is dependent on the surgeon and patient, as well as on the amount of visualization and area of manipulation required. Hospitalization rarely exceeds 3 to 4 days, including the day of surgery. Patients are discharged after bowel sounds have been appreciated and the patient can tolerate a general diet. The bulk of recovery takes place at home with patients gaining full function within 4 weeks if the vaginal approach was used for the procedure, and 5 to 6 weeks if the abdominal approach was used.

NDx Nursing Diagnosis

Deficient Knowledge: Surgical Treatment

Common Related Factors

Unfamiliarity with anatomy and physiology, surgical procedure, recovery process, and menopausal process
Lack of exposure
Lack of recall
Misinterpretation of information
Cognitive limitation
Lack of interest
Fear and anxiety

Defining Characteristics

Verbalized lack of knowledge
Inaccurate follow-through of instructions
Inappropriate or exaggerated behaviors
Request for information
Inability to concentrate or focus on information presented

Common Expected Outcomes

Patient verbalizes understanding of the reason for hysterectomy, surgical procedures anticipated, postoperative recovery, discharge instructions, and follow-up care.
Patient actively participates in planning of care.

NOC Outcomes
Knowledge: Disease Process;
    Knowledge: Treatment Regimen

NIC Interventions
Teaching: Disease Process; Teaching:
    Procedure/Treatment; Teaching:
    Prescribed Activity/Exercise

Ongoing Assessment

Actions/Interventions

■ Assess the patient's understanding of the indications for surgery.
Indications include the following:
  • Severe endometriosis
  • Fibroids or nonmalignant tumors of the reproductive tract that are symptomatic

Rationale

Thorough understanding of indications for the procedure is necessary for informed consent to be given.

■ = Independent; ▲ = Collaborative

Actions/Interventions

- Unresponsive to medical management
- Painful pelvic and abdominal adhesions
- Malignant tumors, including cervical, endometrial, ovarian, or vaginal

Elective indications include the following:
- Family history of reproductive malignancies
- Menstrual irregularities
- Severe dysmenorrhea or premenstrual syndrome
- Termination of reproductive potential

■ Assess the patient's and family's understanding of immediate and long-term postsurgical recovery period.

■ Assess the patient's understanding of ongoing gynecological needs following hysterectomy.

Rationale

The postsurgical recovery period may be difficult and more prolonged than expected.

Patients may assume that the need for yearly or regular gynecological care ceases after hysterectomy.

Therapeutic Interventions

Actions/Interventions

■ Provide the patient with current educational materials about the specific surgical procedure she is about to undergo.

■ Provide preoperative instruction, including rationale for planned surgical approach, explanation of procedures, activity restrictions, and recovery process.

Day of surgery:
- The patient will be NPO (nothing by mouth) until she passes gas and/or bowel sounds are present.
- Have the patient dangle her limbs at bedside the evening of surgery, ambulate in the room, or sit in a chair at the bedside, if tolerated.
- Provide pain medication, as needed.

First postsurgical day:
- Remove the Foley catheter; begin clamp-and-release schedule.
- Allow the patient to ambulate to the bathroom, about the room, and in the hall, as tolerated.
- Advance diet from liquid to soft, to general, as tolerated.
- If laparoscopic procedure was done, the patient may be discharged.

Second postsurgical day:
- Allow the patient to be up ad libitum.

- If an abdominal or vaginal procedure was done, the patient may be discharged.

Rationale

Excellent videos are available that discuss the surgical procedure, indications for, postsurgical recovery from, and psychological adjustments to a hysterectomy. Providing the patient with information in different media formats (e.g., books, pamphlets, approved Internet websites, and videos) will allow her to choose the format that best suits her learning style and needs.

Institutional protocols may vary.

This reduces the risk of aspiration and abdominal distention.

Early ambulation increases peristalsis and circulation.

The patient needs to know about options for pain management.

This reduces the risk for urinary tract infection (UTI) and restores normal urinary elimination.

Ambulation reduces postoperative complications.

The diet is advanced as intestinal function returns to normal.

This surgical approach has few postoperative complications.

Early ambulation reduces complications and helps improve gastrointestinal (GI) function.

Hysterectomy

■ = Independent; ▲ = Collaborative

Hysterectomy—cont'd

Actions/Interventions

- Provide discharge instructions:
  - Abdominal support may be helpful.
  - Avoid lifting heavy objects for about 2 months.

  - Place nothing in the vagina; no penetrating intercourse is permitted for 4 to 6 weeks.
  - Showers, sponge bathing, light activity, and exercise are permitted.
  - Notify the physician of any of the following: increased bleeding, pain, foul-smelling discharge, or symptoms of thrombophlebitis (e.g., leg pain; swelling of calf during ambulation; swollen, red, hot area behind calf).
- Instruct the patient about resuming home activities:
  - Plan brief periods of graduated activity.
  - Minimize or limit climbing stairs.
- Instruct about the need for removal of sutures or staples at postsurgical checkup 7 to 10 days following surgery
- Stress the need to continue with routine gynecological examinations.

Rationale

This prevents strain on the incision line.

This reduces strain on the abdominal muscles and surgical incisions.

These restrictions facilitate healing.

Consider using a shower stool if dizziness and/or weakness is present.

Early assessment facilitates prompt treatment.

Fatigue limits ability to maintain usual household and work activities.

Understanding increases cooperation with routine follow-up procedures.

Periodic examination of the breasts and ovaries and Papanicolaou (Pap) tests are still recommended. Patients on hormone therapy (HT) may be evaluated more often.

NDx Nursing Diagnosis

Deficient Knowledge: Surgical Menopause

Common Related Factors

Unfamiliarity with surgical menopause
Unfamiliarity with HT

Defining Characteristics

Requests information about the expected symptoms of menopause
Questions about the use of HT

Common Expected Outcome

Patient verbalizes knowledge of the effects of surgical menopause and the advantages and disadvantages of HT.

NOC Outcome
Knowledge: Medication

NIC Interventions
Teaching: Disease Process;
    Teaching: Prescribed Medication

Women's Health Care Plans

■ = Independent; ▲ = Collaborative

Ongoing Assessment

Actions/Interventions

■ Assess understanding of menopause.

Rationale

Women who have both uterus and ovaries removed undergo a menopause. Most women have some minimal information about the female climacteric, but few women understand the entire surgical process or the effects of surgical menopause.

■ Assess knowledge about HT.

Individual evaluation is required to determine appropriateness of HT. All women must be given enough information to make an informed choice. Risks are present with and without the use of HT. After hysterectomy, progesterone is no longer required to offset the risk of uterine cancer.

Therapeutic Interventions

Actions/Interventions

■ Describe surgical menopause.

Rationale

With removal of the uterus or removal of the uterus, tubes, and even one ovary, the remaining ovary will continue to function until menopause, when follicular development ceases and the female body goes through a series of changes resulting from estrogen withdrawal. Removal of both ovaries (surgical menopause) results in a sudden, precipitous decrease in hormone levels. The changes that occur are more rapid. Hot flashes begin 1 to 2 days after surgery. Changes in skin and hair occur more rapidly, within months rather than over years.

■ Discuss the benefits and risks associated with estrogen therapy (ET).
Benefits
• Immediate:
  • Reduces hot flashes
  • Relieves vaginal dryness
  • Improves urinary tract symptoms (incontinence and infection)
  • Maintains skin thickness and elasticity
  • Improves sleep
  • Reduces mood swings
• Long-term:
  • Reduces bone resorption
Risks
• Immediate
  • Menstrual symptoms of breast swelling, mood swings
  • Fluid retention
  • Aggravation of migraines
• Long-term
  • Increased risk of cardiovascular problems
  • Increased risk of breast cancer
  • Increased risk of blood clotting
  • Increased risk of gallbladder disease

The decision to take estrogen is based on each woman's personal profile. If surgical menopause results from the hysterectomy/oophorectomy, ET may be prescribed to relieve menopausal symptoms. Usually these symptoms are short-lived, and many women do not require therapy. However, there are significant risks also associated with this therapy. Only short-term therapy may be needed if the outcome is symptom management with the lowest effective dose. Although ET can reduce the risk of osteoporosis fractures, other therapies should be considered given its associated risks.

About two thirds of women who start on HT stop secondary to unpleasant side effects.

Evidence from the Women's Health Initiative (the largest, randomized controlled trial) reports that HT should not be taken for the primary prevention of coronary heart disease, stroke, or dementia. In fact, starting HT may be associated with an increased risk of cardiovascular events for some women. If HT is taken for more than 5 years, there is also an increased risk of breast cancer.

Hysterectomy

■ = Independent; ▲ = Collaborative

Hysterectomy—cont'd

Actions/Interventions	Rationale
Relative contraindications: • History of breast cancer • History of hormone-sensitive cancer • Liver disease • History of blood clotting disorders • History of cardiovascular disease	Each woman needs to evaluate the risks/benefits of treatment based on her personal health history.
■ Describe common HT regimens: • Cyclic hormone therapy versus continuous combined • Systemic versus local	HT needs to be "customized" to the woman, her goals, and any experienced side effects.
■ Describe the role of selective estrogen receptor modulators (SERMs).	SERMs (e.g., tamoxifen and raloxifene) exert tissue-specific effects. They exhibit some of estrogen's beneficial effects on lipid levels and bone metabolism but do not exhibit the adverse effects on breast tissue. Likewise, raloxifene has an adverse effect on endometrial tissue (i.e., cancer) and is the first SERM to be approved for osteoporosis prevention (although its effect is weaker than that of estrogen). The SERMs do increase the risk for thromboembolic events and do not relieve hot flashes (actually, they may intensify them).
■ Counsel the patient to discuss potential ET questions with her health care professional. Examples include the following: • "Is estrogen right for me?" • "How will it benefit my body?" • "What risk might I encounter?" • "What type of regimen is best for me?" • "How long should I take it?" • "What side effects can I expect?" • "Will I be compliant?"	Women need to be comanagers of their health. Only with proper information can they make an informed decision.

NDx Nursing Diagnosis

Acute Pain

Common Related Factors	Defining Characteristics
Incision(s) Verbal complaints of pain Reduced mobility Ineffective pain control	Guarding behaviors Self-focusing and narrowed focus Distraction behavior Facial mask of pain Alteration of muscle tone Autonomic responses

■ = Independent; ▲ = Collaborative

Women's Health Care Plans

Common Expected Outcomes

Patient verbalizes relief or reduction in pain.

Patient is able to perform self-care activities and ambulate with progressive effectiveness.

NOC Outcome

Pain Control

NIC Interventions

Analgesic Administration; Pain Management; Patient-Controlled Analgesia (PCA)

Ongoing Assessment

Actions/Interventions

■ Assess cause of pain:

• Intraoperative position

• Decreased mobility or tension and guarding

• Extreme gas pains

■ Assess level of pain and response to medications.

■ Assess effectiveness of other pain-relief measures:
• Position change
• Backrub
• Heat application
• Relaxation and breathing modifications
• Biofeedback

Rationale

Postsurgical pain may be a result of the incision and manipulation at the surgical site, carbon dioxide remaining in the abdominal cavity following laparoscopy, or other factors. Correct diagnosis of the cause of the pain guides the selection of an appropriate intervention.

Intraoperative positioning may result in intense shoulder pain. This pain responds well to a heating pad or massage.

Manipulation of the intraabdominal contents required to visualize the uterus may cause internal pain related to organ and bowel manipulation in addition to the incisional pain. This may be alleviated with postoperative analgesia, positioning, and abdominal splinting.

These occur from intraoperative manipulation of bowel and from intraoperative and postoperative medications.

Joint Commission on Accreditation of Health Care Organizations (JCAHCO) mandates frequent, regular assessment of pain. Patients have a right to effective pain relief.

Chemical analgesia may not be effective in relieving pain; other methods may be needed.

Therapeutic Interventions

Actions/Interventions

▲ Administer pain medications every 3 to 4 hours in the first 24 hours following surgery. Ask the patient to rate her comfort level and what she feels is necessary. If pain medication is requested before 3 hours, consider a change in medication, dosage, or time.

• Anticipate periods of mobility and administer an analgesic 20 to 30 minutes before.

Rationale

JCAHO mandates frequent, regular assessment and treatment of pain. Patients have a right to effective pain relief. Around-the-clock administration of analgesics on a regular schedule keeps the patient's pain level within a comfortable range.

Decreasing pain levels permits ambulation and improves healing.

Hysterectomy

■ = Independent; ▲ = Collaborative

Hysterectomy—cont'd

Actions/Interventions

- Consider patient-controlled analgesia (PCA) via the epidural or intravenous routes.

- Initiate comfort measures:
  - Position in correct anatomical alignment. Support position with pillows or wedges.
  - Use abdominal splinting during movement.

  - Apply heat or ice as needed.

Rationale

Individual patients react to pain and analgesia differently. Epidural morphine reduces or eliminates incisional pain for 18 to 24 hours. This facilitates early ambulation and prevents many postsurgical complications. PCA provides a continuous basal dose of analgesia while allowing the patient to self-medicate up to a preprogrammed maximum dose/bolus.

This reduces pain and muscle tension.

This supports incision and abdominal muscles, reducing discomfort.

This decreases discomfort by causing vasoconstriction (cold) or vasodilation (heat).

NDx Nursing Diagnosis

Disturbed Body Image

Common Related Factors

Perceived body image changes
Fears of loss of sexual identity or femininity
Loss of childbearing capacity
Effects of surgical menopause on ability to be sexually satisfied

Defining Characteristics

Self-deprecating remarks
Verbalized negative feelings about surgically altered body
Weeping
Decreased attention to grooming

Common Expected Outcomes

Patient is able to identify changes in self, body image, and relationships after hysterectomy.
Patient verbalizes positive statements about body and self.
Patient identifies available resources to aid in coping.
Patient accurately describes effects of hysterectomy as terminating most aspects of reproductive ability.

NOC Outcomes

Body Image; Grief Resolution; Psychosocial Adjustment: Life Change

NIC Interventions

Body Image Enhancement; Grief Work Facilitation; Self-Awareness Enhancement; Teaching: Sexuality

Ongoing Assessment

Actions/Interventions

- Assess knowledge level about loss of reproductive function.

Rationale

After hysterectomy, pregnancy cannot occur because the patient no longer has a uterus to house a developing embryo/fetus. If a woman has a whole or partial ovary remaining, ovulation continues. Reproductive

■ = Independent; ▲ = Collaborative

Actions/Interventions

■ Assess feelings about self and body.

■ Determine ability and comfort in discussing effect of surgery on personal relationships.

■ Assess understanding of the effect of hysterectomy on sexuality and sexual desire and functioning.

Rationale

ability may be maintained through cryopreservation of ovum or embryos for later transplantation in a surrogate. This must be done before surgery.

Loss of reproductive ability may result in lowered feelings of femininity and sexuality. These feelings may be exaggerated by the physical and emotional changes accompanying surgical menopause. Body image changes are affected by age; reason for surgery; religious, cultural, and childbearing expectations; previous childbearing discomfort; history of dysmenorrhea; and previous unpleasant physical or emotional experiences accompanying menstrual cycle.

Open discussion of these issues with partners corrects misconceptions about potential changes in personal relationships. It also identifies specific problem areas to be addressed before and after surgery.

Physical and psychological effects of hysterectomy may alter sexual relations after the 4- to 6-week abstinence required by surgery. Exploration of these feelings promotes more normal adaptation.

Therapeutic Interventions

Actions/Interventions

■ Provide accurate written information about the effect of hysterectomy on reproductive ability, anatomy/physiology, surgical menopause, and cryopreservation of ovum or embryos if desired.

■ Provide anticipatory guidance on management of symptoms and physical changes resulting from surgery.

■ Encourage the patient and significant others to express feelings, ask questions, and correct misconceptions.

■ Explore physiological and emotional influences on sexual functioning:
  • Explain discomforts and fatigue.
  • Explain process of sexual functioning and response.
  • Encourage support from spouse or significant other.
  • Make appropriate referrals for treatments or counseling.

Rationale

It is important not to make assumptions about a woman's acceptance or willingness to permanently end her reproductive ability. Information enables the woman to take control of her life following surgery and elicits her cooperation in decision making and postoperative treatments.

This helps the woman gain control over the situation.

Explanations of surgical menopause may be clarified by comparisons with naturally occurring menopause. Exploration of the most current treatment options to decrease or alleviate symptoms enables the woman to select the options most acceptable to her and her lifestyle.

A woman's response to hysterectomy may range from relief that pregnancy is no longer possible (leading to more enjoyable sexual activity) to sexual difficulties such as difficulty achieving orgasm, painful intercourse (dyspareunia), and conflicts regarding sexual identity. HT and individual or family counseling may provide relief of these symptoms.

• RELATED CARE PLANS

Constipation, p. 46
Impaired urinary elimination, p. 201
Ineffective coping, p. 51

Hysterectomy

■ = Independent; ▲ = Collaborative

Menopause

Perimenopause; Hormone Therapy

Menopause is the point in a woman's life when menstruation stops, as does the ability to reproduce. It is usually confirmed when a woman does not have a menstrual period for 12 consecutive months, in the absence of any biological or physiological causes. It occurs naturally as a part of the aging process. The mean or median age of natural menopause ranges from 48 to 52 years of age. Cancer chemotherapy, cigarette smoking, and surgical trauma to the ovarian blood supply may contribute to the onset of menopause. There may also be a link between heredity and age at menopause.

The 2 to 8 years preceding menopause and 1 year after the final menses is often referred to as the *perimenopause*. Perimenopause begins with the onset of endocrinological, biological, and clinical changes often associated with menopause. Subtle hormonal changes often begin in a woman's 30s. During perimenopause, a woman's oocytes undergo accelerated depletion, which results in cessation of ovulation and changes in serum and hormone levels. The pituitary gland increases the secretion of follicle-stimulating hormone (FSH) to increase ovarian secretion of estrogen, a hormone that decreases during the perimenopause. FSH levels can fluctuate during the perimenopause and may require stopping the use of oral contraceptives before a diagnosis of menopause can be made. Estradiol levels decrease, resulting in insufficient levels to maintain the endometrial lining. Menstrual cycles may become irregular and the intervals between menses may become shorter. This irregularity may result in an unplanned pregnancy until amenorrhea has been present more than 1 year. Abnormal uterine bleeding may result from anovulation, uterine fibroids, abnormalities in the uterine lining, cancer, and blood clotting problems. Pathology must be ruled out before a diagnosis of menopause can be made.

Symptoms during the perimenopause include vasomotor symptoms (e.g., hot flashes or flushes, palpitations, anxiety, and sleep disturbances) and genitourinary effects (e.g., vulvovaginal atrophy and urinary tract conditions). The role of hormone therapy (HT), which encompasses both estrogen therapy (ET) and combined estrogen-progestogen therapy (EPT) in treating these symptoms, is well accepted. Recent evidence from the Women's Health Initiative, the largest randomized, controlled trial, reports that HT should not be taken for the primary prevention of coronary heart disease, stroke, or dementia. In fact, starting HT may be associated with an increased risk of cardiovascular events for some women. If EPT is taken for more than 5 years, there is also an increased risk of breast cancer. Finally, although HT can reduce the risk of osteoporosis fracture, other therapies should be considered given its associated risks. The role of HT for primary prevention of heart disease and other disorders in perimenopausal women is unknown at this time.

NDx Nursing Diagnosis

Deficient Knowledge

Common Related Factors	Defining Characteristics
Unfamiliarity with treatment plans	Asks questions about diagnostic tests and treatment options
Uncertainty about treatment options	Makes statements indicating misinformation
Misinterpretation of information	Expresses inability to make choice about treatment options
Decisional conflict	

■ = Independent; ▲ = Collaborative

Common Expected Outcome

Patient verbalizes understanding of the process of menopause, its diagnosis, and its treatment options.

NOC Outcomes

Knowledge: Disease Process;
Knowledge: Treatment Regimen

NIC Interventions

Teaching: Disease Process;
Teaching: Procedure/Treatment

Ongoing Assessment

Actions/Interventions

■ Assess understanding of perimenopausal symptoms.

■ Assess understanding of the relationship between the normal process of aging and perimenopausal symptoms.

■ Assess understanding of treatment options:
  • Hormone therapy (ET/EPT)
  • Complementary therapies

Rationale

Diagnosis is facilitated by complete reporting of symptoms.

It may be important to emphasize that symptoms are related to "biological" aging, not emotional or attitudinal age.

Most women want a collaborative relationship in the management of this normal biological process and require information about preference for specific treatment options.

Therapeutic Interventions

Actions/Interventions

■ Explain the physiological process of menopause:
  • Cessation of ovulation
  • Hormonal fluctuations
  • Expected symptoms

■ Explain diagnostic tests commonly performed:
  • Blood test for hormone levels
  • Complete physical and pelvic examination
■ Discuss the benefits and risks associated with hormone therapy (ET/EPT).

Benefits
  • Immediate:
    • Reduces hot flashes
    • Relieves vaginal dryness
    • Improves urinary tract symptoms (incontinence/infection)
    • Maintains skin thickness and elasticity
    • Improves sleep
    • Reduces mood swings

Rationale

Women should have accurate information about menopause before its onset. Negative images about menopause have been reinforced by the general public and in the popular media. Women need to understand the physiological process of menopause, its effect on sexuality and reproduction, methods to manage symptoms, and treatment options to promote health and prevent postmenopausal problems such as osteoporosis and heart disease.

This determines level of hormonal fluctuations.

An examination rules out pathology.

The decision to take ET/EPT is based on each woman's personal profile. The primary indication for hormone therapy (ET/EPT) is for relief of menopausal symptoms; however, there are significant risks also associated with this therapy.

Only short-term therapy may be needed if the outcome is symptom management.

Menopause

■ = Independent; ▲ = Collaborative

Menopause—cont'd

Actions/Interventions	**Rationale**

Actions/Interventions

- Long-term:
  - Reduces bone resorption

Risks
- Immediate:
  - Irregular bleeding
  - Menstrual symptoms of breast swelling, mood swings
  - Fluid retention
  - Aggravation of migraines
- Long-term:
  - Increased risk of uterine cancer
  - Increased risk of endometrial cancer

  - Increased risk of heart problems
  - Increased blood clotting
  - Increased risk of breast cancer

Relative contraindications:
- Known or suspected pregnancy
- History of breast cancer
- History of hormone-sensitive cancer
- Unexplained uterine bleeding
- Liver disease
- History of blood clotting disorders
- History of cardiovascular disease

- ■ Describe common HT regimens:
  - Estrogen-progestogen therapy
    - Cyclic EPT (estrogen for 25 days per month, adding progestin on the last 10 to 14 days, followed by no therapy for 3 to 6 days
    - Continuous-cyclic EPT (daily estrogen with progestogen for 10 to 14 days per month)
    - Continuous-combined EPT (daily estrogen with progestogen)
    - Intermittent-combined EPT (daily estrogen with progestogen intermittently)
  - Estrogen therapy
    - Systemic versus local

Rationale

Although ET can reduce the risk of osteoporosis fracture, other therapies should be considered given its associated risks.

About two thirds of women who start on HT stop secondary to unpleasant side effects.

Estrogen therapy increases the risk of endometrial and uterine cancer in women with an intact uterus; however, if combined with progestin, the risk is reduced.

Recent evidence from the Women's Health Initiative (the largest randomized, controlled trial) reports that hormone therapy should not be taken for the primary prevention of coronary heart disease, stroke, or dementia. In fact, starting hormone therapy may be associated with an increased risk of cardiovascular events for some women. If EPT is taken for more than 5 years, there is also an increased risk of breast cancer.

Hormone therapy increases the risk for serious adverse effects in these situations.

ET/EPT needs to be "customized" to the woman, her goals, and any experienced side effects. A woman with an intact uterus needs to take progestogen with estrogen to prevent uterine cancer. Monthly bleeding differs with type of therapy. The current recommendation is the lowest effective dose for the shortest duration to provide symptom relief.

With systemic ET, patch delivers estrogen directly through the skin into the blood, bypassing the liver. This helps reduce problems with blood clots and gallbladder disease. Vaginal creams and rings work locally, yet a small amount of estrogen can circulate in the body. Vaginal ET will not relieve hot flashes and the risks associated with it are unclear.

Women's Health Care Plans

■ = Independent; ▲ = Collaborative

Actions/Interventions	Rationale
■ Describe the role of selective estrogen receptor modulators (SERMs).	SERMs (e.g., tamoxifen and raloxifene) exert tissue-specific effects. They exhibit some of estrogen's beneficial effects on lipid levels and bone metabolism but do not exhibit the adverse effects on breast tissue. Likewise, raloxifene has an adverse effect on endometrial tissue (i.e., cancer) and is the first SERM to be approved for osteoporosis prevention (although its effect is weaker than that of estrogen). The SERMs do increase the risk for thromboembolic events and do not relieve hot flashes (actually, they may intensify them).
■ Counsel the patient to discuss potential HT questions with her health care professional. Examples include the following: • "Is HT right for me?" • "How will it benefit my body?" • "What risk might I encounter?" • "What type of regimen is best for me?" • "How long should I take it?" • "What side effects can I expect?" • "Will I be compliant?"	Women need to be comanagers of their health. Only with proper information can they make informed decisions.
■ Describe some nonpharmacological therapies important for maintaining health and reducing menopausal symptoms: • Proper diet (low fat; increased fruits and vegetables, high fiber)	Menopause is not a medical disease. Regular positive health habits may be adequate to promote good health.
• Weight control	As the body's metabolism slows down and estrogen levels reduce, women are prone to gain weight gradually over the following years. Thus it is important to reduce daily caloric intake by 200 to 400 kcal and increase exercise.
• Adequate calcium intake	Intake of 1200 to 1500 mg daily is required.
• Exercise	Weight-bearing exercise helps stimulate bone growth. Aerobic, strength training, and stretching exercises on a regular basis are all important.
• Smoking cessation	Cessation helps reduce hot flashes and improve HDL profile, as well as reduce risks from blood clotting.
• Other therapies	Clinical trials are currently evaluating the effectiveness of phytoestrogens (plant estrogens) for treatment of menopausal symptoms, primarily hot flashes. Recently, soy-derived isoflavones have been shown to reduce hot flashes for some women, depending on the product. Isoflavones derived from red clover have not been proven effective in the reduction of hot flashes. The evidence for the use of black cohosh is not strong, suggesting that it may be somewhat helpful with mild symptoms. The evidence for the use of vitamin E for symptom relief suggests that it may be a reasonable option for a trial. The use of therapies such as Dong Quai, evening primrose oil, and ginseng are not recommended by the North American Menopause Society (NAMS).

Menopause

■ = Independent; ▲ = Collaborative

Menopause—cont'd

Actions/Interventions

■ Describe other pharmacological therapies used for reducing menopausal symptoms.

Rationale

NAMS recommends antidepressants such as venlafaxine (Effexor), paroxetine (Paxil), and fluoxetine (Prozac) for hot flashes for women who are not candidates for HT, including breast cancer survivors. Nausea and sexual dysfunctions are side effects. Gabapentin (Neurontin) is also recommended by NAMS as a treatment option for hot flashes. Finally, some antihypertensives (e.g., clonidine) have demonstrated moderate efficacy with high adverse effects for treatment of symptoms.

NDx Nursing Diagnosis

Ineffective Coping

Common Related Factors

Hormonal fluctuations
Changing body image
Anxiety
Lowered self-esteem

Defining Characteristics

Labile moods, crying
Restlessness and irritability
Verbalizes fear of losing femininity

Common Expected Outcomes

Patient verbalizes reduced symptom level.
Patient appears comfortable.
Patient expresses satisfaction with therapy and lifestyle.

NOC Outcomes

Anxiety Self-Control; Coping; Social Support

NIC Interventions

Anxiety Reduction; Coping Enhancement; Decision-Making Support; Support System Enhancement

Ongoing Assessment

Actions/Interventions

■ Assess for symptoms of anxiety or ineffective coping.

Rationale

As women progress through menopause, they may experience mood swings, emotional upset, and irritability, which may be attributed only to hormonal fluctuations when other factors (e.g., insomnia and other life stresses) may be the cause. Although menopause itself does not cause depression, women who have a history of psychological disorders (e.g., depression) are vulnerable to recurrent episodes at this time.

■ = Independent; ▲ = Collaborative

Actions/Interventions

- Assess understanding of relationship between hormone fluctuations and normal process of perimenopause and menopause.

- Assess for feelings of optimism and value of self in future.
- Assess for resources and support systems available.

- Assess for impaired memory.

Rationale

Some women may feel incapacitated by the thought of hormonal changes, buying into the "raging hormone" stereotype. Women need to understand that this is a natural process. In some countries, women are revered as they go through this stage.

Not all women view menopause as a loss of sexuality. Many feel excited about their future.

Resources may include family, other women, health care provider, community groups, and spiritual counseling.

Anxiety and labile hormone levels may disrupt ability to remember small details, causing further frustration.

Therapeutic Interventions

Actions/Interventions

- Provide opportunities for the patient to express fears and concerns.
- Encourage the patient to identify her own coping strengths and abilities.

- Identify community resources and support groups (especially women's groups).

Rationale

Verbalization of actual or perceived fears can help reduce anxiety.

Most women, by the time of menopause, have dealt successfully with many complex problems. Opportunities to highlight one's past coping skills can be useful.

Most women rely on one another for both information and understanding. Use of support group networks can be a great source of strength. In addition, such groups can reduce any sense of isolation the woman may experience.

ND_x Nursing Diagnosis

Ineffective Sexuality Patterns

Common Related Factors

Labile hormone levels
Vulvovaginal dryness or atrophy
Misinterpretation of information
Anxiety about loss of femininity

Defining Characteristics

Physical and psychological symptoms that impair sexual feelings
Complaints of painful intercourse
Statements indicating misinformation

Common Expected Outcomes

Patient verbalizes relief of symptoms with correct treatment.
Patient expresses satisfaction with sexual functioning.

NOC Outcomes

Sexual Functioning; Anxiety Self-Control; Knowledge: Sexual Functioning

NIC Interventions

Sexual Counseling; Anxiety Reduction; Teaching: Sexuality

Menopause

■ = Independent; ▲ = Collaborative

Menopause—cont'd

Ongoing Assessment

Actions/Interventions

- Assess understanding of perimenopausal symptoms.

- Assess severity of physical symptoms.

- Assess understanding of possible causes of altered sexuality.

Rationale

Understanding increases comfort with one's perimenopausal body.

Some women may just lose interest in sexual performance, whereas others may experience painful intercourse.

Fluctuating hormone levels contribute to vaginal dryness, sex drive changes, thinning of the vaginal mucosa, and alkalinity of the vaginal secretions. As a result of these changes, a woman may experience dyspareunia, perineal burning and itching, and an increase in vaginal infections. The woman may have concerns about her femininity, sexual attractiveness, and ability to have a satisfying sexual relationship.

Therapeutic Interventions

Actions/Interventions

- Explain physiological changes impacting sexuality:
  - Dryness of vaginal mucosa
  - Hormonal fluctuations causing hot flashes
- Explain sexual treatments to reduce dryness.

- Assist in talking with the woman's partner about personal concerns and feelings.

- Explain the need to discuss with the partner her slower arousal time and need for longer foreplay.

- Explore the use of complementary techniques.

Rationale

Knowledge *normalizes* the process and reduces anxiety. As estrogen levels decline, tissues become thinner, drier, and less elastic.

Vaginal lubricants and moisturizers such as K-Y Jelly and Astroglide may facilitate intercourse. Regular intercourse, likewise, promotes lubrication.

Menopause is a natural process. Sexuality is not tied to intercourse. Starting out with other ways to show intimacy may be helpful.

Longer foreplay is often satisfying to women, and it promotes lubrication. The patient should give herself appropriate time to be aroused.

These may include Lachesis for anxiety, sepia for vaginal dryness, and Natrum Mur for emotional well-being. Supplementation with soy products has been studied, because soy contains high levels of phytoestrogens that bind to estrogen receptors. Positive results have been demonstrated in several studies, but additional research is necessary. Quality and standardization guidelines have not been established.

NDx Nursing Diagnosis

Disturbed Sleep Pattern

Common Related Factors	Defining Characteristic
Labile hormone levels and anxiety causing sleep-altering symptoms Lack of sleep exacerbating other symptoms	Verbalization of loss of sleep related to hot flashes, anxiety, or other symptoms

■ = Independent; ▲ = Collaborative

Common Expected Outcome

Patient verbalizes improved sleep cycles and subsequent decrease in other symptoms.

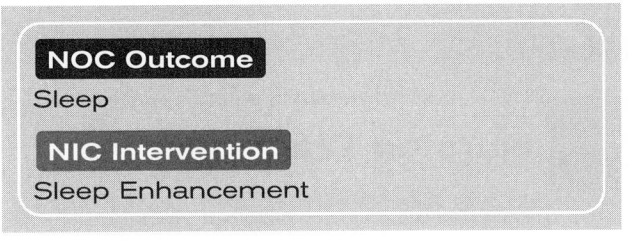

NOC Outcome
Sleep

NIC Intervention
Sleep Enhancement

Ongoing Assessment

Actions/Interventions

- Assess severity of sleep deprivation.

- Determine frequency and severity of night sweats.

- Assess additional factors contributing to sleep loss.

- Assess routines occurring before sleep.
- Assess methods used to alleviate symptoms and their level of effectiveness.

Rationale

Most adult women need 6 to 9 hours of sleep at night. Sleep deprivation is positively correlated with increase in other symptoms. Hot flashes and night sweats can disrupt the usual sleep cycle. This can cause many women to be unable to concentrate at work, further aggravating their response to menopause.

Night sweats are often a consequence of hot flashes. Women commonly awaken with soaking sweats followed by chills.

Environmental temperatures, stresses, caffeinated beverages, and vigorous exercise immediately before sleep can aggravate the situation.

Sleep patterns are unique to each individual.

Information can guide future interventions.

Therapeutic Interventions

Actions/Interventions

- Explain physiological processes resulting in sleep disruption.
- Suggest methods for improving environment and routines to facilitate sleep.

- Provide tips for dealing with night sweats.

- Discuss role of hormone therapy (ET/EPT).

Rationale

Understanding reduces anxiety and fear.

Avoiding alcohol and caffeine and emotional interactions before sleep enhances the environment and is conducive to satisfactory sleep patterns. Maintaining a regular sleep schedule and cooler room temperatures may improve sleep cycles.

Wearing cool cotton clothing to bed and changing bedclothes during the night may be helpful.

HT successfully relieves vasomotor symptoms during menopause.

Menopause

Menopause—cont'd

 Nursing Diagnosis

Risk for Ineffective Health Maintenance

Common Risk Factors

Unfamiliarity with screening routines for menopausal women
Misinterpretation of screening routines

Common Expected Outcome

Patient verbalizes understanding of the appropriate well-woman health monitoring examinations and screenings.

NOC Outcomes

Health-Promoting Behavior; Knowledge: Health Promotion; Participation: Health Care Decisions

NIC Interventions

Health Screening; Self-Responsibility Facilitation; Health Education

Ongoing Assessment

Actions/Interventions

■ Assess understanding of appropriate screening routines.

■ Assess understanding of importance of continued monitoring:
- Mammograms
- Papanicolaou (Pap) smears
- Cardiac screenings

- Osteoporosis screenings

Rationale

Understanding increases cooperation with routine screenings.

Mammograms and Pap smears need to be continued throughout life.

Because risk of heart disease increases with aging, especially after menopause, regular lipid monitoring, exercise stress testing, diabetes testing, and blood pressure monitoring are recommended.

Measurement of bone mineral density is recommended.

Therapeutic Interventions

Actions/Interventions

■ Explain the reason and appropriate schedule for screenings and health examinations.

Rationale

Perimenopausal women need to continue having annual pelvic and clinical breast examinations, Pap smears, and mammograms. They need to do monthly self-breast examinations at the same time each month. Bone density screening provides baseline information about osteoporosis risk. Women many need to continue pregnancy prevention methods for up to 1 year after menstrual periods stop.

■ = Independent; ▲ = Collaborative

Women's Health Care Plans

Actions/Interventions

■ Identify possible barriers to compliance.

■ Promote positive expectation for success.

Rationale

The patient may be unaware of financial reimbursement sources or of free community screenings.

Patients with stronger self-efficacy are more likely to engage in positive behaviors.

• RELATED CARE PLANS

Hysterectomy, p. 1013
Osteoporosis, p. 790

Ovarian Cancer

The cause of ovarian cancer remains unknown. It has been linked to the presence of mutations in the BRCA1 and BRCA2 genes. If mutations are present, a woman's risk for ovarian cancer is 40% greater than for a woman without the genes. About 90% of ovarian cancers develop in the epithelial layer covering the ovaries, most commonly in postmenopausal women and more commonly in white women. Eighty percent of ovarian cancers are first diagnosed in stage 3 or 4 because the early stages are often asymptomatic; this explains the high mortality rate. Later signs of ovarian cancer include increased abdominal girth caused by the tumor size or ascites; abdominal, pelvic, or low back pain; urinary urgency and frequency; and constipation. Treatment depends on the stage at diagnosis. Early stages are treated with surgical removal of the uterus, ovaries, and fallopian tubes, together with the tumor. Later stages are treated with radiation therapy and chemotherapy. A late diagnosis is associated with a poor prognosis. This care plan does not address surgical management.

NDx Nursing Diagnosis

Deficient Knowledge

Common Related Factor

Unfamiliarity with disease and treatment plan

Defining Characteristics

Multiple questions
Lack of questions
Verbalized misinformation

Common Expected Outcomes

Patient verbalizes understanding of the diagnosis and treatment procedures for ovarian cancer.
Patient freely discusses treatment options.

NOC Outcomes

Knowledge: Disease Process;
Knowledge: Treatment Regimen

NIC Interventions

Teaching: Disease Process;
Teaching: Procedure/Treatment

Ovarian Cancer

■ = Independent; ▲ = Collaborative

Ovarian Cancer—cont'd

Ongoing Assessment

Actions/Interventions	Rationale
■ Assess understanding of ovarian cancer and treatment options.	Women may have misinformation about types of female cancers. Previous experience with other women being treated for cancer, or who have died of it, will influence beliefs, some of which may be negative or misconceived. Ovarian cancer has a high mortality rate because of its advanced stage at diagnosis.

Therapeutic Interventions

Actions/Interventions	Rationale
■ Explain that the cause of ovarian cancer is unknown.	Some possible risk factors include family history, advanced age, infertility, ovarian dysfunction, and mutations of the BRCA genes.
■ Discuss clinical manifestations.	No specific symptoms are recognized until the advanced stage, then abdominal swelling and/or pain, bloating and/or feeling of fullness, vague but persistent gastrointestinal complaints, and bowel and bladder dysfunction manifest.
■ Discuss common diagnostic procedures:	Unlike the Papanicolaou (Pap) test for cervical cancer, there is no specific screening test for ovarian cancer. A woman at high risk is recommended to have a pelvic examination, a CA-125 assay, and an ultrasound performed twice a year beginning at 30 years of age and continuing for the rest of her life or until her ovaries are removed.
• Pelvic examination	Pelvic examination is used to assess for masses and growths. This examination can be challenging in obese women.
• CA-125 assay	CA-125 is a tumor marker for ovarian cancer; however, many false-positive results are possible.
•Transvaginal ultrasound	Transvaginal ultrasound evaluates shape and size of ovaries.
• Computed tomography (CT) scan	CT scans provide detailed cross-sectional images.
• Laparoscopy and biopsy	Laparoscopy and biopsy are used to determine the stage and extent of disease, guiding therapy.
■ Discuss staging of ovarian cancer: • I—Confined to one or both ovaries • II—Spread to other areas within pelvic area • III—Spread to lining of abdomen or to lymph nodes within abdomen • IV—Spread to organs beyond abdomen	Staging guides treatment options. Stage III is the most common stage at diagnosis.
■ Discuss common treatment approaches: • Total abdominal hysterectomy and bilateral salpingo-oophorectomy • Chemotherapy • Radiation therapy (external and/or implanted) • Clinical trials	Treatment depends on the stage and extent of disease. For stage I, the usual treatment is total hysterectomy to remove (debulk) as much tumor as possible. In addition, chemotherapy or intraperitoneal radiation implants are usually included. At stage II, external (teletherapy) or internal (brachytherapy) radiation or systemic chemotherapy is used after tumor debulking.

■ = Independent; ▲ = Collaborative

Women's Health Care Plans

Rationale

Stages III and IV are usually treated with chemotherapy. Common drugs include carboplatin, cisplatin, docetaxel, and paclitaxel. Overall, combination therapy is required to treat this malignant disease. Intraperitoneal chemotherapy is also used.

Women are encouraged to participate in available trials either researching new treatments or comparing different treatments. Such participation will provide knowledge about the best way to treat this cancer.

 Nursing Diagnosis

Acute Pain

Common Related Factor

Increased abdominal pressure caused by tumor or metastasis to abdominal structures

Defining Characteristics

Verbal expression of pain
Inability to rest
Guarding of abdominal region
Facial grimacing

Common Expected Outcome

Patient reports absence of pain or tolerable pain.

NOC Outcomes
Pain Control; Pain Level

NIC Interventions
Pain Management; Positioning; Distraction; Relaxation

Ongoing Assessment

Actions/Interventions

- Assess severity, quality, and location of pain.

- Assess factors identified by the patient as precipitating or relieving pain.

- Assess the effect of pain on performance of activities of daily living (ADLs) and activities perceived as meaningful by the patient.

- Assess the effect of psychological factors on pain.

Rationale

Pain is typically abdominal, but may radiate to the back. Pain is caused by pressure on abdominal structures as the tumor enlarges.

Patients may have tried many different therapies and home remedies to manage pain.

Fatigue, anxiety, or depression associated with pain can limit the person's ability to complete self-care activities and fulfill role responsibilities.

Pain is accentuated when the patient feels loss of control and when self-concept or role is threatened. The poor prognosis associated with ovarian cancer may cause grieving in anticipation of death.

Ovarian Cancer

■ = Independent; ▲ = Collaborative

Ovarian Cancer—cont'd

Therapeutic Interventions

Actions/Interventions

■ Suggest positions for comfort.

■ Teach alternative techniques to reduce pain:
  • Imagery

  • Distraction

  • Relaxation
  • Massage of back and shoulders

▲ Administer analgesics as prescribed; develop a schedule for giving pain medications.

Rationale

The following positions are helpful in reducing pain related to pressure: side-lying with knees bent and Fowler's position.

Use mental images and body sense to distract from painful stimuli.

Focus concentration on nonpainful stimuli to decrease awareness and experience of pain.

Techniques using physical and mental awareness increase muscle relaxation and reduce tension and pain.

Ongoing medication alleviates peak pain periods.

NDx Nursing Diagnosis

Risk for Ineffective Breathing Pattern

Common Risk Factor

Presence of ascites (collection of protein-rich fluid in peritoneal cavity)

Common Expected Outcome

Patient maintains an effective breathing pattern as evidenced by absence of dyspnea.

NOC Outcome
Respiratory Status: Ventilation

NIC Interventions
Respiratory Monitoring; Positioning; Medication Administration

---

Ongoing Assessment

Actions/Interventions

■ Assess for signs of ineffective breathing pattern:
  • Altered chest excursion
  • Tachypnea
  • Shallow breathing
  • Verbal complaints of dyspnea
■ Assess for presence of ascites:
  • Measure abdominal girth (be sure to use the same anatomical landmarks each time).

Rationale

Severe ascites secondary to ovarian cancer can impair breathing by limiting full descent of the diaphragm.

This technique provides objective data regarding ascites.

■ = Independent; ▲ = Collaborative

Actions/Interventions

- Percuss the abdomen.

- Check for ballottement.
- Assess the position that the patient assumes for easiest breathing.

- Monitor effect of ineffective breathing pattern on ability to perform ADLs.

Rationale

Percussion over the abdomen sounds dull when fluid is present.

This is a fluid wave caused by shifting of ascitic fluid.

An upright position facilitates breathing because ascitic fluid assumes a gravity-dependent position, relieving pressure on the thoracic cavity.

Ineffective breathing reduces gas exchange and contributes to fatigue and activity intolerance.

Therapeutic Interventions

Actions/Interventions

- Instruct about pacing activities.

- Assist to Fowler's position.

▲ Assist with paracentesis (removal of peritoneal fluids by needle) to relieve significant breathing difficulties.
▲ Facilitate shunt (LeVeen shunt, Denver shunt) function for patients with chronic ascites.

- Apply abdominal binder.

- Encourage use of an incentive spirometer.

- Administer diuretics as prescribed (for patients with a peritoneovenous shunt).

▲ Administer oxygen as prescribed.

Rationale

This reduces episodes of dyspnea from fatigue and excessive oxygen demand.

This relieves pressure from the ascitic abdomen on the thoracic cavity.

This drains ascitic fluid from the peritoneal cavity.

Fluid reaccumulates rapidly following paracentesis. Peritoneovenous shunting returns ascitic fluid to vascular space and provides continuous relief of ascites.

This increases intraperitoneal pressure, causing the valve in the shunt to return fluid into the vascular space.

Inspiring against pressure causes the valve in the shunt to open and shunt ascitic fluid into the vascular space.

This facilitates excretion of excess fluid.

Supplemental oxygen will maximize oxygen saturation.

NDx **Nursing Diagnosis**

Risk for Imbalanced Nutrition: Less Than Body Requirements

Common Risk Factors

Poor appetite secondary to disease, side effects of therapies, and pressure from ascites
Depression
Fear

Common Expected Outcome

Patient maintains an adequate nutritional intake as evidenced by calorie intake of at least 1800 kcal/day.

NOC Outcome
Nutritional Status: Food and Fluid Intake

NIC Interventions
Nutrition Therapy; Nutrition Monitoring

Ovarian Cancer

■ = Independent; ▲ = Collaborative

Ovarian Cancer—cont'd

Ongoing Assessment

Actions/Interventions

- Evaluate weight history and current weight.

- Determine body weight distribution, checking limbs for wasting.

- Assess appetite and factors considered by the patient to influence appetite.

- Assess caloric intake.

Rationale

Ascites may cause a significant increase in overall body weight although the body is actually cachectic.

Weight loss may appear insignificant until the weight of the ascitic abdomen is considered.

Appetite is a complex phenomenon involving physiological well-being and psychological, psychosocial, and environmental factors. Anorexia may result from disease, treatment modalities, complications, and/or emotional turmoil of coping with a potentially terminal disease.

Caloric counts quantify nourishment intake.

Therapeutic Interventions

Actions/Interventions

- Involve the patient and caregiver in selection of calorie-dense, high-protein, high-fiber meal plans.

- ▲ Consult a dietitian for dietary selections palatable to the patient.

- Encourage small, frequent, nutrient-dense meals (at least six per day).

- Encourage activity or exercise as tolerated.

- Suggest mealtime companions and maintenance of a pleasant environment.

- ▲ Give antiemetics as prescribed.

- Educate about oral hygiene.

Rationale

Calories and protein are necessary for strength and healing; fiber combats constipation resulting from inactivity and increased intraabdominal pressure.

Dietitians have a greater understanding of the nutritional value of foods and may be helpful.

Small feedings reduce the work of digestion.

Activity enhances appetite by stimulating peristalsis.

Attention to the social aspects of eating is important in both the hospital and the home setting.

This prevents or alleviates nausea and vomiting.

A clean, moist mouth and mucous membranes may make food more palatable.

NDx Nursing Diagnosis

Risk for Impaired Home Maintenance

Common Risk Factors

Potentially terminal disease
Lack of resources
Inadequate support system

■ = Independent; ▲ = Collaborative

Common Expected Outcome

Patient participates in home care and verbalizes understanding of need for follow-up care.

NOC Outcomes
Family Functioning; Role Performance; Coping; Decision Making

NIC Interventions
Self-Care Assistance; Home Maintenance Assistance; Support System Enhancement

Ongoing Assessment

Actions/Interventions	Rationale
■ Assess perception of ability to care for self and home.	A major stressor can be the woman's role in managing a household and caring for a family. These concerns may supersede her recognition of needing help in caring for herself.
■ Assess available patient resources.	Resources already available to the patient are the basis for determining her need for additional help.
■ Assess need for special equipment in the household.	Equipment may be required to accommodate the patient's needs (e.g., bedside commode).
■ Assess need for a professional caregiver or homemaker.	Assistance may be needed to provide care in the home environment.

Therapeutic Interventions

Actions/Interventions	Rationale
■ Involve patient in arranging and mobilizing support systems. Respect the patient's preferences in arranging assistance.	Assisting the patient in making and carrying out decisions supports self-efficacy and aids in coping with disease, treatment, and outcomes.
■ Initiate referral to a home health nurse or social worker, if needed.	This is important for providing psychosocial support and arranging needed services in advance.
■ Teach the patient the importance of follow-up care.	Patients with ovarian cancer require routine follow-up with a gynecologist or oncologist to monitor progress or recurrence of disease. Advanced ovarian cancer requires chemotherapy and/or radiation therapy to control the disease and its complications. Women who have had ovarian cancer may be at increased risk for breast or colon cancer.
■ Refer to appropriate support groups to meet social and emotional needs (e.g., hospital and community-based organizations or respected Internet support groups).	Living with a serious disease is challenging, carrying a heavy emotional burden. Relationships with persons with common interests and goals can be beneficial.

• RELATED CARE PLANS

Anticipatory grieving, p. 82
Cancer chemotherapy, p. 812
Constipation, p. 46
Hysterectomy, p. 1013
Ineffective coping, p. 51

Ovarian Cancer

■ = Independent; ▲ = Collaborative

Pelvic Inflammatory Disease (PID)

Sexually Transmitted Infection (STI); Salpingitis; Oophoritis

Pelvic inflammatory disease (PID) is an infective process involving the uterus, fallopian tubes, and ovaries, as well as the peritoneum, pelvic veins, and connective tissue. Untreated PID can become a chronic condition; tissue destruction and scarring can cause the formation of abdominal and reproductive adhesions, resulting in infertility or ectopic pregnancy. Treatment includes cultures, diagnosis of infectious agent, and parenteral or intravenous (IV) antibiotics, usually on an outpatient basis. Both the patient and her sexual partner or partners must be treated. Treatment of this problem is complicated by the increasing prevalence of major pathogens such as *Chlamydia* and *Nisseria gonorrhea,* plus syphilis, human papillomavirus (HPV), and human immunodeficiency virus (HIV). STIs have reached epidemic levels, with some pathogens developing antibiotic-resistant strains. There is a positive correlation between the number of sexual partners and the risk for developing PID. Women who use an intrauterine device (IUD) for birth control may be at increased risk of infection because pathogens may ascend via the locator string into the uterine cavity. Women who have recently given birth or had an abortion have an entry portal for infectious agents at the placental site. When other STIs are present, PID must be ruled out. Condoms may be helpful in reducing the incidence of STIs, although research indicates that the microscopic openings in condoms may be larger than some of the infectious organisms. Vaginal spermicides used alone can reduce the risk for cervical gonorrhea and chlamydia. The most effective way to prevent the transmission of STIs is to avoid sexual intercourse with an infected partner.

ND~x~ Nursing Diagnosis

Deficient Knowledge

Common Related Factors

Lack of accurate knowledge about STIs and/or lack of recall or retention of information
Misinterpretation of information
Cognitive limitations
Disinterest in increasing knowledge of STIs
Unfamiliarity with cause of disease, medical management, or prevention
Embarrassment about topic

Defining Characteristics

Verbalization of questions or inaccurate statements
Inaccurate statements or inaccurate follow-through of instructions
Inappropriate or exaggerated behaviors
Lack of attention to teaching, changing subject

Common Expected Outcome

Patient verbalizes an understanding of PID infection, potential complications, medical treatment, and prevention of recurrence.

NOC Outcomes
Knowledge: Disease Process;
Knowledge: Medication

NIC Interventions
Teaching: Disease Process;
Teaching: Prescribed Medications

■ = Independent; ▲ = Collaborative

Women's Health Care Plans

Ongoing Assessment

Actions/Interventions	Rationale
■ Assess knowledge of PID.	Although PID is a frequently encountered infection in women, health care providers cannot assume that all women are knowledgeable.
■ Assess knowledge of the consequences of PID.	Infertility is a major complication. Frequent PID can result in ectopic pregnancy, cervical pathology, and resistance of organisms to antibiotics.
■ Assess past experience with STIs.	Women with gonorrhea or chlamydial infections are at higher risk for PID.
■ Obtain a sexual history.	Incidence of PID increases with multiple sex partners, risky sexual behaviors, and contact with an infected partner.

Therapeutic Interventions

Actions/Interventions	Rationale
■ Remain supportive and nonjudgmental.	The moral stigma of an STI may be an obstacle for those seeking care for a real or suspected STI. Vaginal infections often result in emotional distress. Seeking medical care must not result in a negative response.
■ Explain transmission of PID.	Acute or chronic PID is transmitted during or soon after sexual intercourse or pelvic surgery (e.g., abortion or childbirth). Infections may occur secondary to the use of an IUD. The use of condoms with spermicide reduces the infection rate.

■ Teach the signs and symptoms of PID:
• Early, acute case symptoms include the following:
  • Excessive menstrual cramping
  • Bleeding or spotting outside of the regular menses
  • Painful urination and sexual intercourse
  • Dull abdominal pain or backache
  • Constipation
  • Low-grade fever
  • General malaise
• Late symptoms include the following:
  • Pelvic pain
  • Copious, foul-smelling vaginal discharge
  • Nausea and vomiting
	Symptoms may be absent in women until late in the course of the illness. Symptoms may mimic ectopic pregnancy or appendicitis.

■ Explain common diagnostic tests.	This alleviates apprehension and promotes cooperation.
• Physical examination	Lower abdominal tenderness or pain is a cardinal symptom.
• Gynecologic examination	This rules out other competing diagnoses.
• Laboratory testing	Testing may include erythrocyte sedimentation rate, C reactive protein, white blood cell count, and cultures.
• Pregnancy testing	Ectopic pregnancy mimics PID. Pregnancy status must be determined before treatment with antibiotics.
• Abdominal ultrasound	This is used to rule out other etiologies such as appendicitis.
• Laparoscopy	This permits an optimal view of abdominal and pelvic organs and facilitates culture testing.

Pelvic Inflammatory Disease (PID)

■ = Independent; ▲ = Collaborative

Pelvic Inflammatory Disease (PID)—cont'd

Actions/Interventions	Rationale
■ Explain treatment regimens.	
• Outpatient antibiotic therapy—most common	Treatment options are guided by culture and antibiotic sensitivity results.
• Inpatient antibiotic therapy for high risk	Patients infected with *N. gonorrhoeae* commonly are co-infected with *Chlamydia*. Recommendation is that patients treated for gonococcal infection also be treated routinely with a regimen effective against uncomplicated genital chlamydial infection.
• Treatment of sex partner(s) • Abstinence from sexual intercourse	The patient can be easily reinfected by the sexual partner, who may be infected but asymptomatic.

NDx Nursing Diagnosis

Infection

Common Related Factors

Gram-positive cocci
  • *Chlamydia trachomatis*
  • *N. gonorrhoeae*
  • Streptococcus
Gram-negative cocci
  • *Escherichia coli*
  • *Haemophilus influenzae*
Anaerobes
  • *Gardnerella vaginalis*
  • *Bacteroides*

Defining Characteristics

Edematous vaginal mucosa
Copious, malodorous, greenish-yellow vaginal discharge
Fever
Positive culture or screening test results
Formation of an abscess
Progression to peritonitis

Common Expected Outcome

Patient manifests signs of treated infection as evidenced by absence of fever, absence of pain, absence of vaginal discharge, and negative culture results.

NOC Outcomes
Infection Status; Medication Response

NIC Interventions
Infection Control; Fertility Preservation; Teaching: Prescribed Medication

Ongoing Assessment

Actions/Interventions	Rationale

▲ Assess for presence of minimum criteria for diagnosis of PID
  • Lower abdominal tenderness on palpation
  • Adnexal tenderness
  • Cervical motion tenderness
	The Centers for Disease Control and Prevention (CDC) recommends using a low threshold and minimal criteria to maximize diagnosis of PID due to its potential for serious reproductive damage to women. Treatment is thus instituted on the basis of these criteria after other competing diagnoses are ruled out.

■ = Independent; ▲ = Collaborative

Women's Health Care Plans

Actions/Interventions

▲ Assess for additional criteria to increase specificity of diagnosis.
- Elevated temperature (>38.3° C [>101° F])
- Abnormal cervical or vaginal discharge
- Elevated erythrocyte sedimentation rate (ESR) and/or C-reactive protein
- Positive culture of cervical infection with *N. gonorrhea* or *C. trachomatis.*

■ Assess:
- History of last menstrual period
- Abnormal menses
- Sexual contacts
- Pregnancy status

■ Assess past STI history.

▲ Monitor culture results.

Rationale

According to the CDC, presence of these additional criteria increases specificity of the diagnosis.

The patient's pregnancy status must be known before antibiotics are administered. Certain antibiotics are not safe during pregnancy.

More than one STI may be present at the same time. The presence of a titer elevation may represent an old or a new infection. Serial titers may be required.

Some antibiotic regimens will be implemented before culture and sensitivity results are received. Culture reports must be checked to ensure that organisms are sensitive to the current antibiotic regimen.

Therapeutic Interventions

Actions/Interventions

▲ Institute drug treatment as ordered.
Outpatient regimen:
- Cefoxitin plus probenecid orally, concurrently, or ceftriaxone or equivalent cephalosporin *plus* doxycycline or tetracycline
Inpatient regimen:
- Cefoxitin or cefotetan intravenously *plus* doxycycline

■ Teach importance of proper administration of medications and completion of course of treatment.

■ Stress importance of notifying sexual contacts.

■ Maintain blood and body fluid precautions. If the patient is hospitalized, maintain infection precautions:
- Dispose of soiled items according to infection control policy.
- Maintain strict hand washing for all persons in contact with the patient.
- Cleanse all equipment with disinfectant.
- Use utensils or gloves when handling soiled materials.

■ Instruct about keeping the perineal area clean and dry.

■ Instruct about perineal care after each pad change and after urination or bowel movements.

■ Discourage continuous use of perineal pads. If pads are used during ambulation, change every 1 to 2 hours or more often if needed.

■ Instruct to avoid use of tampons.

Rationale

All patients with PID require antibiotics. Unlike specific STI organisms wherein a single treatment regimen is known, PID represents a complex syndrome that can be caused by a variety of organisms. Thus no single regimen of choice exists for PID. Therefore CDC guidelines are designed to provide broad-spectrum coverage for the most common pathogens.

This will prevent ineffective treatment, recurrence of symptoms, and the development of antibiotic-resistant organisms.

Treatment of partners prevents transmission or reinfection.

These precautions reduce the risk of transmitting infection to others.

Sitz baths may be used to reduce local inflammation. Topical anesthetics may reduce discomfort.

Care prevents skin excoriation.

This reduces the risk of reinfection from exudates on the pad.

Tampons can be a medium for further bacterial growth and may inhibit drainage of pelvic exudates.

Pelvic Inflammatory Disease (PID)

(■ = Independent; ▲ = Collaborative)

Pelvic Inflammatory Disease (PID)—cont'd

Actions/Interventions

- Explain importance of abstaining from sexual intercourse until after follow-up visit.

- Discuss contraceptive use.
  - The CDC makes the following recommendations about the proper use of male condoms:
    - Use a new condom with each act of sexual intercourse.
    - Carefully handle the condom to avoid damaging it with fingernails, teeth, or other sharp objects.
    - Put the condom on after the penis is erect and before genital contact with the partner.
    - Ensure that no air is trapped in the tip of the condom.
    - Ensure that adequate lubrication exists during intercourse, possibly requiring the use of exogenous lubricants.
    - Use only water-based lubricants with latex condoms. Oil-based lubricants can weaken latex.
  - Hold the condom firmly against the base of the penis during withdrawal, and withdraw while the penis is still erect to prevent slippage.
  - The female condom (Reality)—a lubricated polyurethane sheath with a ring on each end that is inserted into the vagina.
- Instruct the patient to notify the physician of the following:
  - Reappearance of severe symptoms
  - Lack of menstruation
  - Nonmenstrual bleeding
  - Severe abdominal cramps
  - Presence of purulent, malodorous vaginal discharge
- Refer to an STI clinic and/or social worker as indicated.

Rationale

Patients may experience pain during intercourse especially if reproductive organs are moved. This pain may result from inflammation of the structures or from the effect of pelvic adhesions.

Condoms may reduce the transmission of certain STIs. Spermicide-coated condoms have been associated with *E. coli* urinary tract infection. Consistent use of condoms, with or without spermicidal lubricant or vaginal application of spermicide, is recommended.

This is an effective mechanical barrier to viruses, including HIV.

Early assessment facilitates prompt treatment.

Risky sexual behaviors may require the implementation of a regular surveillance program (every 4 to 6 weeks or more often).

NDx Nursing Diagnosis

Acute Pain

Common Related Factors	Defining Characteristics
Pelvic cavity inflammation	Pain (expressed or observed pain facies)
Excoriated perineal area	Self- or narrowed focus
Development of abdominal adhesions	Distraction behaviors
	Alteration in muscle tone
	Autonomic responses

■ = Independent; ▲ = Collaborative

Common Expected Outcomes

Patient verbalizes relief or reduction of pain.
Patient appears more comfortable.

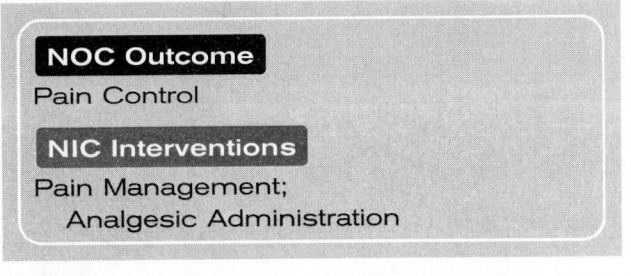

NOC Outcome
Pain Control

NIC Interventions
Pain Management;
  Analgesic Administration

Ongoing Assessment

Actions/Interventions

■ Assess for lower abdominal and back pain.

■ Assess bowel sounds.

■ Assess medication effects and side effects.

Rationale

Pain may be continuous and crampy; bilateral, lower abdominal; or increasing when uterus is moved (e.g., during vaginal examination). Pain may increase with activity.

Cessation of bowel sounds may indicate progression to peritonitis.

Antibiotics are the treatment of choice. Observe for symptoms of allergic reactions.

Therapeutic Interventions

Actions/Interventions

▲ Administer or instruct patients how to self-medicate with oral and topical analgesics, as prescribed.

■ Teach comfort measures:
  • Heat (dry or moist)
  • Positioning with extra pillows
  • Perineal care
■ Encourage a semi-Fowler's position as often as possible.

▲ Administer or instruct the patient on the use of prescribed antibiotics.

Rationale

The patient may experience extreme discomfort requiring narcotic analgesia. Meanwhile, effective antibiotic management will eventually treat causative factors, subsequently relieving pain.

These enhance the effect of pharmacological analgesia and promote comfort.

This promotes drainage of pelvic exudates and prevents development of pelvic abscesses.

Aggressive antibiotic therapy may prevent tubal damage that would otherwise predispose the patient to ectopic pregnancy or infertility.

• RELATED CARE PLANS

Disturbed body image, p. 21
Ineffective coping, p. 51
Ineffective sexuality patterns, p. 170

Pelvic Inflammatory Disease (PID)

■ = Independent; ▲ = Collaborative

12

Endocrine and Metabolic Care Plans

→

Cushing's Syndrome

Hypercortisolism, Cushing's Disease

Cushing's syndrome reflects an excess of glucocorticoids. Depending on the cause of the syndrome, mineralocorticoids and androgens may also be secreted in increased amounts. The syndrome may be primary (an intrinsic adrenocortical disorder, e.g., neoplasm), secondary (from pituitary or hypothalamic dysfunction with increased adrenocorticotrophic hormone [ACTH] secretion resulting in glucocorticoid excess), or iatrogenic (from prolonged or excessive administration of corticosteroids). The syndrome results in fluid and electrolyte disturbances, suppressed immune response, altered fat distribution, and disturbances in protein metabolism. Changes in physical appearance that occur with Cushing's syndrome can have significant influence on the patient's body image and emotional well-being. The focus of this care plan is on the ambulatory patient with Cushing's syndrome.

NDx Nursing Diagnosis

Deficient Knowledge

Common Related Factor

Lack of experience with Cushing's syndrome

Defining Characteristics

Questioning, especially if repetitive
Verbalized misconceptions
Repeated hospital admissions for complications

Common Expected Outcome

Patient verbalizes an understanding of Cushing's syndrome and guidelines for therapy.

NOC Outcomes

Knowledge: Disease Process; Knowledge: Treatment Regimen; Knowledge: Infection Control

NIC Interventions

Teaching: Disease Process; Teaching: Prescribed Diet; Infection Protection

■ = Independent; ▲ = Collaborative

Ongoing Assessment

Actions/Interventions

■ Assess level of knowledge of Cushing's syndrome and the guidelines for therapy.

■ Assess the patient's readiness to learn.

Rationale

An individualized teaching plan begins with assessment of the patient's previous knowledge and understanding of the disorder. The patient or family must understand the disease process and receive specific instructions related to treatment, methods to control symptoms, signs of infections, complications, and indicators of when to notify the physician.

Cushing's syndrome may cause alterations in mental status because of the effects of cortisol on hippocampal neurons. The patient may have impaired memory. This change may limit the patient's ability to learn new information.

Therapeutic Interventions

Actions/Interventions

■ Explain all tests to the patient:

• Urine free cortisol, 17-hydroxycorticosteroids (17-OHCS), 17-ketosteroids (17-KS)

• Dexamethasone suppression tests

• Computed tomography, magnetic resonance imaging, and selected arteriography

■ Anticipate the need to discuss or reinforce the probable treatment in correcting the hypersecretion of hormone:
• If an intrinsic adrenocortical disorder: probable surgery for removal of the adenoma, tumor, or adrenal glands.
• If a disorder secondary to pituitary hypersecretion: transsphenoidal pituitary tumor resection or irradiation.

Rationale

The patient may undergo a variety of diagnostic tests for Cushing's syndrome. Many of the tests require patient cooperation in collecting urine specimens over an extended time period.

To begin the urine collection, the patient is instructed to void and discard this specimen. Then, the patient needs to save all urine for 24 hours. Medications may need to be withheld for several days before urine collection. In Cushing's syndrome, urine free cortisol is elevated. Levels of 17-OHCS (metabolites of cortisol) and 17-KS (metabolites of androgens) are elevated in Cushing's syndrome.

These tests require a combination of urine collections, blood specimens, and administration of dexamethasone. The overnight test is done as an initial screening and does not required urine collection. A prolonged version of the test may be done over 3 days or 6 days. The results help determine the cause of the patient's Cushing's syndrome.

These diagnostic studies are used to identify lesions of the adrenal gland, pituitary gland, or other body organs (lungs, gastrointestinal [GI] tract, pancreas) that are associated with stimulation of cortisol secretion.

Adrenalectomy is the treatment of choice for the patient with an adrenal tumor or adrenal hyperplasia that is causing Cushing's syndrome.

Treatment of pituitary tumors is indicated for patients when the Cushing's syndrome is secondary to ACTH hypersecretion. Surgical therapy usually involves a transsphenoidal hypophysectomy. Radiation therapy may be used as part of the management of these patients.

■ = Independent; ▲ = Collaborative

Cushing's Syndrome—cont'd

Actions/Interventions	Rationale
• If iatrogenic: gradual discontinuation of excessive administration of corticosteroids as the patient's condition permits.	When Cushing's syndrome is secondary to prolonged administration of glucocorticoids, treatment is focused on discontinuing the medication. This approach requires gradual lowering of the dose over time to decrease the risk of adrenal insufficiency if the drug is stopped suddenly. If the patient's condition does not allow for discontinuing glucocorticoids, attempts will be made to adjust the dose and frequency of administration to minimize suppression of the normal hypothalamic-pituitary-adrenal function.
■ Instruct the patient to report signs of localized or systemic infection.	Increase in glucocorticoids inhibits the immune response with a suppression of allergic response, as well as inhibition of inflammation. NOTE: An elevated temperature may not be present with infection because of the decreased immune response. Other signs of infection may be minimized by inhibition of the immune response as well as inhibition of inflammation.
■ Instruct the patient to report areas of skin breakdown and inadequate wound healing.	Wound healing is prolonged in Cushing's syndrome.
■ Reinforce dietary instructions. Instruct the patient in a high-calcium diet.	Cushing's syndrome results in weight gain and calcium and protein loss. A high-calcium diet prevents worsening of osteoporosis.
■ Instruct the patient regarding signs of kyphosis or height loss.	Muscle wasting, fatigue, weakness, and osteoporosis are associated with excess glucocorticoids.
■ Instruct the patient regarding fat distribution.	Chronic cortisol hypersecretion redistributes body fat, with fat from arms and legs deposited on the back, shoulder, trunk, and abdomen.
■ Explain how to obtain a medical identification tag and the importance of wearing it.	The tag can inform others of the patient's condition as a warning so that appropriate treatment will occur in an emergency situation.

 Nursing Diagnosis

Disturbed Body Image

Common Related Factors	Defining Characteristics
Increased production of androgens (giving rise to virilism in women; hirsutism [abnormal growth of hair])	Verbal identification of feeling about altered body structure
Disturbed protein metabolism resulting in muscle wasting, capillary fragility, and wasting of bone matrix: ecchymosis, osteoporosis, slender limbs, striae (usually purple)	Verbal preoccupation with changed body
	Refusal to discuss or acknowledge change
	Change in social behavior (withdrawal, isolation, flamboyancy)
Abnormal fat distribution along with edema resulting in moon face, cervicodorsal fat (buffalo hump), trunk obesity	Compensatory use of concealing clothing

■ = Independent; ▲ = Collaborative

Common Expected Outcome

Patient's body image is enhanced as evidenced by positive patient verbalizations and use of appropriate coping mechanisms.

NOC Outcomes
Body Image; Self-Esteem

NIC Intervention
Body Image Enhancement

Ongoing Assessment

Actions/Interventions

- Assess for changes in personal appearance caused by the glucocorticoid excess.

- Assess for presence of pronounced acne.
- Assess the patient's feelings about changed appearance and coping mechanisms.

Rationale

These may include obesity, thin extremities with muscle atrophy, moon face, red cheeks, buffalo hump, increased body and facial hair. Hyperpigmentation of skin, hair, and mucous membranes occurs as a result of increased levels of melanocyte-stimulating hormones and ACTH.

Acne may result from adrenal androgen excess.

Negative statements about changes in appearance indicate disturbed body image. The patient may withdraw from social interaction. Depression may occur.

Therapeutic Interventions

Actions/Interventions

- Reassure the patient that the physical changes are a result of the elevated hormone levels and most will resolve when those levels return to normal.
- Promote coping methods to deal with the patient's change in appearance (e.g., adequate grooming, flattering clothes).
- Refer to or identify local support groups.

- Provide an atmosphere of acceptance.

Rationale

Information helps the patient develop realistic expectations about the changes in physical appearance.

Learning methods to compensate for changes in appearance enhances the patient's self-esteem.

Talking with people who have experienced similar situations provides social support. Members of a support group offer coping strategies that have proven successful.

Patients look to others for feedback about their appearance. When the nurse responds to the patient in an accepting manner, it supports the patient's adjustment to his or her appearance.

NDx Nursing Diagnosis

Risk for Injury

Common Risk Factors

Poor wound healing
Decreased bone density
Increased capillary fragility

■ = Independent; ▲ = Collaborative

→ **Cushing's Syndrome**–cont'd

Common Expected Outcome

Patient implements measures to prevent injury.

> **NOC Outcomes**
> Knowledge: Fall Prevention; Knowledge: Personal Safety; Risk Control; Fall Prevention Behavior
>
> **NIC Interventions**
> Fall Prevention; Surveillance; Environmental Management: Safety; Bleeding Precautions

---

Ongoing Assessment

Actions/Interventions

Rationale

■ Assess skin for signs of bruising and feces for occult blood.

Patients with Cushing's syndrome will experience loss of collagen tissue that supports the superficial small blood vessels and capillaries. This change makes these blood vessels more susceptible to rupture with minimal trauma. The patient may experience easy bruising and GI bleeding.

■ Assess skin for signs of atrophy and breakdown.

Cushing's syndrome causes thinning of the skin because of loss of collagen and stretching from increased fat deposits. The skin is more easily damaged, with resulting skin breakdown.

■ Ask the patient about problems with slow wound healing.

Increased cortisol levels increase catabolism of peripheral tissues. Impaired nitrogen metabolism associated with Cushing's syndrome contributes to impaired protein synthesis and delayed wound healing.

■ Assess the patient for decreased height and kyphosis.

Hypercortisolism that occurs with Cushing's syndrome causes increased bone resorption, decreased bone formation, increased renal calcium excretion, and decreased calcium absorption from the intestines. These changes lead to decreased bone density and development of osteoporosis. Spinal compression fractures result in decreased height and an exaggerated anterior-posterior curvature of the thoracic spine.

▲ Refer the patient for bone density evaluation.

This diagnostic procedure provides information about the loss of bone density.

Therapeutic Interventions

Actions/Interventions

Rationale

■ Instruct the patient in activities to decrease the risk of bleeding:
  • Use a soft toothbrush.
  • Use an electric razor.

This decreases trauma to the gums.

This reduces the risk of cutting the skin when shaving.

■ = Independent; ▲ = Collaborative

Actions/Interventions

- Eat a high-fiber diet with adequate fluid intake.

- Apply direct pressure over venipuncture sites, injection sites, or wounds for at least 1 minute or longer.

- Instruct the patient about keeping the skin clean and moisturized.

- Instruct the patient about safety measures to reduce the risk of falls and fractures.

- Encourage the patient to increase dietary intake of calcium and vitamin D.

▲ Administer calcium and vitamin D supplements.

- Discuss with the patient safety measures for ambulation and daily activities.

Rationale

These measures decrease the risk of developing constipation, which can result in lower GI bleeding.

Because of capillary fragility, the patient will bleed more easily. Direct pressure helps control bleeding and reduce bruising.

Excessive dryness or excessive moisture increases the risk of skin breakdown.

Cushing's syndrome is associated with loss of bone density and development of osteoporosis. The patient is at risk for pathological fractures as a result of minor stress on the weaker bones.

The patient can add generous amounts of low-fat dairy products and green leafy vegetables to increase calcium intake.

Supplemental calcium and vitamin D are indicated if dietary sources are not adequate.

The patient needs to take precautions with daily activities to reduce trauma that can result in skin trauma, bruising, or bleeding.

NDx Nursing Diagnosis

Risk for Excess Fluid Volume

Common Risk Factors

Retention of sodium and water caused by glucocorticoid excess

Marked sodium and water retention if mineralocorticoids are also in excess

Common Expected Outcome

Patient experiences a normal fluid balance as evidenced by normotensive blood pressure (BP), eupnea, and clear lungs.

NOC Outcomes

Fluid Balance; Electrolyte and Acid-Base Balance

NIC Interventions

Fluid Monitoring; Fluid Management; Electrolyte Management

Ongoing Assessment

Actions/Interventions

- Monitor and record heart rate, BP, and respiratory rate.

Rationale

Cushing's syndrome may result in hypertension caused by expanded fluid volume with sodium and water retention.

■ = Independent; ▲ = Collaborative

Cushing's Syndrome—cont'd

Actions/Interventions

- Assess for signs of circulatory overload: hypertension, weight gain, edema, jugular vein distention, crackles, shortness of breath, dyspnea.
- Monitor weight.

- ▲ Monitor laboratory results (especially potassium and sodium).

- Assess 12-lead electrocardiogram as ordered for changes in rhythm and regularity.

Rationale

Documentation of circulatory overload directs prompt intervention.

Excessive glucocorticoid and mineralocorticoid secretion predisposes the patient to fluid and sodium retention. The patient will experience weight gain.

Excessive glucocorticoids cause sodium and water retention, edema, and hypokalemia. Mineralocorticoids regulate sodium and potassium secretion, and excess levels cause marked sodium and water retention as well as marked hypokalemia.

Unexplained hypokalemia is associated with excessive glucocorticoids, which can result in cardiac dysrhythmias.

Therapeutic Interventions

Actions/Interventions

- Encourage a diet low in sodium with ample potassium.
- Instruct the patient to reduce fluid intake as required by the condition.
- ▲ Administer or instruct the patient to take diuretics.

- Advise the patient to elevate his or her feet when sitting down.
- ▲ Administer or instruct the patient to take antihypertensive medications as prescribed.

Rationale

This helps control development of edema and hypokalemia.

This is necessary to prevent symptoms of circulatory overload.

Diuretics promote sodium and water excretion. Potassium-sparing diuretics may be prescribed to prevent further loss of potassium.

This prevents fluid accumulation in the lower extremities.

Mineralocorticoid excess causes hypertension.

> ### • RELATED CARE PLANS
>
> Activity intolerance, p. 7
> Diabetes mellitus, p. 1050
> Risk for impaired skin integrity, p. 173

Diabetes Mellitus

Type 1, Insulin-Dependent; Type 2, Non–Insulin-Dependent

Diabetes mellitus is a disorder of metabolism in which carbohydrates, fats, and proteins cannot be used for energy. Insulin, a hormone secreted by islet cells of the pancreas, is required to facilitate movement of glucose across cell membranes. Once inside the cell, glucose is the primary metabolic fuel. Type 1 diabetes occurs when the pancreas is no longer able to secrete insulin. This condition occurs as a result of an autoimmune process with destruction of pancreatic beta cells and is usually a condition of children or young

(■ = Independent; ▲ = Collaborative)

adults. Current research suggests that the autoimmune process is triggered by a combination of genetic predisposition and environmental stimuli such as a virus. The result of the insulin deficiency is hyperglycemia. Its onset is abrupt. It represents 5% to 10% of the cases of diabetes. Type 2 diabetes results because of failure of pancreatic beta cells to produce sufficient amounts of insulin as well as resistance of the body to the effects of insulin. This type of diabetes also has a genetic predisposition for insulin resistance in skeletal muscles, fat cells, and liver cells. Type 2 diabetes is characterized by hyperinsulinemia and hyperglycemia. Its onset is slow and gradual, with many individuals having had the disease 10 years before diagnosis. It represents 90% to 95% of the cases of diabetes. This is usually a condition of middle-aged to older individuals, although a recent increase in the incidence of type 2 diabetes has occurred in children.

Diabetes is a major public health problem; more than 16 million individuals, or 6.5% of the population, have the disease. Diabetes causes significant morbidity and mortality. Seventy percent of diabetes-related deaths are from cardiovascular disease. Diabetes is the most common single cause of end-stage renal disease in the United States. Diabetic retinopathy is the most frequent cause of new cases of blindness among adults 20 to 74 years of age. Diabetes is the leading cause of nontraumatic lower extremity amputations in the United States. This care plan concentrates on the care of individuals with type 2 diabetes.

Nursing Diagnosis

Imbalanced Nutrition: More Than Body Requirements

Common Related Factors

Insulin deficiency with inability to utilize nutrients
Excessive intake in relation to metabolic needs
Sedentary activity level

Defining Characteristics

BMI (body mass index) greater than 25 in adults
Frequent urination
Increased thirst
Fatigue
Increased appetite
Hyperlipidemia

Common Expected Outcome

Patient maintains adequate caloric or nutritional intake as evidenced by achieving a reasonable weight, resolving symptoms of hyperglycemia, and maintaining blood glucose and lipid levels within target ranges.

NOC Outcomes

Blood Glucose Control; Knowledge: Medication, Diet, Prescribed Activity; Knowledge: Diabetes Management

NIC Interventions

Nutrition Management; Nutritional Counseling; Weight Reduction Assistance; Hyperglycemia Management; Teaching: Prescribed Activity/Exercise; Teaching: Prescribed Diet; Teaching: Prescribed Medication

---

■ = Independent; ▲ = Collaborative

Diabetes Mellitus—cont'd

Ongoing Assessment

Actions/Interventions	Rationale
■ Weigh the patient on initial and each subsequent contact.	Establish baseline for future comparison. Obesity is a significant risk in the development of diabetes. Nutritional therapy is directed toward weight loss.
■ Calculate BMI.	Evidence suggests a high correlation between BMI greater than 27 and the development of type 2 diabetes.
■ Assess for signs of hyperglycemia.	Hyperglycemia results when inadequate insulin is present to use glucose. Excess glucose in the bloodstream creates an osmotic effect that results in increased thirst, increased hunger, and increased urination.
▲ Monitor blood glucose levels at each office visit and review blood glucose history.	Changes in blood glucose levels, as recorded by the patient, will indicate the patient's success in managing his or her diabetes.
▲ Monitor HbA$_{1c}$-glycosylated hemoglobin.	HbA$_{1c}$ is a measure of blood glucose over the previous 2 to 3 months. Current recommendations are to have HbA$_{1c}$ measured four times each year. The desired goal is to have HbA$_{1c}$ levels less than 6.5% to 7%.
▲ Monitor serum lipid levels to include total cholesterol, low-density lipoprotein (LDL) cholesterol, high-density lipoprotein (HDL) cholesterol, and triglycerides.	Elevated lipid patterns increase the risk for cardiovascular disease in patients with diabetes. Low HDL is also a risk factor.
■ Assess current knowledge and understanding of a "diabetic diet."	Nonadherence to dietary guidelines can result in hyperglycemia. Current guidelines from the American Diabetes Association recommend an individualized plan that promotes healthy eating.
■ Assess pattern of physical activity.	Regular exercise is an important part of diabetes management and reduces the risk of cardiovascular complications. Physical activity has an insulin-like effect and helps lower blood glucose levels.
■ Assess current eating habits.	Knowledge of the patient's food preferences, eating habits, attitudes about food, and financial resources for food purchase is the foundation for developing an individualized nutritional plan.

Therapeutic Interventions

Actions/Interventions	Rationale
▲ Establish goals with the patient for weight loss; glucose, lipids, and HbA$_{1c}$ measurements; and exercise.	*Weight:* Moderate weight loss of 10 to 20 pounds has been shown to improve hyperglycemia, dyslipidemia, and hypertension. *Glucose:* For intensive control, range should be between 80 and 120 mg/dL before meals. *HbA$_{1c}$:* Level should be less than 7%. *Lipids:* LDL cholesterol should be less than 100 mg/dL; HDL cholesterol should be greater than 45 mg/dL in men and greater than 55 mg/dL in women; triglycerides should be less than 200 mg/dL. *Exercise:* Patient should perform 30 minutes of moderate physical activity on most days of the week.

■ = Independent; ▲ = Collaborative

Actions/Interventions	**Rationale**
■ Review progress toward goals on each subsequent visit.	Patient involvement in the treatment plan enhances adherence to treatment regimens. Interest in learning new health behaviors increases when the patient helps set the agenda for change and feels like an active participant.
■ Assist the patient to identify eating patterns that need changing.	This provides the basis for individualized dietary instruction.
▲ Refer to a registered dietitian for individualized diet instruction.	An individualized meal plan based on body weight; blood glucose, and lipid patterns should be developed for each patient. Protein intake is recommended to be 15% to 20% of total calories. Fats are recommended to be no more than 20% of total caloric intake. Saturated fats should be less than 10% of total fat intake. The remaining calories will come from carbohydrates. Current research suggests that type of carbohydrate (sugar or starch) is less important than total carbohydrate intake. Dietary fiber of 20 to 35 g/day is associated with improved glycemic control.
■ Instruct the patient to take oral hypoglycemic medications as directed:	Each category of oral agent acts on a different site of glucose metabolism. Hypoglycemia occurs less frequently with oral agents; however, episodes of hypoglycemia can occur in patients who do not have regular eating habits.
• Second-generation sulfonylureas: glipizide (Glucotrol), glyburide (DiaBeta), glimepiride (Amaryl)	These stimulate insulin secretion by the pancreas.
• Meglitinides: repaglinide (Prandin)	These stimulate insulin secretion by the pancreas.
• D-Phenylalanine derivatives: nateglinide (Starlix)	These stimulate rapid insulin secretion to reduce increases in blood glucose that occur soon after eating.
• Biguanides: metformin (Glucophage)	These decrease the amount of glucose produced by the liver and improve insulin sensitivity.
• α-Glucosidase inhibitors: acarbose (Precose), miglitol (Glyset)	These delay absorption of glucose into the blood from the intestine.
• Thiazolidinediones: pioglitazone (Actos), rosiglitazone (Avandia)	These decrease insulin resistance.
■ Instruct the patient to take insulin medications as directed:	Insulin is required for individuals with type 1 diabetes and for some with type 2 diabetes who develop insulin deficiency over time. Beta cells begin to fail about 10 to 20 years after development of type 2 diabetes.
• Rapid-acting insulin analogs: lispro insulin (Humalog), insulin aspart	Duration of action is 2 to 3 hours for Humalog and 3 to 5 hours for aspart.
• Short-acting insulin: regular	Duration of action is 4 to 8 hours.
• Intermediate-acting insulin: insulin, neutral protamine Hagedorn (NPH), insulin zinc suspension (Lente)	Duration of action is 18 to 26 hours.
• Intermediate and rapid: 70% NPH/30% regular	Premixed concentration has a duration of action similar to that of intermediate-acting insulins.
• Long-acting insulin: insulin, ultralente (Humulin U Ultralente), insulin glargine (Lantus)	Duration of action for ultralente is 36 hours and for glargine is at least 24 hours.
■ Instruct in type, onset, peak, and duration of action of specific insulin.	Characteristics of insulin action determine when injections should be administered.
■ Instruct the patient to prepare and administer insulin with accuracy.	Inconsistencies in technique of insulin preparation and administration can result in elevated blood glucose levels.

■ = Independent; ▲ = Collaborative

Endocrine and Metabolic Care Plans

 Diabetes Mellitus—cont'd

Actions/Interventions	Rationale
• Injection procedures	Absorption of insulin is more consistent when insulin is always injected in the same anatomical site. Absorption is fastest in the abdomen, followed by arms, thighs, and buttocks. The current American Diabetes Association recommendation is to administer insulin into the subcutaneous tissue of the abdomen.
• Rotation of injection within one anatomical site	Injection of insulin in the same site over time will result in lipoatrophy and lipohypertrophy with reduced insulin absorption.
• Storage of insulin	Insulin should be refrigerated at 2° to 8° C (36° to 46° F). Unopened vials may be stored until expiration date. To prevent irritation from injection of cold insulin, vials of insulin may be stored at temperatures of 15° to 30° C (59° to 86° F) for 1 month. Opened vials should be discarded after that time.
• Mixing of insulins: consult manufacturer's guidelines	Mixing of two insulins in one syringe is technically difficult for some patients. Accuracy with this technique is essential. Some insulin products cannot be mixed (glargine) or should be administered shortly after preparation (rapid-acting and ultralente, and rapid-acting and intermediate).
■ Instruct the patient to exercise.	Exercise improves lipid patterns and assists with weight loss.
• Refer the patient to an exercise physiologist or physical therapist, or to a cardiac rehabilitation nurse for specific exercise instructions.	Specific exercises can be prescribed based on any physical limitations the diabetic individual may have.
• Thirty to 60 minutes with warm-up and cool-down periods • Three to four times a week for glycemic control • Five to 7 days a week for weight loss	Warm-ups before exercise and stretching after exercise help prevent muscle injury. Studies have shown sustained improvement in glucose control when a regular exercise program is maintained.
• Instruct on methods to maintain hydration and avoid hypoglycemia during exercise.	Dehydration can hasten hypoglycemia, especially in hot weather. Patients may need to add a snack before exercise if they experience hypoglycemia.

NDx Nursing Diagnosis

Risk for Ineffective Therapeutic Regimen Management

Common Risk Factors

New-onset diabetes
Complex medical regimen
Insufficient knowledge about diabetes and its treatment

■ = Independent; ▲ = Collaborative

Common Expected Outcomes

Patient demonstrates ability to maintain blood glucose levels within defined target range.

Patient demonstrates knowledge of diabetes self-care measures.

NOC Outcomes
Knowledge: Diabetes Management; Blood Glucose Control

NIC Interventions
Mutual Goal Setting; Teaching: Disease Process; Teaching: Individual; Teaching: Prescribed Diet

Ongoing Assessment

Actions/Interventions

- Determine the patient's learning needs.
- Evaluate self-management skills, including ability to perform procedures for blood glucose monitoring.
- Assess the patient's ability and willingness to learn:
  - Cognitive: ability to comprehend and understand instructions
  - Psychomotor: mobility, visual acuity, ability to hear, physical disabilities

- Assess financial resources for health care.

Rationale

These dictate the type and amount of information needed.

This determines the amount and type of education that needs to be provided.

This directs how to present educational information tailored to specific individual needs.

Limited vision may impair the patient's ability to prepare and administer insulin accurately. Limited mobility and loss of fine motor control can interfere with skills needed for insulin administration and blood glucose monitoring. This assessment can lead to appropriate referrals for adaptive equipment.

The cost of medications and supplies for blood glucose monitoring may become barriers to the patient with limited financial resources.

Therapeutic Interventions

Actions/Interventions

- Ensure that the patient has knowledge about symptoms, causes, treatment, and prevention of hyperglycemia.

  - Symptoms: polyuria, polydipsia, polyphagia, weight loss, elevated blood glucose levels, fatigue, blurred vision, poor wound healing
  - Causes: increased food intake, decreased medications, infection, illness, stress
  - Treatment: increased fluid intake, medications to reduce blood glucose levels, identification and treatment of cause

  - Prevention: adherence to dietary guidelines and medical regimen; blood glucose monitoring conducted on a regular basis permits early treatment of hyperglycemia

Rationale

Elevated blood glucose levels in individuals with previously diagnosed diabetes indicate the need to evaluate diabetes management.

The buildup of glucose in the body results in symptoms that can be identified by the patient. Ensure that the patient has been educated regarding these symptoms.

Illness increases counterregulatory hormones that elevate blood glucose levels.

Dehydration causes many of the symptoms related to hyperglycemia. The patient may receive insulin to reduce blood glucose and prevent diabetic ketoacidosis (DKA).

Nonadherence to medical regimen is frequently a cause of hyperglycemia. Effective long-term management of blood glucose levels reduces the risk of vascular complications of diabetes mellitus. These complications include nephropathy, neuropathy, retinopathy, cerebrovascular disease, and coronary artery disease.

■ = Independent; ▲ = Collaborative

Diabetes Mellitus—cont'd

Actions/Interventions

- Ensure that the patient has knowledge about symptoms, causes, treatment, and prevention of hypoglycemia.
  - Symptoms: *autonomic*—trembling, shaking, sweating, pounding heart rate, fast pulse, tingling in extremities, heavy breathing; *neuroglycopenic*—slow thinking, blurred vision, slurred speech, trouble concentrating, fatigue or sleepiness.
  - Causes: *meals*—delayed or missed meals or snacks, irregular timing of meals, irregular carbohydrate content of meals; *medications*—increased dose, medication taken at the wrong time; *activity*—increased physical activity without additional carbohydrate intake.
  - Treatment: 10 to 15 g of carbohydrate for blood glucose levels less than 70 mg/dL; 30 g may be needed for levels less than 50 mg/dL. Examples of 10-g sources include 3 to 4 glucose tablets, 8 to 10 Lifesavers candies, and 4 to 6 ounces of fruit juice.
  - Prevention: adherence to medication and dietary guidelines, regular self-monitoring of blood glucose, accurate medication-taking practices.
- Teach relationship between medication management and blood glucose control.

- ▲ Refer to endocrinologist or diabetes care provider to discuss use of continuous subcutaneous insulin infusion (CSII).

- ▲ Refer to social services for help with financial resources.

- Review current dietary goals for type 2 diabetes with the patient and family: normalize blood glucose and lipid values, improve eating habits, restrict caloric intake, achieve moderate weight loss, maintain consistent carbohydrate intake at meals and snacks, and decrease fat intake.

- Teach the relationship between regular exercise and blood glucose control.

- Review blood glucose monitoring results on each contact with the patient.

Rationale

Frequent episodes of hypoglycemia in individuals with previously diagnosed diabetes indicate the need to evaluate diabetes management.

Autonomic symptoms represent the action of counter-regulatory hormones, initially epinephrine, to the effects of lowered blood glucose levels. Neuroglycopenic symptoms occur because of depletion of glucose in the central nervous system.

All cases of hypoglycemia are caused by excess insulin in relation to available nutrients.

10 to 15 g of carbohydrate should raise blood glucose levels 30 to 45 mg/dL. Glucose-containing products will produce faster results than those containing fat or protein.

Hypoglycemia can largely be prevented by appropriate self-management behaviors.

Approximately 90% of persons with diabetes will require oral antidiabetes medications, insulin, or both. Intensive insulin therapy with multiple daily injections is associated with improved outcomes for blood glucose control and reduced vascular complications.

Insulin infusion devices provide for improved outcomes of blood glucose control compared to multiple daily injections. Use of insulin pumps requires a highly motivated patient to learn how to manage the pump.

Nonadherence to a treatment plan may occur because of limited resources for purchasing medications and blood glucose monitoring supplies. Some costs may not be covered by health insurance.

Successful outcomes for nutritional management require not only active participation by the patient but also participation by family members. The person responsible for meal planning and preparation needs to have a good understanding of nutritional management for diabetes.

Exercise lowers HbA_{1c} levels, improves insulin sensitivity, achieves and maintains weight loss, and decreases cardiac risk factors.

This measures progress to achieving previously set blood glucose goals. Positive feedback on goal attainment helps motivate the patient to continue with health behaviors for effective diabetes management.

■ = Independent; ▲ = Collaborative

Actions/Interventions

- Instruct the patient to increase frequency of blood glucose monitoring during periods of hyperglycemia and hypoglycemia.

- Instruct the patient how to use blood glucose results in overall diabetes management: review basics of pattern management.

- Evaluate effectiveness of previous instruction.

- Instruct the patient on diabetes management during illness.
  - Instruct the patient to take all diabetes medications.

  - Self-monitor blood glucose every 2 to 4 hours.

  - Test urine for ketones every 3 to 4 hours if blood glucose is consistently greater than 300 mg/dL in the presence of abdominal pain, nausea, and/or vomiting.

  - Drink 8 ounces of fluids every 4 hours: sugar-free drinks are recommended when the patient is able to maintain normal carbohydrate intake. Substitute drinks containing sugar when the individual is unable to eat solid food due to anorexia.

- Instruct the patient how and when to take additional rapid- or short-acting insulin as directed.

- Instruct when to contact the primary care provider: blood glucose levels greater than 300 mg/dL, vomiting for more than 2 to 4 hours, failure of urinary ketones to clear within 12 hours, symptoms of dehydration, or symptoms suggesting development of DKA or hyperglycemic hyperosmolar nonketotic syndrome (HHNS).

- Instruct the patient to carry medical identification at all times.

- Instruct the patient about planning for diabetes management when traveling such as putting medications in carry-on luggage.

Rationale

Monitoring allows the patient to identify the onset of side effects of therapy or the onset of complications of the disease.

Instruction allows the patient to identify when therapy adjustments need to be made in diabetes treatment. Blood glucose monitoring results allows the patient to make adjustments in food intake, exercise, and medication dosage in order to maintain therapeutic outcomes for blood glucose levels.

Evaluation provides opportunity to correct any errors in technique. Education is an ongoing process that requires reinforcement over time.

Insulin requirements increase with infection. Secretion of catecholamines, cortisol, and growth hormone in response to the stress of illness results in increased blood glucose levels.

This provides information on response of blood glucose to therapy.

Testing provides for early detection of DKA in patients with type 1 diabetes.

Sufficient fluid intake is needed to prevent dehydration that occurs with hyperglycemia.

Supplements of rapid-acting insulin may be required every 2 to 3 hours to treat hyperglycemia.

Early treatment of hyperglycemia can prevent the occurrence of DKA or HHNS.

It is important for medical personnel to be able to identify the patient as having diabetes to provide appropriate care in an emergency.

Some travel may involve time changes that can disrupt the patient's usual routines.

■ = Independent; ▲ = Collaborative

Endocrine and Metabolic Care Plans

→ Diabetes Mellitus—cont'd

NDx Nursing Diagnosis

Risk for Impaired Skin Integrity

Common Risk Factors

Hyperglycemia
Peripheral sensory neuropathy
Motor function deficit
Autonomic neuropathy
Immune system deficits
Vascular insufficiency

Common Expected Outcome

Patient maintains intact skin by performing daily foot care practices.

NOC Outcomes
Tissue Integrity: Skin and Mucous Membranes; Self-Care: Hygiene; Knowledge: Treatment Regimen

NIC Interventions
Foot Care; Skin Surveillance; Nail Care; Teaching: Individual

Ongoing Assessment

Actions/Interventions	Rationale
■ Assess the general appearance of the foot. Note hygiene.	This provides the basis for future patient education. The patient's feet should be inspected at every visit. The foot is extremely vulnerable to circulatory changes from macrovascular complications of diabetes mellitus. The development of atherosclerosis is accelerated in the patient with diabetes as a result of alterations in lipid metabolism. Foot lesions and associated wound infections are the most common reason for hospitalization of the patient with diabetes.
■ Assess the status of the nails.	Fungal infections in nails serve as a port of entrance for bacteria. The person with diabetes has an increased risk for infection because of impaired immunity. Individuals with thickened, deformed, or ingrown nails should be referred to their primary care provider for appropriate treatment.
■ Assess skin integrity. Note color of skin, presence or absence of ulceration, moisture, quality of the skin, and presence of dermatitis.	Autonomic neuropathy leads to decreased perspiration, causing excessive dryness and fissuring of the skin. Skin breakdown predisposes the patient to infection.
■ Assess for abnormalities in the shape of the foot: pes cavus with prominent metatarsal heads, hammer or claw toes, bunions, and Charcot foot deformity.	Motor neuropathy leads to muscle weakness and atrophy that changes the shape of the foot.

■ = Independent; ▲ = Collaborative

Actions/Interventions

- Note the presence or absence of callus formation or corns.

- Assess the circulatory status of the foot by palpation of peripheral pulses. A Doppler ultrasound transducer can be used when pulses are no longer palpable.
  - Dorsalis pedis
  - Posterior tibial
- Assess for evidence of infection. Local symptoms include redness, drainage, and swelling. Systemic symptoms include fever and malaise, and loss of blood glucose control.
- Assess for edema.

- Assess protective sensation with 5.07 monofilament.

- Examine hosiery and shoes for condition and fit.

- Assess the patient's ability to reach his or her feet and perform self-examination and nail care.

Rationale

Pressure over bony prominences leads to callus formation. This condition can lead to the development of skin breakdown.

Atherosclerosis results in gradual decrease in blood supply to the foot.

Infection may be the initiating event for eventual amputation. Symptoms of pain and tenderness may be absent because of neuropathy.

Edema is a major predisposing factor to ulcerations. Autonomic neuropathy results in loss of vasomotor reflexes and swelling in the foot.

The absence of protective sensation places the patient at high risk for foot injury.

Localized redness over bony prominences indicates the shoe is too tight.

This provides basis for future patient education.

Therapeutic Interventions

Actions/Interventions

- Instruct the patient in principles of hygiene: wash feet daily in warm water using mild soap. Dry carefully and gently, especially between the toes.
- Teach the patient to inspect feet daily for cuts, scratches, and blisters. Use a mirror if necessary to examine the bottom of the foot. Instruct the patient to use both visual inspection and touch.

- Encourage use of moisturizing lotion at least once daily. Avoid area between the toes.

- Report signs of infection immediately to the primary care provider:
  - Area of skin breakdown
  - Increase in temperature as compared with the same location on the opposite foot
  - Discharge that develops an odor
- Teach the patient to inspect shoes daily by feeling the inside of the shoe for irregularities in the lining, sharp objects in the sole of the shoe, or foreign bodies in the shoe.
- ▲ Instruct the patient in appropriate footwear. Have the foot size measured and try shoes on before purchase. Refer patients with hammertoes to a podiatrist or foot care specialist for extra-depth or custom-molded footwear.

Rationale

Maceration between the toes predisposes the patient to infection.

All surfaces of the foot need to be examined, including skin between the toes. Touch will identify skin surface alterations that are not evident by sight.

This replaces moisturizing effects lost by autonomic neuropathy. Select lotion with low alcohol content to prevent further drying of the skin.

Early treatment is essential in prevention of amputation. Clinical studies on amputations have found that as many as 85% of patients have foot ulcers before amputation.

Careful daily assessment reduces risk of injury to the foot. Peripheral neuropathy and loss of protective sensation limits the ability of the patient to feel irregularities that could precipitate an injury to the foot.

Width: The widest part of the shoe must accommodate the widest part of the foot. *Length*: There should be ½ inch of space between the longest toe and the end of the shoe. *Toe box*: The toe box should be high with a rounded toe. *Heel height*: This should be less than 2 inches.

■ = Independent; ▲ = Collaborative

Diabetes Mellitus—cont'd

Actions/Interventions

- Instruct the patient to wear clean, well-fitting stockings made from soft cotton, synthetic blend, or wool.

- Teach the patient to avoid thermal injuries by:
  - Testing the temperature of bath water with the elbow, wrist, or thermometer
  - Avoiding use of heating pads, hot water bottles, or electric blankets
  - Maintaining a safe distance from heat sources such as the fireplace or space heater

- Instruct patients to always wear protective footwear; never go barefoot.

- Instruct the patient to avoid soaking the feet.

- Instruct the patient to trim nails straight across and to file sharp corners to match contour of the toe. Suggest that a family member or podiatrist trim the nails when the patient cannot see well or has difficulty reaching his or her feet.

- Instruct the patient to avoid self-treatment.
  - Do not use adhesive tape, wart treatments, corn plasters, or strong antiseptics.
  - Do not use over-the-counter fungal products without approval of the primary care provider.
  - Avoid "bathroom surgery."

- Stress the importance of maintaining normal blood glucose levels.

- Encourage the patient to stop smoking.

Rationale

Soft cotton or wool absorbs moisture from perspiration and discourages an environment in which fungus can thrive.

Sensory neuropathy may result in loss of normal pain and temperature sensation. These changes increase risk for burns.

This prevents injury to the foot.

Soaking can macerate the skin and increase risk of infection.

This avoids injury to the toes when self-care cannot be provided.

Many over-the-counter agents contain salicylic acid, which can cause ulceration in the diabetic foot.

Over-the-counter products may increase microbial resistance when they are used inappropriately.

Cutting away corns and calluses increases the risk of further foot injury and infection.

Elevated blood glucose or glycosylated hemoglobin levels are associated with risk of foot ulcers. Hyperglycemia impairs wound healing.

Chronic vasoconstriction, caused by smoking, reduces the ability of tissues to heal.

NDx Nursing Diagnosis

Risk for Ineffective Coping

Common Risk Factors

Complex medical regimen
Requirement for changes in lifelong habits
Increasing self-care requirements to maintain blood glucose control

■ = Independent; ▲ = Collaborative

Common Expected Outcome

Patient performs self-care behaviors, identifies stressors that interfere with ability to control diabetes, and develops appropriate action plan to deal with stressors.

NOC Outcomes
Coping; Decision Making

NIC Interventions
Coping Enhancement; Decision-Making Support; Mutual Goal Setting; Self-Modification Assistance

Ongoing Assessment

Actions/Interventions

■ Assess for signs and symptoms of ineffective coping:
  • Nonadherence to regimen
  • Lack of metabolic control
  • Reports or demonstrates symptoms of depression or anxiety: sleep disorders, fatigue, or irritability
  • Evidence of substance abuse: tobacco, alcohol, or recreational drugs

■ Assess current methods of coping with stress. Ask the patient to identify behaviors used in stressful situations.

■ Assess the individual's personal goals regarding diabetes management.

■ Assess readiness for change. Stages of change include the following:
  • Precontemplation: not thinking about change
  • Contemplation: considering change in the near future
  • Preparation: seriously considering change in the near future
  • Action: in process of behavior change
  • Maintenance: continued change for an extended period

■ Assess the ability of the patient to implement self-management behaviors.

Rationale

Inability to adapt to stress results in use of defense mechanisms such as repression, denial, and rationalization. These can interfere with rational decision making and prescribed therapy.

Individuals tend to use behaviors that have worked well for them in the past. Prior coping mechanisms may not be effective in helping the patient cope with long-term health behavior changes.

Focusing on patient goals will increase the likelihood of overall success.

Interventions are more likely to be successful when they are consistent with the person's stage of readiness for change.

Stress can impair the ability of the patient to perform self-care behaviors.

Therapeutic Interventions

Actions/Interventions

■ Assist the patient to identify situations that cause anxiety or increase stress.

■ Help the patient identify thoughts and feelings associated with stressors.

Rationale

A starting point is to ask the patient what he or she finds most difficult to do. The patient may be able to cope with only one health behavior change at a time. Learning to manage medications, diet, and exercise at the same time may leave the patient feeling overwhelmed and anxious.

Feelings of anger, denial, and depression are frequently associated with a chronic disease.

■ = Independent; ▲ = Collaborative

Diabetes Mellitus—cont'd

Actions/Interventions	Rationale
■ Help the patient identify stress-related diabetes problems and issues on which the patient wants to work.	Guiding the patient to view the situation in smaller parts may make coping more manageable.
■ Help the patient identify effective adaptive coping strategies, for example: • Knowing how to make healthy food choices at a dinner party • Knowing when and how to adjust medication dosage to treat hyperglycemic and hypoglycemic episodes • Having a carbohydrate source available during exercise to prevent hypoglycemia	Anxiety can be reduced when the patient has anticipated a stressor and developed a plan to reduce or avoid the stressor.
■ Provide education needed to enable the patient to perform self-management behaviors; for example: • Self–blood glucose monitoring • Medication administration • Adjustment of therapy for exercise and illness • Meal planning • Hypoglycemia management • Hyperglycemia management	Anxiety can be reduced when the patient has the technical knowledge and ability to perform the self-care behaviors required for blood glucose control. Non-adherence to requirements may occur because of patient misunderstanding of information.
■ Assist the patient in examining available resources to meet goals. Review health care resources that are available for use. Provide telephone numbers when possible.	Social support increases the ability of the patient to deal with stress.
■ Provide positive reinforcement for use of adaptive behaviors.	Reinforcement increases the patient's confidence in his or her ability to perform specific behaviors.
■ Acknowledge that change may not be possible.	The patient's level of readiness for change may prevent alterations in behavior.

• **RELATED CARE PLANS**

Deficient knowledge, p. 116
Diabetic ketoacidosis, p. 1062
Ineffective tissue perfusion, p. 198
Risk for infection, p. 108

Diabetic Ketoacidosis (DKA) and Hyperglycemic Hyperosmolar Nonketotic Syndrome (HHNS)

Insulin deficiency causes two conditions of hyperglycemia. Both diabetic ketoacidosis (DKA) and hyperglycemic hyperosmolar nonketotic syndrome (HHNS) are emergency situations and require hospitalization. In DKA, insulin deficiency and elevated levels of counterregulatory hormones result in hyperglycemia, ketonemia, and metabolic acidosis with dehydration and fluid and electrolyte imbalances. Insulin deficiency causes hyperglycemia. To meet the cellular demand for glucose, catecholamines, cortisol, and growth hormone are released. These hormones trigger glycogenolysis and gluconeogenesis from protein catabolism. The insulin deficiency also stimulates breakdown of fats into fatty acids and ketones. The hyperglycemia causes an osmotic diuresis that results in fluid volume deficit. The patient develops hyponatremia, hypocalcemia, hypokalemia, and

■ = Independent; ▲ = Collaborative

decreased levels of magnesium and phosphate. In type 1 diabetes, the onset of DKA can be abrupt and frequently occurs as the result of an infection. DKA also occurs in type 2 diabetes when an acute illness or injury increases the demand for insulin. Careful assessment is required to determine the cause of DKA. Nondiabetic ketoacidosis can occur in alcohol intoxication, severe starvation ketosis, and with the use of drugs such as cocaine.

HHNS is characterized by the presence of severe hyperglycemia, dehydration, and hyperosmolarity. It is usually seen in elderly individuals who develop an infection and are unable to maintain oral intake sufficient to prevent dehydration. They produce enough insulin to minimize ketosis but not to control hyperglycemia. Diagnosis is sometimes made difficult by the presence of neurological symptoms such as hemiparesis, seizures, and coma. These symptoms are related to cerebral dehydration. The major nursing diagnosis for both conditions involves fluid volume deficits. Specific nursing actions are dictated by the degree of fluid volume deficit and resultant fluid and electrolyte disorders.

 ## Nursing Diagnosis

Risk for Deficient Fluid Volume

Common Risk Factors

Hyperglycemic induced osmotic diuresis
Excessive loss of fluids and electrolytes due to vomiting
Decreased intake of fluids and electrolytes due to anorexia and nausea

Common Expected Outcome

Patient achieves adequate fluid balance as indicated by urinary output greater than 30 mL/hr, elastic skin turgor, moist and pink mucous membranes, blood pressure (BP) greater than 90/60 mm Hg, heart rate (HR) 60 to 100 beats/min, and blood glucose levels between 70 and 200 mg/dL.

NOC Outcomes

Fluid Balance; Electrolyte and Acid-Base Balance; Blood Glucose Control

NIC Interventions

Fluid Management; Hyperglycemia Management; Electrolyte Monitoring; Electrolyte Management: Hyperkalemia; Electrolyte Management: Hyponatremia; Acid-Base Management: Metabolic Acidosis; Hypoglycemia Management

Ongoing Assessment

Actions/Interventions	Rationale
■ Weigh the patient daily during hospitalization.	Changes in daily weight can provide information on fluid balance and the adequacy of fluid volume replacement. Weight loss of 2 pounds in 24 hours indicates fluid loss of 1 L.
■ Measure and record intake and output hourly: report urine output less than 30 mL for 2 consecutive hours.	Fluid volume deficit reduces glomerular filtration and renal blood flow causing oliguria or anuria.

■ = Independent; ▲ = Collaborative

Diabetic Ketoacidosis (DKA) and Hyperglycemic Hyperosmolar Nonketotic Syndrome (HHNS)—cont'd

Actions/Interventions

■ Assess the patient for physical signs of volume deficit: loss of skin turgor, dry mucous membranes, or complaints of thirst.

■ Measure and record vital signs every 15 minutes until stable: report HR greater than 120 beats/min; BP less than 90/60 mm Hg or BP decreased greater than 20 mm Hg from baseline; central venous pressure (CVP) less than 2 mm Hg (or <5 cm H_2O).

■ Assess neurological status every 2 hours until the patient returns to baseline: report alterations in mental status, focal neurological signs (hemiparesis or hemianopsia), and seizures.

■ Monitor serum glucose initially every 30 to 60 minutes.

▲ Calculate plasma osmolality:

$$\frac{2\,[\text{Sodium (mEq/L)}] + \text{Glucose (mg/dL)} + \text{Blood urea nitrogen (BUN) (mg/dL)}}{2.8}$$

■ Assess for signs of hypokalemia: fatigue, malaise, confusion, muscular weakness, cramping or pain, shallow respirations, and abnormalities in cardiac conduction with potential for a variety of arrhythmias. Report serum potassium levels less than 3.5 mEq/L.

■ Assess for signs of hyponatremia: muscle weakness, headache, malaise, confusion to coma, poor skin turgor, weight loss, decreased CVP, nausea, abdominal cramps. Report serum sodium levels less than 136 mEq/L.

▲ Assess for increased anion gap.

$$[\text{Na}^+] - ([\text{Cl}] + [\text{HCO}_3])$$

■ Assess for signs of acidosis: drowsiness, coma, confusion, decreased BP, arrhythmias, peripheral vasodilation, nausea, vomiting, diarrhea, abdominal pain, headache, Kussmaul respirations.

■ Assess level of serum ketones: acetoacetate, β-hydroxybutyrate, and acetone.

■ Assess arterial blood gases. Normal values are as follows:

• pH = 7.4

Rationale

This provides baseline data for further comparison. The eyes may appear sunken, and in extreme fluid deficit the eyeballs may be soft to palpation.

Compensatory mechanisms result in peripheral vasoconstriction with weak, thready pulse that is easily obliterated, drop in systolic BP, orthostatic hypotension, hypotension in recumbent position, and reduced CVP.

Severe volume depletion may cause alteration in sensorium secondary to dehydration of cerebral tissue. The patient may present with lethargy and progress to coma.

Diagnostic criteria for DKA: blood glucose greater than 250 mg/dL; for HHNS: blood glucose greater than 600 mg/dL with total serum osmolality greater than 330 mOsm/kg.

Normal is 290 ± 5 mOsm/kg. Elevated osmolality of extracellular fluid produces cellular dehydration.

Osmotic diuresis causes increased excretion of potassium. Insulin therapy results in shifting of potassium intracellularly. Both DKA and HHNS result in a total body deficit of potassium. In the early stages of mild dehydration, potassium levels may be normal or slightly elevated. As the fluid deficit progresses, the potassium level will be low.

Hyperglycemia causes water to be pulled from intracellular fluid and placed in the extracellular compartment, causing dilution of serum sodium. Osmotic diuresis contributes to hyponatremia.

Normal is 8 to 16 mEq/L. DKA is associated with a positive anion gap.

Patients with DKA have metabolic acidosis with arterial pH less than 7.3 and serum bicarbonate less than 15 mEq/L. Acetone is exhaled by the lungs, giving the "fruity" odor to breath.

DKA is associated with elevated levels of ketone bodies in the blood. Urine ketone tests are not reliable for diagnosing or monitoring DKA.

The best way to evaluate acid-base balance is to measure arterial blood gases.

pH reflects H^+ concentration; acidity increases as H^+ concentration increases. pH levels less than 7.35 indicate acidosis; pH levels greater than 7.45 indicate alkalosis.

■ = Independent; ▲ = Collaborative

Actions/Interventions	Rationale
• $Paco_2$ = 40 mm Hg	$Paco_2$ indicates the partial pressure of CO_2 in arterial blood, and is determined by the rate and depth of respiration. Values less than 35 mm Hg indicate respiratory alkalosis; values greater than 45 mm Hg indicate respiratory acidosis.
• Pao_2 = 80 to 100 mm Hg	Pao_2 reflects pressure exerted by dissolved oxygen in arterial blood. Levels less than 80 mm Hg indicate hypoxemia.
• HCO_3 = 24 mEq/L	HCO_3 reflects the concentration of bicarbonate in the blood and is an indication of the metabolic component of acid-base balance.
▲ Assess BUN/creatinine ratio.	Normal BUN/creatinine ratio is 10:1 to 15:1. Ratios greater than 20:1 are associated with dehydration.
▲ Assess for changes in hemoglobin and hematocrit.	Serum hemoglobin and hematocrit may be elevated due to hemoconcentration.
▲ Assess for abnormalities in chest x-ray study and urinalysis.	Pneumonia and urinary tract infections are the most frequent infections causing DKA and HHNS, especially in older adults.
▲ Monitor for effects of intravenous (IV) therapy: report HR greater than 120 beats/min and BP less than 90/60 mm Hg or decreased 20 mm Hg from baseline.	Monitoring provides information on adequacy of circulation, perfusion, and oxygenation of tissues. Hypotension indicates inadequate levels of hydration.
■ Monitor serum glucose initially every 30 to 60 minutes, then hourly as long as insulin infusion continues.	Steady decline in blood glucose of 50 to 75 mg/dL/hr is desired. A decrease in serum glucose to less than 250 mg/dL within the first 24 hours of treatment of HHNS increases the risk of cerebral edema.
■ Notify the physician when serum glucose does not fall by 50 mg/dL from the initial value in the first hour of treatment.	In DKA, blood glucose levels improve faster than does acidosis. Insulin therapy is continued until ketoacidosis is resolved: blood glucose less than 200 mg/dL, serum bicarbonate level of 18 mEq/L or greater, venous pH greater than 7.3, and calculated anion gap of 12 mEq/L or less.
▲ Monitor serum potassium levels. Report serum potassium levels greater than 5.0 mEq/L.	The goal is to maintain plasma potassium levels between 4 and 5 mEq/L.
▲ Report signs of hyperkalemia: irritability, anxiety, abdominal cramping, diarrhea, weakness of lower extremities, paresthesia, irregular pulse, cardiac standstill if hyperkalemia is sudden or severe.	Effects of excess potassium are seen in cardiac, neuromuscular, and smooth muscles.
▲ Monitor and report electrocardiographic signs of hyperkalemia: tall, peaked T wave; widened QRS, prolonged P-R interval, flattened to absent P wave.	Alterations in potassium significantly affect myocardial irritability and rhythm.
■ Monitor administration of IV bicarbonate: monitor for symptoms of hypokalemia during infusion of bicarbonate.	Bicarbonate therapy worsens hypokalemia, causing central nervous system acidosis, and delays ketone body clearance.
▲ Monitor for symptoms of hypoglycemia: blood glucose less than 50 mg/dL, cold and clammy skin, rapid heart rate, emotional changes, headache, nervousness, tremors, faintness, dizziness, unsteady gait, slurred speech, hunger, changes in vision, seizures, coma.	Hypoglycemia may occur during treatment with insulin.

■ = Independent; ▲ = Collaborative

Diabetic Ketoacidosis (DKA) and Hyperglycemic Hyperosmolar Nonketotic Syndrome (HHNS)—cont'd

Actions/Interventions

■ Assess precipitating factors: illness, new-onset diabetes, or noncompliance with medical regimen.

Rationale

These provide the basis for education once hyperglycemia has resolved.

Therapeutic Interventions

Actions/Interventions

IV therapy

▲ Initial IV therapy: infuse isotonic saline (0.9% NaCl) at the rate of 15 to 20 mL/kg/hr or greater for patients without cardiac compromise.

▲ Subsequent IV therapy: Continue administration of IV fluids based on the state of hydration, serum electrolyte levels, and urinary output.

▲ Add dextrose to IV fluid when blood glucose concentrations are less than 250 mg/dL in DKA or less than 300 mg/dL in HHS.

Insulin therapy

▲ Administer IV bolus dose of regular insulin, followed by a continuous infusion of regular insulin.

▲ Decrease the rate of insulin when plasma glucose values reach 250 mg/dL.

Electrolyte therapy

▲ Administer IV potassium, as ordered, typically 20 to 30 mEq/L.

▲ Administer bicarbonate, as ordered, typically 100 mmol NaHCO₃ added to 400-mL sterile water and given at a rate of 200 mL/hr.

Therapy for hypoglycemia

▲ Provide 15 g of quick-acting carbohydrate according to hospital protocol; repeat in 15 minutes if there is no improvement in blood glucose values.

▲ When the patient improves and is alert, provide a long-acting carbohydrate or next scheduled meal to keep blood glucose level within acceptable range.

Rationale

Initial goal is to correct circulatory volume deficit. Isotonic normal saline will rapidly expand extracellular fluid volume without causing a rapid fall in plasma osmolality. The patient may receive 1 L or more of IV fluid in the first hour.

The secondary goal, correction of water deficit, can be accomplished by infusion of a hypotonic solution such as 0.45% normal saline.

Dextrose is added to prevent hypoglycemia and excessive decline in plasma osmolality that leads to cerebral edema.

Subcutaneous and intramuscular injections of insulin are absorbed in an inconsistent manner when the patient is hypotensive. The goal is to reduce serum glucose levels by 75 to 150 mg/dL/hr. Evidence is conflicting about the best protocol to follow to achieve this goal. Both high-dose and low-dose administration have been studied. High-dose protocols are associated with hypoglycemia and hypokalemia.

Reduction of insulin will prevent occurrence of hypoglycemia.

Potassium is added to IV infusions once renal function has been established and serum potassium levels have fallen below 5.5 mEq/L. Administration of insulin to lower blood glucose facilitates movement of potassium into the cells.

This is recommended only in life-threatening hyperkalemia, severe lactic acidosis, and severe acidosis in adults with pH less than 6.9.

Each 5 g of carbohydrate raises blood glucose 20 mg/dL. Avoid use of high-fat foods; fat delays absorption of glucose and prolongs blood glucose response.

Complex carbohydrates sustain blood glucose elevation.

■ = Independent; ▲ = Collaborative

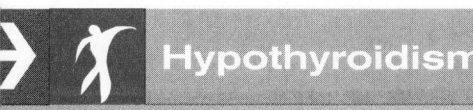 Hypothyroidism

Myxedema; Goiter

Hypothyroidism occurs because of a deficiency in thyroid hormone. Almost every system in the body is affected through a general slowing of metabolic processes. The disorder is common, especially among women older than 30 years of age. In the older adult, hypothyroidism may be overlooked because many of the manifestations are related to changes associated with the normal aging process (constipation, intolerance to cold, decreased activity tolerance, weight gain, lethargy, decreased short-term memory, depression). The most common cause of hypothyroidism is an autoimmune inflammation (Hashimoto's thyroiditis) of the thyroid gland with resulting atrophy of glandular tissue. Hypothyroidism may also develop after a thyroidectomy. Myxedema occurs in hypothyroidism as a result of hyaluronic acid accumulation in tissues. Fluid binds to the hyaluronic acid, producing skin puffiness most noticeable around and below the eyes. Myxedema also causes enlargement of the tongue, which contributes to the impaired speech patterns of the patient with hypothyroidism. When hypothyroidism goes undiagnosed or undertreated, the patient may develop myocardial hypotonic function and ventricular dilation. The patient is at risk to develop decreased cardiac output and systemic tissue and organ hypoxia. This situation is a rare occurrence called myxedema coma and is considered life threatening. Goiter, enlargement of the thyroid gland, may occur when hypothyroidism is the result of decreased hormone synthesis. When hormone production is reduced, thyroid-secreting hormone (TSH) secretion increases owing to lack of negative feedback. The size of the thyroid gland increases as a result of TSH stimulation.

NDx Nursing Diagnosis

Imbalanced Nutrition: More Than Body Requirements

Common Related Factor

Intake greater than metabolic needs

Defining Characteristics

Weight gain
Eating patterns and amount of food intake may be unchanged
Sedentary activity level

Common Expected Outcome

Patient maintains stable weight and takes in essential nutrients.

NOC Outcomes
Nutritional Status: Nutrient Intake;
    Knowledge: Disease Process

NIC Interventions
Nutritional Monitoring; Nutrition
    Management; Teaching: Disease
    Process

■ = Independent; ▲ = Collaborative

Hypothyroidism—cont'd

Ongoing Assessment

Actions/Interventions	Rationale
■ Weigh the patient at regular intervals.	The patient should be weighed under the same conditions each time, using the same scale to monitor changes in body weight. Patients with hypothyroidism experience weight gain related to slowing of metabolic processes and excess fluid volume.
■ Assess calorie and nutrient intake.	Patients with hypothyroidism may actually have decreased food intake owing to decreased energy levels and decreased appetite.

Therapeutic Interventions

Actions/Interventions	Rationale
■ Teach the patient to follow a low-calorie, low-cholesterol, low saturated fat diet.	Because of the decreased metabolic rate, the patient requires fewer calories to support metabolic activity. The patient with hypothyroidism tends to have higher cholesterol levels.
■ Teach the patient and family about the effect of hypothyroidism on body weight.	The patient and family need to understand the inverse relationship between weight gain and appetite in hypothyroidism. When thyroid hormone replacement therapy is initiated, the patient may experience weight loss. However, appetite may increase. This change may require a calorie-controlled diet to prevent additional weight gain.
▲ Consult with a dietitian to determine the patient's caloric needs.	The dietitian can calculate appropriate caloric requirements to maintain nutrient intake and achieve a stable weight.
■ Provide assistance and encouragement as needed at mealtime.	Because of decreased energy levels, the patient may need help with eating to ensure adequate intake of essential nutrients.
■ Encourage the patient to eat six small meals throughout the day.	This approach to eating may promote adequate intake of nutrients in the patient with decreased energy levels.
▲ Administer vitamin and mineral supplements, as ordered.	Nutrient supplements may be indicated to reduce deficiency anemias.

NDx Nursing Diagnosis

Constipation

Common Related Factors	Defining Characteristics
Insufficient physical activity	Abdominal distention
Decreased motility of the gastrointestinal tract	Dry, hard, formed stool
	Hypoactive bowel sounds
	Decreased frequency of defecation

■ = Independent; ▲ = Collaborative

Common Expected Outcome

Patient establishes a regular pattern of bowel elimination.

NOC Outcome
Bowel Elimination

NIC Interventions
Constipation/Impaction Management;
Bowel Management

Ongoing Assessment

Actions/Interventions

- Assess bowel pattern for frequency, consistency of stool, and ease of passage.

- Assess intake of dietary fiber.
- Assess fluid intake.

- Assess bowel sounds and abdominal distention.

Rationale

Constipation occurs in hypothyroidism owing to decreased intestinal motility. The patient may also have decreased appetite and reduced physical activity that contribute to constipation.

A diet low in fiber contributes to constipation.

Inadequate fluid intake results in a fecal mass that is dry and harder to pass.

The patient who is constipated will have hypoactive bowel sounds and a distended abdomen.

Therapeutic Interventions

Actions/Interventions

- Teach the patient about sources of dietary fiber.

- Encourage the patient to drink at least 2 L of water each day.
- Encourage increased physical activity within the patient's tolerance level.
- Instruct in the use of stool softeners and bulk-forming agents as ordered.

▲ Encourage the use of laxatives and suppositories as needed to initiate bowel elimination.

Rationale

Raw fruits, vegetables, and whole grain breads and cereals are good sources of dietary fiber. The fiber attracts water into the fecal mass to keep it soft and easier to pass.

Adequate fluid intake is necessary to maintain a soft fecal mass.

Physical activity promotes peristaltic activity.

Several bulk-forming agents are available over the counter (e.g., Metamucil). These drugs mimic the effect of dietary fiber.

Laxatives should be used with discretion to avoid development of dependency on them for regular bowel elimination.

NDx Nursing Diagnosis

Activity Intolerance

Common Related Factors

Generalized weakness
Sedentary lifestyle
Imbalance between oxygen supply and oxygen demand

Defining Characteristics

Verbal report of fatigue or weakness
Abnormal heart rate or blood pressure response to activity

 = Independent; ▲ = Collaborative

Hypothyroidism—cont'd

Defining Characteristics—cont'd

Exertional discomfort or dyspnea
Unable to complete desired activities

Common Expected Outcome

Patient completes desired activities without fatigue and with normal heart rate and blood pressure responses.

NOC Outcomes

Activity Tolerance; Endurance; Energy Conservation

NIC Interventions

Activity Therapy; Energy Management

Ongoing Assessment

Actions/Interventions

- Assess heart rate, blood pressure, respiratory rate, oxygen saturation, and reports of chest pain before, during, and after activity.

- Assess the patient's energy level, and muscle strength and tone.

Rationale

Patients with hypothyroidism often experience sinus bradycardia and increased diastolic blood pressure. In advanced stages, the patient may develop cardiomegaly and pericardial effusions. The patient is at risk for congestive heart failure.

Slowing of metabolism results in decreased energy levels. Muscles may be weaker and joints stiffer because of mucin deposits in joints and interstitial spaces.

Therapeutic Interventions

Actions/Interventions

- Help the patient identify desired activities and responsibilities.

- Encourage the patient to keep a daily log of energy levels and activities for at least 1 week.
- Teach the patient to alternate periods of rest with periods of activity.
- Encourage the patient to ask for assistance with activities.
- Teach the patient that activity tolerance and endurance will improve in response to thyroid medication.

Rationale

Activities that are important to the patient should be planned during those times of the day when the patient usually has the most energy.

A record of energy levels and activities will help the patient identify periods of peak energy.

Frequent rest periods will promote energy conservation.

This energy conservation technique will help the patient participate in and complete desired activities.

Thyroid hormone supplements will gradually increase cellular metabolism, with a resulting increased energy level. In patients with preexisting cardiac disease, increases in metabolic rate may precipitate angina because of increased demands on the heart.

■ = Independent; ▲ = Collaborative

Nursing Diagnosis

Deficient Knowledge

Common Related Factors

Lack of exposure to hypothyroidism
Unfamiliarity with information resources
New disease process

Defining Characteristics

Verbalizes lack of information about hypothyroidism and its treatment
Limited questioning about hypothyroidism and taking thyroid hormone supplements

Common Expected Outcome

Patient and family members verbalize correct information about hypothyroidism and taking thyroid hormone supplements.

NOC Outcomes
Knowledge: Disease Process; Knowledge: Medication

NIC Interventions
Teaching: Disease Process; Teaching: Prescribed Medication

Ongoing Assessment

Actions/Interventions	Rationale
■ Assess the patient's existing knowledge of hypothyroidism and thyroid hormone replacement therapy.	Patient teaching should begin with what the patient and family members already know about the disease and its treatment.
■ Assess the patient's willingness and readiness to learn new information as well as any barriers to learning (visual, auditory, literacy).	The patient with hypothyroidism may experience impaired memory, decreased attention span, hearing loss, and confusion. These neurological changes can interfere with learning new information.
■ Determine the patient's learning style preferences.	The patient will be more willing to learn new information if it is presented in a manner that is consistent with the patient's learning needs and preferences.

Therapeutic Interventions

Actions/Interventions	Rationale
■ Provide the patient and family with information about hypothyroidism.	Teaching sessions should be planned at times when the patient is best able to concentrate. Information may need to be repeated to facilitate learning. Written information reinforces verbal presentations.
■ Teach the patient and family about taking thyroid hormones. • Review expected benefits and possible side effects. • Encourage the patient to keep follow-up appointments for blood work. • Instruct the patient to take dose in the morning to reduce chances of insomnia.	Thyroid hormone should be taken on a regular schedule to achieve hormone balance. It may take several weeks or longer for a full therapeutic benefit to be noticed. The patient is usually started on a small dose that is gradually increased until a euthyroid state is achieved. Hormone replacement therapy is usually a lifelong commitment.

■ = Independent; ▲ = Collaborative

Hypothyroidism

Hypothyroidism—cont'd

Actions/Interventions

■ Encourage the patient to have medical identification about hormone therapy and to inform all health care providers.

Rationale

Medical identification provides other health care providers with information to guide decisions about care.

> • RELATED CARE PLANS
>
> Disturbed body image, p. 21
> Hypothermia, p. 106

Syndrome of Inappropriate Antidiuretic Hormone (SIADH)

Dilutional Hyponatremia

This syndrome is characterized by the continued synthesis and release of antidiuretic hormone (ADH) unrelated to plasma osmolarity; water retention and dilutional hyponatremia occur. Potential causes include head trauma, brain tumor, and subarachnoid hemorrhage. Systemic cancer and bronchogenic cancer (particularly small-cell carcinoma of the lung) are also potential causes. ADH is synthesized and released by the tumor cells. It is also believed that normal pulmonary tissue can produce and secrete ADH but does not normally do so unless it is damaged. Common causes of pulmonary-induced ADH production include bacterial and viral pneumonias, tuberculosis, fungal pneumonias, pulmonary contusion, and barotrauma. This care plan focuses on the acute and chronic care management of SIADH.

NDx Nursing Diagnosis

Excess Fluid Volume

Common Related Factors	Defining Characteristics
Compromised endocrine regulatory mechanisms	Intake greatly exceeding output
Neurohypophyseal dysfunction	Sudden weight gain
Inappropriate ADH secretion	Cellular edema
Excessive fluid intake	Absence of peripheral edema
Renal failure	High specific gravity
Steroid therapy	Serum hyponatremia: sodium less than 130 mEq/L
	Serum hypoosmolality: less than 275 mOsm/L
	Urine hypernatremia
	Urine hyperosmolality: greater than 900 mOsm/L

■ = Independent; ▲ = Collaborative

Common Expected Outcome

Patient experiences normal fluid volume as evidenced by stable weight, normal serum sodium level, and normal serum osmolarity.

NOC Outcomes
Fluid Balance; Electrolyte and Acid-Base Balance

NIC Interventions
Fluid Monitoring; Fluid Management; Electrolyte Management

Ongoing Assessment

Actions/Interventions	Rationale
■ Carefully monitor intake, output, urine specific gravity, and blood pressure (BP).	Increase in ADH persists even with increased plasma volume and decreased serum osmolality. However, this does not produce edema; instead the plasma volume expands and the BP rises, triggering other compensatory mechanisms that decrease renal sodium and water absorption. Hence, the patient retains water from ADH excess, and then compensatory mechanisms cause loss of both sodium and water. As a result, the serum sodium decreases and water moves into the cells. The kidneys excrete increased amounts of sodium in the urine because of reduced aldosterone; however, elevated ADH levels continue to cause water retention.
■ Weigh the patient daily.	A sudden weight gain of 2.2 pounds can indicate retention of 1 L of water. SIADH patients can retain 3 to 5 L.
■ Assess the patient for signs of hyponatremia: apprehension, confusion, muscle twitches and cramps, convulsions, nausea and vomiting, anorexia, and abdominal cramps.	The decreased serum sodium level causes water to move into the cells, which affects the function of all body systems.
■ Assess for signs of cerebral edema: headache, decreased mental status, seizures, vomiting.	Gradual onset results in mild signs and symptoms. Rapid onset of SIADH may result in severe effects leading to seizures, coma, and death.
■ Check for pitting edema over the sternum.	Pitting reflects cellular edema. Water diffuses from hypo-osmotic intravascular spaces to intracellular spaces.
■ Monitor for symptoms of increased intracranial pressure (e.g., slow, bounding pulse; increased pulse pressure; irritability; lethargy; increased BP; vomiting).	Movement of fluid into brain cells causes cerebral edema and increased intracranial pressure.
▲ Monitor serum sodium level, serum osmolality, urine sodium, and urine osmolality and specific gravity.	Serum sodium level less than 130 mEq/L and serum osmolality less than 275 mOsm/L suggest SIADH. In addition, urine osmolality is usually greater than 900 mOsm/L, with urine sodium inappropriately high compared with the low serum sodium level.
▲ Monitor serum potassium, calcium, blood urea nitrogen (BUN), and creatinine levels.	Hypokalemia and hypocalcemia are present from dilutional effects in SIADH. BUN and creatinine levels are usually normal.

■ = Independent; ▲ = Collaborative

> ## Syndrome of Inappropriate Antidiuretic Hormone (SIADH)—cont'd

Actions/Interventions

▲ Assess the patient's medications for potential drugs that have been known to increase the risk of developing SIADH: chlorpropamide, clofibrate, carbamazepine, cyclophosphamide, isoproterenol, morphine, oxytocin, phenothiazines, thiazide diuretics, tricyclic antidepressants, vasopressin, vincristine.

Rationale

Some drugs may stimulate release of ADH from the pituitary gland. Some drugs may increase renal sensitivity to ADH. Nonsteroidal anti-inflammatory drugs cause decreased renal excretion of water due to suppression of prostaglandin synthesis.

Therapeutic Interventions

Actions/Interventions

▲ Restrict fluid intake to 800 to 1000 mL/day.

■ Provide frequent mouth care.

▲ Administer diuretic agents as prescribed (e.g., furosemide [Lasix]).

▲ Administer hypertonic saline solution (3% sodium chloride) as a sodium replacement, as ordered.

■ Position the patient with head of bed flat, as tolerated.

▲ Administer medications (e.g., demeclocycline hydrochloride [Declomycin]), as prescribed. Lithium carbonate (Lithonate) may also be used, but serious side effects are possible.

Rationale

This prevents further fluid overload and sodium dilution. All sources of fluids need to be considered in calculating fluid intake. Even ice chips need to be included. An 8-ounce glass of ice chips equals approximately 4 ounces of water.

This alleviates thirst.

A potent loop diuretic may help to remove excess water.

Hypertonic saline infusions are indicated when serum sodium levels are very low (<110 mEq/L) and the patient exhibits neurologic symptoms.

Supine position increases atrial pressure through enhancing venous return to the heart and, in turn, decreases ADH release.

These suppress the activity of ADH.

NDx Nursing Diagnosis

Risk for Disturbed Thought Processes

Common Risk Factor

Severe hyponatremia

Common Expected Outcome

Patient's level of consciousness (LOC) and orientation remain normal or without further impairment, and injury is prevented.

NOC Outcomes
Distorted Thought Control; Cognitive Orientation

NIC Interventions
Cerebral Perfusion Promotion; Delirium Management

Ongoing Assessment

Actions/Interventions

- Monitor LOC and orientation; use Glasgow Coma Scale as appropriate.

- Monitor for hostility, decreased deep tendon reflexes, drowsiness, lethargy, and headache.

▲ Assess serum sodium levels (normal: 135 to 145 mg/L).
  - A serum sodium level of 125 to 135 mg/L: the patient may be asymptomatic or experience fatigue and confusion.
  - A serum sodium level of 118 to 124 mg/L: the patient experiences weakness, short-term memory loss, inappropriate behavior, and lethargy.
  - A serum sodium level of 112 to 117 mg/L: the patient may experience seizures, coma, and even death.

Rationale

Hyponatremia results in brain cell swelling and increased intracranial pressure, which can lead to confusion, disorientation, memory loss, seizures, coma, and even death if it continues to progress.

All are signs of a worsening of the patient's condition.

Neurological signs in patients with head injury may be caused by hyponatremia.

Therapeutic Interventions

Actions/Interventions

If the patient is confused:

- Explain reasons for altered thought processes to family or caregivers.

- Maintain bed in low position with side rails up.

- Provide assistance or supervision with activities.

- Reduce stimuli.

▲ Administer hypertonic saline solution as prescribed.

Rationale

This reduces anxiety of caregivers.

This reduces injury potential.

This approach promotes safety and reduces fall risk.

This maintains a calm environment.

This replaces sodium. Typically this is followed by an intravenous diuretic such as furosemide (Lasix) to eliminate free water in an attempt to correct the serum sodium imbalance.

NDx Nursing Diagnosis

Deficient Knowledge

Common Related Factors

New disease process
Unfamiliarity with medications and treatments

Defining Characteristics

Request for information
Verbalized misconceptions

Common Expected Outcome

Patient verbalizes understanding of SIADH and rationale for medications and treatments.

NOC Outcomes
Knowledge: Disease Process; Knowledge: Medication

NIC Interventions
Teaching: Disease Process; Teaching: Prescribed Medications

■ = Independent; ▲ = Collaborative

Endocrine and Metabolic Care Plans

Syndrome of Inappropriate Antidiuretic Hormone (SIADH)—cont'd

Ongoing Assessment

Actions/Interventions

- Assess level of knowledge of SIADH, including understanding of medications and treatments.
- Assess readiness to learn.

Rationale

An individualized teaching plan is based on the patient's prior knowledge.

Neurological changes associated with SIADH can impair the patient's ability to learn new information.

Therapeutic Interventions

Actions/Interventions

- Explain SIADH and treatments in simple, brief terms to the patient, family, and caregivers.
- Instruct the patient on administration of demeclocycline in treatment of chronic SIADH.

- Instruct the patient to wear a medical alert bracelet listing SIADH and the medications that the patient is using.

Rationale

Knowledge assists in patient compliance and reduces the family's anxiety.

Demeclocycline blocks the effect of ADH on the kidney. This effect causes increased renal excretion of water and maintains serum sodium balance.

This allows for prompt intervention in the event of an emergency.

Thyroidectomy

Hyperthyroidism; Thyrotoxicosis; Thyroid Storm

Thyroidectomy is the surgical removal of the thyroid gland performed for benign or malignant tumor, hyperthyroidism, thyrotoxicosis, or thyroiditis in patients with very large goiters, or for patients unable to be treated with radioiodine or thioamides. The surgical procedure may be a total thyroidectomy or subtotal, which is partial removal of the thyroid gland. This care plan focuses on the postoperative management of a patient undergoing a thyroidectomy.

NDx Nursing Diagnosis

Risk for Ineffective Breathing Pattern

Common Risk Factors

Hematoma
Laryngeal edema
Vocal cord paralysis
Tracheal collapse

■ = Independent; ▲ = Collaborative

Common Expected Outcome

Patient's breathing pattern is maintained as evidenced by eupnea and regular respiratory rate or pattern.

NOC Outcome
Respiratory Status: Ventilation

NIC Interventions
Respiratory Monitoring; Airway Management; Oxygen Therapy

Ongoing Assessment

Actions/Interventions	Rationale
■ Observe respiratory rate and rhythm.	Increase in respiratory rate is an early warning sign for changes related to postoperative edema or hematoma formation in the upper airways.
■ Observe for presence of stridor.	Stridor is an upper airway sound that occurs when laryngeal edema is present.
■ Assess for work of breathing, presence of dyspnea, or presence of intercostal rib retractions.	This aids in determining the onset of respiratory distress.
■ Note voice quality.	Edema may result in changes in voice quality, such as hoarseness, for 3 to 4 days after surgery. However, paralysis of the vocal cord may result from recurrent laryngeal nerve damage, which could result in closure of the glottis and the need for emergency tracheostomy.
■ Observe neck for swelling or tightness.	These may be indicative of edema and/or internal bleeding or hematoma formation. The patient may complain of a feeling of fullness at the incision site.
■ Assess wound drains for amount of drainage.	Decreased drainage in the first 24 hours may indicate obstruction of the wound drain. Accumulation of fluid in the wound contributes to edema and possible airway and breathing compromise.
■ Examine the wound for evidence of hematoma or oozing. Assess dressing, both anterior and posterior, and assess behind the neck for pooling.	Gravity tends to pull the drainage posteriorly.

Therapeutic Interventions

Actions/Interventions	Rationale
■ Keep head of bed elevated to 45 degrees.	Elevation limits formation of edema at the surgical site.
▲ Use an ice collar as appropriate.	Cold decreases edema formation.
■ Encourage deep breathing and use of an incentive spirometer every hour.	Deep breathing and use of an incentive spirometer keeps alveoli open and promotes effective breathing.
■ Instruct the patient to cough only as needed.	Coughing clears secretions. It can irritate the incisional area, so it is used only to clear secretions and not as a routine.
■ Suction as needed.	Suctioning clears secretions if the patient is unable to clear the airway.
▲ Administer humidified oxygen as needed.	Humidified oxygen may help with the postoperative hoarseness experienced from intubation and postoperative edema. Increased humidification of inspired air promotes easier breathing and thinner secretions.

■ = Independent; ▲ = Collaborative

Thyroidectomy—cont'd

 Nursing Diagnosis

Risk for Injury: Hypocalcemia

Common Risk Factors

Inadvertent surgical removal of parathyroid glands or trauma to parathyroid glands (hypoparathyroidism)
Damaged blood supply to parathyroids (usually temporary but may be permanent)

Common Expected Outcome

Patient's risk for injury is decreased as evidenced by serum calcium level in normal range and absence of signs of hypocalcemia.

NOC Outcome
Electrolyte and Acid-Base Balance

NIC Intervention
Electrolyte Management: Hypocalcemia

Ongoing Assessment

Actions/Interventions

▲ Monitor serum ionized calcium level. Notify the physician if ionized calcium level is less than 2.1 mEq/L.

■ Assess for presence of circumoral and peripheral (fingers and toes) paresthesia. Instruct the patient to report development of these signs immediately.

■ Observe for tremors in extremities and any seizure activity.

■ Assess for lethargy, headache, and confusion.

■ Check for presence of Chvostek's sign.

Rationale

Postoperative hypocalcemia may occur as a result of inadvertent surgical removal of or trauma to the parathyroid glands. Ionized calcium is the only form of calcium used by the body for muscle contraction, cardiac function, neuron transmission, and blood clotting. The levels of ionized calcium in the body are unaffected by changes in the serum albumin levels compared with the nonionized form of calcium. In the laboratory, ionized calcium levels are adjusted based on the pH of the blood sample. The venous specimen may be drawn in the same syringe used for arterial blood gases. Normal values for ionized calcium are 2.1 to 2.6 mEq/L.

Neuromuscular irritability is an early indicator of hypocalcemia. In addition to paresthesias, the patient may experience muscle twitching, facial grimacing, nausea, vomiting, abdominal cramping, hypotension, and mental confusion.

These changes indicate neuromuscular irritability from hypocalcemia.

These are additional signs of hypocalcemia.

This is assessed by tapping the cheek over the facial nerve; a positive sign results in a twitch of the lip or facial muscles that is indicative of tetany.

■ = Independent; ▲ = Collaborative

Endocrine and Metabolic Care Plans

Actions/Interventions

- Check for Trousseau's sign.

- Assess for laryngeal stridor.
- ▲ Monitor serum potassium and magnesium levels.

Rationale

Carpal spasm is induced by inflation of the blood pressure (BP) cuff 20 mm Hg above the patient's systolic BP for 3 minutes; it is also indicative of tetany.

Stridor may result from tetany.

Hyperkalemia and hypomagnesemia potentiate cardiac and neuromuscular irritability in the presence of hypocalcemia.

Therapeutic Interventions

Actions/Interventions

- ▲ Maintain intravenous access and keep calcium gluconate in near proximity.
- ▲ Administer or monitor infusions of calcium gluconate; also administer oral calcium and vitamin D, as prescribed. Use caution in patients receiving digitalis preparations.
- Institute seizure precautions as appropriate.

Rationale

Treatment is needed for dangerously low serum calcium levels.

Vitamin D enhances intestinal calcium absorption and bone resorption. Calcium enhances the toxic effects of digitalis.

This prevents further injury.

NDx Nursing Diagnosis

Risk for Injury: Thyroid Storm, Hyperthyroidism

Common Risk Factors

Inadequate preoperative preparation (euthyroid state not achieved)
Increased release of thyroid hormone

Common Expected Outcome

Patient is free of thyroid storm as evidenced by vital signs within normal limits and no decrease in mentation.

NOC Outcome
Electrolyte and Acid-Base Balance

NIC Intervention
Electrolyte Management: Hypercalcemia

Ongoing Assessment

Actions/Interventions

- Assess vital signs for presence of increased pulse, dysrhythmias, elevated temperature, and increased BP.

- Assess for presence of heat intolerance.

Rationale

Any increase in temperature and heart rate without a specific known cause should be considered thyroid storm. Thyroid storm can occur postoperatively as the result of increased hormone release from manipulation of the gland intraoperatively.

Heat intolerance is a clinical symptom of thyroid storm.

■ = Independent; ▲ = Collaborative

Thyroidectomy—cont'd

Actions/Interventions	Rationale
■ Assess for gastrointestinal (GI) distress.	Elevated thyroid hormone level increases GI tract motility, possibly resulting in diarrhea.
■ Assess for restlessness and changes in level of consciousness (LOC).	As thyroid storm progresses, LOC decreases and the patient may become comatose.

Therapeutic Interventions

Actions/Interventions	Rationale
■ Provide a quiet environment (control noise level).	Thyroid storm precipitates a hypermetabolic state, which can cause agitation and anxiety.
▲ Maintain intravenous infusion for hydration and electrolyte balance.	The hypermetabolic state increases fluid needs.
▲ Maintain adequate nutritional intake, especially of protein, carbohydrates, and vitamins; avoid caffeine.	Hypermetabolic states increase basal metabolic demand.
▲ Administer sedatives as prescribed.	Administration of sedatives reduces anxiety and agitation.
▲ Protect the patient from adverse effects of excess thyroid hormone.	
• Lower temperature by keeping covers off; use hypothermia blanket; administer nonsalicylate antipyretic agents; give sponge bath.	It is important to use nonsalicylate antipyretics, because salicylates increase free thyroid hormone levels, which would worsen the condition.
• Administer antithyroid drug (iodine).	This inhibits thyroid hormone release.
• Administer β-receptor blocking agent.	This decreases the cardiovascular and neuromuscular effects associated with increased hormone levels.
• Administer adrenal corticosteroid as indicated.	This blocks thyroid hormone secretion.

NDx Nursing Diagnosis

Risk for Acute Pain

Common Risk Factors

Hematoma formation
Improper positioning, movement resulting in excessive strain on suture line
Wound infection

Common Expected Outcome

Patient's pain is relieved or prevented as evidenced by patient verbalization and relaxed appearance.

> **NOC Outcome**
> Pain Control
> **NIC Intervention**
> Pain Management

■ = Independent; ▲ = Collaborative

Ongoing Assessment

Actions/Interventions

- Assess for presence or description of pain.

- Assess the patient's position.

- Assess the neck incision for approximated skin edges, redness, swelling, drainage, and presence of staples or sutures.

Rationale

Pain may be routine postoperative surgical discomfort or may result from pressure of an expanding hematoma. The patient may complain of a sore throat.

Improper positioning can result in pain caused by tension to the surgical site.

Early identification of complications allows for prompt treatment.

Therapeutic Interventions

Actions/Interventions

- ▲ Administer analgesics, throat sprays or lozenges, as needed.
- Give cool liquids and soft foods when the patient begins eating.
- Protect the neck incision by instructing patient to:
  • Avoid neck flexion or hyperextension.

  • Avoid rapid head movements.
  • Support the patient's head with hands when rising.

Rationale

These prevent unnecessary pain.

These techniques lessen difficulty in swallowing.

Neck flexion (bending forward) compresses the trachea. Hyperextension causes pulling or tension on the incision line.

Abrupt movement may cause wound dehiscence.

This prevents suture-line tension.

NDx Nursing Diagnosis

Deficient Knowledge

Common Related Factors

New condition
Lack of familiarity with surgical treatment and medications

Defining Characteristics

Multiple questions
Lack of questions
Expressed need for further information

Common Expected Outcome

Patient and caregiver verbalize understanding of postoperative care for thyroidectomy.

NOC Outcomes
Knowledge: Disease Process; Knowledge: Treatment Regimen

NIC Interventions
Teaching: Disease Process; Teaching: Prescribed Medications

■ = Independent; ▲ = Collaborative

Thyroidectomy—cont'd

Ongoing Assessment

Actions/Interventions

■ Assess knowledge of thyroidectomy and postoperative care.

Rationale

Building on current knowledge prepares for future compliance.

Therapeutic Interventions

Actions/Interventions

■ Instruct the patient to inform the physician if any of the following develop:
- Circumoral or peripheral paresthesia; tremors
- Signs of infection: excessive or continual drainage from the incisional line, incision open and/or red
- Signs of hematoma or increase in edema formation: difficulty in breathing, alteration in voice, sensation of pressure, tightness, fullness in neck
- Signs and symptoms of thyroid storm: temperature greater than 37.8° C (100° F), agitation and anxiety, hot and flushed skin, tachycardia, abdominal pain, nausea and vomiting, diarrhea, anorexia, or systolic hypertension

■ Instruct the patient to avoid abrupt head and neck movements until the suture line heals.

■ Instruct the patient in dosage, schedule, desired effects, and side effects of the medications sent home.

■ Instruct in wound care:
- Incisional care: cleansing; dressings as needed for drainage; keeping wound dry; patient may shower when approved by physician
- Scar appearance and resolution over time: use of scarves and high collars

■ Instruct the patient in range-of-motion (ROM) exercises for the neck.

■ Encourage regular exercise.

■ Instruct the patient to avoid temperature extremes.

■ Instruct the patient who has undergone a partial thyroidectomy in dietary measures.
- Maintain a low-calorie diet.

- Avoid foods that contain thyroid-inhibiting substances (goitrogens): turnips, rutabagas, soybeans.

Rationale

These may result from a low serum calcium level.

Infection may develop 7 to 10 days after surgery.

These symptoms require prompt intervention.

Thyroid storm requires prompt intervention.

Abrupt movement of the head may cause wound dehiscence.

If a total thyroidectomy was done, the patient must develop a basic understanding of the long-term need for thyroid replacement therapy and the consequences of failure to take the medication.

These measures promote wound healing and decrease infection risk.

These camouflage the scar until normal healing occurs. The patient needs to know that the scar will fade in appearance over several months.

Exercises strengthen the neck, return full ROM, and aid in the healing process.

For partial thyroidectomy patients, regular exercise helps stimulate the thyroid gland.

Exposure to hot and cold temperatures promotes thyroid hyperplasia and increases the thyroid levels. The patient may be encouraged to try hot and cold showers, but to avoid high environmental temperatures.

During the hypothyroid period, the patient should reduce caloric intake to prevent weight gain.

These foods inhibit the return of thyroid activity.

• RELATED CARE PLANS

Ineffective airway clearance, p. 11
Risk for infection, p. 108

■ = Independent; ▲ = Collaborative

13

Integumentary Care Plans

 **Burns**

Skin Loss—Partial-Thickness/Full-Thickness; Carbon Monoxide Poisoning; Smoke Inhalation

Although the incidence of burn injury is on the decline, more than 1 million burns still occur in the United States annually. Half of these require hospitalization in one of the specialized burn centers across the country. Thirty-five percent of all burn injuries occur in children. Mortality has improved over the years due to Advanced Burn Life Support, regional burn care, and early excision; overall mortality is 6%. The most common mechanism of injury is thermal, which can be from a flame, scald, or direct contact, but injuries also present due to chemical, electrical, and radiation sources. The pediatric and geriatric populations are most vulnerable because of integumentary and immunological risks. Burn care ranges from major to minor, and care ranges from the emergent through the rehabilitative phase of injury.

NDx Nursing Diagnosis

Impaired Skin Integrity

Common Related Factors	Defining Characteristics
Major burn	Blanching of skin
Minor burn	Redness
	Leathery appearance
	Skin color changes: brown to black
	Blistering, weeping skin
	Pain or absence of pain
	Skin loss

Burns—cont'd

Common Expected Outcomes

Patient's burns are accurately assessed.
Unburned skin remains intact.

NOC Outcomes

Tissue Integrity: Skin and Mucous
Membranes; Wound Healing:
Secondary Intention

NIC Interventions

Wound Care; Wound Irrigation

Ongoing Assessment

Actions/Interventions

- Assess the percentage of body surface burned. Use the Lund-Browder chart (age-appropriate body surface chart).

- Identify and document the location of burns.

- Assess the depth of the wounds:
  - Epidermal: painful, pink, not blistered
  - Partial thickness: painful, red/pink, often blistered
  - Full-thickness: anesthetic (not painful because of destruction of nerves), charred, gray, white
- Note areas where the skin is intact.

- Assess the degree of pain.

- Assess for adherent debris or hair.

Rationale

This is commonly used to determine total body surface area (TBSA) involved. For quick assessment, the "rule of nines" is commonly used to estimate the extent of burn. Another method is that the patient's palm represents 1% TBSA, which is a helpful measuring tool when burns are scattered.

Treatment is determined by TBSA involved and location of burn. Accurate calculation of TBSA is critical in determining fluid replacement therapy.

The deeper the wound, the greater the risk for infection, complications, and wound contractures.

These areas must be cared for and preserved; they may serve as graft donor sites later.

Full-thickness burns are anesthetic (painless) as a result of nerve destruction. Partial-thickness burns can cause severe pain because of exposed nerve endings. The patient may have deeper pain sensations from muscle ischemia.

Wound debris and any remaining surface hair can be sources of contamination. Epithelial migration in the healing wound is delayed if the wound is not clear of devitalized tissue.

Therapeutic Interventions

Actions/Interventions

Major burns:
- Provide a clean sheet.

Rationale

The burn wound is not a sterile wound, so a sterile field is not required.

■ = Independent; ▲ = Collaborative

Actions/Interventions	Rationale

▲ Use hydrotherapy as prescribed.

This aids in cleansing and loosening slough, exudate, and eschar. Wound debridement is necessary to provide a clean area for healing. A shower cart is often used to assist with this procedure.

■ Prevent trauma to the area.

Trauma can increase tissue destruction.

▲ Apply topical bacteriostatic substances (e.g., silver sulfadiazine if the patient is not allergic to sulfa, bacitracin, Neosporin, silver-coated dressings, Sulfamylon), as ordered.

Topicals may be applied directly to the wound or impregnated into the bandage. These substances prevent removal of granulating skin and reduce the risk of infection. Topical agents provide some protection to the wound surface. If an open method of wound care is used, the area is left open to air after ointment application. The risk with this method is increased heat loss.

■ Elevate extremities, if possible.

Elevation reduces swelling.

■ Dress wounds.

Dressings prevent burn-to-burn contact. The closed method of wound care uses gauze dressings to cover burn surfaces. The dressings may be soaked with antimicrobial solutions.

■ Keep body and limbs in correct anatomical position.

This prevents contractures.

▲ Administer analgesics before wound care, debridement, or dressing changes.

Patient comfort and cooperation with wound care are promoted with administration of analgesics.

▲ Treat facial wounds as ordered.

Facial burns may require an open or closed dressing depending on the depth of burn (more superficial burns may be left open to air). Use caution when wrapping over ears to minimize pressure. Place dry gauze in the ear to prevent accumulation of topical agents.

Minor burns:
■ Clean the burn wound with antimicrobial soap and water.

This removes debris and reduces the risk for infection.

▲ Apply topical bacteriostatic and antimicrobial medications as ordered. Cover the wound with dry, sterile dressing.

Applications reduce risk of infection.

▲ Treat blisters as ordered.

If blisters are located on an area that is not limiting mobility and not at a risk of breaking, leave intact; otherwise, debride the wound because blister fluid can be an excellent medium for bacteria.

■ Instruct the patient and caregiver in necessary medical follow-up care.

Healing of burn wounds can take months or longer. Long-term care is required for effective management of the scarring that occurs as the wounds heal.

■ Teach the patient and caregiver about the appearance of a clean, noninfected burn wound. Any deviation from this should be reported to the health care provider.

Clean, noninfected burn wounds are pink and moist, produce clear yellow (serous) drainage, and are odor-free.

Burns

Burns—cont'd

NDx Nursing Diagnosis

Risk for Infection

Common Risk Factors

Impaired skin integrity
Damage to respiratory mucosa
Presence of dead skin
Poor nutrition

Common Expected Outcome

Patient remains free of infection, as evidenced by normal temperature, normal white blood cell (WBC) count, and healing wounds.

NOC Outcomes
Risk Control; Risk Detection; Immune Status

NIC Interventions
Environmental Management; Surveillance; Infection Protection

Ongoing Assessment

Actions/Interventions	Rationale
■ Monitor temperature and notify the physician if temperature exceeds 38.5° C.	Elevated temperature should arouse suspicion of infection.
▲ With each dressing change, monitor the wound for erythema surrounding the burn, change in exudate color or amount, or presence of odor from the dressing. Obtain a wound culture and notify the physician if a change is noted.	The burn patient is at risk of infection. Appropriate topical and or systemic agents can be customized after culture results are obtained.
▲ On ventilated patients, elevate head of bed 30 degrees, provide oral care, and administer H_2 blockers and antacids, as ordered. Suction without the use of instilled saline.	These are Centers for Disease Control and Prevention guidelines for the prevention of nosocomial pneumonia.
■ Monitor endotracheal secretions and obtain a bronchial alveolar lavage specimen if the patient is febrile.	This provides the optimal specimen for culture analysis.
▲ Monitor all invasive lines; use antimicrobial-coated catheters when appropriate. When catheters are removed, send the tips for culture if the patient is febrile.	Indwelling catheters are a source of infection and require meticulous care.
▲ Monitor the effectiveness of the topical agent by culturing the wound, as prescribed.	Vigilant monitoring helps reduce consequences of infection.
■ Observe for disorientation, fever, and ileus.	These may indicate impending septic shock.

■ = Independent; ▲ = Collaborative

Actions/Interventions

▲ Monitor blood glucose.

■ Before discharge, teach the patient or caregiver to monitor wound appearance and drainage.

■ Before discharge, teach the patient or caregiver to monitor body temperature.

Rationale

Goal is less than 110 mg/dL. An elevated level may indicate infection.

A change in drainage color or amount may indicate infection.

Temperature greater than 101.5° F may indicate infection.

Therapeutic Interventions

Actions/Interventions

■ Maintain aseptic technique; wear a mask and sterile gloves for physical contact.

■ Keep the work area clean.

■ Trim or shave hair around the wound (except eyebrows, because this area never grows back).

▲ Treat blisters as ordered.

▲ Apply topical agent (e.g., silver sulfadiazine, bacitracin, Neosporin, Sulfamylon, silver-coated dressing), as prescribed.

■ Implement isolation precautions if needed.

▲ Administer intravenous (IV) antibiotics, which may be prescribed prophylactically but which should be specific to the cultured organism when identified.

■ Provide frequent perineal care, using diversion catheters as needed.

▲ Cover wounds with graft material or dressings as prescribed:

- Xenografts

- Homograft

- Amnion

- Synthetic dressings

Rationale

To prevent nosocomial contamination, the nurse should wear protective coverings when caring for the patient. Gowns, gloves, masks, shoe covers, and hair covers may be needed.

This reduces pathogens in the environment.

This decreases contamination.

Blisters are left intact if they are not impairing mobility and have little risk of breaking. Blister fluid acts as a natural barrier and facilitates healing. However, when a blister is broken, blister fluid is an excellent medium for bacterial growth.

Topical agents provide some protection to the wound surface.

Strict isolation may be necessary if burns become infected. Staff may wear scrubs because they can be changed easily when they become soiled.

IV antibiotics may be useful in treating systemic infection. However, wound infections, especially those near eschar, may be treated more easily with topical agents and debridement.

A Foley catheter or a bowel management system (e.g., Zassi) may be required to divert fecal material for large body surface area burns. Contamination of wounds can lead to infection and impaired wound healing.

Covering burn wounds reduces fluid loss and protects the wound from invasion by bacteria. Early excision and grafting are desirable. Infection is the greatest threat to survival for the burned patient; covering wounds decreases the opportunity for contamination and therefore decreases risk of infection.

These are temporary grafts and generally are skin from another species, typically porcine (pig) skin.

This is skin from another human, typically cadaver skin or banked frozen skin.

This can be used as graft material for 48 hours per application.

These are temporary dressings to cover wounds; types include Op-Site, Tegaderm, and artificial skin.

Burns

(■ = Independent; ▲ = Collaborative)

Burns—cont'd

Actions/Interventions

- Autograft

Rationale

Healthy skin is taken from elsewhere on the patient's body; grafting is carried out in an operating room.

 Nursing Diagnosis

Risk for Deficient Fluid Volume

Common Risk Factors

Inflammatory response to burn with protein and fluid shifts
Massive fluid shifting and circulating volume loss
Hemorrhage; stress ulcer (Curling's ulcer)
Extremes of age

Common Expected Outcomes

Patient maintains normal fluid volume, as evidenced by normal blood pressure (BP), urine output greater than 30 mL/hr, and normal heart rate.
Burn shock is prevented.

NOC Outcomes
Fluid Balance; Electrolyte and Acid-Base Balance

NIC Interventions
Intravenous (IV) Insertion; Fluid/Electrolyte Management; Electrolyte Management: Hyperkalemia; Shock Prevention; Medication Administration

Ongoing Assessment

Actions/Interventions

■ Assess for signs and symptoms of fluid volume deficit.

Rationale

Fluid shifts from the intravascular to extravascular space because of increased capillary permeability; the first 24 to 48 hours are most critical. Also, insensible loss from areas of lost skin are dramatically increased, adding to fluid volume deficit. NOTE: Restlessness, tachycardia, hypotension, thirst (thirst is a sensitive indicator of fluid deficit and hemoconcentration), pale and cool skin, oliguria (urine output less than 30 mL/hr indicating inadequate renal perfusion), and hypoxia (as interstitial spaces fill with fluid, alveolar oxygen exchange is impaired) are common symptoms. Fluid volume deficit is directly proportional to the extent and depth of the burn injury.

■ = Independent; ▲ = Collaborative

Actions/Interventions

▲ Monitor laboratory results for alteration in acid-base balance, catabolism (outpouring of potassium and nitrogen), and altered electrolyte levels.

■ Monitor urine specific gravity every 4 hours.

■ Monitor for signs of bleeding: melena stools, coffee-ground emesis through nasogastric tube.

▲ Evaluate hemoglobin and hematocrit.

■ Weigh the patient daily, taking care to use the same scale and bedding.

Rationale

Decreased tissue perfusion leads to a buildup of lactic acid and metabolic acidosis. Tissue destruction initially causes hyperkalemia. When capillary integrity is restored, excess potassium is eliminated and may lead to hypokalemia.

Very concentrated urine (specific gravity greater than 1.020) indicates fluid volume deficit; a urine output of 30 to 50 mL/hr indicates adequate perfusion.

Severe physiological stress (e.g., with burns) and/or mechanical ventilation can result in gastroduodenal ulceration and life-threatening hemorrhage 48 to 92 hours postevent.

Elevated hemoglobin and hematocrit occur with fluid volume deficit and result in hemoconcentration.

Changes in body weight may be better indicators of fluid balance than intake and output records.

Therapeutic Interventions

Actions/Interventions

▲ Assist with IV and central line placements. Multiple large-bore lines or a central line may be required.

▲ Administer crystalloid solutions as prescribed.

▲ Administer colloid solutions as prescribed.

▲ Administer antacids or H₂-receptor antagonist prophylactically.

Rationale

These are used for rapid fluid resuscitation to prevent circulatory collapse.

Amount and rate are calculated on the basis of TBSA and depth of wound, using the Parkland formula. Over the first 24 hours according to the Parkland formula, give 4 mL of lactated Ringer's solution per percent TBSA burn per kilogram body weight as follows: half in first 8 hours, one fourth in second 8 hours, and one fourth in third 8 hours. After initial fluid resuscitation, 5% dextrose is used to maintain fluid balance.

As capillary permeability is decreased, colloid solutions may be used to restore and maintain vascular volume and correct sodium imbalances.

These minimize the potential for gastric bleeding, which can further add to fluid volume deficit.

Burns

NDx Nursing Diagnosis

Risk for Ineffective Breathing Pattern

Common Risk Factors

Burns to head and neck
Circumferential chest burns
Massive edema
Inhalation of smoke or heated air

■ = Independent; ▲ = Collaborative

Burns—cont'd

Common Expected Outcome

Patient maintains an effective breathing pattern as evidenced by normal arterial blood gases (ABGs).

NOC Outcome
Respiratory Status: Ventilation

NIC Interventions
Airway Management; Respiratory Monitoring

Ongoing Assessment

Actions/Interventions

■ Assess for presence of burns to face and neck.

■ Assess for edema of the head, face, and neck.

■ Assess for history and evidence of smoke inhalation.

■ Assess respiratory rate, rhythm, and depth; assess lung sounds.

■ Assess for dyspnea, shortness of breath, use of accessory muscles, cough, and presence of cyanosis.

▲ Monitor ABGs.

▲ Assess pulse oximetry readings.

■ Observe for confusion, anxiety, and/or restlessness.

▲ Assess hemodynamic pressures if available.

▲ Review chest x-ray study results.

Rationale

Facial burns may indicate that smoke inhalation and possible airway injury have occurred.

As fluid shift begins to occur, the oral airway and trachea become constricted, decreasing the patient's ability to breathe.

Inhalation injury usually occurs when the fire was in a closed space. It can lead to respiratory failure and/or carbon monoxide poisoning (see Risk for Poisoning, p. 1092).

Crackles may be heard if fluid is accumulating from direct burn injury or as a result of fluid shifts associated with fluid resuscitation.

These manifestations suggest progressive hypoxia.

The combined effect of airway edema and accumulation of interstitial fluid results in decreased alveolar ventilation. The patient may be hypoxemic (decreased PO_2) or have metabolic and/or respiratory acidosis.

Pulse oximetry is a useful tool to detect changes in oxygenation.

These are early signs of hypoxia.

Increasing pulmonary pressures may indicate pulmonary edema.

Chest x-ray studies will reflect changing lung status.

Therapeutic Interventions

Actions/Interventions

■ Raise head of bed and maintain good body alignment.

▲ Maintain humidified oxygen delivery system.

▲ Provide chest physical therapy if burns are not to the chest.

Rationale

This promotes optimal breathing and lung expansion by allowing descent of the diaphragm.

Initially patients may receive 100% oxygen. Humidity decreases viscosity of secretions.

This loosens secretions caused by stasis.

■ = Independent; ▲ = Collaborative

Integumentary Care Plans

Actions/Interventions

- Encourage use of incentive spirometer.
- ▲ Be prepared for intubation and mechanical ventilation.

- ▲ Be prepared for escharotomy.

- Manage fear or anxiety. Coach the patient to take deep, slow breaths.

Rationale

This prevents alveolar collapse.

When edema is severe, an artificial airway may be the only means of ventilating the severely burned patient.

Burns of the chest may cause restriction and constriction that decreases chest expansion; escharotomy (cutting through or removing eschar) will be needed to alleviate constricted movement.

This technique enhances coordinated efforts to breathe.

NDx Nursing Diagnosis

Risk for Ineffective Peripheral Tissue Perfusion

Common Risk Factors

Blockage of microcirculation
Blood loss
Compartment syndrome (edema restricting circulation)
Circumferential eschar

Common Expected Outcome

Patient maintains normal tissue perfusion to extremities, as evidenced by palpable pulses in all extremities, and normal sensation in extremity.

NOC Outcomes
Circulation Status; Tissue Perfusion: Peripheral

NIC Interventions
Circulatory Care; Vital Signs Monitoring

Burns

Ongoing Assessment

Actions/Interventions

- Check pulses of all extremities; use Doppler if necessary. Notify physician immediately of noted alteration in perfusion.

- Monitor vital signs (BP, heart rate [HR], and respiratory rate) for abrupt changes.

- Assess color and temperature of extremities.

- Check for pain, numbness, or swelling of extremities.

Rationale

Weak, thready pulses may not be palpable. Also, feeling pulses through extremely edematous tissue or skin covered with eschar may be difficult.

Abrupt drop in BP and HR can indicate decreased blood flow secondary to severe third spacing (movement of fluid into spaces normally without fluid), which impedes venous return.

Cool, discolored extremities indicate compromised tissue perfusion. This situation, if untreated, can result in limb loss.

Circumferential burns with eschar are most likely to cause altered tissue perfusion to extremities, because as fluid shift occurs and eschar cannot stretch, pressure is exerted on tissue, vessels, and nerves.

■ = Independent; ▲ = Collaborative

Burns—cont'd

Therapeutic Interventions

Actions/Interventions

■ Maintain good alignment of extremities. Elevate extremities on pillows or in a specially made sling.

▲ Apply sequential compression device on nonburned extremities.

■ Perform passive range of motion if needed.

▲ Prepare for and assist with fasciotomy or escharotomy.

Rationale

Careful positioning allows adequate blood flow without compression on arteries, also reducing edema.

This improves venous return.

This increases circulation.

This relieves compression of nerves or blood vessels.

NDx Nursing Diagnosis

Risk for Poisoning: Carbon Monoxide

Common Risk Factor

Smoke inhalation

Common Expected Outcome

Patient maintains normal oxygen and carboxyhemoglobin levels.

> **NOC Outcome**
> Respiratory Status: Gas Exchange
>
> **NIC Intervention**
> Oxygen Therapy

Ongoing Assessment

Actions/Interventions

■ Monitor for carbon monoxide poisoning in any burn patient.

▲ Measure carboxyhemoglobin levels on admission to the emergency department.

■ Monitor for dyspnea, headache, and confusion, which may accompany carbon monoxide poisoning.

Rationale

This is seen especially in patients with other signs and symptoms of smoke inhalation or facial burns.

Carbon monoxide has a high affinity for the hemoglobin molecule; when hemoglobin molecules are bound to carbon monoxide, they are not available to transport oxygen.

At low carboxyhemoglobin levels (<10%), the patient may be asymptomatic or complain of a headache. Dizziness, nausea, and syncope occur at carboxyhemoglobin levels above 20%. Seizures and coma develop in patients with carboxyhemoglobin levels above 40%.

■ = Independent; ▲ = Collaborative

Therapeutic Interventions

Actions/Interventions

▲ Administer 100% humidified oxygen. Anticipate administration of hyperbaric oxygen in some cases.

Rationale

The patient may require airway intubation and mechanical ventilation to support an effective airway and gas exchange. According to the American Burn Association's Clinical Practice guidelines, hyperbaric oxygen is indicated if carbon monoxide poisoning is the only injury, because increasing the delivery of 100% oxygen at increased pressure is theorized to reduce the half-life of carboxyhemoglobin.

NDx Nursing Diagnosis

Risk for Imbalanced Nutrition: Less Than Body Requirements

Common Risk Factors

Prolonged interference in ability to ingest or digest food
Increased basal metabolic rate
Loss of protein from dermal wounds

Common Expected Outcome

Patient maintains an adequate nutritional intake, as evidenced by stable weight.

NOC Outcomes
Nutritional Status: Biochemical Measures; Nutritional Status: Food and Fluid Intake

NIC Interventions
Nutrition Therapy; Nutrition Monitoring

Ongoing Assessment

Actions/Interventions

■ Obtain base weight; weigh daily if possible, using same scale and linens.

■ Measure fluid intake and output, including oral and intravenous intake.

■ Closely monitor caloric intake.

▲ Monitor skin test results for cellular immunity.

Rationale

Such consistency facilitates accurate measurement and evaluation.

Changes in fluid balance can be reflected in daily weight changes. All snacks, foods from home, and items that are liquid at room temperature (gelatin, sherbet) should be included as oral intake.

Patients with major burns may require 40% to 100% increase in calorie intake to keep up with hypermetabolic state and wound protein loss.

Anergic patients (those unable to muster a cellular immune response) are seriously nutritionally depleted.

■ = Independent; ▲ = Collaborative

Burns—cont'd

Actions/Interventions

▲ Monitor serum albumin levels.

■ Check for bowel sounds and monitor residuals of enteral feeding.

▲ Monitor nitrogen balance.

■ Determine environmental or situational factors (pain, odors, unpleasant sounds).

Rationale

Serum albumin gives an indication of protein reserve. Levels less than 2.5 g/dL indicate serious protein depletion and are linked to morbidity and mortality.

Early enteral feeding may be started upon admission to prevent paralytic ileus.

If nitrogen output is greater than nitrogen intake, the patient will become nutritionally depleted.

These can diminish appetite.

Therapeutic Interventions

Actions/Interventions

▲ Consult a dietitian to assist in meeting nutritional needs.

▲ Provide nutritional supplementation and replacement as needed.

■ Plan dressing changes or other unpleasant situations away from mealtime.

■ Involve the patient in selection of menu to the extent possible.

▲ Administer tube feeding as ordered.

Rationale

The Curreri formula is used to calculate the caloric needs for the burn patient to support homeostasis and wound healing: (24 kcal $\times$ Usual body weight [in kg]) + (40 kcal $\times$ %TBSA) = Calories. The patient may need 1.5 to 3 g/kg/day of protein to maintain nitrogen balance.

Multivitamins, zinc, vitamin C, phosphorus, magnesium, and calcium are often provided daily or as needed based on laboratory results.

Comfort enhances interest in eating.

This may enhance nutritional intake.

The gastrointestinal tract is the most efficacious route for absorption and use of nutrients.

NDx Nursing Diagnosis

Acute Pain

Common Related Factor	Defining Characteristics
Burn injury	Complaints of pain Increased restlessness Alterations in sleep pattern Irritability Facial grimaces Guarding

Integumentary Care Plans

■ = Independent; ▲ = Collaborative

Common Expected Outcome

Patient verbalizes relief of pain or ability to tolerate pain.

NOC Outcomes
Pain Level; Medication Response

NIC Interventions
Analgesic Administration; Pain Management; Simple Relaxation Therapy; Patient-Controlled Analgesia; Distraction

Ongoing Assessment

Actions/Interventions

- Assess type, location, quality, and severity of pain/discomfort.

- Assess factors that may contribute to an increased perception of pain (e.g., anxiety, fear).
- Assess vital signs.

- Evaluate and document effectiveness of chosen pain control methods.

Rationale

The pain experience varies with extent of the burn injury. As wound healing begins, patient may complain of pruritus. Relief of this discomfort is important because scratching can disrupt fragile new skin or grafts.

Knowing different etiological factors can guide effective therapies.

Increasing pain can cause transient increases in respiratory and cardiac rates, and blood pressure.

Changing effectiveness is expected. Partial-thickness burns are very painful; pain will decrease over time and with healing. Full-thickness burns do not cause pain because of nerve destruction, but as nerves regenerate, pain will increase.

Therapeutic Interventions

Actions/Interventions

▲ Administer sedatives and analgesics prescribed for pain.
- Provide background, procedural, and breakthrough pain control.
▲ Consider use of patient-controlled analgesia.

- Avoid pressure on injured tissues; use a bed cradle.
- Alleviate all unnecessary stressors or sources of discomfort.
- Allay fears and anxiety.
- Turn the patient; obtain a pressure-relieving mattress or bed, as needed.
▲ Premedicate the patient for dressing changes; allow sufficient time for the medication to take effect.
- Saturate dressings with sterile normal saline solution before removal.
- Use distraction and relaxation techniques as indicated.

See also **Acute Pain,** *p. 144.*

Rationale

Intravenous morphine is the drug of choice. Adjuvant drugs such as psychotropics may be added.

Burn patients have pain all the time, so they require three types of control.

This method of analgesic administration increases the patient's sense of control over pain.

This keeps linen off the legs.

A quiet, relaxed environment aids in promoting comfort.

Fear may intensify perception of pain.

These help relieve pressure points and improve circulation to painful areas.

Manipulation of burn surfaces increases the patient's pain.

This eases dressing removal by loosening adherents and decreasing pain.

These complementary therapies can be effective.

Burns

■ = Independent; ▲ = Collaborative

Burns—cont'd

 Nursing Diagnosis

Deficient Knowledge

Common Related Factors
Unfamiliarity with follow-up care
Need for long-term rehabilitation, follow-up care

Defining Characteristics
Questions
Lack of questioning
Verbalized misconceptions
Potential for failure to continue needed care or treatment

Common Expected Outcome
Patient or caregiver verbalizes understanding and ability to care for wound, mobilize resources, get follow-up care, and report signs of complication.

NOC Outcomes
Knowledge: Treatment Regimen; Coping; Family Participation in Professional Care

NIC Interventions
Discharge Planning; Support System Enhancement; Teaching: Disease Process; Teaching: Prescribed Activity/Exercise; Teaching: Psychomotor Skill

Ongoing Assessment

Actions/Interventions

■ Assess the need for ongoing wound or graft site care.

■ Assess the need for continued rehabilitation (occupational therapy [OT], physical therapy [PT], psychosocial support).

■ Assess the patient's perceived ability to care for self after discharge.

■ Assess resources (environmental and human) in the home that can be tapped for assistance.

Rationale

Grafted skin is delicate and at continued risk of breakdown and infection.

A variety of factors (e.g., inability to cope with body image changes; guilt about the injury, or the cause of fire or accident; need for further reconstructive surgery; use of scar prevention garments) may require care for months beyond hospital discharge.

This information may give some perspective on home care needs.

Although family and friends can be great allies, they sometimes may have trouble dealing with the complexities of long-term follow-up.

Therapeutic Interventions

Actions/Interventions

▲ Involve a social worker or case manager early in the course of hospitalization.

Rationale

Discharge planning may be a complicated process requiring a long period of planning.

■ = Independent; ▲ = Collaborative

Integumentary Care Plans

Actions/Interventions

- Instruct the patient or caregiver in wound care of graft sites and donor sites: continue to use aseptic technique until the wound is completely healed; cover open wounds with gauze; keep wounds clean and moisturized with a lanolin-based cream; avoid sun exposure of newly grafted skin.

- Instruct the patient in care and use of scar-prevention garments, which are usually worn at all times (removed for bathing and wound care) up to 18 months after injury.

- Instruct the patient or caregiver to report any of the following: signs or symptoms of wound infection (redness, swelling, pain, unusual drainage); limitation of movement, which can result from delayed contracture formation; inability to cope with disfigurement, role change.

- Encourage the patient or caregiver to maintain a follow-up schedule with the physician, registered nurse, PT, and OT, as well as social services.

- Discuss fire safety or burn prevention.

Rationale

Infection and contractures can occur during the rehabilitative phase of burn recovery.

These may need to be replaced often to maintain elasticity sufficient for their purpose. The use of pressure garments and dressings can control development of hypertrophic scarring.

Early identification of signs of infection or contractures facilitates needed treatment. Difficulty adjusting to home and loss after a burn injury is common. Additional support with coping will be necessary with integration back into society during the rehabilitative phase.

Patients who become co-managers of their care have a greater stake in achieving a positive outcome.

Education regarding safety and prevention is ongoing and based on readiness to learn.

Burns

NDx Nursing Diagnosis

Disturbed Body Image

Common Related Factors

Massive edema
Visible burns
Dressings
Loss of function secondary to burns or burn treatment
Scarring or contractures
Loss of normal skin color
Use of scar-prevention garments

Defining Characteristics

Refusal to look at or care for altered body part
Verbal identification of feeling about altered structure or function of body part
Refusal to discuss change
Focusing behavior on changed body part

Common Expected Outcome

Patient comes to terms with disturbed body image as evidenced by ability to verbalize feelings, participate in self-care, and reintegrate into activities of daily living (ADLs) as capable.

NOC Outcomes

Body Image; Social Involvement; Social Support

NIC Interventions

Grief Work Facilitation; Body Image Enhancement; Coping Enhancement; Active Listening; Presence

Burns—cont'd

Integumentary Care Plans

Ongoing Assessment

Actions/Interventions

- Note the patient's ability to look at burns or dressings and their reactions to them.

- Note the frequency and tone of critical remarks directed toward self, regarding appearance and/or function.
- Assess the perceived impact of actual change on ADLs, social behavior, personal relationships, and/or occupational activities.

Rationale

Denial, looking away, or refusing to participate may indicate body image disturbance or may represent a normal stage of the grieving process.

The extent or severity of response is highly related to value placed on a body part or function affected.

This may give some perspective on any perceived misconceptions that could affect recovery.

Therapeutic Interventions

Actions/Interventions

- Listen and share presence.

- Acknowledge the normalcy of the patient's emotional response to the actual or perceived change in body structure or function.
- Help the patient identify actual changes.

- Assist the patient to identify frightening or worrisome potential situations; role-play responses.

- Encourage attendance at a support group.

Rationale

Health care workers are a "testing ground" for societal reaction to appearance; a supportive relationship facilitates coping with body image disturbance.

Grief, in all its stages, is normal and expected.

This may help minimize perceived changes that are not actually present. Scar maturation may take up to 2 years. Skin appearance may continue to improve during that time.

This gives the patient "practice" in responding to staring, questions, unwanted sympathy, and thoughtless behaviors that he or she may encounter.

Participation in support groups may allow the patient to realize that others have the same problem and that he or she may use this as a means to find suggestions for specific care challenges.

> • **RELATED CARE PLANS**
>
> Deficient fluid volume, p. 71
> Gastrointestinal bleeding, p. 698
> Ineffective coping, p. 51

Plastic Surgery for Wound Closure

Skin Grafts; Flap; Flap Closure; Myocutaneous Flap

Wounds that lack an epithelial base for healing often require closure by plastic surgery. Wounds that may heal over extended periods without surgical intervention may be electively closed to hasten the rehabilitation time, or to protect the vulnerable patient from infection resulting from a long-term open wound. Skin, subcutaneous tissue, fascia, and muscle may all be relocated through a variety of procedures to achieve closure of wounds. Partial- or full-thickness skin grafts may be used to close superficial wounds. Flap closures are performed to close deeper wounds that extend beyond the dermis. Flaps

■ = Independent; ▲ = Collaborative

are categorized either by the source of the blood supply or the area from which they are taken. Myocutaneous flaps are often performed to achieve pressure ulcer closure. These procedures typically require a hospital stay. Older adults are at increased risk for flap or graft failure because of reduced circulation and loss of normal padding and elasticity of the skin.

 Nursing Diagnosis

Risk for Ineffective Peripheral Tissue Perfusion

Common Risk Factors

Skin graft
Flap closure
Anatomical location
Poor circulation
Edema

Common Expected Outcome

Patient maintains adequate tissue perfusion to graft or flap, as evidenced by normal color and warmth of graft or flap and by intact suture lines.

NOC Outcomes
Tissue Perfusion: Peripheral; Tissue Integrity: Skin and Mucous Membranes

NIC Interventions
Pressure Ulcer Prevention; Skin Surveillance

Ongoing Assessment

Actions/Interventions	Rationale
■ Assess skin graft or flap for signs of adequate circulation.	Grafts and flaps that are adequately perfused are similar in color to other skin on the patient's body. The graft or flap should feel warm to touch and should have brisk capillary refill.
■ Assess for history of poor circulation, peripheral vascular disease, decreased cardiac output, or shock.	Any of these situations places the patient at risk for decreased circulation to the skin. The most dramatic complication is loss of viability of the graft or flap.
■ Assess for edema around the skin graft or flap.	Excess edema can impede venous return and compromise arterial perfusion to the area.
■ Assess patency of and output from surgically placed drains.	These drains remove serous fluid from the operative site; up to 100 mL/day for the first 72 hours is normal. The drainage may be sanguinous at first, but it gradually changes to serosanguineous and then serous.
■ Assess intactness of suture lines.	Care should be taken to protect suture lines from disruption. Separation of suture lines may indicate poor tissue perfusion.

■ = Independent; ▲ = Collaborative

Plastic Surgery for Wound Closure

Plastic Surgery for Wound Closure—cont'd

Therapeutic Interventions

Actions/Interventions	Rationale
■ Position the patient off the skin graft or flap.	This eliminates external pressure, which can compromise circulation to the surgical site. Areas where pressure occurs as patient lies in bed or sits in a chair are at risk for impaired perfusion as skin capillaries are compressed.
■ Ensure that dressings are secure but not constrictive.	Dressings over skin grafts may be secured to prevent movement of the graft during the first few days after surgery.
▲ Place the patient on a pressure-reducing cushion or pad when sitting, or in a pressure-reducing bed.	The less pressure on skin grafts or flaps, the better chance the graft or flap has of remaining adequately perfused. Specialized beds support the patient's weight and distribute pressure so that pressure at any point on the body is less than capillary closing pressure (usually considered to be about 32 mm Hg). The occupational therapist can make the best recommendation.
■ Provide an over-bed trapeze.	This reduces friction and shear during movement.

NDx Nursing Diagnosis

Risk for Infection

Common Risk Factors

Surgical graft or flap
Poor nutritional status
Proximity of graft or flap to perineum
Collection of fluid beneath graft or flap
Open donor site (grafts)

Common Expected Outcome

Patient remains free of infection as evidenced by healing graft or flap free of redness, swelling, and purulent drainage, and by normal temperature.

NOC Outcomes
Tissue Integrity: Skin and Mucous Membranes; Risk Control; Risk Detection

NIC Interventions
Infection Protection; Wound Care; Incision Site Care; Nutrition Therapy

■ = Independent; ▲ = Collaborative

Integumentary Care Plans

Ongoing Assessment

Actions/Interventions	Rationale
■ Assess the graft or flap for signs of local infection: redness, swelling, increased pain.	Redness and edema may be expected in the first few days after surgery.
■ Assess the graft donor site and area from which the flap was taken (usually sutured closed) for redness, swelling, and pain.	A transparent dressing may be used to cover the site initially.
■ Assess grafts or flap suture lines for drainage, color of tissue, and odor.	Small amounts of exudate that is clear to straw-colored are normal. Purulent green or yellow drainage typically indicates an infection, as does foul-smelling drainage.
■ Note any separation of suture lines.	Separation may indicate flap or graft failure, which may be associated with infection.
▲ Obtain wound cultures, if available.	Culture determines which pathogens are present and guides antimicrobial therapy.
▲ Monitor white blood cell (WBC) count.	Elevated WBC count is a sign of infection, although in older persons, marrow incompetence results in less elevated WBCs even if an infection is present.
■ Assess nutritional status.	Patients who are seriously nutritionally depleted (e.g., serum albumin level <2.5 mg/dL) are at risk for developing an infection and are unable to heal.
■ Assess for urinary and/or fecal incontinence.	Closure of sacral wounds, because of their proximity to the perineum, are at highest risk for infection caused by urine and/or fecal contamination.
■ Monitor temperature.	Fever is an indication of infection.

Therapeutic Interventions

Actions/Interventions	Rationale
▲ Provide local wound care, using aseptic technique, as prescribed.	Xeroform, a nonadherent bismuth-saturated dressing, is often used for dressing grafts, flaps, and donor sites because it does not stick to the wound and has antimicrobial properties. It may be changed routinely or left in place to dry up and fall off.
▲ Insert a Foley catheter or initiate bowel management system (e.g., Zassi tube).	These systems may be required initially to prevent contamination of the flap or graft site when in close proximity to the perineal area. The systems will prevent any contact with urine or feces while the systems are maintained to promote the healing process.
■ Provide rigorous perineal hygiene after each episode of incontinence.	This minimizes pathogens in the sacral area.
▲ Provide aggressive nutritional therapy.	The skin of malnourished patients is more susceptible to infection and slow healing.
▲ Consult a dietitian for assistance with high-calorie, high-protein diet.	These patients often require enteral or parenteral nutrition to meet nutritional needs for healing.
▲ Administer antibiotics as prescribed.	Early treatment is indicated to reduce compromised healing.

Plastic Surgery for Wound Closure

■ = Independent; ▲ = Collaborative

Plastic Surgery for Wound Closure—cont'd

 Nursing Diagnosis

Risk for Ineffective Health Maintenance

Common Risk Factors

Possible extended healing time
Lack of previous similar experience
Possible need for special equipment

Common Expected Outcomes

Patient or family verbalizes understanding of wound
 care and pressure reduction care.
Patient does not develop new pressure ulcers.

NOC Outcomes
Knowledge: Disease Process; Knowledge:
 Treatment Regimen; Decision Making;
 Coping

NIC Interventions
Discharge Planning; Family Support;
 Teaching: Disease Process; Teaching:
 Prescribed Diet; Urinary Elimination;
 Urinary Catheterization, Intermittent

Ongoing Assessment

Actions/Interventions

■ Assess patient's and caregiver's understanding of long-term nature of wound healing and delicacy of grafted or flapped areas.

■ Assess knowledge of and ability to provide local wound care.

■ Assess for availability of pressure reduction or pressure relief surface.

■ Assess the patient's understanding of and ability to shift position often.

■ Assess understanding of the prevention of further pressure ulcer development.

Rationale

Because grafts or flaps are often done in the sacral area, sitting is limited to brief intervals even after the patient is discharged; the area remains at high risk for breakdown.

Usually by the time of discharge, suture lines and donor sites have healed and require little more than pressure relief, cleaning, and moisturizing.

Patients may take thick, dense foam mattresses home from the hospital to place on their own bed. Rental provision of low–air-loss (e.g., Flexicare, Kinair) beds and air-fluidized therapy (e.g., Clinitron, Skytron, FluidAir) beds may be arranged but often pose financial difficulty because few payer sources will cover the cost of these pressure-relief beds in the home. Patients who use wheelchairs must have adequate pressure reduction or relief surfaces.

It is important to relieve pressure and allow adequate circulation to the grafted or flapped area.

Patients who are incapable of independent movement need frequent repositioning to reduce the risk for breakdown in those areas that are intact.

■ = Independent; ▲ = Collaborative

Integumentary Care Plans

Actions/Interventions

■ Assess understanding of and ability to provide high-calorie, high-protein diet throughout the course of wound healing.

■ Assess understanding of the relationship between incontinence and further skin breakdown or complications of healing.

Rationale

Patients may require enteral feeding (through gastric tube, nasogastric feeding tubes, or the oral route), which requires knowledge of preparation and use of special equipment (e.g., feeding pumps, administration sets).

Managing incontinence may pose the most difficult aspect of home management and is most frequently the reason decisions for nursing home placement are made.

Therapeutic Interventions

Actions/Interventions

▲ Involve the social worker or case manager early in the course of hospitalization.

■ Teach the patient or caregiver the importance of pressure reduction and relief:
  • Use of specialty surface: If provision of a specialty bed is a problem because of reimbursement issues, purchase of a waterbed may be a reasonable alternative
  • Use of pressure reduction or relief surface where the patient sits
  • Turning schedule that does not compromise other body areas

■ Teach the patient or caregiver the signs and symptoms of flap or graft failure and to whom such problems should be reported.

▲ Involve the dietitian in teaching the patient or caregiver how to plan high-calorie, high-protein meals, or how to supplement regular meals with dietary supplements.

■ Teach the patient or caregiver how to manage incontinence:
  • Use of external catheters
  • Intermittent self-catheterization
  • Care of indwelling catheters if no other option is feasible
  • Use of underpads or linen protectors

  • Use of moisture barrier ointments

■ Consider or discuss with the patient or caregiver the need for in-home nursing care or homemaker services.

Rationale

Referrals help in planning for the details of discharge and they help the patient and family determine whether discharge to the home is feasible or whether placement in an extended care facility is more realistic.

Information can foster enhanced adherence to pressure prevention guidelines.

Early assessment of suture line separation, discoloration, and necrosis facilitates prompt treatment.

Specialty expertise may be required to provide an appropriate nutritional plan.

Teaching proper techniques can prevent leakage and skin problems.

Reusable products made of cloth with a waterproof lining are better for the patient's skin and are more economical but require laundering.

These protect intact skin from excoriation.

These may be necessary to provide all or part of the patient's care.

• RELATED CARE PLANS

Acute pain, p. 144
Disturbed body image, p. 21
Imbalanced nutrition: less than body
  requirements p. 134

Plastic Surgery for Wound Closure

■ = Independent; ▲ = Collaborative

Pressure Ulcers (Impaired Skin Integrity)

Pressure Sores; Decubitus Ulcers; Bedsores

Pressure ulcers are defined as any lesion caused by unrelieved pressure that results in damage to underlying tissue. Prolonged pressure occurs when tissue is between a bony prominence and a hard surface such as a mattress. The pressure compresses small blood vessels and leads to ineffective tissue perfusion. Loss of perfusion causes tissue hypoxia and eventually cellular death. In addition to prolonged pressure, friction and shearing force contribute to the development of pressure ulcers. These forces are present when a patient slides down in bed and is pulled up against the surface of the mattress. Pressure ulcers usually occur over bony prominences according to the following distribution: trunk 45%, upper body 20%, and lower extremities 35%. Pressure ulcers are usually staged to classify the degree of tissue damage observed.* Pressure ulcers stage I through III can heal with aggressive local wound treatment and proper nutritional support; stage IV pressure ulcers often require surgical intervention (e.g., flap closure, plastic surgery). Pressure ulcers affect persons, regardless of age, who are immobile, are malnourished, or have contributing conditions (e.g., incontinence, decreased mental status). Reduction of pressure ulcers to no more than 0.8% of nursing home residents was cited as an objective in *Healthy People 2010*. This care plan addresses care issues in hospital, long-term care, or home settings.

---

* Panel for the treatment of pressure ulcers. Treatment of Pressure Ulcers: Clinical practice guideline, No 15, AHCPR Pub No 95-0652, 1994. Agency for Health Care Policy and Research, Public Health Service, U.S. Department of Health and Human Services.

 Nursing Diagnosis

Impaired Skin Integrity

Common Related Factors	Defining Characteristics
Extremes of age Immobility Poor nutrition Mechanical forces (friction, shear, pressure) Pronounced bony prominences Poor circulation Altered sensation Incontinence Environmental moisture Radiation Hyperthermia or hypothermia Acquired immunodeficiency syndrome (AIDS) Chronic disease state	Stage I: • Nonblanchable redness that does not resolve within 30 minutes of relief of pressure • Epidermis intact Stage II: • Blisters (either intact or broken) • Partial-thickness skin loss (epidermis and/or dermis) Stage III: • Open lesion involving dermis and subcutaneous tissue • May have adherent necrotic tissue • Drainage usually present • Typically presents as crater • Undermining is common; does not involve underlying fascia

■ = Independent; ▲ = Collaborative

Stage IV:
- Open lesion involving muscle, bone, joint, and/or body cavity
- Usually has adherent necrotic material (slough)
- Drainage is common
- Infection is common
- Undermining and sinus tract may develop

Common Expected Outcomes

Patient receives stage-appropriate wound care, experiences pressure reduction, and has controlled risk factors for prevention of additional ulcers.
Patient experiences healing of pressure ulcers.

NOC Outcomes

Wound Healing: Secondary Intention; Tissue Integrity: Skin and Mucous Membranes

NIC Interventions

Pressure Ulcer Prevention; Pressure Ulcer Care; Positioning; Pressure Management

Ongoing Assessment

Actions/Interventions

- Use objective tool for pressure ulcer risk assessment:
  - Braden Scale
  - Gosnell Scale
  - Norton Scale
- Assess specific risk factors for pressure ulcers.

  - Determine the patient's age and general condition of the skin.

  - Specifically assess skin over bony prominences (sacrum, trochanters, scapulae, elbows, heels, inner and outer malleolus, inner and outer knees, back of head).
  - Assess the patient's awareness of the sensation of pressure.

  - Assess the patient's ability to move (shift weight while sitting, turn over in bed, move from bed to chair).
  - Assess the patient's nutritional status, including weight, weight loss, and serum albumin levels, if ordered.
  - Assess for history of radiation therapy.

Rationale

These are validated tools for risk assessment. Assessment should be carried out on all patients on admission and every 48 hours in acute care settings, or whenever the patient's condition changes.

Even patients who already have a pressure ulcer continue to be at risk for further injury.

Skin of older patients is less elastic, has less padding, and has less moisture, making for higher risk of skin impairment.

These areas are at highest risk of breakdown due to tissue ischemia from compression against a hard surface.

Normally individuals shift their weight off pressure areas every few minutes; this occurs more or less automatically, even during sleep. Patients with decreased sensation are unaware of unpleasant stimuli (pressure) and do not shift weight, thereby exposing skin to excessive pressure.

Immobility is the major risk factor in skin breakdown.

Albumin level less than 2.5 g/dL is a grave sign, indicating severe protein depletion.

Irradiated skin becomes thin and friable and is at higher risk for breakdown.

Pressure Ulcers (Impaired Skin Integrity)

■ = Independent; ▲ = Collaborative

Pressure Ulcers (Impaired Skin Integrity)—cont'd

Integumentary Care Plans

Actions/Interventions

- Assess for fecal and/or urinary incontinence.

- Assess for environmental moisture (wound drainage, excessive perspiration, high humidity).
- Assess the surface that the patient spends a majority of time on (mattress for bedridden patient, cushion for persons in wheelchairs).
- Assess the amount of shear (pressure exerted laterally) and friction (rubbing) on the patient's skin.

- Assess skin on admission and daily for increasing number of risk factors.
- Assess for history of preexisting chronic diseases (e.g., diabetes, malignancy, AIDS, or peripheral and/or cardiovascular disease).

- Assess and stage pressure ulcers (see Defining Characteristics on the previous page).
- Measure the size of the ulcer and note the presence of undermining.

- Describe the condition of the wound or wound bed:
  - Color

  - Odor

  - Presence of necrotic tissue

  - Visibility of bone, muscle, or joints

- Assess for wound exudate.

Rationale

The urea in urine turns into ammonia within minutes and is caustic to the skin. Stool may contain enzymes that cause skin breakdown. Diapers and incontinence pads with plastic liners trap moisture and hasten breakdown.

These may contribute to skin maceration.

Patients who spend the majority of time on one surface need a pressure reduction or pressure relief device to lessen the risk for breakdown.

Shearing forces are most commonly noted on the sacrum, scapulae, heels and elbows from skin-sheet friction, from semi-Fowler's positioning and repositioning, and from lift sheets.

The incidence of skin breakdown is directly related to the number of risk factors present.

Patients with chronic diseases typically manifest multiple risk factors (see above) that predispose them to pressure ulceration. These include poor nutrition, poor hydration, incontinence, and immobility.

Staging is important because it determines the treatment plan.

The ulcer dimensions include length, width, and depth. An ulcer begins in the deepest tissue layers before the skin breaks down. Therefore the opening of the skin's surface may not represent the true size of the ulcer.

Color of tissue is an indication of tissue viability and oxygenation. White, gray, or yellow eschar may be present in stage II and III ulcers. Eschar may be black in stage IV ulcers.

Odor may arise from infection present in the wound; it may also arise from necrotic tissue. Some local wound care products may create or intensify odors and should be distinguished from wound or exudate odors.

Necrotic tissue is tissue that is dead and eventually must be removed before healing can take place. Necrotic tissue exhibits a wide range of appearances: thin, white, shiny, brown, tough, leathery, black, hard.

In stage IV pressure ulcers, these may be apparent at the base of the ulcer. Wounds may demonstrate multiple stages or characteristics in a single wound (i.e., healthy tissue with granulation may be present along with necrotic tissue).

Exudate is a normal part of wound physiology and must be differentiated from pus, which is an indication of infection. Exudate may contain serum, blood, and white blood cells, and may appear clear, cloudy, or blood-tinged. The amount may vary from a few cubic

■ = Independent; ▲ = Collaborative

Actions/Interventions

■ Assess the condition of surrounding tissue.

■ Assess ulcer healing, using pressure ulcer scale for healing (PUSH) tool.

■ Assess pain level, especially related to dressing changes and procedures.

Rationale

centimeters, which are easily managed with dressings, to copious amounts not easily managed. Drainage is considered "excessive" when dressing changes are needed more often than every 6 hours.

Surrounding tissue may be healthy or may have various degrees of impairment. Healthy tissue is necessary for use of local wound care products requiring adhesion to the skin. Presence of healthy tissue demarcates the boundaries of the pressure ulcer.

This tool provides standardization in measurement of wound healing. It is located at the National Pressure Ulcer Advisory Panel website (www.NPUAP.org).

Joint Commission on the Accreditation of Healthcare Organizations mandates frequent and regular assessment of pain. Prophylactic medications may be indicated.

Therapeutic Interventions

Actions/Interventions

■ Change the patient's position frequently.

■ Use pressure-relieving beds, mattress overlays, and chair cushions.

▲ Provide local wound care as follows:
Stage I

- Apply a flexible hydrocolloid dressing (e.g., Duoderm, Sween-Appeal) or a vapor-permeable membrane dressing (e.g., Op-Site, Tegaderm).
- Apply vitamin-enriched emollient to skin every shift.
- Apply topical vasodilator (e.g., Proderm, Granulex).

Stage II

- Hydrogels (aqua skin, Carrasyn V)

- Hydrocolloids or vapor-permeable membrane dressing
- Alginates (Kalginate, Kaltostat, Sorbsan)

- Gauze with sodium chloride solution

Stage III and IV
- Consult a plastic surgeon to perform sharp debridement (surgical removal of eschar)
- Gauze with sodium chloride solution

Rationale

Position changes relieve pressure, restore blood flow, and promote skin integrity.

These devices redistribute pressure when frequent position changes are not possible.

The goal is to prevent further damage and shearing away of the epidermis.

This prevents friction and shear.

This moisturizes skin.

This increases circulation to skin.

The goal is to prevent further damage and shearing away of the epidermis.

This is used for shallow ulcers without exudates. Promotes wound debridement and healing.

This promotes wound debridement and healing. Do not use with heavy exudate–producing wounds.

These are used for ulcers with exudates or moderate drainage. Avoid in both dry and heavily bleeding ulcers. They can be used in Stage II to IV ulcers.

This maintains a moist environment but requires multiple dressing changes. Dressings must be removed while still wet. Dressings absorb small amounts of drainage.

This surgical procedure removes any necrotic thick eschar to promote future healing.

This maintains a moist environment but requires multiple dressing changes as described for stage II.

Pressure Ulcers (Impaired Skin Integrity)

■ = Independent; ▲ = Collaborative

Pressure Ulcers (Impaired Skin Integrity)—cont'd

Actions/Interventions	Rationale
• Foams	Foams reduce odor and repel bacteria and water. They can be used with moderate to heavy drainage. They may macerate surrounding skin.
• Wound fillers	These are used in conjunction with other dressings. They absorb exudates, fill the wound, and cause autolytic debridement.
• Debridement	See Other therapies.
• Negative pressure wound therapy	See Other therapies.
• Palliative wound care	See Other therapies.

Other therapies

• Enzymatic debridement (collagenase, chlorophyll, papain)	Removal of necrotic tissue aids in healing. These agents work by selectively digesting the collagen portion of the necrotic tissue. Care should be taken to prevent damage to surrounding healthy tissues.
• Autolytic debridement	This uses enzymes already present in the wound to dissolve the necrotic tissue, usually with a hydrocolloid or hydrogel.
• Mechanical debridement	This is painful to the patient. It involves allowing the gauze to dry, then removing it from the ulcer.
• Sharp debridement	This is a surgical procedure that may be done in the operating room or at the bedside. It provides the patient with pain relief.
• Negative pressure wound therapy	This involves a device for draining stage III and IV wounds that would require frequent dressing changes. It decompresses the interstitial fluid in the wound, thus improving blood flow, promoting granulation tissue, and increasing fibroblasts.
• Topical growth factors	Colony-stimulating factors, fibroblast growth factors, and nerve growth factors are currently under study.
• Palliative wound care	This may be an option for a patient with a chronic, non-healing wound. These wounds occur in patients with preexisting debilitating disease. This option requires a comprehensive history as well as evaluation of the patient's goals for comfort and independence. Goals include control of symptoms, control of caregiver strain, and reduction of stress in the patient and family. Education must be conveyed that while the wound is nonhealing and remains open indefinitely, it can remain stable. These cases may require referral to a wound specialist.

Integumentary Care Plans

■ = Independent; ▲ = Collaborative

Nursing Diagnosis

Risk for Infection

Common Risk Factors

Open pressure ulcer
Poor nutritional status
Proximity of sacral wounds to perineum

Common Expected Outcomes

Patient remains free of local or systemic infection, as evidenced by absence of copious, foul-smelling wound exudate.
Patient maintains normal body temperature.

NOC Outcomes
Infection Status; Nutritional Status: Food and Fluid Intake

NIC Interventions
Infection Protection; Wound Care; Nutrition Management

Ongoing Assessment

Actions/Interventions	Rationale
■ Assess pressure ulcers for drainage, color of tissue, and odor.	All wounds produce exudate; the presence of exudate that is clear-to-straw-colored is normal. Purulent green or yellow drainage in large amounts typically indicates an infection, as does foul-smelling drainage. Infected tissue usually has a gray-yellow appearance without evidence of pink granulation tissue.
▲ Obtain wound cultures, if available.	All pressure ulcers are colonized (i.e., will culture out bacteria) because skin normally has flora that will be found in an open skin lesion; however, all pressure ulcers are not infected. Infection is present when there is copious foul-smelling drainage, and the patient has other symptoms of infection (fever, increased pain) and a bacteria count greater than 10,000/mm³.
■ Assess the patient for unexplained sepsis.	When septic workup is done, the pressure ulcer must be considered a possible cause.
■ Assess nutritional status.	Patients who are seriously nutritionally depleted (e.g., serum albumin <2.5 mg/dL) are at risk for developing infection produced by a pressure ulcer. Additionally, patients with pressure ulcers lose tremendous amounts of protein in wound exudate and may require 4000 kcal/day or more to remain anabolic.
■ Assess for urinary and/or fecal incontinence.	Sacral wounds, because of their proximity to the perineum, are at highest risk for infection caused by urine and/or fecal contamination. It is sometimes difficult to isolate the wound from the perineal area.
■ Monitor temperature.	Fever may indicate infection, unless the patient is immunocompromised or diabetic.

■ = Independent; ▲ = Collaborative

Pressure Ulcers (Impaired Skin Integrity)

Pressure Ulcers (Impaired Skin Integrity)—cont'd

Actions/Interventions

▲ Monitor white blood cell (WBC) count.

Rationale

Elevated WBC count may indicate infection, although in very old individuals, WBC count may rise only slightly during an infection, indicating a diminished marrow reserve.

Therapeutic Interventions

Actions/Interventions

▲ Provide local wound care as prescribed (see pp. 1107 to 1108).

■ Provide thorough perineal hygiene after each episode of incontinence.

▲ Consult the dietitian for assistance with a high-calorie, high-protein diet.

▲ Administer antibiotics as prescribed.

▲ Provide hydrotherapy if available.

Rationale

The type and level of wound treatment depends on the staging of the ulcer and the type of infection present.

This minimizes pathogens in the area of sacral pressure ulcers.

These patients, because of their overall condition, often require enteral or parenteral nutrition to meet nutritional needs.

Complicated wounds may develop cellulitis or sepsis, requiring antibiotic therapy.

This is needed to achieve wound cleansing and to promote circulation.

NDx Nursing Diagnosis

Risk for Ineffective Health Maintenance

Common Risk Factors

Need for long-term pressure ulcer management
Lack of previous similar experience
Possible need for special equipment
Impaired functional status

Common Expected Outcome

Patient and caregiver verbalizes understanding of the following aspects of home care: pressure relief, wound care, nutrition, and incontinence management.

NOC Outcomes

Knowledge: Treatment Regimen; Decision Making; Coping; Family Functioning

NIC Interventions

Discharge Planning; Family Support; Decision-Making Support; Teaching: Prescribed Activity/Exercise; Teaching: Prescribed Diet

■ = Independent; ▲ = Collaborative

Integumentary Care Plans

Ongoing Assessment

Actions/Interventions

- Assess the patient's and caregiver's understanding of the long-term nature of wound healing of pressure ulcers and palliative wound care.

- Assess the patient's and caregiver's knowledge of and ability to provide local wound care.

- Assess for the availability of pressure reduction or pressure relief surface.

- Assess understanding of and ability to provide high-calorie, high-protein diet throughout the course of wound healing.

- Assess the patient's and caregiver's understanding of the relationship between incontinence and further skin breakdown or complications of healing.

- Assess the patient's and caregiver's understanding of the prevention of further pressure ulcer development.

Rationale

Pressure ulcers may take weeks to months to heal, even under ideal circumstances. Wounds heal from the base of the ulcer up, and from the edges of the ulcer toward the center. Palliative wound care may be appropriate for clean, chronic, nonhealing wounds.

Patients are no longer kept hospitalized until pressure ulcers have healed. The need for local wound care may continue for weeks to months.

Patients may take thick, dense foam mattresses home from the hospital to place on their own bed. Rental provision of low–air-loss beds (e.g., Flexicare, Kinair) and air-fluidized therapy beds (e.g., Clinitron, Skytron, FluidAir) may be arranged but often pose financial difficulty because few payer sources will cover the cost of these beds in the home.

Patients may require enteral feeding (through gastronomy tube, nasogastric feeding tubes, or the oral route), which requires knowledge of preparation and use of special equipment (e.g., feeding pumps and administration sets).

Managing incontinence may be the most difficult aspect of home management and is often the reason decisions for nursing home placement are made.

Patients who are incapable of independent movement will need frequent repositioning to reduce risk for breakdown in those areas that are intact.

Therapeutic Interventions

Actions/Interventions

- Teach the patient and caregiver local wound care and provide an opportunity for return demonstration.

- Teach the patient and caregiver to report the following signs indicating wound infection: purulent drainage, odor, fever, malaise.
- Provide written instructions with listed resources.

▲ Involve a social worker or case manager.

- Consider or discuss with the patient and caregiver the need for in-home nursing care or homemaker services.

Rationale

This allows the learner to use new information immediately, thus enhancing retention. Immediate feedback allows the learner to make corrections, rather than practice the skill incorrectly.

Early assessment prompts early intervention.

Long-term management requires specific written plans to enhance adherence to treatment. Several Internet resources provide lay education.

Referral helps the patient and family determine whether placement in an extended care facility is needed. Because many patients with pressure ulcers are older, it is often an older spouse who is available to provide care; as a result of the intensive nursing care needs of these patients, discharge to home is often unrealistic.

These provide all or part of the patient's care and can be less costly to the patient. Additionally, keeping the patient in his or her own environment (if possible) reduces the risk of nosocomial infection and keeps the patient in familiar surroundings.

■ = Independent; ▲ = Collaborative

Pressure Ulcers (Impaired Skin Integrity)—cont'd

Actions/Interventions

■ Consider or discuss with the patient and caregiver the possible need for respite care.

■ Teach the patient and caregiver the importance of pressure reduction and relief:
  • Use of specialty surface; if provision of specialty beds is a problem because of reimbursement issues, a waterbed may be a reasonable alternative
  • Use of pressure reduction and relief surface where the patient sits
  • Turning schedule that does not compromise other body areas

▲ Consult a wound specialist to evaluate care in the home.

▲ Include a dietitian in teaching how to plan high-calorie, high-protein meals, or how to supplement regular meals with dietary supplements.

■ Teach the patient and caregiver how to manage incontinence:
  • Use of external catheters
  • Care of indwelling catheters if no other option is feasible

  • Use of underpads or linen protectors

  • Use of moisture barrier ointments

Rationale

Long-term responsibility for patient care in the home is taxing; those providing the care may need help to understand that their own needs for relaxation are essential to the maintenance of health and should not be viewed as "shirking responsibility."

Information can foster enhanced adherence to pressure ulcer treatment guidelines.

Besides evaluating ability to deliver care, the specialist may be useful in securing specialty equipment.

Specialty expertise may be required.

Teaching proper techniques can prevent leakage and skin problems.

Reusable products made of cloth with a waterproof lining are better for the patient's skin and are more economical but require laundering.

These protect intact skin from excoriation.

> • RELATED CARE PLANS
>
> Caregiver role strain, p. 35
> Enteral tube feeding, p. 691
> Imbalanced nutrition: less than body
>   requirements, p. 134

Shingles

Herpes Zoster

Shingles is an infectious viral condition caused by a reactivation of latent varicella zoster virus (VZV), the agent that causes chickenpox. Reactivation usually occurs in individuals with impaired immunity; it is common among older adults. Approximately 20% of people who have had chickenpox will develop herpes zoster. VZV produces painful vesicular eruptions along the peripheral distribution of nerves from posterior ganglia and is usually unilateral. Although VZV typically affects the trunk of the body, the virus may also affect

■ = Independent; ▲ = Collaborative

the eye. Secondary infection resulting from scratching the lesions is common. An individual with an outbreak of VZV is infectious for the first 2 to 3 days after eruption. The incubation period ranges from 7 to 21 days. The total course of the disease is 10 days to 5 weeks from onset to full recovery. Shingles is characterized by burning, pain, and neuralgia. VZV infection can lead to central nervous system (CNS) involvement; pneumonia develops in about 15% of cases. This disease is routinely treated on an outpatient basis unless CNS involvement or pneumonia occur.

 Nursing Diagnosis

Risk for Infection

Common Risk Factors

Skin lesions (papules, vesicles, pustules)
Crusted-over lesions
Itching and scratching

Common Expected Outcomes

Patient remains free of secondary infection.
Risk for disease transmission is minimized.

NOC Outcomes
Knowledge: Infection Control; Risk Control; Risk Detection; Tissue Integrity: Skin and Mucous Membranes

NIC Intervention
Infection Protection; Wound Care

Ongoing Assessment

Actions/Interventions	Rationale
■ Assess for presence and location of skin lesions.	Lesions are fluid-filled, becoming yellow, and finally crusting over, on one side of the trunk or buttock. Lesions follow the path of dermatomes and occur in bandlike strips. Lesions may occur also on the face, arms, and legs if nerves for these areas are involved. As lesions rupture and crust, they take on the appearance of the lesions associated with chickenpox.
■ Assess for lesions around the eye or ear.	Particular attention needs to be given to assessing lesions near the eyes and ears because the virus may cause serious damage to the eyes and ears. This can cause blindness or hearing difficulties.
■ Assess for pruritus or irritation from lesions, and amount of scratching. Assess for signs of localized infection: redness and drainage from lesions.	Secondary infection can occur because scratching opens pustules and introduces bacteria.
▲ Obtain culture and sensitivity test of suspected infected lesions, as ordered.	This provides an indication for appropriate antibiotic therapy.

■ = Independent; ▲ = Collaborative

Shingles

→ **Shingles**—cont'd

Actions/Interventions

▲ Obtain additional cultures, as ordered.

■ Assess the patient and family immunization status and past history of chickenpox.

Rationale

Viral cultures, Tzanck smear, or viral smear may be required for diagnosis.

Patients with shingles are contagious to others who have not had chickenpox. Those who have had varicella vaccine are considered immune but should have varicella titers to confirm immunity.

Therapeutic Interventions

Actions/Interventions

■ Discourage scratching of lesions. Encourage the patient to trim fingernails.

■ Suggest use of gauze to separate lesions in skinfolds.

■ Teach contact isolation.

■ Instruct the patient in the use of systemic steroids, if ordered, for antiinflammatory effect.

■ Instruct the patient in the use of antiviral agents, as ordered.

■ Use universal precautions in caring for the patient to prevent transmission of the disease to self or other patients.

■ Instruct the patient to avoid contact with pregnant women and immunosuppressed individuals.

Rationale

This prevents inadvertent opening of lesions, cross-contamination, and bacterial infection.

This reduces irritation, itching, and cross-contamination.

VZV is spread by contact with fluid from lesions containing viruses.

Use of steroids is controversial; they are most commonly used for severe cases.

Antiviral agents are most effective during the first 72 hours of an outbreak when viruses are proliferating. Drugs of choice are acyclovir, famciclovir, or valacyclovir.

VZV can be transmitted to others and cause chickenpox in the person who has not previously had the disease.

Active lesions can be infectious.

NDx Nursing Diagnosis

Acute/Chronic Pain

Common Related Factor

Nerve pain, most commonly thoracic (55%), cervical (20%), lumbar and sacral (15%), ophthalmic division of trigeminal nerve

Defining Characteristics

Complaints of pain localized to affected nerve
Complaints of sharp, burning, or dull pain
Facial mask of pain
Alteration in muscle tone

Common Expected Outcome

Patient is comfortable as evidenced by minimal complaints of pain and by an ability to rest.

NOC Outcomes
Pain Level; Pain Control

NIC Interventions
Pain Management; Teaching: Prescribed Treatment

■ = Independent; ▲ = Collaborative

Ongoing Assessment

Actions/Interventions

- Assess the patient's description of pain or discomfort: quality, severity, location, onset, duration, precipitating or relieving factors.

- Assess for nonverbal signs of pain or discomfort.

Rationale

The patient may describe the pain as a tingling sensation, a burning pain, or extreme hyperesthesia in one area of the skin. These sensations usually precede the development of skin lesions by several days. Postherpetic neuralgia is a chronic pain syndrome that may continue after the skin lesions have healed. The patient may have constant pain or intermittent episodes of pain.

Each individual has his or her own pain threshold and ways to express pain or discomfort. Some individuals may deny the experience of pain when it is present. Attention to associated signs may help the nurse evaluate pain.

Therapeutic Interventions

Actions/Interventions

- Instruct the patient to do the following:
  - Apply cool, moist dressings to pruritic lesions with or without Burrow's solution several times a day. Discontinue once lesions have dried.
  - Avoid scratching.

  - Take antihistamines for itching as ordered.
  - Use topical steroids (antiinflammatory effect), antihistamines (antiitching effect, particularly useful at bedtime), and analgesics.
  - Avoid rubbing or scratching the skin or lesion.

  - Avoid temperature extremes, both in the air and bath water.
  - Wear loose, nonrestrictive clothing made of cotton.

- ▲ Administer medications as prescribed.

Rationale

This provides relief and reduces risk of secondary infection.

Scratching can increase the possibility of secondary infection.

These may be required for relief of pruritus.

A variety of medications may be required to provide relief.

Scratching stimulates the skin, which in turn increases itchiness.

Tepid water causes the least itching.

Constrictive, nonbreathing garments may rub lesions and aggravate skin irritation. Cotton cloth allows evaporation of moisture.

Analgesics, antidepressants, and antiepileptic medications may be used in the management of postherpetic neuralgia. Topical preparations for postherpetic neuralgia include capsaicin cream (Zostrix) and lidocaine-prilocaine cream (EMLA).

NDx Nursing Diagnosis

Risk for Disturbed Body Image

Common Risk Factor

Visible skin lesions

■ = Independent; ▲ = Collaborative

Shingles—cont'd

Common Expected Outcome

Patient verbalizes feelings about lesions and continues daily activities.

NOC Outcome
Body Image

NIC Interventions
Body Image Enhancement; Coping Enhancement

Ongoing Assessment

Actions/Interventions

■ Assess perception of changed appearance.

■ Note verbal references to skin lesions.

Rationale

Because the course of an outbreak may span several weeks, patients typically need to work and/or carry out their usual routine; they may require assistance coping with changes in appearance.

Scarring may occur with repeated outbreaks or if lesions are infected.

Therapeutic Interventions

Actions/Interventions

■ Assist the patient in articulating responses to questions from others regarding lesions and infectious risk.

■ Suggest use of concealing clothing when lesions can be easily covered.

Rationale

Rehearsal of set responses to anticipated questions may provide some reassurance.

This may help the patient who is having problems adjusting to body image changes.

NDx Nursing Diagnosis

Deficient Knowledge

Common Related Factors

Herpes zoster outbreak
New condition and procedures

Defining Characteristics

Questions
Confusion about treatment
Inability to comply with treatment
Lack of questions

■ = Independent; ▲ = Collaborative

Common Expected Outcome

Patient or caregiver verbalizes needed information about disease, treatment, and possible complications of herpes zoster.

NOC Outcomes
Knowledge: Disease Process; Knowledge: Treatment Regimen

NIC Interventions
Teaching: Disease Process; Teaching: Individual; Teaching: Prescribed Medication

Ongoing Assessment

Actions/Interventions

■ Determine the patient's and caregiver's understanding of the disease process, complications, and treatment.

■ Because of potential infectivity, determine whether the patient's caregiver or family has had chickenpox, varicella vaccine, or is immunocompromised.

Rationale

It is necessary for patients and caregivers to understand that an occult disease may have weakened the patient and allowed expression of the herpes zoster.

Even though varicella vaccine does not confer immunity to shingles, it is less common in varicella-vaccinated adults than those who have had chickenpox.

Therapeutic Interventions

Actions/Interventions

■ Encourage the patient and caregiver to ask questions.

■ Provide necessary information to the patient and caregiver:
  • Description of herpes zoster, including how disease is spread
  • Explanation of need for isolation
  • Need to notify health professionals of signs of CNS inflammation (changes in level consciousness)
■ Discuss future therapies such as vaccination.

Rationale

Specific concerns must be verbalized so they can be addressed and accurate information provided.

Fluid from lesions contains viruses, which are spread by direct contact.

Patient should isolate clothing and linen, including towels.

Early assessment facilitates prompt treatment of complications.

A shingles vaccine is currently under development that may reduce the incidence by 50%.

Skin Cancer

Basal Cell Carcinoma; Squamous Cell Carcinoma; Malignant Melanoma

Tumors of the skin may be benign, premalignant, or malignant. Malignant tumors are categorized as either nonmelanoma cancers (basal cell carcinoma and squamous cell carcinoma) or melanoma. Prolonged exposure to sunlight is the primary cause of all forms of skin cancer. It has been estimated that more than 1 million cases of skin cancer are diagnosed each year. Basal cell carcinoma is the most common form of skin cancer followed by squamous cell cancer. Both of these forms of skin cancer can be cured with early detection and intervention. They rarely metastasize to other parts of the body. Malignant melanoma is the most serious form of skin cancer. The risk of melanoma has

■ = Independent; ▲ = Collaborative

Skin Cancer

> ## Skin Cancer—cont'd

quadrupled in the last 25 years. The 5-year localized survival rate is 98% and the overall 5-year survival rate is 91%. Melanomas can metastasize to regional lymph nodes or to visceral organs if not diagnosed in the early stages. The American Cancer Society estimates that in 2006, approximately 7900 people will die of this disease.

Premalignant skin conditions include actinic keratosis, solar keratosis, and actinic cheilitis. Most premalignant lesions later develop into squamous cell carcinoma. Actinic keratosis occurs most often in older adults. The skin lesions are usually rough, scaly raised growths that range in color from brown to red. The lesions of actinic cheilitis occur on the lower lip, causing dryness, and scaling.

NDx Nursing Diagnosis

Impaired Skin Integrity

Common Related Factor

Tumors

Defining Characteristics

Erosions of the skin with drainage or bleeding
Destruction of the epidermis

Common Expected Outcome

Patient maintains optimal skin integrity within limits of the disease.

NOC Outcome

Tissue Integrity: Skin and Mucous Membranes

NIC Interventions

Skin Surveillance; Chemotherapy Management; Incision Site Care; Wound Care

Ongoing Assessment

Actions/Interventions

■ Assess skin lesions for change in shape, size, color, bleeding, or exudates.
Basal cell carcinoma:
  • An open sore that bleeds, oozes, or crusts and does not heal after 3 weeks
  • A persistent reddish patch on the chest, shoulders, arms, or legs that may crust or itch
  • A shiny nodule that is pearly or translucent and different in color than the surrounding skin
  • A pink growth with elevated borders and a crusted center; blood vessels may be prominent as the growth enlarges

Rationale

Regular inspection of skin that is chronically exposed to the sun is important to identify skin cancers in heir earliest stages. Any change in a preexisting skin growth, development of a new growth, or an open sore that fails to heal may be a precursor to skin cancer. Some skin cancers may resemble psoriasis or eczema in the early stages. These conditions need prompt referral to a physician for further evaluation and diagnosis.

■ = Independent; ▲ = Collaborative

Actions/Interventions

Squamous cell carcinoma:
- A wartlike growth that crusts and bleeds
- A persistent, scaly red patch with irregular borders that crusts or bleeds
- An elevated growth with a central depression that may bleed and grows rapidly

Malignant melanoma:
- Evaluate for changes in existing moles or development of a new pigmented skin lesion paying specific attention to:
  - A *Asymmetry:* Most early melanomas are asymmetrical. A line through the middle does not create matched halves.
  - B *Border:* Borders may be uneven or scalloped.
  - C *Color Variability:* Normal moles are an even brown color. Melanomas may have many colors (brown, black, red, blue, pink).
  - D *Diameter:* Moles greater than 6 mm should be evaluated for removal. This is larger than the eraser on a pencil.

▲ Assist with tissue biopsy.

Rationale

Risk of malignant melanoma is increased in persons with a previous personal or family history of melanoma, or in persons with more than 50 larger or atypical (dysplastic) moles.

Biopsy of any skin growth is necessary to determine the type of cancer.

Therapeutic Interventions

Actions/Interventions

▲ Anticipate and prepare the patient for surgical therapy:

- Cryosurgery

- Mohs microscopic surgery used in nonmelanoma skin cancer

- Excisional surgery

- Reexcision and sentinel lymph node dissection (SLND)
  - The surgical margins for reexcision are determined by the depth of invasion of the original biopsy.
    - 0.5-cm margin—in situ melanoma
    - 1-cm margin—melanoma <1 mm
    - 2-cm margin—melanoma 1.1 to 4 mm
  - Lymphoscintigraphy and SLND are recommended for patients with tumors greater than 1.1 mm. Complete lymph node dissection is indicated for patients with positive sentinel lymph nodes or palpable lymph nodes.

Rationale

Many of the surgical procedures used in the treatment of skin cancer can be done using local or regional anesthesia in an outpatient setting.

Liquid nitrogen is used to destroy the tumor by freezing. This is a bloodless procedure. Redness, swelling, blistering, and crusting may occur in the treatment area. This is primarily used for premalignant lesions.

The surgeon removes a very thin layer of tissue. Each layer is examined under a microscope. Repeated layers are removed and examined until the area is free of tumor cells. This procedure is used in areas of recurring tumors or in areas on the face because it preserves the greatest amount of healthy tissue.

The entire growth is removed with a surrounding border of normal tissue. The incision is closed with sutures.

Lymphoscintigraphy is used to map lymph system drainage and locate the sentinel nodes that are the first one or two nodes that are closest to the tumor. These can be removed and evaluated to detect early micrometastatic disease. Accurate staging and identification of early micrometastasis is important in identifying patients who would benefit from complete lymph node dissection and those eligible for adjuvant immunotherapy.

Skin Cancer

■ = Independent; ▲ = Collaborative

Skin Cancer—cont'd

Actions/Interventions	**Rationale**
▲ Administer immunotherapy (α-interferon, interleukin) or chemotherapy in the adjuvant or metastatic melanoma patient.	For patients diagnosed with stage III or IV melanoma, chemotherapy, immunotherapy, or vaccine therapy may be indicated. These treatments are often used in combination and patients may participate in clinical drug trials. These treatments are rigorous, and patient teaching and nursing and medical support during treatment are critical. Patients often require inpatient hospitalization.
▲ Assist with application of topical chemotherapeutic agents.	Topical application of fluorouracil (5-FU) in a cream or lotion is effective in treating actinic keratosis and cancers that involve only the superficial layers of the skin. Intense inflammation may occur during treatment, but scarring afterward is rare.
▲ Anticipate and prepare the patient for radiation therapy.	Radiation therapy is indicated for patients who are not candidates for surgery because of preexisting health problems. A series of treatments are usually given over several weeks. Permanent changes in skin color and texture may develop in the treatment area.

NDx Nursing Diagnosis

Disturbed Body Image

Common Related Factors

Visible tumor
Surgical scars and grafts

Defining Characteristics

Verbalizes feelings about changes in physical appearance and reactions of others
Negative statements about physical appearance
Denies or avoids talking about changes in physical appearance

Common Expected Outcome

Patient verbalizes positive statements about appearance and continues with daily activities and social interactions.

NOC Outcomes
Body Image; Coping; Social Interaction

NIC Intervention
Body Image Enhancement

Ongoing Assessment

Actions/Interventions	**Rationale**
■ Assess the patient's perception of alteration in appearance.	The nurse needs to understand the patient's attitudes about visible changes in the appearance of the skin that occur with skin cancer and its treatment.

■ = Independent; ▲ = Collaborative

Integumentary Care Plans

Actions/Interventions

■ Assess the patient's behavior related to appearance.

Rationale

Patients with body image issues may try to hide or camouflage their lesions. Their socialization may decrease based on their anxiety or fear about the reactions of others.

Therapeutic Interventions

Actions/Interventions

■ Allow the patient to verbalize feelings regarding skin condition.

■ Assist the patient in identifying ways to enhance appearance.

■ Assist the patient in articulating responses to questions from others regarding lesions.

■ Assist the patient with referral for plastic and reconstructive surgery.

Rationale

Through talking, the patient can be guided to separate physical appearance from feelings of personal worth.

Clothing, cosmetics, and accessories may direct attention away from skin lesions and scars. The patient may need help in selecting methods that do not aggravate skin lesions or healing surgical sites.

Patients may need guidance in determining what to say to people who comment about the appearance of their skin.

Surgical excision of skin cancer of the head and neck may require removal of extensive amounts of tissue. The patient may be a candidate for skin grafting and reconstructive surgery.

Skin Cancer

NDx Nursing Diagnosis

Deficient Knowledge

Common Related Factors

New diagnosis of skin cancer
Lack of information about prevention and sun safety
Unfamiliarity with treatment options

Defining Characteristics

Multiple questions regarding prognosis and risk of metastasis
Lack of questions about preventing skin cancer

Common Expected Outcome

The patient verbalizes knowledge about skin cancer prevention and treatment.

NOC Outcomes

Knowledge: Disease Process; Knowledge: Health Behaviors; Tissue Integrity: Skin and Mucous Membranes

NIC Interventions

Teaching: Disease Process; Teaching: Procedure/Treatment; Skin Surveillance; Skin Care: Topical Treatment

■ = Independent; ▲ = Collaborative

> **Skin Cancer**—cont'd

Ongoing Assessment

Actions/Interventions

- Assess knowledge of diagnosis and treatment options.

- Assess knowledge of skin cancer prevention and sun safety behaviors.

Rationale

The patient needs information about skin cancer and treatment options to make informed decisions about care.

Skin cancers can recur and the patient needs to know about methods to reduce exposure to ultraviolet light.

Therapeutic Interventions

Actions/Interventions

- Provide a comfortable environment for discussion, allowing for questions.

- Dispel or correct any misconceptions or erroneous information that the patient may have.

- Teach the patient about methods to decrease skin exposure to ultraviolet light.
  - Avoid exposure to artificial sources of ultraviolet light such as sunlamps and tanning booths.
  - Practice sun protection and avoidance every day.
  - Limit sun exposure during midday hours (10 AM to 4 PM) when the sun's rays are most intense.
  - Apply sunscreen with an SPF (sun protection factor) of 15 or higher with UV-A and UV-B protection. Apply liberally to all sun-exposed areas and reapply every 2 hours and after swimming or perspiring.
  - Wear sunglasses for eye protection.
  - Wear sun protective clothing with tightly woven fabrics and wide-brimmed hats.

- Teach the patient and a family member to do monthly skin self-examinations.
  - Do examination in a well-lighted room using a full-length mirror and a hand-held mirror.
  - Become familiar with all birthmarks, moles, and skin blemishes. Look for changes in size, shape, or color.
  - Monitor all skin sores that do not show signs of healing after 3 weeks.
  - Look at all body surfaces in the mirror including the front and back of the body, both right and left sides, scalp, between fingers and toes, nail beds, and between skinfolds.
  - Give special attention to all skin surfaces exposed to the sun.
  - Use a comb or blow dryer to move hair on the scalp for better visualization.
  - Ask a family member to examine skin in hard-to-see areas.

Rationale

Patients must feel that no question is trivial and should feel free to express concerns.

Patients must have correct information to make valid choices in their treatment.

Ultraviolet light from natural and artificial sources is the contributing or primary cause of skin cancer. Reducing exposure can prevent recurrence of tumors and development of new lesions.

Early diagnosis of skin cancer is associated with better chances for cure and less disfigurement from surgical interventions. The best time for skin self-examinations is after bathing or showering.

■ = Independent; ▲ = Collaborative

Actions/Interventions

- Instruct regarding importance of annual skin examination by a physician.

- Educate regarding websites with information for health care professionals and patients:
  - Skin Cancer Foundation: www.skincancer.org
  - American Cancer Society: www.cancer.org
  - American Academy of Dermatology: www.aad.org
  - National Institutes of Health: www.nih.gov
  - Melanoma Research Foundation: www.melanoma.org
  - Oncology Nursing Society: www.ons.org

Rationale

Patients who have had a malignant melanoma are seen on a regular follow-up schedule with a physician at 3-, 6-, and 12-month intervals for a complete skin examination and lymph node examination and for additional diagnostic studies, if indicated.

Several Internet resources provide useful lay education.

Skin Cancer

■ = Independent; ▲ = Collaborative

14

Psychosocial Care Plans

Affective Disorders: Depression and Bipolar Disorder

An affective disorder is characterized by feelings of unworthiness, profound sadness, guilt, apathy, and hopelessness. A loss of interest and pleasure in usual activities is evident. Behavioral characteristics may include slowing of physical activity or agitation and alterations in sleeping, eating, and libido. Depression differs from sadness in that it is a disorder rather than a feeling. Depression is diagnosed more often in women than in men, but this is generally because women are exposed to more depression risk factors and are more likely to seek health care, including treatment for depression. The incidence of depression in men is probably underreported. This is presumed to be the case because more men commit suicide, and the method used is usually more lethal than that chosen by women. Men may express symptoms with behaviors not generally associated with depression, such as alcohol and drug use and gambling. Every effort is made to stabilize and treat the depressed patient in an outpatient setting, but a strong indicator for hospitalization would be attempted suicide, active suicide intent, or impulsive suicidal behaviors. Bipolar disorder, also called manic-depressive illness, is a mood disorder that is characterized by shifts in the person's mood, thinking, energy, and functional ability. The mood swings in bipolar disorder can range from severe depression through hypomania and severe mania. Some patients with bipolar disorder may have a mixed bipolar state with symptoms of both mania and depression. Effective treatment can limit the frequency and intensity of mood swings. This care plan addresses two affective disorders: depression and bipolar disorder.

NDx Nursing Diagnosis

Deficient Knowledge

Common Related Factors	Defining Characteristics
Lack of exposure	Verbalization of the problem
Information misconceptions	Inaccurate follow-through of instructions
Lack of interest in learning	Inappropriate or exaggerated behaviors
Unfamiliarity with information resources	Statement of misconception
	Request for information

(■ = Independent; ▲ = Collaborative)

Common Expected Outcome

Patient verbalizes awareness of depression or bipolar disorder, its symptoms, and the available treatment modalities.

NOC Outcomes
Knowledge: Disease Process;
    Knowledge: Treatment Regimen

NIC Interventions
Teaching: Disease Process; Teaching:
    Procedure/Treatment

Ongoing Assessment

Actions/Interventions

■ Assess the patient's awareness of depression or bipolar disorder.

■ Assess the patient's awareness of the various treatments for depression and bipolar disorder

Rationale

Symptoms can reduce awareness of depression. For example, patients may be aware of fatigue, apathy, and insomnia and not recognize these as symptoms of depression. Mania and hypomania may begin as pleasant feelings before becoming distressing.

Patients may have a sense of hopelessness and helplessness, or may experience elation and grandiose thoughts that pervades every aspect of their lives, making it difficult to integrate information even if they have been exposed to it in the past.

Therapeutic Interventions

Actions/Interventions

■ Explain the etiologies for depression or bipolar disorder.

■ Explain the signs and symptoms for depression and bipolar disorder.

Rationale

Depression may be the result of early childhood experiences with or without a trauma component. It may be reactive, occurring in response to situational or environmental stresses such as interpersonal conflict or unemployment. Depressive features are seen in the postpartum and premenstrual periods, as well as in menopause, where hormones may play a role. Depression is often present in drug and alcohol abuse, where the substance use may precede or follow depression. Depression can be one component of bipolar disorder. Patients who are depressed may have additional diagnoses. In this case, depression can be the primary or secondary diagnosis. Bipolar disorder is largely genetic but relatives may differ in their symptoms.

Major depression is a mood disorder in which at least five symptoms present during the same 2-week period. At least one of these five symptoms is depressed mood or a loss of interest or pleasure. Other symptoms are insomnia, weight loss, motor agitation or retardation, inability to concentrate, sense of worthlessness, fatigue, and repeated thoughts of death. Depression can be a component of bipolar disorder that includes episodes of mania; persistently elevated, expansive mood; or irritability present for at least a week. Manic episodes may or may not alternate with or be concurrent with

■ = Independent; ▲ = Collaborative

Affective Disorders: Depression and Bipolar Disorder

Affective Disorders: Depression and Bipolar Disorder—cont'd

Actions/Interventions	Rationale
	periods of depression. In both disorders, mood states can impair social, academic, or occupational functioning. Suicide attempt as well as psychosis can occur with major depression or bipolar disorder.
■ Instruct the patient or significant others about treatment interventions:	
• Antidepressant medication	Four classifications of drugs include the cyclics (drugs that seem to be effective but have greater risks of side effects); monoamine oxidase (MAO) inhibitors, which require rigid compliance with dietary restrictions to prevent potentially life-threatening hypertensive crises; selective serotonin reuptake inhibitors, which are faster acting and have fewer side effects; and atypical drugs (e.g., Wellbutrin, Duloxetine). Despite their overall success rate in effectively treating depression, medications do not work for everyone.
• Mood stabilizer medications	
• Lithium	Lithium is used to stabilize mood by reducing frequency and intensity of mood swings.
• Anticonvulsants	Several anticonvulsant medications have been used to stabilize mood. Medications such as valproate and carbamazepine may be used in combination with lithium and each other to achieve maximum therapeutic effect and mood stabilization.
• Counseling and the support of a therapeutic relationship	Evidence-based treatment guidelines recommend psychotherapy with medication.
• Electroconvulsive therapy (ECT)	This is therapy in which a grand mal seizure and consequently neurotransmission changes are induced in the anesthetized patient by passing extremely small amounts of electrical current to the brain. Usually 6 to 10 treatments over several weeks are needed to achieve full symptom remission.
• Hospitalization	This is required for patients who represent a threat to themselves or to others. A patient may feel guilty about being depressed or may feel such a sense of hopelessness that he or she no longer believes that depression is treatable. Hospitalization is also required for severe symptoms when more comprehensive treatment may be necessary.

NDx Nursing Diagnosis

Situational or Chronic Low Self-Esteem

Common Related Factors	Defining Characteristics
Ineffective or inadequate coping skills	Negative verbalizations about self
Difficulties with relationship	Expressions of shame or guilt

■ = Independent; ▲ = Collaborative

Psychosocial Care Plans

Illness or disability
Significant losses
Decreased level of independence or effectiveness
Inadequate support systems
Cognitive and perceptual distortions

Neglect of appearance and personal needs
Excessive focus on failings and inadequacies
Feelings of helplessness

Common Expected Outcomes

Patient uses positive self-talk to interrupt negative thinking.
Patient uses positive coping behaviors to improve functioning.

NOC Outcome
Self-Esteem

NIC Interventions
Self-Esteem Enhancement;
    Self-Awareness Enhancement

Ongoing Assessment

Actions/Interventions

- Assess for presence of ruminations, negative thoughts, and feelings of inadequacy.

- Assess to what degree the patient is able to carry out normal activities of daily living.

- Determine how gender, race, age, and culture influence self-esteem.

Rationale

Depressed patients describe feelings of hopelessness and helplessness so pervasive that they interfere with the ability to manage relationships and responsibilities.

Patients who are profoundly depressed have difficulty with normal activities.

Social norms affect self-esteem.

Therapeutic Interventions

Actions/Interventions

- Assist the patient in identifying and reviewing negative self-perceptions.
- Identify the patient's positive beliefs and characteristics.
- Encourage the patient to be actively involved in all treatment planning.
- Assist the patient to identify self-limiting behaviors and mental health promotion behaviors.

Rationale

This provides a basis for testing the reality of these perceptions as a first step toward building positive self-perceptions.

These provide supportive feedback and self-validation.

Involvement can reduce the feeling of powerlessness.

The ability to examine one's own behavior and make needed change is a first step in mental health promotion.

NDx Nursing Diagnosis

Social Isolation

Common Related Factors

Maladaptive social behavior
Inadequate resources
Impaired or inadequate personal relationships

Defining Characteristics

Lack of supportive or significant other
Feelings of aloneness imposed by others
Feelings of rejection
Sad, dull affect

Affective Disorders: Depression and Bipolar Disorder

■ = Independent; ▲ = Collaborative

Affective Disorders: Depression and Bipolar Disorder—cont'd

Defining Characteristics—cont'd

Uncommunicative or withdrawn
Preoccupation with negative thoughts
Repetitive meaningless behaviors
Hostility in voice or behavior
Seeking to be alone or existing in a subculture
Lack of significant purpose in life
Behavior unacceptable to significant others

Common Expected Outcomes

Patient develops ways to be more involved with others.
Patient develops satisfying relationships.

NOC Outcomes

Social Involvement;
Social Interaction Skills

NIC Interventions

Socialization Enhancement;
Emotional Support

Ongoing Assessment

Actions/Interventions	**Rationale**
■ Assess mood.	Affect may be flat, unresponsive, or sad.
■ Assess thoughts.	Thoughts may be negative, apathetic, grandiose, or delusional.
■ Assess behavior.	A depressed patient may be underactive or overactive.
■ Assess spontaneity and communication.	A depressed patient may be inhibited and avoidant.
■ Assess interactions with others.	The ability to interact comfortably with others signals remission. Negative thoughts and feelings inhibit the depressed patient's ability to interact.
■ Assess the patient or family for reports of bipolar manic episodes.	Mania can result in unacceptable social behavior. Patients may enter periods of extreme physical activity such as rapid, relentless pacing or talking for hours or days. Patients may spend money with abandon, resulting in financial ruin, or become grandiose or hypersexual. Alcohol abuse is common with depression and mania.

Therapeutic Interventions

Actions/Interventions	**Rationale**
■ Assist the patient in determining socially adaptive behaviors.	The manic patient may engage in behaviors that negatively affect his or her ability to maintain relationships and a sense of belonging in the home or workplace. Some patients with bipolar disorder may insist that the manic phase of their illness gives them a feeling of being powerful, energized, and omnipotent. Consequently, the patient may be reluctant to give up this feeling despite its obvious negative effects.

■ = Independent; ▲ = Collaborative

Actions/Interventions

■ Encourage positive interactions with the patient by spending time with him or her and providing supportive contact.

■ Acknowledge the patient's involvement in activities of daily living (i.e., working, going to school, taking care of own physical needs).

■ Encourage participation in group activities as tolerated.

■ Assist the patient in identifying life interests and people who have meaning to him or her.

■ Provide positive support for the patient's self-esteem.

Rationale

The patient's self-worth is enhanced by consistent support.

Acknowledgment recognizes and reinforces positive efforts.

The patient needs to feel some degree of control. Allow the patient to set his or her own pace in social situations when contact with others can be anxiety provoking.

Patients may have difficulty accessing this information because of their overwhelming feelings of worthlessness.

Positive support recognizes and reinforces positive feelings of self-worth.

NDx Nursing Diagnosis

Risk for Self-Directed Violence

Common Risk Factors

Low self-esteem
Depressed mood
Hopelessness
Perceived or actual failures in life activities
Reality distortion
Alcohol and drug abuse
Mania
Shift from mania to depression

Common Expected Outcomes

Patient verbalizes suicidal thoughts and feelings.
Patient participates in written contract or treatment plan to disclose and take steps to reduce risk of suicidal behaviors.
Patient manages impulsive behaviors that could result in self-harm.

NOC Outcomes

Suicide Self-Restraint; Risk Detection; Risk Control

NIC Interventions

Environmental Management: Violence Prevention; Counseling: Patient Contracting

---

Ongoing Assessment

Actions/Interventions

▲ Assess the patient's potential for self-directed violence. Ask the following:
  • "Have you ever felt suicidal?"

Rationale

Most people who are suicidal remain ambivalent about ending their own life.

Suicide ideation is the process of thinking about or having ideas about killing oneself.

■ = Independent; ▲ = Collaborative

Affective Disorders: Depression and Bipolar Disorder

> ## Affective Disorders: Depression and Bipolar Disorder—cont'd

Actions/Interventions	Rationale

Actions/Interventions

- "Have you ever attempted suicide?"

- "Do you currently feel like killing yourself?"

- "Do you have a suicide plan? What is your plan? Do you have the means to carry out your plan?"

■ Assess for evidence of risk factors that may increase the potential for a suicide attempt.

- History of suicidal attempts
- History of psychiatric hospitalization
- Giving away valued possessions or pets

- Access to firearms
- Newly divorced, widowed, or separated
- Early stage of treatment with antidepressant or mood stabilization medications

■ Assess for manic behavior.

■ Assess the need for hospitalization.

Rationale

Suicidal gestures are attempts to harm oneself that are not considered lethal. Suicidal attempts are potentially lethal actions.

When asked directly, the patient is assured of the staff's comfort in hearing a direct response.

Development of a plan and the ability to carry it out greatly increase the risk of suicide attempt.

It is a myth that suicide occurs without forewarning. It is also a myth that there is a specific type of person who commits suicide. The potential for suicide exists in all people.

Prior suicide attempt increases risk of future attempts.

Hospitalization may represent greater illness severity.

This may represent detachment and disengagement before a suicide attempt.

This is associated with impulsive suicide attempts in males.

This is associated with severe interpersonal distress.

Later treatment benefits may far exceed early benefits.

Manic patients can become belligerent and provocative, resulting in altercations with family, strangers, or law enforcement agencies or in situations when physical harm to others may be a significant risk. Bipolar patients not assessed for mania can appear to be depressed.

Maintaining patient safety is a priority.

> ## Therapeutic Interventions

Actions/Interventions

■ Provide a safe environment.

■ Provide close patient supervision by maintaining awareness of the patient's activities at all times.

■ Develop a verbal or written contract stating that the patient will disclose suicidal impulses. Review and develop new contracts as needed.

■ Encourage recognition of verbalization of negative feelings within appropriate limits.

Rationale

Suicide precautions are taken to create a safe environment for the patient and to prevent the patient from acting on suicidal impulses. These measures include removing potentially harmful objects (e.g., electrical appliances, sharp instruments, belts or ties, glass items).

The degree of supervision is based on the degree of risk that the patient presents.

The patient needs to verbalize suicide ideations with trusted staff. A written or verbal contract also establishes permission to discuss suicide and makes a commitment to take steps to reduce suicidal thoughts and feelings and not to act on suicidal impulses.

Depressed patients need the opportunity to discuss thoughts or intentions to harm themselves. Verbalization of these feelings may lessen their intensity. Patients also need to see that staff are able to discuss suicidal feelings.

Psychosocial Care Plans

■ = Independent; ▲ = Collaborative

Actions/Interventions

- Spend time with the patient and listen.

- Provide safety for the manic patient:
  - Provide for periods of rest, hydration, hygiene, and food if the patient is manifesting excessive activity.
  - Ensure that the activity is not resulting in a deleterious effect.
  - If the patient is provocative, provide limits on behavior; isolate the patient as needed. Decrease stimulation, provide reality checks, and attempt to keep the patient centered on one thought or activity at a time.

Rationale

Time provides opportunity to assess patient safety and support patient self-esteem.

Some patients may experience such a physical frenzy that they can be at risk for hypertensive crisis, stroke, or physical injuries.

> • RELATED CARE PLANS
>
> Disturbed sleep pattern, p. 177
> Hopelessness, p. 101
> Imbalanced nutrition: less than body
> requirements, p. 134
> Impaired home maintenance, p. 99
> Self-care deficit, p. 156
> Spiritual distress, p. 180

Death and Dying: End-of-Life Issues

Dying is part of living. It is an active process, but it is rare when we are able to mark the beginning or the middle of an individual's dying. The end, of course, is death. There are individuals who report having come back from death and who have shared their memories of their experiences, but no one has been able to report on the state of actual death. Because death remains an unknown, it is a source of great mystery and endless speculation. Enabling patients and their families to make quality-of-life and end-of-life decisions to achieve a peaceful death is a daunting task for the health care professional in the context of the twenty-first century.

Still, much is known about dying. The process has been observed from time immemorial. Each person dies in his or her own way. This process is influenced by cultural norms, family traditions, and the people and setting among which a person's death takes place. The patient who is dying may experience both actual and anticipatory losses. Pain, diminished abilities, fear, discomfort, massive dysfunctioning of organ systems (with or without the application of ever more complicated measures to prolong life), and the resounding implications his or her death will have on others require the patient to integrate enormous amounts of information and undergo extraordinarily complicated emotions.

Health professionals who understand the inevitability of a patient's death may seek to provide patients with an opportunity for a "good death," or a positive dying experience. Although the characteristics of a good death will vary, most providers agree that patients should be allowed to die with dignity, surrounded by loved ones and free of pain, with everything having been done that could have been done. A good death includes much more, but this care plan guide addresses the emotional aspects of death and dying. This care plan has been written in accordance with the Hospice and Palliative Nurses Association's (2000) Statement on the Scope and Standards of Hospice and Palliative Nursing Practice.

Death and Dying:
End-of-Life Issues

(■ = Independent; ▲ = Collaborative)

Death and Dying: End-of-Life Issues—cont'd

 Nursing Diagnosis

Fear

Common Related Factors

Threat of death
Pain and anticipation of pain
Anticipation or perceived threat of danger
Unfamiliar environment
Environmental stressors
Separation from support system
Treatments and invasive procedures
Sensory impairment
Phobias and anxieties

Defining Characteristics

Expressions of fear and mixed emotions
Rapid respirations and heart rate
Wide-eyed appearance
Tension, jitteriness, and irritability
Impulsive behavior
Hyperalertness and preoccupation

Common Expected Outcomes

Patient identifies source of fear related to dying.
Patient implements a positive coping mechanism.
Patient verbalizes reduction and absence of fear.

> **NOC Outcomes**
> Fear Control; Coping
>
> **NIC Interventions**
> Presence; Active Listening; Security Enhancement; Spiritual Support; Support System Enhancement

Ongoing Assessment

Actions/Interventions	**Rationale**
■ Help the patient express his or her fears by careful, thoughtful questioning and active listening.	Do not assume that because a patient is dying that his or her fears are limited to death. Fears are patient-specific. Patients may have fears over leaving dependents behind to fend for themselves or fear of embarrassment. Sometimes a fear can be resolved through a specific intervention; at other times the fear simply remains a concern. Being present and being silent are powerful communication techniques. It is also important for the nurse to acknowledge his or her own fears.
■ Assess the nature of the patient's fear and the methods that the patient uses to cope with that fear.	Fear ranges from a paralyzing, overwhelming feeling to mild, nagging concern. Some fears can be resolved by providing the patient with information (reassurance that the patient will have pain medications available and will not suffer intractable pain); other fears can be managed through talking and sharing. The patient's philosophy about death may influence his or her ability to cope.

Psychosocial Care Plans

■ = Independent; ▲ = Collaborative

Actions/Interventions	**Rationale**
■ Document verbal and nonverbal expressions of fear.	This gives care providers the information they need to provide support to the patient. Physiological symptoms and/or complaints will intensify as the level of fear increases. Fear differs from anxiety in that fear is a response to a recognized threat. However, symptoms of fear are similar to those of anxiety.

Therapeutic Interventions

Actions/Interventions	**Rationale**
■ Confirm your awareness of the patient's fear. Validate the feelings the patient is having and communicate an acceptance of those feelings.	In Western culture, there is a great reluctance to discuss death. Loved ones may think that the patient who is dying should be protected from the knowledge that his or her condition is terminal, or the patient may deny death as a possibility until the final moment. This limits the patient's ability to work through emotions.
■ Spend time with the patient.	Care providers may feel they need a reason to be with the dying patient or that they need to be performing a clinical task to justify their presence in the patient's room. However, the simple act of being present can have profound significance. This presence may involve talking or touching, ministering to a physical need, or simply sitting near the bedside.
■ Reframe hope to alleviate fear.	Patients may fear impending hopelessness or abandonment and need reassurance and validation that comfort (palliation) is obtainable.
■ Encourage reminiscing.	This provides reassurance that one's life has meaning and eases the intensity of the present reality.
■ While interacting with the patient, maintain a calm and accepting manner that expresses care and concern.	Patients who are talking about real feelings do not want false reassurances. They do need to feel safe in discussing troubling matters. Some of the social isolation that dying patients feel is the result of trying to protect intimate friends and family members from their need to talk about their impending death and what it means to them.
■ Be aware of the subjects that are difficult for you to discuss. Acknowledge your difficulty to the patient.	Patients may sense the care provider's discomfort and confuse the provider's behavior with the withholding of information or a lack of candor. Professional sensitivity to personal or cultural issues will help demonstrate integrity and truthfulness.
■ Provide continuity of care.	An ongoing relationship establishes trust and is a basis for communicating fearful feelings. The need for continuity of care increases in direct proportion to the intensity of the emotional material on which the patient is working. Patients rarely select a single individual to work on all of their emotional concerns. Rather, patients will share their fears with certain individuals, while sharing anger with others. The care provider will use behavioral and verbal cues from the patient to determine the patient's readiness to begin work on an issue. Continuity in care providers creates an environment in which this can best be accomplished.

Death and Dying:
End-of-Life Issues

■ = Independent; ▲ = Collaborative

Death and Dying: End-of-Life Issues—cont'd

Actions/Interventions

- ■ Confirm that fear is a normal and appropriate response to situations when pain, danger, or loss of control is anticipated or experienced.

- ■ As the patient's fears wax and wane, encourage him or her to explore specific events preceding the onset of specific fears.

- ■ Assist the patient in identifying coping and comfort strategies that were helpful in the past.

- ■ Include family members in care activities.

- ■ Assess sensory stimulation preferences. Remove unnecessary threatening equipment.

- ■ Encourage rest and relaxation.

- ■ Instruct the patient in the performance of self-calming measures:
  - Breathing exercises

  - Relaxation, meditation, or guided imagery exercises
  - Affirmations and calming self-talk exercises

Rationale

This places fear within the scope of normal human experiences.

It is sometimes helpful to recognize what factors precipitate a fear response. This information may be useful in helping the patient cope with her or his feelings.

This helps the patient focus on fear as a real and natural part of life that has been and can continue to be dealt with successfully.

Involvement of family in the care of the dying patient may assist in their sense of worth and decrease their sense of fear and helplessness in the dying process.

Fear may escalate with overstimulation or understimulation. Although staff are comfortable around high-technology medical equipment, many patients are not.

Rest builds inner coping resources. The health care team will need to pace activities (especially for older adults) in order to conserve the patient's energy and offset fatigue.

These reduce fear or make it more manageable.

These reduce the physiological response to fear (i.e., increased blood pressure, pulse, respiration).

These promote relaxation and relieve distress.

These enhance the patient's self-confidence.

 ## Nursing Diagnosis

Anticipatory Grieving

Common Related Factor	Defining Characteristics
Impending death	Expressed feelings regarding potential loss of own life
	Expressed feelings regarding potential loss of significant others
	Expressed feelings regarding potential loss of possessions
	Expressions of guilt, anger, sorrow, or anxiety
	Suppressed feelings
	Changes in sleep, eating habits, libido, level of activity

Psychosocial Care Plans

■ = Independent; ▲ = Collaborative

Common Expected Outcomes

Patient verbalizes feelings regarding pending death. Patient has functional support systems to aid in his or her grieving process.

NOC Outcomes
Grief Resolution; Coping; Caregiver Emotional Health

NIC Interventions
Grief Work Facilitation; Dying Care; Presence; Anticipatory Guidance

Ongoing Assessment

Actions/Interventions

- Identify the patient's grieving process.

- Consistently reassess the phase of grieving being experienced by the patient or significant others.

- Assess whether the patient and significant others are in different phases of grieving.

- Identify available support systems: family, peer support, primary physician, consulting physician, nursing staff, social worker, clergy, therapist, counselor, and professional or lay support group.

- Evaluate the need for referral to hospice, home health, social services, legal consultants, or support groups.

Rationale

Patients will express grief in varied and personal ways. Although the process of grieving has been described as clearly defined phases, grief rarely manifests in a prescribed sequencing of feelings and experiences. Patients and their families revisit the phases of the grief process repeatedly. Grief helps make inevitable loss tolerable.

This allows the care provider to place the patient and family's feelings, which are often turbulent and contradictory, within a framework that is sometimes more understandable. Although the grief is anticipatory, the process is similar to actual grief. Like actual grief, acceptance does not imply that grieving is over.

When appropriate, share this assessment with patients or family members. This may assist their understanding of conflicts or differences in expectations.

Multiple options for help broaden the opportunities for patients and families to personalize their methods of problem resolution.

As more and more patients die in their homes while receiving services from community resources, families are assuming more responsibility for end-of-life care. Although there are compelling financial reasons why this is so, there also seems to be a philosophical shift among consumers to reject extraordinary means to extend life when death is inevitable.

Therapeutic Interventions

Actions/Interventions

- Establish a comfortable connection with the patient and significant others. Listen and encourage the patient and significant others to verbalize feelings.

- Provide a safe space for the expression of grief.

- Maximize privacy.

Rationale

This opens lines of communication and facilitates successful resolution of grief. The patient and family need to complete unfinished business in their relationships through open communication and shared feelings.

This implies that the patient and family feel it is okay to express their feelings.

Privacy facilitates the patient's or family's expression of their feelings and communication without interruption.

■ = Independent; ▲ = Collaborative

Death and Dying: End-of-Life Issues

Death and Dying: End-of-Life Issues—cont'd

Actions/Interventions

■ Anticipate strong emotions.

■ Help significant others to understand that a patient's verbalizations of anger should not be perceived as personal attacks.

■ Provide information about the patient's health status without false reassurances or taking away all hope.

■ Encourage the patient and family to engage in meaningful dialogue.

■ Encourage family members to talk with a patient who may be unresponsive.

■ Facilitate conversations with the patient and significant others on "final arrangements" (e.g., burial, autopsy, organ donation, funeral).

■ Encourage the patient and significant others to share their wishes regarding who should be present at the time of death.

■ Confirm for significant others that not being present at the time of death does not indicate lack of love or caring.

■ Follow unit policies to identify the patient's critical status (e.g., color-coded door marker).

■ Identify needs for additional support systems (e.g., peer support, groups, clergy).

Rationale

Patients whose emotional responses to life have been fairly predictable in the past may experience turbulent and disrupting grief. The use of a bereavement specialist may prove helpful in working through this phase.

It is important for the family to understand that the dying patient is processing a large amount of highly emotional information. Help them understand that anger is part of the process of accepting death.

Hope is a basic survival instinct. Because no one knows the future, allow patients and their families to remain hopeful until death is imminent. After being informed of a poor prognosis, many patients and their families experience a defensive retreat from the shock of what they have been told. During this time, patients may engage in denial and wishful thinking. They may become unwilling to participate in self-care or may become indifferent about it.

Exploring potential reality issues in a nonthreatening manner will lead to informed decision making and assist the patient and family in verbalization of the anticipated loss.

Encouraging family members to talk and visit with the patient, even if they are unresponsive, instills hope. It has been shown that the patient is well aware of his or her surroundings (especially audible) beyond the point of responsiveness.

A clear understanding of the patient's and family's belief systems and cultural differences will help in advocating and facilitating open and honest communication regarding difficult subject matter.

Families and significant others think about this but may feel uncomfortable discussing this issue together.

The moment of death cannot be predicted. It is important to remember that individual needs of each of the bereaved are different yet essential to the process of grieving.

This informs all staff of the patient's status and ensures that staff members do not act or respond inappropriately when encountering the patient or family.

Patients and families often become immersed in their grief and forget to access the resources available to them. Others may require expert help in negotiating grief. In either case, the care provider may be able to offer the observation that additional help is available. The hospice concept offers an interdisciplinary approach and adds a unique dimension to end-of-life care for both patients and families.

■ = Independent; ▲ = Collaborative

Actions/Interventions

■ Facilitate understanding of the nearing death awareness. Attentively and sensitively listen to the patient and affirm the experience.

Rationale

The families and significant others may need assurance and education on the phenomenon of transition from this life.

NDx Nursing Diagnosis

Powerlessness

Common Related Factors

Terminal illness
Irreversible physical decline
Loss of independence
Invasive health care services

Defining Characteristics

Verbal expressions of having lost control or influence over life
Reluctance to participate in decision making
Diminished patient-initiated activities
Submissiveness, apathy
Withdrawal; depression
Aggressive, acting out, irritability
Decreased interest in activities of daily living

Common Expected Outcomes

Patient continues to influence care decisions.
Patient makes important end-of-life decisions.

NOC Outcome
Participation: Health Care Decisions

NIC Interventions
Presence; Decision-Making Support

Ongoing Assessment

Actions/Interventions

■ Assess the patient's need for power and control.

■ Assess for feelings of hopelessness, depression, and apathy.

■ Identify situations and/or interactions that may increase the patient's feelings of powerlessness.

■ Assess the patient's decision-making energy level and ability.

Rationale

Patients can identify those aspects of self-governance that are most important to them.

These feelings may be components of grief. There may be a tremendous guilt associated with any loss of control. Subsequent interventions will be critical to facilitating feelings of well-being and empowerment, especially in older adults.

Many medical routines are superimposed on patients without ever receiving the patient's permission. This can foster a sense of powerlessness in patients. It is important for care providers to recognize the patient's right to refuse procedures. Unresolved loss may trigger feelings of powerlessness and even persist over time.

Powerlessness is not the same as the inability to make a decision. It is the feeling that one has lost the implicit power for self-governance. Energy conservation will help reduce or relieve fatigue so the patient will be better able to use available energy for appropriate decision making.

Death and Dying: End-of-Life Issues

■ = Independent; ▲ = Collaborative

> ## Death and Dying: End-of-Life Issues—cont'd

Actions/Interventions

- Recognize the patient's wishes for information about end-of-life decisions.

- Evaluate the impact of provided information on the patient's behavior and mood.

- Determine whether the patient has an advance directive, a durable power of attorney for health care, or a living will.
  - Advance directive

  - Durable power of attorney for health care

  - Living will declaration

Rationale

This may help differentiate powerlessness from knowledge deficit. Realistic expectations actually decrease distress and worry, once again enhancing the patient's decision making (i.e., empowerment).

A patient simply experiencing a knowledge deficit may be mobilized to act in his or her own best interest after information is given and options are explored. The act of providing information may heighten a patient's sense of autonomy.

This is a legal document that expresses the patient's wishes and desires for his or her health care treatment in case he or she becomes terminally ill and unable to articulate wishes and desires. These directives will act in the place of the patient's verbal requests and serve as assurance that the patient's end-of-life decisions will be honored.

This allows the patient to designate another person to make health care decisions on the patient's behalf. The durable power of attorney for health care becomes effective if the patient becomes unable, either temporarily or permanently, to make his or her own health care decisions. Implicit in this is the fact that the patient has discussed his or her desires with this appointed individual. If the patient becomes able to resume making his or her own decisions, then the durable power of attorney for health care is no longer in effect.

This is a document that contains instructions that a patient be allowed to die if he or she becomes terminally ill and unable to communicate to the extent required by law. It recognizes the patient's desire not to be kept alive artificially and sets parameters on the limits to which health care providers are to go.

Therapeutic Interventions

Actions/Interventions

- Support the patient's sense of autonomy by involving the patient in decision making, by giving and accepting information, and by enabling the patient to control the environment as appropriate.
- Assist the patient in developing an advance directive.

Rationale

The ultimate decision-making authority lies within the patient. However, the goal of the health care professional is to assist patients in identifying and verbalizing their preferences in making authentic choices.

This allows patients to make decisions about their lives even after they are unable to express their own needs and desires.

■ = Independent; ▲ = Collaborative

Actions/Interventions

■ Implement personalized methods of providing hygiene, diet, and sleep. Enhance basic care by offering food, drink, comfort, and security.

■ Encourage comfortable furnishings and surroundings.

■ Provide the patient with acceptable opportunities for expressing feelings of anger, anxiety, and power-lessness.

Rationale

Allowing or helping the patient decide when and how these things are to be accomplished will increase the patient's sense of autonomy.

This enhances the patient's sense of autonomy and acknowledges the patient's right to have dominion over controllable aspects of his or her own life. This gives some normalcy to life during the dying process.

Verbalizing these feelings may diminish or diffuse the patient's sense of powerlessness. The care provider may need to make a special effort to maintain a careful sense of timing and compassion to alleviate the patient's feelings of loneliness or abandonment.

NDx Nursing Diagnosis

Spiritual Distress

Common Related Factors

Terminal illness
Separation from loved ones
Separation from religious and cultural ties
Challenged belief and value system
Pain and suffering

Defining Characteristics

Questions meaning of life and death and/or belief system
Seeks spiritual assistance
Voices guilt, loss of hope, spiritual emptiness, or feeling of being alone
Appears anxious, depressed, discouraged, fearful, or angry

Common Expected Outcome

Patient expresses value and comfort in his or her personal belief system.

NOC Outcomes
Dignified Dying; Spiritual Well-Being

NIC Interventions
Spiritual Support; Presence

Ongoing Assessment

Actions/Interventions

■ Assess history of religious affiliation.

■ Assess spiritual beliefs.

■ Assess the spiritual meaning of illness and death.
  • "What is the meaning of your illness?"
  • "How does grief affect your relationship with God, your beliefs, or other sources of strength?"
  • "Do your illness and grief interfere with expressing your spiritual beliefs?"

Rationale

Information regarding specific religion and importance of rituals or practices may improve understanding of the patient's needs while dying.

Individuals may have other important beliefs besides religion that provide strength and inspiration at the end of life.

These questions provide a basis for understanding the patient's distress. The patient's process of introspection will assist him or her in the process of comprehending the loss.

Death and Dying:
End-of-Life Issues

■ = Independent; ▲ = Collaborative

Death and Dying: End-of-Life Issues—cont'd

Actions/Interventions

■ Assess whether patients need help with unfinished business.

Rationale

Patients may not find peace or acceptance until important affairs are in order. The health care team can provide guidance to patients while assisting in identifying strengths and values pertinent to their system.

Therapeutic Interventions

Actions/Interventions

■ Give understanding and acceptance. Support crying by offering caring touch.

■ Encourage verbalization of feelings of anger or loneliness.

■ Arrange your interventions in terms of the patient's belief system.

■ When requested by the patient, arrange for clergy, religious rituals, or the display of religious objects.

■ If requested, sit with the patient who wishes to pray and arrange for clergy at time of death as requested by the patient.

■ Do not provide intellectual solutions for spiritual problems.

■ Encourage the patient to continue to search for truth by continuing to examine beliefs.

■ Offer opportunities to share feelings verbally, in writing, through art, or through taping (audio or video).

Rationale

Sharing concerns and understanding of the end-of-life journey the patient and family are experiencing will reveal the integrity and professionalism that the care provider holds in helping them through the dying process.

Patients struggle with fears of abandonment.

Patients have a right to their beliefs, even if they conflict with the nurse's beliefs. A neutral-based approach by the nurse allows for unbiased care.

Patients may derive comfort and solace from these intimate spiritual experiences.

Being open to cultural and religious differences will allow the patient's traditions and rituals to be a part of their care while providing comfort and compassion to both the patient and family.

Spiritual beliefs are based on faith and are independent of logic.

Reconstitution and reorganization of beliefs often follow times of questioning a philosophical and spiritual construct.

Leaving an historical legacy can help bring meaning to one's life.

> **• RELATED CARE PLANS**
>
> Acute pain, p. 144
> Caregiver role strain, p. 35
> Chronic pain, p. 149
> Impaired physical mobility, p. 126
> Ineffective coping, p. 51

Substance Abuse and Dependence

Alcohol and Drug Abuse/Dependency and Withdrawal

Substance abuse is a pattern of problem substance use. This pattern includes a single behavior or constellation of behaviors within a 12-month period: failure to fulfill major role obligations (e.g., at work or within family); substance use in dangerous situations

> ■ = Independent; ▲ = Collaborative

(e.g., while driving or operating heavy equipment); substance use that results in legal problems (e.g., arrest for driving under the influence) and social and interpersonal problems (e.g., arguments, domestic violence).

Substance dependence is a pattern of substance use that results in biochemical, psychological, and behavioral changes. This pattern includes at least three of the following maladaptive behaviors within a 12-month period: (1) tolerance (the need for increased amounts of the substance to achieve the desired effect or a diminished effect from use of the same amount of the substance); (2) withdrawal (symptoms occur when the substance is withheld or the substance must be used in specific amounts to prevent withdrawal symptoms); (3) need for greater amounts of the substance over longer periods than was originally intended; (4) failure of efforts to stop substance use; (5) increased time spent in activities that support obtaining, using, and recovering from the substance (drug-seeking behavior); (6) abandonment of activities that were once important (e.g., sports, school) because of substance use; (7) continued substance use despite realization that problems are made worse by the substance use.

The problem of substance abuse and dependence crosses all gender, racial, social, and economic boundaries; it truly is an equal-opportunity killer. Substance disorders may be part of a dual diagnosis in which substance disorder is the primary or secondary problem. Both problems require treatment. A patient may be hospitalized during the initial withdrawal phase of treatment, but treatment must continue on an outpatient basis. Because substance disorders are relapsing disorders, outpatient treatment may continue for many years.

Nursing Diagnosis

Deficient Knowledge

Common Related Factors

Denial of abuse/dependence
No substance abuse education
Cognitive impairment
Apathy

Defining Characteristics

Lack of questions
Lack of recall
Information misinterpretation
Lack of insight

Common Expected Outcome

Patient verbalizes understanding of substance abuse and dependence and their treatment.

NOC Outcome
Disease Process

NIC Intervention
Teaching: Disease Process

Ongoing Assessment

Actions/Interventions

■ Assess readiness to learn. However, do not confuse readiness to learn with readiness to change substance use behavior.

Rationale

Patients experiencing acute withdrawal symptoms will be unable to process new information effectively.

Substance Abuse and Dependence

(■ = Independent; ▲ = Collaborative)

Substance Abuse and Dependence—cont'd

Actions/Interventions

- Identify any significant others with whom the patient will be working during the course of treatment and involve them.
- Assess knowledge of physical and psychological symptoms of substance abuse and dependence.

Rationale

All relationships are affected by the substance use behavior; significant others who also are affected by the substance use may also benefit from support and information.

Many patients are knowledgeable about the substances they use, yet substance use takes place despite this knowledge. It is critical that patients have current and accurate health information regarding substance abuse and dependence.

Therapeutic Interventions

Actions/Interventions

- Provide initial information about substance abuse and treatment in a nonthreatening way, without comment.

- Expect the patient to alternate between acceptance and rejection of information.
- Communicate that with correct information, help, work, and support, the patient can choose detoxification and make decisions that will allow enjoyment of a healthier life. Never attempt to use information to frighten the patient into treatment.
- Instruct on what symptoms to bring to the attention of the health care provider (e.g., withdrawal symptoms, delirium tremens, paranoid feelings, seeing or hearing things that are not there).
- Teach the patient how to access his or her health care provider.

Rationale

How information is presented helps set the tone of the relationship and establishes trust as a basis for therapeutic work together.

Rationalization and denial are strong components of the cycle of substance abuse.

To help the patient remove the substance from his or her life and relationships, this goal must be greatly supported and nurtured.

Acute symptoms of withdrawal, cravings, or intoxication may signal life-threatening events that require professional care.

Therapeutic process is a team effort, with the patient as the key team member.

NDx Nursing Diagnosis

Ineffective Coping

Common Related Factors

Increased vulnerability
Inadequate coping skills
Inadequate support resources
Social relationships all revolve around drugs and alcohol

Defining Characteristics

Inability to meet social role expectations
Inability to meet basic health and safety needs
Inability to problem solve
Destructive behavior toward self and others
Ineffective defense mechanisms
Manipulation
Somatic complaints
Suicide attempts
Impulsive overdoses
Substance abuse or dependence
Frequent psychiatric or medical hospitalizations

■ = Independent; ▲ = Collaborative

Hostility; aggression; physically abusive, lying, anti-social, or criminal behavior

Helplessness and hopelessness

Common Expected Outcomes

Patient daily demonstrates positive coping efforts, one day at a time.

Patient begins to recognize own maladaptive behaviors.

Patient participates in treatment programs.

Patient does not use drug or alcohol, one day at a time.

NOC Outcomes
Coping; Social Support

NIC Interventions
Self-Awareness Enhancement; Coping Enhancement; Therapy Group; Active Presence

Ongoing Assessment

Actions/Interventions

■ Assess substance abuse history.

■ Assess the first and most recent drug use; determine substance taken, amount, routes of administration. Assess amount of last alcohol ingestion and length of alcohol use history.

■ Assess the patient's coping methods.

■ Assess the effects of the patient's coping methods.

Rationale

This is used to determine habituation (repeated use despite the lack of physical dependence), misuse (the drug is used for a purpose other than what it was intended), abuse (the use of a substance that lies outside of the amount tolerated by one's society, which results in negative consequences to one's health and welfare), dependence, as described in the preceding definition, and effects (characterize intoxication state).

Many patients are polydrug users; they may abuse or be dependent on more than one drug.

Early substance use may have resulted from a situational crisis or a long-standing inability to cope.

This is important when attempting to reintegrate these familiar techniques into the patient's repertoire of coping mechanisms.

Therapeutic Interventions

Actions/Interventions

■ Confront the patient's unacceptable substance use behaviors.

■ Affirm the patient's growing awareness of substance abuse behaviors.

■ Confront the patient's effort to blame or explain and reject change.

Rationale

The patient may reflect on the impact his or her behavior has had on persons he or she cares about; the feedback also sets limits on the behaviors others will tolerate.

Positive reinforcement may encourage the patient to work toward greater understanding of his or her own behavior. Keep in mind that insight is only the first step toward sobriety and that insight without follow-through is meaningless.

Allowing rationalizations to be unchallenged sanctions behavior. Patients need to learn to take responsibility for their own behavior.

Substance Abuse and Dependence

■ = Independent; ▲ = Collaborative

Substance Abuse and Dependence—cont'd

Actions/Interventions	Rationale
■ Request participation in support groups for recovery.	Professional and self-help programs have been shown to provide immediate help and lifelong support for patients recovering from experiences with abuse and dependence.
■ Plan for small, steady improvements.	It is realistic to expect patients to refrain from alcohol and drugs one day at a time. However, true recovery from substance abuse may be marked by relapses.
■ Help the patient learn to identify difficult feelings.	Articulating thoughts and feelings sometimes helps diffuse them.
■ Reward positive actions.	This may help sustain them.
■ Spend time with the patient, but avoid reinforcing an already low self-esteem.	These patients experience a sense of pervasive worthlessness, helplessness, and hopelessness. It is important to be realistic about the negative, maladaptive behaviors they have used to support their substance use while still being able to affirm their worth as human beings and their individual value to themselves and others.

NDx Nursing Diagnosis

Risk for Self-Directed/Other-Directed Violence

Common Risk Factors

Acute withdrawal from an abused substance
Toxic reactions to medications
Panic states
Suicidal behavior
Hopelessness
Depression, anxiety, confusion
Psychosis and hallucinations that direct patient to hurt self and others

Common Expected Outcomes

Patient states suicidal or homicidal ideation.
Patient does not act on impulses to harm self or others.

NOC Outcomes
Risk Control; Risk Detection; Impulse Control; Suicide Self-Restraint

NIC Interventions
Environmental Management: Violence Prevention; Counseling

■ = Independent; ▲ = Collaborative

Psychosocial Care Plans

Ongoing Assessment

Actions/Interventions

- Determine suicidal or homicidal risk every 24 hours.

- Assess violent ideation and the means to carry out violent acts.

Rationale

Degree of risk determines amount of supervision required. Some patients will require referral to inpatient psychiatric services.

Having a plan and the ability to carry it out increase the risk of harmful behavior.

Therapeutic Interventions

Actions/Interventions

- Remove dangerous objects from the environment.
- Approach the patient in a helpful manner. Accept the patient's right to refuse procedures.
- ▲ Use medications to modify out-of-control behavior and to treat delusional thinking and symptoms of psychosis.

Rationale

This increases safety for patients who may be impulsive.

Patients who are aggressive may be acting out of a sense of extreme personal fear.

Medications may be useful in the acute stages of stabilization; however, the use of habit-forming medications requires careful analysis of benefits and risks.

NDx Nursing Diagnosis

Ineffective Health Maintenance

Common Related Factors

Impaired communication skills
Impaired judgment
Perceptual or cognitive impairment
Ineffective coping, dysfunctional grieving
Inadequate resources
Alcohol or drug abuse or dependency
Financial or legal problems
Presence of adverse personal habits
Withdrawal from physiological dependence
Lack of appropriate assistive services

Defining Characteristics

Inability to self-manage symptoms
Inability to promote health or well-being

Common Expected Outcomes

Patient begins to participate in healthy self-care.
Patient identifies available professional and community resources.
Patient makes positive choices.

NOC Outcomes

Treatment Behavior: Illness or Injury;
 Health-Promoting Behavior;
 Participation: Health Care Decisions

NIC Interventions

Health System Guidance;
 Self-Responsibility Facilitation

Substance Abuse and Dependence

■ = Independent; ▲ = Collaborative

Substance Abuse and Dependence—cont'd

Ongoing Assessment

Actions/Interventions

- Assess health habits: smoking, poor diet, obesity, hygiene, exercise, and sleep.
- Assess financial problems as a potential barrier to maintaining health.

- Assess mental status functioning.

- Assess health history.

- Assess the relationship between environment, social and family problems, and poor health behaviors.
- Assess the patient for health misconceptions.

- Assess the patient's potential to fail to report changes in health status.

- Assess influences of family and friends.

- Discuss patient ambivalence.

Rationale

History will likely reflect multiple risk factors for health problems.

It takes enormous economic reserves to support the use of a substance over a protracted period. Additionally, irregular attendance at work, frequent illnesses, or the inability to maintain employment compromise one's financial reserves.

Substance use may coexist with other psychiatric, developmental, or cognitive problems. In this case, the patient may carry a dual diagnosis.

Substance abuse is closely related to specific medical complications (e.g., pancreatitis, ulcers for the alcoholic patient).

Substance use presents the patient with problems that pervade virtually every aspect of his or her life.

The patient may deny a relationship between substance use and health problems.

The patient's sense of hopelessness or preoccupation with accessing adequate quantities of the substance may take precedence over any other consideration.

The behavior of significant others may enable the behavior of substance use.

Programs need to be constructed to support success.

Therapeutic Interventions

Actions/Interventions

- Provide self-care education:
  - Cessation of alcohol and drug abuse

  - Regular exercise and rest

  - Proper hygiene
  - Regular physical and dental checkups
  - Reporting of unusual symptoms to health professionals
- Arrange clinic, telephone, and home contacts.

- Arrange methods of contacting health care providers to assist with acute problems or crisis events.

See also **Ineffective Health Maintenance**, *p. 95.*

Rationale

In addition to physical addiction, physical consequences of substance abuse mitigate against continued use.

These manage multiple symptoms such as insomnia, fatigue, and depression.

This promotes self-esteem, appearance, and health.

It is important to treat problems early.

Prompt assessment facilitates early treatment and preventive care.

These foster ongoing relationships and provide patient support.

This facilitates being available for questions or problem solutions to decrease risk of relapse.

■ = Independent; ▲ = Collaborative

Psychosocial Care Plans

Nursing Diagnosis

Noncompliance with Treatment Program

Common Related Factors

Substance abuse and dependency denial
Substance abuse and dependency rationalization
Treatment dropout
New financial, social, personal, and legal problems
Impaired functioning
Blaming attitudes

Defining Characteristics

Behavior indicative of continued substance use
Objective tests, physiological measurement, detection of markers
Evidence of relapse
Failure to keep appointments
Failure to progress
Inability to set or maintain mutual goals

Common Expected Outcomes

Patient follows care plan one day at a time.
Patient substance screens remain negative.

NOC Outcomes

Adherence Behavior; Compliance Behavior; Treatment Behavior: Illness or Injury

NIC Interventions

Self-Responsibility Facilitation; Family Involvement; Therapy: Individual; Group Therapy; Counseling

---

Ongoing Assessment

Actions/Interventions

■ Assess the patient's use of denial, rationalization, and blame to sustain his or her habit.

■ Assess secondary gains from substance abuse.
▲ Perform random substance screens.

Rationale

Substance users have an enormous capacity to compartmentalize the behaviors they use to support substance use.

Perceived gains (e.g., friends, income) promote relapse

Support and rewards for compliance are important to recovery.

Therapeutic Interventions

Actions/Interventions

■ Give the patient all laboratory results.

■ Consider inpatient treatment when physiological withdrawal is severe.

■ Include friends and family members in the care plan.

■ Arrange follow-up calls and provide telephone numbers for crisis intervention lines.

Rationale

Rationalization and denial may obstruct a patient's ability to be honest with care providers. Truth and support form the basis of the therapeutic relationship.

Physical symptoms may require close surveillance during the withdrawal phase. Emotional support will need to be almost constant during this sensitive period.

Friends and family need encouragement not to accept the patient's negative behaviors but to be supportive of positive behaviors.

These resources provide ongoing support.

Substance Abuse and Dependence

■ = Independent; ▲ = Collaborative

Substance Abuse and Dependence—cont'd

Actions/Interventions

- Encourage the patient to participate in a community recovery program.

- Contract with the patient to take medications as prescribed.
- Encourage the patient to redefine and seek out new friendships.

Rationale

These groups are composed of people who come together to derive support during their mutual struggle against substance use. Because recovery is a lifelong process, the relationships to the members and to the program provide a foundation that is ongoing and always accessible.

These may be used to manage symptoms of withdrawal, anxiety, and depression.

These may reduce the opportunity to return to abusive and addictive behaviors.

> **• RELATED CARE PLANS**
>
> Affective disorders, p. 1124
> Caregiver role strain, p. 35
> Disturbed thought processes, p. 189
> Imbalanced nutrition: less than body requirements, p. 134
> Impaired home maintenance, p. 99
> Interrupted family processes, p. 63
> Powerlessness, p. 153

■ = Independent; ▲ = Collaborative

Index

1154 Index